OPEC, ITS MEMBER STATES
AND THE
WORLD ENERGY MARKET

OPEC, ITS MEMBER STATES AND THE WORLD ENERGY MARKET

Compiled and written by

John Evans

A KEESING'S REFERENCE PUBLICATION

Longman

OPEC, ITS MEMBER STATES AND THE WORLD ENERGY MARKET

Published by Longman Group UK Limited, Longman House,
Burnt Mill, Harlow, Essex, CM20 2JE, United Kingdom

Distributed exclusively in the United States and Canada
by Gale Research Company, Book Tower, Detroit,
Michigan 48226, USA

ISBN 0–582–90267–3 (Longman)
      0–8103–2148–3 (Gale)

Library of Congress Catalog Card Number: 86–20075

British Library Cataloguing in Publication Data
Evans, John (Bussell)
    OPEC, its member states and the world energy market.
    1. Organization of the Petroleum Exporting Countries—History
    I. Title
    382′.4482′0601   HD9560.1.066

    ISBN 0–582–90267–3

Library of Congress Cataloging-in-Publication Data
Evans, John (Bussell).
    OPEC, its member states and the world energy market.
    (A Keesing's reference publication)
    Includes index.
    1. Organization of Petroleum Exporting Countries.
    2. Petroleum industry and trade. 3. Gas industry.
    I. Title.   II. Series.
    HD9560.1.066E92   1986   341.7′5472282′0601   86–20075

    ISBN 0–8103–2148–3

Typesetting by The Word Factory, Rossendale, Lancashire, BB4 6HN, UK
Printed and bound by the The Eastern Press, London and Reading, UK

Contents

List of Tables xvi
List of Maps and Diagrams xviii
Introduction xix
List of Abbreviations/Acronyms for Oil Company Names xxii
General List of Abbreviations xxiv

Section A — World Oil and Gas: An Overview
A1   Summary of Basic Facts and Terminology
A1.1   Petroleum Geology 1
A1.2   Natural Gas 2
A1.3   Non-Conventional Hydrocarbons 2
A1.4   Extent of Hydrocarbon Resource Base 2
A1.5   Classification of Reserves 3
A1.6   Main Sectors of the Oil Industry 3
A1.7   Oil Exploration 3
A1.8   Crude Oil Production 3
A1.9   Ownership of Crude Oil
  A1.9.i   Royalty crude 4
  A1.9.ii   Equity crude 4
  A1.9.iii   Participation crude 4
  A1.9.iv   Buy-back crude 4
A1.10   Oil refining 4
A1.11   Specific Gravity and Relative Product Yields of Crude Oils 5
A1.12   Sweet and Sour Crudes 5
A1.13   Oil Stocks 5
A1.14   Measurement of Oil Production 6
A1.15   Measurement of Energy Equivalence 6
A1.16   Petrochemicals 7
A1.17   Oil Pricing Terminology
  A1.17.i   Posted prices (USA) 7
  A1.17.ii   Posted prices (Middle East) 7
  A1.17.iii   Official OPEC selling prices 8
  A1.17.iv   Spot prices 8
  A1.17.v   Netback pricing 9

A2   Commercial Exploitation of Hydrocarbon Resources
A2.1   Oil as a Minor Energy Source (to 1939) 10
A2.2   Oil's Attainment of Dominance in the Energy Market
          (1945 to 1973) 10
A2.3   The Changing Pattern of Oil Demand (post-1973) 11
A2.4   Position of Nuclear and Water Power in the Energy Market 14
A2.5   Natural Gas in the United States and the Soviet Union 14
A2.6   Natural Gas in Western Europe 15
A2.7   Natural Gas in the OPEC Area 16
A2.8   Development of the Petrochemical Industry 18

A3   World Trade in Hydrocarbons
A3.1   Crude Oil and Refined Products
  A3.1.i   Development of mainly product-based trade (to 1945) 21
  A3.1.ii   The shift to mainly crude-based trade (1945 to 1960) 23

A3.1.iii   Growing dominance of eastern-hemisphere exporting countries (1960 to 1970) 25

A3.1.iv   Supply constraints and price rises (1970 to 1973) 28

A3.1.v   Changes in the pattern of trade (1974 to 1979) 29

A3.1.vi   Slump in demand for OPEC exports (post-1979) 31

A3.1.vii   Relative position of refined products in total oil trade, 1973 to 1983 33

A3.2   Natural Gas

A3.2.i   Early pattern of world trade (1960 to 1970) 34

A3.2.ii   Expansion of international gas trade (post-1970) 37

A3.3   Petrochemicals 40

A4   Control over Production and Pricing in the World Oil Industry

A4.1   Extent of Major Oil Companies' Interests at the Time of OPEC's Formation 42

A4.2   Early Company Developments (to 1928) 42

A4.3   "Orderly Marketing", US Prorationing and "Gulf-plus" Pricing 44

A4.4   Venezuelan and Indonesian Oil Concessions 47

A4.5   Middle Eastern Oil Concessions

A4.5.i   Iran and Iraq 47

A4.5.ii   Bahrain, Saudi Arabia and Kuwait 50

A4.6   Nationalization of Mexican Oil Industry – Reform of Government-Company Relations in Venezuela – Introduction of "50-50 Profit-sharing" in the Middle East 52

A4.7   Early Evolution of Middle Eastern and Venezuelan Posted Prices   54

A4.8   Iranian Nationalization Crisis 57

A4.9   Expansion of Independent Oil Companies' International Operations 58

A4.10   Oil Prices in the 1950s

A4.10.i   The price rises of 1953 and 1957 60

A4.10.ii   The move towards mandatory US import controls (mid-1957 to early 1959) 62

A4.10.iii   Background to August 1960 cuts in Middle Eastern postings 63

A4.11   Oil Prices in the 1960s 66

A4.12   Relations between Oil Companies and Exporting Countries in the 1960s

A4.12.i   General position of OPEC 69

A4.12.ii   The "production programming" issue 70

A4.12.iii   Fiscal issues 70

A4.12.iv   New exploration agreements 73

A4.12.v   Pressure for revision of pre-war concession agreements 74

A4.13   Failure of 1967 Arab Oil Embargo – Causes and Effects of 1970 Freight Crisis 75

A4.14   Renegotiation of Middle Eastern and North African Tax Structure   78

A4.15   The Transition to OPEC Control over Crude Pricing

A4.15.i   Emergence of a seller's market for oil 79

A4.15.ii   First unilateral OPEC increase in Middle Eastern crude postings – Subsequent use of Arab oil weapon 83

A4.16   The New Balance of World Oil Power 85

A4.17   The Development of OPEC Pricing Policy, 1975 to 1978

A4.17.i   1975 to mid-1977 89

A4.17.ii   Mid-1977 to December 1978 90
A4.18   The Relationship between OPEC Governments and International
            Oil Companies in 1978 92
A4.19   The Second Oil Price Shock (1979–80) 93
A4.20   The Erosion of OPEC's Market Dominance (1981–82)
A4.20.i   Underlying factors – Position of non-OPEC producers 96
A4.20.ii   Downward pressure on official OPEC prices – Unsuccessful
            attempt to limit OPEC production 98
A4.21   The Breakdown of OPEC Price Administration (1983 to 1985)
A4.21.i   General background 100
A4.21.ii   Further OPEC prorationing initiative to defend reduced
            official prices (1983–84) 101
A.21.iii   From defence of prices to defence of market share (1985) 105
A4.22   The Ascendancy of Market Forces (1986) 109

A5   The Major International Oil Companies
A5.1   Company Profiles 113
A5.1.i   Exxon 113
A5.1.ii   Mobil 114
A5.1.iii   Chevron 115
A5.1.iv   Texaco 116
A5.1.v   Gulf 117
A5.1.vi   Royal Dutch/Shell 118
A5.1.vii   British Petroleum 119
A5.1.viii   Total Compagnie Française des Pétroles 121
A5.2   Major Oil Companies' Operations in the Middle East
A5.2.i   Arabian American Oil Company 121
A5.2.ii   Iranian Oil Participants 122
A5.2.iii   Iraq Petroleum Company 122
A5.2.iv   Interests of IPC group outside Iraq 122
A5.2.v   Kuwait Oil Company 123
A5.2.vi   Other companies 123
A5.3   Major Oil Companies' Operations in OPEC Countries outside the
            Middle East 124

A6   Principal Middle Eastern Pipelines
A6.1   Sumed (Suez-Mediterranean Pipeline) 125
A6.2   Petroline 125
A6.3   Iraq Strategic Pipeline 125
A6.4   Iraq-Dörtyol 125
A6.5   Iraq-Petroline Link 125
A6.6   Iraq-Banias/Tripoli 125
A6.7   Iraq-Haifa 127
A6.8   Tipline (Trans-Israel Pipeline) 127
A6.9   Tapline (Trans-Arabian Pipeline) 127
A6.10   IGAT-1 (Iran Gas Trunkline 1) 127

Section B — International Organizations: Structures and Functions

B1   Organization of the Petroleum Exporting Countries
B1.1   General 129
B1.2   Membership, Staffing, etc. 129
B1.3   Meetings of OPEC Conference 131
B1.4   Other Main OPEC Meetings 132

B1.5   Key Committees of OPEC Conference 133
B1.6   OPEC Fund for International Development 133
B1.7   The OPEC Statute 138
B1.8   OPEC Economic Commission 144
B1.9   Major OPEC Policy Statements
  B1.9.i   Declaratory statement on petroleum policy in member
             countries (June 1968) 146
  B1.9.ii   Policy statement (June 1973) 148
  B1.9.iii   Solemn declaration (March 1975) 149

B2   Organization of Arab Petroleum Exporting Countries
B2.1   Membership, Staffing, etc. 155
B2.2   Formation and Development 155
B2.3   Objectives of OAPEC 156
B2.4   Organs of OAPEC 156
B2.5   OAPEC-sponsored Companies 157
B2.6   Other Joint Ventures 158
B2.7   Co-sponsorship of Arab Energy Conference 158

B3   International Energy Agency
B3.1   Membership, etc. 160
B3.2   Formation, Status and Aims 160
B3.3   Organization 161
B3.4   IEA Principles for Energy Policy 162

Section C — OPEC Member Country Surveys

C1   Algeria
C1.1   Statistical Survey 165
C1.2   Political and Economic Summary 166
C1.3   Oil and Gas Industry
  C1.3.i   Early development (to 1964) 167
  C1.3.ii   New co-operation agreement with France (July 1965) 171
  C1.3.iii   Extension of state control over non-French oil interests 174
  C1.3.iv   Extension of state control over French oil and gas interests 179
  C1.3.v   Oil and gas under state control (post-1971) 184

C2   Ecuador
C2.1   Statistical Survey 189
C2.2   Political and Economic Summary 189
C2.3   Oil and Gas Industry 190

C3   Gabon
C3.1   Statistical Survey 195
C3.2   Political and Economic Summary 195
C3.3   Oil and Gas Industry 196

C4   Indonesia
C4.1   Statistical Survey 199
C4.2   Political and Economic Summary 200
C4.3   Oil and Gas Industry
  C4.3.i   Development of oil industry from earliest exploration work to
             the ending of the concession sytem (1884 to 1963) 201
  C4.3.ii   Oil and gas under state control (post-1963) 205

C5	Iran	
C5.1	Statistical Survey	210
C5.2	Political and Economic Summary	211
C5.3	Oil and Gas Industry	
C5.3.i	From the D'Arcy concession to the overthrow of Mossadeq	212
C5.3.ii	Establishment of IOP consortium	216
C5.3.iii	Developments in Government-IOP relations in the 1960s – NIOC's joint-venture and service-contract agreements with foreign oil companies	218
C5.3.iv	Conclusion of new service contracts under 1974 petroleum law	221
C5.3.v	Iranian Government's 1973 "sales and purchase" agreement with IOP – Subsequent developments in IOP-NIOC relations	222
C5.3.vi	Oil and gas developments after the 1979 revolution	224
C6	Iraq	
C6.1	Statistical Survey	229
C6.2	Political and Economic Summary	229
C6.3	Oil and Gas Industry	
C6.3.i	Concession agreements with foreign oil interests	231
C6.3.ii	Growth of IPC production – Government-company relations in the 1950s	234
C6.3.iii	Inconclusive negotiations leading to Law 80 of 1961	236
C6.3.iv	Developments leading to full nationalization of oil industry (1962 to 1975)	238
C6.3.v	Post-nationalization developments	241
C7	Kuwait	
C7.1	Statistical Survey	243
C7.2	Political and Economic Summary	244
C7.3	Oil and Gas Industry	
C7.3.i	The Gulf/BP concession	246
C7.3.ii	Other companies' concessions in Kuwait and Neutral Zone	247
C7.3.iii	The royalty-expensing issue – Subsequent extension of state control over oil industry	249
C7.3.iv	Post-nationalization developments	252
C8	Libya	
C8.1	Statistical Survey	255
C8.2	Political and Economic Summary	256
C8.3	Oil and Gas Industry	
C8.3.i	From inception to the overthrow of the monarchy (1955–69)	258
C8.3.ii	Intensified campaign for improved state revenue entitlement, leading to signature of Tripoli agreement (1970–71)	262
C8.3.iii	Establishment of state control over production operations (from 1971)	264
C9	Nigeria	
C9.1	Statistical Survey	268
C9.2	Political and Economic Summary	269
C9.3	Oil and Gas Industry	270
C10	Qatar	
C10.1	Statistical Survey	276
C10.2	Political and Economic Summary	276
C10.3	Oil and Gas Industry	277

CONTENTS

C11   Saudi Arabia
C11.1   Statistical Survey 283
C11.2   Political and Economic Summary 284
C11.3   Oil and Gas Industry
C11.3.i   Early development (1933 to 1944) 286
C11.3.ii   Growth of Aramco's output, 1945 to 1950 – Onshore Neutral
Zone concession agreement (1948) 289
C11.3.iii   Agreement with Aramco on 50-50 profit-sharing 291
C11.3.iv   Offshore Neutral Zone concession agreement 292
C11.3.v   Relations between Government and Aramco in the 1960s 293
C11.3.vi   Establishment of Petromin – New agreements with independent
oil interests 295
C11.3.vii   Extension of state control over Aramco's production
operations 296
C11.3.viii   Development of government policy on crude oil production,
pricing and export marketing, 1974 to 1986 297
C11.3.ix   Infrastructural development and downstream diversification in
the Saudi hydrocarbons industry 300

C12   United Arab Emirates
C12.1   Statistical Survey 304
C12.2   Political and Economic Summary 305
C12.3   Oil and Gas Industry
C12.3.i   General 307
C12.3.ii   Early concession agreements in the Trucial States 309
C12.3.iii   Abu Dhabi 310
C12.3.iv   Dubai 313
C12.3.v   Sharjah 314
C12.3.vi   Ras al-Khaimah 315
C12.3.vii   Ajman, Fujairah and Umm al Quwain 315

C13   Venezuela
C13.1   Statistical Survey 316
C13.2   Political and Economic Summary 317
C13.3   Oil and Gas Industry
C13.3.i   General 318
C13.3.ii   Early development (1913 to 1940) 318
C13.3.iii   Hydrocarbons law of 1943 – Introduction of "50-50
profit-sharing" (1948) 321
C13.3.iv   Lifting and subsequent reimposition of ban on new concession
agreements – Strengthening of state role in oil sector (to 1971) 323
C13.3.v   From "reversion" to nationalization (1971 to 1975) – Formation
and development of PDVSA 326
C13.3.vi   Special supply agreements with neighbouring states 329
C13.3.vii   Development of Venezuelan hydrocarbons sector under PVDSA
management 329
C13.3.viii   PDVSA investments in overseas joint ventures 333

Section D — OPEC and the Changing Balance of World Oil Power, 1960–1986

D1   1960 to 1970
D1.1   The Formation of OPEC 335
D1.2   Resolutions of 2nd and 3rd Meetings of OPEC Conference 340

D1.3 OPEC and the Royalty-Expensing Issue, 1962 to 1964

D1.3.i Launching of OPEC campaign for royalty-expensing (1962) – Inconclusive negotiations with producing companies (1963) 341

D1.3.ii Negotiations leading to several member countries' adoption of national agreements on royalty-expensing (1964) 344

D1.4 OPEC and "Production Programming", 1965 to 1966 347

D1.5 Negotiations to eliminate Tax Allowances under the Royalty-Expensing Formula 351

D1.6 The Development of OPEC Policy, 1968 to 1970

D1.6.i General 353

D1.6.ii Decisions of 16th to 20th Conference meetings 353

D1.6.iii Repercussions of increase in Libyan postings – Adoption of resolutions calling for wide-ranging negotiations with foreign oil companies (December 1970) 355

D2 1971

D2.1 Annual Statistical Survey 360

D2.2 Negotiations to implement Main Resolutions of 21st OPEC Conference Meeting

D2.2.i Disagreements between OPEC and foreign oil companies over form of negotiating process 365

D2.2.ii Conclusion of Tehran and Tripoli agreements 368

D2.3 Decisions of 23rd to 26th Meetings of OPEC Conference 371

D3 1972

D3.1 Annual Statistical Survey 374

D3.2 Negotiation of "Geneva I" Agreement to offset Exchange-Rate Losses 379

D3.3 Negotiations on the Participation Issue 380

D3.4 Conclusion of General Agreement on Participation 383

D4 1973

D4.1 Annual Statistical Survey 385

D4.2 Negotiation of "Geneva II" Exchange-Rate Agreement 389

D4.3 Breakdown of Negotiated Agreements on Posted Price Structure 392

D4.4 Gulf Producers' Unilateral Increase in Postings 395

D4.5 Arab Production Cutbacks and Embargo Measures 396

D4.6 Pricing Developments in late 1973 398

D5 1974

D5.1 Annual Statistical Survey 402

D5.2 Ending of Arab Embargo Measures 406

D5.3 Decisions of 37th OPEC Conference Meeting 407

D5.4 Factors Influencing OPEC Pricing Policy in 1974 408

D5.5 Decisions of 38th and 39th Meetings of OPEC Conference 410

D5.6 OPEC Decisions on Prices and Taxes, June to December 1974

D5.6.i Tax and royalty increases based on unchanged postings – Related developments (June to September 1974) 411

D5.6.ii Major reductions in foreign exporting companies' profit margins on Gulf crude (November–December 1974) 414

D5.7 Summary of Price Changes in 1974 416

D5.8 Developments leading to Washington Conference of Major Oil-Consuming Countries 417

D5.9 UN Declaration on the Establishment of a New International Economic Order 419

D5.10	Adoption of Long-Term EEC Energy Targets – Launching of "Euro-Arab Dialogue"	421
D5.11	Modification of Long-Term US Energy Targets	423
D5.12	Establishment of International Energy Agency	423
D5.13	French Proposal for Holding of "Tripartite" Conference on Oil-Related Issues	425
D6	1975	
D6.1	Annual Statistical Survey	427
D6.2	Factors Influencing OPEC Pricing Policy in 1975	431
D6.3	OPEC Ministerial Meetings prior to Summit Conference	434
D6.4	Algiers Summit of OPEC Heads of State	435
D6.5	44th Meeting of OPEC Conference	436
D6.6	Algerian Campaign for Stabilization of Premiums	437
D6.7	Decision on Further OPEC Price Increase – Subsequent Pricing Developments in late 1975	438
D6.8	Agreement to establish OPEC Fund for Developing Countries	441
D6.9	Abduction and Release of OPEC Ministers	442
D6.10	Dakar Conference on Third-World Strategy on Raw Materials and Economic Development	443
D6.11	Developments leading to First Plenary Session of Conference on International Economic Co-operation	444
D6.12	Exclusion of OPEC Countries from US Tariff Preferences – US Energy Policy Developments	446
D6.13	IEA Developments in 1975	447
D7	1976	
D7.1	Annual Statistical Survey	450
D7.2	OPEC Pricing Developments, January to June 1976	454
D7.3	OPEC Pricing Developments, July to December 1976	
D7.3.i	Failure to adopt agreement on differentials – Build-up of pressure for further increase in marker price	457
D7.3.ii	Pressure from importing countries for continued price freeze – The issue of "linkage" with CIEC	458
D7.3.iii	Split decision on pricing at 48th OPEC Conference meeting	460
D7.4	Reactions to Breakdown of OPEC Consensus on Pricing	462
D7.5	Establishment of OPEC Special Fund for Developing Countries	464
D7.6	CIEC Developments in 1976	465
D7.7	IEA Developments in 1976	466
D7.8	EEC Energy Policy in 1976	466
D8	1977	
D8.1	Annual Statistical Survey	467
D8.2	The Market Environment in 1977	472
D8.3	OPEC and Two-Tier Pricing (January to June 1977)	472
D8.4	49th OPEC Conference Meeting	475
D8.5	Prelude to 50th OPEC Conference Meeting	476
D8.6	50th OPEC Conference Meeting	477
D8.7	Meetings of OPEC Finance Ministers in 1977	479
D8.8	Final Session of Conference on International Economic Co-operation	480
D8.9	Adoption of IEA Oil Import Ceiling for 1985	483

D8.10	United States Energy Policy Developments in 1977	
D8.10.i	Policy statement by President Carter	484
D8.10.ii	Commerce Department's energy forecasts	485
D8.10.iii	North Alaskan oil and gas developments	486
D8.10.iv	Creation of Department of Energy	486
D8.11	Statement on Energy Policy by Seven Non-Communist Industrialized Countries	487
D9	1978	
D9.1	Annual Statistical Survey	488
D9.2	The Market Environment in 1978 – Deterioration in OPEC Terms of Trade	493
D9.3	OPEC Developments, January to June 1978	
D9.3.i	Pricing issues – Impact of exchange-rate movements	494
D9.3.ii	Establishment of long-term strategy committee – Continuation of OPEC price freeze	495
D9.4	Upward Pressure on Oil Prices, July to December 1978	496
D9.5	Decisions of 52nd OPEC Conference Meeting	499
D9.6	Statement on Energy Policy by Seven Non-Communist Industrialized Countries	501
D9.7	Enactment of US National Energy Bill	502
D10	1979	
D10.1	Annual Statistical Survey	504
D10.2	Market Reaction to Temporary Suspension of Iranian Oil Exports	509
D10.3	The Development of Prices, January to March 1980	510
D10.4	IEA Initiative to reduce Oil Consumption	512
D10.5	53rd Meeting of OPEC Conference	514
D10.6	Pricing and Production Developments in April and May	515
D10.7	Decisions of IEA Ministerial Meeting	517
D10.8	Subsequent Controversy over US Import Policy	519
D10.9	The Position of the Oil-Importing Developing Countries	520
D10.10	Decisions of 54th OPEC Conference Meeting	521
D10.11	Industrialized Countries' Tokyo Declaration on Oil Policy	524
D10.12	Pricing and Production Developments in the Third Quarter of 1979	525
D10.13	Further Upward Pressure on Prices Leading to Breach of Official OPEC Ceiling (October to early December 1979)	526
D10.14	Further IEA Initiative to stabilize the Oil Market	528
D10.15	Further OPEC Price Increases in December 1979 – 55th Meeting of OPEC Conference	531
D10.16	Increasing Concern over OPEC Price Rises among Oil-Importing Developing Countries	533
D10.17	Start of Phased Decontrol of US Crude Prices – Other US Energy Policy Developments in 1979	534
D11	1980	
D11.1	Annual Statistical Survey	536
D11.2	Pricing and Production Developments, January to March 1980	540
D11.3	Pricing Developments in April – 56th Meeting of OPEC Conference	542
D11.4	Further Round of OPEC Price Increases, May 1980	544
D11.5	IEA Ministerial Meeting, May 1980	544
D11.6	OPEC Finance Ministers' Meeting – 57th Meeting of OPEC Conference	545

D11.7	Statement on Energy by Main Non-Communist Industrialized Countries – Response of OPEC Countries	546
D11.8	OPEC Members' July 1980 Pricing Decisions	548
D11.9	Market Developments and OPEC Activities, July to mid-September 1980	550
D11.10	Initial Impact of Iran-Iraq War (mid-September to November 1980)	553
D11.11	December 1980 Meeting of IEA Governing Board	554
D11.12	Decisions of 59th OPEC Conference Meeting	555
D11.13	Introduction of US "Windfall Profits Tax" – Other US Energy Policy Developments in 1980	557
D11.14	Moves to initiate Global Economic Negotiations	
D11.14.i	Report of Brandt Commission	558
D11.14.ii	UN General Assembly's Special Session on International Development Issues	559
D12	1981	
D12.1	Annual Statistical Survey	561
D12.2	Re-emergence of Oil Supply Surplus during early 1981	566
D12.3	Decisions of 60th meeting of OPEC Conference	567
D12.4	IEA Ministerial Meeting, June 1981	567
D12.5	Major Non-Communist Industrialized Countries' Statement on Energy Questions	568
D12.6	Developments leading to Consultative Meeting of OPEC Oil Ministers	569
D12.7	Achievement of Agreement on OPEC Price Reunification	571
D12.8	Decisions of 62nd Meeting of OPEC Conference	573
D12.9	Formation of Gulf Co-operation Council	574
D12.10	Abolition of Price Controls on US Crude Oil Production – Amendment of Windfall Profits Tax Rates	575
D12.11	Cancún Summit Conference on International Co-operation and Development	576
D13	1982	
D13.1	Annual Statistical Survey	577
D13.2	Market Developments in the First Quarter of 1982	582
D13.3	Decisions of 63rd and 64th Meetings of OPEC Conference – Related Market Developments	583
D13.4	May 1982 meeting of IEA Governing Board	586
D13.5	Breakdown of OPEC Production Programme	587
D13.6	Pricing and Production Developments, August to mid-December 1982	588
D13.7	Failure of 66th OPEC Conference Meeting to agree on New National Production Quotas	589
D14	1983	
D14.1	Annual Statistical Survey	592
D14.2	The Market Environment in 1983	596
D14.3	OPEC Ministers' Failure to agree on National Production Quotas, January 1983	597
D14.4	Intensification of Market Pressure on the OPEC Pricing Structure, February and early March 1983	598
D14.5	Pricing and Production Decisions of 67th OPEC Conference Meeting	601

CONTENTS

D14.6   May 1983 Meeting of IEA Governing Board 603
D14.7   Reaffirmation of OPEC Production Ceiling by 68th Conference
         Meeting 605
D14.8   Pricing and Production Developments, August to December 1983   606
D14.9   Decisions of 69th OPEC Conference Meeting 608

D15   1984
D15.1   Annual Statistical Survey 610
D15.2   The Market Environment in 1984 615
D15.3   Market Developments, January to June 1984 615
D15.4   IEA Decision to strengthen Stock Deployment Policy 617
D15.5   Decisions of 70th OPEC Conference Meeting 618
D15.6   Developments Leading to Nigerian Price Cuts
         (July to October 1984) 620
D15.7   Lowering of OPEC Production Ceiling 622
D15.8   Failure of OPEC's Market Stabilization Measures (November to
         December 1984) 624
D15.9   Decisions of 72nd OPEC Conference Meeting 628

D16   1985–86
D16.1   Initial Estimates of Supply and Demand Trends in 1985 631
D16.2   Developments Leading to Further Realignment of Differentials
         by Most OPEC Countries (January 1985) 633
D16.3   Consequent Price Changes, February–March 1985 638
D16.4   British Pricing Developments (February to April 1985) 639
D16.5   Market Trends, February to June 1985 640
D16.6   OPEC Conference Meetings, July 1985 642
D16.7   July 1985 Meeting of IEA Governing Board 644
D16.8   Developments Leading to 75th Meeting of OPEC Conference 646
D16.9   Market Trends, October–November 1985 648
D16.10   OPEC Developments Leading to 76th Conference Meeting
         (October to early December 1985) 650
D16.11   The Collapse of Oil Prices (December 1985 to April 1986)
   D16.11.i   Prices and production in December 1985 and January 1986 652
   D16.11.ii Prices and production, February to April 1986 655
D16.12   The Politics of the Price War (January–February 1986) 657
D16.13   First Part of 77th OPEC Conference Meeting (March 1986) 662
D16.14   Controversy over US Attitude to Oil Market Developments 663
D16.15   April 1986 Meeting of IEA Governing Board 664
D16.16   Second Part of 77th OPEC Conference Meeting (April 1986) 665
D16.17   Market Developments in May and June 1986 – First Part of 78th
         OPEC Conference Meeting 666
D16.18   Further Price Decline (July 1986) – Strengthening of Market in
         Anticipation of OPEC Production Cutback (August 1986) 668

Oil Company Index 673
Names Index 677

Late Information 679

List of Tables

NB.—This list excludes the separate statistical subsections within Sections C and D, for which see main contents list.

Table 1. Growth and distribution of world oil production, 1860 to 1985 12

Table 2. Cumulative oil production and remaining proved reserves (Dec. 31, 1984) 13

Table 3. OPEC area: natural gas production in 1966 16

Table 4. OPEC natural gas production in 1976 17

Table 5. OPEC natural gas production in 1984 18

Table 6. Regional shares of world refinery capacity, 1949 to 1984 25

Table 7. United States oil statistics, 1960 to 1970 27

Table 8. Natural gas: exports by pipeline in 1983 35

Table 9. Natural gas: imports by pipeline in 1983 36

Table 10. Exports of liquefied natural gas in 1983 36

Table 11. Imports of liquefied natural gas in 1983 37

Table 12. Retail price of oil products in Western Europe, 1969 to 1984 88

Table 13. OPEC: estimated aggregate oil revenues and current-account balance of payments, 1970 to 1984 102

Table 14. Deployment of cumulative OPEC cash surplus in peak year (1982) 102

Table 15. Holders of the post of OPEC Secretary-General 130

Table 16. Cumulative contributions to OPEC Fund at end-1985 136

Table 17. Cumulative commitments and disbursements of OPEC Fund at end-1985 138

Table 18. Distribution of voting power on IEA Governing Board 161

Table 19. World oil production, 1960 to 1970 338

Table 20. World oil consumption, 1960 to 1970 338

Table 21. OPEC oil production, 1960 to 1970 339

Table 22. Calculation of government revenue under the main Middle Eastern concession agreements 345

Table 23. Allocation of "programmed" production among OPEC members 349

Table 24. Actual and "programmed" OPEC production, July 1965 to June 1966 349

Table 25. Posted prices of three Gulf crudes, August 1960 to February 1971 368

Table 26. Evolution of selected east Mediterranean and African postings, August 1970 to January 1972 370

Table 27. Tax-reference values of four Venezuelan crudes, December 1970 to January 1972 370

Table 28. Evolution of selected east Mediterranean and African postings in 1972 380

Table 29. Posted prices of selected Gulf crudes, Jan. 1 to Oct. 1, 1973 392

Table 30. Evolution of selected east Mediterranean and African postings, Jan. 1 to Oct. 1, 1973 392

Table 31. Tax-reference values of four Venezuelan crudes, Jan. 1 to Oct. 1, 1973 392

Table 32. OPEC production of crude oil in September and November 1973 398

Table 33. Posted prices of selected Gulf crudes, Oct. 16, 1973, to Jan. 1, 1974 400

Table 34. Evolution of selected east Mediterranean and African postings, Oct. 16, 1973, to Jan. 1, 1974 400

Table 35. Tax-reference values of four Venezuelan crudes, Nov. 1, 1973, to Jan. 1, 1974 401

Table 36. Posted prices and official selling prices of selected Gulf crudes, Nov. 1, 1974 416

Table 37. EEC energy targets for 1985 422

Table 38. Prices of selected OPEC crudes, Oct. 1, 1975 441

Table 39. OPEC countries' concessional aid disbursements, 1973 to 1975 442

Table 40. Price changes for African and Gulf OPEC crudes, June–July 1976 456

Table 41. Prices of selected OPEC crudes, Jan. 1, 1977 462

Table 42. July 1977 crude prices in Saudi Arabia and United Arab Emirates 475

Table 43. Estimated evolution of OPEC terms of trade, 1970 to 1978 493

Table 44. Evolution of "official" OPEC import price index, 1973 to 1978 494

Table 45. Price changes for selected OPEC crudes from Jan. 1, 1979 501

Table 46. Evolution of official selling prices (inclusive of surcharges) for selected OPEC crudes, April 1 to June 1, 1979 516

Table 47. Prices of selected OPEC crudes, July 1, 1979 523

Table 48. IEA oil import targets for 1980 and 1985 529

Table 49. Evolution of prices for selected OPEC crudes, January to July 1980 549

Table 50. Gross product worth differentials for selected OPEC crudes against Saudi Arabian marker crude, January and September 1980 550

Table 51. Prices of selected OPEC crudes from Jan. 1, 1981 556

Table 52. OPEC members' oil output in August 1981 570

Table 53. Prices of selected OPEC crudes, Jan. 1, 1982 574

Table 54. OPEC members' March 1982 oil output and April 1982 production ceilings 584

Table 55. OPEC members' previous oil output and new quotas, March 1983 601

Table 56. Prices of selected OPEC crudes, April 1, 1983 602

Table 57. Redistribution of OPEC production quotas, Nov. 1, 1984 624

Table 58. OPEC members' estimated monthly oil output in 1984 626

Table 59. Official prices and market values of three OPEC crudes, December 1984 627

Table 60. Jan. 1, 1985, price changes and end-1984 spot values of Saudi Arabian crudes 630

Table 61. OPEC members' estimated monthly oil output in 1985 632

Table 62. OPEC reference prices, Feb. 1, 1985 637

Table 63. Price changes for selected OPEC crudes, February–March 1985 638

Table 64. Official prices and market values of three OPEC crudes, June 1985 640

Table 65. Official prices and market values of three OPEC crudes, November 1985 649

Table 66. OPEC members' estimated oil output, January to June 1986 655

xvii

List of Maps and Diagrams

Fig. **1.** Evolution of nominal OPEC oil prices, 1973 to January 1986 106
Fig. **2.** Evolution of real oil prices, 1973 to January 1986 106
Fig. **3.** Principal pipelines in the Middle East 126
Fig. **4.** Algerian hydrocarbon resources and installations 168
Fig. **5.** Algerian exploration areas and production concessions in 1967 178
Fig. **6.** Ecuadorian hydrocarbon resources and installations 192
Fig. **7.** Gabonese oil resources and installations 197
Fig. **8.** Indonesian hydrocarbon resources and installations 202
Fig. **9.** Iranian hydrocarbon resources and installations 214
Fig. **10.** Principal Iranian oilfields and southern Iraqi oilfields 228
Fig. **11.** Iraqi oil resources and installations 233
Fig. **12.** Oil resources and installations in Kuwait and Neutral Zone 248
Fig. **13.** Libyan hydrocarbon resources and installations 259
Fig. **14.** Nigerian oil resources and installations 271
Fig. **15.** Qatari hydrocarbon resources and installations 279
Fig. **16.** Saudi Arabian hydrocarbon resources and installations 287
Fig. **17.** Aramco's exclusive and preferential oil rights, 1939 to 1963 294
Fig. **18.** Hydrocarbon resources and installations in the United Arab
        Emirates 308
Fig. **19.** Venezuelan hydrocarbon resources and installations 320
Fig. **20.** Evolution of OPEC members' oil output in 1978 498
Fig. **21.** Official price and monthly average spot price of Saudi Arabian 27°
        crude, January 1984 to October 1985 634
Fig. **22.** Official price and monthly average spot price of Saudi Arabian 31°
        crude, January 1984 to October 1985 634
Fig. **23.** Official price and monthly average spot price of Saudi Arabian 34°
        crude, January 1984 to October 1985 635
Fig. **24.** Official price and monthly average spot price of Saudi Arabian 39°
        crude, January 1984 to October 1985 635
Fig. **25.** Evolution of crude oil spot price, December 1985 to August 1986
        (weekly averages for North Sea Brent) 667

Introduction

In the 13 years to 1973, the main concern of the Organization of the Petroleum Exporting Countries (OPEC) was to strengthen the member states' position vis-à-vis the foreign oil companies which dominated their economies. In the 13 years since 1973 the member states, having brought their oil resources under effective national control, have faced the challenge of maintaining a continual compromise between their separate national interests in order to establish agreed OPEC targets in the common interest. Until 1981 these targets were defined solely in pricing terms, without the backing of formal production discipline. Thereafter OPEC's market share declined to a level at which the member states were obliged to turn to co-ordinated production controls as a means of supporting their official pricing system. This increasingly divisive regime was eventually abandoned in late 1985. A subsequent drive to recover market share was accompanied by a fall in real oil prices to pre-1974 levels, and in September 1986 production controls were reintroduced on an interim basis in order to stabilize the market.

OPEC is one of the best known and least well understood international organizations, having often received the credit (or blame) for developments which it did not initiate. There have been countless unfulfilled predictions of its imminent disintegration and many exaggerated assertions of its indispensability. An objective assessment of the Organization must take account of all the factors involved in the complex environment in which it operates. In broad terms, the main considerations include (i) the structure of supply and demand in the world energy market; (ii) the commercial structure of the world oil industry; (iii) the political orientation and economic situation of each OPEC member; and (iv) the global political and strategic issues arising from oil's vital importance as the modern world's principal energy source.

This book's wide-ranging factual coverage of its subject is designed to provide a rounded historical perspective in a format which is easily accessible for reference purposes. The text has accordingly been divided into cross-referenced sections to enable the user to approach specific topics either in detailed context or in a broader context and to move between the general and the particular as required. The overall sequence of the book progresses from the general to the particular, while the material within each separate subsection is organized in chronological sequence as far as is practical and appropriate. Cross-references have been deployed discriminately to indicate the main links between the different sections of the book (each of which is self-contained at its own level of detail). The symbol ◊ is used for forward "see" references and the symbol ◊◊ for forward "see also" references (with ◁ and ◁◁ respectively used for references to earlier sections of the book).

Of the subsections within Section A, **A1** is primarily a detailed glossary of terms, while **A2** provides a historical summary of the role of hydrocarbons as energy sources and industrial raw materials and **A3** outlines the main changes in the patterns of international trade in hydrocarbons. Within subsection **A4**, parts **A4.1** to **A4.10** cover the historical background to OPEC's formation in 1960, with particular reference to the role of the major oil companies and the relationship between oil companies and governments. Parts **A4.11** to **A4.22** provide an overview of developments in the period 1960 to 1986, designed to complement, clarify and summarize the more detailed coverage of OPEC's affairs in Section D. Subsection **A5** contains reference material on the (historically defined) major oil companies, including summaries of company information dispersed throughout other parts of the book. Subsection **A6** and its accompanying map provide a central reference point in respect of the main Middle Eastern pipelines.

Section B deals with the organizational structures of OPEC, of OAPEC (the

Organization of Arab Petroleum Exporting Countries, whose members include all the Arab OPEC countries) and of the IEA (the International Energy Agency, whose members include most of the main oil-importing countries). Subsection **B1**, covering OPEC, includes a full list of the dates of OPEC Conference meetings (**B1.3**), a history of the OPEC Fund for International Development (**B1.6**) and the texts of OPEC's major policy statements (**B1.9**). Section C contains subsections on each of OPEC's 13 member states, comprising uniform statistic surveys as well as political and economic summaries and detailed histories of national oil and gas developments. The accompanying maps provide a general guide to the location of each country's main hydrocarbon resources and installations. Oilfields, gasfields and pipelines are shown in simplified diagrammatic form. No political judgments are implied in the representations of undemarcated or disputed international borders.

Section D contains a detailed chronological account of the development of OPEC policy, with supplementary material on the development of IEA policy from the Agency's formation in 1974. Subsection **D1** covers the period 1960 to 1970. The 14 succeeding subsections (**D2** to **D15**) provide year-by-year coverage of the period 1971 to 1984. The first part of each of these 14 subsections consists of a uniform annual statistical survey showing changes (**i**) in oil production and reserves (world, OPEC countries and selected non-OPEC countries); (**ii**) in oil consumption (world and selected countries); (**iii**) in oil refining (world capacity and throughputs and patterns of product demand in selected markets); (**iv**) in the tonnage of the world oil tanker fleet and the volume and distribution of international trade in oil; (**v**) in the overall pattern of world primary energy consumption; and (**vi**) in world and OPEC natural gas production and reserves. Each survey provides a detailed contextual framework for the developments covered in the subsequent parts of the relevant annual subsection. The final subsection of the book (**D16**) deals with events between the beginning of January 1985 and the beginning of September 1986.

The wide range of sources consulted in the preparation of this book includes specialist periodicals; oil companies' annual reports; material issued by government agencies in various OPEC and non-OPEC countries; and the publications and press releases of international organizations, notably OPEC, the OPEC Fund for International Development, OAPEC, the IEA and the Organization for Economic Co- operation and Development. The full texts of major agreements, including historic concession agreements between oil companies and host governments, have been studied wherever possible.

Mainly because of its breadth of coverage and its regular revisions of past years' figures, the British Petroleum Company's *BP Statistical Review of World Energy* (known until 1980 as the *BP Statistical Review of the World Oil Industry*) has been used as the principal source in compiling a consistent series of annual statistics for the period 1960 to 1984. The main supplementary source was OPEC's *Annual Statistical Bulletin*, whose figures have been preferred for some purposes. Whereas the *BP Statistical Review* for 1985 became available in mid-1986, the OPEC Secretariat's 1985 statistics were not due to be published before the end of 1986. A Section D statistical survey has therefore been omitted for 1985, although the BP estimates of OPEC member countries' 1985 oil production have been included in the Section C statistical surveys. As regards BP's most recent revision of certain 1984 statistics, the updated estimates relating to some OPEC members' oil production have likewise been included in the Section C surveys, while the content of the Section D survey for 1984 (**D15.1**) has been left unchanged.

The *BP Statistical Review*, in common with many other sources, takes account of the broad range of liquid hydrocarbons (i.e. including natural gas liquids and oil derived from shales and tar sands) in its overall production figures for crude oil. The same practice has been followed in the main statistical surveys in this book. In 1983 the narrow definition of crude oil assumed great importance for OPEC members wishing to take maximum advantage of their quotas under the Organization's market stabilization programme, giving rise to considerable blurring of OPEC oil production figures in general and their NGL content in particular. Varying estimates of OPEC members' monthly output, excluding NGL, have been published in specialist periodicals and IEA market reports since compliance with "crude only" quotas became a major political issue within OPEC. "Crude only" estimates published two months in arrears by the British monthly journal *Petroleum Economist* have been used as the principal source in compiling Tables 58, 61 and 66, which together span the period January 1984 to June 1986.

The "economy and trade" sections included in the Section C statistical surveys are based partly on international statistical series compiled by United Nations agencies and partly on OPEC Secretariat estimates where these are more up-to- date. The dollar amounts given in these sections (and in all other sections of this book) refer to US dollars. The status of the 1984 economic statistics for most OPEC countries remained provisional in mid-1986. No reliable economic statistics have been available for Iran and Iraq since 1980, and the 1984 estimates shown for these countries should be treated with particular caution.

It lies beyond the scope of this book to provide detailed information on many of the oil companies mentioned in the text: a comprehensive reference source in this field is the *Financial Times Oil and Gas International Year Book*, published by Longman.

Particular acknowledgment should be made to *Keesing's Contemporary Archives*, whose original coverage of OPEC and related matters provided a starting-point for the content of the present volume and whose standards of objectivity, balance and thoroughness the present author has sought to emulate. Thanks are also due to Allan Lamb of Longman for drawing the maps.

September 1986   *JE*

ABOUT THE AUTHOR. John Evans, a former associate editor of *Keesing's Contemporary Archives*, is a specialist writer on the international energy market, with particular reference to the affairs of OPEC and the oil-producing countries.

KEESING'S REFERENCE PUBLICATIONS. The KRP series of books has been developed as an adjunct to *Keesing's Contemporary Archives* (retitled *Keesing's Record of World Events* from January 1987), the monthly current affairs reference service which over the last 55 years has established an unrivalled reputation for the accuracy and objectivity of its coverage of world events. Other titles available in the series are:

Border and Territorial Disputes (1982)

Political Dissent: An International Guide to Dissident, Extra-Parliamentary, Guerrilla and Illegal Political Movements (1983)

Political Parties of the World (2nd edition, 1984)

State Economic Agencies of the World (1985)

Maritime Affairs—A World Handbook (1985)

Latin American Political Movements (1985)

Communist and Marxist Parties of the World (1986)

Peace Movements of the World (1986)

Treaties and Alliances of the World (4th edition, 1986)

List of Abbreviations/Acronyms for Oil Company Names

Adco	Abu Dhabi Company for Onshore Oil Operations
ADMA	Abu Dhabi Marine Areas
Adma-Opco	Abu Dhabi Marine Operating Co.
Adnoc	Abu Dhabi National Oil Co.
ADOCO	Abu Dhabi Oil Co.
ADPC	Abu Dhabi Petroleum Co.
AGEC	Arabian Gulf Exploration Co.
Agip	Azienda Generali Italiana Petroli
AMIF	Ausonia Minière Française
Aminoil	American Independent Oil Co.
AOC	Arabian Oil Co.
Aramco	Arabian American Oil Co.
BNOC	British National Oil Corp.
BP	British Petroleum
BPC	Basrah Petroleum Co.
BRP	Bureau de Recherches de Pétroles
Casoc	California Arabian Standard Oil Co.
CEPE	Corporación Estatal Petrolera Ecuatoriana
CFP	Compagnie Française des Pétroles
CFPA	Compagnie Française des Pétroles d'Algérie
CPA	Compagnie des Pétroles d'Algérie
CREPS	Compagnie de Recherches et d'Exploitation de Pétrole au Sahara
CVP	Corporación Venezolana del Petróleo
DUMA	Dubai Marine Areas
Dupetco	Dubai Petroleum Co.
Elf	Essences et Lubrifiants de France
ENI	Ente Nazionale Idrocarburi
ERAP	Entreprise de Recherches et d'Activités Pétrolières
Iminoco	Iran Marine International Co.
INOC	Iraq National Oil Co.
IOP	Iranian Oil Participants
Ipac	Iran Pan American Oil Co.
IPC	Iraq Petroleum Co.
Jodco	Japan Oil Development Co.
KNPC	Kuwait National Petroleum Co.
KOC	Kuwait Oil Co.
KPC	Kuwait Petroleum Corp.
Lapco	Lavan Petroleum Co.
MPC	Mosul Petroleum Co.
NEDC	Near East Development Corp.
NIAM	Nederlandsch-Indische Aardolie Maatschappij
NIOC	National Iranian Oil Co.
NNPC	Nigerian National Petroleum Corp.
NOC	National Oil Corp. [of Libya]
Osco	Oil Service Co. of Iran
Partex	Participations and Explorations Corp.
PDTC	Petroleum Development (Trucial Coast)
PDVSA	Petróleos de Venezuela SA
Pertamina	Perusahaan Tambangan Minyak dan Gas Bumi Negara*
Petrogab	Société Nationale Pétrolière Gabonaise
Petromin	General Petroleum and Mineral Organization of Saudi Arabia

Petroven	Petróleos de Venezuela SA
QGPC	Qatar General Petroleum Corp.
QPC	Qatar Petroleum Co.
SN Repal	Société Nationale de Recherches et d'Exploitation des Pétroles en Algérie
SCQ	Shell Company of Qatar
SEHR	Société d'Exploitation du Gaz d'Hassi R'Mel
Sirip	Société Irano-Italienne des Pétroles
Sofiran	Société Française des Pétroles d'Iran
Sofrapel	Société Française des Pétroles Elwerath
Sofrepal	Société Française pour la Recherche et l'Exploitation des Pétroles en Algérie
Sonatrach	Société Nationale de Transport et de Commercialisation des Hydrocarbures†
Sopefal	Société Pétrolière Française en Algérie
SPAEF	Société des Pétroles de l'Afrique Equatoriale Française
Statoil	Den Norske Stats Oljeselskrap
TPC	Turkish Petroleum Co.

*Current name
†Original name

General List of Abbreviations

AFRA	average freight rate assessment
API	American Petroleum Institute
ASCOOP	Association Coopérative [France-Algeria]
ASEAN	Association of South-East Asian Nations
bpd	barrels per day
BTU	British thermal unit
C	centigrade
CFA	Communauté Finançière Africaine
CIEC	Conference on International Economic Co-operation
cif	cost, insurance, freight [= total import cost]
dwt	deadweight tons
ECA	European Co-operation Administration
EEC	European Economic Community
fob	free on board [= export valuation]
FPC	Federal Power Commision
GATT	General Agreement on Tariffs and Trade
GCC	Gulf Co-operation Council
GNP	gross national product
IEA	International Energy Agency
IEFR	International Emergency Food Reserve
IFAD	International Fund for Agricultural Development
IGAT	Iran Gas Trunkline
IMF	International Monetary Fund
IPE	International Petroleum Exchange
km	kilometres
kWh	kilowatt-hour
LDC	less developed country
LNG	liquefied natural gas
LPG	liquified petroleum gas
mcm	million cubic metres
MEEC	Middle East Emergency Committee
MGS	Master Gas System [Saudi Arabia]
mpg	miles per gallon
MSA	Mutual Security Agency
NATO	North Atlantic Treaty Organization
NGL	natural gas liquids
OAPEC	Organization of Arab Petroleum Exporting Countries
OECD	Organization for Economic Co-operation and Development
OPEC	Organization of the Petroleum Exporting Countries
SDR	special drawing right
tmcm	thousand million cubic metres
toe	tonnes oil equivalent
TRC	Texas Railroad Commission
UAE	United Arab Emirates
UNCTAD	United Nations Conference on Trade and Development
WPT	windfall profits tax [USA]

WORLD OIL AND GAS: AN OVERVIEW

A1—Summary of Basic Facts and Terminology

A1.1—Petroleum Geology

Petroleum (literally "rock oil") is generally believed to have originated through the chemical transformation of particles of organic matter which accumulated in prehistoric marine basins and were subsequently incorporated into sedimentary rock structures. Having been created at high temperatures in source rocks situated between about 1,500 and 7,500 metres below the earth's surface, liquid petroleum is forced upwards under pressure through porous rocks and seeps to the surface unless it is blocked by impermeable strata forming one of a number of types of geological "trap". Most reservoirs (i.e. porous strata containing trapped accumulations) have been found at depths of between 600 and 3,000 metres. Although the process of petroleum formation commenced hundreds of millions of years before buried land vegetation began to be transformed into coal, many of the oldest reservoirs were destroyed as a result of the erosion or faulting of overlying strata, and most of the world's known petroleum reserves have been found in 25,000,000- to 210,000,000-year-old rock structures, whereas most known coal reserves were deposited more than 280,000,000 years ago.

Petroleum is composed of hydrocarbon (hydrogen and carbon) compounds, of which many variants exist. Each deposit has unique chemical characteristics, and crudes differ widely in viscosity, colour and odour and in their content of such impurities as sulphur, nitrogen, oxygen, salt and various metals. Oil reservoirs contain varying proportions of associated natural gas, although gas is often found without associated oil. The ratio of liquid to gaseous petroleum in a particular reservoir is determined mainly by the depth (and therefore the temperature) of the original source rocks, the formation of liquid petroleum being less likely to occur as geothermal temperatures increase towards a critical point in the region of 150°C (associated with a depth of about 7,600 metres). At greater depths all petroleum is formed as gas, although ultimately each sedimentary basin has a "hydrocarbon floor" below which the geothermal temperature is too high to support the generation of hydrocarbons.

1

A1.2—Natural Gas

Natural gas contains mixtures of the alkane series of hydrocarbons (whose least complex constituent is methane), and is termed wet if it includes a high proportion of the more complex alkane compounds. Among these more complex compounds, butane and propane (which can be extracted both from wet gas and from crude oil) liquefy at temperatures only slightly below 0°C, remaining liquid under light pressure at normal temperatures. Butane and propane are widely marketed as liquefied petroleum gas (LPG) for fuel purposes. Another compound, ethane, is extracted mainly for use as a petrochemical feedstock. Some reservoirs contain gas which liquefies at atmospheric pressure and normal surface temperatures to form condensate or natural gasoline (a type of light oil containing a high proportion of pentane and other highly complex alkane compounds). Natural gasoline normally has a specific gravity rating (◊A1.11) of between 50° and 65° API. Condensates and LPG are together termed natural gas liquids (NGL) and are often included with crude oil in oil production statistics, although some producers categorize LPG as a refined product. Liquefied natural gas (LNG) is normal dry gas (consisting predominantly of methane) which has been artificially cooled to −161.5°C at atmospheric pressure for transportation and/or storage purposes. Under this degree of refrigeration methane occupies about one six-hundredth of its original volume.

A1.3—Non-Conventional Hydrocarbons

Kerogen (solid organic material which has not matured naturally into petroleum) is found within sedimentary rocks known as oil shales, from which liquid and gaseous hydrocarbons can be extracted by distillation, while heavy oil is sometimes found in the form of tar containing sand, clay and other impurities from which it can be separated using a hot water process. Coal can also be used as a raw material for the manufacture of synthetic petroleum. The production of oil from these sources is more costly than extraction from conventional reservoirs, although there is much research into ways of improving the economic viability of non-conventional oil sources.

A1.4—Extent of Hydrocarbon Resource Base

Suitable geological conditions for the formation of crude petroleum exist in about four-fifths of the world's 57,000,000 square kilometres of sedimentary basins, and many potentially petroliferous regions have yet to be thoroughly explored (although offshore waters and other high-cost exploration areas account for a growing proportion of the remaining potential). There are about 30,000 known oilfields, of which the 17 largest fields (each containing more than 10,000 million barrels of recoverable oil when first brought into production) account for 34 per cent of the total volume of oil discovered, while the 283 next-largest fields (each containing between 500,000,000 and 10,000 million barrels) account for a further 39 per cent of the total.

The great majority of fields containing more than 5,000 million barrels of recoverable oil were discovered before 1970. The average proportion of oil consumption which was "replaced" by reserves in newly discovered fields was about 60 per cent during the 1970s, although total additions to reserves, including new discoveries in known fields, were roughly in balance with current consumption. The discovery rate in the early 1980s showed little change from that of the early 1970s despite an intervening increase of more than 200 per cent in real terms in the level of annual investment in exploration work.

The majority of estimates made in the early 1980s put the world's total recoverable conventional oil resources, including oil already produced (totalling 544,000 million barrels by the beginning of 1985), at between 1,600,000 million and 2,000,000 million barrels. Nearly 40 per cent of the latter total represents projected future discoveries. It is generally agreed that non-conventional oil resources (i.e. in the form of oil shales and tar sands) are in principle many times greater than conventional resources, although in practice their short- and medium-term development potential is limited for technical and economic reasons. Estimates published in the early 1980s put the world's total recoverable natural gas resources, including cumulative production (totalling 38,700,000 million cubic metres by the beginning of 1985) at not less than 222,000,000 mcm, with an energy content equivalent to 1,464,700 million barrels of oil. Over 40 per cent of this estimated resource base consists of projected future discoveries.

A1.5—Classification of Reserves

In respect of known hydrocarbon deposits, the oil and gas reserves which are estimated to be recoverable by conventional means are described either as "proved" (using highly conservative criteria to establish the reasonable certainty of production under existing economic and operating conditions) or as "probable" (representing production which is likely to be achievable as a result of further exploration and development work and/or changed economic and operating conditions). The reserves:production ratio for a particular area at a given time indicates the number of years for which that area's current proved reserves will sustain its current annual rate of production.

A1.6—Main Sectors of the Oil Industry

The location and extraction of crude petroleum constitute the upstream end of the oil industry, while the processing of crude into various refined products, together with the marketing of these products, is known as the downstream end. Trading activities between the extraction and refining stages constitute a "midstream" area, which emerged as a distinct sector of the international oil industry in the late 1970s as increasing volumes of crude came to be marketed outside the formerly dominant "closed circuit" of integrated upstream and downstream interests controlled by the major companies.

A1.7—Oil Exploration

The principal technique used in oil exploration work is reflection seismography, whereby the characteristics of underground rock structures are mapped on the basis of responses to energy pulses transmitted from the surface. Geophysical surveying activity in a potentially oil-bearing area is often quantified in terms of the number of "line kilometres of seismic section" which have been mapped. Drilling for oil is based initially on exploratory or "wildcat" wells (of which an estimated 129,700 were completed in the non-communist world between 1971 and 1980, with an average success rate of about 10 per cent). Appraisal wells are drilled to establish the commercial viability of an oilfield which has been discovered by exploratory drilling, while development wells are drilled to establish an optimum pattern of production from a commercial field.

A1.8—Crude Oil Production

Primary production relies mainly on natural reservoir pressures ("natural drive") to force oil to the surface. Secondary recovery techniques involve the reinjection of associated natural gas or the injection of water in order to maintain these pressures for as long as possible. Gas which is not reinjected is generally burnt off or "flared" where facilities do not exist for its collection and processing.

The proportion of oil in place which can be extracted from a reservoir by primary and secondary techniques varies from 5 to 70 per cent (with a current world average in the range 30–35 per cent), and the use of relatively costly tertiary recovery techniques, including steam injection and chemical flooding, is required to maximize the productive life of a "mature" oilfield. It was estimated in the early 1980s that the world average recovery rate of oil in place could be increased to a maximum level of 40 per cent through the wider use of sophisticated recovery techniques. An oil well which has ceased continuous economic production but which still periodically yields small volumes of oil is known as a stripper well.

The average unit costs of commercial oil production in different regions are normally estimated on the basis of current operating expenses per barrel of production (which are minimal in the case of giant fields requiring relatively simple recovery techniques) plus an allowance for developmental expenditure undertaken to maintain or expand productive capacity in the longer term.

A1.9—Ownership of Crude Oil

A1.9.i—Royalty crude
The owner of the subsoil rights (i.e. the owner of the surface land in the US onshore sector and the national and/or provincial government or the sovereign in virtually all other countries) is entitled to a percentage royalty on crude produced from leased areas, normally payable either in cash or in kind at the discretion of the lessor. Gross production from an oilfield includes royalty crude and oil used in production operations, while net production excludes these elements.

A1.9.ii—Equity crude
Equity crude is that part of its net crude production to which a leaseholding producing company has full ownership rights at the wellhead.

A1.9.iii—Participation crude
The term participation crude was coined in 1972 to denote host-government ownership of a specified proportion of a leaseholding producing company's net crude production under agreements which took effect in several Middle Eastern OPEC countries at the beginning of 1973. Participation agreements involving preferential state purchasing rights over a proportion of net crude production were introduced in Britain in 1976, the exercise of these rights being suspended in 1985 when the state oil corporation was abolished.

A1.9.iv—Buy-back crude
Buy-back crude is participation crude which the producing company or its affiliates are entitled to purchase or repurchase from the host government.

A1.10—Oil Refining

After transportation to a refinery, either by direct pipeline or in the tanks of ships of up to 500,000 deadweight tons, crude petroleum undergoes its downstream transformation into a wide variety of hydrocarbon products. The basic cuts or fractions into which the crude is initially separated in a distillation column are (i) the light, "white" or top-end cuts, (ii) the middle distillates or medium cuts and (iii) the heavy, "black" or bottom-end cuts (also known as the residue). Primary distillation, or "topping", is based on the fact that each fraction has a different boiling point. After further processing the light fractions yield petroleum gases, gasolines and naphtha (the main liquid petrochemical feedstock, which is also obtained from middle distillates). The principal middle distillate products are gas oils (the basis of diesel fuel and higher-grade heating fuel) and kerosene. The bottom-end products include heavy fuel oils (e.g. for industrial plant), bunker oil for shipping, waxes and bitumen.

The products of the lighter refinery fractions thus supply mainly premium markets in which oil has virtually no competition (e.g. the motor fuels market) or in which its main competitor is natural gas (e.g. the synthetic chemicals market). In contrast, the principal heavy product—fuel oil for steam-raising—often faces strong competition from other commercial energy sources and, as a residual product, is less valuable than the crude oil from which it is refined (and which could in principle be burned unrefined as a "general" fuel).

A1.11—Specific Gravity and Relative Product Yields of Crude Oils

Crude oils are broadly categorized as light (paraffinic), medium (mixed-base) or heavy (asphaltic) and are precisely graded on a specific gravity scale devised by the American Petroleum Institute (API). Under this system water is allocated a value of 10° API and crudes lighter than water have progressively higher values (a 30° API rating being equivalent to a specific gravity of 0.876 at a temperature of 60° Fahrenheit). Crudes rated at 40° API and above are very light and those below 22° very heavy; between these values definitions of the gravities which constitute light, medium and heavy grades vary from country to country. For example, a 31° crude is termed "medium" in Saudi Arabia but "heavy" in Iran.

When conventional refining processes are used there is always a close correlation between the gravity of the crude input and the quality of the product output. Thus about 30 per cent of the yield of a typical 44° crude, conventionally refined, consists of the most valuable light fractions, leaving 40 per cent middle distillates and 30 per cent heavy fractions, while a 31° crude yields about 19 per cent light fractions, 31 per cent middle distillates and 50 per cent heavy fractions. Upgraded refining plant is capable of producing higher percentage yields of light fractions from medium and heavy crudes through a process known as cracking (usually involving the use of catalysts), whereby the heavier molecules of the feedstock are chemically reformed into lighter molecules. There was a significant growth in the use of this highly flexible process following the increase in crude oil prices in 1979–80, causing a gradual erosion of traditional "product-worth" differentials between lighter and heavier crudes.

A1.12—Sweet and Sour Crudes

Apart from differences in gravity, an important determinant of the relative worth of different crudes is their content of sulphur, which is costly to remove during the refining process. A crude containing negligible traces of sulphur is termed very sweet. Any crude with a sulphur content exceeding 1 per cent by weight is termed sour, and an exceptionally sour crude might contain as much as 7 per cent sulphur.

A1.13—Oil Stocks

Stocks of crude oil are held by oil companies worldwide and by governments in certain importing countries. Stocks of refined products are held by oil companies and by final consumers. The oil industry's minimum stock requirement includes oil within pipeline systems, oil held at export and import terminals and refiners' basic operating stocks of crude oil and holdings of products to meet seasonal swings in demand. Most Western oil-importing countries and some third-world importers introduced mandatory minimum levels of import cover after experiencing supply disruptions in 1973. Emergency stockholding requirements were in most cases imposed on commercial oil companies rather than being directly assumed by state agencies, and it was estimated that over 90 per cent of state-owned strategic reserves were concentrated in only four countries (the United States, Japan, West Germany and South Korea) at the beginning of 1985.

Commercial oil companies control sufficient storage capacity to carry very large discretionary inventories over and above their operating stocks and mandatory reserves, the utilization rate of this additional capacity being varied in accordance with the prevailing market climate. From 1975 to 1978 short-term swings in discretionary stock levels were closely linked to a cycle of OPEC price increases and freezes, while heavy competition to accumulate stocks was largely responsible for sustaining a progressive rise in prices in 1979–80. Repeated drawings on commercial oil stocks subsequently played a key role in depressing the level of demand for OPEC exports from 1982 to 1985.

Estimates of stock levels cover holdings in land-based storage facilities (and in some cases reserves held in floating storage in non-active oil tankers), but often exclude the vast seaborne stock of oil which is always in transit between exporting and importing countries. Insofar as there has normally been scope for a significant increase in the average steaming speed of the world's active tanker fleet since the mid-1970s, seaborne stocks constitute an effective buffer against limited supply disruptions.

A1.14—Measurement of Oil Production

The normal unit of measurement of oil production by volume is the barrel (originally a wooden container designed to hold 42 US gallons of oil at a temperature of 60° Fahrenheit). One barrel is equivalent to 159 litres or 35 imperial gallons. Average rates of production by volume are expressed in barrels per day (bpd).

To convert volume measurements into accurate weight measurements account must be taken of variations in the density of different crudes and oil products. For example, Algerian crudes, which are very light (42° and 44° gravity), had an average conversion factor of 7.86 barrels per tonne in 1983, while Venezuelan crudes, many of which are heavier than 31°, had an average factor of 6.89 barrels per tonne. The accepted world average conversion factor for crude oil (excluding natural gas liquids) is 7.33 barrels per tonne.

Approximate conversion factors for refined products (in barrels per tonne) include 8.47 for gasolines, 7.63 for middle distillates and 6.66 for fuel oils. Liquefied petroleum gases have a factor of about 11.65 and gas condensates a factor of about 8.5 barrels per tonne.

A1.15—Measurement of Energy Equivalence

Relative energy-use estimates based on the "equivalence" of different primary energy sources are compiled by various organizations applying differing criteria. It is generally accepted that such estimates are likely to contain margins of error of up to 10 per cent and that they should be treated as indicators of broad patterns rather than as definitive data.

Energy equivalence estimates published in the *BP Statistical Review of World Energy* are currently based on calorific values which equate the energy stored in one tonne of oil with that in 1.5 tonnes of coal, 3 tonnes of lignite or 1,111 cubic metres of natural gas. The same publication measures the oil equivalence of nuclear and water power by calculating the inputs required by an oil-fired power station to generate the same amounts of electricity. (An input of one tonne of oil produces about 4,000 kilowatt-hours of electricity in a typical modern power station with an overall generating efficiency of 34 per cent; the primary energy value of one tonne of oil is equivalent to about 12,000 kWh.)

A1.16—Petrochemicals

The main non-energy use of hydrocarbons is as feedstock for the manufacture of synthetic chemicals. The principal organic base petrochemicals are the lower olefins (ethylene, propylene and butylenes) and the aromatics (benzene, toluene and xylenes), while the four main categories of organic end-use petrochemicals are plastics, fibres, elastomers and detergents. The most important inorganic base product of the petrochemical industry is ammonia, which is used mainly in the manufacture of fertilizers. The transformation of base petrochemicals into end-use materials involves a series of intermediate processes during which new compounds are formed by chemical reaction.

The relatively simple production chain for the organic plastic polyvinyl chloride (PVC) involves (i) the separation of ethane from natural gas or refinery gases (or, if a liquid feedstock is used, the isolation of the naphtha fraction of petroleum); (ii) the "cracking" of ethane or naphtha to produce ethylene; (iii) the reaction of ethylene with chlorine to produce ethylene dichloride; (iv) the conversion of ethylene dichloride into a further intermediate compound, vinyl chloride; and (v) the polymerization of the latter compound to form PVC, which then serves as the raw material for the manufacture, by "continuous flow" methods, of a variety of synthetic goods. Stages (i) to (iv) would typically be linked with many related processes within an integrated complex producing an extensive range of base, intermediate and end-use chemicals.

A1.17—Oil Pricing Terminology

A1.17.i—Posted prices (USA)

In the US domestic oil industry posted prices for crude oil are individual refiners' standard wellhead buying prices for piped supplies from local producing fields. US domestic postings have been directly competitive with the export prices of non-US crudes since early 1981, when the Federal Government completed the phasing-out of a system of price controls which had held average domestic crude prices below prevailing world prices since 1973. Before 1973 federal import controls (introduced on a mandatory basis in 1959) had, in conjunction with established systems of output control in Texas and other important oil-producing states, held US domestic crude prices above prevailing world prices.

A1.17.ii—Posted prices (Middle East)

In the Middle East, posted prices for crude oil, as introduced by foreign exporting companies in the early 1950s, were initially these companies' standard fob selling prices for cargoes supplied to "arm's-length" customers (i.e. non-affiliated companies). By the late 1950s all international arm's-length trade was being conducted at discounts from postings, although the posted prices continued to be used to value Middle Eastern crude exports for tax purposes. Cuts in the major oil companies' Middle Eastern postings were the immediate cause of the formation of OPEC in 1960, which deterred the companies from making any further unilateral reductions in these postings despite a continuing decline in arm's-length realizations during the course of the 1960s.

The posted price thus became institutionalized as a tax-reference value rather than an actual selling price for Middle Eastern crudes, although it did indirectly establish a minimum selling price below which the foreign exporting companies could not make a post-tax profit on arm's-length sales. Conversely, the exporting companies stood to gain a higher share of the profits on Middle Eastern crude exports in the event of an increase in realized prices, as was demonstrated in 1972–73 when the companies' arm's-length realizations rose well above the postings which had been negotiated with host governments for tax purposes. This led to the Middle Eastern OPEC members' announcement of a unilateral increase in postings in October 1973.

With the subsequent extension of host-government control over production operations, official government selling prices became the focal point of the OPEC pricing system after the mid-1970s, while postings (derived from official selling prices) played a residual fiscal role in those Middle Eastern and African OPEC countries where the retention of foreign equity interests created a continuing need to apply a tax-reference value to a proportion of exports.

A1.17.iii—Official OPEC selling prices

Official fob export prices, fixed by member governments, were formally adopted as a basis for OPEC price administration from October 1975. Saudi Arabian 34° light crude, fob Ras Tanura, was used as the OPEC marker grade because of its high export volume and average quality, which made it well suited to serve as the central reference point in a differential pricing structure covering all OPEC crudes in the 27° to 44° API gravity range. However, the formulation and implementation of OPEC policy were ultimately dependent on sovereign pricing decisions by each member country (including Saudi Arabia), and the structure was frequently flawed by inconsistencies between individual member countries' official prices or by the non-observance of official prices. The difficulty of maintaining a viable official pricing system increased considerably in 1982, when it became necessary to introduce production controls as a price-support measure, and the system eventually broke down in 1985 after the requirement for both pricing and production discipline had led to acute conflicts of national self-interest within the OPEC area.

A1.17.iv—Spot prices

"One-off" consignments of oil, for prompt delivery on a specified date, are priced on the basis of free bargaining between buyer and seller. This form of trading constitutes the spot market for oil (the term market being used in a very general sense to cover a diverse spread of unregulated transactions). Published spot prices are more or less representative averages calculated by specialist reporting services which monitor a cross-section of open-market dealings.

Before the 1970s spot trading was largely confined to refined products, as virtually all international trade in crude oil consisted either of integrated transfers between upstream and downstream affiliates of multinational companies or of sales under long-term supply contracts. Little direct information was available on arm's-length contract terms when Middle Eastern crude postings began to be widely discounted in the late 1950s, and movements in realized crude prices were therefore monitored mainly on a "netback" basis by deducting estimated refining costs and crude oil shipping costs from the average prices paid by spot buyers for wholesale lots of products at Rotterdam and certain other major refining centres. Such estimates were assumed to provide a tolerably accurate reflection of general price levels in stable trading conditions, although it was recognized that the marginal role of the spot market gave rise to extreme price swings when the balance of supply and demand was disturbed.

The development of a limited volume of spot trade in crude oil during the 1970s exposed OPEC's official selling prices to direct comparison with open-market price trends. Information on spot product prices was meanwhile used in increasingly sophisticated netback calculations incorporating weighted averages of the "gross product worth" of specific grades of crude in different import markets (these calculations being of particular value in assessing the consistency of OPEC price differentials relative to the marker crude). The scale of open-market crude trading began to increase in 1979, when many companies were prepared to pay premium prices for substantial volumes of spot crude following a disruption of established patterns of long-term contract trading. A consequent spot-led escalation of official selling prices continued in 1980, when the developments of 1979 prompted further changes in the pattern of trade.

After 1980 spot crude prices fell below the increased official selling prices, which became subject to sustained downward pressure as international oil companies progressively reduced their dependence on long-term supply contracts to the extent that the spot market became a central trading channel for the first time. It was estimated that more than 40 per cent of international oil trade was routinely conducted on spot terms in the period 1983 to 1985, and that contract trading at discounted official prices accounted for more than half of the remaining trade volume at times when the OPEC pricing structure was badly out of line with spot values. With the decline in the effectiveness of upstream price administration by exporting countries, spot crude prices became increasingly responsive to movements in spot product prices in importing countries.

A1.17.v—Netback pricing

A decisive shift to demand-led contract pricing was initiated by Saudi Arabia in the latter part of 1985, when that country began to export substantial volumes of crude on terms whereby its fob realizations varied in line with the market value of the products refined from that crude, netted back through the supply chain by deducting the importing refiners' agreed profit margins as well as agreed allowances for the costs of shipping and refining. Movements in product values were reportedly assessed partly on the basis of the importing refiners' actual realizations and partly on the basis of published averages of spot product prices, although precise contract terms were not disclosed. The subsequent introduction of netback contracts or comparable market-related pricing formulas by other OPEC countries was accompanied by a significant reduction in the scale of the spot crude trade and a general collapse in oil prices during the first quarter of 1986.

A2—Commercial Exploitation of Hydrocarbon Resources

A2.1—Oil as a Minor Energy Source (to 1939)

Systematic exploration for deep oil reservoirs began in the 1850s following the invention of new mechanical drilling techniques. The main properties of hydrocarbons were well known at this time, some products (notably bitumen) having been used on a small scale throughout recorded history in areas where natural seepages occurred, while liquids had latterly been produced in Europe by distillation from oil shales. The USA's first commercial oil well was drilled in Pennsylvania in 1859, and production increased rapidly thereafter to supply a substantial market for kerosene, which was burned both as a source of illumination (in place of more costly and less efficient animal and vegetable oils) and, to a lesser extent, as a source of heat in place of solid fuels.

The lighter petroleum fractions, including gasoline, did not find a market until the internal combustion engine was developed towards the end of the nineteenth century. The residual fractions came into widespread use in the early twentieth century, when heavy oil began to be used in place of coal as a fuel for steamships. Non-marketable fractions were initially allowed to run to waste, although as production increased it became normal oil industry practice to "reycle" them back into oil wells after the separation of marketable fractions at oilfield topping plants. Considerable progress was made in the development of non-fuel products (e.g. lubricating oils) during the early decades of commercial oil production. By 1900 Russia had (temporarily) overtaken the United States to become the main oil-producing country; minor producers were Burma, Romania, Poland and the Netherlands East Indies. By the outbreak of the First World War production had commenced in Egypt, Iran, Mexico and Peru, while commercial deposits had been discovered in Venezuela.

After the First World War gasoline consumption was greatly stimulated by the growth in motor transport, while kerosene became a relatively less important product, demand for which was increasingly concentrated in the less developed areas. Heavy fuel oil came into wider use in industrial furnaces in those regions of the developed world where it could be obtained more cheaply than coal, although coal remained the dominant general fuel, supplying 80 per cent of the world's primary energy needs in 1929 (as against 95 per cent at the turn of the century). Oil accounted for 15 per cent of world energy consumption in the same year (compared with less than 4 per cent in 1900).

Between 1929 and 1939 there was an overall increase of nearly 50 per cent in the volume of world oil consumption despite a slight fall in demand during the economic depression of the early 1930s, whereas the level of coal consumption (which fell sharply during the depression) showed little overall change over the same period. The main decline in the relative importance of coal occurred in the United States, which relied on oil for over 30 per cent of its energy supplies in 1939 (when it produced 63 per cent and consumed 60 per cent of the world's oil output). West European oil demand (mostly from the transport sector) accounted for less than 10 per cent of the total regional energy demand in the same year.

A2.2—Oil's Attainment of Dominance in the Energy Market (1945 to 1973)

After the Second World War the level of coal production in many industrialized countries was insufficient to fulfil the fuel requirements of the post-war reconstruction programme and the subsequent period of economic expansion. Accordingly, there was

a progressive rise in oil demand which was met by increased output both from established producing countries and the newer producers of the Middle East. By the 1950s world oil consumption had resumed its pre-1930 rate of exponential growth, characterized by a doubling of total demand at intervals of less than 10 years. The main European and Japanese product demand was for fuel oil, while in the United States (where natural gas was an increasingly important general fuel) the main demand was for gasoline.

There was an overall growth in the level of world consumption of coal and other solid fuels of 40 per cent during the course of the 1950s but only 8 per cent in the 1960s, when it became increasingly difficult for West European countries in particular to sustain the existing output levels of their labour-intensive coal industries in the face of a rapid expansion of capacity in many established oil-exporting countries, coupled with the development of major oilfields in new areas (notably north Africa). By the early 1960s oil had become the non-communist world's largest single source of commercial energy (having attained the same position in the United States at the beginning of the 1950s), although fuel demand patterns varied considerably from country to country. In 1965 the degree of dependence on oil in the main importing countries ranged from 57 per cent in Japan to 39 per cent in the United Kingdom, where coal was to remain the dominant energy source until 1970.

By 1967 oil was the largest single commercial energy source in the world as a whole, with a 41.5 per cent share of total consumption as against 38.6 per cent for coal and other solid fuels, although there was a sharp contrast between the consumption pattern in the non-communist world (oil 48 per cent, solid fuels 29.9 per cent) and that in the communist world (oil 23.9 per cent, solid fuels 62.3 per cent). Within the communist bloc, oil became the main contributor to Soviet energy consumption in 1974, but energy use in Eastern Europe and China was still dominated by coal in the mid-1980s. With very few exceptions (notably India, South Korea, Taiwan, Zambia and Zimbabwe, all of which were coal producers) the countries of the Third World depended mainly on oil to fuel their economic development in the post-war period. Oil supplied 54 per cent of the aggregate commercial energy demand of non-oil-exporting developing countries in 1975, over half of the countries concerned being more than 75 per cent dependent on oil. Per-capita oil consumption in most third-world countries was, however, negligible compared with that in the industrialized countries.

In 1970 the overall growth rate of world oil demand was 8.6 per cent, then equivalent to 3,640,000 bpd in volume terms, with local growth rates of 17.8 per cent in Japan (which then accounted for 8.7 per cent of world consumption, as against 3.3 per cent in 1960) and 10.9 per cent in Western Europe (whose share of world consumption had risen from 18.8 per cent to 27.5 per cent between 1960 and 1970). In 1973 there was a record year-on-year increase in world oil consumption of 4,285,000 bpd. An even larger increase in demand was not fully satisfied because the available margin of non-Arab production capacity was insufficient to compensate fully for supply cutbacks by Arab oil-exporting countries during the last quarter of the year.

A2.3—The Changing Pattern of Oil Demand (post-1973)

Large price increases in October 1973 and January 1974 led to a 1.3 per cent fall in world oil consumption in 1974 (this being the first year-on-year decline in consumption since the Second World War). Pricing considerations now exerted a dominant influence on oil demand, which rose again from 1976 onwards (as the impact of the sharp price increases of 1973–74 was eroded by worldwide inflation) but went into a new decline after prices rose again in real terms in 1979–80. In 1980 an unprecedently large fall of 2,510,000 bpd in the level of world oil demand caused the first downturn in the world's total primary energy consumption since the Second World War. Oil now accounted for 43.5 per cent of primary energy use, compared with a peak level of 47.4 per cent in 1973; in 1950 its share had been 25.2 per cent and in 1960 31.2 per cent.

The so-called "oil shocks" of 1973–74 and 1979–80 (the first of which entailed an abrupt rise in expenditure on imported oil from about 0.5 per cent to about 2.5 per cent of gross world product and the second a rise to about 5 per cent of gross world product) prompted a fundamental reassessment of the pattern of energy use in the main consuming countries. Conservation programmes were introduced in many countries to discourage the wasteful and inefficient forms of consumption which had become prevalent during a long period of growing reliance on low-priced oil. A clear distinction was drawn between the "premium" uses of oil—e.g. in transport and in chemical manufacturing—and its use as a general fuel, and efforts were

Table 1 — Growth and distribution of world oil production, 1860 to 1985

Year	Annual world output (million tonnes)	Overall change from previous total (per cent)	Average growth rate per year of previous decade (per cent)	Selected national/regional shares of annual total (per cent)
1860	0.07	—	—	USA 98.
1870	0.8	+1,039	+27.6	USA 91.
1880	4.0	+418	+17.5	USA 88, Russia 11.
1890	10.4	+155	+10.0	USA 60, Russia 38.
1900	20.3	+95	+6.9	Russia 51, USA 43.
1910	44.6	+120	+8.2	USA 64, Russia 21, Eastern Europe 6, Asia 6.
1920	93.7	+110	+7.7	USA 64, Mexico 23, USSR 4, Asia 4, Middle East 2.
1930	199.4	+112	+7.8	USA 63, Venezuela 10, USSR 7, Asia 4, Mexico 3, Middle East 3.
1940	296.9	+49	+4.1	USA 64, USSR 11, Venezuela 9, Middle East 5, Asia 4, Mexico 2.
1950	532.1	+79	+6.0	USA 52, Middle East 17, Venezuela 14, USSR 7, Asia 2, Mexico 2.
1960	1,090.6	+105	+7.4	USA 35, Middle East 25, USSR 14, Venezuela 13, Asia 3, Canada 2.
1970	2,362.5	+117	+8.0	Middle East 29, USA 23, USSR 15, Africa 13, Venezuela 8, Asia 3, Canada 3.
1980	3,081.9	+31	+2.7	Middle East 30, USSR 20, USA 16, Africa 10, Asia 7, Western Europe 4, Venezuela 4, Mexico 3, Canada 3.
1985*	2,777.4	−10	+0.2†	USSR 21, Middle East 19, USA 18, Asia 10, Africa 9, Western Europe 7, Mexico 5, Venezuela 3, Canada 3.

*Estimated.
†Decade 1975 to 1985.

Table 2 — Cumulative oil production and remaining proved reserves (Dec. 31, 1984)

	A Cumulative production to end-1984 (million tonnes)	B* Share of cumulative world production (per cent)	C End-1984 proved reserves† (million tonnes)	D* Share of world reserves (per cent)	E* Reserves (C) as proportion of produc- tion (A) (per cent)
USA	20,575	27.7	4,400	4.9	22.9
Middle East	19,500	26.3	54,200	56.4	278.7
USSR/Eastern Europe/China	13,770	18.6	11,400	11.7	83.0
Latin America/ Caribbean	9,005	12.1	11,700	11.8	126.2
Africa	5,310	7.2	7,500	8.0	142.8
Asia‡/Australasia	2,585	3.5	2,500	2.5	98.2
Canada	1,905	2.6	1,100	1.2	59.4
Western Europe	1,500	2.0	3,300	3.5	224.6
World	74,150	100.0	96,100	100.0	130.1
(of which OPEC)	(30,550)	(41.2)	(64,800)	(67.2)	(212.7)

*Calculated before conversion from barrels to tonnes.
†Excluding oil shales and tar sands.
‡Excluding China.

made to increase the contribution of coal to the general energy market in areas where it had become more competitive with higher-priced oil. The increase in oil demand associated with a 5 per cent economic growth rate in the OECD area was about 2 per cent in the mid-1980s, compared with about 7 per cent in the early 1970s.

World oil consumption in 1983 was only 990,000 bpd higher than in 1973, the level of demand having fallen over this 10-year period by 23 per cent in Japan, 21.7 per cent in Western Europe, 13.8 per cent in the United States and 7.8 per cent in the non-communist world as a whole. (Oil consumption in the communist bloc, which was for the most part insulated from trends in market prices, increased by 39.6 per cent over the same period, with the result that the communist bloc's share of world oil consumption rose from 16.2 per cent in 1973 to 22.7 per cent in 1983.) In terms of product usage, the overall change in non-communist demand comprised a 32.1 per cent fall in fuel oil consumption coupled with a 3.3 per cent rise in consumption of all other products, whose share of non-communist oil consumption rose from 68.5 per cent in 1973 to 76.8 per cent in 1983. Coal consumption rose by 26 per cent over the same period in the world as a whole (25 per cent in the non-communist world), although the extent of the upturn varied considerably between different regions (e.g. from 22.2 per cent in North America to 4.6 per cent in Western Europe).

The "reverse oil shock" of early 1986—a price collapse which cut the net import costs of the main consuming countries by the equivalent of around 0.75 per cent of their aggregate gross national product—seriously undermined the competitiveness of high-cost alternative energy sources (particularly deep-mined coal) and was expected to cause a limited upturn in the use of oil as a general fuel, together with an increase in the rate of growth of oil demand in sectors such as transport. The fall in prices acted as a disincentive to new investment in high-cost oil exploration areas and severely impaired the commercial viability of non-conventional production from oil shales and tar sands (several pilot projects in this field having already been abandoned as uneconomic in the early 1980s).

A2.4—Position of Nuclear and Water Power in the Energy Market

The fastest-growing energy source from the 1960s onwards was nuclear power, which in 1984 supplied 3.9 per cent of total world primary energy consumption and contributed more than 5 per cent of the national energy supply in nine countries. Over 30 per cent of the world's nuclear power was generated in the United States, where it accounted for just under 5 per cent of national energy consumption in 1984. Estimates of the nuclear industry's long-term growth prospects were revised during the 1970s and early 1980s in the light of substantial reductions in the demand forecasts of most electricity generating authorities in the Western industrialized countries. At the same time there was an increase in public concern over the environmental hazards associated with the industry, which became an important political issue in many of these countries. Reassessments of nuclear expansion plans were undertaken in a number of countries following a major accident at a Soviet reactor at Chernobyl (Ukraine) in late April 1986. Water power, the only "non-depleting" energy source in large-scale commercial use, supplied 6.7 per cent of total world primary energy consumption in 1984.

A2.5—Natural Gas in the United States and the Soviet Union

Since the 1920s natural gas has been the world's largest commercial energy source after oil and coal. The marketing of significant volumes of gas produced in association with oil or discovered in the course of exploration for oil began in the United States in the late nineteenth century, when the first iron pipeline systems were built. Although there was a ready demand for this clean and efficient fuel the large-scale expansion of markets did not become feasible until the mid-1930s, when improvements in pipeline technology enabled high-pressure mains to be laid over long distances. The US gas pipeline system was rapidly extended after 1945, and by 1950 (when natural gas supplied over 20 per cent of the country's energy needs) a significant proportion of US hydrocarbons exploration was being undertaken with the primary aim of locating new deposits of non-associated gas.

Natural gas accounted for over 10 per cent of world energy consumption in 1950, although the volume of commercial production outside the United States (mostly in the Soviet Union and Canada) was relatively small. The high capital cost of pipelines acted as a barrier to the marketing of gas in some oil-producing countries, while in others there was no potential domestic market for gas at this time. Non-associated gas wells thus remained capped in many countries, while considerable volumes of associated gas were flared off as an unwanted by-product of oil production.

Within the United States the development of the gas industry was effectively controlled by the Federal Power Commission (FPC), which took responsibility for the supervision of all aspects of inter-state pipeline commerce in 1938. After 1954 (when the US Supreme Court ruled that the Commission had the power to regulate producer prices for inter-state gas supplies) the FPC required the prices charged for long-term contract supplies to industrial users to be fixed at levels related to the cost of pipeline operations (i.e. production costs were equated with operating expenses, without allowing for developmental investment to maintain or expand productive capacity, while producers' sales margins were comparable to those of public utilities). This policy resulted in very low consumer prices throughout much of the United States (with the exception of those regions whose supplies were piped for exceptionally long distances), which caused the country's consumption of gas to grow at a faster rate than that of any other energy source.

Gas displaced coal as the second largest US energy source in the late 1950s and was increasingly used in preference to oil in areas of the general fuel market which it could not have entered if it had been priced on the basis of its relative energy yield. Fuel oil thus accounted for a lower proportion of total product demand in the United States than in any other major oil-consuming country, causing US refiners to maximize their yield of lighter fractions to the extent that many parts of the country were substantially oversupplied with gasoline during the early 1960s. The contribution of natural gas to total US energy consumption rose from 29 per cent in 1961 to a peak level of 34.5 per cent in 1969. In volume terms gas consumption peaked in 1972, by which time supply shortages were already causing many industrial users to switch to fuel oil. Oil's share of total US energy consumption (which had remained at around 41–42 per cent from 1955 to 1970) rose to a peak level of 47 per cent in 1977 before declining to 40.2 per cent in 1984, while gas accounted for only 25.4 per cent of the total by 1984. Coal's share of US energy consumption, which had fallen from 28 per cent in the mid-1950s to a low point of 18 per cent in the early 1970s, stood at 24.1 per cent in 1984. About 40 per cent of the USA's marketed gas output remained subject to federal price controls in 1985, following the completion of a seven-year programme to phase out controls on production from most new wells.

The United States ceased to be the world's largest commercial producer of natural gas in 1983, when its marketed production amounted to 450,184 million cubic metres (29.1 per cent of world marketed output) as against the Soviet Union's 535,950 mcm (34.6 per cent). Soviet output had expanded rapidly since the 1950s, and supplied over 18 per cent of the country's primary energy consumption by the mid-1960s. Gas became a more important energy source than coal in the Soviet Union in 1981, and in 1984 it supplied 33.2 per cent of total Soviet energy consumption, as against oil's 36.1 per cent and coal's 27 per cent.

A2.6—Natural Gas in Western Europe

Natural gas became a minor energy source in Western Europe during the 1950s with the development of non-associated deposits at Lacq in south-western France and in the Po valley in northern Italy. After the discovery in 1959 of the first large-scale West European gas deposits in the Groningen province of the Netherlands, intensive offshore exploration work was undertaken in a wide area of the southern North Sea basin, where the first of many commercial gas fields was discovered in the British sector in 1965. About 11 per cent of the coal consumed in Britain at this time was used for the manufacture of town gas (which had less than half of the calorific value of natural gas), and the initial impact of the subsequent switch to natural gas was therefore borne by the country's coal industry.

Relatively low prices for natural gas in Britain during the mid-1970s caused some fuel-switching away from oil, but by the early 1980s Britain had adopted a policy under which gas was priced as a "premium" fuel. Elsewhere in Western Europe consumer prices for natural gas were generally comparable with oil prices on an energy equivalence basis. In mid-1986 the distribution of piped natural gas was controlled by public-sector enterprises in every European country except West Germany, whose market was open to private companies. (Britain, however, was in the process of legislating to create a private-sector monopoly.) The EEC countries agreed in 1975 to ban the construction of new gas-fired electricity

15

generating plants, with the result that only 12 per cent of West European gas supplies were used by power stations in 1982. The residential and commercial sector accounted for nearly 50 per cent of gas consumption in the same year and the industrial sector for about 30 per cent. The West European pattern of gas usage thus differed significantly from the US pattern of the 1950s and 1960s, which had been dominated by the industrial and power generation sectors.

Western Europe displaced Latin America to become the world's third largest gas producing region in 1967. The West European share of the world's marketed output of natural gas stood at 11.1 per cent in 1984, compared with 13 per cent in 1975 and 2.9 per cent in 1965. Natural gas accounted for 15.2 per cent of West European primary energy consumption in 1984, as against 13.1 per cent in 1975 and 2.3 per cent in 1965. The shares of the other main fuels in the same years were as follows: 1984—oil 47.3 per cent, coal 20.5 per cent; 1975—oil 56.8 per cent, coal 20.1 per cent; 1965—oil 47.4 per cent, coal 40.4 per cent. Gas was the largest single energy source in the Netherlands in 1984, supplying 46.8 per cent of consumption; elsewhere in Western Europe it was the second largest energy source only in Italy (18.9 per cent) and the source of more than 20 per cent of total energy consumption only in the United Kingdom (23.5 per cent).

A2.7—Natural Gas in the OPEC Area

Within the OPEC area Venezuela (then the Organization's largest oil producer) showed the greatest determination to reduce its wastage of associated gas during

Table 3 — OPEC area: natural gas production in 1966

	Gross output (mcm)	Flared* (per cent)	Reinjected* (per cent)	Marketed*† (per cent)	Exported‡ (per cent)
Algeria	4,200	26.8	26.5	46.7	25.4§
Ecuador	—	—	—	—	—
Gabon	—	—	—	—	—
Indonesia	3,162	83.9	—	16.1	—
Iran	17,909	92.2	—	7.8	—
Iraq	5,900	89.7	—	10.3	—
Kuwait	12,767	72.6	8.0	18.6	—
Libya	10,043	68.9	31.1	—	—
Nigeria	2,907	94.0	—	6.0	—
Qatar	1,924	76.8	—	4.3	—
Saudi Arabia	12,966	71.9	19.4	8.7	—
UAE¶	4,200	100.0	—	—	—
Venezuela	41,274	38.1	43.8	14.9	—
Total OPEC	117,252	64.2	22.0	12.2	0.9
(Total non-OPEC)	(851,748)	(0.3)	(6.9)	(84.9)	(1.9)
Total world	969,000	12.4	8.8	76.1	1.8
OPEC volume as percentage of world volume	12.1	62.7	30.4	1.9	6.2

*Percentages may not total 100 due to processing loss ("shrinkage").
†Including exports (if any).
‡Excluding natural gas liquids.
§Liquefied natural gas.
¶ i.e. Abu Dhabi.

the 1960s. The proportion of Venezuelan gas output which was flared off was reduced from 48.8 per cent in 1960 to 38.1 per cent in 1970, while the proportion which was distributed to industrial and residential consumers rose from 5.3 per cent (1,686 mcm per annum) to 15.9 per cent (7,710 mcm) over the same period as the country's pipeline network was progressively extended. The largest share of output (an average 43.7 per cent throughout the 1960s) was reinjected into oil wells to maintain reservoir pressures. Venezuela accounted for 28.2 per cent of OPEC's gross gas output (25.1 per cent of marketed output) in 1970. Of the remaining OPEC countries' aggregate gas output in that year, 68.7 per cent was flared, 18.7 per cent was marketed and 11.3 per cent was reinjected into oil wells.

After the sharp rise in OPEC oil revenues in 1973–74 many member countries made substantial new investments in gas gathering and processing facilities, among which Saudi Arabia's "master gas system" (designed to supply fuel and raw materials to the country's main industrial development areas) was one of the largest gas utilization projects in the non-communist world, with an estimated final cost of at least $15,000 million. Gas played a key role in the economies of several other OPEC countries in the Persian/Arabian Gulf region by the early 1980s, and in 1986 Kuwait began to import associated gas from Iraq in order to offset a shortfall in its own production. (Iraq had previously continued to flare over 80 per cent of its gas production, implementation of a major gas utilization programme having been delayed as a result of the Gulf war.)

About one-fifth of OPEC's aggregate gas output was flared in 1984, although

Table 4 — OPEC natural gas production in 1976

	Gross output (mcm)	Flared* (per cent)	Reinjected* (per cent)	Marketed*† (per cent)	Exported‡ (per cent)
Algeria	24,439	43.6	15.8	31.0	18.8§
Ecuador	288	89.2	—	10.8	—
Gabon	1,826	90.7	—	9.3	—
Indonesia	8,846	59.5	13.9	26.4	—
Iran	50,379	55.4	1.9	39.7	19.3¶
Iraq	13,268	84.1	—	13.6	—
Kuwait	11,208	38.5	11.8	34.5	—
Libya	17,947	23.2	50.2	26.6	23.6§
Nigeria	22,101	97.1	—	2.9	—
Qatar	4,730	68.8	—	23.1	—
Saudi Arabia	47,230	79.2	6.4	9.4	—
UAE	14,309	90.4	—	9.6	—
Venezuela	37,135	8.2	55.2	27.5	—
Total OPEC	253,706	56.6	15.7	23.0	7.1
(Total non-OPEC)	(1,398,449)	(3.2)	(2.4)	(85.1)	(8.2)
Total world	1,652,155	11.4	4.5	75.6	8.1
OPEC volume as percentage of world volume	*15.4*	*76.0*	*54.1*	*4.7*	*13.6*

*Percentages may not total 100 due to processing loss ("shrinkage").
†Including exports (if any).
‡Excluding natural gas liquids.
§Liquefied natural gas.
¶Dry gas.

Table 5 — OPEC natural gas production in 1984

	Gross output (mcm)	Flared* (per cent)	Reinjected* (per cent)	Marketed*† (per cent)	Exported‡ (per cent)
Algeria	93,821	6.1	51.5	37.3	20.3§
Ecuador	513	77.2	7.0	15.8	—
Gabon	2,109	84.3	12.3	3.4	—
Indonesia	43,083	8.7	14.6	76.5	44.1¶
Iran	30,500	21.3	32.8	44.3	—
Iraq	4,900	83.5	—	12.0	—
Kuwait	5,814	11.2	4.3	70.8	—
Libya	12,350	10.1	48.6	37.2	9.1¶
Nigeria	16,251	83.8	3.5	12.6	—
Qatar	6,800	0.7	—	87.2	—
Saudi Arabia	29,050	51.1	4.3	24.6	—
UAE	18,030	37.0	0.2	54.1	15.6¶
Venezuela	32,574	5.4	36.9	53.1	—
Total OPEC	295,795	20.6	28.7	45.0	14.2
(Total non-OPEC)	(1,731,572)	(2.3)	(4.4)	(89.6)	(15.6)
Total world	2,027,367	4.9	7.9	83.1	15.4
OPEC volume as percentage of world volume	*15.2*	*61.0*	*53.0*	*7.9*	*13.4*

*Percentages may not total 100 due to processing loss ("shrinkage").
†Including exports (if any).
‡Excluding natural gas liquids.
§Liquefied natural gas and dry gas.
¶Liquefied natural gas.

utilization patterns differed considerably from country to country, reflecting variations in marketing strategies, oilfield operating practices and gas processing methods. Tables 3, 4 and 5 give details of OPEC natural gas production in 1966, 1976 and 1984.

A2.8—Development of the Petrochemical Industry

The use of hydrocarbons as raw materials for the synthesis of organic chemicals began in the United States during the 1920s, when increasing volumes of feedstock became available in the form of the petroleum gases which were produced by oil refineries as part of the process of gasoline manufacture. Natural gas began to be used as a feedstock for the synthesis of ammonia in the 1930s. Organic chemicals had previously been derived exclusively from animal and vegetable matter or from coal, while the manufacture of ammonia (one of the most widely used inorganic chemicals) had been based exclusively on the use of coke gases as a feedstock.

By 1939 considerable progress had been made in the development of petrochemical manufacturing processes, although traditional raw materials continued to be the dominant source of chemical supplies while such items as lubricants, waxes, tars and asphalt remained the principal non-fuel products of the petroleum industry. Shortages of natural raw materials during the Second World War greatly stimulated the growth of the US petrochemicals industry, which began to manufacture rubber, detergents and various other synthetic products on a large scale and which by 1945 accounted for nearly one-third of the total US output of organic base chemicals.

Petrochemical manufacturing did not develop on any scale in Western Europe until the 1950s, when the European oil refining industry was greatly expanded to supply a regional energy market in which fuel oil demand significantly exceeded gasoline demand, thus enabling substantial volumes of naphtha to be produced from "surplus" light fractions for feedstock purposes. Japan became the third major producing area during the 1960s, when its petrochemical manufacturing capacity was rapidly built up for balance-of-payments reasons (i.e. to provide a source of oil-based export revenue which effectively reduced the net foreign exchange costs of crude oil imports). The average annual growth rate of world output of base petrochemicals rose from 15.5 per cent in the 1950s to 17 per cent in the 1960s as the unit costs of production were progressively reduced through increases in the size and efficiency of the highly integrated manufacturing complexes which were characteristic of the industry. Thousands of new organic compounds (the intermediate and end-use products of the industry) were developed, and synthetics displaced natural materials in the manufacture of an ever-growing range of goods.

During the 1970s the average annual growth rate of base petrochemical production slowed to about 5.3 per cent as a result of substantial increases in production costs at a time of reduced opportunities for market expansion. Apart from benzene, which continued to be produced in large volumes from coal, all of the main organic base chemicals were now produced almost exclusively from oil or natural gas. As regards inorganic chemicals, hydrocarbon feedstocks held an equally dominant position in the production of ammonia and carbon black, while a substantial tonnage of sulphur was produced as a by-product of oil refining and natural gas processing. About 5 per cent of world oil consumption was now used for petrochemical feedstock purposes. Synthetic materials remained competitive with natural materials in most final product markets (the higher costs of petrochemical raw materials in the 1970s being broadly balanced out by competing industries' increased fuel costs), but the scope for the further displacement of traditional materials by synthetics was now far more limited than in the 1950s and 1960s.

North America (which accounted for 42 per cent of world output) remained the largest centre of base petrochemical production in the mid-1970s, the balance of world output being contributed by Western Europe (31 per cent), Japan (14 per cent), communist countries (8 per cent) and other minor producers (5 per cent). Natural gas served as the raw material for a high proportion of North American production, whereas Japanese and West European plants continued to rely mainly on oil-derived feedstocks—it being estimated that 7.5 per cent of Western Europe's total consumption of crude oil was used for petrochemical feedstock purposes at this time. The OPEC countries' negligible contribution to world petrochemical production in the mid-1970s was mainly in the form of ammonia-based fertilizers, whose manufacture from natural gas feedstocks was one of the industry's least complex processes. Only Iran produced significant volumes of organic petrochemicals in 1976 (at a small ethylene/propylene plant fed by petroleum gases from the Abadan oil refinery), Venezuela having failed to overcome serious operational problems at an olefins complex which had been completed in 1973. Algeria completed a gas-based methanol plant during the course of 1976.

There was a sharp and sustained downturn in petrochemical demand in the non-communist industrialized countries after 1979, with the result that the aggregate output of base petrochemicals in North America, Western Europe and Japan fell to around 89 per cent of its 1979 level in 1980–81, with a further decline to 80 per cent of the 1979 level in 1982. A number of older plants were shut down in these areas in the early 1980s in order to bring productive capacity—which had continued to

19

increase as various major projects reached completion—more closely into line with demand.

In contrast, the late 1970s and early 1980s saw an expansion of petrochemical production in the Third World as many countries began to implement industrial development plans which had been drawn up in the early 1970s. Gas-based petrochemical plants were regarded as a logical focus for industrialization in those OPEC countries which had been flaring a high proportion of their output of associated natural gas, the availability of this low-cost feedstock being the key factor enabling such plants to compete with production from industrialized countries, where operating costs were generally lower. The OPEC countries' aggregate capacity to produce ethylene (the most widely used organic base product) stood at 726,000 tonnes per annum in 1981 (about 1.5 per cent of total world ethylene capacity at that time), subsequently increasing to around 1,312,000 tonnes in 1984.

After 1981 the rate of growth of OPEC petrochemicals capacity was governed largely by the availability of financial resources, some member countries being forced to postpone major development projects pending an upturn in their oil revenues while others were able to complete new plants on schedule. Saudi Arabia in particular made massive investments in this sector, and brought a number of major new plants on stream in 1985–86. The kingdom's total capacity to produce base, intermediate and end-use petrochemicals was targeted to reach 6,300,000 tonnes per year (around 4–5 per cent of world capacity) by the end of the 1980s.

The severe recession in world petrochemical demand began to ease in 1983, and in the following year total production of the main organic base chemicals was about 6 per cent higher than the previous peak in 1979. North America accounted for 39.1 per cent of the 1984 total, Western Europe for 32.7 per cent, Japan for 13.6 per cent and all other countries for 14.6 per cent. An estimated 10 per cent of Western Europe's crude oil consumption (and around 25 per cent of its lighter refinery fractions) was used as petrochemical feedstock in the mid-1980s.

A3—World Trade in Hydrocarbons

A3.1—Crude Oil and Refined Products

A3.1.i—Development of mainly product-based trade (to 1945)

Before the First World War international trade in oil was structured around product exports from refineries located in or near the main producing areas. Cross-border movements of crude oil were virtually unknown, not least because of the relatively high cost of transporting crude rather than products at a time when the average product yield per barrel of refinery throughout remained very low. The trade in oil products was initially dominated by the United States, which was exporting over half of its output to worldwide markets by the early 1880s. The Russian oil industry developed a major export capability in the mid-1880s, when the opening of a trans-Caucasian railway made it possible to ship oil from the Black Sea, and Russia subsequently established a dominant position in markets east of Suez while taking a substantial minority share of the European market. Russia's oil exports exceeded those of the United States between 1897 and 1902, when there was a temporary increase in Russian output to a level which was not equalled until the late 1920s (whereas the level of US output rose by more than 900 per cent between 1902 and 1927). The smaller exporters prior to the First World War were Burma and the Netherlands East Indies (which traded within Asia) and Romania (which traded within Europe).

Russian oil production was disrupted by the 1917 revolution, and exports ceased during the initial years of Soviet rule. Exports of refined products were resumed in the early 1920s, mainly to West European markets, and accounted for over 25 per cent of Soviet output and nearly 20 per cent of internationally traded oil by the early 1930s. The volume of Soviet oil exports declined after 1933, although the country continued to play a significant role in the oil market throughout the 1930s (supplying over 10 per cent of West European imports in 1939). The Soviet Union's temporary withdrawal from the world oil market after 1917 coincided with a rapid increase in exports from Mexico, which displaced the Soviet Union as the world's second largest oil-producing country from 1918 to 1926. The Soviet Union lost this position once more in 1928—this time to Venezuela, whose output was to remain either slightly above or slighly below that of the Soviet Union until the early 1940s.

Western-hemisphere producers accounted for over 80 per cent of the world's oil output during the 1920s and over 75 per cent during the 1930s, the United States alone being responsible for nearly two-thirds of the world total throughout the inter-war period. Venezuela and Mexico each exported virtually all of their output. Trinidad, Colombia, Peru and Ecuador were minor exporters, while Argentina and Canada produced only for their own internal markets. The United States continued to export more oil than any other country (supplying about 20 per cent of all the oil consumed in the rest of the world during the 1930s), although these gross exports were now partly offset (and, for a brief period in the early 1920s, were exceeded) by a substantial volume of oil imports. Most imports into the United States were in the form of crude oil (which began to feature in international trade after the First World War), whereas the country's exports continued to consist almost wholly of refined products supplied to European and Asian markets. In terms of its net trade in oil, the United States was displaced by Venezuela as the main western-hemisphere exporter during the course of the 1930s.

The greater part of Mexico's crude output was refined in the United States until the mid-1920s, when a progressive decline in Mexican production began to erode the country's surplus of crude oil over local refining capacity. During the 1930s

Venezuela became an increasingly important source of crude for refineries in the north-east of the United States, which in terms of maritime shipping routes were slightly closer to the southern Caribbean than to Texan oil ports on the Gulf of Mexico. The only refined product imported by the United States was heavy fuel oil (shipped mainly from the Netherlands Antilles, where Venezuelan crude was processed by two major export refineries). In 1939 the level of United States oil consumption was equivalent to about 95 per cent of the country's production, as against 90 per cent a decade earlier, domestic consumption having grown somewhat more rapidly than production during the 1930s while incremental demand in many traditional US export markets had been increasingly met by other producers (notably by Venezuela in West European markets).

Iran played an increasingly important role in eastern-hemisphere oil trade during the inter-war period, becoming a larger producer than the Netherlands East Indies after the early 1920s and a larger exporter than the Soviet Union after 1933. Iran was responsible for nearly two-thirds of Middle East oil production in 1939, the minor producers being Iraq (which had no export capability until 1934, when its first Mediterranean pipelines were completed), Bahrain (which also began exporting in 1934) and Saudi Arabia (where small-scale production began in 1938). Middle East oil was exported to markets throughout the eastern hemisphere. The only African production in 1939 was in Egypt, then a net importer of oil. In Asia the main producer and exporter continued to be the Netherlands East Indies; Burma, Brunei and Sarawak were minor oil exporters, while Japan and India were net importers. The Soviet Union and Romania continued to be Europe's only oil-exporting countries. Minor producers among the net importing countries of Western Europe included Germany and Austria.

There was a gradual increase in the import of crude oil into Western Europe and Japan during the 1930s as oil consumption in several countries began to reach levels which provided a viable basis for the limited introduction of "market-oriented" refining. There was, however, little scope for any major expansion of local refinery capacity so long as the structure of product demand in these markets continued to be heavily biased towards the lighter petroleum fractions (whose large-scale production would have necessitated the unprofitable re-export of considerable quantities of surplus fuel oil). The greater part of the world's refining capacity continued to be concentrated within the main producing areas, and in 1939 North America accounted for over 70 per cent of all capacity outside the Soviet Union and Eastern Europe, while Latin America and the Caribbean accounted for 13 per cent and the Middle East for 6 per cent. Only 6.5 per cent of capacity was located in Western Europe, and refined products constituted three-quarters of the region's 1939 oil imports.

The impact of the Second World War on oil production varied from region to region in accordance with the military situation. An overall increase of 28 per cent in the level of world oil output between 1939 and 1945 reflected the demands of the war economy on oilfields in "secure" areas, whereas many installations in more vulnerable areas were disabled in order to prevent the possibility of their falling into enemy hands in an operable condition. The main destruction of production facilities occurred in connexion with the German invasion of the Soviet Union and the Japanese occupation of the Netherlands East Indies and other Asian producing countries. Seaborne trade in oil was severely disrupted in many regions of the world, and production from Venezuela's "secure" fields fell below its pre-war level in 1940, 1942 and 1943 partly because of wartime constraints on the shipment of exports.

Production in the Middle East declined in 1940 and 1941 but recovered sharply thereafter to stand at 162 per cent of its pre-war level in 1945. The Iranian oilfields came under Allied control in mid-1941, and the capacity of Iran's Abadan refinery was greatly expanded to supply aviation fuel and other products for military use on several fronts. Iraqi production facilities were also placed under Allied military control in 1941 and, despite certain political difficulties in securing effective control over pipeline transit facilities in Syria and Lebanon, were used to supply crude oil to Palestine's Haifa refinery, which had opened in 1939 and was expanded between 1941 and 1944. In Saudi Arabia, whose crude output continued to be processed in Bahrain throughout the war, the construction of the Ras Tanura refinery—regarded as a high military priority by the US Government—commenced in 1944, enabling the plant to start production in late 1945. Wartime conditions permitted little new exploration work in the established Middle Eastern producing countries and precluded any development of the oilfields which had been discovered in Kuwait and Qatar in 1938–39.

A3.1.ii—The shift to mainly crude-based trade (1945 to 1960)

World oil output grew at an average annual rate of 7.8 per cent between 1945 and 1950 in response to heavy post-war demand in the main industrialized countries. The United States, which became a net importer of oil in 1948, was by 1950 importing over five times as much oil as in 1939 (its exports having meanwhile declined to less than 60 per cent of their pre-war level). The volume of US net imports was equivalent to 8.5 per cent of the country's oil consumption in 1950. Venezuela (whose annual oil exports more than tripled in volume during the course of the 1940s) continued to be the main supplier of US imports, although some Middle Eastern crude began to reach the US market in the late 1940s. From 1953 onwards crude was piped to the United States from western Canada, where the first of several major new oilfields had been discovered in 1947.

The Soviet Union, which was obliged to import some refined products from Romania in the immediate post-war period, regained its traditional position as a self-sufficient producer during the late 1940s, when the main focus of its oil development shifted from the long-established fields in the Caucasus to new fields in the Volga-Urals basin. The Soviet Union's total oil output in 1950 was, however, little more than half of that of Venezuela, which was to remain the world's second largest producer throughout the 1950s. The export of Soviet oil in the late 1940s and early 1950s was largely confined to markets within the communist bloc. Although West European import demand continued to be met partly by the main pre-war suppliers (Venezuela and the United States), the region's fastest-growing supply source in the late 1940s was the Middle East. Apart from Iraq, which lost part of its export capacity as a result of the closure of the Haifa pipeline in 1948, all of the established Middle Eastern producing countries greatly expanded their output between 1945 and 1950, while oilfields in Kuwait and Qatar were brought into production for the first time. By 1950 the Middle East had become the world's largest oil-exporting region, although no single Middle Eastern country's exports were to exceed those of Venezuela for a further 20 years.

During the 1950s the level of West European oil consumption increased by about 220 per cent, while the region's share of world consumption rose from 11.6 per cent in 1950 to 18.8 per cent in 1960. The post-war shift towards fuel oil as the main component of regional product demand provided the basis for a considerable expansion of local refinery capacity, which grew by 365 per cent over the same period and accounted for 16.2 per cent of world capacity at the end of 1959, as against 7.4 per cent 10 years earlier. Nearly 90 per cent of West European oil imports were in the form of crude in 1960, product imports having been reduced to the minimum level necessary to compensate for deficits in the output pattern of local refineries. The 1950s saw a similar shift towards local refining in Japan, which provided the world's fastest growing market for crude oil imports and which by 1960 had become the fifth largest oil-consuming country (after the United States, the Soviet Union, the United Kingdom and Canada).

About 80 per cent of the crude oil imported by West European and Japanese refineries in 1960 came from the Middle East, which was then responsible for more than a quarter of world oil production. The region's aggregate output level tripled during the course of the 1950s, when particularly high average growth rates were recorded in Iraq, Kuwait and Qatar (the countries whose productive capacity was expanded most rapidly in the early part of the decade to compensate for the temporary cessation of Iranian exports). Iran, which had produced 38 per cent of Middle Eastern oil output in 1950, accounted for only 20 per cent of the regional total in 1960. The Middle East's two main producers in 1960 were Kuwait (31.2 per cent) and Saudi Arabia (23.7 per cent), each of which also had a half-interest in the output of the jointly held Neutral Zone (some 2.8 per cent of the regional total). Saudi Arabia, whose oil had hitherto been exported only from the Persian/Arabian Gulf, acquired a second export route via the eastern Mediterranean when the trans-Arabian pipeline was opened in late 1950, while Iraq, hitherto wholly dependent on pipeline routes from its northern oilfields to the eastern Mediterranean, began to ship a proportion of its exports via the Gulf when its southern oilfields were brought into production in late 1951. Exports to Europe from the western Mediterranean began in 1958, when Algeria's Saharan oilfields were brought into production. Elsewhere in Africa, oil production began in Gabon in 1957 and in Nigeria in 1958.

The Soviet Union's oil production overtook that of Venezuela in 1960, having grown at an average annual rate of 14.6 per cent during the 1950s. Shipments of crude oil and refined products from the Soviet Union to the non-communist world increased substantially after 1955, and less than one-third of Soviet oil exports were going to other communist-bloc countries by the end of the decade. Nearly 10 per cent of Western Europe's oil imports were supplied by the Soviet Union in 1960, the other main non-communist importers of Soviet oil being Japan and various third-world countries. Indonesia (the former Netherlands East Indies), which remained the only substantial Asian oil exporter in the post-war period, supplied an increasing proportion of its output to the Japanese market during the 1950s. By 1960 China had become the second largest Asian producer, although it continued to rely on imports to supply over a quarter of its very limited oil consumption, then amounting to less than 0.7 per cent of world consumption.

The annual rate of increase in US oil production during the 1950s averaged 2.7 per cent, compared with average production growth of 10.8 per cent per annum in the rest of the world; in the same period consumption increased at average annual rates of 3.7 per cent in the United States and 10.7 per cent in the rest of the world. There was a consequent decline in the US share of total world oil production from 51.9 per cent in 1950 to 35.2 per cent in 1960, coupled with a decline in the US share of world consumption from 60.3 per cent to 44 per cent over the same period. Canada and the Latin American/Caribbean region together accounted for 20.3 per cent of world production and 11.5 per cent of world consumption in 1960 (these shares being slightly higher than in 1950). The western hemisphere as a whole thus produced and consumed 55.5 per cent of the world's oil in 1960 as against 71.5 per cent in 1950.

The United States was the world's largest single importer of oil in the late 1950s, when its import volume was equal to about half of that of the whole of Western Europe. About 10 per cent of US crude oil imports came from Canada, about 27 per cent from the Middle East and most of the balance from Venezuela. Over 40 per cent of the heavy fuel oil used in the eastern United States was imported from

Caribbean refineries using mainly Venezuelan crudes. A mandatory quota system was introduced by the Federal Government in 1959 to regulate the future growth of crude and product imports from all countries other than Canada and Mexico (which was exporting negligible volumes of oil at this time). The aim of this policy was to maintain at around 80 per cent the proportion of US consumption which was met from domestic production.

Table 6 — Regional shares of world refinery capacity, 1949 to 1984 (per cent)

	1949	1959	1969	1979	1984
North America	60.3	46.6	27.9	25.3	23.0
Latin America/Caribbean	12.0	11.6	10.8	10.8	10.6
USSR/Eastern Europe/China	9.7	13.6	15.4	18.5	22.7
Middle East	7.9	5.9	4.8	4.4	4.8
Western Europe*	7.4	16.2	28.6	25.6	21.2
Asia†/Australasia	2.1	3.0	4.9	6.3	7.6
Japan	0.3	2.6	6.1	6.6	6.7
Africa	0.3	0.5	1.5	2.5	3.4
Total world capacity (bpd)	*11,700*	*24,570*	*46,860*	*80,075*	*74,690*
Change from previous total (per cent)	*—*	*+110.0*	*+90.7*	*+70.9*	*−6.7*

*Including Yugoslavia.
†Excluding China and Japan.

A3.1.iii—Growing dominance of eastern-hemisphere exporting countries (1960 to 1970)

The growth rate of the world oil industry during the 1960s was the highest for 50 years. Crude oil was now the most important commodity in international trade, and by 1965 the world's oil tanker fleet (whose total capacity exceeded 90,000,000 deadweight tons, as against 26,670,000 dwt in 1950) accounted for over one-third of all merchant shipping. There was a progressive increase in the capacity of the largest ocean tankers—which had stood at about 32,500 dwt in the early 1950s—as shipowners sought to maximize the economies of scale which could be achieved in the transportation of the ever-increasing volumes of oil which they were handling. The first very large crude carriers of more than 205,000 dwt came into service in 1966, while ultra-large crude carriers of more than 285,000 dwt were introduced in 1970 (by which time the total capacity of the world tanker fleet exceeded 151,000,000 dwt).

The rapid growth of eastern-hemisphere demand for imported crude oil continued to be a dominant feature of the oil market between 1960 and 1970. Over this period Western Europe increased the level of its oil consumption by a further 220 per cent and expanded its refinery capacity by 270 per cent, while Japan increased its consumption by 484 per cent (making it the world's largest oil importer and third largest consuming country) and expanded its refinery capacity by 336 per cent. The level of crude production rose by 165 per cent in the Middle East during the 1960s, while Africa increased its output by more than 2,000 per cent to supersede Latin America and the Caribbean as the world's second largest exporting region. Within the Middle East, Saudi Arabia's production overtook that of Kuwait in 1966, while Iran moved ahead of Saudi Arabia in the following year. Production began for the first time in Abu Dhabi in 1962, in Oman in 1967, in Syria in 1968 and in Dubai in

1969. The main factor in Africa's oil development during the 1960s was the very fast growth of production in Libya, which became the world's sixth largest oil-producing country in 1968, seven years after its entry into the market, and which exported more crude oil than any other country in 1969 (although its exports of refined products were negligible). Nigeria overtook Algeria to become the second largest African producer in 1970. African oil was mainly exported to Western Europe at this time.

A 140 per cent increase in the level of Soviet oil production during the 1960s was accompanied by a major expansion of the Soviet Union's crude oil pipeline network both within its own borders and within neighbouring Eastern European states. At the same time natural gas was developed as an increasingly important component of Soviet energy consumption, thus enabling the Soviet Union to maintain its role as a substantial exporter of oil to non-communist countries. Crude oil, as opposed to products, formed a growing proportion of such exports.

The main developments in oil trade within the communist world in the 1960s were (i) Cuba's switch to dependence on Soviet oil (which replaced imports from Venezuela from 1960 onwards); (ii) the cessation of Soviet oil exports to China in the middle of the decade, which caused China to expand its own oil production to the point of self-sufficiency; and (iii) an overall increase (to rather more than 50 per cent) in the communist bloc's share of total Soviet oil exports. Various official co-operation agreements negotiated in the late 1960s provided for the supply of limited volumes of Middle Eastern oil to East European countries, including Romania (which was now a net importer of oil).

The wide gap between oil industry growth rates inside and outside the United States narrowed very slightly during the 1960s, when production increased by an average 3.4 per cent per annum in the USA, compared with 10 per cent per annum in the rest of the world, while consumption increased at average annual rates of 4.2 per cent within the USA and 10.5 per cent in the rest of the world. Net imports of oil into the United States increased at an average rate of 6.7 per cent per annum, and supplied over 23 per cent of the country's consumption in 1970, as against less than 19 per cent in 1960—a considerably smaller increase than that which could have been expected to occur if import quotas had not been in force. (It was generally estimated, on the basis of comparisons of production costs inside and outside the United States, that up to half of the output of the US oil industry would have been uncompetitive with freely imported oil during the 1960s.) Under the regime of import restrictions, the utilization rate of the US oil industry's productive capacity, which had fallen to a post-war low point of 62 per cent in 1958 in the face of price competition both from imported oil and from domestic natural gas, rose to 89.3 per cent in 1970, while the US reserves:production ratio fell from about 12:1 in the early 1960s to 9.3:1 at the beginning of 1970.

Elsewhere in the western hemisphere, Canada took advantage of its exemption from US import quotas to increase the exports made by pipeline from western Canada to about the same level as eastern Canada's oil imports from the Middle East and the Caribbean region. Venezuela, which was subject to quota restrictions on the growth of its exports to the United States at a time when its oil was facing increasingly keen price competition in other markets, experienced a fall in the average annual growth rate of its exports from 4 per cent between 1960 and 1965 to 1.3 per cent between 1965 and 1970. (This decline was not, however, attributable solely to marketing problems, as the oil industry's production decisions were also influenced by changes in the political and fiscal environment in Venezuela during the 1960s.) Apart from Ecuador, the smaller oil producers of the Latin American/Caribbean region (Mexico, Argentina, Colombia, Brazil, Trinidad, Peru, Chile and Bolivia) all increased their output during the course of the 1960s

Table 7 — United States oil statistics, 1960 to 1970

	1960	1961	1962	1963	1964	1965	1966	1967	1968	1969	1970
Production* (million tonnes)	384.1	392.5	401.0	414.0	420.9	431.2	458.0	487.9	506.7	515.1	537.5
Share of world production (per cent)	35.2	33.8	31.8	30.6	28.8	27.6	27.0	26.8	25.4	24.0	22.8
Consumption (million tonnes)	460.4	478.0	498.2	513.0	527.2	548.9	575.7	595.8	635.5	667.8	694.6
Share of world consumption (per cent)	44.0	42.2	40.9	38.9	37.1	35.9	35.0	33.7	33.0	31.8	30.4
Exports (million tonnes)	10.0	9.0	9.0	11.0	11.0	10.0	10.0	16.0	12.0	12.0	14.0
Imports (million tonnes)	95.0	99.0	108.0	110.0	117.0	127.0	133.0	131.0	147.0	163.0	176.0
Production as proportion of consumption (per cent)	81.2	82.1	80.5	80.7	79.8	78.6	79.6	81.9	79.7	77.1	77.4
Utilization of installed production capacity (per cent)	66.2	66.2	66.7	69.6	69.5	70.1	74.4	78.0	80.5	83.6	89.3

*Including natural gas liquids.

and together accounted for 28.4 per cent of the region's production in 1970 as against 23.7 per cent in 1960. The greater part of their output was, however, consumed internally, and Venezuela remained the region's only substantial net exporter in 1970.

By 1970 the western hemisphere accounted for 39.6 per cent of world oil consumption (USA 30.4 per cent) and 37.3 per cent of world oil production (USA 22.8 per cent), and was absorbing net imports of oil from the eastern hemisphere at an estimated rate of more than 500,000 bpd. The emergence of the eastern hemisphere as the dominant producing and consuming area during the 1960s owed much to the existence of a large surplus of productive capacity which had first become apparent in the late 1950s and which had overhung the main eastern-hemisphere import markets after the introduction of US import controls in 1959. The availability of substantial incremental oil supplies at highly competitive prices greatly accelerated the penetration of oil into the general fuels sector of these markets, and a precipitate rundown of the West European coal industry was prevented only by state intervention of various kinds. (Nuclear power made a negligible contribution to eastern-hemisphere energy consumption at this stage, while significant volumes of natural gas did not begin to become available in eastern-hemisphere oil-importing countries until the late 1960s.) The stimulation of eastern-hemisphere import demand by virtue of the ready availability of low-cost oil supplies continued throughout the 1960s as African oil production was expanded to meet an increasing proportion of incremental consumption in Western Europe. Middle Eastern producers maintained an aggregate production growth rate averaging more than 10 per cent per annum by exporting a higher percentage of their output to Japan.

A3.1.iv—Supply constraints and price rises (1970 to 1973)

During the second half of 1970 there was a downturn in the shipment of "short-haul" crude to Western Europe from Mediterranean export terminals as a result of Libyan production cutbacks and the temporary closure of the trans-Arabian pipeline. Concurrently, the shipment of incremental supplies from the Persian/Arabian Gulf region was hampered by a severe shortage of tankers, relatively few of the new vessels ordered in the aftermath of the closure of the Suez Canal in 1967 having been delivered at this point. This temporary constriction of the flow of oil to Western Europe (the destination of half of all world oil exports) occurred at a time of exceptionally high growth in demand in the eastern hemisphere and provided an opportunity for the OPEC countries (whose share of world oil output was approaching 50 per cent) to use their increased bargaining power to secure significant increases in their unit revenues. The West European supply situation returned to normal during the course of 1971.

By the end of 1972 increasing pressure was being placed on the surplus of productive capacity which had underpinned the expansion of world trade in oil since the late 1950s. The main cause of the erosion of surplus capacity was a radical change in the energy situation in the United States, where domestic production of oil from the lower 48 states had peaked in 1970 while the start of large-scale production in Alaska (from new oilfields discovered in the late 1960s) was delayed until mid-1977. There was an overall decline of more than 14 per cent in the level of US crude output between 1970 and 1976, as against an overall increase in oil consumption of 18.3 per cent which created a considerable additional demand for imported oil. The existing US import quota system was progressively relaxed from 1970 onwards and was ended in May 1973, by which time US domestic producers were operating all available wells at close to 100 per cent of capacity. Net imports increased by 124 per cent between 1970 and 1976, with the highest year-on-year rise of 33.4 per cent occurring in 1973 (when the United States displaced Japan as the largest oil importer). The level of import dependence (expressed as a proportion of US oil consumption) stood at 35.7 per cent in 1973, subsequently reaching a peak of 47.2 per cent in 1977 and remaining above 35 per cent until the early 1980s.

In 1973 net imports of oil from the eastern hemisphere into the western hemisphere averaged an estimated 3,800,000 bpd (about seven times their 1970 level), the western hemisphere's share of Middle Eastern oil exports having risen from less than 5 per cent in 1970 to more than 10 per cent in 1973, while its share of African exports had increased from about 6 per cent to nearly 30 per cent over the same period. There was a 57 per cent rise in the total volume of Middle East oil exports between 1970 and 1973, a 280 per cent increase in the region's exports to the western hemisphere being coupled with a 47 per cent increase in exports to its principal markets in the eastern hemisphere. Part of the incremental volume of Middle East oil imported into Western Europe was required to offset a fall of nearly one-third in the level of European oil imports from Africa between 1970 and 1973. Africa's total oil output fell by 3.3 per cent over this period (mainly because of continuing Libyan cutbacks which more than offset production increases in Nigeria), while African oil exports to the western hemisphere grew by 331 per cent. African oil supplied 13.7 per cent and Middle Eastern oil 13 per cent of the US import market in 1973. Imports into the United States from Canada nearly doubled in volume between 1970 and 1973, making Canada a net exporter of oil and increasing the Canadian share of the US import market from 20.4 per cent to 21.4 per cent. However, a relatively small rise of 27 per cent in US imports from Latin America and the Caribbean caused this region's share of the US market to fall from 62.5 per cent to 43.1 per cent over the same period, the main factor in this decline being a fall of nearly 10 per cent in Venezuela's oil output.

By mid-1973 the world oil industry had very little surplus productive capacity, and there was considerable competition among importers to acquire relatively small additional volumes of crude. The OPEC countries, then responsible for 53.9 per cent of world crude production and 86.9 per cent of world crude exports, announced substantial oil price increases in mid-October, followed by even larger increases in the aftermath of the supply shortages which occurred in the last quarter of 1973 as a result of politically-motivated cutbacks in Arab oil output. The sharp price rises arising from the changes in the balance of market forces during 1973 led to the first reduction in oil consumption in the main non-communist economies since the Second World War. In Western Europe (whose own oil production satisfied only 3 per cent of regional demand in 1973) and Japan (which was able to supply less than 0.3 per cent of its own market in the same year), a decline in oil consumption in 1974 and 1975 was directly linked to a reduction in oil imports, most of which were obtained from OPEC countries.

A3.1.v—Changes in the pattern of trade (1974 to 1979)

Whereas 1973 proved to be the peak year for OPEC oil exports to Western Europe and Japan, the upward trend in the supply of OPEC oil to the United States (mainly from the leading eastern-hemisphere exporters) was not reversed until 1978. Reductions in US oil consumption in 1974 and 1975 were more than offset by reductions in domestic oil production and cutbacks in Canadian export volume, which fell by 41 per cent between 1973 and 1975, restricting Canada's share of the US import market to 13.2 per cent in the latter year. Oil imports into the USA from Latin America and the Caribbean also fell in volume after 1973, and accounted for less than 38 per cent of the market in 1975. Overall, US net oil imports fell by 3.5 per cent between 1973 and 1975, while the country's imports from Africa rose by 54 per cent, its imports from the Middle East by 39 per cent and its imports from all OPEC countries by 11.5 per cent. By 1975 the western hemisphere accounted for

28.7 per cent of world oil production (USA 17.3 per cent) and 37.6 per cent of world consumption (USA 28.1 per cent), the estimated level of net imports from the eastern hemisphere being in excess of 5,000,000 bpd.

The non-communist world's oil consumption began to increase again in the period 1976 to 1979—although at a lower average rate (3.3 per cent per annum) than in the pre-1974 period—and peaked in 1979 at a level 6.8 per cent above that of 1973. The annual growth rate of West European consumption averaged 2.5 per cent from 1976 to 1979, while the region's imports, which rose by 8.8 per cent in 1976, fell at an average rate of 1.6 per cent per annum over the succeeding three years as Norway and the United Kingdom increased their output of North Sea oil, reducing Western Europe's overall dependence on imports to about 84 per cent in 1979. Japan, which was more than 99.8 per cent dependent on imported oil in 1979, increased its consumption by an average 1.1 per cent per annum and its imports by an average 1.3 per cent per annum between 1976 and 1979.

United States oil consumption increased at an average annual rate of 3.2 per cent from 1976 to 1979, while the overall increase in the country's net imports over the same period was equivalent to average growth of 8 per cent per annum (annual increases of about 20 per cent in 1976 and 1977 being partly offset by rather smaller decreases in 1978 and 1979). Middle Eastern oil exports to the United States peaked in 1977 (when they accounted for over 12 per cent of all Middle East oil exports and nearly 29 per cent of all US oil imports), while the Latin American and Caribbean region's share of the US import market fell to a low point of 26.3 per cent in the same year. The US share of African oil exports peaked at nearly 45 per cent in 1977, although the African share of the US import market did not reach its peak level of 29.5 per cent until 1979. The decline in Canadian oil exports to the United States ended in 1979, when Canada's market share reached a low point of 5.4 per cent. The fall in total US import demand after 1977 resulted from the opening of the trans-Alaskan pipeline in that year, which enabled the United States to reverse the prolonged decline in its domestic oil production. US output subsequently remained fairly stable during the period 1978–83 at an average level 4.9 per cent above the low point reached in 1976 and 9.9 per cent below the peak level of 1970.

The US share of world oil production reached its lowest-ever level of 14.9 per cent in 1979, while the western hemisphere's share of production reached a low point of 25.5 per cent in 1977 (when net imports from the eastern hemisphere averaged about 8,000,000 bpd). The fastest growing Latin American producer during the second half of the 1970s was Mexico, which increased its share of western-hemisphere output from 2.7 per cent in 1970 to 9.3 per cent in 1979 as newly discovered fields were brought on stream. Venezuela's share of western-hemisphere output fell from 20.8 per cent to 13.9 per cent over the same period. In 1979 the total oil production of the Latin American/Caribbean region reached a new record level above its previous peak in 1973, the downward trend in Venezuelan output (which was temporarily reversed in 1979) having been offset both by Mexico's re-emergence as a major producer and, to a lesser extent, by an increase in the combined output of Ecuador, Peru, Trinidad, Argentina and Bolivia, which rose by more than 80 per cent between 1970 and 1979. (Brazilian output showed little change over the same period, while production declined in Colombia and Chile.)

The United States ceased to be the world's largest oil producer in 1975, when its output was overtaken by that of the Soviet Union. Soviet production grew at an average annual rate of 5.5 per cent during the 1970s as new fields were developed in western Siberia, while the proportion of production which was consumed within the country fell from 74.5 per cent in 1970 to 72.3 per cent in 1980. The total volume of

Soviet exports to Western Europe was 38 per cent greater in the period 1976–80 than in 1971–75, although deliveries fluctuated considerably from year to year. On average, the Soviet Union supplied 10.5 per cent of West European countries' extra-regional oil imports between 1976 and 1980, compared with an average 7.1 per cent in the first half of the decade. China increased its oil output at an average rate of 14.1 per cent per annum during the 1970s (superseding Indonesia as the largest Asian producer in 1975) and began exporting oil, mainly to Japan, in 1973.

Middle Eastern oil output peaked in 1977, when the region accounted for 36.3 per cent of total world production. Saudi Arabia displaced Iran as the region's largest producer in 1972, while Iraq overtook Kuwait to become its third largest producer in 1976. Iran's production peaked in 1974 and that of Kuwait in 1972 (after which year the Kuwait Government introduced conservation measures). Among the region's smaller producers, Abu Dhabi's output rose by nearly 140 per cent between 1970 and 1977 but was cut back thereafter for conservation reasons, while Qatar's output peaked in 1973. African oil output reached its highest-ever level in 1979. Nigeria overtook Libya to become the continent's largest producer in 1974 (retaining this position in each of the 11 succeeding years except 1978), while Algeria remained the third largest African producer. Egypt became a net exporter of oil in 1976, the other non-OPEC net exporters in Africa in the late 1970s being Angola, Congo, Tunisia and Zaïre. Among the non-communist Asian countries, Malaysia became a net exporter of oil in the late 1970s.

A3.1.vi—Slump in demand for OPEC exports (post-1979)

A major factor in the resumption of growth in world oil consumption after 1975 was the relative stability of the real price of oil, which remained below its 1974 level until 1979 as further OPEC price increases were outpaced by inflation. From late 1978 onwards the disruption of Iranian oil production led to a steep rise in spot oil prices, although the underlying market balance was in many ways less critical than during the last period of temporary shortages in 1973, not least because of the recent downturn in US import demand and the continuing development of new capacity in non-OPEC countries such as Mexico and the United Kingdom. Increases of 13.2 per cent in the aggregate production of OPEC countries other than Iran, of 6.6 per cent in the aggregate production of non-OPEC countries in the non-communist world and of 2.1 per cent in communist production proved adequate to avert a serious oil supply crisis in 1979. However, at the same time the official prices of OPEC crudes began to rise very sharply in line with market prices for marginal supplies as OPEC member countries embarked on a series of "leapfrogging" price increases. This process continued until 1981, when Saudi Arabia (which displaced the United States as the world's second largest producer in 1980 and 1981) was able to end the upward pressure on prices by maintaining an exceptionally high rate of output in a weakening market.

The main effects of the new price rises were (i) to bring about a renewed emphasis on energy conservation and fuel substitution programmes in the main consuming countries, with the result that the non-communist world's oil consumption went into steady decline and had fallen below its 1975 level by 1982; (ii) to stimulate oil production in the non-OPEC countries of the non-communist world, whose aggregate output increased by 26.1 per cent between 1979 and 1985 while OPEC production fell by 45.3 per cent over the same period; and (iii) to alter the pattern of demand for different types of crude as the main exporters upgraded an increasing proportion of their refinery capacity in order to improve the yield of lighter products from heavier crudes. The emergence of a massive surplus of OPEC productive capacity, particularly for lighter grades of crude, forced the Organization (i) to reduce its basic official price in early 1983, (ii) to readjust its gravity differentials during 1985 in the context of further price reductions and (iii) to attempt to defend its pricing structure by restricting production, each member country having an agreed quota (or, in the case of Saudi Arabia, an implied quota) within a collective ceiling. The full utilization of productive capacity in Iraq and Iran had earlier become impossible after the outbreak of war between the two countries in late 1980.

Between 1979 and 1985 oil consumption fell by 16.6 per cent in the United States, by 20.8 per cent in Western Europe and by 24.1 per cent in Japan. The US share of world consumption fell from 27.8 per cent to 25.8 per cent over the same period, while Western Europe's share fell from 23.4 per cent to 20.2 per cent and that of Japan from 8.5 per cent to 7.2 per cent. Net oil imports into the United States, which declined by 45.9 per cent between 1979 and 1985, covered 27.3 per cent of the country's 1985 consumption (this being the lowest level of US import dependence since 1971). The USA's 1985 oil production was equivalent to 93.3 per cent of the peak level recorded in 1970, having risen by 8.3 per cent since 1976. The United States accounted for 17.9 per cent of 1985 world production (its highest share since 1973). Western Europe's net imports fell by 39.1 per cent between 1979 and 1985, a 73.8 per cent increase in North Sea output over this period having helped to reduce the region's level of import dependence to about 65 per cent by 1985. Japan cut its oil imports by 25.2 per cent over the same period while remaining almost wholly import-dependent.

US oil imports from the Middle East fell by 79.9 per cent between 1979 and 1985, while imports from Africa fell by 71.4 per cent and imports from Latin America and the Caribbean by 18.2 per cent. The Latin American/Caribbean and African exporting regions' shares of the US import market in 1985 were, at 41.3 per cent and 14.3 per cent respectively, broadly comparable to the same regions' shares in 1973–74, whereas the Middle Eastern share of 1985 US crude imports (8.5 per cent) was the lowest since 1970. North Sea oil supplied 9.7 per cent of the US import market in 1985, as against 4.2 per cent in 1979, while Canada's market share nearly tripled to 15.2 per cent over the same period. Net exports from the eastern hemisphere to the western hemisphere averaged rather less than 2,000,000 bpd in 1985 (comparable to the level of early 1972), the western hemisphere's share of world oil production having risen to 32.8 per cent by 1985 (close to its 1972 share of 33.3 per cent).

Western-hemisphere oil production showed an overall 3.9 per cent increase between 1972 and 1985, while eastern-hemisphere production increased by 6.2 per cent despite falls of 40.7 per cent in Middle Eastern output and 10.5 per cent in African output. Production in the communist bloc rose by 60.7 per cent over this period to account for 39.8 per cent of the eastern-hemisphere total in 1985 compared with 26.3 per cent in 1972, while Western Europe's production increased by 757 per cent and its share of the eastern-hemisphere total rose from 1.3 per cent in 1972 to 10.2 per cent in 1985. Output in Australasia and non-communist Asia grew by 71.5 per cent between 1972 and 1985, raising the region's share of eastern-hemisphere production from 5.3 per cent to 8.5 per cent, and there were significant increases in the level of self-sufficiency of several of the region's net importing countries over this period (e.g. from 30 per cent to 70 per cent in India and from 55 per cent to nearly 90 per cent in Australia). Mexico overtook Venezuela to become the western hemisphere's second largest producer in 1981 and its largest exporter in 1982.

Soviet oil production stood at 101.5 per cent of its 1979 level in 1985, having gone into decline in 1984 and 1985 after a period of modest growth (averaging 1.3 per cent per annum) between 1979 and 1983. The average volume of Soviet oil exports to Western Europe in the period 1981–85 was 12.9 per cent higher than in 1976–80, while the average volume of West European imports from all external sources was about 30 per cent lower, giving the Soviet Union an average 17 per cent share of the West European market for extra-regional oil imports in the first half of the 1980s. Soviet export volume to Western Europe reached its highest ever annual level in 1984 (when it accounted for 20.9 per cent of extra-regional imports) but then fell by 31 per cent to take a 1985 market share of 14.6 per cent. The 1985 cutback affected mainly crude oil, which had constituted over 60 per cent of the previous year's supplies to Western Europe, whereas Soviet product exports (consisting predominantly of middle distillates) remained fairly stable. Total Soviet oil exports in 1984 (about 52 per cent of which went to other communist countries) were exceeded in volume only by those of Saudi Arabia. It was estimated that around 10 per cent of the 1984 export total consisted of oil obtained by the Soviet Union under trade agreements with non-communist countries (principally Libya, Iraq and Iran).

Established trading patterns in the world oil market were disrupted during the course of 1986 as the OPEC countries engaged in a price war with the aim of recovering some of the market share lost to non-OPEC producers during the first half of the 1980s. The first detailed evidence of the impact of this development came from the United States, whose higher-cost producers were placed in a particularly weak competitive position when prices slumped.

Preliminary US oil trade statistics for the first half of 1986 showed a year-on-year increase in crude imports of 729,000 bpd (22.4 per cent), with Saudi Arabia supplying 68.5 per cent of the incremental volume. Total US crude imports for the period April–June 1986 averaged nearly 4,200,000 bpd, the highest quarterly average for nearly three years. Saudi Arabia displaced Canada to become the second largest supplier of US crude imports (after Mexico) in the first quarter of 1986, but took third place (with a 14.1 per cent share of the market) in the second quarter of the year, when Canadian exporting companies began to undercut Saudi prices. OPEC countries held an aggregate 48.4 per cent share of the US crude oil import market in the first half of 1986, as against 35.3 per cent in the first half of 1985. Other suppliers' first-half shares of this market in 1986 (1985) were as follows: Mexico 16.5 per cent (23.4 per cent), Canada 13.9 per cent (15 per cent), United Kingdom 7.2 per cent (7.9 per cent) and other non-OPEC countries 14 per cent (18.4 per cent).

The US oil industry's average output of liquid hydrocarbons for the January to June period was about 75,000 bpd (0.7 per cent) lower in 1986 than in 1985, higher production of natural gas liquids having partially offset an estimated fall of more than 100,000 bpd in the half-year average for crude oil. By July 1986 the shutting-in of unprofitable oilwells had reduced US liquid hydrocarbons output by more than 200,000 bpd (1.9 per cent) compared with the corresponding month of 1985. A 2 per cent rise in US oil consumption (to 15,980,000 bpd) absorbed rather more than half of the net increase in the country's total oil supply in January–June 1986. Most of the balance of the increase went into a build-up of product stocks as US refiners stepped up their capacity utilization rates in order to take full advantage of the guaranteed profit margins on crude oil imported under netback contracts, while end-users found that they could afford to carry higher inventories.

A3.1.vii—Relative position of refined products in total oil trade, 1973 to 1983

Refined products constituted 31.2 per cent of the total volume of world oil exports (including re-exports) in 1983. This was the highest proportion of products for 20 years, crude oil having made up more than 75 per cent of internationally traded oil throughout the 1970s, with a peak share of 80.8 per cent in 1976. There was an overall increase of 8.9 per cent in the volume of product exports between 1973 and 1983, as against an overall fall of 34 per cent in the volume of crude exports. The OPEC share of world product exports remained fairly constant at an average 23 per cent between 1973 and 1983, whereas the OPEC share of world crude exports fell from 86.9 per cent to 58.4 per cent over the same period. The total volume of international trade in crude oil and refined products (including re-export trade) was equivalent to 53.6 per cent of world crude production in 1983. The corresponding figure for 1973 was 69.1 per cent.

A3.2—Natural Gas

A3.2.i—Early pattern of world trade (1960 to 1970)

Only about 2 per cent of the world's marketed production of natural gas moved across international borders in the early 1960s (when the United States began to import relatively small volumes from Canada and Mexico). The development of trade had for many years been inhibited by the gas industry's dependence on pipeline transportation, which had ruled out the export of gas from any country which lacked a suitable nearby market. It was, moreover, necessary (i) to undertake heavy initial investments in pipeline construction, (ii) to ensure a high utilization rate of pipeline capacity, given the large volume of natural gas relative to its energy yield (the calorific value of a given volume of natural gas being greater than that of manufactured gas but far lower than that of the same volume of oil), and (iii) to operate on the basis of long-term trade agreements which took account of the various special factors involved in the provision of a continuous piped gas supply.

By the end of the 1950s experimental voyages between the United States and the United Kingdom had demonstrated that it was technically feasible to transport individual cargoes of liquefied natural gas for long distances by sea. It was also established, however, that considerable capital investments would be required to install liquefaction facilities in the exporting country and regasification facilities in the importing country and to build specialized cryogenic tankers capable of handling what was an exceptionally dangerous cargo. It was thus apparent that the future development of trade in LNG would depend on the conclusion of long-term supply agreements of comparable scope to those governing trade in directly piped gas, notwithstanding the absence of a fixed conduit between exporter and importer. (This was in contrast to the far more flexible conditions which applied to trade in liquefied petroleum gas, reflecting both the relative ease of shipment of LPG and the fact that its distribution to final consumers was not dependent on pipelines. Demand for LPG began to increase substantially during the latter part of the 1950s, and regular international bulk shipments began in the early 1960s, when facilities for the large-scale production and export of LPG were brought into operation in Kuwait and Saudi Arabia. There was a steady increase during the 1960s in the use of associated natural gas—as opposed to refinery gases—as a basis for LPG production.)

The first commercial exports of LNG were made in 1964 from Algeria to the United Kingdom (where the manufacture of town gas was becoming increasingly uneconomic, while indigenous natural gas had not yet been discovered in commercial quantities). Algeria began exporting LNG to France in 1965. Each of the pioneering Algerian LNG supply contracts was valid for an initial period of 15 years. The USA began exporting LNG from Alaska to Japan in late 1969 (also under a 15-year contract). The inauguration of international trade in LNG during the 1960s took place against the background of a considerable expansion of trade

34

in piped gas. Canada more than doubled its exports to the United States between 1960 and 1970, and remained the world's largest gas exporter throughout the decade. Exports of gas from the recently discovered Dutch fields to other West European countries increased rapidly during the second half of the decade, when the Netherlands became established as the world's second largest exporter.

The Soviet Union greatly expanded its internal pipeline system during the 1960s in order to link its central Asian gasfields to the main Soviet consuming areas, thus acquiring the option to export gas from its Ukrainian fields (which had hitherto constituted the sole supply source of certain of these areas). Exports were initially made to Eastern and Central Europe, where Austria became the first non-communist country to import Soviet gas in 1968 following the construction of a link between the Austrian and Czechoslovakian pipeline systems. Soviet gas exports were partly offset by imports from Afghanistan (which began in late 1967) and from Iran (beginning in 1970).

The world's marketed output of natural gas doubled during the 1960s, while the volume of gas exports quadrupled, with the result that the proportion of output entering international trade had risen above 4 per cent by 1970. More than 90 per cent of all gas exports were made by pipeline in 1970. Algeria's LNG supplies to Britain and France and Iran's piped supplies to the Soviet Union were the only OPEC gas exports in that year, together accounting for 5.4 per cent of world trade in natural gas.

Table 8 — Natural gas: exports by pipeline in 1983

Exporter	Export volume (million cubic metres)	Piped exports as proportion of total marketed gas output (per cent)	Share of world exports* (per cent)	Destination of exports (with percentages where appropriate)
USSR	60,875	11.4	31.0	West Germany 16.7, Czechoslovakia 15.1, Italy 13.9, East Germany 11.0, Poland 9.1, Bulgaria 8.3, Hungary 6.9, France 6.6, Austria 4.3, Yugoslavia 4.3, Romania 2.5, Finland 1.3
Netherlands	37,540	51.4	19.1	West Germany 46.4, France 20.5, Belgium 16.7, Italy 14.3, Switzerland 2.1
Norway	24,236	99.2	12.4	UK 41.7, West Germany 29.7, Netherlands 11.0, France 7.8, Belgium 7.1, Switzerland 2.7
Canada	21,240	30.0	10.8	USA
Algeria	2,572	6.9	1.3	Italy
Afghanistan	2,325	81.6	1.2	USSR
Bolivia	2,220	85.3	1.1	Argentina
Mexico	2,180	7.0	1.1	USA
World total	153,188	9.9	78.1†	

*Piped exports as percentage of total world gas exports, including LNG.
†Independently rounded total.

Table 9 — Natural gas: imports by pipeline in 1983

Importer	Import volume by pipeline (million cubic metres)	Import dependence* (per cent)	Share of world imports† (per cent)	Origin of pipeline imports (with percentages where appropriate)
West Germany	34,830	65.2	17.8	Netherlands 50.0, USSR 29.0, Norway 21.0
USA	22,970	4.5	11.7	Canada 90.7, Mexico 9.3
Italy	15,858	54.9	8.1	USSR 50.8, Netherlands 33.8, Algeria 15.4
France	13,570	77.0	6.9	Netherlands 56.8, USSR 29.1, Norway 14.1
United Kingdom	10,260	20.6	5.2	Norway
Czechoslovakia	9,200	93.8	4.7	USSR
Belgium/ Luxembourg	8,010	100.0	4.1	Netherlands 78.2, Norway 21.8
East Germany	6,750	47.0	3.4	USSR
Poland	5,550	50.4	2.8	USSR
Bulgaria	5,100	98.1	2.6	USSR
Hungary	4,200	39.3	2.1	USSR
Netherlands	2,695	‡	1.4	Norway
Austria	2,640	68.5	1.3	USSR
Yugoslavia	2,630	55.8	1.3	USSR
USSR	2,325	‡	1.2	Afghanistan
Argentina	2,220	17.4	1.1	Bolivia
Romania	1,500	3.2	0.8	USSR
Switzerland	1,480	100.0	0.8	Netherlands 54.4, Norway 45.6
Finland	820	100.0	0.4	USSR
Others	580	—	0.3	various
Total	153,188	—	78.1§	

*Total net imports of piped gas and LNG as a percentage of total gas consumption.
†Gross imports of piped gas as a percentage of total world gas imports, including LNG.
‡Net exporter.
§Independently rounded total.

Table 10 — Exports of liquefied natural gas in 1983

Exporter	Export volume (million cubic metres)	LNG exports as proportion of total marketed gas output (per cent)	Share of world exports* (per cent)	Destination of exports (with percentages where appropriate)
Algeria	16,540	44.5	8.4	France 53.0, USA 22.7, Belgium 13.8, Spain 10.5
Indonesia	12,962	58.9	6.6	Japan
Brunei	7,098	75.6	3.6	Japan
UAE	2,476	31.8	1.3	Japan
Malaysia	1,560	42.2	0.8	Japan
USA	1,375	0.3	0.7	Japan
Libya	1,017	25.1	0.5	Spain 96.4, Italy 3.6
World total	43,028	2.8	21.9	

*LNG exports as percentage of total world gas exports, including pipeline exports.

Table 11 — Imports of liquefied natural gas in 1983

Importer	LNG imports (million cubic metres)	Import dependence (per cent)	Share of world imports* (per cent)	Origin of LNG imports (with percentages where appropriate)
Japan	25,471	92.3†	13.0	Indonesia 50.9, Brunei 27.9, UAE 9.7, Malaysia 6.1, USA 5.4
France	8,760	‡	4.5	Algeria
USA	3,760	‡	1.9	Algeria
Spain	2,720	100.0†	1.4	Algeria 64.0, Libya 36.0
Belgium	2,280	‡	1.2	Algeria
Italy	37	‡	0.02	Libya
Total	43,028	–	21.9§	

*Gross imports of LNG as a percentage of total world imports, including piped gas.
†Imports of LNG as a percentage of total gas consumption.
‡See Table 9.
§Independently rounded total.

A3.2.ii—Expansion of international gas trade (post-1970)

There was a 39 per cent increase in the world's marketed gas output and a 333 per cent increase in the volume of internationally traded gas between 1970 and 1980, some 13.3 per cent of total output being exported in the latter year. An important factor in the growth of the gas trade during the 1970s was the higher level of oil prices, which improved the competitiveness of gas in the world energy market.

Algeria greatly increased its LNG exports to France during the 1970s and had begun to export LNG to the United States by the end of the decade. Several long-term contracts for future Algerian LNG supplies were signed with new customers in Western Europe from 1974 onwards. Brunei began to ship LNG to Japan in 1973, when it became the world's largest LNG exporter, retaining this position until 1978 (after which year its exports were overtaken by those of Algeria and Indonesia). Libya began to export LNG to Spain and Italy in 1971, while Indonesia and the United Arab Emirates each began to export LNG to Japan in 1977.

The main developments in world trade in piped gas between 1970 and 1980 were (i) a significant increase in Canadian exports to the United States between 1970 and 1973, after which Canadian export volume fell back somewhat, with a particularly sharp decline (to about its 1970 level) in 1980; (ii) a considerable expansion of trade within Western Europe, where the Netherlands became the world's largest gas exporter from 1973 (when it overtook Canada) until 1979 (after which it was itself overtaken by the Soviet Union), while Norway, which began exporting its entire output of offshore gas in 1977, overtook Canada to become the world's third largest exporter in 1980; (iii) the construction during the second half of the decade of a new pipeline to Eastern Europe from Soviet gas fields at Orenburg in the southern Urals, which greatly increased the Soviet Union's export capacity (the average rate of increase in Soviet gas exports during the 1970s being in excess of 30 per cent per annum, with particularly rapid growth in exports to West European countries, which accounted for 41 per cent of total Soviet gas exports in 1980); (iv) the cessation in 1980 of Iranian gas supplies to the Soviet Union following a pricing dispute which caused Iran to close its existing export pipeline and to cancel plans to open a second pipeline which was to have been used for the indirect export of

Iranian gas to Western Europe under an exchange agreement with the Soviet Union; and (v) the commencement of a significant export trade from Mexico to the United States at the beginning of 1980. (Virtually all of Mexico's gas production from its existing reserves had been marketed domestically in the early 1970s. An exportable surplus had become available once more in the second half of the decade as newly discovered reserves were brought into production, but no agreement had been reached on the resumption of exports to the United States until late 1979.) Elsewhere in Latin America, Bolivia began exporting gas to Argentina during the 1970s.

World marketed production of natural gas showed an overall increase of 7.5 per cent between 1980 and 1983, strong growth in 1981 having been followed by a small decline in 1982 and virtual stagnation in 1983. Non-communist production showed an overall decline of 5.3 per cent between 1980 and 1983 (the main factor in this decline being an 18.1 per cent fall in US output), while communist production increased by 35 per cent over the same period, reflecting a 42.5 per cent rise in the output of the Soviet Union, which displaced the United States as the world's largest gas producer in 1983. The Soviet Union's main source of new supplies was western Siberia, whose output was rapidly expanded as new pipelines were completed during the early 1980s.

World exports of natural gas declined in 1981 and 1982 before recovering in 1983 to stand at 102.7 per cent of their 1980 level. Exports accounted for 12.7 per cent of world marketed output in 1983. Non-communist exports declined by 1.8 per cent between 1980 and 1983, although there were wide variations in the performance of individual exporting countries (the largest single change in volume terms being an increase of over 200 per cent in Algerian exports and the second largest change a fall of nearly 24 per cent in Dutch exports). The Soviet Union increased its gas exports by 14.3 per cent between 1980 and 1983, an estimated 57.2 per cent of its 1983 exports being supplied to communist countries in Eastern Europe and 42.8 per cent to non-communist countries in Western Europe.

Details of world trade in piped natural gas and LNG in 1983 are given in tables 8, 9, 10 and 11. Notable developments in 1983 were the commencement of non-liquefied exports from Algeria via a new submarine pipeline running from Tunisia to Italy and the commencement of LNG exports (to the Japanese market) from the Malaysian state of Sarawak. OPEC gas exports in 1983 totalled 35,567 million cubic metres from four member countries (Algeria, Indonesia, Libya and the United Arab Emirates), representing an increase of 22.1 per cent over the previous peak reached in 1979 (which had included Iranian exports to the Soviet Union). The OPEC share of world gas exports was a record 18.1 per cent in 1983, compared with 15.7 per cent in 1979.

Preliminary estimates for 1985 indicated that the world's marketed production of natural gas had reached a new record level in excess of 1,770,000 million cubic metres (23 per cent above the 1980 level) following two years of the most rapid growth since the 1960s. Whereas North American production showed virtually no overall change between 1980 and 1985 (increased Canadian output being offset by reduced US output), the Soviet Union recorded an overall increase of 71 per cent over this period, accounting for more than 36 per cent of 1985 world output and more than 80 per cent of the total rise in world output since 1980. Overall production growth in Western Europe amounted to 6.2 per cent between 1980 and 1985. Some 13.2 per cent of marketed gas production was traded internationally in 1985 (10.3 per cent by pipeline and 2.9 per cent as LNG), the estimated export volume of 234,000 mcm being 22.5 per cent greater than in 1980. Denmark entered the pipeline trade for the first time in mid-1985, when it began to supply North Sea gas to Sweden.

38

Movements in gas export prices tended broadly to reflect trends in the prices of crude oil and oil products in the early 1980s, although there were significant variations in the base prices and indexation formulas incorporated in the various bilateral supply agreements through which the gas trade was conducted. Of the main gas-importing countries, Japan had the least complex market, with a heavy dependence on imports (consisting exclusively of LNG) and formal indexation of gas import prices to crude oil prices. Three-quarters of Japan's LNG imports were purchased by the electricity generating sector, whose strong demand for gas arose partly from the country's strict controls on environmental pollution.

US gas imports, although greater than those of Japan, represented only a small proportion of consumption in a highly regulated market whose main feature was for many years the very low average level of prices for domestically produced gas (◊A2.5). The introduction in 1978 of a programme for the partial phasing-out of price controls on domestically produced gas (◊D9.7) was followed in 1979–80 by external pressure for a revision of gas import prices in response to the upward trend in general energy values stemming from the latest increases in the real price of internationally traded oil. The prices paid for piped gas imports from Mexico were indexed to movements in OPEC crude oil prices at the beginning of 1980, while Canadian gas export prices were linked some months later to changes in the cost of eastern Canada's crude oil imports.

US resistance to Algeria's attempts to link the price of its relatively high-cost LNG exports to the price of its crude oil exports under a direct energy-equivalence formula led to the suspension of deliveries to Algeria's largest US customer in April 1980 and to the effective cancellation of the contract concerned in February 1981. Deliveries of LNG under another Algeria's US supply contracts were suspended in December 1983 after a widening of the gap between Algeria's oil-indexed export price and the general level of gas prices in the US market. Suspended US-Algerian contracts accounted for the laying-up of half of the 24 LNG carriers (out of a total world fleet of 69 vessels) which were idle at the beginning of 1986, when the only prospect for an early improvement in the US-Algerian LNG trade appeared to lie in the negotiation of spot sales at market prices for direct delivery to US distributors who had planned to buy Algerian gas from the main US importers. Mexico suspended its gas deliveries to the United States in November 1984 after its existing export price had become uncompetitive in the prevailing weak energy market conditions. Canada, on the other hand, raised its deliveries to the United States by about 22 per cent in 1985 after accepting a substantial price cut.

Western Europe's position as the world's largest centre of international trade in natural gas in the early 1980s was based primarily on the use of an extensive network of cross-border pipelines which provided the main importing countries of the region with access to competing piped supply sources. LNG imports also played a significant role in certain markets. A key factor in the development of regional trade during the first half of the 1980s was the availability of substantial incremental supplies of relatively low-cost gas from the Soviet Union, whose export capacity was greatly expanded at the beginning of 1984 following the completion of a new pipeline from Siberia which had been built in co-operation with West European suppliers of equipment and materials. The base price for exports of Siberian gas was roughly equivalent to the price of fuel oil and was indexed to changes in the market prices of fuel oil and gas oil (which together had an 80 per cent weighting) and crude oil (20 per cent weighting). Dutch gas export prices were normally indexed to movements in fuel oil prices until the end of 1984, after which the prices in some supply contracts were indexed partly to fuel oil and partly to gas oil (each product category having an equal weighting).

It was generally expected that the Soviet Union would supersede the Netherlands as the dominant supplier of West European gas imports during the second half of the 1980s but that excessive dependence on Soviet supplies would be avoided for political reasons, leaving the Netherlands with a substantial market share and a greater flexibility to respond to seasonal peaks in demand for imported gas. Norway, whose proved gas reserves exceeded those of the Netherlands, hoped to establish a dominant position after 1993, when it was due to begin deliveries from newly developed offshore fields under a June 1986 contract with a consortium of West German, French, Dutch and Belgian buyers. The development prospects of one of these fields (Sleipner) had been in doubt since early 1985, when the United Kingdom (which was nearly 80 per cent self-sufficient in natural gas and was not linked to the main European pipeline network) had rejected plans for a major increase in its imports from Norway, stating that the proposed price for supplies from this field was unacceptably high. Also in early 1985, the UK Government announced its rejection on similar grounds of a proposal for the import of gas from the Irish Republic into Northern Ireland, whose uneconomic piped supply of town gas was to be replaced instead by the distribution of bottled LPG.

The prices of Algeria's LNG exports to France and Belgium were fully indexed to crude oil prices under agreements reached in 1981–82 following protracted negotiations with importers in the two countries. The terms of the contract governing the export of piped gas from Algeria to Italy—which were also the subject of lengthy negotiations—included a base price somewhat below Algeria's base export price for liquefied gas but significantly higher than the price which Italy paid for Soviet gas. Spain, whose gas industry was wholly dependent on imported LNG until 1984 (when the country's first indigenous gas field came into production), agreed in 1985 to increase its purchases of Algerian LNG, which had hitherto fallen far short of their contractual level, and to accept a pricing formula similar to that which applied to Algeria's exports to France and Belgium.

The slump in world oil prices during the first half of 1986 prompted a general reassessment of oil-indexation formulas for gas pricing, which operated to the particular disadvantage of LNG exporters in the prevailing market conditions. Both Algeria and Indonesia were involved in negotiations with customers for revised LNG pricing formulas in mid-1986 as crude prices declined towards $10 per barrel (a level at which fully oil-indexed LNG prices would barely cover basic production costs).

A3.3—Petrochemicals

International trade in organic petrochemicals in the early 1980s was concerned mainly with the export of end-use materials from the non-communist industrialized countries. The main functions of the somewhat smaller volumes of trade in base and intermediate petrochemicals were (i) to correct imbalances in the product ranges of different industrialized countries' petrochemical industries (resulting partly from differences in feedstock availability) and (ii) to meet a growing demand from petrochemical processing plants in less-developed countries. Trade in inorganic petrochemicals (i.e. mainly ammonia and associated products) was more diversified, and included a substantial volume of exports from third-world and communist-bloc countries.

The focus of the main industrialized countries' output of organic petrochemicals was expected to shift increasingly towards specialized end-products in the second half of the 1980s in response to an increase in the production of base and intermediate materials by third-world countries (including OPEC members). In view of the slow growth of world petrochemical demand in the mid-1980s some of the main producers had difficulty in adjusting promptly to this significant change in the international supply pattern, the main problem being a continuing surplus of base and intermediate production capacity in the EEC countries, whose tariff-protected market was seen by Saudi Arabia as an important outlet for its rapidly growing exports of ethylene derivatives. Saudi Arabia experienced fewer problems in exporting large volumes of methanol to Japan, where local petrochemical producers had by 1985 taken steps to restructure their own product range in order to accommodate the projected expansion in imports. Having failed to secure increases in duty-free quotas for its petrochemical exports to the EEC, Saudi Arabia indicated in early 1986 that it would seek new outlets in third-world countries.

More than 100 relatively small (6,000 to 15,000 dwt) chemical tankers were built during the first half of the 1980s to cater for the expansion of trade from new exporting regions such as the Persian/Arabian Gulf. Methanol, which had hardly featured in international trade in 1980, was one of the highest-volume petrochemical exports in 1986, when a total of about 5,000,000 tonnes was expected to enter the market. The overall growth of annual world methanol capacity since 1980 (mostly in third-world countries) was estimated to be in the region of 9,000,000 tonnes by mid-1986. The ongoing structural transformation in the scale and the geographical distribution of the international petrochemical trade in the mid-1980s was accompanied by a disruption of established trading practices, involving in particular a growth in the availability of competitively-priced spot cargoes.

A4—Control Over Production and Pricing in the World Oil Industry

A4.1—Extent of Major Oil Companies' Interests at the Time of OPEC's Formation

At the beginning of the 1960s eight companies, known collectively as the international majors (◊A5.1), accounted for more than 80 per cent of all crude oil produced outside the communist bloc and the United States (i.e. mainly in the OPEC area). In addition, these companies owned about 70 per cent of non-US and non-communist refining capacity (a growing proportion of which was located in oil-importing countries) and a similar percentage of non-US and non-communist product distribution and marketing facilities. About 35 per cent of the oil tanker fleet in the same area was directly controlled by the international majors, while a significant proportion of the remaining tonnage was normally chartered to them under long-term agreements with independent shipowners.

Seven of the international majors—the so-called "seven sisters"—were among the world's largest multinational companies, each having an extensive network of subsidiaries operating in distinct functional and/or geographical sectors of the oil industry. Each company's overall corporate structure was designed to accommodate a complex pattern of transfers of oil between upstream and downstream subsidiaries, the degree of vertical integration which was thereby achieved being dependent on the extent to which a particular company's production capacity was in balance with its marketing capacity both in volume terms and in terms of the geographical distribution of company operations.

Five of the seven sisters—Chevron (◊A5.1.iii), Exxon (◊ A5.1.i), Gulf (◊A5.1.v), Mobil (◊A5.1.ii) and Texaco (◊A5.1.iv)—had their headquarters in the United States, while British Petroleum (◊A5.1.vii) was based in the United Kingdom and Royal Dutch/Shell (◊A5.1.vi) was controlled from both the Netherlands and the United Kingdom. The eighth of the international majors, the French-owned Compagnie Française des Pétroles (◊A5.1.viii), operated on a far smaller scale than the seven sisters but nevertheless played an important role in the industry by virtue of its part-ownership of production rights in several countries. There was a high degree of horizontal integration between the majors' upstream operations (◊A5.2), the joint ownership of production rights by two or more of their number being particularly common in the eastern hemisphere. There was also a rather less complex network of downstream links between the majors, several of which marketed part of their output through jointly-owned subsidiaries.

A4.2—Early Company Developments (to 1928)

Exxon, Mobil and Chevron each had their corporate origins in the Standard Oil group founded in 1870 by John D. Rockefeller, which held a position of near-monopoly control over downstream operations in most regions of the United States until 1911, when it was broken up into its 34 constituent companies following litigation by the federal authorities. Standard Oil was responsible for virtually all US oil exports until 1892 (when oil produced by smaller US companies began to reach the seaboard in significant quantities via independent transportation facilities) and was the only substantial supplier of imported oil in most foreign markets until the mid-1880s, when European trading companies began to make large-scale exports from Russia.

Competition for export markets was most intense in Asia, where the development of Indonesia's oil resources by European companies led to an increase in the number of rival suppliers during the 1890s. A series of damaging "price wars" in eastern markets caused Standard Oil's principal European competitors to join forces in a profit-pooling cartel in 1903, when the Asiatic Petroleum Co. was established to regulate both the volume and the destination of supplies from the main Indonesian and Russian exporters (▷C4.3.i). In 1907 two of Asiatic's constituent companies combined to form the Royal Dutch/Shell group, which subsequently became Standard's main rival in the international oil trade.

In 1911 the Standard Oil group supplied rather less than 60 per cent of all internationally traded oil, exclusively in the form of products. Most of its refinery capacity was located in the United States, where up to two-thirds of its crude oil supplies were purchased from non-affiliated producing companies. Much of the group's original strength had stemmed from its control of key links in the US oil industry's crude transportation and product distribution systems, which had prevented many non-affiliated crude producers from "integrating forwards" into the refining and marketing sectors. The dissolution of the Standard Oil group left the former constituent companies in widely differing positions, some having control of reasonably well-integrated domestic operations, others having a concentration of interests in a particular sector of the domestic industry (e.g. production, refining or marketing) and others holding control of various parts of the extensive international marketing network which had handled the group's product exports. The US oil industry subsequently experienced a lengthy series of company mergers and takeovers as former components of the Standard Oil group sought to rectify structural imbalances in their operations, often through "backward integration" into upstream activities.

Whereas the majority of the Standard companies concentrated on the consolidation of their domestic operations after 1911, those companies which owned international marketing facilities became increasingly concerned to gain access to foreign supplies of crude oil, virtually all of which were controlled by European interests at the end of the First World War. The Royal Dutch/Shell group had greatly improved its competitive position in world markets in the 11 years following its formation in 1907 by acquiring or developing new supply sources in Romania, Russia, Sarawak, Egypt, Venezuela, the United States and Trinidad as well as expanding its operations in Indonesia. The group suffered a setback when its Russian properties came under Soviet control after the 1917 revolution, but secured a major new supply source in 1919 when it entered the booming Mexican oil industry (through the purchase of a majority holding in the British-owned Aguila company). In British India (including what was then the province of Burma) oil production was carried out mainly by the British-owned Burmah Oil Co., whose regional marketing activities were informally co-ordinated with those of Royal Dutch/Shell under the terms of a "no-competition" agreement. In Iran oil rights were held by the Anglo-Persian Oil Co. (the predecessor of British Petroleum), whose major shareholders included the British Government and Burmah Oil Co. and whose entry into the oil market was based on a long-term contract for the supply of fuel to the Royal Navy.

Exxon—then known as Standard Oil Co. (New Jersey)—was the largest and most outward-looking of the Standard Oil companies, having acted as the group holding company from 1892 to 1911. The volume of Exxon's refinery throughputs grew by about 200 per cent in the nine years following the end of the First World War, while the extent of the company's dependence on non-affiliated crude supplies was reduced from over 80 per cent to less than 65 per cent over the same period. There was a rapid expansion of proprietary crude production outside the

43

United States, mainly through the acquisition of supply sources in Colombia, Peru and Mexico. Concessions were also under development in Indonesia and Venezuela in the mid-1920s. US refineries were responsible for less than two-thirds of Exxon's output of products for sale in foreign markets in 1927, the main expansion of its foreign refinery capacity since 1918 having occurred in Latin America.

In 1920 Exxon purchased the Branobel company, through which the Swedish Nobel family had controlled about one-third of Russia's oil output prior to October 1917. This investment was apparently undertaken in the expectation of an imminent collapse of Soviet rule, and Exxon was thus eventually obliged to accept that its Russian interests (like those of Royal Dutch/Shell) were of no value except as a basis for the negotiation of some form of compensation and/or co-operation agreement with the Soviet Government. Exxon, Royal Dutch/Shell and other Western oil interests made a number of attempts during the early 1920s to present a joint position to the Soviet Government on a wide range of oil issues, each such attempt being undermined by rivalries and disagreements between the companies concerned. The Soviet oil industry was meanwhile developing the capacity to resume large-scale exports to eastern-hemisphere markets, where oil demand was increasing at a slower rate than the non-communist producers' capacity to supply it in the mid-1920s.

In the winter of 1926–27 Standard Oil Co. of New York (the forerunner of Mobil), which controlled the former Standard Oil group marketing network in Asia but had not yet developed any proprietary crude production outside the United States, contracted to purchase large quantities of relatively low-priced oil products from the Soviet Union, subsequently using this cost advantage to undermine the competitive position of Royal Dutch/Shell in the important Indian market. Royal Dutch/Shell, which alleged that Mobil's Soviet supply contract had been negotiated with the knowledge and the tacit approval of Exxon (notwithstanding Exxon's public solidarity with Royal Dutch/Shell in demanding compensation from the Soviet Union in respect of expropriated oilfields), retaliated by making drastic cuts in its own prices in India as the first stage in a wider "price war" directed at Mobil in particular and the Standard Oil companies in general. The struggle for market shares continued throughout 1927 and into 1928, placing an extreme pressure on oil industry profit margins which some small companies were unable to withstand. The industry's total production capacity was estimated to be equivalent to 160 per cent of current demand in 1928, reflecting the considerable growth in the world's proved oil reserves since the end of the First World War (when exploration activity had been stimulated by fears of an imminent supply shortage).

A4.3—"Orderly Marketing", US Prorationing and "Gulf-plus" Pricing

In September 1928 the president of Exxon, the managing director of Royal Dutch/Shell and the chairman of BP met in Scotland to resolve the inter-company conflict, which had been under discussion at a lower level for some months. The meeting approved seven broad principles as a basis for future inter-company co-operation, details of which were not made public until August 1952, when a subcommittee of the US Senate published a report entitled *The International Petroleum Cartel* (drawn up by the Federal Trade Commission in 1951) describing how these principles had served as a framework for the subsequent development of international trade in oil. The so-called Achnacarry agreement (also known as the "as is" agreement and the pool association agreement) blamed the "tremendous overproduction" of 1927–28 on "excessive competition" in the international oil trade and laid down the following guidelines for the future avoidance of a similar situation:

(1) That each participating company should accept its current market share and should contribute to any future increase in supplies in such a way as to ensure the maintenance of prevailing market shares.

(2) That companies should co-operate where appropriate by making any existing surplus facilities available to one another at cost.

(3) That no new facilities should be added other than those which were required to meet increases in total demand "in the most efficient manner".

(4) That each company should price its oil at the effective ceiling level for each marketing area (calculated according to a formula which reflected the pattern of world oil trade in 1928) while supplying each area from the lowest-cost source which was available to it in accordance with paragraphs (5) and (6) below.

(5) That the industry's transport costs should be kept as low as possible by drawing supplies from the nearest available source of production.

(6) That an inter-company prorationing system should be established by the producers in each geographical region and that steps should be taken to ensure that the operation of a given region's system was not undermined by an influx of surplus supplies from any other region.

(7) That companies should avoid the introduction of any measures which would materially increase costs in the industry.

Each of the participating companies was to use its own commercial judgment in making practical arrangements to meet the objectives of the 1928 agreement, many aspects of which were initially left open to very flexible interpretation. Further inter-company meetings took place at regular intervals to review the effectiveness of the agreement in the light of changing circumstances and to build up a corpus of detailed procedures for its implementation. By the mid-1930s the cartel comprised nearly 20 companies involved in the international oil trade and had achieved a large measure of success in fulfilling its central aim of eliminating price competition in all the main import markets. The Soviet Union had meanwhile built up its own foreign distribution network (mostly in Western Europe) and was no longer seen as a serious threat to market stability, although no formal co-operation agreement was reached with the cartel and no compensation was paid in respect of expropriated oilfields.

The cartel system did not apply to operations within the United States (where most of the participating companies were based) in view of its incompatibility with various US laws and with many aspects of the structure of the US oil industry. However, a strong case already existed for the introduction of controls on the output of US domestic producers in order to put an end to their large-scale wastage of resources.

The inefficient management of US oilfields arose from a code of property rights in that country which stated (i) that ownership of subsoil resources was vested in the owner of the surface land, and (ii) that by virtue of a "rule of capture" mobile resources such as oil and gas belonged to the owner of the land where they were brought to the surface, regardless of the location of the reservoir from which they originated. Under this system the production rights for a single oilfield were frequently held by many different companies or individuals, each of which had a strong incentive to drill a large number of producing wells and to operate them at full capacity in the knowledge that the natural pressure in the common reservoir was vulnerable to depletion by rival producers. This led to the premature exhaustion of reservoirs after the recovery of a relatively low percentage of the total oil in place and to large falls in prices when production ran ahead of demand.

Legislation to control oil production operations existed only in Oklahoma in the 1920s, other oil-producing states having failed to act on this issue. However, a massive "oil rush" to the giant East Texas field following its discovery in late 1930 caused such chaos both in the field itself (where it was necessary to impose martial law for a time) and in the US oil market (where the already low prices of the depression era were driven well below the level of production costs) that mandatory controls on output were soon introduced in Texas and several other states. Federal legislation was subsequently enacted in 1935 to prohibit inter-state trade in oil which had been produced in violation of state laws and to encourage co-operation between the regulatory bodies in the different states. The most important of these bodies was the Texas Railroad Commission, whose monthly decisions on the allowable level of output by Texan producers became the main factor determining the overall level of US output. Although detailed procedures varied considerably between the different oil-producing states which legislated to introduce controls on output, the principal function of most states' prorationing systems was to ensure that the total volume of crude deliveries to refineries did not exceed the prevailing level of market demand for refined products. Decisions on the distribution of allowable production between individual wells and fields were based primarily on resource management criteria.

The consequent stabilization of prices in the US market increased the effectiveness of the international trading companies' cartel agreement, whose pricing provisions were defined with reference to the product prices posted by Texan export refineries at ports on the Gulf of Mexico. (In the case of crude oil, which accounted for a relatively small proportion of international trade at this time, the companies referred to the posted prices at which the same refineries obtained supplies from non-affiliated producers in the Texan oilfields.)

Under the cartel's "single basing point" or "Gulf-plus" system all marketing was conducted on cif terms, foreign oil being valued at the prevailing fob price in Texas for oil of similar quality, to which was added the prevailing cost of shipment between the Gulf of Mexico and the final market, regardless of the actual origin of the oil. Each participating company used the same freight-rate schedule to calculate shipping costs for pricing purposes. The cartel's foreign fob values thus reflected production costs in the United States (which were generally higher than production costs elsewhere in the world because of the US oil industry's low average output per well), while its cif prices included a "phantom freight" element whenever oil was supplied from a producing area situated closer to the final market than the Gulf of Mexico. The Gulf-plus formula was designed to unify prices in each market at the maximum level which could be obtained at the time that the cartel agreement was drawn up (i.e. because the Gulf of Mexico was then the world's dominant oil-exporting region).

The relative importance of the Gulf of Mexico as a source of oil shipments —both to foreign export markets and to US customers on the north-eastern seaboard—declined during the 1930s, not least because the use of Gulf-plus pricing made the Caribbean a more profitable supply centre for the major companies with production interests in Venezuela and refining interests in the Netherlands Antilles. The relative profitability of product exports from the Caribbean was further enhanced by the fact that the companies' local refining operations were based exclusively on the use of their own crude, produced at cost in Venezuela, whereas their Texan operations had become subject to a prorationing regulation which required each refinery in the state to take equal proportions of its crude supplies from all the producing wells which were linked to it, including those operated by non-affiliated companies. The additional profit which could be realized by supplying Venezuelan rather than Texan oil was somewhat higher in West European and Latin American markets than in the north-east of the United States after 1932 as a result of the introduction of US import duties on oil.

A4.4—Venezuelan and Indonesian Oil Concessions

The largest US producer in Venezuela at the beginning of the 1930s was Standard Oil Co. (Indiana), which had begun to operate outside the United States in 1925 following its acquisition of Pan American Petroleum and Transport Co. However, the parent company experienced increasing difficulty in developing adequate marketing outlets for oil produced by its subsidiary during the depression era, and in 1932 Pan American's foreign interests (mainly in Venezuela, Mexico and the Netherlands Antilles) were sold to Exxon, while Standard Oil Co. (Indiana) reverted to its earlier status as one of the largest of the companies operating solely within the US domestic oil industry. Exxon, which had previously acquired additional interests in Venezuela in 1928, thus became the dominant company in that country, where Royal Dutch/Shell was strongly entrenched as the other main producer.

Most of the balance of Venezuela's output was produced by Gulf Oil, an integrated US company which had developed its domestic business independently of the Standard Oil group and had obtained first foreign oil supplies in Mexico during the First World War. By 1937 Gulf was facing marketing difficulties comparable to those which had caused Standard Oil Co. (Indiana) to withdraw from Venezuela five years previously. It therefore entered into arrangements whereby Exxon and Royal Dutch/Shell each acquired a quarter-share in Gulf's Venezuelan concessions, together with powers to determine the level of output from the concessions (◊**C13.3.ii**).

The ownership of Venezuela's subsoil resources—formerly vested in the Spanish crown—was transferred to the republic when independence was achieved in the early nineteenth century. However, the dictatorship which held power during the period when Venezuela's oilfields began to be developed on a large scale did not follow a consistent policy with regard to the terms on which official exploration leases and exploitation concessions were granted to private interests; nor did it act to prevent subsequent private transfers of oil rights. The extensive concessions which the major oil companies had accumulated by the late 1930s thus included numerous small areas which had originally been granted to other companies or individuals on widely varying terms. (An even more confused situation existed in Mexico, where the basic principle of state ownership of subsoil resources was not introduced until 1917, by which date many companies had already acquired US-style oil rights based on the private ownership of surface land.)

In Indonesia the ownership of subsoil resources was vested in the Dutch colonial government, which granted concessions on a uniform legal basis and which itself took a direct stake in several concessions through a joint company formed in partnership with Royal Dutch/Shell in 1921. Royal Dutch/Shell was the sole holder of virtually all of Indonesia's remaining concessions until the late 1920s, when the colonial government relaxed the nationalistic policy under which it had hitherto blocked the direct entry of US companies into the country's oil industry. The subsequent expansion of Exxon's Indonesian production interests provided the basis for the formation in 1933 of a regional partnership with Mobil (◊**C4.3.i**), whose lack of a nearby supply source had recently placed its Asian marketing subsidiaries at a disadvantage relative to Burmah-Shell (a joint company formed by Burmah Oil and Royal Dutch/Shell in 1928 to carry out marketing operations in India in association with BP).

A4.5—Middle Eastern Oil Concessions

A4.5.i—Iran and Iraq

The early development of the oil industry in the Middle East took place against a background of far-reaching political change in which the European powers were deeply involved. The authority of the weak and corrupt regime which held power in Iran at the

47

beginning of the twentieth century was undermined by constant Russian and British interference in the country's internal affairs (culminating in military intervention to ensure that Iran maintained its declared neutrality during the First World War). In 1921 a coup d'état was staged by Col. Reza Khan, who was installed as Shah in 1925 after he had demonstrated his determination to impose strong government and to resist external pressures.

The Ottoman Empire—the world's greatest Moslem state—had meanwhile been destroyed as a result of its alliance with Germany in the First World War. Turkish rule survived only in the north, where the secular republic of Turkey came into being, while the predominantly Arab provinces lying east of the Mediterranean were grouped into three mandated territories administered under League of Nations auspices, with France taking responsibility for Syria/Lebanon and Britain taking responsibility for Iraq and for Palestine/Transjordan. To the south, the Arabian peninsula remained under the political control of independent Arab rulers, although it constituted a British sphere of influence insofar as Britain's strategic maritime interests were safeguarded by a colonial presence in Aden and by treaties with the Arab rulers of various coastal states.

British diplomatic influence was instrumental in securing the D'Arcy oil concession in Iran in 1901 (◊C5.3.i), this being one of a series of monopoly concessions over different areas of economic activity which were granted to European interests by the then Shah and his predecessor as a fund-raising expedient at a time of mounting foreign debt. Iran's northern provinces were excluded from the concession area in order to forestall Russian objections, although Russia did not formally recognize the "British" nature of the concession until 1907. Britain's national interest in the Iranian oilfields was enhanced in 1914 when the British Government acquired a majority shareholding in the company which had been formed to exploit the concession. Shortly thereafter the Ottoman Government agreed in principle to grant an oil concession in Mesopotamia to a company owned 50 per cent by BP, 25 per cent by Deutsche Bank and 25 per cent by Royal Dutch/ Shell (◊C6.3.i). This followed nearly 10 years of complex negotiations in which the British and German governments had become increasingly heavily involved, while the Ottoman Government (which came under the control of radical army officers after 1908) had maintained a cautious attitude which was in marked contrast to Iran's readiness to grant the D'Arcy concession.

The subsequent collapse of Ottoman rule, followed by the inclusion of the proposed Mesopotamian concession area in the British-administered state of Iraq, greatly strengthened the British Government's role when the status of the 1914 agreement-in-principle was re-examined after the First World War. The restructuring of the prospective concessionaire company was initially treated by Britain as a matter to be settled through bilateral discussions with France, and an accord was reached in 1920 whereby France took over the former German shareholding while accepting that the company should remain under British control. The restructured company subsequently signed a formal concession agreement with the Government of Iraq in early 1925, prior to the inauguration of the new state's National Assembly.

The main US oil companies had meanwhile launched their post-war drive to expand their overseas supply sources (◊A4.2), an initiative which gained the strong backing of the US Government. Diplomatic pressure was accordingly brought to bear on the British Government from 1920 onwards with a view to securing US participation in the exploitation of Iraq's oil resources, it being argued that the Anglo-French oil agreement represented an abuse of the mandate system by the two administering powers in the region. Prolonged negotiations involving the British, French and US governments and the various commercial oil companies which had an interest in the issue eventually led to a further reconstruction of the concessionaire company in 1928 to give equal 23.75 per cent shareholdings to BP, Compagnie Française des Pétroles (which had been formed to hold France's interest), Royal Dutch/Shell and a US consortium, with the remaining 5 per cent going to Calouste Gulbenkian, who had been a party to the 1914 agreement with the Ottoman Government. The Iraq Government was not included in these negotiations.

The agreement on the redistribution of shareholdings in what became the Iraq Petroleum Company (IPC) was finalized against the background of the international oil companies' "price war" of 1927–28 and was accompanied by an agreement between the shareholders on future upstream co-operation in the Middle East which predated by nearly two months the Achnacarry agreement on the restraint of downstream competition in world oil markets. IPC's "red line agreement" was modelled on an earlier accord dating from 1914, when each of the joint applicants for the Mesopotamian concession had undertaken not to engage in oil production in any part of the Ottoman Empire (apart from Kuwait and Egyptian-administered territories) except through their joint company. Four of the five US companies which signed the 1928 agreement—Exxon, Mobil, Standard Oil Co. (Indiana) and Atlantic Refining Co.—were former members of the Standard Oil group, while the fifth was Gulf Oil. By the time that oil began to be exported from Iraq in 1934, however, the US shareholding in IPC was held equally by Exxon and Mobil, which had bought out the shares originally taken up by the other US companies.

The terms of IPC's concession had meanwhile been renegotiated with the Iraq Government in 1931 to free the company from its original obligations to develop specific exploration areas within a given time and to allow other companies to bid for sub-leases within the concession area. The Government's basic revenue entitlement under the 1931 agreement was defined as a fixed cash royalty per ton of oil produced, in addition to which IPC was to make an annual capital payment in order to secure exemption from Iraqi taxes. Although IPC accepted a reduction in its existing concession area as part of the 1931 renegotiation, affiliated companies subsequently obtained new concession areas on similar terms, giving the group an effective monopoly over oil development in virtually the whole of Iraq by 1938. Other IPC affiliates obtained monopoly concessions from the rulers of Qatar, Oman and most of the Trucial States between 1935 and 1939 (◊A5.2.iv).

In 1933 Iran (then the Middle East's sole oil-exporting country) secured a radical revision of the term of BP's concession, the original terms granted in 1901 having been repudiated by Reza Shah's government after several years of argument with the company over their interpretation. At the centre of the dispute was a clause in the 1901 concession agreement which defined the state's main revenue entitlement as a fixed percentage of the concessionaire company's net profits (this being one of Iran's normal terms for granting concessions at that time). The 1901 agreement did not, however, set out any precise basis for the calculation of net profits, thus leaving considerable scope for disagreement about the items which were deductible from gross income for accounting purposes and about whether the profits of subsidiary companies operating outside Iran lay within the scope of the agreement. That there was also an element of risk in basing government oil revenues on any profit-sharing formula was brought home to Iran when the company suffered a sharp reduction in its per-barrel income in the depressed oil market of the early 1930s.

Under the 1933 agreement the Iranian Government's principal revenue entitlement was redefined as a fixed tonnage royalty (which was equal in value to the royalty laid down in the 1931 agreement between Iraq and IPC). The main focus of the state's financial interest in the concession thus shifted from the level of the company's profits to the volume of its production, although profits continued to concern the Government insofar as it had the right to receive a percentage of the company's distributed earnings in excess of a specified amount. The revised agreement—which was negotiated only after the British Government had gone to the League of Nations to challenge Iran's repudiation of the 1901 agreement—also provided for an 80 per cent reduction in the size of BP's concession area, to be effected within six years.

A4.5.ii—Bahrain, Saudi Arabia and Kuwait

On the Arab side of the Persian/Arabian Gulf, where the ownership of natural resources was vested in the absolute rulers of the various states, a licence to explore for oil in al-Hasa (which later became the eastern province of Saudi Arabia) was granted to a British-based syndicate in 1923. The same syndicate subsequently acquired exploration rights on the island of Bahrain in 1925. The Bahrain rights were transferred to Gulf Oil in 1927, by which time the syndicate had allowed its al-Hasa rights to lapse after failing to find an established oil company which wished to take them over. Gulf Oil forfeited its freedom of action in Bahrain by signing the "red line agreement" in July 1928 and, having tried without success to persuade the other IPC shareholders to enter into a joint venture on the island, sold the Bahrain rights to Chevron (Standard Oil Co. of California) later in the same year.

Chevron—whose existing interests were mainly within the United States—was subsequently supported by the US Government in its application for full monopoly concession rights in Bahrain, which the company agreed to hold through a Canadian-registered subsidiary in order to satisfy the requirements of the British Government (then in charge of Bahrain's external affairs). Having become interested in the oil potential of the Arabian mainland in the light of its successful exploratory drilling in Bahrain, Chevron entered into negotiations with the king of Saudi Arabia, who granted concession rights over a large area in the east of the Arabian peninsula in 1933 after Chevron had agreed to advance funds to alleviate the kingdom's serious financial problems (◊C11.3.i). The IPC shareholders, whose main concern at this time was not to obtain additional oil supplies but to prevent other companies from entering the region, reacted to Chevron's success in obtaining the east Arabian concession by taking steps to negotiate concession rights for IPC affiliates in other parts of the "red line" area (including western Saudi Arabia).

In Kuwait, which was not covered by the red line agreement, Gulf Oil emerged as the main contender for concession rights in 1927, although negotiations with the ruler of Kuwait were complicated by the fact that any oil agreement would require British government approval. Gulf's position became increasingly uncertain when BP attempted first to obstruct the US company's bid and then to make a counter-bid of its own. The two companies' eventual decision to make a joint bid (which was accepted by the ruler and approved by Britain in late 1934 (◊C7.3.i) arose partly from US diplomatic representations to the British Government and partly from inter-company talks leading to a secret agreement that Kuwaiti oil should be marketed in a "non-disruptive" manner in accordance with the principles laid down in the Achnacarry agreement (◊A4.3).

After the conclusion of the Kuwait concession agreement the only serious threat to the stability of existing inter-company production and marketing arrangements in the Middle East arose from Chevron's unwillingness to create any formal links between its own operations and those of the IPC shareholders (who were themselves unable to agree on a common approach to the "problem" of the Bahrain and east Arabian concessions). However, in 1936 Chevron secured established outlets for its future production from the Middle East (as well as from recently-acquired concessions in Indonesia) by entering into a partnership with Texaco, a US company which had built up a large international marketing network independently of the Standard Oil group. This development was welcome to IPC's shareholder companies insofar as it indicated that Chevron's eastern-hemisphere marketing operations would be conducted in broad conformity with the Achnacarry principles.

The basic financial terms of the Kuwait and Saudi Arabian concessions followed the pattern of the 1931 Iraq-IPC agreement in that royalties were payable at a fixed cash rate per ton, while exemption from local taxation was secured in return for additional fixed payments. The Kuwait concession was valid for 75 years (as were the IPC group's Iraq concessions), while the Saudi concession was valid for 60 years (as was BP's revised Iranian concession of 1933). Gulf Oil and BP had sole rights over the oil development of the whole territory of Kuwait, with no obligation to relinquish unexplored or unexploited portions of their concession area. The IPC group had similar rights over most of the territory of Iraq, as did BP over about 15 per cent of the territory of Iran after the 1933 reduction in the size of its concession area. Chevron and Texaco had full concession rights over more than one-third of the territory of Saudi Arabia, with an option over the rights to an extensive additional area and full discretion in deciding whether and when to select parts of the main concession area for relinquishment to the state.

Gulf and BP set up a jointly-owned operating company (the Kuwait Oil Co., KOC) whose function was to supply them with cost-price oil from the Kuwait concession, similar operating arrangements having previously been adopted by the IPC group in order to enable the profits derived from the sale of jointly-produced Iraqi oil to be attributed to the separate trading accounts of the group's shareholder companies. Chevron and Texaco agreed to exploit the Saudi concession through a US-registered operating company which would supply crude to its parent companies' jointly-owned downstream subsidiaries on a profit-making basis. The accounts of the various joint operating companies in the Middle East were issued only to their respective shareholder companies, while each of the ultimate parent companies (i.e. the international majors) published consolidated accounts in which its total profits were divided between the different sectors of its integrated international operations in such a way as to minimize the company's overall liability to income tax. The use of uniform Gulf-plus product prices ($\Diamond$A4.3), combined with the fact that the companies' financial obligations to Middle Eastern host governments were based on tonnage royalties rather than on the taxation of export profits, provided considerable scope for the flexible application of the internal transfer-pricing systems which were a central feature of the majors' accounting practices.

At the outbreak of the Second World War Kuwait's oil resources had still to be brought into commercial production, while Saudi Arabia had been producing oil for less than a year. However, both countries were known to possess substantial reserves of oil in giant reservoirs whose large-scale exploitation would entail exceptionally low per-barrel production costs, and were thus regarded as highly attractive sources of incremental supplies when market demand began to increase rapidly after the end of the war. The two countries' concession-holders were not themselves equipped to handle the "orderly marketing" of greatly increased volumes of oil, and accordingly concluded various agreements in 1947–48 whereby (i) Texaco and Chevron admitted Exxon and Mobil as additional shareholders in the Arabian American Oil Co. (Aramco, which operated the Saudi Arabian concession), (ii) Gulf Oil contracted to sell Kuwaiti oil to Royal Dutch/Shell on a long-term basis, and (iii) BP contracted to sell either Kuwaiti or Iranian oil to

Exxon and Mobil on a long-term basis. The restructuring of Aramco required the formal cancellation of the "red line agreement", a move which was strenuously resisted for some time by CFP and Calouste Gulbenkian on the grounds that it was detrimental to their own interests as shareholders in the IPC group.

A4.6—Nationalization of Mexican Oil Industry – Reform of Government-Company Relations in Venezuela – Introduction of "50-50 Profit-sharing" in the Middle East

Whereas good relations were generally maintained between concession holders and host governments in the Middle East for some years after the conclusion of BP's revised Iranian concession agreement in 1933, a rather different situation prevailed in the two main Latin American oil-producing countries. In Mexico the assertion of national ownership of subsoil resources in 1917 led to a prolonged dispute between oil companies and successive governments over the introduction of new concession terms, opposition to which on the part of US companies was backed by the US Government until 1928, when Mexico's petroleum law was amended to remove certain "confiscatory" powers which had been declared unconstitutional by the Mexican Supreme Court. By this point Mexico's oil production was undergoing a rapid decline (◊A3.1.i), attributable in large part to the inefficient exploitation of the main oilfields by companies which had established a pattern of "competitive drilling" in shared reservoirs under the country's original US-style concession system and had operated their wells at full capacity in order to maximize their short-term earnings during the dispute which followed the Government's re-pudiation of this system. In keeping with the oil industry's long-established disreg-ard for Mexican sovereignty, some companies sought to further their interests during the dispute by destabilizing the country's internal political situation (mainly through the covert funding of anti-government elements).

The Mexican Government continued to be deeply mistrustful of foreign oil interests throughout the early 1930s, and in late 1936 it gave its backing to demands by the industry's Mexican labour force for improved pay and conditions. The oil companies rejected an arbitration award requiring them to meet most of the workers' demands, a response which effectively nullified an existing collective labour contract and led to a government order that compensation should be paid to the trade unions concerned. The companies' continuing intransigence in the face of strike action caused the Government to order the full nationalization of the country's oil industry in March 1938. The 17 foreign oil companies then operating in Mexico challenged the legality of the nationalization decree, notwithstanding the US Government's public acknowledgement of Mexico's legal right to expropriate foreign oil properties in return for "fair and equitable compensation". The British Government made an official protest to Mexico describing the decree as "in-herently unjustified". The companies subsequently brought pressure to bear on Mexico by depriving the country of export markets, although their claim to legal ownership of oil produced from their former concession areas was eventually undermined when the Mexican Supreme Court upheld the constitutionality of the nationalization decree. A settlement finalized during the Second World War fixed the companies' total compensation entitlement at $180,000,000, payable in in-stalments (which continued to fall due until the early 1960s). The Mexican oil industry remained a state monopoly, managed in accordance with nationalistic policies allowing little scope for the export of crude oil until major new fields were discovered in the 1970s.

The two main companies affected by the Mexican nationalization decree were Royal Dutch/Shell (whose Aguila affiliate had been responsible for rather more

52

than half of Mexico's total output) and Exxon (which had accounted for the largest share of the remaining output). Both companies had ready access to alternative supplies to replace their lost Mexican production, and both had sufficient control over market outlets to ensure the effectiveness of the temporary boycott of Mexican oil exports at the end of the 1930s. One consequence of the companies' uncompromising stand in Mexico was to increase their reliance on Venezuela as a western-hemisphere supply source at a time when the Venezuelan authorities were pressing for stricter controls over oil industry operations, which had come under close scrutiny following a change of government at the end of 1935. The companies' opposition to a new Venezuelan hydrocarbons law (passed four months after the Mexican nationalization decree) strengthened the Government's determination to place all Venezuelan oil concessions on a uniform legal basis, an aim which was finally achieved in 1943 after the companies had agreed to accept the terms of revised legislation drafted with the assistance of mediators nominated by the US Government (◊**C13.3.ii**).

Venezuela's 1943 hydrocarbons law reduced the maximum duration of oil concessions to 40 years and imposed new relinquishment obligations on all concessionaires. Royalties were defined as a percentage of the oil produced (but were normally payable in cash, for which purpose oil was valued on the basis of Texan postings for similar grades of crude), and no exemption was given in respect of general company taxation in Venezuela (which was introduced under separate legislation in the same year). Further income tax legislation was enacted in 1948 to give the Venezuelan Government a minimum 50 per cent share in the net profits of oil company operations, calculated after the deduction of royalties and other contractual payments to the Government. The principle of "50-50 profit-sharing" was soon taken up by host governments in the Middle East, where a new tax formula was negotiated in 1950 between Saudi Arabia and Aramco, whose main concern—as a company wholly owned by US interests—was to secure an entitlement to offsetting tax credits in the United States (◊**C11.3.iii**). The subsequent introduction of the same tax formula into other Middle Eastern concession agreements placed the non-US majors at a competitive disadvantage until equivalent tax allowances were introduced in their home countries during the early 1950s.

The Middle Eastern version of "50-50 profit-sharing" differed significantly from the Venezuelan system (which was based on normal oil industry accounting practices) in that the government tax take in the Middle East was defined as a maximum 50 per cent of net income, with royalties and all other established payments to governments being fully credited against this overall tax liability rather than being deducted as operating expenses for the purpose of calculating taxable profits. The new Middle East tax regulations were, moreover, treated as amendments to the various countries' concession agreements, so that the 50 per cent tax rate was fixed by contract and could not be varied except by negotiation with the concession holders (whereas the Venezuelan Government was contractually obliged to negotiate only over royalties and rentals, having completely separated its income tax system from its concession system). The "submerged" royalty element in the Middle East tax take was redefined during the course of the 1950s as a percentage of output (valued at locally posted prices), with a standard rate of 12.5 per cent (agreed by Iraq and IPC in 1951 and subsequently adopted by the region's other main producing countries) compared with Venezuela's royalty rate of 16⅔ per cent.

A4.7—Early Evolution of Middle Eastern and Venezuelan Posted Prices

Prior to the introduction of the new Middle Eastern tax structure the international oil companies had modified their pricing arrangements to accommodate the growth in the relative importance of Middle Eastern crude exports. The Gulf-plus system (◊A4.3) had ceased to be rigidly applied in the region during the latter part of the Second World War, when the British and US navies challenged the basis of the Gulf-plus cif prices quoted for deliveries of bunker fuel at ports situated close to the main Middle Eastern refineries. In response, the companies had introduced a dual basing point system under which crude oil and bunker fuel became available on an fob basis in the Persian/Arabian Gulf at prices equal to those posted for oil of similar quality at ports on the Gulf of Mexico, thereby eliminating the "phantom freight" element in the charges which had hitherto been made for deliveries of these categories of Middle Eastern oil to nearby customers. Nevertheless, the companies continued to benefit from particularly high profit margins on such oil because of the low cost of production from the Persian/Arabian Gulf oilfields.

After 1945 a sharp rise in US crude prices (which had been controlled by the federal authorities throughout the Second World War) was accompanied by rather smaller increases in Middle East fob prices, creating a differential between the two basing points. By 1948, when the Middle East was firmly established as the dominant source of West European crude imports, while the United States had fallen far behind Venezuela as a supplier of western-hemisphere oil to Europe, a widening of this differential had brought about a westward shift (from the Italian to the British market) in the "equalization point" at which there was notional cif parity between deliveries of Texan and Middle Eastern oil. The proportion of crude in West European oil imports was increasing rapidly at this time in line with the expansion of the region's refinery capacity, prompted partly by a need to minimize the foreign exchange costs of oil products in view of the post-war "dollar shortage".

In 1948 oil prices became subject to systematic monitoring by the European Co-operation Administration (ECA), a US government agency which supervised the disbursement of funds made available under the Marshall Aid programme to finance the economic recovery of Western Europe. Oil accounted for a higher proportion of Marshall Aid funds than any other import category, about 50 per cent of all exports from the Middle East to Western Europe being financed on this basis. One of the early actions of the ECA (which was required under US law to ensure that suppliers charged the lowest competitive prices) was to question the validity of using the Gulf of Mexico as a western-hemisphere basing point, on the grounds that Texas had ceased to be that hemisphere's main source of internationally traded oil. The international oil companies responded by switching their western-hemisphere basing point to the Caribbean, where the prevailing fob prices for Venezuelan crudes were lower than US postings on the Gulf of Mexico by 10 cents per barrel (the amount of the US import duty on crude oil). Middle Eastern fob prices were then adjusted downwards during the second half of 1948 to levels which produced cif parity with Venezuelan crudes in the British market.

By 1949 over 10 per cent of Middle Eastern crude exports were reaching the US market at competitive delivered prices despite the relatively high cost of shipping oil for this distance. This prompted the ECA to press for a reduction in fob prices at the Persian/Arabian Gulf to levels equal to the net realized prices at which companies were exporting to the United States. The companies formally introduced cif parity for Venezuelan and Middle Eastern crudes at importing centres on the east coast of the USA during the second half of 1949. However, the inclusion of an exceptionally low freight element in the new delivered prices meant that the attendant reduction in Middle Eastern fob prices was rather less than that which would have resulted from the application of the equalization formula proposed by the ECA.

Under the companies' formula the net realized price of Middle Eastern crude imported into the United States declined when freight rates rose in 1950–51, while the fob prices posted in the Middle East remained at their end-1949 levels. The US Mutual Security Agency (ECA's successor body) subsequently accused Exxon, Mobil, Chevron and Texaco of overcharging the Marshall Aid programme by a total of $67,341,839 between mid-1949 and mid-1952 by supplying crude oil to Western Europe at fob prices exceeding the net prices realized on the same companies' exports of Middle Eastern oil to the US market. The companies' refusal to make a further reduction in fob prices at the Persian/Arabian Gulf led to the exclusion of Middle Eastern oil from the Marshall Aid programme at the end of August 1952, thus ending the ECA/MSA's active participation in the regional export market.

The fob price of Saudi Arabian light crude exported from Ras Tanura—which was used as a reference point for postings in other Middle Eastern countries—stood at $1.75 per barrel in 1952, compared with prevailing fob postings of $2.75 per barrel on the Gulf of Mexico and $2.57 per barrel in Venezuela for oil of similar quality, while the average cif price of Middle Eastern crude in Western Europe was estimated to be at least 20 per cent lower than it would have been under the pre-war Gulf-plus pricing system. The decline in the fob prices of Middle Eastern crudes relative to those of western-hemisphere crudes did not entail an equivalent change in the relative prices of oil products refined from Middle Eastern crudes, West European ex-refinery prices being fixed at parity with the notional delivered prices of products from Caribbean export refineries (i.e. on the basis of prevailing Caribbean postings plus long-term averages of freight to Europe). The Caribbean pricing structure was itself based on differentials between heavier and lighter products which reflected the pattern of product demand in the United States.

The eight international majors together controlled over 90 per cent of production, refining and marketing outside the United States and the communist bloc in the early 1950s. Six of them (i.e. excluding BP and CFP) together controlled nearly one-third of US crude production and about 45 per cent of total US refining capacity (but up to 60 per cent of capacity in the main east coast importing centres). The initial evolution of crude oil prices in the Middle East after the Second World War was essentially based on adjustments to the major companies' internal transfer-pricing structures, details of which were publicly known only insofar as invoiced crude prices affected cross-border trade and the division of total taxable income between different countries. The general trend of these adjustments was subsequently rationalized by the companies (in terms of the need to maintain "competitive" cif parities) when they were called upon to justify their crude oil pricing policies to the ECA, whose attention was focused on the way in which transfer-pricing (or, very rarely, contract sales to non-affiliated customers) affected import costs in West European countries.

By testing the validity of the companies' rationalizations in the light of such information as it was able to obtain on actual transactions, the ECA accumulated sufficient evidence of discrepancies to make a case for further reductions in Middle East fob prices. The downward adjustment in these prices, which had been initiated by the companies, was thus continued under ECA pressure until in late 1949 they reached the lowest level which the companies were prepared to incorporate into their overall pricing structures. Having established this price level as a reference point for the transfer of crude to their trading subsidiaries, the companies began to publish it as a uniform basis for sales to non-affiliates, the first such postings of

Middle Eastern fob prices being made during 1950. Venezuelan fob prices began to be formally posted in 1952.

The international majors had ceased to meet as an organized cartel by the end of the 1930s, and did not seek to reintroduce any formal arrangements to co-ordinate their marketing activities after the Second World War, not least because US government investigations into their pre-war trading practices (described in detail in the 1951 Federal Trade Commission report ◊**A4.3**) acted as a strong disincentive to collusive behaviour. By this point, however, the interlocking pattern of "legitimate" inter-company relationships, centred on the joint ownership of Middle Eastern concession rights, had become so complex that none of the majors had any need to resort to collusion in order to remain very well informed about the activities of the others or to establish a broad "entitlement" to supply a given proportion of the total oil market. Thus, while the development of post-war pricing was explained to the ECA in terms of competitive market forces, the basic identity of interests between the majors ensured that the system which emerged was in many respects consistent with the anti-competitive Achnacarry principles. In particular, posted prices on the Gulf of Mexico continued to be used as a common reference point to which all postings, upstream and downstream, were ultimately linked, while the new structure of fob differentials between the main exporting centres (and its application in conjunction with standardized freight rates to determine cif equalization points) provided an effective basis for the "orderly marketing" of the greater part of the companies' incremental production of Middle Eastern crude.

The US import market, which offered highly uncertain growth prospects (not least because of the vulnerability of the US prorationing system to disruption by an uncontrolled influx of foreign oil), was treated as a special case, leading to the apparently "disorderly" marketing of Middle Eastern crude in the United States (i.e. by the effective undercutting of European-oriented fob prices in the way which was noted by the ECA). Although the US domestic industry was operating at full capacity when the country became a net importer of oil in 1948, sharp increases in net imports in the two succeeding years were accompanied by the "shutting-in" of over 20 per cent of domestic capacity in accordance with state prorationing regulations, the volume of shut-in capacity in 1949 (a year of abnormally low growth in US oil consumption) being over 3½ times as great as the volume of net imports. Concern about the potential threat to domestic price stability prompted state prorationing authorities and independent US crude producers to use their considerable political influence to secure a number of investigations by congressional committees into the implications of the uncontrolled importation of oil into the United States. This resulted in the publication during 1950 of reports which detailed the geographical and commercial origin of the country's post-war oil imports and which in effect served notice on the majors that their future import levels would be continuously monitored with reference to the overall state of the domestic market.

Having been introduced by the major oil companies in the quite different context of the ECA's campaign to further the short-term interests of European importing countries, Middle Eastern posted prices became the focal point of the companies' long-term financial relationship with the governments of exporting countries under the region's "50-50 profit-sharing" formula, although the companies' acceptance of the principle that crude oil exports should be valued at posted prices for tax purposes was initially qualified by their practice of claiming substantial tax allowances in respect of integrated transfers of crude. By the mid-1950s, however, Middle Eastern host governments had secured considerable reductions in these allowances after a series of bilateral negotiations with their respective concession holders during which the most advantageous financial terms obtained by any one country tended subsequently to become standard features of agreements in other countries of the region.

A4.8—Iranian Nationalization Crisis

While the introduction and consolidation of this new financial relationship was being effected through negotiation in the Arab states, BP was locked in a confrontation with the Iranian Government which led to the severe disruption of the Iranian oil industry from 1951 to 1953 during the premiership of the ultra-nationalistic Dr Mohammed Mossadeq (◊C5.3.i).

The autocratic Reza Shah had abdicated in 1941, shortly after the occupation of his country by British and Soviet troops, and had been succeeded by his eldest son, Mohammed Reza, who announced his intention of ruling as a constitutional monarch. This strengthened the role of Parliament as a focus of Iranian resistance to foreign attempts to obtain new oil concessions during the occupation (culminating in a bid by the Soviet Union which was accepted under duress by the Iranian Government in 1946 but was repudiated by Parliament in the following year). Having secured a statutory ban on the granting of all new concessions, nationalist deputies rejected the terms of a draft agreement, signed by BP and the then Government in 1949, under which the state's revenue entitlement in respect of production from the established concession area would have been substantially increased (although the company would have remained exempt from Iranian income tax). The complexity of the draft agreement—whose overall financial implications were broadly comparable to those of the "50-50 profit-sharing" formula subsequently introduced in Saudi Arabia—rendered it especially vulnerable to attack by its opponents, who were assured of considerable popular support when they presented the issue in terms of a struggle to assert Iran's sovereign rights over the exploitation of its natural resources. A bill was eventually passed to nationalize the company's Iranian operations, while Dr Mossadeq was appointed to lead a government committed to the implementation of this measure.

During the ensuing dispute over the legitimacy of Iran's action, the British Government supported BP's claim to legal title over Iranian oil, while the US Government authorized US oil companies to co-operate with BP in organizing the flow of alternative supplies to export markets which had hitherto been supplied from Iran. The US decision, which was taken on overriding strategic grounds, did much to weaken the impetus of current investigations by the US Justice Department into the legal implications of the Federal Trade Commission's report on past collaboration between the major companies (◊A4.3). The ready availability of crude from Arab countries, coupled with the majors' high degree of control over marketing outlets, ensured the effectiveness of the embargo on Iranian oil exports, although the Mossadeq Government refused to modify its policies in response to this severe economic pressure. Dr Mossadeq was finally removed from office after he had clashed with the Shah, whose authority was restored by a coup carried out with the covert support of US and British intelligence agencies.

The US Government subsequently sanctioned the involvement of all five US majors in the Iranian Oil Participants (IOP) consortium, which was formed in 1954 to take over the operation of the former BP concession area (◊C5.3.ii). The Iranian oil industry remained under state ownership, which was vested in the National Iranian Oil Co. (NIOC), while effective control was exercised by IOP on standard Middle Eastern "50-50 profit-sharing" terms (with certain formal modifications to take account of the fact that IOP's legal status was that of a contractor rather than a concession holder). The consortium's operating subsidiaries functioned as non-profit-making entities under arrangements similar to those adopted by IPC in Iraq

(◊A4.5). The inclusion of all eight international majors as shareholders in IOP —thus completing the network of inter-company links throughout the Middle East (◊A5.2)—reflected the companies' common interest in ensuring that the resumption of large-scale exports from Iran did not result in an uncontrolled supply surplus with disruptive consequences for market stability.

A4.9—Expansion of Independent Oil Companies' International Operations

The outcome of the Iranian nationalization crisis was in most respects a victory for the international majors, not least as a demonstration to other exporting countries that there was little point in taking control over production so long as the companies controlled the majority of marketing outlets and were able to supply them from alternative sources. However, the formation of IOP provided non-affiliated companies with an opportunity to secure US government backing for their entry into the consortium, which was effected in 1955 when the aggregate shareholding of the US majors was reduced from 40 to 35 per cent through the sale of a 5 per cent shareholding to a group of US independents. (The term independent was used in the United States to describe those oil companies not affiliated to the established international majors, ranging from several thousand small-scale crude producers to various former constituent companies of the Standard Oil group which held substantial interests in all sectors of the US domestic oil industry. The vertically integrated operations of between 40 and 50 large independent companies accounted for about the same shares of the principal sectors of the US domestic industry as were held by the international majors in the early 1950s—i.e. nearly one-third of crude production and around 45 per cent of refinery capacity.)

Two of the independent companies which acquired interests in IOP—namely Aminoil (itself a grouping of several US independents) and Pacific Western (later renamed Getty Oil)—already held Middle Eastern concession rights in the onshore area of the joint Kuwait-Saudi Arabian Neutral Zone. A feature of these agreements—concluded between Aminoil and the Kuwait Government in 1948 (◊C7.3.ii) and between Pacific Western and the Saudi Government in 1949 (◊C11.3.ii)—was that they enshrined financial terms far more advantageous to the host governments than those on which the majors were then operating in the Middle East. Oil was discovered in the Neutral Zone in 1953. The rights over Saudi Arabia's interest in the Neutral Zone had previously been held by Aramco, which relinquished them in 1948 in exchange for offshore concession rights in waters adjoining its existing Saudi concession area. Aramco undertook to pay an increased royalty rate for offshore production and also accepted a timetable for the future relinquishment of substantial blocks of territory within its total concession area over a period of 21 years (the precise location of the blocks to be decided by the company).

Post-war interest in the acquisition of offshore rights in the Persian/Arabian Gulf stemmed from the action of governments in extending the limits of their territorial waters and/or claiming jurisdiction over areas of the continental shelf adjoining their territorial waters. (The doctrine of national jurisdiction over the resources of the adjacent continental shelf had first been formulated by the US Government in the 1945 following successful oil exploration work off the coasts of Texas and California.) Whereas Aramco (whose original concession had included "islands and territorial waters") accepted Saudi Arabia's right to negotiate a new offshore agreement in these circumstances, the IPC-affiliated concession holders in Qatar and Abu Dhabi argued that the continental shelf zones claimed by the rulers of these states in 1949 were automatically covered by their existing monopoly concession agreements. The resulting disputes were settled by international arbitrators who declared that the original agreements applied only to territory over which jurisdiction was claimed when the agreements were signed. Both states initially granted separate offshore concessions to a company owned by independent US and British interests but subsequently accepted bids from the majors when this company relinquished its rights, the Qatar offshore concession being obtained by Royal Dutch/Shell in 1952 (◊**C10.3**) and the Abu Dhabi concession by BP and CFP in 1953 (◊**C12.3.iii**). Kuwait's offshore area was excluded from the Gulf/BP concession in 1951 (◊**C7.3.ii**), although the Kuwait Government made no early move to grant offshore rights to another company.

In Venezuela, where existing concession areas covered a far smaller proportion of the national territory than was the case in most Middle Eastern states, the first new concessions to be granted for over 10 years were opened to competitive bidding in 1956–57 (◊**C13.3.iv**). The highest bidders among the many companies which responded were predominantly US independents attracted by the high average rate of return on foreign oil operations (which had doubled relative to the average rate of return in the US domestic oil industry since 1947). Independent companies (some of them acting in partnership with major companies) also obtained a high proportion of Libya's oil concessions, which began to be granted in 1956 under a deliberate policy of dividing the total concession area between a wide variety of interests in order to encourage rapid development (◊**C8.3.i**). Apart from the requirement to pay initial capital premiums, the new Venezuelan concessions were generally granted on that country's standard financial terms, whereas Libya's first concession agreements provided for a modified version of the Middle Eastern "50-50" formula which was more favourable to concession holders than the standard terms in the region's established producing countries.

In addition to the US independents (of which nearly 200 were engaged in foreign oil exploration or production by the end of the 1950s, compared with less than 20 at the end of the Second World War) and a few privately-owned European independents, the non-major companies operating in the international oil industry during the 1950s included various state-owned enterprises established by oil-importing countries. The main proponents of state involvement in the oil industry were France, which embarked on a nationalistic drive to achieve self-sufficiency in oil through government agencies unconnected with CFP (the majority of whose shares were held by French private-sector interests ◊**A5.1.viii**), and Italy, which depended on oil for a higher proportion of its energy needs than any other major West European country and was concerned to minimize the cost of its supplies.

France formed a Bureau de Recherches de Pétroles (BRP) in 1945 to explore for oil within its metropolitan and colonial territories, resulting in discoveries in Algeria and Gabon in 1956 (◊**C1.3.i, C3.3**). The BRP's main Algerian subsidiary, together with CFP, played a leading role in the development of the Algerian oilfields, which was financed mainly by French capital (foreign oil companies being barred from holding concessions except as partners of French companies), while its Gabonese subsidiary operated partly through joint ventures with foreign oil companies after 1958.

Italy's Ente Nazionale Idrocarburi (ENI)—established in 1953 as a holding company for various state oil and gas enterprises, including Agip—made an unsuccessful attempt in 1954 to purchase a shareholding in the IOP consortium in order to gain direct access to foreign crude supplies for its extensive Italian refining and distribution interests. ENI's then president, Enrico Mattei, subsequently became an outspoken critic of the major companies' oligopolistic position in the Middle East and an advocate of co-operative arrangements under which the governments of exporting and importing countries could bypass the majors' integrated trading system to their mutual advantage. Agip finally entered the Iranian oil industry in August 1957, one month after the enactment of Iranian legislation which enabled NIOC to negotiate joint-venture agreements with foreign oil companies (◊C5.3.iii). The Agip-NIOC agreement (which had been under discussion for some months prior to the introduction of the new legislation) gave Iran's national company a 50 per cent equity share in a joint operating company, thus assuring the state of an overall 75 per cent share of net profits at a tax rate of 50 per cent. NIOC would be required to fund its half-share of the operating company's costs only in the event of the discovery of oil in commercial quantities. In 1958 Standard Oil Co. (Indiana), whose post-war re-entry into international operations had hitherto been limited to the western hemisphere, became the first large privately-owned independent to sign a joint-venture agreement with NIOC.

In Japan, whose dependence on imported oil increased dramatically during the 1950s (◊A3.1.ii), electricity generating companies and other industrial oil consumers formed a consortium with Japanese financial interests to bid for offshore concession rights in the Kuwait/Saudi Arabian Neutral Zone, which were granted by the two host governments in 1957–58 (◊C7.3.ii, C11.3.iv). Under these separate but similar concession agreements the consortium's operating company—Arabian Oil Co. (AOC)—undertook to pay tax at rates of 56–57 per cent on the profits of its integrated upstream and downstream operations and to offer 10 per cent equity participation to each of the host governments. Like the provisions of the Agip-NIOC agreement in Iran, these terms contrasted strongly with the majors' Middle Eastern profit-sharing formula and served as a measure of the host governments' growing bargaining power in negotiations with new entrants to the world's cheapest and most prolific producing region. Venezuela, which had no contractual constraints on its freedom to raise income tax rates for established concession holders, introduced tax changes in 1958 which increased the state's overall share of the local oil industry's aggregate profits to about 67 per cent (◊C13.3.iv). This prompted the president of Exxon's Venezuelan subsidiary to issue a thinly-veiled threat to curtail future investment in the country, one apparent intention of his statement being to deter other producing countries from seeking amendments to existing 50-50 agreements.

A4.10—Oil Prices in the 1950s

A4.10.i—The price rises of 1953 and 1957

The major oil companies' crude oil pricing structure (◊A4.7) continued to be centred on the level of postings on the Gulf of Mexico until the late 1950s, increases in US prices in 1953 and 1957 being used as a basis for increases in postings in Venezuela and the Middle East. The differentials between eastern- and western-hemisphere postings were, however, gradually widened. The US price increase of 1953 occurred after the introduction of the first of several schemes intended to prevent imports from disrupting the prorationing system, while the 1957 increase was made during the Suez crisis, when the importation of Middle Eastern oil into the United States was temporarily discontinued. The introduction of the corresponding price changes outside the United States followed the established post-war pattern whereby one of the majors would act as the "market leader", after which the other major companies would fall into line.

The US domestic industry's allowable production under prorationing (◊A4.3) had risen to nearly 89 per cent of capacity in 1951, when strong growth in consumption (arising partly from the demands of the Korean war) coincided with constraints on the availability of foreign crude supplies resulting from the initial interruption of Iranian exports. Net imports began to increase again in 1952, causing allowable production to be cut to 86 per cent of capacity and prompting the Texas Railroad Commission (TRC) to tighten its surveillance of the market. It did this by requiring oil companies to submit regular reports on their planned import volumes, thus enabling the Commission to make a more broadly-based assessment of future trends in the balance between supply and demand and to monitor the accuracy of the companies' import forecasts. (Texas was in effect the main "swing" producer within the United States, accounting for about 50 per cent of national production capacity but for little more than 40 per cent of actual output under prorationing. The Texan oilfields operated at 71 per cent of capacity in 1952.)

The posted prices of crude oil and refined products on the Gulf of Mexico were increased in June 1953, six months after the entry into force of the TRC's import monitoring scheme and two months after the lifting of federal price controls which had been occasioned by the Korean war. The parallel increases which were made in the international majors' Venezuelan postings in June 1953 provided the basis for a general rise in ex-refinery prices in the companies' main non-US import markets under the "Caribbean parity" system of product pricing. Subsequent increases in Middle Eastern crude postings ensured that most of the rise in the overall profitability of the region's oil was attributed to the upstream rather than to the downstream sector, thus limiting the refining profits available to non-affiliated purchasers of Middle Eastern crude produced by the majors. The increases in the prices of Venezuelan and Middle Eastern crudes were unrelated to any changes in local production costs, whereas the US price increase had been occasioned in part by the rising cost of carrying surplus capacity under the prorationing system. An average 17 per cent of US production capacity was shut in during 1953.

In 1954 there was a larger rise in the volume of US net oil imports than in the volume of US consumption, causing a further decline (to less than 77 per cent nationally and less than 54 per cent in Texas) in the utilization rate of domestic productive capacity. A federal cabinet committee, appointed in mid-1954 to inquire into US "energy supplies and resources policy", recommended in early 1955 that a programme of voluntary import controls should be introduced by the federal Office of Defense Mobilization on national security grounds with the aim of stabilizing the ratio of oil imports to domestic output at its 1954 level. Later in 1955 enabling legislation was passed to empower the President to impose mandatory controls on oil imports if voluntary measures were judged to be ineffective. After the introduction of the voluntary programme the major companies maintained a stable level of imports through their own integrated channels in 1955–56 but increased their sales of foreign crude to non-affiliated refiners on the eastern seaboard. Refiners in the west of the country began to step up their purchases of crude from Canada, whose piped exports (which had commenced in 1953) could not be portrayed as a potential threat to national security.

The pressure of imports on the US domestic market was lifted when the Suez Canal was blocked by Egypt from November 1956 to March 1957 in the wake of the Anglo-French occupation of the Canal Zone (which had been secretly planned with Israel as a follow-up to that country's invasion of the Gaza Strip and Sinai). At the same time Syria cut Iraq's pipeline links to Mediterranean export terminals, thereby shutting in production capacity of around 500,000 bpd and leaving the Saudi Arabian Tapline as the only available route for Mediterranean exports of Middle Eastern oil. The price of exports via Tapline was increased during the canal closure to maintain cif parity with westbound tanker shipments from the Persian/Arabian Gulf (now re-routed via the Cape of Good Hope). The loading of Saudi Arabian oil on to British tankers was banned by the Saudi Government, which also suspended supplies to the (US-owned) refinery in the British protected state of

Bahrain. The disruption of Middle Eastern export shipments during the Suez crisis led to serious oil shortages in Western Europe, where most countries were obliged to introduce emergency rationing regulations.

Concern over the security of the Suez Canal supply route following Egypt's nationalization of the (Anglo-French) Suez Canal Co. in July 1956 had prompted the US Government to establish a Middle East Emergency Committee (MEEC) as a forum within which US oil companies could, without violating the country's anti-trust laws, devise a co-ordinated strategy to offset such shortages by shipping large volumes of western-hemisphere oil to Europe and diverting the proportion of Middle Eastern exports which would normally have been shipped to the USA. The work of the MEEC was, however, suspended by the US Government throughout the first month of the supply crisis in order to increase the pressure on Britain and France to effect a speedy withdrawal from Egypt, thus precluding any collaborative action by US oil companies until early December 1956.

Having received federal authorization to launch a joint export initiative as part of the MEEC's European supply strategy, the major Texan producers applied to the TRC for permission to increase their output from oilfields bordering the Gulf of Mexico. They met with a refusal on the grounds that the state prorationing regulations required variations in production to be equitably distributed between all the Texan oilfields, including large inland fields with limited pipeline links to the coast. Texan oil output thus remained at its predetermined level of 52 per cent of capacity in December 1956 and was held at this level by the TRC in January 1957 in order to allow inland producers to run down their existing stocks, despite the fact that the average level of US exports to Europe was thereby restricted to less than 416,000 bpd, compared with the MEEC's January target of 500,000 bpd. Moreover, the proportion of crude in the daily export total fell to as little as 26 per cent at some points as surplus product inventories were reduced in accordance with the requirements of the prorationing system.

This restriction of US crude supplies during January 1957 brought about an increase in posted prices on the Gulf of Mexico, with a corresponding increase in Venezuela. The TRC subsequently sanctioned rises in the level of Texan output to 54 per cent of capacity in February and 58 per cent of capacity in March, while several major companies made reductions in their US refinery runs in order to step up their crude shipments to Europe. In late May 1957, following the resumption of Middle Eastern exports to the USA, upward revisions were made in posted prices on the Persian/Arabian Gulf, with the result that the posting for Saudi Arabian 34° crude fob Ras Tanura reached $2.08 per barrel, some 37 cents (21.6 per cent) higher than the posting for the same gravity in 1952. The posting for Venezuelan 35° crude had risen over the same period by 48 cents (18.7 per cent) to $3.05 per barrel, and that for Texan 36° crude fob Gulf of Mexico by 50 cents (18.2 per cent) to $3.25 per barrel. The average cost of maintaining and expanding production during the 1950s (exclusive of tax and royalty payments) was estimated to be in the region of 16 cents per barrel in the Middle East, 51 cents per barrel in Venezuela and $1.73 per barrel in the United States.

A4.10.ii—The move towards mandatory US import controls (mid-1957 to early 1959)

After the reopening of the Suez Canal oil imports into the United States resumed their upward trend, stimulated both by the recent domestic price increase and by a steep decline in maritime freight rates. Integrated transfers to refining subsidiaries of the five US majors accounted for 40 per cent of the planned east coast imports of crude oil which were notified to the federal authorities for the second half of 1957. Imports planned by six large US independent companies accounted for a further 41 per cent of the total and those planned by eight small US independents for the remaining 19 per cent. A large proportion of the independent companies' imports consisted of Middle Eastern crude purchased from those major companies whose upstream production significantly exceeded their current refining capacity (notably Gulf Oil and BP, which had no agreement to restrict output from the Kuwaiti oilfields ◊**C7.3.i**). Five years previously three-quarters of recorded east coast crude imports had moved within the US majors' integrated channels, while most of the remainder had been purchased from major producers by the six large independents. It was announced by the federal authorities at the end of July 1957 that the administration of the voluntary import control programme was to be strengthened through the drawing up of a formal quota for each importing company. The Government's immediate aim was to secure a cutback in shipments to the seven largest east-coast users of imported crude (i.e. the five US majors plus Atlantic Refining Co. and Sinclair Oil) in order to offset the growth in shipments to the refineries of "new" independent importers.

In 1958 the total volume of US net oil imports rose by 86 per cent despite a fall in Canadian exports to the north-western states, resulting in an increase in the level of the country's import dependence (net imports as a proportion of consumption) to more than 17 per cent, compared with less than 10 per cent in 1957. The proportion of shut-in capacity in the US oil industry exceeded 38 per cent in 1958, compared with less than 27 per cent in 1957. The entry into the east coast import market of at least 14 additional independent companies (including companies which had recently acquired Venezuelan concessions) led to an intensification of existing disagreements over the allocation of market shares under the voluntary control system, which eventually broke down when it became clear that many companies were not prepared to accept their proposed quotas. A mandatory control system, based on the restriction of the share of incremental consumption which could be supplied by imports, was therefore introduced by the Federal Government in March 1959 with the broad aim of stabilizing the ratio of gross imports to domestic production.

The mandatory controls applied initially to crude oil but were extended in the following month to cover residual fuel oil and other refined products. Oil from "sources which would be accessible by overland transportation in the event of an emergency" (i.e. Canada and Mexico) was excluded from the control programme in May 1959 following strong protests from the Canadian Government. No concessions were made in respect of imports from Venezuela and the Netherlands Antilles despite equally forceful representations by the Venezuelan and Dutch Governments.

The initial distribution of quotas within the Government's import ceiling was based on existing importers' last official allocations under the voluntary control system. Subsequent quota reviews gave increasing weight to the overall distribution of US refinery throughputs, companies which received quotas on the basis of inland refining operations being authorized to transfer these quotas to companies with coastal refineries in exchange for supplies of domestic crude. (The resulting transfer agreements were in practice thinly-disguised sales contracts, drawn up in such a way as to ensure that companies which "exchanged" their quotas would gain a financial benefit equal to the current US market value of the right to import the volume of oil covered by the quotas concerned.)

A4.10.iii—Background to August 1960 cuts in Middle Eastern postings

The introduction of mandatory US import controls followed a cut of 15 cents per barrel in the posted price of Texan crude in January 1959, when the price level established in the abnormal market conditions of early 1957 finally became untenable in the increasingly competitive buyer's market which had developed after the end of the Suez crisis. An equal cut was made in Venezuelan postings in early February, while Middle Eastern postings were reduced by 18 cents per barrel (i.e. to slightly less than their end-1953 level) in mid-February. Venezuelan postings were further reduced in early April 1959 by 10 cents per barrel (which fully cancelled the Venezuelan price increase of January 1957) in reaction to the announcement of the US import restrictions, which limited the Venezuelan producers' access to their main export market at a time when their oil was being undercut by Middle Eastern oil in many other markets. Texan crude prices were reduced to their pre-1957 level in early 1960, restoring the differential between Texan and Venezuelan postings to its former level of 20 cents per barrel.

Although the general cuts in posted prices in the first two months of 1959 were triggered initially by the weakness of realized crude prices in the US market, a significant decline in realizations had also occurred in the main non-US import markets. An expansion of independently-owned refining capacity during the 1950s had led to an increase in the volume of crude which was shipped to these markets under negotiated "arm's-length" contracts rather than being transferred through integrated channels or supplied under long-term agreements between major companies (such as that between Gulf Oil and Royal Dutch/Shell regarding Kuwait crude ◊C7.3.i).

In the early years of the decade most arm's-length sales were made at posted prices and thus constituted a form of "orderly marketing" whereby the majors (which then held a virtual monopoly in the supply of internationally traded crude) gained outlets for supplies which exceeded their aggregate refining capacity while ensuring that their customers' acquisition costs were equal to the invoiced acquisition costs of the majors' own refining subsidiaries. By the mid-1950s several major companies were beginning to extend various forms of discount to arm's-length purchasers (including partly-owned affiliates) in order to expand their shares of certain non-US import markets. Discounting was particularly common in Japan, where all refining companies were at least 50 per cent locally-owned and were from 1955 to 1962 subject to foreign exchange controls designed to encourage the purchase of crude supplies at the lowest possible fob prices. The higher posted prices introduced in Venezuela and the Middle East in 1957 were widely discounted in arm's-length sales contracts concluded after the international supply situation had returned to normal. By the end of 1958 virtually all realized fob prices in the international arm's-length crude market were significantly lower than posted prices, although postings continued to be used by the major companies as transfer prices for integrated transactions.

Under the majors' profit-sharing agreements with Middle Eastern host governments, arm's-length sales of crude produced by non-profit-making joint operating companies were deemed to yield the same taxable income per barrel as integrated transfers (which were valued at the full posted price for tax purposes), although Aramco, as a profit-making entity, was authorized to use realized prices to compute its taxable income from third-party sales when a small proportion of its output began to be marketed at a discount in 1958. In Venezuela, where the taxation of oil company profits predated the introduction of locally posted prices, all companies were taxed on their realized income from arm's-length sales and their declared income from integrated transfers of crude, the integrated producers being under no obligation to value such transfers at posted prices if their commercial interests were better served by invoicing their downstream affiliates at lower prices. The reduction in Middle Eastern host governments' per-barrel tax revenues in 1959 was thus directly geared to the cuts in the major companies' posted prices, whereas the fall in Venezuela's per-barrel revenues was partly determined by the rather larger decline in discounted prices. However, Venezuela's higher tax and royalty rates ensured that the Government's unit revenue remained significantly above that of Middle Eastern countries in cash terms.

The growth of discount pricing in the arm's-length crude trade was accompanied by a gradual erosion of the US-oriented "Caribbean parity" system of product pricing (◊A4.7) in the main non-US markets, where refiners began to bring the price differentials between the various product categories into line with local patterns of demand in the late 1950s. Competitively determined prices for marginal supplies began to be quoted at certain West European refining centres, although there was as yet little pressure for a general reduction in the majors' ex-refinery prices in countries where they retained a high degree of market control.

A particularly important influence on the level of oil prices in the most competitive West European import markets (e.g. Italy) in the late 1950s was a build-up of crude and product supplies from the Soviet Union, which was seeking to regain its pre-war share of the regional oil trade (◊A3.1) after a lengthy absence from non-communist markets. These supplies were channelled through the growing number of independent West European marketing outlets, including those owned by state-controlled companies such as ENI (whereas in the 1930s the Soviet Union had been obliged to organize its own foreign distribution networks in order to compete effectively with the international majors). Some export contracts provided for straightforward hard currency payments, while others incorporated a barter element specifying part-payment in particular Western export items. The estimated volume of Soviet exports to Western Europe rose above 100,000 bpd during the Suez crisis and was running at more than four times this level by 1960.

Soviet export prices tended to be pitched at the lowest levels required to build up a reasonable share of particular markets, and were invariably lower than the international majors' current arm's-length prices. The majors were quick to point out that higher prices were charged to communist countries whose oil import trade was monopolized by the Soviet Union and to suggest that Soviet oil was therefore being dumped in non-communist markets. Rather less was heard of this allegation after 1959, when independent US oil companies, faced with a restricted home market for their incremental production from Venezuela and elsewhere, demonstrated that adequate commercial rates of return could be achieved by selling oil in non-US markets at arm's-length prices which yielded a profit margin equal to or lower than the estimated Soviet margin on sales to non-communist countries.

Market reports published in mid-1960 indicated (i) that the international majors were discounting the current posted price of Middle Eastern crude by up to 35 cents per barrel in arm's-length trading; (ii) that Soviet crude was entering the Italian market at cif prices which undercut those of comparable Middle Eastern oil by up to 60 cents per barrel; and (iii) that independent producers were discounting Venezuelan crude postings by as much as 80 cents per barrel. The international majors were, moreover, beginning to come under pressure from governments to reduce their internal transfer prices—and thus to cut national import costs—in certain third-world countries whose markets were supplied exclusively through integrated channels. In the case of India, the Government was able to secure cuts in the cif prices at which the major companies transferred Middle Eastern crude to their local refineries after it had threatened to take up an offer of cheaper supplies from the Soviet Union.

Given that there was no prospect of an early reduction in the post-Suez crude supply surplus or of an early relaxation of US import restrictions, it was clear to the major companies that the maintenance of Middle Eastern postings at existing levels was likely to lead to widespread price discounting on the companies' integrated transfers of Middle Eastern crude to non-US import markets and to a consequent erosion of their post-tax profit margins on such transfers (since Middle Eastern posted prices also served as tax-reference values). The companies were also aware that any reduction in Middle Eastern postings would, by the same token, automatically cut the revenue of the region's host governments, which were beginning to draw up long-term development plans based on their projected income from exports valued at the existing posted prices.

Having been forced to accept the February 1959 reductions in the majors' Middle Eastern postings on the basis that they formed part of a worldwide readjustment of a price structure which had been distorted by the Suez crisis, host governments regarded the stabilization of US postings after early 1960 as a guarantee of stability in local postings, given the traditional role of the Gulf of Mexico as the ultimate reference point in the majors' pricing system. From the companies' viewpoint, however, the effective insulation of the US oil industry from international market trends after March 1959 had removed any remaining basis for a linkage between Texan postings and eastern-hemisphere postings and, by adding to the competitive pressures in non-US markets, had done much to make a reduction in Middle Eastern postings inevitable.

The lead in implementing a round of price cuts was taken by Exxon, which announced reductions in its Middle Eastern postings—amounting to 14 cents per barrel in the case of Saudi Arabian 34° crude—in early August 1960. Exceptionally strong protests were made by host governments, causing the other majors to split into two groups, namely the "economic realists", consisting of companies which supported Exxon's initiative and made identical cuts in their own postings, and the "political realists", consisting of companies which considered both the timing and the magnitude of Exxon's cuts to be ill-considered in view of the known strength of host governments' feelings on this issue. The latter group, led by BP, made rather smaller cuts in their own Middle Eastern postings in mid-August, and in mid-September the "economic realists" realigned their postings at this higher level (thus restoring 4 cents of the original 14-cent reduction in the posting for Saudi Arabian 34° crude). By this time the four leading Middle Eastern producing countries had joined forces with Venezuela to form OPEC (▷**D1.1**), their main initial aim being to secure the full cancellation of the cuts, together with an undertaking from the companies that host governments would be consulted over any future plans to change the level of local postings (such an undertaking having originally been demanded in 1959).

Although the cuts in postings (as finalized in mid-September 1960) were not rescinded, the formation of a united front by the main oil-exporting countries ensured that the majors made no future reductions in the unit revenue of Middle Eastern host governments, regardless of the continuing downward trend in market prices. Middle Eastern posted prices remained unchanged for the rest of the decade, effectively transforming the 50-50 profit-sharing formula into a framework for fixed per-barrel taxation. Venezuelan postings, which had not been changed since April 1959, were also held constant throughout the 1960s, and the Government moved towards a system of fixed tax-reference prices in 1962, when it decided that Venezuela's crude exports should be valued at a minimum level of 90 per cent of postings for tax purposes and that the full cost of any additional price discounts should be borne by the exporting companies.

A4.11—Oil Prices in the 1960s

Between 1957 and 1968 the total volume of internationally traded crude oil grew at an average annual rate of around 9.2 per cent, while the volume of crude sold on an arm's-length basis in non-US import markets increased by an average 13.7 per cent per annum. Such sales accounted for about 1,100,000 bpd (nearly 90 per cent of which was supplied by the international majors and much of the balance by the Soviet Union) out of a total trade of 7,000,000 bpd in 1957. By 1968, when the total crude trade amounted to about 18,500,000 bpd, the volume of crude moving to non-US markets outside integrated channels was estimated at 4,500,000 bpd. Of this, a minimum of 2,700,000 bpd (60 per cent) was sold by the majors, while the balance was made up of (i) about 500,000 bpd of Soviet exports to non-communist countries and (ii) up to 1,300,000 bpd marketed by independent companies.

By far the largest source of non-integrated independent supplies was Libya, from which there was a very rapid build-up of exports as seven producing companies — five of them wholly or partly owned by independent interests—entered the market between 1961 and 1968 ($\lozenge$C8.3.i). The continuing enforcement of US oil import controls throughout the 1960s meant that most Libyan crude was shipped to Western Europe, where the highly competitive prices charged by independent exporters were translated into competitive product prices by a fast-growing independent refining sector (accounting for nearly 40 per cent of the region's total refining capacity by the end of 1966). Among the purchasers of products surplus to such refiners' own distribution capacity were independent traders who, by basing their profit margins on competitively-determined wholesale prices, were able to undercut the relatively high retail prices charged by the majors in certain markets hitherto largely unaffected by competitive pressures. Such markets included the United Kingdom, where the import of Soviet oil was banned by the Government for political reasons and where the majors owned over 90 per cent of local refining capacity in the mid-1960s.

The intensification of price competition in Western Europe's highly fragmented open market for oil (concerned mainly with the wholesaling of barge loads and, to a lesser extent, tanker loads of products in and around large refining centres such as Rotterdam) was monitored by specialized trade publications whose market reports provided an increasingly reliable guide to trends in spot prices from the beginning of the 1960s. In addition to monitoring the wholesaling activities of refiners who had few or no retail interests, these reports took account of a significant volume of open-market sales of heavy fuel oil by fully integrated companies (including the majors) and of the minor spot transactions regularly made by integrated companies in order to correct imbalances in their own requirements for lighter products.

Although open-market spot trading was a marginal activity relative to the far greater volume of product trade conducted through integrated channels, published spot prices tended to reflect the overall level of realized ex-refinery prices with at least 90 per cent accuracy in normal market conditions and, when restated net of known freight costs and estimated refining costs, served as a useful basis for calculating the prevailing level of fob realizations in the arm's-length crude trade. (The volume of spot trade in crude oil was negligible in the 1960s, when virtually all arm's-length sales were based on term contracts, often without public disclosure of the prices involved.)

The wider availability of up-to-date information on the development of the West European oil industry's price structure under competitive conditions led to increased pressure on the majors from contract buyers unwilling to pay more than the accepted "market rate" for arm's-length supplies. The effectiveness of such pressure was dependent on the extent of the majors' vulnerability to competition in particular import markets. In Italy major companies were undercutting the (now rising) cif price of Soviet crude by the early 1960s, Exxon being particularly well placed to compete in this market after its nearby Libyan fields were brought into production in late 1961. After 1963 the lowest prices reported in Western Europe were those for Libyan crudes sold by independent companies, although by the end of 1966 there was some undercutting by major producers supplying crude from the Persian/Arabian Gulf. The integrated transfer prices used by the major companies to invoice crude deliveries to their West European downstream subsidiaries had generally fallen below the level of posted prices by the mid-1960s, although these notional discounts were usually smaller than the reductions made in the same subsidiaries' product prices in order to meet independent competition.

Between mid-1960 and mid-1969 open-market ex-refinery prices in Western Europe showed an overall fall of nearly 20 per cent. The mid-1969 price level was roughly equal to that of early 1967 despite an intervening increase in freight rates caused by the closure of the Suez Canal, and netback calculations therefore indicated an overall decline in average fob realizations for crude oil of rather more than 20 per cent between 1960 and 1969. A general levelling out of variations in average ex-refinery prices in the different countries of the region was accompanied by changes in the relative positions of certain countries, Italy being superseded by West Germany as one of the least profitable import markets, while rising Italian and falling British prices moved closer to the regional average. French ex-refinery prices remained well above the regional average throughout the 1960s because of government regulations requiring local refiners to provide guaranteed access to high-cost franc-zone crude (◊C1.3.i). Average West European fuel oil prices, which had remained at approximate parity with coal prices on an energy equivalence basis throughout the 1950s, began to fall below coal prices after 1959, leading to coal's rapid displacement by oil as the region's dominant general fuel during the first half of the 1960s (◊A2.2). Intervention by governments to protect local coal production was mainly in the form of measures to limit the installation of oil-burning plant by electricity generating undertakings and major heavy industries.

An OPEC analysis of the evolution of the average consumer price of a typical barrel of refined products in 12 West European countries between 1962 and 1969 showed a fall of 10.6 per cent (from $6.14 to $5.49) in the pre-tax retail price and a rise of 1.2 per cent (from $12.90 to $13.05) in the final retail price over this period. Taxation by the governments of the importing countries concerned (mainly in the form of excise duties on motor fuels) thus accounted for 52.5 per cent of the final retail price in 1962, rising to 57.9 per cent in 1969. The average per-barrel tax revenue accruing to OPEC producing governments from the profits of crude oil production was equivalent to 6 per cent of the final price for 1962 and 6.6 per cent of the final price for 1969.

According to the major oil companies, the downward movement in the retail prices of refined products in Western Europe after the late 1950s (net of taxation by the governments of the region) led to financial losses, or at best to an absence of profits, on their local downstream operations. This situation arose out of their continuing use of posted prices to invoice crude deliveries to their downstream subsidiaries at a time when the per-barrel profit margin thereby attributed to upstream production was equal to or greater than the total profit margin available on all stages of the integrated movement of oil from the wellhead to the final consumer. Downstream sales profits were meanwhile being reported by non-integrated refining companies which purchased their crude supplies at arm's-length prices, while the majors themselves displayed no reluctance to reinvest part of their "upstream" profits in the expansion of their "unprofitable" downstream facilities. Pressure from the tax authorities in several importing countries, who began to query the validity of the accounting practices behind the reporting of downstream losses, was partly responsible for the majors' shift towards the use of discounted transfer prices in their more competitive downstream markets during the course of the 1960s.

The scale of the price cuts in the West European oil market during the 1960s was not fully matched in the other main non-US import markets, where the major companies were less vulnerable to price competition from independent suppliers. In particular Japan, which had secured the most advantageous discounts on Middle Eastern crude up to 1962 (when its exchange-control restrictions on refiners were liberalized), was subsequently supplied at contract prices somewhat above the arm's-length prices at which Middle Eastern crude was sold to European customers who would otherwise have purchased Libyan crude (which could not be competitively delivered in Japan). Soviet oil, which supplied less than 5 per cent of the Japanese market in the mid-1960s, did not pose a competitive threat to the majors at existing price levels, while Neutral Zone crude produced by Japan's AOC, which supplied around 10 per cent of the market by 1966, was seen by the majors as a threat to their sales volumes rather than to their prices.

The average realized prices of internationally traded crudes were generally estimated to be between 40 and 50 cents per barrel below posted prices in the late 1960s, with slightly higher realizations in some of the majors' smaller "semi-captive" markets and significantly lower realizations on some sales to highly competitive markets. Posted prices were no longer realizable except in a very small number of fully "captive" markets in third-world countries whose governments lacked the bargaining power to acquire (or to threaten to acquire) cheaper alternative supplies. These developments were in marked contrast to the situation in the US domestic market, where prorationing, combined with import controls, held realized crude prices steady at their 1960 level for most of the decade, with an upturn to the 1957 level in 1969 as the US market began to tighten. The restricted volumes of foreign crude imported into the United States during this period thus produced considerably higher per-barrel profits for integrated companies than were obtainable in other markets. However, despite the widening of the differential between US and foreign oil prices during the 1960s, the profitability of producing low-cost foreign oil mainly for foreign markets remained well in excess of the profitability of producing high-cost US crude for the domestic market, and the number of US independent companies involved in foreign oil ventures continued to increase throughout the decade.

A4.12—Relations between Oil Companies and Exporting Countries in the 1960s

A4.12.i—General position of OPEC
During the 1960s the major oil companies took great pains to avoid direct collective bargaining with OPEC, ostensibly because of the US companies' concern that such action could be held to constitute an infringement of US anti-trust laws. The majors' reluctance to enter into formal dealings with OPEC meant that negotiations on issues of general concern had to be initiated by mandating the host governments of the majors' jointly-owned producing companies to raise particular issues in a national context. This procedure provided the majors with considerable scope to prolong the negotiating process and to exploit potential conflicts of interest between different member countries.

OPEC's objectives were widened during the course of the 1960s to encompass a comprehensive assertion of member countries' sovereign rights over the exploitation of their hydrocarbon resources, while the Organization's ability to negotiate effectively on specific issues was backed up by an extensive body of commissioned research into energy economics and the commercial structure of the world oil industry. However, the prevailing conditions of overcapacity and price weakness in the international oil trade did not provide a favourable environment for rapid progress towards joint objectives, and at certain points these objectives were obscured by rivalry between member countries over their relative shares of the total export market.

A4.12.ii—The "production programming" issue

Only Venezuela, OPEC's largest producer throughout the 1960s, was strongly in favour of a collective agreement to control the rate of growth of member countries' output with a view to supporting the level of oil prices in the world market on the basis of prorationing (as US domestic prices were currently supported and as world prices had been supported by the international oil companies in the 1930s). Middle Eastern countries, which had far higher reserves:production ratios (and far less well developed economies) than Venezuela, were more concerned to maximize their growth rates, knowing that the de facto freeze on posted prices after September 1960 (◊A4.10.iii) had removed the possibility that their unit revenues would be depressed by falling market prices. The major oil companies, which had long-standing shareholders' agreements concerning the "orderly" growth of the output of their joint operating companies in Iraq, Iran and Saudi Arabia, thus came under increasing pressure from host governments to expand their capacity development programmes and to end all restrictive offtake arrangements.

An attempt by OPEC to "programme" the output of each member country for 12 months from mid-1965, undertaken in response to continuing Venezuelan pressure for the adoption of a US-style prorationing scheme, was treated by several other member countries as a means of setting minimum growth targets for their respective producing companies (◊D1.4). It had no impact on market prices and served mainly to highlight the difficulty of reconciling the diverse national circumstances and aspirations of the individual member countries. As well as being undermined by stresses within the Organization, the production-programming experiment also suffered from a lack of co-operation on the part of the producing companies, whose formal position was that they held sole contractual responsibility for decisions on output growth and marketing strategies.

In late 1966 the IOP consortium in Iran became the first producing company to agree to fulfil minimum growth targets laid down by a host government, leading the Iranian Government to incorporate ever more ambitious targets into its subsequent development planning (◊C5.3.iii). Complaints were then made to their own producing companies by Arab governments which felt that Iranian output was being increased at their expense. The international oil companies, which retained ultimate control over the rate of growth of Middle Eastern crude production throughout the 1960s by virtue of their control of export marketing facilities, were thus obliged to perform an increasingly difficult political and economic balancing role. This involved decisions (i) about the overall extent to which production could be expanded without unduly exacerbating the weakness of realized prices, and (ii) about the division of their total incremental requirement among the different producing countries in which they operated, with reference both to host-government pressures and to joint-ownership considerations.

A4.12.iii—Fiscal issues

By effectively ruling out a serious programme of market-oriented prorationing, Middle Eastern governments also ruled out any prospect of an early cancellation of the cuts which had been made in posted prices in 1960. OPEC's formal reiteration in mid-1962 of its demand for the cancellation of the cuts was therefore coupled with a demand that the Middle Eastern "50-50 profit-sharing" formula should be amended to redefine the royalty element as an expense item rather than a credited payment for tax purposes, in accordance with established practice in Venezuela (◊A4.6). Such a move, which was in effect an alternative means whereby host governments could recoup the unit revenue lost through the cuts in postings, was strongly resisted by the majors. Their final offer, made in 1964 after two years of difficult negotiations between Middle Eastern governments and individual producing companies, was based on a compromise formula which failed to win the formal approval of OPEC because of the refusal of a minority of member countries to endorse what they regarded as concessions to the companies on points of principle.

The compromise offered by the companies was nevertheless accepted by the majority of OPEC member countries at national level, and became known as the OPEC royalty-expensing formula notwithstanding the lack of unanimity within the OPEC Conference (◊**D1.3**). The formula was based (i) on the dropping of host governments' financial claims against the companies in connexion with the 1960 cuts in posted prices; (ii) on the amendment of the Middle Eastern "50-50 profit-sharing" terms to provide both for royalty-expensing and for the use of discounted posted prices for tax purposes; (iii) on an understanding that the agreed scale of discounts would be subject to review after three years in the light of trends in the market price of oil; and (iv) on an acceptance by host governments that no producing company which renegotiated its concession agreement to incorporate the new terms would be subject to a heavier per-barrel tax liability than the most-favoured producing company in the same country.

The countries which accepted the royalty-expensing formula thus settled for a lower increase in their unit revenue entitlement than had originally been demanded, while conceding that the possible future attainment of their full claim should be related to market factors. The major companies, for their part, accepted an increase in their unit tax liability at a time of price weakness and accepted the right of host governments to open fresh negotiations on the level of the tax-reference price at a future date. Underlying the royalty-expensing agreement—although not explicitly incorporated into it—was the companies' acceptance of their inability to make unilateral cuts in posted prices. Implementation of the agreement was expected to go some way towards arresting the decline in the market price of oil (i) because the rise in host governments' unit revenues would increase the effective floor price (represented by production costs plus per-barrel payments to host governments) of oil produced by the majors in the countries concerned, and (ii) because the "most-favoured-company" clause would involve the acceptance of an equal or higher floor price by all other producing companies in these countries.

The latter provision was of particular significance in Libya, where the Government had failed to secure its independent concessionaires' acceptance of the standard Middle Eastern taxation formula in 1961, leaving the independents free to base their 50 per cent tax liability not on posted prices but on their far lower market realizations (◊**C8.3.i**). Although the Libyan Government had had little direct involvement in the negotiation of the royalty-expensing terms, it proceeded to conclude implementation agreements with several of the major oil companies in 1965, resulting in a confrontation between the Government and the independents which led to the ending of the realized-price tax base in Libya. This development was welcomed both by OPEC (because of its revenue implications for the Libyan Government) and by most of the major oil companies (because of its cost implications for their independent competitors). (Libyan oil nevertheless remained highly competitive in Western Europe on the basis of tax-paid cost plus freight because of its relatively low fob posting—established by Exxon in 1961—vis-à-vis east Mediterranean crudes.) In Saudi Arabia, where Aramco had been using realized prices as a tax base for arm's-length crude sales, the Government secured an agreement in 1966 that the profits from such sales should, with effect from 1961, be taxed on the standard terms applying to integrated transfers (◊**C11.3.v**).

In 1966 OPEC resolved to seek the full elimination of the discounting of posted prices for tax purposes under the royalty-expensing formula (the terms of which were open to revision after the end of the year). The de facto elimination of the discount in respect of oil shipped from Mediterranean ports was subsequently conceded by the exporting companies after the closure of the Suez Canal in mid-1967, although the resulting increase in the government revenue entitlement was categorized as a "temporary premium" rather than as an amendment to the terms of the royalty-expensing formula. Negotiations on the terms of the formula were complicated by the fact that the discounts included not only a percentage element but also a graduated "gravity allowance" penalizing the lighter grades of crude, this allowance having been included in the formula in order to align the relative tax values of different grades of crude with the structure of product demand in the main non-US import markets in 1964. Agreement was eventually reached in early 1968 on the phasing out of the percentage discounts by 1972 and of the gravity allowance by 1975 (◊**D1.5**).

Between 1962, when royalty-expensing was first proposed by OPEC governments, and 1969, when the final phasing-out of tax discounts was under way, the average per-barrel revenue accruing to the Middle Eastern OPEC governments increased from 76 cents to 85 cents per barrel, thus raising the average tax-paid cost of Middle Eastern oil (assuming a production cost of not more than 20 cents per barrel) from about 96 cents to about $1.05. Average realized prices for Middle Eastern crudes in 1969 were in the region of $1.30 to $1.40 per barrel, which implied an average post-tax profit for the foreign oil companies of 25 to 35 cents per barrel at an effective tax rate of between 71 and 78 per cent. (Other calculations made at the time, using lower estimates of production costs and realized prices, put the effective tax rate at between 74 and 83 per cent.) In Libya, the Government's estimated revenue per barrel, which stood at 62.9 cents in 1964 (when independent companies were still taxed on their realized profits), increased to 87 cents in 1966 (under the original royalty-expensing terms) and to $1 in 1969 (following the introduction of the "Suez premium"). Venezuela, which operated under its own tax system, negotiated the formal introduction of a scale of tax-reference values (fixed initially at a point between posted prices and realized prices) with effect from the beginning of 1967, when its maximum income tax rate was increased to 52 per cent and its effective tax rate (inclusive of an expensed royalty) to about 70 per cent. The Government's per-barrel revenue increased from an average 95.6 cents in 1964–66 to an average 102.4 cents in 1967–69.

Government unit revenues in Venezuela and the Middle East in 1969 were broadly comparable in cash terms to the levels which had been attained before the cuts in posted prices in 1959, the post-tax unit profit margins of the main exporting companies having by 1969 been reduced by virtually the full amount of the intervening fall in realized prices. In real terms, however, the producing countries' unit purchasing power was significantly lower in 1969 than in 1958 because of intervening inflation (averaging about 2.4 per cent per annum) in the prices of imported manufactured goods.

Indonesia, which had refused to grant any new concessions to foreign oil companies after 1951 and had terminated all existing concession agreements in 1963 (◊**C4.3.i**), remained outside the mainstream of OPEC's deliberations on government-company relations and the taxation of profits. Its former concession holders were retained as contractors to the state on profit-sharing terms whereby the Government accepted a market-oriented revenue base and held responsibility for decisions on minimum export prices. (By extending the principle of state control through to the export marketing stage, Indonesia had no grounds for using artificial tax-reference values to determine the state's share of export profits. In Iran, where the formal status of the IOP consortium was also that of a contractor rather than a concession holder, the principle of state control extended only as far as the production stage. The basis of Iran's arrangements regarding the valuation and taxation of export profits was no different in practice to the basis of the arrangements which applied to the main concession holders in other Middle Eastern states.)

A4.12.iv—New exploration agreements

Whereas there had been relatively little state involvement in the oil industries of most of the future OPEC member countries in the late 1950s, every current member except Abu Dhabi and Qatar had formed a state oil company by the end of the 1960s. From October 1966 onwards regular inter-company meetings were organized by OPEC for the discussion of matters of common interest. The state companies were normally empowered to engage in all aspects of the hydrocarbons industry, and in most cases their main initial priorities were to take control of domestic refining and marketing operations and to launch new ventures for the exploration of undeveloped areas. In order to increase the availability of promising exploration territory, new schedules for the immediate and future relinquishment of large undeveloped blocks within concession areas held by the established producing companies were negotiated by the Governments of Qatar (1961), Kuwait (1962), Saudi Arabia (1963) and Abu Dhabi (1965–66), while the IOP consortium accepted a reduction in its Iranian exploration area at the end of 1966.

The terms of new agreements with foreign oil interests in respect of new and/or relinquished exploration areas were progressively improved to the advantage of the governments or state companies concerned. Thus in Kuwait a 1961 concession agreement with Royal Dutch/Shell, covering the country's offshore area, contained an option for 20 per cent government equity participation, whereas a 1967 agreement between the state-controlled Kuwait National Petroleum Company (KNPC) and Spain's recently formed state company Hispanoil provided for 51 per cent KNPC participation and guaranteed access to the Spanish import market (◊C7.3.ii). Iran's NIOC obtained improved financial benefits in respect of six new 50-50 joint-venture contracts concluded in 1965, and in 1966 NIOC employed a subsidiary of Entreprise de Recherches et d'Activités Pétrolières (ERAP)—the holding company for France's state-owned oil interests—on service-contract terms giving NIOC sole title to any oil produced (◊C5.3.iii). In Indonesia a new form of production-sharing contract, entitling the foreign contractor to a minority share of any oil produced, was introduced in 1966 (◊C4.3.ii).

The general trend throughout the OPEC area was away from conventional concessionary arrangements (except in countries which were at an early stage in their hydrocarbon development) and towards contracts giving a wide measure of state control. Increasingly strict time limits and minimum investment obligations were imposed in respect of initial exploration work, while the exploitation rights available in the event of commercial discoveries tended to cover relatively limited areas (to be reduced through regular relinquishment). Foreign companies were invariably required to provide all of the risk capital and were often required to pay large initial premiums to host governments. Agreements were signed by a very wide spectrum of foreign interests, including (i) US independents, (ii) independent companies from various major importing countries, notably Japan (where state financial and technical assistance was available for foreign oil ventures after 1967) and West Germany, and (iii) state-controlled oil companies or investment authorities both from Western Europe and from the Third World (including India and Pakistan). Among the major oil companies, only Royal Dutch/Shell (whose eastern-hemisphere crude production fell far short of its refinery capacity) was prepared to accept the stiffer conditions attached to new ventures in OPEC

73

countries in the 1960s, and entered into a 50-50 joint venture agreement with NIOC in 1965 as well as its Kuwait offshore concession agreement of 1961. (However, Royal Dutch/Shell withdrew from its existing Indonesian contract areas at the end of 1965 following a period of severe political instability in that country.)

A4.12.v—Pressure for revision of pre-war concession agreements

In view of the increasingly favourable financial terms obtainable from new entrants and of the difficult and protracted negotiations which were often required to secure revised terms from established concession holders (e.g. over royalty-expensing), pressure built up steadily within OPEC for radical amendments to "exploitative" provisions of the principal pre-war concession agreements. Feelings were heightened by an epic confrontation between Iraq and IPC which continued throughout the first decade of OPEC's existence, producing an accumulation of unresolved disputes on numerous issues, including the implementation of royalty-expensing in Iraq. A progressively harder line was taken by successive Iraqi military or military-backed regimes, while most of the major oil companies involved were concerned to avoid any compromise on fundamental issues in Iraq which might undermine their established rights elsewhere in the Middle East.

The conflict in Iraq had its origins in the Government's objections to the relatively slow rate at which the IPC group had developed a total concession area covering almost the entire country, held under agreements which made no provision for relinquishment of unexploited blocks (thus depriving the state of the opportunity to invite new exploration investment from alternative sources). The atmosphere at early negotiations concerning relinquishment, the rate of production growth and other issues was soured by the Middle Eastern posted price reductions of 1959–60, causing the Government to widen its demands to include immediate 90 per cent relinquishment and 20 per cent state equity participation. In 1961 the Government took unilateral action to reduce the company's concession area to the blocks containing its existing producing fields (◊C6.3.iii). More than 10 years of deadlock ensued during which the company virtually ceased to invest in its Iraqi fields, thus slowing the rate of capacity development, limiting the growth of Iraq's oil revenues and widening the scope for IPC's parent companies to accede to pressure from other Middle Eastern governments for higher oil output in their own countries. The Iraq National Oil Company meanwhile concluded agreements in 1968 (i) for exploration by ERAP, on service-contract terms similar to those applying to the French company's 1966 Iranian agreement, in an unproved area claimed by IPC, and (ii) for Soviet technical assistance in the development of a proved but undeveloped oilfield originally discovered by IPC (◊C6.3.iv).

In June 1968 (two months after the Iraq Government's controversial decision to proceed to develop the proved North Rumaila field) the OPEC Conference issued a declaratory statement summarizing the main elements in the Organization's general stance on the issue of government-company relations in member countries (◊B1.9.i). When the government of a member country did not possess the capital resources and technical expertise to take sole responsibility for the development of its hydrocarbon resources, foreign companies should (it was stated) be employed subject to the "greatest measure possible" of government control and participation. Existing concession agreements should be open to revision in accordance with the principle of changing circumstances (i.e. rather than continuing unchanged for their full term on the basis of the opposing legal principle of sanctity of contracts). Government revenue entitlements should be based exclusively on posted or tax-reference prices, fixed by the state and adjusted to keep pace with inflation in the prices of internationally traded manufactured goods. The post-tax earnings of foreign producing companies should be restricted to levels "the reasonable expectation of which would have been sufficient to induce the operator to take the entrepreneurial risks necessary".

(By effectively restricting the companies' profits to the minimum levels which would yield a competitive return on capital invested, host governments would receive the whole of the surplus or "rent" attributable to the gap between the actual production costs of their crude and the highest cost at which it was profitable to produce crude at the prevailing market price. A study commissioned by OPEC had shown that companies producing low-cost crude in the Middle East had secured an average annual rate of return on net assets of more than 60 per cent in the second half of the 1950s. In Venezuela, which had higher production costs and a higher effective tax rate, the producing companies' estimated annual returns on net assets were in the 12 to 17 per cent range between 1958 and 1962.)

A4.13—Failure of 1967 Arab Oil Embargo – Causes and Effects of 1970 Freight Crisis

The Suez Canal was blocked by Egypt during the six-day Arab-Israeli war of June 1967; it was to remain closed until June 1975. Representatives of Abu Dhabi, Algeria, Bahrain, Egypt, Iraq, Kuwait, Libya, Qatar and Saudi Arabia, together with representatives of Lebanon and Syria (as pipeline transit countries), decided at the beginning of the 1967 war to halt the export of oil to countries whose actions or policies were deemed to be directly or indirectly supportive of Israel or hostile to the Arab side in the conflict. The main Arab producing countries halted all exports for some days after the announcement of this decision, although in most cases shipments were soon resumed subject to the acceptance by the producing companies of destination embargoes (affecting principally Britain and the United States, and in some instances also West Germany). Saudi Arabia permitted shipments to resume on this basis before the middle of June, and by early July the only remaining general export bans had been lifted by Iraq (which had taken a particularly hard line on the issue) and Libya (whose politically moderate Government had come under strong domestic pressure from radical anti-Western elements).

US oil companies were authorized by the US Government to co-operate in drawing up emergency plans to offset a possible international supply crisis, although in fact no crisis materialized. This was because (i) the embargo on the Arab countries' exports to the USA (which had constituted less than 5 per cent of total US oil consumption in the first five months of 1967) was of largely symbolic significance at a time when a quarter of the productive capacity of the US oil industry was shut in as a result of prorationing; (ii) some stockpiled supplies existed in Western Europe (in accordance with recent OECD recommendations); (iii) the producing countries' destination embargoes were not accompanied by any commensurate ceilings on total export volumes, thus facilitating "swap" arrangements by some exporting companies (although all companies complied with the letter of their host governments' instructions); (iv) the producing companies were able to step up their shipments from the two main non-Arab exporting countries, Iran and Venezuela; and (v) the extent of the Persian/Arabian Gulf exporters' dependence on the Suez Canal supply route for westbound oil shipments had recently begun to decrease with the introduction of a new generation of tankers too large to pass through the Canal.

The fact that the Arab countries could not impose a politically effective embargo in the current oil market conditions without suffering severe revenue losses was rapidly appreciated by the "moderate" producers (led by Saudi Arabia, Kuwait and Libya). This left Iraq (which had favoured a three-month total export ban) in an isolated position among the main Arab exporters. Of the other political hard-liners among the Arab states, Syria stood to lose only transit fees as a result of a total export ban, while Algeria was exporting the greater part of its oil output to France (itself strongly critical of Israel's role in the six-day war).

The combined revenue losses suffered by Saudi Arabia and Kuwait as a result of the destination embargoes were estimated to be as high as $700,000 per day by late June 1967, while the embargoed countries were encountering little difficulty in acquiring alternative supplies from non-Arab sources. Saudi Arabia and Kuwait, together with Libya, therefore secured formal approval for the lifting of oil sanctions when the issue was discussed by a summit conference of Arab heads of state at the end of August 1967. The three countries pledged instead to contribute a total of $378,000,000 per annum to Egypt and Jordan to alleviate the longer-term economic consequences of the six-day war for these countries. Saudi Arabia, Kuwait and Libya subsequently formed OAPEC in January 1968 with the aim (as described by its first Secretary-General, Shaikh Ahmed Zaki Yamani of Saudi Arabia) of "keeping oil activity within the Organization with a view to protecting the member states from precipitous decisions and making oil a genuine weapon to serve the interests of the producing countries and the Arab countries in general" (◊B2.2). At the same time OPEC (whose policies were to be adhered to by OAPEC) was effectively protected from being drawn into Arab politics at times of crisis.

Although the indefinite closure of the Suez Canal caused no insuperable short-term supply problems for importing countries, it did increase Western Europe's dependence on Mediterranean imports (particularly from north Africa) by enhancing their proximity advantage vis-à-vis supplies from the Persian/Arabian Gulf. Spare capacity in the tanker market was rapidly brought into service, and freight rates remained well above their May 1967 level as the volume of trade continued to expand at very high rates. However, an initial rise in the average cif price of crude in Western Europe had been reversed by 1969 as a result of an offsetting decline in fob realizations (estimated netbacks from spot product trading being as much as 55 cents per barrel below the corresponding crude postings at certain points during 1969). The US market was meanwhile beginning to tighten. The annual volume of US oil consumption rose above the level of domestic productive capacity in 1968. The following year net imports exceeded 3,000,000 bpd for the first time, while the capacity utilization rate rose to its highest level since 1952 and the average realized crude price on the domestic market rose to $3.09 per barrel, a post-war high point equalled only in 1957. Libyan crude, which had not previously been shipped to the US market on any scale, began to come into demand on the east coast in 1969 following the introduction of new controls on sulphur pollution.

A section of the trans-Arabian pipeline situated in Israeli-occupied Syrian territory was sabotaged by Palestinian action at the end of May 1969, causing a shutdown of the pipeline until mid-September. This development had little impact on the oil market, mainly because of the continuing rapid expansion of output in Libya, which was OPEC's largest exporter of crude oil in 1969. Exports via the trans-Arabian pipeline were again halted on May 3, 1970, when a different section of the pipeline was (according to the Syrian authorities) accidentally damaged during cable-laying work in Syria. Permission to repair the damage was withheld by the Syrian Government pending the settlement of a claim for sharply increased transit fees. An ensuing political conflict between Syria and Saudi Arabia remained deadlocked until a new Syrian regime took power in November 1970. It was not until late January 1971 that terms were agreed for the repair of the pipeline and the resumption of Mediterranean exports by Saudi Arabia (which was finally achieved on Feb. 8).

Soon after the second shutdown on the trans-Arabian pipeline, the revolutionary regime which had taken power in Libya in September 1969 ordered the country's oil output to be reduced in accordance with new conservation regulations (◊C8.3.ii). These had been introduced as a result of genuine concern about the high rate of reservoir depletion but were now enforced in such a way as to bring the maximum pressure to bear on independent companies which had few alternative supply sources. The Government's immediate aim was to secure an increase in the posted price of Libyan crude on the grounds (i) that it had been underposted relative to east Mediterranean crudes since Libyan exports had begun in 1961, (ii) that the existing Suez premium did not fully reflect Libya's current "short-haul" advantage in West European import markets, and (iii) that no allowance was made in the posting for the low sulphur content of Libyan crude.

(The established posted price structure in the Middle East and north Africa incorporated fixed differentials which reflected the geographical location of different export points on the basis of average long-haul freight rates at the beginning of the 1960s. The structure took account of variations in the gravity of different crudes but made no allowance for any other inherent qualities. Premium prices were, however, beginning to be realized for low-sulphur crudes in arm's-length sales to the United States and other markets where their use obviated the need to invest in desulphurization plant in order to comply with environmental protection legislation.)

The removal from the market of up to 1,250,000 bpd of Mediterranean exports caused the existing shortage of tanker capacity to reach crisis proportions as west-of-Suez importers sought to ship alternative crude supplies from the Persian/Arabian Gulf, driving freight rates for spot charters to four times their 1969 average and pushing up the average cif cost of imported crude oil. Although Persian/Arabian Gulf fob realizations remained unchanged, Mediterranean realizations rose by up to 25 per cent, and at one point a quantity of Libyan crude was sold for more than its posted price for the first time ever.

Whereas West European ex-refinery prices for open-market sales of lighter products rose in line with the general trend in the cif cost of crude imports, the market price of heavy fuel oil showed a far greater increase both in Europe and in other importing regions during 1970 because of the impact of the freight crisis on existing supply problems.

One of the main problems stemmed from a decline in US output of fuel oil during the 1960s, when the country's refining industry, which was reporting returns on investment of as little as 2 per cent, had restructured its capacity in order to give an increasing emphasis to the production of gasoline (the US market price of fuel oil having been driven down to an exceptionally low level as a result of competition from cheap natural gas ◊A2.5). Rising US demand for fuel oil at the end of the 1960s (caused partly by constraints on the supply of natural gas and partly by the iron and steel industry's high demand for coking coal, which reduced the supply of sulphur-free coal to power plants) had therefore led to a build-up of fuel oil imports from West European refineries, which as the principal buyers of Libyan crude were able to compete with established Caribbean suppliers of US fuel oil imports on the basis of the far lower sulphur content of their output.

The deployment of tankers to carry fuel oil from Europe to the United States had reduced the available margin of spare tanker capacity virtually to nil by the time that the Libyan production cutbacks began, with the result that the downturn in Western Europe's supply of short-haul crude affected the availability of fuel oil both in the United States (to the extent that tankers were redeployed to carry Gulf crude to Western Europe) and in Western Europe (to the extent that tankers were not available to transport all of the region's additional requirement for Gulf crude).

The shortage of tankers also ruled out the possibility of shipping fuel oil westwards from refineries on the Persian/Arabian Gulf, whose exports were in strong demand in Japan, where local refineries were operating at close to full capacity in 1970. One ironic aspect of the overall situation was that the current rapid growth in the energy demand of the main industrialized countries (particularly Japan) was attributable in part to the high level of activity in shipyards which were building new oil tankers ordered after it had become apparent that the Suez Canal was likely to remain closed for some time.

A4.14—Renegotiation of Middle Eastern and North African Tax Structure

Given its considerable bargaining power in these circumstances, especially in relation to its independent concession holders, the Libyan Government was able to secure a permanent increase in the posted prices of Libyan crudes in September 1970, with retroactivity to 1965 (normally "bought out" in the form of a higher income tax rate on future export income) and guaranteed escalation of postings to 1975. Overall, the government revenue entitlement was increased by about 25 per cent. The major oil companies, whose ultimate sanction in confrontations with host governments had traditionally been to deny access to export markets (as in Mexico in the late 1930s and Iran in the early 1950s), were unable to threaten such action in Libya, not least because of its unacceptability to the governments of oil-importing countries whose overriding interest was to ensure continuity of supplies, and the threat of an export ban was instead used against the majors by the Libyan Government in order to end their resistance to its demands. (At the same time, the European government which had gone to the greatest lengths to reduce its dependence on the majors as suppliers of crude—that of France—was involved in a separate confrontation with Algeria, which had derived even less benefit than Libya from its "short-haul" advantage because of the preferential fiscal treatment accorded to French oil companies under a 1965 bilateral co-operation agreement ◊**C1.3.ii.**)

The major oil companies' acceptance of Libya's demands did not involve them in any short-term financial loss relative to their position before the freight crisis, since their additional profits on Libyan crude during the crisis were well in excess of their additional tax liabilities. Company resistance to the settlement terms had stemmed largely from the fact that they involved a permanent increase in Libyan postings and a de facto rise in the rate of income tax, setting targets for inevitable "parity" claims by Middle Eastern OPEC countries whose Persian/Arabian Gulf exports had not increased in fob market value during the freight crisis. By the end of 1970 the main Middle Eastern producers had obtained (or had been offered) an increase in the rate of income tax to 55 per cent, together with higher postings not only for crudes exported from east Mediterranean terminals but also for heavy crudes exported from the Persian/Arabian Gulf, while OPEC had resolved to seek a comprehensive revision of the entire posted price structure and had set up a ministerial committee to hold collective negotiations on Middle Eastern oil taxation arrangements (◊**D1.6.iii**).

When it became clear that Libya intended to use a Middle Eastern settlement as a basis for claiming further increases in its own postings, virtually all of the foreign oil companies operating in the Middle East and north Africa entered into a collective agreement to resist country-by-country, region-by-region or company-by-company negotiations on the various OPEC demands, thus totally reversing their long-standing opposition to collective bargaining with the Organization (◊**D2.2.i**). The companies' demand for "global" negotiations covering both Gulf and Mediterranean postings was, however, rejected by the OPEC countries concerned, which were fully aware of their superior bargaining strength at a time when the companies were not in a position to apply pressure by altering the geographical balance of their overall offtake pattern within the OPEC area.

A regional settlement revising the structure of Gulf postings (◊**D2.2.ii**) was therefore concluded in Tehran in February 1971 without prejudice to the terms of a Mediterranean settlement (although with assurances that improved Mediterrancan terms would not be used as a basis for a new "leapfrogging" claim in the Gulf). The Tripoli agreement of April 1971 (◊**C8.3.ii**) subsequently provided the framework for a Mediterranean settlement which widened the fixed differentials between Mediterranean and Gulf postings (including permanent freight and quality premiums) while applying additional temporary freight premiums to Mediterranean exports in the form of an improved "Suez Canal allowance" plus a variable element linked to changes in prevailing average freight rates. All discounting of posted prices for tax purposes was ended, and a schedule was agreed for future increases in postings in the period 1971–75. The Tehran and Tripoli agreements—each concluded under threat of co-ordinated unilateral action by the group of OPEC countries concerned—established the full negotiability of all the elements involved in the determination of government unit revenues, including posted prices and the structure of differentials, and were seen by OPEC as marking the Organization's "emergence as a powerful, internationally recognized oil policy instrument, capable of playing an effective role in the international oil world".

Following this widely publicized renegotiation of taxation arrangements, the international oil companies took the line that their function as exporters was essentially that of "tax collecting agents" for OPEC governments, although at the same time they increased their own arm's-length crude prices by more than the amount of the tax increase. Similar increases were made in the company margin on products marketed through integrated channels, with the result that, after many years of reporting losses or marginal profits, the majors began to record significant levels of profit on their downstream operations in the eastern hemisphere. The formation of an inter-company "policy group" to co-ordinate the process of collective bargaining with OPEC provided scope for regular consultations between oil companies on a scale which had not been possible since the 1930s, while OPEC's role as the perceived agent of change provided an "external" explanation for a general round of price increases which might in other circumstances have been regarded as the result of inter-company collusion. From the companies' viewpoint, the Tehran and Tripoli agreements had many positive implications in that they appeared to offer the prospect of five years of relatively "orderly" marketing as the effective floor price of internationally traded crude gradually rose in line with the OPEC tax take.

A4.15—The Transition to OPEC Control over Crude Pricing

A4.15.i—Emergence of a seller's market for oil

Between the second quarter of 1971 and the third quarter of 1972 sufficient new tanker capacity became available to restore a more normal degree of operational flexibility in the international oil trade, and freight rates fell back to the levels of mid-1969 as dependence on short-haul supply sources became less acute. (One demonstration of the return to flexibility was a cut of 543,000 bpd in the average level of IPC's Mediterranean exports between February and April 1972, which brought the company's conflict with the Iraq Government to a head and led to the nationalization of Iraq's northern oilfields at the beginning of June ◊**C6.3.iv**.) Average fob market prices remained fairly stable at the levels established after the conclusion of the Tehran and Tripoli agreements, subject to changes in the host-government take arising from the operation of these agreements and of supplemental agreements which were negotiated in early 1972 to take account of fluctuations in the exchange rate of the US dollar against other major currencies ($\lozenge$D3.2).

The underlying market situation was, however, far from stable. US oil production began to decline after 1970 ($\lozenge$A3.1.iv), with the result that the utilization rate of domestic productive capacity rose towards 95 per cent in 1971–72, while net imports rose by more than 50 per cent between 1969 and 1972 as quotas were progressively increased in order to step up the supply of eastern-hemisphere oil to the US market (a sharp rise in the country's largely unrestricted imports of Canadian oil having failed to cover the growth in the supply deficit). The decline in the USA's margin of shut-in capacity was offset for a period by the rapid expansion of capacity in certain OPEC countries (particularly Saudi Arabia, where Aramco was the only major Middle Eastern producing company under exclusively US ownership), although by mid-1972 the margin of surplus OPEC capacity was beginning to be seriously eroded. Notable contributory factors (apart from Libya's strict application of its conservation regulations) included the Kuwait Government's decision in April 1972 to veto its concession holders' expansion plans and to announce a "preferred long-range production ceiling" of 3,000,000 bpd. Venezuela introduced a system of government export targets with effect from the beginning of 1973, with financial penalties for companies which over- or under-produced beyond a permissible margin.

US government policy towards the country's growing import dependence was based mainly on strategic considerations and gave priority to the prevention of any decline in the economic viability of high-cost domestic oil production (including future production from the north Alaskan oilfields, whose development had been delayed pending the outcome of legal action by environmental protection groups which objected to the oil industry's pipeline proposals). The narrowing of the gap between the prices of US domestic crudes and imported OPEC crudes in the first quarter of 1971 was therefore welcome to the US Government, which had given clear indications during the run-up to OPEC's Tehran negotiations that its concern was not to keep down the price of imported oil but to ensure security of supply. Because US oilfields were being operated at close to full capacity in order to minimize the growth of import dependence, prorationing could no longer be used as a price-support mechanism, leaving the system of transferable import quotas ($\lozenge$A4.10.ii) as the principal device for "neutralizing" the remaining gap between the US oil price and the OPEC oil price as the volume of imports from OPEC countries increased. The US Assistant Secretary of the Interior for Mineral Resources referred to the strategic function of quotas in May 1972, when he said that the continuing restriction of imports was essential "if we are ever to see the commercial development of synthetic fuel from domestic oil shale and coal".

The other main non-communist oil-importing countries, which had enjoyed a certain competitive advantage over the United States during the 1960s as a result of their manufacturers' access to lower-priced oil (an advantage which was only partially offset by US industry's access to cheap natural gas), were left in little doubt that, as a high-cost oil producer whose long-term security of supply would be enhanced by higher prices, the United States would do nothing to dissuade its importing companies from bidding up the price of oil in the world market if the growing US demand for foreign oil led to a general supply shortage.

The worsening during 1971 and 1972 of localized energy supply problems within the United States, caused mainly by a growing shortfall in fuel oil production as the availability of natural gas became increasingly restricted, served to focus the attention of the US public on energy issues, the credibility of various "crisis" scenarios being heightened by the growth in import dependence. The publication of a number of general studies criticizing the "philosophy of growth" tended to reinforce a general expectation of shortage on the part of both US and foreign consumers, as did warnings by major oil companies concerning the need for the adoption of "balanced" energy policies in the industrialized oil-importing countries.

Increases in spot oil prices signalled a shift to a seller's market during the last quarter of 1972, when the build-up of winter demand in the main importing countries began to cut into the remaining margin of surplus productive capacity. There was a similar upturn in freight rates. Growing competition between the United States and other consuming countries for a limited volume of incremental supplies now seemed inevitable, and a mood of "crisis anticipation" became increasingly apparent among consumers, producers and oil companies alike. OPEC, for its part, placed discussion of "the world energy crisis" on its agenda in March 1973, when member countries began to formulate their conditions for meeting export demand in the changing market environment (◊D4.2). Three months later OPEC issued a policy statement serving notice on the main importing countries that nothing less than a significant change in the balance of world economic power would provide the exporting countries with an adequate incentive to meet the currently-projected medium-term growth in import demand (◊B1.9.ii).

The transition to a seller's market for oil coincided with the finalization of terms for host-government participation in the ownership of production operations in the main Middle Eastern concession areas, which was to begin at the level of 25 per cent from 1973 to 1977, increasing thereafter to reach 51 per cent in 1982 (◊D3.4). Although the major oil companies would handle the export marketing of far more than their equity share of production from the areas concerned for an interim period (e.g. between 93.75 per cent and 97.5 per cent of production in 1973), the fact that the role of the majors was scheduled to diminish year by year ensured that the relatively small volumes of oil which were initially available for direct export by host governments would attract brisk bidding from independent buyers anxious to gain long-term access to supplies from this source.

At the same time, the governments of heavily import-dependent countries began to show a greater concern for their bilateral relations with exporting countries, reflecting the predominant view that government-to-government deals would play an increasingly important role in the future pattern of world oil trade. In contrast, the US State Department indicated during 1972 that it favoured a multilateral approach by the oil-importing countries to the problem of security of supply, on the grounds that unrestrained competition for supplies would merely strengthen the strategic position of OPEC. Other importing countries showed a marked lack of enthusiasm for the US line at this stage, reflecting their awareness that the United States did not share their misgivings about a rise in the cost of imported oil (although for Britain and Norway the issue was less clear-cut, given their medium-term interest in the development of the high-cost oil resources which had recently been discovered beneath the North Sea).

All in all, the way in which conflicting national policies prevented a consensus among the main oil-importers in conditions of shortage was reminiscent of the difficulties which had prevented the exporting countries from introducing an effective prorationing programme in conditions of surplus. In the present circumstances, the United States was virtually the only OECD member which was ready to accept a higher floor price in order to stabilize the supply situation, while in the mid-1960s Venezuela had been virtually the only OPEC member which was ready to accept a lower production ceiling in order to support market prices.

An opportunity for a long-term bilateral deal was presented to the US Government by Saudi Arabia at the end of September 1972, when it was publicly proposed that guaranteed supplies of Saudi oil should be made available to the United States within the context of a "commercial agreement" whereby such supplies would enjoy unresticted duty-free access to the US market, while Saudi Arabia would invest in downstream operations within the USA. An undertaking by the US Government to carry out a "careful study" of this proposal was not followed up because it was held to conflict with the USA's political and strategic interests as an oil-producing country.

The rather different priorities of an almost totally import-dependent country were spelled out as follows by the Japanese Minister of International Trade and Industry on his return from a Middle East tour in May 1973: "I have become strongly aware of the need to approach Middle East oil not simply as tradeable merchandise but as something more deeply politically involved. Oil is a critical resource for Japan and dealings in oil cannot be handled by individual Japanese enterprises or traders alone without the support of the Japanese Government, which will involve itself in strong and continuous petroleum diplomacy in the future. The international oil situation is in a period of transition, with producing nations seeking partners among consuming nations for long-range oil contracts. Establishment of a co-operative relationship between a group of the world's largest oil-producing nations and Japan as one of the world's largest consuming nations will have an important influence over the international oil scene."

During the first nine months of 1973 virtually all the available productive capacity of the world oil industry was brought into use in response to a major surge in demand. By early October the volume of OPEC production was equivalent to more than 119 per cent of its average 1972 level, with a further increase in demand still in prospect as energy use in the main consuming regions built up towards its winter peak.

US crude oil production continued to decline despite the utilization of full capacity after the end of 1972, while US demand for the heavier oil products rose even further above the supply capability of the domestic refining industry (whose total capacity had fallen slightly in 1972) and localized gasoline shortages began to occur as refiners reduced the proportion of lighter products in their output. All quota restrictions on US imports of heating oil were lifted in mid-January 1973. Canada placed controls on its oil exports to the United States at the beginning of March 1973 in order to stem their recent rapid growth rate, and in the following month the US Government announced the ending of all quantitative quota restrictions on oil imports, which instead became subject to a licensing system allowing duty-free entry with effect from the beginning of May. Localized energy supply shortages—exacerbated by the effect of current federal controls on consumer prices—nevertheless became more frequent within the United States, and the introduction of a mandatory allocation system for wholesale supplies of propane gas and middle distillates (including home-heating oil) was announced during the first two weeks of October 1973.

Oil prices and freight rates had meanwhile soared worldwide, with the result that Middle Eastern and north African OPEC crudes, whose market value had been as much as 25 per cent below their tax-reference value in mid-1972, were now commanding as much as or more than the "prices" posted for tax purposes. (By far the highest fob realizations were obtained for short-haul crudes, reflecting the fact that freight rates had reached levels well above the peak recorded during the 1970 freight crisis.) The termination of the US import quota system was therefore effected without any fear of downward pressure on US domestic oil prices, and indeed Canada (which imported mainly OPEC oil to supply its own eastern market) decided in mid-September 1973 to impose an export tax on oil supplied to the USA in order to take account of the sharp rise in the delivered price of Middle Eastern crude in North America.

A4.15.ii—First unilateral OPEC increase in Middle Eastern crude postings – Subsequent use of Arab oil weapon

The principal beneficiaries of the increase in the market price of OPEC oil were the major oil companies, whose post-tax unit profit margins on exports of equity crude rose by between 170 and 500 per cent between the middle of 1972 and the beginning of October 1973 in countries where taxation was based on the posted price structure laid down in the Tehran and Tripoli agreements (◊**D4.3**). The introduction of participation arrangements of one kind or another in virtually all of the countries concerned meant that host governments were exceptionally well placed to monitor market trends (which were reflected in the prices obtained for their own direct exports), and in September 1973 Saudi Arabia began to charge 93 per cent of the posted prices for that part of the state's share of production which was sold to Aramco's parent companies (and which had previously been priced at or below the market rate prevailing at the end of 1972). The overall government share of profits nevertheless remained well below its mid-1972 level.

Indonesia, the only OPEC country which had accepted a market-related revenue base for the past decade, reaped the rewards of this policy when the tightening of the market enabled it to raise its official selling price for 34° crude by 60.5 per cent between Jan. 1 and Oct. 1, 1973. In contrast, the Aramco shareholders' Ras Tanura posting for Saudi crude of the same gravity rose by 16.2 per cent over the same period, the entire increase being attributable to exchange-rate indexation to offset the fall in the value of the US dollar. As at Oct. 1, 1973, the Indonesian selling price was $1.739 higher than the Saudi Arabian posting, whereas in 1970 it had been lower by $0.10. Venezuela, which had fixed its tax-reference prices unilaterally since 1970, increased the reference price of its 35° crude by 41 per cent between Jan. 1 and Oct. 1, 1973.

Dissatisfaction among Middle Eastern and north African OPEC members at their failure to share the full benefit of a strong seller's market was heightened by the fact that the purchasing power of their oil revenues was being seriously eroded by the high rate of price inflation in the industrialized countries, which was running at around 8 to 9 per cent on an annual basis in the third quarter of 1973 (whereas the Tehran and Tripoli agreements had allowed for a fixed 2.5 per cent annual inflation adjustment in posted prices).

Negotiations with the major oil companies opened in early October 1973 on the Gulf OPEC members' demands that the Tehran agreement should be amended to create a link between posted prices and realized prices in a rising market and to provide full indexation against inflation. In view of the implications of the former demand, which would in effect create a "ratchet" mechanism whereby each peak in the market would automatically raise the permanent floor price of Middle Eastern oil, the companies consulted the governments of the OECD importing countries, virtually all of which opposed an agreement along these lines. The possibility of further such consultations was ruled out by the OPEC side, which announced a unilateral 70 per cent increase in postings (said to be equivalent to a 17 per cent increase in the current market price) on Oct. 16 (◊**D4.4**). Control over the floor price of crude oil thus passed into the hands of the producing countries in circumstances which highlighted the current importance of oil pricing as a factor in international economic relations. Since the major oil companies had demonstrated that they could no longer negotiate effectively on taxation without the clearance of the importing countries, negotiability was ended and the companies were left to pass their increased tax liabilities through to the consumer in order to protect their profit margins (a task which they had no difficulty in performing in the current seller's market).

On the following day (Oct. 17, 1973), Arab oil-exporting countries (including non-members of OPEC) announced production cutbacks in support of the Arab cause in the latest Middle Eastern war, which had been launched by Egypt and Syria on Oct. 6 with the declared aim of recapturing the Arab territories occupied by Israel since 1967. Egypt had been attempting throughout 1973 to persuade the US Government to apply diplomatic pressure for an Israeli withdrawal from the occupied territories, and had in August obtained Saudi Arabia's backing for the use of the oil weapon. The US Government had been repeatedly informed of the Saudi Government's grave concern about the US disregard for Arab opinion and had been specifically warned that Aramco's exports would be placed at risk if there was no change in US Middle Eastern policy. This warning was, however, ignored by the United States, which apparently believed that the use of the Arab oil weapon would be no more effective in 1973 than it had proved to be in 1967. (In view of the exceptionally delicate balance of world oil supply and demand in 1973, observers could only account for this belief in terms of the Nixon Administration's failure to consider the issue fully at a time of growing preoccupation with the Watergate scandal.)

Saudi Arabia, for its part, had refused to contemplate the use of oil sanctions until it was certain that there was no possibility of encountering the main obstacle which had existed in 1967, namely an available margin of non-Arab productive capacity large enough to neutralize the effect of Arab cutbacks. The Saudi Government was moreover careful to ensure that the 1973 sanctions were based on the application of progressive across-the-board cutbacks which would produce the widest possible impact on importing countries while severely limiting the scope for the evasion of destination embargoes (which when subsequently imposed were directed principally at the United States and the Netherlands).

The strategy of general cutbacks (which was adopted by all the producers concerned except Iraq) proved to be particularly effective because of the current high growth rate of energy demand, which magnified the impact of each reduction in oil supplies. The financial effect of the cutbacks on the producing countries was minimized by the OPEC tax increase of Oct. 16, which provided scope for production to be cut to less than 60 per cent of its September 1973 level without causing total government revenue to fall below its September level. It was decided by Arab heads of state in late November 1973 that, if necessary, cuts should continue until total government revenue had fallen to 75 per cent of its 1972 level (implying a cut in production to well below 50 per cent of the 1972 level).

Although the total loss of Arab supplies did not exceed 25 per cent of the September 1973 production level when the campaign reached its height in December 1973 (◊**D4.5**), the credibility of the threat to proceed to far greater cutbacks caused importing countries to introduce a wide variety of measures to conserve their existing oil stocks, including the lowering of speed limits on roads, restrictions on the sale of gasoline and the use of motor vehicles, restrictions on non-essential uses of electricity and limitations on the heating of buildings.

In Japan, which was then dependent on Arab oil for about 30 per cent of its total national energy supply, the introduction of measures along these lines on Nov. 16 was followed on Dec. 23 by the declaration of a state of emergency under which stringent energy rationing regulations came into force. The Japanese Government stated that the Arab supply cutbacks had presented the country with its worst crisis since the end of the Second World War. In the United States, the introduction of short-term energy conservation measures was accompanied by the announcement

84

of an ambitious long-term programme ("Project Independence") to achieve self-sufficiency in energy supplies by 1980. It was proposed that $10,000 million of federal funding should be provided for a five-year research and development effort under this programme. In December 1973 the co-ordination of US energy policy was placed under the direction of a new Federal Energy Office (renamed the Federal Energy Administration in May 1974), and in October 1974 a separate Energy Research and Development Administration was established.

In view of the considerable political success of the Arab oil sanctions in ensuring that serious new international initiatives were undertaken to resolve the Arab-Israeli conflict, most restrictions on oil supplies were lifted during the first half of 1974 ($\lozenge$**D5.2**). The supply crisis had drawn attention both to the degree of import-dependence in the main industrialized countries and to the increasingly difficult position of the international oil companies in the buffer zone between producers and consumers. As the effective administrators of the Arab sanctions, the companies had been obliged to observe government instructions in Arab exporting countries, particularly with regard to destination embargoes, while at the same time facing strong pressure from the governments of importing countries regarding access to available supplies of non-Arab oil and non-embargoed Arab oil, the equitable allocation of which was made particularly difficult by the Arab states' decision to subdivide non-embargoed importing countries into different categories after November 1973.

Government-company relations were seriously strained at some points in various West European countries which considered that they were entitled to receive higher import volumes, while in the United States there was a full-scale political backlash against the "disloyalty" of the US majors in enforcing the total embargo on US imports of Arab oil. It was moreover widely alleged that the companies' record earnings during 1973 (attributable mainly to the decline in the effective tax rate in the Middle East prior to Oct. 16) constituted evidence of profiteering at a time of supply shortage and rising consumer prices, and the companies were called upon to justify their conduct before various congressional committees whose detailed investigations did much to illuminate the majors' changing fiscal and operational relationship with the OPEC countries.

A4.16—The New Balance of World Oil Power

Whereas the October 1973 increase in OPEC postings was based primarily on a demand-led tightening of the market, and thus constituted a predictable element in a perceived "energy crisis", a subsequent sharp rise in spot oil prices resulted from the temporary dislocation of normal trading patterns following the imposition of the Arab producers' politically-motivated supply cutbacks. The Gulf OPEC countries, meeting in December 1973 to review market developments for the first time since their assumption of control over pricing decisions in October, found themselves in a very strong position to use this exceptional spot trend as a basis for further large increases in permanent postings, thereby ensuring that the cumulative "price shock" to the world economy was well in excess of all expectations based on the underlying balance of supply and demand.

The main advocate of a drastic shift in world economic power was the Shah of Iran, whose country was not involved in the Arab producers' political campaign. The Saudi Arabian Government, on the other hand, rejected as arbitrary and opportunistic any price increase designed to bring postings fully into line with current spot values, and expressed grave reservations when the meeting eventually adopted a rather smaller compromise increase ($\lozenge$**D4.6**) which more than doubled the host-government take on the foreign exporting companies' offtake of equity crude (to around $7 per barrel, said to be the prevailing cost of developing alternative energy sources). Saudi Arabia had maintained that normal market factors would not justify a government take in excess of $5 per barrel, but was in no position to take a hard line on this issue at a time when its own production cutbacks accounted for a large part of the current abnormality in the marketplace.

The Gulf producers' decision (which was endorsed by the full OPEC Conference in January 1974) placed OPEC at the centre of world economic affairs, serving as it did to invalidate all previous assumptions about trade balances and energy economics and to re-emphasize the vulnerability of import-dependent economies which were still adjusting to the shock of supply disruptions. At the same time, however, the clash between Saudi Arabia and Iran over the extent of the price increase gave some forewarning of OPEC's own vulnerability to internal disagreement now that crude pricing had been taken out of the hands of the foreign oil companies, whose former adversarial role at the negotiating table had provided a powerful stimulus to OPEC unity. A total absence of formal Conference resolutions on pricing issues from October 1973 onwards illustrated OPEC's heightened dependence on compromise between sovereign governments as questions of national self-interest came increasingly to the fore.

The operation of a pricing system based on tax-reference values reached a new level of complexity during 1974 as the governments of the Arabian peninsula, negotiating separately with their respective concession-holders, began to move towards full state control over production operations. (The early abandonment of the general agreement on a nine-year transition to majority state control in the region had become likely in June 1973, when Kuwait announced its intention to seek immediate majority control, and inevitable after the subsequent upsurge of Arab nationalism during the October war.) Kuwait took the lead in establishing a new benchmark of 60 per cent state participation in production operations with effect from the beginning of 1974 (◊C7.3.iii), while Saudi Arabia made it clear that it regarded the 60 per cent level as an interim step towards 100 per cent participation. It was, however, recognized that there was no possibility of achieving similar levels of state control over export marketing in the foreseeable future, with the result that the complicated pattern of overlapping participation negotiations was complemented by a variety of national buy-back arrangements whereby differing proportions of each government's majority share of production were made available to the foreign equity-holders under differing pricing formulas.

Although it was not possible to assess the precise level of the foreign companies' average profit margin on Gulf crudes in these circumstances, it was very clear that the companies had benefited substantially from the increase in postings at the beginning of the year and were well-placed to undercut direct sales by host governments when the market softened after the relaxation of the Arab embargo measures (◊D5.4). Discussion of this problem at successive OPEC meetings during 1974 eventually paved the way for the introduction of a more straightforward pricing system based on official selling prices for state-owned crude, while the margins available on the foreign exporting companies' remaining equity supplies were greatly restricted by increases in tax and royalty rates (◊D5.6.ii). However, strong pressure from Saudi Arabia ensured that the resulting rise in the average government take (to $10.12 per barrel on 34° Saudi crude, which served as OPEC's marker grade) was accompanied by a small cut in the official selling price (to $10.463 per barrel) and by the freezing of prices for the first nine months of 1975.

The existing trend towards the strengthening of bilateral contacts between industrialized oil-importing countries and OPEC countries took on a new momentum in early 1974 as the importers sought both to safeguard their future security of supply in the light of the Arab embargo and to expand their export trade in the light of the vast increase in OPEC oil revenues. As before, the United States distanced itself from the proliferation of government-to-government oil deals, although it did conclude a comprehensive economic and military co-operation agreement with Saudi Arabia in June 1974 with the aim of strengthening the special relationship between the two countries in the aftermath of the "oil shock".

A US diplomatic campaign to form a united front of industrialized oil-importing countries, launched initially at the height of the Arab embargo, was stepped up at the beginning of 1974 amid mounting concern in Washington at the growth in the political influence of the Arab oil exporters and in the economic power of OPEC. However, many differences of opinion emerged at a US-sponsored conference of the main OECD countries in February 1974 (◊**D5.8**), and it was not until November of that year that the International Energy Agency was established to implement a co-ordinated strategy under the auspices of the OECD (◊**D5.12**). The European Economic Community had meanwhile launched a long-term "dialogue" on co-operation with Arab states (◊**D5.10**), while individual EEC members had continued to conclude new bilateral agreements with OPEC countries. Japan had likewise pursued its policy of bilateral "petroleum diplomacy" with renewed vigour.

Having secured agreement on an initial IEA programme of action centred on contingency planning to reduce the member countries' vulnerability to a future disruption of oil imports, the United States proposed in early 1975 that the Agency should adopt a floor price for imported oil in order to guarantee the viability of alternative energy sources whose development would reduce the level of import-dependence in the longer term (◊**D6.13**). This proposal was, however, coolly received by the majority of other members, and a modified "minimum safeguard price" formula was not adopted until January 1976 (when this price was set at $7 per barrel).

The US Government displayed a strongly hostile attitude towards OPEC as an organization during 1974 and 1975 (with the aim, stated in April 1975 by the Assistant Secretary of State for Economic Affairs, of "breaking the cartel"), although it stopped short of explicitly describing the IEA as an intended instrument of confrontation. "Indirect" US government action against the OPEC members included the mounting of a campaign from early 1975 to prevent international credit institutions such as the World Bank from lending money to oil-exporting countries at preferential rates. OPEC was moreover an increasingly common target of public criticism which had previously been focused on the major oil companies (whose perceived role became that of "captive agents" of the exporting countries as state participation was extended), the mood of US public opinion in late 1974 being reflected in the Senate's refusal to extend standard tariff preferences to OPEC countries (◊**D6.12**).

At the same time, however, the US Government's long-term strategic interest in maintaining a high level of energy self-sufficiency was clearly assisted by the increase in OPEC oil prices and the attendant improvement in the economic viability of high-cost energy sources, thus diminishing the credibility of government attacks on OPEC pricing policy. The confusion surrounding US energy policy was compounded by the Government's failure to secure congressional approval for many key aspects of its import-limitation programme, including a proposal to deregulate domestic oil prices (which had become subject to federal controls during the period of supply constraints). Domestic prices were therefore held well below world prices after 1973, and OPEC oil exports to the USA continued to increase at a time when the West European and Japanese markets were contracting as sharp price increases were passed through to consumers (◊**A3.1.v**). (Table 12 shows the evolution of West European consumer prices.)

Table 12 — Retail price of oil products in Western Europe, 1969 to 1984 (dollars per typical barrel)

	1969	1972	1975	1978	1981	1984
Pre-tax retail price	5.49	7.60	17.67	23.65	45.55	39.00
(of which crude oil fob*)	(1.06)	(1.55)	(10.75)	(12.65)	(32.63)	(28.80)
Tax in consuming countries	7.56	8.13	13.30	17.74	22.44	21.00
Post-tax retail price	13.05	15.73	30.97	41.39	67.99	60.00

*Production costs plus government take in producing countries.
Source: OPEC Secretariat.

OPEC, for its part, used its new influence in world affairs to promote the wider interests of third-world commodity exporters, the "oil shock" having given a powerful impetus to a campaign for a "new international economic order" based on a more equitable distribution of resources between the industrialized countries and the rest of the world. A proposal for a United Nations conference on energy issues, put forward by France in January 1974, was rapidly followed by an Algerian proposal for discussion of all aspects of "raw materials and development", Algeria's initiative being instrumental in establishing that all international debate on the broad relationship between oil-exporting and oil-importing countries should be placed in this larger context.

A formal declaration on the establishment of a new international economic order, adopted by a special session of the UN General Assembly in May 1974 (◊**D5.9**), strongly influenced OPEC's own subsequent policy declaration on global economic relations (◊**B1.9.iii**), which was issued by the Organization's heads of government at their only summit meeting in March 1975. France, which had rejected the US policy of confrontation with OPEC and had remained outside the IEA, continued to work for multilateral talks on co-operation between oil-exporters and oil-importers, proposing in late 1974 that such talks should be organized on a "tripartite" basis to include third-world importers as well as OPEC members and industrialized importers (◊**D5.13**). In view of the continuing resistance of OPEC and non-OPEC third-world countries to a primarily energy-related agenda, it was agreed in October 1975 that energy should be discussed in parallel with other issues within the framework of a full-scale Conference on International Economic Co-operation (◊**D6.11**).

OPEC's links with other third-world countries were further strengthened by the establishment in 1976 of a special fund to channel aid to these countries, either directly or through specialized international agencies (◊**B1.6**). It was stressed that the OPEC fund was not designed to supersede member countries' existing national aid programmes and that its own lending programme did not constitute a mechanism to provide "compensation" for higher oil import costs.

Several OPEC members had earlier extended substantial loans to the International Monetary Fund in connexion with the establishment of special borrowing facilities in 1974 and 1975 for the benefit of IMF members with oil-related balance-of-payments deficits. In general, the process of "petrodollar recycling" was effected with minimal disruption to the international monetary system, belying the pessimistic predictions of Western governments which had underestimated both the rate of growth of OPEC countries' spending on imports (◊ Table 13) and the ability of the capital markets to handle the "low-absorbing" oil-exporters' accumulated surpluses (◊◊ Table 14)

A4.17—The Development of OPEC Pricing Policy, 1975 to 1978

A4.17.i—1975 to mid-1977

Although the pattern of sustained growth in the oil consumption of the main non-communist industrialized countries was abruptly reversed in the wake of the oil shock of 1973–74, restocking by importers ensured that total demand for OPEC oil remained relatively strong for some months after the relaxation of the Arab supply cutbacks. During 1975, however, the OPEC countries faced an 11.5 per cent fall in their aggregate oil output, coupled with a sharp decline in unit purchasing power caused partly by high rates of price inflation in the industrialized countries and partly by adverse movements in currency exchange rates (exchange-rate indexation of the dollar oil price having been discontinued at the beginning of 1974). The established structure of price differentials for OPEC crudes, based on relative values applicable at the height of the seller's market, came under severe pressure as demand fell, with "proximity" premiums in particular losing much of their justification at a time of growing overcapacity in the tanker market.

In principle, OPEC was not well-placed to retain control over crude pricing at a time of falling demand, given that the member countries—unlike the members of a true cartel—had no agreement regarding the regulation of their relative market shares, either through prorationing of output or the adjustment of price differentials (collective decision-making being focused on the price of the Saudi marker crude). A number of attempts were made during 1975 to formulate agreed policies on prorationing, price differentials and other issues relevant to the planning of a long-term strategy, each attempt failing because of conflicting national interests within the OPEC Conference. One of the main obstacles to agreement on longer-term issues was the Conference's preoccupation with the existing level of the marker price, which a majority of member countries wished to increase by as much as 25 per cent in order to restore the real purchasing power of their oil exports, whereas Saudi Arabia favoured a prolongation of the nine-month price freeze introduced at the beginning of 1975.

Saudi Arabia's production had been substantially reduced during the period of the freeze, thereby supporting the price of the marker crude at a time when some other members were cutting their premiums or discounting their official prices in response to market forces. The increase in the margin of shut-in capacity in Saudi Arabia was, however, also a strong bargaining counter in the kingdom's campaign to prevent a rise in the marker price, and the threat of a Saudi production increase (coupled with the threat of a unilateral price freeze) proved effective in blocking Iran's call for a minimum price rise of 15 per cent from October 1975. The OPEC Conference instead agreed to make a compromise increase of 10 per cent in the marker price, to be followed by another nine-month freeze (◊**D6.7**).

OPEC's widely publicized disagreements over pricing policy, and the consequent emergence of a freeze-increase-freeze cycle, had a significant impact on the pattern of market demand, causing temporary surges in production before an anticipated price increase, followed by corresponding cutbacks as oil companies disposed of the additional stocks which had been acquired at the lower price. In addition to these commercially-motivated stock movements there was also a gradual increase in the basic level of stocks held by oil companies in the main importing countries (where a growing volume of additional storage capacity was available at new "super-tanker" terminals). The IEA members' target for minimum stock levels—originally agreed as 60 days' coverage of net import requirements—had by late 1976 been increased to 90 days' coverage, to be achieved by the beginning of 1980 (◊**D7.7**).

A strong recovery in oil demand during 1976 provided some compensation for a continuing deterioration in OPEC's terms of trade, and Saudi Arabia argued successfully for a de facto prolongation of the Organization's existing price freeze when it expired in the middle of the year (◊D7.2). Iraq was the only member country to be accused of systematically discounting its official prices to gain market share in 1976, adjustments to differentials in other member countries being designed to reflect changes in the balance of demand (which favoured lighter grades at the expense of heavier crudes). There was serious discussion of a formula to determine "objective" differentials throughout the OPEC area, although implementation was eventually ruled out in the light of unpromising feasibility studies (◊D7.3.i).

Vigorous lobbying by a majority of OPEC members in favour of a year-end increase in the marker price led to heavy stock-building during the last quarter of 1976, boosting OPEC production to an all-time record level in early December (when all grades were trading at a premium on the spot market). With a plenary session of the Conference on International Economic Co-operation scheduled to coincide with OPEC's mid-December ministerial meeting, the United States initiated an intensive diplomatic campaign by the main oil-importing countries to urge OPEC to exercise restraint on the pricing issue, and in particular to refrain from using its pricing powers as a bargaining counter in support of third-world demands within the CIEC (as had been advocated by Venezuela).

Although this controversy over "linkage" was in the event defused by the postponement of the CIEC session, the OPEC Conference meeting nevertheless proved to be highly controversial in view of the strength of the opposition within OPEC to Saudi Arabia's renewed call for price restraint (◊D7.3.iii). No compromise was achieved on this occasion, and a split decision was taken whereby Saudi Arabia and the United Arab Emirates raised their prices by 5 per cent at the beginning of 1977, while the other 11 member countries announced an increase of 10 per cent from the same point, to be followed by an additional 5 per cent increase in the middle of the year (with Saudi Arabian 34° crude being retained as the marker grade in the OPEC majority's pricing structure).

Saudi Arabia subsequently lifted its production ceiling of 8,500,000 bpd (imposed after the end of the Arab sanctions campaign in 1974) with the aim of increasing its market share at the expense of the Gulf producers among the OPEC majority, although the fact that its output was already close to the ceiling level limited the scope for a dramatic upturn. A combination of technical constraints and operational problems restricted Aramco's average output to 9,178,000 bpd over the first half of 1977, as against the Saudi Government's target of 10,000,000 bpd, the impact of this relatively modest increase being strengthened by a fall in demand for OPEC crude in the aftermath of the large-scale stock-building of late 1976. Both Saudi Arabia and the United Arab Emirates took steps to ensure that foreign exporting companies complied with their official pricing policies, particularly in arm's-length trading.

As well as emphasizing Saudi Arabia's dominant role as OPEC's "swing" producer, the advent of two-tier pricing placed the kingdom in a strong position to reopen the question of "linkage" between oil prices and the CIEC by implying that its moderate policy within OPEC would be reconsidered in the event of an unsatisfactory outcome at the postponed CIEC session (which had been rescheduled to open at the end of May 1977). Similar pressure was applied to the US Government with regard to current moves to resolve the Arab-Israeli conflict.

A4.17.ii—Mid-1977 to December 1978

A reunification of OPEC pricing policy was effected in June 1977, when the OPEC majority cancelled their planned mid-year price increase, while Saudi Arabia and the United Arab Emirates brought their prices into line with the majority's existing prices ($\lozenge$**D8.3**). Saudi Arabia's change of policy was presented as a reaction to the final outcome of the CIEC, which had fallen well short of the expectations of the third-world countries and had failed to establish any basis for an institutionalized dialogue between exporters and importers of oil ($\lozenge$**D8.8**).

Between mid-1977 and mid-1978 OPEC's position in the world oil market was weakened by the growth of non-OPEC production, principally in Mexico, Alaska and the North Sea. The broad consensus among forecasters at this time was that non OPEC production would cover the bulk of incremental demand until about 1980, after which point demand for OPEC oil would increase steadily to reach at least 40,000,000 bpd by 1985. Concern over the prospect of increasing dependence on OPEC oil in the 1980s prompted the IEA countries (meeting in October 1977) to establish a group objective regarding the maximum level of IEA oil imports in 1985 ($\lozenge$**D8.9**) and to adopt 12 basic principles for long-term structural change in their energy requirements ($\lozenge$**B3.4**), to be achieved partly through conservation measures and partly through higher indigenous production (with particular emphasis on alternatives to oil).

In the United States, President Carter announced a major new import-limitation initiative in April 1977 ($\lozenge$**D8.10.i**). Legislation was enacted in November 1978 to give effect to a number of his proposals, including the partial decontrol of natural gas prices, although Congress rejected measures which would have raised US oil prices to the world level ($\lozenge$**D9.7**). The Federal Government began to import crude oil in July 1977 for underground storage as a strategic petroleum reserve, which was intended eventually to contain 1,000 million barrels. President Carter's policy towards OPEC was based on an implicit acceptance of the Organization's established status in the international energy market, marking a break with the aggressively "confrontationist" approach which had been taken by Dr Henry Kissinger, the former Secretary of State under Presidents Nixon and Ford. The US Government remained opposed to increases in OPEC oil prices and continued to describe the Organization as a "cartel", but there was now a greater awareness of the pivotal role played by Saudi Arabia's deeply conservative Government in determining the extent to which OPEC could actually function as a cartel.

An understanding between President Carter and the Shah of Iran, reached during talks in Washington in November 1977, was instrumental in altering Iran's stance within the OPEC Conference, where it joined Saudi Arabia in pressing for price restraint. The combined influence of the Organization's two largest producers ensured that there was no alteration in the marker price at the December 1977 Conference meeting ($\lozenge$**D8.6**), and expectations that the price would remain unchanged for some time contributed to a major drawdown of oil company stocks in the opening months of 1978. The consequent fall in demand for OPEC oil forced substantial cuts in the official prices of some OPEC crudes (mainly the light African grades), although prices in the Gulf region were supported by large reductions in Saudi output ($\lozenge$**D9.3.i**). The real price of internationally traded oil fell to a new post-1974 low point as a result of a further sharp deterioration in the value of the US dollar, coupled with continuing price inflation in the industrialized countries, and OPEC's aggregate current-account surplus for 1978 was the smallest since 1970.

OPEC Oil Ministers, meeting informally in Saudi Arabia in May 1978, held their most constructive discussion to date on fundamental policy issues, and established a ministerial committee to draw up a long-term strategy on production and pricing ($\lozenge$**D9.3.ii**). In another significant move towards closer co-operation in the group interest, several member countries entered into a secret agreement in the following month to make voluntary production cutbacks during the remainder of the year if the present market conditions persisted.

Having secured a continuation of the OPEC price freeze into the second half of 1978, together with the shelving of proposals for indexation of the current marker price to reflect movements in the dollar exchange rate (with support from Iran on both issues), Saudi Arabia indicated in August that it would accept a phased price increase, based on a realistic appraisal of underlying market trends, from the beginning of 1979. Moves to rebuild oil company stocks in anticipation of this price increase contributed to a rapid recovery in demand during the closing months of 1978, while on the supply side Iran's production was seriously disrupted by politically-motivated industrial action, the country's oil exports being eventually suspended in late December.

The prevailing tightness of the market—and an attendant surge in spot oil prices—ensured that OPEC's agreed 1979 price increase, announced some days before the suspension of Iranian exports, was somewhat greater than Saudi Arabia had originally intended, although the other member countries accepted Saudi Arabia's proposal that it should be phased in on a quarterly basis in order to produce a gradual and predictable rise in consumers' import costs. A year-on-year rise of 5 per cent in the marker price during the first quarter of 1979 was to increase to 14.5 per cent by the last quarter in such a way as to produce an average rise of 10 per cent over the full year (⬦**D9.5**).

This agreement was seen by Saudi Arabia as the first step in the introduction of a new pattern of planned price administration by OPEC, breaking the freeze-increase-freeze cycle which had proved to be unsatisfactory from the viewpoint of exporters and importers alike. The December 1978 Conference meeting also accepted another aspect of Saudi Arabia's long-term strategy, involving a widening of the differentials between lighter and heavier crudes in order to increase the incentive for importers to invest in upgraded refining plant with a higher proportionate input of heavier grades. It was estimated in late 1978 that such investment was viable on the basis of a light/heavy differential spread of $1.50 to $2 per barrel.

A4.18—The Relationship between OPEC Governments and International Oil Companies in 1978

International oil companies continued to play a dominant role in the export marketing of OPEC oil at the outbreak of the Iranian crisis, notwithstanding their loss of ownership rights over the bulk of OPEC production during the previous five years. An estimated 66 per cent of internationally traded oil was handled by the majors and other present or former concession-holders in 1978 (50 per cent through integrated channels and 16 per cent through arm's-length sales), compared with 92 per cent in 1973 (70 per cent through integrated channels and 22 per cent through arm's-length sales). The 34 per cent share of exports which was handled by producing countries' national oil companies in 1978 comprised rather more commercial arm's-length sales (18 per cent) than government-to-government sales (16 per cent), whereas in 1973 government-to-government sales had accounted for 5 per cent, and arm's-length sales for 3 per cent, within the national companies' 8 per cent share of world oil trade.

The following summary of the arrangements governing the foreign oil companies' "guaranteed" access to OPEC crude in 1978 shows the extent to which foreign equity interests had been reduced or eliminated by this point, leaving many former concession-holders dependent on special purchasing arrangements covering either fixed volumes for limited periods or variable volumes (subject to reduction as direct state exports increased) over longer periods.

Algeria—49 per cent foreign equity interest in fields producing about 22 per cent

92

of total output; *Ecuador*—37.5 per cent foreign equity interest in principal fields; *Gabon*—75 per cent foreign equity interest in principal fields; *Indonesia*—foreign companies handled the marketing of the majority of output from fields operated under "contract of work" agreements giving them a minority profit-sharing interest, while more recent agreements provided for minority foreign production-sharing interests; *Iran*—the IOP parent companies held preferential purchasing rights over the majority of output from the main onshore fields (which were operated by an IOP subsidiary on a contract basis), while offshore fields, accounting for less than 12 per cent of Iran's total production, had 50 per cent foreign equity participation; *Iraq*—no foreign equity interests or special purchase rights; *Kuwait*—BP, Gulf and Shell enjoyed preferential purchasing rights covering around two-thirds of total output under sales contracts expiring in 1980, although there was no foreign operational involvement; *Libya*—minority foreign equity interests (49 per cent or less) in fields producing about 84 per cent of total output; *Nigeria*—45 per cent foreign equity interests in most fields; *Qatar*—sales contracts with former concession-holders (which continued to provide operational services for a per-barrel fee); *Saudi Arabia*—preferential purchasing rights over the majority of output were held by the parent companies of Aramco (which provided operational services for a per-barrel fee); *UAE (Abu Dhabi)*—40 per cent foreign equity interests in main producing fields; 100 per cent foreign equity interests in some smaller fields; *UAE (Dubai)*—former foreign concession-holders were retained on a contract basis with responsibility for production and export marketing; *Venezuela*—the main former concession-holders had two-year purchasing contracts (covering the majority of output); they also provided technical services on a contract basis for a per-barrel fee.

A4.19—The Second Oil Price Shock (1979–80)

Iranian oil exports remained suspended until early March 1979, when their resumption on a much reduced scale was authorized by the revolutionary regime which had overthrown the Shah's Government in the previous month. At the same time the state assumed full control over export marketing, having cancelled the IOP consortium's preferential purchasing rights (◊**D10.3**). The short-term destabilization of the market balance was offset to a limited extent by increases in the output of other producers inside and outside OPEC, although Saudi Arabia restricted its additional output to 1,000,000 bpd during the first quarter of 1979 (i.e. relative to its normal production ceiling of 8,500,000 bpd), apparently because of technical barriers to any further increase at this point. Iran's return to the export market restored a reasonable balance between current supply and current consumption but did little to dispel the deep uncertainty surrounding the oil policy of the revolutionary government, and high spot premiums continued to be paid as importers sought to maximize their stocks with the aim of limiting their exposure to a possible deterioration in the supply situation.

The effects of the rise in spot crude prices quickly worked through into product markets, causing most OPEC members to impose surcharges on their official crude prices in order to restrict the "windfall profits" available to foreign exporters and traders. At the same time the main international oil companies were retaining an increasing proportion of their available supply within integrated channels, obliging many arm's-length customers to compete for direct supplies from producers' national oil companies, often under short-term contracts and in some cases on a spot basis.

The OPEC Conference decided in late March 1979 to bring forward to April the official price increase originally scheduled for October, while leaving the imposition of additional market premiums to the discretion of individual member countries (◊**D10.5**). The Conference agreed that OPEC should attempt to prevent the foreign exporting companies from discriminating against third-world oil-importing countries with regard to the volume and price of deliveries, but took the view that the main responsibility for controlling the market situation rested with the governments of industrialized countries, which were urged to take steps to prevent oil companies from charging more than official OPEC prices. The IEA countries, for their part, had agreed at the beginning of March that their aggregate oil demand should be reduced by 2,000,000 bpd in 1979 (◊**D10.4**), but had not discussed the deployment of mandatory oil stocks as a market-stabilization measure (the Agency's emergency oil-sharing programme being applicable only in the event of a group supply shortfall of at least 7 per cent, whereas the current shortfall was negligible in most member countries).

Saudi Arabia reimposed its 8,500,000 bpd production ceiling on April 1, ostensibly to accommodate a recovery in Iranian production to around two-thirds of its September 1978 level of 6,000,000 bpd. (It was, however, widely believed that the Saudi cutback was also intended to signify disapproval of the recent signature of the US-sponsored peace treaty between Egypt and Israel.) The loss of 1,000,000 bpd of Saudi crude prompted the major oil companies to enter the open market as large-scale buyers in order to fulfil their abnormally high restocking requirement, causing a fresh surge in spot prices during May which led to further general surcharging of official OPEC prices in every member country except Saudi Arabia (which applied a surcharge only to the price of its least important 39° grade).

IEA ministers, meeting in May, reaffirmed their commitment to reduce their countries' aggregate 1979 oil demand but failed to adopt any concrete measures to counter "increasing competition for limited supplies of oil" (◊**D10.7**). The extent of the current disarray within the IEA area was underlined by a subsequent public dispute between the United States and the EEC countries over the introduction of an effective subsidy on US imports of middle distillates in order to meet current stock-building targets (◊**D10.8**). (On the other hand, controls on US domestic crude prices, which had provided a "cost-equalization" subsidy to refiners of imported crude since late 1973, were to be gradually phased out from June 1979, the earliest date on which decontrol could begin without new legislation.)

In an attempt to rationalize OPEC's increasingly chaotic pricing structure, the Conference agreed in June 1979 that the marker price should be fixed at $18 per barrel (about half of the average June spot value of OPEC crudes) but that individual member countries could add market premiums of up to $2 per barrel to their normal differentials, subject to a maximum official price of $23.50 per barrel (◊**D10.10**). This represented a compromise between Saudi Arabia, which was the only member to refrain from surcharging the new marker value, and a hard-line group led by Iran, which favoured a further narrowing of the gap between official prices and market prices. Member countries agreed to "take steps to limit transactions in the spot market".

Saudi Arabia's readoption of a 9,500,000 bpd production ceiling at the beginning of July failed to prevent a further tightening of the market in the last quarter of the year, when a fall in Iran's output was coupled with an Iranian ban on oil sales to US-owned companies (imposed in reaction to the US Government's use of economic sanctions in its campaign to secure the release of US diplomatic hostages in Tehran). The spot price of 34° Saudi crude rose above $40 per barrel in November 1979—by which time OPEC's supposed ceiling price of $23.50 was being treated as a marker value by a majority of member countries—and in mid-December Saudi Arabia increased its official price for the marker grade to $24 in a bid to pre-empt a campaign for a higher price at the December Conference meeting. However, Libya responded by initiating a round of "leapfrogging" increases in the official prices of other OPEC crudes, with the result that the pricing issue was left open at the Conference meeting for want of a consensus (◊**D10.15**).

The IEA, for its part, decided at a ministerial meeting in December (◊**D10.14**) to adopt national import ceilings for 1980 and 1985 (the 1985 group total being 5.4 per cent lower than the target originally agreed in October 1977) and to keep the 1980 ceilings open to adjustment in the light of market developments, which would be closely monitored. In the event, the member countries' imports were held well within the 1980 ceilings as a result of a sharp fall in consumption in reaction to the higher cost of oil (official OPEC prices having risen above their 1974 levels in real terms during the second half of 1979).

Spot oil prices remained high throughout the first half of 1980, underpinned by a continuing build-up of importers' stocks (to the extent that virtually all available storage capacity was filled by September), while the gap between spot values and official OPEC prices was steadily closed as individual OPEC members initiated successive rounds of "leapfrogging". At the same time there was a further shift in marketing patterns as member countries' national oil companies expanded their share of aggregate OPEC export volume to rather more than 50 per cent, as against 45 per cent in 1979, virtually eliminating the foreign exporting companies' arm's-length market. (In the case of Japan, producing countries' national oil companies supplied 47 per cent of oil imports in late 1980, compared with 35 per cent in late 1979 and 20 per cent in late 1978.)

In June 1980, when Saudi Arabia's official price for 34° crude stood at $28 per barrel (more than $7 below Iran's price for the same grade), the OPEC Conference adopted a notional marker value of $32 per barrel and a ceiling price of $37 per barrel (notwithstanding Saudi Arabia's warning that it would freeze its own price and maintain its output at 9,500,000 bpd in an attempt to hasten the stabilization of an already softening market (◊**D11.6**). Spot values finally fell below the prevailing official prices of most OPEC crudes during the course of the third quarter of 1980, strengthening Saudi Arabia's position when OPEC ministers turned their attention in mid-September to a proposed formula for "orderly" price administration, drawn up by the ministerial committee on long-term strategy earlier in the year.)

The formula provided for gradual quarterly increments reflecting the real economic growth rate in the OECD area, with indexation against inflation and exchange-rate fluctuations, and was seen by Saudi Arabia as the most important matter for consideration by an OPEC heads of government meeting scheduled to be held in Baghdad in early November. Saudi Arabia refused to implement the OPEC majority's marker price at the September ministerial meeting, stating that $32 per barrel was an unrealistically high starting point for indexation, but nevertheless agreed to increase its official price for the marker grade to $30 per barrel in order to prepare the ground for a compromise (◊**D11.9**).

Further consideration of long-term planning was, however, abruptly shelved after Sept. 21, when the outbreak of war between Iran and Iraq caused fresh disruption in the oil market and forced OPEC to abandon its summit plans (◊**D11.10**). The other Gulf OPEC states increased their own output to supply some of Iraq's customers during the initial interruption of Iranian and Iraqi exports, while the IEA sought to avert a full-scale market crisis by urging a drawdown of stocks held in the importing countries. Saudi Arabia's production was subsequently held at the higher level of 10,300,000 bpd after the limited resumption of supplies from Iran and Iraq in late November. On the demand side, the IEA countries decided in December to cut their aggregate imports by 2,200,000 bpd in the first quarter of 1981 through a combination of destocking, lower oil use and co-operative action to correct localized imbalances (◊**D11.11**).

The volume of spot trading in the last quarter of 1980 was markedly lower than that recorded in the early part of the year, and a new upturn in spot prices reached its peak in November. This upturn was, however, sufficient to generate renewed pressure for official price increases during OPEC's December Conference meeting, at which Saudi Arabia's acceptance of a $32 price for its 34° crude was accompanied by the adoption of a so-called "deemed marker ceiling" of $36 per barrel (and an overall price ceiling of $41 per barrel) for other members' crudes (◊**D11.12**). The latest increases left the average official price of Saudi crudes about 155 per cent higher than at the end of 1978, while the cumulative increase for non-Saudi OPEC crudes averaged 182 per cent. When restated to take account of changes in the domestic purchasing power of the US dollar, the new Saudi marker price was about 62 per cent higher than in 1974, whereas the 1978 marker price (restated on the same basis) had been about 18 per cent lower than in 1974.

A4.20—The Erosion of OPEC's Market Dominance (1981–82)

A4.20.i—Underlying factors – Position of non-OPEC producers

A process of underlying structural change in the world energy market—originally set in train by the first "oil shock" of 1973–74 but later slowed by the decline in real oil prices—was greatly accelerated in the aftermath of the substantial price rise of 1979–80 and the renewed concern about security of supply which determined the behaviour of buyers during that rise. Export demand for OPEC oil showed an overall fall of around 12,000,000 bpd between 1979 and 1982, an estimated 33 per cent of this decline being attributable to cutbacks in energy consumption in the non-communist industrialized countries, resulting partly from conservation measures and partly from economic recession. A further 25 per cent of the decline was attributable to an increase in the supply of non-OPEC oil, 21 per cent to the use of alternative energy sources and 21 per cent to a shift from stock-building to stock drawdown by oil companies.

OPEC's share of non-communist oil production fell below 50 per cent in August 1981, at which point Saudi Arabia was producing nearly half of the OPEC total, having held its output at 10,300,000 bpd and its marker price at $32 per barrel in a bid to secure an agreement on the reunification and rationalization of the OPEC pricing structure, which had been severely distorted during the undisciplined upward scramble of 1979–80. Within the Gulf region, Saudi Arabia's incremental output had tended increasingly to depress demand for oil from Kuwait, Qatar and the United Arab Emirates, giving rise to a situation in which the ending of war-related constraints on Iranian and Iraqi output would have seriously undermined an already weak market.

It was estimated that around three-quarters of Saudi Arabia's "normal" production of 9,500,000 bpd was going to Aramco's parent companies at this time under long-term purchasing arrangements, the Saudi state corporation Petromin having refrained from entering the private sector of the export market as a direct seller in 1979–80 (although it had increased the volume of its sales to governments and state-owned importing companies). The US majors' continuing dominance in the export marketing of Saudi crude (on terms which excluded unauthorized resale to non-affiliated refiners) contrasted sharply with a continuing decline in the marketing role of former concession holders in other OPEC countries, where the initiative in progressively cutting back long-term contract volumes began to pass from the state sellers to the foreign buyers during 1981.

In deciding to move towards a more flexible acquisition strategy the larger international oil companies took particular account of the downward trend in consumption and the increase in the availability of competitively-priced non-OPEC crude, which had seriously weakened the commercial justification for paying what was in effect a "security of supply" premium for long-term access to non-Saudi OPEC crudes. British Petroleum, whose loss of preferential access to the largest share of the Iranian consortium's offtake had been followed by the nationalization of its Nigerian equity interests in mid-1979, was one of the leaders in this trend, choosing to cancel its remaining purchasing contract with Kuwait in late 1981 in order to widen the scope for spot buying on a scale not previously practised by the majors on a regular basis.

By turning to sources other than "contract crude" to offset their substantial deficit in equity crude, the majors added further diversity to an upstream marketing pattern which had already been fundamentally altered by the disappearance of long-term arm's-length trading between the majors and the smaller companies. Some producing countries were now dealing directly with as many as 40 separate customers, while the total number of customers in the OPEC area as a whole (including importing governments) was estimated to be around 150. Whereas competition between an increasing number of smaller customers had helped to bid up open-market prices in the seller's market of 1979–80, the fact that few of these customers had any strong commitment to a particular supply source placed them in a strong position to bargain prices down in a buyer's market.

A further factor of some importance in the transition to a more open market structure was President Reagan's abolition of all remaining price controls on US crude production in late January 1981 (◊**D12.10**), eight months ahead of the Carter Government's target date for completion of the decontrol process which had begun in mid-1979 (◊**D10.17**). Apart from speeding up the decline in US consumption of imported oil and attracting an inflow of new investment in domestic exploration and development work, full decontrol created the conditions for the direct feedback of price signals from the world's largest consuming country to an international market from which it had been effectively insulated for the past 22 years. This new feedback was of particular significance in conditions of supply surplus because of the downstream sector's role in determining US domestic crude prices (which were posted by the refiner as buyer rather than the producer as seller).

The US Government resumed its own international trading role in 1981 as an importer of crude for the country's strategic petroleum reserve, such imports having been largely suspended while prices were rising in 1979–80. An average acquisition rate of around 335,000 bpd in 1981 more than doubled the size of the reserve, which at the end of the year contained nearly one-third of the revised 1990 target of 750,000,000 barrels. However, the demand impact of US government stockpiling (and of smaller-scale government stockpiling in Japan and Western Europe) was offset by net drawings on commercially-held stocks in the IEA area, where the overall stock-holding requirement was declining because of the downturn in member countries' net import volumes, which were generally used to define mandatory minimum stock levels. Oil companies thus experienced a de facto increase in their already very large discretionary stocks at a time when high real interest rates (introduced as a counter-inflationary measure in the wake of the second oil price shock) were pushing up the cost of financing surplus inventories, and a sustained drawdown became inevitable when the market value of the companies' stocks began to decline in the latter part of 1981.

Non-OPEC exporting countries, which had followed the upward trend in OPEC prices in 1979–80, responded to a subsequent sharp fall in spot values by cutting their official prices in June 1981, thereby gaining additional market share at the expense of non-Saudi OPEC producers (◊**D12.6**). Of particular importance was a cut of $4.25 per barrel by Britain, which was rapidly expanding its net exports following the attainment of self-sufficiency in oil in 1980 and which competed directly with Nigeria in terms both of the quality of its main grade and the location of its principal markets (i.e. in Europe and North America).

Whereas OPEC's official pricing system was based on "administered" selling prices fixed at ministerial level, the British system was based on negotiation between the producing companies and the British National Oil Corporation (BNOC) to establish BNOC's purchase price for crude covered by participation agreements under which the companies were required to sell up to 51 per cent of their output to the state (▷▷**D14.14**). Integrated producing companies normally repurchased most of the participation crude thus acquired from them by BNOC, and therefore had an interest in negotiating a competitive reference price for British crude, while non-integrated producers, having no buy-back requirements, were more concerned to maximize their revenue from sales to the state. As integrated companies played a dominant role in British crude production, BNOC's reference price was subject to strong downward pressure in a soft market, regardless of the fact that BNOC itself had a vested interest in a high crude price until 1982, when its own (non-integrated) upstream equity interests were sold to the private sector. The Norwegian state oil company Statoil followed BNOC's lead on North Sea crude pricing when the process of downward adjustment began in 1981.

There were wide variations in the degree of state involvement in the pricing of non-OPEC oil exports from other regions, with foreign equity holders playing an influential role in several smaller producing countries, while the two high-volume exporters, Mexico and the Soviet Union, each had fully state-owned oil industries. The Soviet Union's official export prices for non-communist customers were notably responsive to short-term spot trends, whereas the Mexican state oil company—which exported much of its output to the increasingly price-sensitive US market—came under some government pressure to delay downward adjustments until customer resistance had built up over a period of time. Mexico's obvious reluctance to relinquish some of the unit revenue gains of 1979–80 stemmed in part from the Government's underlying support for the principle of price administration by third-world countries (although Mexico had in the mid-1970s ruled out the idea of applying for OPEC membership, preferring to retain an independent pricing policy while it re-established itself as a major exporter of oil).

A4.20.ii—Downward pressure on official OPEC prices – Unsuccessful attempt to limit OPEC production

With Saudi Arabia refusing to absorb the impact of the decline in demand for OPEC oil, the June 1981 price cuts by non-OPEC producers led to mounting customer resistance to the official prices of non-Saudi OPEC crudes, particularly the premium grades which were priced at or close to the OPEC majority's ceiling of $41 per barrel. Nigeria was especially vulnerable to this pressure in view of its direct exposure to competition from North Sea oil and its heavy dependence on current oil revenues to meet its substantial development needs, and the Nigerian Government eventually took unilateral action to protect the country's economic interests, announcing a $4 per barrel cut in its maximum selling price in late August. A subsequent cut of $1.50 per barrel at the beginning of October gave Nigeria a price advantage of 50 cents per barrel over competing British crudes.

The Nigerian initiative destroyed the credibility of the OPEC majority's pricing structure (which was also affected by smaller cuts in differentials, together with some concealed discounting, on the part of other countries) and led to renewed efforts to settle the pricing dispute between Saudi Arabia and the rest of the OPEC membership. An agreement was finally reached in late October 1981 under which all members adopted a uniform marker price of $34 per barrel, entailing a $2 increase in the actual price of Saudi Arabian 34° crude and a $2 cut in the other members' "deemed" marker value (◊**D12.7**). It was agreed that the new marker price should be frozen until the end of 1982.

Subsequent adjustments to differentials narrowed the price spread between the lightest and heaviest OPEC crudes and lowered the Organization's de facto ceiling to $37.50 per barrel (although this price was adopted only by Algeria and Libya, while Nigeria fixed its maximum price at $36.50). Saudi Arabia's reimposition of an 8,500,000 bpd production ceiling from Nov. 1 strengthened the impression that OPEC could successfully defend a $34 marker value, and non-OPEC producers generally realigned their prices around the reunified OPEC structure (a particularly significant move being the North Sea producers' establishment of parity with the new Nigerian price).

A further rationalization of OPEC differentials at the beginning of 1982 was followed by renewed downward pressure on market prices as oil companies embarked on a period of heavy stock drawdown, the consequent fall in demand being concentrated on OPEC countries when non-OPEC exporters made fresh price cuts in order to protect their own export volumes. A substantial cutback in Saudi output—which became subject to a 7,500,000 bpd ceiling in early March — was insufficient to relieve the pressure on the smaller OPEC producers, creating a situation in which the Organization had to opt either for an unprecedented reduction in the Saudi marker price or for the introduction of a co-ordinated pro-rationing programme designed to limit each member country's output to a level at which the existing price could be maintained for the duration of what was then expected to be a relatively short-lived crisis.

It was recognized that price maintenance without production discipline would leave the way open to unilateral undercutting by individual member countries (a tactic already adopted by Iran in February 1982). No serious consideration was given to the option of suspending administered pricing altogether in order to conduct a co-ordinated campaign to regain market share from non-OPEC producers, it being felt that such a strategy could only lead to a counter-productive erosion of total revenues.

The OPEC Conference decided on March 20, 1982, to adopt a defensive strategy based on prorationing, national production ceilings being subsequently fixed at levels which would remove nearly 1,000,000 bpd from the market (◊**D13.3**). The marker price remained at $34 per barrel, although the maximum premium for very light crudes was reduced to $1.50. The Conference's refusal to bring official prices into line with non-members' market-related prices caused OPEC production to fall well below the newly agreed ceiling level of 17,500,000 bpd in the aftermath of the meeting. Nigeria suffered a particularly severe shortfall as a result of customer resistance to its new maximum price of $35.50 per barrel, which was grossly uncompetitive with BNOC's current price of $31 per barrel for similar crude.

In a gesture reminiscent of the pre-1974 era, Saudi Arabia and Kuwait each voiced their support for co-ordinated OPEC sanctions against international oil companies which were held to be "penalizing" Nigeria for its application of OPEC pricing policy, although it was far from clear whether any effective sanctions were in fact available to the Organization in the current circumstances. Nigeria remained exceptionally vulnerable to competition from the North Sea producers until the end of the second quarter, when BNOC raised its reference price to $33.50 per barrel.

Whereas prorationing called for an unprecedented degree of unity and co-operation within OPEC, the political cohesion of the Organization was being steadily weakened by the continuing military conflict between Iran and Iraq and the attendant deterioration in relations between Iran and Saudi Arabia. Iran continued to undercut official OPEC prices after the conclusion of the prorationing agreement, stating that it intended to secure a market share about 1,800,000 bpd above its allotted production ceiling, while Iraq, which had lost its Gulf export facilities at the beginning of the war, became unable to fulfil its own OPEC quota (which had been fixed at parity with Iran's) when its 500,000 bpd pipeline links to the eastern Mediterranean were shut down by Syria in April 1982 (◊**C6.3.v**). An increasingly bitter dispute over Iranian and Iraqi quotas (centred on Iran's demand for a substantial increase at Saudi Arabia's expense) coincided with a Saudi campaign for the revision of the price differentials established under the March 20 agreement, which had left the very light African crudes undervalued in relation to the main Gulf crudes.

Failure to agree on these and other issues led to the de facto suspension of the prorationing experiment in July 1982, at which point OPEC's production was already well in excess of the agreed ceiling level (◊**D13.5**). During the second half of the year there was widespread discounting of the official prices of many non-Saudi OPEC crudes as individual member countries sought to increase their market shares, and it was estimated in December that a weighted average discount of $2.35 per barrel was being extended to support a total OPEC production rate of about 19,500,000 bpd (◊**D13.6**). Saudi Arabia's observance of official prices had meanwhile caused its production to fall to around 5,100,000 bpd, restoring the kingdom's proportionate share of the OPEC total to a level equivalent to that of the mid-1970s.

A4.21—The Breakdown of OPEC Price Administration (1983 to 1985)

A4.21.i—General background

Demand for OPEC oil remained severely depressed after 1982 as non-OPEC producers continued to expand their share of a largely static market. Positive energy conservation measures (as opposed to recession-induced cutbacks) played an increasingly important part in the development of non-communist energy demand, which grew by only 1.9 per cent between 1979 and 1985; at the same time, a continuing diversification of energy sources caused oil's share of the non-communist energy market to fall to 44.6 per cent in 1985, as against 52.3 per cent in 1979.

The focus of international trade in oil continued to shift away from transfers between the upstream and downstream affiliates of integrated companies as more of the larger companies became attuned to the commercial advantages of flexible spot trading in a buyer's market. Thus, while the term "spot market" continued to denote a decentralized web of transactions involving a wide range of geographically dispersed buyers, sellers and intermediaries, this informal market was by the end of 1983 regularly handling at least 40 per cent of internationally traded oil and was becoming increasingly involved in forward dealing in "paper barrels" in order to provide a hedging mechanism.

The spot market's evolution from a marginal to a central trading channel was accompanied by considerable improvements in the availability and reliability of information on short-term price trends, notwithstanding the unregulated nature of the market. Moreover, the growth of conventional buyer-seller bargaining and of "trade for the sake of trade" in oil created a wide interest in institutionalized futures dealing through regulated commodity exchanges. An International Petroleum Exchange (IPE) was established in London in 1981 to deal in gas oil contracts, which had been traded on the New York Mercantile Exchange (Nymex) since 1978, while Nymex successfully launched a crude oil contract (for 1,000-barrel lots of the US marker grade, West Texas Intermediate) in March 1983.

The close similarity between West Texas Intermediate and Britain's Brent Blend (the highest-volume crude traded on the spot market) led to a certain amount of direct interaction between formal Nymex trading and unregulated spot trading, involving the use of one market to cover forward positions taken in the other, this being one of a number of links in a strong British-US axis within the oil industry's Atlantic Basin trading area. (An attempt by the IPE to launch a regulated futures contract in Brent crude failed in 1982, partly because of practical difficulties in organizing small trading lots. A restructured form of contract was offered by the IPE in late 1985.)

The international oil industry's rapid abandonment of traditional trading attitudes was accompanied by a thorough reappraisal of operating economics in all sectors, leading to cutbacks and rationalization measures in the least profitable areas and (in the case of the majors) to a withdrawal from many of the non-oil interests which had been acquired under wide-ranging diversification programmes in the 1970s. New acquisitions were concentrated within the oil industry, where a series of multi-billion dollar mergers culminated in the takeover of Gulf Oil by Chevron in March 1984 (◊A5.1.iii). An important consequence of each of the mergers was to increase the successful bidder's holdings of US crude reserves, which could be acquired more cheaply through the stock market than through new exploration work at this time.

Much of the rationalization of existing oil industry operations occurred in the downstream sector, where refining, marketing and petrochemical manufacturing had all been affected by declining demand. Refining capacity in the main consuming areas was considerably reduced between 1981 and 1985 (e.g. by 17 per cent in the United States and 26 per cent in Western Europe), while the remaining capacity was progressively modernized in order to achieve a far higher degree of operational flexibility, with particular emphasis on the capability to obtain high yields of light products either from heavy crudes or from surplus fuel oil produced by conventional refining techniques.

At the same time there was a sustained drive to achieve further reductions in non-mandatory stocks, and in particular to limit the basic operating stocks of crude oil held at upgraded refining plants, whose ability to use a wider range of feedstocks encouraged an increasing reliance on "hand-to-mouth" buying through spot channels. By the end of 1985 the cumulative net drawdown of company stocks in the OECD area since 1981 had reached an estimated 115,000,000 tonnes (although about half as much oil was added over the same period to government-owned stockpiles, which accounted for between 20 and 25 per cent of total land-based stocks at the end of 1985).

While the new flexibility of trading patterns and refining methods provided a sound operational justification for the reduction of commercial inventories, the most important determinant of oil company policy was a belief that a substantial margin of shut-in OPEC capacity would continue to overhang the market for the foreseeable future, providing a reasonable assurance of supply security and precluding any further upward pressure on prices. (A Texaco analysis, published in mid-1983, estimated that irreversible structural changes in the pattern of energy consumption would limit the demand for OPEC oil to 22,900,000 bpd in 1990.) The scale of the inventory drawdown between 1983 and 1985 nevertheless exceeded most forecasts by interested observers of the market, including OPEC Oil Ministers.

Having been cast in the role of residual suppliers to a market rapidly acquiring new mechanisms for free competition, the OPEC countries faced severe problems in maintaining a system of administered pricing which had originally been sustained in the context of a heavy reliance on export outlets controlled by the major oil companies. OPEC's aggregate balance of payments had shown its first current-account deficit for 13 years in 1982 (◊ Table 13), and only the "low-absorbing" Arabian peninsula members had accumulated sufficiently large capital surpluses to be able to participate in a prolonged prorationing initiative without economic hardship. Nigeria's price cuts of

August and October 1981 had already demonstrated the vulnerability of a "high-absorbing" economy, while the short-lived prorationing experiment and subsequent price discounting of 1982 had thrown further doubt on OPEC's ability to operate as a defensive cartel at the low production levels which were currently required to influence free-market prices. Above all, the effective functioning of the Organization was under constant threat from the Gulf war, which poisoned the atmosphere within the Conference while it continued and offered the prospect of a worsening of the supply overhang if it ended.

Table 13 — OPEC*: estimated aggregate oil revenues and current-account balance of payments, 1970 to 1984 (thousand million US dollars)

	A	B	C	D	E	F
Year	Revenues from oil	Exports fob	Imports fob	Visible balance (B–C)	Invisibles, etc. (net deficit)	Current balance (D–E)
1970	7.53	16.88	9.66	7.22	6.44	0.78
1971	11.02	21.57	11.31	10.26	6.95	3.31
1972	13.63	24.69	13.78	10.91	6.80	4.11
1973	22.81	40.07	20.31	19.76	12.74	7.02
1974	89.19	120.81	36.38	84.43	17.43	67.00
1975	90.23	110.44	56.15	54.29	22.87	31.42
1976	107.52	132.44	69.97	62.47	28.52	33.95
1977	122.62	148.68	87.91	60.77	36.92	23.85
1978	114.59	141.66	93.38	48.28	46.63	1.65
1979	192.51	211.59	100.10	111.49	51.37	60.12
1980	274.91	294.58	130.07	164.51	58.20	106.31
1981	249.19	267.12	151.21	115.91	63.55	52.36
1982	201.90	215.69	151.46	64.23	76.02	−11.79
1983	164.59	180.42	135.40	45.02	64.57	−19.55
1984†	157.44	176.97	125.00	51.97	56.05	−4.08

*End-1975 membership basis.
†Provisional.

Table 14 — Deployment of cumulative OPEC cash surplus in peak year (1982)

	thousand million US dollars
United States	86
Eurocurrency	94
United Kingdom	15
Other industrialized countries (including communist countries)	103
Less-developed countries	77
IMF and World Bank	20
Total identified deployed net cash surplus*	395
Residual of unidentified items	72
Total net current-account surplus	467

*OPEC countries' identified external assets include bank deposits, government securities, equity investments and gold. The largest accumulated surpluses are held by Saudi Arabia (which owned about 41 per cent of the identified deployed surplus in 1982), Kuwait (about 20 per cent) and the United Arab Emirates (about 10 per cent).
Source: US Treasury estimates.

A4.21.ii—Further OPEC prorationing initiative to defend reduced official prices (1983–84)

A fresh slump in open-market prices in early 1983, prompted by an unprecedentedly heavy first-quarter drawdown of oil company stocks, led Saudi Arabia to speak out in favour of a cut in the OPEC marker price, adherence to official prices having caused the kingdom's crude production to fall below 4,200,000 bpd (the minimum level required to satisfy domestic demand for associated gas at that time), with some further loss of market share to OPEC producers who were discounting their official prices. The Saudi stance was backed by the Arabian peninsula producers' consultative body (the Gulf Co-operation Council, established in early 1981), which had already given its strong support to Saudi Arabia's campaign for a widening of the official differentials between Gulf and African crudes. The hardening of attitudes within the GCC region followed OPEC's failure to agree on a revision of differentials when Oil Ministers discussed the latest market crisis on Jan. 23 and 24 (◊**D14.3**).

A reduction in the marker price became inevitable after Feb. 20, when Nigeria lowered its maximum selling price by $5.50 per barrel, thereby gaining a 50-cent advantage over BNOC's current reference price (as in October 1981). The Nigerian Government made it clear on this occasion that it would match any future cuts in North Sea prices "cent for cent". The OPEC countries then embarked on three weeks of intensive consultations between themselves and with non-OPEC exporting countries, whose co-operation was seen as essential if OPEC was to re-establish a viable system of administered pricing. Mexico, which was facing worsening debt-servicing problems as a result of the weakening of oil prices, agreed to give its positive support to a realistic OPEC agreement, whereas the British Government expressed a broad interest in avoiding an "exaggerated" fall in prices but refused to place any ceiling on the growth of production from the North Sea or to alter BNOC's system of negotiated pricing. (Britain's non-interventionist policy stemmed partly from the Thatcher Government's ideological commitment to free-market economics and partly from contractual constraints on its freedom to regulate the activities of the North Sea producing companies.)

The OPEC Conference agreed on March 14, 1983, to cut the official price of the marker crude from $34 to $29 per barrel and to keep the maximum premium for African crudes at $1.50 per barrel (thereby increasing the percentage differential vis-à-vis the marker), although Nigeria was to hold its maximum price at $30 per barrel as a "temporary exception" to the differentials agreement (◊**D14.5**). A 17,500,000 bpd production ceiling was reintroduced on the basis of revised national quotas, Iran's quota being twice as large as under the March 1982 prorationing agreement, while Saudi Arabia formally undertook to act as swing producer with an implied national ceiling of 5,000,000 bpd. Iran was allowed to give "official" discounts to compensate its customers for the higher cost of shipping oil from a war zone, but all other forms of discounting were to be avoided.

Mexico immediately aligned its prices with the new OPEC structure and introduced a voluntary ceiling on its own exports. Two weeks of negotiations between BNOC and the North Sea producing companies resulted in the revision of BNOC's pricing formula in order to bring the price of Brent crude into line with that of Nigeria's competing grade, this move being seen as an indication of British government support for the OPEC price stabilization formula. Claims by OPEC that Britain had informally undertaken to restrain its production were, however, strongly denied by the Government.

The strength of consumer demand for oil was generally unaffected by the OPEC price cut (whose impact was progressively neutralized in Western Europe as a result of a subsequent rise in the value of the US dollar). Thus the OPEC Conference decided at the end of 1983 that the agreed production ceiling should remain in force in 1984 despite the mounting economic pressure which some "high-absorbing" member countries were experiencing as they adjusted to the double shock of lower unit revenues and lower output volumes (◊**D14.9**).

Most OPEC crudes were being exported at official prices in late 1983, although the structure of official differentials was becoming markedly out of line with relative values on the open market, which reflected the refining industry's growing shift from lighter to heavier feedstocks. Production discipline was poor, particularly in the last quarter of the year, by which time some member countries' official monthly production figures were being routinely understated in an attempt to conceal overfulfilment of quotas. Saudi Arabia chose to interpret its implied ceiling with reference to its marketed crude production in the latter part of 1983, when a considerable volume of excess production was placed in a government stockpile for future disposal (◊**D14.8**).

Member countries' quotas were held to apply to crude oil only, providing producers of natural gas liquids with some leeway to evade the strict observance of production discipline by exaggerating the claimed NGL content within aggregated official production statistics for liquid hydrocarbons. Exports of refined products were mentioned in the March 1983 agreement only in terms of a general under-taking to refrain from "dumping". In practice, member countries with export refining capacity enjoyed the advantage of flexible decision-making regarding the composition of their oil exports, in which the proportion of market-priced products could be increased to offset a weakness in demand for officially-priced crude. In the case of Venezuela and Kuwait, there was also a direct involvement in the downstream sector in West European importing countries (including access to marketing outlets) by virtue of investments undertaken since late 1982 (◊**C7.3.iv, C13.3.viii**). This form of "forward integration" by OPEC state oil companies clearly required competitive product pricing in the markets concerned and acceptance of the resulting netbacks on crude supplied to wholly- or partly-owned overseas refineries.

By mid-1984 the oil market was beginning to show serious signs of weakness, and the use of concealed discounts was spreading among OPEC producers of lighter crudes (although demand for the heavier grades remained strong, having been boosted by strike action in the British coal industry). It was accepted at OPEC's July Conference meeting that over-quota production totalling about 1,100,000 bpd in June had not enhanced the credibility of the Organization's prorationing pro-gramme, although the main blame for "destabilizing the market" was placed on the North Sea producers, which had increased their average exports by about 377,000 bpd between the first half of 1983 and the first half of 1984. The Conference agreed that Nigeria's continuing economic difficulties warranted a temporary quota in-crease for August and September, to be debited to the Saudi entitlement, and that a further attempt should be made to secure the co-operation of non-OPEC pro-ducers in supporting official oil prices (◊**D15.5**).

A cutback in OPEC production from July, coupled with the announcement of unchanged official prices by all the main non-OPEC exporters except the Soviet Union (which made a cut of $1.50 per barrel from Aug. 1), was sufficient to avert a crisis during the third quarter of 1984, although low spot prices for light crudes continued to encourage discounting by OPEC members on these grades. Among the non-OPEC producers which maintained unchanged official prices, Mexico had remained closely linked to OPEC since March 1983, whereas Egypt had previously tended to react to spot trends. Most significantly, Britain, while refusing to curb its production, had shown a clear reluctance to see BNOC spark a new OPEC price collapse by undercutting Nigeria, and overt government pressure was brought to bear on BNOC's main customers during this latest period of price weakness. The British Government moreover acquiesced in a consequent growth in tax avoidance or "spinning" by integrated North Sea producing companies (involving the transfer of equity crude to downstream affiliates via the spot market in order to establish a spot rather than an official value for tax purposes), together with an increase in BNOC's trading losses on spot sales of participation crude which integrated producers were unwilling to buy back at existing official prices.

BNOC announced a continuation of its price freeze at the beginning of October, but was not on this occasion followed by Norway's Statoil, which ignored its own Government's acquiescence in recent North Sea pricing developments and instead announced a "temporary" switch to monthly market-related pricing from Oct. 12. BNOC was forced to respond with an official price cut of $1.35 per barrel for Brent crude on Oct. 17, thereby provoking a $2 price cut by Nigeria on the following day and throwing OPEC into a new crisis (◊**D15.6**). The other member countries reacted to Nigeria's latest unilateral move by opting to cut their production rather than their official prices, and a reduced production ceiling of 16,000,000 bpd was accordingly introduced from Nov. 1 (◊**D15.7**). Nigeria refused to rescind its price cut or to accept a reduction in its national ceiling (claiming, moreover, that it had a continuing entitlement to the quota increase which had been allotted to it for the month of September). Mexico and Egypt each made voluntary production cutbacks in solidarity with OPEC. An OPEC ministerial committee was established to look into the question of official price differentials for crudes ligher and heavier than the marker, which were now chronically out of line with open-market values.

Nigeria was predictably among the OPEC countries which exceeded their production quotas in the last two months of 1984, when the credibility of the Organization's latest initiative was undermined both by overproduction relative to the new group ceiling and by further recourse to discounting, which was reported to be affecting up to two-thirds of all OPEC exports by early December. Statoil and BNOC came under heavy customer pressure to make further price cuts, but each deferred a decision until after OPEC's year-end Conference meeting (although it was widely reported that BNOC was making preparations for a switch to flexible spot-related pricing).

The Conference resolved on Dec. 29, 1984, to establish an independent auditing system to police member countries' compliance with OPEC production quotas and official prices, this unprecedented incursion into an area of national sovereignty being strongly backed by Saudi Arabia, whose production had slumped to little more than 3,500,000 bpd as a result of undercutting by other OPEC members. However, the Conference was unable to reach a full agreement on the restructuring of differentials, and adopted only a minor readjustment applicable to the Gulf region, where the prices of heavy and medium crudes were increased and those of very light crudes reduced pending a further review of the issue (◊**D15.9**). Algeria and Nigeria refused to endorse this interim readjustment. Brunei and Malaysia joined Mexico and Egypt as observers at the December Conference meeting, during which the two Asian exporters announced voluntary production cutbacks in support of OPEC's prorationing scheme.

A4.21.iii—From defence of prices to defence of market share (1985)

In January 1985 the OPEC countries engaged in an acrimonious debate about price differentials—which would be crucial to the determination of relative market shares if official prices were rigidly adhered to—while current OPEC production fell to 14,850,000 bpd as buyers awaited a Conference decision. Over half of the cut in OPEC output between December and January occurred in Iran, which had made a significant increase in the price of its 34° crude at the beginning of the year and

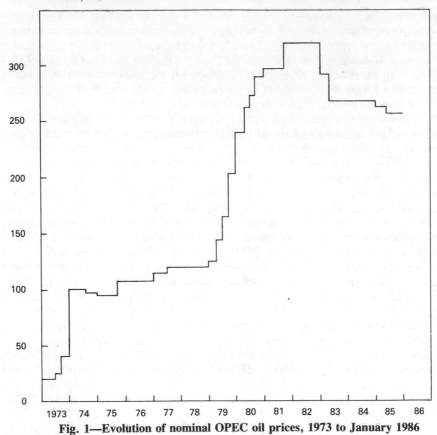

Fig. 1—Evolution of nominal OPEC oil prices, 1973 to January 1986

Based on index (1974=100) of changes in the quarterly average official price (in current dollars) of Saudi Arabian 34° crude fob Ras Tanura.

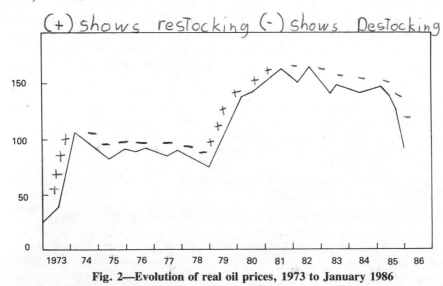

Fig. 2—Evolution of real oil prices, 1973 to January 1986

Based on index (1974=100) of changes in the average price of internationally-traded crude, expressed in special drawing rights and adjusted against movements in OECD export prices.

was strongly opposed to any cut in light crude prices as part of the proposed realignment of differentials, arguing instead that heavy crude prices should be further increased.

In the event, a majority of OPEC members adopted a compromise agreement on Jan. 30 involving an unchanged price for Saudi heavy (27°) crude and cuts in the official prices of all lighter grades, on the basis of which Nigeria finally agreed to rescind part of its unilateral price cut of October 1984. However, the two other main African producers, Libya and Algeria, joined Iran in rejecting this agreement (although Iran subsequently implemented its provisions). Under the agreement the price of Saudi Arabian 34° crude was cut by $1 to $28 per barrel and ceased to be the sole marker value, the new differential framework being instead defined with reference to three Saudi crudes (27°, 31° and 34°) and three non-Saudi OPEC crudes (◊D16.2). Mexico and Egypt were strongly critical of OPEC's failure to reach a unanimous agreement, Mexico's annoyance being signalled both by the cancellation of its November 1984 production cutback and by the undercutting of Saudi Arabia's new price for 34° crude.

Nigeria's new maximum price of $28.65 was deliberately fixed at parity with BNOC's last official reference price, which had ceased to have any contractual validity at the beginning of 1985, the suspension of negotiations on a new British reference price having been extended as a result of OPEC's failure to reach a comprehensive differentials agreement in December. BNOC was thus forced to conduct all its selling activities on spot terms during January, while the suppliers of participation crude made it clear that they expected to receive payment at the end-1984 official price. BNOC's formal acceptance of a $28.65 reference price for the months of January and February was finally announced on Feb. 13, by which point BNOC had incurred massive trading losses for these months. Further losses were incurred in March as a result of the maintenance of an unchanged reference price for the whole of the first quarter.

By this time, however, the British Government had accepted that its recent policy of dissuading BNOC from undermining the official OPEC pricing structure was incompatible with its refusal to impose a North Sea production ceiling, and accordingly announced on March 13 that BNOC was to be abolished in order to end the state's involvement in the fixing of British crude prices, which would be allowed to move in line with the open market (◊D16.4). Norway's Statoil had confirmed its commitment to market-related pricing in mid-January, prior to the announcement of the OPEC differentials agreement. Oman (a member of the Gulf Co-operation Council) was among the smaller non-OPEC exporters which switched to market-related pricing in the second quarter of 1985.

The ending of the year-old British coalminers' strike in March 1985 removed up to 500,000 bpd of heavy fuel oil consumption from an already depressed market, dashing OPEC's hopes of an early upturn in demand and creating a new pattern of open-market values which destroyed the balance of the Organization's differentials agreement as heavier crudes began to trade at substantial spot discounts. With the North Sea producers now responding automatically to monthly changes in market prices, customer pressure for cuts in negotiated non-OPEC prices was concentrated on such exporters as the Soviet Union and Egypt, each of which was obliged to concede lower prices during the second quarter of the year. Mexico's adherence to official pricing led to a slump in exports during May, after which a reduction was made in the price of the country's heavy export grade, which had no counterpart within OPEC's range of agreed differentials. A review of the pricing of Mexico's light grade was, however, postponed in anticipation of a further revision of OPEC differentials (◊D16.5).

OPEC's attempts to restore pricing and production discipline had meanwhile been substantially discredited during the first half of the year as a result of continuing quota violations (leading to breaches of the group ceiling from February to April), followed by a return to widespread discounting of official prices for most non-Saudi crudes as spot prices and export volumes declined during the second quarter. It was clear that many member countries had agreed to the further quota reductions of November 1984 in the expectation of an imminent revival of the market, and were responding to the prolongation of adverse trading conditions by attempting to improve their assured access to export outlets under longer-term barter or semi-barter agreements based on a variety of pricing formulas.

Saudi Arabia continued to be heavily penalized for its consistent adherence to official pricing, whether in occasional barter deals, in spot sales from the government stockpile or in contract sales to Aramco's parent companies, which had retained their now anomalous status as the principal offtakers of Saudi crude. Exports via the US majors were particularly badly hit by the decline in the competitiveness of the kingdom's heavier crudes (which had constituted an increased proportion of Aramco's output since October 1984 ◊**D15.6**), and Saudi production fell below 2,500,000 bpd in June 1985, compared with a maximum entitlement of 4,353,000 bpd under OPEC's current prorationing programme. Total OPEC production averaged 14,070,000 bpd in the same month, when aggregate non-Saudi output was running almost exactly in line with the non-Saudi ceiling of 11,647,000 bpd.

OPEC Oil Ministers met in early July 1985 to discuss the need for revised differentials and the enforcement of strict price discipline, but were unable to overcome the many obstacles to agreement at a time when all member countries were finding increasing difficulty in bearing the economic strain of adherence to OPEC policies (◊**D16.6**). Saudi Arabia reacted to the inconclusive outcome of this meeting by serving notice that its own national interests were now being unacceptably damaged as a result of price competition within OPEC. Mexico, which had displayed a greater practical commitment to price-support measures than most members of OPEC, took immediate action to protect its interests by cutting its official prices for both light and heavy crudes, which became subject to a new system of geographical differentials determined partly by the scale of OPEC discounting in different marketing areas (both Saudi Arabia and Mexico having suffered their greatest loss of competitiveness in Western Europe).

Saudi Arabia formally renounced the role of "swing" producer at the end of July, after the OPEC Conference had accepted only token cuts in the official prices of heavier crudes, with Algeria, Iran and Libya formally objecting to any cuts. The implications of Saudi Arabia's decision became apparent in September, when the kingdom (recognizing its inability to make use of its full quota entitlement at official selling prices) began to conclude agreements to supply crude to Aramco's parent companies on netback terms, thereby abdicating responsibility for upstream price administration and instead accepting fob realizations derived from downstream product values (◊**D16.8**). Similar agreements were subsequently signed with other international oil companies, which were attracted by the offer of guaranteed refining margins in the downstream markets covered by the Saudi netback deals (which at this point excluded Japan). Also in September, Iraq, which had accepted its existing OPEC quota solely because of its limited export capacity, began exporting via a new pipeline link with Saudi Arabia (◊**C6.3.v**), thus eliminating any possibility that total OPEC output would remain within the group ceiling when Saudi Arabia began to utilize its full entitlement.

The collapse of OPEC's ability to defend its official pricing structure was followed by a period of "phoney war" in October and November 1985, when a long-awaited upturn in demand caused spot prices to strengthen significantly despite a steady increase in OPEC output, which was about 2,000,000 bpd above the group ceiling level when the spot market finally began to react to the emergence of a supply surplus in the last week of November (◊**D16.9**). Considerable efforts were made during this period to secure the co-operation of Britain and Norway in averting the outbreak of a full-scale price war, it being stressed by leading OPEC ministers that a market crash was now inevitable without a cutback in North Sea production. These overtures were, however, rejected, as was the idea of a wider agreement on producer-consumer co-operation to stabilize the oil market. This reflected the hard line currently being taken by the United States within the International Energy Agency, where the Reagan Government had made it clear that its free-market ideology excluded any form of dialogue with OPEC (◊**D16.7**).

(OPEC's own objections to a purely oil-related dialogue with consuming countries had evaporated during recent years as the Organization had been forced into a defensive position in the marketplace. There had been no serious discussion of energy issues within the context of a "new international economic order" since the inconclusive Cancún summit conference of October 1981 ◊**D12.11**).

The OPEC countries' 25-year-old commitment to the defence of unit revenues was effectively set aside on Dec. 9, 1985, when the Conference formally agreed that priority should be given to the recovery of market share from non-OPEC producers, notwithstanding the North Sea exporters' stated intention to maintain their own high production levels (◊**D16.10**).

A4.22—The Ascendancy of Market Forces (1986)

According to preliminary estimates, the average level of world oil production was 4.9 per cent higher in the period January–June 1986 than in the first half of 1985, aggregate OPEC output having risen by 15.8 per cent and aggregate non-OPEC output by 0.4 per cent. Within the non-OPEC total, communist-bloc production showed a rise of 2.1 per cent and non-communist production a decline of 0.7 per cent (a 0.6 per cent rise in aggregate British and Norwegian output having been offset by a 0.9 per cent fall in the aggregate output of other non-communist non-OPEC producers). With increased non-OPEC production covering part of the limited growth in oil consumption, the significant rise in the OPEC share of world output—from 29.5 per cent in the first half of 1985 to 32.6 per cent in the first half of 1986—was achieved only by boosting total world output to a level well in excess of the underlying supply requirement. This imbalance precipitated a free fall in real oil prices to their lowest level since the early 1970s, with the result that total OPEC export revenue for the January–June period slumped by more than one-third between 1985 and 1986.

More than half of OPEC's incremental output was contributed by Saudi Arabia (which was "overproducing" by about 1,000,000 bpd relative to its former quota ceiling by the middle of the year) and most of the balance by Kuwait, Iraq, Abu Dhabi and Qatar. For several other OPEC members, including Iran, the fall in unit revenues was accompanied by a decline in market share in the first half of 1986. Non-OPEC exporters which experienced particularly sharp reductions in output volume included Mexico and Egypt. Apart from the United Kingdom (where the Government claimed that the oil sector's revenue losses would be broadly neutralized by the fall in domestic energy costs), every important oil-exporting country acknowledged that its economic position had deteriorated to some degree as a result of the price collapse. In Norway, economic dislocation was accompanied by a political crisis which led to the inauguration in May of a new Government prepared to take positive steps to support a new OPEC market stabilization initiative (◊**D16.17**).

New capital investment in high-cost oil-producing areas (including the North Sea) was seriously jeopardized when open-market crude prices fell below $20 per barrel in January 1986 (◊**D16.11.i**), while a further decline in prices towards $10 per barrel during February and March (◊**D16.11.ii**) caused the shutting-in of the highest-cost North American oilfields and created severe financial problems for those producers whose fields had become barely profitable. The US Government rejected local producers' calls for an import tax on oil, although its announcement in early April of an inquiry into the national security aspects of lower oil prices (◊**D16.14**) was reminiscent of the rationale for the move towards protectionism during the 1950s (◊**A4.10**).

The effects of the price collapse on oil company operations varied according to the spread of these operations within the supply chain. Upstream service companies, whose workload had been contracting for some time because of a general slowdown in exploration activities as prices had weakened, were hit by a severe recession, while non-integrated crude producers suffered a major slump in profits. Integrated producers were able to recoup some of their lost upstream profits at the downstream end of their businesses, but nevertheless faced cash-flow problems and reductions in investment funds for new projects. (Most international oil companies announced cuts of between 30 and 50 per cent in their investment budgets during the first half of 1986.) Independent refiners benefited from reduced feedstock costs but became vulnerable to an intensification of competition for market share from integrated companies.

Intermediaries in the oil trade saw their volume of business decline significantly because of a fall in demand for spot crude as refiners turned increasingly to netback supplies offering secure profit margins. Netback trading was extended into east-of-Suez markets after low North Sea spot prices (forced down by competition in traditional west-of-Suez markets) had begun to draw North Sea crude into Japan in the latter part of January. A rapid growth of Saudi Arabian netback sales in both eastern and western markets was accompanied by a general switch to netback trading on the part of most other OPEC members in the Middle East and Africa. North Sea producers, who continued to trade through established channels, became increasingly reliant on the nearby markets in which they were most competitive. OPEC and non-OPEC exporters in Latin America and Asia adopted varying systems of market-related pricing, the new Latin American prices being generally derived from US domestic crude prices.

While the spread of netback selling exposed the international oil trade to free market forces on a scale not seen since 1928, price transparency was considerably diminished because of the inherent complexities of netback formulas and a paucity of public information on OPEC countries' contract terms. Few representative spot quotations were available for the majority of OPEC crudes because of the widespread shift back to contractual buyer-seller relationships, while the spot trade in non-OPEC crudes was subject to exceptionally large price fluctuations during the course of the dislocation of trading patterns. Unregulated forward dealing was disrupted during the period of very rapid price erosion in January and February, which gave rise to a number of disputes over non-fulfilment of purchasing commitments.

In April 1986 the spot price of North Sea Brent crude averaged $12.25 per barrel (46 per cent of its December 1985 average). The average April netback realization on OPEC crudes was estimated to be in excess of $15 per barrel, product prices having generally fallen less steeply than open-market crude prices in the first quarter of the year. After a limited recovery in May, oil prices resumed their downward trend in June and July, when a growing oversupply of crude oil (averaging as much as 2,600,000 bpd in the latter month) led to a marked build-up of product stocks, while a relative weakening of product prices caused netback realizations to fall below spot values for some crudes. The average spot price of North Sea Brent crude in July 1986 was $9.63 per barrel (36.2 per cent of the December 1985 average). The average July netback realization on OPEC crudes was estimated to be less than $9 per barrel.

As in the 1960s, the extent to which crude oil price cuts were passed through to final consumers varied from country to country, depending on the degree of competition in sectors controlled by oil companies (e.g. gasoline retailing), the degree of protection which was accorded to alternative energy sources in sectors controlled by the state (e.g. electricity generation) and the level of taxation on oil products. The International Energy Agency, meeting in April 1986, stressed the need for continuing observance of energy policies "based on the long-term outlook and not on short-term developments alone" (♢D16.15).

Conflict between OPEC's conservative Arabian peninsula members and the "hard-line" grouping of Algeria, Libya and Iran took on a new intensity during the opening months of 1986, with the hard-liners campaigning vigorously for the re-establishment of administered pricing on the basis of drastic production cutbacks, while the conservatives favoured a further build-up of pressure on the North Sea producers, stating that they were prepared to see prices fall to levels which would force the shutdown of some North Sea fields (♢D16.12). The remaining member countries, which were increasingly alarmed at the implications of an open-ended price war but aware of OPEC's inability to maintain pro-rationing within an unacceptably low ceiling, worked for the introduction of a specific target for the Organization's "fair share" of the market, to be fixed at a level which would stabilize prices without imposing unrealistically low quotas.

The OPEC Conference discussed these issues for a total of 22 days between the middle of March and the end of June, over which period the proposed "fair share" target was progressively raised to 17,600,000 bpd (as an average for the full year) on the basis of forecasts of additional growth in oil consumption under the stimulus of lower prices. It was hoped that a firm OPEC commitment to observe this target would gain sufficient practical support from non-OPEC producers (among which only Britain had continued to oppose the principle of co-operation with OPEC) to secure a recovery of crude prices to between $17 and $19 per barrel (♢D16.17).

However, the OPEC Conference was unable to agree on a redistribution of national quotas when it met in late July to discuss the implementation of the latest market stabilization proposal, with the result that many traders were by Aug. 3 (after a full week of inconclusive OPEC talks) anticipating a further fall in crude prices towards $5 per barrel. The Conference meeting subsequently took a radical new turn when Iran announced its willingness to "depoliticize" the quota issue (insofar as it had been deadlocked by the Gulf war) by ignoring Iraqi overproduction in return for a strict observance of November 1984 quotas by all other OPEC members. On Aug. 5 the Conference announced its unanimous acceptance of this strategy for the months of September and October 1986, although it was stressed that this was a purely interim measure which did not alter OPEC's commitment to "secure for itself a fair market share, consistent with the revenue needed for the economic and social development of member countries" (♢D16.18).

By the time that OPEC's effective production ceiling of about 16,700,000 bpd came into force at the beginning of September, spot crude prices had made a strong recovery (e.g. to nearly $15 per barrel for North Sea Brent) from the low point reached in July, while OPEC producers had benefited from a parallel rise in netback realizations notwithstanding their maintenance of an aggregate production level of more than 20,000,000 bpd during August. Most OPEC members recognized that the impact of the temporary production cutback would be blunted by the existence of a large accumulation of oil stocks in importing countries, and that a failure to agree on further stabilization measures after the end of October would lead to an early resumption of the fall in prices.

A5—The Major International Oil Companies

A5.1—Company Profiles

The term "international majors" is used historically to describe eight oil companies, of which the so-called "seven sisters" (British Petroleum, Chevron, Exxon, Gulf, Mobil, Royal Dutch/Shell and Texaco) came to be so described by virtue of their position as the largest and most geographically diversified companies in the industry, while the smaller Compagnie Française des Pétroles was involved in various joint Middle East production operations as a partner of one or more of these companies. The number of sisters was reduced to six in 1984 through Chevron's takeover of Gulf (◊A5.1.iii).

Chevron, Exxon, Mobil and Texaco are based in the United States (as was Gulf), while Shell (controlled from both the Netherlands and the United Kingdom) and BP (based in the UK) each have large US subsidiaries. Chevron, Exxon and Mobil, together with BP's subsidiary Sohio, were all originally part of the Standard Oil conglomerate which dominated the US oil industry until 1911 (◊A4.2). Another Standard Oil offshoot, Amoco, ranks as a major international oil company on the basis of present-day criteria, but does not fall within the historical definition used in this section. Amoco was known until April 1985 as Standard Oil Co. (Indiana).

The following summaries of the origins and development of the eight companies include details of former corporate names which were used at different times; elsewhere in this book the companies' present names are given except where the use of a former name is considered appropriate to the context. Recent comparative statistics are given for 1983, the last year before the Chevron/Gulf merger and takeovers of large independent companies by Mobil and Texaco. In the tabulated statistics given for each company (i) the total revenues shown are exclusive of excise duties and sales taxes and (ii) the total crude supplies shown are inclusive of all additional purchases which were made to supplement a company's equity production. The five US-based majors are listed first (starting with the three Standard Oil offshoots) and sections on the three European companies follow.

A5.1.i—Exxon

Exxon Corporation has held the position of the world's largest oil company since the late 1930s and currently operates in more than 80 countries. The present corporate name was adopted in 1972 and is used as a trading name in the USA, although the name Esso is widely used in foreign markets. Exxon was originally incorporated in 1882 as Standard Oil Co. of New Jersey. Renamed Standard Oil (New Jersey) in 1892, it acted (from its head office in New York City) as the holding company for Standard Oil operations throughout the United States. These operations had for the preceding nine years been centrally controlled via a trust, but after the enactment of federal anti-trust legislation in 1890 advantage was taken of a New Jersey state law permitting corporations to hold shares outside that state. Standard Oil was nevertheless successfully prosecuted under the anti-trust laws, and was ordered in 1911 to dissolve all functional links between its component companies (although they continued to have many shareholders in common).

The former holding company retained control of most of the Standard Oil export marketing network in Latin America and continental Europe while losing control of most of the domestic crude production used by the refineries which served these markets. It subsequently proceeded to "integrate backwards" by acquiring new sources of crude supply, which to an increasing extent were located abroad. In this context, one of Exxon's most notable achievements was to gain control, through acquisitions made during the period 1928–37, of more than half of the output of Venezuela, then the most important producing country outside the United States (◊C13.3.ii). Exxon regained access to the former Standard Oil regional marketing network in the Far East when it entered into the Standard-Vacuum (Stanvac) partnership with Mobil in 1933 (◊C4.3.i). Exxon's position in the Middle East was greatly strengthened when it joined the Aramco consortium in Saudi Arabia in 1948 (◊C11.3.ii).

During the 1950s the company had a small surplus of equity crude production over refinery throughputs in its eastern-hemisphere operations, while being a significant net buyer of crude in the western hemisphere. The rapid growth of new supplies from Libya in the 1960s (◊C8.3.i) accentuated this regional contrast while bringing the company's overall upstream and downstream production more closely into balance. In 1972, when the company still had full ownership of the greater part of its output from OPEC countries, Exxon's net equity crude production totalled 5,009,000 bpd, of which 46 per cent came from the Middle East and Africa, 25.2 per cent from Latin America, 19.4 per cent from the United States, 4.5 per cent from Canada, 3.8 per cent from Asia and Australasia and 1.1 per cent from Europe. A further 411,000 bpd was purchased under long-term contracts in the Middle East and Africa.

In 1983 Exxon had a net equity crude production of 1,527,000 bpd, of which 51.2 per cent came from the United States, 24.2 per cent from Europe (principally from joint operations with Shell in the UK North Sea), 17.5 per cent from Asia and Australasia, 5.9 per cent from Canada, 0.9 per cent from Latin America and 0.3 per cent from the Middle East and Africa. The balance of Exxon's 1983 supplies consisted of equity crude derived from ventures in which it held minority interests (32,000 bpd), production from oil sands in Canada (23,000 bpd), supplies received under long-term agreements with foreign governments (706,000 bpd) and supplies received under long-term contract (294,000 bpd). Exxon's net proved reserves of crude oil and natural gas liquids totalled 6,478 million barrels at the end of 1983.

Exxon statistics for 1983:

Financial (million dollars)		*Oil (thousand bpd)*	
Total revenues	94,734	Total crude supply	2,582
Net income	4,978	Crude processed	3,266
Total assets	62,963	Products sold	4,085

A5.1.ii—Mobil

Mobil Corporation, which was originally incorporated in 1882 as Standard Oil Co. of New York (Socony), operated mainly as an exporter of refined products from the United States to the Far East prior to 1911. Like Exxon, it chose to "integrate backwards" after the dissolution of the Standard Oil organization in order to secure new supply sources for its established international marketing facilities. During the 1920s a producing company was acquired in Texas and in 1931 Socony merged with the Vacuum Oil Co., a long-established manufacturer of lubricating oils which had also previously been part of the Standard Oil conglomerate. The new Socony-Vacuum Corp. was subsequently named the Socony-Vacuum Oil Co. (1934–55), Socony Mobil Oil Co. (1955–66) and Mobil Oil Corp. (1966–76), "Mobil" being a trade name originally used by the Vacuum Oil Co. Mobil Oil became a wholly-owned subsidiary of a new holding company, Mobil Corporation, in June 1976.

In 1933 Mobil's Far Eastern marketing interests were merged with Exxon's Far Eastern producing interests through the formation of the jointly-owned Standard-Vacuum Oil Co. (Stanvac), this partnership being ended by anti-trust action in 1960 (although the name Stanvac continued to be used by a joint Mobil/

Exxon subsidiary in Indonesia). In 1934 Mobil became the equal co-owner (with Exxon) of the Near East Development Corporation, one of the parent companies of the Iraq Petroleum Company and its affiliates ($\diamond$C6.3.i). Mobil acquired the smallest shareholding in Aramco in 1948 ($\diamond$C11.3.ii) and joined the Iranian Oil Participants consortium in 1954 ($\diamond$C5.3.ii). During the 1950s and 1960s Mobil was a substantial net buyer of crude worldwide, having a small surplus of equity production over refinery throughputs in the eastern hemisphere (where important new concessions were developed in Libya and Nigeria) but a large deficit in the western hemisphere (where production came from the United States, Venezuela and Canada). Additional crude supplies were obtained notably from Kuwait under a long-term contract with BP ($\diamond$C7.3.i).

In 1972 (at which point the company still had full ownership of the greater part of its output from OPEC countries) Mobil had a total net equity crude production of 1,911,000 bpd, of which 51.3 per cent came from the Middle East, 20.6 per cent from the United States, 12.7 per cent from Africa, 6.2 per cent from Latin America, 5.9 per cent from Canada, 1.9 per cent from Asia and 1.4 per cent from Europe. The company's total crude supplies in 1972 were, at 2,399,000 bpd, the lowest of any of the "seven sisters". Mobil's net equity crude production in 1983 totalled 523,286 bpd, of which 53.4 per cent came from the United States, 18.9 per cent from Europe, 9.9 per cent from Canada and 17.8 per cent from other foreign operations. A further 93,150 bpd was received under special arrangements in which Mobil acted as producer. Mobil's end-1983 net proved reserves of crude oil and natural gas liquids comprised 2,148 million barrels held by subsidiaries and 437,000,000 barrels held by virtue of minority shareholdings in affiliates.

In March 1984 Mobil announced a $5,700 million takeover bid for Superior Oil, an independent company whose main producing interests were in the United States and Canada. The bid was approved by the US Federal Trade Commission in May 1984 and by Superior's shareholders in September 1984.

Mobil statistics for 1983:

Financial (million dollars)		*Oil (thousand bpd)*	
Total revenues	58,998	Total crude supply	1,337
Net income	1,503	Crude processed	1,594
Total assets	35,072	Products sold	2,034

A5.1.iii—Chevron

The name Chevron Corporation was adopted in mid-1984 by the Standard Oil Co. of California (Socal or Stancal), which was formed in 1926 through the merger of the Pacific Oil Co. and Standard Oil Co. (California); the latter company was itself formed in 1906 as the successor to the long-established Pacific Coast Oil Co., which had been acquired by the Standard Oil group in 1900 as a source of additional supplies for export to Asian markets. The new merged company, based in San Francisco, was one of the largest crude producers in the United States and tended to concentrate more heavily on upstream than on downstream activities. After the Second World War Chevron recorded a "crude deficit" in respect of its western-hemisphere operations while being a net seller of crude worldwide on the basis of a Middle Eastern output which exceeded its eastern-hemisphere refining capacity.

Chevron has long-established links with Texaco, notably through the two majors' joint ownership of the Caltex group of companies (originally formed in 1936 as an eastern-hemisphere marketing organization when Texaco acquired an interest in Chevron's oil concessions in Bahrain and Saudi Arabia), although in 1967 Caltex's European activities were divided between the two parent companies. Upstream co-operation between Chevron and Texaco in Indonesia—partly through Caltex and partly through other subsidiaries—is co-ordinated by a jointly owned company

115

called American Overseas Petroleum Ltd (Amoseas), which at one time was also a vehicle for co-operation in Libya.

In 1972, when the company still had full ownership of the greater part of its output from OPEC countries, Chevron's net equity production of crude oil and natural gas liquids totalled 3,159,530 bpd, of which 81 per cent came from the eastern hemisphere and 19 per cent from the western hemisphere. In 1983 the company's net equity production of crude oil and natural gas liquids totalled 476,909 bpd, of which 66.6 per cent came from the United States, 13 per cent from Europe, 13 per cent from Canada and 7.4 per cent from other foreign countries. Equity supplies contributed by affiliates in the eastern hemisphere totalled 288,632 bpd (gross), while supplies received under special agreements with foreign governments totalled 506,674 bpd. Chevron's net proved reserves of crude oil and natural gas liquids totalled 1,643 million barrels at the end of 1983.

On March 5, 1984, Chevron announced an agreed takeover bid for Gulf Corporation at a valuation of $13,300 million, making this the largest merger in corporate history. Approval was given by the US Federal Trade Commission on April 26, 1984, subject to the subsequent sale by Chevron of various Gulf refinery, pipeline and retail operations in the United States representing overlapping interests of the two companies. The merger nevertheless made Chevron the largest oil refiner in the United States. The company sold most of its European downstream interests in 1984–85, while Gulf had withdrawn from the European downstream sector prior to the merger (◊**A5.1.v**).

Chevron statistics for 1983:

Financial (million dollars)		*Oil (thousand bpd)*	
Total revenues	29,182	Total crude supply	1,371
Net income	1,590	Crude processed	1,433
Total assets	24,010	Products sold	1,715

A5.1.iv—Texaco

Texaco Inc. traces its origins to the formation in 1901 of the Texas Fuel Co., a production-oriented company whose corporate successors were The Texas Co. (Texas) from 1902 to 1926, The Texas Corp. from 1926 to 1941 and The Texas Co. from 1941 to 1959 (when the current name was adopted). The company's early growth owed much to the absence of a Standard Oil affiliate in Texas, where the state legislature strongly supported the anti-trust cause at an early stage. Texaco's first customers included the Standard Oil organization in the eastern states, but an independent national marketing network was rapidly built up to avoid over-reliance on the established oil companies. Further expansion, including the d evelopment of overseas markets, was largely financed by New York investors, and—its name notwithstanding—the company moved its headquarters from Houston to New York at an early stage in its history.

As mentioned above in the section on Chevron (◊**A5.1.iii**), Texaco is joint owner with Chevron of the Caltex group and various other subsidiary companies, co-operation between the two parent companies having commenced in 1936, when Texaco's equity crude output was insufficient to supply its refining and overseas marketing facilities, while Chevron was in the opposite position. During the 1950s and 1960s Texaco's worldwide crude production and refinery throughputs were more closely balanced than those of the other majors, although in regional terms the company produced a surplus of crude in the eastern hemisphere which offset a deficit in the western hemisphere.

In 1972, when the company still had full ownership of the greater part of its output from OPEC countries, Texaco's equity supplies of crude oil and natural gas liquids totalled 3,296,000 bpd (of which 1,567,000 bpd represented net production by the parent company and its consolidated subsidiaries). About two-thirds of the total was produced in the eastern hemisphere. In 1983 net equity supplies totalled 927,000 bpd, of which 59 per cent came from the western hemisphere (37 per cent from the United States) and the balance from the eastern hemisphere. Eastern-hemisphere supplies under special agreements with foreign governments totalled 559,000 bpd. Net proved reserves of crude oil and natural gas liquids totalled 1,840 million barrels at the end of 1983.

On Jan. 6, 1984, Texaco announced a $10,100 million takeover bid for the independent Getty Oil Co. This merger was approved by the US Federal Trade Commission on Jan. 14 subject to the subsequent disposal by Texaco of certain overlapping interests, and on Feb. 17 Texaco completed the necessary purchases of outstanding shares in Getty. The independent company Pennzoil, which had concluded an agreement in principle to merge with Getty prior to the submission of Texaco's successful higher bid, sued Texaco for breach of contract and was awarded damages totalling $10,530 million by a Texas court in November 1985. This award was contested by Texaco, whose case remained before the US courts in August 1986.

Texaco statistics for 1983:

Financial (million dollars)		*Oil (thousand bpd)*	
Total revenues	41,147	Total crude supply	1,615
Net income	1,233	Crude processed	1,708
Total assets	27,199	Products sold	2,274

A5.1.v—Gulf

Gulf Oil Corporation (formed in 1907 through the amalgamation of two established producing companies) became a wholly-owned subsidiary of a new holding company, Gulf Corporation, in January 1984. The original Gulf company took its name from the Gulf of Mexico, having (like Texaco) struck its first oil in the state of Texas in 1901. Gulf's early development was backed by wealthy investors based in Pittsburgh, including notably the Mellon family, and the company's headquarters remained in that city. By the outbreak of the First World War Gulf had a substantial US business producing oil in the south-western states for sale through its own outlets on the east coast.

During the 1930s the rate of development of new crude sources by Gulf's Venezuelan subsidiary outstripped the parent company's capacity to expand its marketing resources, resulting in the acquisition by Exxon and Shell of 25 per cent interests in Gulf's Venezuelan concessions (◊**C13.3.i**). Gulf again acquired "excess" upstream capacity when Kuwait's oilfields were brought into production after the Second World War, and it sold a higher proportion of its output as crude than any other major oil company (the main contract buyer of part of Gulf's share of Kuwaiti output being Shell, which divided its relevant marketing proceeds with Gulf ◊**C7.3.i**).

By 1960 (when Gulf was producing about as much oil as it refined in the western hemisphere) its eastern-hemisphere production was approximately eight times as high as its eastern-hemisphere refinery throughputs. Eastern-hemisphere refining and marketing operations were substantially expanded during the 1960s and early 1970s. Gulf's net equity output of crude oil and natural gas liquids in 1972 totalled 3,209,600 bpd, of which 58.3 per cent came from the Middle East, 17.5 per cent from the United States, 14.1 per cent from Africa, 6.5 per cent from Latin America and 3.6 per cent from Canada. By 1976 Gulf had lost a higher proportion of its former equity supplies than any other major oil company affected by OPEC participation and nationalization measures, reflecting its heavy dependence on Kuwaiti crude.

Gulf's net equity production in 1983 totalled 506,600 bpd, of which 50 per cent came from the United States, 24.2 per cent from Africa (principally Nigeria, Angola and Zaïre), 15.2 per cent from Canada, 10.2 per cent from Europe (UK North Sea) and 0.4 per cent from Asia. The company's end-1983 net proved reserves totalled 2,046 million barrels. During 1983 Gulf sold its Swiss refining and marketing operations to Shell and its Scandinavian and Benelux operations to the Kuwait Petroleum Corporation, which subsequently purchased Gulf's Italian operations in January 1984 (◊**C7.3.iv**). The company's decision to dispose of its eastern-hemisphere downstream operations followed a fall in its European refinery throughputs from 85 per cent of capacity in 1979 to 48 per cent of capacity in 1982.

As mentioned above in the section on Chevron (◊**A5.1.iii**), Gulf accepted a takeover bid from Chevron in early March 1984. Gulf had previously shown itself to be vulnerable to strong pressure from a group of minority shareholders led by the president of Mesa Petroleum Co. (a Texas-based independent oil company), who were described by Gulf's chairman as being "bent on seeing [Gulf] bought out at a high price or wresting control of it for themselves in order to break it apart and sell the pieces for a quick gain". Chevron's approach to Gulf followed a similar "friendly" takeover bid from the independent Atlantic Richfield Co., which was rejected by Gulf.

Gulf statistics for 1983:

Financial (million dollars)		*Oil (thousand bpd)*	
Total revenues	28,887	Total crude supply	1,500
Net income	978	Crude processed	939
Total assets	20,964	Products sold	1,111

A5.1.vi—Royal Dutch/Shell

The Royal Dutch/Shell Group of companies (often referred to simply as "Shell") came into being in 1907 when the British-based The Shell Transport and Trading Co. (originally formed in 1897 to export Russian oil to the Far East) combined its interests with those of the Dutch-based Royal Dutch Company for the Working of Petroleum Wells in the Netherlands Indies (originally formed in 1890 to develop an oilfield in Sumatra). Each company was already a part-owner of the Asiatic Petroleum Co., formed in 1903 (◊**C4.3.i**).

Under the terms of the 1907 merger Royal Dutch took a 60 per cent interest and Shell a 40 per cent interest in each of two operating companies—NV de Bataafsche Petroleum Mij and the Anglo-Saxon Petroleum Co.—which, together with the Asiatic Petroleum Co., managed the Group's affairs. The name of the Asiatic Petroleum Co. was changed to The Shell Petroleum Co. in 1946 and the business of the Anglo-Saxon Petroleum Co. was vested in The Shell Petroleum Co. in 1955. The Royal Dutch/Shell Group was the largest of the major oil companies for a period preceding the Second World War, and has since then retained the position of second largest.

During the 1950s and 1960s the Group was the largest net purchaser of crude among the major oil companies, having a small shortfall of equity crude in relation to its western-hemisphere refinery throughputs and a substantial shortfall in the eastern hemisphere (where it purchased Kuwaiti crude under a long-term contract with Gulf ◊**C7.3.i**). From 1931 to 1975 Shell and BP owned a joint downstream company, Shell-Mex and BP Ltd, which carried out marketing and some refining activities in a number of countries. An upstream partnership between Shell and BP in Nigeria ended in 1979 when BP's share was nationalized (◊**C9.3**).

In 1972, when it retained full ownership of the greater part of its output in OPEC countries, the Group had a total net equity production of crude oil and natural gas liquids of 4,069,000 bpd, of which 36.9 per cent came from the Middle East, 19.6

per cent from Latin America and the Caribbean, 18.3 per cent from Africa, 15.1 per cent from the United States, 7.2 per cent from Asia and Australasia, 1.9 per cent from Canada and 1 per cent from Europe. A further 912,000 bpd was purchased under long-term contracts. Net equity production in 1983 totalled 1,497,000 bpd, of which 35 per cent came from the United States, 28 per cent from Europe, 12.6 per cent from Asia (mainly Brunei and Malaysia) and Australasia, 11 per cent from Africa, 10.5 per cent from the Middle East (mainly Oman) and 2.9 per cent from Canada. The Group's year-end net proved reserves of 6,681 million barrels were the largest of any oil company in 1983. Reserves totalling a further 418,000,000 barrels were held by virtue of minority shareholdings in associated companies.

The present structure of the Royal Dutch/Shell Group is especially complex because of the retention of separate identities by the Dutch component, with its headquarters in The Hague, and the British component, with its headquarters in London. The Royal Dutch Petroleum Co. (NV Koninklijke Nederlandse Petroleum Mij) and The Shell Transport and Trading Co. plc function as the parent companies and do not themselves form part of the Group. Their income derives from their shareholdings in the group holding companies, Shell Petroleum NV (successor to NV de Bataafsche Petroleum Mij) and The Shell Petroleum Co. Ltd. The group holding companies in turn hold all the shares in nine group service companies (four based in The Hague and five in London) and all or some of the shares in about 300 operating companies located in over 100 countries.

The largest of the operating companies in the US-based Shell Oil Co., 69 per cent of whose shares were held by the Group at the end of 1983. An offer by Shell Petroleum NV to buy out the holders of the 31 per cent minority interest in the Shell Oil Co. was announced at the beginning of 1984 and the buy-out was eventually completed in mid-1985.

Royal Dutch/Shell statistics for 1983:

Financial (£ million sterling)		*Oil (thousand bpd)*	
Total revenues	54,441	Total crude supply	3,913
Net income	2,754	Crude processed	2,927
Total assets	48,784	Crude sold	875
		Products sold	4,184

A5.1.vii—British Petroleum

The British Petroleum Co. plc, which trades under the initials BP in many markets, is the parent company of a group which has subsidiaries or affiliates in 80 countries. BP was originally known as the Anglo-Persian Oil Co., under which name it was incorporated in 1909 to develop an oil concession covering about three-quarters of the territory of Iran (◊C5.3.i). The largest single investor in the new company was initially the Burmah Oil Co. (itself established in 1902 by Scottish business interests), but in 1914 the British Government acquired a majority shareholding in Anglo-Persian and awarded the company a long-term contract for the supply of fuel to the Royal Navy. The company adopted the name Anglo-Iranian Oil Co. in 1935.

The company lost its effective monopoly over Iranian production following the nationalization of that country's oil industry in 1951, although it subsequently became the largest partner (with the other international majors as its main junior partners) in the new producing consortium which was established in Iran in 1954 (◊C5.3.ii). The company's name was changed to British Petroleum in the same year. Production from the company's other main operating areas at that time (Iraq, Kuwait and Qatar) was substantially increased during the period of the Iranian nationalization crisis, and BP subsequently had a large surplus of crude production relative to its refinery capacity, leading it to undertake a major refinery expansion programme in Europe.

The company's downstream operations were centred in Europe and the

Commonwealth during the mid-1960s, while the bulk of its crude production continued to come from the Middle East. Exploration work had, however, commenced in northern Alaska, where BP announced a major discovery in March 1969. In the same month BP purchased a substantial US refining and marketing network (which had become available as a result of the merger of Atlantic Richfield and Sinclair Oil) and on Jan. 1, 1970, it transferred its US upstream and downstream interests to Sohio—the original Standard Oil Company incorporated in Ohio in 1870—in exchange for an initial 26 per cent shareholding in Sohio, which was to increase in line with the growth of the company's Alaskan oil production. BP eventually held a 55 per cent controlling interest in Sohio, which was the largest single producer of US crude (and the holder of the largest US proved crude reserves) for a period at the beginning of the 1980s. The growth of BP's US interests, which provided the company with its first significant oil supplies from the western hemisphere, coincided with a shift in the focus of its upstream operations in the eastern hemisphere towards the UK North Sea, which replaced the Middle East as BP's main source of eastern-hemisphere equity crude after the nationalization of most of its interests in OPEC countries.

In 1972 BP's equity production of crude oil and natural gas liquids totalled 4,618,500 bpd, of which 86.5 per cent came from the Middle East and 12.6 per cent from Nigeria; Sohio produced 50,055 bpd in the same year, all from the lower 48 states of the USA. In 1983 BP's equity supplies, including 100 per cent of Sohio's (mainly Alaskan) output, totalled 1,234,000 bpd, of which 52 per cent came from North America, 41.1 per cent from the United Kingdom and 6.2 per cent from Abu Dhabi. A further 174,000 bpd was purchased under contracts with producing countries' national oil companies. Net proved reserves of crude oil and natural gas liquids held by BP and its majority-owned subsidiaries totalled 4,584 million barrels at the end of 1983. In addition, BP's minority shares in the reserves of producing companies in Abu Dhabi totalled 1,792 million barrels.

The proportion of BP's shares held by the British Government fell to 48.9 per cent in 1967 following transactions connected with BP's purchase of new chemical and plastics interests in the UK, but in 1975 the effective state shareholding increased when the Bank of England acquired a separate 20.15 per cent shareholding in BP from Burmah Oil (which was then in serious financial difficulties). In 1977 the total state shareholding was reduced to its original level of 51 per cent through the sale to the public of part of the Government's holding, and in 1979 the sale of a further part of the same holding made the state a minority shareholder once more. By 1981 the total state shareholding had fallen to 39.04 per cent (21.89 per cent Government, 17.15 per cent Bank of England) following transactions connected with BP's purchase of a UK mining finance house and with a rights issue in which the state shareholders did not take up their entitlement. In late 1981 the Bank of England's shareholding was formally transferred to the Government.

BP's articles of association contain a clause giving the British Government the right to nominate two board members who are entitled to veto any resolution. Undertakings were given when the clause was introduced in 1914 that the Government would not interfere in the company's commercial affairs and would not use its veto unless certain major issues (e.g. of British foreign or military policy) were at stake. The veto has never been used, and the company's commercial independence has always been equal to that of the privately-owned majors.

BP statistics for 1983:

Financial (£ million sterling)		*Oil (thousand bpd)*	
Total revenues	32,979	Total crude supply	2,397
Net income	1,031	Crude processed	1,386
Total assets	27,174	Crude sold	992
		Products sold	2,116

A5.1.viii—Total Compagnie Française des Pétroles

The Compagnie Française des Pétroles (CFP) was originally incorporated in 1924 as a vehicle for the exploitation of the former German interest in Iraqi oil development which was transferred to the French Government in the aftermath of the First World War (◊C6.3.i). The company subsequently acquired interests in other territories in which affiliates of the Iraq Petroleum Company were established (principally Qatar and Abu Dhabi) and became a member of the Iranian Oil Participants consortium which was formed in 1954 (◊C5.3.ii). During the 1950s and 1960s CFP produced a substantial surplus of crude relative to its refinery throughputs, although the overall scale of its operations was far smaller than that of the other majors.

CFP's downstream operations in France were based on a "reserved" market share (first guaranteed by law in 1928), while the company enjoyed a privileged position relative to non-French companies when upstream producing rights were granted in Algeria under French colonial rule in the 1950s (◊C1.3.i). By 1970 the company was producing over 250,000 bpd in Algeria (about 20 per cent of its total crude supply at that time). In 1972, following the 51 per cent nationalization of its Algerian interests (◊C1.3.iv), CFP's net equity crude output totalled 1,247,400 bpd, of which 87.7 per cent came from the Middle East and 11.8 per cent from Algeria.

In 1983 CFP had a total net equity production of 271,110 bpd and made purchases totalling 216,890 bpd under medium- and long-term contracts. Of the combined total of equity and contract supplies, 51.6 per cent came from the Middle East, 19.6 per cent from North Africa and 7.2 per cent from Indonesia. Other regions in which CFP had production operations included the North Sea and North America. Overall, the Total group (for which CFP acts as the holding company) has upstream and downstream interests in nearly 50 countries worldwide. The French Government has a substantial minority interest in CFP (holding 35 per cent of its stock and 40 per cent of the voting rights). The title Total Compagnie Française des Pétroles was officially adopted on June 21, 1985.

CFP/Total group statistics for 1983:

Financial (million French francs)		*Oil (thousand bpd)*	
Total revenues	139,866	Total crude supply	864
Net income	420	Crude processed	619
Total assets	91,755	Products sold	1,032

A5.2—Major Oil Companies' Operations in the Middle East

The main upstream links between the international majors were forged through the joint ownership of companies operating in the OPEC countries of the Middle East (and also in Oman and Bahrain), details of which are summarized below.

A5.2.i—Arabian American Oil Company (Aramco)

Shares in Aramco, which produces the bulk of Saudi Arabia's oil (i.e. with the exception of Saudi Arabia's share of production from the Saudi-Kuwait Neutral Zone), have since 1979 been owned as follows: Chevron 28⅓ per cent, Exxon 28⅓ per cent, Texaco 28⅓ per cent, Mobil 15 per cent. From 1948 to 1974 ownership was 30 per cent by Chevron, 30 per cent by Exxon, 30 per cent by Texaco and 10 per cent by Mobil, but from 1975 Mobil's shareholding was increased by 1 per cent per year over five years through the issue of new stock. Aramco was originally founded in 1933 as the California Arabian Standard Oil Co. (Casoc), a wholly-owned subsidiary of Chevron. Texaco acquired a 50 per cent shareholding in 1936, and the present company name was adopted in 1944. Exxon and Mobil became shareholders in Aramco in 1948.

The Saudi Arabian Government (which does not own any shares in Aramco) acquired 25 per cent of the company's upstream producing assets in 1973, the level of state control being increased to 60 per cent in the following year and 100 per cent with effect from 1976. Aramco continues to operate in Saudi Arabia as a contractor to the state.

A5.2.ii—Iranian Oil Participants (IOP)

The IOP consortium, established in September 1954, was the only Middle East grouping which included all eight international majors, whose shareholdings were distributed as follows from April 1955 onwards: BP 40 per cent, Shell 14 per cent, Chevron 7 per cent, Exxon 7 per cent, Gulf 7 per cent, Mobil 7 per cent, Texaco 7 per cent and CFP 6 per cent. The remaining 5 per cent shareholding in IOP was held by Iricon Agency Ltd, representing a number of US independent oil companies (◊C5.3.ii).

IOP originally acted as a holding company for two subsidiaries, the Iranian Oil Exploration and Producing Company and the Iranian Oil Refining Company, whose nominal status was that of contractors to the state-owned National Iranian Oil Company (NIOC—established upon the nationalization of BP's former concession areas in 1951), although in practice they exercised effective control over production decisions. In 1973 IOP established a new operating subsidiary, the Oil Service Company of Iran, under the terms of a revised agreement with NIOC. This agreement was formally abrogated by the Iranian Government in 1981.

A5.2.iii—Iraq Petroleum Company (IPC)

The Iraq Petroleum Company—established under that name in June 1929 as the successor to the Turkish Petroleum Company—was owned 23.75 per cent by BP, 23.75 per cent by CFP, 23.75 per cent by Shell, 23.75 per cent by Near East Development Corporation (NEDC) and 5 per cent by Participations and Explorations Corporation (Partex). NEDC (originally formed in 1928 by five US oil companies) was owned 50 per cent by Exxon and 50 per cent by Mobil after 1934. Partex was owned by Gulbenkian interests. The IPC shareholders subsequently established two affiliated companies to exploit additional concession areas within Iraq, namely the Mosul Petroleum Company (MPC) and the Basrah Petroleum Company (BPC), all three companies usually being referred to collectively as IPC. The operations of the original IPC company within its own concession area were nationalized in 1972. The MPC's operations were nationalized in 1973. The BPC's operations were 43 per cent nationalized during 1973 (when the Iraq Government expropriated the NEDC and Partex interests and 60 per cent of the Shell interest) and were brought into full state ownership in 1975.

A5.2.iv—Interests of IPC group outside Iraq

The IPC's main "informally affiliated" companies—i.e. companies operating outside Iraq whose ultimate ownership at the time of incorporation was identical to that of IPC—were the **Abu Dhabi Petroleum Company** (ADPC), **Petroleum Development (Oman)** and the **Qatar Petroleum Company** (QPC).

ADPC was established under that name in 1962 after Petroleum Development (Trucial Coast)—its predecessor company, formed in 1936—had relinquished unexploited onshore concessions in Dubai, Ras al-Khaimah and Sharjah. The state-owned Abu Dhabi National Oil Co. took a 25 per cent interest in ADPC's operations in 1973 (increased to 60 per cent in the following year) and in 1978 ADPC (whose share structure remained unchanged) became a 40 per cent shareholder in a new state-controlled operating company.

Petroleum Development (Oman) was established under that name in 1951, having originally been formed in 1937 as Petroleum Development (Oman and Dhofar). The company was restructured as a partnership between Shell (82.6 per cent) and Partex (17.4 per cent) when BP, CFP and NEDC withdrew in 1960 (although CFP subsequently resumed its participation with a reduced shareholding, while Partex's interest reverted to 5 per cent). The Government of Oman acquired a 25 per cent interest in the company's operations in 1973 (increased to 60 per cent in the following year), although the shares continued to be owned by Shell (85 per cent), CFP (10 per cent) and Partex (5 per cent). In 1980 these shareholdings were vested in a new British-registered company, Private Oil Holdings Oman, while Petroleum Development (Oman) became an Omani-registered company owned 60 per cent by the Oman Government and 40 per cent by Private Oil Holdings Oman.

The Qatar Petroleum Company was established under that name in 1953, having originally been formed in 1936 as Petroleum Development (Qatar). The QPC's operations were fully nationalized in 1976, when the former shareholders established a new Dukhan Service Company to operate as a contractor to Qatar's state oil corporation.

A5.2.v—Kuwait Oil Company (KOC)

The London-registered KOC, formed in 1934, was owned 50 per cent by BP and 50 per cent by Gulf Oil. A new state-owned company of the same name (which was registered in Kuwait and subsequently became a wholly-owned subsidiary of the Kuwait Petroleum Corporation) took over the former BP and Gulf assets and concession rights in Kuwait after their full nationalization in 1975.

A5.2.vi—Other companies

Abu Dhabi Marine Areas (ADMA) was established in 1954 under the joint ownership of BP (66⅔ per cent) and CFP (33⅓ per cent) to take up a concession covering offshore areas not included in ADPC's concession. BP's shareholding was reduced to 36⅔ per cent in 1973 through the sale of a 30 per cent interest in ADMA to the Japan Oil Development Co. The state-owned Abu Dhabi National Oil Co. (Adnoc) took a 25 per cent interest in ADMA's operations in 1973 (increased to 60 per cent in the following year), and in 1977 ADMA (whose ownership remained unchanged) became a 40 per cent shareholder in a new operating company, the balance of whose shares was held by Adnoc. Two new companies which were formed in 1971–72 to operate in relinquished parts of the ADMA concession area included major oil company shareholdings; BP and CFP each had a 33⅓ interest in the **Al-Bunduq Oil Co.**, whose remaining shares were held by United Petroleum Development (of Japan), while CFP held a 51 per cent interest in the **Total Abu Al Bakoosh Oil Co.**, whose minority shareholders were three US independent companies.

Dubai Marine Areas (DUMA) was established in 1954 under the joint ownership of BP (66⅔ per cent) and CFP (33⅓ per cent). Conoco acquired a 50 per cent interest in DUMA's offshore concession rights in 1963 (although the ownership of DUMA remained unchanged). BP withdrew from DUMA in 1969, selling its shareholding to CFP, which in turn sold a 50 per cent shareholding to Hispanoil. Operations in the DUMA concession area were placed on a contract basis by the Dubai Government in 1975.

The **Bahrain Petroleum Company** was formed in 1929 as a wholly-owned subsidiary of Chevron, which transferred a 50 per cent interest to Texaco in 1936. The company's upstream producing operations were taken over by the state-owned Bahrain National Oil Co. in 1979. In 1981 the Bahrain Petroleum Company (which had continued to be responsible for refining operations) was reconstituted as a Bahrain-registered corporation, owned 60 per cent by the Bahrain Government and 40 per cent by Caltex (Chevron/Texaco).

The **Shell Company of Qatar** (SCQ), formed in 1953 to develop an offshore concession, was the only Middle Eastern producing company to be wholly owned by a single major oil company during the 1960s. State participation in the company's operations (introduced at the level of 25 per cent in 1973) was increased to 60 per cent in 1974 and 100 per cent in 1977, after which a new Qatar Shell Service Company was established to act as a contractor to Qatar's state oil corporation.

A5.3—Major Oil Companies' Operations in OPEC Countries outside the Middle East

The main upstream operations of the international majors in OPEC countries outside the Middle East are summarized below.

Algeria. The principal "major" producer was CFP, whose upstream interests came under 51 per cent state control in 1971 (extended to 100 per cent in 1981 in respect of CFP's main operations). The only non-French company which held a majority (65 per cent) interest in an Algerian producing company was Shell, whose operations were nationalized in 1970, as were those of Mobil (which had held a minority shareholding in a French-controlled producing company). Shell's minor Algerian interests included a half-share in the Sofrapel company, whose co-owner was Exxon.

Ecuador. Texaco and Gulf operated jointly as producers until 1977, when Gulf withdrew, leaving Texaco as the 37.5 per cent minority partner of the state oil corporation.

Gabon. The only international major with a significant upstream presence in Gabon is Shell, whose local subsidiary (which is 25 per cent state-owned) has a 50 per cent interest in production from certain concession areas held by the French-controlled Elf Gabon company.

Indonesia. Major oil companies which operated as concessionaires in Indonesia prior to the Government's abolition of the concession system in 1963 were Chevron and Texaco (through their jointly-owned Caltex subsidiary), Mobil and Exxon (through their jointly-owned Stanvac subsidiary) and Shell. Thereafter the former concession operations were placed on a contract basis, under which the US majors continued to work for their full contractual periods (normally 20 years) while Shell withdrew in early 1966. In 1986 most of the major oil companies were operating in Indonesia on a production-sharing basis as minority partners of the state oil company.

Libya. Exxon was the only major company to have operated as the sole owner of Libyan production interests. Chevron and Texaco operated in partnership (through Amoseas), while Mobil, Shell and BP each operated in partnership with independent companies (as did Exxon in respect of certain concession areas). The Libyan Government nationalized BP's operations in 1971 and those of Chevron, Texaco and Shell in 1974. The operations of Exxon and Mobil came under 51 per cent state control in 1974. Exxon withdrew from Libya in 1981, while Mobil withdrew at the end of 1982.

Nigeria. The main producing company in Nigeria was a joint venture between BP and Shell (with state participation) until 1979, when BP's share was fully nationalized. Production interests are also held by Chevron and Texaco (in partnership), by Chevron alone (interests held by Gulf Oil until its takeover by Chevron in 1984) and by Mobil. The state oil corporation holds an 80 per cent interest in Shell's current operations and a 60 per cent interest in those of the other majors.

Venezuela. Under the concession system, the dominant producing companies in Venezuela were subsidiaries of Exxon, Shell and Gulf. Texaco, Mobil and Chevron also had local subsidiaries. BP was unable to acquire Venezuelan interests because of a ban on the granting of concessions to companies owned by foreign governments. All foreign oil interests were nationalized at the beginning of 1976.

A6—Principal Middle East Pipelines

A6.1—Sumed (Suez-Mediterranean Pipeline)

Length 320 km, capacity 1,600,000 bpd. Opened early 1977. Links terminals at Ain Sukhna (near Suez) and Sidi Kerir (near Alexandria) which handle tankers too large to navigate the Suez Canal. Became an increasingly important route for westbound exports of Gulf crude after the opening of the Saudi Petroline, and handles a far greater throughput of oil than the Suez Canal. Owned by Arab Petroleum Pipelines Co. (Egypt 50 per cent, Abu Dhabi 15 per cent, Kuwait 15 per cent, Saudi Arabia 15 per cent, Qatar 5 per cent). Kuwaiti shareholding is held by various investment and industrial companies. Other shareholdings are held by respective national oil companies.

A6.2—Petroline

Length 1,269 km, capacity 1,850,000 bpd. Opened 1981. Links Saudi Arabia's Gulf oilfields to the Red Sea port of Yanbu and has attracted some tanker traffic away from the Gulf because of the war risk to shipping using Gulf ports. Up to 500,000 bpd of Petroline's export capacity was made available to Iraq from September 1985.

A6.3—Iraq Strategic Pipeline

Length 650 km. Reversible flow; capacity 880,000 bpd south-north or 1,000,000 bpd north-south. Opened 1976. Links Iraq's central pipeline junction at Haditha to Gulf export terminals at Fao. North-south throughputs were suspended in late 1980 when Iraq's Gulf export terminals were destroyed by Iranian military action. South-north throughputs have been severely limited since Syria's withdrawal of pipeline transit facilities in April 1982.

A6.4—Iraq-Dörtyol

Length 980 km, capacity 1,000,000 bpd. Opened 1977. Runs from Iraq's main northern oilfields to the Turkish Mediterranean port of Dortyöl on the Gulf of Iskenderun. Also linked to the southern Iraqi oilfields via the Strategic Pipeline. Was Iraqi's sole export route for crude oil (except by road) from April 1982 to September 1985.

A6.5—Iraq-Petroline Link

Length 630 km, capacity 500,000 bpd. Opened September 1985. Links Iraq's southern oilfields to the Saudi Arabian Petroline, enabling Iraqi crude to be exported via the Red Sea port of Yanbu.

A6.6—Iraq-Banias/Tripoli

Length: Kirkuk-Banias 893 km, Kirkuk-Tripoli 854 km. Original Tripoli pipeline opened 1934; second Tripoli pipeline 1949; Banias pipeline 1952. The theoretical capacity of the export pipelines crossing Syrian territory totals about 1,400,000 bpd, but not more than 500,000 bpd was available in practice in early 1982 (partly because of a lack of maintenance work at pumping stations and export terminals). After a long history of interruptions to their operation, the pipelines were shut down indefinitely by Syria in April 1982.

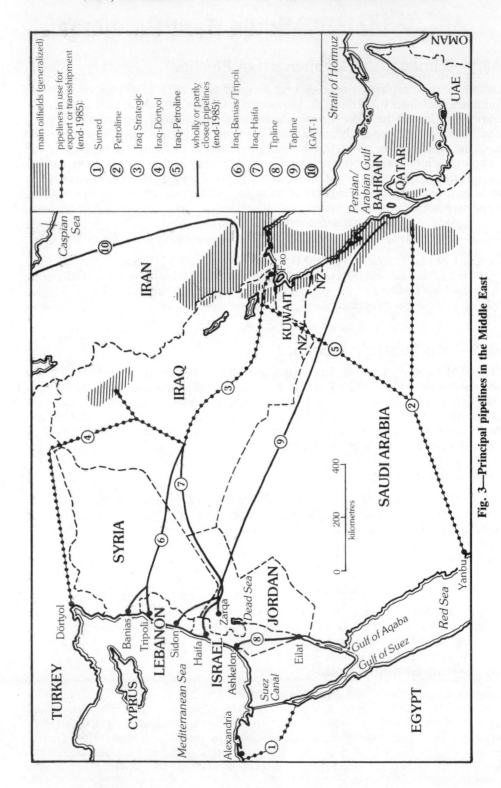

Fig. 3.—Principal pipelines in the Middle East

126

A6.7—Iraq-Haifa

Length 1,000 km, capacity 100,000 bpd. Opened 1934 to link Iraq's Kirkuk oilfield to the Mediterranean port of Haifa (then in British-administered Palestine). Closed in 1948 as a result of the Arab boycott of the new state of Israel. In June 1984 Iraq rejected an Israeli offer to reopen the line.

A6.8—Tipline (Trans-Israel Pipeline)

Length 265 km, capacity 900,000 bpd. Links Israel's Red Sea port of Eilat to the Mediterranean port of Ashkelon. Opened in February 1970, Tipline provided the only route for the movement of oil between the Red Sea and the Mediterranean until the Suez Canal was reopened in June 1975, and continued to provide the only pipeline route until the Sumed line opened in early 1977. However, political considerations severely limited the use of Tipline (which was banned by Arab oil exporters) and Iran was the only exporting country which made open use of it (for transit purposes and for the supply of oil to Israel). The suspension of Iran's oil exports at the end of 1978, followed by the Iranian revolutionary Government's ban on trade with Israel, caused the shutdown of the pipeline in 1979.

A6.9—Tapline (Trans-Arabian Pipeline)

Length 1,312 km, capacity 500,000 bpd. Opened 1950. Links Saudi Arabia's Gulf oilfields to the Lebanese port of Sidon, with a spur to a Jordanian refinery at Zarqa. Exports from Sidon were discontinued in 1975. Supplies to Lebanon's Zahrani refinery were discontinued, and the Lebanese and Syrian sections of Tapline shut down, in 1983. The continued use of Tapline to supply Jordan's Zarqa refinery was in doubt after the end of 1985.

A6.10—IGAT-1 (Iran Gas Trunkline 1)

Length 1,106 km. Export capacity 10,000 million cubic metres per year. Opened 1970. Runs from the south-west Iranian oilfields to join the Soviet gas pipeline system at Astara. Exports discontinued in 1980 following a pricing dispute; subsequently used exclusively for internal gas supply purposes. The pricing dispute was settled in August 1986, when it was announced that exports would resume later that year.

INTERNATIONAL ORGANIZATIONS: STRUCTURES AND FUNCTIONS

B1—Organization of the Petroleum Exporting Countries

B1.1—General

A treaty formally establishing the Organization of the Petroleum Exporting Countries (OPEC) as a permanent intergovernmental organization was published on Sept. 24, 1960, and after ratification by the signatory countries was registered at the United Nations on Nov. 6, 1962. OPEC was officially recognized as an international organization by the UN Economic and Social Council on June 30, 1965, and subsequently became a regular participant in meetings of various UN bodies, including the UN Conference on Trade and Development, and in other international forums.

B1.2—Membership, Staffing, etc.

Founder members .... Iran, Iraq, Kuwait, Saudi Arabia, Venezuela

Subsequent members .... Qatar (January 1961)
Indonesia, Libya (June 1962)
Abu Dhabi (November 1967)
Algeria (July 1969)
Nigeria (July 1971)
Ecuador (associate June 1973, full November 1973)
Gabon (associate November 1973, full June 1975)
United Arab Emirates (January 1974, by transfer of Abu Dhabi's membership)

Headquarters .... Geneva (1961 to August 1965)
Vienna (September 1965 onwards)

Secretariat staffing (1984) .... 52 (department heads and officials)

Annual budget (1985) .... 244,474,500 Austrian schillings (approximately $10,990,100 at January 1985 exchange rate)

Secretary-General (August 1986) .... Vacant (since July 1983)

Deputy Secretary-General .... Dr Fadhil J. Al-Chalabi (Iraq)—current term of office expires October 1987

Table 15 — Holders of the post of OPEC Secretary-General

Name	Country	Period of office	Terms of appointment*
Dr Fuad Rouhani	Iran	Jan. 1961—April 1964	2 years + 1 year extension + 4 month extension
Abdul Rahman Al-Bazzaz	Iraq	May 1964—April 1965	1 year
Ashraf T. Lutfi	Kuwait	May 1965—Dec. 1966	1 year + 8 month extension
Mohamed Saleh Joukhdar	Saudi Arabia	Jan.–Dec. 1967	1 year
Francisco R. Parra	Venezuela	Jan.–Dec. 1968	1 year
Dr Elrich Sanger	Indonesia	Jan.–Dec. 1969	1 year
Omar El Badri	Libya	Jan.–Dec. 1970	1 year
Dr Nadim Pachachi	Abu Dhabi†	Jan. 1971—Dec. 1972	2 years
Dr Abderrahman Khene	Algeria	Jan. 1973—Dec. 1974	2 years
Chief Meshach O. Feyide	Nigeria	Jan. 1975—Dec. 1976	2 years
Ali Mohammed Jaidah	Qatar	Jan. 1977—Dec. 1978	2 years
Rene G. Ortiz	Ecuador	Jan. 1979—June 1981	2 years + 6 month extension
Dr Marc S. Nan Nguema	Gabon	July 1981—June 1983	2 years

*From January 1961 until April 1965, when the posts were separated, the Secretary-General was also Chairman of the Board of Governors. Until June 1970 the Secretary-General's normal term of office was one year. Since then Article 28 of the OPEC Statute ($\flat$B1.7) has provided for a maximum initial period of office of three years, renewable for a further three years, but no appointment has yet been made on these terms.

†Although an Iraqi national and a former cabinet minister in that country (1952–58), Dr Pachachi had since 1966 served in Abu Dhabi as Oil Adviser to the Ruler.

B1.3—Meetings of OPEC Conference

The OPEC Conference, the Organization's policy-making body (at whose meetings member countries' delegations are normally headed by their Oil Ministers), held 78 formal meetings between September 1960 and August 1986 as follows.

Meeting	Status	Location	Dates
1st	Inaugural	Baghdad	Sept. 10–14, 1960
2nd	Ordinary	Caracas	Jan. 15–21, 1961
3rd	Ordinary	Tehran	Oct. 28—Nov. 1, 1961
4th	Ordinary	Geneva	April 5–8 and June 4–8, 1962
5th	Ordinary	Riyadh	Nov. 24–25 and Dec. 24–31, 1963
6th	Ordinary	Geneva	July 6–14, 1964
7th	Ordinary	Jakarta	Nov. 23–28, 1964
8th	Extraordinary	Geneva	April 5–10, 1965
9th	Ordinary	Tripoli	July 7–13, 1965
10th	Ordinary	Vienna	Dec. 15–17, 1965
11th	Ordinary	Vienna	April 25–28, 1966
12th	Ordinary	Kuwait	Dec. 4–8, 1966
13th	Extraordinary	Rome	Sept. 15–17, 1967
14th	Ordinary	Vienna	Nov. 27–29, 1967
15th	Extraordinary	Beirut	Jan. 8–9, 1968
16th	Ordinary	Vienna	June 24–25, 1968
17th	Ordinary	Baghdad	Nov. 9–10, 1968
18th	Ordinary	Vienna	July 8–9, 1969
19th	Ordinary	Doha	Dec. 14–16, 1969
20th	Ordinary	Algiers	June 24–26, 1970
21st	Ordinary	Caracas	Dec. 9–12, 1970
22nd	Extraordinary	Tehran	Feb. 3–4, 1971
23rd	Ordinary	Vienna	July 10, 1971
24th	Ordinary	Vienna	July 12–13, 1971
25th	Extraordinary	Beirut	Sept. 22, 1971
26th	Ordinary	Abu Dhabi	Dec. 7, 1971
27th	Extraordinary	Beirut	March 11–12, 1972
28th	Extraordinary	Bcirut	June 9, 1972
29th	Ordinary	Vienna	June 26–27, 1972
30th	Extraordinary	Riyadh	Oct. 26–27, 1972
31st	Ordinary	Lagos	Nov. 29–30, 1972
32nd	Extraordinary	Vienna	March 16–17, 1973
33rd	Extraordinary	Vienna	May 26, 1973
34th	Ordinary	Vienna	June 27–28, 1973
35th	Extraordinary	Vienna	Sept. 15–16, 1973
36th	Ordinary	Vienna	Nov. 19–20, 1973
37th	Extraordinary	Geneva	Jan. 7–9, 1974
38th	Extraordinary	Vienna	March 16–17, 1974
39th	Extraordinary	Geneva	April 7, 1974
40th	Ordinary	Quito	June 15–17, 1974
41st	Extraordinary	Vienna	Sept. 12–13, 1974
42nd	Ordinary	Vienna	Dec. 12–13, 1974
43rd	Extraordinary	Vienna	Feb. 25–27, 1975
44th	Ordinary	Libreville	June 9–11, 1975
45th	Extraordinary	Vienna	Sept. 24–27, 1975
46th	Ordinary	Vienna	Dec. 20–21, 1975

Meeting	Status	Location	Dates
47th	Ordinary	Bali	May 27–28, 1976
48th	Ordinary	Doha	Dec. 15–17, 1976
49th	Ordinary	Stockholm	July 12–13, 1977
50th	Ordinary	Caracas	Dec. 20–21, 1977
51st	Ordinary	Geneva	June 17–19, 1978
52nd	Ordinary	Abu Dhabi	Dec. 16–17, 1978
53rd	Extraordinary	Geneva	March 26–27, 1979
54th	Ordinary	Geneva	June 26–28, 1979
55th	Ordinary	Caracas	Dec. 17–20, 1979
56th	Extraordinary	Taif	May 7–8, 1980
57th	Ordinary	Algiers	June 9–11, 1980
58th	Extraordinary	Vienna	Sept. 17, 1980
59th	Ordinary	Bali	Dec. 15–16, 1980
60th	Ordinary	Geneva	May 25–26, 1981
61st	Extraordinary	Geneva	Oct. 29, 1981
62nd	Ordinary	Abu Dhabi	Dec. 9–11, 1981
63rd	Extraordinary	Vienna	March 19–20, 1982
64th	Ordinary	Quito	May 20–21, 1982
65th	Extraordinary	Vienna	July 9–10, 1982
66th	Ordinary	Vienna	Dec. 19–20, 1982
67th	Extraordinary	London	March 14, 1983
68th	Ordinary	Helsinki	July 18–19, 1983
69th	Ordinary	Geneva	Dec. 7–9, 1983
70th	Ordinary	Vienna	July 10–11, 1984
71st	Extraordinary	Geneva	Oct. 29–31, 1984
72nd	Ordinary	Geneva	Dec. 19–21 and 27–29, 1984
73rd	Extraordinary	Geneva	Jan. 28–30, 1985
74th	Ordinary	Geneva	July 22–25, 1985
75th	Extraordinary	Vienna	Oct. 3–4, 1985
76th	Ordinary	Geneva	Dec. 7–9, 1985
77th	Extraordinary	Geneva	March 16–24 and April 15–21, 1986
78th	Ordinary	{ Brioni { Geneva	June 25–30, 1986 July 28—Aug. 5, 1986

B1.4—Other Main OPEC Meetings

Summit conference of sovereigns and heads of state
Algiers, March 4–6, 1975

Formal joint meetings of Ministers of Oil, Finance and Foreign Affairs
Algiers, Jan. 24–26, 1975
Vienna, Sept. 15–17, 1980

Meetings of OPEC Finance Ministers/*Ministerial Committee on Financial and Monetary Matters

Vienna, Nov. 17–18, 1975
Paris, Jan. 26–28, 1976
*Paris, May 10–11, 1976
*Vienna, Aug. 5–6, 1976
*Manila, Oct. 6, 1976
*Vienna, Feb. 28—March 1, 1977

*Vienna, Aug. 4, 1977
*Vienna, May 23, 1978
*Vienna, Sept. 27, 1979
*Vienna, Jan. 16, 1980
*Vienna, May 27, 1980

B1.5—Key Committees of OPEC Conference

Ministerial committee on long-term strategy

Established	May 1978
Membership	Algeria, Iran, Iraq, Kuwait, Saudi Arabia, Venezuela

Ministerial committee to monitor the oil market

Established	March 1982
Membership: to December 1984	Algeria, Indonesia, United Arab Emirates, Venezuela
from January 1985	Algeria, Ecuador, Iran, Iraq, Libya, United Arab Emirates
Meetings	25 between April 1982 and June 1986

Ministerial committee on price differentials

Established	October 1984
Initial members	Libya, Saudi Arabia, United Arab Emirates
Additional members (December 1984)	Algeria, Kuwait, Nigeria, Qatar

Ministerial Executive Council on implementation of pricing and production agreement

Established	December 1984
Membership	Indonesia, Nigeria, Saudi Arabia, United Arab Emirates, Venezuela (participation also open to other member countries)
Meetings	Eight between December 1984 and March 1986

B1.6—OPEC Fund for International Development

An agreement to establish a Special Fund for third-world development was signed by OPEC Finance Ministers on Jan. 28, 1976. The preamble to the agreement referred to "the need for solidarity among all developing countries in the establishment of a new international economic order" (◊D5.9) and to the importance of furthering "financial co-operation between OPEC member countries and other developing countries" in accordance with the spirit of the March 1975 solemn declaration by the sovereigns and heads of state of the OPEC member countries (◊B1.9.iii). The Special Fund had the status of a joint international account subscribed by the OPEC member countries to provide a collective aid facility on a temporary basis. Legal title to the resources held by the Fund was vested in the individual contributing countries, which were entitled to receive repayments made by recipients of the Fund's loans.

Existing national aid agencies in OPEC member countries continued to support bilateral and multilateral development programmes outside the framework of the Special Fund, although the Fund played an increasingly important role in ensuring that member countries' national schemes formed part of a co-ordinated pattern of aid flows. (In 1976 Kuwait, Abu Dhabi, Iraq and Saudi Arabia each had their own specialized aid agencies, while Iran and Venezuela had national investment institutions whose responsibilities included external aid. Algerian and Nigerian aid was channelled through special trust funds administered by the African Development Bank.) Each member of the OPEC Special Fund was required to nominate an "executing national agency" (normally the Finance Ministry in countries which did not have specialized aid agencies) to administer that country's agreed transfers of resources to and from the OPEC Special Fund.

The affairs of the Special Fund were overseen by a Governing Committee made up of senior officials appointed to represent the contributing members of the Fund (which comprised all 13 OPEC countries from 1977, when Ecuador and Iraq made their first contributions). The Committee laid down general policies for the utilization of the Fund's resources and was authorized to conclude loan agreements for projects which met with its approval. The Committee was empowered to appoint the Director-General of the Special Fund. Decisions on matters affecting the status of the Fund (e.g. changes in the terms of its agreement and in the size of its total lending programme) were taken by the OPEC Ministerial Committee on Financial and Monetary Matters. The first significant amendment to the provisions of the Special Fund agreement was made in August 1977, when the total amount of the Fund's resources—originally specified as a fixed sum—was redefined in more general terms to include "other contributions made to the Fund by member countries".

The provisions of the agreement were further amended on Sept. 27, 1979, to authorize the Fund to use loan repayments to finance future lending, thus creating a basis for the indefinite continuation of the Fund's existence. It was subsequently agreed on Jan. 16, 1980, to reconstitute the Fund as a permanent multilateral agency with a separate international juridical personality, a change which became effective on May 27, 1980, when it was formally renamed the OPEC Fund for International Development. In order to bring the organizational structure of the Fund into line with the standard pattern adopted by similar international bodies a permanent Ministerial Council—the successor to the OPEC Ministerial Committee on Financial and Monetary Matters—was established as its supreme organ, while the Governing Committee was succeeded by a Governing Board which remained responsible for a wide range of policy decisions. The Ministerial Council became responsible for the appointment of the Fund's Director-General. The terms of reference of the Fund's operations were significantly broadened and its staffing was increased in order to enable it to become directly involved in project appraisal and loan administration (functions which had previously been entrusted either to established international agencies or to OPEC member countries' national aid agencies). The Vienna-based Fund, which had always operated independently of the OPEC Secretariat, was formally recognized by the Austrian Government as a separate international organization on April 21, 1981.

The Director-General of the OPEC Special Fund, Dr Ibrahim F.I. Shihata (Kuwait), continued to serve as Director-General of the OPEC Fund for International Development until August 1983, when he was succeeded by Dr Y. Seyyid Abdulai (Nigeria), who was appointed for a five-year term of office.

The OPEC member countries' aggregate contributions to the Fund were originally fixed in 1976 at $800,000,000. Two subsequent replenishments by the same amount were formally agreed in March 1977 and January 1980, while a third replenishment by $1,600 million was agreed in May 1980, thus increasing the approved contributions to the Fund to a total of $4,000 million. However, the cumulative total of basic contributions which had actually been pledged to the Fund by member countries amounted to only $3,324.3 million at the end of 1985, reflecting the decline in oil revenues which had been experienced by Iran after the 1979 revolution, by Iraq after the outbreak of the Gulf war and by other OPEC countries when demand for their exports weakened after 1981. The voluntary nature of contributions to the Fund was reaffirmed in June 1981, when its Ministerial Council rejected a Venezuelan proposal for compulsory contributions based on each member country's financial circumstances.

Half of the basic contributions which were approved in 1976 consisted of funds pledged by 12 OPEC member countries towards the initial capitalization of the International Fund for Agricultural Development (IFAD), which were to be remitted to that organization via the OPEC Special Fund. Membership of IFAD was divided into three groups with equal voting rights, of which Group 1 comprised the OECD countries, Group 2 the OPEC countries (excluding Ecuador) and Group 3 other developing countries (including Ecuador). The OPEC group initially insisted that its aggregate pledged contribution of $400,000,000 should be two-thirds as large as that of the OECD group, but when it became apparent that the OECD countries' aggregate pledges would not reach the target of $600,000,000 the OPEC group's contribution was raised to $435,500,000 following decisions taken by Iran, Saudi Arabia and Venezuela in December 1976 to increase their initial pledges. IFAD subsequently commmenced operations as a UN specialized agency at the beginning of 1978.

Negotiations for the first replenishment of IFAD's resources began in 1980, when the Group 1 countries made an initial pledge of $650,000,000 and called on the Group 2 countries to pledge an equal amount. The Group 2 countries rejected this request, and in January 1981 the Ministerial Council of the OPEC Fund for International Development announced a Group 2 pledge of $450,000,000, which was conditional on the maintenance of the Group 1 pledge at its existing level. However, the latter pledge was subsequently reduced to $595,000,000, although an increase to $620,000,000 was promised if the Group 2 pledge was maintained at $450,000,000. The Group 2 countries insisted that they were not prepared to pledge more than $430,000,000 to "match" a Group 1 pledge of $620,000,000 (on the basis of the 450:650 ratio proposed in January 1981), causing a deadlock which was resolved by the decision of the OPEC Fund, announced in January 1982, to make a special contribution of $20,000,000 (which was charged to the Fund's grants programme and thus did not form part of the Group 2 pledges made by individual countries through the Fund). The OPEC Fund's initiative enabled IFAD to resume its lending programme, which had been temporarily suspended in September 1981.

A protracted dispute over the respective Group 1 and Group 2 contributions to a second replenishment of IFAD's resources was resolved on Jan. 23, 1986, when the Group 2 contribution was fixed at $184,000,000 and the Group 1 contribution at $276,000,000. With Iran declining to participate in this replenishment, the Group 2 total was made up of the following national pledges: Saudi Arabia $72,600,000, Venezuela $28,000,000, Kuwait $25,000,000, Libya $16,000,000, Algeria $12,000,000, Nigeria $10,000,000, Indonesia $6,900,000, Qatar $5,000,000, UAE $5,000,000, Iraq $2,000,000 and Gabon $1,500,000.

In addition to the basic contributions which were pledged to the OPEC Fund by all its member countries (except Ecuador in the case of Group 2 contributions to IFAD), seven OPEC countries channelled a total of $110,720,833 through the OPEC Fund between 1976 and 1981 for use by the IMF Trust Fund, a temporary account which was established in 1976 to extend concessionary balance-of-payments assistance to low-income developing countries, using resources derived from part of the profits of the sale of gold held by the IMF. A further part of the profits arising from such gold sales was transferred directly to all developing countries which belonged to the IMF—including OPEC countries—in proportion to their IMF quotas. The Finance Ministers of Iran, Iraq, Kuwait, Libya, Qatar, Saudi Arabia, the United Arab Emirates and Venezuela undertook at the October 1976 meeting of the OPEC Ministerial Committee on Financial and Monetary

Table 16 — Cumulative contributions to OPEC Fund at end-1985 (million US dollars)

	Basic contributions (excluding IFAD)		Group 2 contributions to IFAD		Contributions to IMF Trust Fund via OPEC Fund	Total pledged*	Total paid-up*
	Pledged	Paid-up	Pledged	Paid-up			
Algeria	75.1	59.0	25.6	25.6	—	100.7	84.6
Ecuador	5.1	4.1	—	—	—	5.1	4.1
Gabon	3.8	3.0	1.3	1.3	—	5.1	4.3
Indonesia	9.3	7.4	3.2	3.2	—	12.4	10.6
Iran	376.5	126.3	139.6	41.6	17.3	516.2	167.9
Iraq	110.1	18.6	51.1	51.1	10.3	178.5	87.0
Kuwait	270.4	211.8	92.0	92.0		372.7	314.2
Libya	150.1	114.2	51.1	20.0	3.8	205.0	138.0
Nigeria	177.7	147.6	66.5	66.5	—	244.2	214.0
Qatar	67.5	53.0	23.0	23.0	3.2	93.6	79.1
Saudi Arabia	750.9	589.2	261.1	261.1	21.3	1,033.3	871.6
UAE	123.9	97.1	42.2	42.2	2.4	168.4	141.6
Venezuela	342.7	305.0	104.5	104.5	52.4	499.6	462.0
Totals‡	2,463.1	1,736.2	861.1	732.0†	110.7	3,435.0	2,578.9

*Independently rounded; including contributions to IMF Trust Fund.
†Of which 67.8 per cent was remitted in cash and the balance in promissory notes.
‡Independently rounded.

Matters to recommend that their respective Governments' shares of the IMF gold profits should be transferred to the IMF Trust Fund via the OPEC Fund. Qatar and Venezuela acted on this recommendation in 1976, as did Kuwait, Iraq, Saudi Arabia and the United Arab Emirates in 1977 and Libya in 1978. Iran did not contribute to the Trust Fund (which ended its lending programme in early 1981 after the completion of the IMF programme of gold sales).

The Ministerial Council of the OPEC Fund in January 1981 approved contributions totalling $83,560,000 to the UNCTAD Common Fund for Commodities, of which $46,400,000 would constitute a voluntary contribution to the "second account" (for financing measures to improve the structural conditions of world trade in commodities); the remaining $37,160,000 would consist of grants to 35 poorer developing countries to cover their "first account" subscriptions to the basic capital of the Common Fund. (The OPEC member countries' "first account" subscriptions, totalling $16,410,000, were to be paid on an individual basis rather than through the OPEC Fund.) No disbursements had been made to the Common Fund by the end of 1985, when its constituent agreement remained ineffective for want of the minimum number of ratifications required for its entry into force.

Developing countries which were categorized by the United Nations as "least developed" and/or "most seriously affected" accounted for over three-quarters of the OPEC Fund's cumulative loan commitments as at Dec. 31, 1985. Loans were extended (i) for project financing (usually in association with other development agencies, with one of the co-financiers acting as loan administrator), (ii) for general balance-of-payments support and (iii) for programme financing (i.e. to provide foreign exchange for the import of goods fulfilling a specific development purpose). The maximum repayment periods allowed by the Fund were 20 years (including up to 5 years' grace) for project loans, 15 years (including up to 5 years' grace) for programme loans and 10 years (including up to 3 years' grace) for balance-of-payments support loans. Loans were extended either interest-free or at low rates of interest. Each recipient of a balance-of-payments support loan or a programme loan was obliged to raise an equivalent amount of domestic currency (to finance the local costs of development projects) in order to benefit from the full repayment period laid down in the relevant loan agreement.

The OPEC Fund's cumulative loan commitments to Dec. 31, 1985, totalled $1,968.2 million, of which 46.3 per cent was allocated to African countries, 43.1 per cent to Asian countries and 10.6 per cent to countries in Latin America and the Caribbean. Of the Fund's cumulative committed project lending of $1,205.7 million over the same period, 45.4 per cent was allocated for the development of energy resources in a total of 32 countries. Other sectoral allocations were transportation 17.9 per cent (36 countries), agriculture and agricultural industries 14.8 per cent (30 countries), lines of credit to national development banks 7.5 per cent (14 countries), non-agricultural industries 5.3 per cent (7 countries), water supply and sewerage 5 per cent (14 countries), education 3.4 per cent (11 countries), telecommunications 0.4 per cent (two countries) and health 0.3 per cent (one country).

Technical assistance grants were extended by the OPEC Fund mainly to regional or inter-regional organizations carrying out programmes designed to promote economic co-operation and integration among developing countries, including notably a number of projects administered by the United Nations Development Programme. A separate grant account for research and similar intellectual activities was established in 1980. Other items included in the Fund's overall grant programme were (i) a contribution of $25,000,000 committed in 1981 to the International Emergency Food Reserve (IEFR, jointly administered by the World Food Programme and the UN Food and Agriculture Organization); (ii) the $20,000,000 special contribution committed to IFAD in January 1982; (iii) a special "food aid" allocation of $5,000,000 announced in November 1984 to assist the distribution of emergency supplies in 13 African countries; and (iv) contributions to the UNCTAD Common Fund for Commodities. Items not included in the overall grant programme were (i) the OPEC countries' Group 2 contributions to IFAD and (ii) contributions to the IMF Trust Fund.

Table 17 — Cumulative commitments and disbursements of OPEC Fund at end-1985

	Committed	Disbursed
	(million US dollars)	
Loans	1,968.2	1,417.4
of which:		
(project loans)	(1,205.7)	(680.5)
(balance-of-payments support)	(698.4)	(687.7)
(programme loans)	(64.1)	(49.2)
Grant programme	151.0	105.4
of which:		
(food aid)	(5.0)	(5.0)
(IEFR)	(25.0)	(25.0)
(technical assistance)	(69.5)	(54.0)
(special IFAD contribution)	(20.0)	(20.0)
(research)	(1.6)	(1.4)
(UNCTAD Common Fund)	(29.9*)	—
Other	971.8	842.7
of which:		
(Group 2 IFAD contributions)	(861.1)	(732.0)
(IMF Trust Fund)	(110.7)	(110.7)
Total	3,091.1†	2,365.5

*Out of an approved allocation of $83,560,000.
†Independently rounded total.

B1.7—The OPEC Statute

OPEC's original statute was adopted by the Conference at its 2nd meeting in January 1961, various of its provisions being amended at the 3rd, 4th, 5th and 6th meetings. The 8th meeting, in April 1965, revised the entire statute, certain provisions of which were later amended by the 12th, 20th, 24th, 50th, 51st and 57th meetings. At the end of 1985 the current provisions of the statute were as follows.

Chapter I—Organization and Objectives

Article 1. The Organization of the Petroleum Exporting Countries (OPEC), hereinafter referred to as "the Organization", created as a permanent intergovernmental organization in conformity with the resolutions of the Conference of the representatives of the Governments of Iran, Iraq, Kuwait, Saudi Arabia and Venezuela, held in Baghdad from Sept. 10–14, 1960, shall carry out its functions in accordance with the provisions set forth hereunder.

Article 2. (A) The principal aim of the Organization shall be the co-ordination and unification of the petroleum policies of member countries and the determination of the best means for safeguarding their interests, individually and collectively.

(B) The Organization shall devise ways and means of ensuring the stabilization of prices in international oil markets with a view to eliminating harmful and unnecessary fluctuations.

(C) Due regard shall be given at all times to the interests of the producing nations and to the necessity of securing a steady income to the producing countries; an efficient, economic and regular supply of petroleum to consuming nations; and a fair return on their capital to those investing in the petroleum industry.

Article 3. The Organization shall be guided by the principle of the sovereign equality of its member countries. Member countries shall fulfil, in good faith, the obligations assumed by them in accordance with this Statute.

Article 4. If, as a result of the application of any decision of the Organization, sanctions are employed, directly or indirectly, by any interested company or companies against one or more member countries, no other member shall accept any offer of a beneficial treatment, whether in the form of an increase in oil exports or in an improvement in prices, which may be made to it by such interested company or companies with the intention of discouraging the application of the decision of the Organization.

Article 5. The Organization shall have its headquarters at the place the Conference decides upon.

Article 6. English shall be the official language of the Organization.

Chapter II—Membership

Article 7. (A) Founder members of the Organization are those countries which were represented at the 1st Conference, held in Baghdad, and which signed the original agreement of the establishment of the Organization.

(B) Full members shall be the founder members as well as those countries whose application for membership has been accepted by the Conference.

(C) Any other country with a substantial net export of crude petroleum, which has fundamentally similar interests to those of member countries, may become a full member of the Organization, if accepted by a majority of three-fourths of full members, including the concurrent vote of all founder members.

(D) A net petroleum-exporting country which does not qualify for membership under paragraph (C) above may nevertheless be admitted as an associate member by the Conference under such special conditions as may be prescribed by the Conference, if accepted by a majority of three-fourths, including the concurrent vote of all founder members.

No country may be admitted to associate membership which does not fundamentally have interests and aims similar to those of member countries.

(E) Associate members may be invited by the Conference to attend any meeting of a Conference, the Board of Governors or consultative meetings, and to participate in their deliberations without the right to vote. They are, however, fully entitled to benefit from all general facilities of the Secretariat, including its publications and library, as any full member.

(F) Whenever the words "members" or "member countries" occur in this Statute, they mean a full member of the Organization unless the context demonstrates to the contrary.

Article 8. (A) No member of the Organization may withdraw from membership without giving notice of its intention to do so to the Conference. Such notice shall take effect at the beginning of the next calendar year after the date of its receipt by the Conference, subject to the member having at that time fulfilled all financial obligations arising out of its membership.

(B) In the event of any country having ceased to be a member of the Organization, its readmission to membership shall be made in accordance with Article 7, paragraph (C).

Chapter III—Organs

Article 9. The Organization shall have three organs: The Conference; The Board of Governors; and the Secretariat.

The Conference

Article 10. The Conference shall be the supreme authority of the Organization.

Article 11. (A) The Conference shall consist of delegations representing the member countries. A delegation may consist of one or more delegates, as well as advisers and observers. When a delegation consists of more than one person, the appointing country shall nominate one person as the head of the delegation.

(B) Each member country should be represented at all Conferences; however, a quorum of three-quarters of member countries shall be necessary for holding a Conference.

(C) Each full member country shall have one vote. All decisions of the Conference, other than on procedural matters, shall require the unanimous agreement of all full members.

The Conference resolutions shall become effective after 30 days from the conclusion of the meeting or after such period as the Conference may decide unless, within the said period, the Secretariat receives notification from member countries to the contrary.

In the case of a full member being absent from the meeting of the Conference, the resolutions of the Conference shall become effective unless the Secretariat receives a notification to the contrary from the said member at least 10 days before the date fixed for publication of the resolutions.

(D) A non-member country may be invited to attend a Conference as observer, if the Conference so decides.

Article 12. The Conference shall hold two ordinary meetings a year. However, an extraordinary meeting of the Conference may be convened at the request of a member country by the Secretary-General, after consultation with the President and approval by a simple majority of the member countries. In the absence of unanimity among member countries approving the convening of such a meeting, as to the date and venue of the meeting, they shall be fixed by the Secretary-General in consultation with the President.

Article 13. The Conference shall normally be held at the headquarters of the Organization, but it may meet in any of the member countries, or elsewhere as may be advisable.

Article 14. (A) The Conference shall elect a President and an Alternate President at its first preliminary meeting. The Alternate President shall exercise the responsibilities of the President during his absence or when he is unable to carry out his responsibilities.

(B) The President shall hold office for the duration of the meeting of the Conference, and shall retain the title until the next meeting.

(C) The Secretary-General shall be the Secretary of the Conference.

Article 15. The Conference shall:

(1) formulate the general policy of the Organization and determine the appropriate ways and means of its implementation;

(2) decide upon any application for membership of the Organization;

(3) confirm the appointment of members of the Board of Governors;

(4) direct the Board of Governors to submit reports or make recommendations on any matters of interest to the Organization;

(5) consider, or decide upon, the reports and recommendations submitted by the Board of Governors on the affairs of the Organization;

(6) consider and decide upon the budget of the Organization, as submitted by the Board of Governors;

(7) consider and decide upon the statement of accounts and the auditor's report, as submitted by the Board of Governors;

(8) call a consultative meeting for such member countries, for such purposes and in such places as the Conference deems fit;

(9) approve any amendments to this Statute;

(10) appoint the Chairman of the Board of Governors and an Alternate Chairman;

(11) appoint the Secretary-General;

(12) appoint the Deputy Secretary-General; and

(13) appoint the auditor of the Organization for a duration of one year.

Article 16. All matters that are not expressly assigned to other organs of the Organization shall fall within the competence of the Conference.

The Board of Governors

Article 17. (A) The Board of Governors shall be composed of Governors nominated by the member countries and confirmed by the Conference.

(B) Each member of the Organization should be represented at all meetings of the Board of Governors; however, a quorum of two-thirds shall be necessary for the holding of a meeting.

(C) When, for any reason, a Governor is prevented from attending a meeting of the Board of Governors, a substitute ad hoc Governor shall be nominated by the corresponding member country. Such nomination shall not require confirmation by the Conference. At the meetings which he attends the ad hoc Governor shall have the same status as the other Governors, except as regards qualifications for chairmanship of the Board of Governors.

(D) Each Governor shall have one vote. A simple majority vote of attending Governors shall be required for decisions of the Board of Governors.

(E) The term of office of each Governor shall be two years.

Article 18. (A) The Board of Governors shall meet no less than twice each year, at suitable intervals to be determined by the Chairman of the Board, after consultation with the Secretary-General.

(B) An extraordinary meeting of the Board of Governors may be convened at the request of the Chairman of the Board, the Secretary-General, or two-thirds of the Governors.

Article 19. The meetings of the Board of Governors shall normally be held at the headquarters of the Organization, but they may also be held in any of the member countries, or elsewhere as may be advisable.

Article 20. The Board of Governors shall:

(1) direct the management of the affairs of the Organization and the implementation of the decisions of the Conference;

(2) consider and decide upon any reports submitted by the Secretary-General;

(3) submit reports and make recommendations to the Conference on the affairs of the Organization;

(4) draw up the budget of the Organization for each calendar year and submit it to the Conference for approval;

(5) nominate the auditor of the Organization for a duration of one year;

(6) consider the statement of accounts and the auditor's report and submit them to the Conference for approval;

(7) approve the appointment of directors of divisions and heads of departments, upon nomination by the member countries, due consideration being given to the recommendations of the Secretary-General;

(8) convene an extraordinary meeting of the Conference;

(9) nominate a Deputy Secretary-General for appointment by the Conference; and

(10) prepare the agenda for the Conference.

Article 21. The Chairman of the Board of Governors and the Alternate Chairman, who shall assume all the responsibilities of the Chairman whenever the Chairman is absent or unable to exercise his responsibilities, shall be appointed by the Conference from among the Governors for a period of one year, in accordance with the principle of alphabetical rotation. The date of membership in the Organization, however, shall take precedence over the principle of alphabetical rotation.

Article 22. The Chairman of the Board of Governors shall:

(1) preside over the meetings of the Board of Governors;

(2) attend the headquarters of the Organization in preparation for each meeting of the Board of Governors; and

(3) represent the Board of Governors at Conferences and consultative meetings.

Article 23. Should a majority of two-thirds of Governors decide that the continuance of membership of any Governor is detrimental to the interests of the Organization, the Chairman of the Board of Governors shall immediately communicate this decision to the member country affected, who in turn shall nominate a substitute for the said Governor before the next meeting of the Board of Governors. The nomination or such substitute as a Governor shall be subject to confirmation by the following Conference.

Article 24. Should a Governor, for any reason, be precluded from continuing in the performance of his functions on the Board of Governors, the corresponding member country shall nominate a replacement. The nominated Governor shall assume his functions upon nomination subject to confirmation by the following Conference.

The Secretariat

Article 25. The Secretariat shall carry out the executive functions of the Organization in accordance with the provisions of this Statute under the direction of the Board of Governors.

Article 26. The Secretariat of the Organization shall consist of the Secretary-General, the Deputy Secretary-General and such staff as may be required. It shall function at the headquarters of the Organization.

Article 27. (A) The Secretary-General shall be the legally authorized representative of the Organization.

(B) The Secretary-General shall be the chief officer of the Secretariat, and in that capacity shall have the authority to direct the affairs of the Organization, in accordance with directions of the Board of Governors.

Article 28. (A) The Conference shall appoint the Secretary-General for a period of three years, which term of office may be renewed once for the same period of time. This appointment shall take place upon nomination by member countries and after a comparative study of the nominees' qualifications.

The minimum personal requirements for the position of the Secretary-General shall be as follows: (*a*) 35 years of age; (*b*) a degree from a recognized university in law, economics, science, engineering or business administration; (*c*) 15 years' experience, of which at least 10 years should have been spent in positions directly related to the oil industry and five years in highly responsible executive or managerial positions. Experience in government-company relations and in the international aspects of the oil industry is desirable.

Should, in any case, a unanimous decision not be obtained, the Secretary-General, in that case, shall be appointed on rotation basis for a term of two years without prejudice to the required qualifications.

(B) The Secretary-General shall be a national of one of the member countries of the Organization.

(C) The Secretary-General shall reside at the headquarters of the Organization.

(D) The Secretary-General shall be responsible to the Board of Governors for all activities of the Secretariat. The functions of the different departments shall be carried out on his behalf and under his authority and direction.

(E) The Secretary-General shall attend all meetings of the Board of Governors.

Article 29. The Secretary-General shall:

(1) organize and administer the work of the Organization;

(2) ensure that the functions and duties assigned to the different departments of the Secretariat are carried out;

(3) prepare reports for submission to each meeting of the Board of Governors concerning matters which call for consideration and decision;

(4) inform the Chairman and other members of the Board of Governors of all activities of the Secretariat, of all studies undertaken and of the progress of the implementation of the resolutions of the Conference; and

(5) ensure the due performance of the duties which may be assigned to the Secretariat by the Conference or the Board of Governors.

Article 30. (A) The Deputy Secretary-General shall be selected by the Board of Governors from amongst the highly-qualified and experienced national candidates put forward by the member countries, for appointment by the Conference by a vote of two-thirds of full members including the concurrent vote of at least three founder members.

(B) The term of service of the Deputy Secretary-General shall be for a period of three years. It may be extended for a period of one year or more, at the suggestion of the Board of Governors and with the approval of the Conference.

(C) The Deputy Secretary-General shall reside permanently at the headquarters of the Organization.

(D) The Deputy Secretary-General shall be responsible to the Secretary-General for the co-ordination of the research and administrative activities of the Secretariat. The functions of the different departments are exercised under the general supervision of the Deputy Secretary-General.

(E) The Secretary-General may delegate some of his authority to the Deputy Secretary-General.

(F) The Deputy Secretary-General shall act for the Secretary-General, whenever the latter is absent from headquarters.

Article 31. (A) The directors of divisions and heads of departments shall be appointed by the Secretary-General with the approval of the Board of Governors.

(B) Officers of the Secretariat, upon nomination by their respective governments, or by direct recruitment, shall be appointed by the Secretary-General in accordance with the staff regulations. In making such appointments, the Secretary-General shall give due consideration, as far as possible, to an equitable nationality distribution among members, but such consideration shall not be allowed to impair the efficiency of the Secretariat.

Article 32. The staff of the Secretariat are international employees with an exclusively international character. In the performance of their duties, they shall neither seek nor accept instructions from any government or from any other authority outside the Organization. They shall refrain from any action which might reflect on their position as international employees and they shall undertake to carry out their duties with the sole object of bearing the interests of the Organization in mind.

Article 33. (1) The Secretary-General shall be assisted in the discharge of his duties by the Deputy Secretary-General, a Division of Research, a Personnel and Administration Department, a Public Information Department, a News Agency, any division or department the Conference may see fit to create and his own Office.

(2) The OPEC News Agency (OPECNA) shall be a special unit responsible for collecting, producing and disseminating news of general interest regarding the Organization and the member countries and on energy and related matters.

(3) The Office of the Secretary-General shall provide him with executive assistance, particularly in carrying out contacts with governments, organizations and delegations; in matters of protocol; in the preparation for, and co-ordination of, meetings; and other duties assigned by the Secretary-General.

(4) Notwithstanding the provisions of Article 34, and where the efficient functioning of the divisions and departments of the Secretariat so requires, the Board of Governors may, upon the recommendation of the Secretary-General, authorize the Secretary-General to transfer functions or minor units from one division or department to another.

Article 34. (A) The Division of Research shall be responsible for:

(1) conducting a continuous programme of research fulfilling the needs of the Organization, placing particular emphasis on energy and related matters;

(2) monitoring, forecasting and analysing developments in the energy and petrochemical industries; and the evaluation of hydrocarbons and products and their non-energy uses;

(3) analysing economic and financial issues of significant interest, in particular those related to international financial and monetary matters and to the international petroleum industry; and

(4) maintaining and expanding data services to support the research activities of the Secretariat and those of member countries.

(B) The Personnel and Administration Department shall:

(1) be responsible for all organization methods, the provision of administrative services for all meetings, personnel matters, budgets, accounting and internal control;

(2) study and review general administrative policies and industrial relations methods used in the oil industry in member and other countries, and advise member countries of any possible improvements; and

(3) keep abreast of the current administrative policies and/or policy changes occuring in the international petroleum industry which might affect the Organization or be of interest to it.

(C) The Public Information Department shall be responsible for:

(1) presenting OPEC objectives, decisions and actions in their true and most desirable perspective;

(2) carrying out a central public information programme and identifying suitable areas for the promotion of the Organization's aims; and

(3) the production and distribution of publications and other materials.

Article 35. (A) The Secretary-General shall commission consultants, as necessary, to advise on special matters or to conduct expert studies when such work cannot be undertaken by the Secretariat.

(B) The Secretary-General may engage such specialists or experts, regardless of nationality, as the Organization needs, for a period to be approved by the Board of Governors, provided there is a provision for such appointment in the budget.

(C) The Secretary-General may at any time convene working parties to carry out any studies on specific subjects of interest to the member countries.

Chapter IV—Consultative Meetings and Specialized Organs

Article 36. (A) A consultative meeting shall be composed of heads of delegations of member countries or their representatives.

(B) In case a Conference is not in session, a consultative meeting may be convened at any time at the request of the President of the Conference.

(C) The agenda of each consultative meeting shall be prepared by the President of the Conference, unless it has been previously specified by the Conference itself.

(D) The consultative meeting may pass decisions or recommendations to be approved by the next Conference unless otherwise authorized by a previous Conference.

Article 37. (A) The Conference may establish specialized organs, as circumstances require, in order to assist in resolving certain problems of particular importance. The specialized organs shall function in accordance with the resolutions or statutes prepared to that effect.

(B) The specialized organs shall operate within the general framework of the Secretariat of the Organization, both functionally and financially.

(C) The specialized organs shall act at all times in accordance with the principles of the Organization, as set out in the resolutions of the Conference.

Chapter V—Financial Provisions

Article 38. (A) The budget of the Organization shall be drawn up for each calendar year.

(B) The Conference, in accepting any associate member to the Organization, shall ask it to pay a fixed annual subscription to be considered as its financial contribution to the Organization.

(C) Budget appropriations shall be apportioned on an equal basis among all member countries, after taking into consideration the annual subscriptions of the associate members.

Article 39. (A) Each member country shall bear all expenses incurred in sending delegations or representatives to Conferences, consultative meetings and working parties.

(B) The Organization shall bear the travelling expenses and remuneration of the Governors who attend the meetings of the Board of Governors.

Chapter VI—Additional Provisions

Article 40. Amendments to this Statute may be proposed by any member country. Such proposed amendments shall be considered by the Board of Governors which, if it so decides, shall recommend their adoption to the Conference.

Article 41. All resolutions contrary to the context of this Statute shall be abrogated.

Article 42. This Statute shall be applied from May 1, 1965.

B1.8—OPEC Economic Commission

The OPEC Economic Commission was established in accordance with Resolution VII–50 of the OPEC Conference (adopted in November 1964 ⟡**D1.3.ii**), and operates as a permanent specialized organ of OPEC under a separate statute approved (by Resolution VIII–55) in April 1965. Minor amendments were made to certain articles of the statute in December 1965 and December 1979. The Economic Commission Board held 64 meetings between April 1965 and May 1986. The current provisions of the Commission's statute at the end of 1985 were as follows.

Article 1. The OPEC Economic Commission (hereinafter referred to as "the Commission") is established as a permanent and specialized organ of the Organization of the Petroleum Exporting Countries (hereinafter referred to as "the Organization"). . . .

Article 2. The Commission shall assist the Organization in promoting stability in international petroleum prices at equitable levels, in keeping with the spirit and principles set out in particular in the Organization's resolutions I–1 [⟡**D1.1**], IV–32 and V–42 [⟡**D1.3.i**].

Article 3. The Commission shall have the following functions:

(1) to establish the necessary contacts with private and public bodies, in particular the oil industry;

(2) to collect the data and information which it may require for the achievement of its objectives;

(3) to examine the position of petroleum prices on a permanent basis;

(4) to study all economic and other factors that may in any way significantly affect petroleum prices and their structure;

(5) to submit to the member countries of the Organization monthly reports on the position of petroleum prices including relevant economic and other factors, and the current status of the Commission's recommendations;

(6) to formulate and submit to the Conference of the Organization, through its Secretary-General, the relevant recommendations based on its findings and in keeping with its objectives; and

(7) to report through the Secretary-General to every Conference of the Organization on its activities, with a view to enabling the Conference to give the necessary guidance and instructions.

Article 4. In discharging its functions the Commission shall act in accordance with the principles of the Organization as set out in its resolutions and operate within the general framework of the Secretariat of the Organization.

Article 5. The Commission shall be composed of a Commission Board, national representatives and a Commission staff.

Article 6. (1) The Commission Board shall be composed of the Organization's Deputy Secretary-General, the national representatives appointed by the Organization's member countries and a Commission Co-ordinator (who shall be ex officio the director of the research division of the Organization's Secretariat).

The Board shall be responsible to the Conference for the fulfilment of the Commission's functions.

The Organization's Deputy Secretary-General shall be the Chairman of the Board.

The Board shall meet twice a year, at suitable intervals, to be determined by the Board or its chairman in consultation with the Commission Co-ordinator.

The Board meetings shall normally be held at the headquarters of the Organization, but they may also be held in any of the Organization's member countries, or elsewhere, as may be advisable.

An extraordinary meeting of the Board may be convened by its chairman on his own initiative or at the request of a member of the Board.

Each member country of the Organization should be represented at all meetings of the Board; however a quorum of a simple majority of the national representatives shall be sufficient for the holding of a meeting.

Each national representative shall have one vote. The Board's recommendations shall be adopted by simple majority vote, but in no case by less than half of all national representatives.

(2) Each of the Organization's member countries shall appoint one representative, to be known as the "national representative", to serve on the Commission Board and to act as liaison officer between the appropriate petroleum authority in his respective country and the Commission Co-ordinator.

The national representatives shall analyse the position of realized export petroleum prices in their respective countries and provide the Commission, through the Commission Co-ordinator, with all necessary relevant information and data, in particular, periodic price indexes of them.

(3) The Commission staff shall be composed of the Commission Co-ordinator and such other members of the Secretariat staff as may be appointed by the chairman of the Commission Board in consultation with the Commission Co-ordinator.

The staff shall work under the supervision of the Commission Co-ordinator who is directly responsible to the Commission Board.

The staff shall prepare reports designed to assist the Commission Board in examining the position of petroleum prices on a permanent basis and to this end shall collect all data and information it may require, and shall maintain the necessary direct contacts with the Commission's national representatives.

Article 7. The remuneration, travel, and other expenses of the national representatives shall be borne by their respective countries. All other expenses incurred by the Commission in the fulfilment of its functions shall be provided for in the regular budget of the Secretariat.

Article 8. Proposed amendments to this statute may be submitted to the Conference by any member country of the Organization, or, subject to the approval of, and through the Board of Governors, by the Commission Board.

Article 9. This statute shall enter into effect immediately upon its approval by the Organization's 8th Conference.

B1.9—Major OPEC Policy Statements

The following main policy statements have been issued by OPEC: (i) a "declaratory statement on petroleum policy in member countries" adopted at the 16th Conference meeting in June 1968 (◊**D1.6.i**); (ii) a "policy statement" adopted at the 34th Conference meeting in June 1973 (◊**D4.3**); and (iii) a "solemn declaration" issued by sovereigns and heads of state following their Algiers summit conference in March 1975 (◊**D6.4**). The texts of these statements are as follows.

B1.9.i—Declaratory statement on petroleum policy in member countries (June 1968)

The Conference. . . ,

recognizing that hydrocarbon resources in member countries are one of the principal sources of their revenues and foreign exchange earnings and therefore constitute the main basis for their economic development;

bearing in mind that hydrocarbon resources are limited and exhaustible, and that their proper exploitation determines the conditions of the economic development of member countries, both at present and in the future;

bearing in mind also that the inalienable right of all countries to exercise permanent sovereignty over their natural resources in the interest of their national development is a universally recognized principle of public law and has been repeatedly reaffirmed by the General Assembly of the United Nations, most notably in its Resolution 2158 of Nov. 25, 1966;

considering also that in order to ensure the exercise of permanent sovereignty over hydrocarbon resources, it is essential that their exploitation should be aimed at securing the greatest possible benefit for member countries;

considering further that this aim can better be achieved if member countries are in a position to undertake themselves directly the exploitation of their hydrocarbon resources, so that they may exercise their freedom of choice in the utilization of hydrocarbon resources under the most favourable conditions;

taking into account the fact that foreign capital, whether public or private, forthcoming at the request of the member countries, can play an important role, inasmuch as it supplements the efforts undertaken by them in the exploitation of their hydrocarbon resources, provided that there is government supervision of the activity of foreign capital to ensure that it is used in the interest of national development and that returns earned by it do not exceed reasonable levels;

bearing in mind that the principal aim of the Organization, as set out in Article 2 of its Statute, is "the co-ordination and unification of the petroleum policies of member countries and the determination of the best means for safeguarding their interests, individually and collectively";

recommends that the following principles shall serve as basis for petroleum policy in member countries.

Mode of Development

(1) Member governments shall endeavour, as far as feasible, to explore for and develop their hydrocarbon resources directly. The capital, specialists and the promotion of marketing outlets required for such direct development may be complemented when necessary from alternative sources on a commercial basis.

(2) However, when a member government is not capable of developing its hydrocarbon resources directly, it may enter into contracts of various types, to be defined in its legislation but subject to the present principles, with outside operators for a reasonable remuneration, taking into account the degree of risk involved. Under such an arrangement, the government shall seek to retain the greatest measure possible of participation in and control over all aspects of operations.

(3) In any event, the terms and conditions of such contracts shall be open to revision at predetermined intervals, as justified by changing circumstances. Such changing circumstances should call for the revision of existing concession agreements.

Participation

Where provision for governmental participation in the ownership of the concession-holding company under any of the present petroleum contracts has not been made, the government may acquire a reasonable participation, on the grounds of the principle of changing circumstances.

If such provision has actually been made but avoided by the operators concerned, the rate provided for shall serve as a minimum basis for the participation to be acquired.

Relinquishment

A schedule of progressive and more accelerated relinquishment of acreage of present contract areas shall be introduced. In any event, the government shall participate in choosing the acreage to be relinquished, including those cases where relinquishment is already provided for but left to the discretion of the operator.

Posted Prices or Tax-Reference Prices

All contracts shall require that the assessment of the operator's income, and its taxes or any other payments to the state, be based on a posted or tax-reference price for the hydrocarbons produced under the contract. Such price shall be determined by the government and shall move in such a manner as to prevent any deterioration in its relationship to the prices of manufactured goods traded internationally. However, such price shall be consistent, subject to differences in gravity, quality and geographic location, with the levels of posted or tax-reference prices generally prevailing for hydrocarbons in other OPEC countries and accepted by them as a basis for tax payments.

Limited Guarantee of Fiscal Stability

The government may, at its discretion, give a guarantee of fiscal stability to operators for a reasonable period of time.

Renegotiation Clause

(1) Notwithstanding any guarantee of fiscal stability that may have been granted to the operator, the operator shall not have the right to obtain excessively high net earnings after taxes. The financial provisions of contracts which actually result in such excessively high net earnings shall be open to renegotiation.

(2) In deciding whether to initiate such renegotiation, the government shall take due account of the degree of financial risk undertaken by the operator and the general level of net earnings elsewhere in industry where similar circumstances prevail.

(3) In the event the operator declines to negotiate, or that the negotiations do not result in any agreement within a reasonable period of time, the government shall make its own estimate of the amount by which the operator's net earnings after taxes are excessive, and such amount shall then be paid by the operator to the government.

(4) In the present context, "excessively high net earnings" means net profits after taxes which are significantly in excess, during any 12-month period, of the level of net earnings the reasonable expectation of which would have been sufficient to induce the operator to take the entrepreneurial risks necessary.

(5) In evaluating the "excessively high net earnings" of the new operators, consideration should be given to their overall competitive position vis-à-vis the established operators.

Accounts and Information

The operator shall be required to keep within the country clear and accurate accounts and records of his operations, which shall at all times be available to government auditors, upon request.

Such accounts shall be kept in accordance with the government's written instructions, which shall conform to commonly accepted principles of accounting, and which shall be applicable generally to all operators within its territory.

The operator shall promptly make available, in a meaningful form, such information related to its operations as the government may reasonably require for the discharge of its functions.

Conservation

Operators shall be required to conduct their operations in accordance with the best conservation practices, bearing in mind the long-term interests of the country. To this end, the government shall draw up written instructions detailing the conservation rules to be followed generally by all contractors within its territory.

Settlement of Disputes

Except as otherwise provided for in the legal system of a member country, all disputes arising between the government and operators shall fall exclusively within the jurisdiction of the competent national courts or the specialized regional courts, as and when established.

Other Matters

In addition to the foregoing principles, member governments shall adopt on all other matters essential to a comprehensive and rational hydrocarbons policy, rules including no less than the best of current practices with respect to the registration and incorporation of operators; assignment and transfer of rights; work obligations; the employment of nationals; training programmes; royalty rates; the imposition of taxes generally in force in the country; property of the operator upon expiry of the contract; and other such matters.

Definition

For the purposes of the present resolution, the term "operator" shall mean any person entering into a contract of any kind with a member government or its designated agency including the concessions and contracts currently in effect, providing for the exploration for and/or development of any part of the hydrocarbon resources of the country concerned.

B1.9.ii—Policy statement (June 1973)

The Conference,

noting that under the present and expected conditions of the world energy market, member countries should not only strive to attain the appropriate value for their oil, but also negotiate with a view to attaining conditions that would effectively foster the permanent and diversified sources of income within their territories;

taking into account that hydrocarbon resources have constituted an essential factor in the economic development of industrialized countries and that a regular and secure supply of hydrocarbons to these countries is of paramount importance for the continuity of their economic welfare;

bearing in mind that petroleum should not only be a source of finance for the member countries but a primary effective instrument for their economic development;

noting that the inadequate economic conditions to which most developing countries are still subjected, mainly as a consequence of their lack of access to the markets and technology of industrialized countries, hamper the development possibilities of OPEC member countries and of the Third World in general;

reiterating that hydrocarbon resources are of a limited and exhaustible nature and therefore their exploitation must be geared at attaining an accelerated and diversified development of member countries' economies;

bearing in mind that one of the main aims of the Organization is to seek a just valorization of the hydrocarbon resources of member countries and the adequate protection of their revenues;

bearing in mind that it is an objective of OPEC to secure a fair and equitable relationship between the producing-exporting countries and the consuming-importing countries, and not to inflict any damage to the world economy that could result from the interruption of hydrocarbon supplies;

states:

(1) that the exploitation and trade in hydrocarbons from member countries should, in one form or another, be linked to the process of a rational and accelerated economic growth;

(2) that any concerted action undertaken by industrialized-importing countries aimed at undermining OPEC's legitimate aspirations would only hamper the stable relations that have normally existed between these and OPEC member countries, and that to seek a direct confrontation with OPEC may have a damaging effect upon the world economy;

(3) that the governments of member countries should take, or pursue, whatever actions they see fit in the appropriate bilateral or multilateral framework in order (i) to attain greater access to the technology and markets of the developed countries for their present and future industrial products; and (ii) to further strengthen the co-operation with the oil-importing developing countries whose energy requirements are ever-increasing.

B1.9.iii—Solemn declaration (March 1975)

The sovereigns and heads of state of the member countries of the Organization of the Petroleum Exporting Countries met in Algiers on March 4–6, 1975, at the invitation of the President of the Revolutionary Council and of the Council of Ministers of the Democratic People's Republic of Algeria.

(1) They reviewed the present world economic crisis, exchanged views on the causes of the crisis which has persisted for several years, and considered the measures they would take to safeguard the legitimate rights and interests of their peoples, in the context of international solidarity and co-operation.

They stress that world peace and progress depend on the mutual respect for the sovereignty and equality of all member nations of the international community, in accordance with the UN Charter. They further emphasize that the basic statements of this declaration fall within the context of the decisions taken [in 1974] at the Sixth Special Session of the General Assembly of the United Nations on problems of raw materials and development [◊D5.9].

The sovereigns and heads of state reaffirm the solidarity which unites their countries in safeguarding the legitimate rights and the interests of their peoples, reasserting the sovereign and inalienable right of their countries to the ownership, exploitation and pricing of their natural resources and rejecting any idea or attempt that challenges those fundamental rights and, thereby, the sovereignty of their countries.

They also reaffirm that OPEC member countries, through the collective, steadfast and cohesive defence of legitimate rights of their peoples, have served the larger and ultimate interest and progress of the world community and, in doing so, have acted in the direction hoped for by all developing countries, producers of raw materials, in defence of the legitimate rights of their peoples.

They conclude that the interdependence of nations, manifested in the world economic situation, requires a new emphasis on international co-operation and declare themselves prepared to contribute with their efforts to the objectives of world economic development and stability, as stated in the Declaration and Programme of Action for the establishment of a new international economic order adopted by the General Assembly of the United Nations during the Sixth Special Session.

(2) The sovereigns and heads of state note that the cause of the present world economic crisis stems largely from the profound inequalities in the economic and social progress among peoples; such inequalities, which characterize the under-development of the developing countries, have been mainly generated and activated by foreign exploitation and have become more acute over the years due to the absence of adequate international co-operation for development. This situation has fostered the drainage of natural resources of the developing countries, impeding an effective transfer of capital resources and technology and thus resulting in a basic disequilibrium in economic relations.

They note that the disequilibrium which besets the present international economic situation has been aggravated by widespread inflation, a general slowdown of economic growth, and instability of the world monetary system in the absence of monetary discipline and restraint.

They reaffirm that the decisive causes of such anomalies lie in the long-standing and persistent ills which have been allowed to accumulate over the years, such as the general tendency of the developed countries to consume excessively and to waste scarce resources, as well as inappropriate and short-sighted economic policies in the industrialized world.

They therefore reject any allegation attributing to the price of petroleum the responsibility for the present instability of the world economy. Indeed, the oil which has contributed so significantly to the progress and prosperity of the industrialized nations for the past quarter of a century not only is the cheapest source of energy available, but the cost of imported oil constitutes an almost negligible part of the gross national product of the developed countries. The recent adjustment in the price of oil did not contribute but insignificantly to the high rates of inflation which have been generated within the economies of the developed countries basically by other causes. This inflation exported continuously to the developing countries has disrupted their development efforts.

(3) Moreover, the sovereigns and heads of state condemn the threats, propaganda

campaigns and other measures which have gone so far as to attribute to OPEC member countries the intention of undermining the economies of the developed countries; such campaigns and measures that may lead to confrontation have obstructed a clear understanding of the problems involved and have tended to create an atmosphere of tension that is not conducive to international consultation and co-operation. They also denounce any grouping of consumer nations with the aim of confrontation, and condemn any plan or strategy designed for aggression, economic or military, by such grouping or otherwise against any OPEC member country.

In view of such threats, the sovereigns and heads of state reaffirm the solidarity that unites their countries in the defence of the legitimate rights of their peoples and hereby declare their readiness, within the framework of that solidarity, to take immediate and effective measures in order to counteract such threats with a united response whenever the need arises, notably in the case of aggression.

(4) While anxious to satisfy the legitimate aspirations of their peoples for development and progress, the sovereigns and heads of state are also keenly aware of the close link which exists between the achievement of their national development and the prosperity of the world economy. Increased interdependence between nations makes them even more mindful of the difficulties experienced by other peoples which may affect world stability. In view of this, they reaffirm their support for dialogue, co-operation and concerted action for the solution of the major problems facing the world economy.

In this spirit, the OPEC member countries, with increased financial resources in a relatively short period of time, have contributed, through multilateral and bilateral channels, to the development efforts and balance-of-payments adjustments of other developing countries as well as industrialized nations. As a proportion of gross national product, during 1974, their financial support to other developing countries [◊**D6.8**] was several times greater than the average annual aid given by industrialized nations to developing countries during the last development decade. In addition, OPEC member countries have extended financial facilities to developed countries to help them meet their balance-of-payments deficits [◊**A4.16**]. Furthermore, the acceleration of their economic development and the trade promotion measures adopted by OPEC member countries have contributed to the expansion of international trade, as well as balance-of-payments adjustments of developed countries.

(5) The sovereigns and heads of state agree in principle to holding an international conference bringing together the developed and developing countries [◊**D5.13, D6.11**].

They consider that the objective of such a conference should be to make a significant advance in action designed to alleviate the major difficulties existing in the world economy, and that consequently the conference should pay equal attention to the problems facing both the developed and developing countries.

Therefore, the agenda of the aforementioned conference can in no case be confined to an examination of the question of energy; it evidently includes the questions of raw materials of the developing countries, the reform of the international monetary system and international co-operation in favour of development in order to achieve world stability.

Furthermore, this conference may, for reasons of efficiency, be held in a limited framework provided that all the nations concerned by the problems dealt with are adequately and genuinely represented.

(6) The sovereigns and heads of state stress that the exploitation of the depletable oil resources in their countries must be based, first and foremost, upon the best interests of their peoples and that oil, which is the major source of their income, constitutes a vital element in their development.

While recognizing the vital role of oil supplies to the world economy, they believe that the conservation of petroleum resources is a fundamental requirement for the well-being of future generations and therefore urge the adoption of policies aimed at optimizing the use of this essential, depletable and non-renewable resource.

(7) The sovereigns and heads of state point out that an artificially low price for petroleum in the past has prompted over-exploitation of this limited and depletable resource and that continuation of such policy would have proved to be disastrous from the point of view of conservation and world economy.

They consider that the interest of the OPEC member countries, as well as the rest of the world, would require that the oil price, being the fundamental element in the national income of the member countries, should be determined taking into account the following: (i) the imperatives of the conservation of petroleum, including its depletion and increasing scarcity in the future; (ii) the value of oil in terms of its non-energy uses; and (iii) the conditions of availability, utilization and cost of alternative sources of energy.

Moreover, the price of petroleum must be maintained by linking it to certain objective criteria, including the price of manufactured goods, the rate of inflation and the terms of transfer of goods and technology for the development of OPEC member countries.

(8) The sovereigns and heads of state declare that their countries are willing to continue to make positive contributions towards the solution of the major problems affecting the world economy, and to promote genuine co-operation which is the key to the establishment of a new international economic order.

In order to set in motion such international co-operation, they propose the adoption of a series of measures directed to other developing countries, as well as the industrialized nations.

They therefore wish to stress that the series of measures proposed herein constitute an overall programme, the components of which must all be implemented if the desired objectives of equity and efficiency are to be attained.

(9) The sovereigns and heads of state reaffirm the natural solidarity which unites their countries with the other developing countries in their struggle to overcome under-development and express their deep appreciation for the strong support given to OPEC member countries by all the developing nations, as announced in the Conference of Developing Countries on Raw Materials held in Dakar on Feb. 3–8, 1975 [◊D6.10].

They recognize that the countries most affected by the world economic crisis are the developing countries, and therefore reaffirm their decision to implement measures that will strengthen their co-operation with those countries. They are prepared to contribute, within their respective possibilities, to the realization of the UN Special International Programme and to extend additional special credits, loans and grants for the development of developing countries.

In this context, they have agreed to co-ordinate their programmes for financial co-operation in order to better assist the most affected developing countries, especially in overcoming their balance-of-payments difficulties. They have also decided to co-ordinate such financial measures with long-term loans that will contribute to the development of those economies.

In the same context, and in order to contribute to a better utilization of the agricultural potential of the developing countries, the sovereigns and heads of state have decided to promote the production of fertilizers, with the aim of supplying such production under favourable terms and conditions, to the countries most affected by the economic crisis.

They reaffirm their willingness to co-operate with the other developing countries which are exporters of raw materials and other basic commodities in their efforts to obtain an equitable and remunerative price level for their exports.

(10) To help smooth out difficulties affecting the economies of developed countries, the sovereigns and heads of state declare that the OPEC member countries will continue to make special efforts in respect of the needs of these countries.

As regards the supply of petroleum, they reaffirm their countries' readiness to ensure supplies that will meet the essential requirements of the economies of the developed countries, provided that the consuming countries do not use artificial barriers to distort the normal operation of the laws of demand and supply.

To this end, the OPEC member countries shall establish close co-operation and co-ordination among themselves in order to maintain balance between oil production and the needs of the world market.

With respect to the petroleum prices, they point out that, in spite of the apparent magnitude of the readjustment, the high rate of inflation and currency depreciation have wiped out a major portion of the real value of price readjustment, and that the current price is markedly lower than that which would result from the development of alternative sources of energy.

Nevertheless, they are prepared to negotiate the conditions for the stabilization of oil prices which will enable the consuming countries to make necessary adjustments to their economies.

151

The sovereigns and heads of state, within the spirit of dialogue and co-operation, affirm that the OPEC member countries are prepared to negotiate with the most affected developed countries, bilaterally or through international organizations, the provision of financial facilities that allow the growth of the economies of those countries while ensuring both the value and security of the assets of OPEC member countries.

(11) Recalling that a genuine international co-operation must benefit both the developing and developed countries, the sovereigns and heads of state declare that parallel with, and as a counterpart to, the efforts, guarantees and commitments which the OPEC member countries are prepared to make, the developed countries must contribute to the progress and development of the developing countries through concrete action, and in particular to achieve economic and monetary stability, giving due regard to the interests of the developing countries.

In this context, they emphasize the necessity for the full implementation of the Programme of Action adopted by the United Nations General Assembly at its Sixth Special Session, and accordingly they emphasize the following requirements:

(i) Developed countries must support measures taken by developing countries which are directed towards the stabilization of the prices of their exports of raw materials and other basic commodities at equitable and remunerative levels.

(ii) Fulfilment by the developed countries of their international commitments for the second UN Development Decade as a minimum contribution to be increased, particularly by the most able of the developed countries, for the benefit of the most affected developing countries.

(iii) Formulation and implementation of an effective food programme under which the developed countries, particularly the world's major producers and exporters of foodstuffs and products, extend grants and assistance to the most affected developing countries with respect to their food and agricultural requirements.

(iv) Acceleration of the development processes of the developing countries, particularly through the adequate and timely transfer of modern technology and the removal of the obstacles that slow the utilization and integration of such technology in the economies of the developing countries. Considering that, in many cases, obstacles to development derive from insufficient and inappropriate transfers of technology, the sovereigns and heads of state attach the greatest importance to the transfer of technology, which in their opinion constitutes a major test of adherence of the developed countries to the principle of international co-operation in favour of development. The transfer of technology should not be based on a division of labour in which the developing countries would produce goods of lesser technological content. An efficient transfer of technology must enable the developing countries to overcome the considerable technological lag in their economies through the manufacture in their territories of products of a high technological content, particularly in relation to the development and transformation of their natural resources. With regard to the depletable natural resources, as OPEC's petroleum resources are, it is essential that the transfer of technology must be commensurate in speed and volume with the rate of their depletion which is being accelerated for the benefit and growth of the economies of the developed countries.

(v) A major portion of the planned or new petrochemical complexes, oil refineries and fertilizer plants to be built in the territories of OPEC member countries with the cooperation of industrialized nations for export purposes to the developed countries with guaranteed access for such products to the markets of these countries.

(vi) Adequate protection against the depreciation of the value of the external reserves of OPEC member countries, as well as assurance of the security of their investments in the developed countries.

Moreover, they deem it necessary that the developed countries open their markets to hydrocarbons and other primary commodities, as well as manufactured goods produced by the developing countries, and consider that discriminatory practices against the developing countries and among them, the OPEC member countries, are contrary to the spirit of co-operation and partnership.

(12) The sovereigns and heads of state note the present disorder in the international monetary system and the absence of rules and instruments essential to safeguard the terms of trade and the value of financial assets of developing countries.

They emphasize particularly the urgent need to take the necessary steps to ensure the protection of the developing countries' legitimate interests.

They recognize that the pooling of the financial resources of both the OPEC member countries and the developed countries, as well as the technological ability of the latter, for the furtherance of the economy of the developing countries would substantially help in solving the international economic crisis.

They stress that fundamental and urgent measures should be taken to reform the international monetary system in such directions as to provide adequate and stable instruments for the expansion of trade, the development of productive resources and balanced growth of the world economy.

They note that the initiatives so far taken to reform the international monetary system have failed, since those initiatives have not been directed towards the removal of the inherent inequity in the structure of the system.

Decisions likely to affect the value of the reserve currencies, the [IMF] special drawing right and the price and role of gold in the international monetary system should no longer be allowed to be made on a unilateral basis or negotiated by developed countries alone; the developed countries should subscribe to a genuine reform of the international monetary and financial institution, to ensure its equitable representation and to guarantee the interests of all developing countries.

The reform of the monetary and financial system should allow a substantial increase in the share of developing countries in decision-making, management and participation, in the spirit of partnership for international development and on the basis of equality.

With this in mind, the sovereigns and heads of state have decided to promote amongst their countries a mechanism for consultation and co-ordination for full co-operation in the framework of their solidarity and with a view to achieving the goal of a genuine reform of the international monetary and financial system.

(13) The sovereigns and heads of state attach great importance to the strengthening of OPEC and, in particular, to the co-ordination of the activities of their national oil companies within the framework of the Organization and to the role which it should play in the international economy. They consider that certain tasks of prime importance remain to be accomplished which call for concerted planning among their countries and for the co-ordination of their policies in the fields of production of oil, its conservation, pricing and marketing, financial matters of common interest and concerted planning and economic co-operation among member countries in favour of international development and stability.

(14) The sovereigns and heads of state are deeply concerned about the present international economic crisis, which constitutes a dangerous threat to stability and peace. At the same time, they recognize that the crisis has brought about an awareness of the existence of problems whose solution will contribute to the security and well-being of humanity as a whole.

Equally aware of the hopes and aspirations of the peoples the world over for the solution of the major problems affecting their lives, the sovereigns and heads of state solemnly agree to commit their countries to measures aimed at opening a new era of co-operation in international relations.

It behoves the developed countries, which hold most of the instruments of progress, well-being and peace, just as they hold most of the instruments of destruction, to respond to the initiatives of the developing countries with initiatives of the same kind, by choosing to grasp the crisis situation as an historic opportunity in opening a new chapter in relations between peoples.

The anxiety generated by the uncertainty marking relations between those who hold power, coupled with the climate of uneasiness created by the confusion reigning in the world economy, would then give way to the confidence and peace resulting in an atmosphere of genuine international co-operation in which the developing countries would derive the greatest benefit and to which they would contribute their immense potentialities.

At the time when, thanks to man's genius, scientific and technological progress has endowed peoples with substantial means of surmounting natural adversity and of bringing about the most remarkable changes for the better, the future of mankind ultimately depends solely on men's capacity to mobilize their imagination and willpower in the service and interest of all.

153

The sovereigns and heads of state of the OPEC member countries proclaim their profound faith in the capability of all peoples to bring about a new economic order founded on justice and fraternity which will enable the world of tomorrow to enjoy progress equally shared by all in co-operation, stability and peace. They accordingly make a fervent appeal to the governments of the other countries of the world and solemnly pledge the full support of their peoples in the pursuance of this aim.

B2—Organization of Arab Petroleum Exporting Countries

B2.1—Membership, Staffing, etc.

Founder members .... Kuwait, Libya, Saudi Arabia

Subsequent members .... Abu Dhabi, Algeria, Bahrain, Dubai*, Qatar (May 1970)
Egypt†, Iraq, Syria (March 1972)
United Arab Emirates (June 1974, by transfer of membership of Abu Dhabi)
Tunisia (March 1982)

Headquarters .... Kuwait

Secretariat staffing (1984) .... 49 (professional staff)

Annual budget (1985) .... 2,697,000 Kuwaiti dinars (approximately $825,820 at January 1985 exchange rate)

Secretary-General‡ .... Dr Ali Ahmed Attiga (Libya); appointed September 1973; current term of office expires September 1988

*Withdrew from membership in May 1972, but was effectively reinstated (as part of the United Arab Emirates) in June 1974.

†Accession was not formally ratified by Egypt until early 1973; membership was suspended by OAPEC in April 1979.

‡The post of OAPEC Secretary-General was previously held by Shaikh Ahmed Zaki Yamani (Saudi Arabia) in 1968–69 and by Suhail al Sadawi (Libya) in 1970–73.

B2.2—Formation and Development

OAPEC was formed under an agreement signed in Beirut on Jan. 9, 1968, by three OPEC members (see above) representing the "moderate" political tendency within the Arab world (Libya being at that point still under monarchical rule). A non-political constitution was adopted with the main aim of furthering functional co-operation, and it was agreed that member countries' general oil policies would be conducted in accordance with the ratified resolutions of OPEC, which would be binding on any OAPEC member which was not also an OPEC member. Membership of OAPEC was open to Arab countries for which oil was "the main source of national income".

More radical tendencies in Arab politics found expression within OAPEC following the Libyan revolution in 1969 (◊C8.2) and the accession of Algeria to membership in 1970. In December 1971 the Organization's constitution, which as originally framed precluded the membership of Egypt and Syria, was amended to permit them to join (the new economic criterion for accession being that oil should constitute a "significant" source of national income). Their accession was accompanied by that of Iraq, the only Arab OPEC member to have hitherto remained outside OAPEC. The increasing politicization of OAPEC, as an Arab organization functioning in the context of extreme Arab-Israeli tensions in the Middle East, culminated in the OAPEC member countries' use of oil as a political weapon in the aftermath of the October 1973 war (◊D4.5, D5.2). (However, in view of the Organization's non-political constitution decisions on this matter were formally taken by an ad hoc "Conference of Arab Oil Ministers" rather than by the

OAPEC Council of Ministers, although the membership of both bodies was identical.)

Arab politics again influenced OAPEC in 1979, when Egypt's membership was suspended with effect from April 17 of that year as part of the Arab world's hostile reaction to the terms of Egypt's peace treaty with Israel. Bilateral differences between Libya and Tunisia caused the latter country's application for OAPEC membership, originally tabled before the Council of Ministers in December 1981, to be blocked for three months.

Despite OAPEC's inevitable involvement in the Arab-Israeli conflict—one effect of which has been to ensure that this issue has not impinged directly upon the affairs of OPEC, with its important non-Arab membership—the Organization has made considerable progress in fulfilling its functional aims. However, some difficulties have been encountered, including notably rival claims regarding the siting of a dry dock which led to Dubai's temporary withdrawal from OAPEC shortly after it was decided (in March 1972) to construct the dock in Bahrain. Dubai subsequently built its own dry dock to compete with the facilities in Bahrain (◊C12.2, B2.5.ii).

OAPEC participates in the "Euro-Arab Dialogue" which was set in train in early 1974 (◊D5.10) and is conducted under the auspices of a General Commission composed of representatives of the member states of the European Economic Community and the League of Arab States. OAPEC's principal contribution to the process of dialogue is through its representation on a subcommittee on co-operation in the refining and petrochemical industries, established in November 1975. OAPEC also maintains direct contacts with the European Commission, outside the framework of the Euro-Arab Dialogue, on the other matters of common interest.

B2.3—Objectives of OAPEC

The Organization's principal objectives were defined as follows in the constitution of OAPEC: "the co-operation of the members in various forms of economic activity in the petroleum industry; the realization of the closest ties among them in this field; the determination of ways and means for safeguarding the legitimate interests of its members individually and collectively; the unification of efforts to ensure the flow of petroleum to its consumer markets on equitable and reasonable terms; and the creation of a suitable climate for capital and expertise invested in the petroleum industry in the member countries".

In pursuing these objectives, it was required that emphasis be given to the need (i) "to take adequate measures for the co-ordination of the petroleum economic policies of its members"; (ii) "to take adequate measures for the harmonization of the legal systems of the member countries to the extent necessary for the Organization to carry out its activities"; (iii) "to assist members in exchanging information and expertise and to provide training and employment opportunities for citizens of member countries in member countries where such possibilities exist"; (iv) "to promote co-operation among members in working out solutions to problems facing them in the petroleum industry"; and (v) "to utilize the members' resources and common potentialities in establishing joint projects in various phases of the petroleum industry such as may be undertaken by all the members or those interested in such projects".

B2.4—Organs of OAPEC

The Organization's policy-making body is the Council of Ministers, comprising the Oil Ministers of the member countries, which holds at least two ordinary meetings per year (usually preceding the ordinary meetings of the OPEC Conference). The

Council of Ministers held a total of 36 ordinary meetings and six extraordinary meetings between September 1968 and May 1986. The management of OAPEC affairs is overseen by an Executive Bureau made up of senior officials from member states whose functions are broadly equivalent to those of the OPEC Board of Governors (◊**B1.7**). The implementation of OAPEC policies is the responsibility of the General Secretariat, which has departments concerned with finance and administration, documentation, training and manpower development, legal affairs, economic affairs, public information and international relations, petroleum projects and energy resources. The economics and energy resources departments were amalgamated in 1983 to form an Arab Centre for Energy Studies.

OAPEC's fourth organ is its Judicial Tribunal, established under a protocol which took effect on May 8, 1980. The Tribunal, described by OAPEC as "the first Arab court of arbitration among Arab states", is empowered to consider "differences which may arise among the member countries concerning oil issues" and to propose settlement terms designed to "prevent differences from becoming protracted and developing into disputes which could endanger the member countries' interests and the Organization's unity". The Tribunal's nine judges were appointed in 1981, and in the following year they commenced the hearing of their first case, namely a suit filed by Iraq contesting Syria's closure in April 1982 of the pipelines carrying Iraqi oil exports through Syrian territory (◊**C6.3.v**). A second case in progress before the Tribunal in 1985 concerned a claim by AMPTC (◊**B2.5.i**) against the Algerian Government, which had failed to meet its financial commitments as a shareholder in that company.

B2.5—OAPEC-sponsored Companies

Various OAPEC-sponsored companies, in which shares are held by the Governments or state corporations of member countries, have been established under international treaties between the countries concerned, as follows.

B2.5.i—Arab Maritime Petroleum Transport Company (AMPTC)

AMPTC was established in January 1973, with headquarters in Kuwait, to engage in all operations related to the transportation of hydrocarbons. It owned nine vessels in 1983, four of which were laid up in view of depressed market conditions. AMPTC reported a net operating loss of $12,520,000 in 1984 despite a year-on-year increase of 62 per cent in its chartering revenue.

B2.5.ii—Arab Shipbuilding and Repair Yard Company (ASRY)

ASRY was established in November 1974 with headquarters in Bahrain, where construction of a dry dock was completed in December 1977. The company's wider aim is to contribute to the development of the shipbuilding industry in Arab states, particularly by training nationals of OAPEC member states in shipbuilding, repair and maintenance. Its subsidiary companies are ASRYMAR (marketing; wholly-owned), ASRYPROPEC (propellor repairs; owned 67 per cent by ASRY and 33 per cent by the Dutch company Lips) and ASRYWELD (technical welding; owned 60 per cent by ASRY and 40 per cent by the Swiss company Castolin Eutetric). During 1984 ASRY incurred a total loss of $32,500,000 (of which half was an operating loss). The company's ship-repairing business was severely affected by price competition from Dubai (◊**B2.2**), and efforts were being made to diversify into steel processing in order to secure an additional source of income.

B2.5.iii—Arab Petroleum Investments Corporation (APICORP)

APICORP was established in November 1975, with headquarters in Dhahran (Saudi Arabia), to finance petroleum projects and industries and ancillary activities, giving priority to projects in Arab states. APICORP is a minority shareholder in several joint-venture companies in Arab states, and also holds 10 per cent of the shares in the Swiss-based International Energy Development Corporation, which undertakes oil and gas exploration in third-world countries.

B2.5.iv—Arab Petroleum Services Company (APSC)

APSC was incorporated in January 1977 with headquarters in Tripoli (Libya) as a holding company whose main function is to set up Arab companies specializing in petroleum services. The first two subsidiaries to be established, in 1979 and 1982 respectively, were (i) the Libyan-based Arab Drilling and Workover Company, owned 60 per cent by APSC and 40 per cent by Santa Fe International (a US-based company which in December 1981 became a wholly-owned subsidiary of the state-owned Kuwait Petroleum Corporation ◊**C7.3.iv**), and (ii) the Iraqi-based Arab Logging Company (wholly owned by APSC). An agreement was signed in 1984 to set up a Libyan-based Arab Geophysical Exploration Services Company, owned 40 per cent by APSC, 40 per cent by Geosource (UK), 10 per cent by APICORP and 10 per cent by Libya's National Oil Corporation.

B2.5.v—Arab Engineering Company (AREC)

AREC was established in July 1981, with headquarters in the United Arab Emirates, to provide consultancy services aimed at promoting the effective acquisition of modern technology by the Arab oil industry.

B2.6—Other Joint Ventures

The main OAPEC commercial venture under consideration in late 1985 was the proposed establishment of an Arab Drydock Company to serve the Mediterranean region. The OAPEC Council of Ministers gave its approval in principle in 1981 to the formation of such a company to build a dry dock at Mers El-Kebir (Algeria), but implementation of this decision was subsequently delayed when the Algerian Government requested that the dock be sited at an alternative location (Jinjin).

The OAPEC Council of Ministers agreed in May 1978 to establish an Arab Petroleum Training Institute in Baghdad with the main aims of (i) providing comprehensive training courses for managers and engineers; (ii) producing audio-visual aids and other training material; and (iii) carrying out research into oil industry labour and management issues. During the following years some progress was made in setting up the Institute with limited staff in temporary premises. Permanent premises were not expected to be completed before 1987.

B2.7—Co-sponsorship of Arab Energy Conference

In 1979 OAPEC and the Arab Fund for Economic and Social Development inaugurated the Arab Energy Conference, a new forum for the exchange of ideas on all aspects of the energy situation in the Arab world. The original decision to establish the Conference had been taken in May 1977 by the OAPEC Council of Ministers, which subsequently invited the Arab Fund for Economic and Social Development to become its co-sponsor in order to broaden the scope of the Conference to include all Arab countries while placing particular emphasis on the relationship between energy and economic development. The First Arab Energy Conference was held in Abu Dhabi from March 4 to 8, 1979, when it was agreed that future sessions should be organized at three-year intervals and that the Arab League (whose Petroleum Department had organized 10 Arab Petroleum Congresses since 1959 ◊**D1.1**) should discontinue such Congresses and instead become the third co-sponsor of the Arab Energy Conference.

The Second Arab Energy Conference took place in Qatar from March 6 to 11, 1982, with the Arab Industrial Development Organization as an additional co-sponsor. The Conference designated OAPEC as the body responsible for "Arab action in the energy sector" and for the organization of the Arab Energy Conference. The Third Arab Energy Conference was held in Algiers from May 4 to 9, 1985, with the Arab Organization for Mineral Resources as its fifth co-sponsor. The fourth session of the Conference was scheduled to take place in Baghdad in March 1988.

Although attended by ministers from the member countries of the sponsoring organizations as well as by (predominantly Arab) experts on energy issues, the Arab Energy Conference serves primarily as a forum for the dissemination of specialist research findings and the promotion of functional co-operation rather than as a political platform. The main objectives of the Conference are (i) to establish an Arab institutional framework for energy issues in order to develop a pan-Arab energy perspective; (ii) to co-ordinate and strengthen relations among Arab institutions involved in energy issues; (iii) to harmonize energy policies with development planning; (iv) to investigate present and future Arab energy requirements and means of satisfying them; (v) to evaluate existing energy resources in the Arab countries and to co-ordinate and promote efforts to develop these resources; and (vi) to evaluate the impact of international energy policies on the Arab countries.

B3—International Energy Agency

B3.1—Membership, etc.

Founder members .... Austria, Belgium, Canada, Denmark, West Germany, Irish Republic, Italy, Japan, Luxembourg, Netherlands, Spain, Sweden, Switzerland, Turkey, United Kingdom, United States

Subsequent members .... New Zealand, Norway (February 1975)
Greece (May 1976)
Australia (March 1979)
Portugal (April 1980)

Headquarters .... Paris

Executive Director .... Helga Steeg (West Germany)—took office July 1984

Previous Executive Director (November 1974 to March 1984) .... Dr Ulf Lantzke (West Germany)

B3.2—Formation, Status and Aims

The IEA was formally established (i) by a decision of the Council of the Organization for Economic Co-operation and Development (OECD) taken on Nov. 15, 1974, and (ii) by a separate international agreement to develop and implement an international energy programme, which was signed by the founder members of the IEA on Nov. 18, 1974, and took full legal effect on Jan. 19, 1976, after completion of the necessary ratification procedures. The only full members of the OECD which remained outside the IEA in mid-1986 were Finland, France and Iceland.

The OECD itself was formed in 1961 as a co-ordinating body concerned primarily with issues connected with the domestic economic and social policies of its member countries and with their external aid policies towards developing countries. Its 24 full members include all the major non-communist industrialized countries, while Yugoslavia also participates in certain OECD activities as an associate member. The OECD is the successor organization to the Organization for European Economic Co-operation, established in 1948 in the context of the Marshall Plan under which US economic assistance was made available for post-war reconstruction in Europe (◊◊A4.7).

The IEA has the status of an autonomous body within the OECD, at whose headquarters the IEA Secretariat is based. In addition to the individual IEA member countries, the Commission of the European Communities is also represented on the IEA's Governing Board (notwithstanding the non-membership in the IEA of an important EEC member, France). Norway's IEA membership is subject to the terms of a special agreement.

The main aims of the Agency's international energy programme are (i) to bring about, both in the short term and in the long term, "a better world energy supply and demand structure"; (ii) to prepare member countries against the risk of oil supply disruption and to co-ordinate the sharing of remaining oil supplies in a period of severe supply disruption; (iii) to develop alternative energy sources and to increase the efficiency of energy use through co-operative research and development programmes; and (iv) to promote co-operative relations with oil-exporting and oil-importing non-member countries.

160

B3.3—Organization

The IEA's policy-making body is its Governing Board, comprising senior representatives of member countries and of the European Commission. Some meetings of the Board are held at official level and others at ministerial level, national delegations being led in the latter case by ministers responsible for energy. Decisions of the Board are normally taken by consensus, but a complex system of weighted voting (broadly designed to relate each country's voting power to its volume of oil consumption) exists for use when no consensus can be reached on any of over 20 key issues, including aspects of the holding of oil stocks, the sharing and conservation of oil supplies in emergencies and relations between governments and oil companies. Table 18 shows the distribution of votes among the 20 full members (i.e. excluding Norway, which is a non-voting associate member) following Portugal's accession in 1980.

Table 18 — Distribution of voting power on IEA Governing Board

	General votes	"Oil votes"	Weighted total
Australia	3	1	4
Austria	3	1	4
Belgium	3	2	5
Canada	3	5	8
Denmark	3	1	4
West Germany	3	8	11
Greece	3	1	4
Irish Republic	3	0	3
Italy	3	5	8
Japan	3	15	18
Luxembourg	3	0	3
Netherlands	3	2	5
New Zealand	3	0	3
Portugal	3	0	3
Spain	3	2	5
Sweden	3	2	5
Switzerland	3	1	4
Turkey	3	1	4
United Kingdom	3	6	9
USA	3	47	50
Totals	60	100	160

The Governing Board appoints an Executive Director to head a Secretariat responsible for the collection and analysis of energy data, the study of member countries' energy policies and programmes, the preparation of energy use forecasts and the publication of special studies.

Five specialist groups made up of experts from the member countries hold regular meetings and report to the Governing Board on various aspects of the IEA's activities, as follows: (i) the Standing Group on Long-term Co-operation promotes conservation and substitution measures designed to reduce dependence on oil in the long term; (ii) the Standing Group on Oil Market Information analyses international oil market developments and oil companies' activities; (iii) the Standing Group on Emergency Questions is responsible for the development and operation of the IEA's emergency oil-sharing system, which includes procedures for arbitration in disputes between buyers and sellers of oil; (iv) the Standing Group on Relations with Producer and Other Consumer Countries is responsible for the promotion of co-operation with non-member countries on oil matters; and (v) the Committee on Energy Research and Development promotes research into the use of new technologies to increase the efficiency of existing energy use and to develop alternative energy sources through international projects. The IEA has sponsored numerous international energy research projects in such fields as conservation technology, coal technology, enhanced oil recovery, nuclear power, solar energy, geothermal energy, biomass conversion, ocean energy, fusion energy, wind energy and the production of hydrogen from water.

The Standing Group on Emergency Questions is assisted by an industry advisory board made up of senior oil company supply executives. There is also a coal industry advisory board, made up of leaders of coal-related enterprises, which advises the governments of member countries on issues connected with the production, trade and use of coal. In its consideration of nuclear energy questions, the IEA co-operates closely with the OECD's Nuclear Energy Agency (established in 1958, originally with an exclusively European membership but now comprising all the full members of the OECD except New Zealand).

B3.4—IEA Principles for Energy Policy

Some 12 basic policy principles and two appendices were agreed as follows by the Governing Board, meeting at ministerial level on Oct. 5 and 6, 1977. For various reasons the governments of the day in Denmark, the Netherlands, New Zealand, Norway, Spain and Sweden reserved their positions in respect of paragraph (8) dealing with nuclear energy. A detailed coal policy, based on paragraph (6), and a detailed conservation policy, based on paragraph (4), were subsequently adopted in May 1979 and December 1980 respectively.

(1) Further development by each participating country of national energy programmes and/or policies which include the objective, formulated as specifically as possible, of reducing in absolute terms or limiting future oil imports through conservation of energy, expansion of indigenous energy sources and oil substitution.

(2) Constant and careful attention to important environmental, safety, regional and security concerns to which the production, transportation and use of energy give rise, and improvement of the speed and consistency of public procedures for resolving conflicts which may exist between these concerns and energy requirements.

(3) Allowing domestic energy prices to reach a level which encourages energy conservation and development of alternative sources of energy.

(4) Strong reinforcement of energy conservation, on a high priority basis with increased resources, for the purpose of limiting growth in energy demand relative to economic growth, eliminating inefficient energy use, especially of rapidly depleting fuels, and encouraging substitution for fuels in shortest supply, by implementing vigorous conservation measures in various sectors along lines which include the following elements: (i) pricing policies (including fiscal measures) which give incentives to conservation; (ii) minimum energy efficiency standards; and (iii) encouragement and increase of investment in energy-saving equipment and techniques.

(5) Progressive replacement of oil in electricity generation, district heating, industries and other sectors by (i) discouraging the construction of new exclusively oil-fired power stations; (ii) encouraging the conversion of existing oil-fired capacity to more plentiful fuels in electricity, industrial and other sectors; (iii) encouraging the necessary structural adjustments in the refinery sector in order to avoid an excess of heavy fuel oil; and (iv) directing efforts in the reduction of the use of heavy fuel oil as a primary energy source in those sectors where efficiency is low.

(6) Application of a strong steam coal utilization strategy and active promotion of an expanded and reliable international trade in steam coal, composed of the following elements: (i) rapid phasing-in of steam coal as a major fuel for electrical power generation and in industrial sectors; (ii) further development of steam coal policies within producing, exporting

and consuming IEA countries to support increased utilization by enhancing market stability through reliable and increased export and import flows under reasonable commercial terms; and (iii) development of policies to remedy anticipated infrastructure bottlenecks.

(7) Concentration of the use of natural gas on premium users' requirements, and development of the infrastructure necessary to expand the availability of natural gas.

(8) Steady expansion of nuclear generating capacity as a main and indispensable element in attaining the group objectives, consistent with safety, environmental and security standards satisfactory to the countries concerned and with the need to prevent the proliferation of nuclear weapons. In order to provide for this expansion, it will be necessary through co-operation to assure reliable availability of (i) adequate supplies of nuclear fuel (uranium and enrichment capacity) at equitable prices; and (ii) adequate facilities and techniques for development of nuclear electricity generation, for dealing with spent fuel, for waste management, and for overall handling of the back end of the nuclear fuel cycle.

(9) Stronger emphasis on energy research, development and demonstration, including collaborative programmes, more intensive national efforts and greater co-ordination of national efforts, in order to make energy use more efficient and to meet future energy requirements. Each participating country should contribute to energy technology development, with emphasis on (a) technologies which can have relatively near-term impact; (b) policies which facilitate the transition of new energy technologies from the research and development phase to the point of utilization; (c) technologies for broadly applicable renewable energy sources; and (d) investigation of whether there are technological possibilities for significant contributions from other renewable resources, through (i) providing the fullest possible financial support for energy research, development and demonstration; (ii) increasing participation in international collaborative projects to extend the effectiveness of funds available; (iii) encouraging investment in energy technology development by appropriate incentives; and (iv) ensuring that research and development policies remain consistent with and supportive of the objective of on-going energy policy.

(10) Establishment of a favourable investment climate which encourages the flow of public and private capital to develop energy resources by appropriate pricing policies, by minimizing uncertainties about the general directions of energy and other policies such as mentioned in paragraph (2) above and by providing government incentives where necessary, in order to (i) give priority to exploration activities including those in offshore and frontier areas; and (ii) encourage rates of exploration and development of available capacities which are consistent with the optimum economic development of resources.

(11) Providing in energy policy planning for alternative means, other than increased oil consumption, for meeting any development of supply shortfall or failure to attain conservation objectives, taking into account the appropriate requirements of economic development and social progress.

(12) Appropriate co-operation in the field of energy, including evaluation of the world energy situation, energy research and development and technical and financial requirements, with developed or developing countries or international organizations.

Appendix A—Suggested Conservation Measures

Industry. (i) Effective incentives for energy saving investments, including encouragement of the manufacture of more durable goods; (ii) advice service for small and medium industry and energy reporting, auditing and target setting for energy-intensive industries.

Residential/commercial. (i) Building codes with minimum thermal and air-conditioning efficiencies for all new buildings; (ii) effective incentives for retrofitting existing buildings; (iii) education and information programmes; (iv) individual metering of gas/electricity, heat and hot water; (v) minimum energy efficiency standard for appliances.

Transport. (i) Minimum fuel efficiency standard for motor vehicles; (ii) significant taxes on gasoline and progressive taxes on cars according to weight or fuel efficiency; (iii) incentives for public transport; (iv) investments in infrastructure and equipment for public transport; (v) speed limits on roads.

Energy sector. (i) Incentives and regulations for district heating, combined production of heat and power and for the greater use of waste products and waste heat; (ii) full cost tariffs for electricity generation, taking into account the costs of replacement.

Appendix B—Principal Areas of Research, Development and
Demonstration requiring Emphasis

Near- and medium-term technologies. (i) For conservation: improved industrial processes; more efficient transport engines and vehicles; improved means of utilizing waste heat; building insulation. (ii) For supply: enhanced oil recovery; more effective and environmentally acceptable means of coal combustion; solar heating.

Transition technologies. (i) Oil shale, tar sands; (ii) process heat from coal (directly or through conversion to gas); (iii) improved performance of nuclear convertor reactors; (iv) nuclear fuel cycle issues, including safety and waste disposal; (v) coal-derived liquid and gaseous fuels.

Broadly applicable and renewable resources. (i) Large scale direct and indirect solar energy uses; (ii) geothermal energy; (iii) biomass; (iv) breeder reactors and alternative fuel cycles which are economically, politically and environmentally acceptable; (v) fusion.

Investigation of other renewable sources. (i) Wind; (ii) wave; (iii) ocean gradients.

OPEC MEMBER COUNTRY SURVEYS

C1—Algeria

C1.1—Statistical Survey

*1984
†End-1984
‡Revision of 1984 figures given in section **D15.1.i** (see Introduction)

General

Area	2,381,741 sq km
*Population	21,050,000
Capital	Algiers (El Djazair)

Economy and trade

*Gross domestic product	$53,285 million
*Annual exports (fob)	$10,795 million (of which natural gas and gas condensates 49.3 per cent; crude oil and refined products 47.1 per cent)
*Annual imports (cif)	$10,286 million
*Current account balance	+$700,000,000
Foreign exchange reserves	$2,930 million (January 1986)

Oil (upstream)

‡1984 production	1,075,000 bpd (46,100,000 tonnes)
1985 production	1,040,000 bpd (44,800,000 tonnes)
of which: (crude oil)	(635,000 bpd)
(gas condensates)	(405,000 bpd)
†Proved crude reserves	9,000 million barrels
*Reserves:production ratio (crude oil)	38.6 : 1
Production in peak year	1,255,000 bpd (58,500,000 tonnes) in 1979
†Cumulative production (including condensates)	7,966.7 million barrels since 1957 (pre-1957 production negligible)
*Number of producing oil wells	800
Export grades: Saharan Blend	44° API gravity
Zarzaitine	42° API gravity

Oil tanker tonnage
†11 vessels .... 1,079,700 deadweight tons

Oil (downstream)
*Installed refining capacity .... 471,200 bpd
*Output of refined products .... 407,900 bpd
*Consumption of refined products ...... 140,500 bpd

Natural gas (million cubic metres)
*Gross annual production .... 93,821 mcm
   of which: (gas marketed) .... (35,039 mcm)
           (gas reinjected) .... (48,292 mcm)
           (gas flared) .... (5,708 mcm)
           (shrinkage) .... (4,782 mcm)
*Annual exports .... 19,040 mcm
   of which: (liquefied gas) .... (12,040 mcm)
           (dry gas) .... (7,000 mcm)
†Natural gas reserves .... 3,100,000 mcm

C1.2—Political and Economic Summary

The Democratic and Popular Republic of Algeria is a one-party state ruled by the National Liberation Front (FLN), which has been led since 1979 by President Bendjedid Chadli. The FLN is committed both to socialism and the role of Islam as the state religion. President Chadli (the sole candidate) received over 95 per cent of the vote in the 1984 presidential election. National Assembly elections held in 1982 (with three FLN candidates contesting each of the 281 seats) resulted in the return of 68 members of the outgoing Assembly, as against 213 new members.

Formerly under Ottoman rule, Algeria was conquered by France in 1830 and later became subject to colonial government as an "attached territory" of metropolitan France, with a large European settler population holding political and economic power. Independence from France was achieved on July 3, 1962, nearly eight years after the FLN had initiated a war of liberation in which over 1,000,000 people (the majority of them members of the native Moslem population) were killed. The progress of negotiations held during the final two years of the conflict was delayed both by the settlers' often violent campaign against France's belated acknowledgment of the Algerian people's right to self-determination and by unsuccessful French attempts to induce the FLN to agree to the separation of the oil-producing Saharan region from the north of the country in return for the granting of full independence to the north alone.

Algeria is the second largest country in Africa and OPEC's largest member state. Although only a small proportion of its area (mostly in the coastal region) is cultivable there is a wide variety of subsoil resources, including (in addition to oil and gas) iron ore, zinc, lead, mercury, phosphates and coal. The Government's economic development strategy during the 1960s and 1970s was based on the use of oil and gas revenues to finance the rapid growth of capital-intensive state-controlled heavy industries. From 1980 onwards there was a shift of emphasis towards light industry (including privately-owned and labour-intensive enterprises) and towards greater investment in the agricultural sector (aimed particularly at reducing the country's growing dependence on food imports). At the same time the management of many large state enterprises was decentralized. Algeria's external debt of around $15,700 million was the largest of any country in the Arab world at the beginning of 1985, although the structure of its borrowing—which included a high fixed-interest element—placed Algeria in a stronger position than the non-Arab OPEC debtor countries.

The population growth rate is among the highest in the world, and large numbers of Algerian citizens left the country to find work abroad, mostly in France, during the 1960s and 1970s. Arabs form the majority of the population, and there is also a culturally distinct Berber minority. Virtually none of the European settlers chose to remain in Algeria after 1962.

Since independence, and notably under the leadership of President Houari Boumedienne (who held power from 1965, when he led a bloodless coup, until his death in 1978), Algeria has been a prominent member of the non-aligned movement and has generally supported the radical Arab position in Middle Eastern politics. Algeria was OPEC's principal advocate of solidarity with third-world causes from 1974 to 1978, when the Boumedienne Government was at the forefront of the campaign for a "new international economic order".This stance was coupled with a generally moderate approach to pricing questions within OPEC, based on a belief that the adoption of a "responsible" approach to oil-price administration would strengthen the oil exporters' position in global economic negotiations. Under the Chadli Government Algeria adopted a progressively harder line on oil-pricing questions as the "North-South" issue receded into the background of global politics. In the domestic arena, the revolutionary dogmas of the Boumedienne era were superseded by a more moderate brand of pragmatic socialism, this shift being formalized in January 1986 when a revised "national charter" was endorsed by popular referendum after approval by the FLN party congress.

C1.3—Oil and Gas Industry

C1.3.i—Early development (to 1964)

Although France's state-owned Bureau de Recherches de Pétroles (◊A4.9) launched a large-scale oil exploration programme in Algeria in 1947, only minor discoveries (yielding about 24,000 barrels per annum) were made during the first half of the 1950s. However, in 1956 the extensive Hassi Messaoud field was discovered in the Trias basin region of the Sahara desert as a result of joint drilling work carried out in their contiguous exploration areas by Compagnie Française des Pétroles d'Algérie (CFPA) and Société Nationale de Recherches de d'Exploitation des Pétroles en Algérie (SN Repal). Further significant discoveries were made in the same year by Compagnie de Recherches et d'Exploitation de Pétrole au Sahara (CREPS), whose exploration areas were situated in the Polignac basin, near the Libyan border. CFPA and SN Repal together discovered the massive Hassi R'Mel gas and condensate field in 1957. As in neighbouring Libya, the crude oils found in Algeria were of the highest quality, being generally light in gravity and low in sulphur content.

CFPA was owned 85 per cent by CFP and 15 per cent by French investment companies; SN Repal was then owned 50 per cent by the Algerian colonial Government, 48 per cent by the French Government and 2 per cent by other French interests; and CREPS was then owned 51 per cent by the French Government, 14 per cent by other French interests and 35 per cent by Royal Dutch/Shell. The other main holder of Algerian exploration permits was Compagnie des Pétroles d'Algérie (CPA), then owned 65 per cent by Royal Dutch/Shell, 24 per cent by the French Government and 11 per cent by other French interests. Exploration permits were valid initially for five years, after which the permit holder was required to select half of its allocated area for relinquishment to the Government. Production concessions (of up to 50 years' duration) were granted only after the discovery of oil. Apart from CPA (which was categorized as a non-French company by virtue of

Royal Dutch/Shell's majority holding), no non-French company was able to obtain Algerian exploration rights unless it was acting as a minority partner in a consortium controlled by a French company or companies.

In 1958 the Government introduced a Saharan oil code setting out the terms of Algeria's first production concessions. Like the petroleum law which had been adopted by Libya in 1955 (◊**C8.3.i**), the code was a modified version of the Middle Eastern "50-50 profit-sharing" system (◊**A4.6**) and contained various financial incentives intended to stimulate the rapid development of hydrocarbon discoveries. Net oil company income was taxable at the rate of 50 per cent, for which purpose exports were valued at "international market prices". Royalty payments at the rate

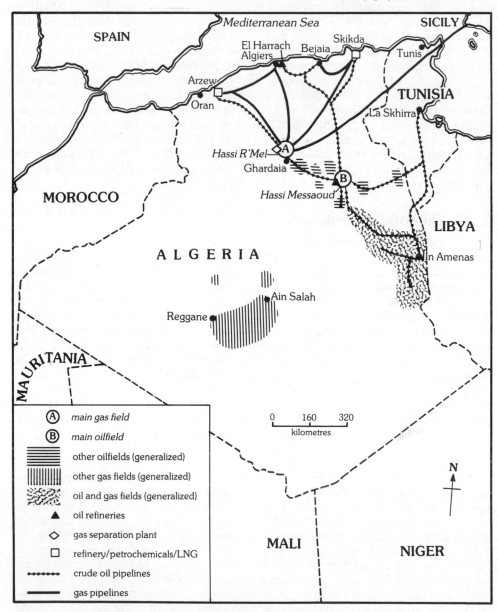

Fig. 4—Algerian hydrocarbon resources and installations

of 12.5 per cent of gross export revenue (fob Algerian ports) were credited against the overall tax liability. The posted prices which were subsequently established by most of the producing companies had no fiscal significance under the 1958 oil code. A depletion allowance enabled producing companies to defer for five years the tax due on 27.5 per cent of their net income (provided that this percentage of net income was reinvested in new exploration work via a "reconstitution fund"), while depreciation allowances were based not on the established accounting conventions of the international oil industry but on the more advantageous conventions of France's standard corporate tax laws.

SN Repal, which was restructured in 1958 to give equal 40.5 per cent shareholdings to the French Government and the Algerian colonial Government (the remaining shares being held by other French interests), obtained a concession covering the south of the Hassi Messaoud field, while CFPA held the production rights over the north of the field. The two companies' output from the field was to be transported to the coast via a pipeline owned 51 per cent by SN Repal and 49 per cent by CFPA. The Hassi R'Mel gas field was to be brought into production by Société d'Exploitation du Gaz d'Hassi R'Mel (SEHR), also owned 51 per cent by SN Repal and 49 per cent by CFPA. Limited commercial production of Hassi Messaoud crude began in early 1958, when the pipeline from the oilfield reached the southern terminal of the Algerian railway system, and large-scale exports became possible in 1960, when work was completed on the extension of the pipeline to the Algerian port of Bejaia. Also in 1960, CREPS completed an export pipeline linking the oilfields in its eastern Algerian concession area to the Tunisian port of La Skhirra. In 1961 SEHR opened a gas pipeline from Hassi R'Mel to the Algerian port of Arzew, the site of a liquefaction plant which was to be operated by a company owned 40 per cent by Conch International Methane Ltd (whose own main shareholders were Shell and Conoco). Pending the completion of the plant—from which the world's first commercial LNG exports were made in October 1964 (◊A3.2.i)—the Hassi R'Mel pipeline was used solely to supply gas to a local pipeline system serving consumers in Algiers and other centres.

At the time of Algeria's independence in 1962 CFPA and SN Repal were producing only from Hassi Messaoud and Hassi R'Mel (although they held exploration permits in other areas), whereas CREPS had expanded its total concession area to include a number of recently discovered oilfields. CPA, which had yet to discover oil within its own exploration area, held production rights in association with CREPS in areas where the two companies had conducted a successful joint exploration programme. Concessions were also held by various small French companies (several of them controlled by the French Government), which usually operated in groups, with one company in each consortium taking responsibility for production activities. Non-French companies holding minority interests in such groups included the following (asterisks denoting those holding operational responsibilities): Mobil*; Sofrapel (a subsidiary of the West German Elwerath company, itself jointly owned by Shell and Exxon); Ausonia Minière Française (AMIF, a subsidiary of the Italian group Montecatini Edison); and the US independent companies Sinclair Oil*, Phillips Petroleum, El Paso Natural Gas Co.*, Getty Oil (through its subsidiaries Tidewater and Veedol) and Newmont Oil.

The Evian agreements of March 1962, which concluded the war of liberation (◊C1.2) and laid the basis for Algerian independence, contained a number of provisions concerning oil and gas. These included (i) the establishment of a joint Franco-Algerian technical organization, in which both countries had equal representation, "to ensure the continuity of the exploitation of the resources of the Sahara"; (ii) the confirmation of all existing exploration and production rights granted under the 1958 Saharan oil code; (iii) the continuation for six years of the existing preference given to French-controlled companies and consortiums when granting exploration permits and production concessions (provided that more advantageous financial terms were not offered by non-French interests); (iv) payment in French currency for all purchases of Algerian hydrocarbons by France or other franc-zone territories; (v) the creation of an international arbitration tribunal to settle disputes between the Algerian Government and its concession holders; and (vi) the transfer to the Government of independent Algeria of the Algerian colonial Government's 40.5 per cent shareholding in SN Repal as well as various minor oil investments held by the colonial authorities.

The new Government thus took over substantial equity interests in Algeria's largest oil and gas fields, and by agreeing to remain within the franc zone was assured that a large proportion of the country's crude exports would continue to enjoy preferential access to the protected French market. (The French refineries of the major oil companies were obliged to purchase a specified proportion of their crude supplies from sources within the franc zone, by far the largest of which was Algeria, whose exports of crude produced by non-integrated French companies were considerably in excess of the capacity of France's public-sector refining interests.) This continuing treatment of Algerian oil as a "national" resource in France, in accordance with the original purpose of the French Government's extensive investments in the Algerian oil industry, ensured that Algeria's post-independence relations with the French producing companies would be inextricably bound up with its bilateral political relations with France.

In 1963 Algeria's oil production reached 500,000 bpd, close to the maximum capacity of existing export pipelines. CREPS was able to accommodate the growing output of the eastern oilfields by adding 70,000 bpd to the capacity of the La Skhirra pipeline in the following year. Most of the oilfields which were being developed by the smaller producing consortiums were, however, dependent on recently constructed links to the Bejaia pipeline, whose capacity was grossly inadequate to handle the full potential output of these new fields in addition to its priority throughout from the Hassi Messaoud field (which accounted for over 80 per cent of total daily deliveries to Bejaia in 1963). The smaller groups (comprising a total of 16 French and non-French companies) accordingly reached an agreement to build a new jointly-owned export pipeline in order to enable them to achieve acceptable production levels. However, the companies refused to accept the Algerian Government's proposal that the state should take a majority shareholding in their pipeline consortium, whereupon the Government withheld permission for the consortium to proceed and instead formed a state enterprise, Société Nationale de Transport et de Commercialisation des Hydrocarbures (Sonatrach) to oversee the construction of a wholly state-owned pipeline. A decree of Dec. 31, 1963, empowered Sonatrach to engage in the transportation of hydrocarbons by land and sea and to buy and sell oil products (it being envisaged at that time that a partly state-owned refinery would be built in conjunction with the pipeline). The new pipeline, running to an export terminal at Arzew, was completed in early 1966, by which time all 16 producing companies had signed transport agreements with Sonatrach.

The constriction of oil output for want of pipeline capacity, coupled with the Government's failure to grant production concessions in respect of post-independence oil discoveries, brought about a sharp fall in exploration activity in 1963 and 1964, when the general investment climate in Algeria was dominated by Western misgivings about the political direction which the country was taking under the increasingly autocratic presidency of Ahmed Ben Bella. The Government, for its part, showed growing concern over the fact that the producing companies (which were not subject to Algerian exchange controls at this time) were retaining an estimated 60 per cent of their export earnings outside the country, most of their new investment being channelled into downstream facilities in France or exploration work outside Algeria.

The Government's unit revenue had, moreover, declined since independence in line with the downward trend in the international market price of Algerian crude. The average market price at which the producing companies valued their Algerian exports for tax purposes in 1964 was around $1.95 per barrel for 44° crude fob Bejaia, compared with the companies' posted price of $2.35 per barrel (which had been cut from $2.65 at the beginning of that year). Only the relatively small volume of Algerian crude which was sold on an arms-length basis by non-French companies actually changed hands at the international market price, the French companies' sales to refineries in France being made at a standard price of $2.26 per barrel in 1964. (This standard "national obligation price", the level of which was negotiated by the French Government and the local refining industry at three-year intervals, was also used by Shell and Mobil to invoice their own integrated transfers of crude from Algeria to France.)

The Government of independent Algeria, unlike the former colonial administration, had no say in determining a fair international market price for Algerian crude, and could not unilaterally secure increases in the per-barrel valuations declared by the producing companies for tax purposes. There was a one-year time limit for inquiries by the tax authorities into the accuracy of the companies' gross revenue declarations, compared with a four-year time limit under colonial rule. These changes had been made in a decree gazetted in February 1962, shortly before the conclusion of the Evian agreements. Another decree gazetted at the same time had authorized concession holders to revalue their balance sheets in such a way as to reduce their future tax liability.

C1.3.ii—New co-operation agreement with France (July 1965)

Negotiations with the French Government for a radical revision of the terms of France's involvement in the Algerian hydrocarbons industry were initiated at the request of the Ben Bella Government in May 1964. In July 1965 (shortly after Ben Bella's overthrow) a comprehensive bilateral agreement, covering both oil and gas and wider industrial co-operation between the two countries, was signed by the new Algerian Government of President Boumedienne. The agreement, which was to be valid for 15 years from 1966, subject to review after five years at the request of either side, was binding on all French companies engaged in Algerian oil and gas operations but did not apply to the operations of non-French companies. (To qualify as "French" in this context a company had either to be registered in France and owned at least 50 per cent by the French Government, by French state-controlled bodies or by persons under French jurisdiction, or, if registered outside France, to be at least 51 per cent French-owned.) The main provisions of the 111-page agreement were as follows:

(1) The tenure of all existing production concessions was confirmed, but their financial terms were altered. A fixed fiscal reference price ($2.08 per barrel fob Bejaia) would be used to value crude exports for tax purposes, while the rate of taxation of net profits would be 53 per cent in 1966–67, 54 per cent in 1968 and 55 per cent from 1969 onwards. The reference price was to be reviewed by the Algerian and French Governments during 1969 in the light of (i) changes in the prices of competing crudes; (ii) changes in Algeria's relative position with regard to freight, quality and tax differentials; and (iii) changes in Algerian production costs. Royalty arrangements would continue unchanged (i.e. payments of 12.5 per cent of gross export revenue would continue to be credited against companies' overall tax liabilities), except that companies were now required to use the new fiscal reference price as a minimum export value when calculating their gross revenue for royalty purposes. The depletion allowance laid down in the 1958 Saharan oil code was abolished, while depreciation allowances were brought more closely into line with the standard allowances in the Middle East.

(The overall improvement in Algeria's unit revenue as a result of these changes fell somewhat short of the Algerian Government's opening demand for fiscal parity with the Middle East. The new fixed reference price was 11.5 per cent lower than the producing companies' current posted price, while the scheduled increases in tax rates were simply an alternative to the implementation of the OPEC royalty-expensing formula (◊**D1.3**.)

(2) Nine new production concessions were to be made available in respect of five oilfields and two gas fields discovered since independence. Concession agreements with French companies would be based on the revised terms outlined above (the Algerian Government having previously refused to grant any new concessions because of its objections to the terms which it had inherited from the colonial period). Two of the concessions were in exploration areas held by CREPS, three in areas held jointly by CREPS and CPA and one in an area held by CPA. The remaining concessions were in areas held by three of the smaller French-controlled consortiums, each of which included non-French minority partners (respectively Phillips Petroleum, El Paso Natural Gas Co., and Mobil and AMIF). Non-French companies would not be subject to any higher tax obligation in the new concession areas than in their existing concession areas.

(3) A Franco-Algerian "co-operative association" (ASCOOP) was established to provide an institutional framework for future French participation in the exploration and development of areas where no hydrocarbon discoveries had yet been made. Directed by an executive council of six Algerian and six French nominees, meeting under Algerian chairmanship, ASCOOP would oversee the operations of a French state-controlled company, described in the agreement as "Company F", and an Algerian state-owned company ("Company A"). The ASCOOP partner-companies were to have exclusive exploration rights (subject to safeguards for existing non-French interests) in four "co-operative zones" covering a total area of 180,000 sq km in regions of Algeria which were considered to have the most promising hydrocarbon potential.

While established production concessions (together with the new concessions which the Boumedienne Government had agreed to grant in respect of the post-independence discoveries) remained in the hands of their existing operators, all exploration permits currently held by French companies, whether inside or outside the co-operative zones, were to be surrendered to ASCOOP. Existing exploration permits held exclusively by CPA (as a company controlled by non-French interests) would remain valid on their original terms. As regards permits held by French-controlled consortiums, the French partners were required to surrender their rights to ASCOOP, while the non-French partners had the option of accepting the ASCOOP companies as their new majority partners (while themselves continuing to operate on their original terms) or surrendering their own rights to ASCOOP. All transfers of existing exploration rights to ASCOOP were subject to the payment of compensation—in the form of crude oil to be delivered at a later date—for work already carried out by the displaced permit holders.

The ASCOOP partner companies were obliged to take up all surrendered exploration permits within the co-operative zones, but could decline to take up surrendered permits outside the zones. Permits which were not taken up would revert to their original holders. Hitherto unallocated areas within the zones were automatically reserved for joint exploration by the ASCOOP partners, provided that they applied for exploration rights within two years of ASCOOP's formation, whereas exploration rights in unallocated areas outside the zones remained open to applications from any company, including either Company A or Company F acting independently. Procedures were laid down for the division of the joint ownership of ASCOOP exploration rights between Company A and Company F, it being envisaged that Company A would hold interests ranging from 10 per cent to 50 per cent in surrendered permit areas within the co-operative zones and from 10 per cent to 90 per cent in all other ASCOOP exploration areas, with Company F holding the balance in each case. Overall, it was intended that the French and Algerian sides should have roughly equal shares of the total ASCOOP area. Operational responsibilities—which would normally be assumed by the majority partner in unequally divided exploration areas—would be allocated to one or other of the partners in equally held areas in such a way as to maintain overall parity. Either company could subcontract its operational responsibilities in a particular area to another Algerian or French company.

The ASCOOP partners' exploration rights in each block within the co-operative zones were valid for 15 years from the start of operations within the block concerned, one-third of the area of the block being subject to relinquishment every five years. The maximum initial area of any block was limited to 10,000 sq km. Exploration rights in blocks outside the zones were valid for five years or for the remaining duration of a permit taken over from a previous holder (if longer). In the event of a commercial discovery being made within an ASCOOP exploration block, production rights would be granted for an initial period of 25 years. Renewal for a further five years would automatically be granted by the ASCOOP executive council at the request of either of the partner companies. The Algerian Government had discretionary powers to grant an additional 10-year extension at the request of both companies.

Each company was responsible for its own share of exploration expenditure, although Company F undertook to advance funds to cover up to 60 per cent of Company A's costs in each block (subject to a ceiling equal to Company F's own share of the costs for the block concerned), such loans being repayable by Company A in the form of crude oil produced within the framework of ASCOOP. The ASCOOP executive council was responsible for drawing up a five-year exploration budget for each block, the fulfilment of which was contractually binding on the partner companies and would be monitored by the Algerian Government. The agreement laid down a minimum average level of spending per square kilometre of ASCOOP's exploration area. Each of the partner companies would have responsibility for marketing its own share of ASCOOP production, although if Company A was unable to market its full share Company F undertook to purchase up to 25 per cent of Company A's share at a "defined commercial price" and to purchase any additional surplus at discounts of up to 20 per cent. The profits of production within the framework of ASCOOP were taxable at the rate of 55 per cent. Royalties and fiscal reference prices were the same as those applying to oil produced by established French concession holders. The currently agreed reference price of $2.08 per barrel was, however, to be maintained for ASCOOP production until such time as that production had reached a cumulative total of 20,000,000 tonnes. Company F was entitled to transfer 40 per cent of its initial profits out of Algeria, to be reduced eventually to 25 per cent.

(4) The development of an oilfield at Haoud Berkaoui, discovered by SN Repal and CFPA shortly before the signature of the Franco-Algerian co-operation agreement, was subject to special arrangements whereby SN Repal withdrew, while CFPA remained as operator of the field and as part-holder of the French rights in the field (which would normally have been held exclusively by Company F under the ASCOOP formula). The final distribution of interests in the field was 50 per cent to Company A, 33.8 per cent to CFPA and 16.2 per cent to Company F.

(5) SN Repal was restructured to give 50 per cent shareholdings to the Algerian and French Governments, to be held through state-controlled companies. In return for its additional 9.5 per cent interest, the Algerian Government agreed (i) to a French takeover of SN Repal's shareholding in the French organization which handled the marketing of franc-zone crude produced by non-integrated French companies and (ii) to the payment of additional compensation to France in the form of specified volumes of Hassi Messaoud crude from the Algerian share of SN Repal's output. The operating structure of SN Repal was reorganized so as to allow each shareholder company to take separate responsibility for marketing (and for paying taxes and royalties on) its own share of output, which would be supplied to it at cost price. Algeria was free to market its half-share of SN Repal's output outside the franc zone, but would continue to enjoy guaranteed access to French outlets for oil which could not be sold more profitably elsewhere. SN Repal's 10 per cent shareholding in Société de la Raffinerie d'Alger (the owner of what was then the country's main oil refinery, which had commenced production near Algiers in 1964) was transferred to the Algerian Government in return for the supply of additional compensatory volumes of crude to France out of the Algerian share of SN Repal's output. It was agreed that SN Repal should be chaired by an Algerian director and should be managed "in the same spirit as ASCOOP", with all decisions being taken by mutual agreement between the French and Algerian sides.

(6) Companies producing natural gas undertook to sell to Algeria, at the wellhead, such quantities of gas as the state wished to purchase for domestic consumption or for export under new contracts (existing long-term contracts with France and the United Kingdom being unaffected by the new arrangements). The state's purchases would be made at prices which gave the producing companies a fixed profit margin—designed to provide "a fair net return on equity capital" plus "a premium to encourage continued exploration activities in

Algeria"—while the state would receive any additional profits resulting from the resale of the gas at full commercial prices. A joint Franco-Algerian company was to be established to implement various new gas liquefaction and transportation projects intended primarily to serve the French import market. The French Government gave an undertaking in principle that France would import an additional volume of Algerian gas totalling at least 1,500 million cubic metres per year from 1968 onwards, "provided that all proper industrial and financial steps be taken in good time".

(7) The French Government would provide financial aid for Algerian industrial development at the rate of 400,000,000 francs per annum (F40,000,000 in grants, F160,000,000 in soft loans and F200,000,000 in credit guarantees to French suppliers) from 1966 to 1970 inclusive. A joint Industrial Co-operation Agency would be established to assess projects proposed by Algeria and to oversee the implementation of approved projects.

In a related agreement signed at the same time, the French Government undertook to establish a second petroleum institute to train Algerian technicians (Algeria's first such institute having been set up with Soviet assistance).

In pursuance of the aims of the new co-operation agreement, the Algerian Government nominated Sonatrach as "Company A" under the terms of the ASCOOP arrangements, as the holder of Algeria's 50 per cent shareholding in SN Repal and as the vehicle for state participation in all other hydrocarbon-related activities (including the marketing of natural gas). The company's full title was formally changed in September 1966 to Société Nationale pour la Recherche, la Production, le Transport, la Transformation et la Commercialisation des Hydrocarbures.

The French Government formed a new company, Sopefal (Société Pétrolière Française en Algérie) to fulfil the role of "Company F" in ASCOOP. Sopefal subsequently became a wholly-owned subsidiary of Entreprise de Recherches et d'Activités Pétrolières (ERAP, formed at the beginning of 1966 as a holding company for France's state-owned oil interests). France's 50 per cent interest in SN Repal was vested in a separate ERAP subsidiary, Sofrepal (Société Française pour la Recherche et l'Exploitation des Pétroles en Algérie). ERAP's other interests in the Algerian oil industry included the French shareholdings (of 65 per cent and 35 per cent respectively) in CREPS and CPA.

C1.3.iii—Extension of state control over non-French oil interests

By establishing revised concession terms only for the French producing companies covered by the July 1965 co-operation agreement, Algeria placed these companies at a disadvantage vis-à-vis non-French companies, which were still entitled to operate (in their predominantly French-controlled concession areas) under the fiscal provisions of the 1958 Saharan oil code. An ordinance was therefore issued in January 1966 to increase the state's share of the profits of non-French oil companies by making them subject to an amended taxation formula, which differed from the formula accepted by the French companies in that (i) the taxable value of "non-French" crude exports was to be based not on a negotiated reference price but on an "assessed international market price" fixed from time to time by the Algerian Government and (ii) no undertaking was given to hold the rate of taxation on non-French companies at 55 per cent after 1969. The initial level of the new fiscal reference price for non-French companies—$2.19 per barrel fob Bejaia—was determined by deflating the companies' posted price of $2.35 by the percentage discount currently allowed by Middle Eastern producing countries under the OPEC royalty-expensing formula (◊ Table 22), and thus enabled the Algerian Government to achieve broad fiscal parity with the Middle East in respect of the taxation of "non-French" exports. The open-market realizations for Algerian crude in early 1966 were about $1.80 per barrel for contract sales and less than $1.70 for sp0178ales.

The non-French producers vigorously contested the validity of the assessed reference price system, accusing the Algerian authorities of unfair discrimination in favour of the French producers (a charge which the Algerian Government rejected on the grounds that the French were entitled to preferential fiscal treatment in view of the investment undertakings which had been made by France in the July 1965 co-operation agreement). Most non-French producers continued to base their tax payments on valuations which were lower than the new reference price (ranging from open-market realizations to the reference price of $2.08 per barrel applicable to French producers), leading the Government to issue an ultimatum in November 1966 requiring the immediate payment of accumulated arrears, failing which the Government would seize company assets to meet its claims. Apart from CPA, the companies involved all met this ultimatum, making it clear that they were complying under protest. The arrears claimed from CPA were removed from the company's local bank account on government instructions.

Further controversy surrounded the non-French companies' rights with regard to the new production concessions which had been promised in July 1965. Draft concession agreements submitted to the companies by the Government in 1966 required them not only to accept the revised tax terms but to agree to refer any disputes to the arbitration of the Algerian Supreme Court (whereas the companies' existing concession agreements provided for international arbitration, as confirmed by the Evian agreements of 1962). French companies were now subject to revised international arbitration procedures, detailed in Algeria's July 1965 co-operation agreement with France, which superseded the previously agreed procedures for all French concession holders and applied also to disputes which might arise within ASCOOP. The non-French companies therefore regarded the lack of recourse to international arbitration under their draft concession agreements as another example of discrimination in favour of French companies, whereas the Algerian Government maintained that equal treatment for non-French companies was not possible since the revised international arbitration procedures formed part of a bilateral agreement with France.

The non-French companies refused to sign the new concession agreements, with the result that the granting of seven of the nine concessions promised in July 1965 remained in abeyance at the end of 1966 (the other two having been granted to the French-controlled CREPS as the sole holder of exploration rights in the areas concerned). While CREPS refused to sign agreements relating to exploration areas held jointly with CPA, all the French members of the consortiums involved in the other potential concession areas signed their agreements despite the opposition of their non-French partners. Royal Dutch/Shell (the majority shareholder in CPA and minority shareholder in CREPS) finally dropped its opposition to the "non-French" arbitration procedures in mid-1967, whereupon the CPA's sole concession and the three joint CREPS/CPA concessions were granted. The situation regarding the granting of the three other outstanding concessions remained deadlocked as a result of non-signature by non-French companies.

In June 1967, as a political gesture in the context of the six-day Arab-Israel war, the Algerian Government banned all exports to the United States and the United Kingdom and placed the Algerian operations of all British and US companies under the supervision of Algerian officials. The export ban, which lasted until early September, did not cause any reduction in oil output (since the increase in the volume of demand for Algerian oil in other markets after the closure of the Suez Canal was greater than the 5 per cent of Algeria's pre-crisis output which had been shipped to Britain and the United States), whereas gas production was cut back in view of the lack of alternative outlets for the two-thirds of Algeria's LNG exports which were normally exported to Britain at this time.

175

State supervision, which was to be maintained for an indefinite period, applied in the hydrocarbons sector to the production operations of Mobil and of the five US independents (Sinclair, Phillips, El Paso, Getty and Newmont) and to the product distribution operations of Mobil and Exxon. The only British company which had been involved in the Algerian hydrocarbons sector, British Petroleum, had withdrawn from its local downstream operations (apart from those in the specialized lubricants market) in January 1967, selling its product distribution facilities and its 10.4 per cent shareholding in the Algiers oil refinery to Sonatrach. (Royal Dutch/ Shell's Algerian interests were initially scheduled for state supervision, but this was not enforced after the authorities decided to disregard the minority British interest in the group.) The US producing companies were ordered to retain 100 per cent of their export earnings in Algeria (as opposed to 50 per cent previously), one of the main functions of the state supervisors being to ensure compliance with this regulation. In 1968 CPA became subject to the same currency repatriation requirement (although not to state supervision) after being accused by the Government of showing a "negative attitude" towards expediture on exploration work.

At the end of August 1967 the Algerian Government nationalized the Algerian refining and product distribution interests of Exxon and Mobil, thereby increasing Sonatrach's total shareholding in the Algiers refinery to 44 per cent and its share of domestic marketing outlets to about 47 per cent. At the same time the Government ordered all foreign producing companies to export their entire output of crude oil in order to give Sonatrach a monopoly over the supply of crude to the local refining industry. It was announced in January 1968 that Sonatrach was to be granted a monopoly over the domestic distribution, storage and transport of petroleum products (including LPG), this objective being achieved through the nationalization in mid-May 1968 of 12 distribution companies, 10 of which were owned by French interests and two by Royal Dutch/Shell. This was the first nationalization measure to affect French interests in the hydrocarbons sector. Compensation was to be paid, although the Government rejected the companies' initial claims as "exorbitant" given the fact that many of the assets involved had already been fully amortized.

Sonatrach's control over downstream oil operations in Algeria was consolidated in November 1968, when it purchased an additional 12 per cent shareholding in the Algiers oil refinery from CFP (the consequent distribution of shares being Sonatrach 56 per cent, Royal Dutch/Shell 24 per cent and CFP 20 per cent). More than two-thirds of the refinery's output was sold within Algeria at prices which were effectively controlled by the Government (which had ordered the then shareholders to cut their profit margin by $1.90 per tonne in 1967).

The Government had meanwhile increased the tax-reference price for crude oil exported by non-French companies to $2.35 per barrel fob Bejaia—the same level as the companies' posted price—in order to bring its revenue entitlement into line with that of Libya and other exporting countries which had secured special premiums on their Mediterranean exports on the basis of the enhanced freight advantage of "short-haul" crude in markets west of Suez following the closure of the Suez Canal in June 1967 (◊A4.13). During the first half of 1968 the Algerian Government invited the US producing companies to negotiate agreements with Sonatrach setting out revised terms for their future operations in Algeria, it being made clear that companies which refused to comply were liable to be subjected to increasingly stringent controls under the June 1967 supervision orders. However, only Getty Oil made a positive response, signing an agreement with Sonatrach in October 1968 on the following terms:

(1) Getty ceded 51 per cent of its Algerian subsidiaries' assets to Sonatrach—the main assets being 11.5 per cent interests in the concession rights to the Rhourde el Baguel oilfield

(current output 92,350 bpd) and in the exploration rights to the proved Mesdar oilfield (in which Sonatrach already held a 30 per cent interest through ASCOOP). In return, Getty was to receive an unspecified proportion of Sonatrach's resulting share of the output of the Rhourde el Baguel field for a period of four years.

(2) Sonatrach transferred to Getty a 49 per cent interest in four exploration permits covering a total area of 11,500 sq km (three of which were already held by Sonatrach, while the fourth was about to be granted). Getty would pay a premium of $2,250,000 for its share of these permits and would invest a minimum of $16,300,000 in a five-year exploration programme. Sonatrach would be liable to meet its share of total exploration expenditure only in the event of a commercial oil discovery, in which case repayments would be made to Getty out of 25 per cent of Sonatrach's share of the oil produced.

(3) The Sonatrach-Getty partnership would be formally structured as a "joint-venture association" (Sonaget) in which Sonatrach, as the majority partner, would hold operational responsibility for exploration work and for the development of any consequent discoveries. Each partner would normally be responsible for marketing its own share of oil produced, although Getty undertook to handle the marketing of part of Sonatrach's entitlement if so requested.

(4) Commercial oil discoveries in Sonaget exploration areas would be exploited under jointly-held 25-year production concessions. Exploitation rights over all natural gas discoveries would be vested solely in Sonatrach.

(5) The posted price of crude exported by Getty was raised immediately from $2.35 to $2.635 per barrel fob Bejaia, while the fiscal reference price used to value the crude for tax purposes was reduced from $2.35 to $2.195. The proportion of export earnings which Getty was required to hold in Algeria was reduced from 100 per cent to 75 per cent.

(6) Arbitration in any dispute connected with the association agreement was to be effected through the Algerian courts.

In March 1969 the Algerian Government rescinded the concession rights held by Sinclair Oil, which had recently merged with Atlantic Richfield, on the grounds that it did not recognize the merger. Sinclair's 28.5 per cent share of the concession rights to the Rhourde el Baguel field (where it had acted as operator) was reallocated to Sonatrach, as was its 28.5 per cent interest in the Mesdar field. Also in March 1969, Sonatrach increased the posted price of its own exports to $2.65 per barrel fob Bejaia, while the Government ordered all foreign producing companies except Getty to increase their postings to the same (pre-1964) level. In the case of the US companies whose operations were under state supervision, the new postings were announced in the companies' names by the supervising officials. CPA, the only non-supervised non-French producing company, refused to announce a similar posting on its own behalf. The Government's action, which had no direct fiscal impact, was seen as a tactical move in the context of Algeria's pending price negotiations with the French Government (◊C1.3.iv) and as a means of increasing the pressure on non-French companies to reach agreements emulating Getty's partnership with Sonatrach (the implied alternative to which was now a full takeover of their interests, as had been experienced by Sinclair).

El Paso Natural Gas Co., which held a 49 per cent interest in the small Rhourde Nouss oilfield, reached an accommodation with Sonatrach in October 1969, when it agreed to make annual purchases of 10,000 million cubic metres of gas from Sonatrach for export to the United States under a long-term contract. It was subsequently established that El Paso's Algerian oil rights would be taken over by Sonatrach when the LNG supply contract was finalized (finalization being dependent on the approval of the US Federal Power Commission, which was eventually given in late 1972).

Royal Dutch/Shell, Phillips Petroleum, Elwerath and Montecatini Edison all rejected formal proposals for 51 per cent Sonatrach participation in their Algerian oil interests, causing the Government to order the full nationalization of these interests in June 1970. As well as taking over Royal Dutch/Shell's 35 per cent

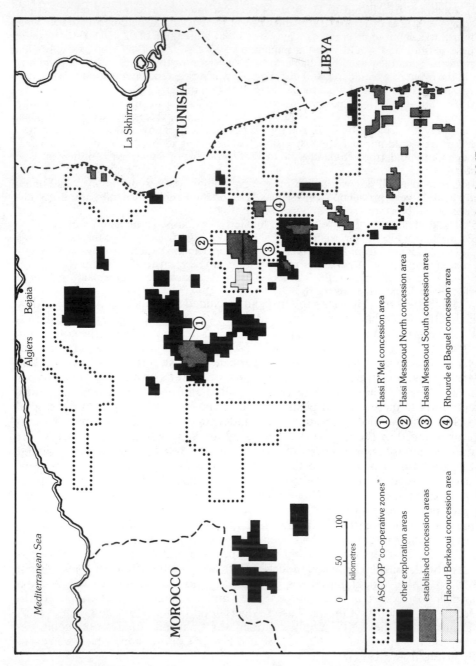

Fig. 5—Algerian exploration areas and production concessions in 1967

shareholdings in CREPS and in the La Skhirra export pipeline and its 65 per cent shareholding in CPA, Sonatrach gained the 24 per cent Royal Dutch/Shell shareholding in the Algiers refinery. Phillips had held a 25 per cent interest in a French-controlled producing consortium, while Sofrapel (Elwerath) and AMIF (Montecatini Edison) had held interests of 20 per cent and 4 per cent respectively in other consortiums. The effects of the June 1970 nationalizations were (i) to increase Sonatrach's crude supplies by about 114,700 bpd (80 per cent of which had hitherto been controlled by Royal Dutch/Shell and most of the balance by Phillips), making the state company the largest single Algerian crude producer, with overall supplies of about 314,000 bpd (nearly one-third of the national total); (ii) to increase the Sonatrach shareholding in the Algiers refinery to 80 per cent and (iii) to increase Sonatrach's overall share in the ownership of Algeria's pipeline capacity to 56 per cent.

In November 1970 the Algerian production interests of Mobil (which had been exporting about 21,600 bpd) and of Newmont were nationalized, apparently with the companies' consent, leaving Getty and El Paso as the only non-French companies in the Algerian hydrocarbons sector. Compensation settlements (calculated on a discounted cash-flow basis) were announced between August 1970 and April 1971 in respect of all the upstream and downstream nationalizations of non-French interests which had occurred since 1967. Sonatrach signed its first major contracts for the supply of crude to former concession holders in December 1970, when Royal Dutch/Shell and Mobil each agreed to purchase about 150,000 bpd for five years.

C1.3.iv—Extension of state control over French oil and gas interests

The progressive extension of state control over non-French oil interests was accompanied by growing Algerian pressure for a revision of the terms of the French companies' operations. Algeria's main grounds for dissatisfaction with the working of its July 1965 co-operation agreement with France were (i) that the ASCOOP arrangements had failed to generate a satisfactory level of spending on exploration and development work, and (ii) that the fiscal reference price fixed in 1965 was unacceptably low in the changed market conditions resulting from the closure of the Suez Canal in mid-1967.

ASCOOP had effectively taken sole responsibility for new exploration work in January 1966 (when existing French permit holders surrendered their rights, while most non-French permit holders suspended their exploration operations pending clarification of their future status). ASCOOP was unable, however, to launch its initial programme for a further seven months because of disagreements between the French and Algerian sides over the drawing up of a budget. By the end of 1968 about 50 exploratory wells had been drilled, involving a total investment 30 per cent above the minimum agreed level. Relatively few new discoveries had been made, the greater part of the cumulative oil production credited to ASCOOP at the end of 1968 (amounting to less than 3,000,000 tonnes) having been lifted from the previously discovered Haoud Berkaoui field. France attributed ASCOOP's poor discovery rate to the fact that one-fifth of the available exploration area had proved to be geologically unpromising, whereas Algeria claimed that there was a general unwillingness on the part of the French to undertake a full exploration programme in all the blocks which were considered to be promising. Sonatrach turned increasingly to the acquisition of exploration permits on its own account, and by the end of 1968 held sole rights over a total of nearly 50,000 sq km outside the co-operative zones reserved for ASCOOP.

A formal review of the effectiveness of the ASCOOP arrangements was initiated in August 1968 following public criticism by the Algerian Foreign Minister of

France's alleged lack of commitment to new exploration work. In April 1969 it was agreed that an exploration budget of F220,000,000 should be adopted for 1969 (as against an initial French proposal of F190,000,000 and an initial Algerian proposal of F300,000,000) and that France's Sopefal company should withdraw from several exploration blocks and reduce the level of its participation in others. Sopefal was to contribute 80 per cent and Sonatrach 20 per cent of the budgeted funds. Sonatrach's recently agreed partnership with Getty Oil (◊C1.3.iii) had meanwhile been purposely styled a "joint-venture association" in order to encourage direct comparison with the ASCOOP arrangements, whose terms were markedly less favourable to Sonatrach.

Although centred on ASCOOP, the controversy over the level of French investment in the Algerian oil industry also extended to the activities of established French producers. The latter were accused of failing to carry out more than a token level of long-term development work in their concession areas while at the same time maximizing their output from existing wells (which had risen considerably since the opening of Sonatrach's Arzew pipeline in 1966 ◊C1.3.i). CREPS in particular was said to be operating one of its fields at an unacceptably high production level, and was ordered during 1968 to close certain wells for conservation reasons. Objections were made to the "unrealistically low" contract prices at which other French companies were exporting some of their output to France, and from September 1968 onwards all French producing companies were required to retain at least $1 per barrel of their export earnings within Algeria.

During 1968 the differential between the fiscal reference price applicable to French producing companies and that applicable to non-French producers reached 27 cents per barrel. About 40 per cent of this was in effect a "co-operation discount" (now considered by Algeria to be unwarranted in view of France's failure to meet Algeria's investment expectations). The balance constituted a "Suez premium", which the French companies were entitled to ignore until their reference price became subject to formal review in 1969. Pending a change in the reference price, the French companies were able to export Algerian crude to France at a competitive delivered cost, whereas before June 1967 their market share had depended largely on the French Government's use of the system of franc-zone preference to restrict imports of cheaper Middle Eastern crudes.

Having informed the French producing companies that it considered their fiscal reference price of $2.08 per barrel to be "provisional" after the end of 1968, the Algerian Government made an official request to the French Government in October 1969 for the opening of bilateral negotiations to determine the taxable value of exports made by the companies after Jan. 1, 1969. The French companies' compliance with Algeria's request for a general rise in postings to $2.65 per barrel (◊C1.3.iii) had meanwhile been authorized by the French Government in April 1969 as a "goodwill gesture" made without prejudice to the renegotiation of the reference price. In July 1969 Algeria became a member of OPEC, clearly signalling the Government's intention to base its demands for an increased revenue entitlement on the situation which prevailed in other major oil-exporting countries, notwithstanding the French Government's contention that the French companies were entitled to continue to receive preferential fiscal treatment in accordance with the spirit of the 1965 co-operation agreement.

When negotiations opened in November 1969 an initial Algerian demand for parity between the fiscal reference price and the current posted price of $2.65 per barrel was countered by an initial French refusal to consider any increase in the reference price, although by June 1970 the French side was willing to accept a reference price of $2.18 per barrel for 1969, rising to $2.30 by 1975. This proposal was rejected by the Algerian Government, which broke off the negotiations and announced in the following month (i) that it was unilaterally increasing the French companies' reference price to $2.85 per barrel fob Bejaia (i.e. the posted price plus freight and quality premiums totalling 20 cents); (ii) that this increase was to be backdated to the beginning of 1969; and (iii) that the French companies would now be required to retain at least $1.80 per barrel of their export earnings within Algeria. However, after much diplomatic activity (during which the French Government indicated its preparedness to exercise its right to international arbitration under the 1965 co-operation agreement) it was announced in August 1970 that Algeria had accepted a French proposal for high-level talks on the overall revision of the 1965 co-operation agreement and had agreed to suspend the implementation of the price increase for the duration of these talks.

The talks opened in late September 1970, by which time Algeria's determination to insist on the adoption of its new reference price had been strengthened by the upturn in open-market crude prices, stemming partly from Libya's recent production cutbacks (◊**A4.13**). The success of the Libyan Government's campaign to increase its share of oil company profits, and the consequent hardening of OPEC's collective line on fiscal issues (◊**D1.6.iii**), meant that a French refusal to accept the Algerian demand for a reference price of $2.85 per barrel was countered by an increase in the Algerian demand; by January 1971 this had escalated to $2.92, with guaranteed future progression to more than $3.20 (although the retroactive tax increase for 1969–70 would continue to be based on a price of $2.85). Algeria also made it clear that it expected France to accept 51 per cent Sonatrach control of all operations covered by a revised co-operation agreement. The French Government's maximum reference price offer in early February 1971 (when the talks were suspended at France's request) was understood to be $2.65 per barrel for 1969–70 and $2.75 for 1971–75. The French companies were authorized at this point to make immediate payments to Algeria totalling F675,000,000 as an "advance" on their additional tax liabilities for 1969–70. These payments (which corresponded to a reference price of approximately $2.50 per barrel fob Bejaia) fell about F525,000,000 short of Algeria's current claim for arrears of taxes.

On Feb. 24, 1971, President Boumedienne announced that Algeria had decided (i) to take majority control, through Sonatrach, of all French oil-producing interests in Algeria; (ii) to take full control of all oil and gas pipelines, all non-associated gas fields and all production of associated gas from oil wells; (iii) to pay compensation for the assets concerned on the same discounted cash-flow basis which had previously been used to compensate non-French oil companies for the nationalization of their Algerian interests; and (iv) to price and tax crude oil exports on the basis of the prevailing OPEC formula for Mediterranean crudes.

Nationalization ordinances published on March 1, 1971, required the transfer to Sonatrach of the following French-held assets: (i) 51 per cent of the local oil interests of CFPA, Petropar (an 84 per cent subsidiary of ERAP), Société Nationale des Pétroles d'Aquitaine (SNPA, a 51 per cent subsidiary of ERAP), Coparex (French private sector), Omnirex (46 per cent CFP, 54 per cent other French interests), Eurafrep (French private sector) and Francarep (French private sector); (ii) a 22 per cent interest in the operations of CREPS (out of the 65 per cent French interest held by ERAP), giving Sonatrach 57 per cent control of CREPS; (iii) 2 per cent of the assets of ERAP's Sofrepal subsidiary, giving Sonatrach 51 per cent control of SN Repal; (iv) Sofrepal's 25.5 per cent share (held through SN Repal) and CFPA's 49 per cent share in the operations of SEHR (giving Sonatrach 100 per cent control over gas production at Hassi R'Mel); and (v) all of the French interests (ranging from 49.75 per cent to 85.5 per cent) in the Algerian operations of four oil and gas pipeline companies. A further ordinance of April 14 gave Sonatrach 2 per cent of the Algerian assets of Sopefal, thus increasing Algeria's

OPEC, ITS MEMBER STATES AND THE WORLD ENERGY MARKET

overall interest in ASCOOP operations to 51 per cent. (In the case of the Haoud Berkaoui field, CFPA's holding was reduced to 33.1 per cent and that of Sopefal to 15.9 per cent in order to achieve 51 per cent Sonatrach control.)

The assertion of majority control over ASCOOP operations was decreed two days after the promulgation of a Fundamental Law on Hydrocarbons which abolished the existing concession system and required all future foreign participation in hydrocarbon exploration and exploitation activities to be conducted through minority holdings in partnerships controlled by Sonatrach. On April 13, 1971, it was announced (i) that total compensation for the nationalized French assets had been assessed by Algeria at F550,000,000 (about $100,000,000); (ii) that tax arrears for 1969–70 were now payable on the basis of a reference price of $2.77 per barrel fob Bejaia, to be applied in accordance with the tax rules laid down in the 1965 co-operation agreement (i.e. with royalties credited against tax payments); (iii) that from the beginning of 1971 oil company taxation (at the rate of 55 per cent) was to be based on posted prices, with an expensed royalty; (iv) that a posted price of $2.70 per barrel was to apply from Jan. 1 to March 19, 1971; (v) that from March 20, 1971 (the effective date of OPEC's Tripoli agreement on Mediterranean postings ◊**D2.2.ii**, **C8.3.ii**), the posting was to rise to $3.60 per barrel, of which 25 cents represented a variable freight premium; (vi) that Algerian postings were to be adjusted thereafter in parallel with Libyan postings; and (vii) that French producing companies were to be required until further notice to retain within Algeria at least $2.95 per barrel of oil exported (thus effectively precluding the export of oil at lower realized prices).

The French Government stated on April 15, 1971, that, as Algeria had chosen to repudiate its special co-operative relationship with France, there was no point in resuming negotiations on a government-to-government basis, and that disputed issues should be settled at company level. French companies had been responsible for producing over 33,000,000 tonnes of Algeria's total crude output of 48,500,000 tonnes in 1970, of which about 25,000,000 tonnes had been exported to the French domestic market (supplying 26.5 per cent of the total French crude requirement of 94,300,000 tonnes). ERAP had obtained 17,400,000 tonnes of crude (about 80 per cent of its total supply) from Algeria in 1970, while CFP had obtained 12,900,000 tonnes (about 20 per cent of its total supply).

Although they were in a relatively weak bargaining position, not least because current market conditions provided Sonatrach with numerous openings to expand its own exports to non-French destinations, the French companies initially resisted the Algerian measures. French imports of Algerian crude were halted in late April 1971, ostensibly on the grounds that it was overpriced, while the French companies issued a general warning to Sonatrach's customers threatening legal action in respect of purchases of "nationalized" crude. There was some disruption of production, arising mainly from ERAP's continuing control over the Tunisian section of the La Skhirra pipeline and from the withdrawal from Algeria of senior production staff employed by ERAP and CFP. The French Government, for its part, contacted both the World Bank (from which Algeria was seeking finance for hydrocarbon projects) and the US Government (which had yet to approve El Paso's LNG export contract ◊**C1.3.iii**) to request that decisions on these matters be deferred until the oil dispute was settled.

By May 1971 Algeria's financial claims against the French companies, mainly for tax arrears, were reported to total as much as F1,400 million, while the companies were counter-claiming up to F4,000 million in compensation for what they regarded as the full nationalization of their Algerian producing assets (it being argued that the remaining French minority interests were "valueless" without Algerian guarantees regarding the companies' future legal and economic rights). The

Algerian Government maintained that it had offered equitable compensation terms in respect of the assets which had actually been taken over and that it was fully prepared to hold constructive discussions on the matter of safeguards for the companies' remaining Algerian production interests; there would, however, be no discussion of the companies' demand for a new international arbitration agreement, which was rejected out of hand. When it had become clear to them that Algeria had no intention of altering its basic position, the French companies modified the basis of their compensation claims and opened negotiations to settle their tax arrears and define the terms of their minority partnerships with Sonatrach. CFP and Sonatrach reached an agreement on June 30, 1971, on the following main terms:

(1) CFP undertook to pay F150,000,000 in settlement of Algeria's claim for tax arrears, while Algeria undertook to pay about F350,000,000 over seven years as compensation for the CFP assets nationalized in February 1971.

(2) Total Algérie, a wholly-owned subsidiary of CFPA, would become the 49 per cent minority shareholder in a joint operating company, Alrep, with Sonatrach holding the balance of the shares.

(3) Total Algérie was to fund 49 per cent of an agreed exploration and development programme, the initial aim of which would be to expand Alrep's production capacity by about one-third.

(4) Total Algérie would pay taxes and royalties on its equity share of Alrep's production on the basis of the new fiscal arrangements introduced in April 1971. It would be obliged to retain within Algeria a minimum sum per barrel exported ($2.75 in 1971–72).

(5) The agreement was valid for 10 years, subject to a review of its financial provisions after five years. In the event of a failure to reach agreement on the financial provisions applicable to the second five-year period Sonatrach would buy out Total Algérie's shareholding in Alrep according to an agreed compensation formula.

Outline agreement on a settlement between Sonatrach and ERAP was announced on Sept. 19, 1971, after talks which had begun on July 19. A detailed 200-page protocol was initialled in mid-November, and after approval by the Algerian and French Governments a "final" agreement between the two state-owned companies was signed on Dec. 15, 1971 (although disputes persisted over certain financial details until January 1974).

ERAP accepted an Algerian claim which assessed the company's tax arrears at F470,000,000 (representing less than half of the total financial claim initially submitted by the Algerian authorities), while its compensation entitlement was reportedly fixed at about F221,000,000. The resulting net tax liability was settled by the transfer to Sonatrach of all of ERAP's remaining interests in the Algerian operations of CREPS, Petropar and SNPA, of its 35 per cent interest in CPA, and of half of its remaining interest in SN Repal. With regard to ASCOOP operations, (i) it was agreed that Sonatrach should have a 51 per cent interest and ERAP a 49 per cent interest in future oil production from ASCOOP concession areas and from exploration areas in which commercial discoveries had already been made; (ii) ERAP accepted the reversion to the state of all other ASCOOP exploration areas; and (iii) Sonatrach undertook to repay to ERAP over five to six years a total of F275,000,000 which had been advanced to Sonatrach for exploration work undertaken within the framework of ASCOOP.

ERAP's future investment obligations as an "associate" of Sonatrach were to be determined in proportion to ERAP's remaining equity interests in the Algerian oil industry (i.e. 24.5 per cent of SN Repal's operations, 15.9 per cent of output from the Haoud Berkaoui field and 49 per cent of ASCOOP production), which it would hold through a new wholly-owned subsidiary, Elf Algérie. Agreed minimum investment targets were laid down for particular exploration and development projects. Fiscal arrangements were similar to those agreed between Sonatrach and

CFP, although ERAP's minimum obligation regarding the retention within Algeria of part of its export earnings was fixed at $2.465 per barrel in 1971–72 (calculated by deflating CFP's "obligation price" of $2.75 fob Bejaia by the cost of pipeline transport from the Algerian border to La Skhirra). All of ERAP's Algerian crude entitlement would, under a "swap" arrangement with Sonatrach, be exported from La Skhirra, with Sonatrach having sole ownership of the Algerian section of the La Skhirra pipeline and ERAP sole ownership of the Tunisian section. Like Sonatrach's agreement with CFP, the ERAP agreement was due to run for 10 years, subject to review of its financial provisions after five years, at which point Sonatrach would buy out ERAP's interests in the event of failure to agree on revised provisions.

The ERAP agreement also provided (i) for the acquisition by Sonatrach of ERAP's minor shareholding in the Arzew gas liquefaction plant; (ii) for the payment of compensation in respect of ERAP's nationalized Algerian marketing interests; and (iii) for the purchase by Sonatrach of ERAP's 50 per cent interest in Algeria's second gas liquefaction plant (then under construction at Skikda as a 50-50 joint venture between Sonatrach and ERAP). Under a separate agreement announced in mid-December 1971, CFP sold its remaining 20 per cent interest in the Algiers oil refinery to Sonatrach (which became the sole owner of the refinery). Sonatrach also acquired CFPA's 9 per cent shareholding in the Arzew liquefaction plant (bringing the plant under 49 per cent Sonatrach ownership).

Eurafrep, Coparex, Omnirex and Francarep all chose to withdraw totally from Algeria under agreements reached with Sonatrach in November and December 1971 whereby their non-nationalized interests were taken over in exchange for the writing-off of net tax liabilities. In 1972 some 77 per cent of Algerian oil production was controlled by Sonatrach (as against 30.8 per cent prior to Feb. 24, 1971), CFP's share having fallen from 25 per cent to 12.9 per cent and ERAP's share from 37.5 per cent to 9.8 per cent. CFP's agreement with Sonatrach subsequently ran for its full 10-year term (after which CFP retained only minor interests in Algeria), while ERAP terminated its agreement after five years.

C1.3.v—Oil and gas under state control (post-1971)

The settlement of the Franco-Algerian oil dispute, and the consequent restoration of normal output levels, placed Sonatrach in an exceptionally strong position as the world's ninth largest crude producer and as one of the largest sellers of non-integrated crude on the world market. Apart from consolidating its control over established foreign oil interests in Algeria, Sonatrach had by the end of 1971 (i) brought to nine the total number of new specialized service companies set up since 1966 with 49 per cent participation by foreign (mostly US) partners; (ii) acquired more than 50 drilling rigs and several tankers; (iii) built a gas pipeline from Hassi R'Mel to Skikda in preparation for the opening in 1972 of the Skikda LNG plant (which had been planned in connexion with a supply contract based on the import commitment made by France in July 1965 ◊**C1.3.ii**); (iv) virtually completed the laying of the country's fourth major oil pipeline, running to a new terminal at Skikda (from which exports began in 1972); (v) initiated the construction of an LPG and condensate pipeline, running from Hassi Messaoud to Arzew via Hassi R'Mel, together with associated processing facilities; (vi) initiated the construction of an oil refinery at Arzew (which came on stream in 1972), while inviting bids for the construction of a further refinery at Skikda; (vii) awarded a contract for the laying of a new gas pipeline from Hassi R'Mel to Arzew, and signed a provisional contract for a new LNG plant at Arzew (planned in connexion with the El Paso supply agreement); (viii) opened an ammonia/nitrogen fertilizer plant at Arzew and awarded contracts for the construction of various organic petrochemical plants;

(ix) secured export contracts for most of its crude output; and (x) negotiated a number of new LNG supply contracts.

By 1980 all of the longer-term projects planned in 1971 had been completed. The second Arzew LNG plant was brought into production in early 1978 (the remaining foreign shareholdings in the original Arzew plant having meanwhile been bought out by Sonatrach in the previous year). A 323,000 bpd refinery was brought on stream at Skikda in 1980, expanding Algeria's total refining capacity by nearly 250 per cent and enabling the proportion of products in the country's total oil exports to be substantially increased. The production of organic petrochemicals, using natural gas as a feedstock, began in 1976 at a methanol and synthetic resins complex at Arzew and was greatly expanded when an ethylene and plastics complex opened at Skikda in 1978.

It was decided in May 1980 that the state-owned hydrocarbons sector had been expanded and diversified to such a degree that the centralized management by Sonatrach of all upstream and downstream activities was no longer appropriate. In July 1981 the company (now styled l'Entreprise Nationale Sonatrach) began to devolve responsibility for certain activities—including refining, domestic product marketing, petrochemical manufacturing and the construction of industrial plant —to newly created state enterprises. By 1986 such enterprises had taken over a total of 13 "peripheral" functions in the hydrocarbons sector, leaving Sonatrach with direct responsibility only for the central business of oil and gas exploration, production, transportation and export marketing.

Foreign oil companies showed relatively little interest in forming new 49 per cent minority partnerships with Sonatrach during the 1970s, and the results of the exploration programmes funded by the few companies which did enter Algeria on this basis were in the main disappointing. Companies which participated in small commercial discoveries included Brazil's Braspetro and Spain's Hispanoil. In 1980 Sonatrach's official contract price for crude oil exports became subject to a temporary $3 per barrel "exploration surcharge", which was to be treated as an advance payment against future investments in Algeria by companies which agreed to conclude exploration contracts with Sonatrach. A total of 14 companies, including the international majors, signed joint-venture agreements after mid-1980 on terms which committed the companies to investing specified sums of risk capital, usually over periods of four years, in return for the right to receive minority shares—ranging from 35 per cent to 42 per cent—in any commercial oil discoveries (although the rights to any gas discovered would belong solely to Sonatrach).

These agreements increased the number of Algerian exploration blocks with foreign participation to 22 at the end of 1981, although Sonatrach (as the holder of 149 blocks) continued to bear sole responsibility for the greater part of Algeria's total exploration programme. No commercial discoveries had been made under the new joint-venture agreements by early 1985 (when several of the contractual exploration programmes had nearly been completed). Algeria's end-1985 proved crude reserves were about 10 per cent lower than the peak level recorded in 1971, having previously declined to 64 per cent of their end-1971 level in 1978.

Sonatrach's share of Algeria's output of crude oil (excluding condensates), which had previously stood at around 80 per cent, rose to about 98 per cent during 1981, when Sonatrach exercised its right to take over CFPA's interest in production from the north of the Hassi Messaoud field. Sonatrach's share of total oil output (including condensates) was even higher, as there was no foreign participation in Algeria's condensate production after 1971 (when Sonatrach acquired its monopoly over the exploitation of natural gas resources). Algeria's low-sulphur crude was produced at an average rate of more than 1,000,000 bpd from 1972 to 1980, over which period export demand was particularly strong in the United States market.

Thereafter there was a sharp fall in crude output as a progressive decline in export demand coincided with the introduction of a long-term strategy to maximize the life of the country's crude oil reserves while relying on increased production of natural gas and gas condensates from the Hassi R'Mel field to prevent a downturn in total hydrocarbon revenues.

Condensates accounted for 37.7 per cent of Algeria's total oil output in 1985, as against 7.7 per cent in 1979, a 47 per cent fall in the volume of crude output over this period having been partly offset by a 283 per cent rise in the volume of condensates produced. The decline in Algeria's total oil output between 1979 and 1985 was thus limited to 17.1 per cent, whereas the other main African OPEC members, Nigeria and Libya (neither of which produced non-associated gas), experienced falls in oil output of 35.9 per cent and 47.8 per cent respectively over the same period. In the absence of any formal OPEC agreement on price levels or production quotas for gas condensates, Algeria followed a highly flexible export marketing policy in this sector which contrasted with its hard line on the use of prorationing to support official crude prices.

Algeria's LNG processing capacity was increased to 29,500 million cubic metres per annum in 1981 through the extension of the Skikda complex and the opening of a third Arzew complex. Total LNG production in 1984 was, however, equivalent to only 41 per cent of this rated design capacity, the 10,000 mcm El Paso supply contract having been abrogated by the US company in 1981 after a prolonged suspension of shipments caused by a dispute over pricing. Disputes had also arisen with most of Algeria's other LNG customers as a result of a campaign by Sonatrach to achieve a substantial increase in its unit revenue from gas exports.

The 1969 El Paso contract—deliveries under which did not begin until 1978—had been drawn up in accordance with Algeria's standard procedure for pricing LNG exports in the 1960s. This procedure was (i) to use a base price up to 50 per cent higher than the originally current crude oil price on an energy-equivalence basis (to take account of the higher production costs for LNG); (ii) to fix between 80 and 85 per cent of the price for the duration of the contract; and (iii) to link the remaining 15 to 20 per cent of the price to an index of prices for manufactures. The inadequacy of this formula became apparent after the oil price rises of the early 1970s, and from 1974 to 1979 Sonatrach negotiated (or sought to renegotiate) contracts in accordance with a formula whereby the fob base price was fixed below the originally current crude oil price but was indexed proportionally to the cif prices of fuel oil and gas oil.

Weaknesses in the revised formula (arising partly from the proportional indexation system, which in practice progressively increased the differential between oil and gas prices) became apparent with the new oil price rises of 1979–80, which had the effect of reducing some Algerian LNG contract prices to as little as one-third of the average export price of crude oil on an energy-equivalence basis. Sonatrach subsequently sought to negotiate or renegotiate LNG export contracts on the basis of initial direct equivalence with the official price of its own premium-grade crudes, followed by direct indexation to price movements for a basket of eight crude oils. After an official inquiry in Algeria had found that heavy financial losses had been incurred in respect of certain LNG contracts signed during the 1960s, Sonatrach in 1980 adopted a policy of suspending supplies to some customers which rejected its new terms. This resulted eventually in most customers' acceptance in principle of the new indexation formula on condition that a basket of crudes was used to fix the original base price. Under renegotiated French contract terms the base price was between $4.77 and $5.12 per million British thermal units in 1982, whereas Sonatrach had originally sought a base price of $6.11 (representing equivalence with Algeria's 1981 crude price). Customer resistance to Sonatrach's new LNG pricing policy arose from the fact that most of the gas consumed in Algeria's export markets (i.e. the United States and various West European countries) consisted of directly piped supplies which were produced at lower cost than LNG and which were generally traded at prices related to those of fuel oils (◊**A3.2.ii**).

Algeria entered continental Europe's increasingly competitive market for directly piped gas in mid-1983 following the inauguration of a trans-Mediterranean pipeline link to Italy (built as a joint venture between Sonatrach and ENI under an agreement of 1977). An offtake schedule covering the first three years of Sonatrach's 25-year supply contract with ENI required the Italian company to increase its annual imports of piped Algerian gas to 9,000 mcm in 1985 (compared with actual imports of 6,560 mcm in 1984). The pipeline's maximum capacity of 12,000 mcm per annum was due to be available by the end of 1986. The price charged to ENI (which was finalized after high-level negotiations between the Italian and Algerian Governments in 1983) was lower than Sonatrach's export price for LNG, although higher than the price at which ENI was importing piped gas from the Soviet Union. A deadlock in the initial price negotiations between ENI and Sonatrach had delayed the opening of the pipeline for over a year. Tunisia was entitled to receive 5.25 per cent of the throughput of the trans-Mediterranean pipeline, or an equivalent cash payment, as a transit fee. Yugoslavia contracted in mid-1985 to purchase 1,000 mcm of Algerian gas per annum, delivery via the trans-Mediterranean pipeline to commence after the construction of a new link between Italy and Yugoslavia.

Algeria's production of liquefied petroleum gas increased significantly after the completion near Arzew in 1984 of a new processing and separation plant with a design capacity of 4,000,000 tonnes per annum. Exports of LPG totalled around 800,000 tonnes in 1985, when hopes of future growth were centred on negotiations for the possible supply of 300,000 to 500,000 tonnes per annum to a consortium of Japanese importers. The Algerian Government's policy of progressively restructuring Algeria's hydrocarbon exports in order to boost the relative contribution of gas and gas products was implemented in parallel with a policy of expanding the utilization of gas as an alternative to oil in all sectors of the Algerian economy. In the transport sector, gasoline prices were increased to West European levels in 1983 following the introduction of a large-scale programme to convert motor vehicles to run on propane gas. Rather more LPG was consumed within Algeria than was exported in 1985.

Sonatrach's main hydrocarbon development projects in the mid-1980s involved the bringing into production of hitherto unexploited gas fields in order to supplement production from Hassi R'Mel. As regards crude oil production, the main priority was to introduce improved recovery techniques in existing fields. Algeria's 1985 hydrocarbon revenues were provisionally estimated as $12,800 million, of which crude oil contributed approximately 26 per cent, natural gas 24 per cent, condensates 24 per cent, refined products 22 per cent and LPG 4 per cent. The Government's initial hydrocarbon revenue forecast of $10,000 million for 1986 was cut to $6,000 million in April in view of Sonatrach's switch to netback crude pricing in the prevailing market conditions.

Natural gas was expected to account for a substantially increased proportion of the 1986 revenue total following moves by Sonatrach to end direct oil-price indexation for LNG exports (such indexation having produced average 1985 fob prices in the range $3.80 to $3.85 per million British thermal units for supplies to France, Belgium and Spain). Sonatrach negotiated a revised price of $3.18 per million BTUs for its customers in these countries with effect from April 1, 1986, whereas direct indexation to the average first-quarter netback values of the previously stipulated basket of crudes would have produced an estimated second-quarter price of $2.70. (At the same time, however, the Belgian Distrigaz company cut the annual volume of its LNG purchases from 5,000 mcm to 3,000 mcm.) Sonatrach's average third-quarter export price for LNG was $2.36 per million BTUs. Agreement was still awaited in mid-1986 on a cut in the fob price of Algerian piped gas supplies to Italy, which had averaged $3.49 per million BTUs in 1985.

C2—Ecuador

C2.1—Statistical Survey

*1984
†End-1984

General
Area	283,561 sq km
*Population	9,110,000
Capital	Quito

Economy and trade
*Gross national product	$11,870 million
*Annual exports (fob)	$2,583 million (of which petroleum 63 per cent)
*Annual imports (cif)	$1,716 million
*Current account balance	−$210,000,000
Foreign exchange reserves	$653,000,000 (January 1986)

Oil (upstream)
1984 crude production	255,000 bpd (12,600,000 tonnes)
1985 crude production	280,000 bpd (13,700,000 tonnes)
†Proved crude reserves	1,400 million barrels
*Reserves:production ratio	14.9:1
Peak production year	1985 (see above)
†Cumulative crude production	1,029.4 million barrels since 1918
*Number of producing oil wells	605
Export grade: Oriente	29.7° API gravity

Oil tanker tonnage
†7 vessels	232,800 deadweight tons

Oil (downstream)
*Installed refining capacity	94,600 bpd
*Output of refined products	90,700 bpd
*Consumption of refined products	69,300 bpd

Natural gas (million cubic metres)
*Gross annual production	513 mcm
of which: (gas marketed)	(81 mcm)
(gas reinjected)	(36 mcm)
(gas flared)	(396 mcm)
†Natural gas reserves	100,000 mcm

C2.2—Political and Economic Summary

Like many of the Latin American republics which came into being after the break-up of the Spanish empire in the early nineteenth century, Ecuador has a post-independence history of political instability in which periods of constitutional government alternated with periods of dictatorship and military rule. The most recent period of military rule lasted from 1972 to 1979, when there was a return to civilian government and party politics. The 1984 presidential elections, held in January and May, were won by Léon Febres Cordero, the candidate of the National Reconstruction Front (a coalition of centre-right parties). The opposition Progressive Democratic Front coalition won a majority of seats in the unicameral Congress elected in January 1984 but subsequently lost its majority in mid-1985 after a number of deputies had switched their party allegiances. The opposition regained control of the Congress in mid-term elections held at the beginning of June 1986.

In the 1970s and early 1980s Ecuador's external policies were based primarily on its membership of Latin American regional and sub-regional organizations, including notably the Andean Group (which promotes economic integration and political co-operation and which in mid-1986 had as its other full members Bolivia, Colombia, Peru and Venezuela). Relations with the other Andean Group countries came under some strain in 1985 as a result of various economic policy initiatives by Febres Cordero administration, including in particular a major liberalization of the regulations governing foreign investment in Ecuador and the repatriation of foreign investors' profits.

Ecuador is currently the third largest oil exporter in Latin America (although it accounted for only 1.6 per cent of total OPEC production in 1985) and the country derives two-thirds of its export revenue from oil, compared with 0.5 per cent in 1971 when it was a net importer of oil. In contrast, the traditional export sector — based on bananas, cocoa and coffee—has tended to stagnate during recent years. Gold mining operations were being expanded in 1985–86 in order to offset part of the decline in unit oil revenues.

Major investments were made, and rapid growth achieved, under an ambitious industrialization programme during the 1970s. However, by 1982 adverse oil market developments, combined with unfavourable trends in the prices of non-oil exports, had contributed to severe problems in financing the country's mounting external debt. The Government subsequently co-operated closely with the International Monetary Fund in drawing up a stringent economic stabilization programme, a policy which led not only to the IMF's approval of standby arrangements for Ecuador but also to the conclusion in 1984–85 of advantageous debt-rescheduling agreements with foreign commercial banks and to the granting in 1986 of a bridging loan from the US Government (with which the Febres Cordero administration had developed particularly cordial relations). The proportion of export earnings required to service Ecuador's foreign debt (of around $7,700 million) was estimated at 30 per cent in 1985, compared with 60 per cent prior to the revision of repayment schedules. However, the effective debt-service ratio rose significantly in early 1986 as a result of the slump in oil revenues, placing the country in severe economic difficulty by the middle of the year. It was reported in June that foreign exchange reserves had fallen to a level which covered only one month's spending on imports.

C2.3—Oil and Gas Industry

Oil was discovered in 1917 in the Santa Elena peninsula, where small-scale commercial production began in 1925. Having reached a level of 9,900 bpd in 1955, output from the Santa Elena fields underwent a gradual decline, and by 1971 (the last year in which the peninsula was Ecuador's sole oil-producing region) the country was dependent on imports for about 85 per cent of its consumption. The Santa Elena concessions were relinquished to the state in 1976, when their output had fallen to around 2,000 bpd. (Since 1919 the main concession holder in this region had been Anglo-Ecuadorian Oilfields Ltd, in which Exxon held a minority shareholding from 1959 to 1963, while Burmah Oil was the majority shareholder from 1963 to 1976.)

Ecuador's first substantial oil discovery was made in April 1967 at Lago Agrio in the north of the Oriente region, where Texaco and Gulf Oil had obtained joint concession rights over large areas of the Amazon basin in 1964. Commercial production began in August 1972 after the completion of a 506 km trans-Andean pipeline (capacity 250,000 bpd) linking Lago Agrio to the port of Balao. The profits of the producing companies were assessed for tax purposes on the basis of "export reference prices" established by the Government under the terms of a hydrocarbons law enacted in September 1971.

Following the establishment in June 1972 of a state oil corporation, CEPE (Corporación Estatal Petrolera Ecuatoriana), negotiations were opened to revise the terms of the Gulf/Texaco consortium's operations. By an agreement of Aug. 6, 1973, the companies relinquished half of their joint concession area, while CEPE obtained the right to market up to 51 per cent of their output and to acquire a 25 per cent interest in their producing operations. CEPE exercised its participation rights in June 1974 (three years earlier than envisaged in the 1973 agreement), leaving Texaco and Gulf each with a 37.5 per cent interest in their remaining concession area.

A dispute subsequently developed between CEPE and Gulf Oil over various issues connected with the operations of the producing consortium, it being alleged by Gulf that CEPE was taking more than its agreed entitlement of oil and was failing to implement an agreed profit-sharing formula. Legal action was threatened by Gulf in connexion with Atlantic Richfield's purchase from CEPE of 900,000 barrels of oil whose ownership was claimed by Gulf as part of its production entitlement. The Ecuadorian Government, for its part, threatened in September 1976 to expropriate Gulf's assets without compensation unless Gulf complied with a deadline for the payment of back taxes which the company had withheld in the context of its dispute with CEPE.

This deadline having been met by Gulf, negotiations were opened in October 1976 for the company's "orderly withdrawal" from Ecuador, which took effect on Jan. 19, 1977, under the terms of an agreement signed on Dec. 31, 1976. After Gulf's withdrawal CEPE held a 62.5 per cent interest and Texaco a 37.5 per cent interest in the former Gulf/Texaco concession area, while CEPE and Texaco each held a 50 per cent interest in the trans-Andean pipeline (which was to come under the sole operational control of CEPE in 1985). The Ecuadorian Government's compensation payments to Gulf were reported to total $115,500,000 (representing the net book value of the assets acquired).

Ecuador's average annual oil production did not significantly exceed its 1973 level of 210,000 bpd until 1983 (having fallen below 200,000 bpd from 1974 to 1977). The trans-Andean pipeline operated at about 95 per cent of capacity in 1983, after which work began to expand this capacity to 300,000 bpd in order to cater for further increases in production from the Oriente region, which were authorized regardless of a cut in the country's agreed OPEC production quota from 200,000 bpd to 183,000 bpd in November 1984. The Government made it clear in 1984–85 that it regarded both of these quotas as unacceptably low in relation to its revenue requirement. The CEPE/Texaco consortium was responsible for 85.8 per cent of Ecuador's 1984 production. CEPE, operating alone, produced a further 12.2 per cent in the Oriente region and 1.6 per cent from the Santa Elena concession areas, which it had taken over in 1976. The remaining 0.4 per cent of output was produced by City Ecuatoriana Production Co. (Cepco, a 51 per cent subsidiary of Clyde Petroleum), acting as operator for a group of small independent companies which held concession rights, in association with CEPE, in the Amazon basin.

Fig. 6—Ecuadorian hydrocarbon resources and installations

Crude oil exports, which stood at 195,100 bpd in 1973, declined steadily thereafter to reach a 10-year low of 90,100 bpd in 1982 before recovering to an average 121,150 bpd in 1983–84. At the end of 1983 CEPE was marketing 75.1 per cent of total crude exports, as against Texaco's 23.7 per cent and the Cepco group's 1.2 per cent. With effect from Dec. 1, 1979, Ecuador adopted a flexible export pricing system under which its "average sales price" (which effectively superseded the official selling price) was reviewed on a monthly basis. This system was in turn replaced by spot-related pricing (⊅**D16.11.ii**) when the market collapsed in early 1986.

Ecuador's proved oil reserves fell from 5,750 million barrels in 1972 to 850,000,000 barrels in 1981, after which they doubled in the course of two years as a result of new discoveries in the Oriente region. The country's end-1985 reserves of 1,700 million barrels were nevertheless equivalent to only 30 per cent of the 1972 level, and secondary recovery techniques were being used in over 80 per cent of producing wells in the mid-1980s in order to prolong the productive life of known resources. Outside the Oriente region the main exploration area was the offshore waters of the Gulf of Guayaquil, where the extensive Amistad natural gas field was discovered in 1970. However, no commercially significant offshore oil finds had been made by the end of 1985.

Although CEPE was empowered under the 1971 hydrocarbons law to enter into new exploration and production contracts with foreign oil companies, it had little success in attracting new investment during the 1970s. By mid-1979 over 35 foreign companies were understood to have rejected opportunities to enter the Ecuadorian oil industry, partly because the financial and operational conditions laid down by the Government compared unfavourably with those in most other Latin American countries and party because the circumstances of Gulf Oil's withdrawal from Ecuador were seen as increasing the political risk factor in the investment climate under the military regime which held power at that time. Ecuador's 87.31 per cent income tax rate for oil companies was among the highest in the world and was levied in conjunction with a standard royalty rate of 18.57 per cent (although the CEPE/Texaco consortium paid royalties on a sliding scale with a minimum rate of 12.5 per cent on production below 30,000 bpd and a maximum rate of 16 per cent on production exceeding 60,000 bpd).

In view of the decline in the country's reserves:production ratio throughout the 1970s legislation was introduced in August 1982 to improve the financial terms offered to new investors. The maximum rate of income tax under a new form of service contract was fixed at 74.4 per cent, of which 44.4 per cent was basic taxation and 30 per cent the maximum rate of an additional progressive tax which increased according to the volume of production in excess of 30,000 bpd. After taking account of a 15 per cent "labour participation fee" (equivalent to a royalty) the overall government revenue entitlement ranged from 53 per cent of net profits on production below 30,000 bpd to 83 per cent of profits on production above 300,000 bpd. The new contracts were to be valid for an initial four-year term, renewable by two-year extensions for a total of 20 years. Exploration work would be financed by the contractor, whose costs would be reimbursed only in the event of commercial discoveries. There would be a guaranteed negotiable rate of return on production operations carried out by the contractor, which could be placed either on a production-sharing or a per-barrel fee basis.

Several exploration areas were opened to bids in 1983, and in early 1985 the first service contract under the new law was concluded between CEPE and Occidental Petroleum, which undertook to spend up to $50,000,000 on exploration in the north-east of the Oriente region and a further $134,000,000 on the development of any commercial discoveries. Subsequent entrants to new exploration areas included an Exxon/Hispanoil consortium and a Texaco/Shell consortium. The stated objective of the Febres Cordero administration was to attract total foreign investment of $1,000 million in 20 new exploration areas with a view to increasing the country's proved reserves to 3,500 million barrels by 1988. CEPE had latterly pursued an intensive exploration programme on its own account—surveying more territory in the 14 months to March 1984 than in the whole of the previous 10 years—but was subject to financial constraints which strengthened the case for a substantial inflow of new foreign investment.

Ecuador's domestic oil consumption increased rapidly during the 1970s (partly because of the low level of government-controlled product prices), and refining capacity was more than doubled in 1977 when CEPE opened a 55,000 bpd plant at Esmeraldas. Refining had previously been centred on two long-established plants at La Libertad, part of whose output had been marketed by CEPE since 1974. CEPE assumed sole responsibility for the domestic marketing of oil products in 1976. The overall configuration of refinery capacity was not fully aligned with the pattern of demand in the early 1980s, and some crude was sent abroad for refining, the light products being repatriated and the heavy products exported. In late 1984 CEPE announced the indefinite postponement of plans to build a new 94,000 bpd refinery in the Santa Elena peninsula, although it was intended to proceed with projects to expand the capacity of the Esmeraldas refinery to 90,000 bpd by 1987 and to build a new 10,000 bpd refinery in the Oriente region (whose existing 1,000 bpd topping plant was designed solely to meet the operational requirements of the oil industry).

Whereas associated gas from the main oilfields was processed at an LPG plant at Shushufindi, little progress had been made by 1985 in bringing the country's offshore resources of non-associated gas into production. Planning was delayed throughout the 1970s as a result of disputes between CEPE (which took over responsibility for gas supplies in 1973) and the private companies which held interests in the Amistad field, and although it was subsequently agreed that the field should be developed within the context of a gas-based industrialization project, centred on a proposed petrochemical complex in the Santa Elena peninsula, implementation of this project was not anticipated until the late 1980s.

C3—Gabon

C3.1—Statistical Survey

*1984
†End-1984
‡Revision of 1984 figures given in section **D15.1.i** (see Introduction)

General
Area	267,000 sq km
*Populaltion	1,130,000
Capital	Libreville

Economy and trade
*Gross national product	$3,320 million
*Annual exports (fob)	$2,018 million (of which petroleum 70 per cent)
*Annual imports (cif)	$880,000,000
*Current account balance	+$150,000,000
Foreign exchange reserves	$213,000,000 (February 1985)

Oil (upstream)
‡1984 crude production	150,000 bpd (7,600,000 tonnes)
1985 crude production	155,000 bpd (7,700,000 tonnes)
†Proved crude reserves	520,000,000 barrels
*Reserves:production ratio	9.2 : 1
Production in peak years	225,000 bpd (11,200,000 tonnes per annum) in 1975 and 1976
†Cumulative crude production	1,091.5 million barrels since 1957
*Number of producing oil wells	231
Export grades: Mandji	28.9° API gravity
Gamba	31.7° API gravity

Oil tanker tonnage
†1 vessel	137,800 deadweight tons

Oil (downstream)
*Installed refining capacity	44,000 bpd
*Output of refined products	23,300 bpd
*Consumption of refined products	31,200 bpd

Natural gas (million cubic metres)
*Gross annual production	2,109 mcm
of which: (gas marketed)	(71 mcm)
(gas reinjected)	(259 mcm)
(gas flared)	(1,779 mcm)
†Natural gas reserves	11,000 mcm

C3.2—Political and Economic Summary

The Republic of Gabon is a one-party state ruled by the Gabonese Democratic Party (PDG) under the leadership of President Omar Bongo, who came to power in 1967. President Bongo was both head of state and head of government until mid-1981 when, following a change in the country's Constitution, he relinquished the latter function to the Prime Minister, Léon Mébiame.

From 1910 to 1957 the country was governed as a province of French Equatorial Africa, becoming an autonomous republic within the French Community in 1958 and a fully independent state on Aug. 17, 1960. Gabon chose to remain within the French Community after independence, and has retained close bilateral links with France while participating in sub-regional affairs mainly through francophone organizations. Gabon uses French as its official language and the CFA franc (tied to the French franc) as its currency, and has a large French expatriate community. The Government pursues a pro-Western foreign policy and a free-market economic policy.

The country possesses an abundance of natural resources and is the richest in black Africa in terms of gross domestic product per capita. It is the only African franc-zone country to record regular surpluses on its trade with France, and needed to use only 15 per cent of its export earnings to cover its debt-servicing requirements in 1985. Petroleum replaced timber as the main source of export earnings during the 1960s, but oil production peaked in the mid-1970s and iron ore is seen as a main mineral export in the future. The development of extensive iron ore deposits in north-eastern Gabon will not, however, be feasible until the completion of a new railway whose construction, which commenced in 1974, constitutes Gabon's largest single development project (accounting for half of the capital budget for infrastructural development in 1986–87). Other mineral resources include manganese (of which Gabon is one of the world's largest exporters), uranium (of which Gabon is the eighth largest world producer) and gold.

Gabon had the lowest oil output and the lowest reserves:production ratio of any OPEC member in the first half of the 1980s. Estimates of Gabon's oil reserves were reduced by 1,535 million barrels (78 per cent) in 1979, and the continuation of the country's membership of OPEC in the longer term will depend on the success rate of new exploration work. The Government accepted a reduction in Gabon's OPEC production quota from 150,000 bpd to 137,000 bpd in November 1984 but made no attempt to enforce the agreed cutback.

C3.3—Oil and Gas Industry

Exploration rights covering an area of more than 115,000 sq km were granted in 1949 to Société des Pétroles de l'Afrique Equatoriale Française (SPAEF) as part of France's initiative to discover new "national" oil resources (◊A4.9). (SPAEF operated under French government control within the framework of what subsequently became the Elf Aquitaine group, whose Gabonese subsidiary company is now known as Elf Gabon.) The first oil strike was made in 1956 near Port Gentil in the central coastal region, where commercial production began on a small scale (3,300 bpd) in the following year.

After 1958 the French company concluded a number of joint-venture agreements with various partners in respect of exploration blocks within its concession area. Of the partner companies which assumed operational responsibilities, Shell discovered two new fields in southern Gabon (Gamba in 1963 and Ivinga in 1967), while Gulf Oil discovered the Lucina field (near the Congolese border) in 1971. Shell and Elf each held a 50 per cent interest in the Gamba and Ivinga fields, while production from the smaller Lucina field was divided between Shell (50 per cent), Elf (20 per cent) and Gulf (30 per cent) until Gulf's withdrawal from Gabon in 1983. Companies which acquired interests in joint ventures for which Elf Gabon took operational responsibility included Murphy Oil (both directly and through its subsidiary Ocean Drilling and Exploration Co.) and Enserch Corporation.

The Gabonese Government decided in 1973 to take a minority interest in the main

196

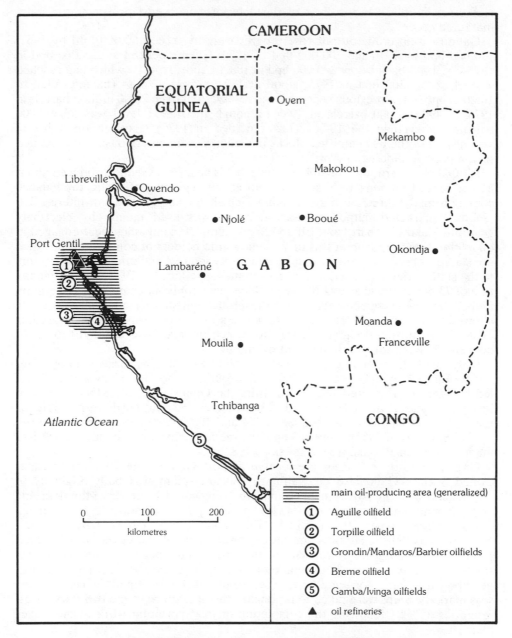

Fig. 7—Gabonese oil resources and installations

operating companies, and had by 1975 acquired 25 per cent holdings in both Elf Gabon and Shell Gabon. A state oil company, Société Nationale Pétrolière Gabonaise (Petrogab), was established in 1979 and started marketing 25 per cent of the country's oil production in October of that year. During 1981 the Government announced its intention to increase its holdings in Elf Gabon and Shell Gabon to between 35 per cent and 41 per cent in the short term and to more than 50 per cent in the longer term. However, no increase from the existing level of 25 per cent had been effected by the beginning of 1986, the Government having apparently reassessed its plans in the light of the deteriorating export prospects for state-marketed crude.

Gabon's total crude output rose progressively to exceed 50,000 bpd by 1967, 100,000 bpd by 1970 and 200,000 bpd by 1974. Having peaked at 225,000 bpd in 1975–76, it fell back below 200,000 bpd in 1980. Crude exports, which had reached a level of 205,300 bpd in 1975, stood at 139,200 bpd in 1984 (having fallen to 105,000 bpd in the previous year). Proved reserves fell from 2,200 million barrels in 1975 to 490,000,000 barrels in 1985 (although their 1985 level was 55,300,000 barrels higher than the 10-year low recorded in 1979). Exploration rights in virtually all of the uncommitted blocks in Gabon's sedimentary basin were opened to competitive bidding in April 1985.

Elf Gabon, operating in mainly offshore fields near Port Gentil, produced about 81 per cent of Gabon's total crude output at the beginning of 1980s, the balance coming from the three southern fields in which Shell Gabon held a half-interest. Elf Gabon's marketed output of associated gas was used mainly by electricity generating plants. Apart from Elf and Shell, about 20 companies were engaged in oil exploration in Gabon at this time, some as the holders of concessions in which the state reserved the right to acquire a minority interest and others as contractors to the state under a production-sharing formula introduced in 1977. An income tax rate of 73 per cent and a royalty rate of 20 per cent applied to companies operating under concession agreements, while the production-sharing contracts generally allowed the contractor to take up to 40 per cent of output until it had recovered its exploration and development costs, after which the state was entitled to receive between 75 per cent and 92 per cent of output.

Only two fields were being operated on production-sharing terms in early 1986, one by Elf Gabon and the other (Oguendjo, south of Port Gentil) by a consortium led by Amoco. Increased production from the Oguendjo field, which had been brought on stream at the rate of 20,000 bpd in late 1983, was partly responsible for the rise in Gabonese output between 1984 and 1985. Companies which reported new discoveries in 1985 included Tenneco, the leader of a consortium which had made several small offshore strikes since 1982.

Gabon's two oil refineries are located at Port Gentil. The 20,000 bpd state-owned Société Gabonaise de Raffinage (Sogara) plant was built originally in partnership with the governments of neighbouring countries to serve the domestic and regional markets, while the 24,000 bpd Compagnie Gabon Elf de Raffinage (Coger) plant, owned 70 per cent by Elf Gabon and 30 per cent by the Government, was built to supply overseas export markets. Gabon's output of refined products fell well short of capacity in the early 1980s, partly because of a contraction of the available regional market (resulting from the opening of a refinery in neighbouring Cameroon) and partly because of a lack of competitiveness in overseas markets. Steps were taken to rationalize the operations of the two Port Gentil refineries in 1984 following the completion of modernization work at the Coger plant.

C4—Indonesia

C4.1—Statistical Survey

*1984
†End-1984
‡Revision of 1984 figures given in section **D15.1.i** (see Introduction)

General

Area	1,904,569 sq km
*Population	159,890,000
Capital	Jakarta

Economy and trade

*Gross national product	$78,110 million
*Annual exports (fob)	$20,991 million (of which crude oil, condensates and refined products 56 per cent, LNG 16.5 per cent)
*Annual imports (cif)	$13,882 million
*Current account balance	−$2,044 million
Foreign exchange reserves	$4,926 million (January 1986)

Oil (upstream)

‡1984 crude production	1,410,000 bpd (68,500,000 tonnes)
1985 crude production	1,310,000 bpd (63,200,000 tonnes)
†Proved crude reserves	8,700 million barrels
*Reserves:production ratio	16.8 : 1
Production in peak year	1,690,000 bpd (83,500,000 tonnes) in 1977
†Cumulative crude production	11,463.7 million barrels since 1893
*Number of producing oil wells	4,570
*Main export grades: Minas	34.1° API gravity
Ardjuna	36.7° API gravity
Attaka	42.1° API gravity
Cinta	33.5° API gravity
Walio	34.3° API gravity

Oil tanker tonnage

†29 vessels	510,800 deadweight tons

Oil (downstream)

*Installed refining capacity	879,700 bpd
*Output of refined products	474,400 bpd
*Consumption of refined products	468,600 bpd

Natural gas (million cubic metres)

*Gross annual production	43,083 mcm
of which: (gas marketed)	(32,969 mcm)
(gas reinjected)	(6,280 mcm)
(gas flared)	(3,750 mcm)
(shrinkage)	(84 mcm)
*Annual exports (liquefied)	18,980 mcm
†Natural gas reserves	1,100,000 mcm

199

C4.2—Political and Economic Summary

Indonesia is a unitary state made up of about 13,700 islands (or, in the case of Kalimantan and Irian Jaya, parts of islands). The capital is located on the island of Java which, together with neighbouring Madura, contains 62 per cent of the total population. An executive President is elected by the People's Consultative Assembly (a partly elected and partly nominated body which is designated under the Constitution as the highest authority of the state). The Constitution enshrines five ideological principles known as the Pencasila, which include "belief in one supreme god" but do not permit the official adoption of a specific state religion. About 90 per cent of Indonesians are Moslems.

Until the Second World War Indonesia was under Dutch rule as the Netherlands East Indies, Dutch colonization of the archipelago having commenced during the seventeenth century. The archipelago came under Japanese occupation in 1942, and after the defeat of Japan an independent republic was proclaimed by Indonesian nationalist leaders in the main islands on Aug. 17, 1945. Attempts to re-establish Dutch rule were unsuccessful, and in December 1949 sovereignty was formally relinquished by the Netherlands in respect of all parts of the territory except Irian Jaya (West New Guinea), which did not become a province of Indonesia until 1963. East Timor (formerly under Portuguese rule) was occupied by Indonesia in 1975 and administratively integrated into its territory in the following year, this development being recognized neither by Portugal nor by the United Nations. Sporadic fighting between Indonesian forces and Timorese nationalists continued to be reported in mid-1986.

Indonesia's first President after independence was Dr Sukarno, under whose increasingly dictatorial rule great emphasis was placed on the pursuit of a strongly nationalistic foreign policy while the domestic economic situation deteriorated. Following his alleged complicity in an abortive communist coup in 1965, President Sukarno was obliged to cede effective power to the military, led by Gen. Suharto. The People's Consultative Assembly formally removed Dr Sukarno from office in 1967 and elected Gen. Suharto to succeed him as President in 1968. President Suharto was elected for further five-year terms of office in 1973, 1978 and 1983.

Indonesia is by far the most populous member of OPEC and the poorest member in terms of gross domestic product per capita, and its economic development programme (the implementation of which has been a main priority of the Suharto Government) has been largely financed by external aid, which was running at an annual rate of $2,400 million in the mid-1980s. Although petroleum and natural gas exports constitute Indonesia's most important source of revenue the economy is predominantly agricultural, with rice as the staple food crop and natural rubber, palm oil and coffee as the main cash crops. There is an important timber industry, while the non-oil mining sector produces tin, bauxite, nickel, copper and coal. Indonesia consults closely with other exporting countries in respect of developments affecting the world markets for copper, tin and natural rubber.

The sharp fall in the volume of Indonesia's oil exports in 1982, followed by the fall in their unit value in 1983, had a serious impact on the country's economy, necessitating a series of emergency measures which included a major currency devaluation and cutbacks in the rate of growth of government spending. Similar corrective measures were taken in response to a further deterioration in oil revenues in 1985, the growth rate of development spending being cut to 1.8 per cent in the fiscal year April 1985 to March 1986. The draft budget for 1986–87, prepared in January 1986 on the assumption of an average oil price of $25 per barrel, incorporated the first reduction in budgeted expenditure for 17 years, amounting to 7 per cent overall and 22.1 per cent for development projects. The subsequent collapse of oil prices raised the prospect of far heavier spending cutbacks in a revised budget, with attendant economic dislocation and worsening unemployment. Debt-servicing absorbed about 21 per cent of export revenue in 1985.

Indonesia is a member of the non-aligned movement, and participates in regional affairs mainly through the Association of South East Asian Nations (whose other members are Malaysia, the Philippines, Singapore, Brunei and Thailand), which has its headquarters in Jakarta. Under an ASEAN oil trade agreement signed in 1986 the three importing members (the Philippines, Singapore and Thailand) undertook to import at least 80 per cent of their crude requirements from the exporting members at times of "market oversupply", while the exporting members undertook to treat the importing members as priority customers at times of world supply shortage. The agreement applied to crude oil imported for domestic consumption, and did not affect the crude input of Singapore's large export-oriented refining sector. As the only Asian member of OPEC, Indonesia has since its accession in 1962 played an important role in broadening the range of viewpoints represented within the Organization.

C4.3—Oil and Gas Industry

C4.3.i—Development of oil industry from earliest exploration work to the ending of the concession system (1884 to 1963)

Exploration work by Dutch interests began in 1884 in north Sumatra, where the first oil strike was made in the following year, although the level of production did not become commercially significant until 1893, when it reached 2,000 bpd. The colonial authorities initially granted relatively small concession areas to a large number of independent companies, which were required to begin drilling within two years of obtaining their concessions. A refinery was built at Pangkalanbrandon in 1892 by the Royal Dutch Company for the Working of Petroluem Wells in the Netherlands Indies, which subsequently became the leading Dutch producing company and established a network of marketing outlets throughout the Far East. Marcus Samuel, a British trader who had been shipping Russian kerosene to the Far East in bulk since 1892, obtained an oil concession in Kalimantan in 1898 and, having brought an oilfield into production, built a refinery at Balikpapan in order to strengthen his competitive position in the regional market.

In 1903 The Shell Transport and Trading Company (established by Samuel in 1897) concluded agreements with the Royal Dutch Company and with the Caspian and Black Sea Petroleum Company (Bnito, controlled by the French Rothschilds) whereby each partner took a one-third share in the newly formed Asiatic Petroleum Co., whose primary function was to control the marketing of Indonesian and Russian oil in the Far East. Shell and Royal Dutch organized the prorationing of Indonesian production through a Committee of Netherlands Indies Producers, while Bnito reached a similar market-sharing agreement with the other main Russian oil producers. Although the Russian connexion was relatively short-lived (ending with Bnito's withdrawal from Asiatic Petroleum in 1917), the joint marketing experiment led to a permanent merger of the interests of Royal Dutch and Shell, which agreed to form the Royal Dutch/Shell Group in 1907 (◊**A5.1.vi**).

Asiatic's success in securing a substantial share of the regional export market, formerly dominated by Standard Oil, prompted Standard to seek its own concession rights in Indonesia. However, strong opposition from Royal Dutch/Shell (whose stance was supported by the colonial authorities) prevented the direct granting of concessions to US companies, and it was not until 1914 that an indirectly-owned Dutch affiliate of Exxon obtained exploration rights in south Sumatra. Oil was discovered in 1922, and in 1928 (after the US Government had

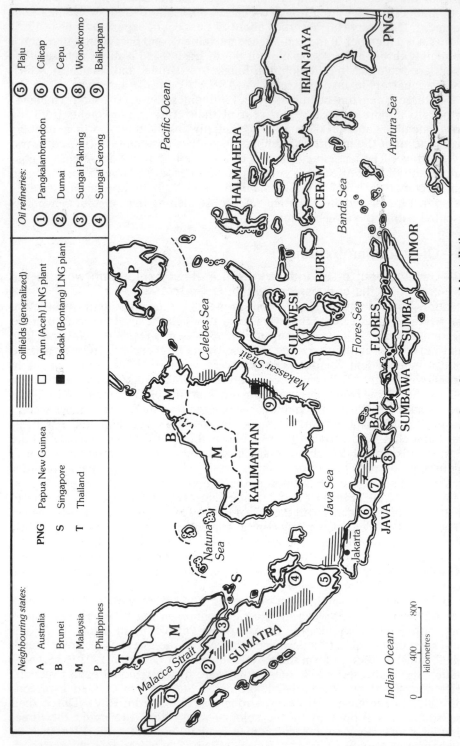

Fig. 8—Indonesian hydrocarbon resources and installations

Neighbouring states:

A Australia	**PNG** Papua New Guinea
B Brunei	**S** Singapore
M Malaysia	**T** Thailand
P Philippines	

oilfields (generalized)

☐ Arun (Aceh) LNG plant

■ Badak (Bontang) LNG plant

Oil refineries:

① Pangkalanbrandon	⑤ Plaju
② Dumai	⑥ Cilicap
③ Sungai Pakning	⑦ Cepu
④ Sungai Gerong	⑧ Wonokromo
	⑨ Balikpapan

lent its support to the company's application) Exxon was granted new concession areas in Sumatra. Having built a refinery at Sungai Gerong, Exxon in 1933 reached an agreement with Mobil (which controlled the former Standard Oil marketing network in the Far East) to form the Stanvac company as an equally owned joint subsidiary which took over its parent companies' upstream and downstream interests in Asia. Chevron had meanwhile become the second US company to obtain Indonesian concession areas, a 50 per cent interest in which was sold to Texaco in 1936 (as part of the agreement whereby the two companies formed their jointly-owned Caltex subsidiary).

Oil concessions granted during the inter-war period were normally valid for 40 years, this being the maximum duration laid down in a 1918 amendment to the country's mining law. The maximum government revenue entitlement was defined as 20 per cent of net profits. The colonial Government held a direct interest in various concessions in south Sumatra and east Kalimantan through a company called Nederlandsch-Indische Aardolie Maatschappij (NIAM), which was established in 1921 as a joint venture between the Government and Royal Dutch/Shell, with the latter holding functional management responsibilities.

Indonesia's average annual production, which had reached 100,000 bpd in 1929 and 170,000 bpd in 1939, fell to a low point of 5,700 bpd in 1946 following extensive wartime damage to oilfield installations. Mainly on the basis of reconstruction work carried out in established fields by Royal Dutch/Shell and Stanvac (the start of which was delayed because of the unsettled political situation in Indonesia), production was restored to its pre-war level in 1952, after which there was a steady increase to more than 400,000 bpd in 1960 as Caltex developed a number of major new fields in central Sumatra. All exploration and development work by the major companies took place in their pre-war concession areas, the Government of independent Indonesia having in 1951 imposed an indefinite ban on the granting of new concessions to foreign oil companies under the existing mining law. As a result of this ban the average level of new investment remained relatively low, while Indonesia's reserves:production ratio began to deteriorate and the country's share of world oil output declined. Oil company profits became subject to a 50 per cent tax rate in the 1950s.

Under the terms of an Oil and Natural Gas Act which came into force in October 1960 (i) all rights over the exploration for and the production, refining, transportation and sale of hydrocarbons were vested exclusively in state enterprises; (ii) state enterprises were empowered to appoint other companies to act as contractors on their behalf; (iii) existing concession arrangements were extended for an interim period pending the appointment of contractors; and (iv) established foreign operating companies were to receive preference when contracts were awarded. The Government subsequently increased the rate of taxation of foreign oil companies' profits from 50 per cent to 60 per cent in August 1961, and in 1962 it was decreed that Indonesia's domestic requirement for petroleum products (then about 95,000 bpd) should be supplied by the major producing companies in proportion to their shares of Indonesia's crude oil output.

Out of a total crude production of 453,400 bpd in 1962 Caltex contributed 227,600 bpd (50.2 per cent), Royal Dutch/Shell 110,600 bpd (24.4 per cent) and Stanvac 69,400 bpd (15.3 per cent). The remaining 10.1 per cent was contributed by three recently established state enterprises as follows: Permina 23,600 bpd (5.2 per cent), Pertamin 18,600 bpd (4.1 per cent) and Permigan 3,600 bpd (0.8 per cent).

Refining capacity at the end of 1962 totalled 256,300 bpd, of which 75,000 bpd was owned by Stanvac (which refined most of its own Indonesian crude output plus some of Caltex's output), 3,000 bpd by Permigan and the balance by Royal Dutch/Shell (which refined all of its own Indonesian crude output plus some of Pertamin's output). Caltex's failure to build a local refinery stemmed from the fact that it had not become a significant crude producer in Indonesia until after the Second World War, when the main growth in export demand was for crude oil rather than products. Notwithstanding the provisions of the decree imposing quota obligations on the major companies in respect of the supply of products to the domestic market (where most sales were made at a loss because of the low level of government-controlled prices), Royal Dutch/Shell remained the leading supplier in mid-1963, while Caltex made a smaller contribution than Stanvac. Product sales by state companies were limited to the immediate areas of their operations.

Permina, originally a military undertaking formed by the Indonesian Army in north Sumatra in 1957, was reconstituted in 1961 as a state enterprise under nominal civilian control. The management of Permina's two producing oilfields (in a former Royal Dutch/Shell concession area which was not returned to the company after the Second World War) was contracted to a Japanese group in 1960, while new exploration work in north Sumatra was subsequently contracted to a North American group led by the Canadian company Asamera. Pertamin was established by the Government in 1961 as the successor to Permindo, a state company which had been formed in 1958 to take control of production operations in the NIAM concession areas (although Royal Dutch/Shell, which supplied technical assistance to Permindo, retained its share in these concessions until their expiry at the end of 1960). In addition to taking over Permindo's rights and assets, Pertamin obtained new concession areas in south Sumatra, and in mid-1962 it appointed a subsidiary of Standard Oil Co. (Indiana) to act as its contractor for the exploration and development of onshore and offshore areas in central Sumatra. Permigan, the smallest of the state enterprises created in 1961, operated in the Cepu area of Java, where a concession area formerly held by Royal Dutch/Shell had come under the control of a workers' co-operative after the Second World War. The division of the state's oil interests between the army-dominated Permina, the government-controlled Pertamin and the communist-dominated Permigan reflected the prevailing "triangle of forces" in Indonesian politics in the early 1960s.

Among the contracts which Permina and Pertamin concluded with foreign oil interests in 1960–62, Pertamin's contract with Standard Oil Co. (Indiana) assumed particular significance as an indication that the terms of the Oil and Natural Gas Act were acceptable to the large independent oil companies, which had not previously operated in Indonesia. However, negotiations to establish a new contractual relationship with the local subsidiaries of the major oil companies made little progress over this period, and in May 1963 the Government announced that if the three established concessionaires did not accept new terms within one month it would act to terminate or restrict their operations. An agreement in principle was subsequently reached on June 1, 1963, after Caltex and Stanvac had held discussions with the US Government, which was reportedly concerned at the possibility that Indonesia might turn to China as a market for its oil. The main provisions of final agreements signed by Caltex, Royal Dutch/Shell and Stanvac on Sept. 25, 1963 (and ratified by Indonesia on Nov. 28 of that year) were as follows:

(1) Each company would relinquish its concessionaire status and enter into 20-year "contracts of work" with a state enterprise for crude oil production from its former concession areas. Its main functions as a contractor would be to provide investment and working capital, to take responsibility for the technical management of oilfield facilities and to handle the export marketing of at least 55 per cent of its output.

(2) Up to 25 per cent of each contractor's crude oil output would be supplied to the domestic market at cost price plus a small per-barrel fee, while the state reserved the right to handle the export marketing of up to 20 per cent of output.

(3) Each contractor would receive oil to cover its costs and depreciation charges and would retain 40 per cent of the net profits arising from its operations, with the proviso that the state's share of profits should not fall below a minimum level equal to 20 per cent of the gross oil yield.

(4) Each company would be able to operate in new areas under 10-year exploration contracts, and would be awarded contracts of work to manage the exploitation of any commercial discoveries in these areas for 20 years after the expiry of the exploration contracts.

(5) Shell and Stanvac were to sell their local distribution and marketing facilities to the state within five years and their refineries within 10 to 15 years. A formula was laid down for the current valuation and future depreciation of refining plant which would effectively reduce its value to nil within 12 years.

(6) Each company was to pay a premium of $5,000,000 to the state upon ratification of its agreement.

(7) Export income was to be assessed for profit-sharing purposes on the basis of prevailing market prices for sales to third-party customers. No special discounts could be granted without the permission of the state, which would closely monitor the level of realized prices.

The Government subsequently pursued a flexible pricing policy under which the use of special discounts was normally sanctioned when it could be shown to be a necessary means of achieving higher export sales in competitive markets. Indonesia's acceptance of a market-related revenue base contrasted sharply with the Middle Eastern system of using constant posted prices for tax-reference purposes, and the Indonesian Government had no direct interest in OPEC's subsequent campaigns to improve the state revenue entitlement under the latter system.

C4.3.ii—Oil and gas under state control (post-1963)

Notwithstanding the ratification of the 1963 agreements—under which Royal Dutch/Shell selected new exploration areas in south Sumatra and east Kalimantan, while Caltex and Stanvac selected new areas in central Sumatra—considerable uncertainty surrounded the future of the companies' operations during the remainder of President Sukarno's tenure of effective power, which saw a significant increase in anti-Western sentiment, fuelled both by the Government's ultra-nationalistic policies and by the growing political influence of the Communist Party. The operations of the three companies were placed under government "supervision and control" in March 1965, after which Royal Dutch/Shell decided to negotiate terms for a total withdrawal from all its existing upstream and downstream interests in Indonesia. Under an agreement of Dec. 30, 1965, the company's local assets were purchased by Permina for $110,000,000, payable (partly in the form of crude oil) over five years. Royal Dutch/Shell's Indonesian crude production at that time was about 68,000 bpd out of a national total of 485,000 bpd. (The company subsequently re-entered the Indonesian oil industry in 1971 on a smaller scale and with a different status.)

One consequence of the destruction of Indonesia's former balance of political forces in the aftermath of the abortive coup attempt of Oct. 1, 1965 (◊C4.2)—which led to the ascendancy of the Army, the removal of nationalist civilian politicians and the suppression of the Communist Party—was a reorganization of the country's state oil enterprises. Permigan was dissolved in 1966 and its operations transferred to the control of Permina, which was subsequently developed as the dominant state oil enterprise while Pertamin's role was progressively reduced. A new form of production-sharing contract was introduced by Permina in 1966 as a basis for future agreements with foreign oil companies, although Caltex and Stanvac (whose full contractual management powers were restored) received assurances that their existing contract of work arrangements would remain valid until the scheduled expiry dates. It was decided in 1967 that production-sharing contractors should normally be required to operate in those (predominantly offshore) exploration areas where state enterprises were least well equipped to operate on their own account.

The main features of the new production-sharing contracts were (i) that the foreign partner would finance all exploration, development and production operations (the costs of unsuccessful exploration being non-refundable); (ii) that Permina (or any successor body established by the state) would exercise control over the management of such operations; (iii) that the foreign partner would be entitled to take up to 40 per cent of oil or gas production until such time as the cumulative value of this benefit was equal to the exploration and development costs which it had incurred in respect of that production; and (iv) that the balance of production would be shared in agreed proportions between the contractor and the state (normally 35 per cent to the contractor and 65 per cent to the state). The contracts were valid for 30 years, provided that commercial discoveries were made within the first 10 years. Over 40 companies (including the international majors) had signed such contracts by 1971, these contractors being responsible for the discovery of many of the 43 new hydrocarbon deposits which were proved in Indonesia between 1968 and 1972.

Pertamin was formally merged with Permina in 1969 to form a single state hydrocarbons corporation, Pertamina (Pertambangan Minyak dan Gas Bumi Nasional). With effect from Jan. 1, 1972, the corporation was renamed Perusahaan Tambangan Minyak dan Gas Bumi Negara (but retained its existing acronym) in accordance with a law of 1971 which confirmed Pertamina's exclusive statutory authority over every stage of the commercial exploitation of Indonesia's oil and gas reserves from exploration to marketing and which set out the terms of reference governing every aspect of its operations. The new law required Pertamina to observe the principle of production-sharing, as opposed to profit-sharing, in all future contractual agreements with foreign oil companies, and expressly ruled out the possibility of any renewal of the remaining pre-1966 contracts of work upon their expiry.

In August 1976 the terms of production-sharing contracts were renegotiated for existing contractors, and revised for future contractors, (i) to reduce the proportion of output which was set aside after the commencement of production in order to cover the foreign partner's exploration and development costs (in respect of which a new amortization formula was introduced) and (ii) to increase Pertamina's share of the balance of oil production from 65 per cent to 85 per cent. The standard production-sharing formula for natural gas was fixed at 70 per cent to Pertamina and 30 per cent to the foreign partner. (The state's share of export profits arising from contract of work operations had earlier been increased by about $1 per barrel in April 1976.) A new form of agreement, the joint venture contract, was introduced in 1977 as an additional basis for foreign investment in the Indonesian hydrocarbons industry. Such agreements provided (i) for all exploration and development costs to be borne equally by Pertamina and the foreign contractor and (ii) for all output to be divided in the proportions which applied to the greater part of output under the standard production-sharing contracts (i.e. 85:15 in favour of Pertamina for oil and 70:30 for gas).

The 1976–77 revisions of contract terms took place against the background of a major financial crisis in Indonesia which followed the revelation that Pertamina had accumulated total foreign debts in excess of $10,500 million in connexion with various operations carried out without the knowledge of the Government. The Government took responsibility for Pertamina's debts and subsequently exercised much closer control over the management of the corporation's affairs. Following the dismantling of the extensive non-oil business empire which it had built up prior to 1975, Pertamina had by early 1979 reverted to its statutory role as an oil and gas enterprise.

Foreign investment in the Indonesian hydrocarbons sector, which fell during the Pertamina crisis, had been resumed at record levels by the early 1980s, expenditure on exploration, development and production being estimated at $3,000 million in 1981. Over 60 production-sharing contracts were in force in 1983, at which point Indonesia's investment terms were generally considered to be more attractive than those currently available in many other oil-producing countries, and increasingly large cash premiums were paid to Pertamina by foreign companies on signature of new contracts. However, the total volume of oil production, which had first exceeded 1,000,000 bpd in 1972, was reduced in the depressed market conditions of 1983 to a level 21 per cent below its 1977 peak of 1,690,000 bpd.

During the period 1979–83 Pertamina, operating on its own account, produced an average 5 per cent of Indonesia's oil output. About half of the balance was produced by up to 20 foreign operators holding production-sharing contracts and half by the four leading US majors from their remaining contract of work operations. Around 38 per cent of the country's oil exports were marketed by Pertamina (which held a half-interest in three trading companies, two of which operated in Japan and the third in both Japan and the United States). About 36 per cent of exports were marketed by foreign companies operating under contracts of work and 26 per cent by production-sharing contractors.

The largest single producing interest was that of the Chevron/Texaco partnership, which was responsible for (i) up to 45 per cent of Indonesia's total oil output through the operations—mainly on contract of work terms—of Caltex, and (ii) about a further 4 per cent through the joint operations—mainly on production-sharing terms—of Calasiatic (California Asiatic Oil Co., wholly owned by Chevron) and Topco (Texaco Overseas Petroleum Co., wholly owned by Texaco). The legal framework governing most of Caltex's operations changed on Nov. 28, 1983, with the expiry of the company's main contracts of work and their conversion into production-sharing contracts (as agreed in principle in August 1971).

The basis of the new Caltex contracts was an 88:12 division of shared oil production in favour of Pertamina—i.e. a somewhat higher state share than the 85:15 division applying to other foreign operators. (Pertamina was reported to have proposed a 95:5 division at the start of negotiations with Caltex in 1982.) It was stated by Pertamina in November 1983 that Caltex had undertaken to invest $3,060 million in Indonesia during the period of the contracts, which were due to expire in 2001. Stanvac's main contract of work areas in south Sumatra, where production had declined since 1963, were taken over by Pertamina when the original contracts expired in 1983.

Apart from Calasiatic/Topco, the main producers under production-sharing contracts prior to November 1983 were Japan Petroleum Exploration Co., Atlantic Richfield, Independent Indonesian American Petroleum Co. (a subsidiary of Diamond Shamrock Corp.), CFP, Mobil and Union Oil of California.

Indonesia has up to 40 potentially petroliferous sedimentary basins, and it was estimated in 1985 that as little as 30 per cent of their total area (mostly in the more easily accessible regions of the archipelago) had so far been geologically explored. During the early 1980s there was an extremely high success rate in exploratory oil drilling operations (e.g. 50 per cent in 1982), and future prospects were considered to be very favourable. Indonesia is particularly dependent on a sustained flow of new investment into both exploration and production activities because the majority of its oilfields are relatively small and require extensive use of secondary recovery techniques to prolong their productive capacity. Offshore oil production commenced in the Java Sea in the early 1970s, since when an increasing proportion of exploration work has been undertaken in offshore areas (which are expected to yield two-thirds of all future oil discoveries).

The level of new oil exploration work reached a peak in 1983, after which there was a shift of emphasis towards the development of existing discoveries. Only four new contracts were concluded with foreign oil companies in 1984–85, compared with an average of 10 per year from 1979 to 1982, this decline being attributed in part to the introduction in 1984 of new tax regulations which effectively eliminated Indonesia's competitive edge over other countries in attracting foreign oil investment. The Government indicated in late 1985 that it was in the process of revising the tax regulations to achieve a "more satisfactory" balance between the provision of adequate incentives for new investment and the protection of the state's revenue base at a time of severe economic difficulty.

Non-associated gas played an increasingly important role in the Indonesian economy as the oil market weakened during the first half of the 1980s. Exports of liquefied natural gas (which began in 1977) contributed $3,800 million (29.7 per cent) to the hydrocarbon sector's total export earnings in 1985, as against $2,510 million (14.2 per cent) in 1981. There are liquefaction plants at Badak (Kalimantan) and Arun (Sumatra) whose construction was financed by Japanese interests in the context of agreements for the supply of guaranteed volumes of gas to Japan under long-term contracts. The combined processing capacity of the two plants in 1984 was 21,500 million cubic metres per annum. Indonesia displaced Algeria as the world's largest LNG exporter from 1980 to 1982, was ranked second behind Algeria in 1983, and regained its predominant position in 1984. LNG export prices were indexed to its official oil prices in 1980. Additional production facilities were being completed at Arun in 1986 to fulfil a 20-year LNG supply contract with South Korea, while a projected expansion of capacity at Badak was dependent on the finalization of a similar contract with Taiwan. Gas condensates constituted nearly 10 per cent of Indonesia's total oil output in the mid-1980s. Pertamina signed a 10-year contract in mid-1986 for the annual supply of 1,950,000 tonnes of liquefied petroleum gas to a consortium of seven Japanese importers.

Indonesia has nine oil refineries, all operated by Pertamina except a small plant at Cepu which forms part of a research and training centre run by the Indonesian Petroleum Institute (Lemigas). Pertamina was unable to supply the full range of domestic product requirements at the beginning of the 1980s, when much of its installed capacity was outdated and inefficient, with a disproportionately high output of residual products (whereas the main increase in domestic demand was for middle distillates). There was a growing reliance during the 1970s on product imports from Singapore (the main regional refining centre) within the framework of a complex pattern of two-way trade in oil between the two countries, a central feature of which was the refining of Indonesian crudes in Singapore. However, between August 1983 and February 1984 major modernization programmes were completed at three Indonesian refineries (at Balikpapan, Cilicap and Dumai) with the aim of eliminating the country's net imports of refined products. The full commissioning of the upgraded capacity was delayed for some time by technical problems, most of which had been resolved by 1986.

Indonesia was OPEC's largest producer of inorganic petrochemicals in the first half of the 1980s, with an average annual output of more than 1,000,000 tonnes of ammonia. Planning for the development of a substantial organic petrochemical industry was seriously disrupted as a result of the deterioration in Indonesia's economic position after 1982, and the prospects for the implementation of the main projects in this sector remained in doubt in mid-1986. A gas-based methanol plant on Bunju Island (off the east coast of northern Kalimantan) was, however, inaugurated in August 1986, three years later than originally planned. The plant had an annual capacity of 330,000 tonnes.

Government planning for the hydrocarbons sector takes account of the fact that a continuing reliance on oil as the main domestic energy source will—given the country's large population and considerable development needs—lead to a progressive reduction in export capacity with adverse balance-of-payments implications. Domestic oil consumption, stimulated by government price subsidies, rose at an average rate of 12 per cent per annum from 1973 to 1980. A sharply reduced average growth rate of 0.8 per cent was recorded during the period 1981–85, when progressive cuts were made in the level of subsidy. The aim of the country's energy planners is to reduce oil's share of domestic energy use from around 80 per cent to around 60 per cent by the end of the 1980s, while increasing the usage of hydro-power, coal, natural gas and geothermal energy.

A notable feature of Pertamina's oil marketing policy in 1985 was the introduction in March of that year of a new export grade, Sumatran Medium, with an initial official selling price of $27.40 per barrel. This move followed a decline in the competitiveness of Indonesia's main light grade (34.1° Minas blend) in upgraded refineries in Japan and Singapore, which had turned increasingly to China's cheaper medium export grade. Sumatran Medium was variously reported to be either a constituent crude of the Minas blend or a new blend of light and heavy crudes. Pertamina was by 1985 handling the marketing of an estimated 56 per cent of Indonesian oil exports.

The state corporation adopted a highly competitive flexible pricing policy during the market upheaval of early 1986, negotiating spot-related discounts on its nominally unchanged official prices rather than entering into netback contracts. The formal retention of official prices (which did not apply to the fiscal valuation of oil exported by foreign producing companies) was generally regarded as a bargaining counter in negotiations on gas prices (hitherto index-linked to official crude prices). Pertamina was reported in mid-1986 to be offering a 20 per cent cut in its end-1985 export price for LNG, whereas its customers were pressing for a cut which more fully reflected the extent of the fall in the market value of crude oil in the first half of 1986.

In the first trade agreement between the two countries since the mid-1960s, China contracted in April 1986 to purchase 1,500,000 barrels of crude from Indonesia at an undisclosed spot-related price which was competitive with the delivered cost in southern China of crude produced in that country's northern oilfields. Further such sales to China were anticipated while crude prices remained at low levels.

C5—Iran

C5.1—Statistical Survey

*1984
†End-1984

General
Area	1,648,000 sq km
*Population	43,410,000
Capital	Tehran

Economy and trade
*Gross national product	$114,920 million
*Annual exports (fob)	$13,979 million (of which petroleum 98 per cent)
*Annual imports (cif)	$16,540 million
*Current account balance	−$2,300 million

Oil (upstream)
1984 crude production	2,195,000 bpd (109,300,000 tonnes)
1985 crude production	2,225,000 bpd (110,500,000 tonnes)
†Proved crude reserves	48,500 million barrels
*Reserves:production ratio	60.5 : 1
Production in peak year	6,060,000 bpd (301,200,000 tonnes) in 1974
†Cumulative crude production	33,027.8 million barrels since 1913
Number of producing oil wells	547 in mid-1979 (extent of subsequent decline not known)

Export grades (onshore):
Iranian Light	34° API gravity
Iranian Heavy	31° API gravity

Export grades (offshore):
Darood	34° API gravity
Foroozan	31° API gravity
Rostam	35° API gravity
Salman	34° API gravity
Sirip Blend	25° API gravity

Oil tanker tonnage
†15 vessels	1,713,400 deadweight tons

Oil (downstream)
*Installed refining capacity	615,000 bpd
*Output of refined products	618,000 bpd
*Consumption of refined products	723,000 bpd

Natural gas (million cubic metres)
*Gross annual production   ....   30,500 mcm
   of which: (gas marketed)   ....   (13,500 mcm)
          (gas reinjected)   ....   (10,000 mcm)
          (gas flared)   ....   (6,500 mcm)
          (shrinkage)   ....   (500 mcm)
†Natural gas reserves   ....   13,600,000 mcm

C5.2—Political and Economic Summary

Iran is the modern successor state to the Persian Empire, the 2,500th anniversary of whose foundation was celebrated in 1971. Imperial rule by the Pahlavi dynasty (which had succeeded the Qajar dynasty in 1925 ◊A4.5.i) ended with the overthrow of Shah Mohammed Reza Pahlavi in 1979, which was followed by the establishment of an Islamic republic in which Ayatollah Ruhollah Khomeini effectively holds supreme political power by virtue of his position as the spiritual leader of the country's Shi'ite Moslems (who make up over 95 per cent of the total population). In ethnic terms, about half of the Iranian population are Persians, slightly more than a quarter are Azerbaizhanis and the remainder are Kurds, Arabs, Baluchis and Turkomans.

Since October 1981 the post of President of the Republic has been held by Hojatolislam Seyed Ali Khameini (a cleric who received his religious training under Ayatollah Khomeini), and that of Prime Minister by Hossein Moussavi (a leading Islamic layman). Members or supporters of the clerically-led Islamic Republican Party form the predominant element in the Islamic Consultative Assembly (Majlis), to which elections were held in 1980 and 1984.

The introduction of a political system founded on Islamic fundamentalism occurred as a reaction to what the country's new leaders regarded as an undermining of traditional values during the rule of the Shah, whose initial modernization programme (launched as the "white revolution" in 1963) had developed into a massive drive to bring about Iran's rapid transformation into one of the world's major industrialized powers. The Shah was the prime mover of the major increase in oil prices at the beginning of 1974 (◊D4.6), and had until mid-1977 remained strongly opposed to Saudi Arabia's more moderate line on OPEC pricing policy.

Within Iran the 1979 revolution was accompanied by political turmoil and considerable economic disruption. Externally, it caused a short-term dislocation of oil supplies which was followed by successive rounds of price increases; it radically altered key aspects of Iranian foreign policy, and in particular destroyed the former close relations with the United States; and it called into question the political stability of "modernizing" governments throughout the Islamic world. There was a progressive breakdown in Iran's relations with Iraq in the aftermath of the revolution, leading eventually to the outbreak of a full-scale war between the two OPEC members in September 1980, when Iraq repudiated a 1975 border agreement.

The basic economic strategy laid down by the republican Government when it first came to power was to restrict Iran's oil production to the minimum level necessary to finance a programme in which a number of larger industrialization schemes were abandoned or scaled down, priority being given instead to broadly-based infrastructural development and to the needs of the agricultural sector. Specific sectoral targets for the five years from 1983 were established in a $169,000 million development plan published in 1982, implementation of which was subsequently impeded by a combination of war-related disruption, adverse oil market trends and factional disputes over economic policy.

By 1985 Iran had sustained total war damage in excess of $100,000 million (according to Western estimates which took account of rebuilding costs and the value of lost output) and was experiencing a growing shortage of foreign exchange for purposes other than military spending and imports of foodstuffs. The collapse of world oil prices in the first half of 1986 greatly increased the economic strain of sustaining the war with Iraq, which after more than five years had given neither side a decisive advantage at the battlefront despite a number of major offensives marked by heavy casualties on both sides. All external mediation initiatives had failed to establish a viable basis for a non-military solution to the conflict, Iran having insisted that no peace negotiations could take place while Sadam Hussein remained President of Iraq.

The bitter conflict between Iran and Iraq had an increasingly serious impact on OPEC affairs as the sharing of a group production ceiling—a highly sensitive issue which had generally been evaded during the 1970s—came to dominate the Organization's agenda from 1982 onwards. Each side in the Gulf war saw the restriction of the other side's oil exports as a key strategic factor in the war. Iraq's Gulf export terminals were destroyed at the start of the conflict, while its Mediterranean outlets were shut down in 1982 by Syria, whose own consequent losses were covered by Iran in the form of free and preferentially-priced oil supplies. Iraq in turn restricted Iran's export capacity by mounting a sustained campaign of aerial attacks on Iranian loading terminals and export routes. Saudi Arabia and Kuwait acted as Iraq's main financial backers, thereby placing their own oil export routes under threat of retaliatory attacks by Iran. Tensions in the Gulf region were heightened by Saudi Arabia's agreement to open up a Red Sea export route for Iraq in 1985 via a new link to its own pipeline system.

In these circumstances, Iranian objections to a formal increase in Iraq's OPEC production quota constituted a major obstacle to the conclusion of a revised agreement on production-sharing in 1985, and it was not until Iran had agreed to ignore Iraq's "overproduction" that the OPEC Conference was able to reach an interim accord on production cutbacks in August 1986. Having lacked the capability to achieve a substantial increase in its own oil exports during 1986, Iran apparently considered that its overriding strategic interest at this point lay in securing a reversal of the recent growth in the Arabian peninsula producers' share of Middle Eastern oil income, which had effectively shifted the regional power balance in Iraq's favour.

C5.3—Oil and Gas Industry

C5.3.i—From the D'Arcy concession to the overthrow of Mossadeq (1901 to 1953)

A 60-year oil concession covering about 1,250,000 sq km—i.e. the whole territory of Iran with the exception of five northern provinces—was granted to William Knox D'Arcy, a British subject, in 1901. (In the context of the regional balance of power at this time northern Persia was regarded as a Russian sphere of influence and southern Persia as a predominantly British sphere of influence.) D'Arcy, in partnership with the Burmah Oil Company, made a major oil find in the southwestern province of Khuzestan in 1908, and in the following year the Anglo-Persian Oil Company (subsequently British Petroleum) was formed to take responsibility for the development of the Iranian concession area. Commercial production commenced in 1913 at the rate of 5,000 bpd after the company had constructed an oil pipeline—the first in the Middle East—to transport crude to a refinery on the island of Abadan in the Shatt al-Arab waterway.

The Iranian Government's main revenue entitlement under the D'Arcy concession agreement was defined as an amount equal to 16 per cent of the net annual profits of the company or companies formed to exploit the concession. (The Government also received an initial cash premium of £20,000, shares in the concessionaire company to the same value and a fixed annual payment equivalent to about $1,800.) After the start of commercial production various disagreements arose between the Anglo-Persian Oil Co. and the Iranian Government which challenged the validity of the company's procedures for calculating its net profits (with particular reference to the accounting treatment of the activities of subsidiaries operating outside Iran).

Following the overthrow of the Qajar dynasty in 1925 there was increasing Iranian pressure on the company for a settlement of disputed issues. Prolonged negotiations led to the conclusion of a draft agreement in early 1932 (the company having meanwhile refused to pay Iranian income tax, introduced under a law of 1930, on the grounds that this was not a feature of the 1901 concession agreement). The company subsequently submitted accounts for 1931 (a year of depressed world oil market conditions) on the basis of which the payment of profits to the Government was to be cut by more than 71 per cent relative to the previous year's payment, although in volume terms Iran's oil production had fallen by only 3.2 per cent (to 121,000 bpd) in the same year.

The Iranian Government rejected both the 1931 royalty calculation and the draft agreement on future accounting practices, and in November 1932 announced the cancellation of the 1901 concession agreement. Iran's right to cancel the concession was challenged both by the company and by the British Government, which referred the matter to the Council of the League of Nations in the following month. In early 1933, however, negotiations were resumed between the company and the Iranian Government, causing the League of Nations to suspend its consideration of the dispute, and in April of that year agreement was anounced on the terms of a new 60-year concession to replace the D'Arcy concession of 1901. The 1933 concession agreement provided (i) for fixed royalty payments of four shillings per ton of oil produced; (ii) for additional payments to be made on a scale related to the volume of oil production in exchange for exemption from Iranian taxes; (iii) for the payment to the Iranian Government of dividends equal to 20 per cent of the amount by which the company's annual distributed earnings exceeded £671,250; (iv) for guaranteed minimum total payments to the Government in any one year; (v) for the reduction of the total concession area to about 250,000 sq km, consisting of blocks within the previous concession area to be selected by the company within six years; and (vi) for a reduction in the prices of oil products supplied to the Iranian domestic market.

The company also undertook (i) to develop the Naft-i-Shah oilfield, situated well to the north-west of its main producing area, (ii) to build a refinery to process crude from the field and (iii) to market the refinery's output of oil products within Iran. The Naft-i-Shah field (the eastern half of a cross-border reservoir whose western half was Iraq's Naft Khaneh field ▷C6.3.i) had been proved by the company in 1927 but had not been brought into production because of its relatively small size and its remoteness from established export facilities. Large areas of northern and central Iran had meanwhile continued to depend on imports of oil products from the Soviet Union pending a northward extension of the fairly limited internal marketing network based on the Abadan refinery (which exported the greater part of its output). The Naft-i-Shah field was brought into production by Anglo-Persian in 1934 to supply crude to a small refinery at Kermanshah.

The Anglo-Iranian Oil Co. (which changed its name from Anglo-Persian in 1935) continued to be responsible for Iran's entire oil output of 214,100 bpd in 1939, no commercial discoveries having been made by the holders of various exploration licences granted in respect of parts of the country outside the company's concession

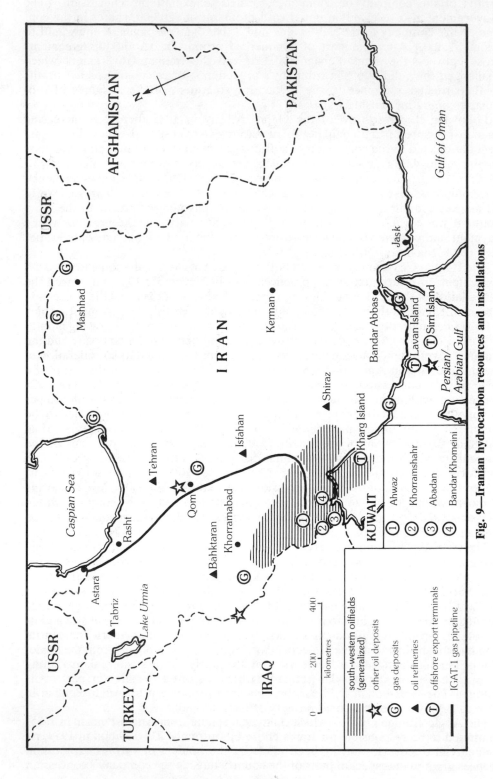

Fig. 9—Iranian hydrocarbon resources and installations

area. During the Second World War, when British, US and Soviet troops were stationed in Iran, oil companies from all three countries made unsuccessful attempts to secure new concessions. A 1946 oil agreement between Iran and the Soviet Union in respect of the northern provinces (which were then under continuing Soviet occupation) was not ratified after the subsequent withdrawal of the Soviet forces. Under an oil law of October 1947 (i) the 1946 agreement was formally declared to be void; (ii) a total ban was placed on the granting of new oil concessions to foreign interests; and (iii) the Government was required to renegotiate the terms of the existing 1933 concession insofar as these were considered to impair Iran's sovereign rights over its natural resources.

In July 1949 a supplemental oil agreement was signed by the Iranian Government and the Anglo-Iranian Oil Co. under which (i) royalty payments were to be increased to six shillings per ton; (ii) the rate of annual "tax exemption" payments was to be increased to a flat one shilling per ton as against the (recently increased) existing rates of one shilling per ton on the first 6,000,000 tons and nine pence per ton thereafter; (iii) the Government was to receive an amount equivalent to 20 per cent of the company's existing general reserve fund and subsequent payments at the rate of 20 per cent of all future allocations to this fund; (iv) there was to be a guaranteed minimum annual payment in respect of dividends and transfers to the general reserve; and (v) the company was to give increased discounts on the price of oil supplied to the Iranian domestic market. The main financial provisions of the agreement were to be retroactive to the beginning of 1948.

Ratification of the agreement by the Majlis (lower house of Parliament) was effectively blocked by opposition members for the remaining period of the current parliamentary term. In June 1950 a newly elected Majlis voted to refer the agreement to a special oil commission, which in November 1950 unanimously recommended against its ratification. The Iranian Government withdrew its existing bill in late December 1950 and announced that it would seek to negotiate improved terms with Anglo-Iranian. Parliament formally accepted the oil commission's report in January 1951 and requested the commission to submit its own recommendations within two months.

Following the assassination in early March 1951 of the Iranian Prime Minister, Gen. Ali Razmara (who had advocated renegotiation of the draft supplemental agreement rather than abrogation of the 1933 concession agreement), the oil commission of the Majlis recommended the nationalization of Anglo-Iranian's operations. A bill for the immediate nationalization of the oil industry was passed in late April, at which time Dr Mohammed Mossadeq, the strongly nationalistic chairman of the oil commission, became Iran's Prime Minister and declared that the implementation of the new law was his Government's main priority. Under the nationalization law the status of the "former" Anglo-Iranian Oil Company's entire local and expatriate staff within Iran was deemed to be that of employees of a new state-owned National Iranian Oil Company (NIOC), which was established to take over the running of the industry. NIOC was to follow a sales policy which gave priority to existing buyers of Iranian oil, and 25 per cent of the new company's profits were to be set aside to meet any compensation claims by Anglo-Iranian.

The then British Labour Government (despite being itself committed to the general principle of nationalization) opposed Iran's action on the legal grounds that it constituted a breach of the 1933 Iranian oil concession agreement, which had provided for the settlement of disputes by arbitration. However, Britain's assertion that Iran had no right under international law unilaterally to abrogate the agreement was countered by an Iranian refusal to recognize the original validity of the agreement, which, it was claimed, had been imposed on Iran under duress. The US Government, which was concerned partly about the strategic implications of an interruption to Iran's oil production, attempted without success to mediate in favour of a negotiated solution. The International Court of Justice, to which the British Government first submitted its case in May 1951, ruled in July 1952 that it had no jurisdiction in the dispute, partly because the 1933 concession agreement did not constitute an international treaty between the British and Iranian Governments.

The Anglo-Iranian Oil Company, for its part, claimed legal ownership of oil produced by NIOC and threatened court action against the buyers of any exported oil. One cargo, en route to Italy, was held in June 1952 in Aden (then a British colony), whose Supreme Court made an interim injunction in Anglo-Iranian's favour pending the International Court's ruling on the British Government's case. Several months after the International Court's ruling the company was granted possession of the Aden cargo, but was unsuccessful in legal actions brought elsewhere (e.g. in Japan and Italy) during 1953 in respect of other oil export shipments from Iran.

However, the total volume of oil which NIOC was able to export during the nationalization dispute was negligible, since all the main international oil companies boycotted supplies from Iran to demonstrate their support for the legal position adopted by Anglo-Iranian. The US majors, together with a number of independent companies, obtained US government approval in June 1951 for an agreement to pool their resources at every stage of the international oil industry "in order to aid friendly foreign countries which might lose their supplies from Iran". A dramatic fall in Iranian oil production—to an average 27,000 bpd throughout 1952 and 1953—was offset largely by increases in the output of concessionaire companies in the other main exporting countries (with Anglo-Iranian's own principal increase occurring in Kuwait). Prior to the dispute Iran had been the Middle East's largest crude producer, with an output in 1950 of 664,300 bpd, about three-quarters of which was processed at what was then the world's largest refinery at Abadan.

Despite the deterioration in Iran's economic position as a result of the virtual cessation of government oil revenues, the Mossadeq Government refused all proposals for a negotiated settlement put forward not only by Britain (with which it broke off diplomatic relations in October 1952) but also by the United States. The situation remained deadlocked until August 1953, when Dr Mossadeq was overthrown in a coup led by supporters of the Shah, who had himself been briefly forced into exile after unsuccessfully attempting to dismiss his Prime Minister. It is now generally accepted that the US Central Intelligence Agency and the British security services played a key role in organizing the coup of 1953.

C5.3.ii—Establishment of IOP consortium

The oil dispute was subsequently settled on the basis of proposals worked out by Anglo-Iranian and the other major oil companies which led to the formation in September 1954 of an eight-member consortium called Iranian Oil Participants (IOP), Anglo-Iranian having accepted that it would not be permitted to resume the position of sole operator. Shareholdings in IOP were initially distributed as follows: British Petroleum (formerly Anglo-Iranian) 40 per cent, Royal Dutch/Shell 14 per cent, Chevron 8 per cent, Exxon 8 per cent, Gulf 8 per cent, Mobil 8 per cent, Texaco 8 per cent and CFP 6 per cent. However, in April 1955 the holdings of Chevron, Exxon, Gulf, Mobil and Texaco were each reduced to 7 per cent in order to permit the acquisition of a 5 per cent shareholding in IOP by Iricon Agency Ltd, owned by US independent oil companies (which had made strong representations to the five US majors and to the US Government regarding the creation of an "independent" shareholding in IOP). Iricon originally represented nine companies, whose number was later reduced through mergers to six, namely Aminoil (16⅔ per cent holding in Iricon), Atlantic Richfield (33⅓ per cent), Conoco (8⅓ per cent), Charter Oil (16⅔ per cent), Getty Oil (16⅔ per cent) and Sohio (8⅓ per cent).

The main features of IOP's settlement with the Iranian Government, which was ratified in October 1954, were as follows:

(1) NIOC was recognized as the owner of Iran's oil deposits and of all installed assets of the Iranian oil industry, as the operator of the Naft-i-Shah oilfield and the Kermanshah refinery and as the sole distributor of refined products within Iran. NIOC would pay BP a total of £25,000,000 sterling over 10 years, commencing in 1957, it being stated that this settlement took into account (i) the current value of the internal distribution facilities and the northern producing and refining assets, and (ii) the various financial claims and counter-claims which had been made by BP and the Iranian Government since the suspension of the company's operations in 1951.

(2) IOP was granted operating rights in respect of exploration for and production of oil within the former Anglo-Iranian concession area, excepting Naft-i-Shah, and the refining of oil at Abadan. The lease conferring these rights was valid initially for 25 years and was renewable for three five-year periods thereafter. Under the terms of the inter-company agreement establishing the IOP consortium, BP was to receive a total of $600,000,000 from its partner companies in respect of their 60 per cent interest in the lease. Initial capital payments to BP totalled $90,000,000 (paid by the other companies in proportion to their shareholdings in the consortium) while the balance was paid at the rate of 10 cents for each barrel of oil exported from Iran by the companies concerned. (These so-called "BP royalty" payments continued until 1970.)

(3) IOP's member companies would be responsible for the export marketing of oil produced under the consortium agreement and would receive the resulting export revenue. The Iranian Government would levy a 50 per cent tax on the net profits of IOP's operations, export revenue being calculated on the basis of posted prices for this purpose. The members of the consortium would purchase oil from NIOC at a wellhead price equal to 12.5 per cent of the posted price, such payments—which were equivalent to the royalty element in concession agreements elsewhere in the Middle East—being fully credited against the overall 50 per cent tax liability. Iran reserved the right to take part of its revenue entitlement in the form of crude oil. IOP would supply NIOC with refined products for the domestic market at a substantial discount.

(4) IOP's London-based parent company held the capital of the Iranian Oil Exploration and Producing Company and the Iranian Oil Refining Company, whose formal status was that of contractors to NIOC. Procurement for the operating companies was handled by another London-based company. The operating companies did not make profits or losses, their expenses being met (at an agreed rate per barrel produced) by the members of the consortium. Each member of the consortium, through a subsidiary trading company, was required to give one year's advance notice of the volume of oil which it intended to lift in Iran, the overall annual production target being the sum of the companies' notified requirements plus NIOC's requirement for the domestic market. Tax was assessed on the profits of the trading subsidiaries.

The consortium agreement thus observed the principle of national ownership of the Iranian oil industry while giving practical control to the IOP member companies through their power to decide the volume of production and to handle export marketing, including the effective fixing of price levels. The state's overall revenue entitlement was equivalent to that currently obtained under concession agreements by other governments in the Gulf region, while in most respects the functions of the IOP members were identical to those of neighbouring countries' concessionaire companies (whose main advantage over IOP lay in the possession of full legal title to the oil which they produced).

The consortium's rules for determining the level of Iranian exports (and thus enabling the majors to balance their supplies from different producing countries in which they operated) were laid down in an additional secret agreement between the IOP companies, full details of which did not become public until the early 1970s. The "aggregate programmed quantity" formula which formed the basis of this

217

agreement effectively gave those member companies with the lowest reliance on Iranian oil (i.e. the companies with the largest access to oil produced in other countries) the greatest influence in fixing a ceiling level on the amount of oil which the consortium could supply to member companies at IOP's standard cost price in any one year. Any member company taking more oil than the quota allocated to it within the overall ceiling (i.e. a quota based on its percentage shareholding in IOP) was obliged to purchase the additional quantity from the other member companies at the full posted price.

C5.3.iii—Developments in Government-IOP relations in the 1960s – NIOC's joint-venture and service-contract agreements with foreign oil companies

Iran's level of oil production reached 1,000,000 bpd during 1960 and 2,000,000 bpd during 1966, somewhat lower than output in Kuwait and Saudi Arabia over the same period ($\lozenge$ Table 21). The Shah of Iran had by 1966 become aware of the existence of IOP's "aggregate programmed quantity" agreement (and of the fact that the price penalty which it imposed on a member company taking more than its "quota" of oil was higher than those imposed under comparable inter-company agreements in other Middle Eastern countries). He accordingly protested strongly to the IOP companies that this policy was restricting the rate of growth of Iranian oil production at a time when a rapid increase in oil revenues was needed to finance the Government's development plans.

In December 1966 IOP agreed to increase production to the level then desired by the Shah, to relinquish at least 25 per cent of the area in which it had exploration rights, and to supply NIOC with 20,000,000 tonnes of crude oil over the next five years for export to Eastern-bloc countries. This was the first time that one of the major Middle East producing groups had entered into a commercial agreement to make part of its output available to a host country's national oil company for export purposes (previous supplies of "royalty oil" to governments having been made available strictly within the context of taxation agreements entitling a government to require payment in kind).

In 1967 Iran once more became the largest Middle East producer, making it increasingly difficult for the majors to continue to meet the Shah's ambitious production targets without compromising their interests in other oil-producing countries. From 1969 onwards the consortium endeavoured to increase the Government's revenue receipts at a rate higher than that of the growth of oil output, notably by changing the dates of its accounting year and by making interest-free advances against revenue from future production. Meanwhile NIOC, acting in accordance with a law enacted in 1957 which empowered it to enter into joint ventures with foreign oil companies in respect of exploration areas other than those leased to IOP, had concluded a number of new oil agreements on terms which were increasingly favourable to Iran.

The main provisions of the July 1957 Petroleum Act were (i) that the territory of Iran outside the existing NIOC and IOP operating areas should be divided into "exploration districts" up to 80,000 sq km in area; (ii) that no new exploration agreement should include an area exceeding 16,000 sq km within any one exploration district; (iii) that NIOC should generally hold at least a 30 per cent interest in any joint venture with another company; (iv) that the maximum initial term of any agreement should be 25 years, with relinquishment of half of the total area concerned after the first 10 years; (v) that NIOC's foreign partner companies should commence exploratory drilling within four years of the signature of a joint venture agreement; (vi) that the foreign partner companies should bear the costs of unsuccessful exploration; (vii) that following a commercial oil discovery NIOC

218

should supply its share of development costs; and (viii) that the profits of joint ventures should be taxed at the rate of at least 50 per cent (thus giving the foreign partner a minority share in the net profits of production—e.g. no more than 25 per cent in the case of a venture in which NIOC held a 50 per cent equity share).

NIOC's first joint venture partner was the Italian company Agip, with which an agreement was concluded in August 1957 to set up the Société Irano-Italienne des Pétroles (Sirip), owned 50 per cent by NIOC and 50 per cent by Agip. (Agip's parent company, the Italian state energy corporation ENI, had in 1954 failed to become a member of the IOP consortium when the major oil companies refused its application to participate in the initial division of shareholdings. In February 1957 ENI had concluded what was then an innovatory joint venture agreement to explore for oil in Egypt.)

Under the August 1957 agreement Sirip was granted exploitation rights, valid for 25 years from the date of the commencement of the sale of oil, over a total area of about 23,000 sq km in three districts. Agip undertook to spend at least $22,000,000 on exploration work, of which at least $6,000,000 was to be spent during the first four years (after which Agip would be obliged to pay to NIOC half of the unexpended balance of $22,000,000 if it wished to discontinue its exploration programme). NIOC and Agip each had the right to purchase 50 per cent of Sirip's production, and any oil which was not purchased by the parent companies was to be offered for general sale at the current posted prices prevailing in the Gulf region. Sirip's net profits were to be taxed at the rate of 50 per cent but the company was not required to pay royalties (although a 12.5 per cent "stated payment", equivalent to a royalty and payable by Agip to NIOC on the basis of a posted-price valuation of 50 per cent of Sirip's output, was later introduced under a supplementary agreement of June 1973).

In June 1958 NIOC signed further joint venture agreements with Standard Oil Co. (Indiana) and with Sapphire Petroleum, a Canadian company (although the Sapphire agreement, which covered an offshore area of less than 1,000 sq km, was cancelled in 1961 after unsuccessful exploration work). The agreement with Standard Oil Co. (Indiana), which concerned a 16,000 sq km area of the Persian/Arabian Gulf, required the US company to pay an initial premium of $25,000,000 (recoverable over 10 years after the commencement of commercial production) and to spend a total of at least $82,000,000 on exploration work during the first 12 years of operations. NIOC and Standard Oil Co. (Indiana) would each own 50 per cent of a joint operating company—the Iran Pan American Oil Co. (Ipac)—whose function was to produce oil on a non-profit-making basis for the account of its parent companies, which would fund its production costs and would be individually taxed on their net income derived from its operations. The state's overall tax entitlement under these arrangements was similar to that applying to the operations of Sirip (a profit-making company).

Following the discovery of offshore oil in the north of the Gulf by Sirip (in 1960) and by Ipac (in 1961), NIOC announced in 1963 that it intended to enter into further joint ventures in other offshore areas. A total of 13 foreign companies or consortiums subsequently agreed to contribute to the costs of carrying out a preliminary seismic survey of the areas concerned (companies which failed to contribute being ineligible to apply for joint venture rights). Six new 50-50 joint venture agreements were signed in 1965 under which NIOC obtained initial premium payments totalling $190,000,000, while its foreign partners undertook to spend a total of over $164,000,000 on exploration work during the first 12 years of operations. In addition NIOC was to receive a "production bonus" from its partner when each venture's output reached an agreed level, its aggregate bonus entitlement if all six ventures reached the specified levels being $51,000,000. The general terms of the new agreements were similar to those of the agreement between NIOC and Standard Oil Co. (Indiana) and provided for the handling of production responsibilities by non-profit-making joint operating companies.

The new joint operating companies formed in 1965 were (i) the Dashtestan Offshore Petroleum Co. (Dopco), in which NIOC's partner was Royal Dutch/Shell; (ii) the Iranian Offshore Petroleum Co. (Iropco)—partners seven US independents led by Tidewater Oil Co. (a Getty subsidiary); (iii) the Lavan Petroleum Co. (Lapco)—partners Atlantic Richfield, Murphy Oil, Sun Co. and Union Oil of California; (iv) the Iran Marine International Co. (Iminoco)—partners Agip, Phillips and the Oil and Natural Gas Commission of India; (v) the Farsi Petroleum Co.—partners three French state-owned companies, together with three small French private-sector companies (which later withdrew); and (vi) the Persian Gulf Petroleum Co. (Pergupco)—partners seven West German companies. Of these companies, Lapco and Iminoco each discovered commercial oilfields in the south of the Gulf (which were linked to an export terminal at Lavan Island), while the remainder were dissolved after unsuccessful exploration work. In 1971 NIOC entered into three new 50-50 joint ventures to be conducted through the following operating companies: (i) the Iran Nippon Petroleum Co. (partners Mobil and four Japanese companies); (ii) the Bushehr Petroleum Co. (partner Amerada Hess); and (iii) the Hormuz Petroleum Co. (partner Mobil). Initial premium payments to NIOC under these agreements totalled $47,000,000, while a total of at least $85,000,000 was to be spent on exploration.

By the late 1960s a growing volume of Iranian crude oil was available for export by NIOC (both through its equity shares in joint ventures and under its December 1966 agreement with IOP) and the company was engaged in securing overseas outlets, notably in Eastern Europe, Asia and Africa. In Eastern Europe the main emphasis was placed on barter agreements under which Iran would import manufactured goods required for its economic development programme. In India NIOC and Standard Oil Co. (Indiana) each took 13 per cent equity shares in a new government-controlled refinery which came on stream in 1969 and which was supplied with crude by Ipac under a long-term contract. NIOC subsequently took a 17.5 per cent interest in South Africa's new Sasolburg refinery (which came on stream in 1971) and signed a 20-year agreement to supply crude to the refinery.

In August 1966 NIOC concluded a 25-year service contract with the French company ERAP under which a new ERAP subsidiary, Sofiran, would carry out geological surveys within an onshore area of 200,000 sq km and an offshore area of 20,000 sq km. These surveys would provide a basis for the selection of a total of 20,000 sq km onshore and 10,000 sq km offshore in which a full-scale exploration programme would be conducted (with a progressive reduction in the size of the exploration areas during succeeding years). ERAP would advance interest-free loans to NIOC to cover Sofiran's surveying and exploration costs (these loans being repayable only in the event of commercial oil discoveries by Sofiran) and would advance interest-bearing loans to finance the development costs of commercial discoveries. Ownership of all oil discovered by Sofiran was vested in NIOC, which was entitled to designate half of the discoveries as a national reserve outside the scope of the service contract.

After the start of commercial production NIOC would sell up to 45 per cent of Sofiran's output to ERAP at cost price plus 2 per cent, using part of the proceeds of these sales to repay (over a maximum period of 15 years) the interest-free loans which had been made by ERAP. The interest-bearing loans which had been made by ERAP would be repaid by NIOC over five years out of revenue derived from exports of the balance of Sofiran's output (which ERAP undertook to market on NIOC's behalf in return for a brokerage fee). ERAP's profits from the export of the oil which it was entitled to purchase from NIOC would be taxed at the rate of 50 per cent, using realized prices rather than posted prices to calculate taxable income. The brokerage fees due to ERAP in respect of exports made on NIOC's behalf would similarly be calculated as a percentage of realized prices. All policy decisions in respect of Sofiran's operations were to be taken by NIOC, while Sofiran would have functional management responsibility. Ownership of all production equipment would be vested in NIOC.

Service contracts on broadly similar terms were subsequently concluded with a consortium known as the European Group of Oil Companies (ERAP/Agip/Hispanoil/Petrofina/Österreichische Mineraloelverwaltung) and with a consortium of US independents (Cities Service Co./Conoco/Phillips).

C5.3.iv—Conclusion of new service contracts under 1974 petroleum law

In July 1974 a new petroleum law was enacted under which a modified form of service contract was introduced as the sole basis for future agreements between NIOC and foreign oil companies in respect of upstream ventures within Iran (although downstream ventures within Iran could still be initiated through jointly-owned companies in which NIOC held at least 50 per cent of the equity). The main features of the contractual relationship laid down by this law were (i) that no service contract should cover an area exceeding 8,000 sq km onshore or 4,000 sq km offshore; (ii) that there should be a maximum exploration period of five years, all exploration work being financed by the foreign contractor and carried out by a non-profit-making subsidiary company registered in Iran by the contractor for this purpose; (iii) that exploration costs should be non-recoverable except in the event of commercial discoveries; (iv) that the development costs of a commercial discovery should be financed by the contractor if NIOC so requested; (v) that when commercial production commenced from any oilfield within an exploration area this field should be excluded from the scope of the service contract for the area concerned and should come under the full operational management of NIOC; (vi) that when NIOC took control of a commercial field it should conclude a sales contract under which the foreign contractor would be entitled to purchase up to 50 per cent of the output of that field for a maximum period of 15 years); (vii) that over the first 10 years of the sales contract the foreign contractor should recover its exploration costs (without interest) and any development costs which it had incurred (plus interest) in the form of appropriate discounts off the current market price of the oil produced; and (viii) that the contractor should be entitled to an additional discount of up to 5 per cent of the market price throughout the duration of the sales contract.

In July and August 1974 NIOC concluded service contracts under this law with Ultramar, CFP, Agip and Ashland as well as with Deminex (which signed two separate contracts for different exploration areas). All of the contracts provided (i) for the payment to NIOC of an initial premium, which was recoverable by the contractor in the event of commercial production (on the same basis and over the same period laid down for the recovery of exploration costs); (ii) for the financing by the contractor of the development costs of commercial discoveries; and (iii) for the conclusion of 15-year sales contracts in the event of commercial production. NIOC was to receive a total of $49,750,000 in initial premium payments from the contractors, whose aggregate minimum expenditure on exploration work was to be $167,000,000. The CFP agreement also provided for non-recoverable production bonuses to be paid to NIOC ($5,000,000 if cumulative output reached 35,000,000 barrels and a further $5,000,000 if output reached 70,000,000 barrels).

C5.3.v—Iranian Government's 1973 "sales and purchase" agreement with IOP – Subsequent developments in IOP-NIOC relations

During 1972 the Iranian Government opened negotiations with IOP with the aim of establishing a timetable both for new investment to increase Iran's oil production to a peak level of 10,000,000 bpd by 1990 and for the progressive extension of NIOC's role at all stages of the consortium's operations. It was envisaged at this time that the 1954 consortium agreement would be extended to 1994 as a framework for the future development of the main oilfields. However, no such timetable had been agreed by January 1973, when the Shah declared that Iran would in no circumstances extend the consortium agreement (i.e. beyond its initial expiry date in 1979), since the IOP member companies had failed to observe a clause in the agreement requiring them to "preserve the interests of Iran".

Of two options presented to the IOP companies in January 1973, one was that they could continue operating on the existing basis—subject to the observance of government revenue and production targets—until 1979, when the companies would cease to have any preferential purchasing rights in Iran. The second was that they should accept the premature termination of the 1954 agreement and establish a new arrangement whereby full operational control would be assumed by NIOC, which would, however, extend long-term preferential purchasing rights to the IOP companies.

Negotiations having commenced on the basis of the second option, a new "oil sales and purchase agreement" between Iran and the IOP, effective from March 21, 1973, was formally ratified on July 24 of that year to replace the 1954 agreement. The principal provisions of the agreement were (i) that NIOC took "full and complete ownership, operation and control in respect of all hydrocarbon reserves, assets and administration of the petroleum industry"; (ii) that IOP set up a new non-profit-making operating subsidiary—the Oil Service Company of Iran (Osco)—to provide technical production skills to NIOC under a contract valid for an initial period of five years; and (iii) that the IOP companies were to have preferential oil purchase rights in Iran for a period of 20 years.

A main aim of the agreement was to ensure that "the total financial benefits and advantages to Iran and NIOC under this agreement shall be no less favourable than those applicable (at present or in the future) to other countries in the Persian Gulf under the [OPEC] General Agreement [on Participation] and related arrangements" (▷**D3.4**). The basic cost to the IOP member companies of crude oil supplied to them by NIOC for export purposes was accordingly made up of the following four elements: (i) the per-barrel operating cost; (ii) a "stated payment" equal to 12.5 per cent of the posted price (i.e. the equivalent of the standard Middle East royalty); (iii) Iranian income tax calculated with reference to the posted price according to the standard regional formula; and (iv) a "balancing margin" designed to produce an overall state revenue per barrel comparable to that obtained by Arabian peninsula countries which had introduced phased buy-back arrangements under the terms of the General Agreement. The IOP companies were also subject to a per-barrel "interest charge" calculated in accordance with a formula designed to limit NIOC's responsibility for interest payments in respect of new capital investment in the production operations formerly financed by IOP to the same level which would apply if NIOC held a participation interest in these operations under the terms of the OPEC General Agreement (i.e. at the level of 25 per cent from 1973 to 1977, 30 per cent in 1978, 35 per cent in 1979, 40 per cent in 1980, 45 per cent in 1981 and 51 per cent in 1982).

The IOP member companies agreed to provide part of the future capital investment in production operations within the former consortium area (which was now NIOC's sole responsibility) in the form of annual prepayments against their future crude oil purchases from NIOC, each prepayment being credited to the companies' oil purchase account over the 10 succeeding years. The proportion of NIOC's investment programme to be funded by prepayments from the IOP companies was fixed at 40 per cent per year for five years, after which it could be altered by the companies provided that NIOC had received two years' written notice of their intentions. The IOP companies were permitted to offset against the cost of oil purchased from NIOC depreciation charges in respect of that portion of the net book value of the assets of the former IOP operating subsidiaries which remained unamortized at the time of the termination of the 1954 agreement.

As regards the level of production, the agreement established a capacity development programme whose aim was to achieve a total installed crude production capacity of 8,000,000 bpd by Oct. 1, 1976, "provided that this is technically feasible and economically justifiable". NIOC's basic export entitlement in respect of oil produced within the areas formerly leased to IOP was fixed at 200,000 bpd in 1973 and 300,000 bpd in 1974, rising subsequently by 150,000 bpd each year until 1978, after which it would rise at the rate of 200,000 bpd each year until it reached 1,500,000 bpd in 1981. Thereafter, NIOC's basic export volume was to be based on the ratio of this 1981 entitlement to the total volume of oil available for export in that year.

The IOP companies had the right to purchase the exportable balance remaining in any year after the allocation of NIOC's basic entitlement, each company's share of this balance being apportioned at the basis of its shareholding in the consortium. The expected amount of each year's exportable balance would be defined in advance by NIOC with reference to the capacity development programme, and IOP would then be required to give notice of its total oil purchase requirement for that year. Any exportable production in excess of this notified requirement would be available for export by NIOC in addition to its basic entitlement. NIOC undertook to refine at Abadan up to 300,000 bpd of the IOP companies' purchases of Iranian crude.

Iran's oil output reached a peak level of 6,060,000 bpd in 1974, but fell back thereafter to average 5,571,000 bpd for the remainder of the period of normal production under the Shah's rule. Although the failure to meet government targets for production growth was mainly attributable to market factors, it had also become clear by 1975 that the targets for increasing the productive capacity of the industry could only be fulfilled on the basis of a massive programme of capital investment in secondary recovery techniques. After 1975 the IOP companies ceased to make prepayments equivalent to 40 per cent of NIOC's capital budget, while NIOC sought to recoup its higher financing costs by reducing the effective price discount of 22 cents per barrel on its oil sales to the companies. A further cause of friction was the companies' failure to purchase consistently the full volume of oil which they had requested in advance from NIOC, it being argued by NIOC, which demanded the payment of compensation, that this was a breach of the 1973 agreement (whereas the companies maintained that they were entitled to vary their purchases in line with market demand). In 1977 NIOC exported 750,000 bpd as its basic entitlement for that year plus an additional 654,000 bpd representing production which was surplus to the IOP companies' purchase requirements.

Negotiations for a comprehensive revision of the 1973 agreement commenced in late 1975 but remained deadlocked three years later. Contentious issues included the procedures for sharing export volume between NIOC and the IOP companies, the procedures for refining oil on the companies' behalf at Abadan, the terms under which the companies were remunerated for operational services provided to NIOC and the duration of a new contract between NIOC and Osco to replace the initial contract which was due to expire in 1978. The estimated productive capacity of the Iranian oil industry in 1978 was about 6,500,000 bpd.

During the nine months preceding the disruption of the industry in late 1978, 88.1

per cent of Iran's oil was produced by Osco (under the terms of its existing contract with NIOC), 6.7 per cent by Ipac, 3.4 per cent by Lapco, 0.8 per cent by Iminoco, 0.7 per cent by Sirip and 0.3 per cent by NIOC (from the Naft-i-Shah field). The IOP companies' purchases of oil produced by Osco accounted for 60 per cent of Iran's oil exports during the same period, while a further 27 per cent consisted of Osco production marketed by NIOC. Offshore joint-venture production, marketed partly by NIOC and partly by its foreign partner companies, made up the remaining 13 per cent of exports. (Offshore production on service-contract terms—by Sofiran—did not commence until 1979.)

C5.3.vi—Oil and gas developments after the 1979 revolution

Strikes by Iranian oil workers, which began in late September 1978 as part of a wider campaign of industrial action to undermine the rule of the Shah, had by the end of the year caused production to fall to 225,000 bpd (less than half of the country's domestic consumption). Exports were halted on Dec. 26, 1978, and did not resume until March 5, 1979, three weeks after the installation of a provisional Islamic revolutionary regime. The new Government immediately ended the purchasing privileges enjoyed by IOP, whose individual member companies became subject to NIOC's standard export contract terms. In the months following the resumption of exports, most of NIOC's additional export sales were made either to IOP member companies or to their former arm's-length contract customers; later in 1979 an increasing proportion of sales was made to non-traditional customers. All remaining aspects of the 1973 agreement with IOP had ceased to have practical effect by the time that the agreement was formally abrogated by Iran on Sept. 8, 1981.

NIOC, which was placed under the direct management of a newly created Ministry of Petroleum in September 1979, formed new production and drilling divisions to take over operations formerly contracted to Osco within Iran. It also set up its own London-based subsidiary company to provide external procurement services formerly contracted to another IOP subsidiary. Before abrogating the consortium agreement the revolutionary Government had in 1980 terminated all of NIOC's joint venture and service contract agreements with other foreign oil interests and had transferred responsibility for the producing ventures to a new national offshore oil company affiliated to NIOC. The National Iranian Gas Company (a NIOC affiliate founded in 1965) and the National Petrochemical Corporation (which was established in 1965 and which after 1979 took over all foreign shareholdings in completed petrochemical projects) also came under the general management of the Ministry of Petroleum.

(By the end of January 1986 compensation agreements had been concluded with BP, Shell, Chevron/Gulf, CFP, Sohio, Aminoil and Charter Oil in respect of their former consortium interests and with Elf Aquitaine in respect of the former service-contract operations of Sofiran. The outstanding compensation claims of the other foreign oil companies which had operated in Iran totalled an estimated $1,600 million.)

NIOC's investment in South Africa's Sasolburg refinery was effectively abandoned when the revolutionary Government severed all relations with South Africa in March 1979. A 50 per cent NIOC shareholding in a new South Korean refinery which came on stream in May 1980 was sold to NIOC's South Korean partner in the following month. NIOC retained its holding in India's Madras refinery.

Having achieved an average production level of 3,175,000 bpd in 1979 (compared with the republican Government's target of around 3,500,000 bpd), Iran suffered a severe decline in output to an average 1,402,500 bpd in 1980–81, followed by a partial recovery to an average 2,437,500 bpd in 1982–83. Factors behind the fall in output in 1980–81 included (i) exceptionally high Iranian export prices during most of this period, (ii) the imposition of trade sanctions by the United States and other leading non-communist industrialized countries during the period of the US-Iranian hostage crisis (November 1979 to January 1981), which affected both exports of oil and imports of oil industry equipment, and (iii) the outbreak of war with Iraq in September 1980, which was followed both by physical damage to oil installations and by interruptions to export trade routes. The partial recovery of output in 1982 was due mainly to substantial official price cuts, a large volume of spot market sales and an increased use of oil in barter trading agreements. Iran accepted a quota of 2,400,000 bpd, based on its 1982 production, as part of OPEC's March 1983 market stabilization initiative.

Iran's oil output averaged about 2,210,000 bpd in 1984–85, having fallen below the country's OPEC quota (reduced to 2,300,000 bpd in November 1984) during eight months of 1984 and seven months of 1985. Repeated Iraqi air attacks on shipping using Iran's main crude oil export terminal at Kharg Island prompted Iran to use its own vessels to provide a transshipment service to an improvised loading terminal at Sirri Island from February 1985 onwards. A subsequent intensification of Iraqi bombing raids on Kharg Island caused serious damage on a number of occasions in the second half of 1985, forcing a reduction in loadings to 200,000 bpd at one point when only two out of 14 berths were usable. Further export loading points for transshipped crude were provided to the south-east of the main war zone in 1986, although the implementation of the latest in a series of plans to build a high-volume "Kharg bypass" pipeline to a safe Iranian port was deferred in late February. Proposals for a crude oil export pipeline to a Turkish port, whose feasibility Turkey had agreed to consider in 1985, had not been translated into a firm project by mid-1986.

Iran suffered a major blow on Aug. 12, 1986, when Iraqi aircraft (apparently using in-flight refuelling techniques) bombed the Sirri Island terminal for the first time, causing extensive damage to tankers using the terminal. NIOC immediately switched its main export operations to its most easterly temporary loading point at Larak Island in the Strait of Hormuz, which enjoyed better military protection (provided by bases at nearby Bandar Abbas) but was poorly protected from disruption by storms in the mouth of the Gulf. The Aug. 12 raid led to a tripling of the war-risk surcharge on insurance premiums for foreign shipping using the Sirri Island terminal, while the new surcharge applicable to Larak loadings was double that which had previously applied to Sirri loadings. The switch from Sirri to Larak meant that NIOC, whose fob prices already contained an overall cost component of around $5 per barrel, had to absorb the extra cost of eastward transshipment for a further 110 nautical miles. A sharp drop in Iranian export volume was reported during the second half of August as a result of adverse weather conditions at Larak.

In 1982 Iran undertook to supply Syria with 180,000 bpd of crude under an agreement linked to Syria's closure of Iraq's Mediterranean export routes in April of that year, 20,000 bpd being provided free of charge and the balance at preferential prices. The total volume covered by the agreement was reduced to 120,000 bpd in 1983. Although Iran rescheduled substantial arrears of payments for preferentially-priced crude in mid-1984, Syria's debts subsequently went well above $1,000 million, prompting temporary suspensions of supplies for periods in 1985 and 1986. The second such cut-off was ended by Iran in July 1986 after Syria had indicated that it was prepared to consider the reopening of Iraq's export pipelines.

The supply of oil products to the Iranian domestic market was seriously disrupted at an early stage in the Gulf war, when damage to some refineries and interruptions in the flow of crude to others reduced the country's effective refining capacity to less than half of its pre-war level of 1,320,000 bpd. The 635,000 bpd Abadan refinery, situated close to the Iraqi border, was irreparably disabled after September 1980, while the small Bakhtaran (Kermanshah) plant was put out of action for four years. Refineries at Tehran (opened in 1968), Shiraz (opened 1973) and Tabriz (opened 1977) all suffered aerial attack in 1980 but continued to operate at reduced levels while damage was repaired. No damage was reported to Iran's newest refinery at Isfahan, which had opened at the end of 1979 and was claimed to be operating at 150 per cent of its design capacity by 1984. The Tehran refinery was again bombed by Iraq in May 1986, apparently causing the shutdown of 100,000 bpd of the plant's 220,000 bpd capacity. Repairs were expected to take up to a year.

In addition to cutting total capacity, the loss of the Abadan plant caused a distortion in the established pattern of output which greatly impaired the operational flexibility of the refining sector. It was necessary to import substantial volumes of certain products, although in many cases these were refined from Iranian crude oil (notably under a 1982 "supply and return" agreement with South Yemen). Rationing of refined products in the domestic market was ended in 1983. In early 1986 substantial volumes of Iranian crude were being shipped to refineries in Singapore and the Mediterranean region under processing deals whereby middle distillates were reimported into Iran, while other products were marketed abroad by NIOC. At the same time an estimated 1,200 bpd of fuel oil began to be transported by road from Iranian refineries for export from the Turkish Black Sea port of Trabzon. Iran's estimated requirement for imported products totalled 80,000 bpd in early 1986, rising to as much as 200,000 bpd after the war damage to the Tehran refinery in May. Bids were invited in mid-1986 for the construction of new refineries at Bandar Abbas and at Shazand (125 km south-west of Qom). It was intended that the two plants, with capacities of 220,000 bpd and 200,000 bpd respectively, should be operational by 1989.

In 1985 Iran had 10 petrochemical plants (including one at Abadan which was closed following the outbreak of the Gulf war) whose combined capacity was insufficient to meet domestic demand. The construction of a $3,500 million petrochemical complex at Bandar Khomeini (formerly Bandar Shahpur), designed to serve both domestic and export markets, was 85 per cent complete in 1979. Six years later, however, little further progress had been made, due partly to disagreements between Iran and its Japanese joint-venture partners and partly to disruption caused by the Gulf war. Plans had meanwhile been announced to build a major new complex at Arak to operate partly in conjunction with the proposed new refinery at nearby Shazand.

From 1982 onwards the republican Government turned its attention to the longer-term development of oil and gas resources, which had been largely disregarded since the 1979 revolution. Some new oil exploration activity commenced, and new investment was authorized in gas reinjection schemes to prolong the productive life of the main oilfields. Work was stepped up on a domestic gas distribution programme (initiated by the Shah), official figures for the laying of new supply pipelines being given as an average of 161 km per year in 1971–78, 500 km per year in 1979–82, 876 km in 1983 and 1,295 km in 1984. Marketed gas output rose from 5,950 million cubic metres in 1981 to 13,500 mcm in 1984. Iran's proved gas reserves (the second largest in the world, after those of the Soviet Union) are nearly twice as large as its proved oil reserves on an energy equivalence basis.

Exports of associated gas to the Soviet Union via Iran's first gas trunkline (IGAT-1), which commenced in 1970 and averaged 7,650 million cubic metres per annum from 1971 to 1979, were halted by Iran in 1980 as a result of a dispute about pricing, while work was cancelled on the export sections of an IGAT-2 pipeline which was to have carried non-associated gas to the Soviet Union under the terms of a formal "exchange" agreement involving the export of equivalent volumes of

Soviet gas to Western and Central European countries. It was announced in August 1986 that Iran had agreed to resume gas exports to the Soviet Union before the end of the year. Details of pricing arrangements were not revealed. Export volume would initially be 1,085 mcm per annum, with the possibility of an increase to 31,000 mcm by 1990. Earlier Iranian proposals for a resumption of gas exports in the late 1980s had envisaged the construction of a new $11,000 million pipeline running to the main European network via Turkey, Greece and southern Italy. The feasibility of this proposal remained to be assessed in mid-1986.

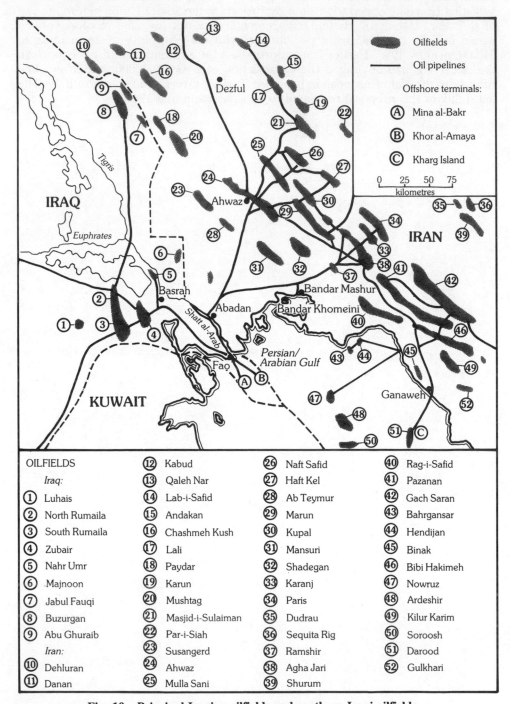

Legend	
	Oilfields
	Oil pipelines
Offshore terminals:	
Ⓐ	Mina al-Bakr
Ⓑ	Khor al-Amaya
Ⓒ	Kharg Island

OILFIELDS	⑫ Kabud	㉖ Naft Safid	㊵ Rag-i-Safid
Iraq:	⑬ Qaleh Nar	㉗ Haft Kel	㊶ Pazanan
① Luhais	⑭ Lab-i-Safid	㉘ Ab Teymur	㊷ Gach Saran
② North Rumaila	⑮ Andakan	㉙ Marun	㊸ Bahrgansar
③ South Rumaila	⑯ Chashmeh Kush	㉚ Kupal	㊹ Hendijan
④ Zubair	⑰ Lali	㉛ Mansuri	㊺ Binak
⑤ Nahr Umr	⑱ Paydar	㉜ Shadegan	㊻ Bibi Hakimeh
⑥ Majnoon	⑲ Karun	㉝ Karanj	㊼ Nowruz
⑦ Jabul Fauqi	⑳ Mushtag	㉞ Paris	㊽ Ardeshir
⑧ Buzurgan	㉑ Masjid-i-Sulaiman	㉟ Dudrau	㊾ Kilur Karim
⑨ Abu Ghuraib	㉒ Par-i-Siah	㊱ Sequita Rig	㊿ Soroosh
Iran:	㉓ Susangerd	㊲ Ramshir	51 Darood
⑩ Dehluran	㉔ Ahwaz	㊳ Agha Jari	52 Gulkhari
⑪ Danan	㉕ Mulla Sani	㊴ Shurum	

Fig. 10—Principal Iranian oilfields and southern Iraqi oilfields

C6—Iraq

C6.1—Statistical Survey

*1984
†End-1984
‡Revision of 1984 figures given in section **D15.1.i** (see Introduction)

General
Area .... 438,446 sq km
*Population 15,360,000
Capital .... Baghdad

Economy and trade
*Gross national product .... $33,190 million
*Annual exports (fob) .... $11,402 million (of which petroleum 98.6 per cent)
*Annual imports (cif) .... $11,591 million
*Current account balance .... −$1,800 million

Oil (upstream)
‡1984 crude production .... 1,225,000 bpd (60,300,000 tonnes)
1985 crude production .... 1,435,000 bpd (70,400,000 tonnes)
†Proved crude reserves .... 44,500 million barrels
*Reserves:production ratio .... 103.9 : 1
Production in peak year .... 3,475,000 bpd (170,600,000 tonnes) in 1979
†Cumulative crude production .... 17,354.8 million barrels since 1928
Number of producing oil wells .... 280 in 1981 (later figures not available)
Export grades: Basrah .... 34° API gravity
      Kirkuk .... 36° API gravity
      Kirkuk Blend .... 34° API gravity

Oil tanker tonnage
†18 vessels .... 1,429,100 deadweight tons

Oil (downstream)
*Installed refining capacity .... 365,500 bpd
*Output of refined products .... 340,000 bpd
*Consumption of refined products .... 234,200 bpd

Natural gas (million cubic metres)
*Gross annual production .... 4,900 mcm
 of which: (gas marketed) .... (590 mcm)
     (gas flared) .... (4,090 mcm)
     (shrinkage) .... (220 mcm)
†Natural gas reserves .... 800,000 mcm

C6.2—Political and Economic Summary

The modern state of Iraq came into existence, under a monarchical constitution, when the Ottoman Empire was dismembered after the First World War (◊**A4.5.i**).

The new kingdom was administered by Britain under a League of Nations mandate until independence was achieved in October 1932. The monarchy was overthrown in 1958, when power was assumed by a strongly nationalistic military regime which ended the pro-Western tendencies in Iraq's foreign policy. Throughout the 1960s Iraq's internal political stability was seriously undermined by factional rivalries, and there were further military coups in 1963 and 1968, with a number of unsuccessful coup attempts in the intervening years. The July 1968 coup was staged by elements of the armed forces sympathetic to the (pan-Arab) Baath Arab Socialist Party.

The country has since been under the rule of a Baathist-dominated Revolutionary Command Council (RCC), although members of the Iraq Communist Party also participated in government from 1972 to 1979. Since July 1979 the posts of chairman of the RCC, President of Iraq and secretary-general of the Baath regional command have been held by Sadam Hussein. Iraq's first elections since 1958 were held in June 1980, when a 250-seat National Assembly was inaugurated. Baathist candidates won nearly three-quarters of the seats in further Assembly elections held in October 1984. Under the 1968 Constitution Iraq is a socialist state with Islam as the state religion. Over half of the population are Shi'ite Moslems, although political power is held by Sunni Moslems.

Although the majority of Iraqis are Arabs, there is an important Kurdish minority in the north of the country. Long-standing Kurdish opposition to rule from Baghdad led the Government to establish a Kurdish autonomous region in 1974 and an elected Kurdish legislative council in 1980. These measures had some effect in appeasing Kurdish opposition, but the key factor in countering a large-scale Kurdish rebellion was Iran's withdrawal of support for the rebels in 1975 in return for Iraqi concessions in a territorial dispute with Iran. Many armed clashes between Kurdish elements and Iraqi government forces were reported in 1984–85.

Partly because of the pan-Arab constitution of the Baath party, Iraqi politics are particularly closely linked with regional politics. Iraq has had notably poor relations with Syria—except for a period in 1978–79 when plans were mooted for a union between the two countries—since a rival wing of the Baath party came to power in that country in 1970. Syria is the only Arab state apart from Libya to support Iran in the current Gulf war (◊C5.2), its main act of support being the closure in April 1982 of the pipelines carrying Iraqi oil exports through its territory. Features of Iraq's wider external relations include membership of the non-aligned movement and good relations with the Soviet bloc (which have, however, been less close since the Iraq Communist Party was excluded from government and banned in 1979). Diplomatic relations with the United States, which had been broken off by Iraq in June 1967, were resumed in November 1984.

Iraq's economy is dominated by state-controlled enterprises, which account for nearly 80 per cent of the gross national product and 90 per cent of import trade. Agriculture is the largest source of employment and the most important sector of the economy after oil. Manufacturing makes a relatively small contribution to the economy, and much investment has been devoted to expanding the country's oil producing and processing capacity. In 1979 and 1980, following the Iranian revolution, Iraq displaced Iran as OPEC's second largest producer, but the events of the Gulf war subsequently led to a drastic fall in oil production and revenues. Since 1981 large grants and loans (totalling an estimated $40,000 million by 1985) have been obtained from Saudi Arabia, Kuwait, Qatar and the United Arab Emirates. Unofficial estimates put the country's foreign exchange reserves at $1,000 million in 1984, compared with $31,000 million in 1980, and many foreign debts have been rescheduled since 1982, with some creditors accepting repayment in the form of crude oil.

Despite its abandonment in 1982 of the current five-year development pro-gramme in favour of year-to-year planning, the Government made strenuous efforts to maintain a high level of investment in infrastructural and industrial projects within the framework of a revised set of priorities dictated by the war with Iran. The most vital projects involved the replacement of lost oil export capacity, in which area considerable progress had been made by the end of 1985, albeit at the expense of compromising the Government's observance of what it described as the "artificially low" OPEC quota allocated to Iraq on the basis of its 1983 export capacity. Hopes that higher oil export volume in 1986 would ease the country's foreign exchange shortage were, however, dashed by the steep fall in unit revenues resulting from the upheaval in the world oil market in the first half of the year. The Government nevertheless took some satisfaction from the fact that Iran, after suffering a far heavier proportionate fall in oil export revenue than Iraq, shifted its stance within the OPEC Conference at the beginning of August 1986 in order to facilitate agreement on a new market stabilization initiative involving Iranian acquiescence in higher Iraqi output.

C6.3—Oil and Gas Industry

C6.3.i—Concession agreements with foreign oil interests

Mesopotamia, a region of well-known natural oil seepages, was recognized as a potential source of commercial production in the early 1900s by Calouste Gulbenkian, an Armenian geologist who subsequently played a major role in bringing together various European groups interested in obtaining concession rights and who acted as an intermediary in negotiations with the Ottoman Government. In March 1914 shareholdings in the Turkish Petroleum Company (TPC), originally formed in 1911 as African and Eastern Concessions Ltd, were agreed as follows: Anglo-Persian Oil Co. (forerunner of British Petroleum) 50 per cent, Anglo-Saxon Petroleum Co. (representing Royal Dutch/Shell) 25 per cent and Deutsche Bank 25 per cent. Gulbenkian was to receive 5 per cent of the profits from TPC's operations, to be transferred from the profits attributable to the Anglo-Persian and Anglo-Saxon companies. It was further agreed that none of the parties concerned would seek oil rights anywhere in the Ottoman Empire (ex-cluding Kuwait and territories under Egyptian administration) except through TPC.

In June 1914 TPC obtained undertakings from the Ottoman Government reg-arding the granting of oil rights in the provinces of Baghdad and Mosul, although the outbreak of the First World War prevented the ratification of a formal agreement. In December 1918 Deutsche Bank's shareholding in TPC was expro-priated by the British Government and placed under the administration of a British trustee. Discussions concerning TPC's future status took place during the 1920 San Remo conference at which Britain and France were granted League of Nations mandates to administer various former Ottoman provinces (◊A4.5.i), and an Anglo-French oil agreement was concluded whereby France took over the former German shareholding in TPC on the understanding that the company would be granted an oil concession by the new British-mandated kingdom of Iraq. The French Government undertook to facilitate the construction of oil export pipelines through French-mandated Syria and Lebanon and to allow oil to pass through them duty-free.

However, the US Government, which had not declared war on the Ottoman Empire and was therefore not represented at the San Remo conference, demanded that US oil interests should be allowed to participate in the proposed concession on the basis of the "open door" doctrine forbidding the introduction of discriminatory international trade policies in mandated territories. (There were at this time wide-spread fears of an imminent shortage of world oil supplies.) Following an initial British offer, made in 1922, to allow 12 per cent US participation in TPC (to be ceded from the share held by Anglo-Persian and paid for out of the proceeds of future oil production) lengthy talks were opened with a number of US oil companies, leading to agreement in 1928 that half of Anglo-Persian's interest should be transferred to the Near East Development Corporation (NEDC), which was formed to represent US oil companies within the TPC. Of the seven US companies which had originally taken part in the negotiations, five took up shares in NEDC in 1928, but Standard Oil Co. (Indiana) and Atlantic Refining Co. (forerunner of Atlantic Richfield) subsequently withdrew in 1930, while Gulf Oil withdrew in 1934, leaving Exxon and Mobil (which had purchased their former partners' shares) as the equal co-owners of NEDC. The Iraq Government had meanwhile granted oil rights over most of the country to TPC in 1925, one condition of this concession being that the company should remain British-registered and under British chairmanship.

It was agreed in 1928 that Gulbenkian's "beneficial interest" in TPC's operations should be converted into a 5 per cent equity share, held through Participations and Explorations Corp. (Partex), resulting in the following overall distribution of shareholdings: Anglo-Persian (BP) 23.75 per cent, Anglo-Saxon (Shell) 23.75 per cent, Compagnie Française des Pétroles (CFP, formed in 1924 to hold the French interest in TPC) 23.75 per cent, NEDC 23.75 per cent and Partex 5 per cent. (Partex's oil entitlement was to be sold to the other shareholders.) The parent companies undertook not to seek new oil concessions throughout most of the Middle East except through TPC, the area covered by this so-called "red line agreement" (which extended from Aden to the Black Sea and included all of today's major Middle East oil-producing countries except Iran and Kuwait) being based on a somewhat arbitrary definition of the territories of the former Ottoman Empire. The red line agreement, which was not formally cancelled until 1948, subsequently had a significant influence on the distribution of oil company interests in the region. TPC was renamed the Iraq Petroleum Company (IPC) in 1929.

As regards the oil concession obtained in 1925, it was envisaged that the IPC should directly develop only 24 blocks totalling about 500 sq km and that after the selection of these blocks by the company the Iraq Government should, through the agency of the company, periodically offer other blocks within the concession area to the highest bidders at public auction, who would in effect become sub-lessees of the company. This arrangement was designed to provide an appearance of conformity both with the "open door" principles espoused by the US Government and with the Iraq Government's sovereign rights over the country's oil resources, although in practice it was capable of implementation in such a way as to ensure that IPC retained effective control over Iraq's oil development. The time limits laid down for the selection and development of the IPC's own initial exploration blocks (which were centred around Kirkuk, where a major discovery was made in 1927) nevertheless proved irksome to the company, and in 1931 a new agreement was reached with the Iraq Government whereby IPC obtained exclusive and unrestricted concession rights (i.e. without any minimum exploration requirements or phased relinquishment obligations) over an area of about 91,000 sq km representing most of northern Iraq east of the Tigris. The concession was valid until the year 2000 (the expiry date of the 75-year concession granted in 1925).

Other features of the IPC concession agreement included (i) an obligation to pay royalties to the Iraq Government at the rate of four gold shillings per ton of oil produced (this rate being fixed for 20 years following the opening of an export pipeline and variable thereafter within certain limits in line with the level of

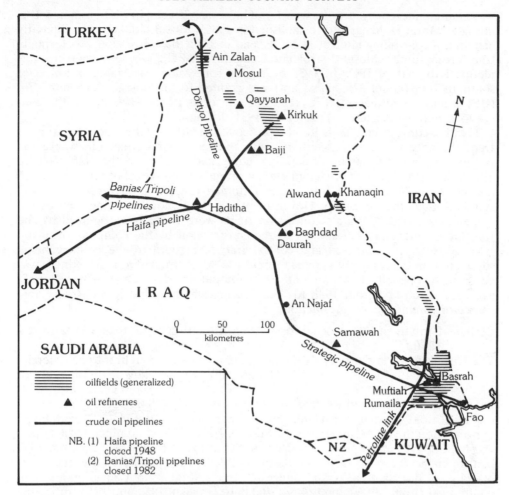

Fig. 11—Iraqi oil resources and installations

company profits), and (ii) exemption from Iraqi taxation in return for annual capital payments to the Government which would increase in line with the volume of oil exports. IPC was constituted as a non-profit-making operational consortium whose function was to make oil available to its shareholder companies at cost price plus a nominal administration charge, and there was no direct legal relationship between the shareholder companies and the host Government. As a closed company IPC had no authority to issue shares to the public, thus rendering meaningless a clause in the concession agreement which required at least 20 per cent of any public offer of new shares to be reserved for sale to Iraqis. (The Anglo-French oil agreement of 1920 had originally proposed that the Government of Iraq should have the right to take a 20 per cent equity interest in any concession granted to TPC.)

One year after the 1931 revision of the IPC concession agreement, the Iraq Government granted a 75-year concession covering northern Iraq west of the Tigris (an area of about 107,000 sq km) to the independent British Oil Development Co., which established a new holding company, Mosul Oil Fields Ltd (MOF) in partnership with Italian, Swiss, German and Dutch interests. The company subsequently encountered financial difficulties and looked to IPC for assistance, which

233

was granted in exchange for the transfer of an equity interest in MOF to a new IPC affiliate, Mosul Holdings Ltd (established in 1936). Mosul Holdings subsequently acquired a controlling interest in MOF, and in 1941 the concession was formally transferred to the Mosul Petroleum Company (MPC), whose ownership was identical to that of IPC. In 1938 a 75-year concession covering the whole of southern Iraq (about 226,000 sq km) was granted to the Basrah Petroleum Co. (BPC), another affiliate of IPC. The general terms of the BPC and MPC concessions were modelled on those of the 1931 IPC agreement.

The IPC consortium thus held oil rights covering virtually the whole territory of Iraq, the only significant exception being an area around Khanaqin where the Anglo-Persian Oil Company, operating alone, had discovered the Naft Khaneh oilfield in 1923. The Naft Khaneh field lay within a small parcel of territory which had been transferred from Iran to the Ottoman Empire in 1913 on the understanding that the Ottoman Government would honour existing concession agreements. Anglo-Persian's concession rights were formally recognized by the Iraq Government in 1925 subject to the construction by the company of an oil refinery to supply northern and central Iraq (the south of the country being supplied from the company's Iranian refinery at Abadan), and a small refinery was accordingly opened at Alwand in 1927. Output from the Naft Khaneh field averaged 2,100 bpd from 1928 to 1933 (during which period it was Iraq's only source of commercial oil production).

C6.3.ii—Growth of IPC production – Government-company relations in the 1950s

The Kirkuk field, in the main IPC concession area, was brought into commercial production in 1934 at the rate of 15,000 bpd after the opening of oil pipelines to Mediterranean export terminals at Tripoli (Lebanon) and Haifa (Palestine). Output from the field reached 100,000 bpd for the first time in 1945, but fell back below this level in 1948 when the Haifa pipeline was permanently closed for political reasons upon the establishment of the State of Israel. A second pipeline to Tripoli was built in 1949 and a pipeline to Banias (Syria) in 1952, by which time the BPC had commenced exports from the southern oilfields via a pipeline to the Iraqi port of Fao on the Shatt al-Arab waterway. Iraq's total output level more than quadrupled (from 139,600 bpd to 581,400 bpd) between 1950 and 1953, reflecting (i) the major oil companies' need to replace supplies from Iran during their boycott of that country's newly nationalized oil industry ($\Diamond$**C5.3.i**), (ii) the fulfilment of undertakings given to the Government in 1951 (see below) and (iii) the fulfilment of agreements which had been made between the IPC shareholder companies in connexion with the cancellation of the "red line agreement" in November 1948 ($\Diamond$**C11.3.ii**).

The IPC companies undertook in August 1950 to increase their royalty payments to the Government from four to six gold shillings per ton produced with effect from the beginning of that year, although no agreement was reached in a long-standing dispute concerning the currency conversion rate applicable to the royalties paid by the original IPC company. In the absence of a clear definition of this matter in its 1931 concession terms, the company claimed the right to base its royalty payments on the "official" gold price quoted by the Bank of England. For its part, the Iraq Government contended that it was entitled to receive royalties based on the considerably higher sterling value of gold sovereigns exchanged within Iraq.

Following the announcement at the end of 1950 of Saudi Arabia's agreement with Aramco ($\Diamond$**C11.3.iii**) in which the taxation of profits took precedence over flat-rate royalties in determining the Government's oil revenue, negotiations opened in Iraq in May 1951 with the aim of similarly revising the financial relationship between the IPC companies and the Baghdad Government. The Government withdrew a legal action in connexion with its claim regarding the valuation of royalty payments, after which the two sides concluded an agreement in August 1951 (with formal ratification in February 1952). Its main provisions, effective from the beginning of 1951, were as follows:

(1) There was to be an overall government revenue entitlement equal to 50 per cent of the consortium's profits, which were defined as the difference between "border values" (calculated with reference to posted prices at seaboard terminals) and the cost of production and internal transportation. The Government was entitled to receive up to 12.5 per cent of the oil available for export, which could either be sold to the IPC shareholder companies at posted prices or marketed directly by the state. The value of this "royalty oil" (calculated at posted prices) constituted part of the state's 50 per cent share of profits. The consortium's three joint operating companies in Iraq continued to function on a non-profit-making basis, and each of the shareholder companies established a new trading subsidiary to which profits could be attributed for tax purposes.

(2) The Government's minimum revenue entitlement was to be equal to 25 per cent of the seaboard value of IPC and MPC output and 33⅓ per cent of the value of BPC output, regardless of the level of the companies' profits.

(3) The combined production of IPC and MPC was to be increased to at least 458,300 bpd from 1954, while the BPC's output was to be increased to at least 166,000 bpd by the end of 1955.

(4) In the event of the interruption of production by force majeure the Government would receive annual payments of at least £5,000,000 sterling for two years.

(5) A most-favoured-nation clause gave the Iraq Government the right to request the IPC companies to match any improved financial terms which any or all of their shareholder companies might offer to the governments of neighbouring countries where they operated under concession agreements.

(6) IPC agreed to supply crude oil at nominal cost to a new state-owned refinery which was to be built at Daurah, near Baghdad.

(7) IPC undertook to assist the education of Iraqi oil technicians and to employ suitably qualified Iraqis in preference to expatriate staff.

The Government subsequently protested to IPC about the subtraction from the selling prices used to calculate the border value of oil for tax purposes of a "marketing discount" averaging 20 per cent, it being argued that IPC did not incur any genuine expenses in selling oil to its own shareholder companies. The discount was reduced to 2 per cent of the selling price under an agreement of March 1955 and further reduced to 1 per cent in 1957 after Iraq had invoked the "most-favoured-nation" clause in the 1951 agreement in connexion with a reduction in Aramco's allowable marketing expenses in Saudi Arabia. IPC initially backdated the application of the 1 per cent discount to the beginning of 1954, rather than to the beginning of 1953 as demanded by Iraq, but subsequently reached an out-of-court settlement when the Government instituted legal proceedings to press this claim.

As regards the Anglo-Iranian Oil Company's separate operations in the Naft Khaneh oilfield (where production was carried out by a subsidiary called the Khanaqin Oil Co.), an agreement was signed in December 1951 and ratified in July 1952 whereby (i) Anglo-Iranian's Alwand refinery and associated product distribution facilities were purchased by the Government, although the company continued to manage them under contract for an interim period; (ii) the company was to operate the new government-owned Daurah refinery under contract for up to 10 years after its inauguration (which subsequently took place in November 1955); (iii) the company immediately built a small refinery for the Government at Muftiah to serve the southern Iraqi market (whose supplies of Iranian oil products had ceased as a result of the nationalization crisis in that country); (iv) following the opening of the Daurah refinery the company was to be relieved of its obligation to supply oil to the Alwand refinery and would be expected to increase its crude production (10,250 bpd in 1952) to a level high enough to justify the commencement of exports (which were to be priced and taxed on the same basis as exports by the IPC companies); and (v) if no such exports had occurred by 1959 the company's concession rights over the Naft Khaneh oilfield would be terminated.

(The Khanaqin Oil Co. did not meet this export deadline, and relinquished its concession rights in November 1958, after which the Government took control over the Naft Khaneh field, using mainly Iraqi personnel assisted by a number of Soviet experts. The Alwand refinery, which continued to process Naft Khaneh crude, was brought fully under government management in April 1959.)

In 1956–57 Iraq's oil exports via Mediterranean terminals were halted for some months when pipeline pumping stations on Syrian territory were severely damaged as a political action in the context of the Suez crisis ($\Diamond$**A4.10.i**). The damage occurred on Nov. 2, 1956, and pumping did not resume until mid-March 1957 after the lifting of bans which the Syrian Government had imposed on the carrying out of repairs and on the export of oil via Syria. Iraqi oil production fell to an average 450,000 bpd in 1957 (the lowest annual average for five years) and the IPC made a substantial prepayment of oil revenues to the Government in order to avert a budgetary crisis.

Iraq's oil output reached 1,000,000 bpd for the first time in 1961, the average rate of growth of IPC's production capacity having slowed after the mid-1950s partly because of the inflexibility of the consortium's investment planning procedures, which required five-year export targets to be agreed by the shareholder companies five years before the start of each target period (e.g. in 1952 for the period 1957–61). This long-range approach was apparently intended to take account of the dependence of the northern oilfields on long-distance export pipelines, the expansion of whose capacity required relatively heavy capital outlays. Collective decisions on the overall volume of output in each target period were reached according to a formula which effectively subordinated the interests of shareholder companies with relatively few alternative supply sources (e.g. CFP) to those of the more broadly based majors. Once the overall output volume was agreed, each company's offtake entitlement was determined in proportion to its shareholding in the consortium, and a company whose entitlement exceeded its anticipated requirements was entitled to contract to sell its surplus to another shareholder company at a "half-way price" between the tax-paid cost and the posted price.

C6.3.iii—Inconclusive negotiations leading to Law 80 of 1981

One month after the overthrow of the monarchy in July 1958 the new military regime in Iraq opened preliminary talks with the IPC companies with the main stated aims of securing (i) acceptance of the principle of relinquishment of undeveloped concession areas; (ii) new commitments regarding the future expansion of crude oil production; (iii) participation by the consortium in a refinery expansion programme; (iv) government control over exports of refined products; (v) the reduction of the six-month notice period required from the Government if it intended to exercise its right to take a proportion of its revenue entitlement in the form of crude oil; and (vi) the further "Iraqization" of company staff at all levels, including the appointment of an Iraqi executive director. Many of these issues had already been raised by the previous Iraqi Government. In May 1960 (by which time several rounds of detailed negotiations had produced agreement only on minor issues) the Government sharply increased the port dues levied on oil exported via Basrah, leading to strong protests from the BPC, which temporarily suspended production from its Rumaila oilfield (although the company denied any retaliatory intention).

236

Negotiations held by the Government and IPC between August and December 1960 proved inconclusive, and after the failure of a further round of talks in early April 1961 the Government ordered the three operating companies to halt immediately all activities outside those parts of their concession areas which had been brought into production or had been proved to have commercial oil reserves.

The scope of the negotiations had by this point been widened to include government demands (i) for the exclusion from the declared operating expenses of MPC and BPC of amounts claimed in respect of rental payments which had been made by the companies prior to the commencement of commercial production (such "dead rents" having been capitalized by the companies for amortization at the rate of 5 per cent per annum, thus depressing the level of taxable profits); (ii) for an increase in the Government's overall share of the profits arising from the activities of all three operating companies in the IPC group; (iii) for the immediate relinquishment by the companies of 90 per cent of their existing concession areas and for the introduction of new concession terms in respect of any unexplored areas retained by them thereafter; (iv) for the reinjection or commercial utilization of associated gas and for payment by the companies for gas which continued to be flared off; and (v) for 20 per cent state equity participation in the companies' operations, in accordance with the original intention of the 1920 San Remo oil agreement (◊**C6.3.i**).

In June 1961 the companies agreed to change their accounting practice regarding "dead rent" payments and offered to relinquish 75 per cent of their concession areas immediately and an additional 15 per cent within seven years. At further talks held between August and October 1961 the Government insisted on the immediate relinquishment of 90 per cent of concession areas, but added that it was prepared to drop its demand for 20 per cent equity participation in return for a higher government revenue entitlement. The companies said that they could not accept lower earnings per barrel in the current over-supplied market conditions (which they had cited as the cause of earlier reductions in posted prices, and thus in government revenue per barrel, in 1959–60 ◊**A4.10.iii**). Moreover, they rejected the basis of the claim regarding government equity participation on the grounds that the TPC had not been a party to the San Remo agreement.

After the latest talks had failed the Government took unilateral action, under Law 80 of 1961 (promulgated on Dec. 11 of that year), to restrict the three companies' concession areas to a combined total of less than 2,000 sq km, with the possibility of extension to double this area in the future. The redefined concession areas, which included all oilfields currently being exploited by the companies, were distributed as follows: IPC—22 blocks at Kirkuk, Bai Hassan and Jambur totalling 747 sq km; BPC—17 blocks at Rumaila and Zubair totalling 1,126 sq km; MPC —eight blocks at Ain Zalah and Butmah totalling 45 sq km.

The blocks in question, covering 0.4 per cent of the territory of Iraq, contained about 60 per cent of the country's end-1961 proved oil reserves of 27,225 million barrels (most of the remainder being in the North Rumaila field within an undeveloped part of the former BPC concession area). The Government said that it expected the companies to expand production from their redefined concession areas and that it would make suitable arrangements for new exploration in the compulsorily relinquished areas, in which connexion the companies were required to submit to the Government within three months all technical records which they possessed regarding these areas. The companies declared that Law 80 constituted a breach of contract on the part of the Iraqi Government, and called for the issue to be put to international arbitration in accordance with the disputes procedure laid down in their concession agreements. The British and US Governments made representations to Iraq in January 1962 calling for the resumption of negotiations with IPC and expressing support for the companies' request for arbitration.

C6.3.iv—Developments leading to full nationalization of oil industry (1962 to 1975)

For the next 10 years the IPC companies increased their oil output at an average annual rate of around 5 per cent, less than half of the rate of increase which occurred elsewhere in the Middle East over the same period (and less than half of that which had occurred in Iraq during the preceding decade). (A fall in Iraq's oil output in 1967 was, however, attributable to two major interruptions in the flow of exports through Syria. The first was caused by a dispute between IPC and the Syrian Government over the level of pipeline transit fees levied by Syria under an agreement of 1955. The second resulted from political action taken by Iraq in connexion with the 1967 Arab-Israeli war ◊**A4.13**.) New IPC investment in the Iraqi oilfields was cut to as little as 3 per cent of its former annual level from 1962 onwards.

In February 1964 the Iraq Government established the Iraq National Oil Company (INOC), which under Law 97 of Aug. 7, 1967, and Law 123 of Sept. 21, 1967, was empowered to carry out exploration work, both on its own account and through contracts with foreign oil companies, in all areas not covered by the reduced IPC concession. The delay in formally granting these rights to INOC arose partly from the fact that intermittent talks had been held with IPC to explore the possibility of reaching a comprehensive settlement of disputed issues. Progress in the talks had been hampered by successive changes of government in Iraq, and a draft agreement of June 1965 was never officially published. (The draft envisaged the return to the IPC group of an area equal to its reduced concession area and the involvement of all the IPC shareholder companies except Exxon in a new joint exploration venture in which INOC would hold a one-third interest.)

INOC's first contract in respect of an undeveloped exploration area (formerly held by BPC) was signed on Feb. 3, 1968, with ERAP. The main provisions of the agreement, which covered onshore and offshore blocks totalling 10,800 sq km, were (i) that ERAP would finance and undertake all exploration work, its exploration expenditure being regarded as an interest-free loan repayable only in the event of commercial oil discoveries (when a proportion of the sales proceeds from future production would be allocated for repayments); (ii) that ERAP's expenditure on the development of commercial discoveries would be regarded as an interest-bearing loan repayable over five years in the form of crude oil; (iii) that ERAP would make non-refundable premium payments to INOC totalling $15,000,000 over the 20-year life of the contract; (iv) that ERAP would release 50 per cent of the exploration area after three years, 50 per cent of the remaining area two years later and, at the end of the sixth year, all other areas which had not been brought into production; (v) that INOC would acquire full operational control of the venture, and would own all the installed equipment, five years after the start of exports; (vi) that 50 per cent of oil discovered would belong to INOC as a "national reserve"; (vii) that 30 per cent of oil produced would be purchased by ERAP (including 12 per cent at a preferential tax-free price); and (viii) that the remaining 70 per cent of production would belong to INOC, which could oblige ERAP to market all or part of its entitlement in return for a flat-rate fee per barrel sold.

(ERAP subsequently discovered oil at Abu Gharab, Buzurgan and Siba, although development work was delayed by disputes between the company and the Government. The commencement of exports was authorized in 1973, when a Japanese consortium acquired a minority interest in the contract. The contract was terminated by Iraq in 1977.)

The main decision facing Iraq concerned the development of the proved North Rumaila field, whose return to IPC had formed part of the settlement proposals drafted in 1965. This option having been specifically ruled out by Law 97 of 1967, negotiations on the development of the field were held with CFP (acting outside the framework of IPC); no agreement was reached, however, and it was later announced on April 10, 1968, that INOC would take sole responsibility for the development of North Rumaila. The state company subsequently signed technical assistance agreements with the Soviet Union in mid-1969, and was able to commence production on April 7, 1972, having secured contracts for the export of oil to Italy, Spain and India as well as to the Soviet Union (which received oil in payment for its role in developing the field).

The export of oil from North Rumaila prompted threats of legal action by BPC, which continued to claim ownership of its compulsorily relinquished concession areas. The start of production by INOC coincided with a reduction in output by IPC, which stated that current market conditions had made it uneconomic to operate its pipelines to the Mediterranean at more than half capacity. However, the then OPEC Secretary-General, Dr Nadim Pachachi (in a statement issued on May 30, 1972, in support of the Iraq Government's position), strongly challenged the consortium's claim, pointing out that IPC's 44 per cent cut in production between February and April 1972 far exceeded the percentage falls both in the volume of Saudi Arabia's pipeline exports to the Mediterranean and in the cost of shipping oil from Gulf terminals over the same period. Dr Pachachi concluded that IPC's action was based not on "commercial considerations or market necessities" but on "a high-level managerial policy decision aimed at punishing Iraq for its independent national oil policy and at exerting pressure to hinder implementation of its development programmes".

The Iraq Government, for its part, had issued an ultimatum to IPC on May 17, 1972, giving the consortium two weeks to increase its output, to draw up a long-term production programme in co-operation with the Ministry of Oil and to respond to government proposals made at the beginning of the year for the final settlement of all outstanding disputes. Amounts claimed by the Government from IPC included additional tax payments based on the OPEC royalty-expensing formula of 1964, which had not been implemented in Iraq because of the deadlock over other issues (◊**D1.3.ii**). IPC, for its part, claimed compensation for the reduction in its concession areas, and in particular for the loss of the proved North Rumaila field, which was said by the consortium to entitle it to receive 7 per cent of future INOC production from the field. (This represented a reduction of an earlier claim for 12.5 per cent of production.) The Government, however, offered compensation based on the net book value of exploration work carried out by BPC before 1961.

The compensation issue was complicated by the fact that the IPC shareholder-companies had in March 1972 (within the framework of wider negotiations between the major oil companies and the Middle Eastern OPEC producing countries) finally accepted the principle of 20 per cent government participation in their own producing operations (◊**D3.3**). Each side was therefore aware that any agreement on a formula for paying compensation in the disputes arising out of Law 80 was likely to be cited as a precedent in the future negotiation of participation terms in Iraq and elsewhere.

On May 31, 1972, IPC responded to the Iraq Government's May 17 ultimatum by offering to increase production substantially over the next five years, although the consortium refused to modify its compensation claim. The Government rejected these terms as inadequate to meet "the minimum legitimate claims of the Iraqi people", and on June 1 announced the full nationalization of the consortium's operations in the IPC's own concession area (but not in the MPC and BPC areas), thus securing control of the country's main oilfield at Kirkuk where the recent production cutbacks had occurred. On the same day the Syrian Government nationalized the IPC pipeline and terminal installations on its territory.

Iraq declared its willingness to supply oil from the nationalized fields to the IPC shareholder companies on an individual basis, and almost immediately entered into negotiations with CFP, which signed a provisional agreement on June 18, 1972, for the purchase over a 10-year period of a volume of oil equal to 23.75 per cent of output (i.e. a share equivalent to the company's former entitlement based on its holding in the consortium). Both OPEC and OAPEC expressed their support for the nationalization measures, and the other OAPEC member countries agreed on June 20 to grant loans to Iraq and Syria to offset any consequent fall in their foreign exchange receipts. Dr Pachachi of OPEC and Jean Duroc-Danner of CFP were accepted by both sides as mediators in compensation negotiations been Iraq and IPC which commenced in July 1972. IPC agreed to refrain from taking legal action in respect of oil exports from the nationalized fields while the talks were in progress (although it was able to block exports via Lebanon by virtue of its continued control of the Tripoli pipeline and terminal facilities).

A comprehensive settlement was formally ratified on March 1, 1973, whereby (i) IPC accepted both Law 80 of 1961 and the nationalization law of 1972; (ii) the consortium agreed to the takeover by Iraq of the operations of MPC (whose modest production of 25,000 bpd had already come under de facto Iraqi control because of MPC's reliance on the Mediterranean export pipelines); (iii) it was agreed to increase BPC's production—currently about 675,000 bpd—to 1,600,000 bpd by 1976; (iv) the consortium agreed to meet Iraq's financial claim for the payment of outstanding royalties; and (v) Iraq undertook to provide the shareholder companies with a total of 15,000,000 tonnes of crude oil in 1973–74 at Mediterranean terminals in settlement of claims for compensation.

During the course of the negotiation of nationalization terms with the consortium Iraq had come into dispute with Syria over pipeline transit fees, a substantial increase having been demanded by Syria following its own nationalization of IPC operations. A compromise agreement was reached in January 1973, although in the same month Iraq formed a special committee to plan the construction of a new pipeline to link the northern oilfields to Iraq's own terminals at the head of the Gulf. The Lebanese Government announced the nationalization of IPC installations on its territory on March 2, 1973, following Iraq's settlement with the consortium, and raised the oil transit fees to Tripoli to a level in line with the new Syrian rates. Iraq subsequently signed an agreement with Turkey on Aug. 27, 1973, for the construction of a new pipeline in order to reduce its dependence on the Syrian and Lebanese installations for the export of oil via the Mediterranean.

In October 1973 Iraq nationalized the 23.75 per cent interest in the assets and operations of the Basrah Petroleum Co. held by Near East Development Corp. (Exxon/Mobil) and also 60 per cent of Shell's 23.75 per cent interest in BPC's assets and operations. This action was taken in the context of the latest Arab-Israeli war and the subsequent Arab campaign against US and Dutch links with Israel. (Royal Dutch/Shell is 60 per cent Dutch-owned and 40 per cent British-owned ◊A5.1.vi.) In a further political gesture in December 1973, Iraq nationalized the 5 per cent interest in BPC held by Participations and Explorations Corp. on the grounds that Gulbenkian Foundation, the ultimate owner of the Panamanian-registered corporation, was itself registered in Portugal, a country which was at that time committed to white minority rule in its African colonies. Iraq held a 43 per cent interest in BPC's assets and operations until Dec. 8, 1975, when it nationalized the remaining (British and French) interests in the BPC concession area, thus ending the major oil companies' role in Iraq. A financial settlement between Iraq and all the former BPC shareholder-companies was announced in March 1979.

C6.3.v—Post-nationalization developments

Between 1971 (the last full year in which the IPC consortium was solely responsible for production) and 1979 (the last full year of production before the outbreak of the Gulf war) Iraq's oil output doubled, making it the second largest producer in OPEC in the aftermath of the Iranian revolution. Moreover, oil transportation and export facilities were greatly improved through the construction of (i) a new deep-water tanker terminal at the head of the Gulf, which was completed in 1975; (ii) a strategic pipeline which in 1976 linked the southern oilfields with the existing pipelines from the northern fields to the Mediterranean and which incorporated a reversible pumping system enabling oil from each producing area to be exported either from the Mediterranean or from the Gulf; and (iii) a new export pipeline from the northern fields to the Turkish Mediterranean port of Dörtyol on the Gulf of Iskenderun, which was completed in January 1977.

The construction costs of the Dörtyol pipeline were met partly by Turkey and partly by Iraq, which guaranteed the supply to the Turkish market of a proportion of the throughput of crude oil. The operation of the pipeline was affected by a number of bilateral disputes, including one which led to its closure by Iraq from January to August 1978 in support of a claim for the settlement of debts owed by Turkey for the supply of oil. However, the availability of the alternative north-south strategic pipeline, through which Kirkuk crude was transported to Gulf terminals, minimized the impact on Iraq's exporting capability. The long-established Mediterranean pipelines running through Syria were closed by Iraq in April 1976 as a result of disputes with both Syria and Lebanon over the revision of transit agreements, supplies to Banias remaining suspended until early 1979 and those to Tripoli until late 1981.

INOC, which had experienced few practical difficulties in taking over the mainly Iraqi-staffed operations of the IPC group, greatly expanded its activities during the 1970s with minimum reliance on foreign oil companies, which from 1977 onwards were permitted to operate only on a service contract basis. (The main service contract, with the Brazilian state company Braspetro, was for the development of the important Majnoon field, discovered in 1976.) INOC operated under the management of the Ministry of Oil and had direct responsibility for exploration and development work, for production operations (with separate management of the northern and southern oilfields), for pipelines, for export marketing and for tanker shipping. Separate organizations within the Ministry of Oil dealt with refining and product distribution, while the creation of a petrochemical industry was entrusted to the Ministry of Industry and Minerals.

Having significantly expanded both its crude oil production (see above) and its refinery capacity (which rose by 66 per cent between 1977 and 1979) Iraq was in 1980 engaged in developing its facilities for processing associated natural gas and in establishing new petrochemical plants using gas as a feedstock. All of the country's oil- and gas-related activities were however severely disrupted following the outbreak of the Gulf war in September 1980, and there was considerable physical damage to installations in southern Iraq.

The export of oil from Gulf terminals in the Shatt al-Arab area (at the centre of the conflict) became impossible, while exports to the Mediterranean via pipelines crossing Syrian territory were halted by Syria on April 10, 1982. Iraq subsequently began proceedings against Syria before the OAPEC Judicial Tribunal, claiming compensation of $20,000,000 per day (◊B2.4). Iraq's crude oil exports were limited to a maximum of around 700,000 bpd (the existing capacity of the Dörtyol pipeline) from April 1982 until early 1984, when the pipeline's rated capacity was increased to 1,000,000 bpd (although it was later proved to be capable of operating at more than 110 per cent of this rating when required). In the downstream sector, the closure of the 140,000 bpd Basrah refinery as a result of war damage was followed by a major expansion of refining capacity at Baiji during 1983, and a significant volume of fuel oil was being exported by road via Jordan and Turkey in 1984. Some crude oil was also road-freighted through Turkey at this time, but there were no reports of crude exports via Jordan until late 1985.

Following the increase in the capacity of the Dörtyol pipeline, Iraq was able to bring its 1984 crude oil output, including production for the domestic market, up to its OPEC quota entitlement of 1,200,000 bpd—i.e. some 34 per cent above the level to which output had fallen in 1981. (Iraq's 1981 output of 895,000 bpd was the lowest since 1959.) Saudi Arabia and Kuwait helped to offset the fall in Iraq's oil export earnings by marketing Neutral Zone crude on behalf of Iraq (which received the resulting revenue), the average volume of these "war relief" supplies being rather more than 300,000 bpd.

At the end of September 1985 up to 500,000 bpd of new export capacity became available to Iraq at the Saudi Red Sea port of Yanbu following the construction over a period of 11 months of a link between the southern Iraqi oilfields and the Saudi Petroline. Saudi Arabia and Iraq subsequently reached an agreement in early 1986 for the expansion to 1,600,000 bpd of Iraq's total export capacity via Saudi Arabia and for the construction of a separate terminal for Iraqi crude some 20 km south of Yanbu, completion of these projects being scheduled for 1987. Work began in the first half of 1986 on a 500,000 bpd expansion of the Iraq-Dörtyol pipeline, with a scheduled completion date of June 1987. These two expansion programmes would bring Iraq's end-1987 export capability via Dörtyol and the Red Sea to 3,100,000 bpd, close to the historical peak level of Iraqi crude exports (3,275,300 bpd in 1979) although about 1,000,000 bpd below the oil industry's installed production capacity in 1985. Proposals to build a 1,000,000 bpd export pipeline from Haditha in central Iraq to the Jordanian Red Sea port of Aqaba were shelved during 1985. Notwithstanding the start-up of Iraqi exports from Yanbu, Kuwait and Saudi Arabia continued to export Neutral Zone crude on Iraq's behalf in the first half of 1986, although it was not clear whether this implied a renewal of the "war-relief" arrangement for 1986 or a completion of supply commitments carried over from 1985.

At the outbreak of the Gulf war five proved oilfields were scheduled for development in Iraq with the aim of raising total production capacity to around 6,000,000 bpd. Implementation of these projects was subsequently deferred because of their proximity to the main war zone, the area containing the largest field (Majnoon) being occupied by Iranian forces for a period until its recapture by Iraq in 1986. Associated gas from the undeveloped fields had featured in the pre-war industrialization programme for the south of the country, based on the manufacture of petrochemicals for export from the Gulf. Having been forced to postpone the completion of its southern programme, the Government proceeded with plans to build a number of smaller petrochemical plants, designed to serve the home market, at more secure locations in the northern half of the country. The proposed construction of a major gas-processing plant near the northern oilfields, from which an annual 3,000,000 tonnes of liquefied petroleum gas would have been piped to the Turkish Mediterranean port of Yumurtalik, was shelved in 1985. A new pipeline was, however, built in 1986 to export gas from the southern Rumaila oilfield to a Kuwaiti processing plant at Shuaiba.

C7—Kuwait

C7.1—Statistical Survey

*1984
†End-1984
‡Revision of 1984 figures given in section **D15.1.i** (see Introduction)

General
Area	17,818 sq km
*Population	1,640,000
Capital	Kuwait City

Economy and trade
*Gross national product	$32,960 million
*Annual exports (fob)	$10,750 million (of which petroleum 95.9 per cent)
*Annual imports (cif)	$7,697 million
*Current account balance	+$5,570 million
Foreign exchange reserves	$4,298 million (January 1986)

Oil (upstream), excluding Neutral Zone
1984 crude production	985,000 bpd (48,900,000 tonnes)
1985 crude production	910,000 bpd (45,000,000 tonnes)
†Proved crude reserves	90,000 million barrels
*Reserves:production ratio	249.6 : 1
Production in peak year	3,055,000 bpd (153,000,000 tonnes) in 1972
†Cumulative crude production	21,385.5 million barrels since 1946
*Number of producing oil wells	329
Export grade	31° API gravity

Neutral Zone (production and reserves shared with Saudi Arabia)
‡Total 1984 crude production	405,000 bpd (21,100,000 tonnes)
Total 1985 crude production	360,000 bpd (18,700,000 tonnes)
†Total proved crude reserves	5,400 million barrels
*Reserves:production ratio	35.7 : 1
Production in peak year	570,000 bpd (29,400,000 tonnes) in 1979
†Cumulative crude production	3,879.7 million barrels since 1954
*Number of producing oil wells	459
Export grades: Khafji	28° API gravity
Hout	35° API gravity

Oil tanker tonnage
†20 vessels	2,108,000 deadweight tons

Oil (downstream, excluding Neutral Zone)
*Installed refining capacity	614,000 bpd
*Output of refined products	477,800 bpd
*Consumption of refined products	83,000 bpd

Natural gas (million cubic metres)

*Gross annual production	....	5,814 mcm
of which: (gas marketed)	....	(4,114 mcm)
(gas reinjected)	....	(250 mcm)
(gas flared)	....	(650 mcm)
(shrinkage)	....	(800 mcm)
†Natural gas reserves	....	900,000 mcm

C7.2—Political and Economic Summary

The state of Kuwait traces its origins to the establishment by Arabian migrants of a settlement on the north-west coast of the Persian/Arabian Gulf. The ruling Sabah dynasty, founded in 1765, was subject to nominal Ottoman sovereignty until 1899, when it entered into a treaty relationship with Britain, which assumed responsibility for defence and foreign policy matters. The treaty was terminated in June 1961, when Kuwait became fully independent. Independence was immediately followed by the assertion of a claim by Iraq (as an Ottoman successor state) to sovereignty over the whole territory of Kuwait. However, this claim was resisted by the remaining members of the Arab League, whose pledge of support for Kuwait's independence was backed by an undertaking to send troops to repel any aggression against Kuwait. Iraq renounced its main claim to Kuwait following the change of regime in Baghdad in 1963 (◊C6.2), although it retained dormant claims to certain border areas. One consequence of the dispute was Iraq's refusal to attend the 3rd, 4th and 5th meetings of the OPEC Conference (◊D1.2, D1.3).

The 6,500 sq km Neutral Zone between Saudi Arabia and Kuwait (which under an agreement of 1922 had constituted an undivided territory subject to joint sovereignty and equal rights over natural resources) was geographically divided between the two countries under the terms of a bilateral agreement signed in 1965, and each country's half of the Zone subsequently came under national administration. However, rights over the natural resources of the Zone remained undivided, and all oil produced within it continued to be regarded as jointly owned for fiscal purposes. The geographical partition of the Zone applied only to its land boundaries. There have been frequent disagreements between Saudi Arabia and Kuwait since 1965 over the procedures for dividing revenue from jointly-owned Neutral Zone hydrocarbons.

Kuwait's first elections were held in December 1961 for a Constituent Assembly, which drew up a Constitution under which the hereditary Amir (as executive head of state) appointed a Council of Ministers, while a National Assembly was established as an elective legislature. Assembly elections took place on a non-party basis in 1963, 1967, 1971 and 1975, but in 1976 the Assembly (which had increasingly asserted its powers to block the passage of legislation ◊C7.3.iii) was dissolved on the grounds that it had been acting against the best interests of the state. The reinstatement of the legislature was decreed by the Amir in 1980 on the basis of a revised Constitution, and a new Assembly elected in 1981 served its full four-year term, fresh elections being held in February 1985. A subsequent renewal of friction between the legislature and the executive—reflecting the success of many radical "opposition" candidates in the 1985 Assembly elections—eventually prompted the Council of Ministers to resign en bloc on July 1, 1986. Three days later the Amir dissolved the Assembly and suspended parts of the Constitution. As in 1976, no date was set for fresh elections.

The title of Amir of Kuwait has been held since the beginning of 1978 by Shaikh Jabir al Ahmad al Sabah, whose heir apparent is Shaikh Saad al Abdullah al Salim al Sabah (the Prime Minister). Islam is the predominant religion in Kuwait, an estimated two-thirds of the country's Moslems (including political leaders) being Sunnis and the remainder Shi'ites. Only about 40 per cent of the total population (and less than one-third of the labour force) are native Kuwaitis, most of the remainder being other Arabs (including many Palestinians), with a minority of Indians, Pakistanis and Iranians. The franchise is restricted to native Kuwaiti males, and persons not born to native Kuwaiti parents have no entitlement to citizenship.

As the holder of a substantial accumulation of "surplus" oil revenues, Kuwait was relatively well placed to withstand the downturn in the world oil market after the early 1980s. The Government's reserves (as opposed to the foreign exchange reserves held by the Central Bank) totalled $76,000 million at the end of 1984, when income from overseas investments was running at an estimated annual rate of $4,700 million. Nominal budget deficits began to be recorded in 1982–83 under a government accounting system which omitted to include investment income on the revenue side (although capital transfers to reserves were included as expenditure items), and it was not until 1984–85 that a real deficit began to develop. The 1985–86 budget estimates provided for a nominal deficit of $1,900 million after allowing for the first annual spending cutback since oil exports began. On the revenue side, allowance was made for a 3.4 per cent decline in revenues in the 12 months from July 1985. Kuwait's oil revenue subsequently showed an estimated year-on-year fall of about 15 per cent in the first half of 1986, when export volume was raised to around 173 per cent of its January–June 1985 level to offset the impact of the slump in per-barrel earnings. Since 1976 statutory transfers of 10 per cent of annual government revenue have been made to a "reserve fund for future generations", created in anticipation of an eventual transition to a non-oil-based economy.

Despite the recession in Kuwait's economy in 1985—marked by a fall of 10.5 per cent in real gross domestic product—living standards remained exceptionally high, reflecting many years of government investment in public works and social welfare projects. The country has a well-developed infrastructure, but there has been relatively little industrial diversification outside the hydrocarbons sector. A main aim of a five-year development plan announced in 1985 was to improve productivity and to reduce the country's heavy dependence on expatriate labour. The public sector was expected to provide 84 per cent of the plan's investment target of nearly $25,000 million. The private sector of the economy was still recovering in 1986 from the effects of the collapse of the country's unofficial stock market (the Souk al Manakh) in 1982, which had left the local financial system in considerable disarray.

Kuwait is one of the world's leading donors of official development assistance to third-world countries—devoting a higher proportion of gross national product to net aid disbursements than any other country in 1982 and 1983—although the amounts disbursed were beginning to decline by the mid-1980s. Kuwait's bilateral aid programme is administered by the Kuwait Fund for Arab Economic Development, which was established in 1961 and empowered in 1974 to support development projects in non-Arab countries. At the end of 1984 the fund's cumulative commitments totalled $4,240 million and its cumulative disbursements $2,682 million.

Kuwait has generally followed a pro-Western foreign policy when compatible with its overriding support for the Arab cause in the Middle East. At the same time, however, Kuwait was until late 1985—when Oman and the UAE followed its long-standing example—the only member of the Gulf Co-operation Council to have full diplomatic relations with the Soviet Union. Kuwait supports Iraq in the Gulf war, important factors in this alignment being the Government's apprehensions concerning the impact of an Iranian victory upon Kuwait (where militant Shi'ites claimed responsibility for terrorist bomb attacks in December 1983) as well as its hopes for the conclusion of a border demarcation agreement with Iraq. Kuwait's internal security was compromised in 1985 by an assassination attempt on the Amir in May and a fatal terrorist bombing in July, which were denounced by the Government as part of a "fierce foreign conspiracy" to destabilize the country. Fears over external security were heightened in early 1986 when Iranian troops occupied areas of Iraq within sight of the Kuwaiti border. During 1985 Iranian forces had frequently boarded shipping in the Gulf to search for military equipment destined for Iraq via Kuwaiti ports.

C7.3—Oil and Gas Industry

C7.3.i—The Gulf/BP concession

A 75-year oil concession covering the whole territory of Kuwait was granted in December 1934 to Gulf Oil Corp. and the Anglo-Persian Oil Co., these two companies having agreed in 1933 to apply for joint concession rights after each had failed (in rival bids) to obtain exclusive rights (◊A4.5.ii). (Anglo-Persian changed its name to Anglo-Iranian in 1935 and to British Petroleum in 1954.) The concessionaires paid an initial premium of 470,000 rupees (about £35,250 sterling) and undertook to make future payments as follows: (i) an annual "dead rent" of Rs 95,000 (£7,125 sterling); (ii) royalties at the rate of three rupees (4s 6d sterling) per ton of oil produced, subject to a minimum total of Rs 250,000 (£18,750 sterling) per annum; and (iii) an additional sum of four annas (4½ sterling) per ton in return for exemption from local taxation. The effective level of the Kuwait royalty was somewhat lower than the prevailing level in neighbouring countries where payment was required to be made in gold pounds rather than in local currency.

Exploratory drilling commenced in 1936, and one of the world's largest oilfields, Burgan, was discovered in 1938. Development work was interrupted by the Second World War, and commercial production did not begin until 1946. A plan to build an export pipeline to a Syrian Mediterranean port was dropped after it had proved impossible to negotiate an acceptable transit agreement with Iraq (which saw the plan as a threat to the expansion of its own oil exports). Kuwait's exports were accordingly shipped only from the Gulf, where a new port was developed at Mina al Ahmadi. Kuwait's oil output reached 1,000,000 bpd in 1955, having doubled since the start of the Iranian nationalization crisis in 1951 (◊C5.3.i).

Production operations were managed by the Kuwait Oil Company (KOC), owned jointly by Anglo-Iranian and Gulf Oil. KOC worked on a non-profit-making basis, transferring oil to its parent companies at prices which covered its costs and interest charges. New capital investment was funded equally by the parent companies to the extent that they derived equal benefit from increased production capacity. Each company was free to make additional capital investments at any time if it wished to increase capacity beyond this point (i.e. to enable it to lift more than 50 per cent of total KOC output), the necessary financial arrangements being made directly between the parent companies without altering the equal division of KOC's share capital. Additional quantities of oil obtained by one of the parent companies in this way were available to that company at KOC's normal cost price.

Under an agreement concluded between the two parent companies in 1933 (i.e. prior to the granting of the Kuwait concession) Anglo-Iranian reserved the right to supply Gulf (at KOC's standard price) with oil produced in Iran and/or Iraq in lieu of oil which Gulf was entitled to take from Kuwait; both companies undertook not to compete with one another directly or indirectly in the marketing of oil obtained through their Kuwait partnership. A further inter-company agreement of 1951 cancelled the latter provision, leaving each of the co-concessionaires with an overall freedom of action which had no parallel within the other major joint operating companies of the Gulf region at that time.

One consequence of KOC's unrestricted production arrangements was that Kuwait became an additional long-term supply source for several oil companies whose own Middle East output was regulated in accordance with inter-company offtake agreements. Anglo-Iranian concluded supply contracts with Exxon and Mobil in 1947–48, each of which took effect for 20 years from 1952 and was fulfilled largely from Anglo-Iranian's Kuwait output (although it was also open to the company to supply Iranian crude). A total of about 800,000,000 barrels was to be supplied to Exxon over the contract period at cost price plus a fixed cash margin, while about 500,000,000 barrels were to be supplied to Mobil at cost plus a variable margin related to market prices. A long-term contract between Gulf and Shell, which took effect in 1947 and was extended in 1956 for the entire remaining life of the Kuwait concession (then expected to be 70 years), provided for the supply by Gulf of large quantities of Kuwaiti crude in return for a percentage of Shell's net profits from this oil. During the 1950s more than half of Gulf's Kuwait output was marketed on this basis.

In December 1951 the Kuwait Government introduced a corporate income tax decree and concluded an agreement for "50-50 profit-sharing" in respect of KOC's operations. These measures followed the pattern established in Saudi Arabia (◊C11.3.iii) and provided for a maximum state revenue entitlement of 50 per cent of net profits, with royalties and other payments fully credited against the overall tax liability. Gulf and Anglo-Iranian each transferred the ownership of their shareholdings in KOC to new wholly-owned trading subsidiaries to which export profits were attributed for tax purposes. Other provisions of the December 1951 agreement excluded Kuwait's offshore waters from the KOC concession area while extending the duration of the onshore concession by 17 years (i.e. a period equal to that for which it had already run) and thus changing its expiry date from 2009 to 2026. A further agreement of October 1955 (i) provided for the use of full posted prices (i.e. without any "marketing allowance") in assessing the taxable profits arising from KOC's operations, and (ii) redefined the royalty element in the state's revenue entitlement as an amount equal to 12.5 per cent of the posted price.

C7.3.ii—Other companies' concessions in Kuwait and Neutral Zone

The KOC parent companies agreed in May 1962 to select a total of 9,622 sq km from the undeveloped parts of their onshore concession area for immediate relinquishment to the state. A further 1,000 sq km was relinquished in 1967 and 1,152 sq km in 1971. (The 1934 concession agreement did not contain any relinquishment provisions.) In 1960 BP and Gulf Oil were among the unsuccessful bidders for concession rights over Kuwait's offshore waters. A 45-year offshore concession was granted to Shell in January 1961 on terms which included an option for the Kuwait Government to acquire a 20 per cent interest in the exploitation of commercial discoveries—this being the first occasion on which one of the major oil companies had agreed to enter into an equity partnership with a Middle Eastern host government. Shell paid an initial premium of £7,000,000 sterling to the Kuwait Government and undertook to make further payments totalling £23,000,000 on specified dates thereafter, but did not succeed in locating any commercially significant hydrocarbon deposits despite extensive survey work and the drilling of several exploratory wells.

Concession rights over Kuwait's half-interest in the Kuwait-Saudi Arabian Neutral Zone remained unallocated until after the Second World War. Whereas Saudi Arabian Neutral Zone rights had been reserved to the main concessionaire company within Saudi Arabia proper (on a preferential basis from 1933 to 1939 and

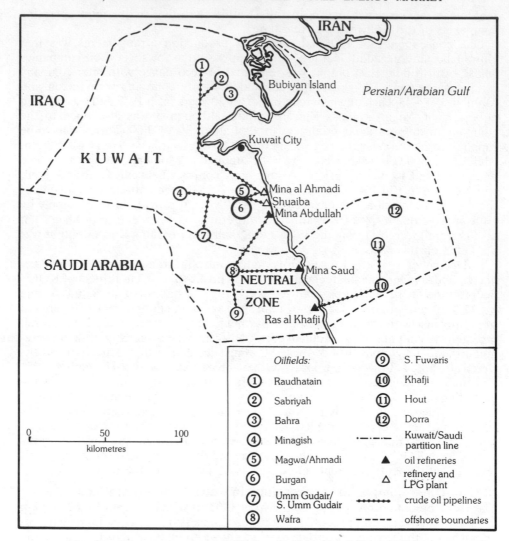

Fig. 12—Oil resources and installations in Kuwait and Neutral Zone

an exclusive basis from 1939 to 1948 ◊C11.3.i, C11.3.ii), it was not possible for any parallel agreement to be made between Kuwait and the KOC parent companies because of the inclusion of the Neutral Zone within the "red line agreement", to which Anglo-Iranian was a party (as was Gulf Oil until 1934 ◊C6.3.i). In late 1946 the Kuwait Government announced its intention to open its Neutral Zone rights to competitive bidding, the successful bid being made by the American Independent Oil Co. (Aminoil), which was formed in 1947 by a consortium of US independent companies among which Phillips Petroleum and Signal Oil and Gas took the largest shareholdings. (Aminoil later became a subsidiary of R.J. Reynolds Industries Inc.)

Aminoil's 60-year onshore Neutral Zone concession agreement, concluded in June 1948, provided (i) for an initial capital payment by the company of $7,500,000; (ii) for a royalty rate of $2.50 per ton (then the highest such rate in the Middle East); (iii) for a guaranteed total annual royalty payment of at least $625,000; (iv) for the payment to the Kuwait Government of 12.5 per cent of locally-made profits;

and (v) for the construction of a local refinery. A concession over Saudi Arabia's half-interest in the Neutral Zone, which was opened to bids after Aramco relinquished its rights in October 1948, was granted in February 1949 (◊**C11.3.ii**) to the Pacific Western Oil Corp. (later renamed Getty Oil). Getty and Aminoil subsequently reached a working agreement under which each of the concessionaire companies retained responsibility for the organization of its own operations (although for fiscal purposes all production was deemed to be shared between Kuwait and Saudi Arabia on the basis of their undivided co-ownership of Neutral Zone resources). Oil was discovered at Wafra in 1953 and exports commenced initially from Aminoil's terminal at Mina Abdullah (within Kuwait proper), a second terminal being opened by Getty in 1955 at Mina Saud (within the Neutral Zone). Refineries were later built near each terminal. During succeeding years the concessionaire companies agreed to improve the co-ordination of their operations by conducting many exploration and production activities on a cost-sharing basis.

Following Saudi Arabia's 1957 concession agreement with the Japan Petroleum Trading Co. in respect of the offshore waters of the Neutral Zone (◊**C11.3.iv**), Kuwait reached an agreement with the same company in May 1958 covering its own half-interest in the offshore area for a total period of 44½ years. There was thus no requirement for a complicated working agreement between separate operating companies, all production activities within the concession area being managed by the Arabian Oil Co. (AOC). The financial provisions of the Kuwait-AOC concession agreement were closely modelled on those negotiated six months earlier by Saudi Arabia, although in certain respects Kuwait obtained marginally better terms (e.g. a 57 per cent share of AOC's profits compared with Saudi Arabia's 56 per cent). Aminoil's 1948 concession agreement was amended in 1961 to provide for an overall government revenue entitlement equal to the higher of (i) 57 per cent of net profits calculated with reference to realized export prices or (ii) 50 per cent of net profits calculated on the basis of posted prices.

The Kuwait National Petroleum Company (KNPC) was formed in 1960, under 60 per cent government and 40 per cent private Kuwaiti ownership, with powers to engage in all phases of the hydrocarbons industry. In 1961 KNPC acquired all rights over the domestic marketing of petroleum products manufactured at KOC's Mina al Ahmadi refinery (which were supplied to KNPC at cost price), and in 1965 it started to build its own export refinery at Shuaiba, to be supplied initially with crude from KOC's Umm Gudair field (discovered in 1962).

In 1967 an agreement was concluded between KNPC and the Spanish company Hispanoil for the joint exploration and exploitation of onshore concession areas which had been relinquished by the KOC parent companies. It was envisaged that Hispanoil's share of production would go to the Spanish import market (a 25 per cent share of which was guaranteed for 15 years) while KNPC's share would go mainly to the Shuaiba refinery. The agreement, which was intended to run for an initial period of 35 years, required Hispanoil to finance all exploration costs, which were recoverable (out of future profits) only in the event of commercial discoveries. A joint operating company, the Kuwait Spanish Petroleum Co. (KSPC), owned 51 per cent by KNPC and 49 per cent by Hispanoil, was formed in 1968 (the same year that the Shuaiba refinery went on stream). Exploratory drilling commenced in 1970 but failed to locate any commercial oilfield, and KSPC was wound up in 1976.

C7.3.iii—The royalty-expensing issue – Subsequent extension of state control over oil industry

The KOC parent companies, which had hitherto maintained a harmonious relationship with the Kuwait Government, free from any serious disputes of the type which had arisen elsewhere in the Middle East in connexion with the terms of concession agreements, were exposed to increasing public criticism within Kuwait after the inauguration of an elected legislature in 1963 (◊C7.2). A fundamental change in the political climate first became apparent in January 1965, when the National Assembly refused to ratify an agreement which had been signed by the Government and the KOC parent companies with the aim of applying the new Middle East royalty expensing formula (◊D1.3.ii) to KOC's operations.

The Assembly's principal objections were (i) to a clause declaring the agreement to be a full and final settlement of all outstanding financial claims against the concessionaire companies (which was criticized on the grounds that it amounted to a tacit acceptance by the Government of the cuts in Middle East posted prices which had been made by the major oil companies in 1959–60 ◊A4.10.iii); (ii) to a clause providing for the settlement of disputes by international arbitration (which was criticized because the companies were currently subject to a 1955 income tax decree which provided for adjudication by Kuwaiti courts); and (iii) to a clause entitling the KOC companies to the enjoyment of fiscal treatment equal to the most favourable treatment accorded to any other concessionaire company in Kuwait (criticized on the grounds that it imposed unreasonable limitations on the Government's freedom of action, particularly with regard to the future development of KNPC's upstream activities). The KOC companies, for their part, were reluctant to accept any amendment of the terms of an agreement which was intended to apply to the Gulf region as a whole.

Continuing opposition to the royalty expensing agreement was spearheaded by radical nationalist elements in Kuwait, who progressively widened the scope of their campaign—conducted both inside and outside the National Assembly—to include criticism of many aspects of the basic KOC concession agreement. Accordingly, the Government in mid-1966 indicated its readiness to take unilateral legislative action to impose revised terms on the concessionaire companies. In November 1966 the companies agreed to compromise on the royalty expensing question (i) by recognizing Kuwait's right to challenge the level of posted prices in the future, (ii) by undertaking to submit disputes connected with Kuwait's tax laws to the Kuwaiti courts, (iii) by accepting the exclusion of KNPC from the "most-favoured-company" clause, and (iv) by backdating the entry into force of the financial provisions of the agreement. The revised agreement was finally ratified by a newly elected National Assembly in May 1967.

In 1968 the Government declared its intention to seek state participation in the operations of KOC, and Kuwait accordingly joined neighbouring OPEC countries in subsequent negotiations with the major concessionaire companies in the Gulf region which culminated in the conclusion of the General Agreement on Participation of October 1972 (◊D3.4). However, having signed a national agreement with the KOC parent companies on Jan. 8, 1973 (which was intended to take effect from the beginning of that year), the Government once more faced strong opposition to its oil policy within the National Assembly.

Ratification was withheld by the Assembly, a majority of whose members maintained (i) that the state should acquire immediate majority control over KOC's operations (whereas the proposed agreement envisaged a gradual increase in the level of state participation, which would not reach 51 per cent until the beginning of 1982), and (ii) that compensation for the acquisition of any state interest in KOC's operations should be based on a net book valuation of the company's assets (whereas the proposed agreement provided for a much higher updated book valuation which would require the Government to pay $150,000,000 for an initial 25 per cent interest). In June 1973 the Government undertook to secure a more acceptable agreement, its new target of immediate 51 per cent state control of

KOC's operations being increased to 60 per cent during the course of negotiations with the parent companies later in 1973.

On Jan. 29, 1974, the companies agreed that a 60 per cent interest in their Kuwait operations should be transferred to the Government in return for compensation of $112,000,000 (calculated at net book value). These terms were ratified by the National Assembly on May 14, 1974, by 32 votes to 2 with 20 abstentions (mainly of members who advocated immediate 100 per cent state control). Under this agreement, which was to be reviewed "prior to the end of 1979", the functions of the London-registered Kuwait Oil Company were taken over by a new Kuwait-registered operating company of the same name, owned 60 per cent by the Kuwait Government, 20 per cent by BP (Kuwait) Ltd and 20 per cent by Gulf Kuwait Co. All operations, rights and facilities of the former parent companies came under 60 per cent state ownership with effect from Jan. 1, 1974, and the companies undertook to pay to the Government an amount equal to that which would have been payable during 1973 "if there had been applied in Kuwait participation arrangements based on those generally applicable in other Arab countries" of the Gulf region.

On March 5, 1975, the Government announced the immediate takeover of the remaining Gulf and BP interests in Kuwait, a detailed agreement on the financial terms of the takeover being reached on Dec. 1, 1975, and ratified by the National Assembly on March 18, 1976. Compensation was based on a $50,500,000 net book valuation of the assets acquired. A separate agreement on the future commercial relationship between the fully nationalized KOC and the former parent companies provided (i) that the companies would guarantee to purchase, and KOC would guarantee to supply at a discount of 15 cents per barrel, an average of 950,000 bpd of oil during the five years 1976–80, BP's "base entitlement" being 450,000 bpd and Gulf's 500,000 bpd; (ii) that any additional purchases above the base entitlement level would be subject to separately negotiated contracts, with no price discount and no guarantee of preferential access to supplies; and (iii) that the companies would ship their purchases of Kuwaiti oil in Kuwaiti tankers when available and would purchase bunker fuel from Kuwait. The companies would not be expected to provide technical services and personnel to KOC in future years except in response to specific requests for particular jobs to be carried out at commercial rates.

In drawing up the five-year preferential sales contracts the Government apparently took account of the volumes of Kuwaiti oil which each of the former concessionaire companies had previously used within its own downstream marketing system (i.e. as opposed to oil which was resold to arm's-length customers). Gulf's long-term supply contract with Shell (◊C7.3.i) had been terminated by mutual agreement between the two companies in January 1975, when it was replaced by a three-year contract between the Kuwait Government and Shell for the supply of up to 400,000 bpd on 60-day credit terms (then equivalent to a discount of 10 cents per barrel). The period of the Shell contract was later extended and its terms revised, and in 1978 the company was purchasing an average 260,000 bpd on 75-day credit terms. A contract of March 5, 1975, between the Kuwait Government and Exxon, providing for the sale of an average 100,000 bpd on 60-day credit terms, was suspended at the end of 1976.

The operations of Aminoil in the Neutral Zone were nationalized by Kuwait on Sept. 19, 1977, after the breakdown of negotiations to draw up an agreed formula for the acquisition of a majority state interest in these operations. Compensation terms and other issues in dispute subsequently became the subject of international arbitration. The Arabian Oil Co. (which had earlier agreed to an increased level of taxation of its profits) was thus left as the only producing company outside full Kuwaiti state ownership, the possibility of which was effectively excluded because of the Saudi Arabian Government's equity interest in AOC.

C7.3.iv—Post-nationalization developments

A plan to create a Kuwait Oil, Gas and Energy Corporation as a holding company for state-owned hydrocarbon enterprises was dropped in July 1976, when it was decided that such enterprises would function for the time being as separate entities under the general management of the Oil Ministry. (The Oil Ministry was itself subject to the policy guidance of a ministerial Higher Petroleum Council which had been set up in August 1974 under the chairmanship of the Prime Minister.) In addition to KOC and KNPC, the main state-controlled enterprises were the Petrochemical Industries Co. (PIC) and, from 1979, the Kuwait Oil Tanker Co. (KOTC). KNPC became 100 per cent government-owned in 1975, while a minority private-sector shareholding in PIC (established in 1963) was similarly bought out in 1976. KOTC, established in 1957 by private Kuwaiti interests, was brought into 49 per cent state ownership in 1976 before being fully nationalized in 1979. The nationalized Aminoil operations were run by a new state company, Al Wafra, until April 1978, when responsibility for production was taken over by KOC and responsibility for refining and marketing by KNPC.

In January 1980 the Kuwait Petroleum Corporation (KPC) was established as a state holding company responsible for the overall management of all aspects of the hydrocarbons industry, with KOC, KNPC, PIC and KOTC as its principal subsidiaries. At the same time the management of KOC's refinery was transferred to KNPC as part of a rationalization under which KOC became solely an exploration and production company and KNPC a refining and distribution company. In 1981 KPC established two new companies, the Kuwait Foreign Petroleum Exploration Co. (a wholly-owned subsidiary empowered to undertake crude oil and natural gas exploration, development and production operations outside Kuwait) and the Kuwait International Petroleum Investment Co. (owned 70 per cent by KPC and 30 per cent by private Kuwaiti investors and empowered to engage in refining and petrochemical operations outside Kuwait).

In April 1980, following the expiry of the five-year oil supply contracts with BP and Gulf which had been negotiated after the full nationalization of KOC, Kuwait introduced new one-year contracts in which price discounts were eliminated, the total volume of oil available to the companies was reduced and premium prices were charged in respect of oil purchased for resale to arm's-length customers (◊**D11.3**). Similar terms were to apply to future purchases by Shell. Kuwait's total contract sales to the three companies, which had previously averaged 1,300,000 bpd, fell to 225,000 bpd under the April 1980 contracts, and were further reduced to 150,000 bpd in April 1981 after the companies had refused to accept the continuation of the premium pricing system (◊**D12.2**). BP and Shell terminated their contracts in November 1981, while Gulf Oil reduced its purchases to 35,000 bpd at the beginning of 1982.

Kuwait's overall level of oil production had meanwhile been substantially cut back from its peak of 3,055,000 bpd in 1972. A law on the conservation of petroleum resources was introduced in 1973, and in 1975, following the nationalization of KOC, a production ceiling of 2,000,000 bpd was imposed in the interests of the optimum long-term exploitation of the country's oil reserves (which were exceeded only by those of Saudi Arabia). This ceiling was breached in 1979 in the aftermath of the Iranian revolution, but was reduced in April 1980 to 1,500,000 bpd and further reduced in April 1981 to 1,250,000 bpd. In March 1983 Kuwait accepted an OPEC production quota of 1,050,000 bpd, which was reduced to 900,000 bpd in November 1984 (each of these quotas being inclusive of Kuwait's share of Neutral Zone output).

Kuwait's combined national and Neutral Zone crude production fell steadily after 1979 to reach about 850,000 bpd—the lowest annual average for 30 years—in

1982. A corresponding fall in production of associated natural gas led to widespread fuel-switching (i.e. to oil) at gas-fired power stations and caused major cutbacks in the country's output of gas products. (Kuwait's main LPG export plant, which opened at Shuaiba in 1979, required a gas input based on oil production of 2,000,000 bpd in order to operate at optimum capacity.) While Kuwait's oil output recovered somewhat after 1982, gas supplies continued to fall far short of demand, and plans to expand the capacity of the petrochemicals sector were scaled down because of uncertainties over the availability of adequate volumes of gas feedstock in the medium term. KOC carried out an onshore deep-drilling programme in 1984 with the aim of locating non-associated gas deposits, but instead struck a new oil-bearing zone containing an estimated 20,700 million barrels of recoverable light crude (whereas heavier crudes predominated in Kuwait's existing proved reserves).

Kuwait became OPEC's only gas-importing country in mid-1986, when the Shuaiba plant began to receive supplies of associated gas from southern Iraq through a new pipeline with an annual capacity of about 2,000 million cubic metres (due to be doubled before the end of the year). A parallel pipeline was planned to carry 40,000 bpd of condensate from Iraq, while the delivery of limited volumes of associated gas from the onshore Neutral Zone oilfields was expected to begin before the end of 1986.

The reduction in Kuwait's crude oil production in the first half of the 1980s was accompanied by an expansion and modernization of the country's mainly export-oriented refinery capacity, the share of product exports in total oil exports being more than 40 per cent by volume and more than 50 per cent by value in 1983. By early 1986 a major upgrading project had been completed at the 270,000 bpd Mina al Admadi refinery, while upgrading and expansion of the 144,000 bpd Mina Abdullah refinery was well advanced. KNPC's main aim in upgrading these plants was to enhance Kuwait's ability to respond rapidly to changes in the pattern of export demand by varying the balance of its refinery output across a wide range of product types, their production operations being closely co-ordinated with those of the company's 200,000 bpd Shuaiba refinery (where highly flexible processing facilities were already installed).

In February 1983 KPC acquired Gulf Oil's marketing and distribution network in the Benelux countries (comprising 750 service stations), together with Gulf's 75,500 bpd Dutch refinery and a lubricating oils plant (both situated at Rotterdam). In the following month KPC took over Gulf's 85,000 bpd Danish refinery at Skaelskor (together with two lubricating oils blending plants) and its 825 service stations in Denmark and Sweden. Under a further agreement with Gulf Oil in January 1984, KPC acquired 1,500 Italian service stations and a 75 per cent interest in an 80,000 bpd refinery at Bertonico (which had closed down in 1982). Other European acquisitions (including the purchase of 53 of Elf Aquitaine's Belgian service stations in mid-1985) placed KPC in a position to market up to 250,000 bpd of Kuwaiti oil through its own overseas retail outlets in early 1986, with some flexibility to choose between refining in Kuwait and refining in Europe according to the prevailing balance of commercial advantage. An important corollary of Kuwait's venture into fully integrated foreign downstream operations was the obligation to accept market-related netbacks at the upstream end of the supply chain, thus blurring the application of the country's official crude price prior to the collapse of the OPEC pricing system at the end of 1985.

KPC's previous foreign acquisitions had included notably the US-based Santa Fe International Corporation, which was taken over in late 1981 and reconstituted as a wholly-owned subsidiary of KPC. Santa Fe's worldwide operations included oil and gas exploration and production (particularly in the United States and the North Sea), onshore and offshore contract drilling, the management of oil industry engineering and construction projects and the provision of a wide range of allied services. KPC was also involved in foreign upstream ventures (mainly in third-world countries) through its ownership of the Kuwait Foreign Petroleum Exploration Co., which by 1984 had progressed from the acquisition of non-operating interests in existing exploration concessions to the acquisition of operating interests and the negotiation of new joint-venture concessions. Other KPC subsidiaries with overseas interests included the Petrochemical Industries Company, which in 1982 acquired a 49 per cent shareholding in a Tunisian fertilizer company.

KPC's net operating revenue in 1985 totalled $13,190 million, 81 per cent of which was derived from the operations of the parent company and of subsidiaries incorporated in Kuwait while the balance was contributed by subsidiaries incorporated outside Kuwait.

C8—Libya

C8.1—Statistical Survey

*1984
†End-1984
‡Revision of 1984 figures given in section **D15.1.i** (see Introduction)

General
Area .... 1,775,500 sq km
*Population 3,620,000
Capital .... Tripoli

Economy and trade
*Gross national product .... $27,200 million
*Annual exports (fob) .... $11,136 million (of which petroleum
                            99.9 per cent)
*Annual imports (cif) .... $6,908 million
*Current account balance .... −$1,930 million
Foreign exchange reserves .... $5,494 million (January 1986)

Oil (upstream)
‡1984 crude production .... 1,105,000 bpd (53,000,000 tonnes)
 1985 crude production .... 1,090,000 bpd (52,100,000 tonnes)
†Proved crude reserves .... 21,100 million barrels
*Reserves:production ratio .... 52.1 : 1
 Production in peak year .... 3,320,000 bpd (159,800,000 tonnes)
                            in 1970
†Cumulative crude production .... 14,491.3 million barrels since 1961
*Number of producing oil wells 961
Export grades: Brega .... 40° API gravity
              Zueitina .... 40° API gravity
              Sirtica .... 40° API gravity
              Sarir .... 38.5° API gravity
              Es Sider .... 37° API gravity
              Amna .... 36° API gravity
              Bu Attifel .... 40° API gravity

Oil tanker tonnage
†11 vessels .... 1,384,900 deadweight tons

Oil (downstream)
*Installed refining capacity .... 350,000 bpd
*Output of refined products .... 128,500 bpd
*Consumption of refined products ...... 109,000 bpd

Natural gas (million cubic metres)
*Gross annual production	....	12,350 mcm
of which: (gas marketed)	....	(4,600 mcm)
(gas reinjected)	....	(6,000 mcm)
(gas flared)	....	(1,250 mcm)
(shrinkage)	....	(500 mcm)
*Annual exports (liquefied)	....	1,130 mcm
†Natural gas reserves	....	600,000 mcm

C8.2—Political and Economic Summary

Formerly under Ottoman rule, Libya was annexed by Italy in 1912 following a war between Italy and Turkey. Colonies of Italian settlers were established by the Fascist authorities during the 1920s and 1930s on expropriated Arab land, and Libyan nationalist forces subsequently supported the Allied armies which won control of Libya during the Second World War. Following a period of joint British and French administration, the country attained independence on Dec. 24, 1951, as the United Kingdom of Libya and, under the rule of King Idris (the former Emir of Cyrenaica), became one of the most conservative and pro-Western Arab states.

Treaties with Britain (valid for 20 years from 1953) and the United States (valid for 17 years from 1954) allowed these countries to maintain large military bases in Libya in return for economic aid which constituted a main source of government revenue prior to the development of the oil industry. Following the commencement of oil exports in the 1960s the treaties became a focus of left-wing opposition to the king, particularly after they were openly denounced by Egypt in 1964. In 1969 a bloodless coup staged by young army officers was followed by the formation of a revolutionary republican Government under Col. Moamer al Kadhafi, who secured the closure of the foreign military bases in the first half of 1970. By September 1970 the Kadhafi Government had achieved its first success in a hard-line campaign for higher oil revenues, thereby weakening the position of international oil companies throughout the OPEC area.

In 1973 Col. Kadhafi launched a "cultural revolution to destroy imported ideologies, whether Eastern or Western", which led to the country being renamed in 1977 the Socialist People's Libyan Arab Jamahiriya ("state of the masses"). Under the 1977 Constitution political power is based on "direct people's authority" expressed through people's congresses, while the social order is based on fundamentalist Islamic principles. (Nearly all Libyans are Sunni Moslems.) The main forum for the expression of the people's views is a General People's Congress, which appoints members of a General People's Committee (formerly the Council of Ministers). Col. Kadhafi ceased to be the secretary-general of the General People's Congress in 1979, although he remained head of state in his role as "revolutionary leader".

Col. Kadhafi's revolutionary zeal has extended far beyond the Libyan domestic scene, to the extent that he has become one of the world's most controversial political figures. Libyan interventions in the affairs of neighbouring countries have often been motivated by his fervent commitment to pan-Arabism, and the failure of Libyan proposals for union with other states has been followed on a number of occasions by periods of intense hostility. During 1985 relations with Tunisia moved into a hostile phase, while Morocco was the current participant in a Libyan merger scheme. Col. Kadhafi had by this point alienated most of the other possible partner countries in the region, and was accordingly turning towards the advocacy of "Arab unity by force". (Morocco subsequently repudiated its planned merger with Libya in August 1986.)

Western allegations that Col. Kadhafi is a leading sponsor of international terrorism are said to be based on conclusive evidence that Libya has trained, armed, financed and provided diplomatic cover for a variety of Palestinian and other extremist groups and has also despatched Libyan "hit squads" to track down exiled political opponents of the regime. These allegations (officially rejected by Libya) have been pursued with particular vigour by the Reagan Government in the United States, which, having severed diplomatic relations with the Kadhafi Government in May 1981, eventually took direct military action against Libya during the night of April 14–15, 1986, when the US Air Force bombed targets in Tripoli and Benghazi in response to a terrorist attack on US military personnel in West Berlin. The air strikes, which caused a number of civilian casualties, gave rise to widespread public criticism of the US Government, notably by moderate Arab governments which had strong political differences with Libya. The 77th OPEC Conference meeting unanimously condemned the US action, describing it as "contrary to international law".

The Reagan Government's severance of all US economic links with Libya, coupled with the Kadhafi Government's failure to secure the opening of negotiations for an economic co-operation agreement with the European Community (along the lines of the Community's agreements with every other non-member state in the Mediterranean region except Albania), tended to enhance the significance of Libya's economic links with the Soviet bloc in the mid-1980s. The Soviet Union's somewhat guarded political relations with Libya were based on past experience of the volatility of Col. Kadhafi's personal brand of non-alignment.

The development of the Libyan oil industry since the late 1950s has drastically transformed an economy which was previously based on subsistence agriculture carried out in an extremely unfavourable natural environment. Oil revenues have been used to finance land reclamation and irrigation schemes with the aim of achieving agricultural self-sufficiency, projects in this sector having been a main feature of development planning since the 1960s. The country nevertheless remained dependent on imports for nearly half of its food requirements at the beginning of the 1980s. State enterprises play a dominant role in the economy, and control by workers' committees is encouraged in all sectors. The economy is heavily dependent on foreign labour, and non-citizens constitute about 18 per cent of the country's total population.

A $62,500 million development plan for the period 1981–85 was designed to achieve overall growth of 9.4 per cent per annum. Annual growth of 21.6 per cent was planned for the manufacturing sector on the basis of investment totalling $13,500 million, while the agricultural sector received the second largest allocation of $10,100 million, with a growth target of 7.4 per cent. However, the financing of the plan was severely disrupted as a result of a progressive decline in annual oil revenues from a peak of $22,600 million in 1980 to around $8,000 million in 1985, obliging the Government to postpone or scale down many projects (most available resources being reserved for a priority scheme to pipe water to the coastal region from deep underground sources in the desert). The availability of certain consumer products began to deteriorate as efforts were made to reduce imports, which were increasingly obtained through oil-barter deals after 1982. Oil was offered in settlement of arrears of payments to foreign contractors working in Libya (who were said to be owed as much as $4,000 million by the end of 1985), although many of these offers were declined while the oil continued to be valued at high official prices.

It was estimated in mid-1986 that Libyan export revenue could fall to as little as $3,500 million in the current year, taking into account the collapse of world oil prices and the growth of "non-earning" exports. It was believed that around

257

150,000 bpd of crude was currently being provided in settlement of arrears owed to foreign commercial creditors and around 100,000 bpd in return for supplies (mainly of weapons) from the Soviet Union. According to Western estimates, Libya obtained arms worth nearly $1,000 million in 1985, mostly from the Soviet Union, whose cumulative arms supplies to the Kadhafi Government were valued at over $12,000 million.

C8.3—Oil and Gas Industry

C8.3.i—From inception to the overthrow of the monarchy (1955 to 1969)

Libya's first oil concessions were granted under a Petroleum Law of April 21, 1955, which provided for 50 per cent taxation of net operating income and a 12.5 per cent royalty rate (royalties and other payments to the Government being included in the overall 50 per cent tax liability). The tax and royalty rates were based on those then current in the main Middle East concession agreements, but whereas these agreements required taxable income to be calculated with reference to posted prices the Libyan law allowed the use of realized export prices for this purpose.

Concession holders were permitted to offset against their tax liability (i) a 20 per cent depreciation charge in respect of all physical assets acquired before the start of commercial production, and (ii) either a "depletion allowance" equal to 25 per cent of gross income or a 20 per cent amortization charge in respect of all pre-production expenses. However, limits were placed on the number of concession areas which could be granted to any one operator and provision was made for the early relinquishment of undeveloped areas. The overall aim of the law was to bring about a high level of investment by a wide range of companies in a short period of time in order to provide a viable basis for the economic development of what was then one of the world's poorest countries.

This strategy was remarkably successful: 51 concessions were granted to 17 companies in the initial round of licensing in 1956; the first oil strike was made in the following year; the first oil exports took place in 1961; and by 1965 production exceeded 1,000,000 bpd with further substantial increases in prospect as new fields were developed. Production was concentrated in the Sirte basin in Cyrenaica, from which five pipelines had been built to coastal terminals by 1968. As in neighbouring Algeria, the crudes produced were of the highest quality, being light in gravity and low in sulphur content. A key element in the rapid development of the Libyan oil industry was the large-scale involvement of independent oil companies with little or no existing international market share, which prevented the major companies from acquiring the effective control over production levels which they enjoyed in the Gulf producing countries.

Exports from Es Sider by the Oasis Oil Co., a consortium of three US independents, commenced in June 1962, nine months after Exxon's wholly-owned Esso Libya subsidiary had exported Libya's first oil shipment from Marsa el Brega. Oasis continued under fully independent ownership (one-third each by Conoco, Marathon and Amerada Hess) until January 1966, when Shell acquired half of the Amerada Hess interest. Meanwhile the Esso Sirte consortium, a partnership between Exxon (50 per cent), Sinclair Oil (25.5 per cent) and Grace Petroleum (24.5 per cent) had begun exporting from Marsa el Brega at the beginning of 1963. (Sinclair subsequently merged with Atlantic Richfield in 1969.) Oasis had established itself as the largest single producer in Libya by the mid-1960s, when it accounted for nearly half of the country's output.

After the first oil discoveries in 1957 the Government sought to obtain more advantageous terms from companies which applied for concession rights. A system of competitive bidding yielded increasingly large premium payments, while depletion allowances and certain other tax incentives included in the 1955 Petroleum Law were modified or omitted when new agreements were negotiated. In July 1961 (when commercial production was about to commence) an amendment to the July 1955 law formally abolished the depletion allowance and provided for all exports to be valued at posted prices for tax purposes.

The Government then opened negotiations to extend the latter provision to existing concession agreements, but encountered strong resistance from the independent companies, which rejected the Government's proposal that tax-deductible marketing expenses should be limited to the level (typically about 2 per cent of the posted price) then prevailing in the main Middle Eastern producing countries. Such resistance was based on the contention that the type of tax allowance cited by the Government was designed primarily to reflect the relatively modest expenses attributed to the marketing of crude through the major companies' integrated systems, whereas the independents could not expect to achieve large-scale production in Libya except by selling a high proportion of their output to non-affiliated European refiners who were able to command substantial discounts on posted crude prices in the highly competitive market conditions of the early 1960s (◊A4.11).

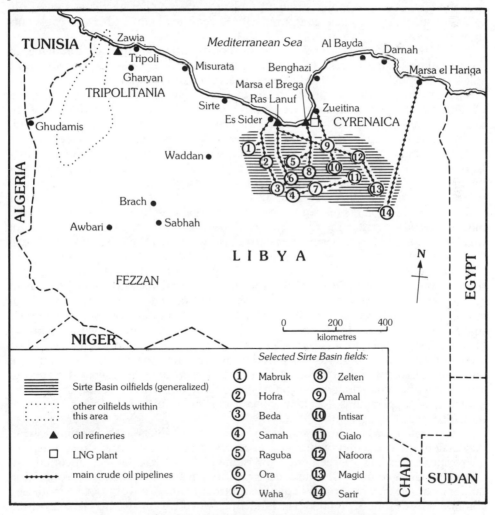

Fig. 13—Libyan hydrocarbon resources and installations

The Libyan Government eventually agreed (i) to add a clause to the 1955 law to the effect that "any amendment to or repeal of" the petroleum legislation in force at the time of the granting of a concession should "not affect the contractual rights of the [concessionaire] company without its consent" and (ii) to accept as an allowable marketing expense for tax purposes "the sum total of rebates, if any, from the posted price which the concession holder is obliged to grant for the purpose of meeting competition in order to sell Libyan crude petroleum to affiliated or non-affiliated customers, provided that the concession holder may be called upon from time to time to demonstrate . . . that any such rebates are commercially reasonable and fair". A decree was issued on Nov. 9, 1961, to safeguard the contractual rights of concession holders, after which the independents formally accepted the amended tax regulations, which were promulgated on Dec. 3, 1961.

Posted crude prices were subsequently heavily discounted by independent companies both in sales to non-affiliates and in transfers to their own refineries (which were themselves reliant on downstream price-cutting to expand their product sales). Thus, although Exxon was declaring much higher taxable profits than the independents, the Libyan Government's average revenue per barrel was relatively low—e.g. 62.9 cents in 1964, compared with 82 cents in Saudi Arabia and 95.4 cents in Venezuela.

During this period Exxon transferred most of its output to affiliated companies at its prevailing posted prices ($2.21 to $2.23 per barrel), from which it deducted a small marketing allowance for tax purposes; it made total payments to the Government of around 90 cents per barrel on the basis of an average taxable realization of $2.16 per barrel (which took account of a relatively small volume of discounted arm's-length sales to non-affiliates). The Oasis companies, on the other hand, priced most of their export sales at less than $1.60 per barrel, representing an average discount of about 30 per cent, and in 1964 (when their pre-production costs were still being offset against tax) they were paying no more than 30 cents per barrel to the Government, of which about 27.7 cents (12.5 per cent of the posted price) represented the basic royalty. It was estimated that the maximum payment which the Oasis companies would be liable to make to the Government in the medium term (i.e. after they had ceased to be eligible for tax relief in respect of their start-up costs) was 60 cents per barrel, assuming that there was no increase in their realized prices and no change in the existing tax regulations.

Some months after its acceptance in principle of the OPEC royalty-expensing formula of late 1964 (◊**D1.3.ii**), the Libyan Government announced its wish to renegotiate the terms of existing concessions with a view to the introduction of revised tax regulations under which the sales revenues of all companies would be uniformly assessed on the basis of posted prices. Realized prices would cease to have any significance for tax purposes, and the only allowable discounts would be those for which provision was made in the royalty-expensing formula. Compliance with the revised fiscal regime—and with a number of other measures designed to strengthen the Government's position—was laid down as a condition for the approval of applications for new concessions in a further licensing round in mid-1965.

Exxon and most of the other major companies which held existing Libyan concessions indicated their willingness to accept the proposed tax changes as part of a royalty-expensing agreement on standard OPEC terms, including a "most-favoured-company" clause designed to ensure that different concession holders were subject to broadly equal fiscal treatment. A government negotiating committee set up in September 1965 failed, however, to secure acceptance of the proposed agreement by a number of (mostly independent) concession holders, who thus effectively blocked the implementation of agreements with other companies. Of the three Oasis companies, only Amerada Hess (which was then negotiating the sale to Shell of part of its interest in Oasis) responded positively to the Government's initiative, which was rejected by Marathon and Conoco.

The Government nevertheless introduced a decree on Nov. 22, 1965, to amend the taxation provisions of the 1955 Petroleum Law, after which most companies' concession agreements were formally amended to bring them into line with the law. (The decree, which was approved by Parliament on Dec. 9, 1965, also provided that each company's acceptance of the tax changes should be followed by the dropping of the Libyan Government's outstanding financial claims against that company in respect of its operations prior to the end of 1964 and by the introduction of international arbitration procedures to settle any future disputes over the terms of that company's concession agreements.) Several companies insisted on their right to disregard the change in the tax regulations on the grounds that, under the decree of Nov. 9, 1961, such a change was not contractually binding without their consent, whereupon the Government made it clear that it was prepared to secure compliance through legislative means.

The Libyan Government's stance was endorsed by the 10th meeting of the OPEC Conference, whose resolution X–63 of Dec. 17, 1965, (i) pledged the full support of other OPEC governments for "Libya's position in safeguarding its legitimate interests"; (ii) recommended that no OPEC government should enter into or continue negotiations for the granting of new oil rights to any company which was withholding acceptance of the new Libyan tax regulations (or to any affiliates or subsidiaries in which such a company held an interest of 10 per cent or more); and (iii) instructed the OPEC Secretary-General to seek the support of non-OPEC oil-producing countries and to explain OPEC's position to the companies concerned and to their stockholders.

A so-called "law of compulsion", unanimously approved by the Libyan Parliament on Dec. 26, 1965, empowered the Government to take whatever steps were necessary to secure the full acceptance of the tax changes, including the banning of production and/or exports by unco-operative concessionaires and, in the event of continuing non-compliance, the expropriation of some or all of the assets of such companies. By Jan. 20, 1966, all of the companies concerned had agreed to amend their concession agreements, making it unnecessary for the Government to carry out its threat to enact the December 1965 law. The last two companies to comply were Gulf Oil (the only major to have resisted the tax changes) and Phillips Petroleum, neither of which had actually discovered oil in their concession areas.

The closure of the Suez Canal in June 1967 (◊A4.13) greatly strengthened Libya's competitive position as a supplier of oil to Western Europe, causing production to be increased to over 3,000,000 bpd by 1969, in which year Libya was OPEC's largest exporter of crude oil. In addition to Esso Libya, Oasis and Esso Sirte, the main producing companies at this time were (i) a partnership between Mobil (65 per cent) and Gelsenberg AG (35 per cent), which commenced exports from Ras Lanuf in December 1964; (ii) a 50-50 partnership between Chevron and Texaco, whose operations were managed by the two companies' jointly-owned Amoseas subsidiary and whose exports, which commenced in 1966, were shipped from the Mobil-Gelsenberg terminal at Ras Lanuf; (iii) a 50-50 partnership between BP and the US independent Bunker Hunt company, which commenced exports from Marsa el Hariga in January 1967; and (iv) Occidental Petroleum, which entered Libya as a sole concessionaire in 1966 and commenced exports from Zueitina in February 1968.

Following the closure of the Suez Canal the Libyan producers paid a "temporary premium" to the Government in recognition of the improvement in the country's freight advantage vis-à-vis the Persian/Arabian Gulf. As agreed in November 1967, the premium (of between 7 and 8 cents per barrel) took the form of the elimination, with effect from July 4, 1967, of the 6.5 per cent discount which the companies had been permitted to deduct from posted prices when declaring their taxable income under the terms of the royalty-expensing formula. The Government was not, however, able to secure a substantive increase in the basic level of posted prices, which under an unamended clause of the tax regulations of Dec. 3, 1961, were defined as those prices posted by the producing companies or their affiliates for the sale of "Libyan crude petroleum available to buyers generally". It was the Government's long-standing claim that Esso Libya had used unrealistically low freight and quality differentials (relative to the east Mediterranean postings for Iraqi crudes) as a basis for its initial Libyan posting in 1961—this being one of the outstanding financial claims which were dropped in respect of the period up to the end of 1964 as part of the royalty-expensing settlement. At the time of the overthrow of the monarchy in September 1969 the posted price for 40° crude remained at its 1961 level of $2.23 per barrel (2 cents higher than the east Mediterranean posting for Iraqi 36° crude), compared with the Government's current claim for a posting of at least $2.33 which was the subject of ongoing negotiations.

C8.3.ii—Intensified campaign for improved state revenue entitlement, leading to signature of Tripoli agreement (1970–71)

The revolutionary Government of Col. Kadhafi set up a special committee to open fresh negotiations for a tax increase with the 21 oil companies then operating in Libya. From May 1970 onwards it ordered a series of production cutbacks by different companies in accordance with new regulations on the conservation of oil resources, resulting in a reduction in total output from a peak level of 3,670,000 bpd in April 1970 to about 2,900,000 bpd in September 1970. The most seriously affected company was Occidental Petroleum, whose initial output of 800,000 bpd was nearly halved over this period. The Government's decision to apply particularly strong pressure on Occidental was based on an awareness that the company was more heavily reliant on Libya for its crude oil supplies than any other concession holder at this time.

Other measures taken by the Government included (i) the establishment in March 1970 of a National Oil Corporation (NOC) as the successor to a General Petroleum Corporation which had been set up in April 1968, the NOC being provided with its own financial resources and empowered to engage in all aspects of the oil industry, including joint ventures with foreign companies; (ii) the initiation in May 1970 of talks on oil co-operation with the Soviet Union and other Eastern-bloc countries; (iii) the blocking in June 1970 of the commencement of exports of liquefied natural gas by Esso Libya, whose export pricing formula was challenged by the Government; and (iv) the nationalization in July 1970 of the Libyan distribution and marketing interests of Exxon, Shell and Agip, which were transferred to the NOC together with the interests of Petro-Libya (hitherto a Libyan private-sector company).

In early September Occidental Petroleum reached a settlement with the Government providing for an immediate increase in its posted price from $2.23 to $2.53 per barrel; for an increase in the rate of taxation, partly to cover a backdating of the increase in the posting (which Libya had claimed from Jan. 1, 1965); and for subsequent posted price increases of 2 cents per barrel in each of the five years 1971–75. Occidental's permitted production ceiling was raised from 425,000 bpd to 700,000 bpd following the conclusion of the agreement. Similar settlements were reached with all of the remaining producing companies by Oct. 16, 1970, the majors having accepted the new terms after the Government had responded to an initial show of resistance on the part of Shell by banning that company from exporting its share of Oasis production. Shell was permitted to resume exports after signing a new agreement with the Government, but apart from Occidental all of the companies which had been ordered to reduce their production levels were obliged to continue operating at the lower levels, which were designed to avoid an excessively rapid reduction in natural reservoir pressures.

Under the agreements of September/October 1970 the de facto rate of taxation was raised from 50 per cent to between 54 and 55.5 per cent for most of the producing companies, although a minority of companies chose to make immediate cash payments in settlement of liabilities arising from the backdating of the increase in postings. The different elements in the overall posted price increase were not explicitly broken down in terms of the factors on which Libya's claims had been based.

The 21st meeting of the OPEC Conference in December 1970 adopted a series of resolutions calling for various increases in host governments' oil revenues, including a general increase in tax rates to 55 per cent to bring other member countries into line with the new situation in Libya. Against this background, the Libyan Government presented further demands to the oil companies on Jan. 3, 1971, as follows: (i) for a 5 per cent increase in the basic rate of taxation, on the grounds that the recent de facto tax increases were concerned mainly with the backdating of posted price increases and had not altered Libya's basic rate of 50 per cent; (ii) for a new "general" posted price increase, to be determined within the framework of separate negotiations by the Gulf OPEC countries; (iii) for a freight premium of 69 cents per barrel, of which 39 cents would represent a permanent increase in the posted price backdated to the closure of the Suez Canal and 30 cents a "temporary and variable" increase backdated to the closure of the trans-Arabian pipeline in May 1970 (◊**A4.13**); and (iv) for the reinvestment in the Libyan economy of 25 cents of the profits made by the operating companies on each barrel of their crude oil exports from Libya (this demand being based on OPEC's Resolution XXI–123 ◊**D1.6.iii**).

In connexion with its demand for a freight premium vis-à-vis oil exported from Gulf terminals (which the oil companies had assumed to be included in the 30 cents per barrel price increase agreed in September/October 1970), the Libyan Government stated that two-thirds of the latter increase had in fact represented a quality premium to reflect the low sulphur content of Libyan crude and one-third a correction of past underpricing by the companies vis-à-vis oil exported from eastern Mediterranean terminals. The latest Libyan demands were revised on Feb. 24 to take account of the terms of the Tehran agreement on tax increases in Gulf OPEC countries (◊**D2.2.ii**) and, after further modification during the course of negotiations with the concessionaire companies, were backed in mid-March by a threat to embargo all Mediterranean exports by OPEC countries. In the face of wider OPEC support for Libya's stance, the companies conceded the following terms, agreed in Tripoli on April 2, 1971, and effective from March 20 of that year:

(1) A substantive posted price increase of 64.7 cents per barrel, of which 35 cents represented a general OPEC increase based on the Tehran agreement, 10 cents a quality premium for crudes with a sulphur content of less than 0.5 per cent, 7 cents a permanent freight premium and 12.7 cents a 1972 annual increment (implemented on March 20, 1971, in lieu of the backdating of the whole agreement to Jan. 1, 1971).

(2) An additional temporary price increase of 25 cents per barrel, of which 12 cents was a "Suez Canal allowance" and 13 cents a variable premium linked to movements in freight rates.

(3) Annual increments in each of the years 1973–75 of 2.5 per cent of the basic posted price, including permanent premiums, plus 5 cents per barrel, in addition to the increments

of 2 cents per barrel agreed in 1970 (which were deemed to be adjustments to the quality premium). The newly negotiated increments (based on the Tehran agreement) were to take effect at the beginning of each of the years in question, while the 2-cent increments would take effect annually on Sept. 1. The 2-cent increment for 1971 was added to the base posting used to calculate the "accelerated" main increment for 1972 (see above), whereas the 2-cent increment for 1972 was to be implemented on its normal due date.

(4) An increase in the basic tax rate from 50 to 55 per cent, and the imposition of a separate supplementary levy (averaging 9 cents per barrel) to cover the backdating of the 1970 increase in postings.

(5) Undertakings by the companies to maintain reasonable levels of new investment in the Libyan oil industry until the end of 1975 (although not as a specified proportion of profits, as had originally been proposed by Libya).

The April 1971 Tripoli agreement increased Libya's per-barrel oil revenue by 47.2 per cent. In a separate agreement with Esso Libya on March 4, 1971, the Libyan Government secured a 65 per cent increase in the price of LNG exports (from 20.6 to 34 cents per million British thermal units), following which exports were allowed to commence on March 14.

C8.3.iii—Establishment of state control over production operations (from 1971)

Nationalizations of Libyan oil producing operations commenced on Dec. 7, 1971, when the Government formed the Arabian Gulf Exploration Co. (AGEC) to take full control of BP's Libyan subsidiary. This action was stated to have been taken on the political grounds that the British Government had failed to prevent Iran's recent occupation of the Tunb islands in the Persian/Arabian Gulf (◊C12.1). Agip, which (as a sole concessionaire) had discovered oil in Libya in 1971, agreed in September 1972 to sell a 50 per cent interest in its producing operations to the NOC following negotiations in which the Italian company was threatened with an export ban. In October 1972 Libya sought a similar participation agreement with the Bunker Hunt company. Bunker Hunt rejected this approach on Dec. 9, causing the Libyan Government to halt the company's operations on May 24, 1973, and to order their full nationalization on June 11, 1973, when the AGEC took over Bunker Hunt's share of the former BP/Bunker Hunt concession areas.

(Both BP and Bunker Hunt received compensation from the Libyan Government, and on Jan. 31, 1975, BP formally withdrew various legal actions which it had taken in support of its claims against Libya. BP then sued Bunker Hunt to recover part of what was claimed to be the US company's disproportionately large share of the benefits arising from the former Libyan joint venture, and was awarded £17,000,000 sterling by the Law Lords when the case completed its final appeal stage in London on Feb. 4, 1982.)

Following the Bunker Hunt nationalization, several other US independent companies, faced with the prospect of a 100 per cent state takeover of their operations, accepted 51 per cent state participation—Occidental Petroleum on Aug. 11, 1973, and Conoco, Marathon and Amerada Hess on Aug. 16. However, the major oil companies—whose offer to concede 25 per cent state participation (on the model of their October 1972 agreement with the Arabian peninsula producers ◊D3.4) had been rejected by Libya—resisted Libya's campaign for 51 per cent participation, and Shell was accordingly banned from exporting its share of the Oasis consortium's output. Shell's interest in Oasis was subsequently fully nationalized on March 30, 1974, leaving the pattern of shareholdings in the consortium as follows: NOC 59.2 per cent, Conoco 16.3 per cent, Marathon 16.3 per cent, Amerada Hess 8.2 per cent.

After the expiry on Aug. 25, 1973, of a deadline for the voluntary acceptance of 51 per cent state participation in the operations of the main producing companies in which there was no existing state interest, Libya unilaterally took 51 per cent control under legislation introduced on Sept. 1, 1973. Texaco, Chevron, Mobil, Exxon, Shell and Atlantic Richfield issued a joint statement on Sept. 7 refusing "to accept terms imposed unilaterally in contravention of valid agreements", but Gelsenberg AG and Grace Petroleum each accepted the Government's action. The operations of Amoseas (which had been ordered to reduce its production by half in mid-August) were fully nationalized on Feb. 11, 1974, as was Atlantic Richfield's holding in Esso Sirte. Control over the operations of Amoseas was transferred to a new NOC subsidiary, the Umm al-Gawabi Petroleum Co.

Exxon and Mobil each accepted 51 per cent state control of their interests on April 16, 1974, the subsequent shareholdings in the operating companies concerned being as follows: Esso Libya—NOC 51 per cent, Exxon 49 per cent; Esso Sirte — NOC 63.5 per cent, Exxon 24.5 per cent, Grace Petroleum 12 per cent; Mobil-Gelsenberg—NOC 51 per cent, Mobil 31.85 per cent, Gelsenberg AG 17.15 per cent. All of the companies whose Libyan assets were nationalized received compensation based on net book value, and those companies which retained minority shareholdings were entitled to a guaranteed profit margin (calculated on the basis of a figure between the tax-paid production cost and the official government selling price) in respect of their equity crude production. Minor producers whose Libyan concessions were not nationalized included the West German company Wintershall AG.

After 1973 various new exploration contracts were granted to foreign oil companies on production-sharing terms (with the NOC usually taking between 81 per cent and 88 per cent of output). Companies which entered into 85:15 production-sharing contracts included Elf Aquitaine (in partnership with Wintershall AG and the Austrian state oil company Österreichische Mineraloelverwaltung), while Occidental Petroleum (which retained a 49 per cent equity interest in its original concessions) concluded an 81:19 contract in respect of new exploration areas. Under the Libyan production-sharing formula, the foreign operating contractor was entitled to take its own minority share of output free of taxes and royalties and to purchase the NOC's majority share at the full official selling price. Although the foreign contractor bore the full cost of all exploration work (including unsuccessful drilling), the development and production costs of commercially viable discoveries were shared between the NOC and the contractor in the same proportions which applied to the sharing of the oil produced.

The management of the state's oil interests was restructured in August 1979, when all operational responsibilities hitherto held by the NOC were devolved to subsidiary companies, leaving the NOC as a holding company with broad powers of planning, supervision and control over a total of 11 wholly-owned subsidiaries. Shortly after its reorganization the NOC negotiated the relinquishment of 138,000 sq km (nearly 20 per cent) of the exploration area covered by existing production-sharing contracts, most of the relinquished blocks being reallocated under new contracts when a second major licensing round began in 1980. An upturn in exploration activity in the early 1980s led to a number of new discoveries, an estimated 20 per cent of current output being replaced by new proved reserves between the beginning of 1980 and the end of 1985. Subsidiaries of the NOC were officially credited with the discovery of 44 per cent of new reserves over this period, as against 28 per cent discovered by foreign production-sharing contractors and 28 per cent by foreign equity holders. Offshore production was scheduled to begin in 1987 from the Bouri field (120 km north of Tripoli) after the completion of development work by Agip (the minority partner in an 81:19 production-sharing scheme with the NOC).

In November 1981 Exxon announced its withdrawal from its Libyan operations, and on Dec. 1 a new NOC subsidiary, the Sirte Oil Co., took over all of Exxon's production concessions and pipeline assets in Libya, as well as its 49 per cent shareholding in the Marsa el Brega gas liquefaction plant. Grace Petroleum continued to hold a 12 per cent interest in the former Esso Sirte concessions. The NOC agreed on Dec. 17, 1981, to pay Exxon a total of $95,000,000 for its relinquished assets (compared with their estimated net book value of more than $120,000,000). Following Exxon's withdrawal Mobil indicated its intention to terminate its Libyan operations, and entered into negotiations to secure agreed compensation terms from the Government. Having failed to reach agreement Mobil handed over its operations to the NOC on Dec. 31, 1982, leaving the question of compensation to be determined by arbitration. Veba Oel AG, which had succeeded Gelsenberg AG as the West German participant in Mobil's Libyan concession areas in 1978, continued to hold a 17.15 per cent interest in these areas. Exxon and Mobil each said that their main reason for leaving Libya was a serious deterioration in the profitability of their local operations. On June 30, 1985, Occidental Petroleum sold one-fourth of both its 49 per cent Libyan equity interest and its 19 per cent Libyan participation interest to Österreichische Mineraloelverwaltung.

In 1984 the overall state share of Libyan oil output was 69.9 per cent, the foreign equity share 28.9 per cent and the foreign production-sharing entitlement 1.2 per cent. The Oasis consortium produced 37.6 per cent of national output, NOC subsidiaries (as sole concession holders) 23.8 per cent and Agip 15.2 per cent. The combined output of fields operated by Occidental Petroleum (including production-sharing areas) accounted for a further 14.9 per cent. Over half of the balance of Libya's output came from the fields formerly operated by Mobil.

Libya's gross output of natural gas, which is produced from associated deposits (although non-associated reserves also exist), fell to 12,350 million cubic metres in 1984, compared with its peak level of 23,470 mcm in 1979. Nearly 50 per cent of the gas produced was reinjected to maintain oil reservoir pressures, while about 10 per cent was flared. The Marsa el Brega liquefaction plant, which commenced operations in 1971 as the world's first LNG scheme based on the utilization of associated gas which was previously flared, exported up to 4,200 mcm of LNG per year to Italy and Spain during the mid-1970s (i.e. over 20 per cent of Libya's gross gas production at that time), but by 1984 exports had fallen to 1,130 mcm (9 per cent of gross production). Liquefied petroleum gas is produced at a plant on the Intisar oilfield from which it is piped to Zueitina.

Libya's refining capacity was expanded to 350,000 bpd in late 1984 through the opening of a new 220,000 bpd refinery at Ras Lanuf. The largely export-oriented refinery operated at very low throughput levels in 1985 as a result of slack demand. The estimated capacity utilization rate in mid-1986 was around 40 per cent. One intended future use for part of the refinery's output was as feedstock for a naphtha-based petrochemical complex under development at Ras Lanuf. In January 1986 the Libyan Arab Foreign Bank purchased a 70 per cent shareholding in the Tamoil group, which had been placed in receivership in 1985. Tamoil's operations were based on Italian downstream assets formerly owned by Amoco—consisting of a 105,000 bpd refinery at Cremona, about 800 km of pipelines and about 1,000 service stations—and provided an important overseas marketing outlet for Libyan oil at a time of excess world supplies.

Western Europe was Libya's dominant oil export market in the mid-1980s, the import of Libyan crude into the United States having been banned by the Reagan Government in March 1982 (by which time US import demand had declined sharply from the very high levels recorded in the 1970s). Subsequent US trade sanctions against Libya included a ban on imports of refined products from November 1985, which was in practice virtually unenforceable with regard to products refined from Libyan crude in third countries. In January 1986 the remaining US producing and service companies in the Libyan oil industry were ordered by the Reagan Government to make immediate arrangements for withdrawal as part of a total severance of US economic links with Libya.

The producing companies concerned (with a current equity offtake of around 300,000 bpd) were initially licensed by the US Government to continue operating on a temporary basis, provided that their profits were placed in escrow, until they had negotiated a "fair market price" for the sale of their assets. The temporary operating licences were, however, later cancelled by the US Government with effect from June 30, 1986, leaving compensation negotiations to be conducted retroactively with the Libyan Government (provided that all such negotiations were held outside Libya). The US withdrawal had virtually no impact on the running of production operations in Libya, although the loss of guaranteed export outlets was expected to create new difficulties for the NOC in the current market environment. Conversely, the prevailing market conditions minimized the impact of withdrawal on the US companies, among which Occidental Petroleum had latterly derived about one-fifth of its total production from Libya.

C9—Nigeria

C9.1—Statistical Survey

*1984
†End-1984
‡Revision of 1984 figures given in section **D15.1.i** (see Introduction)

General

Area	923,768 sq km
*Population	92,040,000
Capital	Lagos (new capital under development at Abuja)

Economy and trade

*Gross national product	$77,330 million
*Annual exports (fob)	$14,124 million (of which petroleum 89.5 per cent)
*Annual imports (cif)	$7,067 million
*Current account balance	+$530,000,000
Foreign exchange reserves	$1,324 million (November 1985)

Oil (upstream)

‡1984 crude production	1,385,000 bpd (68,600,000 tonnes)
1985 crude production	1,475,000 bpd (72,800,000 tonnes)
†Proved crude reserves	16,700 million barrels
*Reserves:production ratio	32.8 : 1
Production in peak year	2,300,000 bpd (114,200,000 tonnes) in 1979
†Cumulative crude production	10,349.7 million barrels since 1958
*Number of producing oil wells	1,050
Export grades: Bonny	36.7° API gravity
Nigerian Medium	25.5° API gravity
Forcados	30.7° API gravity
Brass Blend	44.2° API gravity

Oil tanker tonnage

†1 vessel	272,500 deadweight tons

Oil (downstream)

*Installed refining capacity	247,000 bpd
*Output of refined products	160,200 bpd
*Consumption of refined products	203,300 bpd

Natural gas (million cubic metres)

*Gross annual production	16,251 mcm
of which: (gas marketed)	(2,051 mcm)
(gas reinjected)	(576 mcm)
(gas flared)	(13,624 mcm)
†Natural gas reserves	1,000,000 mcm

C9.2—Political and Economic Summary

Nigeria was formed in 1914 through the amalgamation of territories which had come under British administration during the nineteenth century. The new colony was remarkable for the heterogeneity of its population, which included over 250 ethnic groups with widely differing languages and cultures, the northern peoples being predominantly Moslem and the southern peoples having their own African customs and beliefs (whose influence was being eroded by the spread of Christianity). Until 1946 there was a unitary government structure, but in 1947 a new colonial constitution divided Nigeria into three regions for administrative purposes. Independence was achieved on Oct. 1, 1960, as a federation of the three regions, and in 1963 a fourth region was created in response to political demands. Also in 1963, the Federal Republic of Nigeria was established when the country severed its remaining constitutional link with the British crown.

Increasing political turmoil, fuelled by ethnic rivalries, led to two military coups during 1966, followed by the secession of the Eastern Region in 1967 as the "Republic of Biafra". A large-scale civil war ensued which ended in early 1970 with the re-establishment of the authority of the Federal Government (which had meanwhile divided the country into 12 states in place of the four regions in an attempt to create a more viable federal structure). Gen. Yakubu Gowon, who won wide respect for his handling of the reintegration into Nigeria of the former secessionist territory but who was criticized for delaying a return to civilian rule and for tolerating the spread of corruption in public life, was replaced as head of state by Gen. Murtala Mohammed in a bloodless coup in 1975. Gen. Mohammed was assassinated in an abortive coup in the following year and succeeded by Gen. Olusegun Obasanjo, who implemented his predecessor's programme for a return to civilian rule, which included the creation of seven additional states.

An elected civilian administration headed by Alhaji Shehu Shagari took office in 1979 under a new Constitution which provided for a system of presidential government similar to that of the United States. President Shagari was re-elected in August 1983 amid opposition allegations of ballot-rigging, but was overthrown on Dec. 31, 1983, in a military coup which brought Maj.-Gen. Mohammed Buhari to power as head of state. The new military Government accused the former administration of economic mismanagement, political corruption and "unprecedented" financial corruption. Subsequent inquiries produced a mass of evidence to support these accusations.

As black Africa's most populous nation Nigeria has massive development needs, only a fraction of which had been met by the 1980s despite ambitious government planning. The oil boom of the 1970s was accompanied by persistent price inflation, a decline in the level of agricultural self-sufficiency and a steady increase in spending on imported consumer goods. The downturn in the oil market in the early 1980s, which cut Nigeria's annual oil revenues from $23,405 million in 1980 (their peak year) to $10,155 million in 1983, was accompanied by heavy government borrowing to finance large budget deficits in 1981, 1982 and 1983. The Buhari Government inherited a total external debt in the region of $17,000 million, of which around $11,000 million consisted of long- and medium-term loans, while much of the balance represented arrears of payments for goods imported between 1981 and 1983. There was also a massive public-sector debt to domestic banks and contractors.

The new Government ordered substantial cutbacks in capital spending immediately after taking office, and in early 1985 it announced a scheme to issue five-year promissory notes to the largest domestic creditors. Negotiations were opened with the International Monetary Fund in 1984 for a major loan to support an economic readjustment programme (and to open the way to a refinancing of debts owed to foreign creditor banks). However, this initiative soon ran into difficulty (as had a similar move by the Shagari administration in 1983) because of the Government's reluctance to accept the preconditions for IMF lending to Nigeria, which included a devaluation of the Nigerian currency. In the absence of an agreement on the rescheduling of payments, the Buhari Government expected debt-servicing to absorb 44 per cent of foreign exchange earnings in 1985 and a considerably higher percentage in 1986–87. The rescheduling issue remained unresolved when Maj.-Gen. Buhari was ousted by Maj.-Gen. Ibrahim Babangida in a further coup on Aug. 27, 1985.

The Babangida Government accepted the need for far-reaching economic policy changes but did not make any immediate move towards the introduction of measures recommended by the IMF, preferring initially to encourage a period of "national debate" within Nigeria (which confirmed the existence of deep divisions of opinion on this issue). Disagreements within the military over the future direction of economic policy played a major part in sparking an unsuccessful coup attempt in December 1985. One obstacle to agreement with the IMF was partially removed by the Government in early 1986 when it made a sharp reduction (to 20 per cent) in the level of price subsidy on crude oil supplied to local refineries. The retail price of gasoline was doubled. However, it was not until June 27 that Maj.-Gen. Babangida announced a major reform programme, centred on the introduction of a free-market currency exchange rate for all transactions except government debt repayments. The collapse of world oil prices had by this point thrown the economy into acute crisis, and early agreements with the IMF and with foreign creditors were seen as essential in order to restore a tolerable external payments position.

The country's external policies are mainly oriented towards the Organization of African Unity and other regional groupings, within which Nigeria has been a leading opponent of white minority rule in southern Africa. Nigeria is the only country which is a member both of OPEC and of the Commonwealth.

C9.3—Oil and Gas Industry

Although oil exploration work began in Nigeria before the First World War, it was not until 1956 that the first commercial discovery was made by the Shell/BP Petroleum Development Co. of Nigeria (owned 50 per cent by Shell and 50 per cent by BP), which had embarked on a deep-drilling programme in 1951 within a 103,600 sq km concession area. The company's initial production took place in 1958 from onshore fields in the coastal region of eastern Nigeria. After Nigeria's independence in 1960 (at which point the only other concession holder was Mobil, which had entered the country in 1955), new onshore and offshore concessions were granted to a variety of companies, including (i) Gulf Oil, (ii) a partnership between Chevron (50 per cent) and Texaco (50 per cent), in which Texaco took operational responsibility, (iii) SAFRAP, a French state-owned company which became a subsidiary of ERAP in 1966 and was later renamed Elf Nigeria, and (iv) a partnership between Agip (50 per cent) and Phillips (50 per cent). Taxation of oil company profits (levied at an effective rate of about 35 per cent in the early 1960s) was brought broadly into line with prevailing Middle Eastern OPEC rates in 1967 (although Nigeria did not become a member of OPEC until mid-1971).

Following the commencement of offshore production (by Gulf Oil) and the construction of a tanker terminal linked by pipeline to new onshore fields situated to the west of the original producing area, Nigeria's output reached 420,000 bpd in 1966. It declined in the two succeeding years, however, as a result of the civil war between federal forces and the Biafran secessionists, which caused all the operating companies except Gulf Oil to suspend production. (The extent of federal control over revenue from Nigerian oil—most of which was produced within the former Eastern Region—was a major cause of disagreement between the two sides prior to the outbreak of the war.) Output rose again to 540,000 bpd in 1969, doubled in 1970 following the end of the civil war, and exceeded 2,000,000 bpd in 1973. Production was mainly of light, low-sulphur crudes for which premium postings were negotiated in May 1971 under a five-year agreement with the operating companies (modelled on the Libyan agreement of the previous month ◊**C8.3.ii**).

The Nigerian National Oil Corporation (NNOC), established in April 1971 as a state enterprise empowered to engage in oil exploration, production, refining and marketing, was in February 1972 granted rights over all areas not covered by existing oil concessions and over any areas in which existing concessions were relinquished. All future agreements with foreign oil companies in respect of new exploration areas were based on joint-venture, production-sharing or service contracts with the state corporation.

ERAP agreed in April 1971 to the acquisition of a 35 per cent state interest in SAFRAP as a condition for the resumption of the company's production

Fig. 14—Nigerian oil resources and installations

operations (which had been blocked by the Federal Government in retaliation for France's pro-Biafran stance during the civil war), and in September 1971 the NNOC acquired a 33⅓ per cent interest in the operations of the Agip/Phillips consortium. An agreement on 35 per cent state participation in the upstream interests of the Shell/BP consortium (the main producer), signed in June 1973 to take effect from April 1 of that year, included an option for the state to take 51 per cent majority control by 1982. Nigeria had previously acquired a 60 per cent interest in the consortium's Nigerian refining operations on May 1, 1972.

On May 18, 1974, Nigeria concluded an agreement to increase the level of state participation in the producing operations of SAFRAP, Agip/Phillips and Shell/BP to 55 per cent with effect from April 1 of that year. Mobil and Gulf, in whose operations there had hitherto been no state interest, also accepted 55 per cent participation at this time, but a similar agreement was not reached with the Texaco/Chevron partnership until January 1978 (when it was backdated to May 1, 1975). The level of state participation in all the foreign concessionaire companies was raised to 60 per cent with effect from July 1, 1979, to bring the oil industry into line with a wider policy on the "Nigerianization" of foreign business interests. On July 31, 1979, BP's remaining 20 per cent interest in the Shell/BP consortium was nationalized as a political protest against BP's involvement in international "swap" arrangements to supply oil to South Africa. BP's Nigerian marketing company (already 60 per cent state owned) was fully nationalized at the same time and renamed African Petroleum Ltd. Exxon's local marketing subsidiary had previously been fully nationalized at the beginning of 1977 and renamed Unipetrol (Nigeria) Ltd.

In order to eliminate an unnecessary overlapping of state interests, the NNOC and the Federal Ministry of Petroleum Resources were merged in April 1977 to form the Nigerian National Petroleum Corporation (NNPC). Legislation was passed in 1983 to reconstitute the NNPC as a holding company controlling six operating subsidiaries, namely the National Petroleum Development Co., the National Gas Co., the National Petrochemicals Co., the National Marine Tanker Co., the National Refining Co. and the National Marketing Co. Implementation of this reorganization was still awaited at the end of 1985.

Having reached a peak level of 2,300,000 bpd in 1979, Nigeria's oil output declined sharply in the early 1980s as increasing volumes of directly competing North Sea oil became available to importers in Nigeria's established markets — principally the United States and Western Europe—at a time of depressed demand. Whereas Nigerian crude prices had previously served as the main reference point for North Sea pricing, North Sea prices became the dominant influence on Nigerian prices after mid-1981, causing Nigeria to be regarded as OPEC's "weakest link" in view of the impact of Nigerian price cuts upon the Organization's overall pricing structure.

At the time of its overthrow in December 1983, the Shagari Government, which had accepted a Nigerian quota ceiling of 1,300,000 bpd within the framework of OPEC's market stabilization programme (◊D14.5), was facing growing political pressure within Nigeria for the country's withdrawal from OPEC if an increased ceiling could not be obtained for 1984. The new military regime, while rejecting the possibility of withdrawal, argued vigorously within OPEC for a larger Nigerian quota and, having obtained an increase valid only for the months of August and September 1984 (◊D15.5), later announced that it considered the agreed September ceiling of 1,450,000 bpd to be "to all intents and purposes permanent". This policy was defended on the grounds that no early solution was in sight for the special economic difficulties which had been taken into account when the OPEC Conference approved Nigeria's temporary quota increase.

Of Nigeria's estimated 1985 production of 1,475,000 bpd, about 750,000 bpd (50.6 per cent) was produced from fields in the Shell concession area (now officially styled a joint-venture area) and a total of about 700,000 bpd (47.1 per cent) from the other main joint-venture areas as follows: Gulf Oil of Nigeria (Chevron) 13.5 per cent; Mobil 12.8 per cent; Agip/Phillips 9.4 per cent; Elf Nigeria 6.7 per cent; and Texaco/Chevron 4.7 per cent. Most of the balance was produced by Ashland Oil under a production-sharing contract with NNPC. As the holder of an 80 per cent interest in the Shell joint-venture area and of 60 per cent interests in the operations of the other main producers, NNPC had an overall stake of around 70 per cent in Nigerian production operations, representing a theoretical state offtake entitlement of 1,032,500 bpd in 1985 if total production was divided on a straight-forward pro-rata basis.

In practice, however, it was only between 1980 and 1984 that such a basis was used to determine the respective offtake entitlements of NNPC and its various joint-venture partners. Until 1980 each foreign company's equity entitlement was defined as the applicable share (i.e. 40 per cent in most cases) of a predetermined allowable production volume from the joint-venture area concerned, the validity of this entitlement being unaffected by any shortfall in the final production total (e.g. because of a failure by NNPC to lift the full balance of the allowable total). The strict pro-rata division of actual production, as adopted in 1980, worked against Nigeria's interests when the subsequent transition to a buyer's market led to frequent fluctuations in the volume of NNPC's offtake (which now dictated the overall pattern of production). In October 1984 the Government not only reintroduced the system of reference to an "allowable" production volume to calculate the foreign equity entitlement but also gave foreign equity holders the right to purchase, on equity terms, any crude lifted on NNPC's account which the state corporation was subsequently unable to sell to a third party.

Nigeria's equity terms were based from late 1974 on an 85 per cent tax rate and a 20 per cent royalty rate (i.e. the revised Middle Eastern formula adopted by OPEC from Nov. 1, 1974 ◊**D5.6.ii**), these rates being applied in conjunction with posted prices in such a way as to establish an "official" post-tax profit margin on foreign oil companies' exports of equity crude. The amount of the margin was subject to periodic readjustment in the light of market developments. Following an increase on Feb. 22, 1983 (◊**D14.4**), the official profit margin on equity crude was deemed to be $2 per barrel, and subsequent changes in Nigeria's official selling prices were accordingly accompanied by posted-price adjustments which held the tax-paid cost $2 below the official selling price. Realized profit margins on equity crude were, however, subject to considerable variation (i) because of the use of a fixed tax allowance—amounting to $2 per barrel from February 1983—in respect of pro-duction costs, whereas actual production costs varied from field to field and were often well above $2 per barrel in offshore fields, and (ii) because there was often a discrepancy between the market value of Nigerian crude and the official selling price against which the notional profit margin was allowed.

During 1985 the foreign producing companies pressed for a revision of the established fiscal arrangements in order to reverse a decline in realized margins on equity crude. An initial round of negotiations was held in mid-year with the Buhari Government, which was anxious to ensure a high volume of equity sales in view of the disappointing outcome of several of its recent attempts to expand NNPC's own exports through counter-trade (i.e. barter and semi-barter) deals. The Government was also conscious of the need to provide foreign equity-holders with adequate incentives to maintain a healthy flow of new investment into exploration and development work, which was of particular importance because of the small average reservoir size in the Nigerian oilfields. Negotiations were reopened by the

Babangida Government soon after the Aug. 27 coup, the main company proposal at this point being that the official selling price (e.g. $28.65 per barrel for 36.7° crude) should replace the posted price (currently $29.94 for the same grade) as the effective tax-reference point, thereby raising the official equity profit margin from $2 to $3.14 per barrel.

By the end of 1985, however, the context of the negotiations had been radically altered by the breakdown of OPEC's official pricing system and the spread of netback selling, and the main features of an agreement worked out during the first quarter of 1986 were (i) that the tax-reference point should vary in line with the monthly netback value of Nigerian crudes under a formula which provided an official equity profit margin of $2 per barrel on a netback value of $23, with higher margins on higher values (e.g. $2.85 on a $30 netback); (ii) that a minimum margin of $2 per barrel should be guaranteed on netback values of less than $23; and (iii) that there should be a substantial increase (reportedly to $5 per barrel) in the tax allowance for production costs. At the same time the NNPC's foreign partner companies undertook to market, at a profit margin equal to 50 per cent of the prevailing official margin on equity crude, any state-owned crude which NNPC was unable to sell under its own netback contracts. NNPC was required to give 45 days' notice of the volumes involved. A slump in netback values towards $10 per barrel during the second quarter of the year prompted the Government to press for the introduction of a reduced equity profit margin on netbacks of less than $12.50 per barrel, leading to an agreement (valid initially for six months from Oct. 1) that the margin should be cut to $1.72 on a $10 netback, $1.25 on a $7.50 netback and $0.75 on a $5 netback.

Nigeria's domestic oil demand grew at an average annual rate of 21.3 per cent between 1971 and 1981. Demand reached a record level of 236,300 bpd in 1982, after which there was a sustained downturn (to less than 200,000 bpd in 1985). Part of the pre-1983 demand growth arose not from incremental consumption within Nigeria but from the smuggling of products to neighbouring countries, a practice which was subsequently curbed by the imposition of tighter border controls. Nigeria's pattern of product demand does not correspond to the output pattern of the local refining industry, and significant volumes of lighter products are imported in exchange for crude oil. NNPC's 1986 exchange contract (with CFP) provided for the monthly supply of 120,000 tonnes of gasoline and kerosene in return for 200,000 tonnes of 36.7° crude.

Refineries close to the coastal oilfields were opened at Port Harcourt in 1965 and at Warri in 1978, but it was not until 1980 that a refinery came on stream in the north of the country at Kaduna. A comprehensive network of pipelines and storage depots is under development with the aim of eliminating local shortages of refined products caused by inadequate distribution facilities. Contracts were signed in early 1985 for the construction of a new 150,000 bpd refinery at Port Harcourt, although implementation of this project remained blocked a year later because of difficulties in obtaining external finance. The establishment of a petrochemical industry to serve the domestic market has been an aim of government development planning since 1970, but it was not until 1984 that work began on a limited import-substitution project based on the utilization of feedstock from the Kaduna and Warri refineries. Production of polypropylene was due to begin at Warri before the end of 1986.

Very little progress had been made by the mid-1980s in implementing plans for the commercial exploitation of Nigeria's substantial reserves of associated and non-associated natural gas. Of the 24,552 million cubic metres of gas produced in the oilfields in 1984, 83.8 per cent was flared, 12.6 per cent marketed (mainly for electricity generation) and 3.5 per cent reinjected into oil wells (gas reinjection having begun in Nigeria in 1981). Gas-fired power stations were incurring financial losses at this time because the electricity generating authority's standard tariffs were based on the use of heavily-subsidized fuel oil, while many potential private-sector consumers of piped or bottled gas were deterred from fuel-switching by the heavy price penalties involved. (The retail price of liquefied petroleum gas was estimated to be 2½ times that of kerosene on an energy equivalence basis.)

Contracts were placed in 1984 for the construction of a pipeline system to carry about 6,000 mcm of gas per year from oilfields in the west of the Niger Delta to the Lagos area, where the main use would initially be for electricity generation. The start of pipe-laying work was, however, blocked throughout 1985 pending the authorization of a loan from the World Bank, whose energy experts had helped to draw up the project in 1983. The withholding of the loan authorization was based partly on the Bank's general concern about Nigeria's failure to follow IMF economic policy recommendations and partly on its specific concern about price distortions in the country's domestic energy market. The Bank was reported to be reviewing its attitude to the loan question in early 1986 in the light of the Babangida Government's announcement of a reduction in the subsidy on domestic oil prices.

The construction of a gas-based fertilizer plant at Onne, near Port Harcourt, had by mid-1986 reached a point from which completion could be achieved in 1987 (four years behind schedule) if the Government met its contractual share of development costs.

From 1976 to 1982 the Government collaborated with the main oil companies operating in Nigeria to plan the construction of a $14,000 million plant at Bonny to export liquefied natural gas to the United States and Western Europe, but this project was abandoned after cutbacks in government spending, withdrawals by Western financial backers and difficulties in negotiating US export contracts. NNPC signed an agreement with Shell, Elf Aquitaine and Agip at the beginning of 1986 on collaboration in the planning of a scaled-down LNG export plant with an annual capacity of 4,200 mcm, compared with the 16,000 mcm envisaged in the 1970s. The Government announced some months later that the recent deterioration in Nigeria's economic position had removed any prospect of developing a local LNG industry before the mid-1990s.

Legislation designed to curb the flaring of associated gas was enacted in 1979 to take effect from the beginning of 1984. Implementation was later deferred until the beginning of 1985, by which time the law had been amended to exempt certain categories of oilfield. Non-exempt fields accounted for about 63 per cent of Nigerian gas output in late 1984, although at prevailing oil production levels it was estimated that this proportion could be cut back to about 33 per cent if the larger operating companies reduced their production from non-exempt fields while increasing the level of capacity utilization in exempt fields. Operators who continued to flare gas in non-exempt fields were liable to be fined at the rate of 2.5 US cents per 1,000 cubic feet (28.3 cubic metres).

Gulf Oil of Nigeria stated in early 1985 that, whereas the 90 per cent flaring rate in its oilfields would render it liable to annual fines of up to $1,000,000, the capital cost of switching from water injection to gas reinjection techniques would amount to an unacceptable $156,000,000. The anti-flaring legislation led to some new investment in reinjection facilities by other operators, although many projects were not feasible because of NNPC's inability to fund its majority share of the costs. In mid-1986 the Government announced that it had decided not to demand the payment of gas-flaring fines in view of the constraints on NNPC spending on preventive measures.

C10—Qatar

C10.1—Statistical Survey

*1984
†End-1984

General

Area	11,400 sq km
*Population	290,000
Capital	Doha

Economy and trade

*Gross domestic product	$7,600 million
*Annual exports (fob)	$4,513 million (of which petroleum 93 per cent)
*Annual imports (cif)	$1,714 million
*Current account balance	+$1,513 million
Foreign exchange reserves	$372,000,000 (June 1985)

Oil (upstream)

1984 crude production	425,000 bpd (20,100,000 tonnes)
1985 crude production	310,000 bpd (14,500,000 tonnes)
†Proved crude reserves	3,400 million barrels
*Reserves:production ratio	21.6 : 1
Production in peak year	570,000 bpd (27,300,000 tonnes) in 1973
†Cumulative crude production	3,743.8 million barrels since 1949
*Number of producing oil wells	169
Export grades: Dukhan	40° API gravity
Marine	36° API gravity

Oil tanker tonnage

†2 vessels	197,600 deadweight tons

Oil (downstream)

*Installed refining capacity	62,200 bpd
*Output of refined products	26,800 bpd
*Consumption of refined products	12,400 bpd

Natural gas (million cubic metres)

*Gross annual production	6,800 mcm
of which: (gas marketed)	(5,930 mcm)
(gas flared)	(50 mcm)
(shrinkage)	(820 mcm)
†Natural gas reserves	4,200,000 mcm

C10.2—Political and Economic Summary

The state of Qatar, ruled since the eighteenth century by the al Thani dynasty, has a long history as an independent shaikhdom. During the nineteenth century Qatar became associated with the so-called trucial system under which Britain assumed a

peacekeeping role along the former "pirate coast" of the Persian/Arabian Gulf
($\lozenge$C12.2), and in 1916 the Shaikh entered into a formal treaty relationship whereby
Britain took responsibility for Qatar's defence and foreign relations. In 1968 the
British Government announced its intention to withdraw its remaining military
forces from the Gulf region by the end of 1971 and to terminate the existing
arrangements under which protection was afforded to Bahrain, Qatar and the
seven Trucial States. Negotiations ensued between the nine territories in question
to explore the possibility of forming a federation or union, but Bahrain and Qatar
each eventually decided to retain their separate status. In the case of Qatar, full
independence was achieved on Sept. 1, 1971, when a new treaty of friendship with
Britain superseded the 1916 treaty of protection.

Under the Constitution of Qatar absolute power lies with the hereditary Amir,
who holds the positions of head of state and Prime Minister. An advisory council,
selected from representatives elected by limited suffrage, is empowered to debate
legislation, to request ministerial statements and to make recommendations to the
Government, but there is no parliament and there are no political parties. Almost
all the population (which includes a high proportion of immigrant workers) are
Sunni Moslems. The present Amir is Shaikh Khalifa bin Hamad al Thani, who
deposed his cousin Shaikh Ahmad in a bloodless coup in February 1972.

Qatar is OPEC's smallest member in terms both of area and population, and its
oil wealth has been used to provide the population with an exceptionally high
standard of living. In addition to funding large public works and social welfare
projects, the Government has undertaken a programme of industrialization in both
the oil-related and non-oil sectors. It has also encouraged the revival of the
traditional fishing industry and is sponsoring research into the agricultural development of desert areas. Most major industrial developments are undertaken in
partnership with foreign companies. Heavy industries include a large integrated
steel complex (30 per cent owned by Japanese concerns) which exports most of its
production to Saudi Arabia, Kuwait and the United Arab Emirates.

Qatar was relatively well placed to withstand the adverse oil market trends of the
early 1980s, and the Government drew up deficit budgets from 1983 onwards in
order to maintain a high level of spending on key development projects. A main
aim of cutbacks which were made in other areas was to reduce spending on
imported goods and services, in keeping with a policy of encouraging a higher level
of productivity and self-reliance within Qatar (particularly through the growth of
small- and medium-scale private industry).

Qatar has good relations with the West and is closely associated with the Saudi-
led "moderate" Arab tendency whose main forum is the Gulf Co-operation Council
($\lozenge$D12.9). Like the other OPEC countries in the GCC, Qatar has been a leading
donor of third-world development aid in terms of the percentage of gross national
product devoted to aid programmes.

C10.3—Oil and Gas Industry

An oil concession covering the whole territory of Qatar for a period of 75 years was
granted by the ruler to the Anglo-Persian Oil Company (subsequently British
Petroleum) in May 1935. The company undertook to pay an initial sum of 400,000
rupees and to make subsequent annual payments of 150,000 rupees for five years
and 300,000 rupees thereafter in return for exemption from "all present and future
taxes of any kind whatsoever". The royalty rate was fixed at three rupees per ton of
oil produced (the rate which applied in Kuwait at that time $\lozenge$C7.3.i).

A political agreement of June 1935 between the Anglo-Persian Oil Co. and the
British Government (acting in accordance with its responsibilities for Qatar's

external affairs) precluded the transfer of the concession to any successor company which was not approved by the British Government, registered in Britain and chaired by a British subject. The British Government subsequently approved Anglo-Persian's assignment of its concession rights—under the terms of the 1928 "red line agreement" (◊**A4.5.i**)—to Petroleum Concessions Ltd, a subsidiary of the Iraq Petroleum Company (which had delegated responsibility for the original negotiation of the concession agreement to Anglo-Persian for political reasons). An operating company called Petroleum Development (Qatar) was established in 1936 under the ultimate ownership of the IPC parent companies (BP 23.75 per cent, CFP 23.75 per cent, Shell 23.75 per cent, Mobil 11.875 per cent, Exxon 11.875 per cent, Partex 5 per cent). The operating company was renamed Qatar Petroleum Co. (QPC) in 1953.

The company discovered oil in the onshore Dukhan structure in the west of the peninsula in 1939 and drilled two commercially productive wells in the following year before suspending all development work for the remaining duration of the Second World War. Following the resumption of operations in 1947 the oilfield was linked by pipeline to a tanker terminal at Umm Said on the east coast of the peninsula from which exports commenced in late 1949, reaching an average level of 33,600 bpd during 1950 and increasing to over 200,000 bpd by the mid-1960s.

Under an agreement signed in September 1952 the terms of the 1935 concession agreement were amended to provide for a total government revenue entitlement (including royalties, rentals and other payments) equal to 50 per cent of the net profits arising from the company's exports. Profits were defined as the difference between the "border value" of exports and the costs of production (including amortization and depreciation charges). The initial border value (£4.2s.3d sterling per ton of 40° API crude) was to vary in line with subsequent changes in posted prices. The company guaranteed to make minimum payments to the Government of £1,000,000 per annum during periods of normal production and £750,000 per annum during periods when production was suspended by force majeure. Subsequent amendments to the supplemental agreement of 1952 included the following: (i) the redefinition of the border value of exports as the prevailing posted price less a marketing discount of 2 per cent (August 1955); (ii) the redefinition of the royalty as an amount equal to 12.5 per cent of the posted price (August 1955); (iii) the reduction of the allowable marketing discount to 1 per cent of the posted price (May 1957); (iv) the redefinition of this discount as 0.5 cents per barrel (February 1964) and (v) the treatment of royalties as operating expenses for income tax purposes (December 1964).

The QPC relinquished 4,500 sq km of its concession area in December 1961, 3,200 sq km in July 1963 and 2,860 sq km in July 1965, after which it retained only the Dukhan structure from which all its production was derived.

In 1949 the ruler of Qatar proclaimed his jurisdiction over an area of the continental shelf adjoining the country's territorial waters and granted an offshore concession to the International Marine Oil Company, a partnership between the (US) Superior Oil Co. and the (British) Central Mining Corporation. The validity of this concession was challenged by Petroleum Development (Qatar) but was upheld by an arbitration tribunal, which ruled in March 1950 that the original 1935 concession applied only to territory which came under Qatari jurisdiction at the time that it was granted. The International Marine Oil Co. subsequently relinquished its rights after carrying out initial survey work, and the offshore concession (estimated at 25,900 sq km) was granted in November 1952 to Shell (which thus became the first IPC shareholder company to acquire sole concession rights in an area formerly covered by the "red line agreement").

The 1952 offshore agreement, which was valid for a period of 75 years, provided

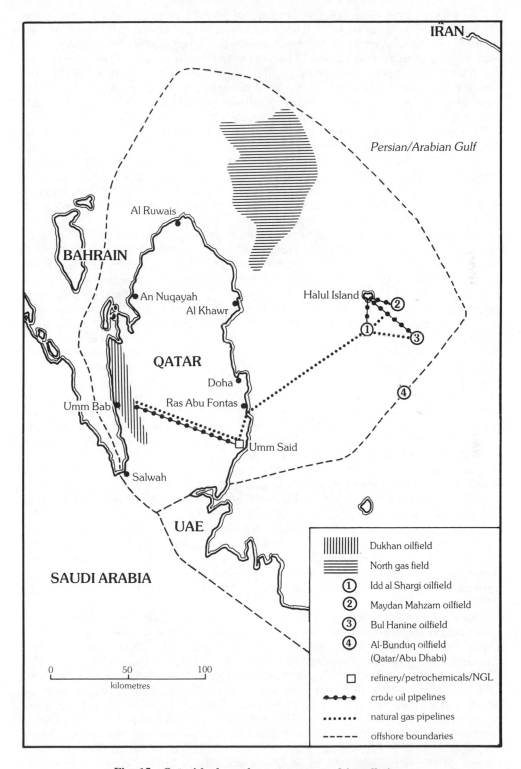

Fig. 15—Qatari hydrocarbon resources and installations

for an initial payment to the Government of £260,000 sterling and for the commencement of exploration work within nine months and of test drilling within two years. The financial terms of the agreement were based on "50-50 profit-sharing" and were subsequently amended in parallel with the terms of the QPC agreement. Shell's offshore operating subsidiary, the Shell Company of Qatar (SCQ), discovered two oilfields in 1960. These were brought into commercial production in 1966 after the construction of storage tanks and other facilities on Halul Island, about 100 km east of the mainland, to which a third offshore field was linked in 1972. Qatar's oil production reached a peak level of 570,000 bpd (more than half of this from SCQ's offshore fields) in 1973.

SCQ relinquished over half of its original concession area in 1963, the relinquished territory being taken over by Conoco, which earlier that year had acquired concession rights over onshore areas relinquished by QPC. Conoco later withdrew from its Qatar concession areas (totalling about 23,300 sq km) after failing to discover any new oil deposits.

As a result of changes in offshore jurisdiction stemming from a maritime boundary agreement with Abu Dhabi, Qatar in 1969 acquired an interest in the Al-Bunduq oilfield, which had been discovered four years earlier by Abu Dhabi Marine Areas Ltd (then owned 66⅔ per cent by BP and 33⅓ per cent by CFP). A new company, Al-Bunduq Oil Co., was established in 1971 to develop this field; ownership was one-third by BP, one-third by CFP and one-third by Japanese interests (which had obtained a 7,500 sq km offshore concession in Qatari territory in 1969). The field was brought on stream in December 1975 but ceased production between mid-1979 and mid-1984 while secondary recovery facilities were installed. The (Japanese) United Petroleum Development Co. acted as operator.

As a signatory of OPEC's General Agreement on Participation (◊D3.4) the Government of Qatar acquired a 25 per cent interest in the operations of the Qatar Petroleum Co. and the Shell Company of Qatar in January 1973. Compensation totalling $43,000,000 was paid to SCQ under an agreement of Jan. 5, while QPC received $28,000,000 under an agreement of Jan. 11, each payment being based on an updated book valuation of the assets acquired. When the Government increased its participation to 60 per cent with effect from Jan. 1, 1974, the compensation terms in respect of the entire state interest (including the 25 per cent acquired in 1973) were placed on a net book value basis, additional payments of $11,000,000 to SCQ and $27,500,000 to QPC being agreed on Feb. 20, 1974. On Dec. 22, 1974, the Government announced its intention to acquire the 40 per cent of the companies' rights, assets and operations which then remained under foreign ownership. An agreement on the full nationalization of QPC's operations (with additional compensation of £18,000,000 sterling) was concluded on Sept. 16, 1976, and a similar agreement regarding SCQ (with compensation of £14,120,000 sterling) on Feb. 19, 1977.

The state's hydrocarbon interests were vested in the Qatar General Petroleum Corporation (QGPC), which was established in July 1974 as the successor to a Qatar National Oil Company set up in April 1972. Following the full nationalization of QPC's operations, a Qatar Petroleum Producing Authority (QPPA) was established in October 1976 as QGPC's operating subsidiary. The QPPA entered into a five-year contract with a new Dukhan Service Company which was formed by QPC's foreign parent companies to provide onshore management and operational services to the QPPA in the Dukhan field in return for a fee per barrel of oil produced (starting at 15 cents and varying thereafter in line with movements in the official price of Qatar's oil). After the subsequent completion of the nationalization of SCQ's operations, a further contract was concluded on a similar basis between the QPPA and a new Qatar Shell Service

Company in respect of the Idd al Shargi, Maydan Mahzam and Bul Hanine offshore fields. Although neither contract was formally renewed upon expiry in 1981–82 the two foreign service companies continued to operate in association with QGPC, which had established separate onshore and offshore operating divisions in place of the QPPA in September 1980.

A 30-year oil concession which had been granted in June 1973 to a consortium of independents led by Wintershall AG (as the operating company), on terms which included a 51 per cent state share option, was cancelled by the Government in April 1976 and replaced by a contractual agreement providing for production-sharing in the event of a commercial oil discovery; the consortium was entitled to recover its exploration and development costs by taking 40 per cent of initial production, while the Government was entitled to take a minimum of 80 per cent of the balance of production. The consortium's only significant discovery, made in 1980, was not of oil but of non-associated gas in the form of a southern extension of the North field (whose main reserves had been located by SCQ in 1972). The Government terminated the consortium's contract at the end of 1985, having declared the North field extension to be unsuitable for separate commercial development.

Sohio was awarded a 25-year contract in June 1985 to explore for hydrocarbons in a 12,000 sq km block off the east coast of Qatar. The company agreed to bear all exploration and development costs in return for a minority share of any production from commercial deposits. A 25-year onshore contract, covering an area of about 7,000 sq km, was awarded to Amoco in February 1986. The state's oil entitlement under these production-sharing contracts ranged from a minimum of 80 per cent at an output level of 20,000 bpd or less to a maximum of 90 per cent at an output level in excess of 90,000 bpd.

Most of Qatar's output of associated natural gas is processed by two natural gas liquids (NGL) plants at Umm Said—one serving the onshore oilfields and the other the offshore fields—which produce liquefied petroleum gas and condensate primarily for export and supply ethane-rich dry gas for use as a feedstock by the Qatar Petrochemical Company (84 per cent owned by QGPC). The Qatar Fertilizer Company (70 per cent owned by QGPC) also uses associated gas as a feedstock. Non-associated gas from a relatively small onshore deposit has been used primarily as a source of fuel for power generation and heavy industry. A crude oil production level of about 450,000 bpd was required to meet Qatar's full demand for associated gas in the first half of the 1980s, and the NGL and organic petrochemical plants experienced some feedstock shortages as a result of the fall in oil output after 1981 (although fertilizer plants were able to use non-associated gas as a substitute feedstock).

According to official figures, Qatar's crude oil output (excluding gas condensates) averaged 308,700 bpd over the period 1982–84, of which slightly more than half came from the onshore Dukhan field. The country's output of natural gas liquids totalled 1,430,000 tonnes in 1984. The Qatar Petrochemical Company produced 204,000 tonnes of ethylene and 149,600 tonnes of low-density polyethylene in the same year, while the Qatar Fertilizer Company produced 631,760 tonnes of ammonia and 734,000 tonnes of urea.

It was expected in the mid-1980s that the extensive offshore reserves of non-associated gas in the North field would displace oil as the main source of Qatar's hydrocarbon revenues in the longer term. Commercial production from the field was due to begin in 1988 upon completion of the first phase of a long-term development project. The object of this phase was to produce about 8,250 million cubic metres per year of gas to supply raw material and fuel requirements within Qatar (with any surplus being injected into the country's greatly depleted onshore gas reservoir). Initial separation into dry gas and condensate was to take place at an offshore treatment platform whose output would be piped to an onshore distribution centre at Ras Laffan (70 km north of Doha).

The proposed second and third phases of the North field project (neither of which could be finalized until firm export contracts had been agreed) envisaged (i) the supply of a further 8,250 mcm per year of piped gas to neighbouring states and (ii) the construction of a liquefaction plant at Umm Said to supply 6,000,000 tonnes per year of LNG to overseas markets in the 1990s. The Qatar Liquefied Gas Company, formed in 1984 to handle forward planning for the LNG project, had as its shareholders in early 1986 QGPC (77.5 per cent), BP (7.5 per cent), CFP (7.5 per cent) and the Japanese company Marubeni (7.5 per cent).

The domestic refining and marketing of oil products in Qatar is handled by the National Oil Distribution Co., a subsidiary of the QGPC. Output from the company's original 12,200 bpd refinery at Umm Said, which came on stream in 1975, was insufficient to meet domestic demand by the early 1980s. A new 50,000 bpd refinery was opened at Umm Said in 1984 in order to eliminate product imports and provide export capacity.

C11—Saudi Arabia

C11.1—Statistical Survey

*1984
†End-1984
‡Revision of 1984 figures given in section **D15.1.i** (see Introduction)

General
Area	2,149,690 sq km
*Population	11,090,000
Capital	Riyadh

Economy and trade
*Gross national product	$98,867 million
*Annual exports (fob)	$46,834 million (consisting almost wholly of petroleum)
*Annual imports (cif)	$36,644 million
*Current account balance	−$13,220 million
Foreign exchange reserves	$13,061 million (January 1986)

Oil (upstream), excluding Neutral Zone (for which see section C7.1)
‡1984 crude production	4,760,000 bpd (233,000,000 tonnes)
1985 crude production	3,600,000 bpd (174,800,000 tonnes)
†Proved crude reserves	169,000 million barrels
*Reserves:production ratio	98.5 : 1
Production in peak year	9,990,000 bpd (493,000,000 tonnes) in 1980
†Cumulative crude production	50,136.5 million barrels since 1938
*Number of producing oil wells	391
Export grades: Berri	39° API gravity
Arabian Light	34° API gravity
Arabian Medium	31° API gravity
Arabian Heavy	27° API gravity

Oil tanker tonnage
†23 vessels	2,658,100 deadweight tons

Oil (downstream, including Neutral Zone)
*Installed refining capacity	1,160,600 bpd
*Output of refined products	878,000 bpd
*Consumption of refined products	531,200 bpd

Natural gas (million cubic metres)
*Gross annual production	29,050 mcm
of which: (gas marketed)	(7,150 mcm)
(gas reinjected)	(1,250 mcm)
(gas flared)	(14,850 mcm)
(shrinkage)	(5,800 mcm)
†Natural gas reserves	3,500,000 mcm

C11.2—Political and Economic Summary

The Kingdom of Saudi Arabia was founded in 1932 by King Abdul Aziz ibn Saud, whose amalgamation of the separate kingdoms of Najd and Hejaz (together controlling most of the Arabian peninsula) formally ended a long history of political and military conflict between rival centres of Arab power in this area. The northern borders of the unified state included those defined in agreements made in 1922 between Najd and Iraq and between Najd and Kuwait, each agreement having established a Neutral Zone under joint sovereignty. The Kuwait-Saudi Neutral Zone was subsequently geographically divided under an agreement of 1965 (◊C7.2), a similar agreement being reached between Iraq and Saudi Arabia in 1975 in respect of the Iraq-Saudi Neutral Zone. Saudi Arabia's southern border with the kingdom of Yemen (present-day North Yemen) was established (but not demarcated) in 1934, when Saudi Arabia asserted its claims by force of arms. The borders between Saudi Arabia and the Aden Protectorates (present-day South Yemen), Qatar, Abu Dhabi and Oman were all disputed at various times, although in each case a practical understanding (which fell short of formal demarcation) was eventually reached without serious incident.

Saudi Arabia contains the two holiest shrines of Islam, at Mecca and Medina, which are the centre of pilgrimage for the world's Moslems. The majority of the Saudi population are Sunni Moslems, with a Shi'ite minority in the east of the kingdom. The Saudi monarch has absolute power to rule according to the laws and precepts of Islam (religious and temporal power being regarded as indivisible); the kingdom has no parliament and no political parties. A committee set up in 1980 to examine the possibility of establishing a form of democratic institution proposed that there should be a nominated "assembly of commoners" with consultative status, but the formation of such an institution was still awaited in mid-1986. Saudi Arabia's present head of state and Prime Minister is King Fahd ibn Abdul Aziz, who succeeded to the throne in June 1982.

By virtue of its possession of the world's largest proved oil reserves and largest export capacity, Saudi Arabia plays a key role both in global politics and in the affairs of OPEC and OAPEC. As a pro-Western country having particularly close relations with the United States, its general policy towards the supply and pricing of oil during the 1970s was to support what it regarded as the equitable demands of the oil exporters while opposing actions which it considered to be excessive in terms of their effect on the world economy. At the same time Saudi Arabia was prepared to make use of its position as the main supplier of the West's oil imports in order to influence Western governments' policies towards the Arab-Israeli conflict. The collapse of oil prices in 1986 followed Saudi Arabia's abandonment of the role of principal guarantor of the stability of the world oil market, fulfilment of this role having led to an unacceptably large contraction of the kingdom's market share during the first half of the 1980s.

Having peaked at $113,406 million in 1981, Saudi Arabia's annual oil export earnings declined to about $28,000 million—their lowest level for a decade—in 1985, while the kingdom's accumulated foreign assets, amounting to about $160,000 million in 1982, were drawn down at an estimated annual rate of $20,000 million from 1983 to 1985. One factor behind the high rate of capital accumulation during the 1970s was the Government's concern to pursue development policies consistent with the preservation of the traditional social order, while the high drawdown rate of the mid-1980s stemmed in part from a desire to avoid the destabilizing impact of a major economic recession.

During the period of Saudi Arabia's first two five-year development plans (1970–75 and 1975–80) the main emphasis was placed on infrastructural development, social welfare projects and non-oil industries, although the share of non-oil manufacturing in the gross domestic product remained negligible in 1980 and was heavily concentrated on the production of building materials and other intermediate goods. A major constraint on the growth of this sector was a severe shortage of skilled Saudi manpower, the country being dependent on expatriates to supply over half of the total workforce. High growth rates in non-productive sectors such as trade and services during the 1970s reflected a steady rise in spending on imports.

Under the Government's industrialization programme, the Saudi private sector has been encouraged to take the lead in creating smaller industries, while state enterprises, in partnership with foreign companies, have taken responsibility for investment in major projects. A mechanism for linking private- and public-sector growth was introduced in 1983, when the Government required all "non-Saudi" companies—i.e. those having less than 51 per cent Saudi equity participation—to sub-contract at least 30 per cent of their work on state-sponsored projects to 100 per cent Saudi-owned companies. The impact of this measure was, however, blunted by subsequent curbs on the growth of public-sector spending.

During the 1980–85 planning period state enterprises were concerned principally with the development of capital-intensive hydrocarbon-based industries designed to reduce the country's heavy reliance on crude oil exports. By the end of this period a number of new oil refineries and gas-based petrochemical plants were on stream or nearing completion, although their short-term export prospects were less favourable than had originally been envisaged (◊C11.3.ix). The main industrial development area was the new city of Jubail, where the state-sponsored plants were seen as the nucleus of a major centre of private-sector manufacturing. Private investment in the state-sponsored plants was encouraged in 1984 through the offer for sale to the public in Saudi Arabia and other Gulf Co-operation Council countries of 30 per cent of the shares in the Saudi Basic Industries Corporation (the main sponsoring body). This exercise was not wholly successful, and no further move had been made by 1986 towards the Government's ultimate target of a 75 per cent privatization of the corporation.

Massive investments have been made in the agricultural sector with the aims of achieving self-sufficiency in food production and of slowing the migration of the rural population into the towns. The most striking result of this policy was an increase in annual wheat production from about 3,000 tonnes in 1975 to about 1,300,000 tonnes (well above the level of consumption) in 1984, the surplus being purchased by the Government at a guaranteed price over five times higher than the current cost of imported wheat. The largest single area of government spending is defence and security, whose allocation (accounting for nearly one-third of the 1985–86 budget) was substantially increased following the outbreak of the Iran-Iraq war. As well as being the main source of financial support for various Arab causes, Saudi Arabia is also one of the world's major donors of aid to developing countries.

The estimated 75 per cent fall in the value of Saudi oil exports between 1981 and 1985 was accompanied by an overall fall of only one-third (from $84,220 million to $55,940 million) in the annual level of budgetary spending as the Government acted to offset part of the slump in current revenues by drawing on its capital reserves. The annual growth target for the non-oil sectors of the economy was trimmed from over 7 per cent to less than 3 per cent over the same period. The 1985–90 development plan, launched in March 1985, envisaged a 30 per cent reduction in total expenditure compared with the previous five-year planning period, with a rather larger percentage fall in investment in new projects in order to accommodate the growing operating costs of completed projects. The Government's main priorities were to increase the productivity of the Saudi workforce, to stimulate the growth of the private business sector and to ensure that an increasing proportion of foreign contractors' profits was reinvested in the Saudi economy.

Revenue projections in both the 1985–86 budget and the 1985–90 development plan were based on the assumption of minimum oil production of 3,850,000 bpd at an average price of $25 per barrel, and it was a fall in average production to little more than 2,500,000 bpd (less than a quarter of installed capacity) between May and August 1985 which prompted the Government to make its radical switch to netback pricing later in the year (◊**D16.8**). With more than half of its capacity still unused, the kingdom was earning an estimated $43,000,000 per day from a substantially increased volume of low-priced oil exports in June 1986, compared with its earnings of $38,000,000 per day from officially-priced exports in June 1985. The value of June 1986 exports in terms of the local currency was boosted by a 2.7 per cent devaluation of the riyal against the US dollar at the beginning of the month, this being the kingdom's largest ever devaluation. The riyal had come under growing pressure from speculators since the Government's announcement that no budget would be drawn up for the fiscal year beginning in March 1986 until such time as it was possible to make a realistic assessment of the outlook for oil revenues.

C11.3—Oil and Gas Industry

C11.3.i—Early development (1933 to 1944)

In May 1933 Chevron (then known as Standard Oil Co. of California) was granted a 60-year oil concession in respect of an "exclusive area" covering about 728,000 sq km of eastern Saudi Arabia. The concession agreement also conferred certain preference rights (i) over a large area situated to the west of the exclusive area, in which the company was permitted to conduct geological survey work, and (ii) in respect of Saudi Arabia's interest in the Kuwait-Saudi Arabian Neutral Zone. (Should concession rights be offered in these "preferential areas", the company had the option to acquire them, if it so wished, by matching the best acceptable terms offered to the Saudi Government—or, in the case of the Neutral Zone, to the Kuwait Government—by any other company.) The Government's royalty income from production operations in the exclusive area was fixed at four gold shillings per ton (or an agreed equivalent in US dollars) and the company was to be exempt from local taxation.

The company was to make an immediate loan to the Government of £30,000 in gold and a further loan of £20,000 in gold 18 months later. The Government had no obligation to repay the first loan during the life of the concession agreement, although the company had the right to recover the amount of both loans through deductions from half of the royalties due to the Government. The company's option rights in the "preferential areas" were to be valid for as long as any loan repayments remained outstanding. The amount of the loans which Chevron undertook to advance was considerably higher than an offer made by the Iraq Petroleum Company (IPC) consortium in a rival bid for concession rights which was rejected by the Saudi Government.

Chevron's only existing Middle East interest was in nearby Bahrain, where it had been granted sole concession rights in 1929 following its acquisition of an option over these rights which was previously held by Gulf Oil. Gulf, which at that time was a shareholder in IPC and thus a party to the "red line agreement" of 1928 (which covered both Bahrain and Saudi Arabia ◊**A4.5**), had itself been unable to acquire the Bahrain concession independently of its IPC partners, who had refused to contemplate a joint bid because of their general scepticism at this time regarding the oil potential of the eastern part of the Arabian peninsula. IPC's attempt to obtain the eastern Saudi Arabian concession in 1933 was prompted largely by Chevron's discovery of oil in Bahrain in the previous year, and the failure of this attempt led the IPC parent companies to set up a new joint company (Petroleum Concessions Ltd) in 1935 as a vehicle for the acquisition of oil rights throughout the remainder of the "uncommitted" area covered by the red line agreement.

In July 1936 Petroleum Concessions Ltd obtained a concession covering a strip of territory about 100 km wide along most of Saudi Arabia's Red Sea coastline (excluding only an area around Mecca), and geological surveys were subsequently carried out by an operating company called Petroleum Development (Western

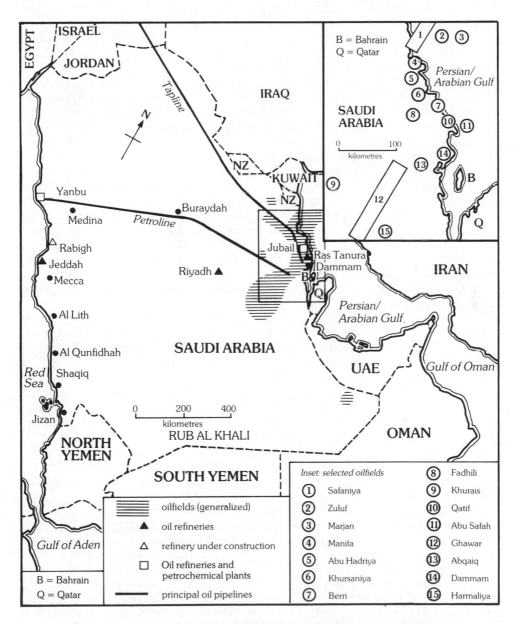

Fig. 16—Saudi Arabian hydrocarbon resources and installations

Arabia) Ltd. Having failed to discover any potentially oil-bearing structures, the company formally relinquished the concession in 1941.

By 1935 a rapid growth of production in Bahrain was placing great pressure on Chevron's limited marketing facilities in the eastern hemisphere. In the following year the company entered into a partnership with Texaco (which had no existing upstream interests in the Middle East) whereby Texaco acquired a 50 per cent share in Chevron's Bahrain production operations while Chevron acquired a 50 per cent share in Texaco's marketing operations east of Suez, which were transferred to the ownership of the jointly-owned California Texas Oil Co. (Caltex). Later in 1936 Texaco acquired a 50 per cent interest in Chevron's Saudi Arabian operating subsidiary, the California Arabian Standard Oil Co. (Casoc), which thus gained additional capital backing for its exploration programme and, in the longer term, a more extensive marketing network to handle any future production. Casoc made its first oil strike in eastern Saudi Arabia in March 1938 and formally declared the discovery of a major commercial field six months later.

In May 1939 Casoc concluded a supplemental agreement with the Government of Saudi Arabia under which the company undertook to make capital payments to the Government (of £140,000 in gold immediately and £100,000 in gold upon the discovery of commercial oil deposits in newly acquired areas) while the Government agreed to grant concession rights to the company in additional "exclusive areas". These were (i) the Kuwait-Saudi Arabian Neutral Zone, hitherto classed as a "preferential area"; (ii) the Iraq-Saudi Arabian Neutral Zone; (iii) an area in the north of Saudi Arabia lying between the western boundary of Casoc's existing exclusive area and the eastern boundary of the coastal concession granted to Petroleum Concessions Ltd in 1936; and (iv) an area of southern Saudi Arabia lying between the western boundary of Casoc's existing exclusive area and the eastern border of the kingdom of Yemen (present-day North Yemen). On the basis of Saudi Arabia's official definition of its undemarcated southern borders, the combined extent of Casoc's new and existing exclusive areas was estimated at up to 1,140,000 sq km. Some of the additional areas in the north and south had hitherto been included in the main preferential area.

The company's concession rights over its additional exclusive areas were to be valid for 60 years from the date of the supplemental agreement, as were its preference rights in the reduced preferential area. The company's entire concession, including the original exclusive area obtained in 1933, was to be free of relinquishment obligations for a period of 10 years (i.e. until 1949); thereafter Casoc was required to relinquish "such portions of the exclusive area as the company may decide not to explore further". Three successive two-year extensions of the expiry dates of the 1933 and 1939 concessions were subsequently granted by the Government (in 1941, 1943 and 1945) to offset the wartime disruption of Casoc's exploration and development programme, each such extension being accompanied by a similar extension of the exemption period with regard to relinquishment. Casoc changed its name to become the Arabian American Oil Co. (Aramco) in 1944.

Wartime constraints limited the company's production to an average 14,500 bpd from 1940 to 1944, with the result that the Saudi Government's income from current oil royalties was not adequate to meet its budgetary needs (the traditional inflow of revenue from Moslem pilgrims having virtually ceased as a result of the war). After 1940 the British Government's financial assistance to Saudi Arabia substantially exceeded the level of aid which was being made available by Chevron and Texaco (in the form of special advances against future rents and royalties), causing the US companies to fear that the post-war security of their concession rights would be endangered by a growth of British influence in the country. As a result of lobbying by the companies, which put forward evidence of Saudi Arabia's considerable potential as a future oil supplier, the US Government agreed in early 1943 to extend "lend-lease" aid to Saudi Arabia on overriding strategic grounds (thus overcoming the objection that, as a neutral country, Saudi Arabia did not fall within the normal scope of the lend-lease programme). This development marked the beginning of a special bilateral relationship between the United States and Saudi Arabia, and gave rise to various proposals on the part of officials in Washington for direct US government involvement in the development of Saudi Arabian oil, either through the purchase of Aramco's concession rights or through a long-term supply agreement. These and other proposals were, however, dropped in the face of opposition within the US oil industry and the US Congress.

C11.3.ii—Growth of Aramco's output (1945 to 1950) – Onshore Neutral Zone concession agreement (1948)

Following the Second World War Aramco's output grew rapidly (by 174 per cent in 1945 and 181 per cent in 1946) and in 1947 Texaco's European and North African marketing operations were transferred to the ownership of Caltex in order to absorb some of the increase. It was, however, already apparent that Saudi Arabia's oil development potential demanded greater capital and other resources than were available to the two parent companies, which accordingly agreed (on the basis of negotiations which had commenced in 1946) to admit Exxon and Mobil as additional shareholders in Aramco. As parties to the red line agreement Exxon and Mobil were technically unable to take this step without the consent of their partners in IPC. This was withheld for some time in the case of CFP and Partex, which saw the prospect of a major growth in Saudi output as a threat to their established interests in the Middle East. Legal proceedings over this issue were withdrawn only after various understandings had been negotiated whereby the smaller companies were assured that Exxon in particular would make substantial investments to increase IPC's production capacity in Iraq.

The red line agreement was finally cancelled in November 1948, allowing the formal redistribution of shareholdings in Aramco to be effected in the following month, with Chevron, Texaco and Exxon each taking 30 per cent and Mobil 10 per cent. Chevron and Texaco were to receive an estimated $500,000,000, payable partly out of future oil production, from the sale of the 40 per cent interest which changed hands. In contrast to most other joint operating companies in the Middle East, Aramco was a profit-making corporation which transferred oil to its parent companies at prices related to export values rather than to production costs. Profits were shared between the parent companies on the basis of a complex formula which gave a higher than average margin per barrel to an Aramco shareholder which "underlifted" oil relative to its proportionate entitlement and a lower than average margin to a shareholder which "overlifted". Aramco's procedures for determining the rate of investment to expand production capacity were not publicly known.

Prior to the change in the company's ownership the Saudi Government concluded an agreement with Aramco in October 1948 under which (i) the company acquired offshore oil rights in all Saudi Arabian waters in that part of the Persian/Arabian Gulf adjoining its existing Saudi concession area (this provision being phrased in such a way as to include offshore areas to which the Government did not formally lay claim until May 1949); (ii) a higher rate of royalty per barrel was established for offshore oil production than for onshore production; (iii) the company guaranteed the payment of offshore royalties totalling a minimum of $2,000,000 per year (payable in advance pending the commencement of offshore production); (iv) the company relinquished its concession rights in the Kuwait-

Saudi Arabian Neutral Zone (which had never been exercised); (v) the company relinquished its preference rights in that part of the preferential area lying west of longitude 46° East; and (vi) a future relinquishment programme was established in respect of the exclusive area.

The relinquishment programme (prepared by Aramco) obliged the company to select one or more blocks totalling 85,470 sq km for relinquishment on each of six specified dates (in 1949, 1952, 1955, 1960, 1965 and 1970). It was agreed that the blocks could include territory falling within Saudi Arabia's southern borders as defined by the Government at the time that concession rights were granted and that "if these boundaries are not correct, and the concession area is reduced, the areas to be relinquished will be reduced proportionately". Part of the territory which was subsequently designated by Aramco for relinquishment under this programme lay in southern areas outside Saudi Arabia's de facto borders as shown on most modern maps.

By 1950 Aramco's production had reached 546,700 bpd (nearly four times the output of Iraq in the same year), while Saudi Arabia's proved reserves amounted to 30,000 million barrels (24.8 per cent of total non-communist world reserves at that time). Development work was facilitated, and routine production costs were reduced to a minimum, by the vast size of the Saudi reservoirs (which enabled Aramco to achieve one of the world's highest rates of output per individual producing oilwell) and by their proximity to the Gulf coast (where the main export facilities were situated). An alternative export route for up to 320,000 bpd of Saudi crude was provided in December 1950 with the opening of the 1,312 km trans-Arabian pipeline (Tapline) which ran north-west from the oilfields to cross Jordanian, Syrian and Lebanese territory, terminating near the Mediterranean port of Sidon. The pipeline, whose capacity was increased to 470,000 bpd during the course of the 1950s, was owned by the Aramco parent companies through a separate joint subsidiary, the Trans-Arabian Pipeline Co.

Aramco's decision to relinquish its rights in the Kuwait-Saudi Arabian Neutral Zone followed the granting of a Kuwaiti Neutral Zone concession to Aminoil in June 1948 on financial terms which were highly advantageous to the Kuwait Government when compared with existing Middle East concession agreements (◊C7.3.ii). (An implied condition of Aramco's 1939 Neutral Zone concession had been that the Saudi Government should not receive less favourable terms than those obtained by the Kuwait Government in the Zone.) Having opened its half interest in the Zone to competitive bidding, Saudi Arabia concluded an agreement in February 1949 under which a 60-year onshore concession was granted to the US independent Pacific Western Oil Corp. (which was renamed the Getty Oil Co. in 1956 and remained an independent producer until 1984, when it was taken over by Texaco).

Notable features of this concession agreement included (i) an initial capital payment of $9,500,000 to the Saudi Government; (ii) a royalty rate of 55 cents per barrel of crude produced (whereas Aramco's unchanged onshore royalty rate was equivalent to 22 cents per barrel in 1949); (iii) a guaranteed minimum annual royalty payment of $1,000,000, payable in advance each year with effect from the signing of the agreement; (iv) an undertaking by the company to begin the construction of a refinery in the Neutral Zone with a throughput capacity of at least 12,000 bpd at such time as its crude oil production in the Neutral Zone had averaged 75,000 bpd for a period of 90 days; (v) the payment to the Saudi Government of 25 per cent of the company's annual net profits from the sale of oil and gas "products and by-products . . . obtained from the Neutral Zone" (excluding oil refined by the company within the Neutral Zone); (vi) the payment to the Saudi Government of 20 per cent of the company's annual net profits from its refining operations within the Neutral Zone; and (vii) an option for the Saudi Government to purchase for domestic use a proportion of the company's output at prices 5 per cent below prevailing market prices.

C11.3.iii—Agreement with Aramco on 50-50 profit-sharing

Having concluded the Pacific Western agreement on what were at that time the most advantageous financial terms (from a government viewpoint) ever to have been incorporated in a Middle Eastern concession agreement, the Saudi Government sought an increase in its revenues from the operations of Aramco. The Government's aim was to emulate Venezuela's recent introduction of "50-50 profit-sharing" (◊C13.3.iii), while the concern of the Aramco parent companies was to minimize the ultimate impact of such a move on their post-tax profits from Aramco's operations. In view of the fact that bona fide income tax payments made by US oil companies to foreign governments could be fully deducted from such companies' US tax liabilities (whereas foreign royalty payments were treated as business expenses and could be deducted only from taxable income) it was recognized both by Aramco and by the Saudi Government during 1950 that the introduction of an appropriate taxation formula in Saudi Arabia would provide a mutually acceptable means of increasing the Saudi Government's oil revenues. The Saudi Arabian "50-50" formula subsequently evolved as follows:

(1) The kingdom's first general tax decree, providing inter alia for the taxation of company profits at the rate of 20 per cent, was introduced in early November 1950. (Taxation in Saudi Arabia had previously been based on Islamic custom rather than on modern laws.)

(2) A further decree of Dec. 27, 1950, imposed an additional tax on the profits of companies engaged in the production of petroleum. Any such company's net operating income—which was defined as gross income less (i) allowable operating expenses and depreciation charges and (ii) income tax payments to foreign governments—was to be "provisionally" assessed for tax at the rate of 50 per cent. The final amount of the additional tax would be calculated after the deduction from this provisional assessment of all other tax, royalty, rental and duty payments to Saudi Arabia.

(3) The terms of Aramco's original concession agreement (which exempted the company from Saudi taxation without its consent) were amended on Dec. 30, 1950, when the company agreed to "submit" to the two recent Saudi income tax decrees, subject to certain conditions. These were (i) that "in no case shall the total of such taxes and all other taxes, royalties, rentals and exactions of the Government exceed 50 per cent of the gross income of Aramco after such income has been reduced by Aramco's cost of operations, including losses and depreciation, and by income taxes, if any, payable to any foreign country", and (ii) that "in all other respects" Aramco's immunity from taxation "shall continue in full force and effect". It was further agreed that "royalties and rentals will not be subject to reduction or recovery by the company should the company suffer an operating loss".

(4) On Feb. 13, 1952, the income tax decree of Dec. 27, 1950, and the agreement with Aramco of Dec. 30, 1950, were each amended (the latter with the company's consent) by deleting the provision allowing foreign income tax liabilities to be deducted from gross income for the purpose of establishing net taxable income in Saudi Arabia. This followed Aramco's receipt of formal confirmation from the US tax authorities that its income tax payments to the Saudi Government were eligible for treatment as tax credits in the United States. The US Treasury and State Departments had consulted closely with Aramco and with the Saudi Government from an early stage in the drafting of Saudi Arabia's tax legislation, whose final effect was to transfer a substantial revenue entitlement from the United States Government to the Saudi Government while leaving the Aramco parent companies with a virtually unchanged post-tax share of the profits attributed to their Saudi operations.

Whereas the Saudi Government had assumed that Aramco's gross income would be based on the sale of oil to its parent companies at the full posted price following the introduction of local postings in 1950 (◊A4.7), it became apparent in due course that various discounts were being granted, thus depressing the company's taxable income. The main general discount was abolished under an agreement between Aramco and the Government of Oct. 3, 1954, which required the company to increase the prices shown in its sales accounts for the period Dec. 31, 1951, to Oct. 6, 1953, by 26.4 cents per barrel and to pay additional taxes totalling $70,014,538 in respect of its profits during the same period. Under a further agreement of June 25, 1956 (which was retroactive to Oct. 6, 1953), Aramco undertook (i) to eliminate a fixed "marketing allowance" equal to 2 per cent of the posted price, which was replaced by an allowance based on the "actual audited marketing expenses incurred in the lifting of crude and products for export", and (ii) to end the practice of granting volume discounts. The company also agreed to end its practice of using fixed "stabilization differentials" and refining fees for accounting purposes and to adopt new formulas which more accurately reflected market realities. Government revenue rose from around 28 cents per barrel in 1951 (when the posted price for Gulf exports was $1.75 per barrel) to around 80 cents per barrel in 1956 (posted price $1.93).

C11.3.iv—Offshore Neutral Zone concession agreement

In December 1957 the Japan Petroleum Trading Company (JPTC, recently formed by a consortium of Japanese industrial interests ◊A4.9) was granted a prospecting licence covering Saudi Arabia's half-share in the offshore waters of the Kuwait-Saudi Arabian Natural Zone, this licence (won on the basis of competitive bidding) being convertible into a 40-year production concession upon the discovery of oil in commercial quantities. After concluding a broadly similar agreement with Kuwait in 1958 (◊C7.3.ii), the JPTC formed a single operating subsidiary, the Arabian Oil Co. (AOC), which entrusted its exploration programme to specialist contractors who discovered oil in January 1960.

The main provisions of the Saudi-AOC concession agreement were (i) for total tax payments equal to at least 56 per cent of the company's net income, including a royalty of 20 per cent of oil and gas produced which the government could elect to take either in cash or in kind; (ii) for the construction of a local refinery or refineries which, once the company's crude oil production had averaged 75,000 bpd for a period of 90 days, should have the capacity to process not less than 30 per cent of that production; (iii) for the offer for sale at par to the Saudi Government, upon the discovery of oil in commercial quantities, of 10 per cent of the company's shares (an identical offer to be made to the Kuwait Government at the same time); (iv) for one-sixth of the AOC's board of directors to be nominated by the Saudi Government and one-sixth by the Kuwait Government; and (v) for the phased relinquishment of unexploited concession areas at five-year intervals commencing on the third anniversary of the first commercial oil discovery. (Had the JPTC failed to obtain a concession covering Kuwait's half-interest in the area concerned, Saudi Arabia would have had the right to acquire 20 per cent of the AOC's shares and to nominate one-third of its board of directors.)

The Saudi-AOC agreement was revised in 1963 to increase the minimum level of tax payments to 57 per cent of net income (the level negotiated by Kuwait in 1958), to provide for the "expensing" of royalties when calculating taxable income and to require the payment to the Government of a non-recoverable bonus of $5,000,000 at such time as the company's production first reached the level of 50,000 bpd (a similar bonus provision having been negotiated by Kuwait in 1958). Under the terms of a further revision in May 1971, which was negotiated with the company by a joint Saudi-Kuwaiti ministerial committee, AOC's tax liability was increased to 62 per cent with effect from Nov. 14, 1970, in respect of income arising from its production, export and local marketing operations. Income from overseas product marketing operations continued to be taxed at the rate of 57 per cent.

The AOC was required by its concession agreement to operate as an "integrated enterprise" responsible for production, refining, transportation and marketing, its operating income for the purpose of Saudi Arabian taxation being defined as "income derived from all the company's activities in the oil industry inside and outside Saudi Arabia". Shaikh Abdullah Tariki, who served in Saudi Arabia's Ministry of Petroleum and Mineral Resources as Director-General from 1954 to 1960 and as Minister from December 1960 to March 1962 (and who played a key role in the formation of OPEC ◊**D1.1**), described the terms of the AOC agreement as an appropriate basis for a "fruitful partnership" between a host government and a concessionaire company. Shaikh Tariki was strongly critical of many aspects of Aramco's operations in Saudi Arabia, although it fell to his successor as Minister of Petroleum and Mineral Resources, the less outspoken Shaikh Ahmed Zaki Yamani, to finalize a series of agreements with the company on disputed issues.

C11.3.v—Relations between Government and Aramco in the 1960s

Agreements were concluded between the Government and Aramco and between the Government and the Trans-Arabian Pipeline Co. on March 24, 1963, regarding the pricing of oil exported via Tapline, a long-standing dispute over which had been put to arbitration at Aramco's request in 1957 but had later been brought back into the realm of direct negotiations between the parties concerned. The price charged by Aramco for oil delivered via Tapline to Aramco's parent companies had hitherto been based on the price posted in the Persian/Arabian Gulf plus the cost of pipeline transport, while the parent companies' Mediterranean export prices were based on Gulf postings plus the (higher) cost of ocean transport to the Mediterranean. According to the Saudi Government, the differential involved (which had fallen from 66 cents per barrel in 1951 to 37 cents per barrel in 1960) should properly be added to Aramco's gross profits, thus increasing the Government's revenue entitlement under the "50-50 profit-sharing" formula. (Tapline had been established under an agreement of 1947 which predated the introduction of this formula.)

The need to settle this dispute had become more pressing during 1962 in view of a clause in the 1947 Tapline agreement which gave the Saudi Government the right to impose transit fees on the pipeline's throughput 15 years after that agreement's entry into force. Under the 1963 agreements Aramco accepted that with effect from Jan. 1, 1963, oil deliveries made to its parent companies via Tapline should be invoiced at the Mediterranean posted price less any discounts approved by the Government; in addition, the company undertook to make additional tax payments for the period Oct. 6, 1953, to Dec. 31, 1962, after its income from Mediterranean deliveries during this period had been restated on the basis of the same pricing formula. Saudi Arabia's per-barrel revenue entitlement in respect of Tapline's throughput after Jan. 1, 1963, was to be the higher of (i) an amount calculated in accordance with the transit fee payable by the Trans-Arabian Pipeline Co. to the Governments of Jordan, Syria and Lebanon (then 1.8 cents per 100 barrel-miles, equivalent to 9.7 cents per barrel within Saudi Arabia), and (ii) 50 per cent of the amount by which the Mediterranean posted price of oil produced by Aramco exceeded the Gulf price plus the cost of transport via Tapline. Item (ii) was payable by Aramco as a tax on its profits. The Trans-Arabian Pipeline Co. was liable to pay only the excess, if any, of item (i) over item (ii), such supplemental payments being non-deductible either by the Trans-Arabian Pipeline Co. or by Aramco for tax purposes.

In addition to issues connected with Tapline, Aramco's financial agreement with the Government of March 24, 1963, also covered the tax treatment of (i) the company's expenditure on exploration and on "intangible development" (e.g. the drilling of dry holes), which was henceforth to be treated as a capital rather than a current item for tax purposes, with amortization phased over a period of years; (ii) the company's US office expenses, 5 per cent of which were disallowed for Saudi

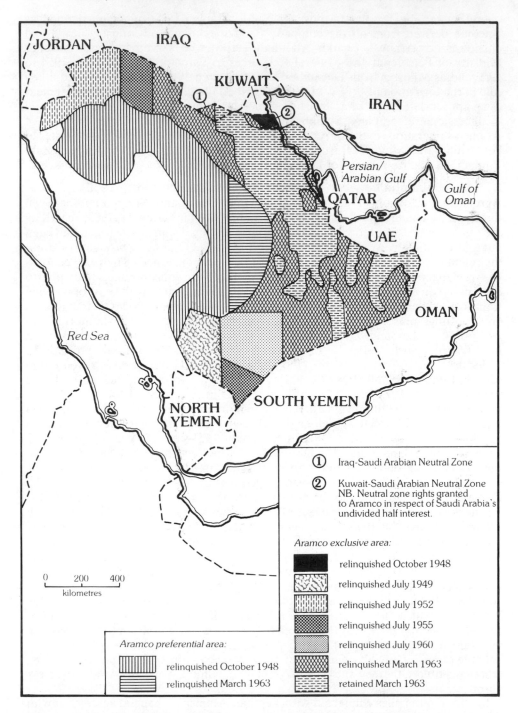

Fig. 17—Aramco's exclusive and preferential oil rights, 1939 to 1963

Arabian tax purposes in the 1960 and 1961 tax years, and (iii) the company's charitable donations, 27.3 per cent of which were disallowed for Saudi Arabian tax purposes in the tax years 1956–61 inclusive. It was agreed in April 1963 that

Aramco's tax-deductible "marketing allowance" based on audited expenses (which amounted to 4.28 cents per barrel in 1962) should be replaced by a fixed allowance of 0.5 cents per barrel.

In a second agreement concluded with the Government on March 24, 1963, Aramco undertook (i) to relinquish immediately all remaining preference rights conferred by its concession agreement, (ii) to relinquish immediately a large proportion of its exclusive area, which was reduced to five blocks totalling 323,750 sq km, and (iii) to implement a revised programme of future relinquishments at five-year intervals which would progressively reduce the size of the exclusive area as follows: 1968—271,950 sq km; 1973—220,150 sq km; 1978—168,350 sq km; 1983—116,550 sq km; 1988—77,700 sq km; 1993—51,800 sq km. The precise areas to be relinquished were to be selected by Aramco.

An agreement on the implementation of the OPEC royalty-expensing formula (◊D1.3.ii) was signed by Aramco on Jan. 25, 1965. Under a further agreement of September 1966 posted prices were used to calculate Aramco's taxable income from export sales to customers other than its parent companies and their affiliates (such sales having previously been taxed on the basis of realized prices). This arrangement was backdated to 1961 for sales of crude and to 1963 for sales of refined products.

C11.3.vi—Establishment of Petromin – New agreements with independent oil interests

A state corporation, the General Petroleum and Mineral Organization (Petromin), was established in November 1962 with a board of directors chaired by the Minister of Petroleum and Mineral Resources. The corporation was given wide powers to engage in all phases of commercial and industrial activity connected with petroleum and minerals both inside and outside Saudi Arabia, either on its own account or in collaboration with other companies or organizations. Petromin's initial operations were mainly in the area of domestic product distribution and marketing, hitherto controlled by Aramco. The Aramco bulk storage and distribution facilities serving western Saudi Arabia were purchased by Petromin in 1964 and the main facilities serving the remainder of the country in 1967. Petromin's first upstream investments took the form of 51 per cent shareholdings in two specialized service companies — the Arabian Drilling Co. and the Arabian Geophysical and Surveying Co.—which were established in 1964 and 1966 respectively in partnership with French interests.

In 1965 Auxirap (a French state-owned company which became a subsidiary of ERAP in the following year) was granted a government exploration licence covering areas of Saudi Arabia's Red Sea coast on the understanding that Petromin would take a 40 per cent shareholding in a new joint company to be established upon the discovery of oil in commercial quantities. The exploration licence was valid initially for two years, with an option for a three-year extension, while a 30-year "exploitation concession lease" was to be granted in the event of commercial discoveries. This lease would be broadly similar to the Arabian Oil Company's Neutral Zone concession agreement (◊C11.3.iv), although many of its detailed provisions were designed further to strengthen the role of the state (e.g. by omitting any reference to a maximum level of taxation). A one-third interest in Auxirap's Saudi operations was acquired by Tenneco in May 1968. In late 1967 Petromin was directly granted two exclusive licences—the first covering other Red Sea coastal areas and the second parts of the Rub al Khali ("empty quarter") in the south-east of the country—on the basis of which it entered into exploration contracts with various foreign oil companies. The exploitation rights over any commercial discoveries would be held by Petromin, which would assign an undivided share of these rights to its contractor. Exploration in the coastal areas concerned was contracted to a Natomas/Sinclair consortium in which the Pakistan Government held a 10 per cent interest, while the Rub al Khali areas were contracted to an Agip/Phillips consortium. None of the above-mentioned ventures resulted in the discovery of oil.

C11.3.vii—Extension of state control over Aramco's production operations

From 1968 onwards a main aim of the Saudi Government's oil policy was to achieve state participation in the upstream operations of Aramco, whose production exceeded 3,000,000 bpd in 1970 (having reached 1,000,000 bpd in 1956 and 2,000,000 bpd in 1965). By February 1972 talks on this subject had led only to an offer by the parent companies to concede 50 per cent state participation in the future development of certain unexploited proved reserves within their concession area, the Government's rejection of which was accompanied by a threat to secure "effective participation" in Aramco's existing operations through unilateral legislative action (◊D3.3). The Aramco parent companies subsequently accepted the principle of minority state participation and entered into wider negotiations leading to the signature in October 1972 of the General Agreement on Participation in respect of oil concessions in Arabian peninsula OPEC countries (◊D3.4). A national agreement between Saudi Arabia and Aramco, concluded on Dec. 20, 1972, provided for 25 per cent state ownership of the company's upstream producing assets with effect from Jan. 1, 1973, to be acquired at a cost of $510,000,000 (representing an updated book valuation of these assets). It was agreed that the ownership of Aramco's shares should remain wholly in the hands of the US parent companies.

Whereas Saudi Arabia's December 1972 agreement envisaged the achievement of 51 per cent majority state control after nine years (i.e. on Jan. 1, 1982), it was clear by mid-1973 that a far more rapid assertion of state control over the operations of concessionaire companies was occurring in other OPEC countries, notably Iraq, Kuwait and Libya. Saudi Arabia, whose gradualist approach was partly based on the view that a phased increase in the level of state participation in the operations of Aramco could provide a basis for negotiating a long-term bilateral oil co-operation agreement with the United States (◊A4.15.i), finally abandoned this approach after the outbreak of the October 1973 Arab-Israeli war, which led to Aramco being ordered to cut off oil supplies to the United States as an expression of Saudi opposition to US Middle East policies (◊D4.5). A new policy of taking "immediate" majority control of Aramco's operations was announced by the Saudi Government in mid-November 1973, and an interim agreement was signed on June 10, 1974, to increase the level of state participation to 60 per cent with effect from Jan. 1, 1974. No additional payments were made to the parent companies at this stage, and negotiations continued with the aim of agreeing terms for full state control.

In late November 1974, after strong pressure from the Saudi Government (◊D5.6.ii), the Aramco parent companies accepted the principle of 100 per cent participation, and by early 1977 they had reached agreement with the Government on the main conditions under which Aramco's role was to be changed to that of a contractor, and its concessionaire status terminated, with effect from Jan. 1, 1976. The parent companies then received additional payments which were understood to represent the difference between the net book value of 60 per cent of Aramco's upstream producing assets and the earlier payments which had been made by Saudi Arabia in August 1973 on the basis of the updated book value of 25 per cent of these assets. Negotiations between the parent companies and the Government on most outstanding issues were completed in 1980, when final payments were received by the companies in respect of the net book value of their remaining 40 per cent interest in Aramco's producing assets. However, no formal agreement was signed, certain unspecified aspects of Aramco's future role being subject to further negotiation.

The following broad principles were understood to apply to Aramco's contract operations: (i) the company retained functional responsibility for oilfield management in return for a per-barrel service fee which varied in line with a monthly IMF index of wholesale prices in various countries; (ii) Aramco's parent companies had preferential access, at official prices, to exportable production which was not required to fulfil state export contracts, with regular reviews of the total volume available and the procedures for its purchase; and (iii) various incentives were introduced to encourage Aramco to share the cost of new investment in exploration work. The individual parent companies' long-term purchasing entitlements were allocated in proportion to their shareholdings in Aramco, anticipation of this arrangement having reportedly been a factor in inter-company negotiations leading to an agreement of April 1975 whereby Mobil's shareholding was increased to 15 per cent by 1979 (◊A5.2.i). Aramco's service contract was understood to cover the whole of its former concession area as defined in 1973 (i.e. some 220,150 sq km in the east of the kingdom, including about 31,000 sq km offshore), within which the company produced around 97 per cent of total Saudi Arabian oil output (with the balance coming from the Saudi share of Neutral Zone production). The world's largest single oilfield (Ghawar) and largest offshore oilfield (Safaniya) together accounted for more than two-thirds of Aramco's output.

C11.3.viii—Development of government policy on crude oil production, pricing and export marketing, 1974 to 1986

Having imposed a normal ceiling of 8,500,000 bpd on Aramco's output in 1974 (◊D5.2), the Saudi Government substantially reduced the scale of the US parent companies' oilfield development programme, which had provided for an expansion of installed production capacity to 13,400,000 bpd by 1976 (and to as much as 20,000,000 bpd by 1983) in order to satisfy the high rates of future demand growth envisaged in the early 1970s. (Aramco's annual output had risen by 135 per cent between 1970 and 1974.) Under the Government's scaled-down programme, which redefined the scope for export growth on the basis of a more acceptable depletion rate, Aramco had by late 1980 installed sufficient extractive capacity to fulfil the Government's highest-ever temporary production ceiling of 10,300,000 bpd on a continuous basis. The maximum possible rate of sustained extraction at this time was believed to be somewhat above this ceiling but well below Aramco's throughput capacity downstream of the wellhead (amounting to about 12,500,000 bpd). Plans to raise Aramco's overall productive capacity to 13,500,000 bpd by the mid-1980s were dropped in view of the sharp decline in export demand after 1981.

In February 1978 the Government instructed Aramco to limit its production of 34° light crude (a grade which constituted about 50 per cent of proved reserves) to 65 per cent of total output, compared with up to 80 per cent previously (◊D9.3.i). A further shift in favour of heavier grades was ordered by the Government in October 1984 in order to bring the average gravity of the country's crude exports more closely into line with the prevailing pattern of demand (◊D15.6).

After the early 1970s Saudi Arabia was able to assume a strategic role as the principal "swing" producer in the world oil trade by virtue of its considerable margin of excess production capacity relative to the output needed to cover the country's basic export requirement (which varied with changes in oil prices and the level of government spending). The basic export requirement originally forecast for the 1980–85 planning period (apparently on the basis of an average oil price of $24 per barrel) was less than 5,300,000 bpd, leaving an initial excess capacity of up to

4,500,000 bpd after domestic oil demand had been met. Fulfilment of the normal production ceiling of 8,500,000 bpd had usually entailed the utilization of rather more than three-quarters of current excess capacity during the second half of the 1970s, providing scope for substantial downward swings in output to defend the country's official prices at times of market weakness. The additional margin of excess capacity above the 8,500,000 bpd ceiling left some leeway for incremental output to dampen upward price pressures which the Government considered to be excessive. The overall aim of Saudi production policy was to maintain a stable market environment and to avoid abrupt price fluctuations.

By absorbing the main impact of periodic troughs in demand, Saudi Arabia played a key role in underpinning the OPEC price administration system from 1974 to 1978, while an increase in exports of lower-priced Saudi crude during the first half of 1977 ensured that an early compromise was reached in OPEC's most serious internal split over pricing policy during this period (▷**D8.3**). However, the two-tier pricing episode of 1977 also revealed the current technical constraints on Aramco's ability to sustain an upward swing from an already high level of capacity utilization —constraints which were to limit the effectiveness of Saudi Arabia's efforts to moderate the upward pressure on prices resulting from the disruption of Iranian oil exports at the end of 1978 (▷**D10.2**). Most other OPEC members subsequently maintained higher official prices than Saudi Arabia from mid-1979 until late 1981, by which time the kingdom had re-established its capability to counteract upward price pressures on the basis of continuous production at the rate of 10,300,000 bpd, as achieved by Aramco between November 1980 and August 1981.

After 1981 Saudi Arabia's ability to defend prices in a weak market was called into question for the first time as falling demand brought Aramco's output progressively closer to the minimum level required to fulfil government oil export targets and associated gas requirements. Market pressures forced an unprecedented reduction in the Saudi marker price in March 1983, at which point the kingdom formally undertook to act as the swing producer within an OPEC quota system giving every other member a fixed entitlement (▷**D14.5**). By mid-1985 Saudi Arabia was experiencing a damaging loss of market share to competing OPEC countries which had largely disregarded Saudi pressure (i) for realistic adjustments to official price differentials, taking into account the changing balance of market demand for different grades of crude, and (ii) for the strict observance of official prices and production ceilings.

Saudi Arabia rejected the role of swing producer at the end of July 1985 and abandoned official OPEC pricing in favour of market-led netback pricing from the beginning of October (▷**D16.8**). The kingdom's decision to concentrate on the defence of its national interest left the other OPEC members with little alternative but to endorse a policy of action to secure a "fair share" of the market from non-OPEC producers (▷**D16.10**), although only Saudi Arabia possessed a large enough margin of shut-in capacity to avoid a dramatic decline in its daily export revenues (relative to their lowest point in 1985) when prices slumped in the first half of 1986.

Whereas most other OPEC countries were marketing a high proportion of their crude exports through their own national oil companies by 1982, Saudi Arabia continued to rely heavily on its long-term arrangements with Aramco's parent companies, leaving Petromin to play a subsidiary exporting role centred on the handling of government-to-government sales. Petromin's exports accounted for nearly 22 per cent of Aramco's output in 1982 (compared with 2.5 per cent in 1973), while about 6 per cent of output went to the Saudi domestic market (which had absorbed less than 1 per cent in 1973). Normal contract purchases by Aramco's parent companies accounted for the balance remaining after the fulfilment of various government contracts for the sale of relatively small volumes of "incentive crude" to foreign companies (including major oil companies) which had invested in new industrial joint-venture projects in Saudi Arabia. (The "incentive crude" scheme had originally been conceived in the unsettled market environment of 1979–80, when security of future supply was at a premium and when Saudi Arabia's official prices were lower than those of most other OPEC countries. The scheme held few attractions in the changed conditions of 1982, and ceased to operate early in the following year.)

Until 1982 Saudi Arabia's export-marketing arrangements worked to the mutual benefit of the Aramco shareholders and the Government, in that the companies enjoyed preferential access to a high-volume supply source and gained some advantage from the kingdom's moderate pricing policy, while the state was able to channel the greater part of its export trade through a small group of long-established buyers on contract terms which guaranteed the strict application of its official prices.

During the latter part of 1982 the balance of the relationship began to shift when the companies' interest as shareholders in Aramco (i.e. in maintaining a high level of output) came into conflict with their role as buyers of Saudi crude in a world market which now offered growing opportunities to obtain favourably priced supplies through the pursuit of highly flexible purchasing policies. The Saudi Government, as a strict adherent to official prices, saw little prospect of securing alternative contract outlets for crude which was surplus to the requirements of the Aramco shareholders, and accordingly opened negotiations with the companies with a view to reaching an understanding regarding minimum purchasing commitments, possibly in return for improvements in the terms of Aramco's service contract. Talks on "certain financial issues and modifications to existing arrangements" continued at regular intervals thereafter against a background of depressed sales to the companies, who made it clear that they were obliged to weigh the value of their special status in Saudi Arabia against the commercial penalties of purchasing uncompetitively-priced crude.

In mid-1983 Petromin formed a new international trading subsidiary, Norbec, to handle the sale of limited volumes of Saudi crude to spot buyers at times when open-market prices were equal to or higher than official prices. Norbec entered the market with sales of up to 500,000 bpd in the third quarter of 1983, and from November 1983 onwards took responsibility for creating a floating stockpile of crude in chartered tankers moored at various locations close to major oil-trading centres. Some land-based stocks were also held at certain centres, mainly in Western Europe and the Caribbean region. Production for the floating stockpile provided some leeway to offset downturns in contract purchases by Aramco's parent companies (and accompanying downturns in the availability of associated gas within Saudi Arabia), while the strategic location of the stocks placed Norbec in a strong position to respond rapidly to favourable market trends. Norbec was permitted to adjust the relative shares of the different Saudi export grades within its total sales volume in order to obtain an average official price (e.g. by balancing spot premiums for heavier crudes against spot discounts for lighter crudes), but nevertheless experienced several periods of negligible or nil spot demand at its minimum selling price.

Norbec's uneven sales pattern was the main cause of frequent fluctuations in the volume of crude held in floating storage, which varied from about 35,000,000 barrels to about 70,000,000 barrels between the first quarter of 1984 and the middle of 1985. Saudi Arabia's subsequent switch to netback pricing for contract exports was accompanied by a switch to fully negotiable pricing by Norbec, whose high volume of spot sales in the last quarter of 1985 reduced the size of the floating stockpile to an estimated 19,000,000 barrels by the end of the year. Spot sales played a less important role in Saudi export policy as the volume of netback trade built up during the first half of 1986, although it was reported in late July that Norbec had begun to replenish its stocks in order to enhance the flexibility of the kingdom's marketing effort. Aramco's parent companies had meanwhile seen their share of Saudi Arabia's contract exports fall significantly as a result of the Government's conclusion of netback deals with a wide range of other international oil companies, this diversification of export outlets having played an important part in raising the level of production.

C11.3.ix—Infrastructural development and downstream diversification in the Saudi hydrocarbons industry

Aramco's main downstream asset, a 450,000 bpd refinery complex located at Ras Tanura (Saudi Arabia's principal oil port), was acquired by the Government in 1980 but remained under the operational management of the company (which had previously retained 100 per cent ownership). The Aramco complex was partly export-oriented, as were the two Neutral Zone refineries at Mina Saud (Getty — capacity 50,000 bpd) and Ras al Khafji (AOC—capacity 30,000 bpd). Purely domestic refineries were operated by Petromin at Jeddah (opened 1968—capacity 90,600 bpd), Riyadh (opened 1975—capacity 120,000 bpd) and Yanbu (opened 1983—capacity 170,000 bpd). The Jeddah refinery was owned 75 per cent by Petromin and 25 per cent by private Saudi interests, while the Riyadh and Yanbu refineries were 100 per cent owned by Petromin. Part of the Jeddah refinery's output was processed by Petromin's nearby lubricating oils base stock plant (Lubref), whose own output of base stocks was blended into finished products by the Petromin Lubricating Oil Company (Petrolube) in factories at Jeddah and Riyadh. Petromin held 70 per cent of the shares in Lubref and 71 per cent of the shares in Petrolube, the balance being held by Mobil in each case.

Petromin entered into three 50-50 joint-venture contracts with foreign oil companies in the early 1980s to build new export-oriented refineries at Yanbu, Jubail and Rabigh, half of the output of each plant to be marketed by Petromin and half by the partner company concerned. Saudi Arabia's official crude prices were to be used as a basis for the supply of feedstock. The Yanbu export refinery (capacity 250,000 bpd, partner Mobil) came on stream in August 1984 and the Jubail refinery (capacity 250,000 bpd, partner Shell) in June 1985. The start of exports from the Jubail plant occurred at a time when Saudi Arabia's official crude prices were being widely undercut by other exporting countries, and very low throughput levels were reported at both plants in the period preceding the introduction of netback crude pricing (which was backdated to the beginning of August 1985 in the case of feedstock for export refineries ◊**D16.8**).

While providing an improved margin on export refining, the revised pricing arrangements left the Saudi refineries in a weak competitive position vis-à-vis overseas refineries which began to receive their own crude oil supplies under netback contracts, with the result that Saudi product exports went into a new decline as the volume of netback crude trade was expanded in the first quarter of 1986. The Jubail plant was shut down in February, by which point Mobil had agreed to market part of Petromin's half-share of the output of the Yanbu plant in return for a brokerage fee. Shell expected to perform a similar role when it became economic to resume product exports from Jubail. The planned opening date of the export refinery under construction at Rabigh (capacity 325,000 bpd, partner Petrola International of Greece) was in early 1986 put back until the third quarter of 1987, about 18 months later than originally scheduled.

A deterioration in projected export demand for refined products had previously led Petromin to suspend initial construction work on a new refinery near Buraydah in the north and to cancel plans to build a refinery at Shaqiq in the south, both decisions being announced in March 1985. The planned refineries, each of 160,000 bpd capacity, were to have been wholly owned by Petromin and were to have supplied Saudi Arabia's own incremental product requirements in the late 1980s (which were to be met instead through domestic marketing of part of the output of the joint-venture plants at Yanbu and Jubail). Uncertain export prospects in the market for lubricating oils base stock had caused the shelving of two specialized refining projects in April 1984. The world's largest lube oil refinery (12,000 bpd) had been planned for Jubail as a joint venture between Petromin (50 per cent), Texaco (25 per cent) and Chevron (25 per cent), while a 5,000 bpd plant was to have been built at Yanbu as a 50-50 joint venture between Petromin and Ashland Oil. Work on an additional Lubref (Petromin/Mobil) plant, under development at Yanbu to serve both domestic and export markets, was suspended in late 1985 for financial reasons.

Yanbu's emergence as a major refining centre followed the completion in 1981 of a 1,269 km trans-peninsular pipeline (Petroline) which had been commissioned by Petromin to pump up to 1,850,000 bpd of crude from the Eastern Province oilfields to the Red Sea coast for export and for use by Saudi refineries. Petroline was Saudi Arabia's only significant non-Gulf export outlet for crude oil in the 1980s (Tapline's sole function after 1983 being to supply crude to Jordan's 91,330 bpd Zarqa refinery ◊A6.9), and its capacity utilization rate varied according to the seriousness of the war risks faced by tankers using Gulf loading ports. From late September 1985 up to 500,000 bpd of Petroline's capacity was made available for the export of Iraqi crude via Yanbu (◊C6.3.v). Work was in progress in 1986 on a major expansion of Petroline's capacity to around 3,000,000 bpd. The sharing of capacity with Iraq was due to cease in 1987 upon the completion of a separate pipeline to carry Iraqi crude through Saudi Arabia.

Running parallel to Petroline was an east-west natural gas liquids (NGL) pipeline forming part of an extensive gas gathering and processing network known as the Master Gas System (MGS). Designed, built and operated by Aramco (as contractor to Petromin), the MGS project was a central feature of the Government's strategy for industrial development based on the utilization, both as a fuel source and as a petrochemical feedstock, of associated gas which had previously been flared. The first phase of the project (1975–82) involved the installation of gas-gathering facilities in the main oilfields and the construction near the oilfields of four processing complexes whose output of NGL was piped to three new fractionation plants (two on the Gulf coast and one at Yanbu). The installed production capacity of the system in 1983 (achievable if crude oil output was running at around 7,400,000 bpd) was (i) 56,000,000 cubic metres per day of methane, available in the Eastern Province for use as fuel and as petrochemical feedstock; (ii) 10,600,000 cubic metres per day of ethane, available from the eastern and western fractionation plants as fuel and as feedstock; (iii) over 315,000 bpd of NGL, available for export (as liquefied petroleum gas and natural gasoline) from terminals near the fractionation plants; and (iv) 3,700 tonnes per day of suphur, produced as a by-product during an initial treatment stage.

(Aramco's existing NGL facilities—which included fractionation plants at Abqaiq and Ras Tanura with a combined production capacity of 370,000 bpd—had been brought into full state ownership with effect from January 1981. Petromin subsequently took sole responsibility for the marketing of NGL exports from the beginning of 1983.)

The second phase of the MGS project was originally planned in terms of an extension of the gathering system to additional oilfields between 1983 and 1985. However, in view of the increasingly serious shortfall in associated gas production caused by the decline in oil output after mid-1982, the scope and duration of this phase were expanded to include the development of non-associated gas deposits situated below the Ghawar and Abqaiq oilfields. Non-associated gas began to be produced in August 1984, and was flowing into the MGS at an estimated rate of 27,200,000 cubic metres per day by the end of 1985. It was hoped that sufficient non-associated gas production would be available by 1987 to maintain supplies to virtually all of Saudi Arabia's gas-using industries regardless of fluctuations in associated gas output. The very low levels of oil production in mid-1985 (prior to the start-up of several of the country's gas-based petrochemical projects) had necessitated some switching to oil by plants which normally used gas as a fuel (mainly for electricity generation and seawater desalination) and had caused the underfulfilment of export contracts for liquefied petroleum gas.

Responsibility for the development of hydrocarbon-based manufacturing was held by the Saudi Basic Industries Corporation (Sabic, established in 1976), whose planning, focused mainly on the new industrial cities of Jubail in the east and Yanbu in the west, was carried out in close co-operation with Petromin. Sabic's investments in the period to 1985, totalling about $10,700 million, were predominantly in gas-based petrochemical plants, the main exception being a 90 per cent interest in a gas-fuelled iron and steel complex which went into production at Jubail in 1983.

Sabic took a 40 per cent interest in the established Saudi Arabian Fertilizer Co. (Safco), which had been operating at Dammam since 1965 and which by 1980 (after completion of an expansion programme) had an annual capacity to produce 330,000 tonnes of urea, 100,000 tonnes of sulphuric acid and 20,000 tonnes of melamine. The balance of Safco's shares was held by Saudi private-sector interests. A National Plastic Co. (Ibn Hayyan), owned 85 per cent by Sabic and 15 per cent by Lucky Group of South Korea, was due to begin operating in 1986 at Jubail with an annual capacity of 300,000 tonnes of vinyl chloride monomer and 200,000 tonnes of polyvinyl chloride. Sabic held a one-third interest in Gulf Petrochemical Industries Co. (an equal partnership with Kuwaiti and Bahraini state corporations), which brought a plant into production in Bahrain in late 1985 with a capacity of 330,000 tonnes of ammonia and 330,000 tonnes of methanol. Also in late 1985, the Saudi Yanbu Petrochemical Co. (Yanpet, a 50-50 joint venture between Sabic and Mobil) went into production at Yanbu with a capacity of 455,000 tonnes of ethanol, 220,000 tonnes of ethylene glycol, 205,000 tonnes of linear low-density polyethylene and 91,000 tonnes of high-density polyethylene.

Sabic's remaining first-phase petrochemical investments were all planned as 50-50 joint-venture projects at Jubail, although one such venture—the development of a 506,000-tonne ethylene plant by the Arabian Petrochemical Co. (Petrokemya)—came under the sole ownership of Sabic after the withdrawal at an early stage of the foreign partner concerned (the US company Dow Chemical). The other Jubail projects were implemented as equal joint ventures by the following companies:

(1) Saudi Methanol Co. (Ar Razi); partner a Japanese consortium led by Mitsubishi; annual capacity 600,000 tonnes of methanol.

(2) National Methanol Co. (Ibn Sina); partners Celanese and Texas Eastern; annual capacity 700,000 tonnes of methanol.

(3) Jubail Fertilizer Co. (Samad); partner Taiwan Fertilizer Co.; annual capacity 500,000 tonnes of urea.

(4) Saudi Petrochemical Co. (Sadaf); partner Pecten Arabian Ltd (an affiliate of Shell's US subsidiary); annual capacity 656,000 tonnes of ethylene, 454,000 tonnes of ethylene dichloride, 295,000 tonnes of styrene, 281,000 tonnes of ethanol.

(5) Jubail Petrochemical Co. (Kemya); partner Exxon; annual capacity 260,000 tonnes of linear low-density polyethylene.

(6) Eastern Petrochemical Co. (Sharq); partner a Japanese consortium led by Mitsubishi; annual capacity 130,000 tonnes of linear low-density polyethylene and 300,000 tonnes of ethylene glycol.

Having brought the bulk of its first-phase petrochemical manufacturing capacity on stream between late 1984 and mid-1986, Sabic hoped to produce about 8.5 per cent of the world's methanol, 7.2 per cent of ethylene glycol, 7 per cent of ethanol and 2.2 per cent of ethylene in the late 1980s. At full production, 25 per cent of the Saudi petrochemical industry's capacity would be used to supply base materials to the more advanced plants and 15 per cent to meet product demand in Saudi Arabia and neighbouring countries. The remaining 60 per cent of output would be exported outside the Gulf Co-operation Council area, with Sabic and its foreign partner companies sharing the responsibility for marketing exports from joint-venture plants.

The country's emergence as a significant exporter during the course of 1985 was marked by excellent results in the fertilizers sector, which achieved very high levels of capacity utilization (mainly on the basis of strong demand in China, India and other Asian markets); by satisfactory progress in securing export outlets for methanol (particularly in Japan and Spain); and by problems in meeting initial export targets for ethylene derivatives, mainly because of tariff barriers in the European Community. According to the Industry Ministry, about 70 per cent of Saudi Arabia's total petrochemical output was exported in the first 10 months of 1985, generating earnings of about $650,000,000. The industry's future earning potential was said to exceed $3,500 million per annum (at 1985 prices) if maximum export volumes were achieved with all first-phase plants in full production.

Talks between the European Commission and the Gulf Co-operation Council in 1985 failed to resolve a dispute over Saudi Arabia's duty-free EEC import quotas for petrochemicals, with the result that import duties were reimposed in early 1986 as soon as Saudi Arabia had exceeded its small annual quotas under the generalized system of preferences. The rates of duty were 12.5 per cent on polyethylenes, 13 per cent on methanol, 11 per cent on urea and 8 per cent on melamine. The European Commission took the view that Saudi Arabia's very low price for the supply of natural gas feedstock to joint-venture plants—fixed at 50 US cents per million British thermal units until such time as the plants had produced a 25 per cent net return on investment—constituted a form of subsidy on export prices. Sabic, for its part, maintained that the Commission was merely seeking to justify a policy of protectionism, since the far greater fixed costs of the new Saudi plants offset their apparent advantage over European plants which paid around nine times more for feedstock. Additional non-European export outlets were being actively sought in mid-1986.

Sabic's investment programme for the 1985–90 planning period envisaged total expenditure of $4,430 million on further downstream diversification in the petrochemicals sector. Product categories under discussion with prospective foreign partners in 1986 included methyl tertiary butyl ether, butadiene and isoprene. However, both Sabic and its propective partners showed a marked hesitancy to commit themselves to firm projects pending reassessments (i) of Saudi spending plans in the wake of the fall in unit oil revenues and (ii) of the export-marketing problems facing Saudi petrochemical plants.

C12—United Arab Emirates

C12.1—Statistical Survey

*1984
†End-1984
‡Revision of 1984 figures given in section **D15.1.i** (see Introduction)

General
Area .... 83,600 sq km
*Population 1,270,000
Capital .... Abu Dhabi Town

Economy and trade
*Gross domestic product .... $28,940 million
*Annual exports (fob) .... $14,103 million (of which petroleum
                                                   87.5 per cent)
*Annual imports (cif) .... $7,592 million
*Current account balance .... +$3,984 million
Foreign exchange reserves .... $1,801 million (September 1984)

Oil (upstream)
‡1984 crude production .... 1,255,000 bpd (60,900,000 tonnes)
1985 crude production .... 1,353,000 bpd (64,000,000 tonnes)
   of which: (Abu Dhabi) .... (890,000 bpd)
                (Dubai) .... (390,000 bpd)
                (Sharjah) .... (64,000 bpd)
                (Ras al-Khaimah) .... (9,000 bpd)
†Proved crude reserves .... 32,500 million barrels
   of which: (Abu Dhabi) .... (30,500 million barrels)
                (Dubai) .... (1,400 million barrels)
                (others) .... (600,000,000 barrels)
*Reserves:production ratios:
   UAE .... 70.5 : 1
   Abu Dhabi .... 99.2 : 1
   Dubai .... 10.5 : 1
Production in peak year .... 2,015,000 bpd (97,200,000 tonnes)
                             in 1977
†Cumulative crude production .... 9,063.7 million barrels
   of which: (Abu Dhabi) .... (7,419 million barrels since 1962)
                (Dubai) .... (1,546.2 million barrels since 1969)
                (Sharjah) .... (96,585,000 barrels since 1974)
*Number of producing wells 530
   Main export grades:
     Murban (Abu Dhabi) .... 39° API gravity
     Umm Shaif (Abu Dhabi) .... 37° API gravity
     Zakum (Abu Dhabi) .... 40° API gravity
     Fateh (Dubai) .... 32° API gravity

Oil tanker tonnage
†12 vessels .... 1,053,500 deadweight tons

Oil (downstream—all production from Abu Dhabi)
*Installed refining capacity .... 180,000 bpd
*Output of refined products .... 145,100 bpd
*Consumption of refined products .... 79,500 bpd

Natural gas (million cubic metres)
*Gross annual production .... 18,030 mcm
       (gas marketed) .... (9,760 mcm)
       (gas reinjected) .... (30 mcm)
       (gas flared) .... (6,670 mcm)
       (shrinkage) .... (1,570 mcm)
*Annual exports (liquefied) .... 2,820 mcm
†Natural gas reserves: Abu Dhabi .... 600,000 mcm
       Dubai .... 100,000 mcm

C12.2—Political and Economic Summary

The United Arab Emirates (UAE) is a federation whose constituent states (in diminishing order of population size) are Abu Dhabi, Dubai, Sharjah, Ras al-Khaimah, Fujairah, Ajman and Umm al Quwain. Abu Dhabi, situated on the Persian/Arabian Gulf east of the Qatar peninsula, accounts for 67,350 sq km of the federation's mainland area, the remaining 10,350 sq km being divided between the six northern Emirates, whose fragmented territories form an interlocking pattern of enclaves in the Musandam peninsula. Numerous small islands add an estimated 5,900 sq km to the total area of the UAE. The mainland consists predominantly of salt flats and desert, with a mountain range in the east.

The seven Emirates share a long history as trading settlements linked by sea with Asia and by land with the interior of the Arabian peninsula. At the end of the eighteenth century their combined naval strength was sufficient to ensure their control over the mouth of the Persian/Arabian Gulf. Clashes with ships of Britain's East India Company led, however, to naval intervention by Britain, culminating in the imposition during the 1820s of a "general treaty for the cessation of plunder and piracy by land and sea". In 1853 a further treaty with Britain, known as the "perpetual maritime truce", was signed by the Rulers of the Emirates, which were thereafter termed the Trucial States and became effectively British protectorates. Britain formally took control over the foreign policy of the Emirates by a treaty of 1892.

Britain's announcement in 1968 of the forthcoming termination of its existing treaties with the Trucial States led to negotiations between the Rulers which resulted in the formation of the UAE, under a provisional federal constitution, on Dec. 2, 1971. However, Ras al-Khaimah, which was critical of some aspects of the constitution, did not accede to the federation until February 1972. (Bahrain and Qatar, whose treaties with Britain were also terminated in 1971, had earlier opted for separate independence rather than participation in the federation.)

Britain's withdrawal from the Gulf prompted Iran to lay claim to the strategically located islands of Abu Musa (hitherto under the jurisdiction of Sharjah) and Greater and Lesser Tunb (hitherto under the jurisdiction of Ras al-Khaimah). The Ruler of Sharjah signed an agreement allowing Iran to station troops on, and to exercise jurisdiction over, a part of Abu Musa, but the Ruler of Ras al-Khaimah refused to relinquish any rights over the other two islands. Iranian troops were nevertheless stationed on all three islands on Nov. 30, 1971 (two days before the independence of the six-member UAE), provoking a major diplomatic dispute during which four Arab states referred the issue to the UN Security Council, while Iraq broke off relations with both Britain and Iran.

Under the 1971 Constitution, the seven hereditary Rulers of the Emirates, meeting as the Supreme Council of the federation, elect a federal President and Vice-President from among their own number. The President appoints a Council of Ministers headed by a Prime Minister (although the separate Abu Dhabi Council of Ministers was not disbanded until the end of 1973). A largely consultative legislative assembly, the Federal National Council, is made up of nominated representatives appointed from each Emirate as follows: Abu Dhabi and Dubai eight members each; Sharjah and Ras al-Khaimah six members each; Ajman, Fujairah and Umm al Quwain four members each. There are no political parties, and within each Emirate the Ruler has absolute power over non-federal matters. The provisional status of the 1971 Constitution was renewed for further five-year periods in 1976 and 1981, reflecting the Supreme Council's inability to reach agreement on the provisions of a permanent instrument.

Moves towards greater political unification of the UAE during the 1970s were advocated by five of the Emirates, led by Abu Dhabi, but were opposed by Dubai with the support of Ras al-Khaimah. Proposals put forward by the majority group in 1979 included the abolition of all internal borders, the unification of income, the full unification of defence forces and the broadening of the role of the federal legislature, whose members should, it was argued, be elected rather than nominated. Resistance to such proposals on the part of Dubai and Ras al-Khaimah was based on fears of the erosion of the individual Rulers' authority in the face of growing political domination by Abu Dhabi. Political tensions were eased somewhat following Kuwaiti mediation in 1979, but acceptable terms for a formal move towards fuller unification remained to be found in early 1986.

Since independence the UAE has had as its President Shaikh Zaid bin Sultan al-Nahayan (Ruler of Abu Dhabi) and as its Vice-President Shaikh Rashid bin Said al-Maktoum (Ruler of Dubai). Shaikh Rashid has also held the post of federal Prime Minister since mid-1979. Virtually the entire population of the UAE are Moslems, and Islam is the basis of the Emirates' political, legal and social systems. The UAE is an active participant in the Gulf Co-operation Council (◊**D12.9**). Of the main GCC members, it had the best bilateral relations with Iran in the mid-1980s, notwithstanding Abu Dhabi's position as a supplier of economic aid to Iraq since the outbreak of the Gulf war.

The UAE had an estimated per-capita gross domestic product of $30,220 at the beginning of the 1980s following a decade of rapid economic development. A striking feature of the development process was the large-scale employment of immigrant workers (predominantly from the Indian subcontinent) to the extent that the total population grew at an average annual rate of 16.6 per cent between 1970 and 1981. It was estimated in 1982 that non-citizens made up as much as 80 per cent of the population and 90 per cent of the labour force. An average population growth rate of about 6 per cent per annum between 1981 and 1984 was accompanied by an average annual decline of 9 per cent in per-capita GDP (to $22,785 in 1984) as the economy experienced the impact of falling oil revenues.

Massive investments were made during the 1970s in the provision of social welfare facilities and in infrastructural development projects, with some duplication of expenditure (e.g. on competing international airports) attributable partly to rivalry between neighbouring Emirates. Industrialization in Dubai, the main centre of commerce, has included the construction of an aluminium smelter and one of the world's largest dry dock complexes (which competes directly with the OAPEC-sponsored shipyard in Bahrain ◊**B2.5.ii**). Abu Dhabi has concentrated mainly on the development of hydrocarbon-based industries.

Annual export earnings from oil peaked at $19,390 million in 1980, subsequently declining to an estimated $12,000 million in 1985. Deficit budgets were prepared from 1982 onwards, with sharp cutbacks in government expenditure from 1983, achieved partly through the cancellation of low-priority capital projects and partly through cutbacks in most current allocations, including funding for the country's programme of third-world aid. (Defence spending, however, was increased in the light of the regional tensions caused by the Iran-Iraq war.) One consequence of this regime of fiscal stringency was to limit the need to draw on the country's accumulated capital reserves (estimated at nearly $40,000 million in 1982), thereby ensuring that the underlying financial position remained very strong.

C12.3—Oil and Gas Industry

C12.3.i—General

Sovereignty over natural resources is vested in the individual Emirates, which have exploration and/or production agreements with a wide range of foreign oil companies. The largest and longest-established producer is Abu Dhabi, whose output exceeded that of Kuwait in 1981–82, while most of the balance of UAE production comes from Dubai, whose output exceeded that of Qatar in 1982–83. Small-scale production has been carried out in Sharjah since 1974 and commenced in Ras al-Khaimah in January 1984. With the exception of Dubai, which placed the operation of its main fields on a contract basis in 1975, the Emirates have not followed the other Gulf OPEC states in bringing upstream production operations under full state ownership.

Abu Dhabi, which introduced a law on the conservation of petroleum resources in July 1978, has sought on the one hand to prolong the life of its established fields by imposing controls on their output pending the implementation of secondary recovery schemes and on the other hand to expand its overall production capacity through the development of new fields. Dubai has maintained a policy of maximizing production from existing fields and, like the other northern Emirates, has encouraged a high level of foreign investment in new exploration work.

An agreement between Abu Dhabi and Dubai on the partial sharing of their oil income within the federation was not reached until 1980, when each Emirate undertook to contribute 50 per cent of its oil revenues to the federal budget (to which Abu Dhabi had previously made a disproportionately large contribution). The preparation of deficit budgets from 1982 onwards gave rise to further disputes over contributions, causing long delays in the disbursement of funds.

In view of the significant degree of political autonomy which has been retained by the individual Emirates, the Federal Ministry of Petroleum and Mineral Resources has only limited control over oil policy outside Abu Dhabi. For OPEC purposes, however, the UAE has been treated as a single entity since it took over Abu Dhabi's individual membership in January 1974 (this transfer being formally ratified by the Federal President in March 1975). When OPEC production quotas were introduced in March 1983 Abu Dhabi was obliged to take the main responsibility for restricting overall UAE production after Dubai had refused to accept a full pro-rata share of the necessary cutbacks.

Federal estimates, based on all the factors involved in UAE oil production (including technical considerations, internal political pressures and the diversity of foreign oil company interests), put the country's minimum production requirement at 1,600,000 bpd in 1983, and the Federal Government took every opportunity to press for an early increase in the country's March 1983 OPEC quota of 1,100,000 bpd. When the continuing weakness of the market led to a further cutback in OPEC production from November 1984 the UAE accepted a new quota of 950,000 bpd while making it clear that its future support for the quota system was dependent on the reform of OPEC's official pricing structure to improve the com-

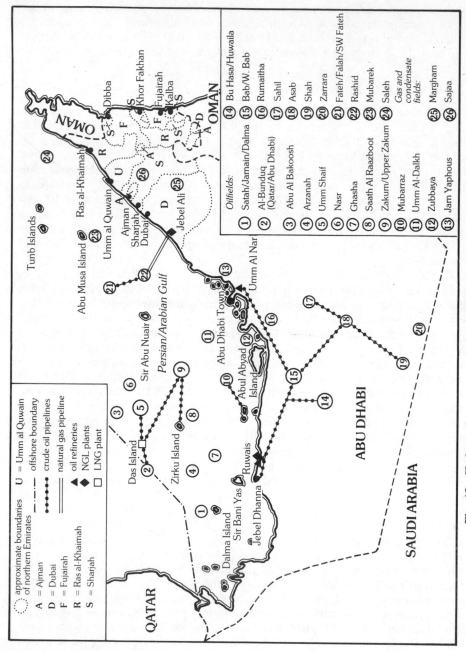

Fig. 18—Hydrocarbon resources and installations in the United Arab Emirates.

petitive position of Abu Dhabi's light crudes. (Dubai, as a producer of a heavier grade of crude and a frequent seller through the spot market, had no direct interest in this issue.) Independent observers reported regular over-quota production by the UAE after November 1984, indicating that Abu Dhabi had ceased to make any attempt to compensate for Dubai's rising output. However, the precise position on quota observance was obscured as a result of the wide latitude claimed by the Federal Government in excluding various sources of production from the quota limit (e.g. condensate fields and fields which were officially at a testing stage).

In July 1984 the Abu Dhabi Government announced the start of survey work in connexion with the proposed construction of a new pipeline to carry oil from Abu Dhabi's main onshore fields to Fujairah (on the Gulf of Oman). An initial capacity of 500,000 bpd was envisaged, with the possibility of rapid expansion to 800,000 bpd. Abu Dhabi's decision in principle to construct the 300 km pipeline, which was subsequently supported by the Federal Government, reflected concern within the UAE about the country's total dependence on oil export terminals in the Persian/Arabian Gulf at a time of frequent attacks on shipping in the context of the Iran-Iraq war (although the UAE's export terminals were situated well away from the main war zone and had suffered very little war-related disruption). Final approval for the pipeline project was still pending in mid-1986.

The UAE became Japan's main source of crude oil imports in 1985, taking over a position held by Saudi Arabia for the previous 20 years. The average volume supplied (713,000 bpd) represented nearly 60 per cent of UAE crude exports and more than 21 per cent of Japanese crude imports in that year.

C12.3.ii—Early concession agreements in the Trucial States
Petroleum Concessions Ltd, a subsidiary of the Iraq Petroleum Company (IPC, owned 23.75 per cent by BP, 23.75 per cent by Shell, 23.75 per cent by CFP, 11.875 per cent by Exxon, 11.875 per cent by Mobil and 5 per cent by Partex), was established in 1935 to acquire concession rights for the IPC shareholder companies in hitherto uncommitted areas of the Middle East which came within the scope of IPC's "red line agreement" of 1928 (◊A4.5.i). As a result of negotiations between Petroleum Concessions Ltd and the rulers of the Trucial States, the IPC companies obtained exclusive concession rights in Dubai and Sharjah in 1937, in Kalba (a small shaikhdom which later merged with Sharjah) and Ras al-Khaimah in 1938 and in Abu Dhabi in 1939. All of these concessions were held by Petroleum Development (Trucial Coast) Ltd (PDTC, formed in 1936 as a subsidiary of Petroleum Concessions Ltd) and were valid for periods of 75 years; PDTC undertook to make small annual rental payments and to pay royalties of three rupees per ton of oil produced (the rate which then applied in Kuwait). The ruler of Ajman granted a five-year exploration licence to PDTC in 1939.

In 1949 the rulers of the Trucial States proclaimed their jurisdiction over areas of the continental shelf adjacent to their territorial waters, leading to claims by PDTC that the oil rights in such areas were covered by its existing concession agreements. It was, however, established in 1951 (as a result of arbitration proceedings arising out of a dispute between PDTC and the Abu Dhabi Government over this issue) that the company's concession rights applied only to those territories which were under the jurisdiction of the state concerned at the time that the rights were originally granted.

PDTC voluntarily relinquished its onshore concession rights in Sharjah in 1959, in Ras al-Khaimah in 1960 and in Dubai in 1962, having drilled only one exploratory well in these territories (in Dubai in the early 1950s) during its period as concession holder. Having reduced its area of operations to mainland Abu Dhabi alone, PDTC was renamed the Abu Dhabi Petroleum Co. (ADPC) in 1962.

C12.3.iii—Abu Dhabi

PDTC, operating under a 75-year concession agreement signed in January 1939, began its first exploratory drilling programme in Abu Dhabi in 1950. Although the Murban structure was discovered in 1953, prolonged delineation and development work was required and onshore commercial production (from the Bab field) did not commence until 1963, when a tanker terminal was opened at Jebel Dhanna. The operating company was, as stated in section **C12.3.ii**, renamed Abu Dhabi Petroleum Co. in 1962.

Concession rights over all offshore areas not covered by the PDTC concession (i.e. about 31,000 sq km of the continental shelf lying outside Abu Dhabi's three-mile territorial waters limit) were granted in 1951 to the International Marine Oil Co., a partnership between the (US) Superior Oil Co. and the (British) Central Mining Corporation. This company relinquished its rights in the following year, and in March 1953 the offshore concession was granted for a period of 65 years to D'Arcy Exploration Co. (a subsidiary of BP), which in 1954 assigned its rights to a newly formed operating company, Abu Dhabi Marine Areas Ltd (ADMA), owned 66⅔ per cent by BP and 33⅓ per cent by CFP. The 1953 concession agreement stipulated that exploration work should commence within one year and test drilling within five years. In 1958 ADMA discovered the Umm Shaif field, from which Abu Dhabi's first commercial production took place in 1962 after the completion of an offshore export terminal on Das Island.

Whereas ADPC was liable to pay flat-rate royalties of three rupees per ton of oil produced, ADMA's concession terms provided for royalties equal to 20 per cent of the value of its oil output (to be determined with reference to the prices of comparable crudes produced elsewhere in the Persian/Arabian Gulf region). Following their initial commercial discoveries both of the producing companies indicated their preference to bring the financial provisions of their concession agreements into line with the standard pattern which had applied in other Middle Eastern countries since the early 1950s (i.e. "50-50 profit-sharing" ◊**A4.6**). However, Abu Dhabi chose not to introduce an income tax on corporate profits until 1965, having stood to gain little if any additional benefit from such a measure while the companies were amortizing their exploration costs during the early years of production. Under an agreement with ADPC, signed in September 1965, the Government's revenue entitlement was redefined as 50 per cent of the company's net operating profits, inclusive of a 12.5 per cent royalty. A royalty-expensing clause on the standard OPEC regional pattern (◊**D1.3.ii**) was subsequently added to this agreement in November 1966. ADMA concluded a 50-50 profit-sharing agreement (which incorporated a royalty-expensing clause) in November 1966.

Under the agreements of 1965–66 ADPC and ADMA each undertook to implement relinquishment programmes requiring them to release parts of their concession areas on specified dates. Responsibility for selecting the precise areas to be relinquished rested with the companies. In the case of ADPC a total of 13,000 sq km was to be relinquished immediately, with subsequent relinquishments at three-year intervals which would leave the company with a total concession area of 21,000 sq km in 1980.

In November 1971 a state corporation, the Abu Dhabi National Oil Co. (Adnoc), was established with powers to engage in all aspects of the oil and gas industry. Adnoc acquired a 25 per cent interest in the operations of ADPC and ADMA with effect from Jan. 1, 1973, the negotiation of the ADMA participation agreement being complicated by BP's announcement on Dec. 26, 1972, of the sale of a 30 per cent interest in ADMA to the Japan Oil Development Co. (Jodco, formed by a consortium of Japanese companies). The Government (as the lessor of the ADMA concession area) withheld its approval of this transaction until March

1973, when it was announced that BP had undertaken to finance the construction of an Adnoc-owned refinery in Abu Dhabi and that ADMA had agreed to increase its production from the concession area.

The Government decided in September 1973 to take early majority control of the operations of ADPC and ADMA, and one year later concluded agreements with the foreign parent companies providing for 60 per cent state ownership of their producing assets with effect from Jan. 1, 1974. Compensation was calculated on the basis of a net book valuation of the entire 60 per cent holding (i.e. including the initial 25 per cent, in respect of which compensation had originally been based on an updated book valuation). The Government indicated in December 1974 that it intended to acquire the foreign oil companies' remaining 40 per cent interests in the operations of ADPC and ADMA. However, this plan was later dropped in April 1975 on the grounds that Adnoc did not yet have the technical or administrative skills to take full operational control of the oil industry (not least because the main potential for future oil discoveries was in technically challenging offshore areas).

In October 1977 the existing 60-40 division of interests was formalized when Adnoc and ADMA formed a locally-registered operating company, the Abu Dhabi Marine Operating Co. (Adma-Opco), with the following shareholdings: Adnoc 60 per cent, BP 14⅔ per cent, CFP 13⅓ per cent and Jodco 12 per cent. A locally-registered Adnoc/ADPC operating company was established in 1978 as the Abu Dhabi Company for Onshore Oil Operations (Adco), in which the shareholders were Adnoc 60 per cent, BP 9.5 per cent, Shell 9.5 per cent, CFP 9.5 per cent, Exxon 4.75 per cent, Mobil 4.75 per cent and Partex 2 per cent. Adnoc had earlier taken 100 per cent control of the domestic marketing of oil products (hitherto controlled by BP, Shell and Caltex) in mid-1973, and had acquired all rights over Abu Dhabi's production of associated and non-associated gas in 1977, when the Government decreed all natural gas reserves to be the property of the state.

Various new concessions in unexploited areas relinquished by ADPC and ADMA were granted to other (mostly independent) oil companies from the mid-1960s onwards. The onshore areas concerned were all relinquished by the new concessionaires during the 1970s after unsuccessful exploratory drilling, but a number of offshore operators discovered small commercial oilfields. These included the Abu Dhabi Oil Company (ADOCO, owned by the Japanese companies Daikyo Oil, Maruzen Oil and Nippon Mining), which was granted a 40-year concession in 1967 and brought the Mubarraz field into production in 1973, and the Total Abu Al Bakoosh Oil Company, which was established in 1972 by CFP (51 per cent), Charter Oil (24.5 per cent), Kerr-McGhee Corp. (12.25 per cent) and Amerada Hess (12.25 per cent) and which brought the Abu Al Bakoosh field—an extension of Iran's Sassan field—into production in 1974. The Arzanah field was subsequently brought on stream in 1979 by a consortium of five US independent companies led by Amerada Hess (41.5 per cent) as operator. The Al-Bunduq field was discovered by ADMA in 1965 in an area which later came under part-Qatari jurisdiction (◊**C10.3**), resulting in the transfer of development responsibilities from ADMA to the Al-Bunduq Oil Co. (BP 33⅓ per cent, CFP 33⅓ per cent, Japanese interests 33⅓ per cent), which brought the field on stream at the end of 1975.

In 1986 two other groups of companies, one led by Attock Oil and one by Deminex, were prospecting in offshore waters, while onshore exploration concessions (granted in 1980) were held (i) by Amoco, (ii) by a Canadian consortium headed by Sceptre Resources as operator, and (iii) by a consortium consisting of Amerada Hess (50 per cent), Occidental Petroleum (33⅓ per cent), Union Texas Petroleum (10 per cent) and Alpha Oil (6⅔ per cent). Abu Dhabi's normal concession terms included a maximum royalty rate of 20 per cent and a maximum tax rate of 85 per cent (applicable in each case when production exceeded 200,000 bpd), with Adnoc having the option to take a 60 per cent interest in successful ventures. The duration of concessions granted in 1980–81 varied from eight to 25 years. The Government did not take any action to secure state participation in the operations of the new offshore companies which commenced production during the 1970s, Adnoc's resources being concentrated instead on the development of other offshore fields in which the European members of the Adma-Opco consortium had declined to invest.

The Upper Zakum field (an extension of Adma-Opco's main Zakum field) was brought into test production in 1982 as a joint investment by Adnoc (88 per cent) and Jodco (12 per cent), with CFP acting as operating contractor through the Zakum Development Company (owned 50 per cent by CFP and 50 per cent by Adnoc). Another 88-12 equity agreement was signed between Adnoc and Jodco in 1978 in respect of the Umm Al-Dalkh offshore field, for which Jodco acted as operating contractor through the Umm Al-Dalkh Development Company (Udeco), owned 50 per cent by Jodco and 50 per cent by Adnoc. This field began producing in mid-1985. Udeco was subsequently awarded a further operating contract in 1980 in respect of the development of the Dalma, Satah and Jarnain fields, production from which was to be piped to a new terminal on Dalma Island (whereas production from the Upper Zakum and Umm Al-Dalkh fields was handled via facilities on Zirku Island). Equity interests in the Dalma, Satah and Jarnain fields were held 60 per cent by Adnoc and 40 per cent by Jodco. The initial development of the Satah field was completed in 1985.

The original aim of the Government's oilfield development programme was to increase Abu Dhabi's total installed production capacity to 3,000,000 bpd by 1985, but this target was abandoned in the light of the downward trend in demand for OPEC oil during the early 1980s. Most ongoing oilfield development projects in Abu Dhabi—including enhanced-recovery schemes for established fields—were being critically re-examined in mid-1986 against the background of the slump in world oil prices, which was of particular importance to the Emirate because of its position as one of the Middle East's highest-cost producers. The first field to be shut in pending a market revival was Adco's Bab field (one of those scheduled for eventual enhanced-recovery operation). The utilization rate of the Bab field's existing capacity of 134,000 bpd had fallen as low as 10 per cent since 1984.

The Upper Zakum field, where production facilities with a design capacity of 500,000 bpd were being developed at a cost of more than $5,500 million, produced up to 120,000 bpd in 1984–85, officially on a test basis (enabling the Government to ignore this output for the purposes of OPEC quota observance). The combined "test" production of the Umm Al-Dalkh and Satah fields was reported to be between 25,000 bpd and 35,000 bpd in early 1986. Officially allowable production of 685,000 bpd from established fields was divided as follows in the first half of 1985: Adco 61.3 per cent (mainly from the Asab and Bu Hasa fields); Adma-Opco 26.3 per cent (mainly from the Umm Shaif field) and smaller offshore operators 12.4 per cent (including Abu Dhabi's half-share of Al-Bunduq output). Compared with Abi Dhabi's peak production year (1977), the respective allowables were equivalent to 41 per cent of Adco's highest output, 35 per cent of Adma-Opco's peak and 80 per cent of the smaller operators' peak.

The post-tax margin on equity crude lifted by the foreign shareholders in Adco and Adma-Opco stood at $1 per barrel in mid-1984, a level said by the shareholders to be too low to generate a positive cash flow in current market conditions. Sharp cutbacks in equity liftings from July onwards (which reduced Adma-Opco's output to as little as 65,000 bpd, compared with its 1984 allowable of 215,000 bpd) led the Government to increase the equity profit margin to $1.80 per barrel in November 1984. Revised margins of $1.625 per barrel for the Adma-Opco shareholders and

$1.375 per barrel for the Adco shareholders were introduced in February 1985 in conjunction with cuts in Abu Dhabi's official prices (◊**D16.2**). The margin on equity crude was increased to $2 per barrel when Abu Dhabi switched to spot-related pricing in early 1986. (Abu Dhabi's "spot-assessed" prices for June 1986, fixed retroactively in July, were in the range $10.75 to $11 per barrel.) Over half of Adnoc's own liftings were sold under contract to Japanese customers, who exerted heavy pressure for price cuts in 1984–85 (particularly after Oman's switch to market-related pricing in early 1985 ◊**D16.5**). Competitive pricing arrangements were introduced for Adnoc's contract customers when the official OPEC pricing system began to collapse in the latter part of 1985.

The Abu Dhabi Gas Liquefaction Co., formed in 1973 by Adnoc (51 per cent), Mitsui (22½0 per cent), BP (16⅓ per cent), CFP (8⅙ per cent) and Bridgestone Liquefied Gas (2⁹⁄20 per cent), opened a plant on Das Island in 1977 to process associated gas from the main offshore oilfields, the output of LNG and LPG being exported to Japan under a long-term contract with the Tokyo Electric Power Corporation. Abu Dhabi's LNG export prices were linked to its crude oil prices with effect from Jan. 1, 1980. An onshore gas-gathering system was completed in 1981 by the Abu Dhabi Gas Industries Co. (Gasco), owned 68 per cent by Adnoc, 15 per cent by Shell, 15 per cent by CFP and 2 per cent by Partex. Consisting of three extraction plants in the main Adco oilfields, connected by pipeline to a fractionation complex and shipping terminal at Ruwais, the system had an annual design capacity of 1,230,000 tonnes of propane, 1,410,000 tonnes of butane and 2,110,000 tonnes of condensates, based on a daily input of 23,000,000 cubic metres of associated gas from oil production of 980,000 bpd. Capacity utilization at the plant fell below 50 per cent in 1983 as a result of low oil production, improving somewhat in 1984–85 as efforts were made to increase the supply of non-associated gas from Abu Dhabi's existing producing gasfields (which acounted for only a small proportion of the Emirate's total reserves of non-associated gas).

Adnoc's first oil refinery, situated at Umm Al Nar, was opened in 1976 with a capacity of 15,000 bpd. Self-sufficiency in refined products was not achieved until 1981, when a second Adnoc refinery was opened at Ruwais with a capacity of 120,000 bpd, more than adequate to meet current demand throughout the UAE. Abu Dhabi's total refining capacity was further increased to 180,000 bpd in 1983 when the original Umm Al Nar plant was superseded by a new 60,000 bpd refinery at the same location. The Ruwais plant was subsequently upgraded by the addition of a hydrocracking unit which came into full production in October 1985. A nitrogen fertilizer plant, owned 66⅔ per cent by Adnoc and 33⅓ per cent by CFP, was commissioned at Ruwais in 1983. Using natural gas as a feedstock, the plant had an annual production capacity of 330,000 tonnes of ammonia and 495,000 tonnes of urea. Production in 1984 (most of which was exported) was 275,000 tonnes of ammonia and 343,000 tonnes of urea.

In May 1984 an International Petroleum Investment Corporation was formed to acquire interests in new petroleum projects outside Abu Dhabi (i.e. in other Emirates and in foreign countries). The corporation was owned 50 per cent by Adnoc and 50 per cent by the Abu Dhabi Investment Authority.

C12.3.iv—Dubai

Following PDTC's withdrawal from Dubai in 1962 (◊**C12.3.ii**), onshore concession rights were granted in early 1963 to Conoco, which formed the Dubai Petroleum Co. (Dupetco) as a wholly-owned operating subsidiary. Offshore concession rights over an area of 3,110 sq km were held by Dubai Marine Areas Ltd (DUMA), an operating company established in 1954 under the ownership of BP (66⅔ per cent) and CFP (33⅓ per cent). Both the DUMA and Dupetco agreements provided for "50-50 profit-sharing" on the standard Middle East terms (◊**A4.6**).

Conoco acquired a 50 per cent interest in DUMA's concession area in mid-1963 (without affecting the ownership of the DUMA company) and in mid-1964 it assigned parts of Dupetco's onshore rights and offshore half-rights to Sun Oil and Deutsche Erdöl AG. Sun Oil acquired a 22.5 per cent onshore interest and a 5 per cent offshore interest, while Deutsche Erdöl (which was later taken over by Texaco in 1966) acquired a 22.5 per cent onshore interest and a 10 per cent offshore interest. Dupetco thus retained a 55 per cent holding onshore and a 35 per cent holding offshore. The DUMA company was reconstituted as an equal partnership between CFP and Hispanoil following BP's withdrawal in 1969, while Dupetco's interest in the DUMA concession area was subsequently reduced to 30 per cent through the transfer of a 5 per cent interest to Wintershall AG.

In June 1966 Dupetco, acting as the operator in the DUMA concession area, discovered the Fateh field, from which Dubai's first oil exports were made in September 1969. Dupetco discovered three further offshore fields between 1970 and 1973, while relinquishing its onshore concession area in 1972. In July 1975 the Government of Dubai announced that it had negotiated 100 per cent state ownership of producing assets in the DUMA concession area (where output had reached 255,000 bpd) and that the formal status of the foreign oil companies holding interests in this concession had been changed to that of contractors to the state. Dupetco retained its position as the operating company and principal participant in what was now referred to as the "Dubai Petroleum Group" (Conoco 30 per cent, CFP 25 per cent, Hispanoil 25 per cent, Deutsche Texaco 10 per cent, Sun Oil 5 per cent, Wintershall 5 per cent). The Government assumed direct responsibility for marketing a proportion of Dubai's output at the end of the 1970s, and was by the mid-1980s exporting large volumes through spot channels.

The Dubai Petroleum Group's crude oil output is exported from offshore storage tanks. Associated gas is piped to the mainland, where a processing plant at Jebel Ali (opened in 1980) produces natural gas liquids for domestic and export markets and residual dry gas for use as industrial fuel, notably by the nearby aluminium smelter. In May 1982 Dubai's first significant onshore hydrocarbon deposit—a gas and condensate field—was discovered at Margham by Atlantic Richfield in a concession area originally granted to that company in 1979 (although Britoil—then part of the British National Oil Corporation—had acquired a one-third minority interest in the concession in 1981). Commercial production from the field began in the first half of 1985 after the construction of gathering and processing facilities linked by pipeline to storage tanks and a loading terminal at Jebel Ali. All of the field's condensate output (about 25,000 bpd in 1985) is exported, while all of its gas output is reinjected to maintain reservoir pressure.

Following the Margham discovery the Government of Dubai invited applications from foreign oil companies for exploration rights in areas not covered by existing concessions, and by early November 1983 agreements were in force in respect of the Emirate's entire territory. Companies or consortiums which obtained new onshore concessions included BP (567 sq km) and the Dubai Petroleum Group (263 sq km).

C12.3.v—Sharjah

Although a variety of oil companies held offshore and onshore exploration concessions from 1962 onwards, it was not until 1972 that the offshore Mubarek oilfield, near the island of Abu Musa, was discovered by a consortium of six US independent companies led by Buttes Gas and Oil as operator. In accordance with an offshore boundary agreement of 1975 between Sharjah and Umm al Quwain and the 1971 agreement on Abu Musa between Sharjah and Iran ($\lozenge$**C12.2**), government revenue from the field was shared between Iran (50 per cent), Sharjah (35 per cent) and Umm al Quwain (15 per cent). Production, which commenced in 1974, peaked at 40,000 bpd in the following year and steadily declined thereafter.

In 1980 an onshore hydrocarbon deposit, the Sajaa gas and condensate field, was discovered by Amoco in a concession area held by that company since 1978. The field was brought on stream in July 1982 and in 1985 produced nearly 60,000 bpd of low-sulphur condensate together with substantial volumes of gas (over 80 per cent of which was flared and the remainder piped into a new gas grid serving industrial users in the northern Emirates). The flaring of gas was greatly reduced in June 1986 upon the commissioning of a processing plant with an annual production capacity of 440,000 tonnes of liquefied petroleum gas and 180,000 tonnes of condensate. LPG exports began in the following month under a 10-year contract for the supply of 300,000 tonnes per year to a group of four Japanese importers.

Sharjah's standard concession terms include a 14.5 per cent royalty rate and a 77 per cent income tax rate. There is no government equity participation.

C12.3.vi—Ras al-Khaimah
The discovery of oil and gas in commercial quantities in the offshore Saleh field was announced in February 1983. Initial production began in January 1984 at the rate of 3,700 bpd following the installation of temporary production facilities, and the first exports from offshore storage tanks took place in July 1984. Production capacity was reported to be 14,000 bpd in late 1985 following the completion of a permanent offshore oil installation. A newly completed onshore gas processing plant, linked by pipeline to the Saleh field, was producing about 1,550,000 cubic metres per day of dry gas, 1,300 bpd of liquefied petroleum gas and 400 bpd of natural gasoline in mid-1986. The Saleh field was developed by a six-member consortium whose operating company was Gulf Oil (25.23 per cent) and whose main shareholder was the Government of Ras al-Khaimah (50 per cent). However, the Government sold its half-share to its foreign partners in 1986. After revision in mid-1986, the royalty rate on Saleh production was 20 per cent and the income tax rate 75 per cent. Onshore exploration, carried out by Gulf Oil in partnership with Amoco, resulted in several discoveries during 1985. No assessment of their commercial viability had been announced by early 1986. (Gulf Oil was taken over by Chevron in 1984 ◊A5.1.iii).

C12.3.vii—Ajman, Fujairah and Umm al Quwain
Exploration work carried out over a number of years by various concessionaires (mostly small independent companies) had failed to produce any commercial discoveries in the three smallest Emirates by early 1986. In 1981 Texaco obtained a 620 sq km concession in Umm al Quwain's offshore waters, 13 km west of Sharjah's Mubarek field.

C13—Venezuela

C13.1—Statistical Survey

*1984
†End-1984

General
Area .... 912,050 sq km
*Population 16,850,000
Capital .... Caracas

Economy and trade
*Gross national product .... $49,500 million
*Annual exports (fob) .... $13,294 million (of which petroleum 91.4 per cent)
*Annual imports (cif) .... $7,307 million
*Current account balance .... +$4,972 million
Foreign exchange reserves .... $8,937 million (December 1985)

Oil (upstream)
1984 crude production .... 1,875,000 bpd (97,500,000 tonnes)
1985 crude production .... 1,745,000 bpd (90,200,000 tonnes)
†Proved crude reserves .... 25,800 million barrels
*Reserves:production ratio .... 37.9 : 1
Production in peak year .... 3,760,000 bpd (195,200,000 tonnes) in 1970
†Cumulative crude production .... 39,088 million barrels since 1917
*Number of producing oil wells 13,405
Main export grades: Tia Juana .... 26° and 31° API gravities
       Oficina .... 34° API gravity
       Centro Lago ...... 37° API gravity
       San Joaquin ...... 42° API gravity
       Boscán .... 10° API gravity
       Bachaquero ...... 17° API gravity

Oil tanker tonnage
†19 vessels .... 773,700 deadweight tons

Oil (downstream)
*Installed refining capacity .... 1,224,200 bpd
*Output of refined products .... 907,800 bpd
*Consumption of refined products ...... 352,100 bpd

Natural gas (million cubic metres)
*Gross annual production .... 32,574 mcm
  of which: (gas marketed) .... (17,300 mcm)
      (gas reinjected) .... (12,030 mcm)
      (gas flared) .... (1,756 mcm)
      (shrinkage) .... (1,488 mcm)
†Natural gas reserves .... 1,600,000 mcm

C13.2—Political and Economic Summary

The Republic of Venezuela was established as a separate state in 1830 after breaking away from neighbouring Colombia, with which it had been associated in a prolonged war of independence to end three centuries of Spanish rule. Dictatorships predominated among the post-independence regimes, and it was not until 1963 that a democratically elected President completed a full term of office. By 1985 Venezuela had experienced 26 years of continuous constitutional government, during which the presidency was held either by the centre-left Democratic Action (AD) party or by the centre-right Christian Social (COPEI) party. Candidates of the AD won the 1958, 1963, 1973 and 1983 presidential elections, and COPEI candidates those of 1968 and 1978. The Venezuelan President's constitutional position is similar to that of the US President, and effective government by one of the major parties has often depended on the support of smaller parties and independent members within the bicameral legislature.

Under the 1961 Constitution Venezuela is a federal republic comprising 20 states, one federal district (which includes the capital), two federal territories and 72 federal dependencies. The current President, inaugurated in February 1984, is Dr Jaime Lusinchi of the AD.

The petroleum sector was the largest single component of Venezuela's gross domestic product in the mid-1980s, generating over 90 per cent of export earnings and about half of government revenue. Non-oil secondary industries contributed about one-fifth of GDP, and there was a relatively well developed infrastructure. The country has important non-oil mineral deposits and produces iron ore on a large scale both for export and for use in domestic steelmaking. Until the end of the 1970s a main aim of development planning was to promote the rapid growth of heavy industries. Thereafter it was decided to devote more resources to agriculture (particularly in view of the country's high level of food imports) and to social welfare projects (in view of the large disparities between the living standards of different groups in society).

Much of Venezuela's economic development during the 1970s was financed by overseas borrowing, and severe repayment difficulties arose when oil demand and prices fell in the early 1980s, causing a shortfall in budgeted revenue. Venezuela's total foreign indebtedness stood at $35,000 million in early 1984, when the new Lusinchi administration introduced a series of austerity measures and announced its intention to negotiate the rescheduling of debts directly with creditor banks without seeking financial assistance from the International Monetary Fund as a basis for such negotiations.

The previous administration had in 1983 rejected IMF loan conditions which included a full currency devaluation, preferring instead to introduce a selective devaluation based on the use of multiple exchange rates. Venezuela's refusal to accept the full programme of stabilization measures recommended by the IMF was in line with the collective position adopted by Latin America's largest debtor countries during 1983, the group's main contention being that the orthodox terms which were being put forward by the Fund as a basis for debt rescheduling were likely to undermine both the economic development and the political stability of Latin America. Terms for the rescheduling of some $20,750 million of Venezuela's public-sector debt were agreed in principle with foreign creditor banks in September 1984 but did not take effect until February 1986 (the total amount covered by the agreement in principle having meanwhile been increased by $450,000,000 in May 1985).

The Government announced in April 1986 that the terms of the public-sector rescheduling agreement would have to be re-examined in the light of the collapse of oil prices, which had caused it to cut its 1986 revenue estimates by about $4,900 million. Subsequent negotiations on this issue were complicated by the Venezuelan Congress's approval in July of a controversial law on the repayment of the private sector's external debt. Under this "exchange compensation fund law"—which reportedly led to retaliatory cuts in credit lines by several US banks—private-sector debt repayments were to be covered by the issue of public bonds, maturing over 15 years and having an effective worth of less than 70 per cent of face value.

Venezuela is a leading member of Latin American regional and sub-regional political and economic organizations, and has taken the initiative (together with Mexico, Panama and Colombia) in launching a diplomatic drive to secure a negotiated solution to the problems of Central America. Venezuela gave its strong support to third-world causes in international forums during the 1970s, but reduced its activities in this field in the 1980s as the Government became increasingly preoccupied with domestic economic difficulties. The country has observer status in the non-aligned movement, its attainment of full membership being effectively blocked pending the settlement of a territorial dispute with Guyana. Venezuela's close co-operation with Mexico on matters of oil policy was instrumental in securing Mexico's support for OPEC's March 1983 market stabilization programme. The two countries established a permanent petroleum co-operation committee in early 1986.

C13.3—Oil and Gas Industry

C13.3.i—General

Venezuela's first hydrocarbon mining leases were granted in the 1860s, mostly in areas which had long been known to contain asphalt deposits and/or natural oil seepages. The first major oil discoveries occurred in 1914, two years after the start of exploratory drilling, and commercial production commenced in 1917. Venezuela attained the position of the world's second largest oil producing country (after the United States) in 1928, when its production exceeded that of the Soviet Union for the first time. However, Soviet output moved slightly ahead again during the 1930s, and Venezuela did not become firmly established as the second largest producer until the mid-1940s (remaining ahead of the Soviet Union until 1960). By 1944 Venezuela had succeeded the United States as the world's largest exporter of oil (having become the leading net exporter during the 1930s), but lost this distinction in 1970 when its exports were overtaken by those of Saudi Arabia and Iran.

C13.3.ii—Early development (1913 to 1940)

The first major foreign oil company to enter Venezuela was Royal Dutch/Shell, through its purchase in 1913 of a 51 per cent shareholding in the Caribbean Petroleum Company, which had recently acquired extensive exploration rights in 11 Venezuelan states. Shell's Venezuelan concessions were later brought under the control of a wholly-owned operating subsidiary. North American interests which acquired options and leases over large areas of Venezuela after the First World War included the Creole Syndicate (established in 1920), whose concessions accounted for over 10 per cent of the country's output by 1927. Gulf Oil acted as drilling contractor to Creole when the syndicate's original concessions were brought into production in 1925, the oil produced on Creole's account being purchased by Gulf under short-term contracts.

In 1928 Exxon acquired a majority shareholding in the Creole Syndicate, which was renamed Creole Petroleum Corporation after its interests had been amalgamated with those of Exxon's existing Venezuelan subsidiaries. Following this amalgamation the company controlled a total concession area of 44,420 sq km, of which 15,800 sq km was subject to eventual relinquishment to the state. Creole's holdings were substantially increased in 1932, when Exxon purchased the Venezuelan assets and concession rights of Standard Oil Co. (Indiana), latterly the leading US producer in Venezuela. At the same time Exxon took over Lago Oil and Transport Co., the subsidiary through which Standard Oil Co. (Indiana) had refined its Venezuelan output on the Dutch island of Aruba.

Gulf Oil, which accounted for 21 per cent of Venezuelan oil production in 1929 following a period of rapid growth in output from its own concession areas, discovered important new reserves of lighter crudes in eastern Venezuela in the mid-1930s. (Most of the country's known reserves had previously consisted of heavier oils, produced mainly in the Lake Maracaibo region in the west.) However, Gulf did not at this time control sufficient marketing outlets to absorb a significant increase in the output of its Venezuelan operating subsidiary (Mene Grande Oil Co.) and accordingly agreed in 1937 to sell an undivided half-interest in Mene Grande's producing operations to the International Petroleum Company, a subsidiary of Exxon.

Having obtained the right to veto Mene Grande's exploration and development programme and to establish a ceiling on the growth of Mene Grande's output relative to that of Creole, Exxon in 1938 sold half of its interest in the Mene Grande concessions to Nederlandse Olie Maatschappij (part of the Royal Dutch/Shell Group). Exxon later transferred the ownership of its remaining 25 per cent interest in these concessions to a new subsidiary, International Petroleum (Venezuela) Ltd, while the 25 per cent Shell interest was eventually transferred to the direct ownership of Shell's main Venezuelan operating company. Gulf Oil continued to hold all the shares in Mene Grande Oil Co. and to manage the company's production operations, which were financed 50 per cent by Gulf, 25 per cent by Exxon and 25 per cent by Shell. The result of the transactions of 1937–38 was to increase Exxon's overall share of Venezuelan oil production to 52 per cent and that of Shell to 40 per cent, while reducing Gulf's share to 7 per cent.

Venezuela's initial rise to prominence as an oil producing country took place under the dictatorship of Gen. Juan Vicente Gómez, who held power from 1909 to 1935. During this period there was little uniformity in the terms on which concessions were granted by the state. Foreign oil companies enjoyed considerable operational autonomy, including freedom to repatriate the greater part of their profits, while much of the oil revenue which did accrue to the Government was misappropriated by the ruling clique. Oil rights (sometimes of questionable validity) were acquired by over 100 companies and individuals, and numerous transfers of rights occurred as the major oil companies gradually consolidated their holdings. The terms of many of these transactions were highly controversial and contributed to a strong and lasting mistrust of foreign oil interests on the part of democratic nationalist politicians in Venezuela.

Prior to 1920 oil concessions were granted under general mining laws on terms which usually defined the Government's royalty entitlement as a fixed sum per tonne of production. The first law dealing specifically with hydrocarbons, introduced in 1920, provided for the payment of percentage royalties (at the rate of 15 per cent of the notional export value of the crude produced); for a maximum concession period of 30 years; for the commencement of drilling within three years of obtaining exploration rights; and for the setting aside of half of each discovery as a national reserve. However, under subsequent amending legislation (enacted in 1922, 1925, 1928 and 1935) many of the provisions of the 1920 law were relaxed, allowing concession periods to be extended while royalty rates were reduced to as little as 7.5 per cent in some cases (although by 1935 there was a minimum rate of 10 per cent for new concessions).

319

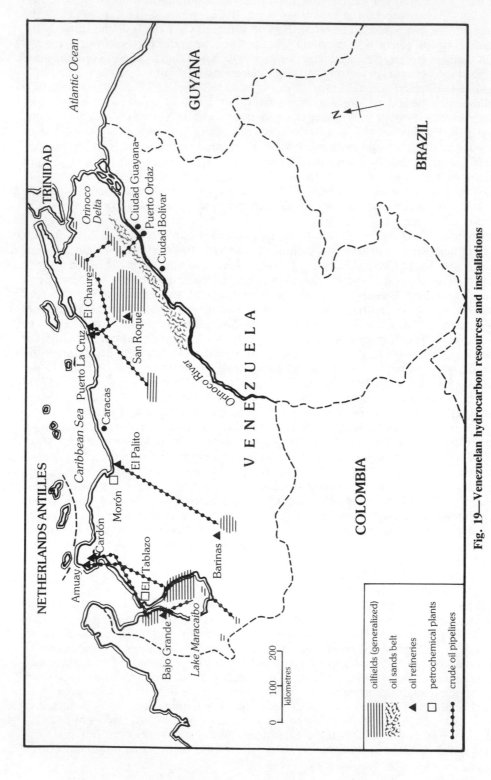

Fig. 19—Venezuelan hydrocarbon resources and installations

Crude oil was valued for royalty purposes by applying a netback calculation based on the prevailing prices of refined products in the United States. Apart from royalties, the main components of the Government's oil revenue were taxes on exploration and initial exploitation, which were levied on concession areas as a fixed sum per hectare of land over which oil rights were held. The 1922 amendment to the hydrocarbons law allowed foreign oil companies to claim exemption from Venezuelan import duties—a provision which was strongly criticized by opponents of the Gómez regime's oil policy, who claimed that the resultant loss of customs revenue was greater than the Government's oil revenue during the 1920s.

Following the death of Gen. Gómez in December 1935, there was a widespread popular reaction against his regime which found political expression under the more liberal military presidencies of his successors. Public condemnation of the Gómez regime's oil policies was accompanied by condemnation of the companies which had benefited from them, and several measures were introduced from 1936 onwards to tighten the government supervision of company operations and to increase the level of the companies' payments to the state. Significantly higher royalty and tax rates were obtained when new concessions were granted on the basis of genuinely competitive bidding in 1936–37, and the holders of the new concessions (including Exxon and Shell) were required to refine specified percentages of their Venezuelan crude output within the country. A detailed analysis of the major companies' declared operating expenses in existing concession areas led to the disallowance of various spurious claims which had been made in order to reduce the royalty value of production; moreover, exemption from import duties was ended in respect of goods which were available within Venezuela (although the companies took legal action to challenge the applicability of the latter provision to existing concession agreements).

A new hydrocarbons law passed in July 1938 provided (i) for higher royalty rates (of 15 to 16 per cent) and greatly increased flat-rate taxes on concessions; (ii) for the payment in gold of taxes and royalties; (iii) for a revision of the system of valuing Venezuelan crude with reference to the prices of products in the US market; (iv) for stricter relinquishment provisions in respect of unexploited concession areas; (v) for a ban on the transfer of concession rights without government approval; and (vi) for the imposition of fines on companies using inefficient production methods (e.g. recovery techniques involving unnecessary wastage of associated gas). At the same time state enterprises were authorized to enter any phase of the oil industry.

The 1938 law proved ineffective in the face of strong opposition from the companies, which refused either to apply for new concessions (which were automatically subject to its provisions) or to agree to the amendment of the terms of their existing concession agreements, then covering a total area of 110,000 sq km. Administrative regulations were issued in 1940 with the aim of extending certain of the provisions of the 1938 law (e.g. the ban on the unauthorized transfer of oil rights) to all concession holders, regardless of the terms of their existing concession agreements. The companies responded by threatening to take legal action to defend their "acquired rights", notwithstanding the Government's assertion that the regulations affected only those rights which were "prejudicial to the public interest".

C13.3.iii—Hydrocarbons law of 1943 – Introduction of "50-50 profit-sharing" (1948)

The deadlock between the Venezuelan Government and the companies was broken in 1943 after unpublicized mediation by the US Government, whose advisers were involved in the drafting of a new hydrocarbons law which comprehensively revised the framework of oil industry operations. Numerous changes were made to concession terms, and all concession holders were required to bring their existing agreements into line with the new standard terms, thus eliminating the many disparities created by past changes in the law. In order to secure acceptance of the new terms the Government agreed to drop all outstanding claims against the oil companies, including claims challenging the validity of long-standing concessions. Following each concessionaire's compliance with the law the concession areas held under existing agreements were re-granted to that concessionaire for a period of 40 years, subject to stricter relinquishment obligations. With regard to future grants of new concessions, it was laid down that there should be a maximum initial term of 40 years and that half of the initial exploration area should be relinquished after three years.

Concession rights over a total area of about 60,000 sq km were re-granted to established concessionaires who brought their agreements into line with the law, the balance of the existing concession areas being relinquished to the state. New concessions covering a total area of about 65,000 sq km were granted in 1944–45 to a variety of bidders (including companies with no existing Venezuelan interests), some of whom agreed to pay more than the legal minimum tax and royalty rates.

Under the 1943 hydrocarbons law various increases were made in the flat-rate taxes levied on each hectare of concession areas; at the same time, royalties were raised to 16⅔ per cent (as a standard rate for existing concessions and a minimum rate for new concessions), Venezuelan crude being valued for this purpose in line with the prices posted in Texas for similar grades of US crude. Foreign oil companies were required to keep the accounts of their local subsidiaries in Venezuela, and the companies' unconditional exemption from the payment of import duties was curtailed. Companies owning pipelines within Venezuela were required to make their transportation capacity available to other companies on a "common carrier" basis. It was laid down that at least 15 per cent of Venezeula's crude oil production should be refined within the country, and (under a separate agreement) the major concession holders undertook to locate within Venezuela any new capacity built by them for the refining of Venezuelan oil in the Caribbean region. (In 1940 Shell and Exxon had an aggregate refining capacity of 495,000 bpd in the Netherlands Antilles and only 45,000 bpd in Venezuela, the bulk of Shell's Venezuelan crude output being refined on the island of Curaçao and that of Exxon on Aruba. Overall, about 95 per cent of Venezuelan crude production was refined outside the country at this time.)

Under a general income tax law introduced at the same time as the 1943 hydrocarbons law, corporate profits became subject to a basic "cedular" tax of 2.5 per cent and, above certain levels, to an additional progressive tax of up to 9.5 per cent (this maximum rate being levied on an income band which in practice included only the profits of the larger oil companies). Specific oil taxes and royalties levied under the hydrocarbons law were treated as deductible expenses for the purpose of assessing taxable income under the general law. The oil companies' liability to pay income tax did not form part of their concession agreements, and the Government thus had no obligation to consult the companies regarding any future changes in the rates of tax. The companies, for their part, could follow flexible export pricing policies in the knowledge that their income tax liability was based on their declared receipts rather than on formal postings. (Export prices nevertheless began to be formally posted by the companies at Venezuelan ports in 1952. Realized market prices began to fall below posted prices in the late 1950s.)

The rates of income tax fixed in 1943 were said by the then Government to be high enough (when applied in conjunction with the financial provisions of the hydrocarbons law) to increase the state's share of aggregate oil company profits to at least 50 per cent (although there would be variations in the effective rates at which individual companies were taxed). In practice, however, this proved to be a gross overestimate, based on an inaccurate assessment of current profit margins in the Venezuelan oil industry.

In October 1945 a coup staged by radical army officers led to the formation of a centre-left Government which included a number of leading civilian advocates of further reform of the oil industry, among whom Dr J. P. Pérez Alfonzo, a specialist in oil economics, held the post of Minister for Economic Development. Three months after taking office the new Government imposed a once-and-for-all tax on corporate profits above a certain level, resulting in a total revenue yield equivalent to $27,000,000, of which 88 per cent was paid by oil companies. The main aim of this measure was to secure an immediate increase to about 50 per cent in the share of oil industry profits received by the Government, whose proportionate revenue entitlement under the 1943 income tax law had declined significantly during the previous year.

The law was subsequently amended to increase the maximum rate of the progressive income tax on corporate profits to 26 per cent, and in 1948 an additional 50 per cent surtax was imposed on any sum by which the net profits from oil operations remaining to any company after the payment of all other revenues due to the Government exceeded the total of those revenues. The state was thereafter guaranteed a minimum 50 per cent share of each oil company's net profits, the actual level of receipts during the early 1950s being around 53 per cent.

Other steps taken by the Government with the aim of strengthening the role of the state vis-à-vis the foreign oil companies included (i) the imposition of a ban on the granting of new oil concessions; (ii) the introduction in 1946 of the country's first collective labour contract for the oil industry; (iii) the exercising in 1947 of the Government's hitherto unused right to receive part of its royalty payments in the form of crude oil (which was marketed by the state at higher prices than those on which the producing companies' cash royalties were based); and (iv) the appointment in early 1948 of a commission to plan the establishment of a national oil company and a state-owned refinery. The interventionist policies adopted by the Government had little effect on the flow of oil company investment into Venezuela, which continued at relatively high levels in 1946–48, when an increase in exports from established fields was accompanied by a major exploration and development programme in the new concession areas obtained in 1944–45.

C13.3.iv—Lifting and subsequent reimposition of ban on new concession agreements – Strengthening of state role in the oil sector (to 1971)

In November 1948, less than a year after the holding of democratic elections, Venezuela returned to military dictatorship following a coup led by "traditionalist" officers. The new regime adopted a policy of positive co-operation with the foreign oil companies, which benefited from such measures as government restrictions on the rights of petroleum workers, the maintenance of tax rates at their 1948 level, the shelving of all proposals to create state-owned petroleum enterprises and the non-enforcement of conservation regulations under which the previous Government had planned to increase the utilization of natural gas. The ban on the granting of new oil concessions was lifted in 1956–57, when rights over a total area of 8,200 sq km were opened to competitive bidding which raised over $700,000,000 in non-refundable premium payments to the Government. The highest premiums per hectare were paid by US independent companies eager to establish themselves in Venezuela for the first time, and in the face of keen competition from this quarter the established majors (i.e. Exxon, Shell and Gulf) were able to obtain only 43 per cent of the total area which was opened to bids. By 1958 the three major companies' combined share of Venezuelan oil production had fallen to 82 per cent, as against 90 per cent in 1952.

The dictatorship of Gen. Marcos Pérez Jiménez was overthrown in January 1958, and free elections held later that year resulted in the formation of a Government led by President Rómulo Betancourt of the Democratic Action party, who took office in February 1959. Faced with a serious budget deficit inherited from the dictatorship, the transitional Government which had overseen the elections issued a decree on Dec. 19, 1958, raising the maximum rate of progressive income tax from 26 per cent to 45 per cent with retroactive effect from Jan. 1 of that year. The Government maintained that the consequent increase (to about 67 per cent) in the state's share of total oil company profits was justified on the grounds that the companies' average rate of return on net assets in Venezuela had risen from 23.4 per cent in 1951 to 32.4 per cent in 1957. The president of Creole Petroleum Corporation strongly criticized the Government for "breaking the 50-50 formula", adding that the new tax decree would "drastically alter the climate for foreign investment" in Venezuela.

The Betancourt Government nevertheless declared its intention both to implement the tax decree and to resume the programme of oil industry reforms which had been initiated in 1945–48 by Dr Pérez Alfonzo (who took the portfolio of Mines and Hydrocarbons in the new Government). The policy of not granting new concessions was reintroduced, and a permanent co-ordinating commission for the conservation and marketing of hydrocarbons was set up to provide expert advice to the Government on the industrial and commercial activities of the oil companies. An important aspect of the commission's work was to monitor the producing companies' realized export prices, with particular reference to the heavy discounting of posted prices by many of the independent producers who had obtained concessions in 1956–57. From 1962 onwards any discount in excess of 10 per cent of the posted price for the grade of oil concerned was challenged by the commission for income tax purposes.

The independent producers' need to offer large discounts on their Venezuelan production arose from a deterioration in Venezuela's market position vis-à-vis the Middle Eastern oil-exporting countries. Whereas the Venezuelan Government's aim was to achieve a rate of increase in annual output based on the country's budgetary needs (expected to increase at a lower rate than world demand for oil), the achievement of even this lower rate was threatened in March 1959 as a result of the imposition of mandatory quota restrictions on the import of oil into the United States (Venezuela's main market) (◊A4.10.ii). Changes in the major oil companies' posted prices in February 1959 (◊A4.10.iii) had already reduced the competitiveness of the companies' exports from Venezuela to other western-hemisphere markets (an increasing proportion of whose supplies were being shipped from the Middle East) and had strengthened the Middle East's existing domination of eastern-hemisphere import markets. Having failed to win concessions from the United States over import quotas, the Venezuelan Government increased its efforts to co-ordinate its oil policies with those of the Middle Eastern producing countries—a strategy which led directly to the formation of OPEC, within which Venezuela was the leading advocate of the prorationing of member countries' output in order to maximize unit revenues (◊D1.1).

In April 1960 the Government established a national oil company, the Corporación Venezolana del Petróleo (CVP), which was empowered to operate in all sectors of the hydrocarbons industry. Initially, CVP was mainly concerned with exploration and development work in concession areas relinquished by private companies, on the basis of which it gradually established a position as one of the country's smaller crude producers. CVP also took responsibility for the running of the first state oil refinery at Morón, whose output was sold on the domestic products market, hitherto controlled by the major oil companies (which were obliged by a government decree of 1963 to relinquish one-third of the market to CVP within five years). The state company also supplied part of the Venezuela's fast-growing residential and industrial consumption of natural gas.

The ban on the granting of new concessions (except to CVP), coupled with a steady decline in investment in the existing concession areas held by foreign oil companies (where the number of exploratory wells drilled fell from nearly 600 in 1958 to fewer than 100 in 1967), contributed to a deterioration in Venezuela's reserves:production ratio from 17.8 : 1 in 1960 to 13.1 : 1 in 1967. In the light of this trend, the Government entered into negotiations with the companies in 1967 to establish a mutually acceptable basis for future foreign investment in new exploration areas. Details were published in 1968 of an agreed formula under which foreign companies would undertake exploration work as service contractors to CVP, but the first contracts were not signed until July 1971, when a total area of 2,500 sq km was divided between Occidental Petroleum (which took up three blocks, representing the company's first venture in Venezuela), Mobil (one block) and Shell (one block). The contractors were required to pay non-refundable initial premiums to CVP and to finance the costs of exploration and development. The ownership of any oil discovered would be vested in CVP, which would reimburse successful contractors from the proceeds of production. The contracts were valid for 20 years, although 80 per cent of each exploration block (consisting of unexploited areas nominated by the contractor) was to be relinquished to CVP after the first three years.

The long delay in finalizing these service contracts (attributable largely to political factors) did not improve the investment climate in the established concession areas. In 1970, when Venezuela's oil production reached its peak level, the reserves:production ratio fell to a record low point of 10.2 : 1 (cumulative production over the previous decade having exceeded additions to proved reserves by some 4,500 million barrels despite a slowing in the average production growth rate to 2.8 per cent per annum, as against 6.8 per cent during the 1950s). The Government's revenue entitlement was meanwhile increased under amendments to the tax laws whereby (i) the maximum rate of progressive income tax was raised from 45 per cent to 52 per cent with effect from Jan. 1, 1967, while the 2.5 per cent "cedular" tax was abolished; and (ii) oil companies became subject to a single income tax rate of 60 per cent with effect from Jan. 1, 1970 (retroactive legislation introducing this increase being enacted in December 1970). The first tax increase raised the state's share of oil company profits to about 70 per cent and the second to nearly 80 per cent.

The impact of each increase was reinforced by measures to strengthen the Government's control over the pricing of oil for income tax purposes. In September 1966, following a prolonged dispute over government claims that realized market prices had been understated by the oil companies as a means of minimizing their tax liability, it was agreed that a system of artificial tax reference prices should be introduced, future changes in these "minimum export values" being a matter for negotiation between the two sides. Under the 1970 tax law, however, the Government took full control over the fixing of minimum export values with effect from March 1971. In order to provide an incentive for new exploration work, provision was made from 1967 onwards for the rate of income tax to be reduced by up to 2 per cent for a company which had significantly increased its capital investment during the relevant tax year.

C13.3.v—From "reversion" to nationalization (1971 to 1975) – Formation and development of PDVSA

In July 1971, shortly after the signature of the first service contracts, a hydrocarbons reversion law was enacted to preclude any extension of the terms of existing concession agreements (which were due to expire from 1983 onwards) and to deter concessionaires from deliberately running down their operations prior to the expiry of their agreements. The main provisions of the law were as follows.

(1) All operating assets within the concession areas would become state property upon the expiry of the concession agreements.

(2) No compensation would be payable in respect of assets which had been fully amortized when a concession was relinquished.

(3) Any concession area which was currently deemed to be inadequately exploited would be liable to be taken over by the state within three years of the entry into force of the reversion law.

(4) Each concessionaire company was required to deposit in a "guaranty fund" administered by the National Bank of Venezuela a security equal to 10 per cent of the value of its operating assets; this would be repayable at the end of the concession period provided that all operating assets were handed over to the state in good condition and that the state had no outstanding financial claims against the company concerned.

(5) No operating assets were henceforth to be changed, moved or dismantled without the written permission of the authorities, who would closely monitor the operations of the concessionaire companies during the period preceding reversion. Infringements of this provision would be punishable with fines of up to $1,000,000.

In August 1971 a law was enacted to bring all natural gas production into state ownership and to give CVP a monopoly over the development of liquefied petroleum gas facilities. CVP was subsequently granted a monopoly over the domestic oil products market under a law of June 1973 (which was to be implemented over a period of three years), while a merchant marine law of 1973 required a specified proportion of oil exports to be carried in Venezuelan tankers. In June 1972 new arrangements were introduced for accelerated tax payments by oil companies, and in October 1972 companies failing to observe government export targets were made liable to tax penalties. In December 1972 oil companies were required to submit annual exploration, production, refining and export programmes for government approval.

In March 1974 Venezuela abandoned its policy of controlled reversion of oil concessions and set up an all-party presidential commission to draft a bill for the early nationalization of the oil industry. The commission's proposals were submitted to the Government at the end of 1974, and a government bill was tabled before Congress in March 1975 after certain of the commission's proposals had been amended (notably through the insertion of a controversial clause permitting the state to enter into joint ventures with private companies after nationalization, subject to the approval of Congress). An "organic law reserving to the state the production and marketing of hydrocarbons" was finally enacted in August 1975, and in the following month a state holding company, Petróleos de Venezuela SA (PDVSA or Petroven), was incorporated to take full control over the oil and gas industry (including the operations of CVP) with effect from Jan. 1, 1976. Pending its formal nationalization the private oil sector was placed under the supervision of government commissioners.

The organic law gave the privately-owned oil companies 60 days to complete their contributions to the "guaranty fund" set up under the July 1971 hydrocarbons reversion law (payments into which had originally been intended to continue in instalments over a number of years). Compensation payments to the companies were to be based on the net book value of their assets as assessed by the Government without negotiation, any sums owed to the state at the time of nationalization being deductible from a company's compensation entitlement and/or its contribution to the guaranty fund. A total compensation entitlement of $1,035.2 million was announced in December 1975, of which $1,012.6 million was divided between 22 principal concession holders (including three small Venezuelan private-sector companies) and the balance between 16 companies holding minority interests in various concession areas. Compensation in respect of oil in stock or in transit was payable in cash within three months of nationalization, and the balance of compensation in government bonds maturing over five years, commencing on Jan. 15, 1977.

The following 11 companies accounted for 94.1 per cent of the total compensation payable: Creole Petroleum Corporation (which was 95.41 per cent owned by Exxon at the time of nationalization)—45.9 per cent; Compañía Shell de Venezuela—24.13 per cent; Mene Grande Oil Company (100 per cent owned by Gulf Oil)—6.68 per cent; International Petroleum (Venezuela) Ltd (through which Exxon held its 25 per cent interest in the operations of Mene Grande)—3.55 per cent; Texaco Maracaibo Inc.—2.98 per cent; Venezuela Sun Oil Company—2.64 per cent; Mobil Oil Company of Venezuela—2.22 per cent; Phillips Petroleum Company—1.92 per cent; Venezuelan Atlantic Refining Company (a subsidiary of Atlantic Richfield)—1.72 per cent; Amoco Venezuela Oil Company—1.23 per cent; and Chevron Oil Company of Venezuela—1.16 per cent. The remaining companies included additional minor subsidiaries of Texaco, Gulf, Sun and Atlantic Richfield as well as subsidiaries of Ashland, Charter, Conoco, Kerr-McGhee, Monsanto, Murphy, Pacific Petroleums (an affiliate of Phillips Petroleum), Petrofina, Tenneco, Texas Petroleum, Ultramar and Union Oil of California. As well as nationalizing the concessionaire companies the Government abrogated the service contracts which had been concluded in July 1971. CVP's contractors were entitled to compensation only in respect of exploration which had resulted in the discovery of commercial oil deposits (none of which had gone into production by the end of 1975).

PDVSA formed 13 new operating subsidiaries, the three largest of which —Lagoven (successor to Creole), Maraven (successor to Shell, with additional responsibility for the former Conoco interests) and Meneven (successor to Mene Grande)—accounted for 82 per cent of total Venezuelan oil production at the beginning of 1976. The remaining 10 companies were based as closely as possible on established divisions of ownership, a major amalgamation of the smaller producing operations being ruled out as unnecessarily disruptive at this point. PDVSA's policy of working initially through existing management structures took account also of the fact that 97 per cent of oil company staff were Venezuelan citizens who had been guaranteed continuity of employment following nationalization. CVP continued to function separately in its existing concession areas with the status of PDVSA's 14th operating subsidiary.

PDVSA also assumed responsibility for Intevep (Instituto Tecnológico Venezolana del Petróleo), a research organization established in 1976, and for the state petrochemical enterprise Pequiven (Petroquímica de Venezuela, originally founded in 1956 as the Instituto Venezolano de Petroquímica). Subsequently established PDVSA subsidiaries included Bariven, which was set up in 1980 to coordinate the oil industry's external purchasing programme, and Interven, which was originally created to oversee the implementation of PDVSA's joint venture with Veba Oel (◊**C13.3.viii**) and later took general responsibility for the management of overseas joint ventures. A separate PDVSA affiliate, Refineria Isla (Curaçao), was formed to manage refining operations in Curaçao under PDVSA's 1985 agreement with the Netherlands Antilles (◊**C13.3.vii**).

The former owners of several nationalized producing companies entered into four-year technical service contracts and renewable two-year export marketing contracts with operating subsidiaries of PDVSA at the beginning of 1976. Under the technical service contracts assistance was provided for production and refining operations on the basis of a per-barrel fee which varied in line with changes in the Venezuelan wholesale import price index (with the proviso that fees could not increase at a faster rate than Venezuelan crude oil prices). Following the expiry of these agreements at the end of 1979 certain companies entered into new contracts, valid initially for periods of up to 30 months, under which fees were separately negotiated for specific tasks on a normal commercial basis without reference to the volume of oil produced. The terms of the largest single contract, between Lagoven and Exxon Services Venezuela Inc., were renegotiated in mid-1981 to eliminate virtually all routine liaison work, the state company having by this point acquired expertise in all but a narrow range of specialized services.

Most of the two-year export marketing contracts between PDVSA and former concessionaire companies were renewed for a further two years at the end of 1977, but at the end of 1979 new one-year contracts were introduced under which the overall volumes of oil sold to the companies were significantly reduced. At the same time less flexibility was permitted in respect of purchasing schedules and price adjustments, while clauses were included to increase the proportion of heavy crudes purchased and to prevent the resale of contract oil on the spot market. Direct export sales by PDVSA to non-traditional customers accounted for about 20 per cent of Venezuela's oil exports in 1976, rising to about 55 per cent in 1980.

In December 1978 the operating structure of the oil industry was rationalized by merging the smaller producing companies into PDVSA's major subsidiaries. Three companies were taken over by Meneven, one by Lagoven and one by Maraven, while CVP (renamed Corpoven) was merged with the remaining five companies. In 1983 various changes were made in the allocation of operating areas in order further to rationalize the geographical distribution of responsibilities between the four consolidated producing subsidiaries. Lagoven accounted for 41.4 per cent of Venezuela's output of crude oil and 47.7 per cent of its operational refining capacity in 1983, the other producing companies' shares being Maraven 28.1 per cent (crude) and 24.6 per cent (refining), Meneven 15.1 per cent (crude) and 15.1 per cent (refining) and Corpoven 15.4 per cent (crude) and 12.6 per cent (refining). The four companies enjoyed a high degree of managerial autonomy and were encouraged to compete with one another in the effective fulfilment of targets laid down by PVDSA. A further reorganization of production operations on June 1, 1986, involved (i) the abolition of Meneven, whose interests were taken over by Corpoven, and (ii) the transfer to Maraven and Lagoven of certain of Corpoven's existing interests.

On the basis of its handling of all stages of the extension of state control over the oil industry PDVSA was widely acknowledged to be one of Venezuela's most efficient companies, being particularly notable among state enterprises for its independent and commercially-oriented style of management. PDVSA's policy objectives were established by the Government, but political involvement in the details of their implementation was actively discouraged in accordance with the company's constitution. The parent company's capital investment funds were derived from a tax-free 10 per cent share of its operating subsidiaries' net income from export sales (these transfers to the parent company being treated as deductible operating costs in determining the tax liability of the subsidiaries). All other income was subject to normal tax treatment, albeit at a somewhat lower rate than that which had applied during the final stages of private control of the oil industry.

(The rate of tax on oil company profits was raised to 63.5 per cent in October 1974 and to 70 per cent in January 1975. In August 1976 the tax rate on the profits of certain smaller private companies whose interests had been nationalized at the end of 1975 was raised to 72 per cent in respect of their outstanding tax obligations, while the tax rate for PDVSA and its operating subsidiaries was fixed at 65.5 per cent for 1976 and 67.7 per cent thereafter. The Government retained its power to determine minimum export values for income tax purposes, although a law enacted in December 1981 provided that these values could not exceed realized export prices by more than 30 per cent in 1982, 25 per cent from 1983 to 1985 and 20 per cent thereafter.)

C13.3.vi—Special supply agreements with neighbouring states

At the beginning of 1976 Venezuela began to supply oil to certain neighbouring countries on favourable financial terms. Under the Puerto Ordaz agreement of December 1975 six Central American states (Costa Rica, El Salvador, Guatemala, Honduras, Nicaragua and Panama) received oil supplies from Venezuela for which there was an initial charge of $6 per barrel, the balance required to make up the prevailing official price being treated as a long-term government-to-government loan. In August 1980 Venezuela and Mexico jointly concluded the San José agreement for the supply of a total of 160,000 bpd to the six states listed above, plus Barbados, Jamaica and the Dominican Republic, an amount equivalent to 30 per cent of receipts from the sale of this oil at official prices being returnable to the importing governments in the form of loans repayable over 10 years at 4 per cent interest. The agreement was extended to cover Belize and Haiti in 1981. In August 1983, however, the worsening financial positions of each of the exporting governments caused them to cut the "concessionary" portion of the oil sales covered by the agreement from 30 per cent to 20 per cent, while requiring new loans to be repaid over 5 years at 8 per cent interest, with the option of conversion to 20 years' repayment at 6 per cent interest if the funds were invested in development projects. It was further announced by Venezuela in July 1984 that half of its future loans would be made in Venezuelan currency and half in US dollars (which had previously been the sole loan currency). Further annual renewals of the agreement in August 1985 and August 1986 covered a total volume of 130,000 bpd.

C13.3.vii—Development of Venezuelan hydrocarbons sector under PDVSA management

The fundamental challenge facing PDVSA in 1976 was to reverse the deterioration which had occurred in Venezuela's position as a major oil producing country during the years preceding nationalization, when the private oil companies had become progressively less inclined to make long-term investments in the industry. Over 90 per cent of Venezuela's producing oilfields had been discovered before 1960 (and the three largest fields before 1930), and an average of only 33 exploratory wells per year had been drilled between 1970 and 1975. An increasing proportion of reservoirs required the use of secondary recovery techniques to maintain operating pressures, and in some cases a need for more advanced recovery processes was likely to arise during the 1980s. Continuous production capacity, which had reached about 4,000,000 bpd by the end of the 1960s, was estimated to have fallen below 2,500,000 bpd by the end of 1975. Export potential was moreover being gradually eroded by a rapid growth in domestic consumption of oil products.

The main aims of PDVSA's initial capital spending programme were (i) to undertake new exploration work, both in the traditional oil-producing regions (i.e. the Maracaibo and Barinas basins in the west, which provided over 80 per cent of Venezuelan output, and the Maturín basin in the east) and in hitherto largely unprospected areas, including the continental shelf; (ii) to achieve improved recovery factors in existing oilfields, particularly those producing lighter crudes (only about 20 per cent of the country's proved reserves in the late 1970s being made up of oils lighter than 29° API, while oils heavier than 22° API accounted for over 50 per cent of the total); (iii) to initiate research into the feasibility of exploiting the 45,000 sq km Orinoco oil sands belt—one of the world's largest known untapped hydrocarbon deposits—which contained an estimated 1,200,000 million barrels of extra-heavy (6° to 14°) crude of which over 200,000 million barrels were believed to be recoverable by steam injection techniques; (iv) to expand the country's natural gas processing facilities and distribution network; and (v) to upgrade refining facilities in order to achieve a higher percentage output of lighter products from a higher percentage input of heavier crudes.

By 1981 a major expansion of exploration and development activity had increased the country's proved oil reserves by nearly 10 per cent since nationalization (although the structure of reserves continued to shift in favour of heavy crudes, which constituted over 60 per cent of the total in 1982). Moreover, initial evaluation work in the Orinoco belt had led to the formulation of plans to invest $8,000 million in developing technologically advanced extraction and treatment facilities by 1988, the relatively high production costs involved being seen as viable in the light of the increases in world oil prices in 1979–80. During 1982, however, the downturn in demand for OPEC oil caused Venezuela's crude oil production to fall below 2,000,000 bpd for the first time since 1954, while combined exports of crude oil and products, at 1,550,000 bpd, were the lowest since 1950. Future investment plans were accordingly reappraised on the basis of reduced revenue forecasts, resulting in the postponement of several costly Orinoco belt projects, the modification of various other investment programmes and a cutback in the current operating budgets of PDVSA's subsidiaries.

In September 1982 the Government ordered PDVSA's accumulated reserve funds (held externally in US dollars) to be transferred to the company's account (in Venezuelan currency) at the Central Bank, thus effectively increasing the Government's foreign exchange reserves by an estimated $6,200 million and strengthening Venezuela's position in debt rescheduling negotiations with foreign creditors. The company's current foreign exchange earnings from oil exports were likewise required to be repatriated until further notice, although up to $300,000,000 could be held abroad to meet immediate requirements. Some $1,750 million of PDVSA's funds was used in December 1982 to repay government debts to state-owned banks, PDVSA being obliged to purchase an equivalent amount of public debt bonds maturing over two to four years.

In the light of these developments PDVSA, which had started to draw on its reserves to finance capital spending earlier in 1982, was obliged to make a further downward revision of its cash-flow projections and to reconsider existing plans to increase Venezuela's crude oil production capacity (2,551,000 bpd in 1983) to 2,800,000 bpd by 1988. Following representations by the company the Government agreed in late 1983 to bring forward the maturity dates of PDVSA's public debt bonds and to require the Central Bank to give priority to the fulfilment of the company's budgeted foreign exchange requirements. Although these measures enabled the company to announce that investment was to be maintained at its 1983 level during 1984, it was noted in PDVSA's 1983 annual report that no significant expansion of upstream or downstream production capacity could now be expected in the period 1984–89, with adverse implications for the company's ability "to continue adapting to market changes that might occur in the future".

Notwithstanding its adoption of less ambitious development targets, PDVSA had made important progress in all of its main areas of activity when it completed its first decade of operations in 1985. Proved reserves of both oil and gas were about 45 per cent greater than at the start of 1976, with a number of recent discoveries still under evaluation. These included major deposits of light and medium crude situated in a Corpoven exploration area about 200 km south-east of Barinas. An even larger discovery of light crude was announced by Lagoven in February 1986 in the Maturín basin, about 500 km east of Caracas. By 1985 the recovery rates for extra-heavy crudes from several established fields in the Maracaibo basin had been doubled (to about 25 per cent) through the introduction of steam-soak techniques, while Orinoco belt production (of crudes ranging from 6° to 20° API gravity) was running at up to 100,000 bpd using a variety of advanced recovery techniques. PDVSA stated in 1985 that it had acquired sufficient technical expertise to develop a capacity of 5,000,000 bpd in the Orinoco belt, given a favourable market environment.

A large gas processing plant was brought into production near the main eastern oilfields in late 1985, and began exporting LPG to Japan in 1986 under an initial one-year contract with Marubeni for the supply of 200,000 tonnes of propane. PDVSA's main gas development project for the second half of the 1980s involved the construction of a new gathering and distribution system (Nurgas) centred on an 800-km east-west trunk pipeline. As well as supplying fuel requirements in Caracas and other population centres, the Nurgas system would enable gas from the eastern oilfields to be injected into low-pressure oil wells in the Lake Maracaibo region. Scheduled for completion in 1989–90, the system was expected to add the equivalent of more than 100,000 bpd of oil to Venezuela's domestic energy supply, thereby increasing the availability of oil for export.

Venezuela's refining capacity was reduced by 215,000 bpd (15 per cent) during the first half of the 1980s through the shutting down of four of the country's older plants and the completion of major modernization programmes at two other plants, including Lagoven's 600,000 bpd Amuay refinery (the largest of the eight refineries which continued to operate). Plans to upgrade two further refineries were shelved following PDVSA's 1982 review of investment priorities. The modernization work enabled PDVSA to bring the supply of products much closer to prevailing patterns of demand on the domestic and export markets while enhancing its ability to respond flexibly to future shifts in demand patterns. The share of the main light and middle-distillate products in PDVSA's overall refinery yield increased from 35 per cent to 61.5 per cent between 1977 and 1984, while the share of fuel oils fell from 60 per cent to 31.4 per cent over the same period. The proportion of residual fractions in Venezuela's total product exports fell from 73 per cent in 1977 to 44.5 per cent in 1984.

The implementation since the late 1970s of refinery upgrading projects in oil-importing countries had meanwhile enabled PDVSA to align Venezuela's relative export volumes of light and heavy crudes more closely with the structure of the country's proved reserves, and grades heavier than 22° API accounted for 72 per cent of total crude exports in 1984, compared with 34 per cent in 1977. The proportion of refined products in total export volume was normally around one-third after 1982, although considerable fluctuations occurred in the second half of 1985, when the first ever monthly excess of product exports (53 per cent) over crude exports (47 per cent) was reported in September.

With effect from Oct. 1, 1985, PDVSA took out a five-year lease on Curaçao's 320,000 bpd export refinery, newly acquired by the Government of the Netherlands Antilles from Royal Dutch/Shell, which had found it impossible to operate the plant at a profit at a time of worldwide overcapacity in the refining industry. (Similar problems had led Exxon to proceed with the closure of its 400,000 bpd Aruba refinery in March 1985 after the Venezuelan Government's rejection of proposals that the plant should be supplied with preferentially priced crude as a means of preserving a guaranteed export outlet while saving the Aruban economy from the damaging impact of a closure.) The Curaçao leasing arrangement, which was open to renewal for two-year periods after 1990, entailed basic annual payments of $11,000,000 by PDVSA, which intended to run up to 150,000 bpd of light and medium crudes through the refinery and expected to gain some benefits in terms of access to processing capabilities complementary to those available in Venezuela (although it was acknowledged that capital investments would be required to improve the plant's economic viability). PDVSA would also enjoy the advantages of Curaçao's deep-water tanker terminal, capable of accommodating far larger vessels than were handled by Venezuela's own oil ports.

PDVSA's principal petrochemical interests were a complex at Morón, whose main product was fertilizers for the domestic market, and a complex at El Tablazo which produced fertilizers for the export market and olefins for use by the domestic petrochemical-based manufacturing sector (which consisted of various partnerships between public and private capital, in most of which Pequiven was a minority shareholder). The establishment of Pequiven as a subsidiary of PDVSA in March 1978 followed 21 years of gross mismanagement of the petrochemical industry by successive political appointees (the estimated cumulative losses of the Instituto Venezolano de Petroquímica being in the region of $910,000,000 at the time of its dissolution). PDVSA agreed to assume responsibility for the industry on condition that the IVP's debts were settled by the Government and that new investment funds were provided by the Government over a 10-year period out of the petroleum royalties received from PDVSA. A major restructuring programme was subsequently carried out under which technical problems were identified and appropriate remedial action taken, while unprofitable operations were closed down or transferred to other state enterprises. The olefins plant at El Tablazo, which had previously operated for only about two months since its completion in 1973, was brought into production in mid-1980, and in 1983 the state-owned petrochemical complexes traded profitably for the first time in their history despite problems caused by a shortage of gas feedstocks arising from the cutback in oil production.

It was widely predicted during 1982–83 that Venezuela's economic problems would lead to a greater degree of government control over the operational management of PDVSA, the transfer of the company's reserves to the Central Bank in September 1982 being seen as the first stage of a "politicization" of the oil industry. This trend continued in August 1983 when Dr Humberto Calderón Berti (hitherto Minister of Energy and Mines in the Christian Social Government of President Luis Herrera Campíns) was appointed president of PDVSA on the retirement of Gen. Rafael Alfonzo Ravard. Gen. Ravard, who had headed PDVSA since its formation, had made major efforts to ensure that the company was run on a strictly commercial basis and had in 1981 strongly resisted government proposals that PDVSA should assume a wider role in the economy by adopting purchasing policies which discriminated in favour of Venezuelan industries and by financing infrastructural development projects in oil-producing areas of the country.

One of the first decisions of the Democratic Action Government which took office in February 1984 was to remove Dr Calderón Berti from the presidency of PDVSA and to appoint in his place a career oilman, Dr Brigido Natera Contreras (hitherto the president of Lagoven). Other recent political appointees were replaced in a subsequent round of management changes which was seen as a move to restore the company's operational independence. The new Government also improved the financial basis of PDVSA's operations by bringing the domestic price of regular-grade gasoline closer to the prevailing world market price. The main effect of gasoline price increases ordered by the previous Government in March 1982 had been on the premium grade, while the price of the regular grade had risen to only about one-third of the world market price. Prior to March 1982 Venezuela's government-controlled gasoline prices were the lowest in any country except Saudi

Arabia, with the result that PDVSA's domestic sales revenues were severely restricted while the availability of oil for export was reduced by a rapid growth in domestic consumption. Gen. Ravard had estimated in 1981 that the average selling price of refined products on the domestic market was only $5 per barrel, equivalent to a subsidy exceeding $100,000,000 per year, and had argued that if this subsidy was to be maintained it should be funded directly by the Government rather than indirectly by PDVSA. The combined impact of price increases and economic recession had reduced Venezuela's oil consumption to an estimated 325,000 bpd by 1985, compared with a peak level of 390,000 bpd in 1981–82.

C13.3.viii—PDVSA investments in overseas joint ventures

In December 1982 PDVSA announced its first foreign investment, involving the purchase of a 50 per cent shareholding in two West German refineries owned by Veba Oel, which were transferred to a new joint-venture company called Ruhr Oel. PDVSA undertook to supply at least 100,000 bpd of crude for processing by the refineries, while Veba Oel undertook to market their output of products. In the longer term, the two companies agreed to co-operate in the development of new processes to refine extra-heavy crudes, with a view to the eventual construction by Ruhr Oel of facilities capable of handling output from the Orinoco belt. PDVSA's decision to invest in West Germany (at an estimated cost of between $200,000,000 and $250,000,000) caused some political controversy in Venezuela, which was revived in early 1984 when it became known that the effective netbacks on crude refined under the agreement were lower than Venezuela's official export prices for the same grades. About one-fifth of the crude processed on Venezuela's account by Ruhr Oel was in fact supplied by the Soviet Union under a bilateral co-operation agreement of November 1976 whereby Venezuelan oil was supplied to "Soviet customers in the Caribbean region" (i.e. Cuba) in return for an equivalent supply of Soviet oil to Venezuelan customers in Europe, thus reducing freight costs.

Despite continuing domestic criticism of the original Ruhr Del deal, PDVSA embarked on a major expansion of overseas downstream interests in early 1986 in order to secure new guaranteed export outlets. Co-operation with Veba Oel was to be broadened through PDVSA's acquisition of 50 per cent of Veba's interests in two further West German refineries, in a West German olefins plant and in certain European oil pipelines. PDVSA was to invest a total of $55,000,000 over five years, and would secure West German outlets for an additional 50,000 bpd of crude.

The acquisition at a cost of $20,000,000 of a 50 per cent shareholding in the Swedish company Nynäs Petroleum (principally a manufacturer of lubricating oils) was expected to assure PDVSA of an outlet for at least 40,000 bpd of heavy crude. The acquisition of a 50 per cent interest in the US company Citgo Petroleum, at a cost of $300,000,000, would provide PDVSA with access to a guaranteed market for 130,000 bpd of crude, with an option to increase deliveries to 200,000 bpd. A further US venture, announced in April 1986, involved the purchase for $30,000,000 of a half-share in a Texan oil refinery owned by Champlin Petroleum. The refinery was expected to take 160,000 bpd of Venezuelan crude, with product distribution through Champlin's own network.

Formal documentation finalizing most of the above transactions remained to be executed in mid-1986. There was some political opposition within Venezuela to PDSVA's so-called "internationalization" strategy (and much criticism of the cost of the Citgo deal), although the Government was able to present a strong case for adopting such a strategy in the present buyer's market for oil. An agreement in principle by PVDSA to purchase a half-share worth $11,000,000 in Steuart Petroleum, a US distributor of refined products, was cancelled without explanation in June 1986, when it was stated that Steuart expected to continue to purchase up to 25,000 bpd of Venezuelan products under existing arm's-length arrangements.

OPEC AND THE CHANGING BALANCE OF WORLD OIL POWER, 1960—86

D1—1960 to 1970

D1.1—The Formation of OPEC

The earliest attempts to co-ordinate certain aspects of the policies of a group of oil-exporting countries were made within the framework of the League of Arab States, which in 1948 (three years after its formation) secured the shutting down of the Iraq Petroleum Company's export pipeline to Haifa (◊**C6.3.i**) in accordance with the League's policy of banning the export of Arab oil to Israel. In 1951 the League formed an Arab Oil Experts Committee, one of whose main functions was to monitor the enforcement of the embargo on supplies to Israel. In 1954 it was decided to establish a permanent Petroleum Department concerned with all aspects of Arab oil policy. The League's Petroleum Department organized 10 Arab Petroleum Congresses between 1959 and 1978, at which representatives of Arab governments and organizations, observers from non-Arab oil-exporting countries and officials of foreign oil companies met to discuss "the technical, economic, legal and political aspects of oil production".

The first Arab Petroleum Congress, held in Cairo in April 1959, provided a forum for the assertion of host governments' rights to exercise greater control over the exploitation of their hydrocarbon resources (and to be consulted before changes were made in exporting companies' posted prices). In retrospect, however, it is clear that the formal proceedings of the Congress were of less significance than a series of informal meetings which took place between a number of Arab delegates and non-Arab observers. The key participants in these meetings were Shaikh Abdullah Tariki of Saudi Arabia (a leading campaigner for greater host-government involvement in the management of the principal Middle Eastern concession areas ◊**C11.3.iv**) and Dr Juan Pablo Pérez Alfonzo of Venezuela (the main architect of his country's programme of oil industry reforms ◊**C13.3.iii, C13.3.iv**). Other participants were the (Iraqi) director of the Arab League's Petroleum Department, officials from Iran and Kuwait, and a representative of the United Arab Republic (Egypt/Syria), which was host to the Congress. The outcome of these meetings was an agreement (full details of which were not publicly revealed until 1961) to recommend the formal establishment of a "petroleum consultation commission" to promote co-operation on issues of common interest to the Governments of Saudi Arabia, Iran, Iraq, Kuwait and Venezuela.

Venezuela was at this time deeply concerned at the restrictions recently imposed on the growth of its oil exports to the US market (◊**A4.10.ii**). These raised the prospect of increased competition with low-cost Middle Eastern oil in non-US markets, notwithstanding the major oil companies' latest reduction in Venezuelan posted prices (announced less than two weeks before the opening of the Cairo petroleum congress ◊**A4.10.iii**). Venezuela's immediate aim in seeking closer co-operation with the Middle Eastern producers was to work towards an agreement on controlled production growth with a view to avoiding unrestricted competition for markets on a scale which, while benefiting the Middle Eastern producers in terms of market share, would harm the interests of all host governments by cutting their unit revenues as prices were eroded. Dr Pérez Alfonzo made it clear that Venezuela would itself accept a lower than average rate of export growth, and that his main concern was to secure wider support for the principle of co-ordinated control over the supply of a non-renewable resource in order to bring the maximum long-term benefit to the producing countries.

The theoretical framework of Dr Pérez Alfonzo's arguments was strongly endorsed by Shaikh Tariki on a personal basis, although Middle Eastern governments (particularly that of Iran, whose market share had fallen substantially since the nationalization crisis of the early 1950s ◊**C5.3.i**) were less convinced of the benefits of taking a long-term approach to the issue of output levels. It was, however, perceived that formal co-operation with Venezuela would enable Middle Eastern governments to press for improved financial terms from their main concession holders with a view to achieving parity with Venezuelan levels of oil taxation. Accordingly, it was agreed during the April 1959 discussions that such a strategy should feature among the aims of the proposed consultation commission.

During the succeeding year Dr Pérez Alfonzo and Shaikh Tariki worked assiduously to bring about the establishment of the commission. In May 1960 they issued a joint declaration calling for an "international petroleum agreement" between the five largest exporting countries, the primary aim of which should be to gear the expansion of aggregate productive capacity to the anticipated growth in export demand. It was envisaged that each participating country's share of incremental production would be prorated according to its share of aggregate reserves, adjusted as necessary to take account of special national circumstances. The major oil companies responded to this initiative by implying, both in publicity campaigns and through contacts with Middle Eastern governments, that the proposed agreement was merely a Venezuelan stratagem to maintain its market share by holding back the output of competing exporters. This argument was most persuasive in Iran, where the misgivings of the Shah remained the greatest obstacle to the conclusion of a viable agreement. The catalyst which finally brought OPEC into being was the announcement in August 1960 of reductions in Middle Eastern posted prices (◊**A4.10.iii**). This caused bitter resentment on the part of the region's host governments (expressed with particular forcefulness in Iran) in view of the producing companies' failure to hold any prior consultations with them.

A meeting held in Baghdad at the invitation of the Iraq Government from Sept. 10 to 14, 1960, resulted in agreement to establish OPEC with Iran, Iraq, Kuwait, Saudi Arabia and Venezuela as its founder members. A delegate from Qatar also attended the meeting with observer status. The preamble to the three resolutions adopted by the inaugural meeting of the OPEC Conference drew attention to the following points: (i) "that the members are implementing much-needed development programmes to be financed mainly from income derived from their petroleum exports"; (ii) "that members must rely on petroleum income to a large degree in order to balance their annual national budgets"; (iii) "that petroleum is a wasting asset and to the extent that it is depleted must be replaced by other assets"; (iv) "that all nations of the world, in order to maintain and improve their standards of living, must rely almost entirely on petroleum as a primary source of energy generation"; and (v) "that any fluctuation in the price of petroleum necessarily affects the implementation of the members' [development] programmes and results in a dislocation detrimental not only to their own economies but also to those of all consuming nations".

Resolution I–1 stated:

"(1) That members can no longer remain indifferent to the attitude heretofore adopted by the oil companies in effecting price modifications.

"(2) That members shall demand that oil companies maintain their prices steady and free from all unnecessary fluctuations; that members shall endeavour, by all means available to them, to restore present prices to the levels prevailing before the reductions; that they shall ensure that if any new circumstances arise which in the estimation of the oil companies necessitate price modifications, the said companies shall enter into consultations with the member or members affected in order fully to explain the circumstances.

"(3) That members shall study and formulate a system to ensure the stabilization of prices by, among other means, the regulation of production, with due regard to the interests of the producing and of the consuming nations and to the necessity of securing (i) a steady income to the producing countries, (ii) an efficient, economic and regular supply of this source of energy to consuming nations, and (iii) a fair return on their capital to those investing in the petroleum industry.

"(4) That if as a result of the application of any unanimous decision of this Conference any sanctions are employed, directly or indirectly, by any interested company against one or more of the member countries, no other member shall accept any offer of a beneficial treatment, whether in the form of an increase in exports or an improvement in prices, which may be made to it by any such company or companies with the intention of discouraging the application of the unanimous decision reached by the Conference."

Resolution I–2 provided for the formation by the participating countries of a permanent Organization of the Petroleum Exporting Countries, "for regular consultation among its members with a view to co-ordinating and unifying the policies of the members and determining among other matters the attitude which members should adopt whenever circumstances such as those referred to in paragraph (2) of Resolution I–1 have arisen". It also provided for (i) the future admission as a new member of "any country with a substantial net export of crude petroleum", subject to the unanimous approval of the founder members; (ii) the Organization to pursue as its principal aim "the unification of petroleum policies for the member countries and the determination of the best means for safeguarding the interests of member countries individually and collectively"; (iii) the holding of meetings of the Conference at least twice a year; and (iv) the appointment of a subcommittee to prepare proposals for the establishment of a permanent secretariat.

The inaugural resolutions were ratified by the governments of the participating countries in September 1960, having apparently been phrased in non-controversial terms in order to ensure that prompt ratification would be forthcoming, particularly from Iran. An intergovernmental treaty establishing OPEC was registered on Nov. 6, 1960. Four days earlier the major oil companies had obliquely responded to the formation of OPEC by making it known, through informal communications with the director of the Arab League's Petroleum Department, that they had decided not to make any future reductions in posted prices without the prior agreement of host governments. (The companies whose postings had been reduced by the greatest margin in August 1960 had already fallen into line with the rather smaller cuts made by other companies, this realignment having been announced on the last day of OPEC's inaugural meeting ◊**A4.10.iii.**)

337

Table 19 — World oil production, 1960 to 1970 (million tonnes)

	1960	1961	1962	1963	1964	1965	1966	1967	1968	1969	1970
Middle East	261.8	280.3	308.1	338.3	380.5	416.1	462.6	495.8	556.9	615.4	691.7
North America	410.5	423.8	436.7	452.2	461.7	475.8	507.2	541.7	564.9	577.3	609.0
USSR/Eastern Europe/China	167.2	186.0	207.8	228.5	247.9	268.8	294.0	316.2	341.8	366.1	398.8
Africa	13.8	24.4	39.2	57.7	82.9	107.6	136.2	151.4	196.1	249.2	299.9
Latin America/Caribbean	194.9	203.4	221.9	226.8	235.1	241.4	239.6	256.0	263.8	264.9	272.7
Asia*/Australasia	27.1	27.6	30.2	30.0	31.1	33.0	35.2	39.0	45.3	54.1	67.6
Western Europe†	15.3	16.8	17.7	19.1	21.6	22.2	22.2	22.7	23.0	23.6	22.8
World total	1,090.6	1,162.3	1,261.6	1,352.6	1,460.8	1,564.9	1,697.0	1,822.8	1,991.8	2,150.6	2,362.5
Total as thousand bpd	*21,980*	*23,485*	*25,510*	*27,405*	*29,520*	*31,745*	*34,450*	*37,035*	*40,380*	*43,820*	*48,125*

*Excluding China.
†Including Yugoslavia.

Table 20 — World oil consumption, 1960 to 1970 (million tonnes)

	1960	1961	1962	1963	1964	1965	1966	1967	1968	1969	1970
North America	500.8	522.0	542.3	560.3	578.7	603.9	633.7	657.5	701.6	736.9	767.6
Western Europe*	196.4	228.0	263.6	303.3	344.5	388.7	425.9	460.3	505.2	565.5	627.0
USSR/Eastern Europe/China	144.3	156.0	174.8	192.7	206.9	222.7	242.6	266.5	283.8	307.8	345.4
Japan	34.1	41.0	48.8	62.6	75.2	87.9	100.0	122.9	142.7	169.0	199.1
Latin America/Caribbean	79.6	86.0	83.7	89.9	94.0	99.2	106.8	110.6	118.9	126.8	134.9
Asia†/Australasia	42.2	47.0	50.6	55.2	61.2	64.1	70.1	83.7	95.0	108.9	116.1
Middle East	29.8	31.0	31.7	32.8	33.0	35.3	39.3	38.9	41.1	47.2	49.5
Africa	18.8	21.0	21.9	23.5	27.0	28.5	30.9	34.7	36.1	38.8	42.1
World total	1,046.0	1,132.0	1,217.4	1,320.3	1,420.5	1,530.3	1,649.3	1,775.1	1,924.4	2,100.9	2,281.7
Total as thousand bpd	*21,100*	*22,890*	*24,760*	*26,880*	*28,835*	*31,120*	*33,550*	*36,125*	*39,100*	*42,800*	*46,440*
Share of oil in world primary energy consumption‡ (per cent)	31.2	32.7	34.0	35.7	37.2	38.8	39.6	41.5	42.0	42.9	44.1

*Including Yugoslavia.
†Excluding China and Japan.
‡Excluding non-commercial fuels.

Table 21 — OPEC oil production, 1960 to 1970 (million tonnes)

(Note – data in parentheses indicate non-membership of OPEC during the year in question. Sub-total A relates to the then current member countries, sub-total B to current non-members and the grand total to the full membership as at end-1975.)

	1960	1961	1962	1963	1964	1965	1966	1967	1968	1969	1970
Algeria	(8.6)	(15.8)	(20.7)	(23.9)	(26.5)	(26.6)	(34.2)	(39.1)	(42.9)	44.5	48.5
Ecuador	(0.4)	(0.4)	(0.3)	(0.3)	(0.4)	(0.4)	(0.3)	(0.3)	(0.2)	(0.2)	(0.2)
Gabon	(0.8)	(0.7)	(0.8)	(0.9)	(1.0)	(1.3)	(1.4)	(3.5)	(4.6)	(5.0)	(5.4)
Indonesia	(20.6)	(21.4)	23.1	22.5	23.3	24.0	23.5	25.2	29.7	37.1	42.2
Iran	52.6	59.4	66.0	73.1	85.4	95.0	105.2	129.6	141.8	168.1	191.3
Iraq	47.5	49.0	49.2	56.7	61.7	64.4	68.1	60.2	73.9	74.9	76.9
Kuwait	81.9	82.7	92.2	97.2	106.7	109.1	114.4	115.2	122.1	131.0	139.1
Libya	—	(0.9)	8.7	22.4	41.4	58.9	72.4	84.1	125.7	149.9	159.8
Nigeria	(0.9)	(2.8)	(3.5)	(3.8)	(6.0)	(13.5)	(20.4)	(15.6)	(7.2)	(26.4)	(52.9)
Qatar	(8.2)	8.3	8.8	9.1	10.2	11.1	13.8	15.5	16.3	17.0	17.7
Saudi Arabia	62.1	69.2	75.8	80.5	86.2	100.6	118.8	129.0	140.9	150.2	178.0
UAE: Abu Dhabi†	—	—	(0.8)	(2.6)	(9.0)	(13.5)	(17.3)	18.3	23.9	28.9	33.4
UAE: Dubai†	—	—	—	—	—	—	—	—	—	(0.5)	(4.3)
Venezuela	148.8	152.3	167.6	170.1	177.4	182.2	177.0	186.1	189.9	188.7	195.2
Neutral Zone*	7.3	9.5	13.0	16.7	18.8	19.4	21.7	21.5	21.0	21.7	26.0
Sub-total A	400.2	430.4	504.4	548.3	611.1	664.7	714.9	784.7	885.2	1,012.0	1,108.1
Sub-total B	(39.5)	(42.0)	(26.1)	(31.5)	(42.9)	(55.3)	(73.6)	(58.5)	(54.9)	(32.1)	(62.8)
GRAND TOTAL (A+B)	439.7	472.4	530.5	579.8	654.0	720.0	788.5	843.2	940.1	1,044.1	1,170.9
Grand total as thousand bpd	8,670	9,350	10,530	11,560	13,010	14,405	15,815	16,910	18,845	21,035	23,625
Sub-total A as percentage of world total	36.7	37.0	39.9	40.5	41.8	42.5	42.1	43.0	44.4	47.0	46.9
Grand total as percentage of world total	40.3	40.6	42.0	42.8	44.7	46.0	46.4	46.2	47.2	48.5	49.5

*Production shared between Saudi Arabia and Kuwait.

†NB — the United Arab Emirates was not formed until 1971; Abu Dhabi and Dubai are grouped together here to facilitate comparison with later years' statistics.

339

D1.2—Resolutions of 2nd and 3rd Meetings of OPEC Conference

The 2nd meeting of the OPEC Conference, held in Caracas from Jan. 15 to 21, 1961, was mainly concerned with the establishment of a permanent organizational structure and the identification of matters on which research should be undertaken in order to strengthen OPEC's position in any future negotiations with the major oil companies.

Resolution II–4 adopted by the Caracas meeting admitted Qatar as the sixth member of OPEC. Resolution II–5 created a Board of Governors to manage the affairs of the Organization, and provided that the chairman of the Board should also hold the office of Secretary-General. Resolution II–6 set out the initial statute of the Organization, which outlined the functions of the Conference (the supreme authority) and of the Board of Governors and the Secretariat. The Secretariat was to be staffed with due regard to ensuring "an adequate geographical distribution among members", although the responsibilities of Secretariat personnel were to be "not national but exclusively international". Resolution II–8 established the initial OPEC budget (to be funded equally by the five founder members) and provided that all member countries should contribute equally to future budgets. Resolution II–9 appointed Dr Fuad Rouhani of Iran as OPEC's first Secretary-General, while Resolution II–10 provided that the Secretariat should be located in Geneva.

Resolution II–11 required the Board of Governors to "prepare a comprehensive study, based on objective research and consultation with experts, concerning the economics of investment in the oil industry by concession-holding companies, in comparison with investment in other enterprises in different countries". Resolution II–12 required each member country to supply documentation regarding "its position in the matter of determination of prices at which its petroleum is paid for by exporting companies, and also the appropriate procedure in regard to the settlement of disputes arising on that matter"; such documentation was to be referred by the Board of Governors to "competent legal advisers for consideration and recommendation as to steps which may be taken in each case with the object of restoring prices to the levels which members consider justified and appropriate". Resolution II–13 required the Board of Governors to carry out a detailed study of the current structure of prices in the world oil market "in order to arrive at a just pricing formula, supported by a study of international proration, should that prove essential".

Resolution II–14 drew attention to "the matter of quotas and other restrictions imposed on the import of oil by friendly countries in order to protect their domestic production and reserves" (i.e. the current US import controls, which were of particular concern to Venezuela). It expressed the hope that consultations would be held with OPEC members on this issue "in order to arrive at satisfactory solutions and thus promote mutual understanding for the protection of the interests both of exporting and importing countries". Resolution II–15 drew attention to "the curtailment of activities in the development of the Venezuelan petroleum industry" (i.e. the fall in the major oil companies' investment in new exploration work which had followed the Venezuelan tax increase of 1958 ◊**C13.3.iv**) and "acknowledged that collective measures should be adopted by OPEC members, in accordance with paragraph (4) of Resolution I–1, to remedy the situation". Resolution II–16 referred to current "difficulties" in negotiations between "some of the members" and their concession holders (i.e. principally in Iraq's current negotiations with the IPC group ◊**C6.3.iii**) and placed on record the OPEC Conference's "earnest hope" that the companies concerned would bring such negotiations to a "prompt and satisfactory conclusion".

The 3rd meeting of the OPEC Conference, originally scheduled to open on Aug. 19, 1961, was postponed for two months in the aftermath of Iraq's assertion of a claim to sovereignty over Kuwait (◊C7.2). Dr Rouhani, the then OPEC Secretary-General, denied that the postponement was politically motivated, stating that the Iraq Government had requested an opportunity to complete its latest round of negotiations with IPC prior to the next Conference meeting. However, when the 3rd meeting was eventually convened in Tehran from Oct. 28 to Nov. 1, 1961, Iraq refused to attend, although its dispute with IPC remained on the agenda of the meeting.

Resolution III–18 expressed OPEC's "full support for Iraq's position in safeguarding its legitimate interests" in the dispute with IPC and "urged the foreign oil companies operating in the territories of OPEC member countries to realize that a spirit of true understanding between them and the member countries is indispensable to securing those healthy conditions in the world oil industry which the furtherance of social justice and international co-operation demands". Resolution III–19 established a petroleum industry information centre within the Secretariat, whose resources were to be made available to member countries as required. Resolution III–20 noted the work of the Venezuelan co-ordinating commission for the conservation and marketing of hydrocarbons (◊C13.3.iv), "particularly in preventing the weakening of crude oil prices", and inaugurated an OPEC study into "the manner in which appropriate and uniform controls may be set up by all the members for the achievement of similar results". Resolution III–26 provided for a study of areas in which it was practicable and desirable to work for "uniformity in the practices, methods and techniques (such as, but not limited to, those of accounting) adopted in the operation of the petroleum industry in different member countries". Resolution III–28 provided for an investigation into reports "that crude oil produced in member countries and elsewhere has been utilized by some oil companies and oil agencies to weaken the price structure of oil in the world market".

D1.3—OPEC and the Royalty-Expensing Issue, 1962 to 1964

D1.3.i—Launching of OPEC campaign for royalty-expensing (1962) – Inconclusive negotiations with producing companies (1963)

Iraq's boycott of OPEC meetings continued throughout 1962 and was not lifted until the Iraqi regime was overthrown in a military coup in February 1963. Indonesia (whose Government was concerned to strengthen its position in current negotiations on the termination of its existing concession agreements ◊C4.3.i) and Libya (whose Government had recently failed to improve its revenue entitlement in respect of oil exported by independent producing companies ◊C8.3.i) were both admitted to OPEC membership on June 4, 1962.

The 4th meeting of the OPEC Conference was held in Geneva in two sessions, from April 5 to 8 and from June 4 to 8, 1962. The main purposes of the intervening break were to allow delegates to consult their governments on various agenda items and to allow the Secretariat to prepare additional briefing papers on key issues under consideration. Indonesia and Libya submitted their membership applications during the break, the existing delegates being authorized by their governments to approve the immediate accession of the two countries upon resumption of the meeting.

The 4th Conference meeting considered the results of several of the studies which had been commissioned by the two previous meetings. It recommended member countries to seek negotiations with their respective producing companies with a view to securing specific improvements in their unit revenue entitlements.

The fiscal changes proposed by OPEC related solely to the Middle Eastern system of oil taxation (◊A4.6), but were of direct interest to Venezuela insofar as their implementation would bring the tax-paid cost of Middle Eastern crude closer to that of Venezuelan crude.

Resolution IV–32 recommended "that member countries should forthwith enter into negotiations with the oil companies concerned, and/or any other authority or body deemed appropriate, with a view to ensuring that oil produced in member countries shall be paid for on the basis of posted prices not lower than those which applied prior to August 1960". It was decided that "if within a reasonable period after the commencement of the negotiations no satisfactory arrangement is reached, the member countries shall consult with each other with a view to taking such steps as they deem appropriate in order to restore crude oil prices to the level which prevailed prior to Aug. 9, 1960". The Board of Governors was to undertake a comprehensive study designed to assist member countries to "jointly formulate a rational price structure to guide their long-term price policy", with particular reference to "the linking of crude oil prices to an index of prices of goods which the member countries need to import".

Resolution IV–33 stated "(i) that the companies enjoying in member countries the right of extracting petroleum, which is a wasting asset, should, in conformity with the principle recognized and the practice observed generally in the world, compensate the countries for the intrinsic value of such petroleum quite apart from their obligations falling under the heading of income tax; (ii) that, under the arrangements at present in force between the member countries and the oil companies, in general no compensation is paid for the intrinsic value of petroleum, royalty or 'stated payment' commitments being treated as credits against income-tax liabilities; and (iii) that the member countries' right to receive compensation for the intrinsic value of petroleum is incontestable". ("Stated payments" were the Iranian equivalent of the standard Middle Eastern royalty ◊C5.3.ii.) The resolution recommended that "each member country affected should approach the company or companies concerned with a view to working out a formula whereunder royalty payments shall be fixed at a uniform rate which members consider equitable, and shall not be treated as a credit against income tax liability".

Resolution IV–34 stated "(i) that neither the OPEC members nor the companies operating in their countries participate in the worldwide marketing operations of the oil companies; (ii) that the bulk of the crude oil produced by the operating companies is marketed through their parents or parent affiliates with no brokerage charges being incurred; and (iii) that one of the member countries [i.e. Kuwait, which had abolished all marketing allowances in 1955 ◊C7.3.i] makes no contribution whatsoever to the selling expenses of the oil companies". It was therefore recommended that "the member countries affected should take measures to eliminate any contribution to the marketing expenses of the companies concerned". Resolution IV–35 recommended that other OPEC member countries should create national institutions with functions similar to those of the Venezuelan co-ordinating commission for the conservation and marketing of hydrocarbons (◊C13.3.iv).

A statement issued by Dr Rouhani after the formal ratification of the resolutions of the 4th Conference meeting emphasized that OPEC was not seeking a confrontation with the major oil companies, and that the resolutions were "in no way motivated by any unfriendly sentiments". The statement went on: "Rather, the discussions contemplated will seek a co-ordination of the interests of the exporting countries with those of the oil companies, which play such an important part in investment and in production and distribution operations, as well as with those of the consuming nations, in a spirit of complete fairness and realism. We are certain that the oil companies, which are especially conscious of their international responsibilities, will react in the same spirit to this manifestation of good will on the part of the exporting countries."

Between July and November 1962 OPEC set out the basis of its claims in three detailed "explanatory memorandums", whereupon the two producing companies with which it was hoped to negotiate new standard terms in the first instance (Aramco in Saudi Arabia and the IOP consortium in Iran) presented their respective host governments with equally detailed rebuttals of many of OPEC's arguments. In justification of its claim for the cancellation of the 1960 cuts in Middle Eastern posted prices, OPEC stressed that the overall decline in postings between the end of 1953 and the end of 1960 (which it put at 7.5 per cent) had been accompanied by a 9 per cent rise in the price index for internationally traded manufactured goods. The producing companies pointed to the widening gap between posted prices and realized prices in their main export markets, which they attributed to the growth in competition from the Soviet Union and from independent oil companies since the late 1950s (◊**A4.10.iii, A4.11**).

In the light of the companies' response, OPEC tacitly accepted that Resolution IV–32 was unrealistic in the current market situation, and instead concentrated its efforts on the campaign for royalty-expensing and the elimination of marketing allowances. Whereas it had been asserted in OPEC's first explanatory memorandum that the minimum "just and equitable" royalty rate for OPEC oil was 20 per cent, this target was likewise seen to be unrealistic in the present circumstances. The main aim of the Saudi and Iranian negotiators was therefore to achieve full expensing of the Middle East's established standard 12.5 per cent royalty, which would bring an increase of around 15 per cent in government unit revenues.

As exploratory talks between Saudi Arabia and Aramco and between Iran and the IOP consortium had produced no concessions from these companies by the time that the 5th OPEC Conference meeting opened in November 1962, the Conference dealt with a number of routine matters and then adjourned the meeting pending further developments. The first half of 1963 brought only an offer by the companies (which was accepted) to reduce their claims for tax-deductible marketing allowances to a uniform 0.5 cents per barrel, as against existing allowances of 1 per cent of the posted price in Iran and about 4.2 cents per barrel in Saudi Arabia. The companies remained obdurate on the issue of royalty-expensing, claiming that market conditions did not justify an increase in their payments to host governments. In July 1963 an OPEC consultative meeting was convened to discuss the possibility of unilateral action on the part of Middle Eastern governments. No consensus was reached regarding immediate measures which might be taken, although a detailed study was begun of the feasible options for future action.

In a further attempt to secure the implementation of Resolution IV–33, the OPEC members agreed in August 1963 to mandate Dr Rouhani (whose term as Secretary-General had been extended in order to ensure continuity in the coordination of OPEC's campaign) to negotiate with the major oil companies on behalf of all the governments concerned. The companies formed a three-man committee (consisting of senior executives of BP, Exxon and Chevron) to meet Dr Rouhani, although it was stressed that the committee was not authorized to act on behalf of any producing company other than the IOP consortium and that the participating companies did not recognize Dr Rouhani's competence to act in any capacity other than that of a representative of the Iranian Government. The committee then proceeded to make what was from OPEC's point of view a meaningless offer to expense Iran's 12.5 per cent "stated payment" in return for (i) a 12.5 per cent discount off posted prices for the purpose of calculating taxable income, (ii) the dropping of all other outstanding financial claims against the consortium, and (iii) a guarantee that no other producing company in Iran would receive more favourable fiscal treatment than IOP. This offer, made in mid-October 1963 after one month of talks and implicitly intended to serve as a standard formula for offers to other Middle Eastern OPEC countries, was rejected by OPEC on the grounds that it would leave the government revenue entitlement unchanged.

In a revised offer, made in November 1963, the companies reduced the amount of the proposed offsetting discount to 8.5 per cent, while adding a further element of conditionality in the form of a requirement that host governments signing royalty-expensing agreements should undertake not to impose any restrictions on the "production or movement of oil". This offer was rejected by OPEC at a consultative meeting held in Beirut in early December 1963, at which a consensus was reported on the desirability of taking unilateral action to impose a royalty-expensing settlement on the companies, to be backed up if necessary by restrictions on company operations. After it had been made known that OPEC's intention was that proposals along these lines should be formally tabled when the 5th meeting of the OPEC Conference resumed in Riyadh later in December 1963 (after an interval of more than one year), Aramco and IOP indicated their preparedness to consider making an improved financial offer with fewer conditions attached. The week-long second session of the OPEC Conference's 5th meeting was marked by prolonged argument between the advocates of immediate unilateral action, led by Iraq and Venezuela, and the advocates of further negotiation, led by Iran.

The moderate viewpoint finally prevailed, and on Dec. 31, 1963, a resolution (V–40) was adopted declaring unilateral action by host governments to be inappropriate in the light of the companies' latest approach. Further negotiations were to be conducted on behalf of all the governments concerned by a three-man committee consisting of Dr Rouhani (whose term of office was extended for a further four months specifically for this purpose), Abdul Rahman Al-Bazzaz of Iraq (whose assumption of office as OPEC's second Secretary-General was delayed for the same period) and Hisham Nazer of Saudi Arabia.

The second session of the 5th Conference meeting also took decisions on certain other matters. Resolution V–41 initiated studies on (i) the compilation of a "code of uniform petroleum laws", and (ii) the establishment of "an inter-OPEC high court for the settlement of all disputes and differences relating to petroleum matters", except disputes involving member countries whose legal systems precluded their participation in the establishment of such a court. (Nothing further was heard of the latter proposal, although a similarly conceived body was eventually established by the OAPEC members in 1980 ◊**B2.4**.) Resolution V–42 directed the Secretariat to draw up proposals for the establishment of a permanent inter-OPEC commission to take responsibility for the continuous monitoring of oil price movements, bearing in mind that OPEC could "in no circumstances cease to strive for an improvement in crude oil prices".

D1.3.ii—Negotiations leading to several member countries' adoption of national agreements on royalty-expensing (1964)

During the first half of 1964 the work of OPEC's negotiating team on royalty-expensing was hindered by the oil companies' continuing insistence on dealing with the issue solely on a country-by-country basis. Offers had now been formally made to their respective host governments by all the main producing companies which operated under the Middle Eastern "50-50 profit-sharing" system. The basic terms and conditions of these various offers were essentially identical for all the countries concerned, although in the case of Iraq the IPC group sought to make its offer conditional on the resolution of all outstanding disputes between the company and the Iraq Government (◊**C6.3.iii**). The fiscal formula proposed by the companies did not differ significantly from that put forward in November 1963. An offer by OPEC to accept the immediate expensing of half of the royalty, with the expensing of the remaining half phased in over an agreed period, was rejected in March 1964.

No further offer was forthcoming from the companies' side until June 1964. It

Table 22 — Calculation of government revenue under the main Middle Eastern concession agreements

(1) The original Middle Eastern "50-50 profit-sharing" formula: royalty treated as tax credit

A.	Posted price*	$1.84
B.	12.5 per cent royalty	$0.23
C.	Production costs*	$0.20
D.	Taxable income (A–C)	$1.64
E.	50 per cent of taxable income	$0.82
F.	Total government revenue per barrel (B credited against E)	$0.82
G.	Tax-paid cost of oil to producing company (C+F)†	$1.02

(2) OPEC's demand for reform: royalty treated as tax-deductible expense

A.	Posted price*	$1.84
B.	12.5 per cent royalty	$0.23
C.	Production costs*	$0.20
D.	Taxable income (A–B–C)	$1.41
E.	50 per cent of taxable income	$0.705
F.	Total government revenue per barrel (B+E)	$0.935
G.	Tax-paid cost of oil to producing company (C+F)†	$1.135

(3) The compromise formula: royalty expensed but posted price discounted

A.	Posted price*	$1.84
B.	12.5 per cent royalty	$0.23
C.	8.5 per cent‡ discount	$0.1564
D.	Discounted posting (A–C)	$1.6836
E.	Production costs*	$0.20
F.	Taxable income (D–B–E)	$1.2536
G.	50 per cent of taxable income	$0.6268
H.	Total government revenue per barrel (G+B)	$0.8568
I.	Tax-paid cost of oil to producing company (E+H)†	$1.0568

* The amounts shown are illustrative and do not relate to a specific country.

† The final upstream profit retained by the producing company is the difference between tax-paid cost and realized fob price.

‡ The 8.5 per cent discount applied to exports made during the first year for which this formula was used (in most cases 1964). For the second year the agreed rate of discount was 7.5 per cent of the posted price for a "base crude" and 7.5 per cent of the posted price, plus a per-barrel "gravity allowance", for lighter grades. For the third year the agreed rate of discount was 6.5 per cent of the posted price, with a doubled allowance for crudes lighter than the base crude. (In the case of Saudi Arabia the "base crude" was defined as oil of 27° API gravity. The second-year gravity allowance was $0.0013235 per API degree above 27°. The third-year allowance was $0.002647 per API degree above 27°.)

345

was then proposed that the expensing of the full royalty should be linked to an 8.5 per cent discount off posted prices for tax purposes in 1964 only (backdated to the beginning of the year), to be followed by discounts of 7.5 per cent in 1965 and 6.5 per cent in 1966 (subject in each case to gravity allowances penalizing lighter crudes). After 1966 the level of discounts would be open to review in the light of trends in market prices. The effect of this formula would be to raise government unit revenues in 1966 to a level slightly below that which would have been achieved by the expensing of half of the royalty without any discounting of posted prices.

The 6th meeting of the OPEC Conference, held in Geneva from July 6 to 14, 1964, decided to treat the companies' latest offer as "a suitable basis for the full implementation of Resolution IV–33, subject to certain improvements and amendments". Resolution VI–47 provided that further negotiations should be held between individual governments and their respective producing companies and that an OPEC consultative meeting should be held within two months for the exchange of information on the progress of these negotiations. The other business of the 6th Conference meeting was to amend certain provisions of the OPEC statute, particularly those concerning the structure of the Secretariat (within which a separate economics department was created).

It was reported that the main changes which host governments agreed to seek in the companies' royalty-expensing offer were (i) a time limit for the full elimination of price discounts for tax purposes, (ii) the removal of all conditionality clauses which sought to link the implementation of royalty-expensing with the dropping of other claims by host governments, and (iii) an undertaking from the companies that benefits offered to one OPEC country should be accorded to all other members. A consultative meeting of the countries involved in the negotiations, convened in Beirut from Sept. 30 to Oct. 4, 1964, reportedly defined the "minimum requirements" which should be incorporated into national agreements, although these requirements were never made public. Talks between representatives of OPEC governments and the major oil companies, held in London in mid-October 1964, led initially to agreement on a compromise formula; however, they were discontinued when the companies reinstated certain "conditionality" clauses. A further consultative meeting of OPEC negotiators (attended also by a Venezuelan observer) took place on Nov. 4, 1964. A fresh round of government-company talks ensued in London, after which final written terms were submitted by the producing companies to their host governments on Nov. 16.

These terms were the subject of bitter disagreements at the 7th meeting of the OPEC Conference, held in Jakarta from Nov. 23 to 28, 1964. Iran, Kuwait, Libya, Qatar and Saudi Arabia all indicated their preparedness to negotiate national agreements based on the companies' offer of Nov. 16, which they considered to be consistent with OPEC's minimum requirements. However, Iraq rejected the terms on the grounds that they did not meet these minimum requirements, adding that it believed "that the non-financial provisions of the companies' offer constitute a clear infringement of Iraq's sovereignty and restrict its freedom of action in the achievement of high common objectives of the Organization". Indonesia and Venezuela supported Iraq's position, stating that "although they were not directly involved in the royalty settlement they were nevertheless concerned with the effects of such a settlement in terms of the common objectives of the Organization".

(Although IPC had dropped its demand that a royalty-expensing agreement should form part of a comprehensive settlement of all outstanding disputes with Iraq, the Iraq Government nevertheless objected to the requirement to grant tax quittances withheld since 1960 as a protest against the cuts in posted prices in that year. It also objected to the "most-favoured-company" clause, which was seen as an encroachment on the sovereignty of the host government, and to a requirement that government-company disputes should be submitted to international arbitration—this requirement having been added to the companies' standard terms and conditions during the final phase of the negotiations. On financial issues peculiar to Iraq, the Government rejected the IPC group's proposal that the royalty on its Mediterranean exports should be based on border values—i.e. seaboard postings deflated by the unit cost of pipeline transportation outside Iraq—rather than on seaboard postings as at present. It also objected to the group's insistence that Iraq should drop its claims for an increase in the posted price of its Persian/Arabian Gulf exports, whose pricing had been in dispute since 1956.)

In order to resolve this impasse, the OPEC Conference adopted a resolution (VII–49) which recorded the incompatible viewpoints expressed by the two groups of member countries and, by formally deleting the royalty-expensing issue from the agenda, left the "moderate" group free to conclude agreements on a national basis. The moderates declared their preparedness "to continue the struggle for the realization of the stand taken on crude oil prices in Resolution IV–32", while all member countries reaffirmed their solidarity, unity and dedication to "the common objectives upheld by the Organization". Resolution VII–50 authorized the establishment of an OPEC Economic Commission as "a specialized body to examine the position of petroleum prices on a continuing basis".

Supplemental agreements whereby royalty-expensing terms were incorporated into existing national concession agreements were subsequently finalized and ratified by Qatar, Iran and Saudi Arabia before Jan. 26, 1965 (the companies having guaranteed to implement the financial provisions of national royalty-expensing agreements with effect from the beginning of 1964 provided that such agreements had been ratified by at least four OPEC countries by the Jan. 26 deadline). Kuwait was unable to secure ratification at this point because of domestic political opposition (◊C7.3.iii), but the retroactivity undertaking was nevertheless honoured by the producing companies in Qatar, Iran and Saudi Arabia on the grounds that the Kuwait Government had sought ratification before the agreed deadline. Libya was not able to finalize supplemental royalty-expensing agreements until early 1966 because of opposition from its independent concession holders (◊C8.3.i). Iraq continued to refuse to accept the IPC group's conditions for a royalty-expensing agreement.

During the numerous rounds of royalty-expensing negotiations the major oil companies made no secret of their "divide and rule" attitude towards the member countries of an organization which they refused to recognize as a collective bargaining agency. This experience served ultimately to reinforce the OPEC countries' awareness both of the importance of unified action in bringing pressure to bear on the companies and of the difficulty of improving government revenues in a "soft" oil market. A report submitted by OPEC to the fifth Arab Petroleum Congress in March 1965 referred to the recent negotiating process as one of the "longest, toughest and most revealing in the history of the international oil industry", representing "a tax [by the major oil companies] on OPEC's time and effort that it obviously cannot afford to pay forever".

D1.4—OPEC and "Production Programming", 1965 to 1966

The 8th (extraordinary) meeting of the OPEC Conference, held in Geneva from April 5 to 10, 1965, adopted Resolution VIII–55 approving the statute of the OPEC Economic Commission (◊B1.8) and Resolution VIII–56 approving a revised and consolidated version of the main OPEC statute, amendments to which included the splitting of the posts of Secretary-General and chairman of the Board of Governors. The Economic Commission had already begun work under Resolution VII–50, which had called for the drawing up of urgent recommendations for action to counter the "continuing erosion of crude and product prices", including, if necessary, measures based on paragraph (3) of Resolution I–1 (dealing with the regulation of production).

The issue of production control, which had been one of the main concerns of Dr Pérez Alfonzo and Shaikh Tariki in their original campaign to establish an oil exporters' organization (◊D1.1), had subsequently been shelved by OPEC pending the conclusion of the royalty-expensing negotiations, not least because the (unpublished) results of an initial study, carried out by specialist US consultants in accordance with Resolution II–13, had reportedly drawn attention to the considerable practical difficulties involved in any attempt to launch an international prorationing scheme in the current market environment. A senior official of the Venezuelan Ministry of Mines and Hydrocarbons had nevertheless put forward fairly detailed theoretical proposals for an OPEC prorationing scheme at the third Arab Petroleum Congress in October 1961, and Venezuela had maintained a strong underlying commitment to the prorationing principle which was in no way diminished by Dr Pérez Alfonzo's retirement from ministerial office (and from direct involvement in OPEC affairs) in 1963. The limited enthusiasm for prorationing among the Middle Eastern members of the OPEC Conference had, however, been seriously weakened in early 1962, when Shaikh Tariki (whose radical principles had enjoyed somewhat qualified support within the conservative establishment in Saudi Arabia) was succeeded as Saudi Minister of Petroleum and Mineral Resources by the more pragmatic Shaikh Ahmed Zaki Yamani.

The results of the OPEC Economic Commission's preliminary inquiry into the use of production controls to stabilize market prices (initiated as a result of strong Venezuelan pressure) were outlined at the 8th OPEC Conference meeting. No decisions were taken on the subject at this meeting because of strong disagreements among delegates regarding the Commission's recommendations for the division of OPEC's projected incremental output among the different member countries.

When the 9th (ordinary) meeting of the OPEC Conference was convened in the Libyan capital, Tripoli, in July 1965, Venezuela succeeded in winning the qualified support of other members for an experimental programme of production planning, having demonstrated its own willingness to accept a far lower share of the "programmed" increase than it would have been entitled to claim purely on the basis of its share of current output (◊ Table 23). Resolution IX–61 stated that the Conference, believing "that one of the contributing factors to the deterioration of crude and product prices is the unrestricted competitive use of excess producing capacity" and recognizing "the need for a steady flow of oil to international markets on the basis of equitable and stable prices", had decided "(i) to adopt as a transitory measure a production plan calling for rational increases in production from the OPEC area to meet estimated increases in world demand and (ii) to submit a production programme to the governments of member countries for approval". Details of the production programme, although never officially released, were widely published in specialist journals after being revealed by representatives of various member countries. The initial programme period was the year beginning July 1, 1965, over which the maximum year-on-year OPEC production increase was to be 10 per cent (as against an 11.5 per cent increase recorded in the calendar year 1964). It was intended that a similar scheme, with appropriately revised targets, should operate in the following year.

Table 23 — Allocation of "programmed" production among OPEC members

	Actual production, 1964–65		"Programmed" increase for 1965–66	
	Volume (000 bpd)	Share of OPEC total (per cent)	Volume (000 bpd)	Share of OPEC total (per cent)
Indonesia	474	3.7	48	3.7
Iran	1,754	13.8	304	23.8
Iraq	1,294	10.2	125	9.8
Kuwait*	2,355	18.6	157	12.3
Libya	1,062	8.4	210	16.4
Qatar	221	1.7	67	5.2
Saudi Arabia*	2,091	16.5	254	19.8
Venezuela	3,445	27.1	115	9.0
OPEC	12,696	100.0	1,280	100.0

*Including share of Neutral Zone output.

Table 24 — Actual and "programmed" OPEC production, July 1965 to June 1966

	Production in 1965–66 (000 bpd)		Increase over 1964–65 (per cent)	
	"Programmed"	Actual	"Programmed"	Actual
Indonesia	522	496	10.0	4.6
Iran	2,058	2,044	17.5	16.5
Iraq	1,419	1,350	10.0	4.3
Kuwait*	2,512	2,351	6.6	−0.2
Libya	1,272	1,344	20.0	26.6
Qatar	288	261	32.0	18.1
Saudi Arabia*	2,345	2,406	12.0	15.1
Venezuela	3,560	3,453	3.3	0.2
OPEC	13,976	13,705	10.0	7.9

*Including share of Neutral Zone output.

The 9th OPEC Conference meeting also approved the removal of the OPEC Secretariat to Vienna with effect from Sept. 1, 1965, in view of the conclusion of a "satisfactory" agreement with the Austrian Government. (Difficulties had previously been encountered in negotiations with the Swiss Government regarding OPEC's request that the legal status of its headquarters staff should be equivalent to that of the staff of other Geneva-based international organizations. OPEC was formally recognized as a bona fide international organization by the UN Economic and Social Council on June 30, 1965.)

A lengthy memorandum issued by OPEC as a "note to Resolution IX–61" provided an indication of the arguments which had been put forward by Venezuela to secure the Middle Eastern producers' participation in a production programme. The memorandum emphasized that while the Organization had no intention of "curtailing supplies of oil to the consumer", it was concerned to ensure that an expanding export market was supplied "on an equitable basis that will benefit both producers and consumers". A brake would be applied to "cut-throat competition among the suppliers of crude who operate in the member countries, . . . which has only been possible because of the surplus of producing capacity". The memorandum cited production statistics showing that a record of steady growth in the Middle East as a whole masked wide variations in the growth of output from the different countries within the region, and referred to the "excessive concentration of power in the hands of a small group of large international companies", which were able to use the existence of surplus capacity to exercise a "wide measure of flexibility in allocating their total requirements as between countries". One aim of the OPEC programme would be to limit this flexibility in order to avoid excessive fluctuations in individual countries' oil revenues. Regarding the usefulness of the programme as a force to stabilize the market price of oil, the memorandum acknowledged that this aim was now of special interest to those OPEC countries which had concluded royalty-expensing agreements providing for market trends to be taken into account in a future review of the use of discounted posted prices for tax purposes (◊**D1.3.ii**).

In practice, the initial one-year production programme proved to be fundamentally flawed, in that it was based on an overestimate of actual demand growth over the period in question and (unlike the US prorationing system) did not provide any agreed mechanism for the interim adjustment of the "allowable" production ceiling in order to correct such an overestimate. It was not clear to what extent the Organization had taken account of export growth in Algeria, Nigeria and Abu Dhabi, none of which had joined OPEC by this point. The OPEC members' programmed national output levels were, moreover, ignored by the producing companies, several of which threatened to seek arbitral rulings on the issue if their host governments took any positive steps to curtail their commercial freedom as concession holders.

As the many disparities between actual and "programmed" production levels began to become apparent (◊ Table 24), so did the reservations of OPEC countries which had no strong commitment to the restriction of their output. Libya made it clear virtually from the outset that it did not wish to see any constraint on its production growth at this relatively early stage in the development of its oilfields. Moreover, Saudi Arabia, having made its support for the programme conditional on an increase in its national production ceiling from the beginning of 1966 and having failed to secure OPEC approval for the desired increase, publicized its effective withdrawal from the programme at that point. Venezuela, as the prime mover of the OPEC programme, was unperturbed by the virtual stagnation of its own production (which increased the scope for other members to exceed their ceilings without breaching the overall OPEC ceiling). However, Iraq and Kuwait were each seriously concerned by substantial shortfalls in their output relative to the levels programmed by OPEC. The lower than average growth rate of Iraq's output was clearly linked to the mounting backlog of disputes between IPC and the Government (◊**C6.3.iv**), while Kuwait saw the fall in its output in 1965–66 as an attempt by its concession holders to bring pressure to bear in connexion with the continuing impasse over the ratification of its royalty-expensing agreement (◊**C7.3.iii**). Iran, which had been allocated the greatest programmed volume increase of any OPEC country on the grounds of its large budgetary requirements and its loss of market share since the nationalization crisis of the early 1950s, made no secret of the fact that it regarded the programmed increase as a minimum target which IOP was expected to meet regardless of the market-oriented principles underlying the production programme.

The 10th meeting of the OPEC Conference, held in Vienna in December 1965, "reviewed the progress of the joint production programme and directed the Secretariat and the Economic Commission to continue their studies on the question of the stabilization of petroleum prices at equitable levels". The 10th meeting also adopted Resolution X–63 (◊**C8.3.i**) supporting the Libyan Government's position in its current confrontation with certain concession holders over the implementation of the OPEC royalty-expensing formula.

The 11th OPEC Conference meeting, held in Vienna in April 1966 and attended by Algeria as an observer, agreed that the joint production programme should be formally extended until the middle of 1967, although in practice the programme had been largely abandoned by the time that the final output figures for the 12 months to June 1966 became available. The fact that the programme had tended to change from a prorationing scheme into a mechanism for establishing minimum output targets was underlined by the adoption in April 1966 of Resolution XI–73, which (i) noted the "unsatisfactory rate of increase in production" in certain member countries, which "could not be ascribed to lack of outlets for their crudes in the international market", and (ii) condemned the "manipulation of production by the oil companies concerned".

Other resolutions adopted by the 11th meeting of the Conference marked a return to the consideration of purely fiscal matters. Resolution XI–71 recommended that member countries which had concluded royalty-expensing agreements should "take steps towards the complete elimination of the allowance granted to the oil companies", OPEC's view being that such action was justified by a "general improvement in the competitive, economic and market outlook of the international oil industry". Resolution XI–72 noted a report by the OPEC Economic Commission to the effect that the application of posted or reference prices for tax purposes would reduce the incidence of "excessive discounting" by exporting companies and recommended "(i) that the governments of the member countries concerned apply posted prices or reference prices for the purpose of determining the tax liabilities of the oil companies operating in their territories, and (ii) that no petroleum rights be granted or contracts entered into by member countries concerning the exploration or exploitation of new areas unless royalty payments and income tax liabilities are calculated on the basis of posted or reference prices, or unless the share to be obtained by the government is no less favourable than that obtained under the existing arrangements based on posted or reference prices, it being understood that current contracts meeting the latter condition are in keeping with the objectives of this resolution". (The first part of the latter resolution was of particular relevance to Venezuela, which was currently involved in negotiations for the introduction of a system of tax reference prices ◊**C13.3.iv.**)

D1.5—Negotiations to eliminate Tax Allowances under the Royalty-Expensing Formula

In August 1966 representatives of Iran, Libya, Qatar and Saudi Arabia held a meeting in Beirut with the then Secretary-General of OPEC, Ashraf T. Lufti, to discuss the implementation of Resolution XI–71. It was decided that negotiations to establish a firm timetable for the elimination of the gap between the effective tax-reference price and the full posting in these countries should be held initially between Saudi Arabia and Aramco, but when talks opened on this basis in late September the company side made it clear that it was not prepared to contemplate a detailed review of market trends until after the end of 1966. OPEC's determination to press for an early agreement was reaffirmed by the 12th meeting of the OPEC Conference in December 1966, and further talks on the same issue were held between Qatar and the Qatar Petroleum Co. during the first half of 1967, when the company side maintained that the current market outlook did not justify any significant reduction in the existing 6.5 per cent discount (and associated gravity allowances) used to deflate posted prices for the purposes of determining taxable income.

At the 13th (extraordinary) meeting of the OPEC Conference, held in September 1967 to review oil market developments in the aftermath of the six-day

351

Arab-Israeli war and the subsequent ineffectual attempts by Arab states to use oil as a political weapon (◊A4.13), resolutions were passed supporting claims by Libya and Iraq that the posted price of oil shipped from Mediterranean terminals should be increased in order to reflect the enhanced locational advantage of such terminals at a time of high freight rates caused by the closure of the Suez Canal. (The meeting also recorded OPEC's support for Libya's separate claim that its posted prices had been fixed at an unjustifiably low level vis-à-vis east Mediterranean postings since the commencement of exports in 1961.) With regard to the lack of progress on Resolution XI–71, the Conference decided that the OPEC members concerned should hold a consultative meeting in Saudi Arabia in early October. This meeting mandated Saudi Arabia to renew its negotiations with Aramco and to report back to a further meeting in early November.

By the time of the second consultative meeting Saudi Arabia had achieved only limited progress in pressing the main demand for a general elimination of the tax allowances arising out of the royalty-expensing formula, but had concluded a national agreement regarding the payment of a temporary "Suez premium" in respect of its Mediterranean exports. Having refused to add a surcharge to the posted price of oil exported via the trans-Arabian pipeline, Aramco instead undertook to increase the government's revenue entitlement by calculating its taxable income from such exports at the full posted price, without any discounts. Similar terms (equivalent to the de facto elimination of "royalty-expensing" discounts on all of its exports) were accepted by Libya in simultaneous talks with its concessionaire companies, while IPC applied an identical calculation to add a premium of between 7 and 8 cents per barrel to Iraq's revenue from Mediterranean exports, notwithstanding the fact that it had no royalty-expensing agreement with the Iraq Government.

The producing companies' aim in adopting a Suez-premium formula which did not entail any increase in the posted prices of Mediterranean crudes was to avoid any weakening of their argument in favour of the retention of significant tax allowances in the main negotiations on the terms of the royalty-expensing formula. At the same time they wanted to ensure that any reduction eventually conceded in the allowances on Gulf crudes would effectively erode the amount of the new differential between the tax-reference prices of Mediterranean and Gulf crudes.

The main negotiations resumed during November 1967 but had progressed very little by the time that the OPEC Conference held its 14th meeting at the end of the month. This caused the Conference to call for the holding of a "final" round of negotiations (to be opened in mid-December by Saudi Arabia and Iran) and to schedule an extraordinary Conference meeting for Jan. 8, 1968, when OPEC would endorse appropriate unilateral measures by host governments if no satisfactory offer had been received from the companies. During the December 1967 negotiations, held in Tehran, agreement was reached on a schedule for the phasing out of the percentage discounts on "base crudes", although serious differences over the more complicated issue of gravity allowances were not resolved until Jan. 6, when an improved offer was submitted by the companies. The 15th (extraordinary) meeting of the OPEC Conference approved the final terms on Jan. 9, 1968, after two days of discussion. Percentage discounts were to be progressively reduced to 5.5 per cent in 1968, 4.5 per cent in 1969, 3.5 per cent in 1970 and 2 per cent in 1971, after which they would cease. Gravity allowances were to be revised in order to lessen the penalty on lighter crudes, and were to cease after 1974.

D1.6—The Development of OPEC Policy, 1968 to 1970

D1.6.i—General

Abu Dhabi was admitted to OPEC membership in November 1967, while Algeria was admitted in July 1969. Nigeria attended the 12th Conference meeting (December 1966) as an observer, but the Government did not make an early application for membership because of its subsequent preoccupation with the civil war (◊C9.2). OPEC's 10 member countries accounted for 46.9 per cent of current world oil output in 1970, as against the 36.7 per cent of current output produced by the five founder members in 1960 (◊ Table 21).

Representatives of national oil companies of OPEC member countries met on five occasions between 1966 and 1970: (i) in Venezuela (October 1966), (ii) in Indonesia (November 1967), (iii) in Iran (October 1968), (iv) in Iraq (October 1969) and (v) in Kuwait (October 1970). Although these meetings served to promote functional co-operation between the various companies, proposals for the institutionalized co-ordination of company policies, particularly in the field of international marketing, were not taken up by the OPEC Conference.

D1.6.ii—Decisions of 16th to 20th Conference meetings (June 1968 to June 1970)

Having dealt with the issue of the phased elimination of tax allowances under the royalty-expensing formula, the OPEC Conference turned its attention to the Organization's broader policy aims. At its 16th meeting in June 1968 it issued, as Resolution XVI–90, a wide-ranging "declaratory statement on petroleum policy in member countries" (◊B1.9.i) whose recommendations included (i) an increase in host governments' oil revenues to the highest level which would leave the producing companies with a "reasonable" return on their investments, (ii) the establishment of full government control over the fixing of tax-reference prices, and (iii) government participation in the ownership of production operations in the main concession areas.

It was made clear by Saudi Arabian and Kuwaiti ministers, in subsequent statements on their national policy objectives, that acceptance of the principle of participation (i.e. acquiescence in partial nationalization) was an essential prerequisite for the continuation of "peaceful operations" by the long-established producing companies in the Arab states, where the extent to which national sovereignty over a key resource was compromised by the traditional concessionary relationships was not politically acceptable in the aftermath of the latest Middle East war (◊A4.13). Shaikh Yamani emphasized that Saudi Arabia did not wish to resort to unilateral nationalization and did not expect the extent of government participation in the operations of Aramco to reach 50 per cent for many years. He also acknowledged that the full nationalization of production operations would not be in the interests of the exporting countries at the present time, since to place the major oil companies in the position of arm's-length buyers of crude in an over-supplied market would merely be to invite a collapse in oil prices.

The reaction of the established producing companies to the concept of host-government participation in existing concession areas was wholly negative. In Iraq, IPC had been resisting a government demand for 20 per cent participation (◊C6.3.iii) throughout the 1960s. In Saudi Arabia Aramco's immediate response to the Government's invocation of the principle of "changing circumstances" was to publish an expert opinion stressing the importance of the principle of sanctity of contracts in Islamic law.

The 17th meeting of the OPEC Conference, held in Vienna in November 1968, adopted three resolutions dealing with matters of general policy.

Resolution XVII–93 recommended that member countries should introduce national regulations based on a "pro-forma regulation for the conservation of petroleum resources" which had been drawn up by the Secretariat in order to assist member countries to protect their "legitimate interests in the conservation of their natural resources" by requiring production operations to be conducted "in conformity with efficient and rational methods".

Resolution XVII–94 recommended that member countries should not grant new oil rights to any company whose home government pursued policies "which may tend to artificially depress petroleum prices in international markets". (The Japanese Government was currently attempting to secure reductions in the price of oil imported into Japan by the major international companies, while the European Commission had recently published draft energy policy guidelines—later approved in principle by the EEC member countries in November 1969—whose main aim was "to ensure security of supply at the lowest possible product price, mainly by means of maintaining competition in the energy market".)

Resolution XVII–95 recommended that "member countries should seek to ensure that the posted or tax-reference prices of their petroleum exports are consistent with each other, subject to differences in gravity, quality and geographic location", and instructed the Secretariat to prepare a report on the extent of existing disparities. The Conference also set up a working party on "government participation in the ownership of the concession-holding companies".

The 18th Conference meeting, held in Vienna in July 1969, discussed the working party's report on participation and the Secretariat's report on price disparities (which was of particular importance to Libya) and ordered further studies to be undertaken on both matters. Other topics under discussion included the accelerated relinquishment of concession areas, which was one of the policy aims adopted in Resolution XVI–90. Noting a deterioration in the terms of trade of OPEC member countries (◊A4.12.iii), the Conference adopted Resolution XVIII–103 instructing the Secretariat "to undertake a study with a view towards linking posted and tax-reference prices to those of manufactured goods of major industrialized countries".

The 19th meeting of the OPEC Conference, held in Vienna in December 1969, adopted two resolutions dealing with developments in north Africa, where both Libya (now under a revolutionary Government) and Algeria were involved in difficult negotiations with concessionaire companies. Resolution XIX–105 expressed OPEC's full support for Algeria's claim for improved fiscal terms from French oil companies (◊C1.3.iv), while Resolution XIX–110 supported Libya's decision (◊C8.3.ii) to introduce controls on production operations (based on OPEC's pro-forma conservation regulation). Each country was assured of OPEC backing for "any appropriate measures taken to safeguard its legitimate interests".

The 20th Conference meeting was held from June 24 to 26, 1970, in Algiers (the venue having been switched from Vienna as a gesture of support for Algeria in its continuing dispute with France). Resolution XX–112 provided for the adoption of a production plan "calling for rational increases in production from the OPEC area to meet estimated increases in world demand during the period 1971–75", which had been prepared by the Economic Commission following renewed Venezuelan pressure for a prorationing initiative. However, a lack of positive commitment on the part of other member countries, particularly Iran, was reflected in the resolution's deferral until the next meeting of the Conference of a "final decision" to proceed with the plan. Resolution XX–113 instructed the Economic Commission "to undertake a comprehensive study with a view to defining the ways and means of effectively implementing integration of the petroleum industry in the economies of member countries, with the understanding that such ways and means should aim at developing within the territories of member countries downstream activities and other industrial activities directly or indirectly related to the hydrocarbon sector, whenever such activities have not yet been integrated". The study should concentrate particularly on means of "ensuring the repatriation in member countries of an adequate portion of the sales proceeds generated from the exploitation of their hydrocarbons, whenever such requirement for repatriation has not been yet provided for in existing agreements".

Resolution XX–114 expressed the Conference's concern at Algeria's failure, in prolonged negotiations, to obtain a satisfactory offer regarding its "well-founded" claim for an increase in the tax-reference price applicable to exports by French oil companies. It declared that OPEC was ready to give its full and active support to any unilateral action which might be taken by the Algerian Government in accordance with paragraph (3) of the "renegotiation clause" section of OPEC's declaratory statement on petroleum policy (◊**B1.9.i**).

Resolution XX–115 criticized the IPC group's production policy in Iraq during recent years, which was said to have been characterized not only by a lack of investment in the development of additional productive capacity but also by a failure "to utilize the existing facilities to their maximum, in accordance with sound economic practices"; it stated the Conference's support for unilateral action by Iraq in pursuance of its demand for the introduction of production policies which ensured "an adequate rate of annual growth". Resolution XX–116 noted Iraq's continuing failure to reach a satisfactory royalty-expensing settlement with IPC and expressed support for "any appropriate measures taken by the Iraq Government to safeguard its legitimate interests in this matter".

D1.6.iii—Repercussions of increase in Libyan postings – Adoption of resolutions calling for wide-ranging negotiations with foreign oil companies (December 1970)

The dramatic tightening of the oil market during the second half of 1970 (◊**A4.13**), caused partly by production cutbacks ordered by the Libyan Government, enabled Libya to press home its long-standing claim for an increase in the posted price of its crude on the grounds of its undervaluation within the international oil industry's overall pattern of postings. The outcome of the Libyan negotiations was a fixed increase of 30 cents per barrel in the posting for the country's (40°) crude (as against the company side's unsuccessful offer of a fixed increase of 10 cents and a variable freight premium of 11 cents), plus guarantees of small additional increases over the next five years. Moreover, by backdating the fiscal effect of the higher posting to the beginning of 1965 (when royalty-expensing was implemented in Libya) the Libyan Government secured an immediate de facto increase in the rate of taxation of the profits of those producing companies which opted to pay off the resulting arrears out of their export earnings over the next five to seven years. Algeria, which had co-operated closely with Libya on matters of oil policy since late 1969, unilaterally increased its tax reference price for French companies in July 1970 (more than a week before the opening of the decisive round of government-company negotiations in Libya in early August) but subsequently agreed to suspend the application of this increase in view of its implications for Franco-Algerian relations. Most of the (comparatively minor) Algerian interests of non-French oil companies were nationalized during 1970 after the companies concerned had refused to accept majority Algerian participation in their operations (◊**C1.3.iii**).

Libya's success in securing acceptance of its new terms by all of its concession holders, including six major oil companies, set off a chain reaction throughout the Middle East. Iran demanded a tax rate of 55 per cent (the approximate level of the new de facto rate in Libya) and a general increase in its posted prices, together with a separate adjustment of the price differential on its heavy (31°) crude to reflect the recent rise in the market price of heavy fuel oil. These claims were backed by a threat to rescind the IOP consortium's production rights in part of its operating area. IOP resisted the claim for a general price increase but conceded the tax increase and agreed to increase the posting for heavy crude by 9 cents per barrel with effect from Nov. 14, 1970. Kuwait then secured identical treatment from KOC, the same terms being offered to the Saudi Government by Aramco. East Mediterranean postings had meanwhile been adjusted by the producing companies in order to realign the overall Mediterranean differential structure in the aftermath of the Libyan increase (which was applied with effect from Sept. 1, 1970). An increase of 20 cents per barrel, effective from the same date, was made in IPC's Mediterranean posting for 36° Iraqi crude, while Aramco announced a similar change in its posting for exports of 34° Saudi Arabian crude via the trans-Arabian pipeline (which was not in fact in use at this time).

The oil companies' refusal to contemplate a general realignment in Middle Eastern crude postings beyond the Mediterranean (i.e. to include crudes exported from Persian/Arabian Gulf terminals) was based on their decision to treat the Libyan price increase essentially as a freight premium reflecting the considerable advantage enjoyed by Mediterranean crudes in the current supply situation, the companies' ability to emphasize this aspect being underpinned by the fact that the final Libyan agreements had not formally defined the basis of the price increase. The Middle Eastern exporting countries therefore decided to avoid negotiations based primarily on demands for a general reactive realignment of Gulf postings (an approach which had proved unsuccessful in Iran) but to press instead for a considerably larger across-the-board increase raising Gulf postings by an amount equal to or greater than the increase in Libyan postings.

High-level political contacts between Middle Eastern governments, notably those of Iran and Saudi Arabia, resulted in an agreement to present a joint demand to the companies at the next OPEC Conference meeting. This would be backed by the threat of co-ordinated unilateral action if an agreed minimum increase was not achieved by a specified deadline (the confidential minimum negotiating target being a 30-cents per barrel rise in Gulf postings). Iran's pledge that it was prepared to cut off supplies to any of IOP's parent companies which refused to accept a unilaterally imposed price increase was in strong contrast to the Iranian Government's previous tendency to give a particularly high priority to the expansion of export volume rather than the improvement of unit revenue.

The principal resolution adopted by the 21st meeting of the OPEC Conference, held in Caracas from Dec. 9 to 12, 1970, laid the ground for wide-ranging negotiations covering a general increase in postings, a realignment of the posted price structure on the basis of the highest OPEC posting and an uplift in the relative valuation of heavy and medium crudes. This last aim was to be achieved by deducting a gravity differential of 0.15 cents per barrel per one-tenth of each API degree below 40°, as against the established gravity differential of at least 2 cents per full API degree. The full text of Resolution XXI–120 was as follows:

"The Conference,
"having heard the statement of the head of the Libyan delegation with regard to the outcome of the negotiations carried out by that member country with its concessionaire companies to correct the unjustifiable basis on which Libyan posted prices had been calculated since their inception;
"having heard the statements of the heads of the Iranian and Kuwaiti delegations with regard to the recent increases made in the posted prices of certain crude oils and the adoption of a uniform 55 per cent tax rate in those member countries, and having also noted the statement of the head of the Saudi Arabian delegation that an offer of a similar nature has been made to his country;

"having noted the recent 20-cents per barrel upward adjustment published by the concessionaire companies in Iraq and Saudi Arabia for the crude oil shipped from east Mediterranean terminals;

"having heard the statement made by the head of the Algerian delegation on the negotiations being held with the French Government concerning the revision of the fiscal terms applicable to the French oil companies;

"having heard the statement made by the head of the Venezuelan delegation on the price situation in that member country, where some of the concessionaire exporting companies have failed to adjust their export prices to take into account prevailing market conditions, as established in existing reference-price agreements, to the eventual detriment of the Venezuelan fiscal revenue;

"recalling Resolutions XIII–80, XIII–81 and XIX–105, where the Organization supported the measures that were being taken by the Libyan, Iraqi and Algerian Governments to safeguard their legitimate interests with respect to the upward revision of posted or reference prices and of fiscal revenue;

"pursuant to the principles established in Resolution XVI–90 (◊B1.9.i), calling for revision of existing agreements as justified by changing circumstances and [stating] that the reference price for the purpose of determining the tax liability of the concessionaire companies should be determined by the governments of member countries;

"having heard the reports presented by the Secretariat concerning the necessity for an immediate elimination of the disparities as well as an upward adjustment of the existing posted or reference prices in all member countries;

"considering the general improvement in the economic and market outlook of the international oil industry, as well as in its competitiveness with other sources of energy;

"resolves that all member countries adopt the following objectives:

"(1) to establish 55 per cent as the minimum rate of taxation on the net income of the oil companies operating in the member countries,

"(2) to eliminate existing disparities in posted or tax-reference prices of the crude oils in the member countries on the basis of the highest posted price applicable in the member countries, taking into consideration differences in gravity and geographical location and any appropriate escalation in future years,

"(3) to establish a uniform general increase in the posted or tax-reference prices in all member countries to reflect the general improvement in the conditions of the international petroleum market,

"(4) to adopt a new system for the adjustment of gravity differentials of posted or tax-reference prices on the basis of 0.15 cents per barrel per 0.1° API for crude oil of 40° API and below, and 0.2 cents per barrel per 0.1° API for crude of 40.1° API and above,

"(5) to eliminate completely the allowances granted to oil companies as from Jan. 1, 1971.

"To this end, all member countries shall establish negotiations with the oil companies concerned with a view to achieving the above objectives and, recognizing the similarity of geographical location and other conditions in Abu Dhabi, Iran, Iraq, Kuwait, Qatar and Saudi Arabia, a committee shall be formed consisting of the representatives of Iran, Iraq and Saudi Arabia who shall negotiate on behalf of Abu Dhabi, Iran, Iraq, Kuwait, Qatar and Saudi Arabia with the representatives of the oil companies operating in said member countries.

"The committee shall establish negotiations with the oil companies concerned in Tehran within a period of 31 days from the date of the conclusion of the present meeting of the Conference and report to all member countries through the Secretary-General the results of the negotiations not later than seven days thereafter.

"Within 15 days of the submission of the committee's report to member countries, an extraordinary meeting of the Conference shall be convened in order to evaluate the results of the committee's and of the individual member countries' negotiations. In case such negotiations fail to achieve their purpose, the Conference shall determine and set forth a procedure with a view to enforcing and achieving the objectives as outlined in this resolution through a concerted and simultaneous action by all member countries."

Although Resolution XXI–120 was intended primarily as a basis for joint action by the Gulf exporting countries, its general applicability, coupled with its implication that the recent increase in Libyan postings was wholly attributable to the correction of past undervaluation, left the way open for a separate Libyan claim for further increases. It was moreover made clear by OPEC that the claims put forward under Resolution XXI–120 were considered to be unrelated to the issue of freight premiums, which was covered separately as follows in Resolution XXI–124:

"Having heard the statement of the head of the Libyan delegation concerning the excessive and windfall profits accruing to the concessionaires as a result of the closure of the Suez Canal and the extraordinary circumstances prevailing in the tanker market, and noting that member countries concerned should obtain a premium reflecting their comparative freight advantage, [the Conference] resolves to support fully any appropriate measures to which the member countries concerned may have recourse in order to safeguard their legitimate interests on this matter."

Apart from Libya, the OPEC members not represented by the Gulf exporters' negotiating committee were Algeria, Indonesia and Venezuela. Of these Algeria was currently involved in negotiations with France and was generally committed to following Libya's lead on pricing; Indonesia already controlled its export prices on a market-related basis (◊**C4.3.i**); and Venezuela had no contractual obligation to negotiate for higher taxation. A bill to increase Venezuela's tax rate and to establish unilateral government control over the level of tax-reference prices was debated by the Venezuelan legislature during OPEC's Caracas Conference meeting, and became law within a week of the end of the meeting (◊**C13.3.iv**).

The third key pricing resolution adopted by the Caracas meeting (Resolution XXI–122) was worded as follows:

"The Conference,
"recalling Resolutions XVI–90 and XVIII–103;
"taking into consideration that the value of the US dollar, the currency in which the posted or tax-reference prices of petroleum are expressed, constitutes an essential element for the determination of the fiscal revenue of member countries;
"taking into consideration that the maintenance of the real level of this revenue is of paramount importance for the successful implementation of the social and economic development programmes undertaken by member countries and constitutes a fundamental objective of the Organization;
"taking into consideration that the purchasing power of the revenue per barrel of member countries has continued to deteriorate due to the continuous inflation in prices felt by the economies of industrialized countries, principal suppliers of the manufactured goods required by member countries;
"taking into consideration that member countries cannot be expected to bear the consequences of decisions or circumstances which are external to them and consequently beyond their control;
"resolves (i) that in case of changes in the parity of monies of major industrialized countries which would have an adverse effect on the purchasing power of member countries' oil revenues, posted or tax-reference prices should be adjusted so as to reflect such changes, and (ii) to direct the Secretary-General to follow up and complete the study called for previously under Resolution XVIII–103 and to prepare a comprehensive report to be submitted to the next Conference meeting for consideration."

Resolution XXI–123 noted statements by various member countries, including Libya, regarding an "unjustifiable slowdown of exploration and development activities by some oil companies operating in their countries". It expressed the Conference's backing for any action taken by governments in support of their "legitimate right to expect concession operators to comply with the highest national interest commanding the undertaking of permanent and extensive exploration and development efforts in order to increase proved and potential hydrocarbon reserves".

Resolution XXI–125 instructed the Secretary-General "to maintain the oil production rates of member countries under continuous surveillance"; to identify concessionaire companies which were practising "discriminatory production policies" in retaliation for the introduction of government measures designed to safeguard member countries' legitimate interests; and "to ask the Conference to study the appropriate measures to be undertaken by all member countries whenever it becomes apparent that the adoption of said discriminatory production policy by concessionaire oil companies noticeably and unjustifiably affects the oil revenue of one or more member countries".

Resolution XXI–121 deferred a final decision on the introduction of a new joint production programme. A standing committee was formed "with a view to determining the relevant factors that must be taken into account for the formulation of a definite and realistic joint production programme for member countries for the period beginning in 1972". It was agreed that the committee's report should be discussed at an extraordinary Conference session to be convened immediately before the next ordinary meeting.

D2—1971

D2.1—Annual Statistical Survey

D2.1.i—Oil production and reserves

World

Total production .... 50,785,000 bpd (2,494.9 million tonnes)
    Change over 1970 .... +5.6 per cent

End-year proved reserves .... 639,200 million barrels
    Change over end-1970 .... +6.7 per cent

Reserves:production ratio .... 34.5 : 1

Regional shares:

	In 1971 world production*			In end-1971 world reserves†		
	Regional total (million tonnes)	Change over 1970 (per cent)	Share of world total (per cent)	Reserves (thousand million barrels)	Change over 1970 (per cent)	Share of world total (per cent)
Middle East	807.7	+16.8	32.4	366.8	+6.7	57.5
North America	606.6	−0.4	24.3	55.6	−2.6	8.7
USSR/Eastern Europe/China	432.0	+8.3	17.3	98.5	−1.5	15.4
Africa	281.1	−6.3	11.2	56.5	+6.8	8.8
Latin America/ Caribbean	266.2	−2.4	10.7	31.4	+19.8	4.9
Asia‡/Australasia	79.4	+17.5	3.2	15.6	+8.3	2.4
Western Europe§	21.9	−3.9	0.9	14.8	+236.4	2.3

*Including production from oil shales, tar sands and natural gas liquids (NGL).
†Excluding oil shales and tar sands; including NGL in North America.
‡Excluding China.
§Including Yugoslavia.

OPEC

OPEC oil production .... 25,525,000 bpd/1,266.3 million tonnes*
                                      (25,280,000 bpd/1,254.1 million tonnes†)
    Change over 1970 .... +8.1 per cent* (*+13.2 per cent†*)
    Share of 1971 world total .... 50.7 per cent* (*50.3 per cent†*)

*OPEC end-year proved reserves .... 430,845 million barrels
    Change over 1970 .... +4.5 per cent
    Share of 1971 world total .... 67.4 per cent

*OPEC reserves: production ratio .... 46.2 : 1

*End-1975 membership basis.
†Current membership basis.

OPEC (continued)

OPEC member countries' production:

	1971 production		Change over 1970 (per cent)	Share of world total (per cent)	Share of OPEC total (per cent)
	(million tonnes)	(thousand bpd)			
Algeria	36.5	780	−24.7	1.5	2.9
Ecuador*	0.2	5	—	—	—
Gabon†	5.8	115	+7.4	0.2	0.5
Indonesia	44.1	890	+4.5	1.8	3.5
Iran	227.0	4,565	+18.7	9.1	17.9
Iraq	83.5	1,700	+8.6	3.3	6.6
Kuwait	148.8	2,975	+7.0	6.0	11.8
Libya	133.1	2,765	−16.7	5.3	10.5
Nigeria	74.7	1,530	+41.2	3.0	5.9
Qatar	20.5	430	+15.8	0.8	1.6
Saudi Arabia	225.0	4,545	+26.4	9.0	17.8
UAE‡	51.1	1,060	+35.5	2.0	4.0
Venezuela	187.7	3,620	−3.8	7.5	14.8
Neutral Zone§	28.3	545	+8.8	1.1	2.2

*Not admitted to OPEC membership until 1973.
†Not admitted to (associate) membership until 1973.
‡Including Dubai (6,200,000 tonnes/125,000 bpd), which was not formally admitted to OPEC membership until 1974.
§Production shared between Kuwait and Saudi Arabia.

Non-OPEC

Selected non-OPEC countries' oil production:

	1971 production		Change over 1970 (per cent)	Share of world total (per cent)
	(million tonnes)	(thousand bpd)		
USA*	530.0	11,160	−1.4	21.2
USSR	377.1	7,630	+6.8	15.1
Canada	76.6	1,585	+7.1	3.1
China	36.7	735	+30.1	1.5
Mexico	23.8	485	−0.4	1.0
Argentina	22.1	425	+8.3	0.9
Egypt	21.0	415	−10.6	0.8
Oman	14.4	285	−13.3	0.6
Norway	0.3	5	n.a.	‡
United Kingdom	0.1	†	—	‡
Total	1,102.1	22,725§	+2.5	44.2

*Of which natural gas liquids 60,100,000 tonnes (1,695,000 bpd).
†Less than 5,000 bpd.
‡Negligible.
§Excluding United Kingdom.

D2.1.ii—Oil consumption

World

Total consumption	49,160,000 bpd (2,413 million tonnes)
Change over 1970	+5.8 per cent

Regional distribution of total:

	1971 consumption		Change over 1970 (per cent)	Share of world total (per cent)
	(million tonnes)	(thousand bpd)		
North America	795.1	16,430	+3.6	33.0
Western Europe*	656.0	13,280	+4.6	27.2
USSR/Eastern Europe/China	377.2	7,620	+9.2	15.6
Asia†/Australasia	342.8	6,920	+8.8	14.2
Latin America/Caribbean	143.5	2,955	+6.4	6.0
Middle East	54.0	1,055	+9.1	2.2
Africa	44.4	900	+5.5	1.8

*Including Yugoslavia.
†Excluding China.

Selected countries

	1971 consumption		Change over 1970 (per cent)	Share of world total (per cent)
	(million tonnes)	(thousand bpd)		
USA	719.3	14,845	+3.6	29.8
USSR	279.2	5,655	+6.2	11.6
Japan	219.7	4,435	+10.3	9.1
West Germany	133.5	2,745	+3.8	5.5
United Kingdom	104.3	2,105	+0.7	4.3
France	102.8	2,090	+9.0	4.3
Italy	93.8	1,875	+7.4	3.9
Canada	75.8	1,585	+3.8	3.1
China	36.7	725	+30.1	1.5
Spain	30.9	635	+10.0	1.3
Total	1,796.0	36,695	+5.7	74.4

D2.1.iii—Oil refining

World

Total refinery capacity	55,295,000 bpd
Change over 1970	+8.3 per cent

Total refinery throughputs	47,905,000 bpd
Change over 1970	+5.6 per cent

Consumption as proportion of capacity	88.9 per cent

Selected markets

Consumption of refined product types and change over 1970:

	USA (million tonnes)	USA (per cent)	Western Europe (million tonnes)	Western Europe (per cent)	Japan (million tonnes)	Japan (per cent)
Gasolines	283.5	+4.0	114.3	+9.8	34.8	+14.5
Middle distillates	177.5	+4.0	214.6	+6.1	36.4	+13.4
Fuel oil	120.3	+5.0	241.9	+2.1	120.2	+7.6
Other	138.0	+1.0	85.2	+1.7	28.3	+13.7
Total	719.3	+3.6	656.0	+4.6	219.7	+10.3

D2.1.iv—Tankers and trade

Tankers

Total world fleet .... 170,900,000 deadweight tons
  Change over 1970 .... +13 per cent

Trade

Total world crude exports
    (including re-exports) .... 25,480,000 bpd (1,257.8 million tonnes)
  Change over 1970 .... +8.3 per cent
OPEC crude exports .... 22,031,700 bpd (1,087.6 million tonnes)
  Change over 1970 .... +8.9 per cent
  Share of 1971 world total .... 86.5 per cent
Total world product exports
    (including re-exports) .... 7,601,500 bpd (387,377,000 tonnes)
  Change over 1970 .... −0.6 per cent
OPEC product exports .... 1,814,500 bpd (92,468,000 tonnes)
  Change over 1970 .... −8 per cent
  Share of 1971 world total .... 23.9 per cent

Regional distribution of world oil trade*:

	Share of 1971 imports (per cent) Crude	Products	Share of 1971 exports (per cent) Crude	Products
USA	7.5	45.8	—	4.9
Canada	2.9	2.4	3.2	1.5
Latin America/Caribbean	3.5	3.0	4.7	45.2
Western Europe	57.4	13.8	0.1	6.1
Middle East	0.6	—	62.7	25.5
North Africa	0.4	1.6	16.6	0.9
West Africa	†	0.4	7.1	0.2
East and southern Africa/ South Asia	3.3	2.6	—	0.2
South-East Asia	3.2	5.9	2.9	3.9
Australasia	1.4	1.5	0.1	0.3
Japan	17.2	16.5	—	0.4
USSR/Eastern Europe/China	0.5	0.3	2.6	10.9
Unspecified	2.1	6.2	—	—
Total	100.0	100.0	100.0	100.0

*Excluding intra-regional trade.   †Negligible.

D2.1.v—World primary energy consumption

Total consumption (excluding
    non-commercial fuels) .... 5,383.6 million tonnes oil equivalent (mtoe)
    Change over 1970 .... +4.2 per cent

Contributions of primary energy sources:

	Consumption (mtoe)	Change over 1970 (per cent)	Share of total (per cent)
Oil	2,413.0	+5.8	44.8
Coal	1,631.6	−0.2	30.3
Natural gas	996.7	+7.3	18.5
Water power	314.3	+4.1	5.9
Nuclear power	28.0	+41.4	0.5

D2.1.vi—Natural gas production and reserves

Marketed production (thousand million cubic metres):

	Regional total (tmcm)	Change over 1970 (per cent)	Share of 1971 world total (per cent)
North America	671.4	+3.4	59.6
Latin America/Caribbean	29.3	−1.4	2.6
Western Europe*	120.4	+61.9	10.7
USSR/Eastern Europe/China	262.1	+7.2	23.3
Middle East	21.4	+11.4	1.9
Africa	7.7	+138.3	0.7
Asia†/Australasia	13.2	+11.6	1.2
World total	1,125.5	+9.3	100.0
(*of which OPEC*)	(*37.0*)	(*+20.5*)	(*3.3*)

*Including Yugoslavia.
†Excluding China.

End-year proved reserves (thousand million cubic metres):

	Regional total (tmcm)	Change over 1970 (per cent)	Share of 1971 world total (per cent)
North America	9,465.5	−2.9	19.3
Latin America/Caribbean	1,902.2	−2.0	3.9
Western Europe*	4,628.2	+12.0	9.5
USSR/Eastern Europe/China	16,077.0	+27.9	32.9
Middle East	9,735.5	−2.9	19.9
Africa	5,452.4	+1.1	11.1
Asia†/Australasia	1,682.4	+11.4	3.4
World total	48,943.2	+8.0	100.0
(*of which OPEC*)	(*15,692.4*)	(*−2.2*)	(*32.1*)

*Including Yugoslavia.
†Excluding China.

D2.2—Negotiations to implement Main Resolutions of 21st OPEC Conference Meeting

D2.2.i—Disagreements between OPEC and foreign oil companies over the form of negotiating process

Following the Libyan Government's presentation on Jan. 3, 1971, of a comprehensive list of new demands based on OPEC's December 1970 resolutions, the major oil companies initiated a series of urgent consultations within the industry aimed at formulating a co-ordinated negotiating strategy to counter what was regarded as Libya's attempt to "leapfrog" the demands of the Gulf OPEC group. Representatives of over 20 companies with concession interests in OPEC countries, including large US independents, Japan's Arabian Oil Co. and most West European independents except ERAP and ENI, met senior executives of the majors in New York on Jan. 11 (the day before the deadline fixed by the OPEC Conference for the opening of negotiations with the Persian/Arabian Gulf members in Tehran). The companies decided to delay the opening of substantive negotiations pending further talks among themselves.

These talks resulted in decisions (i) to seek a settlement covering the whole OPEC area, in order to avoid "leapfrogging" claims by individual countries or groups of countries; (ii) to negotiate collectively from a common position, in order to avoid any attempt by governments to exert pressure on the more vulnerable independent companies (as had happened in Libya in the previous year); (iii) to establish a standing inter-company committee to co-ordinate the negotiating process; and (iv) to seek the co-operation of the US Government in explaining the companies' position to "moderate" OPEC governments. In pursuance of these decisions the companies formed a "London policy group", to be based at the headquarters of BP, while the Libyan producers concluded a secret mutual aid agreement whereby any company which was faced with production cutbacks in Libya would be supplied with crude by the other participating companies at tax-paid cost. The US Government indemnified the US companies against anti-trust proceedings in respect of these arrangements and agreed to despatch an Under-Secretary of State, John N. Irwin, on a week-long mission to Iran, Kuwait and Saudi Arabia.

On Jan. 16, 1971 (the day of Irwin's departure for the Persian/Arabian Gulf), the companies informed the OPEC countries that they were not prepared to "negotiate the development of claims by member countries of OPEC on any other basis than one which reaches a settlement simultaneously with all producing governments concerned". It was the companies' proposal that "an all-embracing negotiation" should take place between a single negotiating team representing the company side (to be led by directors of BP and Exxon) and a single OPEC team mandated to represent all the member countries. The aim of the negotiations would be to reach "an overall and durable settlement" based on a general increase in postings, guarantees of future increases over five years to take account of inflation, and temporary variable freight premiums for "short-haul" crudes. The latest Libyan claims for an effective tax rate in excess of 55 per cent, for backdated premium payments and for "new obligatory reinvestment" were not acceptable to the companies.

Libya and Algeria issued an immediate joint denunciation of the companies' statement, while the Gulf OPEC countries affirmed their interest in the general settlement terms proposed by the companies but emphatically refused to consider "an all-embracing negotiation". The heads of state of the three countries visited by Irwin made it clear that any attempt by the companies to impose their demand for OPEC-wide negotiations would simply cause the Organization to insist on an overall settlement based on the maximum demand of any member country, including Venezuela. If, however, the companies agreed to negotiate a prompt agreement with the "moderate" Gulf OPEC group, this group would honour such an agreement regardless of whether its terms were bettered by those of any subsequent company agreement with Libya (whose own demands were implicitly linked to the prior conclusion of a Gulf settlement).

The Gulf producers' position was accepted as reasonable by Irwin, whose main concern was to safeguard the future security of supplies (◊**A4.15.i**), and the US State Department accordingly advised the companies to modify their stance. The companies then issued a further statement on Jan. 21, 1971, indicating their preparedness to hold what were described as "separate but necessarily connected" negotiations with the Gulf OPEC group and with Libya, the results of which "should form part of a global agreement and should be subordinated to it".

On Jan. 22, 1971, the OPEC Secretariat issued a statement to the effect that the extraordinary Conference meeting foreseen in Resolution XXI–120 (◊**D1.6.iii**) would be convened in Tehran on Feb. 3 to consider the report of the Gulf negotiating committee. The statement added that the merits of the companies' proposals regarding the form of the negotiating process were a matter for discussion by the Conference rather than by the committee. The committee, for its part, advised the companies on Jan. 22 of its wish to open substantive negotiations by Jan. 28 with a view to agreeing terms for a Gulf settlement before the Tehran Conference meeting. The Shah of Iran held a press conference in Tehran on Jan. 24 at which he reiterated his warning that Iran would "follow the maximalists" within OPEC if the companies insisted on adopting a global approach to the negotiating process. He added that a company approach based on "economic imperialism" could be expected to lead "not only to a stoppage of oil exports but to a much more terrible crisis—a rebellion of the have-nots against the haves".

The companies attempted to open simultaneous negotiations in Tehran and Tripoli on Jan. 28, but received a formal rebuff from the Libyan Government which forced them to deal solely with OPEC's Gulf negotiating committee in Tehran. The company representatives nevertheless refused to drop their underlying "global" approach, with the result that much of the discussion in Tehran centred on the nature of the assurances which the Gulf committee was prepared to give regarding the relationship between a Gulf settlement and a future Libyan settlement.

The OPEC side indicated that their position was based (i) on a willingness to stand by the terms of any price agreement in respect of oil exported from Gulf terminals and (ii) a refusal to enter into any agreement in respect of Middle East oil exported from east Mediterranean terminals, the price of which was to be determined in the context of separate negotiations to establish a unified structure of postings and freight premiums for north African and east Mediterranean OPEC crudes. The companies would therefore in effect be obliged to set their east Mediterranean prices in the light of a Libyan settlement, and would not have the option of attempting to impose east Mediterranean terms on Libya. It was eventually established that no government embargoes would be threatened on the export of crude from Gulf terminals in support of future demands for Mediterranean terms which exceeded agreed Gulf terms. In return for undertaking not to attempt to "leapfrog" a future Mediterranean agreement the Gulf exporters would be entitled to receive a limited measure of financial "compensation" from companies which exported both from Libya and the Gulf in the event that a variable freight premium agreed with Libya was not reduced in line with a fall in freight rates (i.e. because of the Libyan Government's failure to honour an agreed formula).

As regards the pricing issue, an initial negotiating gap of 39 cents (between the

OPEC committee's demand for a basic increase in Gulf postings of 54 cents per barrel and an offer from the company side of 15 cents per barrel) was narrowed to a gap of 15 cents (35 cents demanded and 20 cents offered) as the talks progressed. The Gulf states' 35-cent minimum demand formed part of a proposal for a five-year agreement with annual inflation clauses, while 40 cents per barrel was demanded for a one-year agreement. Whereas an "interim" settlement on the basis of the one-year terms was recommended to the London policy group by the companies' Tehran negotiators, continuing dissatisfaction about the exclusion of east Mediterranean crudes from the deal led to the formal rejection of the proposed terms by the company side on Feb. 2. According to a statement issued by the companies, "progress on the many issues involved in both the financial and the contractual area" had been accompanied by failure to secure "realistic assurances" regarding "the problem of spiralling increases in financial demands between some of the major producing countries".

The 22nd (extraordinary) meeting of the OPEC Conference was duly held on Feb. 3 and 4, 1971, and adopted Resolution XXII–131 setting out the following ultimatums to the companies:

(1) "Each member country exporting oil from Gulf terminals shall introduce on Feb. 15 the necessary legal and/or legislative measures for the implementation of the objectives embodied in Resolution XXI–120. In the event that any oil company concerned fails to comply with these legal and/or legislative measures within seven days from the date of their adoption in all the countries concerned, appropriate measures shall be taken by Abu Dhabi, Algeria, Iran, Iraq, Kuwait, Libya, Qatar, Saudi Arabia and Venezuela [i.e. all the members of OPEC except Indonesia], including total embargo on the shipment of crude oil and petroleum products by such company. In case the oil companies operating in the member countries concerned express their willingness to comply with the minimum requirements agreed upon by the six member countries bordering the Gulf on the implementation of the objectives of Resolution XXI–120 before the expiry of the time limit set out above, then the member countries concerned shall refrain from resorting to the legal and/or legislative measures referred to above.

(2) "With regard to Algeria and Libya the necessary legal and/or legislative measures for the implementation of the objectives embodied in Resolution XXI–120 applicable to them shall be introduced at the convenience of their respective Governments. In the event that any oil company operating in these member countries fails to comply, within seven days from the date of their adoption, with the same minimum requirements agreed upon by the member countries bordering the Gulf plus an additional premium reflecting a reasonably justified short-haul freight advantage for [north African] crude oil exports, Abu Dhabi, Algeria, Iran, Iraq, Kuwait, Libya, Qatar, Saudi Arabia and Venezuela shall take appropriate measures including total embargo on the shipment of crude oil and petroleum products by such company."

Resolution XXII–132 expressed the Conference's "full support for measures taken or to be taken by the Libyan Government for safeguarding the legitimate interests of the Libyan people against any collective act that might be exercised by oil companies operating in Libya".

At the same time oil-importing countries were assured in separate statements by Gulf OPEC delegates that the Organization's dispute was solely with the foreign exporting companies, and that if embargo measures were implemented oil supplies would be available to consumers from member countries' national oil companies at prices based on the new postings which the Gulf countries were seeking to agree with the exporting companies. It was emphasized that host governments' unit revenue entitlements under the financial terms proposed by the Gulf states would be equivalent to less than 10 per cent of the current post-tax consumer price of a typical barrel of oil products in the main importing countries (◊◊ Table 12). The preamble to Resolution XXII–131 referred to "the sharp increase and the general

367

firming up of crude oil and product prices in world markets [◊A4.13] coupled with the staggering growth of demand for petroleum in the main consuming countries [◊A2.2]"; this was contrasted with "the continuing erosion in the purchasing power of member countries' oil revenues, due to worldwide inflation and the ever-widening gap between the prices of capital and manufactured goods essential for their economic development and those of petroleum".

D2.2.ii—Conclusion of Tehran and Tripoli agreements

Faced with unanimous OPEC support for the imposition of new financial terms by unilateral legislative action, the foreign oil companies indicated on Feb. 9 that they were now willing to accept the "anti-leapfrogging" assurances which had been offered by the Gulf OPEC committee. Negotiations with the committee on financial issues resumed in Tehran on Feb. 11 and resulted in the conclusion of a five-year agreement on Feb. 14, a matter of hours before the expiry of the time limit laid down in Resolution XXII–131. The principal provisions of the agreement, which applied only to exports from Gulf terminals, were as follows:

(1) The uniform application—backdated as necessary to Nov. 14, 1970—of the 55 per cent tax rate which had already taken effect in several Gulf countries from that date.

(2) The immediate abolition of the 0.5 cents per barrel "marketing allowance" which existed in most OPEC Gulf countries and of all remaining discounts and gravity allowances under the OPEC royalty-expensing formula.

(3) An increase of 35 cents per barrel in the posted price of a 40° "base crude" (Qatari Dukhan), 2 cents of this increase being attributed to "the elimination of existing freight disparities". An across-the-board implementation of the price increase was to incorporate a gravity differential not exceeding 0.15 cents per barrel per 0.1° API for crudes between 30° and 40° (meaning in effect that the amount of the price increase on crudes within this range rose above 35 cents per barrel at the rate of at least 0.5 cents for each degree below 40°, since the previous gravity differential was at least 2 cents per degree). The notional gravity differential on crudes lighter than 40° (which formed a negligible fraction of Gulf output) remained at 2 cents per degree, while the differential on crudes heavier than 30° was subject to national negotiation. Table 25 shows the development of posted prices for three grades of Gulf crude.

The Gulf posting for Iraq's 35° crude was raised by 43.5 cents per barrel on Feb. 15 (6 cents more than the rise due under the OPEC formula) in order to increase its relative value to the level demanded by the Iraq Government. Iraq agreed to sign the Tehran agreement only after receiving a written undertaking from IPC that implementation would not be made dependent on the prior settlement of any current government-company dispute in that country.

(4) There were to be future annual increases in postings of 2.5 per cent plus 5 cents per barrel. The application of the first such increase, due on Jan. 1, 1972, would be brought forward to June 1, 1971, in order to take account of the fact that the new posted price structure was not introduced until Feb. 15, 1971 (i.e. as opposed to Jan. 1, 1971, the companies having argued against formal retroactivity because they did not wish to compromise the basis of their opposition to Libya's demand for backdated freight premiums). Future increases would be applied at the beginning of 1973, 1974 and 1975, and the agreement would expire at the end of 1975. The 2.5 per cent increments represented adjustments for world inflation, while the 5-cent increments represented adjustments to take

Table 25 —Posted prices of three Gulf crudes, August 1970 to February 1971 (dollars per barrel)

	Qatar 40°	Saudi Arabia 34°	Iran 31°
Aug. 16, 1960 to Nov. 13, 1970	1.93	1.80	1.63
Nov. 14, 1970 to Feb. 14, 1971	1.93	1.80	1.72
Feb. 15, 1971	2.28	2.18	2.125

account of increases in the consumer prices of refined products. The intended evolution of the Ras Tanura posting for Saudi Arabian 34° crude under the incremental formula was as follows: June 1, 1971: $2.285 per barrel; Jan. 1, 1973: $2.392; Jan. 1, 1974: $2.502; Jan. 1, 1975: $2.615. An initial rise in this posting of 21.1 per cent on Feb. 15, 1971, would thus be translated into an overall rise of 45.3 per cent over the full five-year term of the agreement. Because of the increased rate of taxation and the elimination of tax allowances, the government unit revenue entitlement for the same crude on Feb. 15, 1971, was 38.9 per cent higher than on Nov. 13, 1970, and was to rise by 1975 to 168 per cent of the Nov. 13, 1970 level.

Saudi Arabia, Iraq and Algeria agreed on Feb. 23, 1971, that the Libyan Government should take responsibility for negotiating a financial settlement with the oil companies in respect of OPEC's Mediterranean exports. If acceptable minimum terms had not been secured within two weeks ministers from the four countries were to consider taking co-ordinated unilateral action, including the possible imposition of an embargo on all Mediterranean exports. On Feb. 24, against the background of Algeria's assertion of state control over its hydrocarbons industry (◊C1.3.iv), the Libyan Government announced a set of opening demands which differed from those made at the beginning of the year mainly in the extent to which they sought to minimize the variable freight element in any increase in postings in order to gain the highest possible fixed increase. The basic increase demanded on the grounds of "parity" with the 35-cent rise in the base Gulf posting was 50 cents per barrel, calculated by treating the Gulf increase as an average percentage rise and applying the same percentage to the existing Libyan posting of $2.53 per barrel. In total, the current Libyan claims amounted to a demand for a new fixed posting of $3.75 per barrel.

Negotiations with a committee representing all the oil companies operating in Libya began on March 1 after the Government had dropped its original insistence on "separate and short" negotiations with the individual companies. Company offers made during the first two weeks of March were designed (i) to maximize the variable freight element in any increase and to obtain firm guarantees that Libya would accept future reductions in postings attributable to movements in freight rates; (ii) to reduce the extent of the greatly increased fixed differential between Libyan and Gulf postings which had resulted from the Libyan increase of September 1970; and (iii) to resist all retroactivity provisions.

On March 15—when the companies' latest proposal was a posting of $3.19 per barrel, including a variable element of 36 cents, while the Libyan Government's latest claim was for a posting of $3.41 per barrel with future annual increments of 5 per cent—the Oil Ministers of Algeria, Iraq and Saudi Arabia held a further meeting with their Libyan counterpart at which minimum acceptable terms were agreed. Any company which failed to reach a settlement consistent with these terms (understood to include a base posting of $3.05 per barrel for Libyan 40° crude, plus appropriate temporary premiums) by a date to be fixed by the Libyan Government would face an embargo on its exports of OPEC oil from all Mediterranean terminals. The Mediterranean exporting countries' main financial demands were subsequently accepted by the companies on March 20 (which became the effective date of an increase in Mediterranean postings). However, a full settlement was not concluded until April 2, the intervening period having been devoted largely to bargaining about terms for the implementation of increments over the period to 1975 and for the dropping of all retroactivity demands. Libya's existing retroactive revenue entitlement, arising out of the backdating of the September 1970 increase in its postings, was taken out of the basic tax structure and redefined as a special national levy in order to establish the general applicability of a 55 per cent tax rate on OPEC's Mediterranean exports.

While the final Tripoli terms (◊C8.3.ii) were rather closer to the Tehran terms than had originally been demanded by Libya, the inclusion of additional fixed freight and quality premiums in the increased Libyan posting widened the underlying fixed differential between Libyan and Gulf postings to more than 80 cents per barrel, compared with about 60 cents in September 1970 and about 30 cents during the 1960s. Of the temporary premiums specified in the Tripoli agreement, the Suez Canal allowance was to be progressively phased out as the canal was reopened to tankers of specified draughts, while the temporary freight premium was subject to quarterly adjustment on the basis of movements in an agreed standard index of world freight rates.

(Independently assessed schedules of average freight rates for different classes of tanker had been published monthly since 1969 by the London Tanker Brokers' Panel. The Panel's "Worldscale Index", or Worldwide Tanker Nominal Freight Scale, was adjusted twice yearly to indicate the notional base tariff for a "standard vessel". Monthly average freight rate assessments—AFRA, based on weighted averages of current charter costs for different classes of vessel—were expressed as percentages of the prevailing Worldscale rate, values below 100 indicating assessment at below the full Worldscale tariff and values above 100 indicating assessment at above the full tariff. OPEC's Tripoli agreement provided for the variable freight premium to move after the end of June 1971 at the rate of approximately 0.058 cents per barrel per one-tenth of each percentage point, between certain limits, by which adjustments were made in the quarterly AFRA for tankers in the range 80,000 to 159,999 deadweight tons. The premium applied in full when this "Large Range 2" AFRA was at or above 92 per cent of Worldscale and ceased to apply when it was below 72 per cent of Worldscale.)

Algeria's unilateral adoption of financial arrangements modelled on those introduced by Libya was announced on April 13, 1971. National agreements for east Mediterranean postings based on the Tripoli terms, adjusted to take account of local freight and quality advantages, were concluded by Iraq on June 7 and by Saudi Arabia on June 23. Nigeria, which was not then a member of OPEC, concluded a similar agreement with its main concession holder on May 10. Table 26

Table 26 — Evolution of selected east Mediterranean and African postings, August 1970 to January 1972 (dollars per barrel)

	Iraq 36°	Saudi Arabia 34°	Libya 40°	Algeria 44°	Nigeria 37°
Aug. 31, 1970	2.21	2.17	2.23	*	2.17
Sept. 1, 1970	2.41	2.37	2.53	*	2.42
March 20, 1971	3.211	3.181	3.447	3.615	3.212
July 1, 1971	3.188	3.158	3.423	3.575	3.195
Oct. 1, 1971	3.166	3.136	3.399	3.552	3.178
Jan. 1, 1972	3.136	3.106	3.386	3.539	3.176

*Not directly comparable with other OPEC (◊C1.3).

Table 27 — Tax-reference values of four Venezuelan crudes, December 1970 to January 1972 (dollars per barrel)

	10°	26°	35°	41°
Dec. 31, 1970	1.429	2.0114	2.339	2.5574
Jan. 1, 1971	1.434	2.0164	2.344	2.5624
March 18, 1971	2.35	2.59	2.725	2.815
Jan. 1, 1972	2.507	2.9009	3.211	3.431

shows the development of postings for African and east Mediterranean crudes up to the beginning of 1972 (which reflected a 14-point decline in the Large Range 2 AFRA during the course of 1971).

Venezuela, which had taken full control over the fixing of its tax reference prices in December 1970, introduced increases on March 18, 1971, to take account of the Gulf states' Tehran agreement. Increments for 1972 were subsequently announced in December 1971. Table 27 shows the development of Venezuela's minimum export values for tax purposes (exclusive of freight and quality premiums) for selected grades of crude. Indonesia's official selling price for 34° crude was raised from $1.70 to $2.21 per barrel on April 1, 1971, with a further increase to $2.56 per barrel on Oct. 1, 1971.

D2.3—Decisions of 23rd to 26th Meetings of OPEC Conference

The 23rd (extraordinary) meeting of the OPEC Conference was held on July 10, 1971, to discuss the matter of a joint production programme, as required by Resolution XXI–121 (◊**D1.6.iii**). The Conference noted the recent improvement in the market price of oil and the favourable outlook for continuing market stability, which was "the basic objective to be achieved through an effective implementation of the principle of production programming". The Conference therefore adopted a resolution (XXIII–133) deferring further consideration of the introduction of a production programme "until such time as the Conference considers it necessary to counteract any element which might lead to instability and deterioration in the oil market". In the meantime, the Economic Commission was to prepare a report on the feasibility of establishing a contingency plan to be put into effect "should the oil market price deterioration reappear".

The 24th Conference meeting, which began two days later, admitted Nigeria to OPEC membership. Following OPEC's success in the recent negotiations with concessionaire companies over fiscal matters, the Conference turned its attention to the Organization's demand for host government participation in the companies' production operations. It was decided (as Resolution XXIV–135) "that member countries shall take immediate steps towards the effective implementation of the principle of participation in the existing oil concessions" and that a ministerial committee should be set up to formulate recommendations regarding a suitable course of action. The committee, consisting of the heads of delegation of Iran, Iraq, Kuwait, Libya and Saudi Arabia, was required to report to an extraordinary meeting of the Conference in September. (An identically constituted committee had already carried out a preliminary study of the issue in accordance with a decision of the 21st Conference meeting.)

The committee subsequently decided to recommend that, in recognition of the extent of the international oil companies' control over downstream marketing outlets and of the likelihood that price stability would be threatened by a large-scale dislocation of established marketing patterns, participation should be phased in on the basis of a "buy-back" formula whereby host governments' "participation crude" would be made available for purchase by the established foreign exporting companies at negotiated prices. It was also decided that compensation for government participation in the ownership of the concessionaire companies' producing assets should be offered on the basis of the net book value of the assets concerned. As regards the extent of participation, the Arab Gulf countries on the committee tended to favour an initial demand for a 20 per cent minority interest, this being the percentage which Iraq had been claiming for the past 10 years in respect of IPC's operations. Iran, which did not have a formal concessionary relationship with IOP, was not strongly committed to the early achievement of participation in the consortium's production operations, although it was prepared to negotiate parallel arrangements based on the Arab Gulf countries' demands. Libya advocated the early achievement of 51 per cent majority state control of production operations (the minimum level achieved by Algeria earlier in the year).

The 25th (extraordinary) meeting of the OPEC Conference, held in Beirut on Sept. 22, 1971, recognized that the issue of participation, like that of tax-reference prices, was best approached through collective negotiations by the six Gulf countries and individual negotiations by other OPEC members, subject to overall co-ordination by the Conference. Resolution XXV–139 called for the establishment of participation negotiations with the oil companies and declared that "in case such negotiations fail to achieve their purpose, the Conference shall determine a procedure with a view to enforcing and achieving the objectives of effective participation through concerted action".

Apart from Libya, the only non-Gulf OPEC member which was known to be interested in opening early national participation negotiations was Nigeria, which had acquired a 33⅓ per cent interest in the operations of one of its smaller concessionaires five days before OPEC's Beirut meeting (◊**C9.3**). Algeria had recently reached an outline agreement which marked the final stage in the consolidation of majority state control of its oil industry (◊**C1.3.iv**), while Indonesia was not involved in the participation issue. Venezuela had enacted "reversion" legislation in July which ruled out the renewal of existing oil concession agreements and envisaged their continuation until their scheduled expiry dates under state supervision but without formal state participation (◊**C13.3.v**).

Although the participation issue had originally been scheduled as the sole agenda item of the 25th Conference meeting, delegates also held urgent discussions regarding the impact on their revenues of the US Government's decision to suspend the free convertibility of the dollar into gold with effect from Aug. 15. This had led to a general appreciation of other major currencies against the dollar and, since crude oil was priced in dollars, to a decline in the overall purchasing power of unit oil revenues. Recalling the concern previously expressed in Resolution XXI–122 (◊**D1.6.iii**), the Conference adopted Resolution XXV–140 calling for negotiations with the international oil companies "with a view to adopting ways and means to offset any adverse effect on the per-barrel real income of member countries resulting from the international monetary developments as of Aug. 15, 1971". The next meeting of the Conference was to decide what "necessary action" should be taken by OPEC if such negotiations had failed to achieve their purpose.

Further action on the issue of participation was held in abeyance during October and November 1971 in view of OPEC's overriding concern with the exchange-rate issue. Representatives of member countries' monetary authorities met in Vienna from Oct. 12 to 14, while the head of the economics department of the OPEC Secretariat visited Washington later in the month for talks with officials of the International Monetary Fund. The oil companies' London policy group (◊**D2.2.i**) met during the third week of October to establish a common negotiating position on both participation and monetary developments, and agreed on Nov. 9 to open talks on the latter issue in the near future with representatives of the Gulf OPEC group. These talks, held at OPEC headquarters in Vienna from Nov. 22 to Dec. 1, began with the rejection by the Gulf states of the companies' initial claim that the 2.5 per cent annual "inflation" increments in postings under the Tehran pricing agreement should be regarded as a sufficient compensation for exchange-rate losses (which were said by the Gulf states to have caused a 5.7 per cent reduction in the current purchasing power of their export revenues). Thereafter the two sides considered various alternative criteria for measuring and offsetting exchange-rate losses, but were unable to agree on a practical formula (not least because of the difficulty of predicting future developments in the international monetary situation at this time).

The 26th meeting of the OPEC Conference, held on Dec. 7, 1971, invited oil company representatives to resume talks with Gulf OPEC ministers in Geneva on Jan. 10, 1972, with a view to "finalizing" an agreement to compensate member countries for the depreciation of the US dollar against other major currencies. The oil companies were also invited to open participation negotiations with the Gulf member countries in Geneva on Jan. 20 (thus effectively establishing a 10-day deadline for completion of the talks on the monetary issue). Unsatisfactory progress on either issue was to lead to the calling of an extraordinary Conference meeting with a view to organizing "concerted action" in support of OPEC's objectives.

D3—1972

D3.1—Annual Statistical Survey

D3.1.i—Oil production and reserves

World

Total production .... 53,540,000 bpd (2,633.8 million tonnes)
   Change over 1971 .... +5.6 per cent

End-year proved reserves .... 635,600 million barrels
   Change over end-1971 .... −0.6 per cent

Reserves:production ratio .... 32.5 : 1

Regional shares:

	In 1972 world production*			In end-1972 world reserves†		
	Regional total (million tonnes)	Change over 1971 (per cent)	Share of world total (per cent)	Reserves (thousand million barrels)	Change over 1971 (per cent)	Share of world total (per cent)
Middle East	898.6	+11.3	34.1	355.3	−3.1	55.9
North America	621.0	+2.4	23.6	52.8	−5.0	8.3
USSR/Eastern Europe/China	461.8	+6.9	17.5	98.0	−0.5	15.4
Africa	282.1	+0.4	10.7	69.2	+22.5	10.9
Latin America/ Caribbean	255.6	−4.0	9.7	32.8	+4.5	5.2
Asia‡/Australasia	92.4	+16.4	3.5	14.9	−4.5	2.3
Western Europe§	22.3	+1.8	0.9	12.6	−14.9	2.0

*Including production from oil shales, tar sands and natural gas liquids (NGL).
†Excluding oil shales and tar sands; including NGL in North America.
‡Excluding China.
§Including Yugoslavia.

OPEC*

OPEC oil production .... 27,315,000 bpd (1,356.8 million tonnes)
   Change over 1971 .... +7.1 per cent
   Share of 1972 world total .... 51.5 per cent

OPEC end-year proved reserves .... 428,592 million barrels
   Change over 1971 .... −0.5 per cent
   Share of 1972 world total .... 67.4 per cent

OPEC reserves:production ratio .... 43 : 1

*End-1975 membership basis.

OPEC (continued)

OPEC member countries' production:

	1972 production (million tonnes)	1972 production (thousand bpd)	Change over 1971 (per cent)	Share of world total (per cent)	Share of OPEC total (per cent)
Algeria	49.8	1,060	+36.4	1.9	3.8
Ecuador*	3.8	80	+1,800.0	0.2	0.3
Gabon†	6.3	125	+8.6	0.2	0.5
Indonesia	53.4	1,080	+21.1	2.0	3.9
Iran	251.9	5,050	+11.0	9.6	18.5
Iraq	72.1	1,465	−13.7	2.7	5.4
Kuwait	153.0	3,055	+2.8	5.8	11.2
Libya	108.2	2,240	−18.7	4.1	8.2
Nigeria	88.9	1,815	+19.0	3.4	6.6
Qatar	23.2	485	+13.2	0.9	1.8
Saudi Arabia	287.2	5,785	+27.6	10.9	21.2
UAE‡	58.2	1,205	+13.9	2.2	4.4
Venezuela	171.5	3,305	−8.6	6.5	12.1
Neutral Zone§	29.3	565	+3.5	1.1	2.1

*Not admitted to OPEC membership until 1973.
†Not admitted to (associate) membership until 1973.
‡Including Dubai (7,600,000 tonnes/155,000 bpd), which was not formally admitted to OPEC membership until 1974.
§Production shared between Kuwait and Saudi Arabia.

Non-OPEC

Selected non-OPEC countries' oil production:

	1972 production (million tonnes)	1972 production (thousand bpd)	Change over 1971 (per cent)	Share of world total (per cent)
USA*	532.2	11,185	+0.4	20.2
USSR	400.4	8,105	+6.2	15.2
Canada	88.8	1,830	+15.9	3.4
China	42.1	845	+14.7	1.6
Mexico	24.8	505	+4.2	0.9
Argentina	22.6	435	+2.3	0.8
Egypt	17.6	350	−16.2	0.7
Oman	14.2	280	−1.4	0.5
Norway	1.6	30	+433.3	0.06
United Kingdom	0.1	†	—	‡
Total	1,144.4	23,565§	+3.8	43.36

*Of which natural gas liquids 62,100,000 tonnes (1,745,000 bpd).
†Less than 5,000 bpd.
‡Negligible.
§Excluding United Kingdom.

D3.1.ii—Oil consumption

World

Total consumption	....	52,765,000 bpd (2,592.4 million tonnes)
Change over 1971	....	+7.4 per cent

Regional distribution of total:

	1972 consumption		Change over 1971 (per cent)	Share of world total (per cent)
	(million tonnes)	(thousand bpd)		
North America	855.1	17,645	+7.5	33.0
Western Europe*	701.8	14,155	+7.0	27.1
USSR/Eastern Europe/China	413.2	8,330	+9.5	15.9
Asia†/Australasia	366.2	7,395	+6.8	14.1
Latin America/ Caribbean	154.5	3,205	+7.7	6.0
Middle East	56.9	1,115	+5.4	2.2
Africa	44.7	920	+0.7	1.7

*Including Yugoslavia.
†Excluding China.

Selected countries

	1972 consumption		Change over 1971 (per cent)	Share of world total (per cent)
	(million tonnes)	(thousand bpd)		
USA	775.8	15,990	+7.9	29.9
USSR	302.9	6,115	+8.5	11.7
Japan	234.4	4,735	+6.7	9.0
West Germany	140.9	2,885	+5.5	5.4
France	114.1	2,315	+11.0	4.4
United Kingdom	110.5	2,230	+5.9	4.3
Italy	98.2	1,965	+4.7	3.8
Canada	79.3	1,655	+4.6	3.1
China	43.1	855	+17.4	1.7
Spain	32.5	655	+5.2	1.2
Total	1,931.7	39,400	+7.6	74.5

D3.1.iii—Oil refining

World

Total refinery capacity	....	59,825,000 bpd
Change over 1971	....	+8.2 per cent

Total refinery throughputs	....	50,540,000 bpd
Change over 1971	....	+5.5 per cent

Consumption as proportion of capacity		88.2 per cent

Selected markets
Consumption of refined product types and change over 1971:

	USA (million tonnes)	USA (per cent)	Western Europe (million tonnes)	Western Europe (per cent)	Japan (million tonnes)	Japan (per cent)
Gasoline	300.8	+6.1	125.3	+9.6	38.3	+10.1
Middle distillates	191.6	+7.9	231.2	+7.7	41.1	+12.9
Fuel oil	133.3	+10.8	256.4	+6.0	124.9	+3.9
Other	150.1	+8.8	88.9	+4.3	30.1	+6.4
Total	775.8	+7.9	701.8	+7.0	234.4	+6.7

D3.1.iv—Tankers and trade

Tankers

Total world fleet	189,500,000 deadweight tons
Change over 1971	+10.9 per cent

Trade

Total world crude exports (including re-exports)	27,779,900 bpd (1,372.5 million tonnes)
Change over 1971	+9 per cent
OPEC crude exports	24,078,500 bpd (1,189.6 million tonnes)
Change over 1971	+9.3 per cent
Share of 1972 world total	86.7 per cent
Total world product exports (including re-exports)	7,939,300 bpd (410,088,000 tonnes)
Change over 1971	+4.4 per cent
OPEC product exports	1,792,300 bpd (92,577,500 tonnes)
Change over 1971	−1.2 per cent
Share of 1972 world total	22.6 per cent

Regional distribution of world oil trade*:

	Share of 1972 imports (per cent) Crude	Share of 1972 imports (per cent) Products	Share of 1972 exports (per cent) Crude	Share of 1972 exports (per cent) Products
USA	9.0	48.3	—	4.4
Canada	3.2	1.6	3.4	4.1
Latin America/Caribbean	7.3	2.8	4.8	49.1
Western Europe	53.6	14.2	—	5.8
Middle East	0.5	—	64.8	17.8
North Africa	0.1	1.7	13.5	0.3
West Africa	0.1	0.3	7.7	0.2
East and southern Africa/ South Asia	3.0	2.5	—	0.1
South-East Asia	3.6	7.5	3.2	5.2
Australasia	0.9	1.6	†	0.2
Japan	16.7	11.4	—	0.4
USSR/Eastern Europe/ China	1.5	0.4	2.6	12.4
Unspecified	0.5	7.7	—	—
Total	100.0	100.0	100.0	100.0

*Excluding intra-regional trade.
†Negligible.

D3.1.v—World primary energy consumption

Total consumption (excluding
    non-commercial fuels) .... 5,625.9 million tonnes oil equivalent (mtoe)
    Change over 1971 .... +4.5 per cent

Contributions of primary energy sources:

	Consumption (mtoe)	Change over 1971 (per cent)	Share of total (per cent)
Oil	2,592.4	+7.4	46.1
Coal	1,629.4	−0.1	28.9
Natural gas	1,045.0	+4.8	18.6
Water power	320.7	+2.0	5.7
Nuclear power	38.4	+37.1	0.7

D3.1.vi—Natural gas production and reserves

Marketed production (thousand million cubic metres):

	Regional total (tmcm)	Change over 1971 (per cent)	Share of 1972 world total (per cent)
North America	679.4	+1.2	58.9
Latin America/ Caribbean	31.5	+7.5	2.7
Western Europe*	120.8	+0.3	10.5
USSR/Eastern Europe/China	274.6	+4.8	23.8
Middle East	24.3	+13.6	2.1
Africa	7.5	−2.6	0.6
Asia†/Australasia	15.9	+20.5	1.4
World total	1,154.0	+2.5	100.0
(of which OPEC)	*(39.0)*	*(+5.4)*	*(3.4)*

*Including Yugoslavia.
†Excluding China.

End-year proved reserves (thousand million cubic metres):

	Regional total (tmcm)	Change over 1971 (per cent)	Share of 1972 world total (per cent)
North America	9,033.7	−4.6	16.8
Latin America/ Caribbean	2,311.3	+21.5	4.3
Western Europe*	5,020.7	+8.5	9.3
USSR/Eastern Europe/China	19,785.1	+23.1	36.9
Middle East	9,749.4	+0.1	18.2
Africa	5,409.7	−0.8	10.1
Asia†/Australasia	2,355.9	+40.0	4.4
World total	53,665.8	+9.6	100.0
(of which OPEC)	*(16,010.3)*	*(+2.0)*	*(29.8)*

*Including Yugoslavia.
†Excluding China.

D3.2—Negotiation of "Geneva I" Agreement to offset Exchange-Rate Losses

By the time that representatives of the Persian/Arabian Gulf group of OPEC countries opened formal negotiations with the oil companies on exchange-rate problems on Jan. 10, 1972, the international monetary situation had been greatly clarified as a result of agreements reached by the major non-communist industrialized countries at a meeting in Washington on Dec. 17 and 18, 1971. Under these "Smithsonian agreements" the dollar price of gold had been increased by 8.57 per cent (i.e. the US dollar had been formally devalued by 7.89 per cent against gold), certain other major currencies had been effectively revalued against the dollar by margins ranging from 8.57 per cent (e.g. the French franc and the pound sterling) to 16.88 per cent (Japanese yen), and wider margins had been introduced for permissible currency fluctuations within the new exchange rate structure. All other countries had then taken steps to define the positions of their currencies within this altered framework.

The company negotiators proposed on Jan. 10 that the posted price of oil should be linked to quarterly movements in an IMF index of export prices for manufactured goods, weighted to reflect the import pattern of the OPEC members, and that such indexation should replace future "inflation" increments under the Tehran agreement of February 1971. The OPEC negotiators' rejection of this formula was announced on Jan. 11, when it was stated by OPEC that the oil companies had gained "substantial windfall profits" in Japan and Western Europe as a result of exchange-rate movements and were attempting to "shift the focus of discussion from the real problem at hand", which could only be solved by an adjustment in postings "to reflect the overall devaluation of the dollar". The form of indexation proposed by the company side was unacceptable because it would not reflect "the actual increase in cost to member countries from such important sectors of their economies as services, investments, military equipment and other government expenditures abroad".

A further company offer, envisaging a modified form of import-price indexation plus retention of the existing "inflation" increments (◊D2.2.ii), was rejected on Jan. 13. The OPEC side stated that the revised formula would bring about an increase of only 4.5 per cent in the Gulf members' dollar revenues in the first quarter of 1972, whereas these countries' loss of unit purchasing power (calculated by relating the recent international currency realignments to their total pattern of trade) was now between 11.5 per cent and 12 per cent. Moreover, the companies' formula could cause a reduction in posted prices in 1973. The Gulf members' minimum demand was stated on Jan. 14 as full compensation for the "actual loss in value of the US dollar in terms of gold". It was pointed out that an 8.57 per cent rise in postings would be in line with a recent increase in dollar freight rates announced by the international maritime conferences and that it would have a neutral impact on industrialized oil-importing countries which had retained unaltered par values for their currencies in terms of gold; moreover, countries which had introduced higher effective revaluations against the dollar would continue to benefit from a lower real import cost for oil.

After further negotiations during which the company side rejected claims for the backdating of a price adjustment to August 1971, an agreement was finally reached as follows on Jan. 20:

(1) There would be an immediate increase in posted prices by a margin (averaging 8.49 per cent) which would produce an 8.57 per cent increase in the government revenue entitlement under the current Middle Eastern tax arrangements.

(2) Posted prices would be subject to future quarterly adjustment under an indexation formula measuring the average change in the composite dollar exchange rate of a basket of

currencies (those of Belgium, France, West Germany, Italy, Japan, the Netherlands, Sweden, Switzerland and the United Kingdom). Starting from an index value of 110.2 (April 30, 1971 composite exchange rate = 100), proportionate corrections were to be made in postings whenever the index moved by more than two full points in any quarter, although downward corrections could not reduce postings to below the level provided for in existing agreements.

(3) The indexation arrangements were to be valid until the end of 1975 and were to be treated as a supplementary provision to the Tehran pricing agreement. The countries covered were the six OPEC signatories of the Tehran agreement (Abu Dhabi, Iran, Iraq, Kuwait, Qatar and Saudi Arabia). The crudes covered were those exported both from Persian/Arabian Gulf terminals and from east Mediterranean terminals.

Similar agreements with concessionaire companies were concluded by Libya on May 4 and by Nigeria in April and June, the initial increase in the Libyan posting being implemented with effect from Jan. 20 and the Nigerian increase with effect from Feb. 15.

After the conclusion of the "Geneva I" agreement there were no exchange rate fluctuations of sufficient magnitude to trigger a change in postings under the indexation formula during 1972. The per-barrel postings established for selected Gulf crudes on Jan. 20 were as follows: Abu Dhabi: 39°—$2.54; Iran: 31°—$2.417, 34°—$2.467; Iraq: 35°—$2.451; Kuwait: 31°—$2.373; Qatar: 40°—$2.59; Saudi Arabia: 31°—$2.373, 34°—$2.479.

A fall in freight rates during the first half of 1972 culminated in the full removal of variable freight premiums after the Large Range 2 AFRA had fallen below 72 per cent of Worldscale. Table 28 shows the resulting decline in the revalued Libyan, Nigerian and east Mediterranean postings during 1972.

Algeria increased its posting for 44° crude by 3.3 per cent to $3.656 per barrel on Jan. 20. Indonesia increased its official selling price for 34° crude by 31 per cent to $2.96 per barrel on April 1. Venezuela, which had fixed its tax-reference values for 1972 in the week following the Smithsonian agreements, did not alter these values during the course of the year (◊**D2.2.ii**), although legislation requiring oil companies to make accelerated tax payments was enacted in June.

Table 28 — Evolution of selected east Mediterranean and African postings in 1972 (dollars per barrel)

	Iraq 36°	Saudi Arabia 34°	Libya 40°	Nigeria 37°
Jan. 20	3.402	3.37	3.673	. . .
Feb. 15	. . .	. . .	. . .	3.446
April 1	3.373	3.341	3.642	3.424
July 1	3.353	3.321	3.62	3.409

D3.3—Negotiations on the Participation Issue

Negotiations on the Gulf OPEC countries' claim for participation in the production operations of the established concessionaire companies opened in Geneva on Jan. 21, 1972, immediately after the conclusion of the exchange-rate agreement. The OPEC side made it clear that the minimum acceptable level of participation was 20 per cent in the first instance, with payment of compensation on the basis of net book value. After the end of January Shaikh Yamani, the leader of the OPEC delegation and the main advocate of government participation in the exploitation of the Middle Eastern concession areas, was mandated by the other Gulf states to continue the participation negotiations at national level with representatives of Aramco in Saudi Arabia.

Aramco reiterated its total opposition to the principle of government participation in producing oilfields, and on Feb. 15 made a counter-proposal for 50 per cent Saudi Arabian participation in the development of unexploited proved oilfields within its concession area. This proposal was seen by Saudi Arabia as an attempt to undermine its commitment to the Gulf states' collective negotiating position and was accordingly rejected on direct instructions from King Faisal, who issued a warning to Aramco on the following day stressing the "imperative" need for the company to co-operate in "the implementation of effective participation" in producing oilfields.

Shaikh Yamani subsequently requested that an extraordinary meeting of the OPEC Conference be convened to consider collective action against the Middle Eastern concession holders in accordance with Resolution XXV–139 (◊**D2.3**). Aramco continued to insist on its established contractual rights until the eve of this meeting, when it finally announced its acceptance of the principle of 20 per cent government participation in its concession area. The 27th (extraordinary) meeting of the OPEC Conference, held on March 11 and 12, acknowledged that Aramco's announcement of March 10 marked "an effective step towards the realization of this important objective" and adopted a resolution (XXVII–145) threatening co-ordinated OPEC sanctions against any oil company which "may attempt to under-mine the solidarity of the Organization by submitting to the demand for participation in some member countries and not in others". The meeting also set up a working party to "prepare a study on the establishment of a fund to assist any member country affected by actions taken against it by oil companies". Shaikh Yamani was mandated to continue participation negotiations with the oil com-panies on behalf of the Gulf OPEC countries.

After the meeting formal acceptance of the principle of 20 per cent participation was conceded by the concessionaire companies in Abu Dhabi, Iraq, Kuwait and Qatar, and representatives of other major oil companies with Middle Eastern concession interests joined the Aramco parent companies in their negotiations with Shaikh Yamani from April onwards. Having accepted the principle involved, the companies began to bargain for favourable participation terms, including com-pensation for "the partial loss of contractual rights to produce and export". This concept was strongly resisted by Shaikh Yamani, who made it clear that, while host governments were prepared to pay compensation based on the companies' past investments in the concession areas, they would not entertain any claims in respect of the companies' loss of future profits from the exploitation of resources in which the host governments had an overriding sovereign interest. This issue was one of the main points of contention between Iraq and IPC, whose latest round of negotiations on outstanding disputes (initiated in mid-January) broke down when IPC refused to drop its claim to a share of future production from the North Rumaila oilfield, which had been discovered by IPC but developed by the state. Threats of legal action by IPC against buyers of North Rumaila crude, which Iraq began to export in April, were accompanied by IPC's introduction of major cutbacks in its own output. This caused a further deterioration in government-company relations, culminating in the full nationalization of IPC's main northern concession areas on June 1 (◊**C6.3.iv**).

The 28th (extraordinary) meeting of the OPEC Conference, held on June 19 at Iraq's request, adopted the following resolution (XXVIII–146) supporting the Iraqi nationalization measures:

"The Conference,

"Having heard the statement of the head of the Iraqi delegation concerning the negotiations with IPC, the failure of which led to the nationalization of the operations of said company by the Government of Iraq;

"Recognizing that the [IPC parent] companies have been adopting discriminatory policies against Iraq for a long time and in a manner that has been causing serious damage to the Iraqi national economy, notably by denying Iraq normal increases in production and other financial rights which would have contributed effectively in accelerating economic growth in that member country;

"Noting that said companies had continually tried to exert pressure in order to influence the outcome of negotiations on outstanding issues, most notably by the recent drastic reduction in the production of the Iraq Petroleum Company, with considerable adverse effects on the implementation of the development plans of Iraq;

"Recalling Resolutions III–18 adopted in 1961, VII–49 of 1964, XI–73 of 1966, XIII–81 of 1967, XX–115, XX–116 and XXI–125 of 1970, which expressed the concern of the Conference over the attitude of the oil companies operating in Iraq and expressed also full support for any appropriate action taken by the Iraq Government to safeguard its legitimate interests;

"Resolves (i) to support the action taken by the Iraq Government to nationalize the operations of the Iraq Petroleum Company as a lawful act of sovereignty to safeguard its legitimate interests; (ii) that member countries shall not allow oil companies to replace the crude exported by IPC at the level of 1970 by oil produced in their territories and/or to substitute that oil in its traditional markets; and (iii) that a committee shall be formed by the heads of delegation of Abu Dhabi, Iran, Libya, Saudi Arabia and Venezuela, assisted by the Secretary-General, to formulate effective ways and means to implement and follow up item (ii) above and report its findings to the Conference."

The circumstances of the IPC nationalization strengthened OPEC's determination to resist the oil companies' demand for a general Gulf compensation formula which took account of the partial loss of access to proved reserves within the concession areas, although Iraq itself now became an interested observer rather than an active participant in the regional negotiating process. (Having eliminated the possibility of phased participation in the IPC group's northern concession areas, the Iraq Government decided not to pursue this option in the group's non-nationalized southern concession areas.) Iran announced its withdrawal from the general Gulf participation negotiations on June 24 in order to pursue national negotiations with the IOP consortium. These were presented as being "parallel" to the Gulf negotiations but were initially centred on the separate issue of the Iranian Government's demands for the accelerated development of the consortium's productive capacity (◊C5.3.v).

At its 29th meeting, held on June 27, the OPEC Conference considered Shaikh Yamani's report on the current status of the Gulf participation negotiations, in the light of which it "confirmed that compensation should be based on the net book value of the assets and refused to consider any other basis for compensation, considering the fact that petroleum reserves belong to the countries". The Conference declared that there should be "full co-ordination" between Shaikh Yamani's negotiations on behalf of Abu Dhabi, Iraq, Kuwait, Qatar and Saudi Arabia and national participation negotiations in Iran, Libya and Nigeria (the main purpose of this declaration being to offset the negative impression which had been created by Iran's withdrawal from the Gulf group). The Conference expressed its concern at the oil companies' delaying tactics in the Gulf negotiations and reaffirmed the member countries' preparedness to take co-ordinated action, as envisaged in Resolution XXV–139, with the aim of securing an early settlement.

After further pressure had been brought to bear on Aramco by King Faisal of Saudi Arabia (who maintained an active interest in the negotiating process), Shaikh Yamani began three weeks of intensive talks with senior oil company executives (representing BP and CFP as well as the four Aramco parent companies) near Beirut in mid-August. "Tangible progress" was reported to have been made when these talks ended in early September, and after further negotiating sessions, held in

Saudi Arabia and in London, Shaikh Yamani stated on Sept. 19 that "the most difficult and critical" problems had been resolved.

During this phase of the negotiations, the companies were understood to have dropped their insistence on compensation for future loss of existing contractual rights and to have accepted the principle of eventual majority state participation. As regards the introduction of buy-back arrangements designed to avoid a damaging dislocation of existing export marketing patterns, the companies made it clear that their aim was to secure access to the highest possible share of host governments' participation crude at the lowest possible price. By September 1972 it had been agreed in principle that the companies should have buy-back rights over the greater part of the government share of output during the early years of participation agreements, with specified minimum entitlements (in recognition of the companies' existing contractual export commitments to arm's-length customers) and specified maximum obligations (in order to provide host governments with additional guaranteed marketing outlets). All buy-back transactions would be effected at market-related prices, with special discounts on those volumes of oil purchased by the companies as an obligation rather than a right.

D3.4—Conclusion of General Agreement on Participation

After further negotiations in New York in early October, it was announced on Oct. 5 that a "General Agreement on Participation" had been concluded setting out the main principles for national agreements between Arab Gulf countries and their respective concessionaire companies. The main features of the agreement were as follows:

(1) Majority state ownership of production operations was to be achieved at the end of a nine-year period during which host government participation in the concession areas would increase as follows: Jan. 1, 1973 to Dec. 31, 1977—25 per cent; Jan. 1, 1978—30 per cent; Jan. 1, 1979—35 per cent; Jan. 1, 1980—40 per cent; Jan. 1, 1981—45 per cent; Jan. 1, 1982—51 per cent.

(2) Compensation payments to producing companies in respect of the state interest in their producing assets were to be based on an inflation-adjusted "updated book value" (roughly equivalent to current replacement cost) which was several times as great as the amortized net book valuation originally offered by the OPEC side.

(3) Host governments were to contribute to capital investment in the concession areas in proportion to their participation interests, and agreed procedures were to be adopted for drawing up investment budgets designed to expand productive capacity in line with the development of export demand.

(4) Each producing company's share of the output from its concession area (i.e. 75 per cent of total production for the first five years of the agreement, declining to 49 per cent in 1982) would be categorized as equity crude, available for disposal by the producing company at the normal tax-paid cost. The balance of production, belonging to the host government, would be known as participation crude. Of this participation crude, a reducing proportion (75 per cent in 1973, 50 per cent in 1974 and 25 per cent in 1975) was categorized as "bridging oil" which would be purchased, as of right, by the producing company at a "quarter-way price" (tax-paid cost plus one-fourth of the difference between tax-paid cost and posted price) plus a negotiable cash margin designed to equate the total buy-back price with the prevailing realized market price. A further proportion of the participation crude was categorized as "phase-in crude", which the producing company was obliged to buy from the host government if the government so required. Phase-in crude was to be priced at the quarter-way price plus a lower cash margin than that which applied to bridging crude—i.e. at a small discount off the prevailing market price. The available volume of phase-in crude in each year was specified as a reducing proportion of the total participation crude (starting at 90 per cent and gradually declining over a period of 19 years), less the volumes of bridging crude specified for the first three years. The remainder of the oil produced (i.e. an initial 10 per cent of the participation crude, equivalent to 2.5 per cent of the total production, in the

first year, and progressively higher proportions in future years) was to be marketed directly by the host government.

The terms of the agreement in principle were discussed by the five Arab Gulf members of OPEC at a meeting in Kuwait on Oct. 17, at which Shaikh Yamani was requested to seek clarification of certain points from the company side (mainly concerning the procedures for fixing the buy-back prices of bridging and phase-in crude). Shaikh Yamani then met the company side in Riyadh on Oct. 19 and obtained new assurances which enabled Abu Dhabi, Kuwait and Qatar to join Saudi Arabia in announcing their approval of the terms of the agreement on Oct. 25. Iraq was represented at the Gulf group's discussions but indicated that it did not intend to negotiate for national implementation of the General Agreement on Participation (not least because this would have placed IPC in a strong position to argue for compensation at updated book value in respect of assets already nationalized). The four countries which had accepted the terms indicated their intention to consult closely with one another, particularly on the pricing question, in their subsequent negotiations to draw up national agreements with their respective concession holders.

The 30th (extraordinary) meeting of the OPEC Conference, held in Riyadh on Oct. 27, 1972, to consider the terms of the draft agreement on participation, acknowledged that the agreement "secures effective participation for the states concerned", although it was noted that Venezuela had formally reserved judgment on the matter. The Conference described "the realization of effective participation" as "an event marking a turning point in the history of the oil industry" and paid tribute to the role which had been played by King Faisal in "eliminating many of the obstacles" which had been encountered during the long negotiations. The meeting also "expressed its solidarity with Iraq, Libya and Nigeria in their efforts to resolve their outstanding issues with the oil companies operating in their territories".

The last phase of the Gulf participation negotiations involved a joint initiative by Abu Dhabi, Kuwait, Qatar and Saudi Arabia (with Iraq acting as an observer) to reach an agreement with the companies on buy-back prices for 1973. In view of the strengthening of realized market prices during the last quarter of 1972 (◊**A4.15.i**), the prices finally agreed in December ($2.25 per barrel for Abu Dhabi's low-sulphur 39° crude, $1.95 for Kuwait's 31° crude, $2.17 for 40° Qatari crude and $2.05 for Saudi Arabian 34° crude fob Ras Tanura) were more than 5 per cent higher than those envisaged when the question had originally been discussed in September. Saudi Arabia and Abu Dhabi signed national participation agreements on Dec. 20. Kuwait and Qatar signed similar agreements in January 1973, the Kuwait agreement being rejected by that country's National Assembly (◊**C7.3.iii**).

The 31st meeting of the OPEC Conference, held on Nov. 30, 1972, reiterated the Conference's support for the Iraqi nationalization measures of June 1, noted a report by the committee set up under Resolution XXVIII–146, and indicated its preparedness to convene an extraordinary meeting, if so requested by Iraq, "to decide on and put into force measures that may be required for the effective implementation of the said resolution".

D4—1973

D4.1—Annual Statistical Survey

D4.1.i—Oil production and reserves

World

Total production .... 58,515,000 bpd (2,871.6 million tonnes)
    Change over 1972 .... +9 per cent

End-year proved reserves .... 634,600 million barrels
    Change over end-1972 .... −0.2 per cent

Reserves:production ratio .... 29.7 : 1

Regional shares:

	In 1973 world production*			In end-1973 world reserves†		
	Regional total (million tonnes)	Change over 1972 (per cent)	Share of world total (per cent)	Reserves (thousand (million barrels)	Change over 1972 (per cent)	Share of world total (per cent)
Middle East	1,052.5	+17.1	36.7	349.7	−1.6	55.1
North America	621.3	+0.05	21.6	51.1	−3.2	8.0
USSR/Eastern						
Europe/China	503.1	+9.0	17.5	103.0	+5.1	16.2
Africa	290.0	+2.8	10.1	67.3	−2.7	10.6
Latin America/						
Caribbean	272.0	+6.4	9.5	31.5	−4.0	5.0
Asia†/Australasia	110.2	+19.3	3.8	15.6	+4.7	2.5
Western Europe	22.5	+0.9	0.8	16.4	+30.2	2.6

*Including production from oil shales, tar sands and natural gas liquids (NGL).
†Excluding oil shales and tar sands; including NGL in North America.
‡Excluding China.
§Including Yugoslavia.

*OPEC**

OPEC oil production .... 31,280,000 bpd (1,547.7 million tonnes)
    Change over 1972 .... +14.1 per cent
    Share of 1973 world total .... 53.9 per cent

OPEC end-year proved reserves .... 421,627 million barrels
    Change over 1972 .... −1.6 per cent
    Share of 1973 world total .... 66.4 per cent

OPEC reserves:production ratio .... 36.9 : 1

*End-1975 membership basis.

OPEC (continued)

OPEC member countries' production:

	1973 production		Change over 1972 (per cent)	Share of world total (per cent)	Share of OPEC total (per cent)
	(million tonnes)	(thousand bpd)			
Algeria	51.2	1,095	+2.8	1.8	3.3
Ecuador	10.2	210	+168.4	0.4	0.6
Gabon*	7.5	150	+19.0	0.3	0.5
Indonesia	66.0	1,335	+23.6	2.3	4.3
Iran	293.2	5,895	+16.4	10.2	18.9
Iraq	99.0	2,020	+37.3	3.4	6.4
Kuwait	140.4	2,810	−8.2	4.9	9.1
Libya	104.9	2,180	−3.0	3.6	6.8
Nigeria	100.1	2,055	+12.6	3.5	6.5
Qatar	27.3	570	+17.7	1.0	1.8
Saudi Arabia	367.9	7,440	+28.1	12.8	23.8
UAE†	73.4	1,525	+26.1	2.5	4.7
Venezuela	179.0	3,460	+4.4	6.2	11.5
Neutral Zone‡	27.6	535	−5.8	1.0	1.8

*Associate member.
†Including Dubai (10,800,000 tonnes/220,000 bpd), which was not formally admitted to OPEC membership until 1974.
‡Production shared between Kuwait and Saudi Arabia.

Non-OPEC

Selected non-OPEC countries' oil production:

	1973 production		Change over 1972 (per cent)	Share of world total (per cent)
	(million tonnes)	(thousand bpd)		
USA*	519.0	10,950	−2.5	18.1
USSR	429.0	8,685	+7.1	15.0
Canada	102.3	2,115	+15.2	3.6
China	54.8	1,100	+30.2	1.9
Mexico	26.9	550	+8.5	0.9
Argentina	22.0	420	−2.7	0.8
Oman	14.7	295	+3.5	0.5
Egypt	13.0	255	−26.1	0.4
Norway	1.8	35	+12.5	0.06
United Kingdom	0.1	†	—	‡
Total	1,183.6	24,405§	+3.4	41.26

*Of which natural gas liquids 61,700,000 tonnes (1,740,000 bpd).
†Less than 5,000 bpd.
‡Negligible.
§Excluding United Kingdom.

D4.1.ii—Oil consumption

World

Total consumption .... 57,050,000 bpd (2,798 million tonnes)
    Change over 1972 .... +7.9 per cent

Regional distribution of total:

	1973 consumption		Change over 1972 (per cent)	Share of world total (per cent)
	(million tonnes)	(thousand bpd)		
North America	901.7	18,625	+5.4	32.2
Western Europe	748.9	15,155	+6.7	26.8
USSR/Eastern Europe/ China	454.6	9,170	+10.0	16.2
Asia†/Australasia	412.8	8,365	+12.7	14.8
Latin America/Caribbean	168.3	3,515	+8.9	6.0
Middle East	62.2	1,210	+9.3	2.2
Africa	49.5	1,010	+10.7	1.8

*Including Yugoslavia.
†Excluding China.

Selected countries

	1973 consumption		Change over 1972 (per cent)	Share of world total (per cent)
	(million tonnes)	(thousand bpd)		
USA	818.0	16,870	+5.4	29.2
USSR	325.7	6,595	+7.5	11.6
Japan	269.1	5,460	+14.8	9.6
West Germany	149.7	3,070	+6.2	5.4
France	127.3	2,585	+11.6	4.5
United Kingdom	113.2	2,300	+2.4	4.0
Italy	103.6	2,070	+5.5	3.7
Canada	83.7	1,755	+5.5	3.0
China	53.8	1,065	+24.8	1.9
Spain	39.1	790	+20.3	1.4
Total	2,083.2	42,560	+7.8	74.3

D4.1.iii—Oil refining

World

Total refinery capacity .... 64,525,000 bpd
    Change over 1972 .... +7.9 per cent

Total refinery throughputs .... 55,075,000 bpd
    Change over 1972 .... +9 per cent

Consumption as proportion of capacity ..... 88.4 per cent

Selected markets
Consumption of refined product types and change over 1972:

	USA		Western Europe		Japan	
	(million tonnes)	(per cent)	(million tonnes)	(per cent)	(million tonnes)	(per cent)
Gasolines	312.7	+3.9	132.6	+5.8	42.8	+11.7
Middle distillates	200.7	+4.7	248.7	+7.6	50.9	+23.8
Fuel oil	148.3	+11.3	269.9	+5.3	142.6	+14.2
Other	156.3	+4.1	97.7	+9.9	32.8	+9.0
Total	818.0	+5.4	748.9	+6.7	269.1	+14.8

D4.1.iv—Tankers and trade

Tankers

Total world fleet	215,600,000 deadweight tons
Change over 1972	+13.8 per cent

Trade

Total world crude exports
    (including re-exports) .... 31,703,900 bpd (1,564.1 million tonnes)
    Change over 1972 .... +14.1 per cent
OPEC crude exports .... 27,547,200 bpd (1,359 million tonnes)
    Change over 1972 .... +14.4 per cent
    Share of 1973 world total .... 86.9 per cent

Total world product exports
    (including re-exports) .... 8,718,400 bpd (447,556,500 tonnes)
    Change over 1972 .... +9.8 per cent
OPEC product exports .... 1,974,400 bpd (101,355,200 tonnes)
    Change over 1972 .... +10.2 per cent
    Share of 1973 world total .... 22.6 per cent

Regional distribution of world oil trade*:

	Share of 1973 imports (per cent)		Share of 1973 exports (per cent)	
	Crude	Products	Crude	Products
USA	11.4	52.6	—	4.3
Canada	3.1	1.9	3.7	5.3
Latin America/Caribbean	6.5	1.8	4.7	45.1
Western Europe	51.0	13.6	—	6.7
Middle East	0.4	0.2	66.4	19.4
North Africa	0.1	1.8	11.4	1.3
West Africa	†	0.1	7.5	0.3
East and southern Africa/ South Asia	2.8	3.7	—	0.2
South-East Asia	3.6	5.9	3.9	4.7
Australasia	0.8	1.5	†	0.7
Japan	17.7	12.4	—	0.4
USSR/Eastern Europe/ China	1.5	0.4	2.4	11.6
Unspecified	1.1	4.1	—	—
Total	100.0	100.0	100.0	100.0

*Excluding intra-regional trade.
†Negligible.

D4.1.v—World primary energy consumption

Total consumption (excluding
   non-commercial fuels) .... 5,908 million tonnes oil equivalent (mtoe)
   Change over 1972 .... +5 per cent

Contributions of primary energy sources:

	Consumption (mtoe)	Change over 1972 (per cent)	Share of total (per cent)
Oil	2,798.0	+7.9	47.4
Coal	1,668.4	+2.4	28.2
Natural gas	1,066.1	+2.0	18.1
Water power	326.3	+1.7	5.5
Nuclear power	49.2	+28.1	0.8

D4.1.vi—Natural gas production and reserves

Marketed production (thousand million cubic metres):

	Regional total (tmcm)	Change over 1972 (per cent)	Share of 1973 world total (per cent)
North America	687.1	+1.1	56.9
Latin America/Caribbean	35.1	+11.4	2.9
Western Europe*	137.6	+13.9	11.4
USSR/Eastern Europe/China	292.9	+6.7	24.2
Middle East	28.3	+16.5	2.3
Africa	8.7	+16.0	0.7
Asia†/Australasia	19.0	+19.5	1.6
World total	1,208.7	+4.7	100.0
(*of which OPEC*)	*(44.9)*	*(+15.1)*	*(3.7)*

*Including Yugoslavia.
†Excluding China.

End-year proved reserves (thousand million cubic metres):

	Regional total (tmcm)	Change over 1972 (per cent)	Share of 1973 world total (per cent)
North America	8,563.3	−5.2	15.4
Latin America/Caribbean	2,469.4	+6.8	4.5
Western Europe*	4,934.1	−1.7	8.9
USSR/Eastern Europe/China	19,707.2	−0.4	35.5
Middle East	11,699.9	+20.0	21.1
Africa	5,330.5	−1.5	9.6
Asia†/Australasia	2,779.6	+18.0	5.0
World total	55,484.0	+3.4	100.0
(*of which OPEC*)	*(18,103.1)*	*(+13.1)*	*(32.6)*

*Including Yugoslavia
†Excluding China.

D4.2—Negotiation of "Geneva II" Exchange-Rate Agreement

The 32nd (extraordinary) meeting of the OPEC Conference was held on March 16 and 17, 1973, at the request of Venezuela, to discuss "the present world energy crisis and all its underlying factors and circumstances". It was now apparent that the industrialized world's growing dependence on imported oil, accentuated by the downturn in US domestic oil output, was placing the OPEC countries in an increasingly strong bargaining position as the available margin of "surplus" installed production capacity began to decline under the pressure of demand (◊A4.15.i).

The meeting examined "the long-term policies which member countries should adopt with a view to securing their accelerated and sustained economic growth and their sources of national income" (accelerated growth being regarded as essential to offset the accelerated depletion of OPEC oil reserves required to meet the industrialized countries' projected import demand). It was agreed that "access to the technology and markets of the developed countries for the present and future industries of the member countries, together with a just valorization for their hydrocarbon resources and an adequate protection of their revenues, are essential objectives of the Organization". A working party was established to examine ways of linking "the exploitation of petroleum and its trade" to "the process of a rational and accelerated economic growth". The Conference expressed its belief that "initiatives regarding the possibility of concerted action on the part of industrialized oil-importing countries are not in the best interests of orderly international trade and could have negative effects on the present energy situation". (This was a reference to recent informal US suggestions that the non-communist industrialized countries should consider forming a "union of oil-consuming countries" to conduct dealings with OPEC on a "bloc-to-bloc basis".)

The Conference also discussed the recent formal devaluation of the US dollar against gold (by 10 per cent with effect from Feb. 13) and noted that it had "adversely affected the purchasing power of oil revenues of member countries". This was because posted prices would not be adjusted until the end of the quarter under the "Geneva I" exchange-rate formula (◊D3.2) and would then, because of deficiencies in the formula, rise by far less than the margin required to offset the full effect of the devaluation. It was therefore decided to convene a special OPEC ministerial meeting on March 22, which in turn mandated a negotiating committee (consisting of the Oil Ministers of Iraq, Kuwait and Libya) to open negotiations with the oil companies for the amendment of the Geneva I agreement "with a view to obtaining full compensation for the devaluation of the US dollar and to avoiding any future loopholes [in the indexation formula]". The composition of the committee indicated a hard-line approach by OPEC, since Libya (which was to chair the committee) and Iraq were each known to favour a full-scale revision of the basic terms of the 1971 Tehran and Tripoli agreements with the oil companies.

The OPEC negotiating committee met oil company representatives in Cairo on April 13 and 14, when a demand was submitted for amendments to the Geneva I formula which would have the effect of increasing posted prices by an average 13.66 per cent relative to their January 1973 level (as opposed to existing second-quarter increases averaging 5.8 per cent in accordance with the provisions of the unamended formula). After requesting some time to hold wider consultations within the industry, the company negotiators met the committee again in Vienna on April 23, when they offered to make minor amendments to the Geneva I agreement to produce an overall 7.2 per cent increase in postings relative to the January 1973 level.

The committee rejected this offer and called for an extraordinary meeting of the OPEC Conference to be convened on May 7, although "the door would be left open" until May 4 for the companies to submit "positive proposals which could form a proper basis for serious discussions". After other OPEC members had agreed to the convening of an extraordinary Conference meeting, the companies submitted further proposals on May 3 which led to the "postponement" of the Conference meeting and to the resumption of the negotiations on May 7 in Tripoli (the intended venue of the postponed meeting). These negotiations ended on May 9 without agreement after the committee had rejected an offer of improved terms which would have produced an overall increase in postings of between 8 and 9 per cent. The committee then called for the postponed Conference meeting to be held on May 21 "to consider further action".

It became apparent at this point that the more moderate members of OPEC, including Iran, Saudi Arabia and Abu Dhabi, considered that Libya and Iraq were injecting an exaggerated element of brinkmanship into the negotiations with a view to securing support within the Conference for an immediate repudiation of the main five-year agreements on the structure of Middle Eastern, Libyan and Nigerian posted prices. A series of inter-OPEC consultations ensued, and on May 18 it was announced that the Conference meeting had been further postponed until May 26. When the 33rd (extraordinary) meeting finally took place on that day the membership of the negotiating committee was widened to include Saudi Arabia and Iran, and it was decided that delegates from the other interested countries not represented on the committee (Abu Dhabi, Nigeria and Qatar) should also attend the next round of negotiations. These were to commence on May 28 in Geneva, the oil companies having indicated their willingness to discuss the issue further (whereas the original OPEC negotiating committee had stated on May 9 that "all possible means to reach an equitable agreement" had been "exhausted to no avail"). If the latest negotiations did not produce an agreement, the extraordinary Conference meeting was to be reconvened "to decide on sanctions to be taken".

A settlement with the companies (known as the "Geneva II" agreement) was subsequently announced on the following terms on June 1:

(1) The Geneva I exchange-rate formula was amended with immediate effect (i) to add the Australian and Canadian currencies to the existing basket of nine currencies (while retaining April 30, 1971, as the base date for the composite exchange-rate index); (ii) to reduce from two percentage points to one percentage point the minimum movement in the composite index which was required to trigger a change in posted prices; (iii) to base the price adjustment mechanism on a revised equation; and (iv) to make monthly rather than quarterly adjustments to posted prices.

(2) The 5-cents per barrel "inflation" increments in posted prices under the 1971 Tehran and Tripoli agreements, as well as the 2-cents per barrel quality increment under the Tripoli agreement, were increased on June 1, 1973, by 8.49 per cent (i.e. the amount by which they would have been increased on Jan. 1, 1973, if they had been index-linked under the Geneva I formula); this calculation was applied to existing postings before they were adjusted on the basis of the amended exchange-rate formula. The corresponding increments due on Jan. 1, 1974, and Jan. 1, 1975, were to be index-linked under the amended formula. The Suez Canal allowance and temporary freight premiums, where applicable, were to be index-linked on a monthly basis.

(3) The level of the Geneva I exchange-rate index on March 1, 1973, was to be re-calculated using amended parities to take account of the floating of the Japanese yen and the Italian lira in February 1973, and additional tax payments based on the notional posted prices resulting from this recalculation were to be made in respect of crude oil exported in April and May 1973.

(4) The agreement constituted a supplement to the Geneva I agreement with Gulf OPEC countries and to the parallel national agreements in Libya and Nigeria, and was thus to remain valid until the end of 1975.

The agreement's entry into force on June 1 increased posted prices in the signatory countries to levels which were an average 11.9 per cent higher than those of Jan. 1, 1973. The postings for selected Gulf crudes between Jan. 1 and Oct. 1, 1973 (reflecting increases in January and April under the Tehran/Geneva I agreements and subsequent changes under the Geneva II formula) are shown in Table 29. Table 30 shows the evolution of postings for selected east Mediterranean and African crudes. Algeria increased the posted price of its 44° crude over the same period as follows: Jan. 1—$3.823 per barrel; April 1— $4.033; June 1—$4.269. Indonesia increased the official selling price of its 34° crude by 26 per cent to $3.73 per barrel on April 1 and by a further 27.3 per cent to $4.75 on Oct. 1. Table 31 shows the evolution of Venezuelan tax-reference values between Jan. 1 and Oct. 1.

Table 29 — Posted prices of selected Gulf crudes, Jan. 1 to Oct. 1, 1973 (dollars per barrel)

	Abu Dhabi 39°	Iran 34°	Iraq 35°	Kuwait 31°	Saudi Arabia 34°
Jan. 1	2.654	2.579	2.562	2.482	2.591
April 1	2.823	2.729	2.711	2.626	2.742
June 1	2.968	2.884	2.865	2.776	2.898
July 1	3.026	2.94	2.291	2.83	2.955
Aug. 1	3.14	3.05	3.031	2.936	3.066
Oct. 1	3.144	2.995	2.977	2.884	3.011

Table 30 — Evolution of selected east Mediterranean and African postings, Jan. 1 to Oct. 1, 1973 (dollars per barrel)

	Iraq 36°	Saudi Arabia 34°	Libya 40°	Nigeria 37°
Jan. 1	3.484	3.451	3.777	3.561
April 1	3.712	3.677	4.024	3.787
June 1	3.921	3.884	4.252	4.003
July 1	4.070	4.003	4.416	4.135
Aug. 1	4.223	4.184	4.582	4.291
Oct. 1	4.243	4.205	4.604	4.287

Table 31 — Tax-reference values of four Venezuelan crudes, Jan. 1 to Oct. 1, 1973 (dollars per barrel)

	10°	26°	35°	41°
Jan. 1	2.54	3.0596	3.3621	3.6145
March 13	2.6005	3.355	3.7683	4.01
Aug. 1	2.9196	3.7667	4.2306	4.502
Sept. 1	3.0133	4.095	4.5993	4.8944
Oct. 1	3.1338	4.2332	4.7546	5.0596

D4.3—Breakdown of Negotiated Agreements on Posted Price Structure

The renegotiation of the Geneva exchange-rate agreement took place against a background of rapid progress towards greater host-government participation in production operations. In March 1973 Iran signed a 20-year "sales and purchase" agreement with the IOP consortium (◊**C5.3.v**), incorporating revenue provisions which took account of the participation terms introduced in Saudi Arabia, Abu Dhabi and Qatar at the beginning of the year (◊**D3.4**). By June the Kuwait Government, under pressure from nationalist politicians, had rejected the General Agreement's provisions for a nine-year phase-in of majority participation and was seeking immediate 51 per cent control of KOC's production operations (◊**C7.3.iii**).

Libya rejected the "General Agreement" terms offered by its main concession holders in January and subsequently launched a campaign for immediate 51 per cent state participation in their concession areas; this was backed by the threat of unilateral legislative action, which was eventually taken on Sept. 1 against companies which had resisted the Government's demands (◊**C8.3.iii**). Iraq's full nationalization of the IPC group's northern concession interests was formally accepted by the group as part of a wider settlement of outstanding issues, agreed at the beginning of March (◊**C6.3.iv**). Nigeria acquired a 35 per cent interest in the operations of its main concession-holder with effect from the beginning of April (◊**C9.3**).

The argument that majority host-government participation should be phased in over a period of years in order to avoid marketing problems (and to prevent an erosion of realized prices) had been weakened during 1972 in view of Algeria's success in negotiating export contracts at normal market prices for the 77 per cent state share of Algerian oil output. During the first half of 1973 the case for phased participation was undermined still further as the shift to a seller's market became more apparent. When negotiating the 1973 buy-back terms for bridging crude at the end of 1972, the Gulf states had finally settled for prices equivalent to about 80 per cent of the January 1973 postings (a ratio of realizations to postings comparable to that which had recently been achieved by Algeria). However, when the first bids for contract purchases of a Gulf government's own share of participation crude were invited by Abu Dhabi in early February 1973, a price equivalent to nearly 90 per cent of the current posting was obtained from the successful bidder (a Japanese company). Subsequent bidding by a wide range of independent companies for the Gulf states' relatively small volumes of state-marketed participation crude reflected a general upward trend in market prices as a proportion of current postings. As a result, Abu Dhabi was able to secure the renegotiation, within five months of signing the contract, of the 1973 price level which had originally been fixed for the full year in its Japanese contract of Feb. 10.

By June 1973 government sales contracts for Gulf crudes were being concluded at prices within a range equivalent to plus or minus 4 per cent of current postings (e.g. slightly below the posting in Iran and slightly above in Qatar). By September the average per-barrel realization on the bulk of the region's output (i.e. crude exported by the foreign concessionaire companies) was at or above the level of the posted price. The convergence of the market price of oil and the posted price used for tax purposes greatly increased the profit margin on the concessionaire companies' equity crude, which was obtained by them at tax-paid cost; moreover, the formula used to determine the buy-back prices of participation crude (i.e. quarter-way price plus a predetermined cash margin) assured the companies of a far higher return on such crude than had originally been intended under the General Agreement on Participation.

Saudi Arabia, having decided in May to define the selling price of its own directly-marketed share of participation crude as 93 per cent of the prevailing posted price, with the requirement that this ratio be maintained throughout the period covered by each sales contract, subsequently pressed Aramco to adopt the same terms for its purchases of both bridging and phase-in crude. Aramco finally accepted this arrangement on Sept. 13 after the Saudi Government had threatened to impose a reduction in the company's production level. Libya had meanwhile announced a buy-back price equivalent to 107 per cent of its current posting.

The radical change in the relationship between posted prices and realized prices, coupled with the upward trend in the rate of price inflation in the non-communist industrialized countries (now running at more than three times the level envisaged in OPEC's five-year posted price agreements), led to a build-up of pressure within the Organization for a fundamental revision of these agreements. The issue was fully discussed at the 34th meeting of the OPEC Conference, held on June 27 and 28. The Conference considered an Iraqi proposal that the agreements should be terminated forthwith by the OPEC side and that the signatory countries should assume sole control over the fixing of tax-reference prices. This proposal was eventually withdrawn when it became clear that the majority of member countries favoured an attempt to renegotiate the agreements, as advocated by Iran, Saudi Arabia and the other "moderate" Gulf countries which had sought to avert a full-scale confrontation with the oil companies over the exchange-rate issue in the previous month.

The 34th Conference meeting adopted, as Resolution XXXIV–155, a formal policy statement (◊**B1.9.ii**) based on the report of the working party established by the 32nd meeting. Whereas the Organization's 1968 declaratory statement (◊**B1.9.i**) had dealt with the relationship between host governments and concessionaire companies, the new policy statement was directed primarily at the governments of industrialized oil-importing countries. Its basic message was that unless the OPEC countries obtained substantial improvements in their terms of trade (in every sense of the phrase) the importing countries could not expect to enjoy guaranteed access to supplies of OPEC oil in a seller's market. A ministerial committee, consisting of the delegates of Iraq, Nigeria and Venezuela, was set up to carry out a "continuous review of the world energy situation" and to commission expert studies on various approaches to "the utilization of oil exports as an instrument to accelerate the economic development of member countries". Ecuador was admitted as an associate member of OPEC by Resolution XXXIV–154 of the 34th Conference meeting.

During August and early September Iraq and other "hard-line" members of OPEC held discussions with the more moderate member countries with a view to obtaining wider support for an uncompromising stand by the Organization in the proposed negotiations with the oil companies to revise the structure of posted prices. Saudi Arabia, which had grown increasingly impatient with Aramco's intransigence in current talks on the revision of the buy-back pricing formula, acknowledged in August that early unilateral action would have to be taken by OPEC if the companies did not accept sweeping changes in existing agreements. Saudi Arabia then secured Iran's support for this position, after which Shaikh Yamani made a public statement in early September to the effect that the agreements were "dead or dying".

The 35th (extraordinary) meeting of the OPEC Conference was held on Sept. 15 and 16 to finalize a negotiating strategy. It was estimated that the rise in realized crude prices had had the effect of reducing the Middle Eastern governments' share of per-barrel profits on the major oil companies' exports of equity crude from about 80 per cent to about 60 per cent. It was also calculated that Saudi Arabia's new buy-back price of 93 per cent of postings would, if applied to all of the 22.5 per cent of output available in 1973 for disposal on buy-back terms in countries which had adopted arrangements based on the General Agreement on Participation, produce a maximum government take equivalent to less than 70 per cent of the average per-barrel profit. Overall, the current average division of per-barrel export profits in the member countries covered by the 1971 Tehran agreement was estimated by OPEC to be 64 per cent to host governments and 36 per cent to the foreign exporting companies.

The Gulf countries agreed that the government take should be increased in order to reverse the recent rise in the company share of profits and that steps should be taken to ensure that future rises in realized prices would not have the effect of reducing the effective tax rate on export profits. It was also agreed that postings should be index-linked to the rate of increase in member countries' import prices. After some discussion as to whether the profit-sharing ratio should be corrected by raising income tax and/or royalty rates or by raising posted prices, the Gulf countries opted for the latter course, as proposed by Saudi Arabia.

Resolution XXXV–160 gave formal notice of the Conference's intention to seek an upward adjustment of the posted prices established under the five-year agreements with the international oil companies. The terms of these agreements were stated to be "no longer compatible" with "the prevailing conditions and expected future trends of the crude oil and product markets as well as the worldwide inflation, especially in the industrialized countries". The oil companies were "reaping high unearned profits" in the current market conditions, while the value of government oil revenues was deteriorating. A ministerial committee comprising the delegates of the six Gulf member countries was therefore formed to open negotiations with the companies on Oct. 8 for a revision of the Tehran agreement, it being understood that Libya and Nigeria would hold separate negotiations in the light of any settlement reached by the Gulf members.

Among the other resolutions adopted by the 35th Conference meeting, Resolution XXXV–159 expressed OPEC's full support for Libya's recent 51 per cent nationalization of foreign oil interests and warned that other member countries were prepared to impose sanctions on any oil companies which might take "individual or collective actions to hinder the implementation of the decision taken by the Libyan Government in the fulfilment of its sovereign right". Resolution XXXV–158 expressed support for a claim by Abu Dhabi that its crudes were undervalued within the general structure of Middle Eastern and north African postings. (A quality premium of about 6 cents per barrel was subsequently added to the posting for Abu Dhabi's 39° crude with effect from Oct. 1 on the basis of its 0.75 per cent sulphur content. This compared with the quality premium of 10 cents per barrel, plus future annual increments, which Libya had negotiated in 1971 for crudes of less than 0.5 per cent sulphur content ◊**C8.3.ii.**)

D4.4—Gulf Producers' Unilateral Increase in Postings

The Gulf negotiating committee made it clear when it met oil company representatives in Vienna on Oct. 8 that any failure to reach an acceptable negotiated settlement would lead to a unilateral increase in postings by the OPEC side. The committee's opening demands were (i) for a doubling of posted prices, (ii) for the establishment of a mechanism to ensure that there would be no future erosion of the effective tax rate (the committee's suggestion being that future increases in realized prices should serve as a trigger for increases in postings), and (iii) for future "inflation" adjustments to postings to be based on quarterly movements in an IMF wholesale price index for the main non-communist industrialized countries (subject to a minimum annual "inflation" increment of 2.5 per cent). The posted price increase demanded by the committee was slightly smaller than the percentage rise which had been recommended in an OPEC report analysing the increase in the international oil companies' per-barrel profits since the beginning of 1971, as measured by the rise in West European ex-refinery prices.

The company side's initial offer of an 8 per cent increase in postings (plus improved indexation to take account of future inflation in the prices of manufactured goods) was raised to 15 per cent on Oct. 9. In rejecting these offers, the OPEC committee stated that its minimum requirement was a 70 per cent increase in postings. It was agreed on Oct. 10 that the talks should be adjourned until Oct. 12 to allow the companies to hold consultations both among themselves and with the governments of the main oil-importing countries. On Oct. 12 a request from the company side for the adjournment to be extended for a further two weeks was rejected by the OPEC committee, which resolved to meet four days later to take a decision on a unilateral posted price increase.

The six Gulf members of OPEC, having met in Kuwait on Oct. 16, announced an immediate 70 per cent increase in the posted price of Saudi Arabian 34° crude fob Ras Tanura, with corresponding increases for other Gulf crudes. The latter increases were subject to the adoption of a new system of quality premiums which would add about 7 cents per barrel for each 0.1 per cent by which the sulphur content of a particular crude fell below the 1.7 per cent sulphur content of Saudi Arabian 34° crude. (This crude was chosen as the "marker" for the Gulf price structure in view of its average gravity and quality and its position as the single most important internationally-traded crude in volume terms.)

The amount of the increase in the Saudi posting had been determined (i) by gathering data on the current realized prices of all OPEC crudes; (ii) by "netting back" each price to a notional Ras Tanura fob value, adjusted for gravity and quality: (iii) by calculating the weighted average market realization for OPEC crudes fob Ras Tanura, which was deemed to be $3.65 per barrel; and (iv) by adding 40 per cent to this figure to produce the new "marker" posting of $5.119 per barrel. The rationale for this last step was that immediately before the conclusion of the February 1971 Tehran agreement the posted price for Gulf exports of Saudi Arabian 34° crude ($1.80) had been 40 per cent higher than the then current fob realization for the same crude ($1.285). The Gulf OPEC committee stated that its new base market value of $3.65 per barrel represented an increase of 17 per cent over the actual market realization for Saudi Arabian 34° crude fob Ras Tanura during the first half of October. If the international oil companies refused to accept the new posted prices, Gulf governments were prepared to take direct responsibility for marketing the companies' share of exports on the basis of the marker crude's deemed market price of $3.65 per barrel.

D4.5—Arab Production Cutbacks and Embargo Measures

A Conference of Arab Oil Ministers met in Kuwait on Oct. 17, 1973, to discuss the use of oil as a political weapon in the context of the latest Arab-Israeli war, which had then been in progress for 11 days (◊A4.15.ii). The participating countries were the seven Arab members of OPEC plus the three non-OPEC members of OAPEC (Bahrain, Egypt and Syria)—i.e. the total membership of OAPEC at that time. (Dubai, which had withdrawn from OAPEC in 1972, did not join the Conference but subsequently complied with its decisions.) The Conference held several of its meetings at OAPEC's headquarters but was formally constituted on an ad hoc basis outside the institutional framework of OAPEC.

The Oct. 17 meeting adopted a Saudi Arabian proposal for an immediate cutback in the Arab states' oil production to no more than 95 per cent of its September 1973 level, to be followed by further geometrically progressing cutbacks at the rate of at least 5 per cent per calendar month. The series of cutbacks was to continue "until Israeli forces have completely withdrawn from all Arab territories occupied in June 1967 and the legitimate rights of the Palestinian people are restored". Although the United States was the main target of the Arab initiative, Saudi Arabia had argued in favour of across-the-board reductions in production rather than selective export embargoes on the grounds that the former approach would provide a more effective means of impressing the urgency and seriousness of the Arab political demands upon "neutral" and "friendly" countries as well as those which were considered to be hostile to the Arab position. Iraq, which had argued in favour of selective action against "hostile" countries, dissociated itself from the policy of general cutbacks, preferring to impose a total embargo on exports to the United States and other "hostile" countries while maintaining normal supplies to all other countries. (Iraq was in fact unable to make any exports via the Syrian port of Banias between Oct. 11 and Nov. 3 because of war damage to the pipeline terminal.)

Following the US Government's announcement on Oct. 19 that a massive new military aid package was planned for Israel, all Arab oil-exporting countries took action to embargo the export of oil to the United States and to US armed forces based abroad. Saudi Arabia and Kuwait each stepped up the level of their across-the-board cutbacks to 10 per cent of the September level and then imposed further cuts equivalent to their normal volume of exports to the United States. The export of oil to the Netherlands was embargoed later in October after the Dutch Government had been accused of following pro-Israeli policies. In Iraq, the embargo on supplies to the United States and the Netherlands was backed up by the nationalization of the US and Dutch interests in the IPC group's remaining concession area (◊**C6.3.iv**). This was followed by the nationalization of the Gulbenkian interest in the same concession after Portugal, together with South Africa and Rhodesia, had been placed on the Arab embargo list in late November as part of a campaign to strengthen political solidarity between black Africa and the Arab world.

On Nov. 4 the Conference of Arab Oil Ministers met again in Kuwait to review the situation, and announced on the following day that a uniform 25 per cent cutback vis-à-vis the September level had been agreed for November (to include reductions made as a result of destination embargoes) and that the resulting production level would be cut by 5 per cent in December. However, it was announced on Nov. 18 that the Arab producers had decided to exempt from the December cutback all the members of the European Communities (except the Netherlands) "in appreciation of the political stand taken by the Common Market countries" in a Middle East policy statement issued by the Communities' Foreign Ministers on Nov. 6. Japan's exemption from the additional December cutback was announced on Nov. 23, the day after the publication of a Japanese government policy statement deploring Israel's occupation of Arab territories.

It was decided at a summit meeting of Arab heads of state, held in Algiers from Nov. 26 to 28 (and boycotted by Iraq and Libya), that the use of oil as a political weapon should be continued on the following basis:

(1) By maintaining a total export embargo against all "hostile" states which supported Israel.

(2) By maintaining cuts in production "to a degree that would not lead to a reduction in the income of the producing states by more than a quarter of their 1972 income".

(3) By forming a Committee of Foreign and Oil Ministers of Arab oil-producing states, which would draw up lists of friendly and neutral countries and "countries supporting the enemy". Any country could be moved from the neutral to the friendly category "in accordance with its commitments to implement the political line decided by the Arab summit, or if it takes a political, economic or military stand in harmony with that political line". Any "neutral" state reclassified as "friendly" would be entitled to receive supplies of Arab oil at its 1972 import levels, subject to a ban on the re-export of such oil either as crude or as products.

The Conference of Arab Oil Ministers decided on Dec. 9 that another 5 per cent production cutback should be made on Jan. 1, 1974, and should be applied to exports to non-embargoed countries classified as "neutral". However, at a further meeting held on Dec. 24 and 25 the Conference modified its policies after hearing a report by the Saudi Arabian and Algerian Oil Ministers on their recent visits to various Western countries, which had led them to conclude that a more positive attitude should be adopted towards "friendly" countries. The Conference agreed (i) that the 5 per cent production cutback planned for Jan. 1 should be cancelled and replaced by a production increase (by a volume equivalent to 10 per cent of the September 1973 level); (ii) that certain "most favoured" friendly countries, including France and the United Kingdom, should be supplied with their full requirements of Arab oil after Jan. 1; (iii) that all other friendly countries should be supplied on the basis of their import requirements in September 1973 (or in any previous month of 1973, if greater); and (iv) that Japan and Belgium should be transferred from the "neutral" to the "friendly" category.

D4.6—Pricing Developments in late 1973

The impact of the Arab states' implementation of general production cutbacks was partly offset by limited production increases in Iran, Nigeria and Indonesia (and by Iraq's refusal to restrict its trade with non-embargoed countries); nevertheless, there was a net loss of nearly 10 per cent of the non-communist world's previously anticipated oil supply during the latter part of 1973. The consequent upward pressure on prices meant that the Gulf OPEC price increase of Oct. 16 (which had been followed by corresponding increases in other OPEC member countries) was rapidly surpassed in routine trading within the framework of established supply contracts. Thus fob realizations on the major oil companies' arm's-length sales reached levels 10 to 15 per cent above the deemed market prices upon which the new OPEC postings were based. Posted prices, on the other hand, showed a slight fall in December in countries which were party to the Geneva II exchange-rate agreement. Freight rates fell sharply as the volume of trade declined.

Spot-market prices soared to record highs, the "netback" value of spot product sales in Western Europe in December being equivalent to a crude oil price in excess of $17 per barrel at the Persian/Arabian Gulf. More significantly, an fob price of $17 per barrel was actually agreed at the Gulf for substantial contract sales of Iranian crude auctioned by NIOC between Dec. 11 and Dec. 14. It was widely reported some days later that bids of up to $22 per barrel had been made for participation crude auctioned by the Nigerian Government, although there was no evidence that any firm contract was concluded at this price.

A meeting between OPEC ministers and oil company representatives was held in Vienna on Nov. 17, at the companies' request, to discuss pricing questions. The company side presented a case for a new long-term pricing agreement, possibly involving the governments of major oil-importing countries as well as OPEC and

Table 32 – OPEC production of crude oil in September and November 1973

	September	November	Change
	Production (thousand bpd)		(per cent)
Arab member countries:			
Abu Dhabi	1,430	1,120	−21.7
Algeria	1,100	900	−18.1
Iraq	2,115	2,150	+1.6
Kuwait*	3,525	2,470	−29.9
Libya	2,285	1,765	−22.8
Qatar	610	475	−22.1
Saudi Arabia*	8,570	6,270	−26.8
(Arab total)	(19,635)	(15,150)	(−22.8)
Non-Arab member countries:			
Indonesia	1,420	1,450	+2.1
Iran	5,830	6,045	+3.7
Nigeria	2,140	2,240	+4.7
Venezuela	3,385	3,380	−0.1
(Non-Arab total)	(12,775)	(13,115)	(+2.7)
OPEC total	32,410	28,265	−12.8

*Including share of Neutral Zone output.

398

the oil companies. The OPEC side responded by emphasizing that the Organization's pricing policy was no longer negotiable. A statement issued at the end of the 36th OPEC Conference meeting, held on Nov. 19 and 20, asserted that the company side had "dwelt vaguely on ideas for pricing petroleum on the basis of a rigid and arbitrarily predetermined procedure divorced from normal market forces". The statement went on: "The Conference is not in agreement with such an approach and believes that the pricing of petroleum, like the pricing of other internationally-traded manufactured goods, commodities and raw materials, should be market-oriented".

The Conference decided that the OPEC Economic Commission should meet four times per year to examine "the structure and determination of oil prices", and that the first such meeting should be held on Dec. 17. The 36th Conference meeting admitted Ecuador as a full member of OPEC and Gabon as an associate member.

A ministerial meeting of OPEC's six Persian/Arabian Gulf members was held in Tehran on Dec. 22 and 23 to review the development of oil prices. The meeting was also attended by delegates from Algeria, Indonesia, Libya, Nigeria and Venezuela, whose function was essentially that of interested observers. The central issue under discussion among the Gulf ministers concerned the extent to which a further increase in postings should reflect the extraordinary market conditions attributable to the Arab production cutbacks. The principal architect of the strategy of across-the-board cutbacks, Shaikh Yamani, took the view that to base a general increase on the highest prices at which oil was currently being sold would be to exploit the short-term market effects of a political initiative whose intention was to alter the Middle Eastern policies of the industrialized countries, not to risk driving their economies into recession to the general detriment of the world economy. A report by the OPEC Economic Commission suggesting that current market conditions would justify a government take of $14 per barrel on equity crude was dismissed by Shaikh Yamani as meaningless in terms of the underlying balance of supply and demand.

On the other hand the Shah of Iran, who made a number of personal interventions in the proceedings of the meeting, stated that his wish was to align the general level of oil prices with the maximum levels attained in recent spot and auction sales in order to secure a massive increase in government unit revenue. An initial Iranian proposal for the implementation of nothing less than the full increase proposed by the Economic Commission (which would have involved raising the Gulf marker posting to about $23 per barrel) was eventually reduced to a demand for a government take of $8 per barrel (equivalent to a marker posting in excess of $13). Saudi Arabia took an equally firm stand in favour of a maximum government take of $5 per barrel, involving a posting of around $8. On the basis of the 1 : 1.4 ratio (of deemed market value to posted price) used by the Gulf OPEC countries in deciding their Oct. 16 price increase (◊D4.4), the Saudi proposal implied a new deemed market value of about $5.70 per barrel, equivalent to an increase of rather more than one-third in the major oil companies' current arm's-length realizations.

A "final" Iranian demand for the introduction of a government take of $7 per barrel (said to be equivalent to the current cost of developing alternative energy sources) obtained the support of a majority of Arab Gulf delegates. Accordingly, Shaikh Yamani indicated that Saudi Arabia was prepared to implement the corresponding marker posting ($11.651 per barrel for 34° crude fob Ras Tanura) in the interests of preserving OPEC unity, although he made it clear that in his view there were no reasonable grounds for this 131 per cent rise in the posting. (On a "deemed market value" basis, using OPEC's 1 : 1.4 ratio, the rise was roughly equivalent to a doubling of the more representative market prices reported during the current supply crisis.) Shaikh Yamani's view was strongly endorsed by King

Faisal, who had not been available for consultation during the final stages of the meeting and whose opposition to the Shah's adoption of a hard line on OPEC pricing policy heralded the start of a lengthy conflict between OPEC's two largest producers over this issue.

A statement issued by the OPEC Secretariat after the Tehran meeting asserted that the Gulf price increase, which would be applied from Jan. 1, 1974, had "already taken into consideration the effect of the Geneva II agreement". (In practice, the Geneva II exchange-rate index, which had begun to fall steadily in November as the value of the US dollar appreciated against other major currencies, ceased to be used by OPEC at the end of 1973 on the grounds that it was an adjunct to the now defunct posted price agreements with the major oil companies.) The statement described the price increase as "moderate" and expressed the hope that industrialized oil-importing countries would "refrain from making further increases in their export prices".

In implementing the increase in postings, the Gulf countries adopted a new scale of gravity differentials based on the deduction of 0.3 cents per barrel for one-tenth of each API degree below 34° and the addition of 0.6 cents per barrel above for one-tenth of each API degree above 34° (as recommended by a committee of Gulf experts appointed after the Oct. 16 meeting of Gulf OPEC countries). The scale of Gulf quality premiums established on Oct. 16 remained unchanged. Libya subsequently adopted the new Gulf gravity differential values, but used 40° rather than 34° as its central reference point.

Table 33 shows the effects of the decisions of Oct. 16 and Dec. 23 (and intervening exchange-rate adjustments) on the postings for selected Gulf crudes. Table 34 shows the development of east Mediterranean and African postings for selected crudes over the same period.

Indonesia increased the official selling price of its 34° crude to $6 per barrel on Nov. 1, 1973, and to $10.80 per barrel on Jan. 1, 1974. Gabon increased the posted

Table 33 — Posted prices of selected Gulf crudes, Oct. 16, 1973, to Jan. 1, 1974 (dollars per barrel)

	Abu Dhabi 39°	Iran 34°	Iraq 35°	Kuwait 31°	Saudi Arabia 34°
Oct. 16, 1973	6.045	5.341	5.061	4.903	5.119
Nov. 1, 1973	6.113	5.401	5.117	4.957	5.176
Dec. 1, 1973	5.944	5.254	4.978	4.822	5.036
Jan. 1, 1974	12.636	11.875	11.672	11.545	11.651

Table 34 — Evolution of selected east Mediterranean and African postings, Oct. 16, 1973, to Jan. 1, 1974 (dollars per barrel)

	Iraq 36°	Saudi Arabia 34°	Libya 40°	Nigeria 37°	Algeria 44°
Oct. 16, 1973	7.213	7.149	. . .	. . .	9.261
Oct. 19, 1973	. . .	. . .	8.925	. . .	. . .
Oct. 20, 1973	. . .	. . .	. . .	8.310	. . .
Nov. 1, 1973	7.293	7.228	9.061	8.404	9.364
Dec. 1, 1973	7.096	7.034	. . .	. . .	9.107
Jan. 1, 1974	*	13.467	15.768	14.691	16.216

*Publication of east Mediterranean posting discontinued.

price of its 31.8° crude ($3.75 per barrel on Oct. 1, 1973) to $7.40 on Oct. 20 and $13.794 on Jan. 1, 1974. Ecuador increased the tax-reference value of its 30.4° crude ($3.60 per barrel on Oct. 1, 1973) as follows: Oct. 17—$5.25; Nov. 10—$7.30; Dec. 15—$10; Jan. 1, 1974—$13.70. The increases in Venezuela's minimum tax-reference values for selected crudes are shown in Table 35.

Table 35 — Tax-reference values of four Venezuelan crudes, Nov. 1, 1973, to Jan. 1, 1974 (dollars per barrel)

	10°	26°	35°	41°
Nov. 1, 1973	5.1454	6.5693	7.1105	7.4098
Dec. 1, 1973	5.4963	6.7697	7.3124	7.67
Jan. 1, 1974	10.8372	11.7972	12.3372	12.6972

D5—1974

D5.1—Annual Statistical Survey

D5.1.i—Oil production and reserves

World

Total production	58,620,000 bpd (2,879.6 million tonnes)
Change over 1973	+0.3 per cent
End-year proved reserves	723,900 million barrels
Change over end-1973	+14.1 per cent
Reserves:production ratio	33.8 : 1

Regional shares:

	In 1974 world production*			In end-1974 world reserves†		
	Regional total (million tonnes)	Change over 1973 (per cent)	Share of world total (per cent)	Reserves (thousand million barrels)	Change over 1973 (per cent)	Share of world total (per cent)
Middle East	1,085.0	+3.1	37.7	403.4	+15.4	55.8
North America	593.2	−4.5	20.6	49.4	−3.3	6.8
USSR/Eastern Europe/China	544.6	+8.2	18.9	111.4	+7.9	15.4
Africa	269.4	−7.3	9.4	68.3	+1.5	9.4
Latin/America Caribbean	254.6	−6.4	8.8	44.1	+40.0	6.1
Asia‡/Australasia	110.2	—	3.8	21.0	+34.6	2.9
Western Europe§	22.6	+0.4	0.8	26.3	+60.4	3.6

*Including production from oil shales, tar sands and natural gas liquids (NGL).
†Excluding oil shales and tar sands; including NGL in North America.
‡Excluding China.
§Including Yugoslavia.

OPEC*

OPEC oil production	31,055,000 bpd (1,538.3 million tonnes)
Change over 1973	−0.6 per cent
Share of 1974 world total	53.4 per cent
OPEC end-year proved reserves	488,540 million barrels
Change over 1973	+15.9 per cent
Share of 1974 world total	67.5 per cent
OPEC reserves:production ratio	43.1 : 1

*End-1975 membership basis.

OPEC (continued)

OPEC member countries' production:

	1974 production (million tonnes)	1974 production (thousand bpd)	Change over 1973 (per cent)	Share of world total (per cent)	Share of OPEC total (per cent)
Algeria	47.1	1,010	−8.0	1.6	3.1
Ecuador	8.7	175	−14.7	0.3	0.6
Gabon*	10.0	200	+33.3	0.3	0.6
Indonesia	67.9	1,375	+2.9	2.4	4.4
Iran	301.2	6,060	+2.7	10.5	19.5
Iraq	96.7	1,970	−2.3	3.4	6.3
Kuwait	116.3	2,330	−17.2	4.0	7.6
Libya	73.3	1,520	−30.1	2.5	4.8
Nigeria	112.2	2,260	+12.1	3.9	7.3
Qatar	24.9	520	−8.8	0.9	1.6
Saudi Arabia	412.4	8,350	+12.1	14.3	26.8
UAE†	81.1	1,680	+10.5	2.8	5.3
Venezuela	158.5	3,065	−11.5	5.5	10.3
Neutral Zone‡	28.0	540	+1.4	1.0	1.8

*Associate member.
†Of which Abu Dhabi 67,700,000 tonnes (1,410,000 bpd), Dubai 12,000,000 tonnes (240,000 bpd), Sharjah 1,400,000 tonnes (30,000 bpd).
‡Production shared between Kuwait and Saudi Arabia.

Non-OPEC

Selected non-OPEC countries' oil production:

	1974 production (million tonnes)	1974 production (thousand bpd)	Change over 1973 (per cent)	Share of world total (per cent)
USA*	496.7	10,480	−4.3	17.3
USSR	458.9	9,290	+7.0	15.9
Canada	96.5	2,000	−5.7	3.4
China	65.8	1,320	+20.1	2.3
Mexico	31.6	640	+17.5	1.1
Argentina	21.6	415	−1.8	0.7
Oman	14.5	290	−1.4	0.5
Egypt	11.5	230	−11.5	0.4
Norway	1.7	35	−5.5	0.06
United Kingdom	0.1	†	—	‡
Total	1,198.9	24,700§	+1.3	41.66

*Of which natural gas liquids 59,900,000 tonnes (1,685,000 bpd).
†Less than 5,000 bpd.
‡Negligible.
§Excluding United Kingdom.

D5.1.ii—Oil consumption

World

Total consumption .... 56,400,000 bpd (2,760.3 million tonnes)
    Change over 1973 .... −1.3 per cent

Regional distribution of total:

	1974 consumption		Change over 1973 (per cent)	Share of world total (per cent)
	(million tonnes)	(thousand bpd)		
North America	867.4	17,935	−3.8	31.4
Western Europe*	699.3	14,165	−6.6	25.4
USSR/Eastern Europe/China........	497.9	10,080	+9.5	18.1
Asia†/Australasia	403.5	8,205	−2.3	14.6
Latin America /Caribbean	174.7	3,660	+3.8	6.3
Middle East...............	67.1	1,320	+7.9	2.4
Africa	50.4	1,035	+1.8	1.8

*Including Yugoslavia.
†Excluding China.

Selected countries

	1974 consumption		Change over 1973 (per cent)	Share of world total (per cent)
	(million tonnes)	(thousand bpd)		
USA	782.6	16,150	−4.3	28.3
USSR	358.5	7,280	+10.1	13.0
Japan	258.9	5,270	−3.8	9.4
West Germany	134.3	2,760	−10.3	4.9
France	121.0	2,460	−4.9	4.4
United Kingdom........	105.3	2,135	−7.0	3.8
Italy	100.8	2,015	−2.7	3.6
Canada......................	84.8	1,785	+1.3	3.1
China	61.9	1,225	+15.1	2.2
Spain	41.1	820	+5.1	1.5
Total	2,049.2	41,900	−1.6	74.2

D5.1.iii—Oil refining

World

Total refinery capacity .... 68,140,000 bpd
    Change over 1973 .... +5.6 per cent

Total refinery throughputs .... 54,590,000 bpd
    Change over 1973 .... −0.9 per cent

Consumption as proportion of capacity   82.8 per cent

Selected markets
Consumption of refined product types and change over 1973:

	USA (million tonnes)	USA (per cent)	Western Europe (million tonnes)	Western Europe (per cent)	Japan (million tonnes)	Japan (per cent)
Gasolines	300.2	−4.0	129.7	−2.2	41.3	−3.5
Middle distillates	195.5	−2.6	222.2	−10.7	50.6	−0.6
Fuel oil	137.8	−7.1	255.7	−5.3	135.7	−4.8
Other	149.1	−4.6	91.7	−6.1	31.3	−4.6
Total	782.6	−4.3	699.3	−6.6	258.9	−3.8

D5.1.iv—Tankers and trade

Tankers

Total world fleet .... 255,800,000 deadweight tons
   Change over 1973 .... +18.6 per cent

Trade

Total world crude exports
   (including re-exports) .... 31,130,600 bpd (1,538.8 million tonnes)
   Change over 1973 .... −1.8 per cent
OPEC crude exports .... 27,258,900 bpd (1,347.4 million tonnes)
   Change over 1973 .... −1 per cent
   Share of 1974 world total .... 87.6 per cent
Total world product exports
   (including re-exports) .... 8,234,800 bpd (419,928,600 tonnes)
   Change over 1973 .... −5.5 per cent
OPEC product exports .... 1,888,800 bpd (96,318,200 tonnes)
   Change over 1973 .... −4.3 per cent
   Share of 1974 world total .... 22.9 per cent

Regional distribution of world oil trade*:

	Share of 1974 imports (per cent) Crude	Share of 1974 imports (per cent) Products	Share of 1974 exports (per cent) Crude	Share of 1974 exports (per cent) Products
USA	12.4	53.3	—	4.5
Canada	2.9	1.0	2.8	5.0
Latin America/Caribbean	7.2	3.0	4.5	44.6
Western Europe	49.7	16.4	—	8.3
Middle East	0.4	0.2	68.2	17.5
North Africa	0.1	1.7	9.0	0.4
West Africa	0.1	0.5	8.9	0.2
East and southern Africa/ South Asia	2.8	3.3	—	0.1
South-East Asia	3.7	6.0	4.2	3.3
Australasia	0.9	1.6	—	0.9
Japan	17.3	10.7	—	0.6
USSR/Eastern Europe/China	1.4	0.5	2.4	14.6
Unspecified	1.1	1.8	—	—
Total	100.0	100.0	100.0	100.0

*Excluding intra-regional trade.

D5.1.v—World primary energy consumption

Total consumption (excluding
    non-commercial fuels) .... 5,945.7 million tonnes oil equivalent (mtoe)
    Change over 1973 .... +0.6 per cent

Contributions of primary energy sources:

	Consumption (mtoe)	Change over 1973 (per cent)	Share of total (per cent)
Oil	2,760.3	−1.3	46.4
Coal	1,691.2	+1.4	28.4
Natural gas	1,088.1	+2.1	18.3
Water power	343.7	+5.3	5.8
Nuclear power	62.4	+26.8	1.1

D5.1.vi—Natural gas production and reserves

Marketed production (thousand million cubic metres):

	Regional total (tmcm)	Change over 1973 (per cent)	Share of 1974 world total (per cent)
North America	656.8	−4.4	53.0
Latin America/Caribbean	36.7	+4.6	3.0
Western Europe*	156.2	+13.5	12.6
USSR/Eastern Europe/China	323.8	+10.5	26.1
Middle East	32.8	+15.9	2.6
Africa	9.4	+8.0	0.8
Asia†/Australasia	23.6	+24.2	1.9
World total	1,239.3	+2.5	100.0
(*of which OPEC*)	(*50.5*)	(*+12.5*)	(*4.1*)

*Including Yugoslavia.
†Excluding China.

End-year proved reserves (thousand million cubic metres):

	Regional total (tmcm)	Change over 1973 (per cent)	Share of 1974 world total (per cent)
North America	8,320.7	−2.8	13.9
Latin America/Caribbean	2,713.2	+9.9	4.5
Western Europe*	5,094.4	+3.2	8.5
USSR/Eastern Europe/China	21,073.6	+6.9	35.1
Middle East	13,942.8	+19.2	23.2
Africa	5,920.2	+11.1	9.9
Asia†/Australasia	2,969.6	+6.8	4.9
World total	60,034.5	+8.2	100.0
(*of which OPEC*)	(*21,124.3*)	(*+16.7*)	(*35.2*)

*Including Yugoslavia.
†Excluding China.

D5.2—Ending of Arab Embargo Measures

After the signature by Egypt and Israel on Jan. 18, 1974, of an initial military disengagement agreement drafted during the course of an intense round of US "shuttle diplomacy" (prompted in large part by the Arab world's use of the oil weapon), Egypt began to exert pressure on Arab oil-exporting countries for the phasing-out of the remaining restrictions on the supply of oil to industrialized countries. A meeting of the Conference of Arab Oil Ministers scheduled for Feb. 14 was postponed at the request of Egypt and Saudi Arabia (the latter supporting the Egyptian view that oil sanctions were now an impediment to further progress towards a political solution in the Middle East) after it had become apparent that Syria intended to argue forcefully against any change in supply policy at this point. Egypt subsequently attempted to organize the holding of the postponed meeting in Cairo on March 10, but abandoned this plan when Algeria, Libya and Syria refused to attend (as did Iraq, which had boycotted every meeting of the Conference after the inaugural session in October 1973).

The meeting was finally convened in the Libyan capital, Tripoli, on March 13, but was adjourned without agreement after several hours. It was reconvened in Vienna on March 17, and on the following day Abu Dhabi, Algeria, Bahrain, Egypt, Kuwait, Qatar and Saudi Arabia announced their decision (i) to lift the embargo on the export of their oil to the United States, and (ii) to treat Italy and West Germany as "friendly" rather than "neutral" countries for oil supply pur-poses. Syria did not assent to the lifting of the embargo against the United States, while Libya assented neither to the lifting of the embargo nor to "any increase in production". Iraq boycotted the meeting.

A statement issued after the Vienna meeting referred to a positive report submitted by the Saudi Arabian and Algerian Oil Ministers regarding their most recent series of visits to oil-importing countries, including Japan, Spain, Italy and West Germany. It was noted that the measures taken by the Conference had "made world public opinion aware of the importance of the Arab world for the welfare of the world economy" and had "led to the gradual isolation of Israel and paved the way for the assumption of political stances which openly condemn Israel's ex-pansionist policy". The Arab states welcomed the "new dimension" which had become evident in US Middle Eastern policy and were "aware of the fact that oil is a weapon which can be utilized in a positive manner in order to lead to results, the effectiveness of which may surpass those obtained if the oil weapon was used in a negative manner".

At a further meeting held in Cairo on June 1 (the day after the signature of a disengagement agreement between Israel and Syria) the Conference of Arab Oil Ministers declared that it had "found no necessity to take any new decisions". However, Algeria unilaterally lifted its embargo on supplies to the Netherlands on the following day, and on July 10 a further Conference meeting (also held in Cairo) formally lifted the collective embargo against the Netherlands in the interests of furthering the process of "Euro-Arab Dialogue" between the European Economic Community and the League of Arab states (◊**D5.10**). The Arab states' collective agreement on the political use of their oil exports effectively lapsed at this point, on the understanding that the embargo against the white minority regimes in Africa (◊**D4.5**) would be maintained on a permanent basis. Libya, however, continued to enforce a national export embargo against the United States until December 1974.

Saudi Arabia and Kuwait each announced national production ceilings after the lifting of politically-motivated cutbacks. The Saudi ceiling was 8,500,000 bpd (2.5 per cent above the September 1973 production level) and the Kuwaiti ceiling 2,500,000 bpd (22.8 per cent below the September 1973 production level). No ceiling was placed on Neutral Zone output.

D5.3—Decisions of 37th OPEC Conference Meeting

The 37th (extraordinary) meeting of the OPEC Conference, held from Jan. 7 to 9, 1974, formally endorsed the increase which had been made in Gulf OPEC postings at the beginning of the year ($\lozenge$**D4.6**). The Gulf members decided, in view of "the recent changes in petroleum market conditions", to "abandon the ratio of 1 : 1.4 between market prices and posted prices" which they had invoked to justify their first unilateral increase in postings in October 1973 ($\lozenge$**D4.4**). The Economic Commission was instructed to "come forward with recommendations on the level of posted prices that would be applicable on April 1, 1974" and to "undertake in the shortest possible time the necessary studies with a view to establishing a price system for crude oil in the long term".

The Conference "expressed its hope that the industrialized countries would adopt the necessary measures to contain the high inflationary trend in their countries and to control the oil companies in the way they increase prices of oil products to end-consumers". It also expressed its interest in "exchange of opinions and information with the consuming countries about matters of common interest". The ministerial committee on the world energy situation (established by the 34th Conference meeting $\lozenge$**D4.3**) was requested to draw up proposals for "the creation of a financial institution for development" to channel OPEC aid to oil-importing developing countries. Abu Dhabi's membership of OPEC was transferred to the United Arab Emirates at Abu Dhabi's request.

D5.4—Factors Influencing OPEC Pricing Policy in 1974

The average realized fob prices of 34° Gulf crudes sold under arm's-length contracts by the major oil companies were in the range of $10 to $11 per barrel during the first nine months of 1974. (Spot prices, netted back to the Persian/Arabian Gulf from West European product markets, remained above contract prices during the early part of the year, moving down to approximate parity as the Arab sanctions were progressively lifted and then declining further after the middle of the year to levels about $1 per barrel below contract prices.) On the basis of the government take of $7 per barrel agreed by the Gulf OPEC countries in December 1973, and assuming a production cost of 16 cents per barrel, the tax-paid cost of the foreign exporting companies' equity share of exports of 34° crude fob Ras Tanura was $7.16 per barrel in January 1974. The exporting companies thus started the year with a post-tax profit margin of between $2.84 and $3.84 per barrel on equity crude and a minimum post-tax profit margin of between $1.92 and $2.92 per barrel on their total offtake (given 25 per cent state participation and the use of a buy-back price of 93 per cent of the posting as per the formula agreed in Saudi Arabia in September 1973 $\lozenge$**D4.3**).

In practice, however, the 25 per cent level of participation became inoperative after the Kuwait Government concluded an agreement on Jan. 29 to acquire a 60 per cent interest in the operations of KOC with effect from Jan. 1, 1974 ($\lozenge$**C7.3.iii**). Agreements on 60 per cent participation were subsequently negotiated by Saudi Arabia ($\lozenge$**C11.3.vii**), Qatar ($\lozenge$**C10.3**) and Abu Dhabi ($\lozenge$**C12.3.iii**). These followed the pattern of the Kuwait agreement with regard to the effective date of the reduction in the foreign interest and to the foreign companies' overall compensation entitlement (net book value of the entire 60 per cent state interest, from which these three countries were to deduct the amount of their earlier compensation payments). The revenue effects of the new Gulf participation arrangements were automatically applied in Iran under the terms of IOP's sales and purchase agreement ($\lozenge$**C5.3.iv**).

With the introduction of 60 per cent state participation the minimum post-tax profit margin available to the exporting companies on their total offtake (assuming unchanged tax and royalty rates on equity crude and buy-back of the entire state share of output at 93 per cent of the posting) was reduced to between $0.635 and

$1.635 per barrel on the basis of the prevailing range of arm's-length realizations. This was in contrast to the average post-tax profit margin of around $0.35 per barrel which had accrued to the exporting companies in mid-1972 before the introduction of host-government participation in the Gulf concessions. Moreover, the arm's-length realization of $10 per barrel which produced the lowest minimum profit margin of $0.635 in the above calculation was some $0.835 below the January 1974 price for direct state exports of participation crude under contracts based on the "93 per cent of postings" formula adopted by the Saudi Government in May 1973.

The Gulf OPEC countries spent much of 1974 working towards new taxation arrangements which would trim the overall company profit margin back to around its 1972 level. A further increase in postings was ruled out as a means to this end because of strong opposition by Saudi Arabia, which had insisted on OPEC's formal renunciation of the 1:1.4 "ratchet mechanism" at the 37th Conference meeting. The issue was complicated by delays in finalizing the buy-back arrangements applicable from Jan. 1, 1974 (with regard both to price and to volume), which were the subject of several months of negotiations at national level between the host governments concerned and their respective foreign partner companies.

The main obstacle to early agreement on buy-back terms was that neither governments nor companies could accurately predict the effect which the Jan. 1 price increase would have on the underlying level of market demand after the lifting of Arab supply restrictions. In the event, exports of OPEC oil increased by 2.5 per cent in the first quarter of 1974 and by 3.7 per cent in the second quarter as most restrictions were phased out; subsequently they declined by 7.5 per cent in the third quarter and by 1.3 per cent in the fourth quarter as the underlying weakness of the market became more apparent. The non-communist world's oil consumption showed an overall fall of 1,565,000 bpd in 1974, the price increase of Jan. 1 having reversed the long-established trend of sustained growth, although the rebuilding of importers' stocks helped to limit the decline in OPEC output to 225,000 bpd.

In these circumstances, there was little incentive for independent buyers to bid up the prices of state-marketed Gulf crudes beyond the levels charged by the major oil companies for arm's-length sales of the same crudes (i.e. between about 86 per cent and 94.5 per cent of postings). Kuwait's royalty crude entitlement for the second and third quarters of 1974 (which could only be profitably sold for more than its full posted price) was offered for sale in February but attracted no acceptable bids, whereupon the Government opted to take its normal cash royalty. Abu Dhabi attempted without success to sell participation crude at prices close to postings on March 6 and March 14, and eventually concluded several contracts at 93 per cent of the posted price on March 27. An attempt by Kuwait to auction its participation crude entitlement for the second half of the year was called off in early July in the face of bids of less than 90 per cent of postings, compared with the Government's target price of 97 per cent of postings. Iran's NIOC was also forced to abandon a mid-year auction after receiving bids no higher than 89 per cent of postings.

Mainly because the Saudi Government was already looking towards the subsequent negotiation of a long-term commercial relationship with Aramco based on full state control, Saudi Arabia did not seek any immediate alteration in its existing buy-back arrangements with regard either to price or to volume when negotiating with Aramco's parent companies during the first half of 1974 on the principle of 60 per cent state participation. Qatar concluded an agreement with its foreign producing companies in April fixing its buy-back price at 93 per cent of postings, the agreed volume of buy-back crude in the second half of 1974 being 60 per cent of the state share of production (i.e. 36 per cent of Qatar's total production).

Buy-back negotiations in Kuwait continued into July, with the Government holding out for the highest possible price while the companies made it clear that insistence on a price in excess of what they considered to be a reasonable market rate would result in reduced purchases by them. The Government was aware (in the light of the bids received in its recent abortive auction) that it could not expect to secure its desired pricing objectives through direct sales in the present market conditions. Accordingly, a compromise was eventually reached in mid-July whereby the foreign companies would purchase 700,000 bpd of participation crude at 94.846 per cent of postings during the third quarter of the year, the fourth quarter's purchases being subsequently agreed as 900,000 bpd priced at 93 per cent of postings. The buy-back volume for the third quarter was equivalent to 46⅔ per cent of the state's maximum possible participation entitlement (i.e. 1,500,000 bpd if total output was running at the current ceiling level of 2,500,000 bpd), while that for the fourth quarter was equivalent to 60 per cent of the same maximum state entitlement. The companies' offtake of participation crude during the first half of the year, whose pricing had hitherto been in dispute, became subject to a retroactive buy-back price of 94 per cent of postings.

The percentages of postings applicable to Kuwait's buy-back transactions throughout 1974 were regarded as new standard rates for the Gulf region under the "most-favoured-country" principle. Thus they were subsequently applied in Qatar and Saudi Arabia as well as in Abu Dhabi (which did not conclude 60 per cent participation agreements with its producing companies until September).

Because of the circumstances in which 60 per cent participation was implemented—involving overlapping negotiations, retroactivity clauses, differing agreements on buy-back volumes and the failure of some state oil companies to lift all of the agreed volumes of crude available for marketing by them—it was not possible to make a precise calculation of the average cost of Gulf crude to the foreign exporting companies during the first nine months of 1974. It was nevertheless clear that the bulk of the output of the countries concerned continued to be marketed through the majors and that equity crude generally accounted for more than half of the majors' total offtake. Thus the effective floor price of Gulf crude was significantly below its theoretical maximum level under 60 per cent participation, notwithstanding the increased buy-back rates chargeable on transactions made before Oct. 1.

The range of post-tax profit margins realized by the foreign exporting companies was therefore higher than the theoretical minimum range cited above, and as long as the income tax and royalty rates on equity crude remained unchanged the majors were in a particularly strong position to undercut state oil companies which offered participation crude for direct sale at prices similar to those applying to buy-back transactions. The main impact of such competition was felt by Algeria, Iraq and Libya, each of which produced substantial volumes of crude from wholly state-owned fields without the safeguard of buy-back arrangements. Reported Libyan realizations on direct sales were between 80 and 85 per cent of postings in mid-May.

D5.5—Decisions of 38th and 39th Meetings of OPEC Conference

The 38th (extraordinary) meeting of the OPEC Conference was convened on March 16 and 17, 1974, to consider a report by the Organization's Economic Commission which stated that the current level of product prices would justify an increase in postings of between 12 and 22 per cent in the second quarter of the year. Delegates were, however, aware that the supply situation was due to ease in the second quarter in view of the fact that a majority of the Arab exporting countries which had made across-the-board cutbacks were about to give their formal approval to a return to September 1973 production levels (i.e. at the March 17 meeting of the Conference of Arab Oil Ministers, held immediately after the conclusion of the OPEC Conference meeting ◁**D5.2**). Few serious objections were raised to Saudi Arabia's proposal that postings should be frozen at their existing level for the second quarter of the year, although the option was left open "to convene an extraordinary meeting at the request of any member country with a view to revising the posted prices". Saudi Arabia made it clear that it would refuse to increase its postings regardless of any decision which might be reached by other OPEC countries.

The 38th Conference meeting also established a working party to prepare draft articles of agreement for the proposed OPEC aid fund for developing countries (◁**D5.3**). The draft articles were submitted to the 39th (extraordinary) Conference meeting, which was held on April 7 with this matter as its sole agenda item. Ministers took a decision in principle that such a fund should be established after seven member countries had ratified a final version of its articles of agreement, the draft articles being referred back to the working party for revision. (Follow-up work was, however, subsequently deferred while OPEC countries explored the feasibility of an Iranian proposal, announced by the Shah on Feb. 21, for co-operation with the industrialized countries to create a joint fund to lend up to $3,000 million per year to oil-importing developing countries.)

D5.6—OPEC Decisions on Prices and Taxes, June to December 1974

D5.6.i—Tax and royalty increases based on unchanged postings – Related developments (June to September 1974)

The 40th meeting of the OPEC Conference was held in Ecuador from June 15 to 17, 1974, in the presence of observers from Bolivia, Colombia, Peru and Trinidad and Tobago. The Foreign Minister of Guyana also attended the meeting to address delegates on behalf of the non-aligned movement, which regarded the OPEC countries' assertion of sovereignty over their natural resources as a victory for all third-world producers of primary commodities in their campaign for a "new international economic order" (▷**D5.9**). (All of the Arab members of OPEC, as well as Gabon, Indonesia and Nigeria, were full members of the non-aligned movement. Ecuador and Venezuela held observer status. Iran did not join the movement until 1979, after the overthrow of the Shah.)

The 40th Conference meeting considered the latest quarterly report of the OPEC Economic Commission, which made further recommendations for an oil price increase. While noting the recent downward trend in open-market spot prices, the Commission drew attention to the "excessive profit margin of the major oil companies" and to the continuing erosion of the purchasing power of oil revenues as a result of price inflation in the main non-communist industrialized countries (now running at an average annual rate of around 14 per cent, of which an estimated 2.4 per cent was attributable to the higher cost of imported oil). Support for a price rise among the OPEC majority was expressed rather more forcefully than at the 38th Conference meeting, and arguments were advanced for increases of up to $1.50 per barrel in the average tax-paid cost of Gulf crude to the foreign producing companies. Saudi Arabia made a counter-proposal for a cut of more than $2 in the marker posting, stating that it was prepared to implement such a cut unilaterally if other member countries increased their postings.

The final decision of the meeting was to increase the royalty rate under the Middle Eastern tax system from 12.5 per cent to 14.5 per cent with effect from July

1, on the grounds that it was desirable to narrow the disparity between this rate and the Venezuelan rate of 16⅔ per cent. (At the same time, member countries not affected by this decision—e.g. Venezuela and Indonesia—were to take alternative steps to achieve an equivalent increase in their revenue entitlement.) Saudi Arabia declined to make any increase in its royalty rate "for the time being" on the grounds that it did not wish to complicate its current negotiations for 100 per cent state control over the operations of Aramco. (An agreement on 60 per cent state participation, concluded five days before the opening of the 40th Conference meeting, had been described by the Saudi Government as an "interim" step towards this end.) The royalty increase raised the government take on marker-grade equity crude by about 10 cents per barrel (a similar increase being subsequently applied to the buy-back price of participation crude with effect from July 1 after Kuwait's national negotiations had established a definitive pattern of Gulf buy-back prices for 1974 ◊**D5.4**). Posted prices were frozen for the third quarter of 1974, and the Conference expressed the hope that the industrialized countries would "take this opportunity" to implement effective counter-inflationary measures.

Having failed to secure support within OPEC for a formal reduction in posted prices, Saudi Arabia announced on July 21 that it intended to auction a quantity of participation crude without setting any reserve price below which it would not sell. Market forces would instead be allowed to determine a "realistic" price level in the current period of slack export demand. According to the *Middle East Economic Survey*, bids were to be invited for a total volume of 1,500,000 bpd of Saudi crude to be delivered over 16 months from September. The Saudi announcement was the subject of urgent consultations between the other Gulf OPEC producers, which made contingency plans for co-ordinated production cutbacks to support the level of market prices if the Saudi Government failed to respond to their appeal for the cancellation of the planned auction.

It was, however, Algeria (whose Oil Minister had worked closely with Shaikh Yamani to monitor the political impact of the recent Arab oil sanctions ◊**D4.5, D5.2**) which made the most effective representations to Saudi Arabia on behalf of the OPEC majority, pledging its support for a continued freeze on posted prices in return for a Saudi undertaking to refrain from action likely to "destabilize" market prices. Implementation of the Saudi auction plan was subsequently "suspended" at short notice in mid-August, and on Aug. 31 the official Algerian news agency reported that Algeria and Saudi Arabia had agreed that posted prices should be maintained, and market prices supported, at their current levels for a "reasonable period of time". The report added that "all recent declarations tending to make the public believe that there should be a reduction in prices" were invalidated by this agreement.

Representatives of OPEC countries' national oil companies and state marketing agencies had meanwhile met in London on Aug. 15 to "examine ways of enhancing co-operation and co-ordination, especially in the field of marketing". The meeting (which was not attended by Saudi Arabia) drew up proposals for an OPEC-wide policy on state oil sales, involving the observance both of a loose system of market-demand prorationing and of minimum selling prices equivalent to 93 per cent of the posting for Saudi Arabian 34° crude fob Ras Tanura after appropriate adjustment for gravity, quality and geographical location. Although a formal agreement embodying these and other proposals failed to secure ratification by a majority of OPEC governments (thus putting an end to efforts to "cartelize" the national oil companies), the recommended official pricing formula subsequently received general acceptance within the OPEC area on an informal basis.

The 41st (extraordinary) meeting of the OPEC Conference was held on Sept. 12

and 13 to consider pricing policy for the last quarter of 1974. The Economic Commission's recommendation was that the "weighted average government take" on marker crude (assuming full buy-back of the 60 per cent state share of output) should be increased by 14 per cent to compensate for the estimated increase in the prices of imported manufactured goods during 1974. The recommended strategy for achieving a higher overall take was to raise the income tax and/or royalty rates on equity crude, the very high post-tax profit margin on such crude having come under increasing criticism from OPEC state oil companies whose own direct sales prices were being undercut by the majors (◊D5.4).

Saudi Arabia secured the backing of Algeria, Iran, Kuwait and Venezuela for the limitation of the increase in the government take to 3.5 per cent, on the basis that an increase imposed in the last quarter of the year should compensate for one-quarter of the annual inflation rate, and for the achievement of such an increase through a combination of higher taxation (to cut the company profit margin) and lower postings (implying a proportionate cut in the price of state-marketed crude). Iran, which had modified its previous hard line on pricing after considering the implications of Saudi Arabi's threat to hold a "free" auction, proposed (i) that a reduced official selling price should replace the posted price as the central reference point in the Middle Eastern tax system, and (ii) that foreign partner companies should receive fixed discounts off this price which would eliminate the scope for "windfall" profits while providing a fair return on the companies' investments as equity holders (or, in Iran, as providers of capital to NIOC).

Most of the remaining member countries supported the scaling-down of the increase in the government take to 3.5 per cent, but a majority of them (led by Iraq and Libya) opposed Saudi Arabia's proposal for a cut in postings and Iran's proposal for a revision of the basis of the tax system. Because of the reduction in the Gulf buy-back price from 94.846 per cent to 93 per cent of postings on Oct. 1 (◊D5.4), it was necessary to increase the government take on marker-grade equity crude by 15.9 per cent (from about $7.09 to about $8.22 per barrel) in order to increase the weighted average take by 3.5 per cent (from $9.41 to $9.74) on the same date. The increased take on equity crude was achieved by introducing a standard OPEC royalty rate of 16⅔ per cent while increasing the income tax rate from 55 per cent to 65⅔ per cent in Gulf OPEC countries where 60 per cent state participation agreements were in force. Other OPEC countries increased their income tax rates by the margins required to secure the 3.5 per cent increase in unit revenue.

Saudi Arabia declined to implement the tax and royalty increases, declaring again that "for the time being" it wished to await the outcome of its ongoing negotiations with Aramco. It insisted that OPEC's press statement on the outcome of the 41st Conference meeting should draw attention to the Saudi view that "the increase in the average government take is justified only on the basis of excess profits realized by the international oil companies" and that "the increases in the rates of tax and royalty should therefore be coupled with a reduction in posted prices".

The press statement also recorded the consensus view of the Conference that the Oct. 1 increase in the foreign oil companies' tax liabilities "should not be passed on to consumers, taking into consideration the excessive margin of profits still being made by the international oil majors in their upstream operations". With regard to what was described as the "alarming" rate of inflation in the industrialized countries, the meeting decided that "as of January 1975 such inflation will automatically be taken into account with a view to correcting any future deterioration in the purchasing power of the member countries' oil revenues". A working party was set up to "study and recommend a new system for long-term oil pricing". The

Conference noted that several OPEC countries had "announced their decision to make a voluntary cutback in their production level" and requested the Secretariat to "carry out a study on the subject of supply and demand".

D5.6.ii—Major reductions in foreign exporting companies' profit margins on Gulf crude (November–December 1974)

In mid-October Saudi Arabia let it be known that it had decided to bring its income tax and royalty rates into line with those in other Gulf OPEC countries (with appropriate retroactivity) as an indication of its impatience at the slow progress of negotiations for 100 per cent state control of the operations of Aramco. Strong opposition to the principle of full state control was nevertheless maintained by Aramco's parent companies. The Saudi Government therefore decided to seek the support of other Gulf OPEC countries for a sharp increase in taxation which would reduce the profit margin enjoyed by the companies under the present 60:40 participation arrangements while demonstrating the Saudi Government's preparedness to take any steps considered necessary to force the companies to open substantive negotiations. A meeting held in Abu Dhabi at Saudi Arabia's request on Nov. 10 and 11 was attended by ministers from Saudi Arabia, Kuwait and the United Arab Emirates, by lower-level delegates from Qatar and Iraq, and by an observer from Iran.

Saudi Arabia, Qatar and the United Arab Emirates announced on Nov. 11 that they had decided to increase their income tax rates to 85 per cent and their royalty rates to 20 per cent with effect from Nov. 1. In keeping with Saudi Arabia's view that increased taxation should be accompanied by reduced postings, an across-the-board cut of 40 cents per barrel was applied to the postings for all grades of crude in the three countries from the same date. The posting for 34° Saudi Arabian crude fob Ras Tanura was therefore reduced to $11.251 per barrel from its January 1974 level of $11.651, while the buy-back price and the government selling price, each of which stood at 93 per cent of postings in Saudi Arabia in October 1974, were cut by $0.372 per barrel (from $10.835 to $10.463). The weighted average government take for the same crude (assuming full buy-back of 60 per cent of output) rose by the slightly higher amount of $0.38 per barrel to reach $10.12. The gap between the government selling price and the tax-paid cost of equity crude was slashed from $2.43 to $0.50 per barrel, while the gap between the government selling price and the foreign exporting companies' average acquisition cost (again assuming full buy-back) fell from nearly $1 to only $0.22 per barrel.

(Implementation of these changes in Saudi Arabia was accompanied by a threat to reduce Aramco's buy-back entitlement to 20 per cent of total output and to increase the buy-back price to 94.8 per cent of postings while reducing the government selling price below 93 per cent of postings. This threat proved adequate to secure the parent companies' prompt acceptance of the principle of 100 per cent state control of Aramco's production operations, thus allowing substantive negotiations to begin on the Saudi Government's proposals for a new contractual relationship broadly similar to that which applied to the operations of the IOP consortium in Iran.)

Iran, Kuwait and Iraq all reserved their positions on the implementation of the measures introduced by the other Gulf OPEC members, on the grounds that it was inappropriate to take a final decision until these measures had been fully discussed by the next OPEC Conference meeting. Iran's view was that the change in the tax structure had paved the way for a formal switch to a pricing system centred on the official selling price, in line with its proposal to OPEC's September Conference meeting (subsequently made public by the Shah on Nov. 2). Kuwait had no objection in principle to the general introduction of the new Saudi Arabian tax structure throughout the Gulf region. Iraq was concerned about the 40-cent cut in postings and the corresponding cut in government selling prices, which it saw as detrimental to the interests of state oil companies, particularly those which were responsible for marketing the entire output of fully nationalized oilfields.

In the event, the 42nd meeting of the OPEC Conference, held on Dec. 12 and 13, endorsed "the financial effect" of the decisions taken by Saudi Arabia, Qatar and the United Arab Emirates on Nov. 11, which were to form the basis of "a new pricing system". However, the Conference did not at this stage formally adopt the government selling price as OPEC's central reference point, which was defined instead as an average government take of $10.12 per barrel on Saudi Arabian 34° crude fob Ras Tanura with effect from Jan. 1, 1975. The structure of posted prices, income tax and royalties established on Nov. 11 remained intact, and was introduced with retroactive effect from Nov. 1 in Gulf countries which had continued to apply the pre-existing arrangements. By focusing not on the details of the changes in the tax structure (which were not mentioned in the announcement of the meeting's decisions) but on their maximum financial impact under 60:40 participation, the Conference deliberately blurred the basis of the new government take calculation. This left individual Gulf countries free to decide whether to establish a fixed take, regardless of the volume of buy-back purchases, or to vary their take according to the extent to which the foreign exporting companies' purchases of participation crude fell below 60 per cent of total output.

Kuwait subsequently applied the agreement in such a way as to establish a fixed company margin relative to the government selling price. The amount of the margin was 22 cents per barrel, equal to the difference between Saudi Arabia's official selling price for Gulf exports of marker crude and the Aramco parent companies' maximum acquisition cost for the same crude (i.e. the average government take as defined by OPEC plus Aramco's average share of production costs, which was deemed to be 12 cents per barrel). Iran, whose revenue entitlement under the sales and purchase agreement with IOP was maintained at the highest level in force under participation agreements elsewhere in the Gulf region (◊C5.3.iv), introduced an identical margin of 22 cents per barrel, which was described as a discount off Iran's official selling price. Saudi Arabia, Qatar and Abu Dhabi continued to allow the profit margins of their foreign producing companies to fluctuate in line with the proportion of participation crude actually bought back. However, OPEC's intention that such arrangements should be the exception rather than the rule was implicitly acknowledged in the press statement issued after the 42nd Conference meeting. This noted that Saudi Arabia was currently negotiating, and that Qatar and the United Arab Emirates intended to negotiate, "a new arrangement which could be made retroactive".

It was agreed that the decision of the 42nd Conference meeting regarding the government take should remain valid until the end of September 1975 (thus nullifying the decision of the previous meeting to introduce a system whereby oil prices would be index-linked to inflation rates in order to protect the purchasing power of OPEC members' export revenues). Iran's representative at the meeting, Dr Jamshid Amouzegar, subsequently stated that the nine-month price freeze, which would halt the series of quarterly price reviews initiated at the end of 1973, was intended "to give the consuming nations a chance to iron out their differences so that we can sit down together for a constructive dialogue".

The OPEC Conference stated its support for "all initiatives towards consultation between various groups of nations, among them developing countries and the industrialized nations", while condemning "all actions and manoeuvres aimed at confrontation". This statement was intended to indicate approval of France's current efforts to convene a "tripartite" conference (◊D5.13) and disapproval of the programme adopted by the recently-formed International Energy Agency (◊D5.12). It was agreed to convene a joint meeting of OPEC Oil and Foreign Ministers in Algiers in January 1975 in order to prepare for a meeting of OPEC heads of state (first proposed by Algeria in October 1974) at which a common position would be agreed in advance of any international conference between oil-exporting and oil-importing countries.

D5.7—Summary of Price Changes in 1974

By the end of 1974 the main process of price and tax adjustments in the principal OPEC producing region (originally set in train by the Gulf OPEC countries' first unilateral price increase on Oct. 16, 1973) was substantially complete, although the fiscal basis of the major oil companies' operations in individual member countries remained subject to further change within the new framework. Compared with the situation at the beginning of October 1973, the posted price of marker crude had undergone an overall rise of 273 per cent; the average government take on marker crude (assuming full buy-back) had increased by 403 per cent; and the average margin by which the government selling price exceeded the foreign exporting companies' overall acquisition cost (based on the same assumption) had been reduced by more than 66 per cent overall (but by more than 85 per cent relative to its peak level in the first half of 1974).

In early 1974 the transfer prices used by the major oil companies to invoice supplies of Gulf crude to their downstream affiliates had (for marker-grade oil) been as much as $2.50 per barrel below the same companies' arm's-length prices. By the end of the year they were virtually the same as these arm's-length prices, which were in turn virtually the same as the official OPEC selling prices for Gulf crudes. This convergence—occuring as it did at a time when spot prices had fallen significantly below contract prices—indicated the extent of the Gulf OPEC countries' control over the market in late 1974. This had been achieved by setting a high floor price (based on the average government take) which could only be undermined by price-cutting on the part of individual OPEC governments anxious to maintain export volume at a time of falling demand. All of the Middle Eastern OPEC countries published official selling prices equal to 93 per cent of their postings fob Gulf ports when implementing the 40-cent cut in their postings with effect from Nov. 1, 1974—the formal establishment of a uniform standard being seen as an important safeguard against competitive price-cutting within the region. Table 36 shows the new price levels applying to selected Gulf crudes with effect from Nov. 1.

Table 36 — Posted prices and official selling prices of selected Gulf crudes, Nov. 1, 1974

	Posted price	Official selling price
	(dollars per barrel)	
Abu Dhabi (39°)	12.236	11.379
Iran (31°)	11.235	10.45
Iran (34°)	11.475	10.67
Iraq (35°)	11.272	10.48
Kuwait (31°)	11.145	10.365
Qatar (40°)	12.014	11.17
Saudi Arabia (27°)	11.041	10.268
Saudi Arabia (31°)	11.161	10.38
Saudi Arabia (34°)	11.251	10.463
Saudi Arabia (39°)	11.951	11.114

Outside the Gulf region, each OPEC member adjusted (or refrained from adjusting) its selling prices or tax-reference values during 1974 in accordance with local export market conditions and the terms of its particular degree of state participation in the ownership of production operations. The most notable trend was towards a reduction in the premiums commanded by African and Mediterranean crudes, whose proximity advantage over Gulf crudes began to disappear as tanker owners, faced with a surplus of capacity resulting from the fall in world oil demand, made progressive cuts in their charter rates.

Algeria ceased to use posted prices in July 1974, when it adopted a system based solely on official selling prices. The official selling price for 44° crude on July 1 was $13 per barrel (slightly above 80 per cent of the last posting). Subsequent reductions brought the price down to $12.30 on Oct. 1 and to $12 on Jan. 1, 1975. Libya and Nigeria published only posted prices over this period. Libya's reported selling prices moved progressively downwards throughout 1974 at a somewhat faster rate than Algeria's, while Nigeria did not start to make significant cuts in its selling prices until demand for its exports began to decline in November. Iraq, which had ceased to publish postings for its (fully nationalized) Mediterranean exports at the end of 1973, did not publish its official selling prices for such exports. Saudi Arabia's Nov. 1, 1974, posting for Mediterranean exports of 34° crude ($13.247 per barrel) was the last to be made, as the trans-Arabian pipeline ceased to be used for export purposes in February 1975 because of the sharp fall in the cost of shipping crude westward from the Persian/Arabian Gulf (◊D6.2).

Ecuador and Gabon held their tax-reference prices constant throughout 1974. Indonesia increased its selling price for 34° crude to $11.70 per barrel on April 1, 1974, and to $12.60 on July 1, 1974. Venezuela increased the minimum tax-reference values for all but its heaviest crudes by 4.5 per cent on July 1, 1974 (taking the reference value for 35° crude to $12.8979 per barrel).

D5.8—Developments leading to Washington Conference of Major Oil-Consuming Countries

The US Secretary of State, Dr Henry Kissinger, speaking in London on Dec. 12, 1973 (11 days before the Gulf OPEC producers announced their second unilateral increase in posted prices ◊D4.6), called upon West European countries, together with Canada and Japan, to join the United States in setting up an "energy action group of senior and prestigious individuals with a mandate to develop within three months an initial action programme for collaboration in all areas of the energy problem". This proposal attracted few positive responses within Western Europe, where most countries took the view that the formation of such a group would be seen as provocative by the Arab exporting countries in the delicately balanced supply situation which existed at that time. The general tendency in Western Europe and Japan in late 1973 was to look towards bilateral agreements with exporting countries as the most realistic means of ensuring long-term security of supply, and France, the leading proponent of such "bilateralism", was also the strongest opponent of the US proposals.

A meeting of EEC heads of state or government, held in Copenhagen on Dec. 14 and 15, 1973, agreed on the need for urgent action to improve the co-ordination of energy policy within the Community and to introduce a "comprehensive Community programme on alternative sources of energy". At the same time, the meeting "confirmed the importance of entering into negotiations with oil-producing countries on comprehensive arrangements comprising co-operation on a wide scale for the economic and industrial development of these countries, industrial investments, and stable energy supplies to the [EEC] member countries at reasonable prices". Such negotiations had been proposed to EEC Foreign Ministers on Dec. 14 by ministers from Algeria, Sudan, Tunisia and the United Arab Emirates, who visited Copenhagen to reiterate the Arab viewpoint on the current Middle East crisis and to make it clear that active EEC support for this viewpoint was a precondition for closer economic co-operation. In an implied rejection of Dr Kissinger's proposal that the importing countries should take joint action outside the framework of existing institutions, the EEC leaders stated that they "considered it useful to study with other oil-consuming countries within the framework of the OECD ways of dealing with the common short- and long-term energy problems of consumer countries".

In the light of the European reactions to the initial US proposals of Dec. 12, a follow-up proposal of Jan. 9, 1974, requesting a conference on the issue, was addressed both to major oil-consuming countries and to the OECD Secretary-General and was accompanied by assurances to OPEC countries. In a message to the heads of government of the other principal consumer nations, President Nixon proposed that a ministerial conference should be held in Washington in the following month to prepare the ground for the formulation of a "consumer action programme" incorporating "new co-operative measures designed to deal with the explosive growth of global energy demand and to accelerate the co-ordinated development of new energy sources". Action should also be taken "to develop a concerted consumer position for a new era of petroleum producer-consumer relations which would meet the legitimate interests of oil-producing countries while assuring the consumer countries adequate supplies at fair and reasonable prices".

In a simultaneous message to OPEC heads of government, President Nixon described the US initiative as "a constructive and positive step, consistent with the views of a number of oil-producing nations which have called for a consultative relationship between producers and consumers". He expressed the hope that the Washington conference would be followed by "an early joint conference of consumer and producer nations".

Whereas the 37th OPEC Conference meeting had stated on Jan. 9 (before the release of the Nixon letters) that the Organization was interested in "exchange of opinions and information with the consuming countries" (◊**D5.3**), Algeria and Iraq each expressed their opposition to the latest US initiative. They called instead for the holding of a world commodity conference under United Nations auspices, stating that the UN was the most appropriate forum for a dialogue between producing and consuming countries. Algeria accused the United States of seeking to "impose a protectorate on oil consumers and producers".

Among the major oil-importing countries, France took the line that the United Nations should play the main role in organizing wide-ranging international consultations on the energy issue. It was announced on Jan. 21 that the French Foreign Minister had formally proposed the "urgent convening" of a UN-sponsored energy conference, a main aim of which should be to draw up "general principles of co-operation between energy producing and consuming countries with a view to ensuring that world needs are met in conditions which are reasonable and equitable for all countries".

When EEC Foreign Ministers met in Brussels on Feb. 4 and 5 to adopt a joint Community mandate for the Washington conference, France sought to limit the scope of the mandate as far as possible, with the result that the final text expressed many reservations which had not appeared in a more positive draft submitted by West Germany (the current holder of the presidency of the EEC Council of Ministers). The French Cabinet decided on Feb. 6 that France's Foreign Minister should attend the Washington conference, but stressed in an official statement that, although France was prepared to participate in an exchange of views on the energy crisis, it could not support the establishment of "an organization of oil-consuming industrialized countries independent of other consuming countries, notably developing countries, and of the oil-producing countries". The statement also referred to the importance of dialogue and co-operation between exporting and importing countries and affirmed the French Government's readiness to engage in all bilateral and multilateral contacts to that end, as for example between the European Community and the Arab states.

The Washington conference took place from Feb. 11 to 13 and was attended by delegations from Belgium, Canada, Denmark, France, West Germany, Irish Republic, Italy, Japan, Luxembourg, Netherlands, Norway, the United Kingdom and the United States, as well as by the President of the European Commission and the Secretary-General of the OECD. National delegations, led by Foreign Ministers, included also ministers responsible for finance, energy, economic affairs and science and technology. The principal decisions of the meeting (which were rejected by France) were officially announced as follows:

"[The non-French delegates] concurred in the need for a comprehensive action programme to deal with all facets of the world energy situation by co-operative measures. In so doing they will build on the work of the OECD. They recognized that they may wish to invite, as appropriate, other countries to join with them in these efforts. Such an action programme of international co-operation would include, as appropriate, the sharing of means and efforts, while concerting national policies, in such areas as: the conservation of energy and restraint of demand; a system of allocating oil supplies in times of emergency and severe shortages; the acceleration of development of additional energy sources so as to diversify energy supplies; the acceleration of energy research and development programmes through international co-operative efforts. . . . They agreed to establish a co-ordinating group headed by senior officials, [which] . . . should: monitor and give focus to the tasks that might be addressed in existing organizations; establish such ad hoc working groups as may be necessary to undertake tasks for which there are presently no suitable bodies; direct preparations of a conference of consumer and producer countries which will be held at the earliest possible opportunity and which, if necessary, will be preceded by a further meeting of consumer countries."

The proposed co-ordinating group was formally established at a meeting held in Washington on Feb. 25 and 26, 1974, between officials from all of the original participating countries except France, which had confirmed its refusal to join the group on Feb. 21, stating that such a body should not be confined to the major oil-consuming countries. The first working session of the co-ordinating group, held in Brussels on March 13 and 14, referred consideration of the following topics to the OECD: (i) ways and means of using energy more efficiently and of reducing demand; (ii) acceleration of research into conventional energy sources; and (iii) establishment of an oil-sharing plan to operate at times of world shortage. Topics referred to working parties of the co-ordinating group itself included (i) co-operation in research into and development of new energy sources; (ii) co-operation in enriched uranium production; (iii) economic and monetary co-ordination to counter the effects of increased oil prices; and (iv) the role of the international oil companies.

D5.9—UN Declaration on the Establishment of a New International Economic Order

A special session of the UN General Assembly (the sixth special session) was held in New York from April 9 to May 2, 1974, to discuss raw materials and development. The holding of the session had been formally requested on Jan. 31 by President Boumedienne of Algeria, who had stated that there was a need for discussion within the UN of all aspects of world trade in primary commodities, and not just of the world energy situation (as had been proposed by the French Government 10 days previously ◊**D5.13**). Algeria's view was that joint action by oil-exporting countries had been too narrowly interpreted in some quarters, and should be placed in the wider context of relations between the developed industrialized nations and the developing countries of the Third World. The Algerian request had secured the backing of the necessary majority of UN member states by Feb. 14.

After wide-ranging debate dominated by representatives of third-world countries, the General Assembly on May 1 approved without a vote a Declaration and Programme of Action for the establishment of a new international economic order. An extract from the text of the Declaration is given below.

"The developing countries, which constitute 70 per cent of the world population, account for only 30 per cent of the world's income. It has proved impossible to achieve an even and balanced development of the international community under the existing international economic order. The gap between the developed and the developing countries continues to widen in a system which was established at a time when most of the developing countries did not even exist as independent states and which perpetuates inequality.

"The present international economic order is in direct conflict with current developments in international political and economic relations. Since 1970 the world economy has experienced a series of grave crises which have had severe repercussions, especially on the developing countries because of their generally greater vulnerability to external economic impulses. The developing world has become a powerful factor that makes its influence felt in all fields of international activity. These irreversible changes in the relationship of forces in the world necessitate the active, full and equal participation of the developing countries in the formulation and application of all decisions that concern the international community.

"All these changes have thrust into prominence the reality of interdependence of all the members of the world community. Current events have brought into sharp focus the realization that the interests of the developed countries and the interests of the developing countries can no longer be isolated from each other; that there is close inter-relationship between the prosperity of the developed countries and the growth and development of the developing countries; and that the prosperity of the international community as a whole depends upon the prosperity of its constituent parts. . . .

"The new international economic order should be founded on full respect for the following principles:

"(a) Sovereign equality of states, self-determination of all peoples, inadmissibility of the acquisition of territories by force, territorial integrity and non-interference in the internal affairs of other states;

"(b) broadest co-operation of all the member states of the international community, based on equity, whereby the prevailing disparities in the world may be banished and prosperity secured for all;

"(c) full and effective participation on the basis of equality of all countries in the solving of world economic problems in the common interest of all countries, bearing in mind the necessity to ensure the accelerated development of all the developing countries, while devoting particular attention to the adoption of special measures in favour of the least developed, land-locked and island developing countries, as well as those developing countries most seriously affected by economic crises and natural calamities, without losing sight of the interests of other developing countries;

"(d) every country has the right to adopt the economic and social system that it deems to be the most appropriate for its own development and not to be subjected to discrimination of any kind as a result;

"(e) full permanent sovereignty of every state over its natural resources and all economic activities. In order to safeguard these resources each state is entitled to exercise effective control over them and their exploitation with means suitable to its own situation, including the right to nationalization or transfer of ownership to its nationals, this right being an expression of the full permanent sovereignty of the state. No state may be subjected to economic, political or any other type of coercion to prevent the free and full exercise of this inalienable right;

420

"(f) all states, territories and peoples under foreign occupation, alien and colonial domination or apartheid have the right to restitution and full compensation for the exploitation and depletion of, and damages to, the natural and all other resources of those states, territories and peoples;

"(g) regulation and supervision of the activities of transnational corporations by taking measures in the interest of the national economies of the countries where such transnational corporations operate on the basis of the full sovereignty of those countries;

"(h) right of the developing countries and the peoples of territories under colonial and racial domination and foreign occupation to achieve their liberation and to regain effective control over their natural resources and economic activities;

"(i) extending of assistance to developing countries, peoples and territories under colonial and alien domination, foreign occupation, racial discrimination or apartheid or which are subjected to economic, political or any other type of measures to coerce them in order to obtain from them the subordination of the exercise of their sovereign rights and to secure from them advantages of any kind, and to neo-colonialism in all its forms, and which have established or are endeavouring to establish effective control over their natural resources and economic activities that have been or are still under foreign control;

"(j) just and equitable relationship between the prices of raw materials, primary products, manufactured and semi-manufactured goods exported by developing countries, and the prices of raw materials, primary commodities, manufactures, capital goods and equipment imported by them with the aim of bringing about sustained improvement in their unsatisfactory terms of trade and the expansion of the world economy;

"(k) extension of active assistance to developing countries by the whole international community, free of any political or military conditions;

"(l) ensuring that one of the main aims of the reformed international monetary system shall be the promotion of the development of the developing countries and the adequate flow of real resources to them;

"(m) improving the competitiveness of natural materials facing competition from synthetic substitutes;

"(n) preferential and non-reciprocal treatment for developing countries, wherever feasible, in all fields of international economic co-operation;

"(o) securing favourable conditions for the transfer of financial resources to developing countries;

"(p) to give the developing countries access to the achievements of modern science and technology, to promote the transfer of technology and the creation of indigenous technology for the benefit of the developing countries in forms and in accordance with procedures which are suited to their economies;

"(q) necessity for all states to put an end to the waste of natural resources, including food products;

"(r) the need for developing countries to concentrate all their resources for the cause of development;

"(s) strengthening through individual and collective actions of mutual economic, trade, financial and technical co-operation among the developing countries, mainly on a preferential basis;

"(t) facilitating the role which producers' associations may play, within the framework of international co-operation, and in pursuance of their aims, inter alia assisting in promotion of sustained growth of the world economy and accelerating development of developing countries."

D5.10—Adoption of Long-Term EEC Energy Targets – Launching of "Euro-Arab Dialogue"

The EEC Council of Ministers resolved in principle on Sept. 17, 1974, to draw up a co-ordinated long-term energy strategy, although certain member countries (notably the United Kingdom, whose offshore oilfields were due to begin commercial production in mid-1975) made it clear that this should be achieved without any encroachment on their control over national energy policies.

In their resolution, the Council of Ministers (i) confirmed that "the world-wide aspects of energy problems necessitate co-operation among the consumer countries and between them and producer countries, in which the Community as such and the member states intend to participate"; (ii) adopted as a guideline in the field of energy demand a commitment to reducing the rate of growth of internal consumption "without jeopardizing social and economic growth objectives"; (iii) adopted as a further guideline the improvement of security of supply by the development of nuclear power, by use of the Community's hydrocarbon and solid fuel resources, by seeking diversified and reliable external sources and by research and technological development; and (iv) decided to hold a further meeting on energy problems before the end of 1974 at which it would "state its position" on target figures for Community energy production and consumption until 1985 and on the "guidelines and action necessary to develop each energy source and the conditions for orderly functioning of the common market for energy".

In a further resolution adopted on Dec. 17, the Council of Ministers established its 1985 targets for the energy sector. The Community's level of dependence on imported energy, which had stood at 63 per cent in 1973, was to be reduced to a maximum of 50 per cent, and if possible to 40 per cent, by 1985. Table 37 shows the Community's 1985 targets for the percentage contributions of different primary energy sources at the reduced levels of import dependence (with actual 1973 percentages and January 1973 projections for 1985 shown for comparison).

Table 37 — EEC energy targets for 1985

	Actual percentage in 1973	1973 projection for 1985	1985 target with 50% import dependence	1985 target with 40% import dependence
Solid fuels	22.6	10	17	17
Oil	61.4	64	49	41
Natural gas	11.6	15	18	23
Water and geothermal power	3.0	2	3	3
Nuclear power	1.4	9	13	16

An overall target for total energy consumption in 1985 was set 15 per cent below the original 1973 projection for that year, "bearing in mind that percentage changes may be different for the various member states and without ruling out the possibility of setting specific objectives, depending on circumstances, for saving energy in the shorter term". An action programme was to be introduced to encourage the "rational utilization" of energy. It was envisaged that 35 per cent of the Community's final energy supply would be in the form of electricity in 1985 as nuclear power in particular was developed in order to reduce dependence on "non-reliable" imports (i.e. of OPEC oil).

The 1985 targets envisaged (i) an unchanged level of annual coal production, at 180 mtoe (million tonnes oil equivalent), together with increased levels of lignite and peat production (30 mtoe) and of coal imports (45 mtoe); (ii) an increase in natural gas production to between 175 and 225 mtoe, to be supplemented by natural gas imports of between 95 and 115 mtoe; (iii) the installation of between 160 and 200 gigawatts of nuclear generating capacity; (iv) an increase in the combined contribution of water and geothermal power, to 45 mtoe; and (v) an increase in EEC oil production to at least 180,000,000 tonnes per annum, and a reduction in oil imports from 640,000,000 tonnes in 1973 to between 420,000,000 and 550,000,000 tonnes in 1985. The proportion of imported oil in total energy consumption was targeted to fall from 61 per cent in 1973 to between 28 and 38 per cent in 1985, while the proportion of imported oil in total oil consumption was targeted to fall from 98 per cent to between 70 and 75 per cent over the same period.

The Council of Ministers agreed in principle on March 4 that a "Euro-Arab Dialogue" should be initiated with a view to strengthening co-operation between the EEC member countries and the Arab states along the lines envisaged by EEC heads of state or government at their Copenhagen summit meeting in December 1973 (◊**D5.8**). It was further agreed on June 10 that the EEC should make a formal offer of long-term economic, technical and cultural co-operation to the member states of the Arab League, and on July 31 European and Arab representatives decided at an initial meeting in Paris to create a permanent General Commission to co-ordinate the process of dialogue. In a related development, the European Commission reached an agreement with OAPEC on Oct. 8 for regular consultation and exchange of technical information. (By June 1975 the Euro-Arab Dialogue had progressed to the stage of setting up joint committees to study specific areas of potential co-operation. The first meeting of the joint General Commission took place in May 1976.)

The EEC's initial decision of March 4, 1974, on the formal establishment of the Euro-Arab Dialogue (for which the French Government had been campaigning since the beginning of the year) had been strongly criticized by the US Government, which objected to the fact that it had not been informed or consulted prior to the adoption of a policy held to impinge on the USA's interest in current negotiations for a political settlement in the Middle East. The further EEC decision of June 10 was therefore coupled with the adoption of a "pragmatic procedure" (proposed by West Germany) whereby any EEC member state could delay a joint decision on a foreign policy issue in order to hold prior consultations with "friendly states".

D5.11—Modification of Long-Term US Energy Targets

"Project Indepence", originally conceived in late 1973 with the aim of making the United States self-sufficient in energy by 1980 (◊**A4.15.ii**), was intended in early 1974 to place the United States in an energy surplus position by 1985, when the total productive capacity of US primary energy sources was targeted to reach 2,720 million tonnes oil equivalent (mtoe), some 660 mtoe (32 per cent) higher than the January 1973 forecast for 1985. At the same time, 1985 consumption was targeted as 2,600 mtoe, some 500 mtoe (16 per cent) below the original 1973 estimate for 1985, thus more than offsetting an originally estimated 1985 import requirement of 1,040 mtoe (85 per cent oil and 15 per cent natural gas). However, by the end of 1974 the US Government had ceased to plan in terms of self-sufficiency by 1980 or surplus by 1985, and was aiming to "end vulnerability to disruption by foreign suppliers by 1985" on the basis of a total import requirement of between 150 and 250 mtoe in that year, when protection against a lengthy supply disruption would be provided by an appropriately large stockpile of oil.

D5.12—Establishment of International Energy Agency – Adoption of Emergency Oil-Sharing System

A draft agreement for the establishment of an International Energy Agency was adopted on Sept. 20, 1974, by the co-ordinating group of 12 industrialized oil-consuming countries which had been set up on Feb. 26 (◊**D5.8**). Of the 12, Norway reserved its position at this stage, subsequently announcing on Oct. 31 that it could not accept the draft agreement in its entirety. The IEA was to function under OECD auspices and membership was to be open to all OECD members and to the EEC as an observer.

The Council of the OECD formally approved the establishment of the Agency on Nov. 15. The 16 OECD members which decided to join the IEA at this stage (Austria, Belgium, Canada, Denmark, West Germany, the Irish Republic, Italy, Japan, Luxembourg, the Netherlands, Spain, Sweden, Switzerland, Turkey, the United Kingdom and the United States) then signed an agreement on Nov. 18 to bring the Agency's initial programme into immediate effect on a provisional basis pending the completion of national ratification procedures. The agreement was valid for 10 years in the first instance, subject to a review of its provisions after the first five years. Member countries could withdraw on 12 months' notice after the agreement had been in operation for at least three years.

The IEA's "international energy programme" included among its aims (◊**B3.2**) the promotion of co-operation with non-OECD oil-exporting countries; suggestions that the Agency was designed to "confront" the OPEC countries were rejected by the chairman of the co-ordinating group which had supervised the drafting of the programme. The role of the Agency in working to reduce member countries' dependence on imported oil was presented as being consistent with statements made by at various times by OPEC members advocating a more rational use of oil resources. Nevertheless, the most widely publicized element in the IEA's programme, dealing with joint action to anticipate and counteract a supply cutback, was an obvious response to the recent use of the Arab oil weapon.

IEA member countries undertook to maintain sufficient oil stocks to cover at least 60 days' net imports and agreed in principle that this requirement should be increased to 90 days' net imports at a later date. In the event of a shortfall of between 7 and 12 per cent in the aggregate oil supply of all member countries, each country would be required to cut back its consumption to 93 per cent of the previous level, drawing down its stocks as necessary to support the reduced level of consumption. In the event of an aggregate supply shortfall of 12 per cent or more, each member country would be required to cut back its consumption to 90 per cent of the normal level and to draw down stocks as necessary.

If an overall supply shortfall of more than 7 per cent affected different countries unequally (e.g. because of the imposition of destination embargoes by exporting countries), the IEA Secretariat was to reallocate a proportion of available oil supplies in order to ensure an equitable distribution of the aggregate cutback between all member countries, using an agreed formula of "supply rights" and "supply obligations" (applicable to deficit and surplus countries respectively). Oil companies would be required to co-operate in this process by supplying full information on the availability of oil supplies and oil transport facilities and by appropriately redeploying their resources. The volume of oil subject to reallocation would not normally exceed 10 per cent of the total available supply from domestic and import sources.

The existence of a supply emergency would be notified by the IEA Secretariat to the Agency's Standing Group on Emergency Questions, which was empowered to call a mandatory meeting of the IEA Governing Board. Unless the Board decided otherwise within 48 hours of being called to meet, the emergency oil-sharing scheme would take automatic effect 15 days after the commencement of an interruption in supplies which had caused the aggregate supply to fall below the "trigger" level of 93 per cent. The automatic activation of the scheme could only be overridden by the Board if such a decision had the backing of a majority of 60 per cent of the total of member countries' "combined" votes, including 75 per cent of the general votes.

(Each of the member countries had three general votes. In addition, there was a total of 100 weighted votes broadly reflecting the member countries' relative shares of IEA oil consumption in 1973. At the formation of the Agency, weighted votes were allocated as follows: United States 48, Japan 15, West Germany 8, United Kingdom 6, Italy 6, Canada 5, Belgium 2, Netherlands 2, Spain 2, Sweden 2, Austria 1, Denmark 1, Switzerland 1, Turkey 1. For most decisions subject to weighted voting, other than a decision to override the activation of agreed emergency procedures, the required majority was 60 per cent of the "combined" votes, including 50 per cent of the general votes. Decisions on matters not covered by the IEA's constituent agreement could only be adopted by consensus.)

Compared with previous contingency planning within the framework of the OECD, the IEA's emergency programme marked a significant change in the policies of the participating countries, in that it brought domestic oil production within the scope of an oil-sharing programme and provided for the observance of obligatory restrictions on consumption. Norway and the United Kingdom were principally responsible for the introduction of mandatory voting procedures to govern the use of several key provisions of the IEA agreement, although as stated above Norway at this stage decided not to adhere to the agreement. This was mainly because it believed that the voting system as finally adopted gave undue weight to member countries' interests as consumers, without adequate safeguards for the interests of net oil-exporters. The Norwegian Foreign Minister said on Nov. 1 that "co-operation on oil-sharing in an emergency is necessary and important for oil-importing countries, but the voting rules of the group are objectionable and do not suit Norway as an oil exporter". He added that Norway, while retaining full sovereignty over its reserves, would be willing to take special measures to supply oil to other Western nations in a future supply crisis.

The effectiveness of many aspects of the IEA's programme depended ultimately on the co-operation of the major oil companies, each of which would be expected to make various categories of information available to the Secretariat on a regular basis. These included details of corporate structure, financial structure (including balance sheets, profit-and-loss accounts and taxes paid), capital investments realized, arrangements for access to crude oil, current production rates and anticipated changes, allocations of available crude supplies to affiliates and arm's-length customers, stocks, cost of crude oil and oil products, and prices (including transfer prices to subsidiaries and affiliates).

D5.13—French Proposal for Holding of "Tripartite" Conference on Oil-Related Issues

Valéry Giscard d'Estaing, who had succeeded the late Georges Pompidou as President of France in May 1974, held a press conference on foreign policy on Oct. 24 at which he announced France's intention to contact the goverments of various oil-exporting countries, industrialized countries and oil-importing developing countries with a view to organizing a conference between representatives of the three groups in early 1975. The French proposal envisaged participation by a total of between 10 and 12 delegations (including an EEC delegation which would provide joint representation for the EEC member countries), whose aim should be to work out a mutually acceptable approach to issues connected with "oil pricing and international inflation in the present phase of adjustment of the world economy". The French Government felt that it was well placed to initiate the process of producer-consumer dialogue in view of its opposition to the formation of the IEA, which it described as "an energy NATO". It was noted that the other countries which had participated in the Washington conference in February had failed to make any progress towards arranging producer-consumer talks.

President Giscard d'Estaing held talks with the US President, Gerald Ford, in Martinique from Dec. 14 to 16, after which a joint communiqué was issued indicating a narrowing of the differences between France and the United States on a number of issues, including the world energy situation. In particular, France accepted the need for a certain measure of "solidarity" among the main oil-importing countries, while the United States gave its qualifid support to the holding of the international conference which had been proposed by President Giscard d'Estaing in October. The US Government's main proviso was that co-operation between the main importing countries should be substantially strengthened as a prerequisite for effective talks with exporting countries.

D6—1975

D6.1—Annual Statistical Survey

D6.1.i—Oil production and reserves

World

Total production .... 55,700,000 bpd (2,733.6 million tonnes)
    Change over 1974 .... −5.1 per cent

End-year proved reserves .... 667,000 million barrels
    Change over end-1974 .... −7.9 per cent

Reserves:production ratio .... 32.8 : 1

Regional shares:

	In 1975 world production*			In end-1975 world reserves†		
	Regional total (million tonnes)	Change over 1974 (per cent)	Share of world total (per cent)	Reserves (thousand million barrels)	Change over 1974 (per cent)	Share of world total (per cent)
Middle East................	975.1	−10.1	35.7	368.3	−8.7	55.2
USSR/Eastern Europe/China	585.2	+7.5	21.4	103.4	−7.2	15.5
North America	557.4	−6.0	20.4	47.1	−4.7	7.1
Africa	248.5	−7.8	9.1	65.1	−4.7	9.8
Latin America/ Caribbean	227.5	−10.6	8.3	36.1	−18.1	5.4
Asia‡/Australasia	109.1	−1.0	4.0	21.4	+1.9	3.2
Western Europe§	30.8	+36.3	1.1	25.6	−2.7	3.8

*Including production from oil shales, tar sands and natural gas liquids (NGL).
†Excluding oil shales and tar sands; including NGL in North America.
‡Excluding China.
§Including Yugoslavia.

OPEC

OPEC oil production .... 27,530,000 bpd (1,361.8 million tonnes)
    Change over 1974* .... −11.5 per cent
    Share of 1975 world total .... 49.8 per cent

OPEC end-year proved reserves .... 450,570 million barrels
    Change over 1974* .... −7.8 per cent
    Share of 1975 world total .... 67.6 per cent

OPEC reserves: production ratio .... 44.8 : 1

*End-1975 membership basis.

OPEC (continued)

OPEC member countries' production:

	1975 production		Change over 1974 (per cent)	Share of world total (per cent)	Share of OPEC total (per cent)
	(million tonnes)	(thousand bpd)			
Algeria.....................	47.5	1,020	+0.8	1.7	3.5
Ecuador	7.9	160	−9.2	0.3	0.6
Gabon	11.2	225	+12.0	0.4	0.8
Indonesia...................	64.6	1,305	−4.9	2.4	4.7
Iran	267.7	5,385	−11.1	9.8	19.7
Iraq	111.0	2,260	+14.8	4.1	8.2
Kuwait......................	94.0	1,885	−19.2	3.4	6.9
Libya	71.3	1,480	−2.7	2.6	5.2
Nigeria......................	88.8	1,785	−20.9	3.2	6.5
Qatar	21.0	435	−15.7	0.8	1.5
Saudi Arabia	343.9	6,970	−16.9	12.6	25.3
UAE*	81.8	1,695	+0.9	3.0	6.0
Venezuela	125.3	2,425	−20.9	4.6	9.2
Neutral Zone†	25.8	500	−7.9	0.9	1.9

* Of which Abu Dhabi 67,300,000 tonnes (1,400,000 bpd), Dubai 12,600,000 tonnes (255,000 bpd), Sharjah 1,900,000 tonnes (40,000 bpd).
†Production shared between Kuwait and Saudi Arabia.

Non-OPEC

Selected non-OPEC countries' oil production:

	1975 production		Change over 1974 (per cent)	Share of world total (per cent)
	(million tonnes)	(thousand bpd)		
USSR	490.8	9,935	+7.0	18.0
USA*	473.9	10,010	−4.6	17.3
Canada......................	83.5	1,735	−13.5	3.1
China........................	74.3	1,490	+12.9	2.7
Mexico......................	39.3	790	+24.4	1.4
Argentina	20.3	390	−6.0	0.7
Oman	17.1	340	+17.9	0.6
Egypt	14.8	295	+28.7	0.5
Norway	9.3	190	+447.0	0.3
United Kingdom........	1.4	30	+1,300.0	0.05
Total	1,224.7	25,205	+2.2	44.65

*Of which natural gas liquids 58,000,000 tonnes (1,635,000 bpd).

D6.1.ii—Oil consumption

World

Total consumption .... 55,720,000 bpd (2,724.8 million tonnes)
    Change over 1974 .... −1.3 per cent

Regional distribution of total:

	1975 consumption		Change over 1974 (per cent)	Share of world total (per cent)
	(million tonnes)	(thousand bpd)		
North America	849.0	17,610	−2.1	31.2
Western Europe*	664.4	13,505	−5.0	24.4
USSR/Eastern Europe/China	526.7	10,545	+5.8	19.3
Asia†/Australasia	390.4	7,995	−3.2	14.3
Latin America/ Caribbean	176.0	3,695	+0.7	6.5
Middle East	66.8	1,320	−0.4	2.4
Africa	51.5	1,050	+2.2	1.9

*Including Yugoslavia.
†Excluding China.

Selected countries

	1975 consumption		Change over 1974 (per cent)	Share of world total (per cent)
	(million tonnes)	(thousand bpd)		
USA	765.9	15,875	−2.1	28.1
USSR	375.1	7,520	+4.6	13.8
Japan	244.0	5,020	−5.8	9.0
West Germany	128.9	2,655	−4.0	4.7
France	110.4	2,255	−8.8	4.0
Italy	94.5	1,895	−6.3	3.5
United Kingdom	92.0	1,875	−12.6	3.4
Canada	83.1	1,735	−2.0	3.0
China	68.3	1,350	+10.3	2.5
Spain	42.7	865	+3.9	1.6
Total	2.004.9	41,045	−2.2	73.6

D6.1.iii—Oil refining

World

Total refinery capacity .... 71,205,000 bpd
    Change over 1974 .... +4.5 per cent

Total refinery throughputs .... 52,930,000 bpd
    Change over 1974 .... −3 per cent

Consumption as proportion of capacity   78.3 per cent

Selected markets

Consumption of refined product types and change over 1974:

	USA		Western Europe		Japan	
	(million tonnes)	(per cent)	(million tonnes)	(per cent)	(million tonnes)	(per cent)
Gasolines	304.5	+1.4	126.8	−2.2	39.4	−4.6
Middle distillates	190.0	−2.8	222.9	−0.3	50.4	−0.4
Fuel oil	129.4	−6.1	230.0	−10.1	125.1	−7.8
Other	142.0	−4.8	84.7	−7.6	29.1	−7.0
Total	765.9	−2.1	664.4	−5.0	244.0	−5.8

D6.1.iv—Tankers and trade

Tankers
Total world fleet .... 291,400,000 deadweight tons
   Change over 1974 .... +13.9 per cent

Trade
Total world crude exports
   (including re-exports) .... 28,521,300 bpd (1,413.3 million tonnes)
   Change over 1974 .... −8.4 per cent
OPEC crude exports .... 24,063,900 bpd (1,192.5 million tonnes)
   Change over 1974 .... −11.7 per cent
   Share of 1975 world total .... 84.4 per cent

Total world product exports
   (including re-exports) .... 7,114,700 bpd (359,146,900 tonnes)
   Change over 1974 .... −13.6 per cent
OPEC product exports .... 1,559,700 bpd (78,733,000 tonnes)
   Change over 1974 .... −17.4 per cent
   Share of 1975 world total .... 21.9 per cent

Regional distribution of world oil trade*:

	Share of 1975 imports (per cent)		Share of 1975 exports (per cent)	
	Crude	Products	Crude	Products
USA	16.0	41.3	†	4.4
Canada	3.2	0.8	2.3	4.3
Latin America/Caribbean	7.9	6.4	4.4	43.9
Western Europe	45.5	20.0	0.2	4.0
Middle East	0.5	2.4	68.9	17.7
North Africa	0.3	1.9	9.2	1.2
West Africa	†	1.0	7.6	0.3
East and southern Africa	1.3	3.1	—	0.8
South Asia	1.2	2.0	—	0.1
South-East Asia	4.5	8.8	4.6	6.0
Australasia	0.9	2.6	—	1.1
Japan	17.8	8.2	—	0.1
USSR/Eastern Europe/ China	0.9	1.5	2.8	16.1
Total	100.0	100.0	100.0	100.0

*Excluding intra-regional trade.
†Negligible.

D6.1.v—World primary energy consumption

Total consumption (excluding
  non-commercial fuels) .... 5,952.7 million tonnes oil equivalent (mtoe)
  Change over 1974 .... +0.1 per cent

Contributions of primary energy sources:

	Consumption (mtoe)	Change over 1974 (per cent)	Share of total (per cent)
Oil	2,724.8	−1.3	45.8
Coal	1,709.1	+1.1	28.7
Natural gas	1,079.4	−0.8	18.1
Water power	353.3	+2.8	5.9
Nuclear power	86.1	+38.0	1.5

D6.1.vi—Natural gas production and reserves

Marketed production (thousand million cubic metres):

	Regional total (tmcm)	Change over 1974 (per cent)	Share of 1975 world total (per cent)
North America	616.5	−6.1	49.5
Latin America/Caribbean	37.1	+1.1	3.0
Western Europe*	161.5	+3.4	13.0
USSR/Eastern Europe/China	356.3	+10.0	28.6
Middle East	34.2	+4.3	2.7
Africa	13.3	+41.5	1.1
Asia†/Australasia	26.9	+14.0	2.1
World total	1,245.8	+0.5	100.0
(*of which OPEC*)	(56.2)	(+11.3)	(4.5)

*Including Yugoslavia.
†Excluding China.

End-year proved reserves (thousand million cubic metres):

	Regional total (tmcm)	Change over 1974 (per cent)	Share of 1975 world total (per cent)
North America	8,075.3	−2.9	13.5
Latin America/Caribbean	2,546.8	−6.1	4.3
Western Europe*	4,423.1	−13.2	7.4
USSR/Eastern Europe/China	21,346.2	+1.3	35.8
Middle East	14,239.6	+2.1	23.8
Africa	5,866.7	−0.9	9.8
Asia†/Australasia	3,219.3	+8.4	5.4
World total	59,717.0	−0.5	100.0
(*of which OPEC*)	(21,455.0)	(+1.6)	(35.9)

*Including Yugoslavia.
†Excluding China.

D6.2—Factors Influencing OPEC Pricing Policy in 1975

After 1974 the OPEC Conference ceased to concern itself with the issue of foreign
exporting companies' profit margins, and therefore with the level of posted or tax-

reference prices and the rates of tax and royalties in individual member countries. The official selling price of the marker crude—hitherto derived from the posted price—accordingly became the initial point from which tax-reference prices were derived in those countries where foreign producing companies continued to hold equity interests in oil output. This development stemmed mainly from the move towards full state control of production operations in several OPEC countries and the attendant divergence of fiscal arrangements within the Gulf region. (Although the phasing-out of the predominant 60:40 Gulf participation pattern was by no means complete by the end of 1975, it became clear during the course of the year that the new government-company relationships under negotiation would vary significantly from country to country.)

Kuwait took full control of KOC's operations with effect from March 1975, subsequently signing an agreement in December whereby its former concession holders were to enjoy preferential purchasing terms, including a fixed discount off the official selling price, for five years from 1976 (◊**C7.3.iii**). Iraq nationalized the remaining foreign concession interests in its southern oilfields in December, without seeking any new form of contractual relationship with its former concession holders (◊**C6.3.iv**). Saudi Arabia continued to negotiate throughout 1975 for 100 per cent state ownership of Aramco's production operations (eventually introducing a formula in 1976 under which Aramco continued to manage these operations—and to sell most of the output to its parent companies at official prices—in return for a per-barrel service fee ◊**C11.3.vii**). Qatar likewise negotiated for 100 per cent state ownership of production operations during 1975 and entered into service-contract arrangements with its former concession holders in 1976, although its per-barrel service fees were calculated on a different basis to Aramco's fees in Saudi Arabia (◊**C10.3**). Abu Dhabi decided in April 1975 to retain its existing 60:40 participation arrangements (◊**C12.3.iii**).

Outside the Gulf region, Nigeria (◊**C9.3**), Gabon (◊**C3.3**) and Ecuador (◊**C2.3**) also retained foreign equity in existing concessions, while Libya (◊**C8.3.iii**) and Algeria (◊**C1.3.iv**) each continued to have a mixture of fully nationalized and majority state-controlled concession areas. Venezuela legislated in August for full state control of production operations from the beginning of 1976, when short-term service contracts, involving per-barrel fees, would be offered to certain former concession holders (◊**C13.3.v**).

Having devoted much of 1974 to the adjustment of the fiscal relationship between host governments and foreign concession holders in the aftermath of the substantial rise in Gulf postings, the OPEC countries were faced in 1975 with the need to adjust the official selling prices of various grades of crude in response to the changing structure of market demand. Against this background attention focused on the relative market shares of the different members of the Organization rather than on the Organization's claims vis-à-vis the international oil companies. The issue of price differentials came to the fore in the context of a major slump in export demand for OPEC oil, the downward pressure on prices being greatest in those member countries which had applied the highest premiums at the beginning of 1974.

Within the Gulf region, Abu Dhabi reduced the gravity differential on its 39° crude to 0.3 cents per 0.1° API above 34° API in February (thus halving the premium for lighter crudes which had been adopted in late 1973 ◊**D4.6**), while cutting the sulphur premium on the same crude by 40 cents per barrel. Both cuts were made relative to the posted price and were backdated to Jan. 1 (the reduced official selling price for Abu Dhabi's 39° crude as of that date being $10.868 per barrel). This action was taken in view of a fall in Abu Dhabi's production to little more than half of its average 1974 level by February 1975 (when total OPEC production was around 12.5 per cent below its 1974 average). However, the basic structure of Gulf postings remained intact, largely because of Saudi Arabia's willingness to accept heavy cutbacks in Aramco's output, which had fallen to around 5,660,000 bpd (nearly one-third lower than the 1974 average) by April. Aramco halted its Mediterranean exports on Feb. 9 after the throughput of the trans-Arabian pipeline had fallen to 11 per cent of capacity.

This left Iraq as OPEC's only east Mediterranean exporter (of oil from the fully nationalized northern Iraqi fields) and as the pace-setter in repeated rounds of price cuts on "short-haul" supplies from Mediterranean and African ports as market resistance to premium pricing intensified. By the middle of 1975 Iraq's (unpublished) selling price for 36° crude fob Mediterranean ports was reported to be in the region of $10.75 per barrel (27 cents above its Gulf selling price for 35° crude). Among the main African exporters, Algeria (also heavily dependent on direct state sales) made the strongest efforts to contain the erosion of short-haul prices, backing up its public criticism of "unjustified" price cuts by Iraq (and parallel cuts by Libya and Nigeria) with a campaign for the introduction of an "objective" OPEC formula for determining price differentials relative to the marker crude and thus establishing a clear dividing line between "justified" and "unjustified" price cuts. The reopening of the Suez Canal in June 1975 (◊A4.13) was of relatively minor significance in the debate about Mediterranean price levels, partly because a deepening depression in the tanker market had accentuated the decline in the relative importance of the freight component in cif prices and partly because of the increasing use in recent years of "super-tankers" too large to pass through the Canal (◊A3.1.iii).

The downturn in OPEC production was most marked in the first half of 1975, when a low point of less than 26,000,000 bpd was reached in April. The second half of the year saw a partial recovery in output to an average of more than 28,000,000 bpd, 5.6 per cent higher than the January–June average (although still well below the annual average for 1974). Much of the fall in demand for OPEC oil was attributable to the fact that the OECD area was in the trough of a recession, marked by a negative economic growth rate in the first half of 1975 (although a real increase of 0.5 per cent was recorded in the OECD countries' aggregate gross national product for the year as a whole). The aggregate OECD unemployment rate reached 5.2 per cent, while price inflation was running at an annual rate of 11.3 per cent, below its peak level of nearly 14 per cent in 1974 but nevertheless well above the levels experienced in previous recessions (leading to the coining of the term "stagflation" to describe the new situation).

In these circumstances, the second main pricing issue to arise within OPEC (i.e. apart from the problem of differentials) was that of protecting unit purchasing power, which had been on the Organization's agenda throughout 1974 but assumed a new urgency as most member countries experienced substantial cutbacks in export volume. Inflationary pressure was, morever, exacerbated by a weakening of the US dollar against other major currencies during the first half of the year. The fact that some member countries were better placed than others to withstand cuts in their oil revenues—and that the largest producer, Saudi Arabia, was among the "low absorbers" of oil revenues into its domestic economy—increased tensions within the Organization over pricing policy and in particular reinforced the tendency towards confrontation between Saudi Arabia and the more "hawkish" member countries. There was, however, an underlying awareness that the effectiveness of OPEC price administration could only be assured through a process of continual compromise which took due account of Saudi Arabia's concern for the economic stability of the industrialized countries, the protection of which was seen by the Saudi Government as a matter of self-interest for the OPEC countries in view of their position as major participants in an interdependent world trade structure.

Saudi Arabia's efforts to secure a moderate OPEC line on the pricing issue were not assisted by the US Government's efforts to strengthen the collective position of the industrialized oil-importing countries. A US drive for new policy initiatives within the International Energy Agency (◊**D6.13**) was generally regarded in OPEC circles as a hostile move and an impediment to dialogue between exporters and importers regarding the supply and price of oil in the longer term. International discussion of such issues was instead linked to discussion of the broader relationship between developed and developing countries (◊**D6.11**), with Algeria playing a leading part in a bid to use the industrialized world's dependence on OPEC oil as a bargaining counter in the Third World's campaign for a new international economic order.

D6.3—OPEC Ministerial Meetings prior to Summit Conference

During the first two months of 1975 OPEC held a series of planning meetings in preparation for the Organization's first summit conference of heads of state, which (as confirmed in February) was to be convened in Algiers from March 4 to 6. A joint meeting of Ministers of Oil, Finance and Foreign Affairs—regarded as the Organization's first "political" meeting—took place in Algiers from Jan. 24 to 26 to discuss various proposals for the summit agenda and to agree broad guidelines for the drafting of a final agenda by a committee of officials. The participation of Finance Ministers in the meeting had been arranged on the initiative of the Algerian Government.

Items under discussion included an Algerian proposal for a medium-term OPEC pricing policy conceived as part of a wider international agreement for a transition to a new international economic order. According to this proposal, there should be an oil price freeze throughout 1975, price increases in 1976–77 at between 80 and 90 per cent of the prevailing rate of inflation in member countries' import costs, and subsequent increases affording full compensation for inflation from 1978 to 1980 (after which consideration could be given to an increase in real terms). In return for guarantees that OPEC would provide secure supplies at predictable prices over this six-year period, the main oil-importing countries would be required to undertake commitments regarding the planned growth of trade in other primary commodities and the acceleration of the economic development of third-world countries through industrialization and transfers of technological and financial resources. "Aggression" by industrialized countries against any OPEC member should be countered by a "global embargo" on oil exports to the countries concerned.

While other OPEC members supported the principle that any discussions between themselves and the industrialized oil-importing countries should cover a wide spectrum of third-world development issues, many reservations were expressed about the proposal that OPEC should offer to forgo an increase in real oil prices until the 1980s. The Algerian pricing plan was therefore dropped from the list of topics to be placed on the final summit agenda.

An OPEC press statement issued on Jan. 26 said that the meeting had "concluded that the present international economic crisis constitutes a growing threat to world peace and stability". The ministers condemned "the propaganda campaigns placing on OPEC member countries the responsibility for this crisis", as well as "threats directed at these countries", and warned that such attitudes could only "create confusion and lead to confrontation". (The reference to "threats" was taken to arise in part from Dr Henry Kissinger's recent refusal to rule out the possibility of military intervention in the Middle East to protect US oil supplies in exceptional circumstances.) The ministers expressed their support for "an international conference, such as that proposed by the Government of France [◊**D5.13**], which will deal with the problems of raw materials and development" and for any form of dialogue between industrialized and developing countries serving "to promote solidarity among all the peoples of the world through a genuine international co-operation".

The 43rd (extraordinary) meeting of the OPEC Conference, held in Vienna from Feb. 25 to 27, 1975, considered the report of the agenda-drafting committee for the forthcoming summit conference. With regard to the current oil-pricing situation, the Conference noted Abu Dhabi's recent problems and formally approved the Government's action in cutting differentials (◊**D6.2**). The Conference "condemned the discriminatory oil-lifting measures adopted by the oil companies operating in the United Arab Emirates". It also considered the decline in the exchange rate of the US dollar since September 1974 (which had prompted Kuwait to call on Feb. 2 for the readoption by OPEC of oil-price indexation against a basket of currencies along the lines of the system which had been abandoned at the end of 1973 ◊**D4.6**). Algeria and Iraq advocated the redenomination of oil prices in a currency other than the dollar, which was described by Algeria as being "constantly subject to manipulations highly prejudicial to OPEC countries". The Conference decided to refer the issue to the OPEC Economic Commission, which was asked to submit recommendations to the next Conference meeting.

It was reported that the 43rd Conference meeting also discussed proposals from certain member countries for co-ordinated action to ensure an equitable distribution of production cutbacks in the current market conditions. Under these proposals (which were not taken up by the Conference) member countries would have been grouped into categories of "high need" (Algeria, Ecuador, Gabon, Indonesia and Nigeria), "medium need" (Iran, Iraq and Venezuela) and "surplus revenue" (Kuwait, Libya, Qatar, Saudi Arabia and the United Arab Emirates).

An informal joint meeting of OPEC Oil, Finance and Foreign Ministers took place in Algiers on March 2 and 3 to finalize the agenda for the summit conference and to make substantial amendments to the texts of a proposed programme of action and declaration of principles.

D6.4—Algiers Summit of OPEC Heads of State

The Algiers summit of March 4 to 6, 1975, was attended in person by the heads of state of eight OPEC countries, while Indonesia, Iraq, Libya, Nigeria and Saudi Arabia were represented by senior members of their governments. Opening the meeting on March 4, President Boumedienne of Algeria reiterated his country's earlier appeals for a new international economic order, calling upon the industrialized countries to "commit themselves explicitly to a huge undertaking of co-operation for the development of the third-world countries" and proposing that OPEC, for its part, should establish a development fund with resources of up to $15,000 million. He issued a warning to the industrialized countries that "the various endeavours to reduce oil consumption, not with the idea of eliminating waste but in the hope of provoking a price fall and weakening us, are false solutions, if only because we in reply can reduce our production in order to maintain the level of our income".

The Shah of Iran, speaking on March 5, ruled out any possibility of a reduction in oil prices while OPEC countries' unit import costs continued to rise, adding that in his view oil prices should be index-linked to the prices of imported goods. He estimated the OPEC countries' loss of unit purchasing power since the end of 1973 as "at least 35 per cent" and criticized the industrialized countries for "not doing anything to check inflation".

The conference discussed the French Government's recent approach to Algeria, Iran, Saudi Arabia and Venezuela in connexion with its proposal for an international conference on "energy and related problems" (◊**D6.11**). It was decided, although with some reservations about its exact terms of reference, to agree in principle to the convening of an exploratory meeting in which the four member countries concerned would participate as sovereign states without any formal commitment to a common OPEC negotiating position.

Apparently because of their inability to reach agreement on specific proposals regarding future OPEC policy on pricing, production, the establishment of a development fund and related questions (all of which were referred back to expert groups for further consideration), the heads of state did not adopt the detailed "programme of action" which ministers had drafted. They did, however, issue a "solemn declaration" outlining the Organization's basic stance on current issues in international economic relations (◊**B1.9.iii**).

OPEC's Algiers summit was the occasion for the announcement (made by President Boumedienne on March 6) of an agreement between the Shah of Iran and the Vice-President of the Iraqi Revolutionary Command Council which "completely eliminates the conflict between the two brotherly countries". A protocol establishing joint committees on border demarcation and border security was subsequently signed by the two countries on March 17.

D6.5—44th Meeting of OPEC Conference

The 44th meeting of the OPEC Conference took place from June 9 to 11 in Gabon (which was admitted as a full member of the Organization). The Conference decided that, "in view of increasing inflation, the depreciation of the value of the dollar and the consequent erosion of the real value of the oil revenues of member countries", OPEC crude oil prices should be "readjusted" on Oct. 1, after the expiry of the current nine-month freeze on the marker price. The Conference took a decision in principle to adopt the International Monetary Fund's special drawing right (SDR) as a unit of account for the pricing of oil, but was unable to reach agreement at this point regarding the reference date which should be used to calculate the depreciation of the US dollar against the SDR (and thus to arrive at a new base valuation for dollar invoicing purposes).

(The SDR—first introduced as an international reserve asset in 1969—had been revalued daily since July 1974 on the basis of a basket of 16 currencies. At the time of OPEC's Gabon meeting the dollar value of the SDR was about $1.25, compared with monthly average rates of $1.2137 in December 1974 and $1.1924 in October 1974. An increase in the relative strength of the dollar after the Gabon meeting brought the dollar value of the SDR back to $1.19 by the end of July 1975, causing OPEC to drop its plans for the implementation of the meeting's decision in principle.)

The Conference declared OPEC's intention "to co-ordinate gas-pricing policies of member countries in such a manner as to be in line with OPEC oil-pricing policy, taking into account the premium attributable to natural gas due to its specific advantages". It also agreed "to create organs and institutions within the framework of OPEC for the promotion of co-operation among the national oil companies of OPEC member countries, particularly in the field of marketing". (The pricing of gas exports—of immediate interest to only a minority of member countries—was subsequently studied by an expert committee but did not become a mainstream Conference issue. Moves towards institutionalized co-operation arrangements between OPEC members' national oil companies, especially in the sensitive area of marketing, met with no more success than in 1974. It was not until April 1978 that the OPEC Secretariat organized a formal meeting of national oil companies' chief executives to discuss the scope for non-institutionalized functional co-operation.)

The 44th Conference meeting considered a report by expert economic advisers which drew attention to the need for an agreed policy on differential pricing in order to avert the "real danger" that continued cuts in individual member countries' premiums could eventually distort the existing price structure to the extent that the basic marker price would come under pressure. It was estimated that "marginal" cuts in premiums had so far caused the weighted average price of all OPEC crudes to fall by 2 per cent during the first half of 1975. Renewed suggestions that an "equitable" prorationing scheme should be adopted as an interim measure to safeguard the existing price structure were again resisted by the majority of member countries; nor was general support given to an Algerian proposal that the differential between Gulf and Mediterranean prices should be narrowed by means of a general increase in Gulf prices in order to prevent a further fall in Mediterranean prices towards the existing Gulf levels. The issue of the adjustment of differentials was instead left to the discretion of the individual member countries until such time as the Conference was able to reach agreement on a comprehensive long-term solution to the problem.

D6.6—Algerian Campaign for the Stabilization of Premiums

Algeria reduced the official selling price of its 44° crude from $12 to $11.75 per barrel on April 1, 1975, in order to remain competitive with other Mediterranean and African exporters. It refused to make a further reduction on July 1 despite third-quarter price cuts by Libya and Nigeria which brought their respective selling prices down to $11.20 for 40° crude and $11.35 for 37° crude (while Iraq was reportedly selling 36° crude fob east Mediterranean terminals for $10.75 per barrel). According to the Algerian Government, some customers of the Algerian state oil company, Sonatrach, had been pressing for a reduction in Algeria's third-quarter price to as little as $11.15 per barrel. Algeria's estimated output in June was 32.9 per cent below the level of June 1974, while Nigeria's output for the same month showed a year-on-year fall of 31.5 per cent, that of Libya a fall of 11 per cent and that of Iraq (including oil produced for export from the Gulf) a rise of 29.1 per cent.

Libya was currently concerned to rebuild its output after experiencing the largest percentage decline of any OPEC member in 1974, owing to its enforcement of an embargo on exports to the United States throughout that year (◊D5.2). Nigeria, having increased its output in 1974 (because of its non-involvement in Arab oil sanctions), was anxious to maintain a high level of exports in order to fulfil the revenue targets of its current development plan. Iraq, while denying allegations that the substantial rise in its overall output was due to "covert" price-cutting on Mediterranean exports, claimed the right to an increased share of OPEC output on the grounds that its production had been held down by its foreign concession holders for many years prior to nationalization. Algeria, for its part, was the only one of the four countries whose current balance of payments had gone into serious deficit during 1975 (spending on imports having been maintained in line with the requirements of an ambitious industrialization programme).

The official Algerian news agency issued a statement on July 4 confirming the country's refusal "to add to the downward price spiral" for Mediterranean and African crudes and expressing the hope that "the other OPEC countries which have made unjustified price reductions will now dissociate themselves from this spiral . . . , which has been brought about by those speculating on the alleged divergences between oil-producing countries with a view to the division or destruction of OPEC". Sonatrach, it was stated, had no intention of reducing its third-quarter price either directly or indirectly (i.e. by extending more than the customary 30 days' credit to contract customers), since its existing selling price was "in line with current prices in the Persian/Arabian Gulf", whereas Nigerian, Libyan and (Mediterranean) Iraqi crudes were "underpriced" relative to Gulf crudes.

Sonatrach subsequently proposed a new "marker-related" pricing system to its contract customers in August, a more detailed version of which was later formally submitted by the Algerian Government for consideration by the OPEC Economic Commission. Under Sonatrach's "replacement value method", an objective structure of OPEC price differentials would have been maintained by measuring the "gross product worth" of each OPEC crude against the gross product worth of the marker crude in the main importing areas. The Algerian formula took into account (i) movements in open-market ex-refinery prices in different trading centres; (ii) the product yields of different OPEC crudes in the markets concerned, based on representative local refinery configurations; (iii) the prevailing cost of shipping different crudes to the markets concerned; and (iv) the relative importance of different markets.in each exporting country's pattern of trade.

Although most attention was focused on the narrowing of differentials between Mediterranean and Gulf crudes because of the close relationship between the two exporting areas, prices were also under pressure in other OPEC countries during the first half of 1975, when balance-of-payments deficits were experienced by both Ecuador and Indonesia. Ecuador suffered a sharp fall in exports during the first half of the year despite offering 120-day credit terms on direct sales, and subsequently cut its official selling price from $10.84 to $10.41 per barrel in July (the amount of this formal reduction being roughly equal to the amount of the earlier de facto reduction). With its sales to Japan adversely affected both by price competition from China and by falling freight rates (which cut the delivered cost of Gulf crudes in Japan), Indonesia was reported in July to be allowing discounts of up to $2 off its official selling price of $12.60 per barrel.

D6.7—Decision on Further OPEC Price Increase – Subsequent Pricing Developments in late 1975

The third quarter of 1975 saw a sharp rise in OPEC oil output, due partly to a gradual upturn in consumption in industrialized countries following the "bottoming out" of the economic recession in the middle of the year (◊D6.2). However, export demand increased at a much faster rate than current consumption because of large-scale stockpiling in anticipation of the unquantified OPEC price increase scheduled for Oct. 1. As a result OPEC output reached a monthly peak for 1975 of 30,500,000 bpd in September before falling to its lowest monthly level of 25,300,000 bpd in October. This so-called "announcement effect" on the level of OPEC production was to be repeated in subsequent years in the months immediately preceding and following an anticipated price increase. The underlying upturn in consumption after the middle of 1975 was biased towards the lighter grades of crude giving high yields of premium products such as gasoline and naphtha, while heavier grades were less in demand as a switch away from the use of heavy fuel oil became more apparent in markets where alternative energy sources were available at competitive prices. The downward pressure on prices was thus eased in the African countries producing lighter crudes, where output moved up steadily from the depressed mid-year level, while a differential pricing problem began to affect producers of heavier crudes, such as Kuwait, whose output now appeared overpriced in relation to the marker.

There was, however, little scope for further discussion of the problem of differentials when the OPEC Conference held its 45th (extraordinary) meeting from Sept. 24 to 27, as the entire meeting was given over to bitter argument about the extent to which the marker price should be increased on Oct. 1. The eventual decision of the meeting was for a 10 per cent increase in the marker price (to $11.51 per barrel) and for a further price review in the middle of 1976. This represented a compromise between the positions of Saudi Arabia, which had argued initially for a continued freeze, and Iran, which had argued initially for an increase of between 15 and 20 per cent.

The Saudi case for moderation was argued on the grounds that any action by OPEC which had the effect of prolonging the recession in the industrialized countries would be counter-productive insofar as it led to a renewed downturn in export demand at a time when a recovery had only recently begun from the "oil shock" of early 1974. OPEC should, it was argued, allow the recovery to continue until the end of the year before considering a limited oil price increase. Saudi Arabia was also anxious to avoid any action which might jeopardize current progress towards a Middle East peace settlement, particularly as congressional approval was then pending on the question of US involvement in the implementation of a second Egyptian-Israeli disengagement agreement signed in Geneva on Sept. 4.

Presenting a different case for moderation, Algeria pointed out the adverse implications of a substantial new oil price rise for the oil-importing developing countries and warned against any action which might undermine OPEC's stated commitment to third-world solidarity shortly before the holding of a new round of preparatory talks on the "North-South dialogue" (◊**D6.11**).

Iran, for its part, maintained that the price increase which it was suggesting fell far short of the rate of increase in OPEC countries' import prices, adding that the impact of higher oil prices on third-world oil importers should be offset by OPEC development aid to such countries. (Iran had previously urged the establishment of a new development fund supported jointly by the industrialized countries and the OPEC countries. The Shah's unsuccessful attempts to win Western support for this proposal had been the main factor in the suspension in mid-1974 of earlier preparations to establish an OPEC aid fund ◊**D5.5**.) The principal supporters of a substantial OPEC price increase were Iraq (which advocated an increase of up to 25 per cent), Libya and Nigeria, while Kuwait, Qatar, the United Arab Emirates and Venezuela associated themselves in varying degrees with Algeria's attempts to secure a compromise between the Saudi and Iranian positions.

During a heated five-hour Conference session on Sept. 25 Saudi Arabia failed to win majority support for a proposal that prices should be increased by 5 per cent on Oct. 1 and by a further 5 per cent on Jan. 1, the latter increase to be valid for the whole of 1976. In this situation Shaikh Yamani secured his Government's authorization to warn the OPEC majority that their adoption of Iran's "minimum" demand for an immediate 15 per cent price rise would lead to a freeze on the price of Saudi oil at its current level, coupled with the lifting of all restrictions on the level of production. In subsequent sessions Saudi Arabia rejected an Iranian proposal for a two-stage 15 per cent increase (10 per cent on Oct. 1 and 5 per cent at the beginning of 1976, with no guaranteed freeze thereafter) and a UAE proposal for an immediate 12 per cent increase, to be followed by a 15-month freeze. The Conference's final decision in favour of a 10 per cent increase, frozen for nine months, was based on a Kuwaiti compromise proposal which was reportedly accepted by Iran only after personal representations had been made to the Shah by the President of Venezuela.

Iran subsequently condemned Algeria's important mediatory role during the meeting, accusing the Algerian Government of "acting in unholy alliance with

Saudi Arabia against the interests of its own economic development". Shaikh Yamani said after the meeting that Saudi Arabia felt that the 10 per cent price increase should be frozen until the end of 1976, and was "prepared for another fight" when the Conference reviewed the freeze in the middle of the year.

In the absence of any agreement on an "objective" structure of differentials, OPEC member countries interpreted the local applicability of the agreed 10 per cent increase in the selling price of the marker crude according to their own market circumstances. The initial increase in the weighted average price of all OPEC crudes was estimated as 9 per cent in October, subsequently falling to between 7 and 8 per cent by December as certain member countries adjusted their premiums with retroactive effect from Oct. 1. Within the Gulf region, most OPEC members tended to follow the basic formula adopted in February by Abu Dhabi in respect of lighter and low-sulphur crudes, involving a gravity differential of 0.3 cents per barrel per 0.1° above 34° API and a quality premium not exceeding 3 cents per barrel for each 0.1 per cent step by which the sulphur content was lower than 1.7 per cent. There was also a move to introduce a sulphur penalty of similar magnitude for crudes with more than 1.7 per cent sulphur content as a means of cutting the prices of heavier crudes relative to the marker.

Kuwait was particularly concerned about the realignment of differentials for heavier crudes and attempted to arrange a Gulf OPEC producers' meeting on Oct. 21 to secure agreement on a new regional price structure. However, it was obliged to call off the meeting after Saudi Arabia had refused to discuss the issue unless the proposed agreement covered Mediterranean as well as Gulf crudes (thereby restricting Iraq's freedom of action with regard to Mediterranean pricing). Kuwait subsequently proceeded to make a downward adjustment in the price of its 31° crude in early November, while Saudi Arabia made corresponding adjustments in the prices of its heavier crudes and at the same time reduced the premium on its lightest grade. Kuwait's initiative in taking a "unilateral decision" on Gulf differentials was publicly criticized by Iraq.

The need for an OPEC-wide agreement on differentials was believed to have been discussed during a consultative meeting of OPEC Oil Ministers held in Vienna on Nov. 18, this issue being adopted as the main agenda item when the 46th meeting of the OPEC Conference opened on Dec. 20. However, no decisions were taken by the latter meeting, which had to be abandoned on Dec. 21 when OPEC's Vienna headquarters was seized by terrorists (◊**D6.9**). Table 38 shows the official selling prices of selected OPEC crudes with effect from Oct. 1 (including backdated adjustments to differentials).

The harshest criticism of the latest OPEC price increase came from within the US Government, which had claimed in the weeks preceding the 45th Conference meeting that a "significant" oil price increase would damage the world economy and would "seriously jeopardize US relations with OPEC countries". US diplomatic activity prior to the meeting had reportedly included a personal approach by President Ford to President Pérez of Venezuela urging a moderate line on the pricing question. Whereas President Ford and Dr Henry Kissinger each acknowledged that the final decision of the meeting reflected the "moderating influence of some oil-producing countries", unqualified condemnation was expressed by the US Federal Energy Administrator, who described the 10 per cent increase as "outrageous". Also critical was the Treasury Secretary, who said that it represented "a purely political decision based on OPEC members' fiscal profligacy".

Among the third-world oil-importing countries (which had hitherto generally refrained from public criticism of OPEC), adverse comments on the price increase were made by ministers in India and Tanzania. The Tanzanian Minister of

Table 38 — Prices of selected OPEC crudes, Oct. 1, 1975

	Dollars per barrel	Percentage increase
Algeria (44°)	12.75	8.5
Ecuador (30.4°)	11.45	10.0
Gabon (31.8°)	11.75	n.a.
Indonesia (34°)	12.80	1.6
Iran (31°)	11.49	10.0
(34°)	11.62	8.9
Iraq (Gulf) (34°)	11.53	10.0
Kuwait (31°)	11.30	9.0
Libya (40°)	12.32	10.0
Nigeria (37°)	12.70	11.9
Qatar (40°)	11.85	6.1
Saudi Arabia (27°)	11.14	8.5
(31°)	11.331	9.2
(34°)	11.51	10.0
(39°)	11.874	6.8
UAE: Abu Dhabi (39°)	11.918	9.7
Dubai (32°)	11.51	n.a.
Venezuela (34°)	12.80*	n.a.

*Initial selling price effective Jan. 1, 1976.

Commerce and Industry said that the OPEC countries were "appearing to turn their backs on the oil-importing developing countries, particularly the least developed, for whom oil products are not luxuries but necessities".

D6.8—Agreement to establish OPEC Fund for Developing Countries

"Pursuant to the directives included in the solemn declaration" issued by OPEC heads of state in March 1975 (◊**B1.9.iii**), OPEC Finance Ministers met in Vienna on Nov. 17 and 18 to consider a formal Iranian proposal for the establishment of a $1,000 million OPEC fund to make interest-free long-term loans to developing countries in connexion with the financing both of balance-of-payments deficits and of economic development projects. The ministers agreed to recommend the establishment of such a fund to their governments and to draw up specific proposals for its operation. It was also agreed to set up a committee to co-ordinate the activities of individual member countries' national aid funds. The meeting noted with "satisfaction" a new report by the UN Conference on Trade and Development showing that OPEC countries' existing financial commitments to other developing countries had approached $15,000 million in 1974 (with a roughly equal division between bilateral and multilateral commitments) and were expected to exceed $21,000 million in 1975. (An earlier report by the OECD had shown that about half of the OPEC countries' 1974 commitments were made on concessional terms.)

The UNCTAD report had, however, noted the OPEC countries' relatively low ratio of disbursements to commitments (attributable partly to the donors' lack of experience in creating large-scale assistance programmes) and the concentration of bilateral aid among a relatively small number of recipient countries. The report showed (i) that some 66 per cent of identifiable OPEC aid disbursements during the period January 1973 to June 1975 had been to Arab countries, as against 19 per cent to non-Arab Asia, 8 per cent to black Africa and 7 per cent to Latin America; (ii) that such aid had represented about 6 per cent of the donors' combined export earnings from oil, and had covered nearly 60 per cent of the increased cost of the recipients' oil imports; and (iii) that the OPEC countries' contribution to the overall flow of official development assistance to the Third World had risen from 10 per cent in 1973 to nearly 23 per cent in 1974.

Table 39 gives the OECD's estimates of OPEC countries' net disbursements of concessional development assistance from 1973 to 1975. The OPEC countries' aggregate net disbursements of non-concessional assistance were estimated as $446,000,000 in 1973, $4,000 million in 1974 and $6,000 million in 1975.

Table 39 — OPEC countries' concessional aid disbursements, 1973 to 1975

	1973	1974	1975
	(million US dollars)		
Algeria	25.4	46.9	40.7
Iran	1.9	408.3	593.1
Iraq	11.1	422.9	218.4
Kuwait	345.2	622.5	976.3
Libya	214.6	147.0	261.1
Nigeria	4.7	15.3	13.9
Qatar	93.7	185.2	338.9
Saudi Arabia	304.9	1,029.1	1,997.4
UAE	288.6	510.6	1,046.1
Venezuela	17.7	58.8	31.0
Total	1,307.8	3,446.6	5,516.9

D6.9—Abduction and Release of OPEC Ministers

The Dec. 21, 1975, attack on OPEC's Vienna headquarters during the 46th Conference meeting (◊D6.7) was carried out by six armed persons whose leader was identified in a subsequent Austrian police report as Ilich Ramírez Sánchez, a well-known international terrorist sometimes known as "Carlos". An Austrian doorman, an Iraqi security guard and a Libyan staff member of the OPEC Secretariat were killed by the attackers, whose hostages included the heads of delegation of all the OPEC countries except the United Arab Emirates (whose minister was not present in the building at the time of the attack). The attackers described themselves as the "Arm of the Arab Revolution", stating that they had acted to thwart "a high-level plot aimed at obtaining recognition for the legality of the Zionist presence on our territory" and "to confront the conspiracy, to strike at its support and to apply revolutionary sanctions to all personalities and parties involved".

The attackers demanded that an aircraft should be made available to fly them out of Austria with their hostages on the following day and that an eight-point statement of their aims should be read out over the Austrian broadcasting media during the intervening period. The statement condemned all negotiations with Israel and other actions which were described as part of "the great Zionist reactionary/American plot against the Palestinian resistance". It also called for the full nationalization of all Arab petroleum resources and "the adoption of national petroleum and financial policies that will enable the Arab people to use its resources for its development, its progress, the safeguard of its national interests and the strengthening of its sovereignty alongside the friendly peoples of the Third World so that they can emerge from their economic stagnation, provided that priority be given to financing the confrontation countries and the Palestinian resistance".

The Austrian Government acceded to the attackers' demands on condition that all Austrian hostages were released and that all foreign hostages were asked to sign declarations that they were willing to leave Austria. A total of 33 foreign hostages, including the 12 OPEC heads of delegation, were then flown out of Austria on Dec. 22 in an aircraft which landed at Algiers on the same day. All the non-Arab hostages except those from Iran (described by the attackers as an "active imperialist tool") were set free at this point. Later on Dec. 22 the aircraft flew to Libya, where several more hostages, including the Algerian and Libyan ministers, were released. Nine remaining hostages (including the Iranian and Saudi Arabian ministers) were flown back to Algiers on Dec. 23 and were released when the attackers gave themselves up to the Algerian authorities.

The attackers were subsequently allowed to leave Algeria for Libya. Algeria's agreement to grant them safe passage was given, with the approval of other OPEC countries, during pre-surrender negotiations punctuated by threats to kill first the Saudi Arabian and then the Iranian minister unless specified conditions were met. The attack on OPEC's headquarters was denounced by the Palestine Liberation Organization, the Popular Front for the Liberation of Palestine and several other Palestinian organizations. The Egyptian Government strongly criticized Algeria for releasing the attackers, while the semi-official Egyptian newspaper *Al Ahram* accused the Libyan Government of financing the organizers of the attack.

D6.10—Dakar Conference on Third-World Strategy on Raw Materials and Economic Development

A conference of 110 developing countries in Africa, Asia and Latin America, organized by the non-aligned movement, was held in Dakar (Senegal) from Feb. 3 to 8, 1975, to discuss problems of raw materials and economic development and approaches to the achievement of a new international economic order.

The Algerian Minister of Commerce called upon all developing countries to agree on a common strategy in their dealings with the industrialized countries in order to secure "the recovery of what is left of their natural resources". To this end he urged the formation of OPEC-style producers' organizations by all third-world exporters of primary commodities.

The conference considered a draft programme for "integrated global action on raw materials" which had been drawn up by non-aligned countries for submission to the UN Conference on Trade and Development. The programme envisaged (i) the creation of a comprehensive system of internationally-financed buffer stocks of different raw materials in order to prevent damaging fluctuations in export prices; (ii) the indexation of the prices of exported raw materials to those of imported manufactured products; (iii) an increase in the number of associations of raw-material producers and the creation of a body to co-ordinate the activities of such associations; and (iv) stronger local control over foreign, and especially multinational, companies operating in the Third World.

On Feb. 7 the conference adopted a resolution expressing solidarity between the oil-importing developing countries and the OPEC member countries, which had been tabled by the Latin American states and supported by Algeria. The resolution demanded that the international conference which had been proposed by France in October 1974 (◊D5.13) should "deal with the problems of raw materials in their entirety" and should not be restricted to consideration of energy questions; that the third-world countries should be represented at this conference "according to their own criteria" (whereas France had recently made specific suggestions that Algeria, Iran, Saudi Arabia and Venezuela should represent the oil-exporters, Japan, the EEC and the United States the industrialized countries and Brazil, India and Zaïre the third-world oil-importers); and that "every measure of economic or other aggression against a developing country or group of countries should entail a concerted response by all other countries". The resolution condemned the "elements of economic pressure and coercion" against developing countries contained in the US Trade Act (◊**D6.12**), as well as "the threats of force uttered against the petroleum-exporting countries". The resolution further expressed the conference's solidarity with all developing countries which acted "to recover their rights by means of nationalizing their natural resources, taking control of foreign enterprises operating on their territory, or fixing the prices of the products which they export".

A "Dakar Declaration" issued at the end of the meeting stated that, while a current need existed for development aid from industrialized countries, the third-world countries should take joint action to reduce their dependence upon "imperialism". It was the view of the conference that third-world countries would "attain economic emancipation only when they succeed in controlling their resources and natural wealth and thereafter achieve economic development".

D6.11—Developments leading to First Plenary Session of Conference on International Economic Co-operation

In pursuance of his proposal of Oct. 24, 1974, for the holding of a "tripartite" conference on "energy and related problems" (◊**D5.13**), President Giscard d'Estaing of France on March 1, 1975, formally invited representatives of the EEC countries (as a bloc) and of nine other countries (individually) to meet in Paris on April 7 to discuss the terms of reference of the proposed conference. The EEC, the United States and Japan were to represent the industrialized countries; Algeria, Iran, Saudi Arabia and Venezuela the oil-exporting countries; and Brazil, India and Zaïre the oil-importing developing countries.

The Paris meeting lasted from April 7 to 15. France provided a "technical president", while officials of the United Nations, the OECD and the IEA attended with observer status. It became clear during the talks that the four OPEC and three non-OPEC developing countries were united in the view that the proposed conference should serve as a framework for a comprehensive "North-South dialogue", as envisaged by the February 1975 Dakar meeting of third-world exporters of primary commodities (◊**D6.10**) and by the March 1975 meeting of OPEC heads of state in Algiers (◊**B1.9.iii**). The industrialized countries, for their part, maintained that "the work programme to be developed here should be concentrated on the specifics of energy and directly related matters, and should not become diluted with parallel discussions of other less germane issues, however important they may be".

The failure of the Paris talks to produce agreement on an acceptable conference agenda was discussed by an IEA ministerial meeting on May 27, when the United States accepted that the industrialized countries should adopt a more flexible approach to the question of "North-South dialogue". The US view was that there was scope for the creation of "parallel" commissions on energy, raw materials and general problems of development, provided that the commission on energy played a dominant role in the dialogue. Representatives of the seven developing countries which had attended the Paris talks met in Geneva from Aug. 9 to 12 at Venezuela's request "to examine the specific conditions for facilitating a dialogue in the context of a sufficiently representative conference dealing with international co-operation in the fields of energy, raw materials, development and financial resources".

On Aug. 21 the French Government made it known that it had drafted a new compromise agenda "designed to ensure a minimum procedural agreement" between the industrialized and developing countries, copies of which had been sent to countries which had participated in the initial round of exploratory talks in April. On the basis of reactions to this initiative, France issued invitations in September for further "preparatory talks" between the same participants, which took place in Paris from Oct. 13 to 16, 1975. These talks resulted in an agreement to convene a full-scale Conference on International Economic Co-operation (CIEC) in Paris on Dec. 16, at which ministers from 19 developing countries and eight industrialized countries (including the president of the EEC Council of Ministers as the representative of all EEC members) were to establish four expert-level commissions whose task would be to draw up specific proposals for submission to a second plenary session of the CIEC at the end of 1976. The subject areas of the commissions were to be (i) energy, (ii) raw materials, (iii) development, and (iv) financial questions.

Disagreement subsequently arose within the EEC over Britain's insistence that the Community's delegation to the CIEC should be mandated to endorse the concept of a "minimum safeguard price" for oil (as advocated by the United States within the framework of the IEA ◊D6.13), failing which the British Government would insist on separate representation at the Conference. A compromise was subsequently reached at a European Council meeting on Dec. 1 and 2, when it was agreed that Britain should be formally represented by the EEC delegation but should have the right to speak separately, both at plenary and commission level, when special UK interests were at stake. The EEC delegation's mandate, as adopted by Community Foreign Ministers on Dec. 9, did not refer to the minimum safeguard price as such, but was nevertheless phrased so as not to exclude the concept.

The "group of 19" developing countries, which included seven members of OPEC, was composed as follows: Algeria, Argentina, Brazil, Cameroon, Egypt, India, Indonesia, Iran, Iraq, Jamaica, Mexico, Nigeria, Pakistan, Peru, Saudi Arabia, Venezuela, Yugoslavia, Zaïre and Zambia. The "group of eight", representing the non-communist industrialized world, consisted of Australia, Canada, the EEC, Japan, Spain, Sweden, Switzerland and the United States. The UN Secretary-General attended the Conference as a guest. Canada and Venezuela acted as co-chairmen of the CIEC.

The CIEC's first plenary meeting, originally scheduled to last from Dec. 16 to 18, was extended to Dec. 19 because of difficulties in establishing the precise terms of reference of the four expert commissions. A "moderate" section of opinion within the "group of 19", led by Saudi Arabia, was prepared to accept the proposal of the "group of eight" that special importance should be attached to the work of the energy commission, whereas more radically-minded governments, including those of Algeria, Nigeria and Peru, advocated equal status for all four commissions in order to promote the campaign for a new international economic order. It was eventually agreed that the co-chairmen of the CIEC should meet the co-chairmen of the four commissions in January 1976 "to establish the terms of reference of the commissions on the basis of the second preparatory meeting of October 1975".

Dr Henry Kissinger, addressing the Conference on behalf of the "group of eight", said on Dec. 16 that higher world oil prices were largely responsible for inflation and unemployment in the Western world and for the deteriorating economic position of oil-importing developing countries; he added that the current international recession was "clouding the prospects of social peace and democratic institutions". Calling for "constructive dialogue" rather than confrontation, he advocated a reduction in OPEC oil prices in order to ease the problems of oil-importing developing countries. Delegates of OPEC countries strongly rejected Dr Kissinger's interpretation of the world economic situation, pointing out that the onset of instability in the established international monetary system (◊D2.3) and of "internally-created" inflation in the industrialized countries had preceded the major increase in OPEC oil prices. They added that the OPEC countries had special development needs of their own connected with their heavy dependence on a depleting resource, and that the industrialized countries should therefore bear the main responsibility for increasing the transfer of financial resources to the oil-importing developing countries.

The composition of the four expert commissions, each of which was made up of 10 members of the "group of 19" and five members of the "group of eight", was as follows:

Energy. Saudi Arabia and the United States (co-chairmen), plus Algeria, Brazil, Canada, EEC, Egypt, India, Iran, Iraq, Jamaica, Japan, Switzerland, Venezuela and Zaïre.

Raw materials. Japan and Peru (co-chairmen), plus Argentina, Australia, Cameroon, EEC, Indonesia, Mexico, Nigeria, Spain, United States, Venezuela, Yugoslavia, Zaïre and Zambia.

Development. Algeria and the EEC (co-chairmen), plus Argentina, Cameroon, Canada, India, Jamaica, Japan, Nigeria, Pakistan, Peru, Sweden, United States, Yugoslavia and Zaïre.

Financial questions. EEC and Iran (co-chairmen), plus Brazil, Egypt, India, Indonesia, Iraq, Japan, Mexico, Pakistan, Saudi Arabia, Sweden, Switzerland, United States and Zambia.

Any participating country could send an observer to the meetings of a commission of which it was not a member. All decisions and recommendations of the commissions were to be based on consensus. The following organizations were invited to send non-voting representatives to meetings of the commissions: UN, OPEC, IEA, UN Conference on Trade and Development, OECD, UN Food and Agriculture Organization, General Agreement on Tariffs and Trade, UN Industrial Development Organization, UN Development Programme, IMF, World Bank and Latin American Economic System.

D6.12—Exclusion of OPEC Countries from US Tariff Preferences – US Energy Policy Developments

On Jan. 3, 1975, President Ford signed the Trade Act 1974, which included a section (inserted by the Senate) whereby all OPEC countries were excluded from the list of beneficiary developing countries whose trade with the United States was eligible for preferential tariff treatment. Such treatment was barred to any country which was "a member of OPEC or a party to any other arrangement of foreign countries and such country participates in any action pursuant to such arrangement the effect of which is to withhold supplies of vital commodity resources or to raise the price of such commodities to an unreasonable level and to cause serious disruption of the world economy". [Despite strong protests from Ecuador and Venezuela, these countries were not exempted from this provision until March 1980. Indonesia was exempted at the same time, but the other non-Arab members of OPEC (i.e. non-participants in the 1973–74 embargo against the United States), namely Gabon, Iran and Nigeria, continued to be excluded from tariff preference along with the Arab OPEC members.]

In mid-January 1975 President Ford announced a series of energy policy proposals, with the short-term aim of reducing US oil imports by 1,000,000 bpd by the end of 1975 (and by 2,000,000 bpd by the end of 1976) and the long-term aims of ending "vulnerability to disruption by foreign suppliers" by 1985 and of developing a net export capability in energy by the end of the century. The main proposals were as follows:

(1) Import fees on crude oil and refined products were to be increased by $1 per barrel on Feb. 1, by $2 per barrel on March 1 and by $3 per barrel on April 1. These increases would constitute "interim administrative actions" pending congressional approval for legislation to impose excise duties and import fees totalling $2 per barrel on imported oil.

(2) Federal price controls which had been imposed on domestic oil production since 1971

were to be phased out after April 1, while legislation was to be requested to impose a "windfall profits tax" on production from all but the smallest wells which had come on stream before 1973 in order "to ensure that oil producers do not profit unduly" from the proposed general increase in domestic prices to world market levels.

(3) Legislation was to be requested to phase out price controls on inter-state trade in natural gas produced from newly discovered fields and to impose a natural gas excise tax.

(4) Legislation was to be requested to authorize commercial production from the Elk Hills oilfield in California, which was owned by the Federal Government as a naval petroleum reserve.

(5) A relaxation of environmental protection legislation was to be sought (i) in order to increase the number of power plants which could be converted from oil to coal (the President having in the previous month vetoed a bill seeking to impose environmental protection restrictions on open-cast coal mining) and (ii) to modify and defer the phased introduction of stricter exhaust emission standards for motor vehicles.

(6) New oil leases were to be granted in areas of the outer continental shelf "where the environmental risks are acceptable" (the exploitation of outer continental shelf resources being under federal control).

(7) Legislation would be requested to allow accelerated licensing procedures and additional tax incentives to the nuclear power industry.

(8) "To provide the critical stability for our domestic energy production in the face of world price instability", legislation would be requested "to authorize and require tariffs, import quotas or price floors to protect our energy prices at levels which will achieve energy independence".

(9) Legislation would be requested to impose mandatory thermal efficiency standards on the building industry and to provide tax incentives to encourage improved insulation of existing buildings.

(10) A "strategic storage programme", covering 1,000 million barrels of oil for normal consumption and 300,000,000 barrels of oil for defence purposes, was planned in order to make the United States "invulnerable to foreign disruption".

(11) Funding would be sought for a research and development programme aimed at achieving the production of 1,000,000 bpd of synthetic fuels and shale oil by 1985.

(12) By 1985 it was intended that the United States should have "200 major nuclear power plants; 250 major new coal mines; 150 major coal-fired power plants; 30 major new oil refineries and 20 major new synthetic fuel plants". Over the coming decade many thousands of new oil wells should have been drilled, some 18,000,000 buildings insulated and millions of motor vehicles constructed to improved standards of fuel efficiency.

Strong congressional opposition blocked the implementation of several of the key fiscal measures proposed by the President, with the result that no action was taken on the general decontrol of domestic producer prices for crude oil and "new" natural gas, while the oil import fee was held at $1 per barrel and subsequently discontinued. The average level of US oil imports in 1975 was 100,000 bpd lower than in 1974, imports from suppliers other than Canada having increased by 125,000 bpd to partially offset a 225,000 bpd reduction in imports from Canada (which had become subject to increasingly tight Canadian export restrictions). By the end of 1975 total US oil imports were running at a higher level than in late 1974. A compromise National Energy Bill enacted in December 1975 contained few of the provisions required to further the Federal Government's previously stated policy objectives, and was acknowledged by President Ford to be no more than "a start in the right direction".

D6.13—IEA Developments in 1975

The Governing Board of the International Energy Agency, meeting in Paris from Feb. 5 to 7, 1975, discussed new US proposals for the introduction of a common IEA floor price for imported oil as a means of encouraging large-scale investment in alternative energy sources. The rationale for taking such a step, and the possible impact on relations between oil-exporting and oil-importing countries, had been outlined as follows by Dr Henry Kissinger in a speech in Washington on Feb. 3:

"If the industrial countries succeed in developing alternative sources on a large scale, the demand for OPEC oil will fall, and international prices may be sharply reduced. Inexpensive imported oil could then jeopardize the investment made in the alternative sources; the lower oil prices would also restimulate demand, starting again the cycle of rising imports, increased dependence and vulnerability.

"Thus paradoxically, in order to protect the major investments in the industrialized countries that are needed to bring the international oil prices down, we must ensure that the price for oil on the domestic market does not fall below a certain level. . . .

"Intensive technical study would be needed to determine the appropriate level at which prices should be protected. We expect that they will be considerably below the current world oil prices. They must, however, be high enough to encourage the long-range development of alternative energy sources.

"These protected prices would in turn be a point of reference for an eventual consumer-producer agreement. To the extent that OPEC's current high prices are caused by fear of precipitate later declines, the consuming countries, in return for an assured supply, should be prepared to offer producers an assured price for some definite period so long as this price is substantially lower than the current price.

"In short, the massive development of alternative sources by the industrial countries will confront OPEC with a choice: they can accept a significant price reduction now in return for stability over a longer period; or they can run the risk of a dramatic break in prices when the programme of alternative sources begins to pay off. The longer OPEC waits, the stronger our bargaining position becomes."

Dr Kissinger called in the same speech for the creation of a synthetic fuels consortium and an energy research and development consortium within the IEA in order to promote the pooling of member countries' resources of capital, manpower and technology, particularly in long-term high-cost projects.

Several member countries expressed reservations about the concept of a floor price for imported oil during the February IEA meeting on the grounds that it appeared to embody a desire for confrontation with OPEC member states. The latter view was taken in particular by several EEC countries, whose representatives pointed out that Western Europe was far more heavily dependent than the United States on oil supplies from OPEC countries.

Discussion of this topic was resumed at a further IEA meeting in Paris on March 6 and 7, at which the US Assistant Secretary of State for Economic Affairs, Thomas Enders, indicated the US Government's willingness, in the absence of general agreement on its floor price proposal, to associate itself with a more general statement of intent, provided that a firm commitment was given to facilitate the effective development of alternative sources of energy. A compromise formula was subsequently approved at a meeting of the IEA Governing Board on March 19 and 20 (although Sweden abstained when the decision was taken).

Under this formula, member countries undertook to protect new investment in the energy sector by reference to what subsequently became known as a "minimum safeguard price" for imported oil, using "measures of their own choice". An agreement that details of the level and operation of the minimum safeguard price should be worked out by July 1 was not fulfilled because of continuing differences of opinion over this issue. It was not until January 1976 that the minimum safeguard price was finally fixed at $7 per barrel within the framework of long-term co-operation programme (◊**D7.7**). The other main IEA decisions in 1975 were as follows:

Reduction of imports. On Feb. 7 the IEA Governing Board agreed that member countries should reduce aggregate oil imports by 2,000,000 bpd (just under 10 per cent) by the end of 1975—half by the United States and half by the other 17 members.

Research into new energy sources. On March 20 the Governing Board agreed (i) to establish an "overall framework" of co-operation for investment in alternative energy sources, particularly synthetic fuels, on a project-by-project basis; and (ii) to establish a co-operative research and development programme.

Contingency oil stocks. At an IEA meeting in Paris on July 28 it was agreed in principle that the emergency oil stocks maintained by participating countries should be increased from 60 days' to 70 days' net imports as from Jan. 1, 1976.

The February 1975 meeting of the IEA Governing Board admitted New Zealand as a full member of the Agency. At the same time an agreement was signed providing for Norway's participation in the IEA's work as a non-voting associate member.

D7—1976

D7.1—Annual Statistical Survey

D7.1.i—Oil production and reserves

World

Total production .... 60,085,000 bpd (2,955.1 million tonnes)
   Change over 1975 .... +8.1 per cent

End-year proved reserves .... 649,600 million barrels
   Change over end-1975 .... −2.6 per cent

Reserves:production ratio .... 29.6 : 1

Regional shares:

	In 1976 world production*			In end-1976 world reserves†		
	Regional total (million tonnes)	Change over 1975 (per cent)	Share of world total (per cent)	Reserves (thousand million barrels)	Change over 1975 (per cent)	Share of world total (per cent)
Middle East...............	1,107.7	+13.6	37.5	365.9	−0.7	56.3
USSR/Eastern Europe/China........	623.4	+6.5	21.1	101.1	−2.2	15.6
North America	539.2	−3.3	18.2	45.1	−4.2	7.0
Africa	285.8	+15.0	9.7	60.6	−6.9	9.3
Latin America/ Caribbean	229.4	+0.8	7.8	32.6	−9.7	5.0
Asia‡/Australasia	124.4	+14.0	4.2	19.4	−9.3	3.0
Western Europe§	45.2	+46.8	1.5	24.9	−2.7	3.8

*Including production from oil shales, tar sands and natural gas liquids (NGL).
†Excluding oil shales and tar sands; including NGL in North America.
‡Excluding China.
§Including Yugoslavia.

OPEC

OPEC oil production .... 31,090,000 bpd (1,540.2 million tonnes)
   Change over 1975 .... +13.1 per cent
   Share of 1976 world total .... 52.1 per cent

OPEC end-year proved reserves .... 441,955 million barrels
   Change over 1975 .... −1.9 per cent
   Share of 1976 world total .... 68 per cent

OPEC reserves:production ratio .... 38.9 : 1

OPEC (continued)

OPEC member countries' production:

	1976 production		Change over 1975 (per cent)	Share of world total (per cent)	Share of OPEC total (per cent)
	(million tonnes)	(thousand bpd)			
Algeria	50.1	1,075	+5.5	1.7	3.2
Ecuador	9.1	185	+15.2	0.3	0.6
Gabon	11.2	225	—	0.4	0.7
Indonesia	74.6	1,505	+15.5	2.5	4.8
Iran	295.0	5,920	+10.2	10.0	19.2
Iraq	118.8	2,415	+7.0	4.0	7.7
Kuwait	98.2	1,965	+4.5	3.3	6.4
Libya	93.3	1,930	+30.9	3.1	6.1
Nigeria	102.9	2,065	+15.9	3.5	6.7
Qatar	23.9	495	+13.8	0.8	1.5
Saudi Arabia	421.6	8,525	+22.6	14.3	27.4
UAE*	94.2	1,945	+15.2	3.2	6.1
Venezuela	122.9	2,375	−1.9	4.2	8.0
Neutral Zone†	24.4	465	−5.4	0.8	1.6

*Of which Abu Dhabi 76,800,000 tonnes (1,595,000 bpd), Dubai 15,600,000 tonnes (315,000 bpd), Sharjah 1,800,000 tonnes (35,000 bpd).
†Production shared between Kuwait and Saudi Arabia.

Non-OPEC

Selected non-OPEC countries' oil production:

	1976 production		Change over 1975 (per cent)	Share of world total (per cent)
	(million tonnes)	(thousand bpd)		
USSR	519.7	10,525	+5.9	17.6
USA*	462.0	9,735	−2.5	15.6
China	83.6	1,675	+12.5	2.8
Canada	77.2	1,605	−7.5	2.6
Mexico	43.6	875	+10.9	1.5
Argentina	20.4	390	+0.5	0.7
Oman	18.4	365	+7.6	0.6
Egypt	16.4	325	+10.8	0.6
Norway	13.8	280	+48.4	0.5
United Kingdom	11.8	240	+742.9	0.4
Total	1,266.9	26,015	+3.4	42.9

*Of which natural gas liquids 57,100,000 tonnes (1,605,000 bpd).

D7.1.ii—Oil consumption

World

Total consumption .... 59,165,000 bpd (2,894.6 million tonnes)
   Change over 1975 .... +6.2 per cent

Regional distribution of total:

	1976 consumption		Change over 1975 (per cent)	Share of world total (per cent)
	(million tonnes)	(thousand bpd)		
North America	908.3	18,770	+7.0	31.4
Western Europe*	710.3	14,465	+6.9	24.5
USSR/Eastern Europe/China	551.5	11,150	+4.7	19.0
Asia†/Australasia	411.3	8,395	+5.4	14.2
Latin America/ Caribbean	181.6	3,755	+3.2	6.3
Middle East	74.7	1,475	+11.8	2.6
Africa	56.9	1,155	+10.5	2.0

*Including Yugoslavia.
†Excluding China.

Selected countries

	1976 consumption		Change over 1975 (per cent)	Share of world total (per cent)
	(million tonnes)	(thousand bpd)		
USA	822.4	16,980	+7.4	28.4
USSR	384.9	7,780	+2.6	13.3
Japan	253.5	5,190	+3.9	8.8
West Germany	138.9	2,855	+7.8	4.8
France	119.5	2,430	+8.2	4.1
Italy	98.8	2,065	+4.6	3.4
United Kingdom	91.4	1,860	−0.7	3.2
Canada	85.9	1,790	+3.4	3.0
China	76.9	1,530	+12.6	2.7
Spain	48.3	970	+13.1	1.7
Total	2,120.5	43,450	+5.8	73.4

D7.1.iii—Oil refining

World

Total refinery capacity .... 74,395,000 bpd
   Change over 1975 .... +4.5 per cent

Total refinery throughputs .... 56,670,000 bpd
   Change over 1975 .... +7.1 per cent

Consumption as proportion of capacity   79.5 per cent

Selected markets
Consumption of refined product types and change over 1975:

	USA		Western Europe		Japan	
	(million tonnes)	(per cent)	(million tonnes)	(per cent)	(million tonnes)	(per cent)
Gasolines	320.4	+5.2	134.4	+6.0	43.6	+10.7
Middle distillates	206.3	+8.6	242.0	+8.6	54.2	+7.5
Fuel oil	146.8	+13.4	244.3	+6.2	125.7	+0.5
Other	148.9	+4.9	89.6	+5.8	30.0	+3.1
Total	822.4	+7.4	710.3	+6.9	253.5	+3.9

D7.1.iv—Tankers and trade

Tankers

Total world fleet .... 320,700,000 deadweight tons
    Change over 1975 .... +10 per cent

Trade

Total world crude exports
    (including re-exports) .... 32,369,000 bpd (1,604.3 million tonnes)
    Change over 1975 .... +13.5 per cent
OPEC crude exports .... 27,462,600 bpd (1,361.1 million tonnes)
    Change over 1975 .... +14.1 per cent
    Share of 1976 world total .... 84.8 per cent
Total world product exports
    (including re-exports) .... 7,715,900 bpd (390,678,500 tonnes)
    Change over 1975 .... +8.5 per cent
OPEC product exports .... 1,870,900 bpd (94,729,100 tonnes)
    Change over 1975 .... +19.9 per cent
    Share of 1976 world total .... 24.2 per cent

Regional distribution of world oil trade*:

	Share of 1976 imports (per cent)		Share of 1976 exports (per cent)	
	Crude	Products	Crude	Products
USA	18.2	38.0	†	4.4
Canada	2.6	0.7	1.3	4.4
Latin America/ Caribbean	8.0	3.6	4.1	42.1
Western Europe	43.8	19.9	0.2	5.3
Middle East	0.6	1.4	68.6	18.3
North Africa	0.2	1.4	10.0	1.3
West Africa	†	0.7	7.7	0.5
East and southern Africa	1.4	0.8	—	0.5
South Asia	1.2	1.9	—	—
South-East Asia	4.4	9.1	4.6	6.4
Australasia	0.8	2.0	—	1.0
Japan	16.3	10.6	—	†
USSR/Eastern Europe/China	1.3	0.4	3.5	15.8
Unspecified	1.2	9.5	—	—
Total	100.0	100.0	100.0	100.0

*Excluding intra-regional trade.   †Negligible.

D7.1.v—World primary energy consumption

Total consumption (excluding
 non-commercial fuels) .... 6,284.2 million tonnes oil equivalent (mtoe)
 Change over 1975 .... +5.6 per cent

Contributions of primary energy sources:

	Consumption (mtoe)	Change over 1975 (per cent)	Share of total (per cent)
Oil	2,894.6	+6.2	46.1
Coal	1,786.7	+4.5	28.4
Natural gas	1,139.8	+5.6	18.1
Water power	358.0	+1.3	5.7
Nuclear power	105.1	+22.1	1.7

D7.1.vi—Natural gas production and reserves

Marketed production (thousand million cubic metres):

	Regional total (tmcm)	Change over 1975 (per cent)	Share of 1976 world total (per cent)
North America	613.2	−0.5	49.1
Latin America/Caribbean	38.4	+3.5	3.1
Western Europe*	170.6	+5.6	13.7
USSR/Eastern Europe/China	346.0	−2.9	27.7
Middle East	35.4	+3.5	2.8
Africa	14.0	+5.3	1.1
Asia†/Australasia	31.1	+15.6	2.5
World total	1,248.7	+0.2	100.0
(*of which OPEC*)	(58.3)	(+3.7)	(4.7)

*Including Yugoslavia.
†Excluding China.

End-year proved reserves (thousand million cubic metres):

	Regional total (tmcm)	Change over 1975 (per cent)	Share of 1976 world total (per cent)
North America	7,767.6	−3.8	12.7
Latin America/Caribbean	2,378.5	−6.6	3.9
Western Europe*	3,885.9	−12.1	6.4
USSR/Eastern Europe/China	23,385.1	+9.6	38.2
Middle East	14,526.2	+2.0	23.8
Africa	5,949.3	+1.4	9.7
Asia†/Australasia	3,255.5	+1.1	5.3
World total	61,148.1	+2.4	100.0
(*of which OPEC*)	(21,926.0)	(+2.2)	(35.9)

*Including Yugoslavia.
†Excluding China.

D7.2—OPEC Pricing Developments, January to June 1976

Average OPEC oil output in the period January-June 1976 was about 4.3 per cent higher than the average for July-December 1975, reflecting a further upturn in economic growth in the OECD countries (which had begun to emerge from recession during the latter part of 1975). The strongest demand continued to be for the lighter crudes (with particularly strong US demand for African crudes). This trend was reflected in a steady rise in the spot prices of African crudes, which in most cases reached levels above the official selling prices during the second quarter of the year. Algeria, using "gross product worth" criteria (◊**D6.6**), increased its official selling price for 44° crude by 10 cents per barrel (to $12.85) on Jan. 1 and by a further 15 cents (to $13) on April 1, thus restoring the price which had applied in the third quarter of 1974.

Open-market realizations for medium-grade Gulf crudes were broadly in line with official contract prices based on the OPEC marker level of $11.51 per barrel established in October 1975, whereas the official prices of the region's heavier crudes were generally discounted in spot trading. Iran, which had not joined Kuwait and Saudi Arabia in making downward adjustments in the official prices of heavier crudes in November 1975, experienced a sharp decline in its exports of 31° crude in January, when this grade accounted for only 28 per cent of total Iranian output as against a normal average of 48 per cent. Iran subsequently cut the selling price of its 31° crude by 9 cents per barrel (to $11.40) on Feb. 14 in order to bring its differential for this grade into line with those applying in Kuwait and Saudi Arabia.

Several attempts were made during the first quarter of the year to convene a special OPEC Conference meeting at which to resume the 46th meeting's unfinished discussion on price differentials. Each such attempt failed, however, because of ill-feeling arising out of current rivalries for market shares, with Iraq in particular coming under criticism from both Algeria and Saudi Arabia for allegedly allowing substantial discounts off its official prices. (The export marketing of Iraq's entire output was now controlled by the state following the nationalization of the remaining foreign concession interests in that country in December 1975 ◊**C6.3.iv**.) By April it had been accepted that consideration of the differentials issue should be deferred until the next ordinary Conference meeting at the end of May, and informal consultations on the agenda for that meeting were held in Geneva on April 22. It was agreed that the principal agenda item should be a review of the level of the marker price after the expiry of the current freeze on June 30, and that differentials should be assessed in the light of the Conference's decision regarding the marker price.

In early May 1976 Saudi Arabia launched an intensive diplomatic campaign to win the backing of other OPEC members, particularly in the Gulf region, for an extension of the current price freeze until the end of 1976. Of particular significance was a visit to Tehran by Shaikh Yamani on May 22 and 23 during which the Iranian Government was reported to have "reluctantly" agreed not to force a full-scale confrontation over the pricing issue at the forthcoming Conference meeting. Shaikh Yamani reiterated the established Saudi position, based on a desire to avoid action which might impede the process of economic recovery in the industrialized countries. Iranian ministers stressed their continuing concern over the erosion of the purchasing power of oil revenues, pointing to recent constraints on the fulfilment of Iran's investment targets for its large-scale economic development plan.

Shaikh Yamani was quoted in the Iranian press on May 24 as saying that the issue of linking oil prices to inflation rates was "of less importance than the question of supply and demand", and that many OPEC members could not afford to take the risk of pricing their oil out of the market at the present time. As regards differentials, Shaikh Yamani reportedly stated that an otherwise viable official pricing structure in the Gulf region was under threat from "dumping" by Iraq.

Largely because of Iran's prior agreement to refrain from forcing a majority decision on a price increase, Saudi Arabia was successful in securing a de facto extension of the existing price freeze at the 47th OPEC Conference meeting, held in Bali (Indonesia) on May 27 and 28. At the start of the meeting a majority of member countries (including Iran) expressed their support for an immediate increase of 15 to 20 per cent in the marker price, based on the OPEC Economic Commission's estimate of member countries' import-price inflation over the previous nine months; on an adjacent tack, Algeria, Kuwait and Venezuela took the line that an increase closer to the average annualized inflation rate within the OECD area (currently about 8.5 per cent) would be more appropriate. Only the United Arab Emirates gave unequivocal support to Saudi Arabia's proposal that prices should remain unchanged until the end of the year. However, with Iran declining to assume the leadership of the "hard-line" faction, it was left to Iraq, backed by Libya and Nigeria, to make an unsuccessful bid to force Saudi Arabia to accept a compromise. The Conference's eventual agreement to leave the marker price unchanged on July 1 was not accompanied by any commitment as to the intended duration of the new freeze.

As regards the differentials issue, the meeting reportedly agreed to instruct the OPEC Economic Commission to draw up proposals for a two-month OPEC-wide trial, prior to the December Conference meeting, of a system based on the Algerian "replacement value method" (◊D6.6). Base prices were to be calculated for 26 main types of crude in four major markets, and a 5 per cent margin of adjustment was to be permitted on either side of the applicable base price for each individual crude. (Readjustments of Mediterranean and Gulf differentials announced after the meeting by certain member countries were apparently based on an informal agreement regarding interim steps to bring prices more closely into line with the current structure of market demand.)

The 47th Conference meeting also expressed OPEC's solidarity with the other members of the "Group of 77" developing countries and "took note of actions being taken by certain consuming countries against the interests of OPEC member countries and decided to take appropriate measures, if necessary, to protect the legitimate interests of the OPEC members". The latter statement was generally taken to be a reference to the International Energy Agency's adoption earlier in the year of a $7 per barrel "minimum safeguard price" for imported oil (◊D7.7), which was seen by OPEC as an implied threat to the maintenance of existing price levels.

Table 40 shows the price adjustments announced by African and Gulf OPEC members after the 47th Conference meeting. The changes in Libyan and Nigerian prices represented "catching-up" increases vis-à-vis Algeria's current market-related price. The cuts in the prices of heavier Gulf crudes continued the process of adjustment begun in November 1975. Iraq's new price for 35° Basrah crude was defined as a "minimum official selling price", the use of this description being regarded as an indication that Iraq had undertaken to put an end to the controversy about covert discounting. Iraq's Mediterranean exports of 36° Kirkuk crude had been suspended in April as a result of disputes over pipeline transit fees, and the initial

Table 40 — Price changes for African and Gulf OPEC crudes, June–July 1976 (dollars per barrel)

	New price	Change	Effective date
Algeria (44°)	13.05	+0.05	June 1
Iran (31°)	11.33	−0.07	June 9
Iraq (35°)	11.43	−0.10	July 1
Kuwait (31°)	11.23	−0.07	June 1
Libya (40°)	12.62	+0.30	July 1
Nigeria (37°)	13.10	+0.40	July 1
Saudi Arabia (27°)	11.04	−0.10	June 1
Saudi Arabia (31°)	11.28	−0.051	June 1

minimum selling price for the same oil fob Gulf terminals was fixed at $11.65 per barrel on July 1 after the opening of the country's new north-south strategic pipeline (◊**C6.3.v**).

D7.3—OPEC Pricing Developments, July to December 1976

D7.3.i—Failure to adopt agreement on differentials – Build-up of pressure for further increase in marker price

During the second half of 1976 OECD economic growth began to slow somewhat, with the result that real gross national product in the OECD area showed an average increase of 5.3 per cent for the year as a whole, compared with an annualized average growth rate in excess of 6 per cent during the period January to June. There was, however, a marked increase in the growth rate of demand for OPEC oil during the latter part of the year, attributable to stockpiling by oil companies following OPEC's 47th Conference meeting, the outcome of which was widely regarded as leaving the way open for discussion of a new price increase at any time. By August production was running at an average 30,700,000 bpd—its highest level since July 1974—and in early December, when a year-end price increase was seen as inevitable, it reached a new peak level of 34,400,000 bpd.

Consultations took place between OPEC member countries during August with a view to convening an extraordinary Conference meeting in the near future to authorize the experimental introduction of the new differential structure which had been discussed in May. However, the OPEC Economic Commission, which met in Vienna from Aug. 23 to 27 to consider the results of detailed feasibility studies submitted by an expert committee, was unable to formulate satisfactory procedures for the implementation of the new system, with the result that the proposed experiment was called off without a Conference meeting being held. The feasibility studies had revealed that many practical difficulties stood in the way of agreement on a workable system, the main problem areas being the gathering of authoritative information on market prices and the selection of criteria for the "objective" interpretation of such information. It was, moreover, clear that any system which relied on the analysis of past market trends would tend to produce differentials which would be out of step with current market developments.

During the last quarter of the year public lobbying in favour of a substantial OPEC price increase gathered momentum among the "hard-line" member states, while a verbal counter-offensive was mounted by the USA and several other industrialized countries wanting a continued freeze. At the same time, however, large-scale stockpiling in these same countries was helping to drive up the open-market prices of OPEC crudes, including the heavier grades, thus adding to the pressure for an OPEC price rise.

(In December, when marker-grade crudes commanded spot premiums of up to 50 cents per barrel, the average open-market premium on all OPEC crudes was estimated to be around 6 per cent relative to official prices. However, only Nigeria and Venezuela made significant adjustments to their differentials during the last quarter. Nigeria raised the prices of its 31°, 37° and 40° crudes by 15 cents per barrel with effect from Oct. 1, when the new price for 37° crude was fixed at $13.25. Venezuela raised its prices on the same date by 40 cents per barrel for 17° crude, 33 cents for 26° crude and 5 cents for 31° and 37° crudes while leaving the prices of other grades unchanged.)

Many different estimates were produced of the extent to which the purchasing power of a barrel of OPEC oil had been eroded by inflation since 1974. The use of an OECD export price index, corrected for fluctuations in the value of the US dollar against the currencies of other OECD member countries, indicated that a 35 per cent increase in the OPEC marker price (to $15.54 per barrel) would be required at the end of 1976 to restore purchasing power to its 1974 level in real terms. It was, however, claimed by OPEC economists that the actual rate of increase in the member countries' import prices (for all goods and services) had been far higher than the rise in average OECD export prices, and would justify a compensatory rise of at least 55 per cent in the marker price.

Statistics produced by Western critics of OPEC's case tended (i) to attribute much of the increase in OPEC import prices to inflationary factors within the OPEC countries (e.g. lack of adequate infrastructural facilities to handle a rapid growth of import trade), and (ii) to demonstrate that relative to a base year of 1972 the oil exporters were still enjoying greatly improved terms of trade. The first of these points received only qualified endorsement from non-partisan analysts, who concluded that there was evidence both of price discrimination against OPEC countries by industrialized exporters and of local factors which tended to increase these countries' costs of trade. The second point was dismissed by OPEC spokesmen as irrelevant at a time when member countries were concerned to finance development plans drawn up on the basis of the purchasing power of a barrel of oil in 1974.

The OPEC Economic Commission's assessment of member countries' average import-cost inflation between October 1975 and the last quarter of 1976 was 26.2 per cent. Iran, which repeatedly stated its intention to press for a minimum oil price increase of 15 per cent at the end of the year, said that its import costs had risen by 40 per cent since the end of 1974. Iraq, which was lobbying for a 25 per cent price increase, claimed that it had experienced an 81 per cent rise in import costs over the same period. Libya said that a 25 per cent price rise would "compensate for inflation", while Algeria (understood to favour a minimum increase of 15 per cent) stated that "whatever increase was decided" by the next OPEC Conference meeting would be insufficient to meet Algeria's development needs.

D7.3.ii—Pressure from importing countries for continued price freeze – The issue of "linkage" with CIEC

The US State Department formally acknowledged on Nov. 11 (just over a month before the scheduled opening of the 48th OPEC Conference meeting on Dec. 15) that it had undertaken a diplomatic campaign—involving "urgent consultations" with other industrialized countries and expressions of "strong opposition" to a price rise in discussions with OPEC countries—to press the view that "any increase would be contrary both to the best interests of the world economy (for which OPEC must accept a major responsibility) and the interests of the oil-producing countries themselves". State Department spokesmen claimed that a 15 per cent rise in OPEC oil prices would add about $15,000 million to the aggregate import bill of the seven major importing countries (the USA, Japan, West Germany, France, the UK, Italy and Canada) and would increase their inflation rate by about 1.5 per cent and reduce their growth rate by about 1 per cent, while severe economic problems would also arise for many developing countries.

It was reported on Nov. 17 that, following consultations within the membership of both the European Economic Community and the International Energy Agency, the major non-communist industrialized countries had agreed to express their concern regarding the possibility of a significant price increase in their bilateral dealings with oil-exporting countries. (However, EEC heads of government subsequently failed to agree on a joint statement on this issue and confined themselves to authorizing publication of a European Commission statement that "the price of oil should not increase, or only be subject to a moderate increase".) Among the European oil-importers, a forthright position on oil prices was taken by West

Germany, where the Federal Chancellor stated on Nov. 14 that although his country, like the United States, "was capable of absorbing" a 15 per cent increase, many other countries in both the developed and developing worlds would suffer "a serious aggravation" of their inflation and balance-of-payments problems.

While Saudi Arabia expressed broad agreement with the contention that a substantial oil price rise would jeopardize world economic recovery, other members of OPEC maintained that the Western diplomatic initiative was aimed at discrediting the Organization in the eyes of oil-importing developing countries, particularly within the Conference on International Economic Co-operation (CIEC), which was then scheduled to hold its second plenary session on Dec. 15. In the context of the CIEC, the participating oil-importing developing countries were reported to have made strong representations to the OPEC members regarding the impact of higher oil prices on the poorer third-world countries. The question of "linkage" between the forthcoming OPEC Conference and the scheduled simultaneous CIEC meeting was widely discussed during November, and until the CIEC meeting was itself postponed to 1977 (◊D7.6) it was planned to put back the opening of the OPEC meeting to Dec. 20 so that OPEC could take account of the industrialized countries' position in the CIEC talks before fixing the new oil price.

A forceful statement in favour of "linkage" with the CIEC was made by President Pérez of Venezuela in an address to the UN General Assembly on Nov. 16. He said that OPEC had "made the historic opening towards a new power of negotiation which, for the first time, is in the hands of the countries of the Third World"; the raising of oil prices did not represent "selfish purposes of OPEC, for the sole benefit of its members", but an "irreversible decision to dignify the terms of trade, to confer true value on the raw materials and other primary commodities of the nations of the Third World". President Pérez added that "the North-South dialogue is a clear expression of this new reality, and we do not want even to think about what would happen if this effort were to fail". In a subsequent interview he said that "any future oil price increase will be directly connected with the decisions at the North-South talks and the price of manufactured goods imported by the developing countries".

The US attitude to "linkage" was set out by Dr Henry Kissinger in a confidential telegram (dated Nov. 22) which was sent through the Dutch Foreign Minister to the EEC delegation at the CIEC and published in *The Sunday Times* of Dec. 12 (which reported that the US move had contributed to the EEC's subsequent failure to agree on a common approach to the scheduled CIEC meeting). Extracts from the text of the telegram are given below:

"The United States believes it would be dangerous for the industrialized countries to strengthen the linkage between CIEC and OPEC. A number of OPEC spokesmen have been publicly attempting to make clear that the final decision on oil prices by OPEC will depend in large measure on concessions extracted from the industrialized countries in CIEC. This would reverse the linkage we would be seeking, and would strengthen OPEC ties to other LDCs [less developed countries]. . . .

"We are convinced that there is no negotiable CIEC package which the industrialized countries could accept and which would also represent sufficient inducement to OPEC to refrain from a substantial oil price increase over several years, given the lack of leverage by consumers over oil prices. . . .

"We have been relatively successful in CIEC in intensifying LDC restraints on OPEC. A strategy linking the two would negate these gains and confirm the effectiveness and utility of the OPEC-LDC alliance.

"The outcome [of OPEC's forthcoming meeting] has not yet been determined and we continue to believe a price increase is not inevitable. Linking the two now could result in OPEC's maintaining that it had been planning a large increase but is willing to reduce it in exchange for costly concessions on resource transfer in CIEC. In other words, actual increases in oil prices would not necessarily be any different from what OPEC would have arrived at without CIEC, but the cost to the industrialized countries would be higher. . . ."

An additional political factor bearing on OPEC's December Conference meeting was the prevailing uncertainty regarding future US foreign policy in the aftermath of President Ford's defeat in the recent presidential election. As well as sharing OPEC's general interest in possible changes in US policy towards international economic co-operation, some Arab members of OPEC were particularly concerned about President-elect Carter's attitude towards a Middle East peace settlement, taking the view that Arab interests in this matter might be adversely affected if the OPEC Conference did not take due account of US opposition to a significant oil price increase.

James E. Akins, a former US ambassador to Saudi Arabia who toured Arab countries on Jimmy Carter's behalf in late November, said in Kuwait on Nov. 23 that both the Middle East situation and the oil price question were "most important issues which have reached a perilous stage". The UAE Oil Minister, who was attending an OAPEC meeting in Kuwait on the same day, was quoted as saying that OPEC "should not hit President-elect Carter with a hard line on oil prices, because if we do we would be doing exactly what the Zionists want us to; we should give him a chance to assume power and handle the problems realistically".

Jimmy Carter himself was quoted on Dec. 3 as having told the foreign relations committee of the US Senate that he saw the current campaign within OPEC for a substantial price rise as the main exception to the "dormant" phase through which most international relationships were currently passing in the period between his election and his inauguration as President. Also contained in the transcript of this meeting (which had taken place the previous week) was a statement by Senator Charles H. Percy that he had received a personal assurance from the Saudi Arabian Foreign Minister, Prince Saud al Faisal, that his country was opposed to any price increase at the present time, and would not support an OPEC increase exceeding 5 per cent.

D7.3.iii—Split decision on pricing at 48th OPEC Conference meeting

The much-heralded 48th meeting of the OPEC Conference took place in Doha (Qatar) from Dec. 15 to 17, 1976. The formal opening speech by the Ruler of Qatar, Shaikh Khalifa bin Hamad al Thani, reflected the attitude of the majority of member countries. Shaikh al Thani said that the sole aim of OPEC's pricing policy was to maintain "a fair and reasonable balance between oil prices and the prices of commodities manufactured by that oil and our countries' imports from the industrial countries" in order to further the Organization's "efforts to establish a new and fair international economic system". He denied that there was any "serious relationship" between recent rises in oil prices and world economic recession, and said that "strictly objective scientific studies have proved that OPEC's import-cost inflation was 110 per cent between 1973 and 1976".

OPEC's recent price freezes had, he went on, been applied "regardless of the wide-ranging assistance given by the OPEC countries to the industrialized nations, and despite the latter countries' negative and provocative attitudes towards the OPEC countries' demand to link oil prices to the rate of world inflation in order to maintain the purchasing power of their main and only financial source", which had been "continually lowered". The attempt by "certain industrial countries, fearing an increase in our oil prices which would make up for only a small part of our losses, . . . [to] return to the era of threats which has gone for ever" would "keep us from tackling economic problems through a constructive discussion and objective dialogue and hinder our efforts to find just solutions to problems affecting the interests of all sides".

During the first day of the meeting, discussion centred on the following minimum price increases advocated by different member countries: Iraq and Libya 25 per cent; Iran, supported by Algeria, Ecuador, Gabon, Nigeria and Qatar, 15 per cent; and Kuwait, supported by Indonesia and Venezuela, 10 per cent (which was also the maximum acceptable to the UAE). Saudi Arabia's case for a continuation of the price freeze for the first half of 1977 was outlined by Shaikh Yamani, who had said on his arrival in Doha that "developments in the past month have shown that the world economic recovery is not as strong as we thought".

Negotiations to reach a compromise effectively broke down after two hours on the second day of the meeting, when Shaikh Yamani flew back to Saudi Arabia for talks with Crown Prince Fahd (First Deputy Prime Minister), returning to Doha 10 hours later to inform delegates that 5 per cent was the maximum price increase acceptable to his Government. This position was endorsed by the UAE Oil Minister, Dr Maneh Said al Oteiba, but was rejected by the heads of the remaining 11 delegations, who finalized their own position (reflecting Iran's proposal for a 15 per cent increase but delaying its full application for six months to take account of the Kuwaiti position) in a series of informal meetings late on the same day. A press statement announcing a "split-level" price increase was issued on Dec. 17 after the proceedings had been formally reconvened for a final morning session, at which Shaikh Yamani and Dr al Oteiba were represented by their deputies.

The statement noted that Saudi Arabia and the UAE had "decided to raise their prices by 5 per cent only", whereas the remaining 11 member countries had "decided to increase the price of $11.51 (former price of the marker crude) to $12.70 per barrel as of Jan. 1, 1977, and to $13.30 as of July 1, 1977; the price of all other crudes shall be increased by the same amount".

The Jan. 1 marker value adopted by the OPEC majority would thus be 10.3 per cent higher than the 1976 OPEC marker price, rising by a further 4.7 per cent on July 1 to produce a cumulative increase of 15.55 per cent. (These amounts were generally represented in subsequent reporting of the decision as 10, 5 and 15 per cent respectively). Saudi Arabia's 5 per cent increase on Jan. 1 would increase the actual selling price of 34° Saudi crude to $12.09 per barrel, some 61 cents (5 per cent) below the "majority" marker value. The "majority" increase scheduled for July 1 would leave an unchanged Saudi price some $1.21 (10 per cent) below the new "majority" marker value.

Although the phrasing of the "majority" decision appeared to provide for uniform price increases on all crudes, most of the new selling prices announced by the 11 countries concerned incorporated market-related adjustments to differentials. The largest increase was made by Ecuador, which in effect increased its existing price by 9.8 per cent and then added the 43 cents by which it had reduced its price in July 1975 (◊D6.6). The smallest increase among the OPEC majority was made by Indonesia, which claimed that it was compensating for a past overvaluation (despite the fact that it had previously made a far smaller increase than other OPEC members in October 1975 ◊ Table 38). The main factor in Indonesia's policy was reported to be an awareness of vulnerability to competition from Saudi and UAE crudes in the Japanese market.

Saudi Arabia and the UAE decided to apply increases of approximately 5 per cent to their premium-grade crudes, which under normal market-related criteria would have merited rather larger percentage increases relative to the increase in the marker. However, Saudi Arabia took full account of the negative differentials on its heavier crudes, and in particular maximized the gap between the price of its own 31° crude and the 31° crudes produced by Kuwait and Iran (each of which was subject to a 10.2 per cent price increase). As regards Neutral Zone crudes, Saudi Arabia's Jan. 1 price for the 28° grade was $11.38 per barrel, as against Kuwait's

Table 41 — Prices of selected OPEC crudes, Jan. 1, 1977

	New price (dollars per barrel)	Increase (dollars)	Percentage increase
Algeria (44°)	14.30	1.25	9.6
Ecuador (30.4°)	13.00	1.55	13.5
Gabon (31.8°)	13.00	1.25	10.6
Indonesia (34°)	13.55	0.75	5.9
Iran (31°)	12.49	1.16	10.2
(34°)	12.81	1.19	10.2
Iraq (35°)	12.58	1.15	10.1
(36°)	12.77	1.12	9.6
Kuwait (31°)	12.37	1.14	10.2
Libya (40°)	13.92	1.30	10.3
Nigeria (37°)	14.31	1.06	8.0
Qatar (40°)	13.19	1.34	11.3
Saudi Arabia (27°)	11.37	0.33	3.0
(31°)	11.69	0.41	3.6
(34°)	12.09	0.58	5.0
(39°)	12.48	0.606	5.1
UAE: Abu Dhabi (39°)	12.50	0.582	4.9
Dubai (32°)	12.09	0.58	5.0
Venezuela (34°)	13.99	1.19	9.3

price of $12.242 for the same oil. For 35° Neutral Zone crude Saudi Arabia charged $12.08 per barrel and Kuwait $12.69. Table 41 shows the Jan. 1 prices announced for selected OPEC crudes after the 48th Conference meeting.

D7.4—Reactions to Breakdown of OPEC Consensus on Pricing

Shaikh Yamani announced at a press conference immediately after OPEC's Doha meeting that the Saudi Government, which had allowed liftings to rise to an average of about 9,000,000 bpd in recent weeks, would in 1977 formally lift the 8,500,000 bpd ceiling imposed since mid-1974 (◊D5.2) on Aramco's production, the level of which would "for the time being" be determined "solely by market forces". This development greatly increased tensions within OPEC, although Shaikh Yamani dismissed "talk of the collapse of OPEC" as "wishful thinking". He said that he expected that as a result of increased Saudi output "the [average] increase in the world price of crude will not be larger than 5 per cent", and reiterated his Government's view that any greater increase would be "harmful to the world economy", and would have "caused suffering in certain industrialized countries, such as Britain, France, Italy and Spain", as well as affecting the developing world. He added: "We live in a small world, and if the world suffers then, no matter how much money we have, we suffer with it, with the international community."

Shaikh Yamani stressed, however, that he expected Western governments, and especially the new US Administration, to "show their appreciation" of Saudi Arabia's moderate stance at the Doha meeting by working for progress during the coming months "on two different fronts: first, the North-South dialogue in Paris, and second the Arab-Israel conflict; there must be peace in that area". Dr al Oteiba fully associated the UAE with these aims, stating with regard to the Middle East situation that the whole world was being asked "to play a positive role in putting pressure on Israel to pull out of the occupied territories and acknowledge the rights of the Palestinian people", and that it was inadvisable to impose a substantial increase in the cost of oil imported by Western countries at a time when the Arab nations "need their co-operation in searching for a peaceful settlement".

Iran's representative at the Doha meeting, Dr Jamshid Amouzegar, denied that the two-tier pricing system threatened the unity of OPEC, or that Saudi Arabia would be able to undermine the majority price increase by raising its production, since "the world could not live without" the 20,000,000 bpd produced by the 11 "majority" countries. Nor, he said, would Iran have proposed a 15 per cent increase "had we not believed the industrialized countries capable of absorbing it". Iran was prepared to assist countries with particularly vulnerable economies on a bilateral basis by, for example, depositing surplus oil funds with them and increasing purchases of their exports. According to Iranian estimates, the majority price increase would not add more than 0.3 to 0.6 per cent to the inflation rate in industrialized countries. While Dr Amouzegar did not directly criticize Saudi Arabia, the Iranian press subsequently made repeated personal attacks on Shaikh Yamani, which were regarded as reflecting an official policy of publicizing the Government's opposition to Saudi Arabia's position on the oil price question without formally impairing relations with the Saudi monarchy.

Iraq's Minister of Petroleum and Mineral Resources, Tayea Abdel-Karim, said on his return to Baghdad from Qatar on Dec. 18 that Saudi Arabia was acting "in the service of imperialism and Zionism" to "render the oil weapon ineffective", and constituted "a defeatist and compromising reactionary cell working inside and outside OPEC against the interests of its people and against the interests of the oil-producing and other developing states". However, Iraq was confident "that the Saudi plans will not succeed and that Saudi Arabia will be forced to follow the overwhelming majority of OPEC states under the pressure of the liberated world and Arab public opinion, and under the pressure of the liberation forces of our people in Saudi Arabia and the Arab homeland".

The head of the Algerian delegation at Doha, Belaid Abdessellam (Ministry of Industry and Energy), criticized the Saudi position on the grounds that OPEC "cannot favour the industrialized countries indefinitely on the pretext that some of them are in uncertain health", although he did not see "how, after having refused to harm the developed countries, Saudi Arabia could agree to harm the Third World" through a production increase which, if implemented, would "constitute an act of direct political aggression against OPEC".

The Libyan Minister of Petroleum, Ezzedine al Mabrouk, said that Saudi Arabia had felt that it could impose its point of view at Doha simply by virtue of its position as OPEC's largest producer, but that the survival of the Organization without Saudi Arabia "was one possibility". He did not believe that Saudi Arabia would implement a major production increase, but said that if this did happen the majority countries could react by making a proportionate cutback in their own output.

Statements by the three countries regarded as the "moderates" within the OPEC majority (Kuwait, Indonesia and Venezuela) tended to minimize the significance of the split within the Organization, described by President Pérez as "a mere incident which will not affect the unity of OPEC as an organization in the service of the Third World".

Among industrialized oil-importing countries, the United States laid greatest stress on the split within OPEC. President Ford drew a distinction between on the one hand Saudi Arabia and the UAE, which had shown "international responsibility and concern for the adverse impact of an oil price increase on the world economy", and on the other hand the remaining members of OPEC who, "citing artificial economic justification and ignoring the destructive consequences of their actions, chose to take a course which can only be termed irresponsible". President-elect Carter praised the "courageous and statesmanlike" policy of Saudi

Arabia and the UAE, but declined to comment on the majority price increase. With regard to the Middle East question, he said that "we clearly want a peaceful and fair resolution in the common interest", but denied that he had given any specific undertakings to Saudi Arabia.

The Commission of the European Communities issued the following statement on Dec. 17: "OPEC's decision to raise crude oil prices imposes a considerable burden on the world economy, including that of the member countries of the Community. It comes on top of other uncertainties as regards economic revival; it will reinforce the already marked tendency towards inflation and aggravate balance-of-payments difficulties. Close co-operation at international and Community level will be needed to minimize the harmful effects of this decision as far as possible. The rise in the price of oil again demonstrates the need for a Community energy policy aimed at making a more efficient use of energy and developing new sources as alternatives to imported oil."

India, Jamaica and Zambia were among the third-world countries which publicly deplored the new OPEC price rise (which was then expected to add up to $1,500 million to the non-oil-producing developing countries' aggregate balance-of-payments deficit in 1977).

D7.5—Establishment of OPEC Special Fund for Developing Countries

OPEC Finance Ministers, meeting in Paris from Jan. 26 to 28, 1976, signed an agreement to establish an OPEC Special Fund "to provide interest-free long-term loans" to other developing countries. The meeting (originally scheduled to last two days) was prolonged by disagreements over the size of individual member states' voluntary contributions to the Fund. It was finally agreed that the target figure for the total resources of the Fund should be $800,000,000 for one year (whereas Iran and Venezuela in particular had pressed for a total commitment to the Fund of $1,000 million per year for five years).

At a further meeting in Paris on May 10 and 11, OPEC Finance Ministers noted "the advanced stage of the process of ratification" of the Fund's constituent agreement, and "provisionally constituted themselves as the Governing Committee of the Special Fund so that it may be operational as early as possible". It was agreed that the Fund should allocate $400,000,000 of its resources to the proposed International Fund for Agricultural Development, provided that at least $600,000,000 was pledged to IFAD by the developed countries. (OPEC countries had been the strongest advocates of the creation of IFAD when the need for such an organization was debated at the UN World Food Conference in November 1974.)

OPEC Finance Ministers met in Vienna on Aug. 5 and 6 as the Ministerial Committee on Financial and Monetary Matters, which had been established to hold responsibility for basic policy decisions affecting the status of the Special Fund. It was "noted with satisfaction" that the Special Fund was "now in operation" and would soon be in a position to implement "a comprehensive programme for providing financial support to other developing countries". The ministers noted the OECD countries' failure to meet OPEC's target for their contributions to IFAD, and urged that this target be met as soon as possible. (A formal agreement on the establishment of IFAD had been reached at an international conference held in June.) They reviewed the work of the Conference on International Economic Co-operation and "expressed concern about the lack of practical progress due to the reluctance of some developed countries to negotiate seriously on issues of importance to the developing countries".

The Ministerial Committee on Financial and Monetary Matters met again in

Manila on Oct. 6, when the Finance Ministers of eight OPEC member countries agreed to recommend that their governments should make voluntary contributions to the IMF Trust Fund for developing countries out of the profits accruing to them from IMF gold sales (◊**B1.6**). At the same time, the Committee urged the industrialized countries "to come forward with significant voluntary contributions to the IMF Trust Fund".

The 48th OPEC Conference meeting expressed the Organization's "full harmony and solidarity with the efforts of developing countries to attain the objectives of the new international economic order" and decided that the resources of the Special Fund should be increased by an additional $800,000,000 and that part of the additional resources should be available for allocation to the proposed UNCTAD common fund for commodities. This decision was taken at the behest of the 11 countries which had opted for the higher 1977 oil price increase, and was regarded by Western observers as a means of minimizing these countries' exposure to criticism from third-world oil importers. Saudi Arabia and the UAE placed on record their view that decisions on the status of the Special Fund lay "within the jurisdiction of Ministers of Finance".

The Special Fund's initial bilateral lending programme was concerned with the allocation of a total of $200,000,000 in balance-of-payments support, the first six loan agreements under this programme being signed on Dec. 23. By the end of January 1977 a total of 30 such agreements had been signed, and by May 1977 the programme's resources were fully committed to a total of 49 countries. The 48th OPEC Conference meeting recommended that "early measures be taken for the Special Fund to assist developing countries in the furtherance of their own economic development" (reflecting an awareness within OPEC that, because of its initial emphasis on balance-of-payments support loans, the Fund had been widely portrayed merely as a channel for the payment of "compensation" for the increase in the Third World's oil import costs). The Fund's first annual report emphasized that many non-oil-related factors had contributed to the deterioration in the Third World's terms of trade during recent years and that OPEC's "preferred approach" was "to consider the resource gap for development in the totality of its causes and to contribute to its closing, especially in the most seriously affected countries, irrespective of the ways in which the gap arises".

D7.6—CIEC Developments in 1976

The Venezuelan and Canadian co-chairmen of the Conference on International Economic Co-operation met the co-chairmen of the CIEC's four expert commissions in Paris on Jan. 26 and 27, 1976, to finalize the commissions' terms of reference. It was agreed that the commissions should meet in February, March, April, June and July with a view to submitting recommendations to a plenary session of the CIEC on Dec. 15. However, the work of the commissions progressed at a slower pace than had been anticipated during 1976 because of disagreements over their agendas and difficulties in reaching a consensus on many issues, and it was announced by the French Government on Dec. 9 that the plenary session had been postponed until 1977.

Other factors in the postponement included the forthcoming change in the US presidency, resulting from Jimmy Carter's victory over Gerald Ford in the election of Nov. 2, and the failure of EEC heads of government to agree on a common position when they discussed the CIEC on Nov. 29 and 30 (the main disagreements being over various aspects of the Community's policy on third-world aid).

D7.7—IEA Developments in 1976

A detailed policy document, setting out a long-term co-operation programme which included the observance of a "minimum safeguard price" of $7 per barrel for imported oil (◊D6.13), was approved by the Board of Governors of the International Energy Agency on Jan. 30, 1976. The programme established a formal framework for the co-ordination of member countries' national efforts (i) to promote the conservation of energy, (ii) to accelerate the development of alternatives to imported oil, and (iii) to "encourage and promote new and beneficial technologies for the efficient production and utilization of energy". The member countries undertook to work towards the removal of "legislative and administrative obstacles and discriminatory practices" which might impede the realization of these objectives. It was agreed that medium- and long-term targets should be established from time to time for "the reduction of the dependence of the group as a whole on imported oil" and that progress towards the fulfilment of targets should be monitored on a country-by-country basis.

Greece's application for IEA membership was approved by the Governing Board on May 20. In July the IEA published its first comprehensive review of member countries' energy conservation programmes. In October and November the Agency carried out the first test of its emergency oil-sharing procedures. The Governing Board agreed at a meeting on Nov. 8 and 9 that member countries' emergency oil stocks should be increased to levels equivalent to 90 days' net imports by the beginning of 1980.

D7.8—EEC Energy Policy in 1976

Little progress was made during 1975 in furthering the energy policy aims adopted by the EEC Council of Ministers in December 1974 (◊D5.10), a situation which was attributed by the European Commission to an "absence of political will on the part of the member countries". The Commission submitted wide-ranging proposals in January 1976 for the adoption of joint Community policies on several energy issues, including the sharing of oil resources within the Community in the event of a supply emergency, the promotion of energy conservation, the protection and development of Community energy resources and the adoption of a $7 per barrel "minimum safeguard price" for crude imports in order to "create a safety net against the uncertainties affecting the world price of oil".

Endorsement of the "minimum safeguard price" concept—accepted in January 1976 by all EEC member countries except France within the framework of the IEA's long-term co-operation programme (◊D7.7) and strongly advocated by Britain in particular—continued to be withheld by the Council of Ministers at France's insistence. The Council of Ministers also failed to agree on an emergency oil-sharing programme. Policy decisions taken by the Council of Ministers on March 25 dealt (i) with improved efficiency of energy use, in which connexion five of the Commission's recommendations were adopted; (ii) with the improvement of information-gathering and consultation procedures on oil price levels within the EEC, on which a directive was issued; and (iii) with the disbursement of EEC funds to support projects in the energy sector, funding being approved for 34 oil and gas projects in 1976–77.

Statistics published by the European Commission in March 1976 showed that EEC oil imports in 1975 were 11.1 per cent lower than in 1973, while oil consumption was 7.4 per cent lower and energy consumption 3.4 per cent lower. The overall level of dependence on imported energy was 55 per cent in 1975 as against 63 per cent in 1973.

D8—1977

D8.1—Annual Statistical Survey

D8.1.i—Oil production and reserves

World

Total production .... 62,560,000 bpd (3,066.9 million tonnes)
   Change over 1976 .... +3.8 per cent

End-year proved reserves .... 653,500 million barrels
   Change over end-1976 .... +0.6 per cent

Reserves:production ratio .... 28.6 : 1

Regional shares:

	In 1977 world production*			In end-1977 world reserves†		
	Regional total (million tonnes)	Change over 1976 (per cent)	Share of world total (per cent)	Reserves (thousand million barrels)	Change over 1976 (per cent)	Share of world total (per cent)
Middle East................	1,114.1	+0.6	36.3	365.8	−0.03	56.0
USSR/Eastern Europe/China........	659.5	+5.8	21.5	98.0	−3.1	15.0
North America	542.6	+0.6	17.7	43.4	−3.8	6.6
Africa	304.7	+6.6	9.9	59.2	−2.3	9.0
Latin America/ Caribbean	238.5	+4.0	7.8	40.2	+23.3	6.2
Asia†/Australasia	137.8	+10.8	4.5	19.7	+1.5	3.0
Western Europe§	69.7	+54.2	2.3	27.2	+9.2	4.2

*Including production from oil shales, tar sands and natural gas liquids (NGL).
†Excluding oil shales and tar sands; including NGL in North America.
‡Excluding China.
§Including Yugoslavia.

OPEC

OPEC oil production .... 31,690,000 bpd (1,564.5 million tonnes)
   Change over 1976 .... +1.6 per cent
   Share of 1977 world total .... 51 per cent

OPEC end-year proved reserves .... 439,755 million barrels
   Change over 1976 .... −0.5 per cent
   Share of 1977 world total .... 67.3 per cent

OPEC reserves:production ratio .... 38 : 1

OPEC (continued)

OPEC member countries' production:

	1977 production		Change over 1976 (per cent)	Share of world total (per cent)	Share of OPEC total (per cent)
	(million tonnes)	(thousand bpd)			
Algeria	53.5	1,150	+6.8	1.7	3.4
Ecuador	9.1	190	—	0.3	0.6
Gabon	11.1	220	−0.9	0.4	0.7
Indonesia	83.5	1,690	+11.9	2.8	5.3
Iran	283.5	5,705	−3.9	9.2	18.1
Iraq	115.2	2,350	−3.0	3.7	7.4
Kuwait	91.5	1,835	−6.8	3.0	5.9
Libya	99.4	2,065	+6.5	3.2	6.4
Nigeria	103.6	2,085	+0.7	3.4	6.6
Qatar	21.6	445	−9.6	0.7	1.4
Saudi Arabia	455.0	9,235	+7.9	14.8	29.1
UAE*	97.2	2,015	+3.2	3.2	6.2
Venezuela	119.5	2,315	−2.8	3.9	7.6
Neutral Zone†	20.8	390	−14.8	0.7	1.3

*Of which Abu Dhabi 80,000,000 tonnes (1,665,000 bpd), Dubai 15,800,000 tonnes (320,000 bpd), Sharjah 1,400,000 tonnes (30,000 bpd).
†Production shared between Kuwait and Saudi Arabia.

Non-OPEC

Selected non-OPEC countries' oil production:

	1977 production		Change over 1976 (per cent)	Share of world total (per cent)
	(million tonnes)	(thousand bpd)		
USSR	545.8	11,055	+5.0	17.8
USA*	466.9	9,865	+1.1	15.2
China	93.6	1,880	+12.0	3.1
Canada	75.7	1,610	−1.9	2.5
Mexico	53.7	1,085	+23.2	1.7
United Kingdom	37.5	765	+217.8	1.2
Argentina	22.5	430	+10.3	0.7
Egypt	21.0	415	+28.0	0.7
Oman	17.1	340	−7.1	0.6
Norway	13.5	275	−2.2	0.4
Total	1,347.3	27,720	+6.3	43.9

*Of which natural gas liquids 57,400,000 tonnes (1,620,000 bpd).

D8.1.ii—Oil consumption

World

Total consumption .... 61,230,000 bpd (2,985.9 million tonnes)
    Change over 1976 .... +3.2 per cent

Regional distribution of total:

	1977 consumption		Change over 1976 (per cent)	Share of world total (per cent)
	(million tonnes)	(thousand bpd)		
North America	951.5	19,735	+4.8	31.9
Western Europe*	697.3	14,225	−1.8	23.4
USSR/Eastern Europe/China	577.8	11,740	+4.8	19.3
Asia†/Australasia	427.7	8,750	+4.0	14.3
Latin America/ Caribbean	193.4	4,010	+6.5	6.5
Middle East	78.9	1,565	+5.6	2.6
Africa	59.3	1,205	+4.2	2.0

*Including Yugoslavia.
†Excluding China.

Selected countries

	1977 consumption		Change over 1976 (per cent)	Share of world total (per cent)
	(million tonnes)	(thousand bpd)		
USA	865.9	17,925	+5.3	29.0
USSR	399.6	8,125	+3.8	13.4
Japan	260.4	5,350	+2.7	8.7
West Germany	137.1	2,855	−1.3	4.6
France	114.6	2,350	−4.1	3.8
Italy	96.1	1,920	−2.7	3.2
United Kingdom	92.0	1,885	−0.7	3.1
Canada	85.6	1,810	−0.3	2.9
China	82.0	1,630	+6.6	2.7
Spain	45.5	930	−5.8	1.5
Total	2,178.8	44,780	+2.7	72.9

D8.1.iii—Oil refining

World

Total refinery capacity .... 75,885,000 bpd
    Change over 1976 .... +2 per cent

Total refinery throughputs .... 58,630,000 bpd
    Change over 1976 .... +3.5 per cent

Consumption as proportion of capacity   80.7 per cent

Selected markets

Consumption of refined product types and change over 1976:

	USA (million tonnes)	USA (per cent)	Western Europe (million tonnes)	Western Europe (per cent)	Japan (million tonnes)	Japan (per cent)
Gasolines	329.5	+2.8	132.8	−1.2	44.6	+2.3
Middle distillates	224.2	+8.7	244.3	+0.9	55.7	+2.8
Fuel oil	160.8	+9.5	227.1	−7.0	128.9	+2.5
Other	151.4	+1.7	93.1	+3.9	31.2	+4.0
Total	865.9	+5.3	697.3	−1.8	260.4	+2.7

D8.1.iv—Tankers and trade

Tankers

Total world fleet	332,500,000 deadweight tons
Change over 1976	+3.7 per cent

Trade

Total world crude exports (including re-exports)	32,909,100 bpd (1,625.9 million tonnes)
Change over 1976	+1.7 per cent
OPEC crude exports	27,641,100 bpd (1,365.7 million tonnes)
Change over 1976	+0.6 per cent
Share of 1977 world total	84 per cent
Total world product exports (including re-exports)	8,053,000 bpd (407,953,400 tonnes)
Change over 1976	+4.4 per cent
OPEC product exports	1,751,000 bpd (88,703,100 tonnes)
Change over 1976	−6.4 per cent
Share of 1977 world total	21.7 per cent

Regional distribution of world oil trade*:

	Share of 1977 imports (per cent) Crude	Share of 1977 imports (per cent) Products	Share of 1977 exports (per cent) Crude	Share of 1977 exports (per cent) Products
USA	22.2	40.9	0.2	4.4
Canada	2.3	0.9	0.9	5.5
Latin America/Caribbean	7.6	3.3	4.0	39.0
Western Europe	41.3	20.4	0.4	6.5
Middle East	0.2	1.8	66.9	18.2
North Africa	—	1.4	10.5	1.6
West Africa	†	2.1	8.0	0.5
East and southern Africa	1.4	1.0	—	0.3
South Asia	1.3	1.9	—	—
South-East Asia	4.6	7.2	5.2	6.1
Australasia	0.8	2.0	—	1.1
Japan	16.6	10.9	—	0.1
USSR/Eastern Europe/China	1.1	2.3	3.9	16.7
Unspecified	0.6	3.9	—	—
Total	100.0	100.0	100.0	100.0

*Excluding intra-regional trade.
†Negligible.

D8.1.v—World primary energy consumption

Total consumption (excluding
    non-commercial fuels) .... 6,480.2 million tonnes oil equivalent (mtoe)
    Change over 1976 .... +3.1 per cent

Contributions of primary energy sources:

	Consumption (mtoe)	Change over 1976 (per cent)	Share of total (per cent)
Oil	2,985.9	+3.2	46.1
Coal	1,830.1	+2.4	28.3
Natural gas	1,161.9	+1.9	17.9
Water power	371.9	+3.9	5.7
Nuclear power	130.4	+24.1	2.0

D8.1.vi—Natural gas production and reserves

Marketed production (thousand million cubic metres):

	Regional total (tmcm)	Change over 1976 (per cent)	Share of 1977 world total (per cent)
North America	618.7	+0.9	47.9
Latin America/Caribbean	41.8	+8.9	3.2
Western Europe*	172.5	+1.1	13.4
USSR/Eastern Europe/China	369.6	+6.9	28.6
Middle East	38.1	+7.6	2.9
Africa	12.4	−11.4	1.0
Asia†/Australasia	38.8	+24.8	3.0
World total	1,291.9	+3.5	100.0
(of which OPEC)	(64.0)	(+9.8)	(5.0)

*Including Yugoslavia.
†Excluding China.

End-year proved reserves (thousand million cubic metres):

	Regional total (tmcm)	Change over 1976 (per cent)	Share of 1977 world total (per cent)
North America	7,557.4	−2.7	11.2
Latin America/Caribbean	2,996.2	+26.0	4.4
Western Europe*	3,924.8	+1.0	5.8
USSR/Eastern Europe/China	23,196.3	−0.8	34.5
Middle East	20,394.2	+40.4	30.3
Africa	5,891.5	−1.0	8.8
Asia†/Australasia	3,337.6	+2.5	5.0
World total	67,298.0	+10.1	100.0
(of which OPEC)	(27,733.9)	(+26.5)	(41.2)

*Including Yugoslavia.
†Excluding China.

D8.2—The Market Environment in 1977

The annual rate of real economic growth in the OECD area fell to 3.7 per cent in 1977, compared with 5.3 per cent in 1976, while the average OECD inflation rate rose slightly to 8.9 per cent. A downturn in the annual growth rate of non-communist oil consumption to 2.8 per cent (as against 6.6 per cent in 1976) was accompanied by a 6.6 per cent increase in non-communist oil production outside the OPEC area. Britain began to establish itself as a substantial producer, Mexico began to step up its output from new fields and (in the third quarter of the year) the United States began to obtain supplies from northern Alaska, thus ending a prolonged decline in US output which had broadly balanced out non-US production increases outside the OPEC area in the previous three years. In these circumstances the OPEC majority were obliged to reassess their ability to withstand a "production war" with Saudi Arabia over the level of the 1977 marker price. By the latter part of the year (after a compromise had been achieved within OPEC on the pricing question) the main concern of most member countries was to minimize the erosion of their existing price levels in the face of a world supply surplus of around 2,000,000 bpd.

D8.3—OPEC and Two-Tier Pricing (January to June 1977)

OPEC oil output, which had been greatly stimulated by consumer stockpiling in the last quarter of 1976, fell by 6.5 per cent in the first quarter of 1977 (although the reduced level was still 11.6 per cent above the average for January–March 1976). Production in January 1977 was some 5,800,000 bpd (16.9 per cent) below the December 1976 average (although 7.1 per cent above the January 1976 average). The aggregate output of Iran, Iraq and Kuwait, the three OPEC members most vulnerable to price competition from Saudi Arabia, fell by an average 4,900,000 bpd between December 1976 and January 1977 and by an average 2,400,000 bpd between the last quarter of 1976 and the first quarter of 1977. First-quarter production in Iran and Iraq was higher in 1977 than in 1976, whereas Kuwait's output underwent a small year-on-year decline, reflecting the country's total reliance on 31° crude, a grade on which Saudi Arabia enjoyed a particularly strong price advantage. In the joint Kuwait-Saudi Arabian Neutral Zone, where the administration of two-tier pricing posed acute practical problems (◊**D7.3.iii**), output plunged to 10 per cent of capacity in January.

Saudi Arabia announced in early January 1977 that it had authorized Aramco to raise its production to an average 10,000,000 bpd in the first quarter of the year and was prepared to introduce an even higher ceiling thereafter. In the event, however, Aramco's average first-quarter output reached only 9,150,000 bpd (about 2 per cent above the average for the last quarter of 1976), having built up from 8,350,000 bpd in January to 9,680,000 bpd in March. The main constraint on Saudi production in January and February was a period of adverse weather conditions at Ras Tanura, which greatly increased tanker loading times, while in March technical difficulties began to be encountered in maintaining reservoir pressures under conditions of high-volume extraction. Shaikh Yamani claimed in an interview published on March 6 that a daily output of more than 13,000,000 barrels had recently been achieved at some points.

Shaikh Yamani said in the same interview that some Gulf countries within the OPEC majority were already finding it necessary to discount their official prices. In particular, he alleged that Iraqi oil was being sold at only 7 per cent above its 1976 price and that Iran was using barter deals and extended credit terms as a means of providing concealed discounts. Shaikh Yamani warned, however, that Saudi

Arabia would not continue to accept an accelerated depletion of its oil reserves in order to undermine the OPEC majority's price increase unless there were clear signs of "appreciation" from the industrialized countries in the form of progress towards a Middle East peace settlement and a satisfactory "North-South" agreement within the Conference on International Economic Co-operation.

The Saudi Government had earlier taken steps to prevent the resale of Saudi crudes for more than their official export prices. Aramco's parent companies were required to submit audited sales reports specifying fob prices, destinations and transport costs, and were required to sell incremental output directly to refiners rather than through brokers. It was subsequently reported that each of the Aramco parent companies had undertaken to make its third-party sales of incremental output to one of four designated European companies (Shell, BP, CFP and ENI) under a "pairing" system. The Saudi Government also declared its intention to seek the co-operation of the governments of importing companies in order to prevent any "exploitation" of consumers. The UAE did not permit its production to rise above its existing level of 2,000,000 bpd while two-tier pricing was in force (despite a reported Saudi request that it should allow a temporary increase), but did announce its intention to monitor exporting companies' compliance with its official prices. Spot prices of marker-grade Gulf crudes were meanwhile fluctuating at levels rather higher than the mid-point between the two OPEC marker values.

Whereas the public stances of Saudi Arabia and Iran remained inflexible during the first quarter of the year, intensive "behind-the-scenes" consultations took place within OPEC with a view to securing a compromise on the pricing deadlock. The Qatari Oil Minister, who held the presidency of the OPEC Conference at this time and was thus at the centre of these consultations, said on March 1 that he hoped that an extraordinary ministerial meeting could be arranged to resolve the issue before the scheduled implementation of the second stage of the "majority" price increase on July 1 (the agreed opening date of the next ordinary Conference meeting being July 12).

Shaikh Yamani had earlier stated on a number of occasions that Saudi Arabia would not oppose the holding of an extraordinary Conference meeting, provided that it had been "well prepared", but had also pointed out that the OPEC statute did not give the Conference any power to question an individual member country's sovereign right to determine its own price levels. Iran had indicated its willingness to attend any extraordinary meeting which was called to consider proposals "acceptable to the other OPEC states". Kuwait, Venezuela and Indonesia were all known to be strongly in favour of an early compromise, it being stated by the Kuwaiti Oil Minister that two-tier pricing posed a serious threat to OPEC's continued existence.

The introduction of two-tier pricing had little impact on the output of most non-Gulf producers. Libya, Algeria and Nigeria all experienced firm underlying demand for their light crudes at official prices, and Nigeria announced a 30-cents per barrel price increase with effect from April 1, taking its 37° crude to $14.61 per barrel. Venezuelan exports held up well during the early part of the year, when US demand for heavier products was boosted by an exceptionally harsh winter, while Indonesia (whose oil was in any case competitively priced) benefited from above-average seasonal demand in Japan (also related to adverse weather).

Saudi Arabia finally achieved an average output of 10,000,000 bpd in April and early May, but on May 11 serious fire damage to oilfield installations (caused by the structural failure of a corroded pipeline) forced a cutback to less than 8,000,000 bpd for a May average of 8,250,000 bpd. Production in June averaged 9,350,000 bpd. Saudi Arabia's average output for the entire second quarter was less than 1 per cent higher than the first quarter's average, and the average for the first six months of the year was nearly 9 per cent below that Government's 10,000,000 bpd target. Iran and Iraq each experienced production declines of between 6 and 7 per cent between the first and second quarters of the year, while Kuwait's average output increased by about 5 per cent relative to its exceptionally low level in the first quarter.

At the same time that Aramco's production difficulties were helping to delay the exercise of Saudi Arabia's full potential to exert market pressure on the other main Gulf producers, efforts were stepped up within OPEC to find a price reunification formula, the main initiative being taken by Venezuela. The Venezuelan President, Carlos Andrés Pérez, visited Saudi Arabia, Iran, Iraq, Kuwait, Qatar, Algeria and the UAE between April 20 and May 5, and on May 4 became the first OPEC head of state to visit the Organization's Vienna headquarters, where he conferred with other OPEC countries' ambassadors and heads of mission in Austria. An OPEC press statement issued on this occasion described it as "a symbolic visit to all those member countries he was unable to include on his journey, and a demonstration of the solidarity existing among member countries".

According to the *Middle East Economic Survey* of May 13, President Pérez had obtained the full support of Kuwait and Qatar, the "reluctant" support of Iran and the "very reluctant" support of Iraq for a proposal that the OPEC majority should cancel the supplementary price increase planned for July. However, while Saudi Arabia and the UAE were reported to have agreed in principle to raise their prices in July as a reciprocal gesture, Saudi Arabia was said to be unwilling at this stage to give a firm undertaking to bring its prices fully into line with the level adopted by the majority in January and to have indicated a preference for a unification of prices at 8 per cent rather than 10.3 per cent above the 1976 level.

Saudi Arabia and the UAE nevertheless announced on June 19 that they were now prepared to raise their prices on July 1 by the full 5 per cent required to bring them into line with the majority countries, provided that the latter group cancelled the price increase planned for that date. This decision was presented by Saudi officials as a reaction to the inconclusive outcome of the final meeting of the Conference on International Economic Co-operation (◊**D8.8**). However, it was reported by *The Financial Times* on June 22 that a firm decision had been taken "towards the end of May" and stemmed mainly from a "desire to heal the breach in OPEC".

In a formal statement issued through the OPEC Secretary-General on June 29, nine of the majority countries—Algeria, Ecuador, Gabon, Indonesia, Iran, Kuwait, Nigeria, Qatar and Venezuela—announced that, "in the interest of the unity and solidarity of OPEC", they had "resolved to forgo" the application on July 1 of the additional 4.7 per cent increase (from $12.70 to $13.30 per barrel) in their notional marker value. Of these nine countries, Indonesia had unilaterally cancelled its July price increase on May 20, while Ecuador was reported to have had no plans for a July increase after encountering some customer resistance to its existing price. The two members of the majority not mentioned in the June 29 statement, Iraq and Libya, subsequently indicated that they would cancel their July price increases only after Saudi Arabia and the UAE had formally and unconditionally committed themselves to a price rise.

Such a commitment was subsequently announced by Saudi Arabia and the UAE on July 3, in a statement which also referred to "their firm belief that OPEC should be one united front, and their firm desire that in future there should be a moderate attitude by all while discussing oil prices".

As a result of the settlement of the pricing dispute, the overall increase in OPEC oil prices for the whole of 1977 was expected to average between 8.5 and 9.5 per cent, compared with between 10 and 11 per cent if there had been no settlement. The average price rise under two-tier pricing in the first half of the year was variously estimated at between 7 and 8.5 per cent.

Table 42 shows the new selling prices announced by Saudi Arabia and the United Arab Emirates with effect from July 1. The new Saudi price for 31° crude still left this grade somewhat underpriced relative to the same grade of crude in Kuwait and Iran when judged against the differentials which had applied at the end of 1976. Saudi Arabia increased its price for 35° Neutral Zone crude to $12.69 per barrel (the existing price charged by Kuwait), but raised its price for the 28° grade to only $12.10, as against Kuwait's price of $12.242.

The following adjustments were made to other OPEC members' differentials with effect from July 1: (i) an increase of 15 cents per barrel by Algeria, taking the price of 44° crude to $14.45 per barrel; (ii) a cut of 10 cents per barrel on Gabon's 27° grade (from $12.80 to $12.70) and (iii) an increase of 28 cents per barrel, to $14.20, for Libyan 40° crude.

Table 42 — July 1977 crude prices in Saudi Arabia and United Arab Emirates

	Dollars per barrel	Increase (per cent)
Saudi Arabia (27°)	12.016	5.68
(31°)	12.323	5.41
(34°)	12.704	5.08
(39°)	13.225	5.97
UAE: Abu Dhabi (39°)	13.26	6.08
Dubai (32°)	12.64	4.55

D8.4—49th OPEC Conference Meeting

In view of the settlement of the dispute over the level of the marker price, the 49th OPEC Conference meeting, held near Stockholm on July 12 and 13, 1977, was devoted mainly to the discussion of differentials, and the only formal decision of the meeting was to establish a ministerial committee "to discuss this issue further and reach a solution thereon". The membership of the committee was subsequently announced as Iran, Iraq, Kuwait, Saudi Arabia and Venezuela. The main focus of attention at this time was on the level of Gulf differentials for heavier crudes, in which connexion Iran, Iraq and Kuwait pressed Saudi Arabia to raise its prices for 27° and 31° crudes by between 10 and 15 cents per barrel.

However, Shaikh Yamani argued that Saudi Arabia's recently announced prices for these grades were realistic in relation to current market conditions. He also maintained that it was in the Gulf countries' long-term interest—given that reserves of lighter crudes were being depleted at a faster rate than the region's larger reserves of heavier crudes—to give importers a financial incentive to restructure their refinery capacity in order to achieve higher yields of lighter products from heavier crudes. In this context he pointed out that the growth in the relative importance of lighter products within the overall pattern of Japanese and West European product demand was expected to accelerate as fuel oil was progressively displaced by alternative energy sources. A subsequent report (commissioned by a subcommittee of the US Senate and published in April 1979) suggested that the Saudi Government's policy on this issue was based on conclusions drawn from Aramco's attempt to achieve near-capacity output during the first half of 1977, when the main technical problems had occurred in fields producing 34° crude.

When interviewed in Stockholm about OPEC's two-tier pricing experience, Shaikh Yamani said that it had been "very helpful", and was unlikely to be repeated as it had proved to be in the interests neither of producers nor consumers.

He said that Saudi Arabia favoured the maintenance of oil prices at their current levels until at least the end of 1978, subject to review only on the basis of market-related criteria, "coupled with an awareness of the political situation in our area" (in respect of which the Saudi Government had no criticism of the Middle East policy so far pursued by the new US Government). Shaikh Yamani said that Saudi Arabia would not be considering the reimposition of its former production ceiling until later in the year (i.e. after the expiry of existing supply contracts for additional volumes).

Dr Jamshid Amouzegar, the head of Iran's delegation to the Stockholm meeting, acknowledged that his country's decision to compromise on the pricing issue (which had been the key factor in OPEC's reunification agreement) marked a fundamental change in Iranian policy. He expressed broad agreement with Shaikh Yamani's forecast of an OPEC price freeze throughout 1978, stating that he accepted the importance of market forces in determining prices at a time when the market was beginning to experience a supply surplus. He said that Iran was concerned at the state of the world economy, including the high levels of unemployment in the industrialized countries, and felt that the rate of economic growth in these countries should be a major factor in OPEC's pricing decisions for 1978. On Iran's long-standing advocacy of the indexation of oil prices to those of goods imported from industrialized countries, Dr Amouzegar said that "having failed to win the support of all our OPEC colleagues for such a system, we will not insist on pursuing the matter further".

Dr Amouzegar added, however, that he did not expect the current surplus of oil supply over demand to persist beyond the end of 1978, and warned that "in about three years' time" OPEC would cease to serve a useful purpose as a price-fixing organization because "the laws of supply and demand will ensure that oil prices stay high".

The 18-month price freeze foreseen by both Saudi Arabia and Iran (and also advocated by the UAE) was criticized by the delegates from Libya, Iraq and Algeria, and Ezzedine al Mabrouk of Libya was quoted as saying on July 13 that failure to agree on a 10 per cent price increase at the beginning of 1978 could result in another period of two-tier pricing.

D8.5—Prelude to 50th OPEC Conference Meeting

While the average level of OPEC production showed little change in July–December 1977 as against January–June 1977, it was well below the average for July–December 1976. Whereas the second half of 1976 had brought large-scale stockpiling in anticipation of an OPEC price increase ($\Diamond$**D7.3.i**), the availability of substantial incremental supplies from non-OPEC sources eliminated this factor in 1977. The underlying weakness of the market was demonstrated by a fall in spot prices to well below official prices for all grades of crude.

In these conditions, price differentials came under increasing pressure, and on Sept. 8 Kuwait was obliged to cut the price of its 31° crude by 10 cents per barrel, to $12.27, following a fall in its production from 1,700,000 bpd to 1,400,000 bpd between July and August and a consequent shortfall in the supply of associated gas for consumption within Kuwait. The price reduction was initially announced as a temporary measure in exchange for guaranteed purchasing commitments by contract buyers for the remainder of 1977, but was subsequently retained on an official basis after the end of the year. The price cut restored the differential between Saudi and Kuwaiti 31° crudes to its end-1976 level. Also on Sept. 8, Kuwait reduced its price for 28° Neutral Zone crude to $12.10 with retroactive effect from July 1. These changes preceded any meeting of OPEC's new ministerial committee on differentials.

Widespread discounting of official prices by other OPEC producers—particularly on African light crudes—was reported from September onwards, although no other

OPEC member made a formally announced price cut during the latter part of 1977. Saudi Arabia reimposed its 8,500,000 bpd production ceiling on Aramco's output during December, when Shaikh Yamani stated that there was "no danger facing OPEC" in the present situation, since Saudi Arabia, as a "surplus revenue" country currently producing at a level close to its ceiling, had considerable leeway to make production cuts to defend the marker price. As regards the prospect of renewed pressure for a price increase at the next OPEC Conference meeting, Saudi Arabia's stated position in October was that in the interests of OPEC unity it would not oppose a "token" increase. Iran's position at this time was that it would take a "strictly neutral" line on prices at the next Conference meeting.

However, on Nov. 16 the Shah of Iran stated during a visit to Washington for talks with President Carter that the President's arguments in favour of an oil price freeze had "convinced him to modify his policy of neutrality" and that Iran would therefore positively oppose any increase in OPEC prices at the beginning of 1978. (Western observers noted that Iran had strong political motives for not wishing to sour its relations with the United States, notably in connexion with current arms supply negotiations.) Dr Amouzegar (who had become Prime Minister of Iran in August) said that an oil price rise in 1978 "could adversely affect the balance of payments in developing countries and would not be advisable during a serious glut of oil throughout the world which was forcing some OPEC members to sell crude at below agreed levels".

Following Iran's declaration of its position, Saudi Arabia (supported by the United Arab Emirates) adopted a firmer line in pressing for a price freeze both publicly and through diplomatic efforts aimed at achieving a consensus within OPEC in advance of the opening of the 50th Conference meeting on Dec. 20. Qatar and Kuwait eventually agreed to support a price freeze, but Iraq refused to abandon a claim for an increase of up to 23 per cent to compensate for inflation in its import prices. The Iraqi Minister of Petroleum and Mineral Resources, Tayea Abdel-Karim, announced on Dec. 14 (during a meeting of the OAPEC Council of Ministers) that he would not attend the for-thcoming OPEC meeting in view of the "collusion" of the other Gulf members on the pricing issue.

Algeria and Libya associated themselves with Iraq's call for a substantial price rise, while the other non-Gulf members supported a price increase of between 5 and 8 per cent, as advocated by President Pérez of Venezuela on Nov. 20. The US Secretary of State, Cyrus Vance, was unsuccessful in putting his country's case for a price freeze to President Pérez during talks in Caracas on Nov. 23, and intensive contacts subsequently took place between the Venezuelan Minister of Mines and Hydrocarbons, Dr Valentín Hernández Acosta, and his counterparts in other OPEC countries with the aim of securing a compromise agreement on prices based on the Venezuelan proposal. It was widely reported during the week preceding the meeting that Venezuela, as the host country, had called for its postponement to avoid a possible repetition of the December 1976 split on prices but that this suggestion had been rejected by other OPEC members.

D8.6—50th OPEC Conference Meeting

The 50th meeting of the OPEC Conference was held near Caracas on Dec. 20 and 21, 1977. The meeting opened with a speech by Qatar's Oil Minister (as the outgoing Conference President), who said that the delegates had three realistic options on the pricing issue—to extend the freeze, to make a nominal increase or to delete the issue from the agenda in the interests of maintaining OPEC unity. President Pérez then delivered a formal opening address in which he departed from convention by making a direct appeal for the adoption of his own proposal for a price increase of between 5 and 8 per cent.

He said that this proposal was made purely "for the benefit of humanity" and was linked to a plan to use the additional revenues which would be generated by such a price increase during the year 1978—estimated at between $7,000 million and $11,000 million—to set up a fund for the alleviation of the international indebtedness of the poorer third-world countries. The detailed operation of the fund should be decided in consultation with the "Group of 77" developing countries and the International Monetary Fund. President Pérez said that there had been an "alarming and dramatic" growth in third-world indebtedness from $40,000 million in 1973 to $180,000 million in 1977, with 40 per cent of the current total (as opposed to 20 per cent 10 years earlier) representing "very expensive monies supplied by the commercial banks".

"Each day," he continued, "developing countries which lack oil have less possibility of servicing the debt already contracted and at the same time see their purchasing power decrease. A vicious circle without solution in sight is driving the world towards catastrophe. The sinking of the economies of the developing countries makes the possibility of recovery of the industrial economies even more precarious." President Pérez said that OPEC should set up the proposed fund to alleviate this situation because the Third World "continues to recognize in OPEC the pioneering instrument of its cause", although that the Organization could not assume all the responsibilities of the industrialized countries, whose aid commitments should reflect the size of their economies. He accused the industrialized countries of showing "selfishness and incomprehension" at the final session of the CIEC (◊**D8.8**) and at other recent meetings concerned with the problems of developing countries.

President Pérez condemned the pressure which he said had been exerted on OPEC member countries "from the highest summits of world economic power" in order to secure a freeze in oil prices until there was an improvement in the world economy. It was his view that, when account had been taken of the need to conserve the world's remaining oil resources and develop alternative energy sources, "maintaining the prices of petroleum at their present level can be perceived at this moment as more harmful to the world economy". He concluded by calling for a discussion of his proposals by a summit conference of OPEC heads of state.

The press statement issued by ministers on Dec. 21 noted that President Pérez had "made proposals stressing the role of OPEC vis-à-vis other developing countries" and that it had been "agreed that member countries will consult among themselves with a view to making new efforts towards strengthening the solidarity among the developing nations in the establishment of a new international economic order". "In this connexion," the statement went on, "the Conference expressed its disappointment with respect to the lack of progress concerning the establishment of the [proposed UNCTAD] common fund for commodities despite the clear commitments made by the developed countries during the CIEC negotiations in Paris. The conference reaffirmed its full support, including financial contributions, towards the early establishment of the common fund as a key institution of the integrated programme for commodities."

The statement made no mention of the specific nature of the Venezuelan proposals, of their dependence on an oil price increase or of President Pérez's call for a special OPEC summit meeting to consider them.

When the meeting discussed the pricing question, Shaikh Yamani and Mohammed Yeganeh (the current head of Iran's Conference delegation) repeated their countries' firm intention of freezing prices, while presentation of the "hardline" case for a substantial increase was weakened by the non-attendance of Tayea Abdel-Karim of Iraq, who was represented by his chief official adviser. In these circumstances the advocates of a moderate price increase were unsuccessful in presenting their position as a valid basis for a compromise agreement, and when the proponents of a price freeze indicated that they would not insist on any formal commitment to a specified period of price stability the moderates accepted a Kuwaiti proposal that prices be frozen on a de facto basis through the post-ponement of any decision until a future meeting. It was accordingly announced that "the Conference considered the question of a price readjustment, but the member countries were unable to reach a common consensus on this issue".

Although there was some public criticism of the de facto price freeze by delegates from "hard-line" countries—Ezzedine al Mabrouk being quoted as saying that "the big conservative oil producers" had violated OPEC's statute by "imposing their will for political reasons"—it was noted by observers that no country wished to see a repetition of the open split in the unity of the Organization which had led to two-tier pricing a year earlier. Shaikh Yamani was reported to have given a general assurance that Saudi Arabia was prepared to adjust the level of its oil production "to safeguard the interests of OPEC" as long as member countries continued to be affected by the current oversupply of oil on the world market (thereby removing any pressure on the Organization to consider a co-ordinated prorationing pro-gramme). On the question of the relative values of medium and heavy crudes, ministers decided that a meeting of the OPEC differentials committee (◊**D8.4**) should be held within three months.

Regarding the preservation of the real value of member countries' earnings from oil, it was announced that "the Conference considered the losses in purchasing power of export earnings of member countries resulting from continued imported world inflation and expressed its great concern over the accumulated effect of such inflation". The Conference also considered "the situation created by the weakening position of the US dollar" and instructed the Secretariat to draw up recom-mendations for "remedial measures" as a matter of urgency.

The question of the decline in the exchange rate of the dollar vis-à-vis other major currencies during 1977 had been a matter of increasing concern to OPEC countries during recent months, estimates produced by the OPEC Economic Com-mission having indicated that they had suffered an aggregate loss of up to $2,500 million as a result of the denomination of oil prices (and of most of their overseas investments) in dollars. The benefit to oil-importing countries had varied from the effective neutralization of the whole of the increase in OPEC prices during 1977 for Japan to the neutralization of the July 1977 increase at the end of two-tier pricing for France, West Germany, Italy, the Netherlands and the United Kingdom, while the United States had benefited to the extent that oil import prices remained stable at a time when other US import prices were rising in dollar terms.

D8.7—Meetings of OPEC Finance Ministers in 1977

On March 1, 1977, the Ministerial Committee on Financial and Monetary Matters formally endorsed the decision of the 48th OPEC Conference meeting regarding the doubling of the resources of the OPEC Special Fund (◊**D7.5**). The committee called for the speedy ratification of the constituent agreement of the International Fund for Agricultural Development and expressed its strong support for the appointment of Saudi Arabia's nominee as IFAD's first president and for the location of IFAD's headquarters in Tehran. No alternative proposals had been submitted by other participating developing countries.

At a further meeting of the committee on Aug. 4, a resolution was adopted providing for the doubling of the OPEC Special Fund's resources to be effected on the basis of the same national contributions as had been made to the Fund's initial capital. It was confirmed that part of the new resources would be available to support the proposed UNCTAD common fund for commodities. Ministers discussed the outcome of the Conference on International Economic Co-operation and reiterated their appeal for ratification of the constituent agreement of IFAD in order to allow that organization to begin operating before the end of the year. (IFAD was subsequently able to hold its inaugural meeting in mid-December, when Saudi Arabia's nominee was elected as its president. It was decided that the Fund—described as "the first important institution of the new international economic order"—should be based in Rome.)

D8.8—Final Session of Conference on International Economic Co-operation

The second plenary session of the Conference on International Economic Co-operation, originally scheduled for mid-December 1976 (◊**D7.6**), took place in Paris from May 30 to June 2, 1977. During the preceding months the US Government of President Carter (who had taken office on Jan. 20) had adopted a more conciliatory attitude towards the demands of the "group of 19" developing countries than that which had been shown by Dr Henry Kissinger under the Ford Government, while the EEC countries had succeeded in reaching a common negotiating position on certain key issues. These developments had helped to speed up the work of the CIEC's four expert commissions, which had progressed sufficiently by late March for a firm date to be fixed for the second plenary session, notwithstanding the fact that the final reports of the commissions seemed certain to reflect many disagreements between the "group of 19" and the "group of eight" industrialized countries.

The EEC's position at the plenary session, as agreed by EEC Foreign Ministers on May 3, included (i) a proposal for the creation by the industrialized countries of a $1,000 million "special action" aid fund for the poorest third-world countries; (ii) a commitment in principle to the establishment of a common fund to stabilize international trade in primary commodities, as had been recommended by the fourth ministerial session of the UN Conference on Trade and Development (UNCTAD IV), held in Nairobi in May 1976; and (iii) a recommendation that the appropriate international institutions should examine the possibility of creating a worldwide guarantee arrangement for individual developing countries' earnings from commodity exports, based on the EEC's own guarantee system for a group of African, Caribbean and Pacific countries (consisting predominantly of former British and French colonies).

US support for these proposals was indicated in an address to the Conference on May 30 by the new Secretary of State, Cyrus Vance, who concentrated primarily on development issues and indicated the US Government's commitment to "a new international economic system" which would provide an equitable basis for growth. Vance did not give undue emphasis to energy questions, although he did note "an urgent need for reliable energy supply, strict energy conservation and a shift to new energy resources", a need for stable energy prices and a need "to find ways to transfer appropriate energy technology to oil-importing developing countries" which were currently facing "acute problems".

It was reported that the "group of eight" considered that their new proposals for development aid and commodity price stabilization provided the basis for a "trade-off" involving acceptance by the "group of 19" of the establishment of an institutionalized forum for international discussions on energy, including the supply and price of internationally traded oil. Although a prior agreement in principle on this matter was believed to have been reached by the US and Saudi Arabian Governments, the Conference was unable to accept such a trade-off because other

OPEC members were opposed to any arrangement which might restrict their freedom of action over pricing decisions. For their part, oil-importing developing countries were opposed to the separation of the energy issue from other "North-South" issues, not least because they considered the industrialized countries' general trade and aid proposals to be inadequate.

In the latter context spokesmen for the "group of 19" pointed out that the $1,000 million special action aid pledge would cover less than one year's debt servicing for the poorest developing countries and that no commitment had been given by the "group of eight" on the size of the proposed UNCTAD common fund for commodities. Although there were differing views on these issues within the "group of 19" countries, in general they pressed for a commitment to a common commodities fund totalling $6,000 million, and for a moratorium on the debts of the poorest developing countries and the rescheduling of those of others. In addition, they sought a specific undertaking from the "group of eight" that the industrialized countries would, within five years, all meet the long-standing UN target of 0.7 per cent of gross national product in respect of the transfer of official development aid. (OECD statistics showed that among OECD members only Sweden and the Netherlands were currently meeting this target.)

With the two sides in a state of deadlock on several key issues, the Conference (which had originally been scheduled to end on June 1) was extended for another day to enable further negotiations to take place between officials. However, when the session finally ended on June 2 a wide range of differences still separated the two groups, including the refusal of the "group of 19" to agree to the creation of a permanent energy forum. Of the points of agreement, the most significant were a commitment in principle to the negotiation within UNCTAD of a common commodities fund and the pledge by the "group of eight" concerning the special action aid fund.

The final report of the CIEC included abbreviated lists of the points of agreement and disagreement on the detailed negotiating agendas of the four expert commissions. The points of agreement were given as follows:

"**Energy**. (1) Conclusion and recommendation on availability and supply in a commercial sense, except for purchasing power constraint [subject to certain reservations on the part of some members of the "group of 19", including Egypt, Iran, Iraq and Venezuela].

"(2) Recognition of depletable nature of oil and gas. Transition from oil-based energy mix to more permanent and renewable sources of energy.

"(3) Conservation and increased efficiency of energy utilization.

"(4) Need to develop all forms of energy.

"(5) General conclusions and recommendations for national action and international co-operation in the energy field.

"**Raw materials and trade**. (1) Establishment of a common [commodities] fund with purposes, objectives and other constituent elements to be further negotiated in UNCTAD.

"(2) Research and development and some other measures for natural products competing with synthetics.

"(3) Measures for international co-operation in the field of marketing and distribution of raw materials.

"(4) Measures to assist importing developing countries to develop and diversify their indigenous natural resources.

"(5) Agreement for improving generalized system of preferences schemes; identification of areas for special and more favourable treatment for developing countries in multilateral trade negotiations; certain other trade questions.

"**Development**. (1) Volume and quality of official development assistance.

"(2) Provision by developed countries of $1,000 million in a special action programme for individual low-income countries facing general problems of transfer of resources.

"(3) Food and agriculture.

"(4) Assistance to infrastructure development in developing countries with particular reference to Africa.

"(5) Several aspects of the industrialization of developing countries.

"(6) Industrial property; implementation of relevant UNCTAD resolutions on transfer of technology; [holding of proposed] UN Conference on Science and Technology.

"**Finance**. (1) Private foreign direct investment, except criteria for compensation, transferability of income and capital and jurisdiction and standards for settlement of disputes.

"(2) Developing countries' access to capital markets.

"(3) Other financial flows (monetary issues).

"(4) Co-operation among developing countries."

The final report listed the points of disagreement under the four headings as follows:

"**Energy**. (1) Price of energy and purchasing power of energy export earnings.

"(2) Accumulated revenues from oil exports.

"(3) Financial assistance to bridge external payments problems of oil-importing countries.

"(4) Recommendations on resources within the [UN] Law of the Sea Conference.

"(5) Continuing consultations on energy.

"**Raw materials and trade**. (1) Purchasing power of developing countries.

"(2) Measures related to compensatory financing.

"(3) Aspects of local processing and diversification.

"(4) Measures relating to interests of developing countries in: world shipping tonnage and trade; representation on commodity exchanges; a Code of Conduct for Liner Conferences; other matters.

"(5) Production, control and other measures concerning synthetics.

"(6) Investments in the field of raw materials.

"(7) Means for protecting the interests of developing countries which might be adversely affected by the implementation of the [UNCTAD] integrated programme [on commodities].

"(8) Relationship of integrated programme to new international economic order.

"(9) Measures related to trade policies, to institutional framework of trade, to aspects of the generalized system of tariff preferences, to the GATT multilateral trade negotiations and to conditions of supply.

"**Development**. (1) Indebtedness of developing countries.

"(2) Adjustment assistance measures.

"(3) Access to markets for manufactured and semi-manufactured products.

"(4) Transnational corporations.

"**Finance**. (1) Criteria for compensation, transferability of income and capital, and jurisdiction and standards for settlement of disputes.

"(2) Measures against inflation.

"(3) Financial assets of oil-exporting developing countries."

The summary section of the final report then referred in general terms to the outcome of the CIEC and went on to state that the participants had agreed to submit its results to the UN General Assembly and "to all other relevant international bodies for their consideration and appropriate action". These passages were worded as follows:

"**Group of 19" reaction**. "The participants from developing countries in CIEC, while recognizing that progress has been made in CIEC to meet certain proposals of developing countries, noted with regret that most of the proposals for structural changes in the international economic system and certain of the proposals for urgent action on pressing problems have not been agreed upon. Therefore, the "group of 19" feels that the conclusions of CIEC fall short of the objectives envisaged for a comprehensive and equitable programme of action designed to establish the new international economic order.

"**Group of eight" reaction**. "The participants from developed countries in CIEC welcomed the spirit of co-operation in which on the whole the Conference took place and expressed their determination to maintain that spirit as the dialogue between developing and developed countries continues in other places. They regretted that it had not proved possible to reach agreement on some important areas of the dialogue such as certain aspects of energy co-operation.

"**Future action**. "The participants in the Conference think that it has contributed to a broader understanding of the international economic situation and that its intensive discussions have been useful to all participants. They agreed that CIEC was only one phase in the ongoing dialogue between developed and developing countries which should continue to be pursued actively in the UN system and other existing, appropriate bodies.

"The members of the Conference agreed to . . . recommend that intensive consideration of outstanding problems be continued within the United Nations system and other existing, appropriate bodies.

"The participants in the Conference pledged themselves to carry out in a timely and effective manner the measures for international co-operation agreed to herein. They invite the countries which did not participate in the Conference to join in this co-operative effort."

D8.9—Adoption of IEA Oil Import Ceiling for 1985

The Governing Board of the International Energy Agency, meeting in Paris at ministerial level on Oct. 6, 1977, adopted (i) 12 "principles for energy policy" (◊**B3.4**) and (ii) the following resolution on the fixing of "group objectives" regarding future oil import volumes.

"The Governing Board, considering:

"That the world is confronted with the serious risk that as early as the 1980s it will not have sufficient oil and other forms of energy available at reasonable prices unless present energy policies are strengthened;

"That such a situation would have severe economic, social and political repercussions in all IEA countries and throughout the world;

"That IEA countries must help reduce this risk by a strong and sustained policy response designed to make more effective use of energy resources and put more emphasis on less depletable energy sources;

"That prompt action in this regard should be a major and essential element of IEA countries' energy policies in the development of their general economic strategy, taking into account environmental and safety aspects of the use of energy resources;

"That the policy response of IEA countries should be concerted, having regard to the consequences of action in individual IEA countries for energy supply and demand in other countries, and taking into account the provisions of the agreement on an international energy programme and the long-term co-operation programme;

"Decides:

"(1) That, in order to maintain equilibrium in energy market conditions, it will be the objective of IEA countries as a group to hold their total oil imports, [excluding bunkers], to not more than 26,000,000 bpd in 1985; and that they will establish group objectives for successive periods;

"(2) That, in order to achieve the group objectives, IEA countries will reinforce their present efforts:

"(a) by endorsing the Agency's principles for energy policy, which IEA countries are determined to follow in the establishment and implementation of national energy policies;

"(b) by contributing, as individual IEA countries, to the achievement of the group objectives through the energy policies and measures which they adopt;

"(c) by reviewing systematically each year within the review process of the International Energy Agency: (i) the contribution of IEA countries to the achievement of the group objectives referred to in paragraph (1); (ii) the continuing validity of the group objectives; and (iii) the need for establishment of objectives for later years, taking account (i) of IEA countries' individual circumstances (including the timing considered appropriate for the implementation of energy policies), (ii) of the IEA principles for energy policy and (iii) of the need for ensuring equivalence of effort among all IEA countries;

"(d) by accepting the need to further strengthen—by national action supplemented where appropriate by concrete measures for international co-operation and solidarity with due regard for the financial and technological implications—their policies and measures as may be necessary to meet the group objectives, taking into account the results of the reviews in the International Energy Agency."

D8.10—United States Energy Developments in 1977

D8.10.i—Policy statement by President Carter

President Carter made a nationwide address on April 18, 1977, drawing attention to the consequences of continued failure to implement a comprehensive national energy plan of similar scope to the plans proposed by Presidents Nixon and Ford in the aftermath of the oil supply constraints and price rises of 1973–74 but subsequently largely abandoned for want of backing within Congress ($\Diamond$**D6.12**). Urgent action was, he said, required to balance US energy demand with "our rapidly shrinking resources" if the country was to control its future "rather than letting the future control us". Domestic oil and gas production had, he said, been "dropping steadily at the rate of about 6 per cent a year", while imports had doubled over the past five years, with the result that "our nation's independence of economic and political action is becoming increasingly constrained". Unless immediate action was taken to cut back the growth rate of oil and gas consumption and to develop alternative energy sources, the United States could expect a 33 per cent increase in its energy consumption by 1985 and an annual oil import bill of $550,000 million in that year.

The main targets of President Carter's energy plan for the period to 1985 were outlined as follows: (i) to reduce the growth rate of US energy demand to less than 2 per cent per annum; (ii) to reduce annual gasoline consumption to 90 per cent of its 1977 level; (iii) to reduce the level of US oil imports to 6,600,000 bpd (compared with a currently projected level of 11,500,000 bpd in 1985); (iv) to increase US coal production by about 66 per cent, to more than 1,000 million tonnes per annum; (v) to insulate 90 per cent of the existing housing stock and all new buildings; (vi) to install solar energy systems in more than 2,500,000 houses; and (vii) to establish a strategic petroleum reserve of 1,000 million barrels (equivalent to more than six months' net imports). (Legislation to create a strategic petroleum reserve had been enacted in 1975. Oil began to be imported to fill strategic storage facilities—i.e. underground caverns in Texas and Louisiana—in July 1977).

On the following day (April 19) President Carter released a report by the US Central Intelligence Agency which predicted that by 1985 (i) the Soviet Union and Eastern Europe would have an oil requirement of between 3,500,000 bpd and 4,500,000 bpd (as against a current export capability of around 1,000,000 bpd); (ii) China would have a negligible oil export capability; and (iii) no potential for increased oil export capacity would exist in OPEC countries other than Saudi Arabia.

On April 20 President Carter presented his detailed energy policy proposals to Congress. The President said that one of the fundamental principles of his energy policy was that the price of energy should reflect its true replacement cost. He therefore proposed to allow the price of newly discovered oil to rise, over a three-year period, to the 1977 world market price, with allowances for inflation, and to "phase in a wellhead tax on existing supplies of domestic oil, equal to the difference between the present controlled price of oil and the world price, and return the money collected by this tax to the consumers and workers of America". The phasing-in of this "crude oil equalization tax" should begin on Jan. 1, 1978. As regards natural gas, the President called for an increase in the federally-controlled ceiling price for inter-state supplies and for the extension of price controls to cover intra-state supplies.

After outlining proposed fuel-switching measures to increase the use of coal, he added: "As a last resort we must continue to use increasing amounts of nuclear energy." In particular he said: "We now have 63 nuclear power plants, producing about 3 per cent of our total energy, and about 70 more are licensed for construction. Domestic uranium supplies can support this number of plants for another 75 years. Effective conservation efforts can minimize the shift towards nuclear power. There is no need to enter the plutonium age by licensing or building a fast-breeder reactor. . . . We must, however, increase our capacity to produce enriched uranium for light water nuclear power plants, using the new centrifuge technology, which consumes only about one-tenth the energy of existing gaseous diffusion plants."

Pointing out that the rate of energy waste in the transportation sector (which currently accounted for 26 per cent of US energy consumption) was as high as 50 per cent, and that Congress had already adopted fuel-efficiency standards requiring new cars to average 27.5 miles per US gallon by 1985 (as against the current average of 18 mpg), the President proposed a graduated excise tax for new cars which did not meet these standards. The proceeds of this tax would be returned to consumers in the form of price rebates on cars whose fuel efficiency surpassed the set standard. For a car doing only 15 mpg the proposed tax would rise from $180 in 1978 to $1,600 in 1985, while for a car doing 11 mpg the tax would rise from $450 to $2,500 over this period.

Other proposals included (i) a standby tax designed to restrain the growth of gasoline consumption; (ii) the removal of a 10 per cent excise tax on inter-city buses (to encourage the use of public transport); (iii) tax credits for home insulation (of 25 per cent on the first $800 spent and 15 per cent on the next $1,400); (iv) tax credits for the installation of solar energy equipment, and expenditure (of up to $100,000,000 over the next three years) for its installation in government buildings; (v) mandatory standards for domestic appliances to increase their efficiency; (vi) the abolition of discounts for large users of electricity; and (vii) lower off-peak domestic rates in certain circumstances.

A final step towards conservation, President Carter said, was to encourage the expansion of "cogeneration" projects to utilize much of the steam currently wasted in generating energy; in the United States, he added, only 4 per cent of the final energy supply came from cogeneration (as against 29 per cent in West Germany).

Further details of the proposed standby gasoline tax were given by the White House energy staff as follows: "If gasoline consumption nationwide in 1978 exceeds the target set for 1978 by 1 per cent or more, a 5 cents per gallon tax will be imposed on Jan. 15, 1979. In any subsequent year, the tax will amount to 5 cents per gallon for each [percentage point] that consumption in the prior year exceeded the target, except that the tax could not be increased or reduced more than 5 cents per year. The tax will rise, remain the same, or fall, depending on the prior year's record. The cumulative amount of taxes applicable in any one year may not exceed 50 cents per gallon. Any funds collected would be rebated to the American people progressively through the federal income-tax system and by direct payments to people who do not pay taxes."

D8.10.ii—Commerce Department's energy forecasts

A new and detailed forecast of US energy developments, prepared by a special task force at the US Department of Commerce, was published early in May 1977. The forecast was based on the assumption that energy consumption in the United States would, in the coming 20 years, grow at the rate of roughly 2 per cent per annum (i.e. at about half the rate of the last few years, and as aimed at by President Carter). In the expectation that conservation efforts and the replacement of oil and gas by coal and nuclear power would produce savings of 11,400,000 barrels of oil equivalent per day in 1985 and nearly 32,000,000 by the year 2000, the report said that total US energy consumption (which was 35,200,000 barrels of oil equivalent per day in 1976) was likely to reach 41,300,000 in 1985 and 54,800,000 in 2000. It was forecast that US oil production would fall to no more than 6,200,000 bpd by 2000, with imports continuing to run at 45–50 per cent of US needs. Natural gas production would also be falling.

The report concluded that there would be no choice other than a massive programme of coal and nuclear power expansion. As electricity would account for more than half of all energy consumption by the year 2000, and requirements until 1985 necessitated the construction of 129 new 1,100 megawatt power plants, another 545 would have to be built in the last 15 years of the century to meet this demand (or one every 12 days between 1978 and 2000).

The report contained a warning that the coming energy challenges would "pose a serious test of the existing institutional structure for handling capital funding and environmental procedures", and it estimated capital requirements for electricity generating capacity alone at almost $500,000 million by the end of the century. It also forecast that by the year 2000 some 26,000,000 cars would have to be powered by something other than gasoline, or that alternative means of transport would have to be provided.

D8.10.iii—North Alaskan oil and gas developments

US energy supply projections made in early 1977 took account of the imminent opening of the trans-Alaskan pipeline (running from the North Slope oilfields to the ice-free port of Valdez). Offloading from the Valdez pipeline terminal commenced on July 29, and the first shipment of Alaskan oil to the lower 48 states was delivered on Aug. 5. The final cost of the 1,284-kilometre pipeline (whose construction had been expedited by the Nixon Government in November 1973) was in the region of $7,700 million, as against an original estimate of $900,000,000. The pipeline had an initial capacity of 1,200,000 bpd (to be increased to 2,000,000 bpd).

Under the November 1973 legislation, the President was empowered to ban the export of oil transported via the pipeline, such a ban being imposed by President Carter in July 1977, partly on the grounds that it was necessary to ensure that the oil industry had an incentive to build new long-distance pipelines running inland from the west coast of the lower 48 states. An oil industry proposal for the export of Alaskan oil to Japan (in exchange for the import into the USA of Middle Eastern oil which would otherwise have been shipped to Japan) was moreover held to be unacceptable on both political and technical grounds. It was, however, announced by the Federal Energy Administration on Aug. 12 that North Slope oil would be treated as imported oil for pricing purposes, and could therefore be invoiced to refiners in the lower 48 states at the prevailing world market price.

On Sept. 21 the US and Canadian Governments signed an agreement for the construction of a pipeline system to link the extensive North Slope natural gas deposits to the gas distribution networks in Canada and the lower 48 states of the USA. Described as "the largest industrial project in the non-communist world", the system was originally scheduled for completion by the second half of the 1980s. (However, subsequent financing problems caused completion to be put back until the 1990s.)

D8.10.iv—Creation of Department of Energy

Legislation to create a new Department of Energy within the Federal Government, in accordance with proposals submitted by President Carter on March 1, was passed by Congress on Aug. 2 and signed by the President on Aug. 4. Under this legislation the Federal Energy Administration, the Energy Research and Development Administration and the Federal Power Commission were to be abolished as independent agencies, while energy-related responsibilities held by the Department of the Interior, the Bureau of Mines, the Department of Housing and Urban Development, the Commerce Department and the Defense Department were to be wholly or partly taken over by the new Energy Department.

The Energy Department was empowered to gather energy data and to order energy companies to supply information on their reserves and production levels; to supervise all energy conservation programmes and to order compliance with mandatory conservation measures; to exercise jurisdiction over oil pipelines, nuclear waste management, federal energy research and development programmes and strategic petroleum reserves; to administer emergency fuel allocation and rationing programmes; and to play a part in determining the rate of production of energy resources from the outer continental shelf and other federally-administered areas. The fixing of inter-state natural gas prices, which would have come under the Department's direct control if the original government bill had been adopted unchanged, was (as a result of congressional amendments to the bill) vested in an independent regulatory commission within the Department. The commission also took responsibility for the fixing of inter-state electricity supply tariffs. Responsibility for controls on domestic crude oil prices was shared between the regulatory commission and the Secretary of Energy.

D8.11—Statement on Energy by Seven Non-Communist Industrialized Countries

The heads of government of the United States, Japan, West Germany, France, the United Kingdom, Italy and Canada met in London on May 7 and 8, 1977, to discuss current international economic developments. A joint statement issued after the meeting included the following section on energy:

"We welcome the measures taken by a number of governments to increase energy conservation. The increase in demand for energy and oil imports continues at a rate which places excessive pressure on the world's depleting hydrocarbon resources. We agree, therefore, on the need to do everything possible to strengthen our efforts still further.

"We are committed to national and joint efforts to limit energy demand and to increase and diversify supplies. There will need to be greater exchanges of technology and joint research and development aimed at more efficient energy use, improved recovery and use of coal and other conventional resources, and the development of new energy sources.

"Increasing reliance will have to be placed on nuclear energy to satisfy growing energy requirements and to help diversify sources of energy. This should be done with the utmost precaution with respect to the generation and dissemination of material that can be used for nuclear weapons. Our objective is to meet the world's energy needs and to make peaceful use of nuclear energy widely available, while avoiding the danger of the spread of nuclear weapons. We are also agreed that, in order to be effective, non-proliferation policies should, so far as possible, be acceptable to both industrialized and developing countries alike. To this end we are undertaking a preliminary analysis, to be completed within two months, of the best means of advancing these objectives, including the study of terms of reference for international fuel cycle evaluation.

"The oil-importing countries have special problems both in securing and in paying for the energy supplies needed to sustain their economic development programmes. They require additional help in expanding their domestic energy production and to this end we hope the World Bank, as its resources grow, will give special emphasis to projects that serve this purpose.

"We intend to do our utmost to ensure, during this transitional period, that the energy market functions harmoniously, in particular through strict conservation measures and the development of all our energy resources. We hope very much that the oil-producing countries will take these efforts into account and will make their contribution as well.

"We believe that these activities are essential to enable all countries to have continuing energy supplies now and for the future at reasonable prices consistent with sustained non-inflationary economic growth; and we intend through all useful channels to concert our policies in continued consultation and co-operation with each other and with other countries."

D9—1978

D9.1—Annual Statistical Survey

D9.1.i—Oil production and reserves

World

Total production .... 63,050,000 bpd (3,092.9 million tonnes)
  Change over 1977 .... +0.8 per cent

End-year proved reserves .... 649,300 million barrels
  Change over end-1977 .... −0.6 per cent

Reserves:production ratio .... 28.2 : 1

Regional shares:

	In 1978 world production*			In end-1978 world reserves†		
	Regional total (million tonnes)	Change over 1977 (per cent)	Share of world total (per cent)	Reserves (thousand million barrels)	Change over 1977 (per cent)	Share of world total (per cent)
Middle East	1,058.8	−5.0	34.2	369.6	+1.0	56.9
USSR/Eastern Europe/China	697.7	+3.1	22.6	94.0	−4.1	14.5
North America	562.5	+3.7	18.2	42.0	−3.2	6.5
Africa	295.9	−2.9	9.6	57.9	−2.2	8.9
Latin America/ Caribbean	251.4	+5.4	8.1	41.5	+3.2	6.4
Asia‡/Australasia	137.0	−0.6	4.4	20.0	+1.5	3.1
Western Europe§	89.6	+28.6	2.9	24.3	−10.7	3.7

*Including production from oil shales, tar sands and natural gas liquids (NGL).
†Excluding oil shales and tar sands; including NGL in North America.
‡Excluding China.
§Including Yugoslavia.

OPEC

OPEC oil production .... 30,275,000 bpd (1,494.6 million tonnes)
  Change over 1977 .... −4.5 per cent
  Share of 1978 world total .... 48.3 per cent

OPEC end-year proved reserves .... 445,165 million barrels
  Change over 1977 .... +1.2 per cent
  Share of 1978 world total .... 68.6 per cent

OPEC reserves:production ratio .... 40.3 : 1

OPEC (continued)

OPEC member countries' production:

	1978 production		Change over 1977 (per cent)	Share of world total (per cent)	Share of OPEC total (per cent)
	(million tonnes)	(thousand bpd)			
Algeria	57.2	1,230	+6.9	1.8	3.8
Ecuador	10.0	205	+9.9	0.3	0.7
Gabon	10.5	210	−5.4	0.3	0.7
Indonesia	81.0	1,635	−3.0	2.6	5.4
Iran	262.3	5,275	−7.5	8.5	17.5
Iraq	125.7	2,560	+9.1	4.1	8.4
Kuwait	97.0	1,945	+6.0	3.1	6.5
Libya	95.5	1,985	−3.9	3.1	6.5
Nigeria	93.9	1,895	−9.4	3.0	6.3
Qatar	23.6	485	+9.3	0.8	1.6
Saudi Arabia	409.8	8,315	−9.9	13.2	27.4
UAE*	88.8	1,830	−8.6	2.9	5.9
Venezuela	115.4	2,235	−3.4	3.7	7.7
Neutral Zone†	23.9	470	+14.9	0.8	1.6

*Of which Abu Dhabi 69,700,000 tonnes (1,450,000 bpd), Dubai 18,000,000 tonnes (360,000 bpd), Sharjah 1,100,000 tonnes (20,000 bpd).
†Production shared between Kuwait and Saudi Arabia.

Non-OPEC

Selected non-OPEC countries' oil production:

	1978 production		Change over 1977 (per cent)	Share of world total (per cent)
	(million tonnes)	(thousand bpd)		
USSR	572.5	11,595	+4.9	18.5
USA*	488.1	10,270	+4.5	15.8
China	104.1	2,090	+11.2	3.4
Canada	74.4	1,575	−1.7	2.4
Mexico	66.0	1,330	+22.9	2.1
United Kingdom	53.3	1,095	+42.1	1.7
Egypt	24.2	480	+15.2	0.8
Argentina	23.6	455	+4.9	0.8
Norway	17.2	350	+27.4	0.5
Oman	15.8	315	−7.6	0.5
Total	1,439.2	29,555	+6.8	46.5

*Of which natural gas liquids 55,700,000 tonnes (1,565,000 bpd).

D9.1.ii—Oil consumption

World

Total consumption .... 63,140,000 bpd (3,083 million tonnes)
  Change over 1977 .... +3.3 per cent

Regional distribution of total:

	1978 consumption		Change over 1977 (per cent)	Share of world total (per cent)
	(million tonnes)	(thousand bpd)		
North America	975.7	20,090	+2.5	31.7
Western Europe*	716.5	14,660	+2.8	23.2
USSR/Eastern Europe/China	602.8	12,225	+4.3	19.6
Asia†/Australasia	442.3	9,080	+3.4	14.3
Latin America/ Caribbean	201.4	4,175	+4.1	6.5
Middle East	81.5	1,620	+3.3	2.7
Africa	62.8	1,290	+5.9	2.0

*Including Yugoslavia.
†Excluding China.

Selected countries

	1978 consumption		Change over 1977 (per cent)	Share of world total (per cent)
	(million tonnes)	(thousand bpd)		
USA	888.8	18,255	+2.6	28.8
USSR	419.2	8,480	+4.9	13.6
Japan	262.7	5,420	+0.9	8.5
West Germany	142.7	2,960	+4.1	4.6
France	119.0	2,445	+3.8	3.9
Italy	99.8	2,015	+3.9	3.2
United Kingdom	94.0	1,930	+2.2	3.1
Canada	86.9	1,835	+1.5	2.8
China	84.7	1,705	+3.3	2.7
Spain	46.4	955	+2.0	1.5
Total	2,244.2	46,000	+3.0	72.7

D9.1.iii—Oil refining

World

Total refinery capacity .... 78,575,000 bpd
  Change over 1977 .... +3.5 per cent

Total refinery throughputs .... 60,675,000 bpd
  Change over 1977 .... +3.5 per cent

Consumption as proportion of capacity 80.4 per cent

Selected markets

Consumption of refined product types and change over 1977:

	USA		Western Europe		Japan	
	(million tonnes)	(per cent)	(million tonnes)	(per cent)	(million tonnes)	(per cent)
Gasolines	338.3	+2.7	145.9	+9.9	45.7	+2.5
Middle distillates	232.1	+3.5	254.4	+4.1	60.2	+8.1
Fuel oil	158.4	−1.5	224.5	+1.1	124.5	−3.4
Other	160.0	+5.7	91.7	−1.5	32.3	+3.5
Total	888.8	+2.6	716.5	+2.8	262.7	+0.9

D9.1.iv—Tankers and trade

Tankers

Total world fleet	....	328,500,000 deadweight tons
Change over 1977	....	−1.2 per cent

Trade

Total world crude exports (including re-exports)	....	31,787,800 bpd (1,571.3 million tonnes)
Change over 1977	....	−3.4 per cent
OPEC crude exports	....	26,088,700 bpd (1,289.6 million tonnes)
Change over 1977	....	−5.6 per cent
Share of 1978 world total	....	82.1 per cent
Total world product exports (including re-exports)	....	8,308,100 bpd (423,019,300 tonnes)
Change over 1977	....	+3.2 per cent
OPEC product exports	....	1,888,100 bpd (96,166,000 tonnes)
Change over 1977	....	+7.8 per cent
Share of 1978 world total	....	22.7 per cent

Regional distribution of world oil trade*:

	Share of 1978 imports (per cent)		Share of 1978 exports (per cent)	
	Crude	Products	Crude	Products
USA	21.5	40.7	0.5	4.7
Canada	2.1	1.0	0.8	4.3
Latin America/Caribbean	8.5	4.4	5.2	41.1
Western Europe	41.1	23.9	0.9	5.5
Middle East	0.3	1.0	65.5	15.6
North Africa	0.2	1.6	10.9	2.1
West Africa	†	1.5	7.2	1.2
East and southern Africa	1.6	0.8	—	0.2
South Asia	1.4	1.1	—	0.1
South-East Asia	5.3	6.4	5.0	5.6
Australasia	0.8	2.4	—	1.1
Japan	16.5	10.9	—	0.3
USSR/Eastern Europe/China	0.2	1.5	4.0	18.2
Unspecified	0.5	2.8	—	—
Total	100.0	100.0	100.0	100.0

*Excluding intra-regional trade.
†Negligible.

D9.1.v—World primary energy consumption

Total consumption (excluding
non-commercial fuels) .... 6,704.8 million tonnes oil equivalent (mtoe)
Change over 1977 .... +3.5 per cent

Contributions of primary energy sources:

	Consumption (mtoe)	Change over 1977 (per cent)	Share of total (per cent)
Oil	3,083.0	+3.3	46.0
Coal	1,863.0	+1.8	27.8
Natural gas	1,206.2	+3.8	18.0
Water power	403.1	+7.1	6.0
Nuclear power	149.5	+13.3	2.2

D9.1.vi—Natural gas production and reserves

Marketed production (thousand million cubic metres):

	Regional total (tmcm)	Change over 1977 (per cent)	Share of 1978 world total (per cent)
North America	614.8	−0.6	45.9
Latin America/ Caribbean	45.9	+9.8	3.4
Western Europe*	177.0	+2.6	13.2
USSR/Eastern Europe/China	402.6	+8.9	30.0
Middle East	39.9	+4.7	3.0
Africa	15.3	+23.4	1.1
Asia†/Australasia	45.2	+16.5	3.4
World total	1,340.7	+3.8	100.0
(of which OPEC)	(72.9)	(+13.9)	(5.4)

*Including Yugoslavia.
†Excluding China.

End-year proved reserves (thousand million cubic metres):

	Regional total (tmcm)	Change over 1977 (per cent)	Share of 1978 world total (per cent)
North America	7,342.8	−2.8	10.8
Latin America/ Caribbean	3,230.9	+7.5	4.7
Western Europe*	4,053.2	+3.3	5.9
USSR/Eastern Europe/China	24,287.1	+4.7	35.5
Middle East	20,752.2	+1.8	30.4
Africa	5,249.0	−10.9	7.7
Asia†/Australasia	3,450.6	+3.4	5.0
World total	68,365.8	+1.6	100.0
(of which OPEC)	(27,315.7)	(−1.5)	(40.0)

*Including Yugoslavia.
†Excluding China.

D9.2—The Market Environment in 1978 – Deterioration in OPEC Terms of Trade

In the first half of 1978 demand for OPEC oil was depressed both by the continuing growth of non-OPEC production and by a substantial decline in the level of importing companies' inventories, it being estimated that stocks were being drawn down at around twice the normal seasonal rate (of up to 2,000,000 bpd) at some points during the first three months of the year. Average OPEC production of 28,680,000 bpd in the period January–June 1978 was 8.7 per cent below the average for January–June 1977. There was, however, a progressive increase in demand from July onwards, and OPEC's average daily output over the whole year was equivalent to 95.5 per cent of the 1977 level.

The rate of price inflation in the OECD area averaged 8 per cent in 1978, while the effective exchange rate of the US dollar against other major currencies declined during the course of the year by about 11 per cent, bringing the cumulative depreciation of the dollar since mid-1977 to nearly 20 per cent. The OPEC countries, which in the third quarter of 1977 had become net borrowers of new funds from the international banking system for the first time since 1973, recorded their smallest aggregate balance-of-payments surplus on current account for eight years in 1978 (◊ Table 13), reflecting the reductions which had occurred both in the volume and in the unit purchasing power of their oil exports. Conversely, the fall in the real cost of OPEC oil contributed to an improvement in the aggregate balance-of-payments position of the OECD countries, which showed a current-account surplus of $9,500 million in 1978, as against a deficit of $24,800 million in 1977.

While the OPEC marker price remained unchanged in current dollars between July 1977 and December 1978, estimates published in the US journal *World Oil* indicated a fall in the real value of OPEC oil over this period amounting to 15.2 per cent in terms of the special drawing right, 24.8 per cent if the US dollar was excluded from the SDR "basket" (in which it then had a 33 per cent weighted share) and 17.9 per cent when set against variations in industrialized countries' export prices. Table 43 gives a nine-year index of OPEC terms of trade—calculated by offsetting changes in the average government revenue entitlement/official selling price for marker crude against changes in the wholesale prices of industrialized countries' non-food exports, weighted by these countries' share of OPEC imports —as published by the (US) Morgan Guaranty Trust Company at the end of 1978. According to the OPEC Secretariat, a 360 per cent increase in OPEC countries' aggregate spending on imports between 1973 and 1978 was accompanied by an increase of only 70 per cent in annual import volume. The evolution of OPEC's own index of member countries' unit import costs is shown in Table 44.

Table 43 — Estimated evolution of OPEC terms of trade, 1970 to 1978 (1974=100)

	Oil price index	Import price index	OPEC terms of trade
1970–72	19.0	66.0	28.0
1973	31.0	84.0	37.0
1974	100.0	100.0	100.0
1975	98.4	112.8	87.2
1976	105.7	114.6	92.2
1977	113.9	125.2	91.0
1978 (Jan–Dec.)	116.6	144.0	81.0
1978 (Oct–Dec.)	116.6	151.5	77.0

Table 44 — Evolution of "official" OPEC import price index, 1973 to 1978

Year	Base 1973 = 100*	Base 1974 = 100†
1973	100.0	75.4
1974	132.6	100.0
1975	169.1	127.5
1976	221.0	166.7
1977	262.0	197.6
1978	324.1	244.4

*As published by OPEC.
†Restatement of OPEC figures for comparative purposes.

D9.3—OPEC Developments, January to June 1978

D9.3.i—Pricing issues – Impact of exchange-rate movements

A substantial production cutback by Saudi Arabia—accounting for over half of the drop in OPEC's January–June 1978 output relative to the average for January–June 1977—relieved the downward pressure on OPEC's central marker price in the early months of 1978. By May spot-market realizations for Saudi Arabian 34° crude (which had fallen to around $12.65 per barrel at the end of 1977) were equal to or slightly above the official price of $12.704 per barrel. However, heavy discounting persisted in the spot trade in premium-grade African crudes, and the producers concerned, led by Nigeria (whose economy was particularly vulnerable to a drop in oil revenues), twice cut their official selling prices in response to strong pressure from contract buyers.

Reduced official prices introduced with effect from Jan. 1—involving cuts of 20, 23 and 30 cents respectively for the main Algerian, Libyan and Nigerian crudes—were by March being discounted by up to 25 cents per barrel in spot trading; on April 1 the official prices of the same crudes were further reduced by 15, 12 and 21 cents respectively. The new Algerian price was 20 cents below the January 1977 level, while the Nigerian and Libyan prices were respectively 21 cents and 7 cents lower than in January 1977. Spot prices for African crudes remained stable throughout the second quarter of 1978 (when the average spot realization for Libyan crude was about 15 cents below the new official price).

In South America, Ecuador cut the official selling price of its 30.4° crude by 35 cents per barrel on Jan. 1 and by a further 28.5 cents on April 1. The latter reduction brought the price to $12.365, some 4.9 per cent lower than in January 1977. Venezuela made some downward adjustments in the prices of heavy and extra-heavy crudes during the first half of 1978 but did not alter the prices of its medium and light grades.

Official prices for all grades of Gulf OPEC crude remained unchanged throughout 1978, it being confirmed by Kuwait on Jan. 17 that its reduced price for 31° crude (effective since Sept. 8, 1977 ◊**D8.5**) would continue to apply for the foreseeable future. The OPEC ministerial committee on differentials reviewed the relative prices of medium and heavy crudes at its first meeting on Feb. 1, when ministers noted Kuwait's "special circumstances and difficulties" as a single-grade exporter. Later in February, the Saudi Government ordered Aramco to limit its production of 34° crude to 65 per cent of total production, compared with the previous level of 70 to 80 per cent, as the first phase of a long-range plan to restructure the country's oil exports so as to include a higher proportion of the heavier crudes which made up nearly half of Saudi Arabia's proved reserves.

The most important pricing issue for the OPEC countries during the first half of

1978 concerned the denomination of oil prices in US dollars and the heavy foreign exchange losses which this had entailed since mid-1977 (◊**D9.2**). There was strong pressure for the indexation of the dollar oil price to movements in a basket of currencies (the system used in 1972 and 1973 and proposed, but not implemented, in 1975), while some member countries maintained that any introduction of exchange-rate indexation should be based on a formula under which the dollar would be dropped altogether for invoicing purposes. Kuwait, Iraq and the UAE were at the centre of attempts made in the opening weeks of 1978 to secure support within OPEC for the holding of an extraordinary Conference meeting on oil price indexation.

Saudi Arabia, however, was opposed to any formal OPEC initiative on the exchange rate issue, on the grounds that this would cause a further loss of confidence in the US currency, with disruptive consequences for the world economy. Individual OPEC governments were instead urged to make bilateral representations to the US Government calling for appropriate remedial action to be taken by the US monetary authorities. The Saudi Government made it known in mid-March that King Khaled had sent a "toughly worded" letter to President Carter warning that, while Saudi Arabia would continue to support the maintenance of dollar pricing for OPEC oil, any further deterioration in the value of the dollar might lead the Saudi Government to reconsider its stated opposition to an OPEC price increase in 1978.

D9.3.ii—Establishment of long-term strategy committee – Continuation of OPEC price freeze

It was announced by the OPEC Secretariat on April 18 that Oil Ministers would meet informally in the following month in Taif (the Saudi summer capital, near Mecca) for discussions "without any agenda". A proposal for an informal meeting on matters of long-term strategy (which could not be adequately dealt with at regular OPEC Conference sessions dominated by more immediate issues) was understood to have come originally from Venezuela, but ministers from those countries most strongly in favour of reforming the oil pricing system had made it clear that they intended to raise the (immediate) question of the dollar's decline as the major issue at the meeting.

Two earlier dates had previously been announced for the meeting, which was to have taken place in Geneva. The change of plans was widely attributed to strong pressure from Saudi Arabia, whose main reasons for wishing to delay the meeting and to transfer it to a venue on its own territory were given in the Western press as (i) continuing apprehensions about the international consequences of a "hasty decision" on the role of the dollar, arising in part from the fact that Saudi Arabia had substantial investments in the United States, and (ii) a desire to maintain good bilateral relations with the United States, in view particularly of a pending purchase of US military aircraft (which was subsequently approved by the US Senate on May 15).

Despite a strengthening of the dollar's exchange rate against other major currencies from April 20, following the announcement that auctions of official gold holdings were to be organized by the US Government, some OPEC members continued to maintain that they would press the exchange-rate issue at the Taif meeting, leading Saudi Arabia to issue statements giving the meeting's agenda as "future oil prices against the background of international variables" and specifically excluding any consideration of current pricing problems. It was however stressed by Shaikh Yamani in an interview published on May 1 that, while his Government's oil policies were based principally on economic considerations, its "enthusiasm to help the West and co-operate with the US" would be affected by the outcome of the US Senate's forthcoming vote on aircraft sales to Saudi Arabia.

In the event, the more militant OPEC members were obliged to accept the exclusion of immediate issues from the agenda of the Taif meeting, which took place on May 6 and 7 and concentrated on long-term policies. Shaikh Yamani presented a lengthy justification of the current Saudi Arabian position and went on to forecast the elimination of the current world oil supply surplus by the end of 1979, to be followed by a period of several years of market equilibrium (whose duration would depend partly on the effectiveness of conservation measures by consumers), after which there would be a growing excess of demand over supply and the rate of reserve depletion permitted by OPEC members would become a major issue. Shaikh Yamani was reported to have proposed the introduction, upon the re-emergence of more favourable market conditions, of a system of gradual quarterly OPEC price increases which would "prepare the world for future energy shortages".

It was decided at the end of the meeting to set up a committee of ministers from six member countries—Saudi Arabia, Iran, Iraq, Venezuela, Kuwait and Algeria —to study OPEC's long-term pricing and production strategy. The then Secretary-General of OPEC, Ali Mohammed Jaidah, said that the establishment of the committee, which would "develop a set of principles to guide us through the difficult times of shortage ahead", marked the start of an important new stage in OPEC's development.

The meeting's failure to deal with the immediate problems facing member countries was strongly criticized by the official Algerian news agency in a statement issued on May 13. This condemned "certain member countries" for permitting an erosion of real oil revenues which jeopardized the development plans of Algeria and some other OPEC members, and for displaying more concern for the economic interests of the industrialized countries than the latter countries had displayed towards OPEC in particular and the Third World in general.

At the 51st OPEC Conference meeting, held in Geneva from June 17 to 19, Saudi Arabia (supported principally by Iran and the UAE) argued successfully in favour of a continuing price freeze and against any change in OPEC's pricing system, despite the fact that the US dollar was currently undergoing a further decline after recovering some of its value between mid-April and mid-May. The main advocates of immediate OPEC action on pricing issues were on this occasion Iraq, Libya and Algeria. A brief press statement issued after the meeting made no mention of prices, although it did stress OPEC's "deep concern" regarding "the situation related to the fluctuation in international exchange rates", which was to be studied by a "high-level committee of experts" chaired by the Kuwaiti Oil Minister (as the current President of the Conference).

One session of the 51st Conference meeting was devoted to a discussion of the scope for co-ordinated production cutbacks in support of market prices, although in view of its sensitive nature this topic did not form part of the formal agenda of the meeting. The fact that it had been discussed remained secret for some months until several delegates chose to reveal that a "non-binding six-month agreement" had been reached under which some member countries had indicated their willingness to make voluntary production cuts in order to hasten the elimination of the current supply surplus.

The inaugural meeting of OPEC's long-term strategy committee took place immediately after the end of the full Conference meeting. According to the Venezuelan delegate, the questions considered by the committee included the opening of discussions with the major oil-importing countries on the long-term supply and pricing of oil.

D9.4—Upward Pressure on Oil Prices, July to December 1978

During the third quarter of 1978 OPEC production rose to an average 30,400,000 bpd in response to a sustained upturn in export demand. Spot prices exceeded the official prices for all grades of OPEC crude by August, removing any pressure for the implementation of the voluntary price support measures which had been informally discussed during the 51st Conference meeting. The largest spot premiums were realized for light crudes, a significant influence on the market being an unexpectedly large increase in gasoline consumption (particularly in the United States) at a time when the availability of incremental supplies of light crude was limited by Saudi Arabia's recently-imposed proportionate output ceiling for its 34° grade (◊**D9.3.i**).

An acceleration of the rate of increase of world oil demand became apparent towards the end of the third quarter as importers began an unusually early pre-winter build-up of their oil stocks, which had been heavily depleted during the first half of the year (◊**D9.2**). Stock-building was further stimulated (i) by additions to strategic reserves (particularly in the United States and Japan) and (ii) by expectations of an OPEC price increase at the beginning of 1979. In the latter respect, Saudi Arabia had indicated during August that it was prepared to accept an increase in order to reduce the tensions which had built up within the Organization as a result of Saudi opposition to an OPEC initiative on the exchange-rate issue.

The special OPEC committee on exchange-rate fluctuations, comprising over 30 financial experts representing every member country except Algeria, held its first meeting in London from July 14 to 17 under the chairmanship of Kuwait's Oil Minister, Shaikh Ali Khalifa al Sabah. It was followed immediately by the second meeting of the ministerial committee on long-term strategy. Subsequent press reports indicated that the exchange-rate committee had formally recommended the indexation of oil prices to movements in a basket of currencies, but that Shaikh Yamani (who chaired the meeting of the long-term strategy committee) had made it clear to Shaikh Ali Khalifa al Sabah (who was responsible for assessing OPEC governments' reaction to this recommendation) that Saudi Arabia would continue to oppose the calling of an extraordinary Conference meeting on this issue. Similar opposition to any action which might result in a further erosion of international confidence in the US dollar was reportedly expressed by the Iranian member of the long-term strategy committee (the maintenance of close relations with the United States being a matter of considerable importance to the Shah's increasingly beleaguered Government).

Clear signals that Iran and Saudi Arabia would accept an OPEC price increase after the end of 1978 were given in statements made by the Shah on Aug. 10 and by Shaikh Yamani on Aug. 20. At the same time Shaikh Yamani indicated the Saudi Government's preference that such an increase should be planned on the basis of longer-term market projections and should be implemented in phases.

In September average OPEC production reached 32,000,000 bpd, 7 per cent above the level of August 1978 and 2.5 per cent above that of September 1977. During the remainder of 1978 there was a progressive decline in OPEC's average monthly output (which stood at around 30,550,000 bpd in December), although the fourth-quarter average remained above that for the third quarter. At the same time world oil demand continued to increase, and by November was beginning to approach the level of available supplies.

OPEC's export capacity was adversely affected by disruptive action on the part of Iranian oil workers, who assumed an increasingly important role in the campaign to overthrow the Shah's regime (◊**C5.3.vi**). Iranian production, which had reached an average 6,060,000 bpd in the month to Sept. 23, was at first subject to fairly moderate cutbacks when small-scale disruption commenced on the following day. Heavy cutbacks began to occur at the end of October, after which the country's output fluctuated considerably, generally at levels well below normal, until on Dec. 26 it fell to less than half of Iran's domestic requirement and all oil exports ceased (a call for the halting of exports having been made on Nov. 23 by the then-exiled Ayatollah Khomeini).

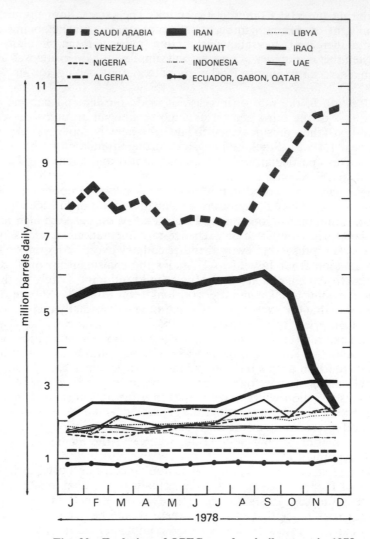

Fig. 20—Evolution of OPEC members' oil output in 1978

In Saudi Arabia, Aramco was authorized to treat its official production ceiling of 8,500,000 bpd as an average for the whole of 1978, and accordingly increased its output (which had averaged 7,670,000 bpd over the first nine months of the year) to 8,882,600 bpd in October, 9,645,700 bpd in November and 10,020,000 bpd in December. Smaller production increases were made in several other OPEC countries where surplus capacity was available (◊ Fig. 20). Outside the OPEC area, north Alaskan output had already reached the current throughput limit of the trans-Alaskan pipeline (◊**D8.10.iii**), while existing capacity development programmes in the Mexican and North Sea oilfields provided little scope to effect a sudden production increase in response to an unforeseen tightening of the market.

Spot-market premiums, which had averaged around 10 cents per barrel for both Gulf and African crudes during September, had reached levels of around $2.25 per barrel for Gulf crudes and more than $2.50 per barrel for African crudes by early December. Correspondingly large upward revisions were made in most Western forecasts of the likely extent of OPEC's year-end price increase, in which connexion it was widely noted (i) that Saudi Arabia's ability to impose a policy of price moderation had been undermined by the virtual elimination of the country's surplus production capacity and (ii) that the Shah's Government in Iran was now anxious to maximize its unit oil revenues in order to finance the higher wages promised to strikers in many sectors and to offset some of the current loss of export earnings. It was further noted that the signature on Sept. 17 of the US-sponsored Camp David agreements, which provided the basis for a peace treaty between Egypt and Israel, had led to a cooling of relations between the United States and Saudi Arabia, and that Saudi Arabia's participation in the subsequent Arab summit conference on the agreements, held in Baghdad from Oct. 24 to 26, implied a strengthening of its relations with the more radical Arab states, including Iraq and Libya (the leading advocates of a substantial OPEC price rise).

Statements calling for a continued OPEC price freeze were nevertheless made by representatives of major oil-consuming countries, among whom Dr Guido Brunner, the European Community's Commissioner for Energy, was reported on Oct. 27 as saying that "a price increase at this stage is not warranted by the market situation" and that the decline in the international value of the US dollar was "not on its own a good enough reason for a rise in prices in the oil sector". In the United States, President Carter said on Nov. 20 that "any unwarranted increase" in oil prices would have "a destabilizing effect on inflation throughout the world", adding that through domestic anti-inflation proposals which he had put forward on Oct. 24, together with dollar support measures which had been announced on Nov. 1, the US Government would take the lead in correcting the international currency instability which had been cited by OPEC members as one major ground for a substantial price rise.

Immediately prior to the 52nd OPEC Conference meeting Saudi Arabia and other "moderate" members sought to strengthen the basis for a compromise on pricing designed to avert a renewed confrontation with the more militant members. The main features of the compromise were understood to have been finalized during a meeting of the OAPEC Council of Ministers, held in Abu Dhabi on Dec. 12. They involved Saudi Arabia's acceptance, on the basis of prevailing market conditions, of the minimum overall increase for 1979 acceptable to the most militant members, while the latter accepted Saudi Arabia's proposal (supported in particular by Venezuela and Kuwait) that such an increase should be implemented in gradual stages during the year and agreed to defer any action on the exchange-rate issue.

D9.5—Decisions of 52nd OPEC Conference Meeting

The main sections of the press statement issued at the conclusion of the 52nd OPEC Conference meeting (held in Abu Dhabi on Dec. 16 and 17) were as follows:

"The Conference reviewed the report of the Economic Commission Board and noted with great anxiety the high rate of inflation and dollar depreciation sustained over the last two years, and hence the substantial erosion in the oil revenues of the member countries, and its adverse effects on their economic and social development. However, in order to assist the world economy to grow further, and also in order to support the current efforts towards strengthening the US dollar and arresting the inflationary trends, the Conference has decided to correct only partially the price of oil by an amount of 10 per cent on average over the year 1979. Moreover, as a gesture of goodwill, the Conference has decided that this correction be broken down into the following quarterly adjustments on a cumulative basis: 5 per cent on Jan. 1, 1979; 3.809 per cent on April 1, 1979; 2.294 per cent on July 1, 1979; and 2.691 per cent on Oct. 1, 1979.

"For example, the application of those adjustments on the marker crude would yield the following prices: $13.335 [per barrel] as from Jan. 1; $13.843 as from April 1; $14.161 as from July 1; and $14.542 as from Oct. 1.

"The Conference, on the other hand, notes that should inflation and currency instability continue, thus adversely affecting the oil revenues of member countries and encouraging the wasteful use of this important but depletable resource, the Conference will find it imperative to adjust fully for the effects of such inflation and dollar depreciation."

The average marker price planned for 1979 was thus $13.968 per barrel, the scheduled fourth-quarter price of $14.542 being about 14.5 per cent above the current official price of $12.704 for Saudi Arabian 34° crude. Spot-market prices for the same crude were approaching $15 per barrel at the time of the 52nd Conference meeting.

The meeting was also understood to have discussed the question of relative values and to have reached a broad agreement in principle to apply the 1979 price increases to individual grades of crude in such a way as to widen the differentials between heavier and lighter grades. It was stated by Shaikh Yamani on Dec. 17 that importers would be well advised to "reconsider [their] investment policies and build refineries which can process heavy crudes, since these will become progressively less expensive than lighter grades".

Shaikh Yamani also said that the planned quarterly phasing-in of the 1979 price increase would prevent both "a sudden shock to the world economy" and also "speculation at the end of the year, when certain oil companies resort to over-lifting". He indicated Saudi Arabia's willingness to defend the new price levels by "bearing the burden alone" if an OPEC production cutback was needed during 1979 in consequence of any renewed supply surplus which might emerge after the stabilization of the political situation in Iran.

Although OPEC's planned 1979 price increase was smaller than had been forecast by some Western observers, it was strongly criticized in industrialized countries.

In the United States the White House issued the following statement on Dec. 17: "We regret OPEC's decision and hope that it will be reconsidered before the next steps take effect. Market conditions do not warrant price increases of this magnitude, since the current tightness in the world oil market is a temporary situation that does not reflect underlying demand forces. This large price hike will impede the programmes to maintain world economic recovery and to reduce inflation. Responsibility for the success of these programmes is shared by the oil-producing countries."

A matter of some concern to industrialized countries (particularly the United States) was reported to be OPEC's adoption of a system of phased quarterly increments, which was seen as the possible precursor of a mechanism for the automatic linkage of oil prices to an inflation index; on the other hand some governments, including that of France, welcomed the incremental approach as allowing smoother economic adjustment to the increase.

In an interview with the official Kuwait news agency on Dec. 21, the OPEC Secretary-General-elect, Rene G. Ortiz, described the Conference's pricing decision as "a very moderate and responsible move" made "after a thorough study of the economic situation in both the industrialized and OPEC nations", and added that further action could be taken by OPEC ministers at any time "if the international economy deteriorates rapidly". Also on Dec. 21, Shaikh Yamani said that industrialized countries' criticisms of OPEC were "unjustifiable" and that the increased price of oil would "provide a strong incentive towards exploration in new areas".

Table 45 shows the increases in official selling prices announced by individual OPEC member countries with effect from Jan. 1, 1979, when the new marker price became $13.339 per barrel (and not $13.335 as announced in OPEC's Dec. 17 press statement, which had given examples based on a 1978 marker value of $12.70).

Table 45—Price changes for selected OPEC crudes from Jan. 1, 1979

	December 1978	January 1979	Increase
	(dollars per barrel)		(per cent)
Algeria (44°)	14.10	14.805	5.0
Ecuador (30.4°*)	12.365	13.03	5.4
Gabon (31.8°)	13.03	13.67	4.9
Indonesia (34°)	13.55	13.90	2.6
Iran (31°)	12.49	13.06	4.6
(34°)	12.81	13.45	5.0
Iraq (35°†)	12.58	13.21	5.0
(36°)	12.77	13.41	5.0
Kuwait (31°)	12.27	12.83	4.6
Libya (40°)	13.85	14.69	6.1
Nigeria (37°)	14.10	14.80	5.0
Qatar (40°)	13.19	14.03	6.4
Saudi Arabia (27°)	12.016	12.511	4.1
(31°)	12.323	12.886	4.6
(34°)	12.704	13.339	5.0
(39°)	13.225	14.06	6.3
UAE: Abu Dhabi (39°)	13.26	14.10	6.3
Dubai (32°)	12.64	13.27	5.0
Venezuela (34°)	13.99	14.69	5.0

*29.7° API with effect from Jan. 1, 1979.

†34° API with effect from Jan. 1, 1979.

D9.6—Statement on Energy Policy by Seven Non-Communist Industrialized Countries

The heads of government of the United States, West Germany, France, Japan, the United Kingdom, Italy and Canada, whose previous economic summit conference had taken place in London in May 1977 (◊D8.11), held a further such meeting in Bonn on July 16 and 17, 1978, at which the European Commission was also represented. A joint statement issued at the end of the meeting included the following section on energy issues:

"In spite of some improvement, the present energy situation remains unsatisfactory. Much more needs to be done.

"We are committed to reduce our dependence on imported oil.

"We note that the European Community has already agreed at [a heads of government meeting held in] Bremen [on July 6 and 7] the following objectives for 1985: to reduce the Community's dependence on imported energy to 50 per cent, to limit net oil imports and to reduce to 0.8 the ratio between the rate of increase in energy consumption and the rate of increase in gross domestic product." [A report published in October by the European Commission made it clear that progress to date towards the achievement of the Community's import dependence target for 1985—which had first been set in December 1974 ◊D5.10—had occurred as a result of economic recession rather than specific action to limit oil imports.]

"Recognizing its particular responsibility in the energy field, the United States will reduce its dependence on imported oil. The US will have in place by the end of the year a comprehensive policy framework within which this effort can be urgently carried forward. By year-end, measures will be in effect that will result in oil import savings of approximately 2,500,000 barrels per day by 1985. In order to achieve these goals, the US will establish a strategic oil reserve of 1,000 million barrels; it will increase coal production by two-thirds; it will maintain the ratio between growth in gross national product and growth in energy demand at or below 0.8; and its oil consumption will grow more slowly than energy consumption. The volume of oil imported in 1978 and 1979 should be less than that imported in 1977. In order to discourage excessive consumption of oil and to encourage the movement toward coal, the US remains determined that the prices paid for oil in the US shall be raised to the world level by the end of 1980.

"We hope that the oil-exporting countries will continue to contribute to a stable world energy situation.

"Looking to the longer term, our countries will review their national energy programmes with a view to speeding them up. General energy targets can serve as useful measures of the progress achieved.

"Private and public investment to produce energy and to use it more efficiently within the industrialized world should be increased. This can contribute significantly to economic growth.

"The further development of nuclear energy is indispensable, and the slippage in the execution of nuclear power programmes must be reversed. To promote the peaceful use of nuclear energy and reduce the risk of nuclear proliferation, the nuclear fuel cycle studies initiated at the London summit should be pursued. The President of the United States and the Prime Minister of Canada have expressed their [countries'] firm intention to continue as reliable suppliers of nuclear fuel within the framework of effective safeguards. The President intends to use the full powers of his office to prevent any interruption of enriched uranium supply and to ensure that existing agreements will be respected. The Prime Minister intends that there shall be no interruption of Canadian uranium supply on the basis of effective safeguards.

"Coal should play an increasingly important role in the long term.

"Joint or co-ordinated energy research and development should be carried out to hasten the development of new, including renewable, energy sources and the more efficient use of existing sources.

"In energy development, the environment and human safety of the population must be safeguarded with greatest care.

"To help developing countries, we will intensify our national development assistance programmes in the energy field and we will develop a co-ordinated effort to bring into use renewable energy technologies and to elaborate the details within one year. We suggest that the OECD will provide the medium for co-operation with other countries.

"We stress the need for improvement and co-ordination of assistance for developing countries in the energy field. We suggest that the World Bank explore ways in which its activities in this field can be made increasingly responsive to the needs of the developing countries, and to examine whether new approaches, particularly to financing hydrocarbon exploration, would be useful."

D9.7—Enactment of US National Energy Bill

Several related pieces of energy legislation were enacted on Nov. 9, 1978, after 18 months' congressional consideration of the energy plan submitted by President Carter in April 1977 (◊D8.10.i). Five separate bills were approved by the Senate between July 18 and Oct. 15, 1978, all five bills—known collectively as the National Energy Bill—being approved by the House of Representatives on Oct. 15. Many of the detailed legislative proposals originally submitted by the President had been substantially accepted by the House of Representatives in August 1977 but had been significantly amended during their subsequent passage through the Senate. According to the Federal Energy Department, the effect of the new legislation would be to reduce the country's 1985 oil imports (originally projected as 11,500,000 bpd) by between 2,400,000 and 2,900,000 bpd, compared with the President's target of a saving of 4,900,000 bpd. The main provisions of the National Energy Act were as follows:

Natural gas. Federal price controls on "new" gas were to end at the beginning of 1985. Until the end of 1984 price controls were to be extended to cover intra-state as well as inter-state gas sales, and the ceiling price of new gas would increase as follows: on enactment from $1.50 per thousand cubic feet (28.3 cubic metres) to about $2.09, and thereafter annually by an amount equal to the inflation rate plus 3.7 percentage points until April 20, 1981, and from then until Dec. 31, 1984, annually in accordance with the inflation rate plus 4.2 percentage points. During a two-year period from July 1985 the President or Congress would be able to reimpose controls for up to 18 months if deregulation appeared to be resulting in unduly rapid increases in gas prices.

"New" gas was defined as that produced since April 20, 1977, either 2.5 miles (4.1 kilometres) away from, or 1,000 feet (308 metres) deeper than, an existing well, or from a reservoir which had not produced gas in commercial quantities. Offshore gas would be treated as new if it came from a lease acquired after April 20, 1977.

[Inter-state sales of natural gas had been subject to federal price controls since 1954 ($\Diamond$**A2.5**). "Old" gas had recently sold for as little as 9 cents per thousand cubic feet — equivalent to an oil price of 54 cents per barrel—under some long-term contracts.]

The Act also contained provisions designed to make large industrial users pay most of the cost of the higher gas prices, with the aim of lessening the economic impact on domestic users, hospitals and schools, and to give industry an incentive to switch to other forms of energy.

Utility tariffs. The regulatory authorities in the individual states were urged to ensure that the energy supply tariffs of public utilities conformed to conservationist criteria (e.g. by incorporating differential rates for the supply of electricity at times of peak and off-peak demand). Utilities whose tariff structures were queried on conservation grounds would be required to justify their policies (although the federal authorities had no power to impose tariff changes). In certain circumstances the Energy Department was to have the authority to order power-sharing arrangements between different utility companies.

Fuel-switching. Most electricity generating plants whose construction had begun since April 20, 1977, were required to use a fuel other than oil or gas. Existing gas-burning plants were required to switch to coal by 1990. The Energy Department was authorized to ban the use of oil by power plants which had the capability to switch to coal.

Conservation. The Energy Department was authorized to set new efficiency standards for 13 types of appliance, including air conditioners, refrigerators, furnaces and dishwashers. Other provisions were: increased penalties on car manufacturers whose products did not meet federal fuel efficiency standards; grants and low-interest loans to help low- and moderate-income families to insulate their homes; a three-year aid programme of $900,000,000 to help schools and hospitals to make their facilities more energy-efficient and an additional $65,000,000 for the same purpose in respect of public buildings; and additional money for federal buildings to demonstrate solar energy equipment. Public utilities were required to give customers information about energy-saving equipment.

Taxation measures. A graduated excise tax was imposed on motor manufacturers whose cars, starting with 1980 models, did not meet federal fuel-efficiency standards. In 1980 the tax would be $200 for a car doing between 14 and 15 miles per gallon; $300 for one doing between 13 and 14 mpg; and $550 for one doing less than 13 mpg. The mileage threshold would rise annually from 17 mpg for 1981 models to 22.5 mpg for 1986 and later models, while by the latter date the tax on a car which averaged less than 12.5 mpg would be $3,850. The Act also provided a 15 per cent tax credit for the first $2,000 spent by home owners and tenants in installing insulation or other energy conservation equipment. Other tax credits were authorized for the installation of solar, geothermal or wind energy equipment.

President Carter's proposals for the accelerated decontrol of domestic crude oil prices and for the introduction of a standby gasoline tax and a crude oil equalization tax were rejected by Congress.

D10—1979

D10.1—Annual Statistical Survey

D10.1.i—Oil production and reserves

World

Total production	65,775,000 bpd (3,225.4 million tonnes)
Change over 1978	+4.3 per cent
End-year proved reserves	649,800 million barrels
Change over end-1978	+0.08 per cent
Reserves:production ratio	27.1 : 1

Regional shares:

	In 1979 world production*			In end-1979 world reserves†		
	Regional total (million tonnes)	Change over 1978 (per cent)	Share of world total (per cent)	Reserves (thousand million barrels)	Change over 1978 (per cent)	Share of world total (per cent)
Middle East	1,081.0	+2.1	33.5	361.8	−2.1	55.7
USSR/Eastern Europe/China	712.2	+2.1	22.1	90.0	−4.3	13.8
North America	564.7	+0.4	17.5	40.8	−2.9	6.3
Africa	328.6	+11.1	10.2	57.1	−1.4	8.8
Latin America/ Caribbean	280.0	+11.4	8.7	57.1	+37.6	8.8
Asia‡/Australasia	142.4	+3.9	4.4	19.4	−3.0	3.0
Western Europe§	116.5	+30.0	3.6	23.6	−2.9	3.6

*Including production from oil shales, tar sands and natural gas liquids (NGL).
†Excluding oil shales and tar sands; including NGL in North America.
‡Excluding China.
§Including Yugoslavia.

OPEC

OPEC oil production	31,470,000 bpd (1,552.8 million tonnes)
Change over 1978	+3.9 per cent
Share of 1979 world total	48.1 per cent
OPEC end-year proved reserves	436,245 million barrels
Change over 1978	−2 per cent
Share of 1979 world total	67.1 per cent
OPEC reserves:production ratio	38 : 1

OPEC (continued)

OPEC member countries' production:

	1979 production		Change over 1978 (per cent)	Share of world total (per cent)	Share of OPEC total (per cent)
	(million tonnes)	(thousand bpd)			
Algeria	58.5	1,255	+2.3	1.8	3.8
Ecuador	10.5	215	+5.0	0.3	0.7
Gabon	10.2	205	−2.9	0.3	0.6
Indonesia	78.8	1,590	−2.7	2.4	5.1
Iran	158.1	3,175	−39.7	4.9	10.2
Iraq	170.6	3,475	+35.7	5.3	11.0
Kuwait	113.2	2,270	+16.7	3.5	7.3
Libya	100.7	2,090	+5.4	3.1	6.5
Nigeria	114.2	2,300	+21.6	3.5	7.3
Qatar	24.7	510	+4.7	0.8	1.6
Saudi Arabia	469.9	9,555	+14.7	14.6	30.2
UAE*	88.6	1,835	−0.3	2.7	5.7
Venezuela	125.4	2,425	+8.7	3.9	8.1
Neutral Zone†	29.4	570	+23.0	0.9	1.9

*Of which Abu Dhabi 70,300,000 tonnes (1,465,000 bpd), Dubai 17,600,000 tonnes (355,000 bpd), Sharjah 700,000 tonnes (15,000 bpd).
†Production shared between Kuwait and Saudi Arabia.

Non-OPEC

Selected non-OPEC countries' oil production:

	1979 production		Change over 1978 (per cent)	Share of world total (per cent)
	(million tonnes)	(thousand bpd)		
USSR	586.0	11,870	+2.4	18.2
USA*	480.9	10,135	−1.5	14.9
China	106.1	2,130	+1.9	3.3
Canada	83.8	1,770	+12.6	2.6
Mexico	80.8	1,630	+22.4	2.5
United Kingdom	77.9	1,600	+46.2	2.4
Egypt	26.5	525	+9.5	0.8
Argentina	24.5	470	+3.8	0.7
Norway	18.8	385	+9.3	0.6
Oman	14.8	295	−6.3	0.5
Total	1,500.1	30,810	+4.2	46.5

*Of which natural gas liquids 56,200,000 tonnes (1,585,000 bpd).

D10.1.ii—Oil consumption

World

Total consumption .... 64,125,000 bpd (3,125 million tonnes)
Change over 1978 .... +1.4 per cent

Regional distribution of total:

	1979 consumption		Change over 1978 (per cent)	Share of world total (per cent)
	(million tonnes)	(thousand bpd)		
North America	958.1	19,825	−1.8	30.7
Western Europe*	733.1	15,010	+2.3	23.4
USSR/Eastern Europe/China	619.2	12,560	+2.7	19.8
Asia†/Australasia	459.1	9,435	+3.8	14.7
Latin America/ Caribbean	214.2	4,440	+6.4	6.9
Middle East	75.4	1,495	−7.5	2.4
Africa	65.9	1,360	+4.9	2.1

*Including Yugoslavia.
†Excluding China.

Selected countries

	1979 consumption		Change over 1978 (per cent)	Share of world total (per cent)
	(million tonnes)	(thousand bpd)		
USA	868.0	17,910	−2.3	27.8
USSR	427.0	8,640	+1.9	13.7
Japan	265.1	5,485	+0.9	8.5
West Germany	147.0	3,050	+3.0	4.7
France	118.3	2,440	−0.6	3.8
Italy	103.2	2,080	+3.4	3.3
United Kingdom	94.5	1,950	+0.5	3.0
China	91.1	1,835	+7.6	2.9
Canada	90.1	1,915	+3.7	2.9
Spain	49.1	1,015	+5.8	1.6
Total	2,253.4	46,320	+0.4	72.2

D10.1.iii—Oil refining

World

Total refinery capacity .... 80,075,000 bpd
Change over 1978 .... +1.9 per cent

Total refinery throughputs .... 61,920,000 bpd
Change over 1978 .... +2.1 per cent

Consumption as proportion of capacity ...... 80.1 per cent

Selected markets
Consumption of refined product types and change over 1978:

	USA (million tonnes)	(per cent)	Western Europe (million tonnes)	(per cent)	Japan (million tonnes)	(per cent)
Gasolines	323.5	−4.4	147.0	+0.8	46.2	+1.1
Middle distillates	231.2	−0.4	256.7	+0.9	61.5	+2.2
Fuel oil	148.5	−6.3	231.8	+3.3	123.7	−0.6
Other	164.8	+3.0	97.6	+6.4	33.7	+4.3
Total	868.0	−2.3	733.1	+2.3	265.1	+0.9

D10.1.iv—Tankers and trade

Tankers

Total world fleet .... 327,900,000 deadweight tons
Change over 1978 .... −0.2 per cent

Trade

Total world crude exports
   (including re-exports) .... 33,427,400 bpd (1,652.8 million tonnes)
   Change over 1978 .... +5.2 per cent
OPEC crude exports .... 26,793,200 bpd (1,324.8 million tonnes)
   Change over 1978 .... +2.7 per cent
   Share of 1979 world total .... 80.2 per cent
Total world product exports
   (including re-exports) .... 8,560,600 bpd (429,749,000 tonnes)
   Change over 1978 .... +3 per cent
OPEC product exports .... 2,070,000 bpd (103,915,700 tonnes)
   Change over 1978 .... +9.6 per cent
   Share of 1979 world total .... 24.2 per cent

Regional distribution of world oil trade*:

	Share of 1979 imports (per cent) Crude	Products	Share of 1979 exports (per cent) Crude	Products
USA	21.4	38.8	0.8	5.5
Canada	2.0	0.3	0.9	3.6
Latin America/ Caribbean	8.4	3.7	5.5	41.6
Western Europe	40.1	18.8	1.0	4.5
Middle East	0.2	2.6	64.4	18.2
North Africa	0.2	1.9	10.4	3.1
West Africa	†	1.6	8.6	1.0
East and southern Africa	1.5	0.8	—	0.2
South Asia	1.2	2.2	—	0.8
South-East Asia	5.3	7.4	5.1	6.1
Australasia	0.7	2.9	—	0.4
Japan	16.3	12.3	—	0.2
USSR/Eastern Europe/China	1.7	0.4	3.3	14.8
Unspecified	1.0	6.3	—	—
Total	100.0	100.0	100.0	100.0

*Excluding intra-regional trade.   †Negligible.

D10.1.v—World primary energy consumption

Total consumption (excluding
non-commercial fuels) .... 6,940.5 million tonnes oil equivalent (mtoe)
Change over 1978 .... +3.5 per cent

Contributions of primary energy sources:

	Consumption (mtoe)	Change over 1978 (per cent)	Share of total (per cent)
Oil	3,125.0	+1.4	45.0
Coal	1,975.7	+6.0	28.5
Natural gas	1,273.4	+5.6	18.3
Water power	413.4	+2.6	6.0
Nuclear power	153.0	+2.3	2.2

D10.1.vi—Natural gas production and reserves

Marketed production (thousand million cubic metres):

	Regional total (tmcm)	Change over 1978 (per cent)	Share of 1979 world total (per cent)
North America	634.9	+3.3	44.5
Latin America/Caribbean	52.5	+14.4	3.7
Western Europe*	184.0	+4.0	12.9
USSR/Eastern Europe/China	428.9	+6.5	30.1
Middle East	48.3	+21.1	3.4
Africa	26.0	+69.9	1.8
Asia†/Australasia	51.1	+13.1	3.6
World total	1,425.7	+6.3	100.0
(of which OPEC)	(97.7)	(+34.0)	(6.9)

*Including Yugoslavia.
†Excluding China.

End-year proved reserves (thousand million cubic metres):

	Regional total (tmcm)	Change over 1978 (per cent)	Share of 1979 world total (per cent)
North America	8,113.1	+10.5	10.9
Latin America/Caribbean	4,127.4	+27.7	5.6
Western Europe*	4,057.2	+0.1	5.5
USSR/Eastern Europe/China	26,926.0	+10.9	36.4
Middle East	21,043.2	+1.4	28.4
Africa	5,934.9	+13.1	8.0
Asia†/Australasia	3,837.3	+11.2	5.2
World total	74,039.1	+8.3	100.0
(of which OPEC)	(28,455.6)	(+4.2)	(38.4)

*Including Yugoslavia.
†Excluding China.

D10.2—Market Reaction to Temporary Suspension of Iranian Oil Exports

The halting of Iranian oil exports on Dec. 26, 1978, and the subsequent intensification of political unrest in Iran (culminating in the overthrow on Feb. 11, 1979, of the Bakhtiar Government appointed by the Shah) led to mounting concern over the security of supplies. Most international oil companies took steps to limit the rundown of their existing stocks (e.g. by cutting back deliveries to non-affiliated customers) as a precaution against a prolonged suspension of Iranian exports. Although a limited resumption of exports was authorized by Iran's revolutionary Government on March 5, continuing uncertainties about the new regime's production and marketing policies ensured that the oil market's so-called "crisis of anticipation" persisted for some time thereafter.

OPEC's average production during the first quarter of 1979 was estimated at 29,703,000 bpd, some 3.5 per cent higher than in January–March 1978 but about 5.7 per cent lower than in the last quarter of 1978. Comparisons of various member countries' production levels in the first quarters of 1978 and 1979 showed increases of 39.7 per cent by Iraq, 35.3 per cent by Nigeria, 34.4 per cent by Kuwait, 28.1 per cent by Venezuela and 23.3 per cent by Saudi Arabia. The fall in OPEC's average monthly output between December 1978 and January 1979 was around 2,000,000 bpd, reflecting both the full impact of Iranian developments and, to a lesser extent, the effect of a decision by Saudi Arabia in mid-January to apply a temporary production ceiling of 9,500,000 bpd for the first quarter of 1979, which although 1,000,000 bpd above Aramco's normal ceiling was lower than the actual production level reached in December. It was subsequently reported that the main reason for this decision was that the maintenance of December production levels in certain oilfields had been ruled out pending the resolution of continuing technical problems associated with their near-capacity operation.

Statistics released in August by the OECD showed that world oil production averaged 63,180,000 bpd during the first five months of 1979, compared with 62,230,000 bpd in January–May 1978; that during the same period the main OECD importing countries' oil imports had risen by 2.3 per cent compared with the previous year; and that by May 1979 these countries' stocks were nearly 3 per cent higher than a year earlier.

While oil companies were taking steps to minimize their drawdown of stocks in early 1979, strong winter demand was evident in the major consuming countries, many of which experienced exceptionally cold weather conditions. At the same time the geographical balance of the world oil trade became subject to distortions which reflected the varying degrees of dependence upon Iranian exports and which contributed to a rapid "bidding up" of prices on the spot market. Minor market distortions included Iran's own temporary need to import oil products during the period of greatest disruption to its own industry.

One effect of the sharp rise in spot market prices was to introduce further distortions into the pattern of trade, including the diversion of some marginal supplies away from importing countries where government price controls operated in respect of oil products, thus contributing to the creation of some localized shortages. It was also widely alleged, notably by OPEC member countries, that in the generally confused state of the oil market the widening gap between spot prices and the official OPEC prices which had taken effect on Jan. 1 was being exploited for speculative gain by independent traders (mostly in crude oil) and, to a lesser extent, by the large integrated oil companies (which were accused in particular of "hoarding" refined products).

In order to restrict the opportunities for "windfall profits" to be made through the resale of crude originally purchased at official OPEC prices, many member countries introduced surcharges on their contract sales to foreign oil companies while taking steps to expand the marketing activities of their own national oil companies (including some direct selling through the spot market). Most non-OPEC exporters' contract prices, hitherto closely aligned with official OPEC prices, had already been increased from Jan. 1 by rather more than OPEC's basic 5 per cent first-quarter rise—e.g. by 11 per cent in the case of British North Sea oil.

D10.3—The Development of Prices, January to March 1979

During the first quarter of 1979 the monthly average spot price paid for all grades of OPEC crude rose from $16.75 per barrel in January to $23.15 in February and $23.23 in March; for marker-grade Gulf crudes, the average spot premium above Saudi Arabia's official first-quarter price of $13.339 per barrel increased from $2.90 in January to over $9 in February and March. The volume of spot trading in the early part of the year was generally estimated to be between 500,000 bpd and 1,000,000 bpd (representing between 1.5 and 3 per cent of the total oil trade, as opposed to the normal level in recent years of between 4 and 5 per cent). By mid-March, however, between 15 and 20 per cent of world oil trade in oil was being transacted on spot terms, a notable factor in this upturn being Iran's very heavy dependence on spot sales for several weeks after the resumption of export shipments.

As regards monthly average spot prices for refined products, these reached $322.41 per tonne for premium-grade gasoline and $133.25 per tonne for fuel oil in Western Europe in February, representing price rises of 134.5 per cent over January 1978 and 53.5 per cent over December 1978 in the case of the former (53.7 per cent and 37.4 per cent respectively in the case of the latter).

During January spot sales took place in what *Petroleum Intelligence Weekly* described as "a totally irrational market climate" characterized by "hysteria reminiscent of the 1973 oil crisis", with premiums of up to $4 per barrel over the new OPEC prices being paid for some cargoes by the end of the month. This occurred despite an announcement during the month by the IEA that its 19 member states had started the year with total oil stocks of 377,000,000 tonnes, representing about 120 days' net imports, and that the Iranian situation would have "no real practical impact on oil availability until March" (by which point winter demand would have passed its peak).

Although no changes were made in official OPEC prices during January 1979 some member countries used normal spot-market channels to sell relatively small volumes of state-owned crude which had not been committed to contract buyers, while in Abu Dhabi the national oil company invited competitive bids at the end of the month for about 2,000,000 barrels of incremental production during February. Up to $18.60 per barrel was reportedly paid by Japanese bidders in this auction, which was widely compared to that held in Iran in the strong seller's market of December 1973 (◊**D4.6**).

Political influences on the oil market included an appeal made in early February by Yassir Arafat, the leader of the Palestine Liberation Organization, for Arab OPEC countries to "exert economic pressure on the United States in order to bring about changes in US policies towards the Middle East". It was subsequently stated on March 4 by Dr Maneh Said al Oteiba of the United Arab Emirates (the current President of the OPEC Conference) that the willingness of Arab exporting countries to increase their output to offset the loss of Iranian oil depended on the co-operation of Western importing countries in working for "a just solution" to the Palestinian question.

The initial move towards applying official producer surcharges to the price of OPEC oil was reported in the first week of February as a limited step by Saudi Arabia. In order to emphasize that it regarded the increase in Aramco's production ceiling to 9,500,000 bpd during the first quarter of 1979 as a "borrowing" from future production to offset the current Iranian shortfall, the Saudi Government announced that its scheduled fourth-quarter prices (e.g. $14.546 per barrel for 34° crude) would be charged in respect of the temporary 1,000,000 bpd production increase.

The first "across the board" surcharges on all current contract sales were subsequently announced on Feb. 15 by Qatar and the UAE, which imposed immediate price increases ranging from 6.8 to 7.5 per cent for various grades of crude.

In the case of the UAE, the official price of Abu Dhabi's 39° crude rose by $1.02 to $15.12 per barrel (compared with a current spot value of up to $25 per barrel), and a schedule of further planned price increases in April, July and October was issued which envisaged a "surcharged" fourth-quarter price of $16.32 per barrel (over 23 per cent above the December 1978 price). Dubai increased its official selling price by $1 per barrel. Qatar (which increased the price of its 40° crude to $15.05 per barrel while announcing that its pricing policy after the end of the first quarter would depend on OPEC decisions) also gave notice of an auction of 500,000 barrels of crude with a reported floor price for bids of $23 per barrel.

This action by two smaller Gulf members which were normally grouped among the "moderates" in OPEC pricing discussions was widely regarded as an initiative to test market reaction to official surcharges, it being noted that Dr al Oteiba had recently visited Saudi Arabia and Kuwait for consultations on OPEC matters. During these visits, he had strongly criticized the alleged "exploitation" of the Iranian situation by the international oil industry, and had said that inflated trading profits should be "returned to their rightful owners", as the current high prices being paid for oil "were severely affecting the developing countries".

In response to growing pressure from many member countries for an early reconsideration of OPEC's 1979 pricing policy in the light of recent market trends, Dr al Oteiba announced on Feb. 19 that a special consultative meeting of the OPEC Conference would be held in Geneva on March 26.

Also on Feb. 19, Algeria was reported to have opened negotiations with its customers for a 15 to 20 per cent price increase from April 1, it being stated by that country's official news agency that the current level of spot market prices "proved that the international oil market is perfectly capable of paying much higher prices than those fixed by OPEC". Libya made an immediate price increase of 68 cents per barrel on Feb. 21, and Venezuela on Feb. 26 announced a surcharge of $1.20 per barrel on most of its exports, originally scheduled to take effect from March 1 but subsequently postponed until April 1 for contractual reasons. Also on Feb. 26, Kuwait announced a $1.20 per barrel (9.35 per cent) surcharge, which was backdated to Feb. 20 and was to be reviewed monthly in the light of market conditions.

However, Saudi Arabia (which was understood to have insisted on the consultative status of the forthcoming OPEC meeting in order to preclude a formal revision of the 1979 price structure) issued a statement on Feb. 27 announcing that it would maintain its first-quarter prices at their January levels in respect of production up to Aramco's normal ceiling of 8,500,000 bpd, and also proposing urgent consultations between oil producers and consumers "to regulate demand and stabilize prices in the interests of the world economy".

On Feb. 28 the OPEC Secretariat issued the following statement on member countries' current pricing policies: "Conference decisions in setting crude oil prices do not prevent member countries from making an upward adjustment in the light of their prevailing circumstances. Therefore the decisions taken by member countries, either by adjusting their prices upwards or by choosing other courses of action or further consultation, certainly fall within the framework of the [OPEC] statute and are strictly in accordance with their sovereign rights. . . . In the present circumstances, the actions of member countries in exercising their sovereign rights cannot be construed as prejudicing the solidarity and unity of OPEC."

Also in late February, the new Government of Iran announced that it would shortly be in a position to resume oil exports, although initially on a small scale and without any firm indication at this stage of government policy regarding the optimum export volume which it was planned to achieve. It was, however, made clear that NIOC would hold sole responsibility for the operation of Iran's oilfields and the marketing of its oil exports and that future access to Iranian supplies by the constituent companies of the IOP consortium would be subject to the negotiation of individual contracts on non-preferential terms. Pending the negotiation of new contracts, almost all of NIOC's export trade was conducted on a spot basis, initially by inviting competitive bids in the range of $18 to $20 per barrel. Early buyers on these terms included Royal Dutch/Shell (IOP's second largest shareholder). The new Government banned the export of Iranian oil to Israel and South Africa (both of which had obtained a high proportion of their oil imports from Iran under the Shah's Government).

In early March (i) Ecuador announced the renegotiation of oil export contracts "to take account of world market prices" and subsequently increased its official selling price by 36.3 per cent (to $17.76 per barrel) with effect from March 1; (ii) Iraq imposed a $1.20 per barrel surcharge with effect from March 1, and was reported to be selling a large proportion of its substantial increase in output on the spot market; (iii) Libya increased its surcharge to $1.38 per barrel with effect from March 3, and announced a cutback "for technical reasons" of up to 18 per cent in the volume of oil supplied under certain contracts from April 1; (iv) Venezuela announced price increases of up to 45 per cent with effect from April 1 for its exports of refined products; (v) Algeria was reported to have significantly increased the level of the surcharge which it planned to introduce on April 1, while requesting a "voluntary" cutback by oil companies of 10 to 15 per cent in their contractual purchases from the same date; (vi) Indonesia (which had indicated that it was deferring a decision on pricing until after the forthcoming OPEC consultative meeting) was reported to have notified its Japanese customers of a 10 per cent cutback in contract supplies during the second quarter; and (vii) Nigeria notified its customers of a planned $2.50 per barrel (nearly 17 per cent) price increase with effect from April 1.

Later in March it was estimated that up to 45 per cent of OPEC exports were being marketed either on spot terms or at surcharged official prices. Spot prices remained generally stable during the latter part of the month as NIOC increased its export volume (which was approaching 2,000,000 bpd by early April) and began to place some of its sales on a contract basis.

D10.4—IEA Initiative to reduce Oil Consumption

At a meeting at official level of the Governing Board of the International Energy Agency held in Paris on March 1 and 2, 1979 (at which Australia was admitted as the 20th member of the IEA), agreement was reached on the adoption of policies designed to reduce member countries' oil consumption by 2,000,000 bpd in view of the "serious risk" of a supply shortfall of this magnitude in 1979. The main features of this initiative to stabilize the world oil market—one objective of which was reported to be to counterbalance the case for a major official price increase which some producing countries were expected to make at the forthcoming OPEC meeting in Geneva—were outlined as follows in a press statement issued on March 2.

"[It was] agreed that IEA countries will contribute to a stabilization of the world situation by reducing their demand for oil on the world market. The reduction would be of the order of 2,000,000 bpd, which would correspond to about 5 per cent of IEA consumption. Each participating country will regard this as guidance in the policies it will pursue to achieve its contribution to this reduction. These policies are expected to yield equivalent results in participating countries.

"[It was] agreed accordingly that each participating country will take short-term action by promptly applying effective and adequate methods appropriate to its individual circumstances to:

"(1) Reduce demand for oil (i) by more efficient use of energy and avoidance of energy consumption which is not essential for maintaining a high level of economic activity and (ii) by utilizing existing possibilities for short-term fuel switching away from oil, replacing it wherever possible by alternative forms of energy;

"(2) Maintain and develop indigenous energy production at high levels;

"(3) Take into account the potential to shift to non-premium grades of crude oil, adjusting regulatory systems wherever possible and advisable; and

"(4) Adopt, where necessary, domestic pricing policies which would support the achievement of the above objective."

The measures decided upon by the IEA were described both by officials of the Agency and by members of the US delegation to the Paris meeting as "a positive response" to Saudi Arabia's recent call for consultations between oil importing and exporting countries (◊**D10.3**).

The final paragraph of the IEA announcement was aimed particularly at the United States, whose current rate of oil consumption was described on March 19 by the European Community's Commissioner for Energy, Dr Guido Brunner, as "barely tolerable" in the present circumstances. Dr Brunner said that immediate action should be taken by the US Government to decontrol domestic oil prices as "a token of its commitment to the rest of the industrialized world".

The heads of government of the nine EEC countries, for their part, decided at a European Council meeting held in Paris on March 12 and 13 to "pursue a policy designed to reduce oil consumption [in 1979] to 500,000,000 tonnes, i.e. around 25,000,000 tonnes less than estimated".

It was reported in mid-March that the major international oil companies were beginning to cut back their crude deliveries to downstream affiliates in oil-importing countries, and were placing increasing emphasis on historic consumption levels (rather than import levels) as the basis for calculating percentage reductions in supplies through integrated channels. According to *The New York Times* of March 15, this approach had been adopted in particular by Exxon, whose allocations to affiliates were said to be based on an (as yet unenforced) IEA formula for mandatory oil-sharing.

The uniform application of this formula would have ensured that cutbacks bore more heavily on consuming countries which met a substantial proportion of demand from domestic production (e.g. the United States) than on those countries (such as Japan) which were almost totally dependent on imported oil. In practice, however, the non-renewal by the majors of many of their supply contracts with non-affiliated refiners produced an extremely uneven pattern of cutbacks throughout the world. In Japan an estimated 5 per cent of the country's oil imports were affected by such non-renewal on the part of Exxon, whose action was described by Japanese oil officials as "the most drastic step ever taken by a major oil company".

D10.5—53rd Meeting of OPEC Conference

Despite the IEA countries' commitment to attempt to stabilize the world oil market through curbs on the growth of consumption, a number of OPEC countries made it clear during March 1979 that, given the current state of the market, they intended to seek a change in the consultative status of the Conference meeting scheduled for March 26, which, they argued, should be turned into an extraordinary session with decision-making powers on pricing.

Algeria, Libya and Iraq were among the leading proponents of the formal amendment of the 1979 pricing structure adopted in December 1978, and Algeria made it widely known that Sonatrach was currently involved in negotiations with its contract customers for an April 1 price rise of about 25 per cent. Iran's revolutionary Government indicated its strong backing for a hard line on OPEC pricing policy, in contrast to the moderate approach which the Shah's Government had followed since mid-1977 (◊D8.4). Moreover, it was stated by Shaikh Yamani on March 25 that, while Saudi Arabia "would not apply pressure for a formal OPEC price rise" because "this would not be in the interest of world economic stability", he nevertheless expected oil prices to rise further in response to market forces regardless of the policies adopted by OPEC. These remarks were widely regarded as an indication that Saudi Arabia would not now seriously challenge proposals for an OPEC price increase, a policy which was seen by the Western press as arising partly from opposition to the US-backed Egyptian-Israeli peace treaty to be signed in Washington on the following day.

A formal proposal to convert the status of the Geneva meeting into the 53rd (extraordinary) session of the OPEC Conference was unanimously adopted by delegates on March 26 "in view of the current situation and the important developments which have been taking place in the oil industry", and wide-ranging discussions subsequently continued on March 27, the following press statement being issued by ministers on that day:

"The Conference, after reviewing recent developments in the international oil market, expressed its high concern over the interests of both producers and consumers, especially those of the developing countries. The Conference analysed the difficulties being experienced by the latter group of countries, whether in relation to their supplies of oil or to the exceptionally high prices they were being charged by the oil and trading companies.

"The Conference examined possible measures which could be taken to guarantee the requirements of developing countries, as well as ways and means of ensuring that the prices they were charged were consistent with prices set by OPEC member countries.

"It was agreed that all member countries would take steps to instruct lifting companies to guarantee the quantities supplied to developing countries, and to take such measures as would secure strict compliance by the companies with this agreement.

"The Conference also agreed to monitor continuously the prices charged by the lifting companies to developing countries in order to guarantee that no such levies would be imposed on the developing countries concerned over and above the prices decided upon by [OPEC] member countries.

"The Conference also discussed the current market situation and the developments in the OPEC price structure and expressed high concern about the price speculation practices on the part of the major and trading oil companies in the open market, to the detriment of both producers and consumers, by reaping unjustified windfall profits which are not warranted by the OPEC prices. The Conference furthermore expressed its deep concern for the lack of necessary measures that should be taken by the industrialized developed countries with a view to controlling the market situation.

"In spite of the large gaps that currently exist between prices prevailing in the open market and the OPEC official selling prices, the Conference decided to undertake only a moderate and modest adjustment in the price by bringing forward the price adjustment of the fourth quarter 1979, decided upon by the 52nd meeting of the Conference in Abu Dhabi in December 1978 [◊D9.5], and applying it as of April 1, 1979. The application of this adjustment on the marker crude would make its price $14.546 with effect from April 1, 1979. Besides this adjustment, it is left for each member to add to its price market premiums which it deems justifiable in the light of its own circumstances.

"The modest adjustment referred to above is intended to confirm OPEC member countries' responsibility to help maintain the appropriate conditions for a continued and sustained growth of the world economy.

"In so doing, the Conference calls upon all consuming countries to take such measures as to prevent oil companies from charging them prices beyond the price decided upon by OPEC countries."

The statement's emphasis on the needs of the developing countries followed indications that the especially disadvantaged position of the oil-importing Third World in the current oil market situation was threatening to undermine OPEC's established policy of solidarity with these countries. In particular, four Latin American states (Bolivia, Colombia, Costa Rica and the Dominican Republic) had, together with Spain, issued a declaration on March 12 criticizing what were described as "constant indiscriminate oil price increases". According to *Le Monde*, this was "the first occasion since 1973 on which several third-world countries have jointly made an open declaration which does not accord with the policy of solidarity with OPEC followed by the 'Group of 77'".

As regards the pricing decisions of the 53rd Conference meeting (which were described by the US State Department as "untimely and unjustified"), the abandonment of the phased introduction of the prearranged quarterly increments for 1979 meant that the April 1 increase in the official price of marker crude was just over 9 per cent instead of 3.8 per cent as originally planned, and that the average increase for 1979 as a whole would be about 12.1 per cent rather than 10 per cent if the new price remained in force throughout the remainder of the year. The complete discretion given to individual member countries to impose unspecified "market premiums", however, confirmed that official OPEC prices were now regarded only as floor prices, and that the actual price rise would be strongly influenced by free market forces.

Saudi Arabia, which announced that it would increase the price of its own oil only to the new official level (thus effectively creating a two-tier OPEC price structure), was understood to have agreed to give its formal acceptance to the operation of surcharges by other member countries after the latter had agreed to drop demands to raise the basic marker price to at least $17.50 per barrel. Shaikh Yamani said after the meeting that the only way in which the major oil-importing countries could avoid the development of a "free-for-all" in the operation of surcharges was by swift and substantial cutbacks in demand, affecting both current consumption and the rebuilding of stocks.

It was widely reported that a major item on the agenda of the Geneva meeting concerned the co-ordination of production policies in order to ensure that the build-up of exports from Iran was balanced by cutbacks in the production increases made by other member countries to offset the Iranian shortfall, and that an informal understanding had been reached to this end, with Saudi Arabia in particular indicating that it would reimpose its normal production ceiling of 8,500,000 bpd as Iranian output increased further during the second quarter of the year. The meeting was, however, understood to have rejected an Iranian proposal for a 5 per cent cutback in overall OPEC production designed to prevent the consumption cutback planned by the IEA (◊**D10.4**) from undermining official price levels.

D10.6—Pricing and Production Developments in April and May

Total OPEC production was estimated at 30,700,000 bpd in April 1979 and 31,200,000 bpd in May. Iranian output reached an average 4,100,000 bpd during the month April 21 to May 21, of which 760,000 bpd went to domestic refineries. Thereafter NIOC was instructed by the Iranian Government to observe a production ceiling of 4,000,000 bpd. Meanwhile Saudi Arabia had reimposed its normal ceiling of 8,500,000 bpd on Aramco's production after the end of the first quarter, and in the light of these developments OPEC's May production level was regarded as indicative of the maximum output which member countries were willing to maintain in the current circumstances.

The monthly average spot price for all OPEC crudes, which had fallen slightly to $22.03 per barrel in April, rose to $29.52 in May following the commencement of regular large-scale spot purchases by the major oil companies (including in particular Aramco's parent companies). Average spot prices for refined products in Western Europe rose to a new monthly highs of $368.62 per tonne for premium-grade gasoline and $141.99 for fuel oil in May.

The revised OPEC pricing structure which had taken effect on April 1 was seriously undermined during May as most members responded to the renewed upturn in spot prices by adding "market premiums" to their official contract prices (although the Saudi Arabian marker price was held at its April level). There was little or no prior consultation between neighbouring producers regarding the level of surcharges, which tended to be determined through a reactive process whereby an initiative by one OPEC member prompted either matching or "leapfrogging" increases by others. Details of OPEC's April price structure and of the effective dates of subsequent price increases to June 1 are given in Table 46.

Saudi Arabia's decision to add a $1.40 surcharge to the price of its 39° crude (which then accounted for less than 6 per cent of Aramco's output) was announced on May 31

Table 46 — Evolution of official selling prices (inclusive of surcharges) for selected OPEC crudes, April 1 to June 1, 1979

	April 1	May 1	May 15	May 16	May 17	May 27	June 1
	(dollars per barrel)						
Algeria (44°)	18.546	—	—	21.00	—	—	—
Ecuador (29.7°)	19.09	20.24	—	—	—	—	26.63
Gabon (31.8°)	16.42	—	17.22	—	—	—	18.52
Indonesia (34.1°)	15.65	16.15	—	—	—	—	—
Iran (31°)	16.04	—	16.64	—	—	—	17.74
(34°)	16.57	—	17.17	—	—	—	18.47
Iraq (34°)	15.50	16.20	—	—	—	—	16.94
(36°)	15.82	16.42	—	—	—	—	17.16
Kuwait (31°)	15.80	16.40	—	—	—	—	—
Libya (40°)	18.25	—	—	18.95	—	21.26	—
(40.5°)	18.30	—	—	19.00	—	21.31	—
Nigeria (37°)	18.50	—	—	20.96	—	—	—
(40°)	18.60	—	—	21.06	—	—	—
Qatar (40°)	17.04	—	—	—	17.84	—	—
Saudi Arabia (27°)	13.643	—	—	—	—	—	17.172†
(31°)	14.052	—	—	—	—	—	17.547†
(34°)	14.546	—	—	—	—	—	18.00†
(39°)	16.47	—	17.87*	—	—	—	21.324†
UAE: Abu Dhabi (39°)	17.10	—	—	—	17.90	—	—
Dubai (32°)	16.286	—	—	—	17.086	—	—
Venezuela (26°)	15.76	—	—	16.36	—	—	—
(31°)	16.70	—	—	17.30	—	—	—
(34°)	17.21	—	—	17.81	—	—	—

*Retroactive implementation of decision taken at end-May.
†Retroactive implementation of decision taken at end-June.

(the date on which Iran announced its June 1 prices). No increases were envisaged at this point in the official prices of Saudi Arabia's other grades—now the only OPEC crudes which were still being sold at April prices—despite the fact that the Government was currently forgoing a potential incremental revenue of around $20,000,000 per day by refusing to follow the prevailing pattern of surcharges in the Gulf region. Because of Saudi Arabia's policy of price restraint the weighted average official price of all OPEC crudes, which had reached $16.74 per barrel in April, rose by only 54 cents in May.

D10.7—Decisions of IEA Ministerial Meeting

The Governing Board of the IEA held a meeting at ministerial level—the first such meeting since October 1977—on May 21 and 22 at which the 2,000,000 bpd target for the reduction in member countries' demand for oil (adopted at official level in March ◊**D10.4**) was endorsed as the main short-term element in the IEA's policy objectives. In an opening address the OECD Secretary-General referred to "doubts whether the IEA programme will be fully implemented, in which case conditions in the world oil market will tighten further", and warned that "inadequate energy and economic policies would almost inevitably lead to a new inflationary recession of the kind experienced in 1974–75".

Referring to the medium-term outlook, he said: "OECD growth at only 3½ per cent per year over the period to 1985 would require an increase in demand for OPEC oil of around 5,000,000 to 6,000,000 bpd. Events over the last six months suggest the need for considerable caution in assessing future production levels, as OPEC countries revise their assessment of revenue needs and reconsider their pricing and sales policy. I think it is appropriate to say that there is reason for serious doubt whether this amount will in fact be available."

Sweden, which was currently experiencing a supply shortfall in excess of 7 per cent, made a formal request at the meeting for the activation of mandatory oil-sharing measures, while Denmark proposed a voluntary allocation scheme. However, despite some support for these proposals from other smaller importers, including Greece, New Zealand and the Irish Republic, they were not adopted by the meeting. The majority view was that the Agency should adhere to its agreed programme, under which oil-sharing measures would take effect only in the event of a shortfall of more than 7 per cent in the aggregate oil supply of all member countries (◊**D5.12**).

The principal passages of the press statement issued after the meeting were as follows:

"Ministers reviewed world energy prospects for both the short and long term. They agreed that energy supply and demand problems are serious and likely to continue, and that immediate and strong action is urgently required. Following events in Iran, market developments (particularly supply limitations and price increases) have caused current difficulties and cast further doubt upon medium- and long-term prospects. . . .

"As to the short term, ministers concluded that the international oil market has evolved rapidly into a situation of overall supply stringency, which has affected different countries in different ways, and that this situation is likely to continue into 1980. They expressed particular concern about the large and rapid increase in crude oil and product prices.

"Ministers therefore confirmed the decision by IEA countries to reduce their demand for oil on the world market in the order of 2,000,000 bpd which would correspond to about 5 per cent of IEA consumption, and decided that:

"(1) IEA countries will take immediate and particular steps to bring about effective implementation of measures to achieve that result, including appropriate pricing polices; strengthened voluntary programmes; and mandatory action where necessary to reinforce the effect of other measures. Ministers will keep in mind the problem of product imbalances and especially that high consumption of gasoline in summer would in most countries add to supply difficulties for heating oil in the winter.

"(2) IEA countries will pay particular attention to oil stock levels, keeping in mind both the advantages of flexible stock policies in the present situation and the fact that stocks, which have already undergone an unusually heavy drawdown in the first quarter, will to some extent have to be replenished during the course of 1979 for the next winter heating season.

"(3) Measures to reduce the demand of IEA countries for oil on the world market will also be necessary for 1980, and the Governing Board at official level will take detailed and co-ordinated action in good time for the necessary measures to be continued or put into effect.

"(4) The appropriate bodies of the IEA will undertake an analysis of (i) the impact of a fragile market situation on spot prices; (ii) the impact of spot prices on the overall price structure; (iii) changes in oil market structures; and (iv) the effect of increasing competition for limited supplies of oil. The purpose of such analysis will be to improve understanding of the operation of the oil market.

"Ministers reviewed progress made by the IEA countries in implementating the principles for energy policy [◊B3.4] adopted at the last ministerial meeting in 1977. They noted that the group objective of limiting oil imports to 26,000,000 bpd in 1985 seemed capable of realization, but expressed deep disquiet that the achievement of this objective might result principally from a lower level of economic growth than had been assumed when the objective was established. They agreed that a group objective for 1990 should be considered and that in that context the 1985 group objective should be reviewed. They agreed that all IEA countries should give much higher priority to the development of effective long-term policy measures designed to achieve the group objective, and that the effectiveness of these measures should continue to be monitored closely by the IEA. They noted the important contribution which would need to be made by IEA countries with larger economies.

"Ministers considered the medium- and long-term energy outlook and concluded that if nothing is done to change present trends, available energy supplies will not be sufficient to support even moderate economic growth.

"Ministers reviewed the prospects for world oil production and concluded that there are only limited possibilities for expansion of exports from OPEC countries or elsewhere and that continued dependence on oil to meet growing energy demand can no longer be viewed as a satisfactory option, even in the medium term. They therefore decided that solutions must be sought in other directions—principally conservation, coal, nuclear and natural gas—and that greater emphasis must be placed on new and renewable energy sources that hold considerable promise for the long term.

"**Coal**. Ministers agreed that greatly increased coal use is required to meet growing energy demand in the medium and long term, and that this is both desirable and possible in light of the world's abundant coal reserves and the economic advantages which coal already has over oil in many energy markets. . . .

"**Conservation**. Ministers agreed that energy conservation and fuel-efficiency efforts must be intensified and accelerated as a matter of high priority, in order to further reduce the overall energy/economic growth ratio in IEA countries. The main measures which have already contributed to improvement—pricing, investment incentives, consumption standards and public information—should be continued and reinforced. . . .

"**Nuclear**. Ministers noted that nuclear projections have been lowered repeatedly in recent years. They also noted that the recent accident at Harrisburg has renewed public concern about safety. [A serious accident had occurred at a nuclear power station in Pennsylvania, USA, on March 28, 1979.] However, they also recognized that oil or other alternative energy sources would not be sufficient to meet growing energy demand in the short and medium term and that undesirable economic and social consequences would therefore result if more nuclear power is not available. They therefore agreed on the need for projected additions to nuclear power supply to be realized in timely fashion and exceeded wherever possible, having due regard to legal and constitutional provisions. They also agreed on the urgent need for effective national and international efforts to ensure that safety systems are sufficient to minimize the possibility of nuclear plant accidents and their consequences, and to adequately inform the public of the results. They also recognized the need to bring the

International Nuclear Fuel Cycle Evaluation [a technical and analytical study launched by 40 countries in October 1977 on the basis of an original initiative announced by seven non-communist heads of government in May of that year ◊**D8.11**] to a successful conclusion by early 1980, and to ensure that effective action is taken to resolve long-term waste disposal and non-proliferation questions.

"**Natural Gas**. Ministers stressed the importance of natural gas as the most readily available alternative fuel, and agreed on the need to encourage both indigenous production and international trade in natural gas.

"**Oil**. Ministers considered that oil exploration and development and enhanced recovery techniques, within IEA and worldwide, should be strongly encouraged by policies which promote the development of reserves on a timely basis, under sound economic and reservoir management practices, and by appropriate pricing policies. In this regard, ministers welcomed the World Bank's decision [announced on Jan. 17, 1979] to expand lending for conventional energy exploration and development in developing countries, which should serve to accelerate investment in these activities. Ministers agreed that in order to use future crude oil production more effectively, the appropriate bodies of the IEA should examine the capability of refineries in IEA countries to increase the yield of light products and the need for policies designed to achieve a better balance between future crude oil availability and refinery configuration.

"**Research and Development**. Ministers stressed the contribution which could be made by intensified research and development and commercialization activities for conventional and non-conventional energy technologies, including continued work on electricity technologies and additional efforts on technologies to provide liquid and gaseous fuels for transportation and for domestic and industrial uses where direct substitutions for oil are possible, as well as technologies which can significantly improve energy efficiency. . . .

"Ministers recognized that most forms of energy production, transportation and utilization involve health, safety and environmental problems, to which acceptable solutions must be found in developing energy policies.

"Ministers agreed that more progress is necessary on energy price structures which encourage conservation and promote indigenous production, and noted with satisfaction the recent decision by President Carter for decontrol of domestic crude oil prices (◊**D10.17**).

"Ministers agreed that in general added momentum must be given to programmes of public information stressing the reality and the seriousness of the energy situation; the direct links between energy and the public's overall economic well-being; practical means for using energy more efficiently; and the potential cost savings associated with conservation measures.

"Ministers reaffirmed that it is the objective of IEA countries to make a positive and constructive contribution to international energy co-operation [and] stressed the willingness of IEA countries to . . . discuss energy questions of mutual interest with oil-exporting and oil-importing developing countries. . . .

"Ministers agreed, finally, that in view of the dangers which the world energy situation poses for the world economy, IEA countries will keep energy policy at a high national priority and strengthen their co-operation within the IEA with the objective of making an even greater contribution toward stabilizing global energy supply and demand. They also expressed their willingness to meet more frequently in order to keep the situation under review."

D10.8—Subsequent Controversy over US Import Policy

At the May 1979 IEA meeting certain member countries were understood to have made representations to the US Energy Secretary concerning recent US spot purchases in West European oil markets, which were seen as having increased the upward pressure on prices. Nevertheless, the US Government on May 25 announced an extension of the federal "crude oil entitlement system" (◊**D10.17**) to cover imports of the middle distillate range of refined products (i.e. mainly home-heating oil and diesel fuel). Under the new measures imports of such products would attract an effective subsidy of $5 per barrel from the entitlement fund, to operate from May 1 (i.e. retroactively) until Aug. 31. This arrangement was strongly criticized in Western Europe, where it was viewed as contrary to the spirit of the recent IEA agreement in that it was likely both to divert supplies away from other importing countries and to contribute to a further rise in spot market prices.

The European Community's Energy Commissioner, Dr Brunner, on May 30 accused the United States of "trying to export its energy problems to Europe", and critical statements were also made by Danish, Dutch, French, British and West German ministers. The French Foreign Minister, Jean François-Poncet (the current chairman of the Council of Ministers of the European Community) said at a press conference in Washington on June 5 that the major industrialized countries would be "committing energy suicide" if they did not adopt a concerted policy to end competitive bidding on the spot market.

US spokesmen denied that the new measures (which did not involve direct government funding) constituted an import subsidy. Michael Blumenthal (then Treasury Secretary) stated on June 3 that the United States was "under the threat" that supplies of middle distillates from Caribbean refineries would be "diverted" to Europe, and that "under our system of entitlement we are merely making sure that we continue to receive our normal supplies". (US stocks of middle distillates, which had fallen in February to a level 21 per cent lower than a year earlier, subsequently returned to normal by the end of August, but their inclusion in the entitlement system was then nevertheless extended for a further two months.)

The Executive Director of the IEA, Ulf Lantzke, said in a speech in London on June 20 that whereas "we have basic agreement among industrialized countries as to the basic energy outlook and the required action", governments remained unwilling to make the political and national sacrifices to achieve the common objective of less dependence on imported oil. He said that in the longer term the "chain reaction" of political and economic problems arising from the Iranian revolution was likely to prove far more serious than the effects of the 1973 oil crisis, and that in the short term the main immediate problem was that of the spot market, where "higher and higher prices have begun to affect OPEC pricing decisions and general economic activity" to the extent that it was now "time for governments to step in" to regulate transactions on this market.

D10.9—The Position of the Oil-Importing Developing Countries

Notwithstanding OPEC's declaration of March 27 that member states would take steps to protect oil-importing developing countries from supply shortfalls and "unauthorized" price increases, deep concern at the rise in world oil prices continued to be expressed, particularly by Latin American countries.

A resolution stressing the severity of the balance-of-payments effects of oil price increases, tabled by five Central American countries, was adopted by the 18th session of the UN Economic Commission for Latin America, held in Bolivia in April, it being stated by the Guatemalan delegate that the oil importers were seeking an "act of solidarity" from Latin American oil exporters (i.e. principally Venezuela and Mexico). However, a group of 11 oil-importing Latin American countries, led by Colombia and Costa Rica, failed in a subsequent attempt to secure the inclusion of a reference to the oil price question in a draft resolution put forward by the "Group of 77" (developing countries) to the fifth session of the UN Conference on Trade and Development (UNCTAD V, held in Manila in May) after it had become apparent that there was general support among African and Asian countries for OPEC's opposition to such a move and that Venezuela's position was one of solidarity with OPEC.

At the same time, however, Venezuela made it clear that it would maintain its own bilateral aid to Latin American countries and would also put forward proposals within OPEC (i) for the creation of a new fund to give budgetary and balance-of-payments assistance to developing countries adversely affected by oil price increases and (ii) for the conversion of the existing OPEC Special Fund into a development bank with liberalized rules on eligibility and with authority to finance energy-related projects in less developed countries.

Among other OPEC members which put forward suggestions for action to alleviate the difficulties experienced by oil-importing developing countries, Iraq proposed on May 11 during UNCTAD V that the oil-exporting and the industrialized countries should co-operate in setting up a special fund to compensate the Third World for inflation. Under such a scheme the former would increase their aid "by the amount added to third-world inflation by higher oil prices", while the latter would increase their aid "to compensate the amount of inflation directly exported by them annually to the developing countries and according to the reflected prices of goods and services imported by these countries".

D10.10—Decisions of 54th OPEC Conference Meeting

Although there was a further rise in the market price of oil after June 1, no OPEC member sought to pre-empt the proceedings of the forthcoming mid-year Conference meeting by initiating another round of increases in official prices. The purpose of the only mid-June increase (by Indonesia, which raised the price of its 34.1° crude to $18.25 per barrel from June 15) was to bring that country more closely into line with the existing situation. The average official price of all OPEC crudes was estimated to be between $17.50 and $18 per barrel in late June, although the overall monthly average subsequently rose to $18.82 after Saudi Arabia's retroactive implementation of a June 1 price increase (for which see below). An intensification of stock-building activity contributed to a June increase of $6.58 in the monthly average spot price for all OPEC crudes (taking this average to $36.10 per barrel), while West European spot product prices averaged $397.40 per tonne for premium-grade gasoline and $156.19 per tonne for fuel oil.

Total OPEC production in June averaged 30,950,000 bpd, following notably a 200,000 bpd drop in Iranian output to 3,900,000 bpd in the month May 22–June 20, and overall OPEC production for the first half of 1979 was estimated at 30,110,400 bpd (5 per cent higher than in the corresponding period of 1978). Excluding Iran, OPEC's aggregate production for the first five months of the year was 18.6 per cent higher than in 1978, with five countries (Venezuela, Algeria, Nigeria, Ecuador and Gabon) utilizing more than 90 per cent of their maximum capacity.

Prior to the opening in Geneva on June 26, 1979, of the 54th meeting of the OPEC Conference, Oil Ministers made it clear that their main priority was to seek a formula for the re-establishment of a unified official price structure. Nevertheless, major differences emerged between Saudi Arabia, which favoured the dropping of surcharges and the adoption of the current average official price as the new marker price, and a group of "hard-line" members led by Iran, which favoured a marker price of $20 and continuing scope for the addition of surcharges.

Intensive negotiations took place on June 26 and 27 with the initial aim of restoring an orderly differential pricing relationship between the various grades of OPEC oil, but remained deadlocked as a result of the conflict between Saudi Arabia and Iran over the basic price level, despite mediation efforts by Venezuela, Kuwait and Algeria. In a third day of talks on June 28 the ministers accordingly acknowledged the impossibility of agreement on a unified pricing policy and instead adopted what Shaikh Yamani described as a "confusing and complicated" compromise formula which in effect established an official marker price of $18 per barrel, a surcharged reference price of $20 and an overall ceiling price of $23.50. Member countries also undertook to "limit transactions" in the spot market.

The meeting discussed at length the various proposals which had been put forward for the improvement of OPEC aid to oil-importing developing countries (◊D10.9) and recommended an increase of $800,000,000 in the resources of the OPEC Special Fund (in addition to its existing resources of $1,600 million). OPEC's long-term strategy committee was requested to consider Iraq's proposal for a new "inflation compensation" fund to be operated in conjunction with industrialized countries. It was further agreed to study the feasibility of establishing an international news agency to emphasize OPEC's positive role in world affairs, stressing particularly the Organization's policy of solidarity with the Third World (this proposal being subsequently discussed at official level at a meeting in Vienna on Sept. 10).

Details of these decisions were given in the following press statement issued on June 28.

"The Conference expressed concern for the problems being faced by developing countries, especially in the light of the continued lack of readiness on the part of the industrialized countries to face up to their responsibilities towards the problems of the Third World. For their part, OPEC member countries have in the past proved their strong solidarity with the Third World and have contributed in many ways to alleviating the problems of other developing countries. The member countries of the Organization of the Petroleum Exporting Countries once again act in accordance with their invariable solidarity towards the other third-world countries by agreeing to step up their aid to them. It was agreed to recommend to the governments of the member countries that they approve the further replenishment of the resources of the OPEC Special Fund by an additional amount of $800,000,000. Within the same context, the Conference also looked into another proposal for a long-term fund to be set up jointly by the industrialized countries and OPEC member countries to compensate developing countries for imported inflation, on the one hand, and any increases in crude oil prices on the other, and has decided to refer this subject for further study by the ministerial committee on long-term strategies.

"The Conference takes this opportunity to invite the industrialized countries to take a more positive stand towards the problems of the third-world countries, whether in regard to grants, aid and other forms of financial support as well as the restructuring of the international economic order, so as to give developing countries a better chance of solving their problems.

"The Conference expressed its continued willingness to discuss energy matters along with other problems of concern for developing countries, of which OPEC is an integral part. It took note of proposals for dialogue between OPEC and industrialized countries. Some of these proposals, however, seem to suggest that a meaningful dialogue can be carried out only on energy matters, in isolation from other global, economic and structural problems. The Conference wants to take this opportunity to restate its categorical rejection of any dialogue which does not look into the various problems faced by the world community and especially the developing countries, taking into account the problems of development, the acquisition of advanced technology, the financial and monetary reforms, world trade and raw materials, along with the various aspects of the energy problem.

"The Conference, conscious of the efforts undertaken individually and collectively by the member countries in co-operating with other developing countries, and of the need to inform other countries of the world of the true scope and magnitude of such efforts, as well as of other news of general interest regarding the Organization and the member countries, and in order to counteract the manipulation of information by some of OPEC's detractors, has given general support to the idea of establishing an international news agency—OPEC News. For this purpose, it has been decided to refer this matter to a committee of experts of the member countries to study the most effective means of implementing this idea, and to submit its report to the Conference, through the Board of Governors.

"This Conference expressed its great concern over the continuation of abnormal conditions prevailing in the international oil market. Demand has continued to be a source of pressure on the price structure, resulting in several phenomena which generated difficulties for both producers and consumers, especially the developing countries. The Conference once again calls upon the major industrialized consuming countries to control their total demand, whether for consumption or stock build-up, so that the adverse effects of the present market situation can be avoided. The Conference also takes this opportunity to warn the oil companies of the irresponsible practice of taking advantage of the present situation to reap unwarranted profits and calls upon them to play a more constructive role in connexion with guaranteeing supplies to developing countries, and to prevent price speculation.

"In an endeavour to bring some stability to the market, the Conference decided on the following: (i) to adjust the marker crude price from the present level to $18 per barrel; (ii) to allow member countries to add to the prices of their crude a maximum market premium of $2 per barrel over and above their normal differential, if and when such a market premium was necessitated by market conditions; and (iii) that the maximum prices that can be charged by member countries shall not exceed $23.50 per barrel, whether on account of quality and location advantage or market premiums. It was also agreed that member countries would take steps to limit transactions in the spot market in a collective effort to stop the present price spiral.

"The Conference expressed concern on the movement of the US dollar vis-à-vis the major international currencies with a view to eroding the real price of oil and further reducing the purchasing power of the OPEC barrel [the dollar having undergone a marked depreciation during June, reversing the trend of the previous three months], and has decided that should such movement indicate a further erosion in the real value of OPEC revenues, an extraordinary meeting of the Conference shall be called upon to decide on shifting to a basket of currencies as a means of compensating OPEC countries for resulting losses and further protecting the purchasing power of those revenues."

Table 47 — Prices of selected OPEC crudes, July 1, 1979

	Price at July 1, 1979	Increase over Dec. 31, 1978
	($ per barrel)	(per cent)
Algeria (44°)	23.50	66.7
Ecuador (29.7°*)	23.41	89.3
Gabon (31.8°)	22.50	72.7
Indonesia (34.1°)	21.12†	55.9
Iran (31°)	19.90	59.3
(34°)	22.00	71.7
Iraq (34°‡)	19.96	58.7
(36°)	21.25	66.4
Kuwait (31°)	19.49	58.8
Libya (40°)	23.45	69.3
(40.5°)	23.50	69.1
Nigeria (37°)	23.47	66.5
(40°)	23.50	66.3
Qatar (40°)	21.42	62.4
Saudi Arabia (27°)	17.172	42.9
(31°)	17.547	42.4
(34°)	18.00	41.7
(39°)	21.324	61.2
UAE: Abu Dhabi (39°)	21.56	62.6
Dubai (32°)	19.93	57.7
Venezuela (26°)	19.31	52.0
(31°)	20.90	54.4
(34°)	22.45	60.5

*30.4° API prior to Jan. 1, 1979.
†Price at July 15, 1979.
‡35° API prior to Jan. 1, 1979.

The pricing decisions of the Geneva meeting were widely compared in press reports to the formal two-tier structure in force during the first half of 1977. Nevertheless, the price increases subsequently announced for various grades of OPEC oil showed that, although Saudi Arabia was alone in observing the official marker value of $18 per barrel (except in respect of its 39° Berri crude, which was already subject to a surcharge ◊**D10.6**), the absence of an overall agreement on the restoration of "historic differentials" meant that there was little uniformity in the extent of other member countries' price increases.

Moreover, Saudi Arabia's own position was further modified by its decision to backdate its application of the new official marker price to June 1, and also to cut its credit period for oil sales from 60 to 30 days with effect from July 1, thus increasing the effective cost of its oil by about 1 per cent at current interest rates. Similar alterations in credit terms were subsequently announced by various other OPEC countries.

Algeria, Libya and Nigeria each increased the surcharged price of their top grade to the new OPEC ceiling level of $23.50 per barrel, while Ecuador reduced its June surcharge by $3.22 per barrel in order to bring its price—latterly the highest in the OPEC area—within the ceiling.

Table 47 shows member countries' new price levels and the overall percentage increase in each case since 1978.

D10.11—Industrialized Countries' Tokyo Declaration on Oil Policy

The 54th OPEC Conference meeting was followed immediately by an economic summit (held in Tokyo on June 28 and 29) attended by the heads of government of seven major non-communist industrialized countries (Canada, France, West Germany, Italy, Japan, the United Kingdom and the United States) and by the President of the European Commission. The proceedings of the summit were dominated by discussion of oil market developments, and the final declaration issued on June 29 included the following reference to OPEC oil-pricing policies: "We deplore the decisions taken by the recent OPEC Conference [meeting]. We recognize that relative moderation was displayed by certain of the participants. But the unwarranted rises in oil prices nevertheless agreed are bound to have very serious economic and social consequences. They mean more worldwide inflation and less growth. That will lead to more unemployment, more balance-of-payments difficulty and will endanger stability in developing and developed countries of the world alike. We remain ready to examine with oil-exporting countries how to define supply and demand prospects on the world oil market."

The declaration also gave details of agreement on a common strategy to reduce oil consumption and to hasten the development of alternative energy sources, stemming largely from proposals endorsed by EEC heads of government at a European Council meeting held in Strasbourg on June 21 and 22.

Regarding the level of oil imports in the immediate future, (i) it was noted in respect of the four EEC member countries whose leaders participated in the Tokyo summit that the European Council had decided at its March meeting to restrict member countries' aggregate 1979 oil consumption to 500,000,000 tonnes (◊**D10.4**) and at its June meeting to maintain Community oil imports between 1980 and 1985 at an annual level not higher than that of 1978 [i.e. about 470,000,000 tonnes]; and (ii) in respect of Canada, Japan and the United States, it was noted that these countries had undertaken to adjust their 1979 import levels in the light of the IEA decision confirmed by ministers in May (◊**D10.7**) and that they undertook to maintain their 1980 imports at levels not higher than those of 1979.

The following broad import targets for 1985 were adopted by the latter three countries: (i) for Canada, 600,000 bpd (involving a reduction of 1 per cent in the average annual rate of growth of oil consumption, given a projected decline in domestic oil production); (ii) for Japan, between 6,300,000 and 6,900,000 bpd; and (iii) for the United States, an import level not exceeding the levels either of 1977 or the then current target for 1979 (i.e. 8,500,000 bpd). (The US import target for 1979 was subsequently revised to 8,200,000 bpd, as announced by President Carter on July 15.)

The participating countries urged other industrialized countries "to set similar objectives for themselves" and stated that in fulfilling the commitments outlined above "our guiding principle will be to obtain fair supplies of oil products for all countries, taking into account the differing patterns of supply, the efforts made to limit oil imports, the economic situation of each country, the quantities of oil available, and the potential of each country for energy conservation".

The Tokyo declaration also proposed the following measures to stabilize world oil prices.

"We agree to take steps to bring into the open the working of oil markets by setting up a register of international oil transactions. We will urge oil companies and oil-exporting countries to moderate spot market transactions. We will consider the feasibility of requiring that at the time of unloading crude oil cargoes, documents be presented indicating the purchase price as certified by the producer country. We will likewise seek to achieve better information on the profit situation of oil companies and on the use of the funds available to these companies.

"We agree on the importance of keeping domestic oil prices at world market prices or raising them to this level as soon as possible. We will seek to minimize and finally eliminate administrative action that might put upward pressure on oil prices that result from domestic underpricing of oil and to avoid new subsidies which would have the same effect.

"Our countries will not buy oil for governmental stockpiles when this would place undue pressure on prices; we will consult about the decisions that we make to this end."

D10.12—Pricing and Production Developments in the Third Quarter of 1979

Following the undertakings to reduce oil consumption given by industrialized countries at the Tokyo summit, Saudi Arabia on July 2, 1979, announced an unspecified "temporary increase" in Aramco's 8,500,000 bpd production ceiling, officially for the purpose of generating additional revenue (a relatively small budget deficit in the 1978–79 fiscal year having been financed by drawing on the country's substantial capital reserves). It was however subsequently reported that a major consideration in authorizing the increase—later specified as 1,000,000 bpd, effective until the end of 1979—had been a request from President Carter for Saudi Arabia's co-operation in stabilizing world oil prices by further easing the pressures on supplies.

A White House statement of July 9 emphasized that "while the increased production will be helpful in the short term, it does not relieve the United States or other oil-consuming nations of the necessity for firm action to reduce significantly their dependence on imported oil". It became known during September that the US Government had itself refrained from resuming purchases for its strategic petroleum reserve (which had been halted in November 1978) in the light of both the Tokyo declaration and of high-level representations from Saudi Arabia.

Following the Saudi production increase a more conciliatory attitude towards OPEC became apparent in US Government statements on the world oil situation, and it was acknowledged by President Carter on Oct. 18 that OPEC countries were currently producing "at maximum levels" and that Saudi Arabia's output in particular was in excess of the upper limit dictated by that country's national interests. (According to estimates published on July 11 by the US Central Intelligence Agency, Aramco's increased production level of 9,500,000 bpd was currently the maximum which it was technically possible for the company to achieve on a sustained basis.)

Saudi Arabia's action was taken despite opposition to such a production increase on the part of several other OPEC members, which was understood to have been expressed at the 54th OPEC Conference meeting notably by Iraq and Libya. It was in addition strongly criticized by several Palestinian leaders, including Georges Habash of the Popular Front for the Liberation of Palestine, who was quoted in the Lebanese press on July 9 as saying that "the pressure which the oil-exporting countries can exert on the United States [in the context of current political developments in the Middle East] is a function of the volume of oil production rather than the level of oil prices".

On the basis of an estimate by Shaikh Yamani of an overall 800,000 bpd shortfall in oil supplies at the beginning of July, the effect of Saudi Arabia's 1,000,000 bpd production increase was to restore equilibrium in world oil trade, albeit within very narrow margins, and the third quarter of 1979 saw an appreciable easing of the supply problems which had recently been experienced by some importing countries and of the upward pressure on the level of prices. Increases in official OPEC prices during this period were confined (i) to a rise of 75 cents per barrel in the price of Iraq's 36° crude, which was brought into line with that of Iran's 34° crude (i.e. $22 per barrel) with effect from Aug. 1, and (ii) to various adjustments in Venezuelan differentials for heavy and extra-heavy crudes (also with effect from Aug. 1).

The monthly average spot price of Saudi Arabian 34° crude, which had reached $35.40 per barrel in June, fell to $33.13 in July and remained fairly stable (at $33.80) in August before rising to $35 in September. The monthly average spot price of light African crudes evolved as follows over the same period: $37.86 (June), $36.71 (July), $37.43 (August), $38.17 (September). The volume of spot trade fell appreciably during July and August, when the effect of the increase in Saudi output was reinforced by the seasonal trough in oil consumption. The impression that the spot market was reverting to its traditional marginal role in international oil trade was, however, gradually dispelled during September, which brought an upturn in demand for spot cargoes as (for the second successive year) the oil industry began an unusually early build-up of winter stocks.

Statistics published by the European Commission as part of a policy of closer surveillance of oil market activities in the European Community showed a fall in a composite index of Rotterdam spot prices for a range of crude oil and imported finished products (end-1978 = 100) from 213 points on July 2 to 193 points on Sept. 24, with a low point for the third quarter of 189 points on Aug. 13. An index of pre-tax consumer prices in EEC member countries (calculated from the same base date for the same range of products) rose progressively from 135 points on June 25 (i.e. prior to OPEC's mid-year price increase) to 157 points on Sept. 24, while an index of the average fob price of the Community's external crude oil supplies, based on oil exporters' official prices, remained at 157 points throughout the third quarter (having stood at 135 points on June 25).

D10.13—Further Upward Pressure on Prices Leading to Breach of Official OPEC Ceiling (October to early December 1979)

During the last quarter of 1979 international oil trade was dominated by renewed anxieties about the security of future supplies, causing buyers to seek a rapid build-up of stocks regardless of the stress which this placed on the current fragile balance between supply and demand. Uncertainty about future supply prospects continued to stem mainly from the situation in Iran, whose exports—which had fallen well below the government ceiling of 3,300,000 bpd during the first half of October—were felt to be at constant risk in view both of the country's general political instability and of various technical and managerial problems which had become apparent in the oil industry after the departure of senior foreign personnel. Matters were further complicated by a US government ban on the import of Iranian oil (announced on Nov. 12), which was followed by an Iranian ban on the sale of oil to US-owned companies, regardless of the destination of the oil. Several OPEC countries which had raised their 1979 production ceilings in order to offset the shortfall in Iranian supplies (including notably Kuwait) had meanwhile made it clear that these higher ceilings were unlikely to be maintained in 1980.

In a strong seller's market, the average monthly spot price of Saudi Arabian 34° crude rose to $38 per barrel in October and $41 in November and December, while the averages for light African crudes were $40.66 in October, $43.73 in November and $43.25 in December. A round of reactive increases in official OPEC prices was initiated on Oct. 8 by Kuwait, which raised the price of its 31° crude by 10 per cent, to $21.43 per barrel, with effect from Oct. 1. On Oct. 15 Iran announced that the price of its own 31° crude would rise to $22.77 per barrel and the price of its 34° crude to $23.50 (i.e. the OPEC ceiling level and the prevailing official price of the most expensive African crudes), these increases being likewise backdated to Oct. 1. The OPEC ceiling was then breached when Libya increased its prices by $2.77 per barrel in order to re-establish a differential vis-à-vis Iran. Libya's decision was announced on Oct. 15 and took effect on that date.

Prior to the resumption of the upward trend in official prices, most OPEC countries had expressed renewed concern at a continuing decline in the international value of the US dollar. Thus at the annual meeting of the International Monetary Fund the Saudi Arabian Minister of Finance and National Economy, Shaikh Muhammed Ali Abu al Khail, stated on Oct. 3 that "it would be naive to pretend that a continuous erosion of our financial resources through inflation and exchange depreciation could not evoke reaction".

Shaikh Yamani said on Oct. 17 that the world oil market was now "going out of control" despite his country's current increased production, and could in the present circumstances only be stabilized through reduced demand for oil. He also criticized the operation of the spot markets in what was understood to be a reference to the preparedness of purchasers to bid for supplies at record price levels; yet it was noted in press reports that some OPEC countries were continuing both to divert oil to these markets (with Iran in particular reportedly making up to 15 per cent of its exports on this basis) and to charge prices approaching spot levels for a proportion of their sales to established customers as a prerequisite for the renewal of long-term supply contracts at official prices (a practice reported to have been adopted notably by Iran, Iraq, Algeria and Libya).

Iraq increased its official prices with effect from Oct. 20 (to $21.96 per barrel for 34° crude and $22.18 for 36° crude), while Algeria and Nigeria each adopted a new maximum price of $26.27 per barrel (Algeria with effect from Oct. 24 and Nigeria with effect from Nov. 6) in order to restore parity with Libya. Gabon increased its prices by $2.50 per barrel with effect from Nov. 9, while Indonesia raised its prices to a uniform $23.50 per barrel for all grades with effect from Nov. 17. The price of Ecuador's 29.7° crude, which had been fractionally reduced to $23.28 per barrel on Oct. 1, was sharply increased to $30.57 with effect from Nov. 1. (After the end of November Ecuador retained a purely notional official selling price, switching for practical purposes to a more flexible system of monthly "average sales prices".

Ecuador's average sales price for December was, at $32.09 per barrel, higher than any other OPEC country's official selling price.)

In early December Qatar, Saudi Arabia, the United Arab Emirates and Venezuela were the only OPEC producers whose official selling prices had remained unchanged since the third quarter of 1979. Iran's price of $23.50 per barrel for 34° crude was now generally regarded as OPEC's de facto marker value, and had been used as a reference point for the upward revision of several non-OPEC countries' official export prices.

D10.14—Further IEA Initiative to stabilize the Oil Market

The Governing Board of the IEA met in Paris on Dec. 10, 1979, to consider further measures designed to stabilize the world oil market. The Board heard a report on earlier discussions which had taken place in Paris on Sept. 26 between the energy ministers of the seven countries represented at the Tokyo summit conference (◊D10.11), the purpose of these discussions (which were also attended by the European Community's Energy Commissioner) being to evaluate the implementation to date of the energy policy undertakings which had been made at the summit.

The Sept. 26 meeting had dealt in particular (i) with each participating country's confirmation of its oil import target for 1985, and (ii) with the introduction of procedures for monitoring imports of crude oil, which it was agreed should be recorded on a monthly basis, with consideration being given to the feasibility of more frequent monitoring of selected transactions. It was agreed to set up a high-level committee to supervise the implementation of the Tokyo summit objectives and agreed in principle to set up an international energy technology group to review the measures taken or planned by participating countries for marketing promising energy technology and to report on the need for international co-operation, including financial requirements.

As regards the nine member countries of the European Community, the Council of (Energy) Ministers had at meetings held on Oct. 9 and Dec. 4 respectively set out the 1985 and 1980 import targets of each member country within the overall annual limit of 472,000,000 tonnes (i.e. equivalent to the 1978 total) which the Community had undertaken to observe during the period 1980–85. Details of these targets are shown in Table 48 as reaffirmed in the context of the IEA meeting by eight Community members; France, the only Community member which did not belong to the IEA, adopted oil import targets of 117,000,000 tonnes in 1980 and 111,000,000 tonnes in 1985. It was also agreed at the Dec. 4 meeting of the Council of (Energy) Ministers to establish a quarterly monitoring procedure to assess progress in fulfilling the agreed targets.

A proposal by the United States that the major IEA importing countries should undertake to restrict their 1980 imports to levels significantly lower than those proposed at the Tokyo summit was rejected by the IEA Governing Board following opposition particularly from the European Community ministers, who were not prepared to consider the further adjustment at this stage of their own countries' recently agreed import targets. The press statement issued at the conclusion of the Dec. 10 meeting was worded as follows.

"Ministers noted with concern the turbulent development of the world oil market in 1979 and the continuing uncertainties about oil supplies which pose a severe threat to the health of the world economy. The IEA countries are determined to make their contribution to restoring order and reducing pressures on the world oil market so as to avoid further sharp price increases. Their actions are aimed not only at the immediate situation, but also at accelerating and facilitating the medium- and long-term transition to an oil-scarce world economy. They expressed their determination to overcome any shortfall of supply in a spirit of full solidarity.

"Ministers underlined their concern and recognition of the fact that development policies might be compromised if developing countries do not have sufficient energy resources at reasonable prices and stressed the need for energy-specific action to help developing countries in meeting their energy requirements.

"Ministers further recognized the importance of oil-producing countries for their part in pursuing policies which contribute to stabilization of conditions in the world oil market and in the world economy. They feel certain that such countries will be influenced by this consideration. Solution of the world's serious energy problems requires a common approach by producing and consuming countries, both developed and developing. IEA countries would welcome more opportunities to discuss these issues with oil-producing countries.

"Ministers agreed on the importance of keeping domestic oil prices at world market levels or raising them to these levels as soon as possible, and that action must be taken within individual IEA countries to transform short-term conservation measures into permanent long-term gains in energy efficiency, and to accelerate the development of alternative energy sources [through] rapid medium-term substitution of natural gas for oil; much greater world-wide production and use of coal; steady expansion of nuclear power wherever possible and having due regard to legal and constitutional provisions; and pursuit of new energy technologies for the long term. The effect of measures taken should be sufficient to achieve acceptable balance between available supply and demand and to give a substantial contribution to meeting IEA countries' need to reduce their dependence on imported oil.

"Ministers undertook to assure that their countries take serious and effective energy policy action to restrain demand for oil on world markets in 1980.

"All IEA countries firmly committed themselves to limit their oil imports in 1980, and to pursue goals for their oil imports in 1985, as set forth below [see Table 48].

Table 48 — IEA oil import targets for 1980 and 1985

	1980	1985
	(million tonnes)	
Australia	13.5	17.0
Austria	11.5	13.5
Belgium	30.0	31.0
Canada	7.4	29.4
Denmark	16.5	11.0
West Germany	143.0	141.0
Greece	14.8	16.5
Irish Republic	6.5	8.0
Italy	103.5	124.0
Japan	265.3	308.66
Luxembourg	1.5	2.0
Netherlands	42.0	49.0
New Zealand	4.2	4.4
Norway	−15.5	−18.3
Spain	51.0	52.9
Sweden	29.9	29.0
Switzerland	14.0	14.5
Turkey	17.0	25.0
United Kingdom	12.0	−5.0
United States and Territories	437.2	436.0
IEA Total	1,205.3*	1,289.56*

*The totals shown in Table 48 were also expressed in barrels per day as follows: for 1980, 24,500,000 bpd, of which 1,400,000 bpd represented bunker fuel for shipping; for 1985, 26,200,000 bpd, including 1,600,000 bpd for bunkers.

"Ministers agreed upon a monitoring process to cover energy policies and developments in the short, medium and long term:

"(1) The Governing Board will meet again at ministerial level within the first quarter of 1980 to begin the process of monitoring, to review all aspects of the situation and the outcome of the work commissioned today, including adjustment of the 1980 oil import ceilings to the extent which proves necessary on the basis of oil supply and demand developments;

"(2) Thereafter the IEA Governing Board will review quarterly the results achieved by each country in meeting its 1980 ceiling and its goal for 1985, and will determine whether the specific measures in place in each country are adequate and are being effectively implemented, and whether additional measures are necessary;

"(3) The IEA Governing Board will review quarterly oil supply developments and whether the 1980 ceilings and the 1985 goals are adequate in light of these developments;

"(4) Ministers will meet promptly to consider what corrective action is necessary if the performance of countries in keeping within their import limitations is not satisfactory, or if there is a major change in the supply situation.

"The Governing Board at official level will develop plans to meet any deterioration of the supply/demand situation which may arise in the coming months, including a system for adjusting national oil import ceilings and goals which, taking account of the 1980 and 1985 oil import targets, promotes equitable burden-sharing and which also takes account of each country's continuing performance in accordance with the IEA principles for energy policy [◊B3.4]; its economic growth and overall economic structure; its development needs; the structure of its energy economy, including consumption levels, energy prices, and changes therein; and opportunities for and achievements in conservation, fuel switching and indigenous production.

"IEA countries will take the measures necessary within their national responsibility to ensure that they keep within their oil import ceilings and goals.

"Ministers agreed that the overall group objective for oil imports by IEA countries as a group in 1985 will be lowered to 24,600,000 barrels per day plus bunkers, as compared to the former group objective [◊D8.9] of 26,000,000 bpd plus bunkers. Each country will adjust its energy programmes to assure that this revised group objective for 1985 will be met.

"Ministers agreed that because stock movements are an essential element in determining market conditions, IEA member countries should increase their ability to influence stock levels. As a first step they directed the Governing Board to elaborate on an expedited basis an improved information system on stock movements, adding information on stocks at sea, stocks in bonded areas and consumer stocks.

"Ministers agreed on the necessity of improving understanding of and ability to cope with changing oil market structures by (i) expanding the list of oil companies which report oil flows directly to the IEA; (ii) extending the new international register of crude oil transactions [which it had been agreed to establish at the Tokyo economic summit] to include oil products; (iii) obtaining more information regarding state-to-state transactions; and (iv) effectively discouraging unnecessary recourse to spot market purchases by both government-related and private companies.

"Ministers also agreed that the Governing Board at official level should (i) seek to develop a system of consultation on stock policies among governments within the IEA and between governments and oil companies; evaluate the 90-day emergency reserve level [i.e. the IEA member countries' agreed target of acquiring by 1980 national oil stockpiles equivalent to 90 days' net imports]; and develop other proposals for an effective and flexible stock policy; and (ii) consider additional measures leading to a more co-ordinated approach to spot market activities by member country governments, companies and individuals, which might include developing a system for registration of entities trading oil into or from IEA countries, in order to identify the participants in changing market structures; developing a 'code of conduct' as a basic standard for desired behaviour of market participants; and preparing measures and procedures designed to 'cool off' oil markets under overheated trading conditions."

The then US Energy Secretary, Charles Duncan, said after the meeting that it was "a very positive achievement" to have reached agreement on a framework for taking rapid co-operative action in response to changing market conditions, although it was noted in press reports that the United States had failed to win endorsement for its proposals to reduce further the agreed import targets and to devise a system for penalizing IEA countries which exceeded their targets (e.g. by excluding such countries from the Agency's emergency oil-sharing arrangements). Other proposals which were understood to have been rejected by the meeting included one for immediate action by governments to regulate the operation of the spot markets, which was reported to have been pressed particularly by the United Kingdom.

D10.15—Further OPEC Price Increases in December 1979 – 55th Meeting of OPEC Conference

In an unexpected development on Dec. 13, 1979, Saudi Arabia increased the prices of its 27°, 31° and 34° crudes by $6 per barrel, thus adopting a new marker value of $24, some 50 cents above the de facto OPEC marker value which had been established by Iran in October ($\lozenge$**D10.13**). Simultaneous across-the-board price increases of $6 per barrel were announced by Qatar and the United Arab Emirates. The price of Saudi Arabia's 39° crude was raised by $3.397, to $24.721 per barrel. All of the above increases were backdated to Nov. 1. Later on Dec. 13, Venezuela announced price increases ranging from $2.60 to $5.40 per barrel for its various grades of oil; for 34° crude, the increase was $4.30 and the new price $26.75. The Venezuelan increases took effect on Dec. 14.

Shaikh Yamani said on Dec. 14 that his country's pricing initiative had been taken in the light of the current state of the world oil market (and had been backdated in order to prevent foreign oil companies from retaining the "windfall profits" which had accrued as a result of the relatively low prices previously charged), and would form the basis of an attempt by him to secure the agreement of other countries' Oil Ministers to a reunified pricing structure when the OPEC Conference next met on Dec. 17. He added that Saudi Arabia intended to maintain Aramco's production ceiling at 9,500,000 bpd beyond the end of 1979.

Libya nevertheless challenged the Saudi initiative on Dec. 16, when it increased its prices by $3.73 per barrel with effect from Dec. 13, taking the price of its 40.5° crude to $30 per barrel. The new Libyan prices (of which 50 cents per barrel was to be allocated to the OPEC Special Fund for developing countries) were estimated to be equivalent to a marker value of between $26 and $27 per barrel after allowing for freight and quality differentials. In announcing the price increases, Libya's Oil Minister criticized Saudi Arabia for attempting to "impose" its own new marker value of $24 on the OPEC Conference. Other member countries which announced price increases at this point were Indonesia (by between $1.80 and $4.40 per barrel—$2 for its main 34.1° grade—with effect from Dec. 17) and Iran (by $5 per barrel, with retroactive effect from Dec. 1).

The 55th meeting of the OPEC Conference, which opened in Caracas on Dec. 17, 1979, ended on Dec. 20 without any agreement on pricing (which was to be the subject of a subsequent extraordinary meeting), and the press statement issued by the Secretariat gave prominence instead to the question of OPEC members' co-operation with other developing countries.

The greater part of the meeting was nevertheless devoted to the pricing issue, in respect of which the OPEC Economic Commission had recommended reunification on the basis of a marker price of $24–$25 per barrel. Saudi Arabia, supported by Qatar and the UAE, urged the implementation of this recommendation, but Libya and Iran defended their own most recent increases, with Iran proposing a further increase in the marker price to as much as $35 per barrel. It therefore proved impossible to reach agreement on a compromise proposal put forward by Venezuela, Iraq, Kuwait, Algeria, Indonesia and Gabon for a marker price of $26 per barrel, including a $2 surcharge. The main sections of the press statement issued on Dec. 20 were as follows:

"The Conference noted with appreciation the invitation of His Excellency the President of the Republic of Iraq to sovereigns and heads of state of OPEC member countries to hold their second summit conference in Baghdad in 1980, the year coinciding with the commemoration of the 20th anniversary of the Organization.

"The Conference centred its discussions on measures of co-operation with the other developing countries in the areas of economic co-operation and development, as a means of strengthening the solidarity among countries of the Third World. For this purpose, it decided to recommend to the governments of OPEC member countries to replenish the OPEC Special Fund by an amount of up to $1,600 million, in addition to the $800,000,000 already agreed upon in Geneva in June 1979 [◊**D10.10**]. These total contributions of $2,400 million, which would bring the total amounts given to the OPEC Special Fund since its establishment to $4,000 million, are to be considered as a transitory and urgent measure of financial co-operation with other developing countries while a more permanent mechanism for financial co-operation is established. In this respect, the Conference agreed in principle to convert the OPEC Special Fund into a development agency with its own legal personality. In this respect, [a joint] Algerian and Venezuelan proposal was referred to the long-term strategy committee to be studied together with the Iraqi proposal presented to the 54th meeting of the Conference held in Geneva in June 1979 with a view to presenting a definite recommendation as to the implementation of such proposals to an extraordinary meeting of the Conference to be held as soon as possible.

"Furthermore, the Conference decided to accord priority to the other developing countries in securing the supply of oil for their domestic requirements, on the basis of member countries' official prices, and reaffirmed its commitment to ensure that these countries do not incur prices beyond those official OPEC prices.

"The Conference examined the report of the 50th meeting of the Economic Commission Board, which dealt with the market trends and oil prices but did not take any decision thereon. However, an extraordinary meeting of the Conference would convene to review the various positions with regard to prices adopted by member countries.

"Consideration was given to the report of the committee of member countries' experts on the establishment of an OPEC news agency. The Conference decided in this respect to set up a special unit within the Secretariat, and instructed the Secretariat to expedite its creation so that it would become operational as soon as possible during 1980.

"While recognizing the fact that the OPEC member countries are entitled to derive direct economic advantages for their peoples by benefiting from lower energy prices, the Conference expressed its concern regarding the prevailing situation in the internal markets for oil products [which had been unaffected by recent increases in member countries' export prices] and the increasing domestic consumption in the OPEC countries. In this respect, the Conference agreed that it is necessary for all member countries to adopt internal energy policies that take into account the ever increasing scarcity of our exhaustible oil resources. In particular, it urges all the member countries to adopt an internal pricing structure for their oil products which will foster the conservation of such resources, and which will favour the rationalization of domestic consumption of energy."

Retroactive price increases were announced as follows by OPEC members in the aftermath of the 55th Conference meeting: (i) Algeria and Nigeria aligned their prices with Libya's (i.e. with a new maximum of $30 per barrel), the former with effect from Dec. 14 and the latter with effect from Dec. 17; (ii) Iraq increased its prices by $4 per barrel, $2 of this increase being retroactive to Nov. 1 and the remaining $2 to Dec. 1; and (iii) Kuwait raised the price of its 31° crude by $4.07 per barrel with effect from Nov. 1. Identical increases were made in Kuwait's prices for Neutral Zone crudes (taking these prices to $25.202 per barrel for the 28° grade and $26.004 for the 35° grade). Kuwait's 1979 price increases for Neutral Zone crudes, which had paralleled the increases for exports from Kuwait proper, had previously been formally matched by Saudi Arabia, notwithstanding the fact that they had since February been out of step with movements in the price of oil exported from Saudi Arabia proper. From the Nov. 1 increase onwards, however, changes in Neutral Zone prices were announced solely by Kuwait.

D10.16—Increasing Concern over OPEC Price Rises among Oil-Importing Developing Countries

The recommendation of the 55th Conference meeting that the resources of the OPEC Special Fund should be further increased came less than three months after OPEC Finance Ministers (meeting in Vienna on Sept. 27, 1979) had formally endorsed the previous increase recommended at the 54th Conference meeting in June.

International Monetary Fund estimates, published after the announcement of the OPEC countries' mid-year price adjustments, had shown that oil-importing developing countries could expect their annual oil import costs to rise by $12,000 million in 1979 if OPEC prices remained at their July 1 levels throughout the second half of the year. Many of these countries had subsequently increased their pressure for a new OPEC aid initiative, and had in particular used a summit meeting of non-aligned states, held in Cuba from Sept. 3 to 7, as a forum within which to pursue this issue on both a formal and an informal basis.

It became clear during the non-aligned summit that the preference of the most seriously affected third-world importers was for some form of direct compensatory financing to offset the increase in the cost of their oil imports (although it was also suggested that OPEC's "surplus revenue" members should transfer some of their external financial holdings and equity investments from the developed to the developing countries). However, the only OPEC member to address the issue directly on a bilateral basis at this point was Iraq, whose President told the summit on Sept. 4 that his Government would grant interest-free long-term loans to offset the impact of increases in Iraq's official oil prices for the period June 1 to Dec. 31, 1979, on "the poor developing countries already linked by direct oil contracts with Iraq".

It was, however, stressed that Iraq retained as its longer-term objective the establishment of an aid mechanism whereby the industrialized countries would assume a joint responsibility with the OPEC countries for the alleviation of third-world balance-of-payments problems (◊**D10.9**). Other OPEC members reiterated the Organization's established policy that oil prices could not be considered without reference to wider economic issues, this policy being reflected as follows in the non-aligned summit's final declaration: "The heads of state or government emphasized that the international energy issue should be discussed in the context of global negotiations within the United Nations with the participation of all countries and in relation with such other issues as the problems of development of developing countries, financial and monetary reforms, world trade and raw materials, all of which have an important bearing on the establishment of the new interntional economic order."

The line taken by the OPEC countries was generally regarded in the West as a "diversionary tactic" designed to prevent the Organization from becoming the principal focus of criticism in the Third World as the poorer oil-importing countries' terms of trade continued to deteriorate. Criticism of OPEC nevertheless became more frequent as the upward movement in official oil prices gathered momentum during the last quarter of 1979, although at the same time talks were held between oil-importing and oil-exporting non-aligned countries with a view to drafting a formal proposal for "global negotiations" under UN auspices.

Black African concern over the impact of OPEC price increases tended to impede progress towards closer Afro-Arab co-operation (a wide-ranging co-operation programme having been adopted in March 1977 at a conference of African and Arab heads of government organized by the Arab League and the Organization of African Unity). A weakening of Afro-Arab solidarity was apparent during the non-aligned summit meeting, when several black African oil-importing countries failed to give their full backing to certain aspects of the Arab League's stance on current Middle Eastern political issues.

D10.17—Start of Phased Decontrol of US Crude Prices – Other US Energy Policy Developments in 1979

President Carter announced on April 5, 1979, that he had decided to order the phasing out of federal controls on domestic crude oil prices, which had been introduced in 1971 and were currently applied under the terms of the Emergency Petroleum Allocation Act of 1973. This Act, which was due to expire on Sept. 30, 1981, empowered the President to begin a phased decontrol process on June 1, 1979. Under the existing controls, whose administration required what was described by President Carter as an "almost unbelievably complicated" system of "federal bureaucracy and red tape", two-thirds of US oil output was classed either (i) as lower-tier or old oil (from wells which had been brought into production before 1973) or (ii) as upper-tier or new oil (from non-exempt wells brought into production from 1973 onwards). The one-third of output which was currently exempt from price controls included oil from "stripper" wells producing less than 10 bpd, production from the Alaskan North Slope and production from federally-owned reserves.

Lower-tier oil was currently priced at around $6 per barrel and upper-tier oil at around $13 per barrel, while exempt oil commanded the full world price. US refiners' acquisition costs were equalized under a "crude oil entitlement system", whereby the proceeds of a levy on refiners whose throughput included a high proportion of lower-priced crude were used to subsidize refiners whose throughput included a high proportion of higher-priced crude (the practical effect of this system being to encourage a high level of dependence on "subsidized" imports among non-integrated refiners).

President Carter's decontrol schedule was announced as follows:

"As of June 1, 1979, newly discovered oil will be permitted to receive the world market price. While only a small amount of oil will be included in this category at first, newly discovered oil will contribute increasingly to US supplies as new reserves are found and developed. The Department of Energy has promulgated a rule under which, as of June 1, 1979, 80 per cent of all production from 'marginal' wells may be sold at the upper-tier price. Marginal wells are those wells which produce below a certain volume of oil per day depending upon the depth of the well. . . . On Jan. 1, 1980, the remaining 20 per cent of production from marginal wells will be released to the upper-tier price. Effective June 1, 1979, any incremental new production from wells employing specified enhanced recovery techniques (e.g. tertiary recovery) may receive the world price. Beginning on Jan. 1, 1980, producers who invest in enhanced recovery projects may release specified volumes of lower-tier oil to the upper-tier price in order to finance that investment. Beginning on Jan. 1, 1980, the upper-tier oil price will increase in equal monthly increments until it reaches the world price on Oct. 1, 1981. The Department of Energy has today promulgated a rule under which, as of Jan. 1, 1980, lower-tier oil will be permitted to decline at a rate of 3 per cent per month. Between June 1, 1979, and Jan. 1, 1980, the decline rate will equal 1½ per cent per month, a rate equal to the natural decline rate experienced by lower-tier wells in 1978. . . . The President retains the authority to adjust price controls in any way necessary."

A request for legislation to impose a tax on increases in oil company profits attributable to the phasing out of price controls was submitted to Congress by President Carter on April 26. The proceeds of the proposed tax were to be placed in an "energy security fund". On June 28 the President requested legislation to establish a special bank (using resources from the proposed energy security fund) which would disburse $150,000,000 per year in interest subsidies on loans taken out for the purpose of installing solar energy systems in residential and commercial buildings. New tax credits were proposed for certain users of solar energy systems (and for those who installed airtight woodburning stoves in principal residences), while it was proposed that gasohol (gasoline mixed with alcohol) should be permanently exempted from the federal excise tax on gasoline.

On July 15 President Carter announced a six-point energy plan, the cost of which would be covered by the proposed energy security fund. The plan envisaged the following measures:

(1) The establishment of a "clear goal" for US energy policy, namely that oil imports should never exceed their 1977 level (of between 8,700,000 and 9,000,000 bpd) and should be halved by 1990.

(2) The establishment of oil import quotas for 1979 and 1980 below the ceiling level of 8,500,000 bpd which had been agreed by President Carter at the recent Tokyo economic summit meeting (◊**D10.11**). (The quota for 1979 was subsequently fixed at 8,200,000 bpd.)

(3) Legislation to require utility companies to halve their use of oil by 1990, mainly by switching to coal.

(4) Legislation to introduce a "bold conservation programme", including mandatory conservation measures, standby gasoline rationing authority and the expenditure of an additional $10,000 million on public transportation during the 1980s.

(5) Legislation to create an energy security corporation—an independent government-sponsored corporation with a congressional charter—to oversee an $88,000 million programme of investment in the development of synthetic hydrocarbons and other alternative energy sources. The corporation's central objective would be to secure the production of sufficient "new" energy to displace 2,500,000 bpd of imported oil by 1990. Investment would be mainly in coal conversion, shale oil, peat and biomass conversion.

(6) Legislation to create an energy mobilization board, which would be empowered to establish binding schedules to expedite the development and construction of "critical energy facilities" (including non-nuclear power plants).

Legislation was enacted on Nov. 5 to empower the President to draw up a standby gasoline rationing plan and to implement it during an emergency. Such a plan would take effect 30 days after its submission, unless rejected by a joint resolution of both Houses of Congress. The President could veto such a resolution, but his veto could in turn be overridden by a two-thirds majority vote in both Houses. In the event of a 20 per cent or greater fuel shortage existing for 30 days the President could take the plan off its standby status and implement it, although either House could prevent such a move by a resolution of disapproval. However, if the shortage was less than 20 per cent, both Houses would have to give their positive approval. The legislation also laid down that motorists in each state should have the same percentage reduction in gasoline and that the standby plan must recognize the relative needs of users.

D11—1980

D11.1—Annual Statistical Survey

D11.1.i—Oil production and reserves

World

Total production	62,745,000 bpd (3,081.9 million tonnes)
Change over 1979	−4.4 per cent
End-year proved reserves	656,500 million barrels
Change over end-1979	+1 per cent
Reserves:production ratio	28.6 : 1

Regional shares:

	In 1980 world production*			In end-1980 world reserves†		
	Regional total (million tonnes)	Change over 1979 (per cent)	Share of world total (per cent)	Reserves (thousand million barrels)	Change over 1979 (per cent)	Share of world total (per cent)
Middle East	927.4	−14.2	30.1	362.0	+0.06	55.1
USSR/Eastern Europe/China	727.6	+2.2	23.6	86.3	−4.1	13.2
North America	565.8	+0.2	18.3	39.2	−3.9	6.0
Africa	301.7	−8.2	9.8	55.1	−3.5	8.4
Latin America/ Caribbean	298.5	+6.6	9.7	71.1	+24.5	10.8
Asia‡/Australasia	135.3	−5.0	4.4	19.6	+1.0	3.0
Western Europe§	125.6	+7.8	4.1	23.2	−1.7	3.5

*Including production from oil shales, tar sands and natural gas liquids (NGL).
†Excluding oil shales and tar sands; including NGL in North America.
‡Excluding China.
§Including Yugoslavia.

OPEC

OPEC oil production	27,450,000 bpd (1,357.7 million tonnes)
Change over 1979	−12.6 per cent
Share of 1980 world total	44.1 per cent
OPEC end-year proved reserves	435,935 million barrels
Change over 1979	−0.07 per cent
Share of 1980 world total	66.4 per cent
OPEC reserves:production ratio	43.5 : 1

OPEC (continued)

OPEC member countries' production:

	1980 production		Change over 1979 (per cent)	Share of world total (per cent)	Share of OPEC total (per cent)
	(million tonnes)	(thousand bpd)			
Algeria	52.2	1,120	−10.8	1.7	3.8
Ecuador	10.0	205	−4.8	0.3	0.7
Gabon	8.8	175	−13.7	0.3	0.7
Indonesia	78.3	1,575	−0.6	2.5	5.8
Iran	73.7	1,480	−53.4	2.4	5.4
Iraq	130.2	2,645	−23.7	4.2	9.6
Kuwait	71.5	1,430	−36.8	2.3	5.3
Libya	88.4	1,830	−12.2	2.9	6.5
Nigeria	102.3	2,055	−10.4	3.3	7.5
Qatar	22.4	460	−9.3	0.7	1.7
Saudi Arabia	493.0	9,990	+4.9	16.0	36.3
UAE*	82.6	1,705	−6.8	2.7	6.1
Venezuela	115.9	2,235	−7.6	3.8	8.5
Neutral Zone†	28.4	545	−3.4	0.9	2.1

*Of which Abu Dhabi 64,700,000 tonnes (1,345,000 bpd), Dubai 17,400,000 tonnes (350,000 bpd), Sharjah 500,000 tonnes (10,000 bpd).
†Production shared between Kuwait and Saudi Arabia.

Non-OPEC

Selected non-OPEC countries' oil production:

	1980 production		Change over 1979 (per cent)	Share of world total (per cent)
	(million tonnes)	(thousand bpd)		
USSR	603.0	12,215	+2.9	19.6
USA*	484.1	10,170	+0.7	15.7
Mexico	107.3	2,155	+32.8	3.5
China	105.8	2,125	−0.3	3.4
Canada	81.7	1,725	−2.5	2.6
United Kingdom	80.5	1,650	+3.3	2.6
Egypt	29.8	590	+12.5	1.0
Norway	25.8	525	+37.2	0.8
Argentina	25.7	490	+4.9	0.8
Oman	14.4	285	−2.7	0.5
Total	1,558.1	31,930	+3.6	50.5

*Of which natural gas liquids 56,000,000 tonnes (1,575,000 bpd).

D11.1.ii—Oil consumption

World

Total consumption .... 61,615,000 bpd (3,002 million tonnes)
   Change over 1979 .... −3.9 per cent

Regional distribution of total:

	1980 consumption		Change over 1979 (per cent)	Share of world total (per cent)
	(million tonnes)	(thousand bpd)		
North America	881.7	18,315	−8.0	29.4
Western Europe*	681.6	13,955	−7.0	22.7
USSR/Eastern Europe/China	626.6	12,670	+1.2	20.9
Asia†/Australasia	435.4	8,950	−5.2	14.5
Latin America/ Caribbean	222.8	4,615	+4.0	7.4
Middle East	82.0	1,625	+8.8	2.7
Africa	71.9	1,485	+9.1	2.4

*Including Yugoslavia.
†Excluding China.

Selected countries

	1980 consumption		Change over 1979 (per cent)	Share of world total (per cent)
	(million tonnes)	(thousand bpd)		
USA	794.1	16,460	−8.5	26.5
USSR	436.0	8,795	+2.1	14.5
Japan	237.7	4,935	−10.3	7.9
West Germany	131.1	2,725	−10.8	4.4
France	109.9	2,265	−7.1	3.7
Italy	97.9	1,975	−5.1	3.3
China	88.0	1,765	−3.4	2.9
Canada	87.6	1,855	−2.8	2.9
United Kingdom	80.8	1,670	−14.5	2.7
Spain	52.2	1,070	+6.3	1.7
Total	2,115.3	43,515	−6.1	70.5

D11.1.iii—Oil refining

World

Total refinery capacity .... 81,130,000 bpd
   Change over 1979 .... +1.3 per cent

Total refinery throughputs .... 59,945,000 bpd
   Change over 1979 .... −3.2 per cent

Consumption as proportion of capacity ... 75.9 per cent

Selected markets
Consumption of refined product types and change over 1979:

	USA (million tonnes)	USA (per cent)	Western Europe (million tonnes)	Western Europe (per cent)	Japan (million tonnes)	Japan (per cent)
Gasolines	305.7	−5.5	138.9	−5.5	42.1	−8.9
Middle distillates	207.9	−10.1	237.4	−7.5	59.9	−2.6
Fuel oil	133.0	−10.4	211.3	−8.8	103.5	−16.3
Other	147.5	−10.5	94.0	−3.7	32.2	−4.5
Total	794.1	−8.5	681.6	−7.0	237.7	−10.3

D11.1.iv—Tankers and trade

Tankers

Total world fleet .... 324,800,000 deadweight tons
  Change over 1979 .... −0.9 per cent

Trade

Total world crude exports
  (including re-exports) .... 29,824,700 bpd (1,480.1 million tonnes)
  Change over 1979 .... −10.8 per cent
OPEC crude exports .... 22,843,700 bpd (1,133.7 million tonnes)
  Change over 1979 .... −14.7 per cent
  Share of 1980 world total .... 76.6 per cent
Total world product exports
  (including re-exports) .... 8,635,000 bpd (433,701,700 tonnes)
  Change over 1979 .... +0.9 per cent
OPEC product exports .... 2,017,000 bpd (101,305,900 tonnes)
  Change over 1979 .... −2.6 per cent
  Share of 1980 world total .... 23.4 per cent

Regional distribution of world oil trade*:

	Share of 1980 imports (per cent) Crude	Products	Share of 1980 exports (per cent) Crude	Products
USA	19.7	28.8	1.1	5.6
Canada	2.2	0.8	0.8	4.5
Latin America/Caribbean	10.0	5.7	7.1	38.2
Western Europe	39.1	27.3	1.2	2.9
Middle East	0.3	3.7	61.9	20.0
North Africa	0.3	0.7	9.9	3.4
West Africa	†	1.8	8.8	1.5
East and southern Africa	1.6	0.7	–	0.2
South Asia	1.8	2.7	–	0.7
South-East Asia	6.2	7.0	5.0	6.4
Australasia	0.7	3.0	–	0.3
Japan	16.7	9.4	–	0.1
USSR/Eastern Europe/China	0.6	3.5	4.2	16.2
Unspecified	0.8	4.9	–	–
Total	100.0	100.0	100.0	100.0

*Excluding intra-regional trade.   †Negligible.

D11.1.v—World primary energy consumption
Total consumption (excluding
non-commercial fuels) .... 6,896.2 million tonnes oil equivalent (mtoe)
Change over 1979 .... −0.6 per cent

Contributions of primary energy sources:

	Consumption (mtoe)	Change over 1979 (per cent)	Share of total (per cent)
Oil	3,002.0	−3.9	43.5
Coal	2,006.4	+1.6	29.1
Natural gas	1,296.8	+1.8	18.8
Water power	421.6	+2.0	6.1
Nuclear power	169.4	+10.7	2.5

D11.1.vi—Natural gas production and reserves
Marketed production (thousand million cubic metres):

	Regional total (tmcm)	Change over 1979 (per cent)	Share of 1980 world total (per cent)
North America	620.9	−2.2	43.2
Latin America/ Caribbean	62.7	+19.4	4.3
Western Europe*	180.9	−1.7	12.6
USSR/Eastern Europe/China	455.4	+6.2	31.7
Middle East	41.2	−14.7	2.9
Africa	20.2	−22.3	1.4
Asia†/Australasia	56.9	+11.4	3.9
World total	1,438.2	+0.9	100.0
(of which OPEC)	(86.2)	(−11.8)	(6.0)

End-year proved reserves (thousand million cubic metres):

	Regional total (tmcm)	Change over 1979 (per cent)	Share of 1980 world total (per cent)
North America	8,108.0	−0.1	9.9
Latin America/ Caribbean	4,598.9	+11.4	5.6
Western Europe*	4,604.4	+13.5	5.6
USSR/Eastern Europe/China	31,821.4	+18.2	38.8
Middle East	23,121.9	+9.9	28.2
Africa	5,890.3	−0.8	7.2
Asia†/Australasia	3,861.4	+0.6	4.7
World total	82,006.3	+10.8	100.0
(of which OPEC)	(30,474.1)	(+7.1)	(37.2)

*Including Yugoslavia.
†Excluding China.

D11.2—Pricing and Production Developments, January to March 1980

There was a general downward trend in oil consumption in the main importing countries throughout 1980 as the growing impact of energy conservation and fuel-switching measures was reinforced by the onset of economic recession. The significance of these underlying factors was least apparent during the first quarter of the year, when an abnormally low seasonal peak in consumption was attributed primarily to mild winter weather conditions. There was a correspondingly low gross drawdown of importers' substantial opening inventories, the rapid replenishment of which was effected without placing any additional upward pressure on free- market prices. The net drawdown of oil company stocks between Jan. 1 and March 31 was estimated as 330,000 bpd (compared with a first-quarter average of 2,750,000 bpd over the four preceding years), while spot oil prices had by March fallen back to levels comparable to those which prevailed in the third quarter of 1979 (◊**D10.12**).

Overall demand for OPEC oil was further depressed by increases in non-OPEC production, and OPEC's average monthly output underwent a sharp decline of around 1,200,000 bpd between December 1979 and January 1980, with the result that the exports of most member countries other than Saudi Arabia (including several countries which had reduced their production ceilings on Jan. 1) fell well short of the planned volumes. OPEC's January output averaged 29,500,000 bpd (its lowest level since early 1979), the average for the entire first quarter of 1980 being 29,300,000 bpd.

In the absence of an OPEC consensus on pricing, member countries' official contract prices continued to rise towards the prevailing level of spot prices. On Jan. 1 Libya imposed an additional market premium of $4.72 per barrel (which was subsequently incorporated into the country's basic prices, taking them to a maximum of $34.72), while Algeria began to levy a separate "exploration fee" of $3 per barrel, refundable to contract customers who agreed to invest in new oil exploration ventures in Algeria (◊**C1.3.v**). Iran imposed a $3 per barrel premium in respect of half of each contract customer's purchases (i.e. an effective price increase of $1.50 per barrel). Also with effect from Jan. 1, (i) Gabon increased its prices by between $3.50 and $4 per barrel, with a new maximum of $29 for its 31.7° (formerly 31.8°) grade; (ii) Ecuador's average sales price rose by $4.32 to $36.41 per barrel; (iii) Indonesia increased its prices by between $1.60 and $2.95 per barrel (taking the price of its 34.1° grade, which rose by $2, to $27.50 per barrel); and (iv) Venezuela raised the prices of 31° and lighter crudes by $2 per barrel and the prices of heavier grades by between $1.20 and $1.72 per barrel.

On Jan. 28 Saudi Arabia increased the official price of its 34° crude by $2 per barrel (8.3 per cent) with retroactive effect from Jan. 1, while raising the prices of its other grades by amounts ranging from $1.83 (7.9 per cent) for 27° crude to $2.80 (11.3 per cent) for 39° crude. Saudi Arabia's adoption of a marker value of $26 per barrel represented a belated acceptance of the compromise proposal put forward by certain member countries during the 55th OPEC Conference meeting (◊**D10.15**), and was apparently intended to provide a reference point for the reintroduction of "historic differentials" throughout the OPEC area. However, all the other Gulf OPEC countries except Iran responded by making across-the-board increases of $2 per barrel in their own official prices, these increases —among which Kuwait's was most clearly intended as a "leapfrogging" move —being announced on Jan. 29 and backdated to Jan. 1. Across-the-board increases of $2 per barrel were subsequently announced (i) by Indonesia with effect from Feb. 4, (ii) by Venezuela (except for crudes heavier than 31°, which were subject to smaller increases) with effect from Feb. 6 and (iii) by Gabon with effect from Feb. 8. Algeria and Nigeria each increased their prices by $4.21 per barrel with effect from Feb. 4. Iran had meanwhile increased its basic official prices by $2.50 per barrel with effect from Feb. 1 while retaining its de facto surcharge of $1.50, thus taking its effective prices to $32.50 per barrel for 34° crude and $31.77 per barrel for 31° crude. Ecuador's average sales price for

February was reduced to $34.796 per barrel, at which level it remained the highest price in the OPEC area.

Following the substantial decline earlier in the year, export demand for OPEC crudes was fairly stable during March (as were spot prices). OPEC countries' selling prices remained unchanged throughout the month, save for a fractional increase by Ecuador. Several members, including Kuwait, Libya, Algeria, Iran and Venezuela, announced reductions in their production ceilings for the second quarter of the year, but Saudi Arabia confirmed on March 25 that Aramco's ceiling would remain at 9,500,000 bpd, regardless of the impact on other members' exports in the current market climate (Saudi Arabia's conservative pricing policy having led to a progressive increase in Aramco's share of total OPEC output).

D11.3—Pricing Developments in April – 56th Meeting of OPEC Conference

Iran increased the basic selling price of its 34° crude by $2.50 per barrel on April 1, 1980, while retaining its existing premium of $1.50 (now formally incorporated into the official price) and adding a new "credit charge" of 37 cents per barrel. At a total cost of $35.37 per barrel (only 38 cents below the current spot value) contract supplies of this crude on normal credit terms were now the most expensive in the OPEC area. The total cost of Iran's 31° crude on the same basis was raised to $34.37 per barrel (35 cents less than Libya's current maximum price for 40° crude). There was, however, no immediate reactive move by African producers to restore their differentials, the only April 1 adjustment in the official prices of African crudes being an increase of 51 cents per barrel by Nigeria which brought that country fully into line with Libya'a first-quarter prices. Kuwait introduced a selective premium of $5.50 on April 1, chargeable on each barrel of Kuwaiti crude which, having been supplied under contract at the official price, was subsequently resold to third-party customers rather than being marketed through the contract buyer's integrated channels. Ecuador's average sales price was reduced by $3.212 to $31.663 per barrel in April.

Iran's second-quarter price increase was strongly resisted by the Japanese and West European oil companies which had taken the bulk of the country's oil exports since the suspension of trade with US companies in November 1979, and Iranian export volume fell to as little as 500,000 bpd in early May. A temporary rise in spot prices during the latter part of April was attributed to purchases by Japanese companies which had cancelled their Iranian contracts on April 21 but had not yet completed negotiations for new contracts with alternative suppliers.

As continuing divergences of opinion among member countries had effectively ruled out the implementation of the OPEC Conference's December 1979 decision to hold an extraordinary meeting on current pricing policies, the 56th (extraordinary) meeting of the Conference, held in the Saudi summer capital of Taif on May 7 and 8, was devoted solely to longer-term issues. The main focus of discussion was a report by the ministerial committee on long-term strategy (whose most recent meeting had taken place in London on Feb. 21 and 22).

In an OPEC press statement on the outcome of the 56th Conference meeting (which was not attended by Nigeria) it was noted (i) that the central recommendations of the report on long-term strategy had been accepted by the Conference subject to "some reservations" on pricing questions by three member countries; (ii) that the Conference had "fully adopted" that part of the report which dealt with "OPEC member countries' relations with the other developing countries"; and (iii) that it was proposed to refer the question of OPEC's relations with the industrialized countries to a joint meeting of OPEC Ministers of Foreign Affairs, Finance and Oil (which subsequently took place in September ♭**D11.9**).

It was also stated (i) that "the Conference reaffirms the intention of member countries not to replace Iran's exports [i.e. exports lost through trade sanctions against Iran] in the international oil market" and (ii) that the Conference had "recommended" that natural gas prices should be aligned with crude oil prices on an energy-equivalence basis. (The latter issue, which had assumed particular importance for gas-exporting countries in the context of the steep rise in oil prices since early 1979, was raised by Algeria, Libya and Iran, which had held joint discussions in late March.)

The substance of the Conference's debate on long-term strategy was detailed in subsequent press reports based on information supplied by representatives of individual OPEC countries. As regards the longer-term development of prices, the report of the strategy committee was understood to have proposed a system of quarterly adjustments which took account of movements (i) in an index giving a two-thirds weighting to the prices of OECD merchandize exports and a one-third weighting to OECD domestic consumer prices (which would be taken to represent the prices of exported services); (ii) in an exchange-rate index based on a basket of 12 major currencies; and (iii) in the real growth of gross national product in the OECD area. The first and second elements in this formula were designed to prevent the erosion of the real purchasing power of oil exports, while the third element was intended to serve as a basis for increases in the real price of oil. The committee expected the application of the formula to produce nominal price increases exceeding 10 per cent per annum, equivalent to real increases of around 3 per cent per annum, in normal market conditions.

The countries which had expressed reservations about the proposed indexation formula were identified as Libya, Algeria and Iran (notwithstanding the latter two countries' membership of the long-term strategy committee). These countries' delegates to the Taif meeting were understood to have advocated the measurement of inflation in terms of an OPEC import price index rather than an OECD export price index and to have maintained that real price increases should be determined in the light of various additional criteria which could be expected to produce a faster rate of increase than would occur through straightforward linkage to OECD economic performance.

The long-term strategy committee was understood to have put forward various proposals for the defence of official prices at times of supply surplus but to have failed to make any recommendation that OPEC members should undertake to act to stabilize market prices during temporary supply shortages. As regards the avoidance of competitive price-cutting in a weak market, the recommended strategy depended ultimately on the ability of OPEC's "surplus revenue" members to provide financial assistance—possibly in the form of oil-indexed bonds—to those members which were less well placed to withstand a fall in export earnings.

Other sections of the committee's report were understood to include recommendations (i) that OPEC should be prepared to offer "a certain degree of assurance" to industrialized oil-importing countries regarding security of supplies, on the assumption that such countries would reciprocate by "ceasing to argue about price"; (ii) that increases in the level of OPEC aid to less developed countries should be linked to increases in oil prices; and (iii) that a "dialogue" should be opened with industrialized oil-importing countries in which OPEC's aims should include free duty-free access to Western markets for petrochemicals and refined products, access to advanced technology, the location of energy-intensive industries in OPEC countries and the lifting of trade barriers affecting OPEC member countries' non-oil exports.

543

D11.4—Further Round of OPEC Price Increases, May 1980

During the Taif meeting of the OPEC Conference, Shaikh Yamani and other members of the Saudi Arabian Cabinet were quoted as stating their country's "implacable resolve" to maintain its production at 9,500,000 bpd in the present circumstances as part of "a political/oil plan designed to serve, rather than to hurt, the economy of the world". As regards longer-term pricing policy, they criticized the stance taken by Algeria, Libya and Iran on the indexation issue, stating that these countries' only interest was in "large price increases", whereas Saudi Arabia "would like the increases to be predictable for the consuming nations". Having defined its production policy, Saudi Arabia made a further attempt to provide a basis for reunified OPEC pricing by announcing on May 14 an across-the-board increase of $2 per barrel, backdated to April 1, in its own official prices (taking the marker value to $28 per barrel).

Once more, however, a Saudi price adjustment served to precipitate a new round of increases by other OPEC members, which began with announcements by Libya, Algeria and Indonesia on May 19. Libya and Indonesia each raised their prices by $2 per barrel, the former with effect from May 15 and the latter from May 20, while Algeria imposed an increase of $1 per barrel with effect from May 16. By May 22 increases of $2 per barrel had been announced by Iraq, Kuwait, Qatar and the United Arab Emirates (all with effect from May 1) as well as by Gabon (effective May 15) and Nigeria (effective May 22), while Venezuela had announced increases of up to $3.50 per barrel (for crudes of 31° and lighter) with effect from May 26. Ecuador's average sales price for May rose by $4.417 to $36.08 per barrel. Iran's prices remained at the levels fixed on April 1.

This fresh round of increases raised the weighted average of OPEC official prices to nearly $32 per barrel, as against an average spot market price of less than $36 per barrel in late May. By early June the spot premiums for some light African crudes had declined to around $1 per barrel, while several OPEC countries were experiencing reductions in export volume as a result of customer resistance to their new official prices.

D11.5—IEA Ministerial Meeting, May 1980

The Governing Board of the IEA met at ministerial level in Paris on May 22, 1980, to review a wide range of issues, with particular reference to the development of the oil market over the previous five months. The ministers "expressed their concern about the level of oil prices which confronts the world economy with declining economic activity, having serious negative results for all countries", and referred to the official price increases announced since the end of 1979 as having "occurred despite falling oil demand [and having appeared] to be made without taking into account their adverse impact on the world economy". The meeting discussed the 1979 annual review of IEA countries' energy policies and programmes, and agreed that, in formulating future energy policies, account would be taken of the review's findings regarding the extent to which individual countries had acted in accordance with the Agency's principles for energy policy. Agreement was reached on the desirability of medium-term structural change (designed to reduce both total energy demand and oil's share of the reduced total) and of further action to provide protection against short-term market disruptions.

In view of the potential both for reductions in oil consumption and for increases in oil production within the IEA area, it was agreed that member countries should aim to reduce their aggregate net oil imports in 1985 by about an extra 4,000,000 bpd below the ceiling of 26,200,000 bpd agreed in December 1979 (◊**D10.4**), and to aim to reduce the share of oil in their total energy demand to about 40 per cent by 1990, compared with the present level of 52 per cent. It was agreed that there was scope for the reduction of the the ratio between the rate of increase in energy consumption and the rate of economic growth in the IEA area to about 0.6 by 1990 if current IEA policies were fully implemented at national level. The meeting noted that the IEA's coal industry advisory board (established in July 1979) had recently held its first meeting, and invited the board to submit "concrete recommendations on action needed to double coal production and use by 1990". It was also noted that the expansion of nuclear power was "indispensable for ensuring structural change in the medium term".

Agreement was reached on the tightening of monitoring procedures in order to enhance the ability of member countries "to limit the damaging economic effects of short-term price or volume disruptions which could occur in the oil market". To this end it was decided to establish "a system for consultations between governments within the IEA and between governments and the oil industry on stock policies, which will be used to respond to oil market conditions beginning in 1980". The meeting reaffirmed that the IEA's existing policy on the minimum level of oil stocks (i.e. that each member country should hold sufficient reserves to cover 90 days' net imports) "appears to provide reasonable protection against future emergencies". Ministers also discussed the "flexible use of [additional] stocks (over and above the 90-day emergency reserve requirement and normal working stocks) to meet short-term market disruptions".

The meeting reviewed the Agency's oil import monitoring exercise for the first quarter of 1980, which showed that no member country expected to exceed its agreed ceiling, and decided that at present it did not appear necessary to agree any ceilings for 1981. If a situation arose in which "tight market conditions appeared imminent", however, ministers would meet at short notice to decide on the use of oil import ceilings which would "represent a political commitment stating the degree of self-restraint which individual countries [were] willing to impose upon themselves" in these circumstances. The ministers reaffirmed their belief in the importance of international co-operation in dealing with world energy issues, and restated their willingness to discuss these issues with oil-exporting countries.

D11.6—OPEC Finance Ministers' Meeting – 57th Meeting of OPEC Conference

OPEC Finance Ministers, meeting in Vienna on May 27, 1980, "alternately in their capacities as the Ministerial Council of the OPEC Fund and as the OPEC Ministerial Committee on Financial and Monetary Matters", gave their formal approval (i) to the $1,600 million increase in the resources of the OPEC Special Fund which had been recommended by the OPEC Conference in December 1979 (◊**D10.15**), and (ii) to a comprehensive revision of the Fund's constituent agreement, whereby it was renamed the OPEC Fund for International Development and was restructured as a permanent multilateral agency operating within an independent institutional framework (◊**B1.6**). Iran was understood to have made it clear that it expected to bear a reduced share of the latest increase in the Fund's resources in view of the reduction in its share of OPEC oil output since 1978.

The 57th OPEC Conference meeting, held in Algiers from June 9 to 11, 1980, discussed the feasibility of reunifying the Organization's pricing structure, but eventually adopted what was in effect an "agreement to disagree" as follows: (i) "to set the level of oil price for a marker crude up to a ceiling of $32 per barrel" with effect from July 1; (ii) to restrict to a maximum of $5 per barrel the total value differential which could be added to this marker ceiling "on account of quality and geographical location"; and (iii) to review the resulting price structure at OPEC's forthcoming "tripartite meeting" (of Foreign Affairs, Finance and Oil Ministers). By failing to designate a specific marker crude, by introducing the concept of a marker ceiling and by omitting any reference to market premiums, the Conference was able to indicate a range of maximum prices preferred by the majority of members while allowing scope for other members to fix their prices above or below this range without breaking the letter of the agreement. The agreement was described by the Conference as "a further endeavour by OPEC member countries to stabilize the international oil market" and in particular to achieve "an equilibrium between supply and demand in order to avoid further stockpiling which is harmful to producers and consumers alike".

The Conference reiterated the determination of OPEC's gas-exporting members to align their natural gas prices with crude oil prices on an energy-equivalence basis as part of a "coherent marketing policy for their hydrocarbons" (◊**D11.3**). It called upon gas-importing countries "to consider oil-gas equivalency as a necessary incentive to develop gas resources economically and thus to allow gas to contribute substantially to the satisfaction of world energy needs."

As regards the preparation of a "plan of action for the long-term strategy of OPEC", Shaikh Yamani (as the chairman of the long-term strategy committee) was requested to draw up recommendations for the consideration of the forthcoming tripartite meeting. The Conference adopted a resolution (LVII–217) to provide funding for the planned OPEC news agency (which subsequently commenced operations on Nov. 3 as a special unit within the OPEC Secretariat). The Secretariat was instructed to carry out a feasibility study for the creation of an OPEC institute of higher education whose main objective would be "to help other developing countries in forming and promoting highly qualified scientific, social and technological development of human resources".

D11.7—Statement on Energy by Main Non-Communist Industrialized Countries – Response of OPEC Countries

The 1980 summit meeting of seven non-communist industrialized countries took place in Venice on June 22 and 23. Delegations were led by the French and US Presidents, the West German Federal Chancellor, the Canadian, British and Italian Prime Ministers and the Japanese Foreign Minister, while the President of the European Commission participated in discussions on issues within the competence of the European Communities. The summit declaration issued on June 23 dealt with energy issues at considerable length, and in particular welcomed the decisions of the previous month's IEA meeting regarding the establishment of medium- and long-term targets for structural change (◊**D11.5**). The IEA members represented at the summit (i.e. all the participating countries except France) reaffirmed their commitment to the fulfilment of these targets. Selected passages of the Venice summit declaration are given below.

"In this our first meeting of the 1980s, the economic issues that have dominated our thoughts are the price and supply of energy and the implications for inflation and the level of economic activity in our own countries and for the world as a whole. Unless we can deal with the problems of energy, we cannot cope with other problems.

"Successive large increases in the price of oil, bearing no relation to market conditions and culminating in the recent decisions by some members of the Organization of [the] Petroleum Exporting Countries at Algiers, have produced the reality of even higher inflation and the imminent threat of severe recession and unemployment in the industrialized countries. We believe that these consequences are increasingly coming to be appreciated by some of the oil-exporting countries. The fact is that the industrialized countries of the free world, the oil-producing countries and the non-oil developing countries depend upon each other for the realization of their potential for economic development, but only if all work together, and with the interests of all in mind. . . .

"We must break the existing link between economic growth and consumption of oil, and we mean to do so in this decade. This strategy requires conserving oil ard substantially increasing production and use of alternative energy sources. To this end, maximum reliance should be placed on the price mechanism, and domestic prices for oil should take into account representative world prices. Market forces should be supplemented, where appropriate, by effective fiscal incentives and administrative measures. Energy investment will contribute substantially to economic growth and employment. . . .

"To conserve oil in our countries: (i) we are agreed that no new base-load, oil-fired generating capacity should be constructed, save in exceptional circumstances, and that the conversion of oil-fired capacity to other fuels should be accelerated; (ii) we will increase efforts, including fiscal incentives where necessary, to accelerate the substitution of oil in industry; (iii) we will encourage oil-saving investments in residential and commercial buildings, where necessary by financial incentives and by establishing insulation standards. We look to the public sector to set an example.

"In transportation, our objective is the introduction of increasingly fuel-efficient vehicles. The demand of consumers and competition among manufacturers are already leading in this direction. We will accelerate this progress, where appropriate, by fuel efficiency, by gasoline pricing and taxation decisions, by research and development, and by making public transport more attractive.

"We must rely on fuels other than oil to meet the energy needs of future economic growth. This will require early, resolute and wide-ranging actions. Our potential to increase the supply and use of energy sources other than oil over the next 10 years is estimated at the equivalent of 15,000,000–20,000,000 barrels a day of oil. We intend to make a co-ordinated and vigorous effort to realize this potential. To this end, we will seek a large increase in the use of coal and enhanced use of nuclear power in the medium term, and a substantial increase in production of synthetic fuels, in solar energy and other sources of renewable energy over the longer term.

"We shall encourage the exploration and development of our indigenous hydrocarbon resources in order to secure maximum production on a long-term basis. . . .

"We are deeply concerned about the impact of the oil price increases on the developing countries that have to import oil. The increase in oil prices in the last two years has more than doubled the oil bill of these countries, which now amounts to over $50,000 million. This will drive them into ever-increasing indebtedness, and put at risk the whole basis of their economic growth and social progress, unless something can be done to help them.

"We approach in a positive spirit the prospect of global negotiations in the framework of the United Nations and the formulation of a new international development strategy. In particular, our object is to co-operate with the developing countries in energy conservation and development, expansion of exports, enhancement of human skills, and the tackling of underlying food and population problems.

"A major international effort to help these countries increase their energy production is required. We believe that this view is gaining ground among oil-exporting countries. We ask the World Bank to examine the adequacy of the resources and the mechanisms now in place for the exploration, development and production of conventional and renewable energy sources in oil-importing developing countries; to consider means, including the possibility of establishing a new affiliate or facility, by which it might improve and increase its lending programmes for energy assistance; and to explore its findings with both oil-exporting and industrial countries."

The OPEC countries' collective response to the Venice summit declaration was contained in the following statement issued by the OPEC Secretary-General on June 25, 1980:

"The summit of seven industrial nations in Venice has ended with OPEC once again being made the scapegoat for their economic ills and the rest of the world's. At the same time, leaders of the major oil and energy consumers have announced plans for energy conservation—something which OPEC has repeatedly urged upon the industrialized nations.

"Notwithstanding the unjustified criticism of oil prices, the industrialized countries are directly to blame for their current high inflation and unemployment, because of fiscal and monetary mismanagement and an unwillingness to accept the rational use of energy. Inflation and recession generated by and in the industrialized countries are in turn exported worldwide, with shattering consequences for the poor nations.

"The modern wasteful style of energy consumption, coupled with traditional purchases of cheap raw materials, has led governments in the industrialized world to seek easy solutions, satisfying among other things short-term electoral needs, which have led the world to high rates of inflation and which have ultimately deteriorated the terms of trade of that great majority gathered within the so-called Third World.

"It is widely realized that even if there was a doubling of oil prices, it would only increase inflation by between 1.5 and 2 per cent, depending on the country and its energy imports. Therefore it is unjust to hold OPEC responsible for the current double-digit inflation running in countries like the United States.

"The past plans and promises of investment to develop alternative sources of energy have been shelved. OPEC welcomes the statement from the summit that conservation and alternative energy policies will now apparently be seriously implemented.

"OPEC also rejects the misplaced accusation that it is to blame for the economic problems of developing countries. It must be remembered that OPEC countries are themselves developing nations, totally dependent in most cases on one rapidly dwindling resource. The Organization has been a constant advocate for a new international economic order and for aid to promote rapid economic growth of other developing countries. The Organization welcomes the pledge of the summit to contribute more to the aid of developing countries, which has been grossly inadequate, given the capacity of the industrialized world.

"It has been widely recognized that it is in fact due to the inflation in the industrialized countries and other endemic economic problems that an atmosphere of economic injustice has been created. The main damage has thus been caused to OPEC and other developing countries as they are expected to pay more for the goods and services they import, while allowing their vital and rapidly dwindling resources to be wasted and underpriced in real terms.

"OPEC aid to developing countries in relation to GNP far outstrips that of the rich industrialized nations. According to OECD statistics, countries like Qatar, Kuwait, the United Arab Emirates and Saudi Arabia are giving untied official development assistance relative to their GNP which is 15 to 20 times higher than that given by any Western country. The OPEC Fund for International Development is also a major channel of multilateral aid to the other developing nations, towards which OPEC has reaffirmed its solidarity."

D11.8—OPEC Members' July 1980 Pricing Decisions

When reassessing their existing price levels in the light of the pricing formula adopted by the 57th Conference meeting, individual OPEC members took account of the fact that OPEC's production in the April–June quarter had averaged only 27,400,000 bpd (1,900,000 bpd down on the January–March average), while net additions to importers' stocks had been running at an estimated rate of 2,825,000 bpd (compared with an average second-quarter build-up of 1,670,000 bpd over the preceding five years). Moreover, Saudi Arabia, whose below-average export prices had enabled it to maintain a production rate of 9,500,000 bpd throughout the first half of the year, had made it clear during the Conference meeting that it had no intention either of increasing its prices or reducing its production in the near future.

Of the other Gulf producers (i.e. the group of countries which were most directly exposed to price competition from Saudi Arabia), Iraq, Kuwait and Qatar all decided to increase their prices by $2 per barrel on July 1, taking them to levels which represented approximate alignment with a notional marker value of $32 but were between $3 and $4 below prevailing spot realizations for the crudes concerned. Iran, whose prices were already above the agreed marker ceiling, made no changes on July 1. The United Arab Emirates announced its intention to follow Saudi Arabia in freezing its official prices, regardless of neighbouring states' increases, although this policy was observed only by Abu Dhabi, while Dubai followed Iraq, Kuwait and Qatar in making a $2 price increase.

Libya, Algeria and Nigeria all increased their maximum prices to the agreed OPEC ceiling level of $37 per barrel on July 1, regardless of the fact that spot prices for light African crudes had by this point fallen to $37.50 per barrel for some of the grades concerned, rendering the new official prices highly vulnerable to downward market pressure given a continuing decline in export demand. Algeria, whose maximum price had been held below Libya's during the first half of 1980, indicated its intention to phase out its additional $3 "exploration fee" (◊D11.2) by the end of September. Of the remaining OPEC members, Gabon and Indonesia chose not to alter their prices on July 1, while Venezuela made minor increases and Ecuador a minor reduction.

Table 49 shows the new prices introduced on July 1 by all member countries except Saudi Arabia, Abu Dhabi, Gabon, Indonesia and Iran, together with a summary of previous price changes for selected OPEC crudes during the first half of 1980. All prices are given inclusive of standard market premiums and surcharges (but Algeria's prices exclude that country's exploration fee).

Table 49 — Evolution of prices for selected OPEC crudes, January to July 1980

Normal type indicates prices announced and implemented during the relevant month (although not necessarily from the beginning of that month—see text for details); bold type indicates unchanged December 1979 prices; italic type indicates backdating to April of increases announced in May.

	January	February	April	May	July
		(dollars per barrel)			
Algeria (44°)	**30.00**	34.21	—	35.21	37.00
Ecuador (29.7°)*	36.41	34.796	31.663	36.08	35.004
Gabon (31.7°)	29.00	31.00	—	33.00	—
Indonesia (34.1°)	27.50	29.50	—	31.50	—
Iran (31°)	29.27	31.77	34.37	—	—
(34°)	30.00	32.50	35.37	—	—
Iraq:Mediterranean (34°)	29.29	—	—	31.29	33.29
(36°)	29.50	—	—	31.50	33.50
Gulf (34°)	27.96	—	—	29.96	31.96
(36°)	28.18	—	—	30.18	32.18
Kuwait (31°)	27.50	—	—	29.50	31.50
Libya (40°†)	34.72	—	—	36.72	37.00
Nigeria (36.7°‡)	**29.97**	34.18	34.69	36.69	37.00
(44.2°§)	**30.00**	34.21	34.72	36.72	37.00
Qatar (40°)	29.42	—	—	31.42	33.42
Saudi Arabia (27°)	25.00	—	*27.00*	—	—
(31°)	25.454	—	*27.454*	—	—
(34°)	26.00	—	*28.00*	—	—
(39°)	27.52	—	*29.52*	—	—
UAE:Abu Dhabi (39°)	29.56	—	—	31.56	—
Dubai (32°)	27.93	—	—	29.93	31.93
Venezuela (26°)	25.20	26.78	—	29.28	29.88
(31°)	26.90	28.90	—	32.40	33.00
(34°)	28.75	30.75	—	34.25	34.85

*"Average sales price", adjusted monthly (March — $34.875; June — $35.26).
†Zueitina (40.5° API until end-1979).
‡37° API until end-1979.
§40° API until end-1979.

D11.9—Market Developments and OPEC Activities, July to mid-September 1980

During the third quarter of 1980 a further decline in average OPEC output (to around 26,750,000 bpd) was accompanied by a further build-up of importers' stocks (at the rate of over 2,000,000 bpd). At the end of September non-communist oil stocks on land were estimated to have reached a record 4,622 million barrels, close to the maximum capacity of available storage facilities. The estimated decline in the average level of non-communist oil consumption between the first and third quarters of the year was, at 6,300,000 bpd, greatly in excess of the normal seasonal downturn in oil use. Major oil companies which had suspended supplies of crude to non-affiliated customers in 1979 began to negotiate a limited number of new short- term third-party contracts in July 1980, this development being attributable to a fall in the majors' own refinery throughputs rather than to any reversal of the trend towards increased state control of export marketing in the OPEC area (◊**A4.19**).

The limited resumption of arm's-length contract sales by the majors helped to depress the volume of spot trade in crude oil, which remained at very low levels for much of the third quarter. By the second week of September spot prices had fallen below the official prices in force at that time in all OPEC countries except Saudi Arabia and Abu Dhabi. The largest spot discounts (of around $4.50 per barrel) were recorded for very light African crudes, whereas spot quotations for other grades were generally far closer to official prices (e.g. within 25 cents for Iraqi crudes and within 50 cents for Kuwaiti crude). The changing structure of spot differentials served to highlight a fundamental weakening of relative demand for the lightest grades of crude, which were beginning to

Table 50 — Gross product worth differentials for selected OPEC crudes against Saudi Arabian marker crude (dollars per barrel)

	January 1980	September 1980
Algeria (44°)	+4.208	+3.133
Ecuador (29.7°)	+0.624	+0.389
Gabon (28.9°)	−1.812	−1.038
Indonesia (34.1°)	+0.925	+1.098
Iran (31°)	−1.201	−0.588
(34°)	+0.208	+0.184
Iraq (34°)	−0.268	−0.178
(36°)	+1.033	+0.625
Kuwait (31°)	−2.138	−1.207
Libya (40°)	+3.534	+2.515
Nigeria (36.7°)	+4.592	+3.719
Qatar (40°)	+1.843	+1.093
Saudi Arabia (27°)	−3.161	−1.958
(31°)	−2.042	−1.053
(34°*)	0.000	0.000
(39°)	+1.475	+0.788
UAE (Abu Dhabi 39°)	+2.651	+1.700
Venezuela (26°)	−1.521	−0.993
(34°)	+2.256	+1.906

*Marker crude: gross product worth calculated by OPEC as $33.91 per barrel in January 1980 and $29.55 per barrel in September 1980.

be displaced by heavier crudes as upgraded processing capacity came on stream in the main refining centres.

An OPEC analysis of the gross product worth of member countries' crudes in the main refining centres, carried out with the aid of an updated computer model of the "replacement value method" (◊**D6.6**), illustrated the underlying change in the relative values of light and heavy crudes over the first nine months of 1980. Table 50 shows the gross product worth differentials of other OPEC crudes vis-à-vis Saudi Arabian 34° crude in January and September. In the same OPEC analysis, the netback value of Saudi Arabian crude (i.e. the fob value at Ras Tanura derived from gross product worth calculations) was estimated as $30.56 per barrel in January and $25.95 in September.

The only changes to be announced in official OPEC prices between July and mid-September were minor cuts of between 5 and 50 cents per barrel for three of Iran's six offshore crudes with effect from July 13. (Offshore production accounted for about 400,000 bpd out of Iran's officially claimed total production of up to 2,000,000 bpd in July.) There were, however, several reports during this period of substantial unannounced reductions in market premiums by Iran and certain other OPEC members whose official prices were considered by customers to be excessive in the current market conditions. Ecuador, operating under its own overtly market-oriented system of monthly adjustments, cut its average sales price by $1.151 per barrel on Aug. 1 and by a further $1.663 (to $32.22) on Sept. 1.

During July and August OPEC governments began to define the positions which they intended to adopt at the Organization's second summit conference of heads of state, whose venue had been agreed as Baghdad by the 55th Conference meeting, while the opening date had been provisionally fixed as Nov. 4 by the 57th Conference meeting. Saudi Arabia in particular was concerned that the planned summit should serve as the occasion for the formal adoption of the long-term strategy which had been outlined in the report discussed at the 56th Conference meeting (◊**D11.3**). The Saudi Government's efforts to secure an OPEC consensus on potentially divisive aspects of the report were, however, coolly received by some more radical member countries which resented Saudi Arabia's current campaign to hold down the level of official OPEC prices. Iran voiced the strongest criticism of the fact that Saudi Arabia's share of total OPEC production had risen above 35 per cent in the third quarter, and made a public threat on Sept. 2 to block the adoption of a long-term strategy so long as disunity persisted within OPEC over current policies. At the same time Iran called for the dropping of the plan to hold the summit in Iraq, relations between the two countries having deteriorated dramatically since the end of 1979 as outbreaks of fighting became more frequent in border areas.

The second formal joint meeting of OPEC Oil, Finance and Foreign Ministers was held in Vienna from Sept. 15 to 17 to prepare the ground for the planned Baghdad summit (the only previous formal "tripartite" meeting having been concerned with preparations for the Organization's 1975 Algiers summit ◊**D6.3**). According to precedent Iraq, as the host country of the planned summit, should have assumed the chairmanship of the meeting, but Iranian objections to this arrangement resulted in a compromise whereby the Algerian Foreign Minister took the formal chairmanship while the Iraqi Oil Minister (as alternate chairman) presided over the working sessions of the meeting.

On behalf of OPEC's long-term strategy committee, Shaikh Yamani submitted a draft plan of action covering (i) "the long-term hydrocarbon pricing policy of OPEC", (ii) "OPEC's relationship with the developing countries, with a view to strengthening solidarity with the Third World, of which OPEC is an integral part, including ways and means to increase financial and economic co-operation with those countries", and (iii) "OPEC's relationship with the industrialized countries and its positive contribution to the success of the global negotiations between the North and the South, with a view to promoting the new international economic order".

Algeria indicated its willingness to drop its earlier objections to the recommended long-term price indexation system in return for certain modifications of other aspects of the price administration proposals. Specific matters which were reportedly discussed on Algeria's initiative included an understanding that official price increases of up to 5 per cent above the prevailing indexed level would be acceptable during supply shortages and that co-ordinated production cutbacks would be made at times of supply surplus. Whereas Libya was understood to be satisfied with Algeria's proposals for compromise on the indexation issue, Iran hardened its position, stating that any discussion of future price administration of OPEC was a "joke" in view of the member countries' inability to agree on short-term pricing policy and that the concept of phased price increases should be abandoned in favour of immediate increases to levels reflecting the development costs of alternative energy sources.

Notwithstanding Iran's objections in principle, the tripartite meeting held detailed discussions on the possibility of introducing a price indexation system at the beginning of 1981. In this context most member countries insisted that their initial prices at the beginning of the indexation period should be no lower than the maximum levels established at the 57th Conference meeting—i.e. a marker ceiling of $32 per barrel and an additional value differential of up to $5 per barrel. Saudi Arabia, however, refused to contemplate an increase in the official price of its 34° crude to $32 per barrel in the present market climate, stating that the latest OPEC estimates of the gross product worth of member countries' crudes (◊ Table 50) showed that any marker value above $30 would be unrealistic.

On Kuwait's initiative, Oil Ministers met alone on Sept. 17 (i.e. immediately after the end of the tripartite meeting) "with a view to examining the present market situation". It was agreed to convert what had begun as a consultative session into the 58th (extraordinary) meeting of the OPEC Conference, which announced its unanimous decision (i) to increase the official price of the Saudi marker crude to $30 per barrel, and (ii) to freeze the official prices of all other OPEC countries' crudes at their present levels until the next ordinary Conference meeting. This formula was seen as a possible basis for the introduction of indexation at the beginning of 1981, provided that the freeze on other member countries' prices was maintained until such time as index-linked adjustments had raised the Saudi marker price to the level which would permit reunification of the OPEC price structure (i.e. $32 per barrel).

The tripartite meeting was apparently unable to reach agreement on OPEC's long-term aid policy towards developing countries, in which connexion Algeria and Venezuela favoured the establishment of a full-scale investment bank with resources of $20,000 million and powers to borrow in international capital markets. At the same time Iraq continued to advocate negotiations with industrialized countries to establish a joint "compensatory fund" (◊D10.9), while Saudi Arabia, Kuwait and other major Arab aid donors maintained that OPEC aid should be channelled through the existing OPEC Fund for International Development.

It was agreed at the tripartite meeting (i) that the subject of development aid should be further considered at a meeting of OPEC Finance Ministers on Oct. 6, (ii) that oil price indexation and related matters should be further considered at a consultative meeting of Oil Ministers on Oct. 14, and (iii) that a further tripartite meeting should be held immediately before the Baghdad summit in order to finalize the ministers' submissions to heads of state on these and other issues.

D11.10—Initial Impact of Iran-Iraq War (mid-September to November 1980)

In the event, however, all of the planned ministerial meetings had to be cancelled, and the summit conference itself "indefinitely postponed", following the outbreak of a full-scale war between Iran and Iraq on Sept. 21, 1980, four days after Iraq's abrogation of the June 1975 "reconciliation treaty" between the two countries (itself stemming from an agreement announced after the first OPEC summit conference ◊D6.4). All discussion of long-term co-operation ceased as OPEC entered a period of heightened political tension (one manifestation of which was Saudi Arabia's severance on Oct. 28 of its diplomatic relations with Libya, the only Arab OPEC member which came out in support of Iran). Concurrently, the transition to a buyer's market for oil was interrupted when exports totalling up to 4,000,000 bpd (about 70 per cent from Iraq and the balance from Iran) were halted within days of the outbreak of the Gulf war.

However, the overall fall in average OPEC output between the third and fourth quarters of 1980 did not exceed 2,500,000 bpd, reflecting the following factors: (i) a joint decision by Saudi Arabia, Kuwait, Qatar and the United Arab Emirates to increase their aggregate output by around 1,000,000 bpd, most of this incremental volume being earmarked for sale to state-owned oil companies (mainly in third-world countries) whose contracts with Iraq had been suspended on grounds of force majeure; (ii) a rather smaller rise in the aggregate production of OPEC countries outside the Middle East; and (iii) the limited resumption of exports from Iran and Iraq in late November. Saudi Arabia's additional output volume fluctuated during October and early November as Aramco tested the current limit of its sustainable capacity, which was eventually established as 10,300,000 bpd. Saudi output was held at this level after the partial resumption of Iranian and Iraqi exports, whereas the smaller production increases which had been authorized elsewhere in the Gulf region were mostly rescinded at this point.

Apart from Turkey, which had obtained a relatively high proportion of its oil imports from Iraq, IEA member countries were largely unaffected by the initial disruption of Iranian and Iraqi exports. A substantial fall in fourth-quarter demand for OPEC oil had been generally anticipated in view of the high level of importers' stocks and the downward trend in consumption, and press reports published shortly before the outbreak of the Gulf war indicated that most OPEC countries apart from Saudi Arabia had originally planned to cut their fourth-quarter output by 10 per cent in order to support their current official prices. The IEA, whose member governments were anxious to avoid a repetition of the "bidding-up" of oil prices which had followed the Iranian revolution, reacted swiftly to the interruption of supplies from Iraq and Iran. A statement issued by the Agency on Oct. 1 (some days before production increases were agreed by other Gulf OPEC countries) drew attention to the strong stock position in the IEA area, adding that member governments had agreed to make every effort to dissuade "both private and public market participants" from undertaking "any abnormal purchases on the spot market" pending the outcome of intergovernmental and government-company consultations on the use of stocks to prevent local supply shortfalls.

While the underlying market balance was subsequently maintained through net drawings on non-communist countries' oil stocks at an average rate of 1,675,000 bpd during the fourth quarter of 1980 (compared with net additions to stocks of 1,000,000 bpd in the same quarter of 1979), the IEA's appeal for calm in the spot market was widely ignored during the early stages of the Gulf war, when trading was dominated by fears that the military situation might develop in such a way as to disrupt the shipment of neighbouring countries' oil exports. Spot prices for all

OPEC crudes rose sharply, peaking in November at levels similar to those recorded a year earlier, although the volume of trade was significantly lower than in November 1979.

There were no immediate reactive increases in OPEC countries' official selling prices, which remained at the levels fixed in July (and later frozen until the end of the year) save for (i) an across-the-board incease of $2 per barrel by Saudi Arabia (i.e. the increase accepted by Shaikh Yamani during the 58th OPEC Conference meeting), which was backdated to Aug. 1, (ii) a consequent increase of $2 per barrel by Abu Dhabi (announced on Oct. 16 and backdated to Sept. 1), which restored that state's differentials vis-à-vis Saudi Arabia, and (iii) a temporary surcharge of $2 per barrel on Saudi Arabia's production in excess of 9,500,000 bpd, introduced in October to bring the price of this incremental output broadly into line with the Gulf export price of the Iraqi oil which it replaced. Ecuador (whose pricing system was effectively outside the scope of the current OPEC price freeze) raised its average sales price to $34.802 per barrel on Oct. 1, $37.313 on Nov. 1 and $39.51 ($2.51 above the official OPEC ceiling) on Dec. 1. These increases closely reflected the trend in the average spot value of OPEC crudes, which showed an overall rise of between $7 and $8 per barrel between late September and the beginning of December.

D11.11—December 1980 Meeting of IEA Governing Board

The IEA Governing Board, meeting at ministerial level in Paris on Dec. 9, devoted most of its attention to recent oil market developments and agreed that additional steps should be taken to counter the upward pressure on prices. The Board's decisions were announced as follows:

". . . Ministers welcomed the increase in oil production undertaken by certain oil producers in order to help consumer countries most affected and assist in balancing overall supply and demand on the world oil market. Ministers expressed their determination that difficulties caused by the current situation will receive priority attention by their governments and that every effort will be made by industrialized countries to manage it effectively.

"Ministers assessed the overall situation in the world oil market, and concluded that for the first quarter of 1981 a combination of high stock levels, declining consumption and additional production should make the situation manageable. They noted that the net supply shortfall resulting from the Iraq-Iran conflict has so far been managed largely through drawing on stocks on land and at sea, but that total stocks on land in IEA countries at the end of 1980 will still be higher than at the end of 1979; and that in the first quarter of 1981 further stock draw could reduce IEA stocks to a level still somewhat higher than at April 1, 1979. They also recognized that, within this overall pattern, the position of individual countries and companies could vary considerably.

"Ministers concluded that under these conditions, industrialized countries in the aggregate can maintain adequate oil supplies to their economies by continuing to draw on stocks. However, they also recognized the need to discourage purchases which place unnecessary pressure on markets and prices; to keep oil consumption under control; to manage the country and company imbalances which uneven distribution of stocks and of supply could produce; and to achieve high levels of indigenous production from existing facilities. . . .

"Ministers agreed that the objective of IEA countries is to remove serious potential market pressures which unnecessarily lead to higher prices, thereby damaging the world economy. They agreed that (i) each IEA country will contribute to achieve this result; (ii) IEA countries in a more favourable position will contribute to easing pressures on those countries less favourably situated, in order to avoid potential imbalances which could increase market pressure; and (iii) there is a need to correct serious imbalances between countries and companies which remain despite national efforts to correct internal imbalances and which are likely to result in undue market pressures on price.

"So as to achieve this objective, governments will in an equitable manner take the measures outlined below:

"(1) Draw on stocks as necessary to maintain a balance between oil supply and demand in the world market during the fourth quarter of 1980 and the first quarter of 1981. Countries with relatively high stocks or supply will also permit their stocks to be drawn down taking into account deficits in other countries more seriously affected.

"(2) Discourage undesirable purchases of oil at price levels which have the effect of increasing market pressures, with a view to removing as much buying pressure as possible on a broad basis including elements of price, volume and timing, all in relation to the buyer's overall current position (supply, stocks, anticipated demand, etc.) and past practices.

"(3) Take further action to pursue and implement energy policies which encourage the rational use of oil and its replacement by other forms of energy without constraining economic growth, in order to support and extend the considerable progress already made by consumers in industrialized countries in constraining oil consumption in 1980 (about 6 per cent less overall than in 1979).

"(4) Follow policies for the efficient use of existing facilities which encourage and support high levels of indigenous oil and gas production in their countries.

"(5) Contribute to correcting severe imbalances in accordance with the decision attached as Annex 1 [which outlined a limited and voluntary oil-sharing system between IEA member countries and between oil companies operating in those countries, based on monitoring by and advice from the IEA Secretariat, to take effect from Dec. 9 and to remain in force initially during the first quarter of 1981].

"The collective result of these actions, as estimated by the Secretariat, would be to reduce demand of IEA countries for oil on the world market to 238,000,000 tonnes, as compared with otherwise estimated requirements of 264,000,000 tonnes, in the first quarter of 1981, as the IEA's contribution to stabilizing the world oil market and heading off an economically damaging increase in world energy prices.

"They recognized the Secretariat estimate that this reduction would amount to 2,200,000 bpd, in addition to normal stock draw of 2,000,000 bpd. All IEA countries will contribute to this commitment. . . .

"Ministers further agreed that in order to ensure implementation of the above measures: (i) governments of IEA countries will make greater efforts, at an appropriate high level, to attain the support of oil companies which is necessary to successful implementation; (ii) the Secretariat will consult closely with oil companies in assessing the seriousness of imbalance situations and identifying possible solutions; (iii) the Secretariat and all governments will monitor oil market developments closely, in order to ensure the effectiveness of these measures; and (iv) ministers are prepared to meet again on short notice if this appears necessary.

"Ministers agreed to keep the situation under review, and if necessary to consider further action, including the possible use of oil import ceilings in the manner they agreed in May 1980 [◊D11.5]."

D11.12—Decisions of 59th OPEC Conference Meeting

The 59th meeting of the OPEC Conference took place on the Indonesian island of Bali on Dec. 15 and 16, 1980, amid unprecedented political tensions arising out of the Iran-Iraq war, heightened by the fact that the then Iranian Oil Minister, Mohammed Tondguyan, was currently being held in captivity in Iraq. Tondguyan's deputy used the Conference meeting as an occasion to call for the minister's release and to accuse Iraq of torture and other atrocities. The Conference rejected an Iranian request that the Gulf war should be considered as a formal agenda item, although it publicly endorsed an appeal by the President of Indonesia for an early peaceful settlement of the Iran-Iraq conflict.

Ministers were unwilling to impose any additional stress on the cohesion of OPEC in the prevailing political circumstances, and the Conference therefore made no attempt to resume its consideration of the Organization's long-term strategy or to resolve the continuing disagreement between Saudi Arabia and other member countries over current pricing policy. The Conference decided after a relatively brief discussion that the current price freeze should be lifted at the end of the year and that consequent increases should be consistent with a revised "agreement to disagree" whereby the official price of Saudi Arabian 34° crude would rise by $2 to $32 per barrel; other member countries were to observe a "deemed marker ceiling" of $36 per barrel and an overall ceiling of $41 per barrel, inclusive of differentials. Whereas the new "deemed marker ceiling" was well below the prevailing spot value of marker-grade Gulf crudes (around $40.60 per barrel), the new overall ceiling for official prices was only 35 cents lower than the current average spot value of the lightest African and Gulf crudes.

The 59th Conference meeting also decided to pursue further the feasibility study for an OPEC institute of higher education whose creation had been proposed in June (◊D11.6).

After the meeting Saudi Arabia announced that its own $2 per barrel price increase would be backdated to Nov. 1, while other OPEC members announced varying increases to take effect from the beginning of January 1981. Libya, Qatar, Kuwait, Iraq and Dubai all applied across-the-board increases of $4 per barrel (equal to the rise in OPEC's "deemed marker ceiling"), while Abu Dhabi, Nigeria, Algeria and Gabon opted for increases of $3 per barrel. Other member countries' increases were generally in the $3 to $4 range, with some variations between different grades of crude. Iran, which recognized that its main export terminal was

Table 51 — Prices of selected OPEC crudes from Jan. 1, 1981

	Price from Jan. 1, 1981	Increase since Dec. 31, 1978
	(dollars per barrel)	(per cent)
Algeria (44°)	40.00	183.7
Ecuador*(29.7°)	40.07	224.1
Gabon (31.7°)	36.00	176.3
Indonesia (34.1°)	35.00	158.3
Iran (31°)	36.00	188.2
(34°)	37.00	188.8
Iraq† (34°)	37.28	185.9
(36°)	37.50	183.3
Kuwait (31°)	35.50	189.3
Libya (40°)	41.00	196.0
Nigeria (36.7°)	40.00	183.7
(44.2°)	40.00	183.1
Qatar (40°)	37.42	183.7
Saudi Arabia‡ (27°)	31.00	158.0
(31°)	31.454	155.2
(34°)	32.00	151.9
(39°)	33.52	153.5
UAE: Abu Dhabi (39°)	36.56	175.7
Dubai (32°)	35.93	184.3
Venezuela (26°)	32.88	158.9
(31°)	36.00	165.9
(34°)	38.06	172.1

*"Average sales price".
†Mediterranean.
‡Prices applied with effect from Nov. 1, 1980.

now regarded as a war risk zone by tanker operators, announced that an increase of $3.50 per barrel in its basic official prices would be accompanied by the abolition of the $1.50 market premium and the $0.37 credit charge hitherto incorporated into these prices (producing a net increase of $1.63 per barrel).

Table 51 gives details of the official selling prices of selected OPEC crudes with effect from Jan. 1, 1981, together with the percentage price increase for each crude since the end of 1978.

D11.13—Introduction of US "Windfall Profits Tax" – Other US Energy Policy Developments in 1980

A Crude Oil Windfall Profit Tax Act became law on April 2, 1980, nearly one year after President Carter had requested legislation to tax the additional profits accruing to oil companies as a result of the phased decontrol of domestic crude oil prices, which had commenced on June 1, 1979 (◊D10.17). The "windfall profits tax" (WPT)—so-called for domestic political reasons rather than for the purpose of accurate description—was a special excise tax on petroleum revenues which applied (albeit at a lower rate) to newly-discovered high-cost oil as well as to "old" oil whose production had become more profitable as a result of the relaxation of federal price controls.

The WPT took effect on March 1, 1980, and was to be phased out either from the beginning of 1988 or from the month after the cumulative revenue from the tax reached $227,300 million, whichever was later, provided that the 33-month phase-out period should begin no later than 1991. Of the target revenue of $227,300 million, it was intended that $204,770 million should be contributed by larger integrated producers and the balance by the smaller independent producers and royalty owners. The proceeds of the WPT were to be used to finance cuts in other federal taxes (including personal income tax), to assist the less well-off to meet higher energy costs and to finance energy development and mass transportation programmes.

The rates of tax ranged from a minimum of 30 per cent on new oil (discovered after 1978) to a maximum of 70 per cent on old oil (discovered before 1973), the average effective rate being about 60 per cent. The tax was levied on the difference between the actual selling price per barrel and an "exempt base" ranging from $12.81 per barrel for old oil to $16.55 per barrel for new oil in 1980 (these base levels being increased in each succeeding year by the rate of inflation plus 2 per cent). The effect of the WPT was to cut the producing companies' profits (net of royalties and existing state and federal taxes) from an average 42 per cent of gross revenue to an average 19 per cent of gross revenue (the highest post-tax margin, equivalent to 27 per cent of gross revenue, being derived from "new" oil).

A proposal by President Carter to impose a licence fee of $4.62 on each barrel of imported oil (and thereby to curb gasoline consumption through a consequent price increase of 10 cents per US gallon) was rejected by both Houses of Congress on June 4. President Carter's announcement on the following day of a veto on the relevant congressional resolutions prompted further resolutions (passed by the requisite two-thirds majority in each House) to override the veto, and the proposal was formally withdrawn on June 19. President Carter had been forced to seek legislative authority to impose the fee after a US district court had declared that the President's existing powers to control oil imports could not be used for the purpose of imposing a "conservation tax" which would affect the price of all gasoline, regardless of whether it was refined from domestic or imported crude. The President said that failure to implement his proposal would "encourage more domestic energy consumption, add to our intolerable oil import bill, hinder our efforts for

557

energy security, obstruct our fight against inflation and be inconsistent with our responsibility for leadership among the oil-consuming nations".

On June 27 the Priority Energy Bill, calling for the creation of the energy mobilization board proposed by President Carter in July 1979 (◊**D10.17**), was defeated in the House of Representatives. On June 30 the Energy Security Bill was enacted to create (i) a Synthetic Fuels Corporation (originally proposed by President Carter as the "energy security corporation"), (ii) a solar energy bank and (iii) an alcohol fuel production programme. The Synthetic Fuels Corporation had an initial spending authority of $20,000 million (to be drawn from an energy security reserve fund) and was to receive additional future resources of up to $68,000 million, subject to congressional approval of its annual budgets. The Corporation's targets for synthetic hydrocarbons output were 500,000 bpd by 1987 and 2,000,000 bpd by 1992. A total of $1,450 million was allocated for the alcohol fuels programme.

A standby gasoline rationing plan, which had been submitted to Congress on June 12, took effect on July 30. The cost of establishing the emergency rationing procedures authorized under the plan was estimated as $103,000,000.

D11.14—Moves to initiate Global Economic Negotiations

Two attempts were made in 1980 to draw up an agenda for fresh negotiations on the topics which had been discussed to little effect by the Conference on International Economic Co-operation between 1975 and 1977 (◊**D6.11, D7.6, D8.8**). An Independent Commission on International Development Issues, which had been established in 1977 under the chairmanship of Willy Brandt (the former West German Federal Chancellor), published a wide-ranging report entitled *North-South: A Programme for Survival* in February 1980, while the same range of issues was debated by the UN General Assembly in August and September.

D11.14.i—Report of Brandt Commission

The Independent Commission on International Development Issues, whose formation at the end of 1977 had been seen as a reaction to the ineffectiveness of the Conference on International Economic Co-operation, was made up of 21 persons (17 ordinary members and four office-holders) drawn from 10 third-world and nine OECD countries, with each participant serving in an individual capacity rather than as a representative of his or her government. Members drawn from within the OPEC area were the director of Kuwait's development aid fund, the Vice-President of Indonesia and a former Algerian Trade Minister. The Commission's report called for "a review of the present system of negotiations to see whether more flexible, expeditious and result-oriented procedures can be introduced without detracting from co-operation within established groups" and for "the occasional use of limited summit meetings to advance the cause of consensus and change".

On energy issues, the Commission emphasized the need for an "orderly transition from high dependence on increasingly scarce non-renewable energy sources". The report added that "prices which reflect long-term scarcities will play an important role in this transition" and stressed the benefits to the world economy of "orderly and predictable price changes". The Commission recommended that an "international strategy on energy" should be drawn up in the context of an emergency programme to accelerate the economic development of the Third World; that the energy supplies of the poorest countries should be subject to "special arrangements, including financial assistance"; that established international and regional lending agencies should provide substantially increased funding for the development of renewable and non-renewable energy resources in third-world countries; and that a "global energy research centre" should be set up under UN auspices.

Another section of the report drew attention to "the emergence of capital-surplus developing countries" whose financial resources could be combined with the technological resources of industrialized countries to establish "tripartite" development projects in the poorer third-world countries. Developing countries were urged "to give special attention to the establishment and extension of payments and credit arrangements among themselves to facilitate trade and to ease balance-of-payments problems".

The Commission's suggestion that its recommendations should be considered by a summit meeting of the leaders of about 25 countries (representing a balanced cross-section of the major world groupings) was taken up by President López Portillo of Mexico, whose agreement to host such a meeting in 1981 was announced by Willy Brandt in May 1980.

D11.14.ii—UN General Assembly's Special Session on International Development Issues

The UN General Assembly's 11th special session, held in New York from Aug. 25 to Sept. 15, was devoted to the discussion of (i) the procedures and agenda for global negotiations on international economic co-operation and development and (ii) the text of an international development strategy for the next decade. The inauguration during 1981 of a round of global negotiations under UN auspices had been recommended by the General Assembly in a series of resolutions based on the Declaration and Programme of Action for the establishment of a new international economic order, adopted by the sixth special session in 1974 (◊D5.9). (The possible implementation of the Programme of Action had been debated in detail at the seventh special session in September 1975.)

Several of the opening speeches delivered at the 11th special session included expressions of concern about the impact of oil price increases on the international economy. The US Secretary of State, Edmund Muskie, said that OPEC members had a "unique responsibility" in the international economy, which they could meet by pursuing "stable" pricing policies, concluding secure supply agreements with importing countries and ensuring that their oil revenues were recycled to the benefit of other developing countries. The President of Bangladesh called for increased OPEC investment in oil-importing third-world countries and for direct aid to offset half of the oil import costs of the least developed countries.

The special session reached agreement on the text of a UN development strategy for the next decade, which was formally adopted in December during the General Assembly's regular session. The strategy proposed the following initiatives in the energy sector: (i) immediate measures to rationalize energy consumption, particularly in the industrialized countries; (ii) the promotion of exploration for, and rational exploitation of, conventional and non-conventional energy resources, according to the national plans and priorities of each country; (iii) facilitation of the fullest possible access by developing countries to scientific and technological processes for energy development, including nuclear technology; (iv) establishment of medium- and long-term national programmes on new and renewable sources of energy; (v) greater participation in energy projects by international, national and regional financial institutions; (vi) improvements in the investment climate in developing countries with a view to increasing the inflow of foreign capital into energy projects; and (vii) co-operation, assistance and investment in conventional as well as non-conventional projects in energy-deficient developing countries.

As regards the procedures for initiating global negotiations on international economic co-operation, delegates to the 11th special session were in general agreement that the five main topics for negotiation should be energy, food, the transfer of technology, development aid, and the international monetary system. The finalization of a detailed agenda and timetable was however blocked as a result of a fundamental procedural disagreement between the developing countries (including OPEC members), which maintained that negotiations on all of these topics should be conducted within the framework of a single UN conference, and certain leading industrialized countries, which insisted that negotiations on topics falling within the competence of specialized UN agencies (e.g. the International Monetary Fund) should be conducted under the auspices of the agencies concerned. Yugoslavia put forward a compromise proposal whereby a UN conference would have held responsibility for the overall co-ordination of a negotiating process which respected both the procedures of the General Assembly and the autonomy of the specialized agencies, this proposal being accepted by the developing countries, the communist bloc and most OECD members but rejected by the United States, West Germany and the United Kingdom.

D12—1981

D12.1—Annual Statistical Survey

D12.1.i—Oil production and reserves

World

Total production .... 59,375,000 bpd (2,903.7 million tonnes)
  Change over 1980 .... −5.8 per cent

End-year proved reserves .... 677,300 million barrels
  Change over end-1980 .... +3.2 per cent

Reserves:production ratio .... 31.3 : 1

Regional shares:

	In 1981 world production*			In end-1981 world reserves†		
	Regional total (million tonnes)	Change over 1980 (per cent)	Share of world total barrels)	Reserves (thousand million barrels)	Change over 1980 (per cent)	Share of world total
Middle East	789.2	−14.9	27.2	362.6	+0.2	53.5
USSR/Eastern Europe/China	727.6	—	25.1	85.5	−0.9	12.6
North America	555.7	−1.8	19.1	44.4	+13.3	6.6
Latin America/ Caribbean	317.5	+6.3	10.9	84.6	+19.0	12.5
Africa	239.7	−20.6	8.3	56.2	+2.0	8.3
Asia‡/Australasia	140.1	+4.8	4.8	19.1	−2.6	2.8
Western Europe§	133.9	+6.6	4.6	24.9	+7.3	3.7

*Including production from oil shales, tar sands and natural gas liquids (NGL).
†Excluding oil shales and tar sands; including NGL in North America.
‡Excluding China.
§Including Yugoslavia.

OPEC

OPEC oil production .... 23,390,000 bpd (1,150.3 million tonnes)
  Change over 1980 .... −15.3 per cent
  Share of 1981 world total .... 39.6 per cent

OPEC end-year proved oil reserves ...... 436,090 million barrels
  Change over 1980 .... +0.04 per cent
  Share of 1981 world total .... 64.4 per cent

OPEC reserves:production ratio .... 51.1 : 1

OPEC (continued)

OPEC member countries' production:

	1981 production		Change over 1980 (per cent)	Share of world total (per cent)	Share of OPEC total (per cent)
	(million tonnes)	(thousand bpd)			
Algeria	46.3	1,035	−11.3	1.6	4.0
Ecuador	10.3	210	+3.0	0.3	0.9
Gabon	7.6	150	−13.6	0.3	0.7
Indonesia	82.2	1,680	+5.0	2.8	7.1
Iran	65.8	1,325	−10.7	2.3	5.7
Iraq	44.0	895	−66.2	1.5	3.8
Kuwait	48.2	965	−32.6	1.7	4.2
Libya	58.7	1,220	−33.6	2.0	5.1
Nigeria	71.0	1,440	−30.6	2.4	6.2
Qatar	20.2	425	−9.8	0.7	1.8
Saudi Arabia	491.3	9,985	−0.3	16.9	42.7
UAE*	72.8	1,505	−11.9	2.5	6.3
Venezuela	112.5	2,180	−2.9	3.9	9.8
Neutral Zone†	19.4	375	−31.7	0.7	1.7

*Of which Abu Dhabi 54,500,000 tonnes (1,135,000 bpd), Dubai 17,800,000 tonnes (360,000 bpd), Sharjah 500,000 tonnes (10,000 bpd).
†Production shared between Kuwait and Saudi Arabia.

Non-OPEC

Selected non-OPEC countries' oil production:

	1981 production		Change over 1980 (per cent)	Share of world total (per cent)
	(million tonnes)	(thousand bpd)		
USSR	609.0	12,370	+1.0	21.0
USA*	482.8	10,180	−0.3	16.6
Mexico	128.3	2,585	+19.6	4.4
China	101.0	2,035	−4.5	3.5
United Kingdom	89.4	1,835	+11.1	3.1
Canada	72.9	1,545	−10.8	2.5
Egypt	34.1	690	+14.4	1.2
Argentina	25.5	490	−0.8	0.9
Norway	24.9	505	−3,5	0.9
Oman	16.4	325	+13.9	0.6
Total	1,584.3	32,560	+1.7	54.7

*Of which natural gas liquids 57,100,000 tonnes (1,610,000 bpd).

D12.1.ii—Oil consumption

World

Total consumption .... 59,910,000 bpd (2,902.8 million tonnes)
Change over 1980 .... −3.3 per cent

Regional distribution of total:

	1981 consumption		Change over 1980 (per cent)	Share of world total (per cent)
	(million tonnes)	(thousand bpd)		
North America	827.7	17,310	−6.1	28.5
Western Europe*	633.7	13,085	−7.0	21.8
USSR/Eastern Europe/China	631.3	12,800	+0.8	21.8
Asia†/Australasia	422.3	8,740	−3.0	14.6
Latin America/ Caribbean	227.2	4,725	+2.0	7.8
Middle East	84.7	1,685	+3.3	2.9
Africa	75.9	1,565	+5.6	2.6

*Including Yugoslavia.
†Excluding China.

Selected countries

	1981 consumption		Change over 1980 (per cent)	Share of world total (per cent)
	(million tonnes)	(thousand bpd)		
USA	746.0	15,550	−6.1	25.7
USSR	444.1	8,985	+1.9	15.3
Japan	223.9	4,690	−5.8	7.7
West Germany	117.6	2,465	−10.3	4.1
France	99.0	2,060	−9.9	3.4
Italy	95.7	1,940	−2.2	3.3
China	84.8	1,705	−3.6	2.9
Canada	81.7	1,760	−6.7	2.8
United Kingdom	74.7	1,555	−7.5	2.6
Spain	50.4	1,040	−3.4	1.7
Total	2,017.9	41,750	−4.6	69.5

D12.1.iii—Oil refining

World

Total refinery capacity .... 81,670,000 bpd
Change over 1980 .... +0.7 per cent

Total refinery throughputs .... 57,590,000 bpd
Change over 1980 .... −3.9 per cent

Consumption as proportion of capacity   73.4 per cent

563

Selected markets
Consumption of refined product types and change over 1980:

	USA (million tonnes)	(per cent)	Western Europe (million tonnes)	(per cent)	Japan (million tonnes)	(per cent)
Gasolines	297.9	−2.6	133.5	−3.9	39.8	−5.5
Middle distillates	199.2	−4.2	224.6	−5.4	60.6	+1.2
Fuel oil	110.6	−16.8	186.6	−11.7	91.2	−11.9
Other	138.3	−6.2	89.0	−5.3	32.3	+0.3
Total	746.0	−6.1	633.7	−7.0	223.9	−5.8

D12.1.iv—Tankers and trade

Tankers
Total world fleet .... 320,200,000 deadweight tons
Change over 1980 .... −1.4 per cent

Trade
Total world crude exports
(including re-exports) .... 25,642,700 bpd (1,273.2 million tonnes)
Change over 1980 .... −14 per cent
OPEC crude exports .... 18,424,000 bpd (914,796,400 tonnes)
Change over 1980 .... −19.3 per cent
Share of 1981 world total .... 71.8 per cent
Total world product exports
(including re-exports) .... 8,694,900 bpd (432,152,000 tonnes)
Change over 1980 .... +0.7 per cent
OPEC product exports .... 1,934,100 bpd (96,128,000 tonnes)
Change over 1980 .... −4.1 per cent
Share of 1981 world total .... 22.2 per cent

Regional distribution of world oil trade*:

	Share of 1981 imports (per cent) Crude	Products	Share of 1981 exports (per cent) Crude	Products
USA	18.8	29.2	1.0	7.5
Canada	2.4	1.3	0.7	5.6
Latin America/ Caribbean	9.5	3.7	10.0	39.1
Western Europe	37.9	27.7	2.2	4.6
Middle East	0.5	4.8	59.7	11.7
North Africa	0.1	1.0	8.5	3.5
West Africa	†	2.0	7.2	0.7
East and southern Africa	1.9	0.7	—	0.3
South Asia	2.0	2.6	—	0.9
South-East Asia	7.3	6.8	5.5	7.2
Australasia	0.9	2.0	—	0.2
Japan	16.9	9.1	—	0.1
USSR/Eastern Europe/China	0.9	3.2	5.2	18.6
Unspecified	0.9	5.9	—	—
Total	100.0	100.0	100.0	100.0

*Excluding intra-regional trade.   † Negligible.

D12.1.v—World primary energy consumption

Total consumption (excluding
   non-commercial fuels) .... 6,857 million tonnes oil equivalent (mtoe)
   Change over 1980 .... −0.6 per cent

Contributions of primary energy sources:

	Consumption (mtoe)	Change over 1980 (per cent)	Share of total (per cent)
Oil	2,902.8	−3.3	42.3
Coal	2,002.9	−0.2	29.2
Natural gas	1,320.7	+1.8	19.3
Water power	431.6	+2.4	6.3
Nuclear power	199.0	+17.5	2.9

D12.1.vi—Natural gas production and reserves

Marketed production (thousand million cubic metres):

	Regional total (tmcm)	Change over 1980 (per cent)	Share of 1981 world total (per cent)
North America	(613.6	−1.2	39.6
Latin America/ Caribbean	65.1	+3.8	4.2
Western Europe*	187.8	+3.8	12.1
USSR/Eastern Europe/China	543.0	+19.2	35.0
Middle East	52.5	+27.4	3.4
Africa	29.5	+46.0	1.9
Asia†/Australasia	58.6	+3.0	3.8
World total	1,550.1	+7.8	100.0
(of which OPEC)	(107.1)	(+24.2)	(6.9)

*Including Yugoslavia.
†Excluding China.

End-year proved reserves (thousand million cubic metres):

	Regional total (tmcm)	Change over 1980 (per cent)	Share of 1981 world total (per cent)
North America	8,258.4	+1.9	9.7
Latin America/ Caribbean	4,983.2	+8.3	5.8
Western Europe*	4,470.6	−2.9	5.2
USSR/Eastern/ Europe/China	34,282.3	+7.7	40.0
Middle East	23,449.1	+1.4	27.4
Africa	5,943.5	+0.9	6.9
Asia†/Australasia	4,234.7	+9.7	5.0
World total	85,621.8	+4.4	100.0
(of which OPEC)	(30,867.3)	(+1.3)	(36.1)

*Including Yugoslavia
†Excluding China.

D12.2—Re-emergence of Oil Supply Surplus during early 1981

Average OPEC output, which had fallen to around 24,250,000 bpd in the last quarter of 1980, rose by up to 400,000 bpd in the first quarter of 1981 as Iran and Iraq brought more of their capacity back into production (the marketing of Iran's exports being facilitated by the lifting of trade sanctions after the release in January of US citizens who had been held hostage in Tehran). Saudi Arabia continued to produce at the rate of 10,300,000 bpd, representing more than 40 per cent of the OPEC total, the possibility of a cutback in 1981 having been ruled out by the Saudi Government until such time as other OPEC members agreed to adopt "realistic" pricing policies. Saudi production up to Aramco's basic ceiling of 9,500,000 bpd was marketed at official prices, while the company's incremental output of 800,000 bpd was subject to a $4 per barrel surcharge from Jan. 1 in order to retain broad parity with current Iraqi prices.

On the spot market, the spate of panic buying which had occurred during the suspension of Iranian and Iraqi exports gave way to calmer trading conditions as the underlying downward trend in oil consumption—stemming from fuel-switching and energy conservation measures and from a continuing economic recession in the OECD area—again became the dominant influence on demand. In these circumstances the estimated net rate of stock drawdown in the IEA area was close to what the Agency had described in December 1980 as the "normal" first-quarter level of 2,000,000 bpd. The stabilization of the supply situation in the Persian/Arabian Gulf region coincided with a substantial upturn in non-OPEC output, and most estimates indicated that world oil production was running ahead of demand by around 2,000,000 bpd at the beginning of the second quarter.

The official prices of most light African crudes were being discounted on the spot market within a month of OPEC's Jan. 1 price increase, while most non-Saudi Gulf crudes had ceased to command spot premiums by late March. In the light of this trend the US Government, which had resumed its programme of imports for the country's strategic petroleum reserve, was able to conclude several large purchase contracts on advantageous spot terms in February and March. Ecuador's market-oriented average sales price fell from $40.07 per barrel in January to $39.375 in February, $38.239 in March and $36.223 in April. No changes were made in other OPEC producers' official selling prices, although by April all remaining surcharges on these prices had either been formally dropped or had become inoperative when customers refused to renew surcharged contracts. A notable case of customer resistance occurred in Kuwait, whose announcement that its selective premium on oil supplied for resale to third parties would be retained after the end of March — albeit at a reduced rate of $3 per barrel—caused its foreign customers to discontinue such purchases at that point.

During the second quarter of 1981 there was increasing evidence of customer resistance to OPEC countries' basic official prices, particularly in view of price cuts by several non-OPEC exporters (e.g. Malaysia and Mexico). With the main impact of the decline in oil demand concentrated on OPEC producers, the Organization's aggregate production fell below 24,000,000 bpd during April, and averaged 23,300,000 bpd over the whole second quarter (1,350,000 bpd lower than in the first quarter of 1981 and 4,100,000 bpd lower than in the second quarter of 1980). The steepest falls were experienced by the producers of light African crudes, which had an average spot value in mid-May of around $35.50 per barrel ($5.50 below Libya's maximum official selling price and $4.50 below that of Nigeria and Algeria). The average spot quotation for marker-grade Gulf crudes was at this point $33.75 per barrel, some $2.25 below OPEC's "deemed marker ceiling".

Shaikh Yamani, who had held informal discussions on pricing questions with other members of the OPEC Conference on various occasions in early 1981 (notably at a secret meeting in Geneva in February with the Oil Ministers of Algeria, Indonesia, Kuwait, Nigeria and Venezuela), made a series of increasingly blunt statements on Saudi oil policy. Speaking on US television on April 19, he said that "we engineered the [oil] glut, and we want to see it in order to stabilize the price of oil", adding that the latest round of price increases by other OPEC members had "gone too far" and was "not in the interests of the international economy". Some days later Saudi Arabia reduced the surcharge on Aramco's "incremental" production to $2 per barrel with effect from April 1, thus intensifying the downward pressure on other members' official prices.

D12.3—Decisions of 60th Meeting of OPEC Conference

Saudi Arabia's campaign to reunify the OPEC price structure was the main topic of discussion at the 60th Conference meeting, held in Geneva on May 25 and 26, 1981. Shaikh Yamani indicated his country's willingness to increase the official price of its 34° crude by $2 per barrel if other OPEC members accepted a $2 cut in their own marker value (i.e. the "deemed marker ceiling") and a consequent trimming of value differentials. This proposed structure should, he said, be maintained unchanged until the end of 1982.

The Saudi proposals were rejected by the Conference, which decided "in the light of the prevailing circumstances to maintain the deemed marker crude price at a ceiling of $36 per barrel, with a maximum OPEC price of $41 per barrel, until the end of the year". Shaikh Yamani made it clear that this decision meant that Saudi Arabia would continue to exert direct pressure on the oil market by holding its own marker price at $32 per barrel and its production ceiling at 10,300,000 bpd, a stance which prompted a further decision by "a majority of member countries" to cut their production by "a minimum of 10 per cent" from June 1. This announcement — signalling the first formal OPEC initiative on the co-ordinated restriction of member countries' output levels since the "production programming" experiment of 1965–66 (◊**D1.4**)—was treated by market analysts as a largely symbolic gesture when it became known (i) that Iran and Iraq did not form part of the OPEC majority for this purpose and (ii) that cutbacks were to be calculated with reference to planned output levels for the first half of the year, which for most of the 10 participating countries were significantly higher than the levels which had actually been achieved.

The Conference also decided to request a further report from the ministerial committee on long-term strategy "as soon as possible".

D12.4—IEA Ministerial Meeting, June 1981

The IEA Governing Board held a meeting at ministerial level in Paris on June 15 at which consideration was given both to the short-term oil market outlook and to the Agency's programme to expedite medium- and long-term structural change in IEA countries' energy economies. The ministers noted "encouraging improvement" on both fronts, and identified areas where "further strengthening of policy is necessary".

The current stability of the oil market was described as "fragile", and it was stated that continuing stability would depend both on "avoidance of complacency" by importing countries and on "significant levels of supply from several major producing countries". Ministers expressed the determination of their governments to maintain and strengthen procedures for continuous monitoring of market trends in order to ensure prompt intervention "to prevent a disruption in oil supply from again resulting in sharply higher prices and severe economic damage".

As regards the medium-term outlook, the meeting "noted that the Secretariat has indicated a potential for limiting IEA net oil imports to between 19,000,000 bpd and 21,000,000 bpd in 1990 and even lower by the end of the century, if appropriate policies are carried through" and agreed that "still stronger efforts arc required to improve energy efficiency in IEA countries, despite the progress which has been achieved".

The ministers also noted "the encouraging response by industry to the new opportunities provided by coal" and reiterated the need for "stronger action to realize the full potential for expansion of coal production and use on an economic basis". They endorsed the on-going work of the Agency's coal industry advisory board and agreed to make greater efforts, in co-operation with industry, to clarify the potential for and constraints on coal production, trade and use in their countries.

They stressed that "nuclear power will have to play a major and increasing role in many countries in order to achieve the necessary structural change which all IEA countries have agreed upon", and that this would be facilitated by better conditions for the "timely growth of nuclear power". IEA countries should therefore "take prompt national and international action to increase public understanding of reactor safety; implement waste management and disposal programmes; streamline licensing procedures to shorten lead times with continued emphasis on safety; ensure that regulatory practices do not unnecessarily constrain investment; and reinforce the reliability and predictability of international trade in nuclear fuels and technology under appropriate safeguards, in order to enhance public acceptance of and confidence in nuclear power, including advanced reactor technology".

D12.5—Major Non-Communist Industrialized Countries' Statement on Energy Questions

The heads of government of Canada, France, West Germany, Italy, Japan, the United Kingdom and the United States held their 1981 summit meeting in Ottawa from July 19 to 21. Energy questions (which had dominated the agendas of the 1979 and 1980 summits) were treated on this occasion as a subsidiary topic of discussion within a broader review of economic policy. The section of the summit declaration dealing with energy questions was worded as follows:

"We are confident that, with perseverance, the energy goals we set at Venice for the decade (◊D11.7) can be achieved, enabling us to break the link between economic growth and oil consumption through structural change in our energy economies.

"Recognizing that our countries are still vulnerable and energy supply remains a potential constraint to a revival of economic growth, we will accelerate the development and use of all our energy sources, both conventional and new, and continue to promote energy savings and the replacement of oil by other fuels.

"To these ends we will continue to rely heavily on market mechanisms, supplemented as necessary by government action.

"Our capacity to deal with short-term oil market problems should be improved, particularly through the holding of adequate levels of stocks.

"In most of our countries progress in constructing new nuclear facilities is slow. We intend in each of our countries to encourage greater public acceptance of nuclear energy, and respond to public concerns about safety, health, nuclear-waste management and non-proliferation. We will further our efforts in the development of advanced technologies, particularly in spent-fuel management.

"We will take steps to realize the potential for the economic production, trade and use of coal and will do everything in our power to ensure that its increased use does not damage the environment.

"We also intend to see to it that we develop to the fullest possible extent sources of renewable energy such as solar, geothermal and biomass energy. We will work for practical achievements at the forthcoming United Nations Conference on New and Renewable Sources of Energy [held in Nairobi from Aug. 10 to 21, 1981].

"We look forward to improved understanding and co-operation with the oil-exporting countries in the interests of the world economy."

568

D12.6—Developments leading to Consultative Meeting of OPEC Oil Ministers

Spot oil prices continued to decline in June 1981, when the available supply of OPEC oil remained well ahead of demand despite the cuts which were made in most member countries' official production ceilings at the beginning of the month. By July even Saudi Arabian 34° crude was (for the first time since April 1978) trading at a small spot discount relative to its basic official price, and there was a slight fall in the volume of Aramco's surcharged "incremental" output.

Among major non-OPEC exporting countries, Mexico cut its export prices by $4 per barrel (to an average $30.60) on June 1 and subsequently encountered strong customer resistance when $2 of this cut was rescinded on July 1 following domestic political criticism which had led to the resignation of the head of the state oil company. The British National Oil Corporation (BNOC) proposed in early June to cut the basic reference price of British North Sea crude by $2 to $37.25 per barrel with effect from July 1, but subsequently acceded to pressure from the major integrated producers for a reduction to $35 per barrel with effect from June 15. (The average spot value of British North Sea oil in June was $32.38 per barrel.) This reduction was BNOC's first significant departure from its previous policy of aligning official British prices with those of African OPEC crudes. Reductions in oil export prices were also announced during June by the Soviet Union, Malaysia, China, Brunei, Oman, Syria and Egypt, while parallel falls occurred in US domestic crude prices (which had been brought fully into line with world prices earlier in the year ◊**D12.10**).

The reduction in the official prices of British (and shortly afterwards of Norwegian) North Sea crudes increased the pressure of African OPEC countries to reduce the widening differentials between the spot and official prices of their own crudes, and the Algerian, Libyan, Nigerian and Gabonese Oil Ministers met in Algeria on June 22 to discuss the current situation. Notwithstanding a statement by the ministers that they would "take all necessary measures to support the present price structure and act in accordance with OPEC decisions", it was subsequently reported on June 29 that Nigeria had concluded a two-year contract for the sale of 100,000 bpd at a "temporary discount" of $2.50 per barrel below its official price of $40. Libya reduced its maximum selling price from $41 per barrel (the current OPEC ceiling level) to $40 with effect from July 1 in order to bring its official pricing structure into line with that of Algeria and Nigeria, although this cut did not prevent the non-renewal of third-quarter contracts by several customers.

Iraq had meanwhile cut its official selling prices fob Mediterranean ports by 57 cents per barrel with effect from June 1, giving new prices of $36.93 for 36° crude and $36.71 for 34° crude. These cuts were presented in terms of an adjustment to Iraq's pipeline tariff. At the same time Iraq's Japanese customers (who had been supplied from Gulf terminals prior to the Iran-Iraq war) were allowed 60 rather than 30 days' credit in order to offset their additional transport costs. Venezuela, whose crude oil prices remained unchanged, announced cuts of between $2.25 and $3.75 per barrel in its fuel oil export prices on June 11. Ecuador's average sales price was cut from $34.223 in May to $32 in June (remaining at this level throughout the third quarter of the year).

Although open-market prices recovered slightly during August, taking the spot value of Saudi Arabian 34° crude back above the official price (by an average margin of 30 cents per barrel) and reducing the average spot discount on light African crudes to $3.90 per barrel, OPEC oil was increasingly displaced by competitively-priced contract supplies from non-OPEC exporters, to the extent that OPEC's share of non-communist oil output fell below 50 per cent for the first time since the early 1960s. Saudi Arabia's share of total OPEC output had meanwhile risen to nearly 50 per cent (◊ Table 52), and certain of the least competitive OPEC producers were beginning to experience economic difficulties as a result of the sharp falls in their oil revenues (falls which had been only partially mitigated by a recent strengthening in the exchange rate of the US dollar). Statistics published some months later by the Bank for International Settlements showed that the OPEC countries as a group had during the third quarter of 1981 become net borrowers of funds from the international banking system for the first time since 1978. The most seriously affected OPEC member was Nigeria, whose net monthly oil revenues had declined from $2,306 million in January to $609,000,000 in August, when Nigeria was superseded by Britain as the second largest supplier of US crude oil imports.

Table 52 — OPEC members' oil output in August 1981 (with 1980 annual averages for comparison)

	August 1981	Year 1980
	(thousand barrels daily)	
Algeria	600	1,120
Ecuador	200	205
Gabon	150	175
Indonesia	1,600	1,575
Iran	1,100	1,480
Iraq	800	2,645
Kuwait	630	1,430
Libya	700	1,830
Nigeria	708	2,055
Qatar	295	460
Saudi Arabia	10,200	9,990
United Arab Emirates	1,476	1,705
Venezuela	1,960	2,235
Neutral Zone*	246	545
Total	20,665	27,450

*Production shared between Kuwait and Saudi Arabia.

The Nigerian Government conducted a vigorous diplomatic campaign from June onwards to press the case for an early end to the pricing dispute between Saudi Arabia and other OPEC members, and having called for an extraordinary meeting of the OPEC Conference it indicated in early August that it was prepared if necessary to make a unilateral price cut of $3 per barrel in order to restore the competitiveness of its exports. The Saudi Government then stepped up its own diplomatic efforts to secure acceptance of its price reunification proposals, which it agreed to submit to a consultative meeting of the OPEC Conference (apparently in the belief that a prior consensus had been achieved). When this meeting opened in Geneva on Aug. 19, however, it became clear that no such consensus existed, and the meeting ended in deadlock on Aug. 21 after consultations between Oil Ministers and their respective heads of government had failed to produce any acceptable compromise.

The Saudi reunification formula envisaged (i) a $2 increase in the price of Saudi Arabian 34° crude, taking it to $34 per barrel (which, according to Shaikh Yamani, was $6 higher than the "correct" marker value which would apply if OPEC's proposed price indexation system had been in force since 1974); (ii) a $2 reduction, to $34 per barrel, in the OPEC majority's "deemed marker ceiling"; (iii) a $4 reduction, to $37 per barrel, in OPEC's overall ceiling price; and (iv) a price freeze to last until the end of 1982 at the earliest. Shaikh Yamani also spoke in favour of the early introduction of oil price indexation as a means of stabilizing world oil markets, pointing out that the current decline in demand was not due solely to economic recession in the OECD area but formed part of a process of structural change—accelerated by the 1979–80 price rises—which would progressively reduce oil's share of world energy consumption.

The main objection to the acceptance of the Saudi price reunification formula came from Venezuela, whose Minister of Energy and Mines told the Conference that, while he supported a lengthy price freeze, he could not accept a reduction in OPEC's deemed marker ceiling at a time when his country was experiencing little difficulty in marketing its crude oil at existing official price levels. He added that Venezuela was regarded as a reliable supplier by its customers (mainly in the United States), and had never sought to exploit market conditions by imposing high premiums or by selling oil at inflated spot prices. Iran and Iraq (and initially also Libya and Algeria) were reported to have raised various other objections to the Saudi proposals, and much of the meeting was devoted to an attempt to secure Saudi Arabia's acceptance of a compromise whereby prices would have been reunified on the basis of a $35 marker value.

After the meeting Shaikh Yamani said that Saudi Arabia would hold its marker price at $32 per barrel and that he would refuse to attend any future special meeting of the OPEC Conference until firm guarantees were secured from other member countries to accept a uniform $34 marker value. He announced a 1,000,000 bpd reduction in Aramco's production for the month of September as a "goodwill gesture", but added that the primary aim of this step was to defend Saudi Arabia's current prices, and that the future level of Aramco's output would be reviewed each month.

D12.7—Achievement of Agreement on OPEC Price Reunification

In view of the failure of the Geneva talks, Nigeria announced on Aug. 26 that its official prices were being cut by $4 per barrel since "the Federal Government deems it necessary to take immediate action to ensure that the national interest is preserved in the face of adverse developments in the oil markets". A further reduction of $1.50 per barrel was announced on Oct. 1, taking Nigeria's maximum price to $34.50 per barrel (and thus undercutting the current official price of British North Sea oil by 50 cents). Algeria and Libya made no changes in their official prices, although both countries were reported to be allowing effective discounts on oil exported under barter agreements. Gabon, however, announced a price cut of $1 per barrel with effect from Oct. 1. Iraq cut its Mediterranean export prices by $2 per barrel on the same date, while Kuwait introduced 90-day credit terms whose effect was equivalent to a third-quarter price reduction of around $1 per barrel. Indonesia, whose principal crudes were in strong demand at their existing prices, made minor cuts of up to 50 cents per barrel in the prices of some of its less important grades on Sept. 10.

During September aggregate OPEC output fell below 20,000,000 bpd at some points following Saudi Arabia's 1,000,000 bpd cutback, while the average price of OPEC oil fell below $33 per barrel as a result of overt or covert reductions in uncompetitive official prices. World oil supplies were estimated to be outrunning current demand by between 1,500,000 bpd and 2,000,000 bpd, while non-communist oil stocks on land at the end of the month totalled 4,522 million barrels (only 2.2 per cent below the all-time peak recorded at the end of September 1980 ◊**D11.9**).

In view of Saudi Arabia's refusal to attend a further Oil Ministers' meeting without prior agreement on price reunification, Kuwait took the initiative in early September to launch a fresh round of informal consultations to this end. The Saudi Government authorized an increase in Aramco's production from around 9,200,000 bpd in September to slightly over 9,600,000 bpd in October, this being regarded as a means of bringing additional market pressure to bear on other OPEC members.

The Venezuelan Government indicated on Oct. 13 that it was now prepared to accept an OPEC majority decision on pricing, and on Oct. 20 the OPEC Secretariat announced that Oil Ministers would hold a "short meeting" in Geneva on Oct. 29 (implying an intention to give formal endorsement to a prior consensus). Having agreed to designate the meeting as the 61st (extraordinary) session of the OPEC Conference, ministers formally adopted a pricing structure based largely on the proposals previously put forward by Saudi Arabia in August (◊**D12.6**), thus restoring a unified structure for the first time since early 1979. The decisions of the meeting were announced on Oct. 29 as follows:

"The Conference, after examining the prevailing conditions in the oil market and recognizing the necessity to adopt a unified pricing system for OPEC crudes in order to create the right conditions for stability in that market, has resolved to set the official price of the marker crude—Arabian light 34° API fob Ras Tanura—at $34 per barrel effective not later than Nov. 1, 1981, and to abide by that price until the end of 1982.

"The Conference has also agreed to a set of value differentials for the pricing of all other OPEC crudes in accordance with their respective qualities and geographical locations.

"The Conference is aware that this decision will have an evident positive effect on the economy of the world through the organization of the oil market which, in turn, will contribute also to the consolidation of OPEC as the main hydrocarbon supplier to the international market, thus maintaining its relevance as an energy source.

"In compliance with its decision taken at the 60th meeting of the Conference in May 1981, the Conference has decided that the ministerial committee on long-term strategy will continue its work and report to the Conference in its next ordinary meeting."

Subsequent press statements by individual ministers indicated that value differentials had been readjusted on an interim basis pending further refinement after the next meeting of the Conference, most of the Oct. 29 meeting having been taken up by discussion of the new ceiling prices for light African crudes (which would have been set at $37 per barrel under the formula put forward by Saudi Arabia in August). Algeria and Libya were understood to have made it clear that they considered the proposed ceiling level to be too low in relation to their current price of $40, while Nigeria took the view that it was too high relative to its own current price of $34.50. This led to a compromise whereby the new African ceiling price was fixed at $37.50 per barrel on the understanding that Nigeria would for the time being set the price of its own main (36.7°) grade $1 lower at $36.50 per barrel. It was also accepted that Nigeria should honour all binding contracts which had already been concluded at lower prices.

The new Libyan and Algerian prices of $37.50 per barrel and the new Nigerian price of $36.50 per barrel took effect on Nov. 1. On the same day (i) Iran cut the price of its 34° crude by $2.40, to $34.60 per barrel, and that of its 31° crude by $2.60, to $33.40 per barrel; (ii) Kuwait cut the price of its 31° crude by $2.50, to $33 per barrel; (iii) Qatar cut its prices by an average of $1.75 per barrel (by $1.77 for 40° crude, taking the price of that grade to $35.65); (iv) Abu Dhabi cut its prices by a flat $0.86 per barrel, taking the price of its 39° crude to $35.70 per barrel; (v) Dubai cut the price of its 32° crude by $2.07, to $33.86 per barrel; and (vi)

Venezuela cut the prices of its 31°, 34° and 37° crudes by $1 per barrel, while leaving the price of its 26° crude unchanged and increasing the prices of extra-heavy crudes by up to $0.54 per barrel.

Saudi Arabia backdated the $2 per barrel increase in the price of its 34° crude to Oct. 1 and announced price increases of $0.50 for 27° crude, $1.546 for 31° crude and $2.08 for 39° crude from the same date. Gabon, Indonesia and Iraq maintained their existing official prices after the 61st Conference meeting. Ecuador's average sales price, which had risen to $34.638 per barrel on Oct. 1, was cut to $34.24 in November and December. According to the IEA, the net effect of the OPEC price changes was to raise the weighted average price of OPEC oil by 1 per cent to $34.19 per barrel. Reactive price adjustments in non-OPEC countries included an increase of $1.50 per barrel for British North Sea oil (to establish parity with Nigeria's new price of $36.50).

On Nov. 1 Saudi Arabia restored Aramco's production ceiling to 8,500,000 bpd for the first time since June 1979, and announced its preparedness to lower or raise the ceiling at any time in order to defend the new OPEC marker price against market pressures (i.e. including any upward pressure which might lead other OPEC members to consider breaching the agreed price freeze). Shaikh Yamani said that he expected oil prices to remain under downward market pressure for around six months, but that he hoped that the cutback in Saudi production would bring supply and demand back into "a more normal balance" by the middle of 1982.

D12.8—Decisions of 62nd Meeting of OPEC Conference

During the last two months of 1981 the spot oil market was relatively stable, and most quotations for OPEC crudes were close to the prevailing official prices of the crudes concerned. Total OPEC production was running at around 21,400,000 bpd in December, giving an average for the whole fourth quarter of just over 21,000,000 bpd.

The 62nd OPEC Conference meeting, held in Abu Dhabi from Dec. 9 to 11, was devoted mainly to the task of rationalizing the value differentials for crudes heavier and lighter than the marker grade in order fully to correct the various distortions which had been introduced since 1979 as a result of repeated rounds of flat-rate price increases. Studies of the current structure of market demand indicated that the official prices of the lightest Gulf and African crudes incorporated excessive premiums relative to the marker value, while the negative differentials for heavier Gulf crudes were unrealistically small. Ministers from the countries concerned agreed to make appropriate downward price adjustments, which in the case of the most expensive Algerian and Libyan crudes amounted to 50 cents per barrel. However, Nigeria refused to increase its own prices to the new Algerian and Libyan ceiling level.

The Conference noted a progress report in connexion with its proposal to establish an OPEC institute for higher education (◊D11.6) and also reviewed the work of the ministerial committee on long-term strategy (whose price-indexation proposals had been placed in suspense pending an assessment of the medium-term market reaction to OPEC's current price levels).

The press statement issued after the meeting made no reference to the Conference's agreement that certain price differentials should be adjusted with effect from Jan. 1, 1982, ministers having decided that the announcement of the consequent price changes (which reduced the weighted average price of OPEC crude by an estimated 50 cents per barrel) should be left to individual member countries. Table 53 shows the extent of the price adjustments for selected OPEC crudes. (NB—both Nigeria and Venezuela made cuts in their prices for grades heavier than those listed in this table for these countries.)

Table 53 — Prices of selected OPEC crudes, Jan. 1, 1982

	End-1981 price	Price from Jan. 1, 1982
	(dollars per barrel)	
Algeria (44°)	37.50	37.00
Ecuador† (29.7°)	34.24	33.05
Gabon (31.7°)	35.00	*
Indonesia (34.1°)	35.00	*
Iran (31°)	33.40	32.30
(34°)	34.60	34.20
Iraq‡ (34°)	34.71	34.21
(36°)	34.93	*
Kuwait (31°)	33.00	32.30
Libya (40°)	37.50	37.00
Nigeria (36.7°)	36.50	*
(44.2°)	36.60	*
Qatar (40°)	35.65	35.45
Saudi Arabia (27°)	31.50	31.00
(31°)	33.00	32.40
(34°)	34.00	*
(39°)	35.60	35.40
UAE: Abu Dhabi (39°)	35.70	35.50
Dubai (32°)	33.86	*
Venezuela (26°)	32.88	*
(31°)	35.00	*
(34°)	37.06	*

*No change.
†Average sales price.
‡Mediterranean.

D12.9—Formation of Gulf Co-operation Council

The Foreign Ministers of Bahrain, Kuwait, Oman, Qatar, Saudi Arabia and the United Arab Emirates, meeting in Saudi Arabia on Feb. 4 and 5, 1981, agreed to establish a Co-operation Council of the Arab Gulf States which would provide a framework for the co-ordination of all government policies between the member countries with a view to safeguarding security and stability in the Persian/Arabian Gulf.

Following a further meeting of Foreign Ministers in Oman on March 9 and 10, the heads of state of the six countries met in Abu Dhabi on May 25 and 26 to approve the statutes of the Council, whose aims were defined as follows:

"(i) To achieve co-ordination, integration and co-operation among the member states in all fields in order to bring about their unity; (ii) to deepen and strengthen the bonds of co-operation existing among their peoples in all fields; (iii) to draw up similar systems in all fields . . . including economic and financial affairs, trade, customs and transport, educational and cultural affairs, health and social affairs, information and tourism, and judicial and administrative affairs; and (iv) to promote scientific and technical progress in the fields of industry, minerals, agriculture, sea wealth and animal wealth and to establish scientific research centres and collective projects and to encourage the private sector's co-operation for the good of the peoples of the member states."

The heads of state declared that they had agreed to form the Council because of their "awareness of their special ties and common characteristics and the similarity of the regimes governing them on the basis of the Islamic faith", their "belief in the common destiny and aim uniting their peoples", their "desire to achieve co-ordination, integration and co-operation" which they believed would serve "the sublime objective of the Arab nation", and "a desire to continue efforts in all vital fields concerning their peoples and to achieve their aspirations for a better future and unity".

It was agreed that the Council, the headquarters of which was to be in Riyadh, would be composed of a Supreme Council, a Ministerial Council and a General Secretariat, these three bodies being able to establish auxiliary organs as required.

The Supreme Council of heads of state would hold two ordinary sessions a year. Additional extraordinary meetings could be convened at the request of at least two member countries. The Ministerial Council of Foreign Ministers or their representatives would normally meet once every three months (additional extraordinary meetings being called in the same manner as for the Supreme Council). The General Secretariat would comprise the Secretary-General aided by assistant secretaries-general and by "employees whom he may need", and would have a budget "towards which all member states will contribute in equal proportions". The Secretary-General would be appointed by the Supreme Council for a renewable three-year term but would nominate his own assistants and choose other employees of the Secretariat from the member countries.

It was agreed on May 26 to establish standing committees on (i) economic and social planning; (ii) financial, economic and trade co-operation; (iii) industrial co-operation; (iv) oil; and (v) social and cultural services.

The oil committee, made up of the member countries' Foreign, Oil and Finance Ministers, would be responsible for policy co-ordination regarding "all stages of drilling, refining, marketing and pricing" of oil, as well as "transporting and exploiting natural gas and developing sources of energy". In addition, the oil committee would draw up a "unified oil policy and joint stands towards the outside world and international organizations".

D12.10—Abolition of Price Controls on US Crude Oil Production – Changes in Windfall Profits Tax Rates

With effect from Jan. 28, President Reagan ordered the lifting of all federal price controls on US crude oil production and on a range of hydrocarbon products, including gasoline, heating oil and propane gas. Phased decontrol of oil prices had originally been due to end on Sept. 30. (The existing schedule for the phased decontrol of the wellhead price of natural gas, which could not be varied by executive order, remained in force.) President Reagan described his action as "a positive first step towards a balanced energy programme, free of arbitrary and counter-productive constraints and designed to promote prudent conservation and vigorous domestic production". More than nine years of price controls had, he said, "held US oil production below its potential, artificially boosted energy consumption, aggravated our balance-of-payments problem and stifled technological breakthroughs". The effect of the refining industry's crude oil entitlement system (◊D10.17) had been to provide "a subsidy for the importation of foreign oil" and to increase US dependence on OPEC. Immediate decontrol would reduce US oil consumption by up to 100,000 bpd and would increase gasoline prices (which currently averaged $1.22 per US gallon) by up to 5 cents per gallon.

The US Energy Department stated in July that the influence of free market forces would play a central role in US energy policy under the Reagan Administration. The Government was opposed to the imposition of a "windfall profits tax" on natural gas production after the ending of federal price controls on "new" gas at the beginning of 1985 (◊D9.7). The commercial production of synthe-

575

tic fuels should depend largely on private investment, and public funds (other than for research and development) should not be used to support the production of uncompetitive high-cost alternatives to imported oil. Energy companies should have "broader access" to federal lands. The annual level of US primary energy consumption was expected to undergo an overall increase of 28 per cent between 1980 and 2000, while oil's share of total energy consumption was expected to fall from 43 per cent to 25 per cent over the same period.

Under the Economic Recovery Act of 1981, independent producers' crude output from small wells was exempted from the windfall profits tax (◊**D11.13**), while a schedule was established for a progressive reduction in the rate of windfall profits tax on "new" oil (currently 30 per cent), which would come down to 15 per cent by 1986. The cumulative revenue target of the tax was not, however, reduced.

D12.11—Cancún Summit Conference on International Co-operation and Development

In accordance with a proposal made in February 1980 in the report of the Independent Commission on International Development Issues (◊**D11.14.i**), a 22-nation summit conference was held in the Mexican city of Cancún on Oct. 22 and 23, 1981, to discuss the economic relationship between industrialized and developing countries. The countries represented (16 of them by heads of state or government and the remainder by senior cabinet ministers) were Austria, Canada, France, West Germany, Japan, Sweden, the United Kingdom and the United States as members of the industrialized world and Algeria, Bangladesh, Brazil, China, Guyana, Ivory Coast, India, Mexico, Nigeria, Philippines, Saudi Arabia, Tanzania, Venezuela and Yugoslavia as members of the developing world. The Soviet Union refused an invitation to attend the conference.

Although the Cancún summit was itself expressly designated as a forum for discussion rather than negotiation, its stated aim was to bring about a "positive political impetus" towards the holding of global negotiations on international economic co-operation, particularly in the areas of energy, food, trade and finance. In the event, however, each participating country took up the same position with regard to global negotiating procedures as it had adopted during the 11th special session of the UN General Assembly in the previous year (◊**D11.14.ii**), with West Germany, the United Kingdom and the United States continuing to insist that any negotiations should be "compartmentalized" within the relevant UN specialized agencies, while the remaining participants argued that the UN General Assembly should exercise ultimate authority over the negotiating process. The summit thus served to reinforce rather than to remove the political barriers to a resumption of substantive "North-South" negotiations.

Discussion of energy issues at the Cancún summit centred on a Mexican proposal for the introduction of a global energy policy designed to "promote an orderly dialogue about the energy problems which all nations have to face and none can solve alone" and on a proposal put forward by oil-importing developing countries (and opposed in particular by the United States) that the World Bank should establish an affiliated agency to finance exploration for oil and other energy resources in the Third World.

D13—1982

D13.1—Annual Statistical Survey

D13.1.i—Oil production and reserves

World

Total production .... 57,020,000 bpd (2,785.9 million tonnes)
    Change over 1981 .... −4.1 per cent

End-year proved reserves .... 677,800 million barrels
    Change over end-1981 .... +0.1 per cent

Reserves:production ratio .... 32.6 : 1

Regional shares:

	In 1982 world production*			In end-1982 world reserves†		
	Regional total (million tonnes)	Change over 1981 (per cent)	Share of world total (per cent)	Reserves (thousand million barrels)	Change over 1981 (per cent)	Share of world total (per cent)
USSR/Eastern Europe/China	734.2	+0.9	26.4	85.1	−0.5	12.6
Middle East	652.2	−17.4	23.4	369.0	+1.8	54.4
North America	554.5	+0.2	19.9	43.9	−1.1	6.5
Latin America/ Caribbean	330.5	+4.1	11.9	78.5	−7.2	11.6
Africa	229.7	−4.2	8.2	58.4	+3.9	8.6
Western Europe‡	150.7	+12.5	5.4	23.2	−6.8	3.4
Asia§/Australasia	134.1	−4.3	4.8	19.7	+3.1	2.9

*Including production from oil shales, tar sands and natural gas liquids (NGL).
†Excluding oil shales and tar sands; including NGL in North America.
‡Including Yugoslavia.
§Excluding China.

OPEC

OPEC oil production .... 19,943,000 bpd (978,000 million tonnes)
    Change over 1981 .... −15 per cent
    Share of 1982 world total .... 35.1 per cent

OPEC end-year proved reserves .... 445,150 million barrels
    Change over 1981 .... +2.1 per cent
    Share of 1982 world total .... 65.7 per cent

OPEC reserves:production ratio .... 61.2 : 1.

OPEC (continued)

OPEC member countries' production:

	1982 production		Change over 1981 (per cent)	Share of world total (per cent)	Share of OPEC total (per cent)
	(million tonnes)	(thousand bpd)			
Algeria	45.8	1,045	−1.1	1.6	4.7
Ecuador	10.4	210	+1.0	0.4	1.1
Gabon	7.7	155	+1.3	0.3	0.8
Indonesia	69.0	1,415	−16.1	2.5	7.0
Iran	119.8	2,410	+82.1	4.3	12.2
Iraq	49.6	1,010	+12.7	1.8	5.1
Kuwait	34.9	705	−27.6	1.2	3.6
Libya	54.7	1,140	−6.8	2.0	5.6
Nigeria	63.5	1,285	−10.6	2.3	6.5
Qatar	16.3	340	−19.3	0.6	1.7
Saudi Arabia	327.9	6,695	−33.3	11.8	33.5
UAE*	60.7	1,253	−16.6	2.2	6.2
Venezuela	101.3	1,965	−10.0	3.6	10.3
Neutral Zone†	16.4	315	−15.5	0.6	1.7

*Of which Abu Dhabi 42,500,000 tonnes (885,000 bpd), Dubai 17,800,000 tonnes (360,000 bpd), Sharjah 400,000 tonnes (8,000 bpd).
†Production shared between Kuwait and Saudi Arabia.

Non-OPEC

Selected non-OPEC countries' oil production:

	1982 production		Change over 1981 (per cent)	Share of world total (per cent)
	(million tonnes)	(thousand bpd)		
USSR	612.2	12,430	+0.5	22.0
USA*	484.5	10,200	+0.4	17.4
Mexico	149.4	3,005	+16.4	5.4
United Kingdom	103.4	2,125	+15.7	3.7
China	101.7	2,050	+0.7	3.6
Canada	70.0	1,485	−4.0	2.5
Egypt	34.9	705	+2.3	1.2
Argentina	25.6	490	+0.4	0.9
Norway	24.6	500	−1.2	0.9
Oman	16.2	325	−1.2	0.6
Total	1,622.5	33,315	+2.4	58.2

*Of which natural gas liquids 55,000,000 tonnes (1,550,000 bpd).

D13.1.ii—Oil consumption

World

Total consumption .... 58,420,000 bpd (2,824.8 million tonnes)
    Change over 1981 .... −2.7 per cent

Regional distribution of total:

	1982 consumption		Change over 1981 (per cent)	Share of world total (per cent)
	(million tonnes)	(thousand bpd)		
North America	778.4	16,330	−6.0	27.6
USSR/Eastern Europe/China	632.0	12,820	+0.1	22.4
Western Europe*	604.9	12,525	−4.5	21.4
Asia†/Australasia	407.9	8,475	−3.4	14.4
Latin America/ Caribbean	235.4	4,900	+3.6	8.3
Middle East	87.9	1,745	+3.8	3.1
Africa	78.3	1,625	+3.2	2.8

*Including Yugoslavia.
†Excluding China.

Selected countries

	1982 consumption		Change over 1981 (per cent)	Share of world total (per cent)
	(million tonnes)	(thousand bpd)		
USA	705.5	14,765	−5.4	25.0
USSR	448.5	9,075	+1.0	15.9
Japan	207.8	4,395	−7.2	7.3
West Germany	112.2	2,355	−4.6	4.0
France	91.5	1,915	−7.5	3.2
Italy	90.7	1,845	−5.2	3.2
China	82.4	1,660	−2.8	2.9
United Kingdom	75.6	1,580	+1.2	2.7
Canada	72.9	1,565	−10.8	2.6
Spain	47.8	990	−5.2	1.7
Total	1,934.9	40,145	−3.8	68.5

D13.1.iii—Oil refining

World

Total refinery capacity .... 79,090,000 bpd
    Change over 1981 .... −3.2 per cent

Total refinery throughputs .... 55,700,000 bpd
    Change over 1981 .... −3.3 per cent

Consumption as proportion of capacity ... 73.9 per cent

Selected markets

Consumption of refined product types and change over 1981:

	USA (million tonnes)	USA (per cent)	Western Europe (million tonnes)	Western Europe (per cent)	Japan (million tonnes)	Japan (per cent)
Gasolines	294.4	−1.2	134.2	+0.5	38.6	−3.0
Middle distillates	186.6	−6.3	215.5	−4.1	58.0	−4.3
Fuel oil	90.8	−17.9	165.4	−11.4	78.8	−13.6
Other	133.7	−3.3	89.8	+0.9	32.4	+0.3
Total	705.5	−5.4	604.9	−4.5	207.8	−7.2

D13.1.iv—Tankers and trade

Tankers

Total world fleet .... 303,700,000 deadweight tons

   Change over 1981 .... −5.2 per cent

Trade

Total world crude exports

   (including re-exports) .... 22,337,200 bpd (1,109.6 million tonnes)

   Change over 1981 .... −12.9 per cent

OPEC crude exports .... 14,202,800 bpd (705,554,000 tonnes)

   Change over 1981 .... −22.9 per cent

   Share of 1982 world total .... 63.6 per cent

Total world product exports

   (including re-exports) .... 9,068,900 bpd (450,069,500 tonnes)

   Change over 1981 .... +4.3 per cent

OPEC product exports .... 2,231,100 bpd (110,725,000 tonnes)

   Change over 1981 .... +15.4 per cent

   Share of 1982 world total .... 24.6 per cent

Regional distribution of world oil trade*:

	Share of 1982 imports (per cent) Crude	Share of 1982 imports (per cent) Products	Share of 1982 exports (per cent) Crude	Share of 1982 exports (per cent) Products
USA	17.3	28.0	1.2	11.5
Canada	1.7	1.1	1.0	5.0
Latin America/ Caribbean	9.0	5.4	12.2	30.6
Western Europe	38.4	30.6	3.0	6.7
Middle East	0.6	3.9	54.5	12.8
North Africa	0.3	0.8	9.3	4.9
West Africa	†	1.1	7.3	0.7
East and southern Africa	2.0	1.7	—	0.4
South Asia	2.1	2.5	0.1	0.7
South-East Asia	7.9	7.2	5.3	7.5
Australasia	1.0	2.2	—	0.5
Japan	18.1	9.4	—	0.2
USSR/Eastern Europe/China	0.8	2.4	6.1	18.5
Unspecified	0.8	3.7	—	—
Total	100.0	100.0	100.0	100.0

*Excluding intra-regional trade.   †Negligible.

D13.1.v—World primary energy consumption

Total consumption (excluding
non-commercial fuels) .... 6,857.7 million tonnes oil equivalent (mtoe)
Change over 1981 .... +0.01 per cent

Contributions of primary energy sources:

	Consumption (mtoe)	Change over 1981 (per cent)	Share of total (per cent)
Oil	2,824.8	−2.7	41.2
Coal	2,047.1	+2.2	29.8
Natural gas	1,315.5	−0.4	19.2
Water power	451.6	+4.6	6.6
Nuclear power	218.7	+9.9	3.2

D13.1.vi—Natural gas production and reserves

Marketed production (thousand million cubic metres):

	Regional total (tmcm)	Change over 1981 (per cent)	Share of 1982 world total (per cent)
North America	577.3	−5.9	37.3
Latin America/ Caribbean	71.0	+9.1	4.6
Western Europe*	176.4	−6.1	11.4
USSR/Eastern Europe/China	580.0	+6.8	37.5
Middle East	40.5	−22.9	2.6
Africa	35.1	+19.0	2.3
Asia†/Australasia	66.0	+12.6	4.3
World total	1,546.3	−0.2	100.0
(of which OPEC)	(101.4)	(−5.3)	(6.6)

*Including Yugoslavia.
†Excluding China.

End-year proved reserves (thousand million cubic metres):

	Regional total (tmcm)	Change over 1981 (per cent)	Share of 1982 world total (per cent)
North America	8,453.3	+2.4	9.4
Latin America/ Caribbean	5,259.5	+5.5	5.8
Western Europe*	4,635.1	+3.7	5.2
USSR/Eastern Europe/China	36,576.1	+6.7	40.5
Middle East	24,021.5	+2.4	26.6
Africa	6,425.8	+8.1	7.1
Asia†/Australasia	4,870.2	+15.0	5.4
World total	90,241.5	+5.4	100.0
(of which OPEC)	(31,902.8)	(+3.4)	(35.4)

*Including Yugoslavia.
†Excluding China.

D13.2—Market Developments in the First Quarter of 1982

During 1982 the most important underlying factor in the market environment was (for the third successive year) a decline in oil consumption in the OECD area, attributable both to ongoing changes in the structure of energy demand and to the effects of economic recession. The recessionary influence was particularly severe in 1982, when real gross national product in the OECD area showed an overall fall of 0.3 per cent after two years of low growth (averaging 1.2 per cent per annum). At the same time there was continuing growth in the supply of non-OPEC oil, not only from recently developed oilfields in areas such as Mexico and the North Sea but also from such established major producers as the United States (where oil companies had benefited from the deregulation of domestic crude prices in the previous year ◁**D12.10**) and the Soviet Union (whose exports to the world market had been stimulated by the price rises of 1979–80).

With Saudi Arabia now seen to be in a strong position to guarantee a secure supply of OPEC oil at stable prices, the holding of exceptionally high commercial inventories (as opposed to strategic stocks) became a liability to importers, with the result that stocks were drawn down at a net rate of up to 4,000,000 bpd during the first quarter of 1982, further depressing the demand for OPEC oil. This was the highest rate of stock drawdown since the first quarter of 1978 (during a previous OPEC price freeze ◁**D9.2**). OPEC production fell below 21,000,000 bpd in January, below 20,000,000 bpd in February and below 19,000,000 bpd in March, a large part of the decline being borne by Saudi Arabia, whose output had fallen below 7,500,000 bpd by mid-February. At the same time there was an increase in the proportion of OPEC output sold on the spot market, where the official prices of marker-grade Gulf crudes were being discounted by nearly $4 per barrel in February and over $5 per barrel in March.

A round of cuts in non-OPEC contract prices began in January when Mexico reduced the price of its heavy grade by $2, to $26.50 per barrel, while maintaining the price of its light grade at $35 per barrel (equivalent to a $1 per barrel cut for its main export blend, which then comprised a 50:50 mixture of the two grades). On Feb. 8 the British National Oil Corporation reduced the basic reference price of British North Sea oil by $1.50 to $35 per barrel, a similar reduction being subsequently announced by Norway. Price cuts were also made in February by Egypt and by United States domestic producers.

Within the OPEC area, Iran (which was anxious to increase its output in order to finance heavy military expenditure arising from the Gulf war) exported substantial volumes of oil to spot buyers at prevailing market prices while cutting its official selling prices to contract customers by a total of $4 per barrel during the course of February (by $1 on Feb. 5, $1 on Feb. 12 and $2 on Feb. 21). These cuts left the official price of Iranian 34° crude $3.80 lower than the Saudi marker price, while Iranian 31° crude was priced $4 below Kuwaiti crude of the same gravity.

On March 1 Mexico cut the price of its heavy grade by another $1.50, to $25 per barrel, and the price of its light grade by $2.50, to $32.50 per barrel, the new prices being applied in conjunction with an altered light:heavy export ratio of 60:40. On the same day Venezuela made cuts of $2.50 per barrel in the prices of its extra-heavy crudes, which were not considered to fall within the main structure of OPEC differentials.

Pressure intensified within OPEC during February for the holding of an extraordinary Conference meeting to consider the introduction of co-ordinated production cutbacks, as advocated in particular by Libya, Algeria and Iraq. Libya, whose relations with Saudi Arabia remained strained despite the restoration of diplomatic links at the end of 1981, publicly blamed the current weakening of the oil market on Saudi "overproduction". However, Shaikh Yamani (speaking after consultations with the Oil Ministers of Kuwait and the United Arab Emirates) said on Feb. 9 that he saw no need for such a meeting, since production levels should be "defined by market forces". He also attacked price reductions and concealed discounting by some OPEC members who, he said, had "lost the confidence of their clients" by overpricing their oil in 1979–80 and were now "paying the price for what they did" in the form of reduced exports.

Specific proposals to convene an extraordinary OPEC Conference meeting on Feb. 27 were dropped after objections from Saudi Arabia, but on March 2 efforts to organize such a meeting were resumed as a matter of urgency following the announcement by BNOC of a $4 cut in the reference price of British oil to $31 per barrcl, $5.50 below the price of similar Nigerian crude. This cut was made in response to strong pressure on BNOC from integrated North Sea producers who had been making heavy losses on their refining operations at the previous price level. The British price cut was matched by Norway. Other non-OPEC exporters which subsequently announced price cuts in early March included Egypt (by $1 per barrel) and the Soviet Union (by $4 per barrel for oil exported to Western Europe).

The then President of the OPEC Conference (Dr Maneh Said al Oteiba of the United Arab Emirates) announced on March 3 that a majority of OPEC members had agreed to an early "consultative meeting", detailed discussions on the timing and agenda of which commenced on March 6 in Qatar, where seven OPEC ministers who had gathered for a regular meeting of the OAPEC Council were joined for informal talks by the Oil Ministers of Indonesia and Nigeria. Following the announcement of a reduction in Saudi Arabia's production ceiling to 7,500,000 bpd, these talks (during which the Oil Ministers of the four remaining non-Arab OPEC countries were consulted by telephone) centred on plans to defend the existing OPEC pricing structure through a co-ordinated restriction of production, and ended with Shaikh Yamani's withdrawal of his previous objection to the holding of a formal OPEC ministerial meeting.

Dr al Oteiba said after the Qatar talks that the recent price cuts by Britain and other non-OPEC producers could only be regarded as "hostile" to OPEC, which took the view that since the non-OPEC producers benefited from OPEC price increases they should support the Organization's attempts to maintain its price structure in the current market conditions. It was estimated in mid-March that non-OPEC supplies totalling nearly 13,000,000 bpd had been reduced in price by an average $1.90 per barrel since the beginning of 1982, while the average price of OPEC oil had fallen by only 30 cents per barrel.

D13.3—Decisions of 63rd and 64th Meetings of OPEC Conference – Related Market Developments

Consultations between OPEC Oil Ministers in Vienna on March 19 and 20 were designated as the 63rd (extraordinary) meeting of the OPEC Conference after the ministers had achieved a consensus on the following points: (i) to reaffirm OPEC's $34 per barrel marker price; (ii) to restore value differentials for light African and Gulf crudes to the levels prevailing in 1978 (the new maximum African differential above the marker price being set at $1.50); (iii) to place a ceiling of 18,000,000 bpd on OPEC's aggregate production with effect from April 1, to be reviewcd at the next meeting of the Conference; and (iv) to establish a monitoring committee, comprising the Oil Ministers of Algeria, Indonesia, Venezuela and the United Arab Emirates, which would keep market developments under constant review and make recommendations to the Conference.

Algeria and Nigeria reduced their maximum prices to the agreed African ceiling level of $35.50 per barrel with effect from March 20, while Libya's maximum price was cut to $35.40 on April 1. Iraq cut the price of its 36° crude (fob Mediterranean terminals) by 10 cents to $34.83 per barrel on March 20. The producers of light Gulf crudes cut their prices on the same day as follows: (i) Qatar, by $0.96 (to $34.49) for 40° crude and by $1 (to $34.30) for 36° crude; (ii) Saudi Arabia, by $0.88 (to $34.52) for 39° crude, with retroactive effect from March 1; and (iii) Abu Dhabi, by $0.94 for all grades (taking the price of 39° crude to $34.56).

Details of OPEC members' national production ceilings (released to the press by individual ministers) showed that these totalled 17,500,000 bpd, the Saudi Government having delayed the announcement of a 500,000 bpd cut in Aramco's ceiling until after the Conference meeting in order to emphasize that this cut—like all Saudi production decisions—was regarded as a sovereign act outside the formal scope of any OPEC agreement. Table 54 shows each member country's production ceiling from April 1, together with its actual output in early March.

Table 54 — OPEC members' March 1982 oil output and April 1982 production ceilings

	March output	April ceiling
	(thousand barrels daily)	
Algeria	700	650
Ecuador	200	200
Gabon	150	150
Indonesia	1,450	1,300
Iran	1,200	1,200
Iraq	1,200	1,200
Kuwait	775	650
Libya	600	750
Nigeria	1,300	1,300
Qatar	350	300
Saudi Arabia	7,325	7,000
UAE	1,250	1,000
Venezuela	1,700	1,500
Neutral Zone*	250	300
Total	18,450	17,500

*Production shared between Kuwait and Saudi Arabia.

The credibility of OPEC's production programme was undermined shortly after the conclusion of the Conference meeting, when Iran made clear its intention to continue to undercut the prices of other Gulf crudes with a view to maximizing its exports regardless of the OPEC production ceiling allocated to it. Libya, for its part, again voiced strong public criticisms of Saudi Arabia's oil policy. Despite the hopes expressed by several OPEC ministers that non-members would now bring their prices into line with OPEC prices, the British Secretary of State for Energy said on March 21 that the British Government saw no reason for BNOC to reduce its reliance on market forces as a major factor in pricing North Sea oil.

The member country most vulnerable to market pressure under the new OPEC strategy was Nigeria, with a production ceiling nearly 1,000,000 bpd below the level required to finance current government spending and an official price some 14.5 per cent higher than the $31 price of directly competitive North Sea oil. Within days of the 63rd Conference meeting Nigerian oil output fell by about 50 per cent to 630,000 bpd, and on March 23 the Nigerian Government announced emergency measures, including severe import restrictions, to protect its economy, which had suffered a monthly visible trade deficit of up to $600,000,000 even before the latest fall in oil production.

Saudi Arabia, supported by Kuwait, responded immediately by making it clear to the foreign producing companies which had reduced or suspended their Nigerian liftings that it was prepared to call for a further extraordinary meeting of the OPEC Conference to discuss appropriate joint action in support of Nigeria. Speaking on March 31 (the same day that Nigeria announced that a shortfall in oil revenues would necessitate the rescheduling of its five-year development plan), Shaikh Yamani said that such a meeting could be called under Article 4 of the Organization's statute (◊B1.7), which was intended to deter international oil companies from penalizing a particular member country because of its application of Conference decisions. He added that OPEC's policy of defending its existing pricing structure was based on the premise that the current supply surplus was a temporary phenomenon caused by "massive" oil company destocking and that a more balanced market situation would be restored within a matter of months.

Following several rounds of confidential negotiations between oil company representatives and Nigerian officials, which were accompanied by conflicting public claims from both sides about the causes of the current crisis, a compromise was reached which enabled Nigeria's production to increase to 950,000 bpd by mid-April. However, most producing companies reserved the right to decrease their liftings again unless market conditions improved during the coming weeks.

The Nigerian Government accepted this increase in the country's oil production as the maximum obtainable through informal OPEC pressure on the international oil companies, and did not press for the holding of an extraordinary Conference meeting. However, the first meeting of the OPEC monitoring committee, held in Vienna on April 21, paid special attention to Nigeria's situation and reaffirmed OPEC's intention to support any member country whose adherence to OPEC policies was threatened by international oil companies (Ecuador being mentioned as another member country which was experiencing customer resistance, forcing a cut of $1.85, to $31.20, in its average sales price for April). The committee's chairman, Dr al Oteiba, said that OPEC's current aggregate production level had fallen to 15,850,000 bpd, indicating the Organization's capability to restrain output in order to defend its pricing structure.

It was, however, noted by market analysts that up to 500,000 bpd of Iraq's export capacity had been cut off on April 10 by Syria's closure of the pipelines carrying Iraqi oil through its territory (in accordance with Syria's support for Iran in the Gulf war); that spot oil prices, despite an upturn during April, still remained below official OPEC prices; and that Iran was increasing its sales of low-priced oil, while certain other member countries were known to be offering covert discount arrangements.

During the first week of May talks took place between Saudi Arabian and Nigerian ministers, reportedly concerning a request by Nigeria for a $1,000 million loan to support the Nigerian economy in the short term, while Venezuela agreed to refine and market up to 100,000 bpd of Ecuadorian oil at higher prices than could be obtained through Ecuador's own available outlets. (Ecuador's average sales price subsequently rose to $32.80 in May and $33.20 in June.) During the second week of May spot oil prices reached levels equivalent to official OPEC prices for the first time since January (although they later declined again), leading to further expressions of optimism about a revival of demand when the OPEC monitoring committee held its second meeting in Venezuela on May 18. The current OPEC production level was stated by the committee to be about 16,500,000 bpd.

The 64th meeting of the OPEC Conference, held in Quito on May 20 and 21, decided that the present ceiling on total OPEC production should be maintained, subject to continuing surveillance by the monitoring committee. Heated exchanges were reported during the meeting over Iran's non-compliance with its production ceiling, which was strongly criticized by Iraq. Iran, however, stated that it intended to increase its production towards a target of 3,000,000 bpd (of which 2,500,000 bpd would be exported), and demanded a formal increase in its quota, to be achieved within the overall OPEC ceiling by cutting Saudi Arabia's quota (which Saudi Arabia, for its part, continued to regard as self-imposed and not subject to alteration by OPEC). It was estimated that Iran was at that point exceeding its quota by between 600,000 and 800,000 bpd, while Saudi Arabia was producing around 500,000 bpd less than its ceiling of 7,000,000 bpd.

D13.4—May 1982 Meeting of IEA Governing Board

The Governing Board of the International Energy Agency met in Paris at ministerial level on May 24. The main sections of the ministers' final communiqué were worded as follows:

"**General**. Ministers considered the prospects for the oil market in the light of the recent changes in oil prices, as well as the contribution that energy conservation and progress in switching away from oil has made towards the continued fall in oil demand. They welcomed the progress so far but were aware of the risk of complacency and noted the need for continuing progress in bringing about a better energy mix. They emphasized the important role that market forces, supplemented where appropriate by government action, could continue to make towards these ends. Ministers furthermore underlined the importance they attach to the need for timely development on an economic basis of IEA countries' energy resources, thereby improving the overall security of their energy supply.

"Ministers noted that substantial improvements have been made in increasing energy efficiency and substituting other fuels for oil, as a result of market reaction to higher prices, supplemented by effective government policies. Thus considerable *progress has been made towards achieving the objectives* agreed upon in the IEA ministerial meeting in May 1980 (◊**D11.5**) and also at the Venice summit of June 1980 (◊**D11.7**). Although low economic growth has contributed to this result, the link between overall economic activity and oil consumption has weakened considerably. However, they also concluded that despite the current more relaxed oil market situation, *considerable uncertainties continue to exist* about energy developments. The political situation in the Middle East carries with it the underlying and ever-present risk of oil supply interruptions. Furthermore, concentration on short-term oil market conditions, particularly under present economic conditions, is deterring producers and consumers from taking the investment decisions necessary to meet probable long-term trends. Recognizing that *sustained improvement in the level and structure of energy use* is a critical element for revitalizing IEA economies in the medium term, ministers reconfirmed the IEA objective of improving overall energy efficiency and bringing about a more balanced energy mix, and agreed to pursue policies to that end.

"Ministers noted that progress has also been made in *improving preparations for supply interruptions*, including the development of procedures for consultation and co-ordination in responding to oil supply interruptions of less than 7 per cent and the establishment of a new short-term information system. They noted that study of stocks is continuing. Ministers noted that the fourth test of the emergency allocation system will be conducted in 1983 to continue to develop the operational readiness of the system and called for full participation by all member countries in the test.

"**Short-term oil market assessment.** Ministers welcomed the *reduced current demand for oil* and noted the resulting weakening of oil prices. However, they recognized that there could be a turnaround in overall demand on short notice when the existing drawdown of oil stocks ends or if a strong upturn in economic activity occurs, and that the risk of a price shock caused by political disturbances remains. They concluded that the present situation should be viewed as a temporary one which does not necessarily indicate probable future developments based on underlying trends. They therefore agreed to continue to watch closely future developments, particularly in stock movements and oil consumption.

"**Structural change.** Ministers agreed that *recent movements in world oil prices*, as well as bringing a welcome relief from inflationary pressures, provide an important opportunity to

586

revitalize the world economy. However, their assessment of long-term energy prospects confirms the need for measures to sustain and improve upon progress made in reducing the growth of total energy requirements and dependence on oil. They reconfirmed that this could be achieved through further improvement in energy efficiency, and by relying on other energy sources such as coal, nuclear, natural gas, and, in the very long term, renewable sources of energy to provide greater shares of the energy supply mix.

"Ministers emphasized the importance of *energy pricing* in bringing about these changes. They agreed to give particular attention to energy pricing issues when developing national energy policies, including the need for oil prices to consumers to reflect world market prices; for electricity tariffs that encourage efficiency and permit utilities to finance new capacity; and to avoid those subsidies of consumer prices and other interventions which discourage conservation, high levels of domestic production and substitution away from oil. They also recognized the need to take account of energy policy objectives in determining energy taxation.

"Ministers noted that past increases in prices have made *energy conservation even more economically attractive*. They agreed that further efforts are required to improve energy efficiency in IEA countries, particularly in areas where government action can remove barriers to the operation of market forces, or is needed to supplement market forces. Ministers agreed, therefore, to keep their national energy conservation programmes under review in order to ensure their full implementation and maintain their effectiveness. . . .

"**International energy relations.** Because of the *global nature of energy questions*, ministers agreed on the importance of all countries recognizing the nature of energy as a decisive element for progress in the world economy and, in particular, for the development of the poorer countries . . . Ministers noted that many developing countries have promising energy resources, but that their expeditious development will require finance, expertise and technology. While external financial support provided for energy development in developing countries has risen significantly, continued weight will be given to energy in both multilateral and national aid programmes. They agreed upon the need for better understanding of constraints affecting energy investment in developing countries, and for co-operative participation by enterprises with significant financial and technological resources as well as by governments and international organizations. Ministers noted the various contacts which are underway between oil producer and consumer countries, and stressed the need to enhance such exchanges in order to improve mutual understanding of the oil and energy situation. Ministers believe this will contribute to greater stability in the world energy situation which is vital to future development of the world economy as a whole."

D13.5—Breakdown of OPEC Production Programme

Following the 64th OPEC Conference meeting Britain and Norway announced oil price increases, BNOC's basic reference price being raised from $31 to $33.50 per barrel on June 1. (North Sea oil had been traded at a premium on the spot market since early April, placing strong pressure on the profit margins of non-integrated producing companies.) Iran's official prices, which had remained at $30.20 per barrel for 34° crude and $28.30 for 31° crude since Feb. 21, were raised by $1 with effect from July 1, the new price levels being close to the prevailing spot market rates for the same crudes. Ecuador's average sales price fell in July to $30.25 per barrel (its lowest level since that country's adoption of market-oriented pricing in late 1979).

OPEC's aggregate production during June was officially stated to be at least 18,200,000 bpd, although unofficial estimates put it as high as 18,700,000 bpd (both Libya and Iran, which were known to have substantially exceeded their quotas, having failed to submit production figures to OPEC). Nigeria acknowledged that it had exceeded its daily production ceiling during June, but maintained that its average output for the whole of the second quarter remained within its quota. The June production figures created considerable tension within

OPEC, with some member countries calling for a redistribution of quotas within the existing ceiling and others advocating either a higher ceiling or an end to all restrictions on output.

Saudi Arabia, whose average June production (some 6,477,000 bpd) had remained substantially below its ceiling, maintained that the premium of $1.50 per barrel which had been applied to African crudes since March 20 was now too low in terms of the current product worth of these crudes and was adversely affecting sales of its own and other Gulf crudes. (Market reports suggested that the pattern of demand in the second quarter was heavily influenced by selective restocking of light "short-haul" crudes, whereas stocks of heavier Gulf crudes continued to be drawn down in the expectation of a further decline in the open-market prices of these grades.)

The OPEC monitoring committee, meeting in Vienna on July 7, recommended that the 17,500,000 bpd production ceiling should remain in force, but as a monthly rather than a quarterly average, on the grounds that whereas there was as yet no indication of any significant upturn in oil consumption there was evidence that the June increase in OPEC output had contributed to the softening of spot oil prices during that month. Members of the committee expressed some concern about certain member countries' "overproduction" relative to their ceilings, it being made clear by the Venezuelan Minister of Energy and Mines that his country (which had had to turn away buyers in order to abide by its own production ceiling) would feel free to disregard that ceiling if such violations continued.

The 65th (extraordinary) meeting of the OPEC Conference opened in Vienna on July 9 to consider the monitoring committee's recommendations. Differences over the economic issues involved were, however, sharpened by political tensions, and on July 10 the meeting was suspended after reaching deadlock (thus effectively suspending the validity of the Organization's production programme).

The main issues which caused the breakdown of the meeting were Saudi Arabia's refusal to accept a lower production ceiling in order to permit the raising of Iran's ceiling, and the refusal of Libya and the other African producers to accede to Saudi Arabia's request to raise their maximum differentials by $1.50 per barrel. Iran's case was put forward in terms which implied a clear challenge to Saudi Arabia's dominant position within OPEC and with a degree of harshness attributable to the politics of the Gulf war (in which Saudi Arabia supported Iraq). Libya's strong political opposition to Saudi Arabia on most Middle East issues was also a factor in its unwillingness to compromise at the meeting. Iran claimed that there was wide support at the meeting for the principle of an increase in its quota to 3,000,000 bpd and that this represented a "moral triumph" over Saudi Arabia.

Venezuela, which had unsuccessfully attempted to achieve a compromise at the meeting on the basis of an increase in the overall OPEC production ceiling, announced on July 17 that since the quota system had now collapsed it would increase its output to about 1,800,000 bpd (20 per cent above its former quota) for the remainder of the year.

D13.6—Pricing and Production Developments, August to mid-December 1982

It was reported in mid-August that Saudi oil output had fallen to 5,500,000 bpd, its lowest level for a decade, following a sharp reduction in Aramco's sales to its parent companies. The spot value of Saudi Arabian 34° crude was now more than $3 below its official price of $34 per barrel. The Saudi Government's preferred minimum production level for domestic budgetary purposes was believed to be over 6,000,000 bpd at this time. According to official OPEC estimates, the decline in Saudi output contributed to a reduction in overall OPEC output in mid-August to 16,900,000 bpd.

The OPEC monitoring committee, meeting in Vienna on Aug. 20, acknowledged that its earlier forecasts of a substantial upturn in demand for OPEC oil were exaggerated, and reduced its estimate of the likely year-end demand by 10 per cent (to between 19,000,000 and 20,000,000 bpd), the continuing slackness of demand being attributed to a further net drawdown of importers' stocks. A further meeting of the committee, held in Abu Dhabi on Sept. 20, recommended the observance of a production ceiling of 17,500,000 bpd until a clear upturn in demand occurred, but was unable to agree on any recommendation concerning the differentials between African and Gulf crudes. Kuwait's Oil Minister said in London on the same day that OPEC must now be considered as a "marginal" (i.e. residual) supplier of oil, and that its marker price should be frozen until 1985 and should not increase by more than the rate of inflation for several years thereafter.

The Oil Ministers of Saudi Arabia, Kuwait, the United Arab Emirates and Qatar met in Oman on Oct. 14, together with their counterparts from Bahrain and Oman, under the auspices of the Gulf Co-operation Council (◊D12.9). A statement issued after the meeting strongly criticized overproduction and price-cutting by OPEC members, the refusal of African producers to raise their price differentials and the undercutting of OPEC prices by Mexico and by North Sea producers, all of which were described as destabilizing influences on the oil market.

Indonesia cut its official prices by between 47 cents (for its main 34.1° grade) and $1.60 on Nov. 11 in an attempt to improve its market position. The country had suffered a fall of around $2,000 million in its foreign exchange reserves since the introduction of OPEC quotas in April, and was facing a record budget deficit. This action by a major OPEC producer was seen as further evidence of the weakness of the OPEC pricing structure, and was followed by a steady decline in spot market prices after several weeks of relative stability. Ecuador maintained its average sales price within 50 cents of $32 between August and December.

It was announced on Nov. 12 that the ordinary December meeting of the OPEC Conference, which had been planned to take place in Nigeria, would be moved to "an alternative venue felt by some member states to be more appropriate" (indicating the Gulf producers' wish to press their case for an increase in African differentials in a politically neutral location). The date of the meeting was subsequently put back from Dec. 9 to Dec. 19 in response to requests from several member countries for an extension of the time available for prior consultations in the light of the growing pressures upon "several countries facing severe financial difficulties".

OPEC's production level in mid-December 1982 was estimated to be up to 19,500,000 bpd, of which Saudi Arabia contributed about 5,100,000 bpd, Iran up to 2,500,000 bpd, Venezuela over 2,200,000 bpd, Libya 1,800,000 bpd (about the limit of its current capacity) and Nigeria about 1,400,000 bpd. It was reported on Dec. 9 that because of widespread discounting the weighted average price of all OPEC crudes had fallen to $31.75 per barrel, from $32.90 in June. This compared with a theoretical weighted average—if all official prices were observed—of $34.10 per barrel.

D13.7—Failure of 66th OPEC Conference Meeting to agree on New National Production Quotas

Following several weeks of intensive consultations between member countries, the 66th meeting of the OPEC Conference was held in Vienna on Dec. 19 and 20 under the chairmanship of the Nigerian delegate, Alhaji Yahaya Dikko (Special Adviser on Petroleum and Energy to the Nigerian President).

In his formal opening address to the meeting, Alhaji Dikko said that member countries should "close ranks, share the production in some rational and equitable manner, set differentials at levels that enable each partner to sell its export quota and voluntarily agree to abide by these limits". In a clear reference to the proceedings of the October meeting of the Gulf Co-operation Council (during which Shaikh Yamani had warned of Saudi Arabia's preparedness to cut its prices and increase its production if other exporters "persisted in their misguided actions"), Alhaji Dikko said that "threats are never a basis for co-operation", adding that there was an urgent need for OPEC to "act with resolve in order to prevent this period of difficulty from becoming a time of crisis which could conceivably engulf us all".

The meeting was confined almost entirely to prolonged discussion of individual countries' production ceilings, and ended after it had become clear that no basis existed for a compromise on this question at this point. A new aggregate production ceiling of 18,500,000 bpd was agreed only as an annual average for 1983, and it was acknowledged by the Conference that "agreement on establishing national quotas for the distribution of that total amount would require further consultations among the respective governments". A subsequent meeting would be held in the light of these consultations, pending which member countries were exhorted to make "every effort to preserve the price structure and to stabilize the market conditions".

The main obstacle to agreement was the continuing unwillingness of Saudi Arabia and Iran to seek a means of reconciling their conflicting production targets in a depressed market. Iran argued that the four "logical criteria" for the establishment of national production quotas should be each country's historical output levels, size of oil reserves, size of population and extent of current economic and social needs—on which basis Iran now claimed a quota of 3,200,000 bpd, of which 700,000 bpd would be for domestic consumption. At the same time Iran stated its support for an overall OPEC ceiling of 17,500,000 bpd and called for a cut in Saudi Arabia's output to below 5,000,000 bpd.

Other countries which put forward cases for increases in their national production quotas included Venezuela (whose 1983 budget provided for a minimum production level of 1,900,000 bpd), Libya, Indonesia and Nigeria. Iraq demanded a quota increase equal to any increase obtained by Iran, but this was regarded as a purely political gesture, given Iraq's current inability to fulfil its existing quota. Among the moderate Gulf producers, the United Arab Emirates requested a 35 per cent increase in its former quota, to 1,350,000 bpd. Overall, the national quota demands put forward at the meeting totalled 23,400,000 bpd.

Venezuela (one of several OPEC members which broadly supported Iran's contention that its former quota was "imposed and unfair") advocated a compromise on the basis of an aggregate OPEC ceiling of 19,000,000 bpd, to include Saudi Arabian production of about 5,600,000 bpd. Saudi Arabia, however, maintained that current market conditions would not permit aggregate production of more than 18,200,000 bpd, within which Saudi Arabia's minimum production level should be 6,000,000 bpd (although the country intended to retain its formal production ceiling of 7,000,000 bpd).

Because of its preoccupation with production questions, the meeting did not discuss Saudi Arabia's request for an increase of $2.30 per barrel in the maximum differential for Algerian, Libyan and Nigerian crudes, which would have raised the African ceiling price to $37.80 per barrel.

Iran said that the meeting marked the end of an era in which one OPEC member (i.e. Saudi Arabia) could "unilaterally" impose its policy on production matters, while Algeria said that member states were now "free to fix their own production". Saudi Arabian radio broadcasts on Dec. 21 stated that "so long as there is no definitive and binding system of quotas, there will be new troubles" within OPEC, adding that the member countries responsible for the Organization's present problems were Iran, Libya, Venezuela and Nigeria.

D14—1983

D14.1—Annual Statistical Survey

D14.1.i—Oil production and reserves

World

Total production	56,705,000 bpd (2,768.7 million tonnes)
Change over 1982	−0.6 per cent
End-year proved reserves	677,700 million barrels
Change over end-1982	−0.01 per cent
Reserves:production ratio	32.7 : 1

Regional shares:

	In 1983 world production*			In end-1983 world reserves†		
	Regional total (million tonnes)	Change over 1982 (per cent)	Share of world total (per cent)	Reserves (thousand million barrels)	Change over 1982 (per cent)	Share of world total (per cent)
USSR/Eastern Europe/China	742.0	+1.1	26.8	84.3	−0.9	12.4
Middle East	596.1	−8.6	21.5	369.7	+0.2	54.5
North America	558.5	+0.7	20.2	42.4	−3.4	6.3
Latin America/ Caribbean	326.0	−1.4	11.8	81.7	+4.1	12.1
Africa	230.2	+0.2	8.3	56.9	−2.6	8.4
Western Europe‡	171.1	+13.5	6.2	23.7	+2.2	3.5
Asia§/Australasia	144.8	+8.0	5.2	19.0	−3.6	2.8

*Including production from oil shales, tar sands and natural gas liquids (NGL).
†Excluding oil shales and tar sands; including NGL in North America.
‡Including Yugoslavia.
§Excluding China.

OPEC

OPEC oil production	18,500,000 bpd (906,900,000 tonnes)
Change over 1982	−7.3 per cent
Share of 1983 world total	32.7 per cent
OPEC end-year proved reserves	448,300 million barrels
Change over 1982	+0.7 per cent
Share of 1983 world total	66.1 per cent
OPEC reserves:production ratio	66.4 : 1

OPEC (continued)

OPEC member countries' production:

	1983 production		Change over 1982 (per cent)	Share of world total (per cent)	Share of OPEC total (per cent)
	(million tonnes)	(thousand bpd)			
Algeria	42.3	965	−7.6	1.5	4.7
Ecuador	11.9	240	+14.4	0.4	1.3
Gabon	7.6	150	−1.3	0.3	0.8
Indonesia	65.3	1,345	−5.4	2.4	7.2
Iran	122.4	2,465	+2.2	4.4	13.5
Iraq	54.1	1,105	+9.1	2.0	6.0
Kuwait	44.7	900	+28.1	1.6	4.9
Libya	54.4	1,135	−0.5	2.0	6.0
Nigeria	61.0	1,235	−3.9	2.2	6.7
Qatar	14.7	310	−9.8	0.5	1.6
Saudi Arabia	255.8	5,225	−22.0	9.2	28.2
UAE*	59.5	1,240	−2.0	2.1	6.6
Venezuela	97.0	1,875	−4.2	3.5	10.7
Neutral Zone†	16.2	310	−1.2	0.6	1.8

*Of which Abu Dhabi 40,800,000 tonnes (860,000 bpd), Dubai 16,900,000 tonnes (345,000 bpd), Sharjah 1,800,000 tonnes (35,000 bpd).
†Production shared between Kuwait and Saudi Arabia.

Non-OPEC

Selected non-OPEC countries' oil production:

	1983 production		Change over 1982 (per cent)	Share of world total (per cent)
	(million tonnes)	(thousand bpd)		
USSR	616.3	12,520	+0.7	22.3
USA*	486.8	10,245	+0.5	17.6
Mexico	146.6	2,950	−1.8	5.3
United Kingdom	114.9	2,360	+11.1	4.1
China	106.0	2,135	+4.2	3.8
Canada	71.7	1,515	+2.4	2.6
Egypt	38.3	775	+9.8	1.4
Norway	30.5	620	+24.0	1.1
Argentina	24.9	475	−2.7	0.9
Oman	19.6	390	+21.0	0.7
Total	1,655.6	33,985	+2.0	59.8

*Of which natural gas liquids 55,500,000 tonnes (1,565,000 bpd).

D14.1.ii—Oil consumption

World

Total consumption .... 58,040,000 bpd (2,801.4 million tonnes)
    Change over 1982 .... −0.8 per cent

Regional distribution of total:

	1983 consumption		Change over 1982 (per cent)	Share of world total (per cent)
	(million tonnes)	(thousand bpd)		
North America	773.1	16,215	−0.7	27.6
USSR/Eastern Europe/China	634.8	12,895	+0.4	22.7
Western Europe*	586.6	12,240	−3.0	20.9
Asia†/Australasia	408.1	8,480	—	14.6
Latin America/Caribbean	229.0	4,760	−2.7	8.2
Middle East	90.5	1,805	+3.0	3.2
Africa	79.3	1,645	+1.3	2.8

*Including Yugoslavia.
†Excluding China.

Selected countries

	1983 consumption		Change over 1982 (per cent)	Share of world total (per cent)
	(million tonnes)	(thousand bpd)		
USA	704.9	14,745	−0.1	25.2
USSR	450.5	9,115	+0.4	16.1
Japan	207.2	4,390	−0.3	7.4
West Germany	110.8	2,340	−1.2	3.9
France	89.4	1,880	−2.3	3.2
Italy	89.2	1,820	−1.7	3.2
China	84.7	1,705	+2.7	3.0
United Kingdom	72.5	1,535	−4.1	2.6
Canada	68.2	1,470	−6.4	2.4
Spain	47.8	1,010	—	1.7
Total	1,925.2	40,010	−0.5	68.7

D14.1.iii—Oil refining

World

Total refinery capacity .... 76,375,000 bpd
    Change over 1982 .... −3.4 per cent

Total refinery throughputs .... 55,245,000 bpd
    Change over 1982 .... −0.8 per cent

Consumption as proportion of capacity ... 76 per cent

Selected markets

Consumption of refined product types and change over 1982:

	USA (million tonnes)	USA (per cent)	Western Europe (million tonnes)	Western Europe (per cent)	Japan (million tonnes)	Japan (per cent)
Gasolines	298.4	+1.4	137.3	+2.3	39.5	+2.2
Middle distillates	189.0	+1.3	216.8	+0.6	59.6	+2.8
Fuel oil	78.6	−13.4	142.1	−14.1	76.4	−3.0
Other	138.9	+3.9	90.4	+0.7	31.7	−2.2
Total	704.9	−0.1	586.6	−3.0	207.2	−0.3

D14.1.iv—Tankers and trade

Tankers

Total world fleet	283,200,000 deadweight tons
Change over 1982	−6.8 per cent

Trade

Total world crude exports (including re-exports)	20,920,900 bpd (1,039.5 million tonnes)
Change over 1982	−6.3 per cent
OPEC crude exports	12,220,800 bpd (607,245,000 tonnes)
Change over 1982	−13.9 per cent
Share of 1983 world total	58.4 per cent
Total world product exports (including re-exports)	9,494,900 bpd (464,980,400 tonnes)
Change over 1982	+4.7 per cent
OPEC product exports	2,191,300 bpd (107,311,500 tonnes)
Change over 1982	−1.8 per cent
Share of 1983 world total	23.1 per cent

Regional distribution of world oil trade*:

	Share of 1983 imports (per cent) Crude	Share of 1983 imports (per cent) Products	Share of 1983 exports (per cent) Crude	Share of 1983 exports (per cent) Products
USA	17.6	30.1	0.9	11.7
Canada	1.4	1.2	1.4	4.9
Latin America/Caribbean	8.8	5.6	14.1	25.5
Western Europe	36.6	32.5	2.4	7.0
Middle East	0.4	2.1	50.6	14.7
North Africa	0.3	1.7	9.8	6.0
West Africa	—	1.3	7.3	0.9
East and southern Africa	2.2	1.0	—	†
South Asia	2.0	2.1	0.1	0.5
South-East Asia	8.5	7.1	5.8	6.0
Australasia	0.7	1.9	†	0.7
Japan	19.0	10.4	—	0.1
USSR/Eastern Europe/China	1.5	2.3	7.6	22.0
Unspecified	1.0	0.7	—	—
Total	100.0	100.0	100.0	100.0

*Excluding intra-regional trade.

†Negligible.

D14.1.v—World primary energy consumption

Total consumption (excluding
non-commercial fuels) .... 6,943.2 million tonnes oil equivalent (mtoe)
Change over 1982 .... +1.2 per cent

Contributions of primary energy sources:

	Consumption (mtoe)	Change over 1982 (per cent)	Share of total (per cent)
Oil	2,801.4	−0.8	40.3
Coal	2,101.0	+2.6	30.3
Natural gas	1,325.5	+0.8	19.1
Water power	475.0	+5.2	6.8
Nuclear power	240.3	+9.9	3.5

D14.1.vi —Natural gas production and reserves

Marketed production (thousand million cubic metres):

	Regional total (tmcm)	Change over 1982 (per cent)	Share of 1983 world total (per cent)
North America	520.9	−9.8	33.7
Latin America/Caribbean	70.6	−0.6	4.6
Western Europe*	180.2	+2.2	11.6
USSR/Eastern Europe/China	615.9	+6.2	39.8
Middle East	38.9	−4.0	2.5
Africa	47.8	+36.2	3.1
Asia†/Australasia	72.7	+10.2	4.7
World total	1,547.0	–	100.0
(*of which OPEC*)	(*112.8*)	(*+11.2*)	(*7.3*)

*Including Yugoslavia.
†Excluding China.

End-year proved reserves (thousand million cubic metres):

	Regional total (tmcm)	Change over 1982 (per cent)	Share of 1983 world total (per cent)
North America	8,169.5	−3.4	8.7
Latin America/Caribbean	5,329.5	+1.3	5.6
Western Europe*	5,220.3	+12.6	5.5
USSR/Eastern Europe/China	39,431.9	+7.8	41.7
Middle East	24,680.1	+2.7	26.1
Africa	6,381.3	−0.7	6.8
Asia†/Australasia	5,287.4	+8.6	5.6
World total	94,500.0	+4.7	100.0
(*of which OPEC*)	(*33,654.5*)	(*+5.5*)	(*35.6*)

*Including Yugoslavia.
†Excluding China.

D14.2—The Market Environment in 1983

The changing structure of energy demand in the non-communist industrialized countries was clearly illustrated in 1983, when a marked upturn (to 2.5 per cent) in the average rate of real economic growth in the OECD area was accompanied by falls of 0.4 per cent in OECD energy consumption and 1.7 per cent in OECD oil consumption. As in 1982, demand for OPEC oil exports was affected not only by reduced consumption in the main markets but also by further growth in non-OPEC oil output and by a further drawdown of importing countries' commercial inventories which was only partially offset by additions to strategic stocks. Although the average net drawdown rate of non-communist oil stocks was, at 600,000 bpd, only about half as great as in 1982, an exceptionally high proportion of the 1983 drawdown occurred between January and March, when stocks were liquidated at a record rate of 4,250,000 bpd, as against a maximum rate of 4,000,000 bpd in the first quarter of 1982.

D14.3—OPEC Ministers' Failure to agree on National Production Quotas, January 1983

A shift from limited stock replenishment to heavy stock drawdown by importers caused average OPEC output to fall by around 2,000,000 bpd between mid-December 1982 and mid-January 1983. Saudi Arabia's production declined to little more than 4,000,000 bpd (severely restricting the country's supply of associated gas) as a result of further cutbacks in purchases by Aramco's parent companies, which had in early January informed the Saudi Government of their commercial objections to the fulfilment of purchase contracts at official prices which were far in excess of prevailing spot values (e.g. by about $3.25 per barrel for 34° crude). Moreover, the netback value of the marker crude, extrapolated from product prices in the main refining centres, was more than $4 below the official price of $34 per barrel in early January.

Following a meeting of the oil committee of the Gulf Co-operation Council in Bahrain on Jan. 15 and 16, during which Oman reportedly described the OPEC pricing structure as unrealistic and threatened to reduce the official export price of its own crude by $2.50 per barrel, the four OPEC members of the GCC (Saudi Arabia, Kuwait, Qatar and the United Arab Emirates) held a separate round of talks in Bahrain with representatives of Nigeria, Indonesia, Iraq and Libya. It was recognized that importers could be expected to minimize their forward purchasing commitments in OPEC countries while uncertainty persisted over the OPEC pricing structure, now regarded by most oil analysts as untenable without the backing of national production quotas. It was accordingly decided on Jan. 16 (with the concurrence of the five remaining OPEC members) that a full OPEC ministerial meeting should be convened as soon as possible with a view to revising the overall OPEC production ceiling and to resolving existing disagreements over the distribution of national quotas.

OPEC Oil Ministers subsequently met in Geneva on Jan. 23 and 24 on a purely consultative basis, with no agreement being adopted to justify the designation of these talks as an extraordinary Conference meeting. Press reports indicated that a tentative understanding was reached to reduce the aggregate OPEC production ceiling to between 17,000,000 and 17,500,000 bpd and to allocate national quotas within these proposed limits, but that deadlock ensued when Saudi Arabia and Kuwait, supported by Qatar and the United Arab Emirates, made their acceptance of quotas conditional upon an increase in the value differentials for light African crudes and the ending of all discounting of official prices by OPEC members.

Kuwait's Oil Minister, Shaikh Ali Khalifa al Sabah, said that production quotas were meaningless without realistic price differentials, while Shaikh Yamani said that the African producers' continuing rejection of an increase in their premiums could leave the Gulf producers with no option but to cut their own prices by a corresponding amount. Saudi Arabia had previously maintained a consistent public commitment to defend OPEC's $34 marker price.

D14.4—Intensification of Market Pressure on the OPEC Pricing Structure, February and early March 1983

The official Kuwait news agency reported on Feb. 1, 1983, that Kuwait, Saudi Arabia, Qatar and the United Arab Emirates (together with the two non-OPEC GCC members) were considering a $4 per barrel cut in their oil prices unless other OPEC members adhered to a realistic agreement on production quotas and price differentials. Saudi Arabian 34° crude was then being traded at a $4.75 discount on the spot market, where prices had dropped abruptly following OPEC's abortive consultative meeting. It was revealed on the same day that Nigeria's oil production had declined to an average 800,000 bpd in January and that the country's foreign-exchange reserves were sufficient to cover less than one month's imports.

In separate developments on Feb. 1, the Soviet Union (whose net oil exports to Western Europe currently averaged 1,500,000 bpd, compared with 1,300,000 bpd at the beginning of 1982) announced a cut of $2.25 per barrel, to $29.25, in the contract price of its Urals crude, while United States domestic producers cut their prices by $1 per barrel, to between $30 and $31.35. The Soviet price reduction was strongly criticized by the then OPEC Secretary-General, Dr Marc Nan Nguema, who described it as an attempt to "engineer a price cut and gain a bigger share of the world oil market".

On Feb. 3 Egypt reduced its oil price by $3 per barrel, while within OPEC Nigeria reported that it had exported no oil for five days and Saudi Arabia announced that its current oil revenues were no longer sufficient to finance its economic development programmes. OPEC's aggregate production had fallen to 15,000,000 bpd by Feb. 7, when Venezuela's Minister of Energy and Mines, Dr Humberto Calderón Berti, was quoted as saying that OPEC "might find it difficult to continue as an organization" with such a low level of output.

Shaikh Yamani said on Feb. 10 that a cut in the OPEC marker price was now "inevitable" and that Saudi Arabia "will no longer play the role of defending the benchmark and will let others bear the responsibility of their mistakes". Iran, Venezuela, Libya and Algeria all issued statements criticizing the new Saudi Arabian stance, and both Libya and Iran called for a further OPEC consultative meeting to discuss current developments.

On Feb. 14 further cuts of $1 per barrel were made in US domestic crude postings, increasing the pressure on Mexico to reduce its export prices. On Feb. 18 the British National Oil Corporation, which had recently been forced to sell North Sea oil at a loss on the spot market because of a sharp fall in producing companies' repurchases of participation crude at official prices, announced a cut (backdated to Feb. 1) of $3 per barrel, to $30.50, in the basic price of British crude. BNOC's cut was immediately matched by Norway. Nigeria on Feb. 20 cut its ceiling price by $5.50, to $30 per barrel (also with effect from Feb. 1), in order to undercut the new North Sea price, and on Feb. 22 agreed to increase the official profit margin on foreign producing companies' exports of equity crude by 40 cents per barrel (◊C9.3).

The Nigerian member of the OPEC Conference, Alhaji Yahaya Dikko, said that "the North Sea price reductions have shown that there is no longer a basis in today's market for a price structure based on Arabian light crude priced at $34 a barrel"; he added that "the restoration of stability and the defence of crude oil markets is a responsibility of both OPEC and non-OPEC exporters alike". Any further reduction in North Sea prices would, he said, be matched "cent for cent" by

Nigeria. Venezuela and Indonesia stated that they would not cut their oil prices unilaterally, but would await developments within the context of OPEC.

The Oil Ministers of Saudi Arabia, Kuwait, Qatar and the United Arab Emirates held talks in Riyadh on Feb. 22 and 23 within the framework of the GCC oil committee. It was subsequently announced by Shaikh Yamani that these four countries had agreed in principle to reduce their oil prices by an unspecified amount and that their decision had been communicated to and approved by Iraq and Indonesia and would shortly be discussed with Libya and Venezuela. Meanwhile Venezuela took the initiative in contacting Mexican, British and Norwegian oil officials with a view to reaching an informal understanding designed to avert an "international oil price war". The Venezuelan and Mexican Oil Ministers visited BNOC's London office on Feb. 24 before travelling to Paris for talks with their Kuwaiti and Algerian counterparts.

Dr Calderón Berti said in Paris on Feb. 24 that Britain, as a major oil exporter and also a member of the International Energy Agency, could act as "a bridge between OPEC and the consumers". (Britain's oil production of up to 2,300,000 bpd—including about 1,400,000 bpd for domestic consumption—was now higher than that of any OPEC member except Saudi Arabia and Iran.) The British Government, however, made it clear that it was not prepared to change its established oil production or pricing policies in order to alleviate OPEC's current crisis. Mexico, on the other hand, agreed as a gesture of co-operation with OPEC to postpone a $2.50 per barrel price cut which had been planned for Feb. 25; Mexico's oil production was running at around 2,600,000 bpd (compared with 3,275,000 bpd in January), of which about 1,500,000 bpd was exported. A delegation of Venezuelan officials visited Norway on Feb. 25, while Dr Calderón Berti himself travelled to Riyadh for talks with Shaikh Yamani.

The UAE Oil Minister, Dr Maneh Said al Oteiba, said on Feb. 26 that total OPEC output had now dropped to 13,400,000 bpd, with Saudi Arabia contributing less than 4,000,000 bpd, and that the Arab Gulf producers would implement a drastic price cut unless a new OPEC agreement was reached within one week. (Average OPEC output for the whole of February amounted to 14,400,000 bpd, 58 per cent below the peak monthly output level recorded in December 1976.)

Dr Calderón Berti held further talks in Paris on Feb. 28 with the Oil Ministers of Kuwait (representing the Arabian peninsula producers) and of Algeria (which was in contact with Libya and Iran), following which it was stated that some progress was being made towards the establishment of a new OPEC price structure. It was reported from Saudi Arabia on the same day that there was a virtual consensus on a reduction in the marker price but that quotas and differentials were still under discussion. However, non-co-operation by Britain was regarded by OPEC as a serious threat to the effective implementation of any agreement, and from March 2 onwards OPEC's main consultations took place in London, this choice of venue being regarded as a means of bringing the maximum pressure to bear on BNOC and the British Government.

Ministers from Saudi Arabia, Kuwait, the United Arab Emirates, Venezuela, Algeria, Nigeria, Indonesia and Libya held five hours of talks in London on March 3. Consultations also took place with a Mexican delegation which remained in London during the talks without directly participating in them, while several OPEC ministers had what were described as "informal bilateral meetings" with the UK Energy Secretary. Public statements made by the UK Energy Department on the same day indicated that the British Government did not intend to modify its existing policy (adopted in June 1982) of deferring any consideration of a North Sea production ceiling until 1985 at the earliest, nor did it intend to give BNOC any directions on the pricing of British crude (which was officially held to be a matter for the corporation's commercial judgment).

(BNOC—whose former equity interests in North Sea production had been transferred to majority private ownership in 1982 through the formation of a new company,

Britoil—was responsible for the trading of crude acquired under 51 per cent state participation agreements with North Sea producing companies. BNOC's official buying price for participation crude was normally fixed quarterly in advance. The state corporation owned no storage facilities or downstream outlets, and had always depended on buy-back arrangements with producers or term contracts with other oil companies to dispose of the bulk of its crude entitlement. In a weak market, integrated producing companies were able to exert downward pressure on BNOC's reference price by reducing their repurchases of officially-priced buy-back crude, forcing BNOC to sell a proportion of its entitlement at a loss through spot channels. However, in the context of total state revenue from the oil sector the impact of trading losses incurred by BNOC in order to defend its official prices was softened by the fact that these prices were used by the British tax authorities to value the North Sea producing companies' output of equity crude traded within integrated channels.)

After a second meeting among themselves on March 4, the eight OPEC ministers announced that they would continue their discussions on the following two days and that they had invited the five remaining OPEC members (Ecuador, Gabon, Iran, Iraq and Qatar) to join them in London for a full informal meeting on March 7 (notwithstanding Iran's denunciation of the previous limited talks as "a plot to bring us to our knees"). At the same time it was widely reported that BNOC was under heavy pressure from a majority of its customers to increase the size of its recent price cut in view of the fact that the new North Sea reference price exceeded the current spot value of British crude by $2.25 per barrel.

The Iranian Oil Minister, Mohammed Gharazi, arrived in London on March 7, when he was informed that the Arab Gulf States were now willing to drop their previous demand for an increase in African differentials in order to facilitate the acceptance of a compromise agreement based on a new marker price of $29 to $30. Gharazi, however, indicated his country's opposition to any reduction in the existing marker price, stating moreover that a production ceiling of 3,000,000 bpd should be imposed on Saudi Arabia. As a result the full OPEC talks planned for March 7 were postponed until the following day, although informal meetings continued between various groups of Oil Ministers. A series of full meetings finally began on March 8, when Nigeria cast further doubt upon the possibility of reaching a viable compromise by insisting that it would reject any pricing formula which did not permit it to continue to undercut the price of North Sea oil.

British Petroleum (one of the integrated producing companies currently pressing for a further reduction in BNOC's prices) issued a public statement on March 10 warning that it would be "economically unrealistic" for OPEC to adopt the range of differentials which was currently being proposed, particularly by Nigeria. This led the British Government (which held a 39.04 per cent shareholding in British Petroleum ◊A5.1.vii) to declare on March 11 that Britain shared with OPEC "a desire not to see an exaggerated fall in the world oil price now which would inevitably be followed by a sharp and damaging rebound later on", a declaration which was interpreted by OPEC ministers as an undertaking that BNOC's reference price would not be cut again to a level below Nigeria's (as had been implied in BP's statement).

The Soviet Union on March 9 cut the price of its Urals crude by $1.25, to $28 per barrel. Within OPEC, Ecuador's market-oriented average sales price for March had fallen to $26.20 per barrel (from $28.45 in February and $29.60 in January).

D14.5—Pricing and Production Decisions of 67th OPEC Conference Meeting

The London consultations between all 13 OPEC members lasted from March 8 until March 13, 1983, when a compromise agreement was finally reached on an informal basis. The delegates met again formally on March 14, when the 67th (extraordinary) meeting of the OPEC Conference endorsed the following decisions: (i) to reduce the official price of Saudi Arabian 34° marker crude to $29 per barrel; (ii) to "maintain the existing differentials among the various OPEC crudes at the same level as agreed . . . in March 1982 [◊D13.3], with the temporary exception that the differentials for Nigerian crudes should be $1 over the price of the marker crude"; (iii) to establish an aggregate production ceiling of 17,500,000 bpd, to be observed as an average for the remainder of 1983, and to allocate quotas to each member country except Saudi Arabia, "which will act as a swing producer to supply the balancing quantities to meet market requirements"; and (iv) "that member countries shall avoid giving discounts in any form whatsoever and refrain from dumping petroleum products into the world oil market at prices which will jeopardize the crude-oil pricing structure".

It was further agreed that "the recommended oil prices are floor prices and the national production quotas are ceiling figures". It was noted that Iran accepted its production quota but formally "reserved its position on the decision to reduce prices". The "co-operative efforts of some non-OPEC exporters in resolving the present difficulties" were welcomed by the Conference.

Details of individual members' production quotas (disagreement over which was reported to have been the most contentious issue in the final days of the London talks) were subsequently disclosed by individual ministers (◊ Table 55), the Saudi "quota" being an implied ceiling marking the upper limit of the Saudi "swing". The estimated output of each member country immediately prior to the London talks is shown in Table 55 for comparative purposes.

In addition to the basic formula endorsed at the 67th Conference meeting, the London agreement was believed to involve the following main understandings: (i) that official prices could be raised by 50-cent increments, subject to the observance of a maximum marker value of $30 per barrel, if there was a sufficient improvement in market conditions; (ii) that Iran would be allowed to continue to

Table 55—OPEC members' previous oil output and new quotas, March 1983

	Previous output	New quota
	(thousand barrels daily)	
Algeria	525	725
Ecuador	190	200
Gabon	130	150
Indonesia	1,200	1,300
Iran	2,000	2,400
Iraq	750	1,200
Kuwait*	650	1,050
Libya	800	1,100
Nigeria	900	1,300
Qatar	250	300
Saudi Arabia*	3,500	(5,000)
United Arab Emirates	800	1,100
Venezuela	1,700	1,675
Total	13,395	17,500

*Including share of Neutral Zone output.

pitch its official prices significantly below those of competing Gulf crudes, although only to the extent that this was necessary to compensate customers for the additional costs of shipping oil from a war-risk zone; (iii) that Iraq's quota would be subject to upward revision in the event of the reopening of export pipelines running via Syria, and would in the meantime be deemed to cover crude marketed on Iraq's behalf by Saudi Arabia and Kuwait; and (iv) that the United Arab Emirates would be given priority treatment if an upward revision of OPEC's aggregate ceiling became possible in the last quarter of the year.

Price cuts were announced as follows by OPEC members in the aftermath of the 67th Conference meeting: (i) Saudi Arabia, Qatar and Kuwait made across-the-board reductions of $5 per barrel, of which the first $4 was applied retroactively from Feb. 1 and the remaining $1 from March 15; (ii) Algeria and Iraq made cuts of $5 per barrel with effect from March 15; (iii) $5 cuts were backdated to Feb. 23 by Libya and to March 1 by the United Arab Emirates; (iv) Indonesia backdated a $5 price cut for its main grades to Feb. 23, which was also the effective date for slightly larger reductions in the prices of other grades; (v) Gabon's prices for 28.9° and 31.7° crude fell by $1 and $1.30 respectively with effect from Jan. 1 and by a further $4 from March 15; (vi) Iranian price cuts of $3.20 for 34° crude and $2.40 for 31° crude took effect from March 15; and (vii) Venezuela reduced its prices on March 15 by amounts ranging from 50 cents for 10° crude to $6.08 for 42° crude (with a $5 cut on its 26° grade). Iraq subsequently trimmed its Mediterranean export prices by a further 40 cents per barrel with effect from April 1. Ecuador's average sales price for April rose by 85 cents to $27.05 per barrel. Table 56 shows the official prices of selected OPEC crudes on April 1.

Table 56—Prices of selected OPEC crudes, April 1, 1983

	Dollars per barrel
Algeria (44°)	30.50
Ecuador* (29.7°)	27.05
Gabon (31.7°)	29.70
Indonesia (34.1°)	29.53
Iran (31°)	26.90
(34°)	28.00
Iraq‡ (34°)	28.81
(36°)	29.43
Kuwait (31°)	27.30
Libya (40°)	30.40
Nigeria (36.7°)	30.00
(44.2°)	30.00
Qatar (40°)	29.49
Saudi Arabia (27°)	26.00
(31°)	27.40
(34°)	29.00
(39°)	29.52
UAE: Abu Dhabi (39°)	29.56
Dubai (32°)	28.86
Venezuela (26°)	27.88
(31°)	29.84
(34°)	31.09

*Average sales price.
‡Mediterranean.

Following the announcement of the OPEC agreement, Mexico on March 15 announced price cuts of $3.50 per barrel, to $29, for its light crude and of $2 per barrel, to $23, for its heavy crude, bringing them into line with the new OPEC marker value. It was also revealed that Mexico had reached an informal agreement with OPEC to limit its exports to 1,500,000 bpd for the remainder of 1983 and to consult closely with Venezuela on pricing questions. Smaller oil exporters which realigned their prices after the OPEC meeting included Egypt, Malaysia and Brunei.

The main focus of attention, however, was on BNOC, which had not yet been able to formalize its February 1983 price cut because of continuing customer pressure for a still lower price. OPEC, for its part, had since March 14 intensified its strong public demands for BNOC to enforce its originally announced price of $30.50 per barrel, it being stressed by OPEC ministers that any new undercutting by BNOC of Nigeria's $30 ceiling price would make OPEC's pricing agreement unworkable and cause a new crisis in world oil markets.

BNOC's response to these conflicting pressures was to announce on March 30 a formula whereby its February transactions would be based on the $30.50 reference price already announced, but from March 1 a range of further price cuts would be applied, with the price of 37.4° Brent crude falling by 50 cents to $30 per barrel and the price of 36.5° Forties crude (the previous main reference grade) falling by 75 cents to $29.75 per barrel. The prices of all other British North Sea crudes were cut by 75 cents. The effect of this formula was to establish parity with Nigeria in respect of the most widely traded British grade (Brent crude accounting for about one-third of total British production). The Nigerian Government acknowledged BNOC's conciliatory intention and announced that it would not adjust its own price, while BNOC's customers dropped their demands for a larger North Sea price cut and Norway realigned its prices with Britain.

Following the North Sea price settlement spot values rose to levels close to the new OPEC prices, and OPEC's market monitoring committee, meeting in London on April 18, expressed its confidence that the oil market had now stabilized. All members of OPEC were said to be abiding by the March 14 agreement on production and pricing, and aggregate production had recovered to 15,250,000 bpd from its exceptionally low level of early March. A claim by Dr al Oteiba that Britain, as well as Mexico, had given an informal undertaking to OPEC to maintain its exports at the present level for the remainder of 1983 was, however, categorically denied by the British Government.

The committee nevertheless announced that it would continue to seek Britain's co-operation in OPEC's attempts to maintain stable oil prices, along with that of Mexico and Norway. The Soviet Union, which had recently been stepping up the volume of its oil exports in a drive to increase hard currency earnings, would be approached by Algeria on OPEC's behalf, while among consuming countries Japan's co-operation would be sought on pricing questions. (Japanese companies, as purchasers of substantial quantities of heavily discounted Iranian oil prior to the March 14 agreement, had shown some resistance to the revision of supply contracts on the basis of Iran's new official prices.)

The Soviet Union's official export price was on April 25 raised by 50 cents to $28.50 per barrel. Egypt increased its prices by between 25 and 50 cents on the same day.

D14.6—May 1983 Meeting of IEA Governing Board

Following a meeting at ministerial level in Paris on May 8, 1983, the IEA Governing Board issued the following press statement summarizing its discussions on a range of energy issues (which were covered in greater detail in an annex to the statement).

"The current energy situation. Ministers assessed the current energy situation and particularly world oil markets. They welcomed the relief provided to the world economy by today's conditions, characterized by price adjustments which take account of reduced economic activity worldwide. They believe that these developments also reflect growing efficiency in energy use and production from a widening range of sources. However, they recognized that conditions could change in the future, as the world economy picks up and the current stock drawdown comes to an end. They expressed concern that sharply lower oil prices and uncertainty about future oil market developments could slow down investment in energy efficiency, hydrocarbon development and alternative energy sources, thus creating over the longer term the possibility of renewed instability in energy and oil markets, with adverse effects on the world economy. They agreed that the easing of the oil market was no reason to change the agreed objectives of energy policies, given remaining uncertainties about short-term developments and the underlying trends pointing towards tighter market conditions in the longer term. They therefore reaffirmed their intention to fulfil the policies of oil substitution, energy conservation, and energy research and development. They instructed the Governing Board at official level to follow developments in the world oil market closely, particularly further movement of oil inventories.

"Energy requirements and security. Ministers assessed energy requirements and security for the next two decades, bearing in mind the importance of adequate and secure energy supplies to the prospects for sustained economic growth and considering the study *Energy Requirements and Security* prepared by the Secretariat. They recognized the continued likelihood of heavy reliance on imported energy, particularly oil, and for the first time addressed the question of natural gas in detail. They reached the conclusions set forth in Annex 1 regarding the need for strong and cost-effective energy policies, reconfirming previous action taken within the IEA and emphasizing the need for a balanced approach which puts each aspect of energy policy into its proper perspective, including:

"(1) improved energy efficiency and appropriate pricing and fiscal regimes;

"(2) further expansion of the production, use and trade of coal and other solid fuels;

"(3) a major and increasing role for nuclear power in many countries;

"(4) obtaining the advantages of increased use of gas on an acceptably secure basis;

"(5) continuation of efforts to improve energy security in the case of oil, which will remain by far the most important factor in energy imports; and

"(6) development of new and renewable sources of energy.

"Coal industry advisory board. Ministers considered a report from the special committee of the coal industry advisory board (CIAB) on the current status of developments in coal and its prospects for the future. They noted the special committee's concern that the present oil market situation could jeopardize the effectiveness of coal in meeting the objectives set forth in the IEA principles for action on coal. Ministers requested the Governing Board at official level and the CIAB to give prompt and active consideration to these matters, taking account of the conclusions reached at the meeting concerning coal. . . .

"Ministers also agreed on the desirability of promoting the development and increased use of other solid fuels, such as lignite and peat which have specific geographical importance.

"International energy relations. Ministers emphasized that energy remains a decisive element for progress in the world economy, and is particularly important for developing countries. Ministers welcomed the contribution which the various contacts between oil producing and consuming countries are making to improved understanding by all parties of world oil and energy markets. They again stressed the importance of enhanced exchanges for greater stability in the world energy situation and an improved world economy."

As stated above, this was the first time that international trade in natural gas had been considered in detail by IEA ministers, its discussion on this occasion having been facilitated by the settlement in November 1982 of a dispute between the United States and West European countries concerning the participation of the latter in the construction of a new Soviet export pipeline (◊**A3.2.ii**). The annex to the Board's statement included the following outline of the meeting's approach to issues involved in the international gas trade:

"Ministers agreed that gas has an important role to play in reducing dependence on imported oil. They also agreed, however, on the importance of avoiding the development of situations in which imports of gas could weaken rather than strengthen the energy supply security and thus the overall economic stability of member countries. They noted the potential risks associated with high levels of dependence on single supplier countries. Ministers stressed the importance of expeditious development of indigenous OECD energy resources. They noted that existing contracts are currently insufficient to cover expected gas demand by the mid-1990s, and agreed that in filling this gap steps should be taken to ensure that no one producer is in a position to exercise monopoly power over OECD and IEA countries."

D14.7—Reaffirmation of OPEC Production Ceiling by 68th Conference Meeting

From May to July 1983 there was a steady increase in demand for OPEC oil, attributable mainly to the partial replenishment of commercial inventories following the heavy drawdown earlier in the year ($\Diamond$**D14.2**). Demand was particularly firm for Africa's (predominantly light) short-haul crudes and also for other regions' medium and heavy grades, whose relative product worth was steadily increasing in line with the expansion of upgraded refinery capacity. Spot transactions, which had accounted for up to one-third of the volume of international oil trade in the first quarter of 1983, continued to play a major role in the market, and spot prices were by the end of July marginally higher than the official prices of most crudes, indicating that the supply of OPEC oil was being held slightly below the level of demand. OPEC's current production rose above the Organization's "average ceiling" level of 17,500,000 bpd during July, although the cumulative production rate (i.e. the daily average since March 14) remained below the ceiling until October.

Statistics collated by Western oil analysts (which from mid-1983 onwards were regarded as more reliable than most OPEC countries' official output figures) showed that OPEC's average monthly production had increased sharply from 15,850,000 bpd in April to 17,420,000 bpd in May, rising slightly to 17,450,000 bpd in June. In July there was another sharp increase to 18,585,000 bpd, nearly 700,000 bpd of the additional output being attributed to Saudi Arabia, whose current production exceeded its implied average quota ceiling by 435,000 bpd. Other OPEC members whose July production exceeded their average quota ceilings were Ecuador and Gabon (by 20,000 bpd in each case), Iran (by 300,000 bpd), Kuwait (by 35,000 bpd), Nigeria (by 400,000 bpd), the UAE (by 75,000 bpd) and Venezuela (by 10,000 bpd). Indonesia, Libya and Qatar were producing at their average ceiling levels, while Algeria's output (excluding gas condensates) was 25,000 bpd below its ceiling and that of Iraq 200,000 bpd below its ceiling.

Nigeria and Iran—each benefiting from lower official prices than competing OPEC producers—had first raised their output to levels well above their average quota ceilings in May. All of Kuwait's "excess" production in July consisted of crude marketed on behalf of Iraq (which also accounted for part of Saudi Arabia's "excess").

The 68th OPEC Conference meeting, held in Helsinki on July 18 and 19, 1983, "recorded with satisfaction the positive indicators of stability in the world oil market and the successful implementation of [the] decisions [taken on March 14]", which would continue to be applied "in order further to strengthen the balance of oil supply and demand" (the maintenance of unchanged aggregate and national production ceilings having been recommended by the market monitoring committee at a meeting on June 8). OPEC's optimistic assessment of the market outlook was emphasized by Alhaji Yahaya Dikko, who said in his keynote address (as outgoing President of the Conference) that "OPEC's basic problem is not how to share a dwindling market, but one of organizing itself to share with non-OPEC exporters any incremental demand as it materializes".

The delegates agreed that OPEC's long-term strategy committee, which had last reported to the Conference in December 1981, should resume its work, with particular reference to future pricing strategy, co-operation with non-OPEC producers, relations with oil-consuming countries and relations with other developing countries. (Shaikh Yamani, the committee's chairman, had stated on July 6 that Saudi Arabia believed that OPEC should freeze its $29 marker price until at least the end of 1985.)

Dr Marc Nan Nguema having completed his two-year term as OPEC Secretary-General on June 30, the Conference left the post vacant when a unanimous decision on the appointment of a successor was made impossible by disagreements between Iran and Iraq. (Since OPEC's formation in 1960 each of the 13 member countries had supplied one Secretary-General. Article 28A of the OPEC statute provided for appointments to be made "on rotation basis" in the absence of a unanimous Conference decision, but did not further define the meaning of "rotation" in this connexion. If rotation was taken to mean repetition of the previous sequence of national representation, Iran, which had nominated the first Secretary-General, would also have been entitled to nominate the fourteenth.)

D14.8—Pricing and Production Developments, August to December 1983

Year-on-year increases in OECD oil consumption of 0.8 per cent in the third quarter of 1983 and 0.6 per cent in the fourth quarter of the year (the first such increases to be reported for four years) were attributable largely to a strong upturn in economic activity in the United States, and had little impact on the underlying level of consumer demand for OPEC oil, which remained close to 17,500,000 bpd. (US consumption was stimulated in part by the fall in dollar oil prices during 1983, the impact of which had been offset in Western Europe by a rise in the international value of the US currency.) Total export demand was bolstered by limited stock replenishment during the third quarter, when importing companies were influenced (i) by fears that all oil shipments from the Persian/Arabian Gulf might be halted if the Gulf war developed along the lines currently being threatened by Iraq and Iran and (ii) by forecasts that the reversal of the decline in US oil demand would soon be paralleled in other non-communist industrialized countries.

OPEC production increased to 18,800,000 bpd in August and 18,900,000 bpd in September and October, taking cumulative production since March 14 slightly above the agreed average production ceiling for the 8½ months to Dec. 31. However, not all of OPEC's incremental output was being exported, as Saudi Arabia (whose October output level of 6,000,000 bpd took its cumulative average since March to 5,060,000 bpd) was placing substantial volumes of crude into storage, having stated that its main motive in keeping its current production rate above 5,000,000 bpd was to satisfy its domestic requirement for associated natural gas.

Relative demand for heavier crudes continued to be boosted by the introduction of upgraded refining plant, enabling Iran to raise the official price of its 31° grade by 20 cents, to $27.10 per barrel, on Aug. 10, while Venezuela made successive increases in the prices of its extra-heavy grades on Aug. 1 and Oct. 2 (by $1 per barrel for 17° crude on each occasion and by $1.50 in August and $1.25 in October for 10° crude). Mexico made parallel increases in the prices of comparable crudes. Ecuador's export price, which averaged $27.69 per barrel from May to August, rose to \$28.35 in September. The export price of (31°) Soviet crude was increased by 50 cents per barrel on Aug. 15 (having previously been increased by the same amount on July 1). Egypt announced price increases on July 1 and Aug. 27.

The share of spot trade in the total world market for crude oil had by the latter part of 1983 stabilized at around 40 per cent (◊**A4.21.i**), with some of the major integrated companies now regularly obtaining over half of their crude supplies on spot terms. Spot crude prices peaked during the first half of August, after which the prices of lighter grades gradually fell below official OPEC levels, while those of heavier grades weakened to levels either slightly above or slightly below their official prices. (The average December spot quotations for Saudi Arabia's four main grades incorporated discounts of \$1.02, \$0.74 and \$0.11 respectively for 39°, 34° and 31° crude, as against a premium of \$0.29 for 27° crude.) The Soviet Union's market-oriented export price was cut by \$0.50 per barrel in November and by the same amount in December, the effect of the second cut being to restore the price of Urals crude to its May–June level of \$28.50 per barrel.

The main factor in the softening of the market during the last quarter of the year was overproduction within the OPEC area relative to the Organization's "average ceiling" of 17,500,000 bpd, which would have had to be observed as a current ceiling after October in order to comply with the Conference decision of March 14. In practice, however, OPEC's aggregate output (as monitored by Western oil analysts) reached a peak level of 19,100,000 bpd in November, falling back to 18,630,000 bpd in December to give an average of approximately 18,000,000 bpd for the period March 15 to Dec. 31 and an average for the full year of 17,480,000 bpd. (These estimates were at variance with OPEC's own subsequently published production figures, which indicated an average of just under 17,500,000 bpd for the last nine months of the year within a 12-month average of 16,992,300 bpd. Neither the independent estimates nor the OPEC statistics took account of member countries' output of natural gas liquids, which is included in the higher OPEC production figures given in section **D14.1.i**.)

Saudi Arabia, which accounted for about 300,000 bpd of OPEC's average excess production over the full quota period, was producing at estimated rates of 5,915,000 bpd in November and 5,825,000 bpd in December, although it was claimed by Shaikh Yamani that the country's "real" overproduction relative to its implied ceiling of 5,000,000 bpd amounted to only 35,000 bpd after allowances had been made for oil which had either been stockpiled or marketed on behalf of Iraq. Saudi Arabia's land-based storage facilities had been filled to capacity by November, when a decision was taken to create an additional "floating stockpile" in the tanks of chartered ships, which held an estimated 29,000,000 barrels by the end of the year. Most of these tankers were moored beyond the Strait of Hormuz (which Iran had threatened to blockade in the event of an Iraqi attack on its main export terminal), a fact which contributed to a downturn in precautionary stockbuilding by importers during the last two months of 1983.

The non-observance of average quotas by Saudi Arabia and several other member countries during the fourth quarter occurred despite an appeal for restraint from OPEC's market monitoring committee following a meeting in Vienna on Sept. 15. The committee recommended the maintenance of existing policies on the grounds that the market outlook was "not healthy enough" to justify either increased quotas or higher prices during the fourth quarter, and expressed particular concern about the continuing growth of oil production in most non-OPEC exporting countries (excluding Mexico, which had adhered to its own voluntary export ceiling). Britain in particular ignored OPEC's call for non-members to contribute to the maintenance of market stability—a call which was repeated at the next meeting of the monitoring committee on Oct. 27—and it was announced in

November that output from British North Sea oilfields had reached a new record level of around 2,500,000 bpd.

OPEC's long-term strategy committee met in London on Nov. 15 and 16 but was unable to reach agreement on key issues. The main difference of opinion was between Saudi Arabia, which maintained that official prices should remain frozen at their present levels for about three years in order to stimulate demand for OPEC oil, with the production ceiling being gradually raised as demand recovered, and Iran, which argued in favour of an early price rise backed by a lowering of the production ceiling. Saudi Arabia was supported by Kuwait and Iraq, while Iran was supported by Algeria and Venezuela.

Algeria and Venezuela, in their capacity as members of the market monitoring committee, nevertheless concurred in that committee's recommendation, announced after a meeting on Dec. 6, that the present price levels and production quotas should be retained beyond the end of 1983 in view of the recent softening of spot prices.

D14.9—Decisions of 69th OPEC Conference Meeting

At its 69th meeting, held in Geneva from Dec. 7 to 9, 1983, the OPEC Conference reviewed the level of production quotas in the light both of the market monitoring committee's recommendations and of the financial difficulties experienced by several member countries during 1983. The political sensitivity of this issue was highlighted by the Nigerian Senate's adoption on Dec. 7 of a motion (which was not binding on the Government) calling for Nigeria to withdraw from OPEC membership if it was not granted a higher production ceiling. Indonesia and Venezuela were also known to be seriously concerned about the impact of falling oil revenues on their domestic economies, while among the economically stronger OPEC members the United Arab Emirates was anxious to secure a higher production ceiling (the onus of complying with the existing UAE quota having fallen upon Abu Dhabi because of Dubai's refusal to adopt an output ceiling ◊**C12.3.i**).

During the run-up to the Conference meeting much publicity had been given to demands by Iran for an increase in its production ceiling to 3,200,000 bpd and for an increase in the OPEC marker price to its former level of $34 per barrel. Iraq had indicated on Nov. 30 that it would seek a 600,000 bpd rise in its production ceiling in view of the imminent expansion of the capacity of its Dörtyol export pipeline (which, while enabling Iraq to produce up to its existing ceiling for the first time, would leave it without any additional quota entitlement to take account of the capacity of other export routes which were currently closed as a direct or indirect result of the Gulf war ◊**C6.3.v**). Both countries' demands were treated by the meeting as largely political gestures.

All of the delegates eventually accepted that no revision of existing national quotas could be achieved within the existing aggregate ceiling and that this ceiling could not be increased in the present market climate without inviting further downward pressure on prices (notably in the context of current negotiations between BNOC and North Sea producers to fix a British reference price for the first quarter of 1984). The Conference therefore "confirmed its adherence" to its March 14 decisions on pricing and production and made provision for an extraordinary meeting to be called should it prove necessary to "discuss and adopt appropriate measures for the defence of the OPEC price structure in the spirit of the said decisions". The absence of any reference to the averaging of quotas over a specified period implied that the 17,500,000 bpd ceiling was intended to apply on a current basis until further notice. Nigeria's commitment to remain within

OPEC and to support its policies was subsequently affirmed by the military government which took power at the beginning of 1984 (◊**C9.2**).

The 69th Conference meeting failed to resolve the deadlock over the appointment of a new OPEC Secretary-General, and the post remained vacant "pending further consultations".

D15—1984

D15.1—Annual Statistical Survey

D15.1.i—Oil production and reserves

World

Total production	57,800,000 bpd (2,826.1 million tonnes)
Change over 1983	+2.1 per cent
End-year proved reserves	707,200 million barrels
Change over end-1983	+4.3 per cent
Reserves:production ratio	33.5 : 1

Regional shares:

	In 1984 world production*			In end-1984 world reserves†		
	Regional total (million tonnes)	Change over 1983 (per cent)	Share of world total (per cent)	Reserves (thousand million barrels)	Change over 1983 (per cent)	Share of world total (per cent)
USSR/Eastern Europe/China	746.9	+0.7	26.5	83.8	−0.6	11.7
Middle East	577.7	−3.1	20.3	398.4	+7.8	56.4
North America	567.7	+1.7	20.1	42.8	+0.9	6.1
Latin America/ Caribbean	338.0	+3.7	11.9	83.3	+2.0	11.8
Africa	248.8	+8.1	8.9	55.6	−2.3	8.0
Western Europe‡	186.5	+9.1	6.5	24.7	+4.2	3.5
Asia§/Australasia	160.5	+10.9	5.8	18.6	−2.1	2.5

*Including production from oil shales, tar sands and natural gas liquids (NGL).
†Excluding oil shales and tar sands; including NGL in North America.
‡Including Yugoslavia.
§Excluding China.

OPEC

OPEC oil production	18,380,000 bpd (901,800,000 tonnes)
Change over 1983	−0.6 per cent
Share of 1984 world total	31.9 per cent
OPEC end-year proved reserves	476,300 million barrels
Change over 1983	+6.2 per cent
Share of 1984 world total	67.2 per cent
OPEC reserves:production ratio	71 : 1

OPEC (continued)

OPEC member countries' production:

	1984 production		Change over 1983 (per cent)	Share of world total (per cent)	Share of OPEC total (per cent)
	(million tonnes)	(thousand bpd)			
Algeria	43.2	990	+2.1	1.5	4.8
Ecuador	12.6	255	+6.3	0.4	1.4
Gabon	7.8	155	+2.3	0.3	0.9
Indonesia	70.0	1,440	+7.2	2.5	7.8
Iran	109.3	2,195	−10.7	3.9	12.1
Iraq	57.5	1,170	+6.3	2.0	6.4
Kuwait	48.9	985	+9.5	1.7	5.4
Libya	53.5	1,115	−1.8	1.9	5.9
Nigeria	69.4	1,405	+13.9	2.5	7.7
Qatar	20.1	425	+36.8	0.7	2.2
Saudi Arabia	229.6	4,690	−10.2	8.1	25.5
UAE*	60.5	1,260	+1.7	2.1	6.7
Venezuela	97.5	1,875	+0.4	3.5	10.8
Neutral Zone†	21.9	420	+35.5	0.8	2.4

*Of which Abu Dhabi 39,800,000 tonnes (840,000 bpd), Dubai 17,800,000 tonnes (365,000 bpd), Sharjah 2,600,000 tonnes (50,000 bpd), Ras al-Khaimah 300,000 tonnes ((5,000 bpd).
†Production shared between Kuwait and Saudi Arabia.

Non-OPEC

Selected non-OPEC countries' oil production:

	1984 production		Change over 1983 (per cent)	Share of world total (per cent)
	(million tonnes)	(thousand bpd)		
USSR	613.0	12,415	−0.5	21.7
USA	494.0	10,385	+1.5	17.5
Mexico	150.0	3,010	+2.3	5.3
United Kingdom	125.9	2,580	+9.6	4.5
China	114.5	2,300	+8.1	4.1
Canada	73.7	1,555	+2.9	2.6
Egypt	45.2	915	+18.0	1.6
Norway	35.0	710	+15.0	1.2
Argentina	24.3	465	−2.5	0.9
Oman	21.0	420	+7.3	0.7
Total	1,696.6	34,755	+2.4	60.1

D15.1.ii—Oil consumption

World

Total consumption .... 58,870,000 bpd (2,844.5 million tonnes)
   Change over 1983 .... +1.5 per cent

Regional distribution of total:

	1984 consumption		Change over 1983 (per cent)	Share of world total (per cent)
	(million tonnes)	(thousand bpd)		
North America	791.4	16,600	+2.4	27.8
USSR/Eastern Europe/China	632.4	12,780	−0.4	22.2
Western Europe*	591.0	12,335	+0.8	20.8
Asia†/Australasia	422.9	8,790	+3.6	14.9
Latin America/Caribbean	229.5	4,775	+0.2	8.1
Middle East	94.9	1,890	+4.9	3.3
Africa	82.4	1,700	+3.9	2.9

*Including Yugoslavia.
†Excluding China.

Selected countries

	1984 consumption		Change over 1983 (per cent)	Share of world total (per cent)
	(million tonnes)	(thousand bpd)		
USA	723.9	15,150	+2.7	25.4
USSR	447.8	9,040	−0.6	15.7
Japan	214.6	4,550	+3.6	7.5
West Germany	110.9	2,340	+0.2	3.9
United Kingdom	88.7	1,835	+22.3	3.1
France	86.2	1,820	−3.5	3.0
China	85.8	1,720	+1.4	3.0
Italy	84.7	1,735	−5.0	3.0
Canada	67.5	1,450	−1.0	2.4
Spain	44.2	945	−7.5	1.6
Total	1,954.3	40,585	+1.5	68.6

D15.1.iii—Oil refining

World

Total refinery capacity .... 74,690,000 bpd
   Change over 1983 .... −2.2 per cent

Total refinery throughputs .... 56,165,000 bpd
   Change over 1983 .... +1.7 per cent

Consumption as proportion of capacity ... 78.8 per cent

Selected markets
Consumption of refined product types and change over 1983:

	USA (million tonnes)	(per cent)	Western Europe (million tonnes)	(per cent)	Japan (million tonnes)	(per cent)
Gasolines	304.1	+1.9	137.5	+0.1	40.6	+2.7
Middle distillates	201.0	+6.4	219.0	+1.0	64.7	+8.5
Fuel oil	75.7	−3.7	141.9	−0.3	76.2	−0.2
Other	143.1	+2.9	92.6	+3.0	33.1	+4.4
Total	723.9	+2.7	591.0	+0.8	214.6	+3.6

D15.1.iv—Tankers and trade

Tankers

Total world fleet	269,700,000 deadweight tons
Change over 1983	−4.8 per cent

Trade

Total world crude exports (including re-exports)	21,205,600 bpd (1,053.6 million tonnes)
Change over 1983	+1.4 per cent
OPEC crude exports	11,840,000 bpd (588,295,500 tonnes)
Change over 1983	−3.1 per cent
Share of 1984 world total	55.8 per cent
Total world product exports (including re-exports)	9,491,000 bpd (464,789,400 tonnes)
Change over 1983	−0.04 per cent
OPEC product exports	2,428,000 bpd (118,903,000 tonnes)
Change over 1983	+10.8 per cent
Share of 1984 world total	25.6 per cent

Regional distribution of world oil trade*:

	Share of 1984 imports (per cent) Crude	Products	Share of 1984 exports (per cent) Crude	Products
USA	18.2	32.6	1.0	10.2
Canada	1.4	1.3	2.0	4.7
Latin America/Caribbean	8.4	3.8	13.8	24.8
Western Europe	36.2	30.4	2.9	5.2
Middle East	0.2	2.4	47.2	16.3
North Africa	0.1	1.1	10.0	6.9
West Africa	0.1	0.4	8.5	1.1
East and southern Africa	2.0	1.4	—	0.3
South Asia	1.6	3.0	0.1	0.5
South-East Asia	9.0	5.8	5.9	8.3
Australasia	0.6	1.9	0.2	0.3
Japan	19.7	10.4	—	0.2
USSR/Eastern Europe/China	1.6	2.4	8.4	21.2
Unspecified	0.9	3.1	—	—
Total	100.0	100.0	100.0	100.0

*Excluding intra-regional trade.

D15.1.v—World primary energy consumption

Total consumption (excluding
   non-commercial fuels) .... 7,201.6 million tonnes oil equivalent (mtoe)
   Change over 1983 .... +3.7 per cent

Contributions of primary energy sources:

	Consumption (mtoe)	Change over 1983 (per cent)	Share of total (per cent)
Oil	2,844.5	+1.5	39.5
Coal	2,179.6	+3.7	30.3
Natural gas	1,409.9	+6.4	19.6
Water power	485.4	+2.2	6.7
Nuclear power	282.2	+17.4	3.9

D15.1.vi—Natural gas production and reserves

Marketed production (thousand million cubic metres):

	Regional total (tmcm)	Change over 1983 (per cent)	Share of 1984 world total (per cent)
North America	565.7	+8.6	33.5
Latin America/Caribbean	77.5	+9.8	4.6
Western Europe*	187.2	+3.9	11.1
USSR/Eastern Europe/China	669.3	+8.7	39.7
Middle East	46.4	+19.3	2.8
Africa	51.1	+6.9	3.0
Asia†/Australasia	89.2	+22.7	5.3
World total	1,686.4	+9.0	100.0
(*of which OPEC*)	*(134.6)*	*(+19.3)*	*(8.0)*

*Including Yugoslavia.
†Excluding China.

End-year proved reserves (thousand million cubic metres):

	Regional total (tmcm)	Change over 1983 (per cent)	Share of 1984 world total (per cent)
North America	8,270	+1.2	8.4
Latin America/Caribbean	5,350	+0.4	5.4
Western Europe*	5,600	+7.3	5.7
USSR/Eastern Europe/China	41,000	+4.0	41.7
Middle East	25,610	+3.8	26.1
Africa	6,370	−0.2	6.5
Asia†/Australasia	6,100	+15.4	6.2
World total	98,300	+4.0	100.0
(*of which OPEC*)	*(35,100)*	*(+4.3)*	*(35.7)*

*Including Yugoslavia.
†Excluding China.

D15.2—The Market Environment in 1984

Real economic growth in the OECD area in 1984 averaged 4.6 per cent, the highest annual rate since 1976. The upturn was strongest in the United States (6.6 per cent) and Japan (5.1 per cent), as against an average of 2.3 per cent for the European OECD members. Primary energy consumption rose by 4.7 per cent in the United States, 5.8 per cent in Japan and 2.4 per cent in Western Europe, the corresponding growth figures for oil consumption being markedly lower at 2.7 per cent, 3.6 per cent and 0.8 per cent respectively. For the United States, this was the first year-on-year increase in oil consumption since 1978; for Japan and Western Europe, the first since 1979. The European figures were, however, distorted by an exceptionally large upturn in UK oil consumption to offset the effects of strike action in the British coalfields (which began in March and was still in progress at the end of the year), and the aggregate oil consumption of West European countries other than the United Kingdom showed a fall of 1.5 per cent compared with 1983. The whole of the year-on-year increase in overall OECD oil consumption occurred in the period January to September, the final quarter's consumption being more than 2 per cent lower than in the corresponding period of 1983.

An important influence on the relative strength of demand in Western Europe during 1984 was a 12.2 per cent rise in the effective value of the US dollar which increased the price of oil in local currencies, continuing a trend which had begun in the second quarter of 1983. (According to the International Energy Agency, the average price of imported oil in European IEA members' local currencies at the end of 1984 was about 34 per cent higher than in April 1983.) The exchange-rate factor brought about an improvement in OPEC countries' terms of trade during 1984, the real increase in the unit purchasing power of oil exports being estimated by the OPEC Secretariat as 4.2 per cent. However, OPEC's annual export volume underwent a small decline, all of the incremental demand for oil being met by non-OPEC producers.

Total OECD oil stocks on land increased at an average net rate of 211,000 bpd during 1984, net drawings of 49,000 bpd on commercial inventories being out-weighed by a build-up of importing governments' strategic stocks (principally in the United States and Japan) at the rate of 260,000 bpd.

D15.3—Market Developments, January to June 1984

Spot crude prices, which had been in decline since August 1983, moved upwards during January 1984, subsequently remaining relatively stable until May. Spot quotations for light short-haul crudes were close to official prices during this period (Nigeria's main grade being traded at a small premium from February to May), whereas there was a rather more limited reduction in the level of spot discounts for the lighter Gulf crudes. There was a general strengthening of existing spot premiums for heavier crudes as refiners continued to reduce their proportionate requirement for lighter grades of feedstock, and the main non-OPEC exporters were able to make small upward adjustments in the official contract prices of heavier grades (e.g. by $0.50 for Soviet 31° crude on March 1, by $0.25 for Egyptian 26° crude on Feb. 1 and March 1 and by $0.50 for Mexican 24° crude on May 1). The basic reference prices of light North Sea crudes were maintained unchanged in the first and second quarters of 1984.

The average level of OPEC's first-quarter production (excluding natural gas liquids) was independently estimated as 17,770,000 bpd, compared with the Organization's quota ceiling of 17,500,000 bpd and member countries' officially reported output of 16,740,000 bpd. The main factors behind the market's absorption of this level of OPEC production were (i) the limitation of average drawings on importers' commercial inventories to between 1,000,000 and 1,500,000 bpd, well below the exceptionally high first-quarter drawdown rates of the two preceding years (when far larger opening inventories had been available), and (ii) a strong upturn in consumption, caused partly by higher industrial oil use (particularly in the United States) and partly by severe winter weather in the United States and Japan. Minor factors on the non-OPEC supply side included a reduction in Soviet exports to Western Europe in February and March.

OPEC's market monitoring committee, meeting in Vienna on March 9, acknowledged that member countries' aggregate output was currently "close to the ceiling level" and stressed the importance of maintaining the ceiling at 17,500,000 bpd in order to defend the existing official price structure. Replying to reporters' questions about quota violations by individual member countries, the committee's chairman (Dr Maneh Said al Oteiba of the United Arab Emirates) said that he was not aware of any evidence of overproduction, adding that compliance was being monitored on the basis of quarterly averages. Press reports indicated that the committee had chosen to disregard a recent increase in Nigeria's output in view of public assurances by the new Nigerian Oil Minister (who attended the meeting as an observer) that his country would observe its agreed ceiling during the second quarter and would not request a formal quota increase before the mid-year meeting of the OPEC Conference.

Although production cutbacks in April by Nigeria and several other member countries were largely offset by a rise in Saudi output, it was claimed by Dr al Oteiba on May 6 (at the conclusion of the market monitoring committee's second meeting of the year) that OPEC output had remained "within the ceiling". He said that the oil market was "still sensitive" but that there might "hopefully" be an increase in demand for OPEC oil to between 19,000,000 and 19,500,000 bpd in the second half of the year. Subsequent evidence of a slowdown in the rate of growth of IEA members' oil consumption during the second quarter led, however, to progressive downward revisions of both OPEC and IEA demand forecasts for the latter part of 1984.

Spot crude prices, which had begun to weaken slightly in early May, recovered in the middle of the month in response to a further escalation of the Iran-Iraq war, the extent of the upward movement being well within the limited range of price fluctuations recorded earlier in the year. (The launching in February of a new Iranian land offensive along the border with south-eastern Iraq had led to an intensification of Iraqi aerial attacks on shipping using Iran's Kharg Island terminal and to threats that the terminal itself would be destroyed. Iran responded in May by attacking Kuwaiti- and Saudi-owned tankers in areas to the south of the Iraqi-declared "war zone" at the head of the Gulf, stating that "if the Kharg route is not to be secure, then no other [oil export] routes in the Gulf will be secure". Iran was reported in late May to have offered substantial increases in its "war risk" discounts to customers facing massive increases in the insurance premiums on tankers sailing to the Kharg terminal, while the GCC countries agreed in mid-June to compensate their own customers for any export cargoes lost as a result of the "tanker war".)

The oil market's generally calm reaction to developments in the Persian/Arabian Gulf served to illustrate the reduced importance of the Gulf oil ports at a time when considerable shut-in capacity existed elsewhere in the OPEC area and when Saudi Arabia was capable of exporting more than one-third of its implied OPEC production quota via its Red Sea pipeline (which was now operating at near-peak capacity for the first time since its opening at the end of 1981 ◊**A6.2**). Importers' inventories had already been partially replenished after the first-quarter drawdown, while Saudi Arabia's "floating stockpile" was estimated to have increased to around 70,000,000 barrels by early April.

Despite a relatively low demand from importers for additional "precautionary" stocks (and despite a recovery in Iran's June output to the equivalent of 92 per cent of its OPEC quota ceiling, as against 83 per cent in May), every other OPEC country except Venezuela increased its production in June, boosting the Organization's monthly output by more than 1,000,000 bpd to 18,600,000 bpd and taking the second quarter's group average to just over 18,000,000 bpd. Saudi Arabia was responsible for 40 per cent of OPEC's June overproduction and for 35 per cent of its second-quarter overproduction relative to the group ceiling, although the kingdom's average output over the first half of the year was roughly in line with its implied quota ceiling of 5,000,000 bpd. The result of the surge in OPEC's June output was a general decline in spot prices, which for most crudes had fallen by the end of the month to levels comparable to those which had prevailed at the beginning of January.

D15.4—IEA Decision to strengthen Stock Deployment Policy

The Governing Board of the International Energy Agency, meeting at official level in Paris on July 11, 1984, took a decision in principle that government oil stocks should be mobilized to avert the bidding-up of prices during the early stages of a significant supply disruption and that consultations on co-ordinated stock deployment should be open to all OECD members (i.e. including France). Government-owned or government-controlled stocks in the OECD area were at this point sufficient to cover 18 days' forward consumption, while a further 79 days' consumption was covered by oil companies' inventories; in 1979 government and company stocks had been sufficient to cover four and 76 days' consumption respectively.

Government-owned strategic stocks were concentrated mainly in the United States (where the Federal Government's strategic petroleum reserve now contained a total of 404,000,000 barrels), in Japan (whose National Oil Corporation held over 90,000,000 barrels in offshore tanker storage) and in West Germany (where a federal agency held about 60,000,000 barrels). In most other OECD countries emergency oil stocks took the form of mandatory minimum holdings by commercial oil companies.

At the beginning of 1984 no clear national procedures existed within the IEA area for the "pre-emptive" mobilization of strategic stockpiles, the US Government in particular having displayed a marked reluctance to consider the adoption of an interventionist policy aimed at preventing sudden price rises. In the latter connexion, the Reagan Administration's argument during its first three years in office was that the federal stockpile existed to safeguard security of supply in the last resort, and that prices should be determined by market forces until such time as a particular supply disruption became sufficiently serious to warrant the formal declaration of a national emergency.

In early 1984, however, the US Government began (i) to consider proposals for a flexible national drawdown policy whereby reserve supplies could be released to commercial oil companies either by auction or through the advance sale of uniformly-priced options (to be exercised in the event of an interruption of normal supplies), and (ii) to approach other IEA members with a view to formulating a group policy on the co-ordinated deployment of strategic stocks (discussion of which had been effectively blocked since Reagan's accession to the presidency). The change of emphasis in US policy was welcomed by Japan (which was particularly vulnerable to a major disruption of supplies from the Persian/Arabian Gulf), it being stated by the Japanese Prime Minister on May 23 that discussion of a co-ordinated drawdown policy should be a main priority of the 1984 economic summit meeting of the principal non-communist industrialized countries. The issue was accordingly raised at that meeting (held in London on June 8 and 9), and was covered in very general terms in the following section of the summit declaration:

"We [the heads of government of Canada, France, West Germany, Italy, Japan, the United Kingdom and the United States] have considered the possible implications of a further deterioration of the situation in the Gulf for the supply of oil. We are satisfied that, given the stocks of oil presently available in the world, the availability of other sources of energy, and the scope for conservation in the use of energy, adequate supplies could be maintained for a substantial period of time by international co-operation and mutually supportive action. We will continue to act together to that end."

After the London summit several rounds of detailed talks took place at official level between selected members of the IEA in order to draft proposals for consideration by the Governing Board at its July 11 meeting, the outcome of which was made public in the following press statement by the Agency's newly-appointed Executive Director, Helga Steeg:

"The Governing Board of the International Energy Agency met today with stock policy as the main agenda item. Member governments have agreed that oil stocks, and particularly government or government-controlled stocks, should be used early on in a significant supply disruption if this is judged necessary to calm the oil market.

"The IEA has extended its range of responses to oil supply disruptions in this way because it is determined to protect member countries from the severe economic damage that can be caused by exaggerated market reaction to a supply shortfall. The intention of governments to co-ordinate their response, and to use their stocks quickly if need be, should help to calm psychologically-induced fears and prevent panic buying.

"You will note that there is no attempt to set down the precise circumstances that would justify a co-ordinated drawdown of stocks. This is quite deliberate. We want our response to be flexible, and to be based entirely on the situation at the time of the shortfall, and the nature of the shortfall itself. The objective is timely and co-ordinated action, and I stress the word 'timely' because any hesitation or delay in some highly volatile supply emergency could negate our efforts.

"The Governing Board has also set out clear procedures for prompt decisions on use of stocks and other complementary measures. The Governing Board would determine what action should be taken under existing IEA agreements. Those countries that have significant stocks available would consult together on the timing, amounts and method of using them. The consultations would be open to all OECD countries, should they wish to participate, and would be an integral part of the Governing Board's decision. This will ensure that the IEA as a whole is directly involved.

"I wish to stress that today's decision does not supersede existing IEA emergency provisions. The emergency system, which includes oil-sharing arrangements and provides for the holding of emergency stocks, remains in full force. That system may be triggered if there is a disruption of 7 per cent or more of expected supplies.

"In making its decision today, the Governing Board had very much in mind the oil shocks of 1979 and 1980, when limited shortfalls of brief duration produced an oil price increase of 160 per cent. This, in turn, provoked a new bout of inflation, recession and higher unemployment.

"Since that time, available stocks—and particularly those owned by governments—have increased considerably. The IEA governments are now in a position to bring significant amounts of oil on to the market, and thus exercise a calming effect. I regard today's decision as a major extension of the IEA's ability to shield its members from the adverse consequences of any interruption in their supplies of oil."

D15.5—Decisions of 70th OPEC Conference Meeting

The 70th meeting of the OPEC Conference, held in Vienna on July 10 and 11, 1984, was preceded by a meeting of the market monitoring committee on July 9. The committee acknowledged that OPEC's second-quarter output had significantly exceeded the agreed ceiling level (notwithstanding the fact that member countries' official production returns showed an average aggregate output of only 17,200,000 bpd) and that several member countries were now effectively discounting their official export prices. Dr al Oteiba said at the end of the meeting that it was necessary for the Conference to "give confidence to the oil market by asking the member countries to abolish quota violations and direct and indirect price discounting". He recognized that OPEC oil was regarded as a residual supply source in the world energy market and said that if OPEC could not "hold the market from collapsing" a price war with non-OPEC producers was "the only alternative".

The current President of the OPEC Conference, Kamel Hassan Maghur of Libya, said in his opening address to the 70th meeting that the member countries needed "to demonstrate our sense of discipline, solidarity and responsibility towards a world oil situation that poses a challenge". He criticized Britain and Norway for "destabilizing the market" by increasing their output by about 13.5 per cent during the period January–May 1984 (i.e. relative to the corresponding period in 1983), whereas total non-OPEC output, including net exports from the communist bloc, had increased by only 3.2 per cent. Mexico was praised for its "responsible international behaviour" in maintaining its voluntary export ceiling of 1,500,000 bpd, adopted in March 1983 "with a view to supporting OPEC's price structure". As well as calling upon other non-OPEC producers to emulate Mexico's example in "sharing the sacrifices" required to defend current price levels, Maghur called for producer-consumer co-operation "to cope with the structural changes in the world supply and demand of oil", stating that developments over the previous 10 years had shown "the need for better producer-consumer relations in an atmosphere devoid of suspicion".

In endorsing the recommendations of the market monitoring committee, the Conference agreed that there should be "strict adherence" to the decisions of the 67th Conference meeting (◊D14.5), to which end OPEC delegations were to make formal representations to each member government to secure the "further consolidation" of the group commitment to control production and to defend official prices. It was also decided "to establish contacts" with non-OPEC exporters whose increased production had "greatly contributed to the recent market situation". In view of the impossibility of raising the overall OPEC production ceiling without inviting a collapse in market prices, no formal request for an increased quota was made on this occasion by any of the member countries which had expressed dissatisfaction about their existing entitlements. Nigeria was, however, authorized by the Conference to make "some adjustments to its quota within OPEC's overall production ceiling" in view of the country's "special circumstances". Nigeria's additional quota entitlement was subsequently specified as 100,000 bpd in August and 150,000 bpd in September, to be balanced in each case by temporary reductions in Saudi Arabia's implied ceiling.

There was no serious discussion of proposals which had been put forward prior to the meeting for an increase in the OPEC marker price to $34 per barrel (advocated by Iran), for a restructuring of price differentials relative to the existing $29 marker price (advocated by the United Arab Emirates) and for the indexation of OPEC prices to movements in the interest rates charged on OPEC members' borrowings from foreign commercial banks (advocated by Ecuador and Venezuela).

The 70th Conference meeting heard a "progress report" from the long-term strategy committee, whose recommendations were not made public. A fresh attempt to select a new OPEC Secretary-General was deferred pending further consultations, although it was agreed that the term of office of the present Deputy Secretary-General (Dr Fadhil J. Al-Chalabi of Iraq) should be extended for three years from Oct. 7. (Similar deferrals of the selection process by subsequent Conference meetings meant that the post of Secretary-General remained vacant in August 1986.)

After the meeting Kamel Hassan Maghur took responsibility for leading an OPEC delegation to African and Latin American member countries for discussions on the rigorous implementation of Conference policy on production and pricing, while Dr al Oteiba undertook to head a delegation to Indonesia and the Middle Eastern member countries. Shaikh Yamani was to play a prominent role in efforts to secure closer co-operation with non-OPEC producers.

D15.6—Developments Leading to Nigerian Price Cuts (July to October 1984)

On July 13, 1984, BNOC, which had delayed a decision on the level of its third-quarter reference price until after the OPEC Conference meeting, announced that this price would remain unchanged at $30 per barrel despite forecasts of a further decline in the spot value of North Sea oil if Nigeria fulfilled its additional quota entitlements for August and September. Texaco announced a cutback in its contract purchases from BNOC on July 19 (when the spot discount for Brent crude was, at nearly $2 per barrel, larger than at any time since the fixing of the $30 official price in March 1983), while other customers reserved the right to request the revision of the reference price if there was no improvement in the spot market over the coming weeks. Customer resistance intensified during the latter part of July as spot prices continued to move sharply downwards (by a further $1.50 per barrel for Brent crude, taking its spot value below that of Saudi Arabia's 34° grade). The market was further depressed by the Soviet Union's announcement of a $1.50 per barrel cut in the official export price of Urals crude with effect from Aug. 1, although Egypt (which normally followed the Soviet Union in responding to spot trends) announced an unchanged price for August.

The credibility of OPEC's market stabilization programme—hitherto strengthened by a substantial fall in OPEC production from its June peak—was seriously undermined on July 29, when it became known that Saudi Arabia had agreed to supply up to 36,000,000 barrels of oil to the Boeing and Rolls-Royce companies as a barter payment for a fleet of 10 airliners. No clarification was offered by either side to dampen speculation among traders that this oil would be (or already had been) placed on the world market at spot prices over a short period of time.

Shaikh Yamani, speaking in Britain on July 30, said that the key to market stability in August and September 1984 was continued resistance by BNOC to pressure for a cut in its reference price. The same point had earlier been put to the British Energy Secretary by Shaikh Yamani during informal private talks, and on Aug. 1 the British Energy Department took the unprecedented step of sending formal written requests to BNOC's major customers urging them to end their criticism of the corporation's official third-quarter price. The British Government's intervention—which was seen as a form of tacit co-operation with OPEC—helped to relieve the downward pressure on spot prices, which began to recover during the course of August. Other factors contributing to the recovery included a sharp cutback in OPEC production, principally in Iran (which had reduced its "war risk" discounts following a temporary easing of tensions in the Persian/Arabian Gulf) and Saudi Arabia. Nigeria, far from being able to use its temporary additional entitlement, was unable to fulfil its basic OPEC production quota in August despite the partial shutdown of two major British oilfields for maintenance work in the middle of the month.

The relative slackness of demand for light crudes sold at official prices—which was also noticeable in Abu Dhabi—was due in part to an unavoidable overproduction of lighter products by refineries supplying heavy fuel oil to replace coal in British power stations. At the same time, however, strong British import demand for OPEC's heavy crudes helped to keep the spot value of these grades above the corresponding official prices.

Dr Maneh Said al Oteiba on Aug. 9 praised Britain, Norway and Egypt for "their refusal to cut their official prices in response to unreal market conditions", adding that some OPEC members had indicated their willingness to introduce lower production ceilings if the underlying demand for OPEC oil did not improve in the near future. Intensive discussions were by this point underway between member countries with a view to preventing any repetition of the overproduction of recent months. By the end of August spot prices had improved sufficiently to warrant a 25-cent increase in the official Soviet export price for September, a similar increase being implemented at the beginning of October (by which point the spot quotations for most crudes were similar to those recorded in the latter part of June).

OPEC's market monitoring committee, meeting in Vienna on Sept. 26, announced that it did not consider that the market had improved sufficiently to warrant any increase in the Organization's production ceiling. Dr al Oteiba told a press conference that the strong downward pressure on spot prices at the beginning of August had been "partially of an artificial nature and intended by certain consuming countries and certain oil companies to place us in the same circumstances as prevailed in early 1983".

When asked at the same press conference about the viability of OPEC's price differentials, given the continuing contrast in the strength of spot prices for light and heavy crudes, Dr al Oteiba said that this "rather complicated issue" required "further study" by experts before any decisions could be reached. Some days later, however, the issue became more urgent when Saudi Arabia authorized Aramco to alter the balance of its export production from the beginning of October to comprise between 40 and 45 per cent light (predominantly 34°) crudes, about 35 per cent heavy (27°) crude and between 20 and 25 per cent medium (31°) crude. The lighter grades had latterly accounted for about 60 per cent of Saudi contract exports and the heavy and medium grades each for about 20 per cent (although the state-owned marketing company Norbec had been offering "packages" containing a higher proportion of 27° crude in order to secure an "average official price" for its total sales to spot buyers ◁**C11.3.viii**).

The change in Saudi policy was presented as an aid to OPEC's light crude producers (by reducing the country's output of lighter grades); however, because of the prevailing structure of market demand, it served in practice further to emphasize the weak competitive position of these producers. Dr al Oteiba (speaking in his capacity as UAE Oil Minister) said at the end of September that Abu Dhabi, which produced exclusively light crudes, was prepared if necessary to make a unilateral cut in its quality premiums in order to maintain a reasonable export volume.

Whereas BNOC (reportedly acting on the advice of the British Government) announced on Oct. 1 that it did not intend to cut its reference price for the last quarter of 1984, it became known on Oct. 15 that the Norwegian national oil company Statoil had on Oct. 12 effectively abandoned the use of its own quarterly reference price and was instead offering new one-month contracts to its customers at market-related prices. Norway's main (42°) Ekofisk grade, which was officially priced at $30.10 per barrel but had traded at an average of about $28.60 on the spot market during September, was to be supplied under contract at the latter price throughout October, while Statoil's November contract price would be decided after the company had taken account of market trends during October. This system of allowing so-called "temporary discounts" on a theoretically unchanged official price was to continue on a monthly basis for as long as it was considered to be warranted by market conditions. Taxation would be based on a market-related "standard price" fixed quarterly in arrears.

Statoil—which had producing and refining interests as well as holding responsibility for marketing the state's royalty crude entitlement—had previously followed a reactive pricing policy in line with the Norwegian Government's preference that BNOC should act as the effective "market leader" for North Sea oil. The new policy was introduced without prior consultation with the Norwegian Government (which was politically embarrassed by this development) or with BNOC, and clearly took the oil market by surprise. Spokesmen for Statoil said, however, that the company's intention was not to lead the market but rather to formalize an existing situation which had been disguised by the use of "unreal" official prices.

Market analysts noted in this connexion that BNOC's adherence to a "politically motivated" reference price of $30 had forced the corporation to dispose of a growing proportion of its entitlement through spot channels, while the British Government had recently accepted a de facto cut in its tax take on integrated producing companies' equity output, which had increasingly been sold on the spot market for repurchase by downstream affiliates rather than being transferred directly to them at official prices. The use of various forms of concealed discounting had meanwhile become increasingly common in OPEC countries' official sales contracts for lighter crudes.

Despite the relatively small volume of production from the Norwegian sector of the North Sea, Statoil's initiative made BNOC's pricing policy untenable (not least because certain oilfields straddled the boundary between the British and Norwegian sectors), and it was announced on Oct. 17 that the official price of Brent crude had been cut by $1.35 to $28.65 per barrel for the remainder of the year. The price of BNOC's slightly heavier (35°) Ninian crude was cut by $1.20, to $28.40 per barrel.

Nigeria in turn reacted on Oct. 18 by reducing its ceiling price for light crudes by $2 to $28 per barrel, undercutting the new British reference price by 65 cents. Smaller cuts (e.g. of $1, to $27 per barrel, for 25.5° crude) were made on heavier grades. The Nigerian price changes were decided at the highest political level without any prior consultation with the other members of OPEC, who were informed that the Nigerian Government "could not afford to take the costly risk" of defending uncompetitive official prices in a highly volatile market climate, since "failure to take appropriate action would mean immediate loss of export customers". Spot crude prices, which had undergone a general decline in the third week of October (with North Sea crudes falling by as much as $2 per barrel), strengthened again in the following week, when Brent was traded at a discount of 65 cents against its new official price, while Nigeria's directly competing Bonny grade was traded at a premium of 50 cents.

D15.7—Lowering of OPEC Production Ceiling

Nigeria's price cuts were announced shortly after the OPEC Secretariat had confirmed that Oil Ministers were to meet on Oct. 29 to consider their collective response to the North Sea pricing developments. Ministers from several Gulf OPEC countries reacted to the unilateral Nigerian move by reaffirming their intention to defend OPEC's $29 marker price (although it was acknowledged that some quality differentials might have to be adjusted), and Saudi Arabia took the lead in convening a round of preparatory talks with Algeria, Libya, Kuwait, the United Arab Emirates and Venezuela. These talks, held in Geneva on Oct. 22 and 23 and attended also by Egyptian and Mexican delegations, resulted in an agreement that the six OPEC countries concerned would take a firm stand at the forthcoming Conference meeting in favour of production cutbacks rather than price reductions and that the two non-OPEC countries would take no action on prices before that meeting.

The Oil Ministers of Saudi Arabia, Venezuela and Mexico visited Lagos on Oct. 24 to urge the Nigerian Government to rescind its price cuts. Shaikh Yamani went on to visit Oslo on Oct. 26 for talks with Norwegian ministers, who assured him that

Norway had a strong interest in high and stable oil prices but pointed out the commercial reasons for Statoil's current pricing policy. Shaikh Yamani said that the talks had provided useful clarification of recent developments, and had in particular served to confirm that the Norwegian pricing initiative had not been politically inspired. Statoil subsequently announced that its monthly contract price for Ekofisk crude would rise in November by 35 cents to $28.95 per barrel (as against an average spot value of $27.88 in October).

OPEC's market monitoring committee, meeting in Geneva on Oct. 28, formally recommended a strategy of production cutbacks to defend the existing marker price, Indonesia having endorsed the decision already taken by Algeria, the United Arab Emirates and Venezuela. It was, however, stated on the same day by Nigeria's Federal Commissioner for Petroleum and Energy, Prof. Tam David-West, that his country would not accept a lower production quota and would not rescind its recent price cuts until such time as they ceased to be necessary to meet the competition of North Sea oil.

A consultative meeting of OPEC Oil Ministers opened in Geneva on Oct. 29 and continued until Oct. 31, when it was designated the 71st (extraordinary) meeting of the OPEC Conference. Agreement was reached on the first day of the meeting that the OPEC production ceiling should be cut by 1,500,000 bpd with effect from Nov. 1, proposals for the national distribution of reduced quotas being drawn up on Oct. 30 for submission to governments. The final day was given over to the establishment of definitive national quotas. The meeting failed to take any action on price differentials despite strong pressure from the United Arab Emirates, although it was agreed that a ministerial committee should be formed to draw up proposals for consideration by the December Conference meeting. The countries represented on this new committee were Saudi Arabia (which held the chair), Libya and the United Arab Emirates. One barrier to the immediate adjustment of differentials was Nigeria's flat rejection of all requests for the immediate cancellation of its Oct. 18 price cuts. The Conference was also obliged to accept Nigeria's objection to any reduction in its production quota (the only other member country which was exempted from a cutback being Iraq, in view of its drastically reduced export capacity resulting from the Gulf war).

The main section of the press statement issued by the OPEC Secretariat on Oct. 31 was worded as follows:

"The Conference reviewed with great concern the recent developments in the world oil market following the price cuts undertaken by Statoil of Norway and the British National Oil Corporation of the United Kingdom, as well as by member country Nigeria. The Conference believes that the present oil price structure should be maintained and market stability restored as a means to secure healthy world energy balances and to stimulate world trade. Beneficiaries of such stability are not OPEC countries alone but the international community at large, producers and consumers alike. The Conference is therefore determined to defend the price of its marker crude at the level of $29 per barrel and to consolidate market stability. For this purpose the Conference decided to cut, as from Nov. 1, 1984, and on a temporary basis, the global production ceiling of OPEC from 17,500,000 bpd to 16,000,000 bpd."

The 1,500,000 bpd reduction in the group production ceiling was to be shared unequally as shown in Table 57.

The OPEC Secretariat's official tabulation of these changes was given solely in terms of volume reductions, a form of presentation which, given Saudi Arabia's continuing status as "swing" producer, allowed for ambiguity as to the size of the Nigerian quota. For its part, the Nigerian Government indicated that it regarded the special 150,000 bpd increment conceded to it for the month of September (and used in practice during October) as a permanent addition to its official 1,300,000 bpd ceiling.

Table 57—Redistribution of OPEC production quotas, Nov. 1, 1984

	Quota at Oct. 31	Quota from Nov. 1	Reduction
	(thousand barrels daily)		(per cent)
Algeria	725	663	8.55
Ecuador	200	183	8.50
Gabon	150	137	8.66
Indonesia	1,300	1,189	8.54
Iran	2,400	2,300	4.16
Iraq	1,200	1,200	—
Kuwait*	1,050	900	14.28
Libya	1,100	990	10.00
Nigeria	1,300	1,300	—
Qatar	300	280	6.66
Saudi Arabia†	5,000	4,353	12.94
United Arab Emirates	1,100	950	13.63
Venezuela	1,675	1,555	7.16
OPEC	17,500	16,000	8.57

*Including share of Neutral Zone output.
†"Implied" ceilings, including share of Neutral Zone output.

Several OPEC ministers said after the meeting that they did not expect the reduction in the group ceiling to be necessary beyond the end of the year, it being predicted by the Saudi Arabian and Kuwaiti Oil Ministers that crudes currently selling at a discount on the spot market would be traded at parity with official prices within a matter of weeks as seasonal oil demand increased. Iran and Algeria were, however, known to have argued in favour of the removal from the market of supplies totalling between 2,500,000 and 3,000,000 bpd, while the chairman of the economic and financial affairs committee of Kuwait's National Assembly described the agreed level of cutback as "futile" in the face of growing non-OPEC output. Non-OPEC co-operation with the Organization's latest prorationing initiative was limited to export cutbacks of 100,000 bpd and 30,000 bpd respectively by Mexico and Egypt, which had attended the 71st Conference meeting as observers.

D15.8—Failure of OPEC's Market Stabilization Measures (November to December 1984)

During the last two months of 1984 spot crude prices moved steadily downwards. Demand was depressed by a decline in the underlying level of OECD oil consumption, by unusually warm weather conditions in the main importing countries and by the liquidation of the net additions which had been made to oil companies' commercial inventories over the first nine months of the year. The estimated commercial drawdown rate reached a peak level of more than 1,500,000 bpd in mid-December, although the overall rate of stock drawdown for the fourth quarter (after taking account of additions to government stocks in the IEA area) was limited to an average 700,000 bpd.

On the supply side, North Sea output reached a new record level—the December average for Britain being 2,730,000 bpd (including natural gas liquids) and that for Norway 817,775 bpd—while aggregate OPEC output exceeded the Organization's new ceiling level by an estimated 510,000 bpd in November and 680,000 bpd in December. This occurred despite a progressive cutback in Saudi production, which dropped below the country's implied quota ceiling by a margin of about 763,000 bpd (17.5 per cent) during December.

Among the OPEC members which ignored their agreed quota limits, Nigeria benefited strongly from its October price cuts (despite the fact that the $28 official price of its main export grade was being discounted on the spot market by late November). Iran, which had been producing well below quota for the previous three months, was able to fulfil its November quota and to achieve an above-ceiling output level in December after offering substantial discounts, reportedly of $1.60 per barrel for 34° crude and $0.80 for 31° crude. Concealed discounting and barter trading became more prevalent elsewhere in the OPEC area, and it was estimated in early December that as little as one-third of the Organization's total output was being exported at official prices.

The further weakening of the market led to pressure for further cuts in North Sea contract prices, attention being focused initially on Statoil, whose December price review would have to take account of the fact that the gap between the contract price and the monthly average spot value of Ekofisk crude had widened from 72 cents in October to $1.15 in November (35 cents of this increase being attributable to the rise in the contract price on Nov. 1, introduced in the expectation of an upward movement in spot values). The weekly average spot discount for the same crude relative to its November contract price of $28.95 had, moreover, increased from 75 cents to $1.85 per barrel between the opening and closing weeks of that month, the closing spot value ($27.10) being only 60 cents above the 1984 low recorded in the third week of October.

Given the probability that a decision to maintain an unchanged contract price in December would lead to a loss of customers, while a significant price cut could be expected to spark off a fresh round of cuts by its competitors, Statoil eventually announced on Dec. 5 that no decision would be taken on the pricing of its December deliveries until after the end of the year, when a "fair and competitive" price would be fixed retroactively.

Responsibility for "market leadership" in the North Sea was thus effectively passed back to BNOC, which had reported record trading losses in November, when over half of its total sales had been made on the spot market because of intensified customer resistance to the official fourth-quarter prices fixed on Oct. 17. (BNOC's total crude sales amounted to about 800,000 bpd in late 1984.) A thorough reassessment of BNOC's role in the oil market was initiated by the British Government in early December, at which time it was widely reported that the corporation had agreed to open negotiations on customers' requests for a switch to the use of monthly sales contracts at market-related prices from the beginning of 1985. However, Britain was no more willing than Norway to run the risk of precipitating a new crisis in the oil market during the run-up to the December meeting of the OPEC Conference, and it was made clear by the British Government that no firm pricing decisions would be taken before the end of the month. BNOC, for its part, formally notified the producing companies of its inability to meet a Dec. 15 deadline for the announcement of its first-quarter purchase price for participation crude.

Other non-OPEC net exporters followed the North Sea producers' lead in deferring any pricing decisions until after the OPEC Conference meeting, notwithstanding a further weakening of average spot values for all grades of crude during December. Adjustments to contract prices during November and December were thus confined to the US domestic market, where the trend was firmly downwards as refiners (who determined the level of US crude prices) sought to minimize their acquisition costs against a background of severely depressed product prices and substantial downstream overcapacity. The decline in US product prices produced particularly low netback values for imported crudes, large refining losses being recorded on all grades (including heavy crudes which commanded spot

Table 58 — OPEC members' estimated monthly oil output in 1984 (thousand barrels daily, excluding natural gas liquids)*

Note — italic type indicates apparent underproduction, and bold type apparent overproduction, relative to current (monthly) or average (annual) OPEC ceiling; figures in parentheses are shown for comparative purposes.

	Jan.	Feb.	March	April	May	June	July	Aug.	Sept.	Oct.	Nov.	Dec.	Full year	Average ceiling	"Official" output†
Algeria	650	600	600	600	650	700	650	650	650	650	650	600	637	(715)	(695)
Ecuador	245	245	250	260	255	265	262	260	260	250	260	260	255	(197)	(256)
Gabon	150	150	150	150	150	160	160	160	160	160	150	150	155	(148)	(157)
Indonesia	1,470	1,575	1,560	1,600	1,470	1,520	1,400	1,410	1,400	1,430	1,300	1,450	1,465	(1,281)	(1,280)
Iran	2,000	2,350	2,400	2,250	2,000	2,200	2,400	1,750	1,800	2,000	2,300	2,500	2,160	(2,383)	(2,032)
Iraq	1,150	1,000	1,200	1,120	1,200	1,225	1,200	1,250	1,300	1,200	1,250	1,250	1,200	(1,200)	(1,221)
Kuwait‡	1,130	1,235	1,290	1,200	1,100	1,135	1,100	1,100	1,190	1,090	990	990	1,130	(1,025)	(1,053)
Libya	1,100	1,100	1,100	1,100	1,150	1,180	1,100	1,000	1,000	1,000	1,000	1,000	1,070	(1,081)	(1,080)
Nigeria	1,350	1,560	1,460	1,300	1,200	1,300	1,230	1,100	1,300	1,450	1,580	1,650	1,370	(1,323)	(1,388)
Qatar	440	340	380	325	350	450	430	400	450	400	280	260	375	(297)	(325)
Saudi Arabia‡	5,130	4,260	4,700	5,120	5,000	5,435	5,000	4,500	4,090	4,090	3,990	3,590	4,576	(4,870§)	(4,079)
UAE	1,200	1,200	1,205	1,205	1,200	1,225	1,090	980	1,110	1,060	1,060	1,210	1,150	(1,075)	(1,069)
Venezuela	1,710	1,815	1,830	1,800	1,840	1,805	1,850	1,820	1,850	1,800	1,700	1,770	1,800	(1,655)	(1,695)
OPEC	17,725	17,430	18,125	18,030	17,565	18,600	17,872	16,380	16,560	16,580	16,510	16,680	17,343	(17,250)	(16,330)

*Based mainly on *Petroleum Economist* time series.
†As recorded in *OPEC Annual Report 1984*.
‡Including share of Neutral Zone output.
§"Implied" ceiling, adjusted downwards to offset formal Nigerian quota increase for August and September.

premiums). West European netback values had also fallen below crude prices across the board by December, although the divergence was not as wide as in the United States, especially for heavy crudes.

Table 59 shows the estimated average netbacks for three OPEC crudes in Western Europe (Rotterdam) and the United States (north-eastern seaboard) in December, together with the official prices and monthly average spot values of the same crudes. Given that the "correct" official price of Nigeria's light crude within the OPEC pricing structure was between $30 and $30.50 per barrel at this time, these comparisons indicate the extent of the basic divergence between market values and OPEC differentials in late 1984. OPEC's three-member committee on differentials held discussions on the issue in Kuwait on Dec. 8 and in Geneva on Dec. 18, the outcome of the second meeting being an agreement to recommend a limited narrowing of the existing $4.50 gap between the official prices of heavy Gulf crudes and light north African crudes.

Table 59—Official prices and market values of three OPEC crudes, December 1984

	Official	Spot	Netback (W. Europe)	Netback (USA)
	(dollars per barrel)			
Saudi Arabia (27°)	26.00	26.29	25.50	23.74
Saudi Arabia (34°)	29.00	27.78	25.18	24.59
Nigeria (36.7°)	28.00	27.84	26.46	25.94

The first meeting had established that the OPEC pricing structure should continue to be centred on Saudi Arabian 34° crude, with an unchanged marker value of $29 per barrel, a decision which was regarded by independent oil analysts as a wholly unrealistic starting point in view of OPEC's failure to implement production cutbacks of sufficient magnitude to support such a structure. According to press reports, Dr Maneh Said al Oteiba associated himself with this decision (which left little scope for a meaningful cut in the premiums for the lightest Gulf crudes) only because Abu Dhabi had already acted in mid-November to reduce the effective cost of its crudes by means of tax cuts on the offtake of foreign producing companies (◊C12.3.iii).

Confidence in OPEC's ability either to implement its existing policies or to reach agreement on effective price reforms was not enhanced by the repeated attempts which were made during November 1984 by prominent Oil Ministers (notably Shaikh Yamani and Shaikh Ali Khalifa al Sabah) to "talk up the market" by predicting imminent supply shortages on the basis of inflated estimates of demand growth and stock depletion in the industrialized countries. However, in the first half of December, when it was clear that the impact of Saudi Arabian production cutbacks was being neutralized by increases in the output of other OPEC members, Shaikh Yamani instead emphasized the OPEC countries' ability to flood the market with low-cost oil if the North Sea producers chose to start a "price war". This threat had the desired effect of guaranteeing the postponement of changes in British and Norwegian pricing policy, although at the same time it provoked strong criticism from Iran and Algeria, which said that if OPEC allowed itself to be drawn into competitive price-cutting it would merely be "succumbing to a conspiracy by non-OPEC countries". OPEC members which backed the Saudi stance included Venezuela and the United Arab Emirates.

D15.9—Decisions of 72nd OPEC Conference Meeting

The 72nd OPEC Conference meeting opened in Geneva on Dec. 19, 1984, the market monitoring committee having met on the previous day, when it was decided to recommend the maintenance of the existing production ceiling and marker price and the adoption of a flexible approach to differentials, which should, the committee said, be open to regular review in the light of market conditions.

In his formal opening address to his ministerial colleagues, the current President of the OPEC Conference, Dr Subroto of Indonesia, directly attacked Britain and Norway for "indulging in pricing practices which can only affect our determined struggle to strengthen the oil market, the most recent deplorable example of this [being] the intended shift towards the linking of the price of their crudes to the spot market". He said that the North Sea producers had "the highest oil investment costs in the world and unprecedentedly high rates of depletion of oil reserves" and could not expect to sustain their production, especially from newly developed fields, "without a reasonably stable international price structure". It was "patently unfair" for non-OPEC producers to increase their own market share at the expense of OPEC countries whose observance of self-imposed restrictions on production had led to cutbacks in "vital" economic development programmes. He therefore called upon the North Sea producers, "in the name of OPEC and indeed of global economic stability", to give their positive backing to the Organization's market stabilization measures.

The only firm decisions taken on the first day of the Conference meeting were that OPEC should retain a 16,000,000 bpd production ceiling and a $29 marker price. Several delegates expressed deep concern about the Organization's diminishing credibility in the marketplace, in which connexion there was much blunt criticism of various members' non-compliance with Conference decisions. Saudi Arabia, as the designated "swing producer", saw the tightening of production discipline as the single most important issue for discussion, it being stated by Shaikh Yamani that "until we can have agreement on how our production quotas are adhered to there is no point in discussing the matter of price differentials".

In an unexpected development on Dec. 20, the Conference formed a ministerial working party to draft a set of guidelines for the introduction of what Dr Subroto described as "machinery for the enforcement and policing" of OPEC's market stabilization programme. Formal proposals for the close surveillance of each member country's future compliance with this programme were finalized by the full Conference on Dec. 21, whereupon the meeting was adjourned to allow delegates to put the proposals to their respective governments.

During the second part of the 72nd Conference meeting (Dec. 27 to 29) the 13 member countries gave their backing to a decision to establish an "internal control system" for the surveillance of OPEC trade in petroleum. Algeria recorded a reservation about one unspecified aspect of the decision, subsequently explaining that it objected to the monitoring of its exports of gas condensates, which did not fall within the scope of the established quota system.

The opening section of Resolution LXXII–251, giving formal effect to the decision, was worded as follows: "The Conference, in view of the necessity to provide complete internal transparency of information concerning member countries' petroleum sales, as a means to enhance credibility of implementing OPEC's decisions, decides to establish a system of internal control on production, exports and prices in order to ascertain compliance with the Organization's decisions." The establishment and operation of the system were to be overseen by a Ministerial Executive Council, comprising the Oil Ministers of Saudi Arabia (which would hold the chair), Indonesia, Nigeria, the United Arab Emirates and

Venezuela. Participation in the Council's work would be open to any other OPEC Oil Minister at any time.

The Council would have an allocation of $3,000,000 of OPEC funds to spend at its discretion, would establish its own rules and procedures, and was "empowered to take any measures it deems necessary to fulfil its tasks". It would be "assisted by one or more reputable international auditing firms to provide a check on member countries' petroleum sales, tanker nominations, shipments, prices, quantities, etc.", the auditing firm being "empowered to send its representatives to member countries to check the books, invoices or any other documents that are deemed necessary by the firm in the fulfilment of its tasks". The Council could in addition "choose any other means of check and control, such as tanker tracking methods, to be undertaken by consulting firms" and could "send its representatives to pay visits to the ports and loading terminals of member countries to provide check and control" in addition to the checks carried out by outside auditors. Each member country undertook "to make available to the auditors, their representatives and the representatives of the Council, all the required documents" and "to send all the information on tanker nominations to the OPEC Secretariat".

The resolution defined petroleum as "crude oil, refined products and condensates". The term "petroleum sales" included "barter deals, processing agreements, government-to-government agreements, exchange and direct sales, equity oil, participation oil, etc.". "Terminals" meant "all loading terminals in member countries or outside member countries from which petroleum is loaded" and covered also "loading from depots outside member countries".

The Conference went on to discuss the need to adjust OPEC's differential pricing structure, which was acknowledged to have contributed to the deterioration of discipline within the Organization insofar as it had placed the producers of lighter crudes at a strong disadvantage in the marketplace. However, the Conference's determination to maintain an unchanged marker price (and thus to leave crudes of 34° and above substantially overpriced in relation to prevailing spot values) meant that no "equitable" realignment of official prices could be achieved without introducing an equivalent degree of overpricing for heavier crudes, and Nigeria's response to renewed pressure for its return to marker-related pricing was therefore to demand increases of up to $1.50 per barrel in the official prices of heavy crudes. This approach found some support among other producers of light crudes but was rejected by the producers of heavy crudes, who were willing to eliminate the spot premiums for these grades but reluctant to raise official prices significantly above spot values. The heavy crude producers claimed in particular that the present spot premiums were "artificially" high because of the British coal strike.

Eleven member countries eventually endorsed an interim agreement covering limited changes in the differentials for Gulf crudes from Jan. 1, 1985, when a cut of 25 cents per barrel in the prices of very light grades was to be accompanied by increases of 50 cents and 25 cents respectively in the prices of heavy and medium grades, thereby trimming the overall spread of official prices in the Gulf region by 75 cents. For Saudi Arabia, the new spread between the prices of heavy and very light crudes amounted to $2.77, as against a spread of $1.75 in the corresponding spot values during the last week of 1984. Table 60 gives details of the official price changes and the prevailing spot values for Saudi Arabia's four export grades.

The amended Gulf differentials were to be "applicable temporarily" pending a review of the whole range of OPEC price differentials "not later than the end of January 1985". It was agreed that Algeria, Kuwait, Nigeria and Qatar should join Saudi Arabia, Libya and the United Arab Emirates as members of the ministerial committee on price differentials (◊D15.7), which was to remain under the chairmanship of Shaikh Yamani. Algeria and Nigeria had each refused to endorse

Table 60—Jan. 1, 1985, price changes and end-1984 spot values of Saudi Arabian crudes

	Official price, Dec. 31, 1984	Official price, Jan. 1, 1985	Average spot value, Dec. 24–31
	dollars per barrel		
Heavy (27°)	26.00	26.50	26.50
Medium (31°)	27.40	27.65	27.00
Light (34°)	29.00	29.00	28.00
Very light* (39°)	29.52	29.27	28.25

*Berri.

the Jan. 1 realignment of Gulf differentials, thus effectively blocking any wider OPEC realignment at that point. Algeria described the Gulf formula as "a cosmetic adjustment which will damage the credibility of OPEC".

The 72nd Conference meeting also decided to change the membership of OPEC's market monitoring committee, with Ecuador, Iran, Iraq and Libya replacing Indonesia and Venezuela. Algeria and the United Arab Emirates continued to be represented on the committee, which remained under the chairmanship of Dr al Oteiba of the UAE. This decision was adopted unanimously by means of a formal resolution (LXXII–252), whereas the decision to expand the membership of the differentials committee and the split decision on changes in Gulf differentials had been taken under the less formal procedure applicable to substantive price changes (OPEC policy on which was ultimately subordinate to member countries' national policies).

Mexico, Egypt, Brunei and Malaysia held observer status at the 72nd Conference meeting. Brunei and Malaysia announced on Dec. 28 that they would cut their current rates of oil production by 9,000 bpd (5.3 per cent) and 40,000 bpd (8.7 per cent) respectively from the beginning of 1985 in order to lend support to OPEC's market stabilization programme.

D16—1985-86

D16.1—Initial Estimates of Supply and Demand Trends in 1985

According to year-end estimates, the average rate of real economic growth in the OECD area slowed to 2.8 per cent in 1985, mainly because of a marked decline (to below the group average) in the US growth rate, while OECD oil consumption fell by 1.5 per cent compared with 1984. Quarterly estimates of the evolution of OECD oil consumption showed year-on-year falls of 2 per cent, 3.4 per cent and 1.4 per cent respectively in the first, second and third quarters of 1985, as against a year-on-year increase of 0.7 per cent in the fourth quarter. When adjusted to take account of the return to normal working in the British coal industry after the beginning of March 1985, the OECD oil consumption figures indicated an underlying annual decline of 1 per cent in 1985, with year-on-year falls of 3.2 per cent, 2.4 per cent and 0.3 per cent respectively in the first, second, and third quarters, followed by an upturn of 2.3 per cent in the fourth quarter.

OECD oil stocks on land fell at an estimated average rate of 253,000 bpd in 1985. The estimated net drawdown of commercial inventories averaged 393,000 bpd, while government stocks were built up at an average rate of around 140,000 bpd. In view of the ready availability of oil for "hand-to-mouth" spot purchase, oil companies' stocks were kept fairly close to the minimum seasonal operating requirement throughout the year, and were sufficient to cover only 73 days' forward consumption in the OECD area at the end of December. Government stocks were by this time sufficient to cover a record 21 days' consumption. A slowdown in the growth of government stocks in 1985 was caused mainly by cutbacks in purchases for the US strategic petroleum reserve, which by September contained nearly 490,000,000 barrels, sufficient to offset the loss by the United States of over 100 days' net imports.

The overall change in commercial inventories was based on net drawdowns averaging 2,100,000 bpd and 300,000 bpd respectively in the first and third quarters of the year, as against partial replenishments of 500,000 bpd and 300,000 bpd respectively in the second and fourth quarters. When restated net of normal seasonal factors, these figures indicated underlying drawdowns averaging 700,000 bpd, 400,000 bpd and 1,100,000 bpd respectively in the first, second and third quarters, followed by a partial replenishment at an average rate of 600,000 bpd in the fourth quarter.

Preliminary estimates of world production of crude oil (including natural gas liquids) in 1985 indicated an overall decline of 1.7 per cent from the 1984 level (◊D15.1.i), with non-communist non-OPEC production rising by 2.3 per cent, communist production falling by 0.6 per cent and OPEC production falling by 7.8 per cent. The non-communist non-OPEC share of the 1985 total was put at 43.4 per cent (1984: 41.6 per cent), the OPEC share at 29.9 per cent (31.9 per cent) and the communist share at 26.7 per cent (26.5 per cent). The OPEC countries accounted for about 50 per cent of world crude exports in 1985.

The output of the world's largest producer, the Soviet Union, fell by an estimated 2.9 per cent in 1985 (its second successive annual decline) as a result of technical problems and managerial shortcomings in the west Siberian oilfields, where the situation was exacerbated by adverse weather conditions during the first three months of the year. Soviet exports to non-communist countries, which were subject to erratic fluctuations from month to month, fell by around 31 per cent (500,000 bpd) over the year as a whole. The level of US production was virtually unchanged in 1985, as was that of Mexico. Britain and Norway increased their

Table 61 — OPEC members' estimated monthly oil output in 1985 (thousand barrels daily, excluding natural gas liquids)*

Note — italic type indicates apparent underproduction, and bold type apparent overproduction, relative to OPEC quota ceiling.

	Jan.	Feb.	March	April	May	June	July	Aug.	Sept.	Oct.	Nov.	Dec.	Full year	(Quota ceiling)
Algeria	*600*	*650*	*650*	*650*	*600*	*600*	*600*	*600*	*650*	*650*	**680**	*650*	*632*	(663)
Ecuador	**260**	**270**	**280**	**280**	**280**	**250**	**285**	**280**	**280**	**280**	**290**	**290**	**278**	(183)
Gabon	**150**	**150**	**150**	**150**	**150**	**150**	**150**	**150**	**160**	**160**	**160**	**160**	**154**	(137)
Indonesia	**1,300**	**1,330**	**1,300**	**1,200**	**1,200**	*1,020*	**1,300**	**1,250**	**1,200**	**1,260**	**1,350**	**1,250**	**1,246**	(1,189)
Iran	*1,300*	*2,100*	*2,200*	**2,400**	*2,000*	*2,200*	*2,300*	**2,600**	*2,200*	*2,300*	*2,200*	**2,400**	*2,183*	(2,300)
Iraq	**1,250**	**1,250**	**1,200**	**1,300**	**1,300**	**1,365**	**1,450**	**1,400**	**1,600**	**1,650**	**1,700**	**1,650**	**1,427**	(1,200)
Kuwait†	**990**	**1,125**	**1,085**	**970**	**940**	**920**	**940**	**940**	**980**	**1,060**	**1,150**	**1,110**	**1,017**	(900)
Libya	**1,000**	**1,000**	**1,000**	**1,000**	**1,100**	*970*	*900*	*900*	**1,000**	**1,200**	**1,200**	**1,300**	**1,124**	(990)
Nigeria	**1,400**	**1,700**	**1,690**	**1,600**	**1,430**	*1,100*	*1,000*	*1,200*	**1,500**	**1,680**	**1,760**	**1,620**	**1,471**	(1,300)
Qatar	*280*	**290**	**310**	*260*	**290**	**300**	**320**	**320**	**295**	**300**	**300**	**335**	**300**	(280)
Saudi Arabia†	*3,490*	*4,025*	*3,835*	*3,470*	*2,590*	*2,420*	*2,740*	*2,340*	*2,980*	*3,910*	*4,200*	**4,680**	*3,385*	(4,353‡)
UAE	**1,160**	**1,160**	**1,215**	**1,215**	**1,220**	**1,105**	**1,155**	**1,200**	**1,285**	**1,255**	**1,245**	**1,225**	**1,202**	(950)
Venezuela	**1,670**	**1,700**	**1,700**	**1,670**	**1,670**	**1,670**	**1,670**	**1,670**	**1,670**	**1,670**	**1,670**	**1,670**	**1,675**	(1,555)
OPEC	*14,850*	*16,750*	*16,615*	*16,165*	*14,770*	*14,070*	*14,810*	*14,850*	*15,800*	**17,375**	**17,905**	**18,340**	*16,094*	(16,000)

*Based mainly on *Petroleum Economist* time series.
†Including share of Neutral Zone output.
‡"Implied" ceiling.

annual output by 1.7 per cent and 9.5 per cent respectively, raising the principal North Sea producers' combined share of world output to a record 6 per cent.

Around 87 per cent of the fall in OPEC output in 1985 occurred in Saudi Arabia, most of the remaining reduction being shared by Indonesia, Kuwait, Venezuela and Qatar. Iraq was able to increase its annual output by around 20 per cent as a result of the opening of a new export route via Saudi Arabia in the latter part of the year (◊C6.3.v). Ecuador, Nigeria and the United Arab Emirates all recorded significant increases in output, while there was little change in Algeria, Gabon, Iran and Libya. OPEC's October–December production was substantially higher in 1985 than in 1984, with the result that the year-on-year decline in the Organization's average output for the last six months of 1985 was limited to 2.5 per cent, compared with a year-on-year decline of 12.7 per cent during the first half of 1985.

The sustained rise in the effective value of the dollar (◊D15.2) was reversed after February 1985. The exchange rate of the US currency declined by 13.6 per cent over the year as a whole, reducing the cost of imported oil in West European countries' own currencies and adversely affecting the purchasing power of OPEC countries' unit oil revenues.

D16.2—Developments Leading to Further Realignment of Differentials by Most OPEC Countries (January 1985)

Apart from Saudi Arabia, only Iran, Kuwait, Qatar and Abu Dhabi were directly affected by the Jan. 1 realignment of Gulf differentials, as Iraq remained unable to export via the Gulf, while Dubai's 32° crude was considered to be "light" rather than "medium" for official pricing purposes.

Qatar and Abu Dhabi duly cut the official prices of their (very light) crudes by 25 cents per barrel, while Kuwait increased the price of its 31° crude by the same amount. Iran raised its official prices by $1.11 (to $29.11 per barrel) for 34° crude and by 45 cents (to $27.55 per barrel) for 31° crude, thereby bringing them into line with Saudi Arabia's December prices for crudes of light and medium gravity (with full restoration of the traditional differentials between the two countries). Iran's new price for 31° crude was, however, about 27 cents below the level required to match Saudi Arabia's January price for this grade on the same basis. Also on Jan. 1, Iran discontinued its existing discounts—which had reduced the effective prices of its 34° and 31° grades to $26.40 and $26.30 respectively in late 1984—and substituted a standard "war risk" allowance of $2 per barrel against the new official prices, producing an overall increase of 71 cents in the effective price of its 34° grade and an overall cut of 75 cents in the effective price of its 31° grade.

Customer resistance to the increased cost of Iran's 34° crude was partly responsible for an estimated fall of 1,200,000 bpd (48 per cent) in the average level of Iranian production between December 1984 and January 1985. Among the remaining members of OPEC, only Qatar recorded an increase (of 20,000 bpd) in its January output, while significant reductions were reported in Indonesia (by 150,000 bpd), Nigeria (250,000 bpd), Saudi Arabia (100,000 bpd), the United Arab Emirates (50,000 bpd) and Venezuela (100,000 bpd). OPEC's aggregate monthly output therefore fell below 15,000,000 bpd for the first time since March 1983, despite the fact that a majority of member countries were reported to be exceeding their quota ceilings (◊ Table 61).

Market reaction to the outcome of OPEC's December 1984 Conference meeting was generally sceptical, not only because of the limited scope of the agreed changes in official prices but also on account of the Conference's failure to provide for sanctions to be imposed on member countries in connexion with any breaches of discipline which might be revealed by the planned audits of production and pricing.

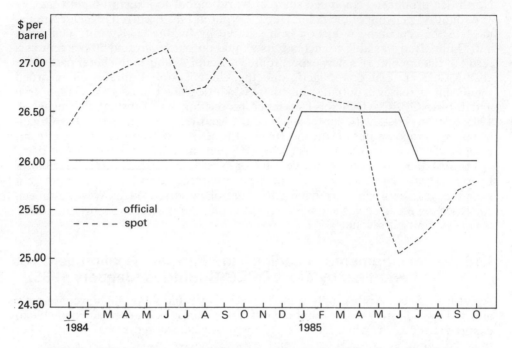

Fig. 21—Official price and monthly average spot price of Saudi Arabian 27° crude, January 1984 to October 1985

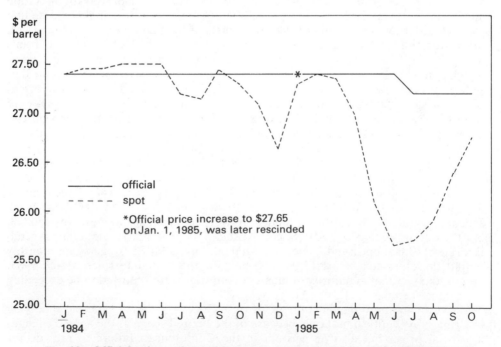

Fig. 22—Official price and monthly average spot price of Saudi Arabian 31° crude, January 1984 to October 1985

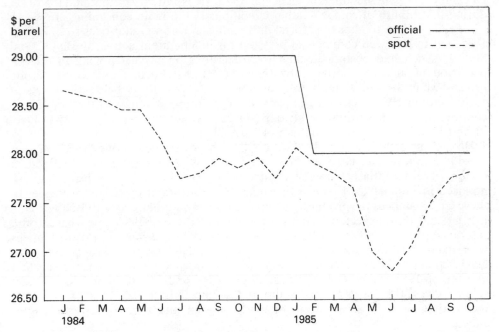

Fig. 23—Official price and monthly average spot price of Saudi Arabian 34° crude, January 1984 to October 1985

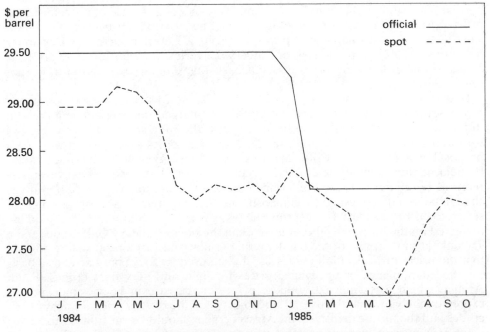

Fig. 24—Official price and monthly average spot price of Saudi Arabian 39° crude, January 1984 to October 1985

Spot prices remained weak during January, when the monthly average quotations for most crudes were similar to or only slightly above the levels reported for December, notwithstanding the sharp fall in OPEC's January output and the onset during that month of colder weather conditions in the main consuming areas.

OPEC's failure to alter the official differentials for non-Gulf crudes from Jan. 1, 1985, led to renewed commercial pressure for independent action by BNOC and Statoil, which had postponed their own decisions on official pricing in the expectation of an early initiative by OPEC (◊**D15.8**). Further cuts in US crude prices—which by mid-January were as much as $4 per barrel below the levels of early October 1984—served to emphasize the uncompetitiveness of the last official contract prices for North Sea oil (i.e. BNOC's price for the period Oct. 17 to Dec. 31 and Statoil's price for the month of November).

BNOC nevertheless complied with a British government policy decision that consideration of price changes should be further delayed until after OPEC's next review of differentials, with the result that no official reference price was announced in January for BNOC's first-quarter purchases of participation crude. In these circumstances the producing companies which supplied crude to BNOC made it clear that they expected to receive payment at the end-1984 rates (based on a reference price of $28.65 per barrel for Brent crude) until such time as new prices were fixed, it being indicated by some companies that they were prepared to take legal action if BNOC attempted to introduce a retroactive price cut for the first quarter of 1985. Since BNOC's official purchase prices determined its contract selling prices, the corporation's failure to announce a first-quarter reference price meant that all of its sales had to be made on spot terms from the beginning of January.

Statoil, which had been supplying its contract customers at unspecified prices since the beginning of December, did not clarify its policy on the retroactive pricing of these supplies until Jan. 14, when it announced the opening of separate negotiations with individual customers on "market-related" prices for December and January, adding that it had now formally abandoned the use of predetermined official prices in favour of contract-by-contract negotiations. It became known on Jan. 18 that Statoil's negotiated prices averaged $27.80 per barrel for December deliveries and $27.35 per barrel for January deliveries. Statoil's effective price for January was virtually the same as BNOC's average January realization from spot sales.

Informal talks took place in Riyadh on Jan. 20 and 21 between experts from six of the seven countries represented on OPEC's enlarged ministerial committee on differentials (the absent member being Libya) with a view to preparing the ground for a full committee meeting on Jan. 27. The main topics of discussion were (i) a proposal by Kuwait that the official prices of medium and heavy Gulf crudes should be held at their January levels and the prices of the light and very light crudes reduced by 50 cents per barrel, while the wider structure of price differentials should be realigned using a "composite marker" system based on a range of selected OPEC crudes; (ii) a proposal by Nigeria that differentials should be realigned on the basis of a 50-cent increase in the prices of heavy Gulf crudes and a 75-cent cut in the price of the Saudi marker crude; and (iii) a proposal by Algeria that the prices of heavy Gulf crudes should be raised by $1.50 per barrel as a basis for the maintenance of unchanged prices for light and very light crudes. Saudi Arabia, which was known to oppose a further increase in heavy crude prices, expressed the view that the overall spread between the official prices of heavy Gulf crudes and the most expensive light African crudes should be cut from $4 to $2.50.

OPEC's market monitoring committee, meeting in Geneva on Jan. 26, recommended that the spread of OPEC differentials should be substantially reduced on the basis of an unchanged marker price (five of the countries represented on this committee—Algeria, Iran, Iraq, Libya and the United Arab Emirates—being known advocates of further increases in heavy crude prices, while the sixth, Ecuador, had little involvement in the debate on this issue). The ministerial committee on differentials met as planned in Geneva on the following day but was unable to reach agreement on the submission of any clear proposal to the full Conference. In a separate meeting on Jan. 27, the Ministerial Executive Council drew up proposals for the implementation of the auditing scheme approved by the last Conference meeting and agreed to recommend that a Dutch accounting firm, Klynveld Kraayenhof (whose existing clients included Royal Dutch/Shell, Statoil and the European Commission), should be engaged to carry out the audits.

The 73rd (extraordinary) meeting of the OPEC Conference, held in Geneva from Jan. 28 to 30, endorsed the recommendations of the Ministerial Executive Council, "reviewed" the report of the market monitoring committee and "discussed" a report by the committee on differentials. The meeting opened in an atmosphere of considerable tension generated by the strong disagreements which had become apparent within OPEC during the various preparatory discussions on differentials, and its proceedings were punctuated by a number of heated exchanges between proponents of incompatible pricing schemes. Iran and Algeria took a particularly hard line in arguing for the maintenance of the existing official prices of light and very light crudes, while the supporters of cuts in these prices were split initially into two tendencies, one favouring Saudi proposals which would have narrowed the overall price spread between heavy Gulf crudes and the most expensive African crudes to $2.90 and the other favouring Nigerian proposals which would have narrowed that spread to $2. A working group consisting of the Oil Ministers of Indonesia, Kuwait, Libya, Nigeria and Qatar played an important part in the Conference's efforts to achieve a compromise.

On Jan. 30, when it had become clear that no consensus position could be reached, nine member countries—Ecuador, Indonesia, Iraq, Kuwait, Nigeria, Qatar, Saudi Arabia, the United Arab Emirates and Venezuela—agreed to adopt a new pricing structure with effect from Feb. 1, while Algeria, Iran and Libya formally "dissociated themselves from this decision" and Gabon abstained. The main provisions of the majority agreement were (i) that Saudi Arabian 34° crude should be reduced in price by $1 per barrel and should lose its status as OPEC's marker crude, thereby opening the way for greater flexibility in the adjustment of differentials; (ii) that the Gulf floor price (i.e. for Saudi Arabian 27° crude) should be held at the level established on Jan. 1 (◊ Table 60); and (iii) that the effective African ceiling price (i.e. in Nigeria, as the only African producer which endorsed the agreement) should be fixed at parity with the last official price of Britain's Brent crude. On this basis, the official price spread between Africa and the Gulf region amounted to $2.15, although the participating countries also stated that the

Table 62—OPEC reference prices, Feb. 1, 1985

	Official price at Jan. 31	Official price from Feb. 1
	(dollars per barrel)	
Saudi Arabia (27°)	26.50	26.50
Saudi Arabia (31°)	27.65	27.40
Saudi Arabia (34°)	29.00	28.00
Abu Dhabi (39°)	29.31	28.15
Indonesia (34.1°)	29.53	28.53
Nigeria (36.7°)	28.00	28.65

maximum spread should in principle be "of the order of $2.40", thus indicating that Algeria and Libya would be expected to adopt a ceiling price of no more than $28.90 per barrel if they subsequently decided to fall into line with the majority.

Table 62 gives details of the six OPEC crudes selected as reference grades for the establishment of the new pricing framework. In addition to implementing the agreed Feb. 1 price changes, Saudi Arabia reportedly rescinded the 25-cent increase in the price of 31° crude exported during January.

D16.3—Consequent Price Changes, February–March 1985

Iran, which had on Feb. 3 denounced the cut in the former OPEC marker price as "another deadly blow to the Organization", announced five days later that it had after all brought its official prices into line with the new OPEC differentials structure with effect from Feb. 1. Algeria cut its price by $1 per barrel with effect from March 20 (whereas a cut of $1.60 would have been required to achieve full alignment with the new structure). Libya held its ceiling price at $30.40 per barrel throughout 1985. Details of the new Iranian and Algerian prices and of the changes introduced on Feb. 1 for a selection of other OPEC crudes (excluding the reference grades listed in Table 62) are given in Table 63.

Table 63—Price changes for selected OPEC crudes, February–March 1985

	Official price at Jan. 31	New official price*
	(dollars per barrel)	
Algeria (44°)	30.50	29.50
Iran (31°)	27.55	27.35
(34°)	29.11	28.05
Iraq (36°)	29.43	28.18
Kuwait (31°)	27.55	27.30
Qatar (40°)	29.24	28.10
Saudi Arabia (39°)	29.27	28.11
UAE: Dubai (32°)	28.86	27.86
Venezuela (26°)	27.88	27.60
(31°)	29.84	28.25
(34°)	31.09	28.80

*Effective Feb. 1 for all countries except Algeria (March 20).

Price changes introduced from Feb. 1 by non-OPEC producers included a cut of $1.25 per barrel, to $27.75, for Mexico's 34° crude (ending a period of parity with Saudi Arabia's 34° grade which had lasted since March 1983) and a cut of 50 cents per barrel, to $27.50, in the price of Egypt's 33° crude. Both of these countries had (together with Brunei and Malaysia) sent observers to OPEC's 73rd Conference meeting, although the Egyptian Oil Minister had walked out at the beginning of the second day, stating that his Government had lost patience with OPEC's internal disagreements and would reconsider its policy of co-operation with the Organization's market stabilization programme. Mexico also expressed public criticism of OPEC's latest display of disunity, and presented its own February price cut as an "autonomous" decision, based on "national self-interest" at a time of growing pressure from US customers. It was announced at the same time that Mexico's voluntary export ceiling was to revert to its October 1984 level of 1,500,000 bpd.

D16.4—British Pricing Developments (February to April 1985)

In agreeing to increase its official ceiling price in accordance with the OPEC majority's revised differential pricing formula, Nigeria gave no guarantee that it would maintain the new price in the event of any future erosion of its competitive position, it being stated by Prof. Tam David-West that his country had "two feet in OPEC but two eyes on the North Sea". He made it clear that the onus was now on Britain to underpin the OPEC pricing formula by affirming BNOC's adherence to its former reference price of $28.65 per barrel, which had been deliberately matched by Nigeria to give "a warning that the oil market should not be destabilized".

On Feb. 1 BNOC began to honour invoices from producing companies for the supply of participation crude at $28.65 per barrel during January, although it described these payments as "provisional" pending the formal fixing of a January reference price. A firm decision was finally announced on Feb. 13, when BNOC informed its suppliers that a reference price of $28.65 per barrel would apply for both January and February. At the same time the British Government informed the House of Commons of its intention to seek supplementary funding to cover BNOC's trading losses over this period. Although the spot price of Brent crude was then higher than the official price (having risen to an average $28.90 in the second week of February, as against $28.25 in the first week), BNOC's crude entitlement for February had already been committed to spot buyers at an average $27 per barrel, taking the corporation's estimated trading loss for the first two months of 1985 to around £50,000,000.

In an unexpected development on March 13, the British Government announced its intention to introduce legislation to abolish BNOC within six months in view of "the major change in the structure of the oil market away from term contracts and towards spot and similar short-term contracts" (◊A4.21.i), a trend which was "unlikely to be reversed in the near future". The main effect of abolition would be to suspend indefinitely the producing companies' obligation to sell 51 per cent of British North Sea output to the state, while relieving the state of the obligation to operate an official pricing system. State participation agreements would remain in place under the aegis of BNOC's successor body, the Government Oil and Pipelines Agency (GOPA), although the Government did not envisage the reactivation of the state purchasing entitlement except during a supply crisis. GOPA's main functions would be to market royalty crude (when this was taken by the state in preference to a 12.5 per cent cash royalty) and to manage the state-owned pipeline system.

After holding its reference price at $28.65 per barrel during March, BNOC informed its suppliers in early April that its purchase prices for participation crude during the forthcoming winding-up period would be determined by its average realizations from crude sales (using one month's realizations to fix the next month's purchase price). The April purchase price for Brent crude was accordingly fixed at $27.50 per barrel (compared with an average spot quotation of $28.50 for the same grade during the first week of April). This move effectively reinforced a government campaign to encourage producing companies to make rapid cutbacks in their sales of participation crude to BNOC (complete termination of individual companies' supply agreements being possible from May 1 onwards).

Initial OPEC reactions to the phasing out of the established British pricing and marketing system were generally positive, the publicly stated view of most member countries being that the direct disposal of British crude by the producing companies was preferable to the channelling of participation crude through BNOC in a weak market. It was hoped that smaller non-integrated producing companies in particular would have less incentive to maximize their output in the future. Prof. David-West said on March 20 that "OPEC will no longer have to worry about what BNOC's next price move will be", while Dr Subroto said that "in the longer term you have one destabilizing factor less".

D16.5—Market Trends, February to June 1985

Spot crude prices strengthened significantly in February, when realizations for many OPEC crudes were, for at least part of the month, close to or above the new official prices introduced on Feb. 1. However, the market was at this time subject to a number of short-term influences, including a sharp fall in Soviet exports to non-communist countries (◊D16.1), and the medium-term outlook (as indicated by open-market quotations for forward selling in the second and third quarters of the year) was for a downturn in prices. Spot realizations drifted downwards over the next two months, weakening markedly during the latter part of April, when an increased volume of Soviet exports began to enter markets still in the process of adjusting to a steady decline in UK oil consumption after the ending of the protracted coalminers' strike (fuel-switching at power stations having boosted UK fuel oil demand by up to 500,000 bpd above its normal level during the winter of 1984–85).

The Soviet Union cut the official export price of Urals crude (cif north-western Europe) by $1 to $27 per barrel with effect from May 1, but found few contract buyers at the new price and was therefore obliged to sell a high proportion of its May exports on spot terms for an average $26.55 per barrel. On May 1 Egypt cut the price of its 33° crude by 75 cents, to $26.75 per barrel, this cut being later backdated to April 1 following pressure from contract customers.

The downward trend in spot prices accelerated sharply in May and June, when heavy crudes were subject to particularly large falls (to well below their official OPEC prices) as the market absorbed the full impact of the drop in UK fuel oil demand. Table 64 shows the extent of the average spot discounts for three OPEC crudes in June 1985, together with the estimated average netback values of the same crudes at refining centres in Western Europe (Rotterdam), the United States (north-eastern seaboard) and Japan.

BNOC, which was by early June handling less than 300,000 bpd of crude, announced that its remaining suppliers would be paid $26.65 per barrel for June deliveries, as against $27.90 for May deliveries.

The decline in spot crude prices in May and June was accompanied by sharp falls in the level of OPEC production, which had previously exceeded the aggregate ceiling of 16,000,000 bpd by an average 505,000 bpd from February to April. Non-Saudi OPEC production had over the same period exceeded the collective quota ceiling of the 12 countries concerned by an average 1,087,000 bpd, with Nigeria accounting for one-third of the average excess.

It became increasingly apparent during the first four months of 1985 that the downward trend in oil demand in the main importing areas was unlikely to be

Table 64—Official prices and market values of three OPEC crudes, June 1985

	Official	Spot	Netback (W. Europe)	Netback (USA)	Netback (Japan)
			(dollars per barrel)		
Saudi Arabia (27°)	26.50	25.05	22.52	22.95	20.50
Saudi Arabia (34°)	28.00	26.79	23.21	25.23	22.97
Nigeria (36.7°)	28.65	26.53	26.18	27.67	n.a.

reversed in the near future, whereas OPEC had been relying on a moderate upturn in consumption (and in underlying stock levels) to enable it to defend its official price structure on the basis of existing production quotas. Only Saudi Arabia continued to sell all its crude exports at official prices when spot values began to weaken after February. The state oil companies in Kuwait and Venezuela each maintained their official prices for non-affiliated purchasers while enjoying some flexibility in the pricing of crude supplied to their own overseas refining affiliates. (Venezuela, moreover, had full discretion in the official pricing of extra-heavy crudes excluded from the OPEC price structure.) A growing proportion of exports from other OPEC member countries entered the market at effectively discounted prices under barter deals and various other special trading arrangements.

The shift towards such arrangements gathered momentum during May and June, and it was estimated that no more than one-third of OPEC crude exports (and no more than a quarter of all internationally-traded crude) were being sold at official prices by the middle of the year. The scale of the discounts available in the OPEC area was believed to range from $1 to $3 per barrel at this time.

The main impact of the slump in OPEC production after April was felt by Saudi Arabia, whose export customers were turning increasingly to lower-cost supply sources inside and outside the OPEC area to fulfil their currently declining crude requirements. Thus in June, when total OPEC production averaged little more than 14,000,000 bpd (the lowest aggregate output recorded by the current OPEC members since 1964), non-Saudi OPEC output was almost exactly equal to the combined quota ceiling of the countries concerned, albeit with a somewhat uneven division of the total between five under-producers and seven over-producers (♢Table 61). In the same month Saudi Arabia was able to produce only 2,420,000 bpd, its estimated revenue-earning export sales (after deducting domestic consumption and oil exported for the benefit of Iraq) having fallen to between 1,000,000 and 1,500,000 bpd because of cutbacks in contract purchases by Aramco's parent companies. The Saudi production total was equivalent to only 56 per cent of the kingdom's full balancing entitlement within the OPEC quota ceiling (or 63 per cent of its notional pro-rata share of the current OPEC production total) and was lower than total North Sea output for the second consecutive month.

Saudi Arabia's economic planning targets for 1985–86 were based on minimum average oil production of 3,850,000 bpd (with an implied crude oil export target of at least 2,500,000 bpd at current official prices), while most other OPEC members were under heavy pressure to maximize their own production in order to limit the deterioration in their economic position. It was therefore clear in early June that the Organization's market stabilization programme was in danger of imminent collapse, and there was a fresh upsurge of speculation within the oil industry at this time regarding the likelihood of a major fall in oil prices (which had first been widely predicted in early 1983).

The need for stricter adherence to the stabilization programme had been emphasized at meetings in Geneva of OPEC's market monitoring committee (April 23) and Ministerial Executive Council (March 19 and April 30/May 1). The last of these meetings reportedly focused on the recent performance of individual member countries, in which connexion Nigeria and Ecuador were understood to have come under particularly strong criticism for non-observance of production ceilings. Nigeria subsequently cut back its output, whereas Ecuador claimed the right to continue to ignore its ceiling on the grounds that the country would be "committing economic suicide" by lowering its oil exports at this point.

A further meeting of the Ministerial Executive Council, held in the Saudi summer capital on Taif on June 3, was attended not only by ministers representing the permanent council members (Saudi Arabia, Nigeria, Venezuela, Indonesia and the United Arab Emirates) but also by ministers from Ecuador, Iran, Iraq and Kuwait (which, like the four remaining OPEC members, had the right to take part in council meetings) and from Mexico (which had been invited to attend as an observer).

Shaikh Yamani made it clear to his OPEC colleagues that Saudi Arabia would feel obliged to reconsider its status as the "swing" producer within the OPEC quota system if other member countries continued to flout agreed Conference policies on pricing and production, this stance being formally endorsed by King Fahd in a personal message to the delegates. Shaikh Yamani also pointed out that Saudi Arabia's position as a strict observer of official prices had been made especially difficult by the recent change in the structure of open-market differentials, which had severely affected the kingdom's exports of heavier crudes. It was agreed that the points put forward by Saudi Arabia, together with related issues raised by other countries, should be discussed by a special meeting of the full Conference (provisionally scheduled to open on June 30).

Mexico announced on June 17 that the price of its 22° crude (a grade too heavy to fall within the scope of OPEC's differentials structure) had been cut by $1.50, to $24 per barrel, with retroactive effect from June 1, while a possible change in the price of its 34° grade was being deferred until after the special OPEC Conference meeting (the opening date of which had by this point been put back to July 5). As the principal non-OPEC exponent of strict adherence to official prices, Mexico had seen its crude exports fall to around 800,000 bpd (53 per cent of the country's voluntary export ceiling) since the beginning of May.

China on June 16 cut the official export price of its 33° crude by 65 cents, to $26.75 per barrel, with retroactive effect from April 1. Oman, which had recently gone over to monthly pricing, based on average open-market realizations for each preceding month, cut its June contract price for 34° crude to $25.90 per barrel, as against $26.15 in May, taking the cumulative reduction for this grade since the beginning of the year to $2.65 per barrel. The Soviet Union cut the July contract price of Urals crude to $25.50 per barrel, compared with $26 in June.

D16.6—OPEC Conference Meetings, July 1985

The special mid-year meeting of the OPEC Conference was preceded by an attempt to avert a clash between the producers of light and heavy crudes over the issue of differentials. Saudi Arabia's proposal for cuts in the official prices of heavier grades was opposed in particular by the north African producers, whose very light crudes had recently become more competitive. An ad hoc "mediation team", comprising ministers from Kuwait, Venezuela and Mexico, visited Algeria and Libya on June 29 and 30 respectively to put the case for compromise on this issue, the team's talks in Algeria being attended also by the Nigerian Oil Minister. According to British press reports, a series of informal meetings took place in London at the beginning of July between ministers from Nigeria, Venezuela and several Arab Gulf states (including Saudi Arabia) to discuss a possible reduction in OPEC's production ceiling.

The various rounds of preparatory talks served only to emphasize the lack of agreement within OPEC on measures to resolve the Organization's current crisis, and the market monitoring committee, meeting on July 4, was unable to draw up any formal recommendations for submission to the special session on the full Conference, which took place in Vienna from July 5 to 7. The Conference's discussions on future strategy proved to be equally fruitless, and ministers found no basis for upgrading the status of the session beyond the purely consultative level. The Mexican Energy Minister, who attended the consultations as an observer, delivered a message from the President of Mexico on July 5 stating his Government's intention "fully to defend its national interests" if the Conference failed to take "decisive action" to stabilize the oil market. Moreover, Shaikh Yamani warned the other OPEC members on July 7 that Saudi Arabia would have to take steps to safeguard its own interests if the present deadlock was not resolved at the ordinary session of the Conference later in July.

According to subsequent statements by individual ministers, the only positive initiative to emerge from the Vienna consultations was an agreement in principle that OPEC members should, before the forthcoming ordinary Conference session, disclose full details of all existing supply arrangements involving "discounting and other malpractices" and should formally commit themselves to phase out such arrangements by the end of 1985. Six member countries were said to have rejected a proposal (tabled by Kuwait) calling for the level of the OPEC production ceiling to be varied from quarter to quarter in line with projected seasonal fluctuations in demand, the suggested margin of flexibility being 7 per cent above or below 16,000,000 bpd, with a recommendation that an across-the-board cutback of 7 per cent should be made in existing national quotas during the third quarter of 1985. At least seven member countries were said to have rejected a formal proposal by Saudi Arabia for cuts in the official prices of heavier crudes.

The Mexican Government reacted to the inconclusive outcome of the OPEC consultations by authorizing unilateral price cuts for the country's 34° and 22° export grades on July 10, stating that Mexico "cannot tolerate a situation in which it watches itself be progressively displaced from its traditional markets through widespread recourse to irregular commercial practices by other exporters". Mexico's initiative "to re-establish competitiveness in foreign markets" involved (i) a retroactive cut of $1, to $26.75 per barrel, in the price of 34° crude exported during June, and (ii) the introduction, with retroactive effect from July 1, of a "zoned" pricing structure which took account of variations in the degree of price competition in the principal markets for imported oil. Under this structure Mexico's 34° grade was priced at $26.75 per barrel for US importers, $26.50 for Asian importers and $26.25 for European importers, while the official fob price of the 22° grade (hitherto $24 per barrel in all markets) fell to $23.50 (USA), $23 (Asia) or $22.50 (Europe). On July 17 Egypt made an across-the-board cut of $1.50 per barrel in the export prices for all grades of crude, backdated to July 1.

Notwithstanding its effective withdrawal of support for OPEC's existing official pricing structure, Mexico accepted an invitation to hold observer status at the 74th meeting of the OPEC Conference, which took place in Geneva from July 22 to 25. In his opening address to the meeting, Dr Subroto of Indonesia made a fresh appeal for the support of non-OPEC producers in stabilizing the market, stating that OPEC had "reached the extreme limiting level in its capacity to continue supporting prices with production cuts". Delegates were, however, informed by OPEC's Deputy Secretary-General that the British and US Governments had declined invitations to attend a forthcoming OPEC seminar on the current state of the oil market, whereupon the Conference agreed that the seminar should be indefinitely postponed.

Faced with formal requests for quota increases from Ecuador, Gabon, Qatar and Iraq, the Conference decided to defer all discussion of national and group production ceilings until early October, when a further Conference meeting would be convened for this purpose. The 74th Conference meeting instead centred its discussions (i) on the issue of adherence to existing market stabilization policies, and (ii) on the need for a further realignment of price differentials.

The Ministerial Executive Council informed the Conference that five OPEC members had declined to co-operate fully with the auditing procedures approved by the 73rd Conference meeting (◊**D16.2**), and made various recommendations for improving the effectiveness of these procedures. The five countries concerned (which were not publicly named) agreed to open their books to the auditors in future and joined the other member countries in approving a strengthening of the Council's monitoring methods. The Conference did not, however, accept a proposal by some member countries that the Council should be empowered to recommend the imposition of sanctions on countries where "malpractices" were revealed as a result of independent audits.

The ministerial committee on price differentials, having failed to reach agreement at its pre-Conference meeting on July 21, met again on the two succeeding days, finally presenting three alternative proposals to the full Conference on July 24. These were (i) that the official prices of heavier crudes should be cut and those of lighter crudes left unchanged; (ii) that a price cut for heavier crudes should be accompanied by an equal price increase for lighter crudes; and (iii) that a price cut for heavier crudes should be accompanied by a smaller price increase for lighter crudes. After heated debate, a majority of member countries agreed on July 26 that differentials should be readjusted on the basis of a cut of 20 cents per barrel (to $27.20) in the price of Saudi Arabia's 31° crude and a cut of 50 cents (to $26) in the price of Saudi Arabia's 27° crude, with no changes in the prices of lighter crudes. Algeria, Iran and Libya "disagreed with the reduction and dissociated themselves from this decision".

Kuwait subsequently backdated to July 1 a 20-cent reduction (to $27.10) in the price of its 31° crude, and it was generally assumed that the agreed Saudi cuts had been similarly backdated. The official price of Iran's 31° grade remained unchanged at $27.35. Venezuela cut the price of its 31° grade by 20 cents (to $28.05) with effect from Aug. 1, while reducing the prices of its heavy and extra-heavy grades (which fell outside the scope of the OPEC differentials structure) by up to $2 per barrel in order to restore broad parity with comparable Mexican grades. Similar cuts were made at the same time in the prices of Indonesia's heavier crudes.

It was noted by market analysts that the new prices for heavy and medium Gulf crudes remained significantly above the prevailing spot prices for the same grades (i.e. $25.25 for Saudi Arabian 27° crude and $25.75 for Saudi Arabian 31° crude) and were therefore unlikely to be of any great assistance in countering the slump in export demand for officially-priced Saudi crude.

D16.7—July 1985 Meeting of IEA Governing Board

The Governing Board of the International Energy Agency met in Paris on July 9, 1985, this being its first meeting at ministerial level since May 1983. The ministers avoided any formal discussion of the short-term outlook for oil prices, while proposals by some member countries for the opening of a dialogue between the IEA and OPEC were dropped in the face of strong opposition from the United States. Supporters of such a dialogue were believed to include Austria, Japan, Sweden and the Netherlands, while the European Commission (which held observer status) was known to favour "practical co-operation" with oil-exporting countries.

The US Energy Secretary, John Herrington, said that his Government saw "no advantage—and even the possibility of serious disagreements—in formal or informal multilateral dialogues between producing and consuming countries". The chairman of the meeting, G.M.V. van Aardenne (Minister of Economic Affairs of the Netherlands), acknowledged that the Agency's existing policies were designed primarily to cope with conditions of supply shortage and rising prices, but said that the Governing Board saw no reason to discuss the possibility of a major collapse in oil prices in an oversupplied market, which remained a "hypothetical question".

Discussion of immediate oil trade prospects was therefore narrowly concentrated on the growth in exports of refined products from new refineries in Saudi Arabia and other OPEC countries, in which connexion Japan yielded to strong pressure from the United States and the main West European importers for a relaxation of its highly protectionist policies on product imports. The meeting "recognized the interest of developing countries in valorizing their exports", and agreed that imported refined products should be allowed "to go to the markets of the different IEA countries and regions on the basis of supply and demand as determined by market forces without distortions".

The ministers reviewed the development of the energy market over the previous 10 years and reaffirmed their commitment to the original objectives of the IEA, with particular reference to medium-term supply and demand forecasts which had been published by the IEA Secretariat on June 17. The Secretariat's annual energy review had included a warning that member countries' oil production had "probably reached its peak" and that their requirement for imported oil could be expected to increase by 10.5 per cent by 1990. Moreover, natural gas production within the IEA area was expected to go into decline after 1990. The Secretariat therefore concluded that "unless the IEA countries achieve further big improvements in the efficiency with which energy is used, together with expansion in the production of energy resources, they could once again become vulnerable to oil supply disruption in the 1990s". The Governing Board recognized the dangers of complacency in "the current slack oil market" and called in particular for prompt remedial measures by "member countries whose oil stocks presently are at lower levels in relation to current net imports than would permit them to make a meaningful contribution to a co-ordinated drawdown".

The opening sections of the final communiqué issued by the Governing Board on July 9 were worded as follows:

"**The past decade.** Ministers reviewed the energy results of the past decade, characterized by two sharp oil price increases, each of which contributed to a serious economic recession. They welcomed the extensive structural adjustments by which the energy sectors of IEA countries' economies have responded to the consequences of higher oil prices, including (i) the reduced amount of energy, especially oil, needed for each unit of GDP, thereby holding total energy consumption level while their economies grew by 29 per cent; (ii) major changes in the fuel mix, reducing the share of oil from 53 per cent to 42 per cent; and (iii) an increase in indigenous energy production by the equivalent of over 10,000,000 bpd of oil.

"They attributed these changes to the effects of sharp price increases working through the market mechanism, and also to government policies addressed to energy security, conservation, market-oriented pricing, energy research and development, open international trade and, in general, toward greater indigenous production, growing efficiency and public awareness of energy problems. They recognized the importance of dynamic energy industries capable of responding to the need for structural change and of open, flexible and transparent energy markets. They also recognized the crucial importance of international energy co-operation within the IEA in achieving these results.

"They noted the severe economic losses caused by the recessions which followed the oil price increases. They believe, however, that structural adjustments in energy economies contributed to subsequent recovery and helped to prevent GDP losses and unemployment from being greater than they were. Further structural adjustment in energy sectors will be necessary to sustain economic activity in the future.

"They noted that the current oil market situation is characterized by relatively weak demand, considerable overcapacity (much of which, however, is concentrated in the Gulf region) and downward pressure on prices.

"Looking ahead, ministers found major challenges facing energy consumption and every major fuel, and concluded that the present oil market situation is not to be expected to extend far into the next decade and beyond. Secretariat analysis indicates that within 10 years (or earlier if weakness appears in any alternative fuel or in efficiency gains), world demand for oil could approach levels close enough to anticipated available production capacity to produce upward price pressures and to restore the condition of vulnerability to supply disruptions which existed in 1973–74 and 1979–80.

"If that were the case, the consequences for the world economy could be severely adverse. Despite the inherent difficulties of forecasting energy developments, given the wide range of unpredictability concerning many of the underlying factors, ministers therefore agreed that it would be imprudent and even dangerous for IEA countries to ignore forecasts of the IEA, governments and industry which point to tightening energy markets in the 1990s, especially for oil. Instead, they reaffirmed that providing adequate and secure energy sources in a way which complements efforts to promote economic growth remains the major objective which governments have for the IEA. They therefore forcefully underlined the importance of reducing future risks by maintaining the energy policy directions already well established in the IEA and continuing their vigorous implementation, especially in the areas referred to below.

"**Structural change within the market system.** Against this background, ministers agreed that one requirement for energy policy is flexible, open and resilient markets within which the different fuels can compete vigorously and find their levels of demand and supply through operation of the price mechanism. Another requirement, since governments are directly and indirectly concerned with energy activities, is that governments must also carry out policies which accomplish their objectives and at the same time supplement an effective market system in a manner which is consistent with the national circumstances of each country, such as the following approaches in overall policy: (i) energy pricing policies which permit consumer prices to reflect world market prices (and where world markets do not exist to reflect long-term costs of energy supply), and which interfere as little as possible with operation of market forces (with particular reference to direct controls or subsidies for natural gas, electricity and coal); (ii) actions regarding national energy resources which contribute to increased indigenous energy production; (iii) tax, royalty and trade regimes which are conducive to efficient use of energy, indigenous energy production and energy imports, exports, and finance; and (iv) the particular energy policy areas referred to below."

The energy policy areas covered in detail in the remaining sections of the communiqué were conservation; oil refineries and product trade; electricity, coal, nuclear power and natural gas; energy and the environment; and oil emergency preparedness.

D16.8—Developments Leading to 75th Meeting of OPEC Conference

Saudi Arabia's oil output, which had risen to 2,740,000 bpd in July 1985 following the chartering of additional tankers for the purposes of "floating storage", dropped to an average 2,340,000 bpd (a new 20-year low) during August. Total OPEC output had meanwhile recovered from its June low to reach 14,850,000 bpd in August, much of the upturn being attributable to an improvement in Iranian production and to a drive by Iraq to fill its new link with the Saudi Arabian pipeline system prior to the scheduled start of Iraqi exports from the Saudi Red Sea port of Yanbu in September (◊C6.3.v).

Spot crude prices, which had stabilized or improved during July, strengthened further in August, particularly for lighter grades, although they remained significantly below official OPEC prices. Factors in this improvement included (i) a temporary cutback in British output while annual maintenance work was carried out on offshore production platforms, and (ii) the return to the market of some buyers who had deferred purchases during July in anticipation of significant OPEC price cuts. The Soviet Union increased the price of its Urals crude from $25.90 to $26.90 in three stages between the beginning of August and the middle of September. The price of Oman's 34° crude rose by 20 cents to $26.10 per barrel in July and by a further 82 cents to $26.92 in August. Egypt increased its export prices on Aug. 1 by amounts ranging from 40 cents for 33° crude to 25 cents for crudes heavier than 26°.

The Saudi Government, which had made it clear on July 31 that it intended to abandon the role of swing producer within the OPEC quota system (and would therefore observe a fixed, rather than an "implied", ceiling of 4,353,000 bpd), began to conclude a series of sales agreements with major oil companies in early September on terms which would make the kingdom's exports competitive with discount-priced oil from other OPEC members. This radical change in pricing policy was understood to have been under discussion at the highest political level within Saudi Arabia for several months, while the arrangements for its implementation had been under negotiation for some weeks with Aramco's US parent companies (three of which—Exxon, Texaco and Mobil—were to purchase a total of about 820,000 bpd under the first round of agreements).

The fob price of the crude supplied under these agreements was to vary in line with the crude's product worth to the companies' downstream affiliates, thereby assuring them of a guaranteed profit margin on refining operations. The agreements, valid initially for six months from Oct. 1, were understood to stipulate that the oil should be sold only through integrated channels and in particular markets (with Japan being specifically excluded on account of its system of government controls on product prices).

Because of the inherent complexities of "netting back" fob crude prices from ex-refinery realizations (a process which had to take account of such variables as the structure of product demand and processing capacity in each market), no precise information was available on the overall level of discounting under the new agreements. It was, however, known that most of the crude was destined for West European markets, where the weighted average netback value of Saudi crudes in early October was estimated to be around $2.50 per barrel below the weighted average official price.

In separate deals covering feedstock for export refineries within Saudi Arabia, the Saudi authorities agreed in mid-September that netback pricing should (with retroactive effect from Aug. 1) apply to crude supplied to the new refineries at Yanbu and Jubail, in which 50 per cent interests were held by Mobil and Shell respectively (◊C11.3.ix). The two plants had recently been operating at less than one-third of their combined capacity of 500,000 bpd, having encountered serious export marketing problems because of their poor competitive position when processing officially-priced crude.

The *Middle East Economic Survey* (generally regarded as a source of accurate information on Saudi government thinking) reported in mid-September that "from now on the restoration of Saudi Arabia's market position and the maintenance of Saudi production at an acceptable level will be the linch-pin of the Government's oil policy". The switch to market-related pricing was intended "as a warning to other oil-exporting countries", and the prospects for a return to administered pricing in Saudi Arabia after the end of March 1986 would depend very much on the willingness of OPEC and non-OPEC producers to adopt a more positive commitment to market stabilization measures.

Saudi Arabia's average monthly production rose by 640,000 bpd in September (i.e. before the entry into force of the new crude oil export contracts), while total OPEC production increased by nearly 1,000,000 bpd over its August level. The other main contributors to this upturn were Nigeria, which restored its output to a level in excess of its quota ceiling following the coup of Aug. 27 (◊C9.2), and Iraq, which began exporting from Yanbu during the last week of September. On the other hand, Iran's average production fell sharply to a level below its quota ceiling following a series of damaging Iraqi bombing raids on the Kharg Island terminal during the second half of September, while outside the OPEC area there were further major interruptions in the flow of Soviet oil to non-communist countries (◊D16.1). Against this background spot crude prices, which (despite constant fluctuations in nervous trading) had shown little overall change during the first

647

three weeks of September, rose strongly in the last week of the month, when the average quotations for many OPEC crudes were close to or higher than the corresponding official prices.

OPEC's market monitoring committee, meeting in Vienna on Oct. 2, concluded that the current strength of spot prices was unlikely to be more than a "temporary phenomenon" in a "fragile market", and accordingly recommended that the OPEC production ceiling should be held at 16,000,000 bpd. The Ministerial Executive Council met on the same day but made no public statement on its discussions. The 75th (extraordinary) meeting of the OPEC Conference, held in Vienna on Oct. 3 and 4 with Mexico again holding observer status, unanimously endorsed the retention of a 16,000,000 bpd ceiling but failed to agree on any redistribution of national quotas within this ceiling.

Ecuador, Gabon, Iraq, Qatar and the United Arab Emirates had all requested formal increases in their quotas at the outset of the Conference meeting in order to "legitimize" their existing overproduction, while Iran had demanded a higher quota for itself if any increase was made in the Iraqi quota. Iraq made it clear for some months that it would treat the throughput of its new 500,000 bpd pipeline link to Yanbu as an additional entitlement, affording partial compensation for the earlier war-related losses of export capacity which had caused its OPEC quota to be fixed at an "artificially low" level. The new ceiling requested by Iraq was believed to be 2,000,000 bpd (an increase of 800,000 bpd). Iran, for its part, threatened to increase its own output by two barrels for every incremental barrel produced in Iraq.

Nigeria, while not requesting a formal quota increase, said that it still considered its ceiling to be 1,450,000 bpd (i.e. including the additional entitlement of 150,000 bpd which had been intended by the Conference to apply only during September 1984 ◊**D15.5**). Ecuador, which followed Iraq in declaring its intention to maximize its exports regardless of its quota ceiling, pointed out that its oil revenues were "being used for peaceful purposes, not to sustain a war", and threatened to "reconsider" its membership of OPEC if the Conference continued to "impugn the honour of the country" by categorizing it as an over-producer relative to an "inadequate" ceiling.

Shaikh Yamani, however, made it clear that Saudi Arabia had no intention of modifying its claim to a fixed production ceiling of 4,353,000 bpd in order to accommodate increases in other countries' quotas within the unchanged group ceiling (although he did indicate that the kingdom would not necessarily produce its entire entitlement "unless the market demands"). He provided the Conference with a detailed account of Saudi Arabia's netback pricing formula, which, he said, would enable the kingdom to operate "on an equal footing" with discount pricing practices elsewhere in the OPEC area. None of the other delegates were able to suggest a strategy for an early return to observance of the official OPEC pricing structure, the de facto suspension of which was implicitly acknowledged in public statements by several Conference delegates. The President of the Conference, Dr Subroto, told reporters after the meeting that, although netback pricing was technically in breach of OPEC guidelines, "not all malpractices are negative". He added that he could see "nothing bad" in the market-related pricing system which had been adopted by the North Sea producers.

D16.9—Market Trends, October–November 1985

In mid-October Saudi Arabia concluded a netback supply agreement with Chevron, the only one of Aramco's parent companies which had not adopted the new pricing system at its inception. By late November six further agreements had been negotiated with various major and independent oil companies, taking the total volume of the kingdom's netback crude exports to about 1,860,000 bpd. In a separate development during November, the Saudi Arabian state-owned marketing company Norbec began selling crude at "negotiated spot prices" from Saudi stockpiles in Western Europe and the Caribbean region, although the degree of discounting was negligible in view of the strength of spot prices for most of the month.

Saudi Arabia's average monthly crude output increased by nearly 1,000,000 bpd in October and by a further 290,000 bpd in November to reach 4,200,000 bpd (96.5 per cent of the kingdom's OPEC quota) in the latter month. The aggregate output of the other 12 OPEC members increased by 645,000 bpd in October and 240,000 bpd in November, with the result that the Organization's total November output was estimated to be 1,905,000 bpd above the group ceiling of 16,000,000 bpd. Apart from Saudi Arabia, only Iran was producing within its national ceiling in November, war damage to the Kharg terminal having prevented the country from carrying out its threat to increase its output twice as fast as Iraq (whose own "excess" production relative to its ceiling reached 500,000 bpd in November). Iran had, however, managed to produce its full quota in October and 95.6 per cent of its quota in November by stepping up the transfer of oil to an improvised export terminal at Sirri Island, which had first come into use in February 1985 (◊**C5.3.vi**).

Spot crude prices, which had weakened slightly in early October in reaction to the outcome of the 75th OPEC Conference meeting, recovered during the first three weeks of November, when there was a particularly strong upturn in quotations for very light grades, which reached their highest levels of the year in the third week of that month (subsequently suffering the sharpest falls when prices began to decline in the fourth week). Table 65 shows the extent of the average spot discounts for two Saudi crudes (and the spot premium for Nigeria's main export grade) during November, together with the estimated average netback values of the same crudes in Western Europe (Rotterdam) and the United States (north-eastern seaboard).

As indicated by the firmness of prices for spot cargoes, OPEC's "excess" output was until late November closely balanced by incremental demand, arising partly from a limited upturn in current consumption and partly from pre-winter additions to the exceptionally low commercial inventories held in the main importing countries at the beginning of the fourth quarter of 1985 (◊**D16.1**). Open-market quotations for forward delivery were, however, significantly lower than current spot values, reflecting a general expectation that a supply surplus would build up during the coming months, and the market was quick to react to the first reports of unsold cargoes during the last week of November. Thus the average quotation for spot cargoes of the most widely-traded crude, North Sea Brent, fell from $30.80 to $29 per barrel between Nov. 25 and Nov. 29, while the average quotation for January delivery fell by $30 to $28.40 over the same five-day period. By Dec. 4 Brent was being quoted at $27.75 for December delivery and $27.60 for January delivery, the reported cause of the latest slide in the market being a high volume of crude sales by the Saudi company Norbec.

Several non-OPEC exporters announced price increases during and immediately

Table 65—Official prices and market values of three OPEC crudes, November 1985

	Official	Spot	Netback (W. Europe)	Netback (USA)
	(dollars per barrel)			
Saudi Arabia (27°)	26.00	25.81	25.60	23.26
Saudi Arabia (34°)	28.00	27.86	26.31	26.86
Nigeria (36.7°)	28.65	30.33	29.42	29.70

after the period of strong spot values. In Egypt, the export price of 33° crude rose by 45 cents to $26.10 per barrel on Oct. 1 and by a further 60 cents to $26.70 from Dec. 1, the prices of heavier grades being increased by smaller margins on each occasion. Mexico increased the "zoned" prices of its 34° crude as follows: Nov. 1— USA $27.50, Asia $26.90, Europe $26.75; Dec. 1—USA $27.80, Asia $27.45, Europe $27.60. (However, the price of Mexico's 22° crude was cut by a uniform 40 cents per barrel in all markets on Nov. 1, prompting an equal cut in the prices of similar Venezuelan grades on Nov. 5.) The Soviet Union increased its export price to $27.60 on Nov. 1 and $28.15 on Dec. 1. Oman's 34° crude was priced at $27.37 in September, $27.20 in October and November and $27.35 from Dec. 1.

D16.10—OPEC Developments Leading to 76th Conference Meeting (October to early December 1985)

Kuwait's Oil Minister, addressing a meeting of the oil committee of the Gulf Co-operation Council in Riyadh on Oct. 21, said that there was a need for an "immediate and serious effort" by the GCC member countries to step up co-operation between themselves and with other oil producers "to meet the challenge of a weak oil market". Moreover, Dr Subroto made a number of statements during the latter part of October urging non-OPEC producers and major importing countries to "start talking" with OPEC members on an informal basis with a view to arranging "broader discussions on action to protect our mutual interests".

Notwithstanding the fact that he was received in his capacity as a member of the Indonesian Government rather than as the current President of the OPEC Conference, Dr Subroto put the case for co-operation with OPEC to the British Energy Secretary, Peter Walker, during informal talks in London on Oct. 23. He was, however, informed that the British Government saw no reason to move towards such co-operation (particularly as the idea of dialogue with OPEC had recently been shown to lack majority support within the IEA ◊ **D16.7**) and did not intend to impose cutbacks on production from the North Sea. The Norwegian Energy Minister, speaking in Oslo on the same day, said that Norway was planning to achieve a 40 per cent increase in its oil production by 1990.

In a speech to an oil conference in London on Oct. 24, Dr Subroto said that OPEC's most realistic option in the current circumstances might be to defend its market share, if necessary through seasonally-adjusted production quotas, while accepting a defined range of market-related price movements. A blunt acknowledgment of the present pricing situation came on Nov. 1 from Dr al Oteiba of the United Arab Emirates, who said that "since the last OPEC Conference meeting, each producing country either inside or outside OPEC has full freedom to fix the prices it feels are suitable for its oil".

Shaikh Yamani said in an interview published by the *International Herald Tribune* on Nov. 7 that "very violent" oil price fluctuations could be expected in 1986 if non-OPEC producers did not restrain their output, adding that if a price war did occur these producers might "realize the facts of life" (i.e. accept the case for stabilization measures) by the third quarter of 1987. As regards the restriction of OPEC output, he said that Saudi Arabia had "abandoned the policy of carrying the burden alone", and was prepared to produce above its ceiling if other OPEC members continued to exceed their own quotas, the Saudi Government's current attitude being that "if it's free for some, it's free for all". He expressed broad agreement with Dr Subroto's views regarding OPEC's "realistic" course of action in the short term.

The Venezuelan Energy Minister, Dr Arturo Hernández Grisanti (who had said in early November that Venezuela "will defend OPEC, but this does not prevent us from acting to defend our own interests"), announced on Nov. 29 that detailed proposals for a new market stabilization formula had been approved by President Lusinchi for submission to the OPEC Conference. It was believed that Venezuela, while broadly accepting the case for concentrating on the defence of OPEC's market share in the short term, was anxious to minimize any consequent erosion of price levels.

Dr Subroto, Dr Hernández Grisanti and Shaikh Yamani were among several OPEC ministers who travelled to Geneva on Dec. 4 in order to hold preparatory talks in advance of the next round of formal OPEC meetings, which began with pre-Conference sessions of the market monitoring committee and the Ministerial Executive Council on Dec. 6. The 76th Conference meeting took place from Dec. 7 to 9, with Mexico and Malaysia holding observer status.

Dr Subroto began his opening address to the Conference meeting by highlighting the sharp downturn in spot oil prices since late November (◊**D16.9**), caused primarily by the emergence of a supply surplus. He asserted that market stability was "of the utmost importance to all segments of the interdependent world economy" and listed the main reasons why, in his opinion, the industrialized countries had a "particularly high stake" in such stability.

These were (i) the heavy investments which had been made by commercial banks in the development of oil resources and alternative energy sources; (ii) the large upstream investments made by the commercial oil companies themselves on the assumption that amortization would be geared to high and stable unit revenues; (iii) the positive implications of stable oil prices for the wider structure of international trade, in view of the close link between the level of the third-world exporting countries' oil revenues and the level of their spending on imports of goods and services; and (iv) the fact that several OPEC and non-OPEC oil-exporting countries could be expected to face insurmountable problems in servicing their heavy foreign debts in the event of a collapse in oil prices.

Dr Subroto said that OPEC had "had to assume the responsibility of a swing producer in the world oil trade" over the past two years in order to prevent a significant fall in oil prices, although OPEC was "not the sole beneficiary of a stable market". He repeated his recent appeal for "trilateral co-operation" whereby "OPEC unity and discipline" would be backed (i) by a commitment on the part of the industrialized countries "to achieve higher rates of economic growth that would be reflected in a higher level of oil consumption" and (ii) by a commitment to output controls on the part of non-OPEC oil producers. Supportive action by the main importing countries should, he said, be based on the modification of trade practices and fiscal policies which were "deliberately geared to preventing an increase in oil demand and to reducing the share of oil—and in particular OPEC oil—in the overall energy mix".

Dr Subroto called for a "reawakening of the spirit of solidarity" within OPEC, and urged the member countries "not to sacrifice long-term interests for short-term gains" by overproducing in the "very difficult" months ahead, since to do so would only "play into the hands of those whose idea of a fair price for oil is one that would encourage wasteful consumption of energy".

The main decisions of the 76th Conference meeting were announced on Dec. 9 as follows: (i) "to secure and defend for OPEC a fair share in the world oil market consistent with the necessary income for member countries' development"; (ii) to establish a special ministerial committee "to examine the ways and means to achieve this objective and to recommend to the Conference the course of action to be taken in this respect"; and (iii) to "reaffirm all previous resolutions". The special committee was to be chaired by Dr Hernández Grisanti (the newly elected President of the OPEC Conference) and was to include also the Oil Ministers of Indonesia, Iraq, Kuwait and the United Arab Emirates.

The Conference's decision to switch to a "market share" strategy was tantamount to a formal acknowledgment of OPEC's inability to implement its official pricing policy on the basis of a quota system which, having originally been agreed as a temporary expedient pending an expected increase in demand for OPEC oil in 1985, had broken down when that increase had failed to materialize. The reference to the "reaffirmation of all previous resolutions" was freely acknowledged by delegates to indicate a purely symbolic retention of existing official prices and production quotas.

The failure of the Conference to quantify OPEC's "fair share" of the market reflected the absence of a clear consensus on this issue, although several delegates subsequently maintained that a decision was being deliberately deferred until OPEC was able to assess the implications of any changes in the policies of non-OPEC producers. Most delegates said after the Conference meeting that a main aim of the new OPEC strategy was to force the non-OPEC producers to take positive steps to halt the erosion of oil prices (i.e. by cutting their own market share in order to accommodate OPEC's current level of production). Some ministers stressed that their countries were fully prepared to fight a price war to defend their existing market shares, and in particular Prof. David-West said that Nigeria would "match the North Sea producers barrel by barrel and cent by cent".

The strongest reservations about the dangers of a price collapse were expressed by Algeria and Iran, each of which had declined to be represented on the special committee set up to elaborate the "fair share" strategy. Shaikh Yamani, for his part, had declined to accept the chairmanship of the committee, apparently in order to emphasize Saudi Arabia's intention to reserve all its options regarding its own production policy.

The full Conference was understood to have reached a virtually unanimous agreement that OPEC's minimum share of the market should be 16,000,000 bpd, but to have been divided on the issues of seasonal flexibility and maximum market share, with some members arguing that 16,000,000 bpd should be treated as an annual average rather than an absolute floor level, while others maintained that production should be allowed to rise as high as 20,000,000 bpd. Moderate opinion was reported to favour an annual average of about 17,000,000 bpd, within which there would be seasonal peaks of around 18,000,000 bpd and seasonal troughs of around 16,000,000 bpd.

D16.11—The Collapse of Oil Prices (December 1985 to April 1986)

D16.11.i—Prices and production in December 1985 and January 1986

The decisions of the 76th OPEC Conference meeting had an immediate impact on open-market prices as oil traders attempted to assess the implications of the Organization's unquantified "fair share" strategy. The daily average quotation for 15-day spot delivery of British Brent crude slumped by $2.85 to $24.40 per barrel on Dec. 10, this fall being partially reversed in succeeding days to give a weekly average value of $26.14 (some $2.29 below the average for the first week of December). Within the OPEC area, the average spot value of Nigeria's main export grade declined by $2.60, to $27 per barrel, between the first and second weeks of December, while the weekly average quotations for most Gulf crudes fell by around $1 per barrel. In the latter part of the month spot prices weakened further but remained significantly above the low point reached on Dec. 10.

The average spot value of Brent crude for the whole of December 1985 was $26.62 per barrel, some $3.38 below the average for November and $1.30 below the average for the first 11 months of the year. The average December spot price for Saudi Arabia's 34° light crude ($26.92 per barrel) was 94 cents below the November average and 64 cents below the January–November average.

Aggregate OPEC output in December was estimated to be 18,340,000 bpd (the highest monthly average since June 1984), boosting the fourth quarter's OPEC average to 17,873,000 bpd and the full year's average to just over 16,000,000 bpd. Estimated Saudi production for December amounted to 4,680,000 bpd, taking the kingdom's October–December average to 4,264,000 bpd (89,000 bpd below its OPEC ceiling). Saudi Arabia's July–December average was estimated as 3,473,000 bpd (377,000 bpd below the level required to meet government revenue targets on the basis of official prices ◊**D16.5**) and its 1985 annual average as 3,385,000 bpd. Non-Saudi OPEC output fell in December by an estimated 45,000 bpd from its November peak of 13,705,000 bpd, but continued to exceed the combined quota of the 12 countries concerned by more than 2,000,000 bpd. Iran, Libya and Qatar all increased their output in December, when Algeria was the only OPEC member to produce less than its full entitlement under the moribund quota system. Full-year averages indicated that Algeria, Iran and Saudi Arabia were the only under-quota producers during 1985 as a whole (◊ Table 61).

A significant supply-side factor in the levelling off of December's decline in spot prices (and a subsequent minor upturn in early January) was a fall of 207,000 bpd in the average output of the two main North Sea producers between November and December. In the latter month British output was trimmed by 184,000 bpd to 2,537,000 bpd mainly for the purpose of keeping the annual averages for two major fields within pre-planned targets for 1985, while Norway's output fell by 23,000 bpd from the record monthly rate of 913,000 bpd reached in November. Other non-OPEC countries which involuntarily helped to offset the impact of the 435,000 bpd increase in OPEC output in December included Mexico, whose production declined by 64,000 bpd; this was largely because of the growth of customer resistance to the higher Mexican export prices introduced on Dec. 1 (which became increasingly uncompetitive in the US market as US domestic crude prices weakened in line with the spot trend).

During January 1986 the pressure of surplus supplies on price levels intensified amid increasing competition for shares of a largely stagnant market, the main demand factors in the first quarter of 1986 (as estimated by the International Energy Agency in early April) being (i) a year-on-year fall of 0.8 per cent in OECD oil consumption (equivalent to an underlying increase of 0.5 per cent when the figures were restated to take account of the abnormally high level of UK oil demand in early 1985), and (ii) a drawdown of about 1,400,000 bpd from commercial oil stocks on land. Minimal additions were made to the oil stocks held by OECD governments.

The aggregate output of the main North Sea producers increased by an estimated 218,000 bpd in January, when British production recovered to around 2,800,000 bpd (2.9 per cent above its November 1985 level) while Norway's production was around 45,000 bpd lower than in December. The January 1986 North Sea total was 1.9 per cent higher than that for the corresponding month of 1985, a year-on-year fall in UK production having been more than offset by higher Norwegian output. Estimated OPEC production in January 1986 averaged 17,350,000 bpd, some 990,000 bpd below the previous month's average but 2,500,000 bpd above that for January 1985. Saudi Arabia's "excess" production relative to its notional quota ceiling fell from 327,000 bpd in December to 97,000 bpd in January, while Libya's "excess" fell from 310,000 bpd to 110,000 bpd. Notional quota entitlements were underfulfilled in Nigeria and Iran, whose output levels declined by 420,000 bpd and 300,000 bpd respectively in January. Indonesia increased its output by an estimated 150,000 bpd, while the production of the eight remaining OPEC members showed little or no change between December and January.

The volume of open-market trading in most OPEC crudes dwindled to negligible proportions during the course of January as Saudi Arabia expanded its netback trade and other member countries began to negotiate their own netback supply contracts with foreign refiners in order to secure guaranteed export outlets. In addition to threatening the market shares of those producers who remained heavily dependent on spot selling and other established arm's-length trading practices, this development served further to diminish price transparency within the OPEC area, to the extent that the spot value of North Sea Brent crude became the principal reference point for monitoring short-term price trends in the international crude trade.

Declining demand from established customers meant that January's high volume of North Sea production was achieved only by selling at progressively lower prices as the market crashed under the pressure of the supply overhang both in Western Europe (which had experienced the main influx of Saudi netback crude) and North America (which imported most of the balance at this time). The average Brent spot price fell from more than \$26 to less than \$19 per barrel between the first and last weeks of January, for an overall monthly average of \$22.13 (\$4.49 below the previous month's average), the price levels of late January being low enough to enable North Sea crudes to compete in the Japanese import market for the first time. However, Saudi Arabia reacted swiftly to the latter development by speeding up existing negotiations for the introduction of the first netback contracts with Japanese refiners, the Saudi Government's basic target for netback exports having been defined during January as 2,000,000 bpd in west-of-Suez markets and 1,000,000 bpd in east-of-Suez markets.

The January collapse in spot crude prices undermined the level of spot product prices in all refining centres, although the proportionate price falls were rather smaller for products than for crude, resulting in significant increases in the apparent refining margins on openly-traded crudes. According to estimates based on weighted averages of spot product prices, the netback value of Brent crude at north-west European refineries was \$23.74 per barrel at the end of January, compared with a current Brent spot price of \$18.42, while the most widely-traded US grade (40° West Texas Intermediate) had an end-month netback value of \$21.92 at refineries on the Gulf of Mexico, as against its end-month spot price of \$19.60.

Similar estimates for Dubai's 32° grade (the only Gulf OPEC crude to be traded in any volume on the spot market during January) showed an end-month netback value of \$21.96 per barrel at European refineries, as against a spot price of \$18.50. Among the crudes which had disappeared from the spot market, Saudi Arabia's 34° grade had an estimated netback value of \$21.47 in north-western Europe in late January, compared with a notional spot value of around \$18.75. Among the non-Gulf OPEC crudes which entered the spot market intermittently and in low volume during January, Nigeria's 36.7° grade was quoted at \$19.50 per barrel—\$5 below its estimated European netback value—at the end of the month.

Whereas the North Sea producers had opted to sacrifice price stability in order to protect their market share following OPEC's own switch to a "fair share" strategy, Mexico retained an official pricing structure during January, albeit at the following lower rates (backdated to the beginning of December 1985): (i) 34° crude—USA and Asia \$26.25, Europe \$25.85; (ii) 22° crude—USA \$22.10, Asia \$21.75, Europe \$21.40. These initially competitive prices were soon undercut as a result of the collapse of the open market, and Mexican production consequently fell in January by 295,000 bpd (9.7 per cent) to reach its lowest monthly average since March 1983.

An initial cut of \$1 per barrel in Egypt's January export price for 33° crude was increased to \$4 in the last week of the month, for a final January price of \$22.70 per barrel. Corresponding reductions were made in the prices of heavier crudes. It was announced on Jan. 27 that Egypt's production would be cut by between 100,000 bpd (11.5 per cent) and 150,000 bpd (17.2 per cent) as a price-support measure.

Official Soviet export prices were reportedly trimmed during January to reflect a progressive fall in the spot value of Urals crude from around $26.50 to around $19.50 per barrel, although relatively low volumes were exported because of production difficulties similar to those experienced at the beginning of 1985.

Of the OPEC countries where production declined between December and January, Nigeria suffered a 26 per cent cutback as a result of intensified competition from North Sea crudes, implementation of the Government's policy of maximizing market share having been hampered by delays in finalizing netback-related terms with foreign equity holders (◊C9.3). The cutbacks in Iranian and Libyan output were consistent with the two countries' stated commitment to the defence of prices rather than market share (◊D16.12), although it was noted that Iran was in any case facing continuing war-related problems in maintaining its export capacity.

D16.11.ii—Prices and production, February to April 1986

Competition for market share between OPEC countries and the North Sea producers continued unchecked in February and March 1986, driving open-market crude prices down to levels which (in real terms) had not been seen since before the first "oil shock" of 1973–74. The estimated North Sea and OPEC production averages for the first quarter of 1986 were little changed from the levels recorded in January (being 0.2 per cent higher for OPEC and 0.5 per cent lower for the North Sea). Adjustments of national shares within the OPEC area (◊ Table 66) included a cutback in Saudi output in March which reduced the kingdom's "excess" production for the first quarter to 57,000 bpd relative to its notional quota ceiling.

The monthly average spot price of Brent crude fell by $4.87, to $17.26 per barrel, in February and by a further $3.52, to $13.74 per barrel, in March, the weekly average having fallen by $5.98, to $12.25 per barrel, between early February and late March. The cumulative fall in the Brent spot price since early December 1985 was thus of the order of 55 per cent by the end of the first quarter of 1986.

Except in the Far East, product prices continued to fall more gradually than crude prices in spot trading during February and March, boosting apparent refining margins to record levels at the end of the quarter. The estimated end-March

Table 66 — OPEC members' estimated oil output (excluding natural gas liquids), January to June 1986

	January	February	March	April	May	June
	(thousand barrels daily)					
Algeria	650	550	600	600	600	600
Ecuador	290	290	300	300	300	300
Gabon	160	160	160	160	160	170
Indonesia	1,400	1,300	1,300	1,340	1,425	1,355
Iran	2,100	1,900	1,800	2,000	2,100	2,200
Iraq	1,650	1,650	1,650	1,500	1,700	1,800
Kuwait*	1,100	1,300	1,515	1,520	1,510	1,650
Libya	1,100	900	900	900	1,100	1,200
Nigeria	1,200	1,400	1,600	1,700	1,600	1,540
Qatar	360	325	350	180	360	430
Saudi Arabia*	4,450	4,685	4,115	4,720	4,360	5,250
United Arab Emirates	1,220	1,365	1,365	1,315	1,465	1,565
Venezuela	1,670	1,670	1,670	1,670	1,670	1,690
OPEC	17,350	17,495	17,325	17,905	18,350	19,750

*Including share of Neutral Zone output.

netback values of Brent and Dubai crudes at north-west European refineries — $18.95 and $17.74 respectively—were around $7.20 per barrel higher than the corresponding crude spot prices, while the end-March netback value of West Texas Intermediate crude on the Gulf of Mexico was $5 higher than the same crude's spot price of $11.35 per barrel. A far steeper fall in product prices in Singapore (the centre of the Far Eastern spot trade) produced netback values which were virtually equal to prevailing spot crude prices at the end of March; however, this development had little direct effect on OPEC producers' realizations under netback contracts with customers in the region, which were mostly linked to movements in north-west European product prices.

It was reported in late March that Saudi Arabia had so far concluded netback agreements with a total of 24 oil companies for the supply of 1,750,000 bpd of crude to west-of-Suez markets and 900,000 bpd to east-of-Suez markets, while the country's own product exports had fallen to negligible proportions, causing the shutdown of the Jubail refinery (◊**C11.3.ix**). Of the other Gulf OPEC states, Iran, Iraq, Kuwait and Qatar all adopted netback pricing for the bulk of their crude exports during the course of the first quarter of 1986, whereas Dubai continued to export mainly through the spot market and Abu Dhabi adopted a system of flexible contract pricing based on "assessed spot prices". The four African OPEC producers each evolved netback formulas appropriate to their own circumstances.

An Indonesian policy of "linkage" with movements in the spot prices of a basket of crudes was officially confirmed on Feb. 20. Venezuela, which formally adopted a "commercially flexible" pricing policy on Feb. 10, subsequently used the price of an appropriate US grade (33° West Texas Sour) as the main reference point in a market-related indexation formula. Ecuador (whose sales price had averaged $26 per barrel from January to November 1985, $24.60 in December 1985 and $24.20 in January 1986) switched in February to a policy of direct alignment with the spot price of 27° Alaskan North Slope crude cif Gulf of Mexico (which stood at about $11 per barrel in late March).

Among the main non-OPEC exporters, Mexico cut its average official price by $4 at the end of January (with effect from Jan. 1) and by $4.68 in mid-February (with effect from Feb. 1), subsequently switching to a system of flexible market-related pricing from the beginning of March. Egypt cut the price of its 33° grade to $19 in February and $14 in March, although its export volume was believed to be negligible following the production cutbacks ordered in late January. Arm's-length trading in North Sea crudes continued to be conducted mainly on established spot-related terms, with virtually no switching to netback contracts.

Spot quotations for delivery in future months (which had remained below quotations for prompt delivery throughout the first quarter's slide in prices) fell to less than $10 per barrel for the first time at the beginning of April in the markets for British and US crudes, which were dominated by expectations of further growth in the supply overhang when demand underwent its normal second-quarter downturn. However, the market was subsequently steadied by a three-week shutdown of Norwegian oil production from April 6 (caused by an industrial dispute) which blunted the impact of a 580,000 bpd increase in OPEC production and an upturn in Soviet oil exports during April.

The daily average spot quotation for 15-day delivery of Brent crude, which had fallen to a low point of $10.30 per barrel on April 1, reached $13.85 in the first week of the Norwegian shutdown and ended the month at $12.37. The average Brent spot price for the last five trading days of April ($12.43 per barrel) was virtually the same as the average for the corresponding period of March, while the average for the whole of April ($12.25 per barrel) was $1.49 below that for March, this being by far the smallest monthly decline since the start of the upheaval in the oil market in late 1985. Forward spot prices moved in parallel with 15-day prices during the course of April, stabilizing at levels above $10 (e.g. around $12 per barrel for end-April contracts relating to delivery in June).

D16.12—The Politics of the Price War (January–February 1986)

While the high level of current OPEC production was the primary factor in the decline of oil prices during the first quarter of 1986, prolonged uncertainty over the future direction of OPEC policy gave much additional momentum to the decline, particularly after the supposed "barrier" of $20 per barrel was breached during the second half of January without affecting Saudi Arabia's commitment to the "fair share" strategy. Many observers had expected the Saudi Government to reconsider the validity of the strategy at that point because of the diminishing benefit to the kingdom—and the escalating cost to most other OPEC members—of gaining market share at prices below $20. It was, however, stated by Shaikh Yamani on Jan. 23 that a further "unlimited downward spiral" in prices could be expected unless non-OPEC producers, and "above all Britain", reached a "realistic" market-sharing agreement with OPEC.

The British Government responded by reaffirming its free-market stance in the price war and ruling out any dialogue with OPEC, it being stated on Jan. 28 by the Prime Minister, Margaret Thatcher, that recent price falls had not altered the Government's rejection of output controls on North Sea producing companies. (The other main North Sea producer, Norway, had meanwhile indicated on Jan. 22 that it would only consider the introduction of output controls in the context of a general agreement supported by Britain.) It was known that both countries' oilfields would remain profitable at far lower prices than those currently prevailing and that Britain (unlike Norway) was particularly well-placed to withstand a price war with the third-world exporters because of the oil sector's relatively small size within the country's total economy.

Estimates published in late 1985 had indicated that up to 95 per cent of North Sea crude output came from fields with operating costs of less than $5 per barrel and that no producing field had an operating cost of more than $11 per barrel. Moreover, the considerable expense of shutting down offshore platforms provided a disincentive to the early closure of any field which became only marginally unprofitable. The oil sector of the British economy accounted in 1985 for around 8.5 per cent of government tax revenues, 8 per cent of export earnings and 5 per cent of gross national product, and Treasury forecasts suggested that the overall economic impact of lower oil prices would be broadly neutral in view of Britain's position as a major oil-consuming country.

In terms of cost thresholds, the United States oil industry was more vulnerable to falling prices than the North Sea industry, the costs of production from "stripper" wells (which accounted for about 15 per cent of US crude output) being as high as $18 per barrel, while north Alaskan oil had an estimated production cost (inclusive of pipelining and shipment to the lower 48 states) of $11 to $12 per barrel. Break-even points of as much as $20 per barrel were reported for certain US oilfields using enhanced recovery techniques. The Reagan Government nevertheless adopted a non-interventionist policy on the pricing issue, pressure from domestic producers for an oil import tax being resisted on the grounds that the US economy as a whole would experience a net benefit from lower oil prices. It was estimated that at least 250,000 bpd of US production capacity could be shut in if prices stabilized at $15 per barrel, and around 1,000,000 bpd if prices stabilized at $10 per barrel (assuming that the north Alaskan fields were kept in production at the latter price level).

OPEC's special ministerial committee on the implementation of the "fair share" strategy (◊**D16.10**) held its first meeting in Vienna on Feb. 3 and 4, 1986, by which time it was clear that several member countries took the view that the strategy should be abandoned on the grounds that OPEC producers and "friendly" non-OPEC producers had been the main sufferers from a price slide which had failed to secure any concessions from the North Sea producers. A campaign for an alternative strategy of "short, sharp cutbacks" in OPEC output (backed if necessary by a boycott of imports from Britain and Norway) was initiated in late January by Iran and was immediately supported by Libya. The two countries made informal joint representations to Saudi Arabia, Kuwait and the United Arab Emirates (which were regarded as the principal advocates of a full-scale price war) in the days immediately preceding OPEC's Vienna committee meeting.

Venezuela, which was to chair the OPEC meeting, held bilateral summit talks with Mexico on Jan. 30 at which the two main Latin American exporters agreed to establish a petroleum co-operation committee to "co-ordinate their oil marketing policies and their position in any negotiations aimed at restoring stability to the market". It was agreed in this context that "flexible policies of pricing and trading" should be applied in order to defend market share. The two countries expressed their "deep concern" about the deteriorating revenue prospects of heavily indebted oil-exporting countries and warned that "internal economic adjustments alone could not take the strain of a loss of income of such magnitude".

Although all the countries represented at the Vienna OPEC meeting (i.e. Venezuela, Indonesia, Iraq, Kuwait and the United Arab Emirates) accepted that the Organization's "fair share" of the world oil market should be greater than the former production ceiling of 16,000,000 bpd, no agreement was reached on a higher target figure and no specific proposals were put forward for the implementation of the strategy.

Venezuela and Indonesia made differing proposals for the upward revision of the production target (arguing respectively for levels of 17,250,000 bpd and 18,000,000 bpd) and called for an intensification of diplomatic efforts to open a dialogue with the North Sea exporters. Iraq and the United Arab Emirates backed Kuwait's contention that OPEC should refrain from setting any specific production target and should aim instead to take the maximum possible market share until such time as falling prices forced a cutback in North Sea output. Kuwait's Oil Minister said after the meeting that the committee's unanimous rejection of the old production ceiling of 16,000,000 bpd had formally "freed member countries from their obligations under quotas".

The abandonment of the "fair share" strategy had meanwhile been discussed by the Oil Ministers of Libya, Iran and Algeria at a rival meeting which was held in Tripoli from Feb. 3 to 5 to plan a joint drive to "foil the plot to reduce oil prices". The three countries agreed in particular to press for an OPEC production ceiling of less than 16,000,000 bpd.

Saudi Arabia made its views known on Feb. 3 through an article in a Saudi newspaper which quoted Shaikh Yamani as saying that "OPEC cannot by itself reduce production to a low enough level to maintain prices" and that "no possibility of reaching an agreement with non-OPEC producers is visible on the horizon". Shaikh Yamani said that the question of how OPEC should define and defend a fair share of the market had been studied by "a thousand ministerial committees" in the past.

Mexico's Oil Minister arrived in Vienna immediately after the OPEC committee meeting to launch a co-ordinated diplomatic initiative with his Venezuelan counterpart, starting with a joint visit to Cairo on Feb. 6 to seek Egypt's views on the oil market situation. They were reportedly informed that Egypt (which had already cut back its own production ◊**D16.11.i**) was strongly opposed to the Arab

Gulf producers' policy of "flooding the market". The Mexican and Venezuelan ministers subsequently visited Riyadh on Feb. 8 for talks with Shaikh Yamani, going on to Geneva on the following day to meet Norway's then Minister of Petroleum and Energy, Kåre Kristiansen.

The Norwegian minister made it clear that his country had no plans to introduce output controls or to enter into a market-sharing agreement, and had agreed to the meeting in order to exchange views rather than to discuss co-operation. The fact that the meeting had taken place was nevertheless interpreted by some sections of the press as an initial move towards co-operation with OPEC, and led the US Government to seek reassurances from Norway on this point.

In an article published on Feb. 11, the Soviet newspaper *Izvestia* criticized the campaign by "some OPEC members" to force down the price of oil and accused Western governments and multinational oil companies of encouraging the collapse of the market. The appearance of the article coincided with an official visit to Moscow by the Oil Minister of Kuwait (Saudi Arabia's principal ally in the "fair share" campaign). The Kuwaiti minister had earlier stated (in a British television interview broadcast on Feb. 9) that a cutback of at least 300,000 bpd in British oil production was required to prevent crude prices from falling below $10 per barrel.

The UAE Oil Minister, who visited neighbouring Oman on Feb. 17 for talks on the oil market situation, was told that the sultanate would co-operate in any general market-sharing agreement between OPEC and non-OPEC producers.

The policy dispute within OPEC entered a new phase on Feb. 18, when the Oil Ministers of Algeria, Iran and Libya (acting in their capacity as the heads of their countries' delegations to the OPEC Conference) issued a joint statement consisting largely of thinly-veiled criticisms of Saudi Arabia's oil policy, while the official Algerian newspaper *El Moudjahid* published a full-page article explicitly accusing Saudi Arabia of playing "a very active role in the degradation of the international market in crude". The text of the joint ministerial statement (adopted at the end of a two-day meeting in Algiers between the three countries' Oil, Finance and Foreign Ministers) was worded as follows:

"The three delegations consider that the present situation prevailing in the world oil market is adversely affecting the economies of oil-exporting countries and is not the result of ordinary market forces, but a consequence of a planned strategy designed to deprive them of their achievements and the revenues necessary for their economic and social development.

"In this context, the three delegations express their regret and concern about the parties who have contributed to the deterioration of this situation.

"They believe that OPEC is not the only target of this planned strategy, which is also aimed at preventing developing countries from exercising sovereignty over their natural resources.

"With due regard to the statute of OPEC [◊B1.7], the OPEC Solemn Declaration of Algiers in 1975 [◊B1.9.iii], and the OPEC resolutions of March 1983 [◊D14.5], which call for defending the price structure that secures steady revenues, the three countries consider that all are binding. Therefore, they call upon all member countries to strictly adhere to all OPEC decisions and resolutions as their contribution to the restoration of the market situation.

"They reaffirm that the only way to safeguard the supreme interests of the petroleum exporting countries is through defending the price and purchasing power of oil.

"Emphasizing the importance of the contribution of OPEC to the cause of development of all petroleum exporting countries as well as the world economy, the three delegations are of the opinion that the unity of OPEC calls for safeguarding common interests in collective action.

"They call upon the member countries of OPEC to refrain from any individual action and to take further responsibility to strengthen the solidarity of OPEC through collective measures.

"Therefore all member countries should abandon any market-related pricing mechanism and excessive production which have created, and contributed to, the glut and led to a drastic price fall. Member countries should return to the official pricing system and adopt an adequate production policy in conformity with the OPEC resolution of March 1983 in order to remove the existing glut.

"The three delegations urge non-OPEC oil-exporting countries to join OPEC members in their efforts to shoulder the responsibility of restoring the stability of the oil market as their economies have been affected by the present situation.

"While expressing their determination to maintain solidarity among OPEC member countries and adherence to this objective, the three delegations consider that OPEC in unison is highly beneficial to the world economy. Hence short-term considerations aimed at destabilizing this Organization will have grave consequences for the world economy and its financial stability.

"Due to the gravity of the situation and in order to take the necessary measures for stabilizing the oil market through extensive consultations, they invite other petroleum exporting countries to hold an urgent ministerial meeting to achieve the above-mentioned objective."

The three countries' disquiet about Saudi oil policy was based in part on a growing belief that the kingdom, having seen spot crude prices fall to their present levels (e.g. around $17 per barrel for Brent crude) without any effect on current North Sea production policy, now favoured the stabilization of prices at these levels for several years as a means of securing a "fair" market share in the longer term. Such a strategy would rely both on the choking off of new investment in exploration and development work in the North Sea and other high-cost producing areas (which could rarely be justified at an oil price of less than $20 per barrel) and on the displacement from the energy market of high-cost alternatives to oil, and would operate to the particular benefit of countries with vast oil reserves, exceptionally low production costs and substantial capital resources (i.e. the conservative Arab Gulf states). This interpretation of Saudi Arabia's long-term policy aims was broadly accepted by many Western oil analysts.

In response to the radical OPEC members' public criticism of Saudi Arabia's role in the collapse of prices, the Saudi Ministry of Petroleum and Mineral Resources issued the following official statement to the OPEC News Agency on Feb. 22:

"To start with, we should recall that the continuing drop in consumption, due to repeated hikes in oil prices, and accompanied by a continuous annual increase in oil production by non-OPEC producers, led to a continued drop in OPEC's share in the world oil market, affecting financial conditions of OPEC member states which were forced to offer price discounts in order to be able to produce their quotas.

"Some OPEC member states even exceeded their quotas by giving more discounts. Consequently, price levels started to deteriorate. The kingdom was the only OPEC member state whose production fell by 50 per cent of its set quota and whose export simultaneously dropped to one-third due to its adherence to OPEC's official price structure.

"Other OPEC member states had been able to market their oil either through giving discounts or because they owned refineries whose products could be sold at market prices, not subject to the OPEC pricing system, or for some other countries, to sell some of their crude production at prices which did not fall within the OPEC pricing system.

"The kingdom had frankly approached its colleagues in the Organization and informed them of the difficulty in continuing this situation, and made them feel repeatedly and in various clear ways that the kingdom would be forced to follow the same practices which they adopted, unless the situation was corrected.

"Since other OPEC member states failed to abandon those practices because of their difficult financial situation, and in the face of the refusal of non-OPEC oil producers to give up part of their share in the market, there was no other way but for the kingdom to adopt a sales policy related to market prices in order to enable it to sell its entire quota or thereabouts. In this respect, however, we have adopted a careful and decisive policy aimed at preserving oil prices from a deterioration from whose adverse consequences nobody would be saved.

"Three months passed with this market-related sales policy without any negative repercussions on prices, which not only maintained their levels, but also continued to increase.

"When the [76th OPEC Conference meeting] unanimously decided to secure and defend for the Organization a fair oil market share, speculative sales in the market began to push oil prices downwards as it became clear to all that if non-OPEC states did not revise their policies and give up some part of their market share to OPEC, there would be a production surplus which would lead to a fall in oil prices.

"At this point, some of the media began to forget all clear market facts and realities and tried to give the impression that the present market situation was created by Saudi Arabia, while others even went as far as saying that the kingdom had an interest in what was taking place or it was conspiring with major industrialized countries to weaken the oil market.

"For all these reasons, it becomes necessary to issue a statement emphasizing the following facts:

"(1) What happened in the market was a result of circumstances which were imposed on all oil-exporting countries, as previously described, and which are beyond the control of any individual governments which have found their financial resources shrinking rapidly, causing an unbearable and unacceptable budget deficit.

"(2) What has taken place will harm all oil exporting countries, including Saudi Arabia and its colleagues in the Gulf Co-operation Council. It will likewise result in known adverse effects on consumers in the short, medium and long terms.

"(3) In order to put an end to the present deteriorating situation, the oil producers outside OPEC must co-operate with OPEC member states, as it has become clear that those latter countries cannot alone shoulder the burden of defending the price structure.

"(4) The kingdom will not abandon its oil policy, adopted since the early 1970s, which opposes rapid fluctuations in oil prices, downwards or upwards. The kingdom's position was known in the past when it objected to the repeated increases in oil prices which ultimately led to the current situation.

"Furthermore, our subsequent position was known when we agreed to reduce our oil production from 10,000,000 bpd to little more than 2,000,000 bpd, to the point that the wheels of our national economy were about to come to a standstill. It is unjust to distort facts about the kingdom and to depict the state of affairs untruthfully. What was said by Venezuelan Energy Minister, Dr Arturo Hernández Grisanti, the current President of the OPEC Conference, on Saudi television during his recent visit to the kingdom, is the best evidence of the truth of our position.

"(5) The kingdom will spare no efforts to correct the situation and to bring prices back to an acceptable and just level, and co-operate with every sincere effort to safeguard our economies from massive damage and to protect the international community from another energy crisis in the not-too-distant future."

Commenting on this statement on Feb. 25, Shaikh Yamani said that an "acceptable" level of prices would "be defined by all concerned parties inside and outside OPEC"; that prices "might go lower" before recovering to higher levels than at present; and that such a recovery might take years rather than months.

The Oil Ministers of Algeria, Gabon, Libya and Nigeria, meeting in Algiers on Feb. 24 and 25, adopted a proposal for the establishment of an "African Hydrocarbon Association" to "establish and foster co-operation among African oil producing and exporting countries", and agreed to consult their colleagues in other net oil-exporting African countries (i.e. Angola, Egypt, Tunisia and Congo-Brazzaville). It was stated that the proposed association was "not intended to duplicate or be in conflict with any organization to which members belong". The African OPEC members "expressed grave concern at the impact of the deterioration of oil prices on their respective economies", and issued the following appeal for corrective measures:

"The recent oil price collapse since December 1985 once more underlines the need for OPEC to take concerted action to restore market stability. To this end, the ministers reaffirmed the need to strengthen the Organization with a view to taking appropriate action to protect their collective interest. Therefore, the ministers agreed that OPEC should once more take the initiative of setting and defending the price of oil. The present market-related pricing practice is chaotic and does not serve OPEC's interest. The ministers urged non-OPEC producers to join OPEC in sharing the responsibility of restoring stability to the oil market."

D16.13—First Part of 77th OPEC Conference Meeting (March 1986)

The 77th (extraordinary) meeting of the OPEC Conference opened in Geneva on March 16 against a background of continuing tension between the conservative Arab Gulf states and the "hard-line" group consisting of Iran, Algeria and Libya. The oil committee of the Gulf Co-operation Council, meeting in Riyadh on March 8, had referred to the "unacceptable level of deterioration" in the oil market but had taken the view that it would be "difficult, if not impossible" for OPEC to support the price of oil without the full co-operation of non-OPEC producers, including Britian and Norway. Iran, on the other hand, had called in late February for the reassertion of control over the market by means of a two- to four-week suspension of all OPEC exports and the subsequent adoption of a drastically reduced production ceiling, stating that this strategy had the backing of Algeria and Libya.

Among the non-Gulf OPEC producers which had recently taken steps to safeguard their own market share, Nigeria indicated on March 12 that it supported the principle of output restraint within a lower OPEC ceiling, maintaining that an agreement within OPEC to remove 2,000,000 bpd of crude from the market would boost prices to between $20 and $25 per barrel. This price range was also considered to be "fair" by Indonesia, which drew up various compromise proposals for consideration by the Conference. Dr Subroto said on March 13 that Mexico, Malaysia, Egypt, Brunei, China and the Soviet Union could all be expected to "help to stabilize world prices" if OPEC held its own output at a "realistic" level. Kuwait, however, warned that the main Arab Gulf exporters could not be expected to accept a new OPEC production ceiling without firm guarantees that all member countries would adhere strictly to "sensibly allocated" national quotas.

Dr Hernández Grisanti, whose position as President of the Conference was unsuccessfully challenged by the hard-line group on March 16 on the grounds of his alledged bias towards the conservative group, said on the same day that all member countries were "interested in maintaining and defending a reasonable level of prices and avoiding any possibility of an abrupt decrease in prices". In a brief plenary session on March 17, the Conference noted the latest report of the market monitoring committee (which foresaw an average demand for OPEC oil of 16,360,000 bpd in 1986, with a seasonal low of less than 15,000,000 bpd in the second quarter of the year) and instructed the Secretariat to produce detailed estimates of the revenue implications of six different ratios of OPEC to non-OPEC output. The ministers devoted the remainder of the day to informal bilateral consultations.

On March 18 the Secretariat's revenue estimates were used as the starting point in the Conference's preparations for talks with five non-OPEC producers (Angola, Egypt, Malaysia, Mexico and Oman) which had agreed to send delegations to Geneva to discuss market stabilization measures. March 18 also saw the publication in London of 1986–87 UK budget estimates incorporating the assumption that the price of North Sea oil would average $15 per barrel over the coming year. In the strongest ministerial statement to date on non-co-operation with OPEC, the British Chancellor of the Exchequer (and former Energy Secretary), Nigel Lawson, asserted that "the whole outstanding success of the North Sea has been based on the fact that it is the freest oil province in the world, in which decisions on levels of output are a matter for the companies and not for the Government". There was, he said, "no question whatever, and never has been any question, of the UK cutting back its oil production in an attempt to secure a higher oil price".

Any possibility of sharing the burden of production cutbacks with the North Sea producers was therefore firmly excluded from the options considered at OPEC's first round of talks with the five "friendly" non-OPEC producers on March 19, which was devoted to a general review of the current state of the market. The two sides then met separately on March 20 to draw up specific proposals for cutbacks, obliging the OPEC Conference to address itself once more to the highly contentious matter of establishing a specific OPEC production target and redistributing national quotas within it. The immediate focus of attention was moreover the target for the second quarter of the year, which would have to be set below 16,000,000 bpd to have any impact as a price-support measure. In these circumstances deadlock was reached almost immediately when several member countries repeated their existing claims for increased shares of the group total (◊**D16.8**), Iraq's claim being subject once more to bitter criticism by Iran, which had launched a major new military offensive across Iraq's borders in February.

The Conference was thus unable to give any assurances about the possible level of OPEC cutbacks when (on March 21) it submitted a request for a 20 per cent cutback in the production of the five non-member countries, this request being immediately rejected on the grounds that it was both premature and excessive. Further talks took place between the two sides later on the same day, but yielded only an agreement in principle recording the willingness of the non-OPEC states to lend their support to any OPEC initiative designed to stabilize the market and ultimately to "restore and defend the former marker price of $28 per barrel".

Over the three succeeding days the OPEC countries failed in a further attempt to agree a second-quarter production target, notwithstanding the strenuous mediation efforts of Dr Subroto, who tabled successive proposals for the allocation of national quotas within group ceilings of 14,000,000 bpd and 14,400,000 bpd. Under these proposals, Ecuador, Gabon, Iraq, Nigeria and the United Arab Emirates would each have seen their percentage shares of the group total increase by one-eighth relative to their existing shares of the 16,000,000 bpd ceiling, while Saudi Arabia would have borne the greater part of the offsetting reduction. However, only the Kuwaiti, Indonesian and Qatari ministers indicated their unqualified acceptance of their countries' proposed quotas. Most other heads of delegation (including Shaikh Yamani) said that the proposals would have to be referred to their respective governments, while the Iranian minister totally rejected any agreement which would give Iraq a higher share of total OPEC output.

It was decided on March 24 to adjourn the 77th Conference meeting until April 15, thus leaving the "fair share" strategy in place and ensuring that the use of netback contracts and other market-related trading practices would extend into the second quarter of the year. Pessimistic comments were made in late March by several of the ministers who had participated in the nine days of inconclusive talks. Among the non-OPEC delegates, Egypt's Oil Minister said that there was a poor outlook for co-operation with an organization which "talks much and does little". Among the OPEC delegates, Dr al Oteiba of the United Arab Emirates said on March 31 that he had not so far seen "any worthwhile efforts or contacts among OPEC members and non-members to lay the groundwork for the success" of the second part of the 77th Conference meeting, adding that without an agreement on production cutbacks there was nothing to prevent oil prices from falling as low as $5 per barrel.

D16.14—Controversy over US Attitude to Oil Market Developments

On April 1, when spot crude prices dipped below $10 per barrel for the first time since the start of the current market upheaval (◊**D16.11.ii**), the US Vice-President,

George Bush, expressed serious concern about the prospect of any further erosion of price levels. Speaking to reporters in Washington before his departure to visit Saudi Arabia and other Gulf states, Vice-President Bush said that "it is essential that we talk about stability and do not have a continued free-fall like a parachutist jumping out without a parachute". He said that it was his belief that a strong domestic oil industry was vital to the security of the United States, adding that he would be "selling very hard" to convince the Saudi Government on this point.

The desirability of an early stabilization of the market had been stressed on the previous day by the US Energy Secretary, John Herrington, at an informal meeting with US reporters. According to Herrington, Saudi Arabia's policy of "forcing prices down by excess production" had "ramifications among its allies", and it would be timely for the Saudi Government to consider the "political implications" of the current dislocation of the market.

Although the Reagan Government moved swiftly to deny that there had been any change in its non-interventionist approach to the oil price question, while Vice-President Bush was accused by opposition politicians of seeking primarily to promote the commercial interests of US oil producers, the statements by Bush and Herrington were widely taken to indicate that the fall in prices to $10 per barrel had revealed the underlying "threshold of concern" in the United States, particularly regarding the national security aspects of the price collapse. This impression was strengthened by the announcement on April 3 that a government task force had been established to look into the security implications of the situation, one of the options under review being the purchase of US crude for the strategic petroleum reserve, possibly at premium prices.

The main consequences of Vice-President Bush's controversial remarks were (i) to neutralize the short-term impact of the recent pessimistic comments by OPEC ministers (particularly those made by Dr al Oteiba on March 31 ◊**D16.13**), thereby contributing to a market rally which was subsequently underpinned by the shutdown of Norwegian production (◊**D16.11.ii**); (ii) to ensure that the US Vice-President received a markedly cool reception when he visited Saudi Arabia for talks with King Fahd and other leaders from April 5 to 7, it being emphasized by both sides after the visit that the US and Saudi Governments held widely differing views on the state of the oil market; and (iii) to strengthen the US Government's efforts to ensure continuing support from other OECD oil producers for a free-market approach to oil pricing.

President Reagan, speaking on April 9, denied that the Vice-President's controversial remarks were inconsistent with a free-market approach, since the fact that the oil industries of "some foreign countries" were under state control meant that "we must keep our eyes open to see that no one starts playing tricks for some kind of illicit future gain".

D16.15—April 1986 Meeting of IEA Governing Board

The Governing Board of the International Energy Agency, meeting in Paris at official level on April 10, decided that recent oil market developments did not call for any change in established IEA policies or for any new policy initiative by the Agency. The Agency's Executive Director, Helga Steeg, said after the meeting that there had been no discussion of the possible activation of the 1976 agreement on a "minimum safeguard price" of $7 per barrel for imported oil (◊**D6.13, D7.7**). A spokesman for the IEA Secretariat had said some days earlier that a triggering of the safeguard price was "not politically on the cards at the moment" in view of the IEA members' non-interventionist approach to the current market situation. The following statement was issued after the April 10 meeting:

"The Governing Board reviewed the current world oil market situation in the light of the satisfactory progress which has been obtained over the past decade in moving towards a better balance of supply and demand through market forces and sound energy policies. They took note of the volatility and relative lack of transparency in day-to-day oil market conditions. They also noted the Secretariat's estimate that crude oil transactions [i.e. including OPEC netback transactions] are currently taking place in substantial volumes at price levels of around $15 to $16 per barrel fob and that [spot] prices in some markets for smaller volumes are lower.

"They noted that current economic analysis shows that lower oil prices than those experienced in recent years will, on balance, produce significant macroeconomic benefits in member countries and for the world economy, which they welcomed.

"At the same time they recognized that there will be negative impacts for some member countries and that debt and other economic problems of certain oil-exporting countries will be aggravated.

"In the long term, neither concerns about energy supply security nor the need for continuity in energy policy objectives have been removed by lower oil prices. On the contrary, a prolonged period of relatively low oil prices might intensify those concerns and bring forward the period when tighter energy markets can be expected.

"The energy policy objectives which have been agreed upon by all member countries to meet those long-term objectives remain valid under today's circumstances. Their purpose is to achieve the better balance of underlying energy supply and demand which is most conducive to long-term stability of energy market conditions and energy supply security.

"Consequently the Governing Board decided:

"(1) That the energy policy objectives referred to above can best be achieved through flexible, open and resilient markets, supplemented by government policies consistent with the national circumstances of each country and based on the long-term outlook and not on short-term developments alone. The decisions taken by the Governing Board in May 1983 [◊D14.6], in July 1984 [◊D15.4] and in July 1985 [◊D16.7] regarding, among other things, energy conservation and efficient use of energy, energy security, stocks and other measures, international energy trade, and diversification of energy supply are therefore reconfirmed and their implementation will continue with whatever adjustments the Governing Board may later decide are necessary. No new IEA action in the area of energy policy is required at the present time. The IEA will exercise continued vigilance as to future developments.

"(2) That, for this purpose, an updated assessment of the medium- and long-term energy outlook will be developed to serve as a basis for seeing whether energy policy objectives are likely to be achieved under current and future market conditions. More and better information as to oil market developments will assist in this assessment.

"(3) That the Governing Board's 1984 decision on stocks and supply disruptions is reconfirmed. The Governing Board stressed the importance of maintaining adequate stock levels and noted that the current oil market situation affords an advantageous opportunity to increase stock levels.

"(4) That reducing barriers to energy trade, and facilitating development of indigenous energy resources, would also contribute to achieving IEA policy objectives.

"(5) That internal adjustments may be necessary in some member countries to meet pressing regional, sectoral or other national requirements. These should take account of IEA energy policy objectives, international energy trade and the energy situation and policies in other member countries.

"Active consultation between member countries, especially on the part of those contemplating national policy action, will continue. Sound energy policies in member countries and in other countries will contribute strongly to improvement of world economic conditions."

D16.16—Second Part of 77th OPEC Conference Meeting (April 1986)

OPEC's Geneva Conference meeting reconvened on April 15 to face the same obstacles to agreement which had caused it to be adjourned on March 24, no fresh initiatives having been taken during the intervening period. The opening days were taken up with renewed debate about the advisability of retaining the "fair share" strategy, with the hard-line group of Iran, Algeria and Libya again urging the adoption of a policy of drastic production cutbacks. Plenary sessions tended to reach deadlock after short periods of repetitive argument, and delegates spent an increasing proportion of their time in informal bilateral or group consultations.

It was decided on April 17 to reappraise the market outlook for OPEC oil on the basis of updated statistics, including a full range of projections showing the estimated impact of different price levels on demand and on supply from high-cost non-OPEC producers. However, estimates submitted by a committee of economic experts on April 18 were rejected by the Conference as unsatisfactory (on the grounds that they contained insufficient detail and allowed unacceptably large margins of error), and serious discussion did not begin until April 20, when revised statistics became available. With the exception of Algeria, Iran and Libya, all member countries agreed to use the latest demand forecasts as a basis for setting a "realistic" production target under the fair-share strategy, although all discussion of the revision of national quota ceilings within the group total was to be deferred until the next Conference meeting, which was to be convened on June 25 with a view to finalizing a new quota agreement for implementation from July 1.

The 77th Conference meeting ended on April 21, when it was announced that the OPEC majority, having taken account of the need to restore market stability, had concluded that OPEC's average market share for the whole of 1986 should be 16,700,000 bpd, with quarterly averages of 16,300,000 bpd from July to September and 17,300,000 bpd from October to December. Algeria, Iran and Libya had, however, taken the view that the market could only be stabilized if OPEC production was limited to 14,000,000 bpd in the second quarter, 14,500,000 bpd in the third quarter and 16,800,000 bpd in the fourth quarter of the year. The OPEC majority requested the Oil Ministers of Indonesia, Kuwait, Nigeria, Saudi Arabia and Venezuela to take all necessary steps to secure the co-operation of non-OPEC producers in measures to stabilize the market. Delegates from the majority countries said after the meeting that a "gradual adjustment" of production levels could be expected during the course of May and June, and that strict observance of the proposed ceilings for the second half of the year could eventually stabilize prices at around $18 to $20 per barrel, which was now regarded as an acceptable medium-term range.

D16.17—Market Developments in May and June 1986 – First Part of 78th OPEC Conference Meeting

Far from being adjusted downwards, OPEC production underwent a further increase in May and June (◊ Table 66), giving an estimated second-quarter average of 18,660,000 bpd and an average of just over 18,000,000 bpd for the first half of the year. There was an estimated average excess of production over consumption of around 1,700,000 bpd in the second quarter, indicating a substantial build-up of stocks in importing countries. More than 300,000 bpd of high-cost North American productive capacity had been shut in by the end of June, at which point oil drilling activity in the United States was reported to have fallen to its lowest level since 1942.

The monthly average spot price of Brent crude rose by $1.90 to $14.15 per barrel in May, this being the first month-on-month increase in 1986. The relative buoyancy of the spot crude market in May was attributed to a temporary shortfall in the US refining industry's output of gasoline and middle distillates—a situation which was rectified by the end of the month. A subsequent sharp fall in product

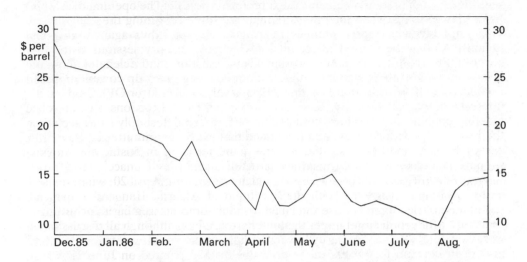

Fig. 25—Evolution of crude oil spot price, December 1985 to August 1986
(weekly averages for North Sea Brent)

prices led to a renewed weakening of the crude oil spot market in June, when the monthly average price of Brent crude fell by $2.56 to a new 1986 low point of $11.59 per barrel. Mainly because of the leading role played by the product markets in the latest decline, netback values fell slightly below spot crude prices in most markets during June (e.g. to around $10 per barrel for medium-grade Gulf OPEC crudes refined in Western Europe). Increasing price competition in its main export markets had earlier prompted Saudi Arabia to revise its netback contract terms at the beginning of May to allow additional discounts of between 50 cents and $1.50 per barrel, varying in accordance with the volume of purchases between agreed minimum and maximum levels.

Norway's Conservative-led coalition Government resigned at the end of April after Parliament had rejected key parts of an austerity programme involving substantial tax increases to offset a damaging fall in the state's oil revenues. It was succeeded by a minority Labour Government whose programme, presented to Parliament on May 13, included a pledge to "contribute to price stability" in the oil market "if OPEC nations reach agreement in measures which can stabilize prices at a reasonable level". The Norwegian Finance Minister appealed on the following day for Britain to "co-operate in a sensible dialogue with OPEC", stating that a market stabilization initiative by the North Sea producers need not necessarily involve mandatory restrictions on output from existing producing fields. However, the British Government dissociated itself from the shift in Norwegian policy, making it clear on May 18 that it remained opposed to any move towards co-operation with OPEC.

The Norwegian Prime Minister, Gro Harlem Brundtland, subsequently met the current President of the OPEC Conference, Dr Hernández Grisanti, in Venezuela on June 19, while Norway's new Minister of Petroleum and Energy, Arne Øien, met his Saudi counterpart, Shaikh Yamani, in Italy on June 22. The Norwegian side was understood to have indicated a willingness to give limited support to a realistic agreement on OPEC production controls by making "some modifications in the level of increase" in Norway's production, with the proviso that such support would be withdrawn if North Sea crude prices rose above $20 per barrel.

The first joint meeting of the five OPEC ministers who had agreed in April to seek closer co-operation with non-OPEC producers was held in Taif (Saudi Arabia) from May 23 to 25, when the ministers reported some progress in recent bilateral talks (notably with representatives of Angola, Egypt, Malaysia, Mexico and Oman). Among the non-OPEC countries which had not participated in the first part of OPEC's 77th Conference meeting, China had indicated in early May (on the occasion of a visit to Kuwait by a high-level trade delegation) that it was prepared to freeze its 1986 oil exports at their 1985 level of around 600,000 bpd in the interests of market stability. OPEC's "group of five" held a pre-Conference meeting on June 24 to review the outcome of further bilateral contacts, including the recent talks with Norway, and concluded that every significant net oil exporter except Britain could be expected to lend some measure of formal or informal support to a credible new initiative by the OPEC countries.

The 78th OPEC Conference meeting, which opened on the Yugoslavian island of Brioni on June 25, adjourned on June 30 without adopting a new quota agreement. Delegates to the Brioni talks spent much of their time reassessing the third- and fourth-quarter production targets adopted by the OPEC majority in April, which were now felt to be unnecessarily low in the light of the latest projections of future growth in demand for OPEC oil at prices below $20 per barrel. (The IEA's oil demand forecasts for the non-communist world had been subject to progressive upward revision throughout the year, and were by June indicating an annual increase of up to 2.5 per cent in 1986.)

Statements by individual delegates indicated that the majority countries (whose number was apparently reduced to nine through a decision by Gabon to back the line taken by Iran, Libya and Algeria) were in broad agreement that OPEC production averaging 17,400,000 bpd in the third quarter, 17,900,000 bpd in the fourth quarter and 17,600,000 bpd over the full year would secure a recovery in prices to a target range of $17 to $19 per barrel. These production levels were said to assume voluntary production cutbacks totalling between 500,000 bpd and 700,000 bpd by non-OPEC exporters. However, the Conference was unable to reach any agreement on the redistribution of national quotas within the higher group ceilings, and deferred further discussion of this issue until July 28.

An official press statement issued by OPEC on June 30 referred to the need for further consultations between each delegation and its respective government "in view of the crucial importance of these matters", but made no reference to any of the specific proposals discussed at the meeting. It was announced that the long-term strategy committee was "to resume its work as soon as possible with a view to defining the right strategies to be adopted by OPEC in all areas of interest".

D16.18—Further Price Decline (July 1986) – Strengthening of Market in Anticipation of OPEC Production Cutback (August 1986)

Having weakened significantly in reaction to the inconclusive outcome of OPEC's Brioni meeting, oil prices declined further during the course of July as OPEC production rose above 20,000,000 bpd for the first time since January 1982. Preliminary estimates published at the beginning of August by the *Middle East Economic Survey* indicated an aggregate OPEC output of 20,260,000 bpd (more than one-third greater than in July 1985), shared among the member countries as follows: Algeria 680,000 bpd, Ecuador 285,000 bpd, Gabon 170,000 bpd, Indonesia 1,325,000 bpd, Iran 2,200,000 bpd, Iraq 1,900,000 bpd, Kuwait 1,725,000 bpd, Libya 1,200,000 bpd, Nigeria 1,600,000 bpd, Qatar 450,000 bpd, Saudi Arabia 5,525,000 bpd, UAE 1,500,000 bpd and Venezuela 1,700,000 bpd. Outside the OPEC area, British North Sea production, which had averaged 2,609,000 bpd in

May, returned to a similar level in July after being cut back to around 2,200,000 bpd while seasonal maintenance work was carried out in June. Spot crude prices fell to their lowest levels of the year, the July average for North Sea Brent being $9.63 per barrel, $1.96 below the previous month's average and $16.99 (63.8 per cent) below the December 1985 average. Middle Eastern OPEC producers' average July realizations under netback contracts were estimated to range between $7 and $8.50 per barrel, having roughly halved over a period of three months.

Estimates compiled by the OPEC Secretariat in late July indicated that the OPEC countries' aggregate oil export revenues totalled around $36,760 million in the first half of 1986, some $19,540 million (34.7 per cent) below the total for the first half of 1985. Given that first-half OPEC production was about 2,500,000 bpd higher in 1986 than in 1985, the fall in revenues was equivalent to an average loss of about $43 for each incremental barrel exported. Independent estimates of the monthly trend in OPEC oil revenues in 1986 indicated an overall decline of 46.5 per cent (from $325,000,000 per day in January to $174,000,000 per day in June) and a per-barrel decline of 53 per cent during the first half of the year. The fall in revenue between January and June was equivalent to an average loss of about $63 per incremental barrel exported.

Revenue trends in individual member countries varied widely in line with changes in the volume of exports. Thus Kuwait, which was estimated to have increased its first-half exports by about 73 per cent in 1986, experienced a fall in revenue of around 15 per cent compared with the first half of 1985, whereas Iran experienced a small decline in first-half export volume and a decline of over 50 per cent in revenue. Saudi Arabia's estimated export volume for the period January–June 1986 was about 56 per cent higher, and its revenue about 22 per cent lower, than in the same period of 1985. Saudi revenue for the month of June was reported to be about 13 per cent higher in 1986 than in 1985, reflecting the severity of the decline in Saudi export volume in mid-1985.

The second part of the 78th OPEC Conference meeting opened on July 28 in Geneva, where the long-term strategy committee had met on the previous day. The Conference began by hearing member countries' reactions to proposals for the allocation of national quotas within an annual production ceiling of 17,600,000 bpd (the proposals in question having been drawn up by Indonesia's Dr Subroto at the end of June for consideration by governments during the Conference's recess). Discussion of the Subroto plan reached early deadlock when proposed quotas were rejected by several countries, among which Iraq which demanded parity with Iran, while the United Arab Emirates demanded a minimum entitlement of 1,500,000 bpd (equivalent to 8.5 per cent of the proposed group ceiling, as against the UAE's 5.9 per cent share of the former 16,000,000 bpd ceiling).

The main focus of debate shifted on July 29 to a proposal by Saudi Arabia, Kuwait, Venezuela, Nigeria and Indonesia that the Conference should attempt to reach an informal agreement on voluntary production cutbacks rather a formal agreement on binding quotas. Algeria, however, called for further consideration of a return to a fixed quota system, suggesting in particular that the inability of Iran and Iraq to agree on their respective entitlements should not prevent the other 11 member countries from adopting national quota ceilings for their own output. On July 31, by which time "nine or ten" OPEC countries were said to have pledged voluntary cutbacks totalling 1,925,000 bpd, the Conference agreed to discuss the Algerian proposal in detail while retaining the voluntary cutback scheme as a fall-back strategy. The plan for a 11-country quota system was subsequently withdrawn by Algeria on Aug. 2 after the Arabian peninsula producers had rejected specific quota proposals which fell far short of what they considered to be a fair market share.

It had meanwhile become clear that several member countries had used inflated estimates of current production as their starting point for offers of voluntary cutbacks. Ministers were therefore requested to provide forecasts of their countries' remaining production after the implementation of proposed cutbacks, the reported sum of these forecasts being significantly above 19,000,000 bpd, compared with the total of about 18,335,000 bpd which would have resulted if pledged cuts had been applied to July output levels. The latter total was itself significantly higher than the targets envisaged by the OPEC majority during the Brioni talks in June (i.e. 17,400,000 bpd in the third quarter of the year and 17,900,000 bpd in the fourth quarter). Attempts were made on Aug. 3 to find a basis for a realistic voluntary agreement to cut total OPEC production to between 18,000,000 bpd and 18,500,000 bpd with a view to halting the decline in prices (although it was accepted that a cutback of this order would not be sufficient to reverse the decline).

In practice, the scope for effecting cutbacks was heavily concentrated in the hands of the four Arabian peninsula members, which together accounted for 63.8 per cent of OPEC's estimated "excess" July output relative to the former production ceiling largely of 16,000,000 bpd, while Iraq accounted for a further 16.4 per cent (consisting largely of crude exported via Saudi Arabia). Saudi Arabia in particular had strengthened its position in July by maintaining an output level well in excess of its former quota ceiling while reportedly preparing contingency plans to increase its floating stockpile of oil. A statement issued by the Saudi Cabinet on Aug. 3 stressed that the kingdom had no intention of reducing its oil output below the (unspecified) level needed to meet its national "requirements and responsibilities"; at the same time it had "no objections to any country producing as much as it needs". This pointed reaffirmation of the "fair share" principle was apparently intended to quash any expectation that Saudi Arabia might make special concessions in the negotiation or the observance of an agreement on voluntary cutbacks.

On Aug 4, when the talks on voluntary cutbacks appeared to be moving towards an unconvincing compromise, Iran unexpectedly modified its hard line on the issue of Iraq's entitlement under an OPEC quota regime, thereby removing a central obstacle to agreement on the readoption of binding quotas. The Iranian proposal called for the application of a "shock" to the market by means of a temporary return to November 1984 quotas by all member countries except Iraq, which would be free of any quota restriction. The effective OPEC ceiling would therefore be 16,000,000 bpd plus Iraq's excess output (currently 700,000 bpd) relative to its former quota. The Iranian plan quickly gained support from other OPEC members, who recognized its significance both as a major concession on an issue of political principle and as a means of forcing oil prices back above $10 per barrel in the near future. Iran, for its part, was in urgent need of additional export earnings to ease a worsening foreign-exchange shortage, and felt that a return to quota ceilings by the pro-Iraqi Arabian peninsula producers would provide an important strategic compensation for its own acquiescence in quota-free production by Iraq.

After an intensive round of high-level contacts between member countries (during which Saudi Arabia and Iran each pressed the President of the UAE to set aside his country's claim for a higher quota), the Conference was able to announce on Aug. 5 that it had unanimously decided to reintroduce the former quota ceilings for non-Iraqi OPEC production during the months of September and October. Iran had originally proposed the reintroduction of quotas from mid-August, but accepted that other member countries had entered into binding supply contracts for the whole of that month. In agreeing to cut back their output, Saudi Arabia and Kuwait made it clear that they had not altered their basic commitment to secure a "fair share" of the market, while Iran made it clear that its decision to ignore Iraq's over-quota output should not be taken to imply any formal recognition of Iraqi claims or formal abandonment of Iranian claims on the quota issue.

At the insistence of Saudi Arabia and Kuwait, it was agreed that quota observance by the 12 participating countries should be rigorously monitored by the OPEC Secretariat. Kuwait stressed that it would react immediately to any indiscipline on the part of other participating members, while Saudi Arabia emphasized the temporary status of the agreement and warned that its willingness to limit its output after the end of October would depend on whether OPEC had succeeded in adopting a realistically updated quota system by that point. Saudi Arabia also drew attention to the continuing need for co-operation from non-OPEC producers in creating a stable market environment. A carefully-worded OPEC press statement of Aug. 5 included the following passages:

"After having reviewed with concern the market developments and the continuing deterioration in the oil price structure, the Conference felt that this situation had been caused, inter alia, by the continued overproduction of the oil-producing countries outside OPEC and the recent excessive production of OPEC itself beyond the level which it considers a fair market share.

"For this reason, it was thought that an interim action should be taken as a means of strengthening the oil price structure and moving prices up to reasonable levels by temporarily cutting OPEC's production by an amount necessary to remove the surplus in the oil market. Consequently, the Conference decided that OPEC's production for the months of September and October 1986 should be fixed on the basis of the ceiling of 16,000,000 bpd, as decided in October 1984 [◊D15.7], distributed among member countries with the same national quotas, with the exception of Iraq, and that all other member countries should strictly abide by those quotas during this interim period.

"In this context it should be emphasized that this temporary measure should not prejudice the discussion in the Conference concerning new national quotas for its members and OPEC's appropriate and rightful total production. While OPEC will continue its endeavour to secure stability in the world oil market, it will also pursue its efforts to secure for itself a fair market share, consistent with the revenue needed for the economic and social development of member countries.

"Furthermore, in taking this temporary measure to stabilize the oil market, the Conference calls upon the oil-producing countries outside OPEC to contribute sizeably in cutting production, with a view to shouldering, together with OPEC, the burden of defending market stability. Failing such contribution, OPEC will not be committed to defending the price structure alone. In this connexion, the Conference will be convened again in order to consider the production level for the subsequent period.

"The Conference also agreed on a system for controlling member countries' production to ensure compliance with these decisions."

The announcement of the impending temporary cutback in OPEC output produced an immediate positive reaction in oil markets which had previously anticipated a early slide in prices towards $5 per barrel. Spot quotations for North Sea Brent crude, which had averaged $9.40 per barrel on Aug. 1, touched $14 per barrel on Aug. 5, while the weekly average Brent spot price rose above $14 (for the first time in three months) after the middle of August. The average Brent spot price for the whole of August was $13.51 per barrel, some $3.88 above the July average and only $0.64 below the May average. When the OPEC cutbacks took effect at the beginning of September, Brent was trading at nearly $15 per barrel for September delivery, with a small premium for October delivery. August netback realizations on Middle Eastern and African OPEC crudes were estimated to range between $10 and $13 per barrel.

In the absence of any reports of significant voluntary reductions in current OPEC output, the rally in the oil market during August was sustained by clear evidence that individual member countries were taking action to cut back their supply commitments for September. Direct action by producers on pricing included the withdrawal with effect from Sept. 1 of the additional discounts which had been offered on Saudi crude since May in order to boost netback exports. While other OPEC members were benefiting from the combination of high production levels and firmer prices during August, Iran sustained a damaging Iraqi attack on its export facilities (◊C5.3.vi) which virtually halted the outflow of Iranian oil from Aug. 12 to 17 and severely limited the flexibility of loading operations thereafter. Iran was thus very poorly placed to use its full entitlement when OPEC quotas were reimposed on Sept. 1, a situation which was especially ironic in view of an earlier Iranian threat to control Iraq's output by military means when the OPEC cutbacks came into force.

Outside the OPEC area, Mexico announced on Aug. 6 that it would lower its oil export ceiling by 10 per cent, to 1,350,000 bpd, during September and October in solidarity with the latest OPEC initiative. Other "friendly" non-OPEC exporters in the Third World indicated their intention to take similar supportive action. Talks in Moscow in mid-August between the Soviet Prime Minister and the Iranian Oil Minister were followed by an announcement that the Soviet Union had agreed to co-operate with OPEC by making a cut of 100,000 bpd in its oil exports to non-communist markets (currently running at between 1,300,000 bpd and 1,500,000 bpd). The Norwegian Government welcomed OPEC's Aug. 5 agreement and subsequently opened talks with North Sea producing companies to explore the possibility of limiting the future growth rate of Norwegian oil exports by delaying the start of production from newly developed fields. Britain maintained a policy of opposition to any form of co-operation with OPEC.

Oil Company Index

Abu Dhabi Company for Onshore Oil Operations, 311–313
Abu Dhabi Marine Areas, 123, 280, 310–311
Abu Dhabi Marine Operating Co., 311–312
Abu Dhabi Oil Co., 311
Abu Dhabi National Oil Co., 310–313
Abu Dhabi Petroleum Co., 122, 123, 309–311
Agip, 59, 60, 219, 221, 262, 264, 265, 266, 270, 272, 273, 275, 296
Aguila (Mexican Eagle Oil Co.,), 43, 52
Al-Bunduq Oil Co., 123, 280, 311, 312
Alpha Oil, 311
Amerada Hess, 220, 258, 261, 264, 311
American Independent Oil Co. (Aminoil), 58, 216, 224, 248, 249, 251, 252, 290
American Overseas Petroleum (Amoseas), 116, 124, 261, 265
Amoco, 113, 198, 266, 281, 311, 315, 327; see also Standard Oil Co. (Indiana)
Anglo-Ecuadorian Oilfields, 190
Anglo-Iranian Oil Co., 213, 215, 216, 235; see also British Petroleum
Anglo-Persian Oil Co., 43, 212, 213, 231, 232, 234, 277, 278; see also British Petroleum
Arab Maritime Petroleum Transport Co., 157
Arab Petroleum Investments Corp., 157
Arab Petroleum Pipelines Co., 125
Arab Petroleum Services Co., 158
Arab Shipbuilding and Repair Yard Co., 157
Arabian American Oil Co. (Aramco), 51, 52, 53, 58, 64, 71, 80, 83, 84, 90, 93, 96, 108, 114, 115, 121, 234, 288–301, 343, 344, 351, 352, 353, 356, 380, 381, 382, 393, 394, 409, 412, 413, 414, 415, 432, 433, 462, 472, 473, 474, 475, 494, 498, 509, 511, 516, 525, 526, 531, 542, 553, 566, 567, 569, 571, 572, 583, 588, 597, 621, 641, 647
Arabian Drilling Co., 295
Arabian Geophysical and Surveying Co., 295
Arabian Gulf Exploration Co., 264

Arabian Oil Co., 60, 69, 249, 251, 292, 293, 300, 365
Arco—see Atlantic Richfield
Asamera, 204
Ashland Oil, 221, 273, 301, 327
Asiatic Petroleum Co., 43, 118, 201
Atlantic Refining Co., 49, 63, 232
Atlantic Richfield, 118, 120, 177, 191, 207, 217, 220, 258, 265, 314, 327; see also Atlantic Refining Co.
Attock Oil, 311
Ausonia Minière Française, 169, 172, 179
Auxirap, 295
Azienda Generali Italiana Petroli—see Agip

Bahrain National Oil Co., 123
Bahrain Petroleum Co., 123
Basrah Petroleum Co., 122, 234–240
Branobel, 44
Braspetro, 185, 241
British National Oil Corp., 98, 99, 103, 104, 105, 314, 569, 582, 583, 584, 587, 598, 599, 600, 603, 608, 620, 622, 623, 625, 636, 639, 640
British Petroleum, 42, 43, 47, 48, 49, 50, 51, 57, 63, 66, 93, 97, 115, 118, 119–20, 122, 123, 124, 176, 216, 217, 224, 231, 246, 251, 252, 261, 264, 270, 272, 278, 280, 282, 309, 310, 311, 313, 314, 343, 365, 382, 473, 600
Britoil, 314
Bunker Hunt, 261, 264
Bureau de Recherches de Pétroles, 59, 167
Burmah Oil, 43, 47, 119, 120, 191, 212
Bushehr Petroleum Co., 220
Buttes Gas and Oil, 314

California Arabian Standard Oil Co., 121, 288
Caltex, 115, 116, 123, 124, 203, 204, 205, 207, 288, 289, 311
Central Mining Corp., 278, 310
Champlin Petroleum, 333
Charter Oil. 217, 224, 311, 327
Chevron, 42, 50, 51, 55, 101, 115–116, 118, 121, 122, 123, 124, 203, 207, 216, 224,

261, 265, 270, 272, 273, 286, 287, 288,
289, 301, 315, 327, 343, 648
Cities Service Co., 221
Citgo Petroleum, 333
City Ecuatoriana Production Co., 191, 192
Clyde Petroleum, 191
Compagnie de Recherches et
d'Exploitation des Pétroles au
Sahara, 167, 169, 170, 172, 174, 175,
179, 180, 181, 183
Compagnie des Pétroles d'Algérie, 167,
169, 172, 174, 175, 176, 177, 179, 183
Compagnie Française des Pétroles—see
Total Compagnie Française des Pétroles
Compagnie Française des Pétroles
d'Algérie, 167, 169, 173, 181, 183, 185
Conch International Methane, 169
Conoco, 123, 169, 217, 221, 258, 261, 264,
280, 313, 314, 327
Coparex, 181, 184
Corporación Estatal Petrolera
Ecuatoriana, 191–194
Corporación Venezolana del
Petróleo, 324–328
Corpoven, 328, 331
Creole Petroleum Corp., 318, 319, 324, 327

Daikyo Oil, 311
Dashtestan Offshore Petroleum Co., 220
Deminex, 221, 311
Den Norske Stats Oljeselskrap—see Statoil
Diamond Shamrock Corp., 207
Distrigaz, 188
Dubai Marine Areas, 123, 313–314
Dubai Petroleum Co., 313–314
Dubai Petroleum Group, 314
Dukhan Service Co., 123, 280

El Paso Natural Gas Co., 169, 172, 176,
177, 179, 182, 184, 186
Elf Algérie, 183
Elf Aquitaine, 196, 224, 253, 265, 275
Elf Gabon, 124, 196–198
Elf Nigeria, 270, 273
Elwerath, 169, 177, 179
Enserch Corp., 196
Ente Nazionale Idrocarburi, 59, 65, 187,
219, 365, 473
Entreprise de Recherches et d'Activités
Pétrolières, 73, 74, 174, 181, 182, 183,
184, 220, 221, 238, 270, 271, 295, 365
Esso Libya, 258, 261, 262, 264, 265
Esso Sirte, 258, 261, 265, 266
Eurafrep, 181, 184
Exxon, 42, 43, 44, 47, 49, 51, 52, 53, 55, 60,
66, 67, 71, 113, 114, 121, 122, 124, 169,
176, 190, 193, 201, 203, 216, 232, 238,
247, 251, 258, 260, 262, 265, 266, 272,

278, 289, 302, 309, 311, 318, 319, 321,
322, 323, 327, 328, 331, 343, 366, 647

Farsi Petroleum Co., 220
Francarep, 181, 184

Gelsenberg AG, 261, 265, 266
General Petroleum and Mineral
Organization of Saudi Arabia—see
Petromin
Getty Oil, 58, 117, 169, 176, 177, 179, 180,
217, 220, 249, 290, 300
Grace Petroleum, 258, 265, 266
Gulf Oil, 42, 47, 49, 50, 51, 59, 63, 64, 93,
101, 116, 117, 118, 122, 123, 124, 191,
193, 196, 216, 224, 232, 246, 247, 251,
252, 253, 261, 270, 271, 272, 273, 286,
315, 318, 319, 323, 327

Hispanoil, 73, 123, 185, 193, 221, 249, 314
Hormuz Petroleum Co., 220

Independent Indonesian American
Petroleum Co., 207
International Energy Development
Corp., 158
International Marine Oil Co., 278, 310
International Petroleum (Venezuela)
Ltd, 319, 327
Iran Marine International Co., 220, 224
Iran Nippon Petroleum Co., 220
Iran Pan American Oil Co., 219, 220, 224
Iranian Offshore Petroleum Co., 220
Iranian Oil Participants, 57, 59, 70, 72, 93,
115, 121, 122, 216, 217, 218, 222, 223,
224, 343, 344, 350, 356, 372, 382, 392,
408, 415, 512
Iraq National Oil Co., 74, 238, 239, 241
Iraq Petroleum Co., 49, 50, 51, 52, 53, 58,
74, 79, 115, 121, 122, 232–241, 278, 286,
287, 289, 309, 340, 341, 344, 346, 347,
350, 352, 353, 355, 368, 371, 381, 382,
384, 393, 397
Iricon Agency, 122, 216

Japan Oil Development Co., 123, 310, 312
Japan Petroleum Exploration Co., 207
Japan Petroleum Trading Co., 249, 292

Kerr-McGhee Corp., 311, 327
Khanaqin Oil Co., 235, 236
Kuwait Foreign Petroleum Exploration
Co., 252, 254
Kuwait International Petroleum Investment
Co., 252
Kuwait National Petroleum Co., 73, 249,
250, 252, 253
Kuwait Oil Co., 51, 123, 246–253, 356, 392,
408, 432

Kuwait Petroleum Corp., 118, 123, 158, 252–254
Kuwait Spanish Petroleum Co., 249

Lago Oil and Transport Co., 319
Lagoven, 327, 328, 331, 332
Lavan Petroleum Co., 220, 224

Marathon Oil, 258, 261, 264
Maraven, 327, 328
Marubeni Corp., 282, 331
Maruzen Oil, 311
Mene Grande Oil Co., 319, 327
Meneven, 327, 328
Mesa Petroleum Co., 118
Mobil, 42, 44, 47, 49, 51, 52, 55, 114–115, 121, 122, 124, 169, 171, 172, 176, 179, 203, 207, 216, 220, 232, 247, 261, 265, 266, 270, 272, 273, 278, 289, 297, 300, 301, 302, 309, 311, 325, 327, 647
Monsanto, 327
Montecatini Edison, 169, 179
Mosul Petroleum Co., 122, 234, 235, 237, 240
Murphy Oil, 196, 220, 327

National Iranian Oil Co., 57, 60, 73, 122, 215–226, 398, 409, 512, 515
National Oil Corp. (of Libya), 158, 262, 264–267
Natomas, 296
Near East Development Corp., 115, 122, 123, 232, 240
Nederlandsch-Indische Aardolie Maatschappij, 203, 204
Newmont Oil, 169, 176, 179
Nigerian National Petroleum Corp., 272–275
Nippon Mining, 311
Norbec, 299, 300, 621, 649
Nynäs Petroleum, 333

Oasis Oil Co., 258, 260, 261, 263, 264, 266
Occidental Petroleum, 193, 261–267, 311, 325
Österreichische Mineraloelverwaltung, 221, 265, 266
Omnirex, 181, 184

Pacific Western Oil Corp., 58, 249, 290
Pan American Petroleum and Transport Co., 47
Participations and Explorations Corp. (Partex), 122, 123, 232, 240, 278, 289, 309, 311, 313
Pennzoil, 117
Permigan, 203–205
Permina, 203–206

Permindo, 204
Persian Gulf Petroleum Co., 220
Pertamin, 203–206
Pertamina, 206–209
Petrobrás Internacional SA—see Braspetro
Petrofina, 221, 327
Petrogab, 197
Petrola International, 300
Petróleos de Venezuela SA, 326–333
Petroleum Concessions Ltd, 278, 287, 309
Petroleum Development (Oman), 122, 123
Petroleum Development (Qatar), 123, 278
Petroleum Development (Trucial Coast), 122, 309, 310, 313
Petroleum Development (Western Arabia), 287
Petromin, 96, 295, 298–302
Petropar, 181, 183
Phillips Petroleum, 169, 172, 176, 177, 179, 220, 221, 248, 261, 270, 272, 273, 296, 327
Private Oil Holdings Oman, 123

Qatar General Petroleum Corp., 280–282
Qatar Petroleum Co., 123, 278, 280, 351
Qatar Shell Service Co., 124, 280

Royal Dutch/Shell, 42, 43, 44, 47, 48, 49, 51, 52, 59, 64, 73, 74, 93, 117, 118–119, 122, 123, 124, 167, 168, 169, 171, 175, 176, 177, 179, 193, 196, 198, 201, 203, 204, 205, 216, 220, 224, 231, 232, 240, 247, 251, 252, 258, 261, 262, 263, 264, 265, 270, 272, 273, 275, 278, 280, 300, 302, 309, 311, 313, 318, 319, 321, 322, 323, 325, 327, 331, 473, 512, 647
Ruhr Oel, 333

Sante Fe International, 158, 253
Sapphire Petroleum, 219
Sceptre Resources, 311
Shell Co. of Qatar, 123, 280
Shell Group—see Royal Dutch/Shell
Shell Oil Co., 119
Signal Oil and Gas, 248
Sinclair Oil, 63, 120, 169, 176, 177, 258, 296
Sirte Oil Co., 266
Société d'Exploitation du Gaz d'Hassi R'Mel (SEHR), 169, 181
Société des Pétroles de l'Afrique Equatoriale Française, 196
Société Française des Pétroles Elwerath (Sofrapel), 124, 169, 179
Société Française des Pétroles d'Iran, 220, 221, 224
Société Française pour la Recherche et l'Exploitation des Pétroles en Algérie (Sofrepal), 174, 181

Société Irano-Italienne des Pétroles, 219, 224
Société Nationale de Recherches et d'Exploitation des Pétroles en Algérie (SN Repal), 167, 169, 170, 173, 174, 181, 183
Société Nationale des Pétroles d'Aquitaine, 181, 183
Société Nationale Pétroliére Gabonaise— see Petrogab
Société Pétrolière Française en Algérie (Sopefal), 174, 180, 181,
Sohio, 113, 120, 217, 224, 281
Sonatrach, 170, 174, 176, 177, 179–188, 437, 438, 514
Standard Oil Co.—see Sohio
Standard Oil Co. (Indiana), 47, 49, 60, 113, 204, 219, 220, 232, 319
Standard Oil Co. (New Jersey), 43, 113; see also Exxon
Standard Oil group, 42, 43, 44, 49, 51, 58, 113, 116, 201
Standard Oil Co. of California, 50, 115, 286; see also Chevron
Standard Oil Co. of New York, 44, 114; see also Mobil
Standard-Vacuum Oil Co. (Stanvac), 114, 124, 203, 204, 205, 207
Statoil, 98, 105, 107, 621, 622, 623, 625, 636
Stewart Petroleum, 333
Sun Co., 220, 314, 327
Superior Oil, 115, 278, 310

Tamoil, 266

Tenneco, 198, 295, 327
Texaco, 42, 51, 55, 101, 115, 116–117, 121, 122, 123, 124, 191, 192, 193, 203, 207, 216, 261, 265, 270, 272, 273, 288, 289, 301, 314, 315, 327, 620, 647
Texas Petroleum, 327
Tidewater, 169, 220
Total Abu Al Bakoosh Oil Co., 123, 311
Total Algérie, 183
Total Compagnie Française des Pétroles, 42, 49, 52, 59, 121, 122, 123, 124, 167, 176, 182, 183, 184, 207, 216, 221, 224, 232, 236, 239, 240, 274, 278, 280, 282, 289, 309, 310, 311, 312, 313, 314, 382, 473
Trans-Arabian Pipeline Co., 290, 293
Turkish Petroleum Co., 122, 231, 232, 233, 237

Ultramar, 221, 327
Umm Al-Dalkh Development Co., 312
Umm al-Gawabi Petroleum Co., 265
Union Oil of California, 207, 220, 327
Union Texas Petroleum, 311
United Petroleum Development Co., 123, 280

Veedol, 169
Veba Oel AG, 266, 333

Wintershall AG, 265, 281, 314

Zakum Development Co., 312

Names Index

Aardenne, G.M.V. van, 644
Abdel-Karim, Tayea, 463, 477, 478
Abdessellam, Belaid, 463
Abdulai, Y. Seyyid, 134
Akins, James E., 460
Amouzegar, Jamshid, 415, 463, 476, 477
Arafat, Yassir, 510
Attiga, Ali Ahmed, 155

Babangida, Maj.-Gen. Ibrahim, 270
Badri, Omar El, 130
Bakhtiar, Shapour, 509
Bazzaz, Abdul Rahman Al-, 130, 344
Ben Bella, Ahmed, 170, 171
Betancourt, Rómulo, 324
Blumenthal, Michael, 520
Bongo, Omar, 195
Boumedienne, Houari, 167, 171, 419, 435, 436
Brandt, Willy, 558, 559
Brundtland, Gro Harlem, 667
Brunner, Guido, 499, 513, 520
Buhari, Maj.-Gen. Mohammed, 269, 270
Bush, George, 664

Calderón Berti, Humberto, 332, 598, 599
Carter, James E. (Jimmy), 91, 460, 463, 465, 477, 480, 484, 485, 486, 495, 499, 502, 519, 525, 534, 535, 557, 558
Chadli, Bendjedid, 166
Chalabi, Fadhil J. Al-, 129, 619

D'Arcy, William Knox, 212
David-West, Tam, 623, 639, 652
Dikko, Alhaji Yahaya, 590, 598, 605
Duncan, Charles, 530
Duroc-Danner, Jean, 240

Enders, Thomas, 448

Fahd ibn Abdul Aziz, King, 284, 461, 642, 664
Faisal ibn Abdul Aziz, King, 381, 382, 384, 400
Febres Cordero, Léon, 190
Feyide, Chief Meschach O., 130

Ford, Gerald R., 91, 425, 440, 446, 447, 460, 463, 465
François-Poncet, Jean, 520

Gharazi, Mohammed, 600
Giscard d'Estaing, Valéry, 425, 444
Gómez, Gen. Juan Vicente, 319, 321
Gowon, Gen. Yakubu, 269
Gulbenkian, Calouste, 49, 52, 122, 231, 232

Habash, Georges, 526
Hernández Acosta, Valentín, 477
Hernández Grisanti, Arturo, 650, 651, 661, 662, 667
Herrera Campíns, Luis, 332
Herrington, John, 644, 664
Hussein, Sadam, 212, 230

Idris, King, 256
Irwin, John N., 365, 366

Jaidah, Ali Mohammed, 130, 496
Joukhdar, Mohamed Saleh, 130

Kadhafi, Col. Moamer al, 256, 262
Khail, Shaikh Muhammed Ali Abu al, 527
Khaled ibn Abdul Aziz, King, 495
Khameini, Hojatolisam Seyed Ali, 211
Khene, Abderrahman, 130
Khomeini, Ayatollah Ruhollah, 211, 497
Kissinger, Henry, 91, 417, 418, 434, 440, 445, 448, 459, 480
Kristiansen, Kåre, 659

Lantzke, Ulf, 160, 520
Lawson, Nigel, 662
López Portillo, José, 559
Lufti, Ashraf T., 130, 351
Lusinchi, Jaime, 317, 651

Mabrouk, Ezzedine al, 463, 476, 479
Maghur, Kamel Hassan, 619
Maktoum, Shaik Rashid bin Said al-, 306
Mattei, Enrico, 59

Mébiame, Léon, 196
Mohammed, Gen. Murtala, 269
Mossadeq, Mohammed, 57, 215, 216
Moussavi, Hossein, 211
Muskie, Edmund, 559

Nahayan, Shaikh Zaid bin Sultan al-, 306
Nan Nguema, Marc S., 130, 598, 606
Natera Contreras, Brigido, 332
Nazer, Hisham, 344, 679
Nixon, Richard M., 84, 91, 418

Obasanjo, Gen. Olusegun, 269
Øien, Arne, 667
Ortiz, Rene, G., 130, 500
Oteiba, Maneh Said al, 461, 510, 511, 583,
    585, 599, 603, 616, 619, 620, 621, 627,
    630, 650, 663, 664

Pachachi, Nadim, 130, 239, 240
Pahlavi, Shah Mohammed Reza, 57, 85,
    91, 93, 211, 216, 218, 222, 336, 366, 399,
    400, 435, 436, 439, 477, 497, 499, 509,
    512, 514
Parra, Francisco R., 130
Percy, Charles H., 460
Pérez, Carlos Andrés, 440, 459, 463, 474,
    477, 478
Pérez Alfonzo, Juan Pablo, 323, 324, 335,
    336, 348
Pérez Jiménez, Gen. Marcos, 324

Ramírez Sánchez, Ilich, 442
Ravard, Gen. Rafael Alfonzo, 332
Razmara, Gen. Ali, 215
Reagan, Ronald, 97, 109, 575, 617, 664
Reza Khan, Shah, 48, 49, 57
Rockefeller, John D., 42
Rouhani, Fuad, 130, 340, 341, 342, 343, 344

Sabah, Shaikh Ali Khalifa al, 497, 597, 627
Sabah, Shaikh Jabir al Ahmad al, 244
Sabah, Shaikh Saad al Abdullah al Salim
    al, 244
Sadawi, Suhail al, 155
Samuel, Marcus, 201
Sanger, Elrich, 130
Saud, Abdul Aziz ibn (King Ibn Saud), 284
Saud al Faisal, Prince, 460
Shagari, Alhaji Shehu, 269
Shihata, Ibrahim, F. I., 134
Steeg, Helga, 160, 618, 664
Subroto, 628, 640, 643, 648, 650, 651, 662,
    663, 669
Suharto, 200
Sukarno, 200, 205

Tariki, Shaikh Abdullah, 293, 335, 336,
    348
Thani, Shaikh Khalifa bin Hamad al, 277,
    460
Thatcher, Margaret, 103, 657
Tondguyan, Mohammed, 555

Vance, Cyrus, 477, 480

Walker, Peter, 650

Yamani, Shaikh Ahmed Zaki, 76, 155,
    293, 348, 353, 380, 381, 382, 384, 394,
    399, 412, 439, 440, 455, 461, 462, 463,
    472, 473, 475, 476, 477, 478, 479, 495,
    496, 497, 500, 514, 515, 521, 526, 527,
    531, 543, 546, 551, 566, 567, 570, 571,
    573, 582,   585, 590, 597, 598, 599,
    606, 607, 620, 622, 627, 628, 629, 642,
    643, 648, 650, 651, 652, 657, 658, 659,
    661, 663, 667, 679
Yeganeh, Mohammed, 478

Late Information (October 1986)

The 79th (extraordinary) meeting of the OPEC Conference was held in Geneva from Oct. 6 to 22. It was agreed on Oct. 7 to establish ad hoc committees to examine the basis for a permanent redistribution of production quotas and the restoration of acceptable oil price levels. The member countries represented on the quotas committee were Nigeria (chairman), Indonesia and the United Arab Emirates. The prices committee comprised Kuwait (chairman), Ecuador and Libya. After it had become clear that no agreement could be achieved at this meeting on a permanent redistribution of quotas, the Conference sought a formula for the extension of OPEC's existing temporary quota arrangements until the end of 1986, subject to minor increases in some national ceilings. Finalization of the terms of the extension was impeded for some days by disagreements over Kuwait's quota demands.

It was eventually decided on Oct. 22 that the aggregate production ceiling for the 12 participating countries (i.e. excluding Iraq, which continued to be exempted from the interim quota system) should be raised to 14,961,000 bpd in November and 15,039,000 bpd in December. Saudi Arabia and the United Arab Emirates retained their existing national quota ceilings of 4,353,000 bpd and 950,000 bpd respectively. The other participating countries were allocated increased November ceilings as follows: Algeria 669,000 bpd, Ecuador 221,000 bpd, Gabon 160,000 bpd, Indonesia 1,193,000 bpd, Iran 2,317,000 bpd, Kuwait 921,000 bpd, Libya 999,000 bpd, Nigeria 1,304,000 bpd, Qatar 300,000 bpd and Venezuela 1,574,000 bpd. Indentical ceilings were to be observed in December except by Kuwait, which obtained a December allocation of 999,000 bpd. Norway welcomed the agreement, stating on Oct. 22 that it intended to implement a decision in principle (first announced on Sept. 10) to make a 10 per cent cutback in Norwegian oil exports in November and December by withholding state-owned royalty crude from the market.

The most experienced and influential member of the OPEC conference, Shaikh Ahmed Zaki Yamani, was dismissed from the post of Saudi Arabian Minister of Petroleum and Mineral Resources on Oct. 29. Oil traders saw this development as a signal of Saudi Arabia's intention to shift away from a market-share strategy, and the Brent spot price accordingly rose sharply from $13.15 per barrel on Oct. 29 to $14.80 on Oct.31. The Saudi Planning Minister, Hisham Nazer, who took additional responsibility for petroleum (as acting minister), called on Oct. 30 for an urgent meeting of OPEC's ad hoc prices committee to consider means of raising oil prices to at least $18 per barrel in the near future.

1987 - AUG 3 $22.2   24 $19,70
         OcT   12 $20,3   nov 9 $19,8
         Dec   16 $16,0
Graph   87- 11/25 - P6